League Express

LEAGUE
Publications Ltd

RUGBY LEAGUE
2016-2017
A coming of age

League Publications Ltd

First published in Great Britain in 2016 by
League Publications Ltd, Wellington House, Briggate, Brighouse, West Yorkshire HD6 1DN

Copyright © League Publications Ltd

A CIP catalogue record for this book is available from the British Library
ISBN 978-1-901347-33-3

Designed and Typeset by League Publications Limited
Printed by H Charlesworth & Co Ltd, Wakefield

Contributing Editor
Tim Butcher

Statistics, production and design
Daniel Spencer

Contributors

Thomas Alderson
Malcolm Andrews
Matt Annis
Peter Bird
Alex Black
Aaron Bower
Martin Butcher
Michael Butcher
Phil Caplan
Joshua Chapman
George Clarke
John Cox
John Davidson
Richard de la Riviere
Andy Donnelly
John Drake
Steve Fox
Ian Golden
Ryan Gould
Adam Gray
Sean Hayes
Phil Hodgson
Ash Hope
Andrew Jackson
Chris Jackson
Gareth Jones
Steve Kilmartin
David Kuzio
John Lawless
Lorraine Marsden
Tommy Marsden

Paddy McAteer
Keith McGhie
Joe Mills
James Oddy
Michael Park
Dave Parkinson
Josh Pay
Arindam Rej
Huw Richards
Ian Rigg
Lee Rowley
Mike Rylance
Martyn Sadler
David Saffer
Matthew Shaw
Steve Slater
Ryan Sparks
Alex Spindler
James Stott
Gareth Walker
John Walsh
James Whaling
Ricky Wilby
Chris Wilson
Gavin Wilson
Ian Wilson
Peter Wilson

Pictures

Matthew Merrick
Peter Morley
Magi Haroun
Steve Gaunt
Action Photographics
(Australia)
Glenn Ashley
Bob Brough
Paul Butterfield
Paul Clayton
Graeme Crowther
Peter Green
Steve Jones
Richard Land
Ian Lovell
Lewis Mitchell
Dave Murgatroyd
Bernard Platt
Kevin Read
Pascal Rodriguez
John Rushworth
Laurent Selles
Alain Soula
Ken Sparks
Dave Walker
Mal Walker
Simon Wilkinson
Dean Williams

Main cover picture
Steve Gaunt

CONTENTS

ACKNOWLEDGEMENTS

Rugby League 2016-2017 is the 21st of League Publications Ltd's annual series of Rugby League Yearbooks.

In compiling this historical record of the Rugby League year, we rely on the hard work and dedication of all the contributors to *Rugby Leaguer & Rugby League Express* and *Rugby League World* magazine. Without their efforts this yearbook would not be possible.

We are able to include some wonderful action photography provided by, in particular Matthew Merrick, Peter Morley, Magi Haroun and Steve Gaunt.

Thanks also to the Rugby Football League for their help during the year and to the historians and statisticians at clubs who help us resolve any anomalies.

Acknowledgement also to the Rothmans Yearbook 1999, compiled by our late friend Ray Fletcher, the British Rugby Records Book from London Publications, and to the club officials, and some supporters, who helped us verify records.

The comprehensive statistical review was put together meticulously, as always, by Daniel Spencer, who also designed the book.

Special thanks to Matthew Shaw and Malcolm Andrews, who respectively wrote the Championship and NRL sections.

Thanks also to Opta Sportdata, who compiled the Opta Index Analysis in our statistical section.

TIM BUTCHER
Contributing Editor

INTRODUCTION

Whether the sport of Rugby League came of age after 21 years of summer rugby and Super League is open to vigorous debate.

The radical re-structure of the league system made in 2015 went into its second year. And in 2016 it produced the result it was designed for when Leigh Centurions managed to gain promotion to Super League by winning six of their seven Super Eights Qualifiers games, beating Salford Red Devils, Huddersfield Giants and Hull Kingston Rovers to finish second in the eight-team table.

The Centurions' promotion was one of the big stories of the 2016 season with their larger-than-life chairman Derek Beaumont cleverly playing the Rugby Football League's adjustment of the salary cap to assemble a Super League quality team by the end of the regular season. With their marvellous stadium at Leigh Sports Village they will add an intriguing new dimension to Super League.

Alas, one club and its supporters had to experience the despair of relegation and that was Hull KR, after a ten-year stay in Super League. And the difference between top-flight survival and the Championship was a 45-metre field goal, kicked in golden-point extra-time by Salford fullback Gareth O'Brien in the Million Pound Game at Rovers' KC Lightstream Stadium. Some Robins supporters may never get over seeing their team lose after leading by eight points with only two minutes of the game remaining.

It was cruel on Hull KR, as it would have been on any team, the repercussions close to incalculable.

Still it gave Salford Red Devils owner Marwan Koukash the chance to have his photograph taken on the pitch holding a giant-sized cardboard cheque for one million pounds made out to his club signed by 'Big Nigel', a taunt at RFL chief executive Nigel Wood, whose organisation had deducted six league points in April for historical salary cap breaches. Without that sanction the Red Devils wouldn't have been in the Middle Eights.

One of the more compelling dimensions to the 2016 season was the demise of Leeds Rhinos in a matter of months from treble-winning club of 2015 to a bottom-four side which faced the ignominy of having to play-off in the last seven weeks of the season to retain its place in Super League. One of the big unknowns going into the new season was how the Rhinos would cope without the bedrocks of their success, Kevin Sinfield and Jamie Peacock. The answer was not very well, although the Rhinos' injury crisis was foretold in the first game of the season when new captain Danny McGuire became the first of a series of injuries that derailed their chances of beating North Queensland Cowboys in the World Club Challenge.

The expanded three-match World Club Series also enjoyed its second year but Warrington and Wigan joined Leeds in being well beaten at home by Australian opposition. The Super League general manager Blake Solly insisted the competition had a future but within two months he was himself leaving to take up a job in Australia.

Wigan and Warrington both went on to have much more successful seasons than Leeds, although the Rhinos sailed through the Middle Eights at the end of the season.

Warrington and Wigan take to the field at Old Trafford for the Super League Grand Final

The Wolves and the Warriors met in the Super League Grand Final and, despite both having injuries to some key players, produced a tough, exciting game that Wigan edged 12-6.

It was Warrington's second defeat in a final, the Wolves having lost by an even smaller margin to Hull FC in the Challenge Cup Final at Wembley in August. Hull FC had spent hard in the build-up to the new season and this year it paid benefits as they not only won the Cup, but also established themselves as a top-four side. The Wembley final provided an unbearably exciting finish courtesy of Danny Houghton's last-minute tackle on Ben Currie. Houghton was one of the most popular choices as Super League Man of Steel at the end of the year.

Widnes, Catalans and Castleford threatened to shake the hegemony of the big clubs early in the season. The Vikings led the table for four weeks up until Easter before going off the boil, finishing seventh and making the Super 8s, without ever having much chance of making the play-offs.

The Tigers never got higher than fourth spot and suffered from a big injury list. At one stage they couldn't buy a win at home but intermittently through the year registered some cracking victories. Their winger Denny Solomona was also one of the stories of the year. The Samoan, first brought to England from Melbourne Storm by London Broncos, ended the campaign with a total of 40 tries in Super League and 42 in all competitions, seeing him overtake Danny McGuire and Lesley Vainikolo's 2004 record of 38 tries in a Super League campaign.

Introduction

The Dragons celebrated ten years In Super League after an off-season recruitment campaign of high-profile seasoned Australian players and seemed almost certain to threaten the play-offs after a run of 14 matches that included only two defeats - one by two points, one by a single point. They then lost their 15th match of that run, again by two points at Warrington and it all went downhill from there, off-field indiscipline contributing to them finishing sixth before an end-of-season clear-out.

St Helens were the major beneficiaries of Catalans' collapse, a 23-4 win at Wigan in the last round of the regular season promising a run to Old Trafford, although they fell at the semi-final stage.

Wakefield were almost everyone's prediction to finish rock bottom and their goose looked well and truly cooked when coach Brian Smith, who had steered them to Super League safety the year before, resigned and went home to Australia five games and one win into the season.

But, astoundingly, local lad Chris Chester, himself let go by Hull KR weeks before, took over and the Wildcats won nine of their next ten games. Their run around Easter and through April, including a 62-0 home win over Wigan, gave them enough points to finish eighth.

The honour of the wooden spoon went surprisingly to Huddersfield Giants, who had spent the previous ten years establishing themselves as a top club. They only made their Super League status safe and avoided the Million Pound Game with a Danny Brough field goal at Hull KR in the ultimate week of the Qualifiers.

There were, once again, near the end of the season plenty of dead rubbers with some teams having little to play for after 23 of the 30 rounds and a complicated end-of season play-off system in the different divisions. But wherever there is Rugby League there is drama and passion. We are sure you will enjoy reliving the 2016 season.

* Because of this year's print deadlines, full details of the 2016 Four Nations tournament will be included in next year's edition.

The 21st League Express Yearbook contains the full story of the domestic year, the Australian NRL season and match facts for all Super League, Challenge Cup games involving professional teams, Championship and League One games. Every player who has played Super League is also listed along with those players to have made their debuts this year. We have also selected five individuals who we judge to have made the biggest impact on Rugby League in 2016. There are scoring and attendance records for every club. League Publications publishes the weekly newspaper Rugby Leaguer & Rugby League Express, as well as the monthly glossy magazine Rugby League World and the UK's most popular League website 'totalrl.com'.

TIM BUTCHER
Contributing Editor

1
THE 2016 SEASON

DECEMBER & JANUARY
One fine night

December 2015

RFL chief executive Nigel Wood described Kevin Sinfield as one of the greatest players in Rugby League history after his second-placed finish in the end-of-year BBC Sports Personality of the Year award.

Tennis player Andy Murray won the public vote, as Sinfield created further history by becoming the first ever Rugby League player to earn a placed finish in the list of twelve nominees.

There was a moving contribution to the awards night, held in Belfast, when Lizzie Jones, the widow of Danny Jones, who died when he went into cardiac arrest playing for Keighley Cougars at London Skolars in May 2015, sang 'Danny Boy' in front of thousands of sports stars and spectators. Lizzie came on stage during the section of the show dedicated to honouring and remembering sportspeople who had died over the past 12 months. Husband Danny was included in the tribute.

The Cougars were voted Club of the Year in the 2015 League Express Readers' Poll, scooping 48.3% of the total vote, for the way the club coped with the tragic loss of Danny Jones.

Overall, treble winners Leeds were the big winners in the end-of year poll. Rhinos fullback Zak Hardaker, the Man of Steel, was the League Express Player of the Year, taking 51.2% of the available votes in that category. And, in other categories, Brian McDermott was the Coach of the Year, Danny McGuire the Mature Player of the Year, Adam Cuthbertson the best new recruit for Super League in 2015 and Kevin Sinfield the Captain of the Year.

Sinfield was also voted the player who would be most missed in 2016, while new Leeds recruit Keith Galloway took the vote as the best signing for 2016.

Wigan Warriors' halfback George Williams, who broke into the England team in the Test series against the Kiwis, won the vote for Young Player of the Year.

The winter's longest-running transfer saga had come to a close at the end of November when a former Man of Steel and Albert Goldthorpe Medal winner, Rangi Chase, signed a two-year deal with ambitious Championship club Leigh Centurions.

The club that no longer wanted Chase, Salford Red Devils were having mixed luck with wingers. Having failed in an attempt to bring released Warrington flanker Joel Monaghan to the AJ Bell Stadium for 2016, they instead took Justin Carney on a season-long loan. Carney was unwanted by Castleford after being suspended earlier in the year. Although that suspension was officially lifted by the club soon afterwards, the episode had left bad feeling between the Australian and the rest of the Tigers squad. The Tigers signed Joel Monaghan, along with Wigan fullback Ryan Hampshire on a season-long loan.

Warrington Wolves, keen to get back at the top table after a modest season by their recent standards, made two late signings, both props - the rangy Jordan Cox, released by Hull KR, and former Leeds prop Ryan Bailey, who had short and unsatisfying spells at Hull KR and Castleford after leaving Headingley. Wolves coach Tony Smith said Bailey was on a 'one strike' policy with the club.

Former New Zealand international Frank Pritchard arrived in Hull from the NRL's Canterbury Bulldogs, despite late interest in him from the New Zealand Warriors. Pritchard joined five other new signings at the KCOM Stadium for 2016, fellow NRL stars Sika Manu, Mahe Fonua and Carlos Tuimavave and home-based players Scott Taylor and Danny Washbrook.

Ambitious Hull had also been linked with former Leeds fullback Ben Jones-Bishop after his release by Salford but surprisingly he opted to sign for Wakefield Trinity Wildcats. Jason Walton followed him to Belle Vue from the Red Devils.

Widnes Vikings signed Newcastle Knights forward Chris Houston and confirmed that Danny Tickle had been involved in an incident at a Wigan nightclub that required hospital treatment, but that he was expected to make a full recovery.

The Vikings released young Academy produced winger Jack Owens, who was promptly snapped up by neighbours St Helens.

Huddersfield and England forward Brett Ferres was facing an uncertain future after his suspension from the club, with his days at the Giants looking numbered. The Sun on Sunday claimed that Ferres was allegedly caught by his wife with the wife of a team-mate.

A number of clubs were already believed to be interested in taking Ferres from the Giants, but he had four years remaining on his contract, meaning a hefty transfer fee would be involved.

Prop Keith Galloway made his first appearance in Leeds colours in the club's Boxing Day clash against Wakefield. Galloway and fellow new recruit Beau Falloon, who was knocked out twice during the game, both played in the 14-6 defeat to the Wildcats.

In other festive friendlies, Castleford proved too strong for Featherstone, winning 42-28 and Batley Bulldogs beat Dewsbury Rams 12-4.

And Tony Smith hailed the 'sensational' Kurt Gidley as he shone on the last Sunday of the year in Warrington's 40-0 win against a youthful Widnes side at the Select Security Stadium.

* St Helens dominated the voting for Super League's 20-year Dream Team decided by a League Express Readers' Poll at the end of 2015.

Of the 13 players who were selected by League Express readers, who cast several thousand votes, seven were St Helens players. Jamie Lyon and Lesley Vainikolo were the only two overseas players to be represented in the Dream Team.

THE SUPER LEAGUE 20-YEAR DREAM TEAM

1 Paul Wellens (St Helens)
2 Ryan Hall (Leeds Rhinos)
3 Jamie Lyon (St Helens)
4 Keith Senior (Leeds Rhinos/Sheffield Eagles)
5 Lesley Vainikolo (Bradford Bulls)
6 Tommy Martyn (St Helens)
7 Sean Long (Hull FC/St Helens/Wigan Warriors)
8 Jamie Peacock (Leeds Rhinos/Bradford Bulls)
9 Keiron Cunningham (St Helens)
10 James Graham (St Helens)
11 Andy Farrell (Wigan Warriors)
12 Gareth Ellis (Hull FC/Leeds Rhinos/Wakefield Trinity Wildcats)
13 Paul Sculthorpe (St Helens/Warrington Wolves)

January 2016

The New Year began with the immediate future of England second-rower Brett Ferres settled, after he had been placed on the transfer list the previous autumn by Huddersfield. Ferres revealed that he had offers from teams on both sides of the world to continue his career, but described the opportunity to sign for Super League Champions Leeds Rhinos - initially on a one-year deal - as a 'no-brainer'.

The Rhinos appointed Danny McGuire as their new captain ahead of the 2016 season prior to their 74-6 win against the USA in Jacksonville at the end of a pre-season training camp. McGuire took over the job from Kevin Sinfield, becoming only the sixth permanent captain of the club in the Super League era. McGuire, the leading Super League try-scorer of all time, had captained the team in 2015 when Sinfield was absent.

Rugby League got the thumbs up from the north-east in a poll run by the Newcastle Chronicle newspaper. 'Magic Weekend takes North East award as fans fall in love with

Rugby League', said the headline as the Chronicle revealed the results of its readers' poll on the most popular events to hit the city in 2015. The Magic Weekend beat off competition from the Great North Run and the Rugby Union World Cup to be voted the best North East event of 2015 at the Chronicle People's Choice Awards. The Magic Weekend was to return to St James Park in Newcastle in 2016.

Former St Helens centre Josh Jones's spell in rugby union lasted a matter of weeks. Jones, 22, left St Helens at the end of the 2015 Super League season to join Exeter RUFC in rugby union's Aviva Premiership. But in early January he returned north because his partner was expecting the couple's first child and wanted to be near her family in the northwest. Salford were the beneficiaries, with Jones admitting that the presence of Red Devils Director of Rugby Tim Sheens was a crucial factor in persuading him to return to Rugby League at the AJ Bell Stadium.

Tommy Lee was made Red Devils captain for SLXXI but Salford were hit by a training injury to star signing from the NRL, winger Daniel Vidot. The former Brisbane Broncos player vowed to recover quickly from shoulder surgery.

Salford weren't the only club with injury concerns even before the start of the new season. Hull Kingston Rovers coach Chris Chester confirmed that the club would be without French international Kevin Larroyer for three months after he underwent surgery on his shoulder after the Robins were thumped 60-20 by cross-city rivals Hull FC in the Clive Sullivan Trophy match. Hooker Shaun Lunt was also due to miss the start of the season after ankle surgery, with doubts still lingering over the fitness of Terry Campese.

Among other friendlies, Denny Solomona scored four tries in Castleford's 32-6 home victory over Wakefield, while Widnes Vikings retained the Karalius Cup with a hard-earned 30-16 win over St Helens at Langtree Park.

St Helens were one of four clubs set to compete in a new reserves competition, alongside Wigan, Warrington and Hull FC. The four clubs had pressured the RFL for a third tier and offered to run the competition themselves, insisting the dual-registration system was not providing enough opportunity for non-selected and players returning from injury to get game time.

Former Super League referee Steve Ganson was appointed the RFL's new Head of Match Officials.

At the end of the month Paul Rowley resigned as Leigh Centurions head coach, ten days before the start of the new Championship season. Leigh had been tipped to be promoted into Super League in 2015 but performed badly in the Middle Eights. In the off-season they had signed Super League players such as Rangi Chase, Corey Paterson, Harrison Hansen and Willie Tonga ahead of the 2016 campaign.

It meant a number of Super League clubs were chasing their halfback, 2015 Championship player of the year Ryan Brierley. There was a clause in Brierley's contract which allowed him to leave the Centurions if Rowley departed the club.

LADBROKES CHALLENGE CUP - ROUND 1

Saturday 30th Janury 2016
Aberdeen Warriors 16 Northumbria University 42
East Leeds 0 Oulton Raiders 32
Egremont Rangers 62 Blue Bulls 0
Hull Dockers 8 Thornhill Trojans 6
Kells 30 Nottingham Outlaws 0
Leigh Miners Rangers 14 Underbank Rangers 20
London Chargers 14 Shaw Cross Sharks 22
Millom 32 University of Hull 14
Normanton Knights 18 Distington 31
Royal Navy 18 Featherstone Lions 20
Stanningley 16 Pilkington Recs 28
Thatto Heath Crusaders 16 Hunslet Club Parkside 23
Wath Brow Hornets 26 Royal Air Force 4
West Bowling 0 Castleford Lock Lane 16
Widnes West Bank 20 Rochdale Mayfield 38
York Acorn 36 Sharlston Rovers 10

Sunday 31st January 2016
British Army 4 Siddal 30
West Hull 36 Great Britain Police 4

LADBROKES CHALLENGE CUP - ROUND 2

Saturday 13th February 2016
Egremont Rangers 22 Rochdale Mayfield 26
Hull Dockers 12 Featherstone Lions 14
Hunslet Club Parkside 18 West Hull 19
Kells 42 Underbank Rangers 6
Millom 12 Pilkington Recs 46
Shaw Cross Sharks 6 Castleford Lock Lane 40
Siddal 18 Northumbria University 16
Wath Brow Hornets 30 Oulton Raiders 4
York Acorn 28 Distington 10

FEBRUARY
England 0 Australia 3

Round 1

Super League XXI kicked off on the first Thursday of
February with a rip-roaring contest at Headingley, as the
reigning champions Leeds were edged by Warrington
12-10.

The Wolves fielded six debutants, the focus on
their new halfback pairing of Kurt Gidley and Chris
Sandow, with the latter having failed to impress in his
spell at the end of the previous season.

But the pair secured the points for Warrington.
Sandow's arcing run from ten metres brought the first
try of the season, on 36 minutes, when it seemed as
though the opening half would end as a stalemate.
And when his side had fallen behind, it was Sandow's
beautifully flighted chip kick out wide that created
Warrington's second score for winger Kevin Penny,
thanks to the catch and pass of gamestar Ben Currie.

Gidley kicked both goals, but it was his game-high 45 tackles that summed up
Warrington's desire to protect their line, especially in the light of a 6-0 penalty count
against them in the second half.

Zak Hardaker missed a late kickable penalty to tie it up after tries from Brad
Singleton and Ryan Hall - after a superb break and offload by Joel Moon - just after half-
time had put Leeds into a 10-6 lead in a period of dominance, but Penny's try and the
subsequent conversion from the touchline by Gidley put Warrington into a lead they
would not surrender.

Brett Ferres made his debut for the Rhinos, but the new Leeds captain Danny
McGuire had to leave the field on 31 minutes with a knee injury, which ruled him out until
the beginning of April. Signing from Gold Coast Titans, hooker Beau Falloon was missing
with a broken toe.

Currie's pass for the winning try was far from being his only contribution. He pulled
off two try-saving tackles, the first on Rob Burrow in the 73rd minute when the Leeds star
broke clear and looked almost certain to score, on the end of a glorious move involving
Carl Ablett, Jordan Lilley, Adam Cuthbertson and Liam Sutcliffe. And with 30 seconds of
the match remaining Currie tackled Kallum Watkins into touch when the Leeds centre
threatened to break down the right to rescue the game for the Rhinos.

The following night's live TV game was a huge disappointment in the wake of the
opening game, almost solely down to the mudbath of a pitch at DW Stadium. The horrible
spectacle had critics pointing out that when Super League began in 1996, the first match
had been staged at the end of March, not in the middle of winter.

Much was expected of the visitors Catalans with their high-profile recruitment but they never got the chance to show their true wares, continually spilling possession as they tried to play dry-weather football, with the Warriors winning 12-6.

Wigan led 10-0 at the break with two tries from hooker Michael McIlorum, on the back of handling errors from the Dragons, the first when Krisnan Inu spilled the ball on his own line in a tackle by Ben Flower. The Dragons showed plenty of resolve in defence as the Warriors threw a lot at them in first half and they did well only to concede two tries.

Catalans' only points of the game came after a towering Pat Richards kick-off that won possession for the Dragons, with Justin Horo grabbing a four-pointer from a Richie Myler stab into the in-goal on his debut, while Wigan's only points of the second half came from a Matty Smith penalty.

Wigan coach Shaun Wane made a surprise call before the game, as he named skipper Sean O'Loughlin at prop, despite having three front-rowers on the bench in Tony Clubb, Taulima Tautai and Ryan Sutton. Dan Sarginson was back in the starting line-up after surgery on a hamstring had cut short his 2015 season. He started at centre with Oliver Gildart missing out, while Willie Isa was handed his debut in the second row.

Former Wigan star Richards was on the wing for the Dragons in his 200th Super League appearance, while Myler, Paul Aiton, Glenn Stewart and Horo were all making their debuts. Another of the Catalans' big signings, Dave Taylor, was named on the bench.

Aiton's debut lasted only 12 minutes as he injured a biceps and was sidelined until round seven.

On the same night St Helens fought out a tough 30-16 season-opening victory over an injury-depleted Huddersfield at Langtree Park, where the pitch was in much better condition than at the DW Stadium, despite the heavy rain.

The boot of Luke Walsh was the difference, as Saints handled the wet conditions better than the Giants and got their 2016 Super League campaign off positively.

The Giants lost three key players to injury, including one, Joe Wardle, before kick-off, when he picked up a quad tear on the eve of the game. Danny Brough had a deadleg and failed to appear in the second half, while Scott Grix dislocated his shoulder and left the field after 61 minutes. Grix didn't make a return until the Magic Weekend at the end of May.

Saints had their own injury concerns, with skipper James Roby leaving the field on 59 minutes after suffering a bang on the ribs and he did not return for the rest of the game, although coach Keiron Cunningham allayed concern over the injury.

Both teams featured several new signings, and there were unhappy debuts for NRL recruits Sam Rapira and Ryan Hinchcliffe, although Saints' debuting trio Lama Tasi, Dominique Peyroux and Jack Owens all gave solid performances. The Giants never led and the outstanding Luke Thompson's 60th minute try snuffed out any chance of a comeback.

The Giants were already in the midst of an injury crisis and were close to securing a deal to bring former St Helens and Bradford winger Jamie Foster to the John Smith's Stadium for 2016.

Hull FC kicked off their Super League campaign with an emphatic eight-try, 42-20 home demolition of a disappointing Salford Red Devils. Hull, another club who had recruited some big names for 2016, blew the Red Devils away for the first hour of the match.

The Hull forward pack, led superbly by captain for the night Danny Houghton and bolstered by the addition of Frank Pritchard, the outstanding Sika Manu and Scott Taylor, battered the Red Devils' middle, and allowed them to take complete control of the first half, which they ended 26-6 in front. By the 53rd minute when Jamie Shaul scored a try, it was 42-6, before Salford rallied.

Mahe Fonua and Carlos Tuimavave also had fine debuts for the Airlie Birds, although Fonua suffered a knee injury and was out until Easter. Hull tried to sign former

Leeds and Wakefield star Lee Smith. But salary cap pressure meant Smith signed for Leigh Centurions.

In east Hull on the Sunday, Hull KR snatched a dramatic late 16-all draw against Castleford. Josh Mantellato, who had only one functional eye after an earlier bang to the face, secured a point for the Robins with a late touchline conversion of his own try - his second spectacular finish in the corner.

Robins coach Chris Chester praised his side's response after a pre-season which saw them lose heavily to both Hull FC and Huddersfield. His Tigers opposite Daryl Powell hit out at a third-man tackle from Hull KR hooker John Boudebza that put captain Michael Shenton out for the season with an ACL injury.

The tackle was placed on report after Shenton was helped off the field and the French hooker Boudebza was charged with a dangerous tackle and suspended for four matches.

Shenton's replacement Jake Webster scored two second-half tries for Castleford and winger Denny Solomona was superb, registering a wonderful winger's try down the left to open the scoring.

The game drew an encouraging attendance at the KC Lightstream Stadium of 11,011.

Andy Bell, famous for his time at the head of pop band Erasure, was the guest of honour, attending his first ever game at the stadium after the club invited him along. He had struck up a relationship with the Robins, much publicised on social media, after the club adopted their biggest hit, A Little Respect, on the terraces at the KC Lightstream Stadium.

Rhys Hanbury helped get Widnes Vikings off to a winning start, by 24-16, on a cold, blustery opening day at Wakefield. Fullback Hanbury set the tone for his performance with a long-range break on the very first play of the game and scored one try and made another as the Wildcats paid the price for a sloppy first half.

The Wildcats trailed 18-4 at the break following a number of handling errors. Although they improved in the second half, a genuine comeback never quite looked on. Lloyd White's second-half try helped keep the Vikings at arm's length.

Both sides handed debuts to five players, including a second debut for Wildcats halfback Liam Finn. Ben Jones-Bishop, Anthony England, Tinirau Arona and Anthony Tupou were the others for Wakefield.

Of those, Jones-Bishop started brightly but made three crucial handling errors, England ran strongly throughout and Tupou caught the eye after emerging from the bench.

Making their bows for the visitors were Corey Thompson, Chris Bridge, two-try Setaimata Sa, Connor Farrell and Chris Houston, impressive after only being in the country for a matter of days.

* In the first week of February, the RFL announced that England coach Steve McNamara would not be offered a new contract and would be replaced by Australian Wayne Bennett on a two-year contract.

Round 2

Salford Red Devils set the competition alight with a 44-10 Thursday night TV hammering of St Helens at the AJ Bell Stadium, their first win of the season after a disappointing opening night in Hull.

Ian Watson and Tim Sheens' side took their opponents apart with a thrilling brand of attacking rugby spearheaded by stand-off Robert Lui, who looked every inch the top-level NRL halfback that thrived under Sheens at Wests Tigers before falling out of favour at North Queensland.

February

Lui scored two superb tries and was the fulcrum of a right-side attack that looked dangerous every time it got the ball, with Ben Murdoch-Masila, Justin Carney and Niall Evalds all impressing too. At halfback, Michael Dobson proved Lui's perfect foil, while up front Craig Kopczak led a tremendous effort against a much bigger Saints pack.

Saints had young hooker Morgan Knowles on Super League debut, in the absence of James Roby, and Theo Fages also on debut on the bench against his former club. But, substitute prop Alex Walmsley apart, they struggled to have any impact on an enthusiastic Salford defence, while they couldn't handle what the Red Devils threw at them in attack, not a good augur for the following week's World Cub Series match with Sydney Roosters.

The writing was on the wall for Saints by the twelfth minute, at which stage the Red Devils held a stunning 18-0 lead. Dobson created the first try, kicking twice in a matter of seconds for Greg Johnson to score, before the impressive Kopczak crashed over from close range. The Red Devils were three scores in front when Lui brushed off Luke Thompson and crossed directly from a scrum.

The introduction of Walmsley off the bench briefly stemmed the tide, and the big prop powered over to reduce the deficit to 12 points. But Dobson kicked a penalty goal and by the break it was a 26-point deficit, as the Red Devils ran riot in the closing ten minutes of the half.

Luke Walsh was sin-binned for tackling a try-bound Lui from an offside position after a superb Justin Carney break off his own line and, although Salford wasted that chance, they crossed twice in his absence.

Both tries came down that destructive right side, and were both launched by Lui. The first saw Murdoch-Masila and Carney combine to send Niall Evalds over, before Lui himself finished following more crisp work, with fullback Gareth O'Brien this time involved. The Red Devils left the field to a standing ovation, with Saints hearing boos ringing in their ears from the considerable travelling support.

Any hopes of an unlikely Saints comeback ended within two minutes of the restart when, after a Knowles forward pass, Adam Walne stretched over for Salford's sixth.

More bad news for Saints was that Mark Percival was carried off having sustained a medial ligament injury and would be out for two months.

The incident was recognised by the RFL's disciplinary panel on Monday but the contact from the Salford forward Adam Walne on Percival's leg was judged to be accidental.

Wigan fared better the following night, coming away from Huddersfield with an 18-13 win. Twice the Warriors were forced to come from behind, finally pinching the points through a try from Josh Charnley with less than three minutes remaining, to make it two wins out of two

It was harsh justice for a makeshift Huddersfield side - who gave a try-scoring debut to winger Jamie Foster - shorn of half of the players they would normally have expected to field in only the second round of matches, but battling bravely enough to come so close to toppling the Grand Finalists of the last three years. Danny Brough (dead leg), Eorl Crabtree (groin) and Scott Grix (shoulder) were added to a casualty list already containing Craig Huby, Joe Wardle, Kyle Wood and Jared Simpson.

And Luke Robinson had announced his retirement from the game earlier in the week due to a recurring hip injury.

Wigan struggled to find any fluency, also missing a few big guns, with the Tomkins brothers joined on the sidelines during the previous week by Dom Crosby and George Williams. That enabled Greg Burke to play his first game for the Warriors since July 2014, after having spent the previous season out on loan to Hull KR.

And with just a few minutes to play, the Giants, with Foster, who had been playing rugby union for Hull union club, and Dewsbury Celtic teenage product Sam Wood thrust straight into the starting line-up, led 13-12. Charnley's late winner was tough to take.

18

Jamie Shaul missed the birth of his son to star for Hull FC as the Airlie Birds produced their first league win in Perpignan since 2010 on the Saturday evening, by 38-10. Gamestar Shaul found out that his partner, Chloe, had given birth to a baby boy as he boarded the bus to head to the stadium.

The game was nicely poised at 10-10 after 22 minutes, with Pat Richards having scored two tries on his home Catalans debut. But it was 22-10 by the break, after converted tries from Josh Bowden and Jack Logan

Even the sin-binning of Leon Pryce for an off-the-ball challenge on 51 minutes couldn't stop the flow and when he returned to the field Hull had scored a further eight points and had broken the spirit of the Dragons.

On the Sunday at Castleford, Wakefield hooker Stuart Howarth scored the first try of the game for the second week running.

That, though, was about as good as it got for the visitors as Castleford, with scrum-half Luke Gale, fullback Luke Dorn and winger Denny Solomona particularly impressive behind a dominant Tigers pack, cut loose to finish 40-6 winners.

Gale, thriving on being captain with Michael Shenton likely to be out for the season, marshalled the Tigers in the style of 2015 and landed six goals from seven attempts for good measure. Oliver Holmes' try two minutes into the second half helped Castleford build on an 18-6 interval lead and ended Wakefield's hopes of a recovery.

That week the Wildcats had been fined £20,000 for racial chanting by a group of their fans during the Super 8s play-off match against Bradford at Belle Vue in August 2015. Half of the fine was suspended until the end of the 2016 season, but the tribunal also ordered the club to pay a £1,000 fine which had been suspended following a previous incident of misconduct, when two smoke canisters were thrown from the away end during Wakefield's fixture at Castleford on the opening weekend of 2015.

The RFL tribunal praised Wakefield for the steps taken after the match to address the issue, but felt the punishment should reflect the serious nature of the incidents.

Tom Lineham scored a hat-trick on home debut in Warrington's 38-8 win over Hull KR, with Chris Sandow in great form for the second week running.

Before the opening quarter had finished Warrington were 12-0 up, Ben Currie and Joe Westerman the try scorers as the Wolves opened up a commanding lead they never looked like losing. Kurt Gidley was sin-binned right on half-time for obstructing a quick restart, but even without him on the field, the Wolves' defence still stood firm.

Ironically, it wasn't until Gidley returned that Warrington conceded their first points but, by that stage, they had extended their lead further with a miraculous finish from Lineham.

Hull KR fought hard after that score though and they got a try their efforts deserved when Iain Thornley finished well after some sustained pressure on the Wolves' line. Soon after though, Lineham was in again with another astonishing finish and that essentially put the game to bed. Lineham's third was slightly more straightforward after a sublime break from Sandow in midfield allowed him the opportunity to stroll home unchallenged.

Hull KR coach Chris Chester's injury problems worsened. The Robins, already without a string of big names including captain Terry Campese, Shaun Lunt, Josh Mantellato, with a tear in his retina, and Kevin Larroyer, lost forward James Donaldson until the end of April to a dislocated wrist.

Widnes Vikings were the surprise Super League leaders on points difference, following their 56-12 victory over 2015 treble winners Leeds Rhinos at the Select Security Stadium on the Sunday.

Australian winger Corey Thompson scored a hat-trick of tries on his home debut and Rhys Hanbury kicked eight goals to help the Vikings to a second win in two games, leaving them with a points difference of 52, two ahead of second-placed Hull FC. Lloyd White and Hanbury were once again outstanding for the Vikings.

February

Leeds - bottom of the Super League table after two successive defeats - suffered three serious injuries to disrupt their preparations for the World Club Challenge against the North Queensland Cowboys the following Sunday at Headingley.

The Rhinos went into the game at the Select Security Stadium without Danny McGuire, Jamie Jones-Buchanan, Stevie Ward and their new signing Beau Falloon. And during the first half they lost winger Tom Briscoe, fullback Ashton Golding and second-rower Carl Ablett with leg injuries, with none of the three returning to the pitch.

World Club Series

Super League General Manager Blake Solly was refusing to panic after the Super League clubs' failure in the second World Club Series. Leeds Rhinos, Wigan and St Helens scored 28 points between them, while the Sydney Roosters, Brisbane Broncos and North Queensland Cowboys scored 118 points, with the Cowboys winning the World Club Challenge Trophy for the first time. Solly admitted that he was disappointed by the outcome, but was determined to develop the concept further.

Inspired by the world's best player, Johnathan Thurston, North Queensland Cowboys won their first World Club Challenge with a convincing 38-4 win over depleted Leeds Rhinos.

Leeds stood toe to toe with the world's best and looked their equal during a pulsating first 40 minutes. But ultimately their youthful squad couldn't keep the tempo up at a packed Headingley Carnegie.

It was 34-0 in the second half as the Cowboys blitzed Leeds and effectively tore them to shreds - with six out of the seven members of their back line scoring tries.

The preparations of the two sides could not have been more different. Leeds, without their three heroes, Kevin Sinfield, Jamie Peacock and Kylie Leuluai, from the 2015 Grand Final as well as current first-team players Danny McGuire, Tom Briscoe and Carl Ablett, were very much up against it with the numbers.

Coach Brian McDermott handed a debut to Anthony Mullally from the bench - but he didn't appear until after the interval as Leeds opted to use just one sub in the first period in prop Mitch Garbutt.

As for North Queensland, their coach Paul Green had the luxury of naming the exact same 17 that won the Grand Final against Brisbane, something which hadn't been seen in the WCC for years.

A majestic handling move unlocked Leeds' defence on 21 minutes, with Thurston freeing half-back partner Michael Morgan for the game's opening score.

Any fears that the opening try would have prompted Leeds' waters to break were unfounded though - and the Super League champions battled back to go in at the interval level. Liam Sutcliffe was growing in confidence opposite Thurston as the game wore on and it was his remarkable interception from the Golden Boot winner which laid the platform for the game-levelling try. Sutcliffe picked off Thurston's pass mid-air, raced 80 metres downfield and Leeds kept their composure two tackles later, with a superb offload

DACIA WORLD CLUB CHALLENGE

Sunday 21st February 2016

LEEDS RHINOS 4 NORTH QUEENSLAND COWBOYS 38

RHINOS: 1 Zak Hardaker; 22 Ash Handley; 3 Kallum Watkins; 4 Joel Moon; 5 Ryan Hall; 14 Liam Sutcliffe; 25 Jordan Lilley; 8 Keith Galloway; 7 Rob Burrow (C); 10 Adam Cuthbertson; 15 Brett Delaney; 26 Brett Ferres; 16 Brad Singleton. Subs (all used): 17 Mitch Garbutt; 18 Jimmy Keinhorst; 20 Anthony Mullally (D); 21 Josh Walters.
Try: Burrow (33); **Goals:** Lilley 0/1.
Dismissal: Garbutt (73) - fighting.
COWBOYS: 1 Lachlan Coote; 2 Kyle Feldt; 3 Justin O'Neill; 4 Kane Linnett; 5 Antonio Winterstein; 6 Michael Morgan; 7 Johnathan Thurston (C); 8 Matt Scott (C); 9 Jake Granville; 10 James Tamou; 11 Gavin Cooper; 12 Ethan Lowe; 13 Jason Taumalolo. Subs (all used): 14 Rory Kostjasyn; 15 John Asiata; 16 Scott Bolton; 17 Ben Hannant.
Tries: Morgan (21), Linnett (41), Feldt (48), Coote (61), Thurston (64), O'Neill (69, 77); **Goals:** Thurston 5/7.
Sin bin: Tamou (73) - fighting.
Rugby Leaguer & League Express Men of the Match:
Rhinos: Jordan Lilley; *Cowboys:* Johnathan Thurston.
Penalty count: 12-6; **Half-time:** 4-4;
Referee: Richard Silverwood; **Attendance:** 19,778
(at Headingley Carnegie).

No way through for Leeds' Brett Ferres during the Rhinos' World Club Challenge defeat to North Queensland

from Adam Cuthbertson putting Rhinos captain Rob Burrow over to make it 4-4.

Jordan Lilley also missed the conversion from a modest position, but Leeds were worth every inch of their half-time share of the spoils.

However, the second half could not have started worse for the Rhinos. The first set of the half saw Thurston hoist a towering bomb towards winger Ash Handley and, when the youngster spilled it, the ball was passed wide for Kane Linnett to score. This time Thurston would not fail from the kicking tee.

Tries from Kyle Feldt, when he shrugged off Ryan Hall on his way to the right corner, Lachlan Coote, Thurston and two from Justin O'Neill followed, with Thurston donating his kicking tees to awe-struck youngsters in the crowd after every conversion attempt.

To compound it all, Garbutt was sent off in the 73rd minute for punching James Tamou, who had slapped Keith Galloway at a play-the-ball. Garbutt was suspended for two matches.

Sydney Roosters thumped St Helens 38-12 in the opening match of the series on the Friday night.

Missing James Roby and Mark Percival, Saints were out of the contest by half-time when they trailed 22-0 and, although centre Dominique Peyroux scored his first tries for the club in an improved second-half display, there wasn't much for the 14,008 crowd to celebrate.

From Dylan Napa's shot on Alex Walmsley in the second minute that almost broke the giant prop in half to Luke Walsh squandering possession on half-way, unaware that international rules did not allow a 'free-play' that operated in Super League, Saints were only hanging on.

Teenager Jayden Nikorima, in the absence of suspended halfback Mitchell Pearce, had a blinder and, although he was forced off after only three minutes after taking a knock to the head, he returned after a concussion test to play a major role in his side's seven-try rout. Dale Copley's try on the stroke of half-time put the game out of Saints' reach.

New England coach Wayne Bennett witnessed his club side Brisbane Broncos make short work of Wigan, posting a 42-12 victory, on the Saturday night.

Brisbane, on their first competitive run-out of the year were terrific, with their talented halfbacks Anthony Milford and Kodi Nikorima (Ben Hunt was suspended from the 2015 season) at the fulcrum of their crisp attack.

Out wide they were brutally efficient, with Corey Oates scoring two tries and former Castleford, Huddersfield and Hull KR man Greg Eden one.

Wigan had their absences. Sam and Joel Tomkins, Josh Charnley and Lee Mossop would normally all feature in their first choice 17, while Michael McIlorum - their leader in defence - was stretchered off with a broken ankle in the 16th minute. In addition, Matty Smith and Willie Isa couldn't finish the game because of knee complaints. Even so, the Warriors were thoroughly outplayed.

Round 11

Two Super League games were played on the Sunday of the weekend of the World Club Series, featuring the previous year's bottom four clubs who would be involved in the fifth round of the Ladbroke's Challenge Cup in April.

DACIA WORLD CLUB SERIES

Friday 19th February 2016

ST HELENS 12 SYDNEY ROOSTERS 38

SAINTS: 22 Jack Owens; 2 Tom Makinson; 18 Dominique Peyroux; 3 Jordan Turner; 5 Adam Swift; 12 Jon Wilkin (C); 7 Luke Walsh; 8 Alex Walmsley; 6 Travis Burns; 16 Andre Savelio; 20 Joe Greenwood; 11 Atelea Vea; 13 Louie McCarthy-Scarsbrook. Subs (all used): 10 Kyle Amor; 14 Lama Tasi; 17 Luke Thompson; 28 Morgan Knowles.
Tries: Peyroux (41, 63); **Goals:** Walsh 2/2.
ROOSTERS: 1 Blake Ferguson; 2 Daniel Tupou; 3 Dale Copley (D); 4 Latrell Mitchell; 5 Shaun Kenny-Dowall; 6 Jayden Nikorima (D); 7 Jackson Hastings; 8 Kane Evans; 9 Jake Friend (C); 10 Dylan Napa; 11 Aidan Guerra; 12 Mitch Aubusson; 24 Sio Siua Taukeiaho. Subs (all used): 13 Sam Moa; 14 Isaac Liu; 15 Vincent Leuluai; 16 Ian Henderson (D).
Tries: Evans (17), Guerra (22, 54), Ferguson (26), Copley (37), Kenny-Dowall (52), Tupou (67); **Goals:** Hastings 5/7.
Sin bin: Napa (61) - high tackle on Swift.
Rugby Leaguer & League Express Men of the Match:
Saints: Dominique Peyroux; *Roosters:* Jayden Nikorima.
Penalty count: 5-2; **Half-time:** 0-22;
Referee: Ben Thaler; **Attendance:** 14,008 *(at Langtree Park).*

Saturday 20th February 2016

WIGAN WARRIORS 12 BRISBANE BRONCOS 42

WARRIORS: 22 Lewis Tierney; 20 Oliver Gildart; 3 Anthony Gelling; 4 Dan Sarginson; 5 Dominic Manfredi; 6 George Williams; 7 Matty Smith; 13 Sean O'Loughlin (C); 9 Michael McIlorum; 10 Ben Flower; 12 Liam Farrell; 25 Willie Isa; 14 John Bateman. Subs (all used): 15 Tony Clubb; 16 Sam Powell; 19 Taulima Tautai; 21 Ryan Sutton.
Tries: Sarginson (22), Williams (76); **Goals:** Smith 1/1, Powell 1/1.
BRONCOS: 1 Darius Boyd (C); 5 Corey Oates; 4 James Roberts (D); 3 Jordan Kahu; 2 Greg Eden (D); 6 Anthony Milford; 7 Kodi Nikorima; 10 Adam Blair; 9 Andrew McCullough; 15 Josh McGuire; 12 Matt Gillett; 11 Alex Glenn; 13 Corey Parker. Subs (all used): 8 Sam Thaiday; 14 Jarrod Wallace; 16 Joe Ofahengaue; 17 Travis Waddell (D).
Tries: Oates (9, 53), Nikorima (17, 57), Gillett (32), Wallace (39), Eden (66); **Goals:** Parker 6/6, Kahu 1/1.
Rugby Leaguer & League Express Men of the Match:
Warriors: John Bateman; *Broncos:* Anthony Milford.
Penalty count: 7-4; **Half-time:** 6-24;
Referee: Matt Cecchin; **Attendance:** 19,103 *(at DW Stadium).*

Wakefield Wildcats beat Hull KR 14-12 at a blustery KC Lightstream Stadium, with Brian Smith's side doing a hefty amount of defending to survive and claim the two points after being outscored three tries to two.

Wakefield scrum-half Liam Finn was a dominant figure, landing three goals from as many attempts and having a major hand in one of the Wildcats' touchdowns.

Rovers winger Kieran Dixon, by contrast, was off target with a couple of efforts, both from wide out, while young substitute Ryan Shaw, on debut, was unable to land what would have been a levelling conversion of Ken Sio's try as the game entered the final quarter.

Shaw was also denied what could have been a match-winning touchdown, nine minutes from time, by a superb tackle by young Trinity winger Tom Johnstone, who somehow got across to bundle the bench man into touch.

Johnstone was then thwarted at the other end of the field in attempting to dive over for the clincher in a highly dramatic clash that went down to the wire.

Rovers coach Chris Chester could have pointed to the controversial sin-binning of stand-off Maurice Blair on 54 minutes for obstruction as a key factor in the defeat, in a game in which 15 penalties were awarded to the home side and 11 to the visitors.

Salford weathered a spirited fightback and the 20th-minute sin-binning of Gareth O'Brien to steal a thunderous home game with Widnes by 28-20.

Both sides further enhanced their Super League credentials over 80 minutes in damp and difficult conditions, with the Red Devils storming into a 22-point lead, only for Widnes to claw the deficit back to two points.

A timely Tommy Lee 40/20 steadied the Salford ship, which was really rocking with ten minutes to play before Mark Flanagan charged over for his second and the decisive try four minutes before the end

Round 3

A Sunday afternoon 36-18 win at Huddersfield, which ended a 20-year hoodoo, put Widnes Vikings on top of the Super League table at the end of February.

Kevin Brown returned to his former club with a stellar 80-minute performance, although he was pipped to the gamestar honour by in-form Lloyd White as Widnes overcame the injury-hit Giants in great style.

With the Giants' last fit halfback, Jamie Ellis, forced out of the game on 26 minutes - Widnes already led 16-nil at that stage - MacGraff Leuluai's try right on half-time made it 22-6 and killed off Huddersfield's hopes.

Chris Chester became the first coaching casualty of the season when his departure, by mutual consent was announced by Hull KR on the last Tuesday of February.

Willie Poching stated that he wanted the job on a permanent basis, after being appointed as the club's interim coach, but the Robins were believed to be keen on former England coach Steve McNamara, assistant coach at Sydney Roosters, becoming their new man.

Poching took charge for the following Friday night but, with the continued absence of club captain Terry Campese and hooker Shaun Lunt, Rovers were beaten at home 31-22 by St Helens, their first victory at Craven Park, now known as KC Lightstream Stadium, in Super League, since 2007.

The key ten minutes came straight after half-time, at which stage the Robins led 16-10 thanks to tries from Ben Cockayne, Maurice Blair and James Green.

But with Albert Kelly back in his suit during the second half, having suffered a hamstring injury, Saints began to impose themselves with the return of James Roby in the 48th minute. Roby produced the spark which helped Saints turn the game around, having missed St Helens' defeats against Salford and Sydney Roosters with a rib problem.

Luke Walsh's kicking put lots of pressure on Rovers and it was after a kick from him when the match went beyond the home side, as he slotted over a penalty which gave Saints a 14-point lead with nine minutes left on the clock.

Catalans Dragons got off the mark with a 32-28 win over Leeds Rhinos in Perpignan on the Saturday.

The Dragons gave former Tonga and Australia giant prop Willie Mason a debut after they signed him on a one-year contract. But it was another former Kangaroo forward, Dave Taylor, who played the major role in that hard-fought win, with two tries and a power-packed performance.

The Rhinos were still in the middle of a major injury crisis with captain Danny McGuire, Tom Briscoe, Beau Falloon, Carl Ablett and Jamie Jones-Buchanan all injured and Mitch Garbutt also out suspended, so it was a much better display from them, Pat Richards' penalty to put the Catalans two scores ahead with nine minutes remaining finally ending their challenge. Jodie Broughton also made his Dragons debut.

Wigan coach Shaun Wane revealed he was disappointed with his side's performance on the Thursday night, despite extending a perfect start to the new Super League season.

Dom Manfredi's late try consigned Salford to a narrow 20-16 loss at the DW Stadium, a ground at which they had never won. However, a knock-on from Taulima Tautai at the play-the-ball in the build-up to Manfredi's late score was missed by referee George Stokes and his officials.

Salford had conceded defeat in the battle to land Luke Burgess, who looked set to stay with Manly Sea Eagles.

Castleford Tigers emphasised their top-four credentials after a match-winning Luke Gale field goal saw them edge out an unbeaten Hull FC side that had also been touted to be contenders in 2016, by 31-24.

Gale's sensational 40 metre field goal six minutes from time, in addition to a Denny Solomona hat-trick, eventually saw the Tigers home in one of the most thrilling games of the season so far.

Ben Crooks returned to Hull to face his old club and was outstanding. And there was a notable two-try debut - the first after 90 seconds - for Aussie wing partner Jy Hitchcox, signed from Featherstone and drafted in at the last minute to replace Joel Monaghan, who was injured in the warm-up. Jamie Shaul was once again excellent for Hull and bagged two tries.

Warrington were level top as they also held a 100 per cent record after a 34-16 home win over Wakefield.

Tries for Ben Currie and Kevin Penny gave the Wolves an early lead before Craig Hall and Anthony Tupou touched down for Wakefield either side of a Kurt Gidley try for Wire.

But two tries from Chris Sandow and one from Currie secured a home win, despite Jon Molloy's late try for the Wildcats. The other halfback Kurt Gidley was also a key performer but was helped from field just after the hour mark with concussion.

FIRST UTILITY SUPER LEAGUE
Sunday 28th February

	P	W	D	L	F	A	D	Pts
Widnes Vikings	4	3	0	1	136	74	62	6
Warrington Wolves	3	3	0	0	84	34	50	6
Wigan Warriors	3	3	0	0	50	35	15	6
Castleford Tigers	3	2	1	0	87	46	41	5
Hull FC	3	2	0	1	104	61	43	4
Salford Red Devils	4	2	0	2	108	92	16	4
St Helens	3	2	0	1	71	82	-11	4
Catalans Dragons	3	1	0	2	48	78	-30	2
Wakefield Trinity Wildcats	4	1	0	3	52	110	-58	2
Hull Kingston Rovers	4	0	1	3	58	99	-41	1
Huddersfield Giants	3	0	0	3	47	84	-37	0
Leeds Rhinos	3	0	0	3	50	100	-50	0

MARCH
Beware the Vikings

Round 4

Super League Champions Leeds picked up their first win of the season on the first Friday night of March when they saw off Huddersfield at Headingley by the slender margin of 20-16.

In a nervy encounter, it took the Rhinos until the 68th minute to take the decisive lead when Jimmy Keinhorst just about touched down a kick to the line by teenage halfback Jordan Lilley. Referee Richard Silverwood called no-try but went to the video-referee Phil Bentham, who overturned his decision on what looked to be slender evidence

Danny Brough returned to the Giants side after being out with a dead leg since round one, although Ryan Hinchcliffe remained captain, and Brough scored his side's first try on 14 minutes, after Joel Moon had given the Rhinos an eighth-minute lead when Ryan Hall tapped back Zak Hardaker's lofted kick to the corner. Jermaine McGillvary's try on the half-hour and Jamie Foster's second conversion made it 12-6 to the Giants at half-time.

Moon failed to return after the break after succumbing to a hamstring injury as Liam Sutcliffe and Michael Lawrence swapped tries before Keinhorst was awarded his scratchy try that Lilley converted before slotting a penalty five minutes from time.

The result meant four losses from four for the Giants at the start of the new season and they remained the only team in Super League without a point. They also suffered a blow when starting prop Daniel Smith was forced off after only three minutes with a foot injury. Former Leeds junior Smith needed surgery and missed the rest of the season.

Only one other team was without a win and that was Hull KR, who lost 30-16 at an ice-cold Widnes on the Sunday.

Scrum-half Joe Mellor was at the heart of the Widnes win, scoring two fine tries and having a hand in the other three. Rovers battled hard but Corey Thompson's try early in the second half took the game away from them as the Vikings remained top of the table on points difference.

Without eight regulars in all, caretaker Rovers coach Willie Poching handed teenage forward Kieran Moran his debut on a youthful bench. Rovers were unable to call upon the services of suspended James Green, banned for one match for a spat with Travis Burns in the home defeat by St Helens, with Albert Kelly and acting captain Graeme Horne added to the lengthening injury list.

Following the game, Rovers football manager Jamie Peacock confirmed James Webster's return to the club as interim coach for the remainder of the season, taking over from Poching. Webster had been in charge of the merged City of Hull Academy and it was a return to Super League coaching for the Australian for the first time since leaving Wakefield the previous year. Steve McNamara was still the Robins' preferred target for 2017.

Rovers had moved to secure the services of ever-present George Lawler after the promising 20-year-old forward penned a new long-term contract to the end of the 2019 campaign.

March

The Vikings had played an extra game to the two sides with 100 per cent records, Wigan and Warrington.

Chris Sandow was the star for the Wolves in an amazing Thursday TV game, producing a mesmerising second-half performance as his side overturned a 30-12 deficit just before the hour to win 31-30 at Salford, with Sandow kicking a winning 40-metre field goal out of the mud on the final hooter.

Warrington had looked destined to settle for a draw when Sandow missed a 78th-minute penalty, which was understandable in conditions that had become more treacherous as the match went on. Salford's Michael Dobson and Robert Lui had both been unable to get field-goal attempts far off the ground. Sandow's all-round kicking performance in the second half was central to a win that made it four in a row for the Wolves.

Salford centre Junior Sa'u got the opening score as he powered past four defenders directly from a tap penalty. Penalties also led directly to tries from back-rowers Jack Hughes and Ben Currie and the Wolves almost scored again through Matty Russell, only for Kevin Penny to put a foot on the touchline. But the remainder of the half belonged to the Red Devils.

They were level when Dobson kicked smartly for Josh Jones to touch down, before the try scorer provided the break that led to Greg Johnson diving over from dummy-half. A Gareth O'Brien 40/20 against his former club then allowed Dobson to kick again, this time for Sa'u's second, and when Josh Griffin slid over in the left corner on 33 minutes the home side were suddenly 28-12 ahead.

That was extended by a further two points with an O'Brien penalty early in the second half before the tide began to turn.

Both sides had a man sin-binned - Currie for patting Ben Murdoch-Masila on the back of the head after a second skirmish between the two, and Justin Carney for becoming involving in the ensuing melee.

Warrington moved level with a stunning spell of 18 unanswered points in seven minutes. Ryan Atkins touched down twice before Chris Hill's break led to Ashton Sims levelling the scores. The longest scoreless spell of the game ensued - fully 14 minutes - before Sandow produced his moment of magic.

The only major negative for the Wolves was yet another serious injury to the unlucky Gary Wheeler, who snapped his Achilles.

Wigan remained unbeaten after another nailbiter, this time at Hull FC on the Friday, Matty Smith's field goal a minute from time sealing a 26-25 win. Four minutes earlier Smith had given the Warriors a one-point lead, only for Marc Sneyd to cancel it out with a one-pointer of his own.

Wigan had a significant injury toll, but they came up with the goods despite a last-minute withdrawal by captain Sean O'Loughlin with an infection, whilst Hull had the notable absence of marquee man Frank Pritchard with a shoulder injury.

Ben Flower's second-minute try was added to by George Williams for the Warriors, with Steve Michaels crossing as Hull FC trailed 14-6 at the break. The excellent John Bateman extended the lead 14 minutes into the second half but tries from Leon Pryce, Sika Manu and Steve Michaels - all converted by Sneyd - pushed the hosts ahead 24-20. Josh Charnley levelled it at 24-24 before the drama of the three field goals.

Also on the Friday night, St Helens' superior kicking game, Luke Walsh, Jon Wilkin and Jordan Turner all helping turn the screw, won them a 28-22 home victory over unbeaten Castleford.

Saints applied the early pressure with six goal-line drop-outs, but the Tigers came up with the game's first points as Grant Millington crossed with their first meaningful attack. After Adam Swift pounced, fine work from Ben Crooks sent Mike McMeeken in for the Tigers' second try, but two tries in five minutes from Atelea Vea and Matt Dawson saw Saints lead 16-14 at half-time.

A Crooks penalty goal restored parity, but that was as good as it got for the visitors as Louie McCarthy-Scarsbrook and Dawson tries gave Saints a comfortable lead before Adam Milner added a consolation score. The Tigers' chances went with key injuries, as Ben Roberts, Junior Moors and Grant Millington all went off and didn't return to the field.

Catalans won their second game on a row, a 42-28 win at Wakefield. For the opening 25 minutes, the Dragons, and the huge figure of Dave Taylor in particular, were breathtaking in taking a 26-0 lead. They looked a class apart from the moment Todd Carney's inch-perfect pass got centre Krisnan Inu into a half gap and he sent winger Jodie Broughton over for his first try for the club after only five minutes. A hefty defeat looked on the cards for Wakefield.

But the Wildcats staged an incredible comeback after Anthony Tupou crashed over on the angle. When Broughton spilled a towering kick from Liam Finn two minutes later, the ball was shifted well for Joe Arundel to touch down in the right corner. Finn converted both tries and suddenly, at 26-10, it was game on.

The game tightened further at the start of the second half. A walk-in for Reece Lyne after Catalans had stopped playing, sensing a knock-on in back play, was followed by a brilliant try from Tom Johnstone, who leaped high to claim Finn's latest marvellous kick.

But when Finn missed the goal to leave it 26-22 and Wakefield spilled possession on halfway, momentum changed again as Richie Myler's try on 54 minutes gave Catalans breathing space.

The following Tuesday, head coach Brian Smith told the Wildcats players he was leaving and heading home to Australia.

Round 5

Salford beat Castleford Tigers 32-16 at the Jungle on the Sunday after the Red Devils had received allegations by the RFL that the club had breached the salary cap in 2014 and 2015. Owner Marwan Koukash had held a press conference in which he denied the club had done anything wrong, although he conceded that he could have made some mistakes.

Gareth O'Brien, the former Warrington halfback who had been playing fullback for Salford, was the man of the match with a couple of try-saving tackles, having a hand in three of his side's tries, and he landed six goals from as many attempts, four from wide out.

The game was decided in the last six minutes with the Tigers, battling back to 20-16 down having trailed 20-6 on the hour mark, threatened with a break in midfield by bench hooker Paul McShane. McShane had forward Nathan Massey in support, but Red Devils second row Ben Murdoch-Masila got a hand to the attempted pass to avert the danger. The visitors made the most of the territory, O'Brien feeding centre Josh Griffin, who crashed over in the corner.

And a notable victory was duly wrapped up by Justin Carney, who chased a kick to the corner by scrum-half Michael Dobson, outflanking Adam Milner, the hooker having been switched to the wing when the Tigers had to reshuffle following a hamstring injury sustained by fullback Luke Dorn.

It was Carney's second try of the game, cruel on Castleford as the winger was still a Castleford player, on loan for the season after an acrimonious off-field indiscretion. The bad feeling erupted after four minutes of the game when Carney and Nathan Massey were sin-binned after a fracas.

Cas stand-off Ben Roberts missed the game after picking up a foot injury in the defeat at St Helens, but signed a three-year contract extension until the end of the 2019 season.

Widnes Vikings had cemented their position at the top of Super League on the Thursday night by hammering Hull FC 46-6 at home. Kevin Brown was the man of the match as the Vikings scored 46 unanswered points, after Hull had taken an early 6-0 lead through a Frank Pritchard try, to consign their opponents to a third straight defeat. It was an amazing performance by Brown, who had been on a drip 24 hours before the game due to illness.

His halfback partner Joe Mellor was still in great form too, as was fullback Rhys Hanbury, with Stefan Marsh finishing with a hat-trick, as the Vikings put on a breathtaking attacking display.

It was a humiliation for big-spending Hull, whose coach Lee Radford and his staff were locked out of the team's dressing room as his players had a hard-hitting after-match talk.

The night after, Wigan made it five wins from five to stay level on points at the top, beating defending champions Leeds at home in a rematch of the previous year's Grand Final by 28-6. It was solid display from the Warriors, who lost stand-off George Williams in the warm-up, meaning a shift into the halves for captain Sean O'Loughlin.

Despite only leading 6-0 at half-time - the only try of the first 40 minutes was scored by John Bateman after he took full advantage of a long break from Dom Manfredi - Wigan were already looking comfortable and managed to shut out the Rhinos' limited attacking opportunities. Manfredi raced 80 metres and shrugged off a number of defenders before being hauled down by Zak Hardaker. Bateman was quickest to react and forced his way over from dummy-half.

After the break it was all Wigan and they managed to cross for four more tries with Oliver Gildart, Manfredi, the barnstorming Tony Clubb and Anthony Gelling all going over. However, the Rhinos were spared the embarrassment of being nilled for the first time since 1998 when Hardaker went over in the dying stages. Winger Ryan Hall suffered an ankle injury that kept him out for three months.

Warrington prop Mitchell Dodds suffered a broken leg on the Saturday evening in the Wolves' 30-20 victory over Catalans Dragons in Perpignan. The former Brisbane Broncos player suffered the season-ending injury in the 37th minute and underwent surgery in Perpignan on the Sunday morning on both his tibia and fibula. It was only his second game for the Wolves, having made his debut off the bench in the win at Salford the week before.

The Wolves' perfect start to the season continued thanks to a last-gasp double try salvo - from George King and Chris Sandow - in the final four minutes of a game in which they had never led until that point. Matty Russell really upped his game in the second half and was pivotal to Warrington securing the two points. His evasive running style created space for Rhys Evans' second try on the hour and the match-clinching score of King.

Saints winger Adam Swift sustained an ankle injury which sidelined him for two months, after only six minutes of the 44-4 home win over Wakefield on the Friday night. Wildcats prop Tinirau Arona was banned for two matches the following Tuesday for dangerous contact.

It wasn't vintage Saints but they methodically ground down Wakefield, who had caretaker coach Stuart Dickens in charge, with Brian Smith on his way back home to Australia. Kyle Amor led an outstanding pack performance against his former club, while Luke Walsh pulled the strings of some impressive midfield combinations and extended Super League's longest scoring streak to 18 games with six conversions from eight attempts.

Win-less Huddersfield Giants welcomed back Eorl Crabtree, Kyle Wood and Joe Wardle in Sunday's 38-6 home win against Hull KR, as well as handing a debut to on-loan-from-Wakefield Jordan Tansey, a result which lifted them off the bottom of the league.

Terry Campese was back in a Robins shirt after nine months out with a ruptured anterior cruciate ligament suffered against Castleford in June the previous year. He was brought on after 17 minutes but his comeback lasted just 42 minutes before he went off with a hamstring complaint.

Danny Brough was back to his best - he controlled the game all afternoon with a majestic performance beginning with the kick that led to Tansey's try after three minutes and ending with the kick that created a try for Ukuma Ta'ai just before the final whistle.

Round 6

Widnes Vikings became the first away team to win in Super League at the DW Stadium since June 2014 when they came back from an 8-0 half-time deficit to beat Wigan 18-12 in the Thursday TV game. Fullback Rhys Hanbury again caught the eye as Widnes retained their position at the top of Super League in style with their sixth win from the seven opening games.

As well as Hanbury, captain Kevin Brown, Joe Mellor and Aaron Heremaia provided a structured attack that yielded three second-half tries to Matt Whitley, Stefan Marsh and Charly Runciman, a penalty from Hanbury in the final ten minutes sealing the points for Widnes.

Wigan were missing three key members of their spine in Sam Tomkins at fullback, George Williams at stand-off and Michael McIlorum at hooker and only their doggedness helped them create that 8-0 half-time lead through an 80-metre interception from Liam Farrell and a Josh Charnley try against the run of play.

Centre Runciman's 62nd minute try off a searing Hanbury break was a beauty that signalled the Vikings would be continuing their lightning start to the season.

It had been St Helens that had last won at the DW Stadium - by 16-12 on June 27th 2014.

Neighbours Warrington were level again on points with Widnes 24 hours later after they hammered Castleford 56-12 at the Halliwell Jones Stadium to maintain their 100 per cent start. Scrum-half Chris Sandow was magnificent alongside fellow Australian Kurt Gidley in the halves, the addition of the pair giving the Wolves an edge they had lacked in 2015.

The contest was over by the break with the Wolves leading 38-0. Sandow, Ben Currie, on his 100th career appearance, and Tom Lineham all collected try-doubles.

In the Friday TV game, champions Leeds looked like they had steadied the ship with their second win of the season, a 30-18 success over St Helens at Headingley.

Leeds shot into a 16-0 lead by the tenth minute. But it was the Rhinos' second-half defence that saw them home, with 40 points scored in the opening 40 minutes, Leeds leading 22-18, and only eight after the break, all to the hosts through an Ash Handley try and two Liam Sutcliffe goals.

Even without Danny McGuire who, although recovered from the knee injury that had kept him out from round one, had his return delayed by a calf strain in training, Leeds looked far more structured than in previous games, much of that down to the first start and home debut of recognised hooker Beau Falloon. Carl Ablett was masterful, especially when scoring his try just before half-time when he shrugged off the clutches of Shannon McDonnell and Luke Walsh, which was a turning point, whilst Jamie Jones-Buchanan - on his 300th Super League appearance - made 41 tackles, topped only by James Roby.

Off the field St Helens had hit back at their former player Lance Hohaia, following an article in the New Zealand Herald newspaper. In it Hohaia accused the club of having treated him badly when he suffered repeated bouts of concussion during the season following the notorious incident in the 2014 Super League Grand Final, when Wigan's Ben Flower was dismissed and subsequently suspended for six months.

Hohaia, who now lived in the United States, suggested St Helens hadn't supported him as they should have. He was forced into early retirement in 2015 as he continued to have memory loss, headaches and blackouts, and St Helens granted him a release from his contract.

Hull KR coach James Webster admitted his side took some big steps forward in their 44-30 home win against Salford on the Sunday, his first home game in charge. Already down to their remaining 18 fit players, the Robins lost both James Greenwood and Graeme Horne in the course of the match.

Rovers withheld a strong second-half comeback from the Red Devils - who trailed

30-6 at the break - to hang on and finally score a victory at the seventh attempt this season. A key moment came when Niall Evalds made a stunning break after the Red Devils had fought back to 30-24. But he chose to pass infield rather than to the easier option of Greg Johnson on his left and the move broke down. The Robins made Salford pay as Ryan Shaw scored the crucial try shortly after.

Former Giants winger Jodie Broughton scored an 11-minute hat-trick on the same afternoon to help Catalans Dragons to successive away wins after Huddersfield's Joe Wardle was shown a red card in the 49th minute for a high tackle on Rémi Casty.

The Dragons led 24-20 at that stage, and continued with a dominant third quarter that effectively decided the game. During that period - which included all three of Broughton's tries - Catalans had six successive penalties and at one stage the home side didn't hold the ball for fully 12 minutes.

That effectively decided another madcap afternoon of Super League rugby, as 0-12 went to 20-12 to 20-40, the final score 46-26.

There was no appearance for Ryan Brierley, the halfback having penned a four-and-a-half year contract with the Giants after the club agreed a transfer fee with Leigh Centurions. Wardle was subsequently banned for two games, a blow for the Giants who remained just above Wakefield on the bottom of the table on points difference.

The Wildcats' new coach Chris Chester insisted the squad he inherited was more than capable of Super League survival in 2016, after watching Wakefield's 22-4 defeat at Hull FC on the Friday night. Chester also admitted he was relishing the challenge of working with John Kear, currently coaching Championship side Batley, who was set to join the club as Head of Rugby in 2017.

It was a key victory for the Airlie Birds, still missing Leon Pryce, Carlos Tuimavave filling in well at stand-off, after a run of three consecutive defeats, the last one a humiliation at Widnes eight days before. In a strong pack Mark Minichiello put in a professional performance and was rewarded with two tries.

Round 7

In the first game of the Easter weekend, Castleford ended their three-game losing run by beating Leeds 18-14 at home on the Thursday, with 2015 Albert Goldthorpe Medal winner Luke Gale having a hand in all three of their tries, two of them to centre Jake Webster.

With injuries keeping key men Luke Dorn and Ben Roberts out, Grant Millington, Paul McShane and Andy Lynch played superbly, while Webster was particularly outstanding.

Gale's second conversion after Andy Lynch and Webster tries put the Tigers 12-0 ahead after 13 minutes, but from there Leeds started to perform and by half-time they were ahead.

Joel Moon steadied the ship for Leeds following a superb move down the left involving a Brett Ferres kick and clever Ash Handley pass. Liam Sutcliffe converted from the touchline and on 24 minutes Carl Ablett brushed off a number tackles before passing to Kallum Watkins to dive in. Five minutes before the break Leeds hit the front. A lovely move involving Hardaker, Watkins and Josh Walters culminated in Tom Briscoe scoring a walk-in on his return to the team, leaving the score 12-14 at the interval.

The second half was an exciting affair despite a lack of tries. Both teams had their chances; Zak Hardaker produced a magnificent cover tackle on Denny Solomona, while at the other end Jy Hitchcox superbly hauled back Briscoe, pushing him into touch by the corner flag as he raced to the line.

Castleford won it with six minutes to go as Gale's cut-out pass made space for Webster, who stepped his way to the line to score.

The Archbishop of York, Dr John Sentamu, blessed Hull KR's KC Lightstream Stadium ahead of the Good Friday derby, as part of a six-month pilgrimage of prayer, witness and blessing across Yorkshire.

On the day, God smiled on the Black and Whites as they produced a remarkable comeback in the final 20 minutes to snatch victory from the jaws of defeat. Seemingly dead and buried at 20-0 down after almost an hour, Hull FC clicked into gear and registered 22 unanswered points in the closing stages to stun the Robins, who had looked to be home and dry after a solid display.

Rovers wing Ryan Shaw opened the scoring and Ken Sio's interception try and Josh Mantellato's two goals gave the hosts a 12-0 half-time lead. Hull KR looked to be heading for back-to-back wins under interim head coach James Webster when Iain Thornley's try was added to by Josh Mantellato's penalty goal to put them 20-0 up on 58 minutes.

But Jamie Shaul's long-range score, from a brilliant Kirk Yeaman offload, began a burst of four tries in the final quarter. After Danny Houghton capped a fine team move and Mahe Fonua burst over from close range straight from a tap penalty, Australian winger Steve Michaels side-stepped his way over on the right five minutes from time. Marc Sneyd's conversion provided the winning margin.

It was a seventh Easter loss in a row against Wigan for St Helens, who were left to rue an opening quarter in which, despite heavily dominating possession and territory, they didn't score a single point. A purple patch from Wigan yielded three tries in ten minutes at the end of the first quarter and, at 16-0 down at the break, Saints never recovered, eventually losing 24-12.

Wigan winger Dom Manfredi had an absolutely stunning game, scoring the first try on 21 minutes and then setting up position for the second as Sam Powell collected his own grubber to the posts. When Joel Tomkins charged through several tackles down the right, Wigan's win looked assured.

Catalans made it three wins from four away from home as they registered their first ever win at the AJ Bell Stadium with a 26-12 victory over Salford Red Devils. Never trailing, the Catalans made it three away wins in a row after victories at Wakefield and Huddersfield thanks to a brace of tries from former Australian international Dave Taylor. Todd Carney controlled a game that the Catalans would have potentially lost in previous years, after Greg Johnson's second-half brace brought the Red Devils back to 18-12.

Wakefield hooker Scott Moore made a return to the field after nearly four months out with a biceps injury suffered at Leeds on Boxing Day and helped the Wildcats to their second win of the season - a 36-22 victory over Huddersfield at Belle Vue.

Two late tries from Tom Johnstone and Nick Scruton secured the valuable points which enabled the Wildcats to jump off of the foot of the table by leapfrogging over the now-bottom Giants and Hull KR.

Huddersfield, who went ahead after nine minutes and came close to regaining their lead at one stage, were never convincing, with high-profile new recruit Ryan Brierley making an unexceptional debut.

The game was in the balance until Johnstone virtually sealed the victory on 72 minutes with a spectacular 90-metre breakaway try after collecting a loose ball deep in his own half and busting several tackles. There was a superb show from 18-year-old fullback Max Jowitt, whose non-stop effort in defence and imaginative free running in attack was rewarded with a fine try.

Warrington's perfect start continued and they went two points clear at the summit of Super League after seeing off in-form local rivals Widnes at home by 28-10.

The top-of-the-table clash drew a stadium record crowd of just over 15,000 and the weather to match the excitement. It was an absorbing clash that was in the balance until the final twelve minutes. Widnes didn't give an inch and neither did the Wolves, who managed to be more clinical with the ball in the second half to keep their winning streak going.

Widnes, without playmaker Kevin Brown, led 10-0 after 23 minutes following tries from deputy scrum-half Tom Gilmore and fullback Rhys Hanbury. But two tries in as many minutes from scrum-half Chris Sandow and winger Tom Lineham, helped by a Kurt Gidley penalty, made it 10-all at the break.

Gidley, a controlling influence, Ryan Atkins and Ben Currie all scored after the break. Gidley landed all three second-half conversions to complete a 12-point individual haul

Round 8

Hull FC lowered the colours of Warrington Wolves for the first time this season in an Easter Monday thriller at the KC Stadium. And it took a late try by Curtis Naughton just five minutes from time to secure a dramatic 26-24 win, which was Hull's third in a row.

In a match that was tightly fought throughout, both sides scored five tries, but Hull halfback Marc Sneyd kicked three conversions, while Warrington's Chris Sandow and Stefan Ratchford could only manage one each.

At half-time, however, that didn't look as though it would matter, as Warrington held a 20-10 lead after first-half tries from Ryan Atkins, Tom Lineham, Kevin Penny and Sandow, with Hull having registered tries from Sneyd and Jamie Shaul.

But Hull started the second half well and Naughton scored his first after a break by Danny Washbrook, with Sneyd's conversion reducing Warrington's lead to four points. And when Shaul put through a smart kick for Kirk Yeaman to score, Sneyd's goal gave Hull a two-point lead with 20 minutes remaining.

Rhys Evans sent Lineham over for his second, before Naughton clinched the winning score to the acclaim of the Hull supporters.

Catalans made it two wins out of two over Easter with a convincing 41-22 victory over Castleford Tigers at the Stade Gilbert Brutus, with Todd Carney playing a key role in their success.

Two younger players also caught the eye, with Morgan Escaré getting his first run of the year for the Dragons and Greg Minikin making his first start for the Tigers. Escaré and Minikin both scored two tries and they made more ground than any other players on the pitch, with Minikin registering 197 metres and Escaré clocking up 164 metres in what was a very satisfying return to the team for his fans in the five-figure crowd.

Salford sneaked home 26-24 in an encounter at Huddersfield that was nip and tuck all the way, the lead changing hands six times. Ryan Brierley made his home debut for the Giants in the unaccustomed position of fullback and he acquitted himself well, with Kyle Wood moving to halfback to partner Danny Brough.

In a match that featured several tries that could have qualified for a highlights reel, the pick of the bunch was Salford's first of the second half, when Mason Caton-Brown raced clear down the right and gave a smart pass inside to Josh Griffin to touch down.

With the game going into its third quarter the Giants led 24-18, but the Red Devils shocked their hosts with two tries in as many minutes from Justin Carney and Niall Evalds, and they held on over the last nine minutes.

Trouble erupted at the end of the game at the away fans' end. A supporter threw a flare onto the pitch and two Salford fans leapt over the barrier, before being escorted back off the pitch by stewards. Some other Red Devils fans rushed from the back to the front of the stand, near to where some of the wives and children of Salford players and coaching staff were sitting, with several Salford players jumping over the barrier into the stand to try to protect their families.

Wakefield earned their first victory at Headingley since 2007, by 20-16, with a late try by Craig Hall, who ran almost the length of the field down the right after former Rhinos player Ben Jones-Bishop dislodged the ball from Leeds winger Ash Handley's grasp in a heavy tackle.

Each side scored one try in the first half, with Matty Ashurst scoring for Wakefield before Joel Moon went over for the Rhinos. Liam Finn kicked a penalty goal to give the

Wildcats a two-point lead at the break.

When Tom Johnstone offloaded for Jacob Miller to race clear and score a stylish touchdown they had established an eight-point lead. But Tom Briscoe touched down for the Rhinos, and they were able to take advantage of the sin-binning of Scott Moore as Mitch Achurch got over the line and Liam Sutcliffe converted to put the Rhinos ahead for the first time.

Wakefield got back on level terms when Finn added another penalty and, after Moore returned, Hall pounced on Handley's dropped ball to secure the points.

St Helens shook off their Good Friday horror-show against Wigan by winning 20-12 at high-flying Widnes Vikings in a performance that smacked of a traditional Easter Monday hangover.

Saints had the touches of quality throughout, with victory secured thanks to an impressive first-half showing, Luke Walsh showing glimpses of his very best.

Walsh's halfback partner Theo Fages set up the first score, putting Joe Greenwood over. Walsh converted to make it 6-0, and, although Widnes responded with a Rhys Hanbury try seven minutes later, Saints doubled their lead following a barnstorming run and touchdown from Louie McCarthy-Scarsbrook.

Patrick Ah Van's error allowed Saints more field position, his hesitation allowing Tommy Makinson to touch down for try number three.

Walsh missed the conversion, but at 6-16 Saints were comfortable in a game with little energy. He would kick two more penalties in the second half, and although Hanbury got his second late on, it was nothing more than a consolation.

Saints were hit by an injury to Makinson that refuelled the argument surrounding the safety on Widnes Vikings' i-Pitch. The winger's year was ended after he ruptured his anterior cruciate ligament.

Josh Charnley scored a second-half hat-trick as Wigan made it a perfect Easter, although they had to fight back from an unexpected 4-10 half-time deficit to win 30-16 at home against an Hull KR side giving debuts to three young players.

The Warriors had taken an early lead with a try from Lewis Tierney, but they were shocked by two tries in the final three minutes of the first half from Graeme Horne and former Wigan centre Iain Thornley, with Kieran Dixon converting the first.

Two early second-half tries for Charnley put the Warriors back in control, but Thornley added another try on 51 minutes to put the Robins back in the lead and with the prospect of an unlikely victory.

Wigan had to wait until the final 15 minutes, with quick-fire tries from Dom Manfredi and Oliver Gildart, to confirm their victory, with Charnley completing his hat-trick to make it seven wins from eight in 2016.

FIRST UTILITY SUPER LEAGUE
Monday 28th March

	P	W	D	L	F	A	D	Pts
Warrington Wolves	8	7	0	1	253	132	121	14
Wigan Warriors	8	7	0	1	170	112	58	14
Widnes Vikings	9	6	0	3	252	156	96	12
Catalans Dragons	8	5	0	3	223	196	27	10
Hull FC	8	5	0	3	205	181	24	10
St Helens	8	5	0	3	193	174	19	10
Salford Red Devils	9	4	0	5	238	233	5	8
Castleford Tigers	8	3	1	4	177	217	-40	7
Wakefield Trinity Wildcats	9	3	0	6	144	256	-112	6
Leeds Rhinos	8	2	0	6	136	200	-64	4
Hull Kingston Rovers	9	1	1	7	160	249	-89	3
Huddersfield Giants	8	1	0	7	173	218	-45	2

APRIL
Wildcats go wild

Round 9

On the Friday night after they lost their first points of the season at Hull FC, Warrington managed to withstand a second-half fightback from Wigan at the DW Stadium to extend their lead at the top of the Super League to two points. A blistering seven-minute spell in the first half saw the Wolves take a stranglehold on the game with three unanswered tries and they went on to record a 28-16 win.

Chris Sandow had a hand in three of Warrington's tries as he ran the show. First he offloaded for Ben Currie to open the scoring before floating out a long ball for Tom Lineham to score after Liam Farrell had been sin-binned. The Australian then produced a measured kick to the corner for Kevin Penny to grab their third try of the night.

Sandow's involvement did not last much longer, however, as he was replaced just as Stefan Ratchford extended their lead to 14-0 with a penalty after he had picked up a hamstring injury that sidelined him until early June.

Wigan did manage to get a try back before the break through Dom Manfredi, but they were second best for the majority of the opening 40 minutes and it showed, as an eight-point try - Farrell lunging with his knees as Ratchford scored the Wolves' third try, for which he later got a one-match ban - saw the Wolves go in 22-4 up at the break.

The Warriors did show plenty of spirit after the break, though Ryan Atkins try on 43 minutes extended the lead to 26-4, outscoring Warrington two tries - both to Manfredi - to one in the second half, but it was never going to be enough.

Wigan had announced in the week that Dan Sarginson would be joining the NRL's Gold Coast Titans at the end of the season while Josh Charnley would play rugby union for Sale Sharks.

Wolves coach Tony Smith insisted that his players' welfare was at the forefront of his mind rather than the result after three games in eight days. Warrington not only lost Sandow but a shoulder injury saw Rhys Evans leave the action in the first half.

On the same Friday night Leeds Rhinos suffered a 30-10 home defeat to Hull Kingston Rovers, who they had defeated 50-0 at Wembley in the 2015 Challenge Cup Final.

That August afternoon, Kieran Dixon had a torrid 80 minutes. It was fitting, then, that he should score a 70-metre try at the start of the second half that ensured the Robins would retain the upper hand.

A second successive home defeat for Leeds to a side who in 2015 finished in the bottom four, was in danger of putting the defending champions out of the running to retain their trophy even before the campaign reached its half-way stage.

Rovers backed up one of Easter's most heroic displays in a narrow defeat at Wigan four days earlier with another cohesive performance. Two tries in the first half went to former Headingley favourite Shaun Lunt, who was called into action off the bench early and changed the game, though Terry Campese's first start in over 300 days lasted barely a quarter of an hour as he suffered a recurrence of his hamstring injury, which bought Lunt into the action.

Castleford Tigers coach Daryl Powell heaped praise on hat-trick hero Jy Hitchcox following Sunday's 38-34 home win against Huddersfield.

After a nip-and-tuck first hour the Giants led 30-22 following a Sam Rapira try but Australian Hitchcox scored twice, sandwiched by a Jake Webster try, to see the Tigers lead 38-30 before Jermaine McGillvary completed the scoring with his hat-trick try.

Giants coach Paul Anderson admitted his side was in a battle to avoid the bottom four in 2016 after their eighth loss in nine games left them rooted to the bottom of the table.

Catalans recorded their third win in nine days as early pacesetters Widnes fell to a third successive defeat in Perpignan by 21-8. It was tougher than expected for the Dragons, whose preparations were disrupted two hours before kick-off when Louis Anderson left the stadium to cross the road to the hospital to be at his wife's bedside to welcome the arrival of their sixth child. Depleted Widnes gave debuts off the bench to Sam Brooks and Jordan Johnstone.

Pat Richards scored the only points of the first half, crossing after two minutes but missing the conversion. Rhys Hanbury missed a penalty to leave Catalans 4-0 ahead at the break, before Vincent Duport widened the gap. Corey Thompson and Hanbury drew Widnes level, but tries from Dave Taylor, quickly becoming a cult hero in Perpignan and having a hand in three of the Catalans' four tries, and Eloi Pelissier and a Thomas Bosc field goal sank Widnes late on.

Chris Chester's honeymoon at Belle Vue continued on the Saturday afternoon as Wakefield recorded their third straight win with a gritty 32-18 triumph over Salford.

Tom Johnstone claimed a hat-trick to take his tally to six tries this season. Johnstone's first came at the end of a half in which Trinity had given up a 12-0 lead - the Red Devils coming back through Gareth O'Brien and Matt Sarsfield tries, and stopped Salford going in level at the break.

Johnstone scored again before the visitors reduced the arrears through Justin Carney, who shortly after was withdrawn with an ankle injury. With Salford enjoying back-to-back penalties and momentum, they looked likely to snatch the lead, but some desperate Wakefield defending kept them at bay.

Junior Sa'u looked certain to score on 73 minutes but a cover tackle from Ben Jones-Bishop drove him into touch. The Wildcats then turned defence into attack, as Reece Lyne burst through and dummied past some weak tackles to finally put the Red Devils to the sword. The crowd cheered and, with three minutes left, Johnstone stepped inside to add his third and Wakefield's final try.

Wakefield were a form side going into April, as were Hull FC and they moved into joint third in the table after Marc Sneyd's 76th-minute field goal gave them a 17-16 win at St Helens, a fourth straight Super League win.

Saints led 16-10 at half-time through Joe Greenwood, Matty Dawson and Jordan Turner tries, but failed to score after the break and the visitors capitalised.

Danny Houghton and Curtis Naughton crossed for Hull before the break and they levelled through Kirk Yeaman after 58 minutes. And Sneyd's 40-metre kick inflicted a second straight home defeat on Saints.

Round 10

Wakefield moved to the cusp of the top eight after one of the most amazing blow outs in Super League history, a 62-nil home victory over Wigan.

With long-term injury victim Sam Tomkins still to make his second Warriors debut, captain Sean O'Loughlin and John Bateman injured and Liam Farrell suspended as part of ten front-line absentees, Wigan lacked leadership. Two youngsters made their Wigan bows - Joe Bretherton and Jack Wells, both from the bench - but no-one expected this scoreline.

April

It was an exceptional Wakefield performance, the first 40 minutes in particular some of the finest rugby the Belle Vue faithful had seen in years. It was 22-0 at the break after four home tries - and they had three tries ruled out - the last one the try of the game - and a contender for the try of the season. With Wakefield penned inside their own half, Scott Moore's diagonal grubber seemed a gamble, but Tom Johnstone collected out wide, raced away and swatted off Lewis Tierney before offloading to Joe Arundel. From there, Arundel only needed one man to support him and that man was Jacob Miller, who collected and raced home from halfway to bring Belle Vue to its feet.

Miller finished with a try hat-trick and three Albert Goldthorpe points as the Wildcats registered their fourth straight win under new coach Chris Chester. After their heaviest loss in the league since the 70-0 thumping at Leeds in 2005, Warriors coach Shaun Wane insisted he wasn't stressed one little bit.

St Helens had done neighbours Wigan a favour by preventing Warrington going four points clear at the top of the table with a 25-22 win at the Halliwell Jones Stadium, although the Wolves still led Super League after eight victories in ten outings.

It was a thrilling nine-try contest which ebbed and flowed in front of the Friday night TV cameras right until the last minute. Warrington weren't as creative without halfback Chris Sandow, whose hamstring injury against Wigan was to keep him sidelined for almost two months. Saints, who had lost three of their last four games, were shorn of several stars with Joe Greenwood and Dominique Peyroux the latest casualties to be added to Atelea Vea, Travis Burns, Adam Swift, Mark Percival and Lama Tasi. Tommy Makinson was also missing with a season-ending injury suffered on Easter Monday. Coach Keiron Cunningham called up youngsters Jack Ashworth and Jake Spedding, with winger Spedding making his debut.

Theo Fages was the gamestar, involved in everything Saints did well and with a superb kicking game to match. Youngster Morgan Knowles' converted try on 70 minutes put Saints 24-14 up and Luke Walsh's field goal minutes later looked to have ended the contest. But Warrington mounted a late rally.

A line break up the middle of the field from young Frenchman Benjamin Jullien was farmed out to the left for Ben Currie, who sent in Kevin Penny from 20 metres out for his second try. Kurt Gidley missed the kick and it was now 25-18 and Walsh's field goal was looking very pertinent as Warrington toiled in the rain as the clock ticked down.

But there was anxiety for Saints on 78 minutes when Stefan Ratchford floated a kick out to the right which was gobbled up by Tom Lineham who touched down in the corner. Warrington turned down the conversion attempt, but Saints held on for a well deserved win, despite scoring four tries to the Wolves' five.

Both Hull FC and Catalans finished the weekend in joint second with Wigan, two points behind Warrington. The Dragons hammered Hull KR 40-0 in the Thursday TV game at the KC Lightstream Stadium, their fifth successive win in the league. They were almost faultless in a first half that saw them lead 28-0 and although their standards dropped a little after the break, they still had far too much for a tired Hull KR.

Their forwards bullied their opponents for much of the game, and out wide the likes of Tony Gigot and Jodie Broughton had a field day. Richie Myler led his side superbly and produced a masterful kicking display throughout, including a 40/20 in the first set of the game.

Hull FC produced an impressive second-half display the night after at the KCOM Stadium to make it five successive wins, leaving Huddersfield Giants rooted to the foot of the table, recording a 37-20 victory.

With the game in the balance at half-time, Hull scored three unanswered tries after the break, inspired by an in-form Marc Sneyd. The 55th-minute sin-binning of Danny Brough for dissent after a dubious-looking try from Danny Houghton, proved crucial. Jamie Shaul got his second try, and Curtis Naughton also crossed before Brough's return with the score at 36-16.

The game marked milestones of 350 club appearances for Kirk Yeaman and 100 for Liam Watts, and the home faithful were once again treated to Hull's huge forward pack laying the platform for victory

Castleford overturned an 18-point deficit to win 34-24 at a blustery Select Security Stadium and in the process condemn Widnes to a fourth consecutive defeat, despite the return of captain Kevin Brown.

It was a remarkable comeback after an opening quarter in which the Tigers could barely put a foot right but, inspired by the brilliant Luke Gale and the potent left-wing pairing of Jake Webster and Danny Solomona, who finished with a try hat-trick, they dominated most of the last hour, making light of a growing injury list.

Salford remained in the top eight over the weekend after a first home victory against Leeds since 1993, winning 14-10 at a wet AJ Bell Stadium.

The Red Devils ground the Rhinos down, taking a slender 8-0 lead into half-time with a converted Logan Tomkins try and a penalty from Michael Dobson, before edging ahead with a converted try by Robert Lui in the second half. Leeds staged a late rally and almost stole a win through Keith Galloway and Ashton Golding tries, but that would have been unfair on Salford.

The Red Devils' league position was still in doubt with the hearing into their alleged salary cap breaches set to take place on April 25th.

Challenge Cup Round 5

Oldham, promoted from League One at the end of 2015, secured the shock result of the season so far when they travelled to the previous year's Challenge Cup finalists Hull Kingston Rovers on the Saturday and gained a 36-22 victory. Chairman Chris Hamilton said that it was the best day in the history of the Oldham club since it was re-formed from the ashes of the defunct Oldham Bears 19 years before.

Rovers chairman Neil Hudgell promised to 'smoke out the dishonest people at the club' in a tweet following the defeat.

The re-structured Challenge Cup once again saw the previous season's bottom four Super League clubs enter the fray and the other three progressed.

The Vikings thumped Rochdale Hornets at Spotland 62-6 in a largely one-sided encounter; Salford won at League One Hunslet 50-14 and Wakefield knocked out Sheffield at Belle Vue by 44-10. The last remaining amateur club, Castleford Lock Lane exited the competition after an 80-4 defeat at Halifax.

One result of note was Toulouse's 10-8 win over Championship leaders Leigh at Stade Ernest Argelès, the 35-metre match-winning penalty from Toulouse fullback Mark Kheirallah coming 11 minutes from the end.

Round 11

Warrington were brought back to the chasing pack as Huddersfield breathed life into their ailing 2016 Super League campaign with a deserved 11-0 victory at a wet John Smith's Stadium.

The Giants recorded their first win since their only two points of the season over Hull KR in round five with a gritty and disciplined performance, one powered by a brilliant kicking display from Danny Brough and some determined defence. They took a 4-0 lead into half-time - through an Aaron Murphy try on 35 minutes - and held on, adding a second try through Leroy Cudjoe late in the game.

It was the Wolves' third loss in four games, though they remained on top of the Super League table on equal points with the Catalans and Wigan.

Warriors coach Shaun Wane praised his side's character and toughness following a difficult week because of illness and injury as they bounced back from successive losses to defeat Castleford Tigers at home by 26-12 on the Friday night.

The Warriors had seen a sickness bug run through the squad and the Wigan coach admitted again that some players were backing up from the previous Sunday still suffering from illness. John Bateman was one of the worst affected and was apparently sick at half-time, but he managed to recover and was rewarded with two tries as the Warriors ran out winners despite trailing 12-8 until the hour mark and Bateman's first try. Nick Gregson's first try for the club in the 70th minute started to take the game away from the Tigers.

Castleford refused to lie down and fought hard until the final whistle. But Wigan deserved the victory in the end and they made the scoreline more flattering with Bateman touching down in the dying seconds as he chased his own kick to the line.

Leeds picked up their first victory in five matches on the Friday as they defeated Hull FC 20-18, a victory that moved them up to tenth in Super League. Jamie Jones-Buchanan twisted out of Curtis Naughton's tackle on a last-tackle power play close to the Hull line to give Leeds a two-score advantage going into the closing minutes, a cushion they needed as Danny Houghton's converted try made for a nervous last three minutes.

Keiron Cunningham described his side's performance against Catalans Dragons on the Thursday as one that looked like an 'under-16s side', Saints going down 30-12, their third defeat in a row at Langtree Park.

It was another fine win on the road for the Dragons, making it five successive away wins for Laurent Frayssinous' improving team and six in total, placing them firmly among Super League's front runners.

The Dragons were brimming with confidence and scored some more fine tries with crisp backline moves, with Jodie Broughton the main beneficiary with four, which included him passing his 100-career tries milestone.

Round 12

Hull Kingston Rovers went some way to laying to rest the memory of the previous week's defeat at the hands of Oldham with a stunning Sunday afternoon 58-16 win at Castleford.

Scrum-half Albert Kelly was the star of the show as Rovers built on a 20-16 interval lead, the side as a whole responding emphatically to chairman Neil Hudgell's call after the cup defeat for more honesty. Centre Thomas Minns closed with a hat-trick in an 11-try mauling. Minns' try a minute into the second half gave Rovers, with Ben Cockayne's touchline conversion, a 10-point cushion and seemed to knock the wind out of Castleford's sails.

St Helens coach Keiron Cunningham revealed that Jonny Lomax's dream return moved him to tears during his side's thrilling 38-34 home win over Leeds Rhinos on the Friday.

The fullback had not played first team for over a year after a knee reconstruction - already the second one of his career. But he showed little sign of that in scoring two well-taken first-half tries. There were brilliant individual performances, in particular from Rob Burrow and Theo Fages.

And there were brutal hits, with Kyle Amor's on Zak Hardaker likely to live long in the memory. Amor touched down after hitting Hardaker with a huge hit as he tried to clear his line, which was described by Leeds coach Brian McDermott as 'a fantastic Rugby League tackle.' Hardaker, whose head was already bandaged and was wearing a headguard following a deep first-half cut, received lengthy treatment before regaining his feet to retire to the sidelines.

In a game that swung one way and then the other, Liam Sutcliffe's high bomb to the corner in the 72nd minute was taken by Ash Handley. He passed to Jimmy Keinhorst, who touched down for his second.

But the Rhinos just couldn't find a winner in the desperate closing stages, with the last throw of the dice coming when Ash Golding passed to Kallum Watkins, but he was pushed into touch by Fages, before Percival caught a final Rhinos kick to complete a thrilling match.

Hull FC captain Gareth Ellis led his team to a 46-28 victory at Wakefield on the Sunday, after signing a one-year extension to his contract to the end of the 2017 season. Jamie Shaul and Leon Pryce also returned to the Hull side and both played a telling role as the Black and Whites made it six wins from seven.

Fetuli Talanoa was the major beneficiary with four tries, in a game Hull led 24-6 after 24 minutes, only to see the Wildcats draw level by half-time, thanks to an Ashley Gibson hat-trick, and then lead 28-24 as captain Danny Kirmond scored a fine try five minutes into the second half.

But Hull looked good after that and Talanoa's fourth try six minutes from time killed off Wakefield, suffering a first defeat under coach Chris Chester.

Hull remained fourth as the top three sides all recorded victories.

Warrington came back with a bang at Widnes, as they put on arguably their best attacking display of the season in a 48-16 win, halfbacks Stefan Ratchford and Kurt Gidley running the show. Joe Westerman's second try just before half-time gave Warrington a 30-6 lead, and Widnes never looked capable of pulling that back.

Kevin Brown and centre Chris Bridge both limped off during the Vikings' fifth consecutive loss, with Brown being pictured leaving the stadium on crutches after sustaining a blow near the end of the defeat. The pair missed a month of action.

John Bateman captained Wigan on the same Friday night in the absence of senior figures Sean O'Loughlin, Michael McIlorum and the Tomkins brothers. And he played a key role in the 26-19 home win over Huddersfield.

Ryan Brierley's first three tries in Super League for the Giants counted for nothing as Wigan once again showed their fighting spirit to come from behind. The result was in doubt right until the final hooter, with three field goals being knocked over in the final ten minutes, until a late score from Dan Sarginson settled matters. Giants prop Craig Huby faced ten weeks out after tearing a pectoral muscle.

And on the Saturday in Perpignan, Catalans came from behind to register their seventh win in a row, although the 42-32 success over Salford was closer than the scoreline suggested, with the Dragons scoring eight points in the closing five minutes of the game, Pat Richards' try and Thomas Bosc's goal being followed by a Richards penalty.

Junior Sa'u scored a hat-trick for the Red Devils and Niall Evalds a brace in Salford's six tries, but they proved to be in vain as the Catalans scored seven tries of their own in a bitterly contested match in which tempers flared.

* That week the Rugby Football League confirmed that a side from Canada, Toronto Wolfpack, would be granted entry into League One from next season.

Round 13

On the 25th April, Salford were found guilty of breaching the Super League salary cap in 2014 and 2015 and docked six league points, sinking them into the competition's bottom four. Owner Marwan Koukash confirmed that an appeal would be lodged. 'I'm really shocked and very disappointed,' said Koukash. 'We did not breach the salary cap and are still penalised. It's their court, their rules and we can't argue against that.'

The following Saturday afternoon, the Red Devils midfield trio of Gareth O'Brien,

April

Robert Lui and Michael Dobson pulled all the right strings as the Red Devils ended a difficult week with a 44-26 home win over Hull KR. Such were the trio's performances, that hat-trick centre Junior Sa'u missed out on any Albert Goldthorpe points, despite finishing off their midfield work smartly.

Rovers paid the full price for two key spells - falling 16-0 behind early on and then conceding twice just before half-time. But the likes of Shaun Lunt, Maurice Blair and youngster Joe Wardill caught the eye at different stages in a spirited showing.

Salford's win had them level on six league points with Huddersfield and Leeds after the Giants climbed off the foot of the table with a 28-20 home win over the Rhinos on the Friday night.

The Giants were forced to come from behind three times before sealing only their third win of the season with two tries in the last seven minutes, to Jake Connor and Eorl Crabtree, of a see-saw encounter against the youthful but tenacious Rhinos.

Danny Brough tortured Leeds fullback Ashton Golding with towering bombs amid a commanding display. And Gene Ormsby scored a try in his last game on loan before returning to Warrington, while Leeds handed a debut to 17-year old Cameron Smith, the younger brother of sidelined Huddersfield forward Daniel, and Luke Briscoe started his first game in Rhinos colours for two years.

The Giants' first win in six games against the Rhinos might have been more comfortable but for some hugely committed goal-line defence from the visitors and a couple of questionable decisions from the officials. Coach Paul Anderson's body language implied that he too was occasionally perplexed but, having been fined for comments the previous week for criticising the referee after the defeat at Wigan, he remained tight lipped.

Wakefield drew level with Widnes on twelve points from thirteen games with an 18-16 win at the Select Security Stadium on the same Friday night. Chris Chester, the Wakefield coach, labelled it 'a crazy game', with Widnes counterpart Denis Betts describing the performance of match referee Joe Cobb as 'the worst refereeing performance I've seen in 30 years'. Betts was convinced Cobb had wrongly disallowed a late try that would have ended the contest. Instead the result was settled in the last minute by a try from one-time Vikings loanee Craig Hall.

It was six Super League losses on the bounce for Widnes as they had three players sin-binned and one dismissed. Dummy-halves Aaron Heremaia and Scott Moore were both sent off for fighting following a fracas caused by Moore's high tackle on Patrick Ah Van on 20 minutes. Ah Van had just come back on the field after spending ten minutes in the sin bin for a spear tackle on Ashley Gibson.

The fall out continued for weeks. Ah Van was suspended for five games; Gibson was out for at least three months with a dislocated shoulder; Stefan Marsh got two games for tripping, Heremaia NFA, both on Early Guilty Pleas. Moore faced four charges. He got no further action on an EGP for 'contrary behaviour' for his reaction to Ah Van's tackle on Gibson; NFA was ruled for his part in the later fight but he got a two-match ban for the high tackle on Ah Van. And then two weeks later he was found guilty of gouging Heremaia in the fight and was banned for a further four games.

Keiron Cunningham praised St Helens' spirit as they picked up their second win in a row. Saints produced a late fightback to win at Castleford 30-20, after trailing 20-12 as the game entered the final quarter. Then tries for Kyle Amor, Joe Greenwood, his second, and Jonny Lomax secured two points that kept them in touch with the top four.

The Tigers were suffering injury-wise. With recent signings Larne Patrick and Danny Tickle both unavailable, Daryl Powell's resources were so stretched that he was forced to hand a debut to Academy forward Conor Fitzsimons, the 17-year-old eventually making his debut from the bench during the closing stages. And Cas suffered another blow during the warm-up when centre Jake Webster pulled out, meaning Denny Solomona went from fullback to the wing, Joel Monaghan moved to centre and prop Grant Millington went to stand-off.

At the KCOM Stadium, Hull FC held off a Catalans Dragons side that had recently been unbeatable by 28-26, in a pulsating and entertaining encounter that could have gone either way right until the end. The Airlie Birds were never behind, but were made to defend desperately late on to survive numerous attacks from the dangerous Dragons, proving their ability to grind out tight games.

A disastrous 60 seconds for Catalans in the 56th minute was crucial. Remi Casty was sin-binned for repeat team offending and then the Dragons conceded a try to Scott Taylor, which gave them a mountain to climb in the final quarter.

Thomas Bosc made his 200th Super League appearance for the Catalans as Danny Houghton proved himself the key man for Hull from dummy-half.

League leaders Warrington recorded a 40-10 home victory over a patched up Wigan on the Thursday. For the first 28 minutes there was no real indication that the margin would be so great. Wigan had created a superb try for Josh Charnley after 18 minutes, six minutes after Warrington winger Tom Lineham had left the field concussed from a tackle by Wigan's Tony Clubb.

Charnley's try came from a beautifully worked move coming soon after Daryl Clark had conceded a penalty, with Dan Sarginson giving the final pass.

Warrington drew level through Clark shortly after Taulima Tautai conceded the first of three penalties, this one for a high tackle on Ashton Sims. Clark, coming into real form, sold a dummy to Greg Burke and fended Sarginson before touching down.

Kurt Gidley kicked the goal to give them the lead, and when Tautai committed his second high tackle, this time on Kevin Penny, the Wolves had the green light to score their second try, with Ben Westwood, newly arrived off the bench, bursting past four tacklers to touch down.

Tautai's mistake again was the precursor to Warrington's third try, when he was pulled up for a forward pass. Matty Russell made a great break downfield and Penny scored from a Gidley bomb, catching the ball superbly in the face of Charnley to make it 18-4.

In the second half the competitive nature of the contest faded as the Wolves asserted themselves and gradually pulled away.

FIRST UTILITY SUPER LEAGUE
Sunday 1st May

	P	W	D	L	F	A	D	Pts
Warrington Wolves	13	10	0	3	391	210	181	20
Catalans Dragons	13	9	0	4	382	276	106	18
Hull FC	13	9	0	4	351	291	60	18
Wigan Warriors	13	9	0	4	248	273	-25	18
St Helens	13	8	0	5	314	297	17	16
Widnes Vikings	13	6	0	7	316	277	39	12
Wakefield Trinity Wildcats	13	6	0	7	284	336	-52	12
Castleford Tigers	13	5	1	7	297	389	-92	11
Hull Kingston Rovers	13	3	1	9	274	359	-85	7
Salford Red Devils *	13	6	0	7	346	343	3	6
Huddersfield Giants	13	3	0	10	285	339	-54	6
Leeds Rhinos	13	3	0	10	230	328	-98	6

* Six points deducted for salary cap breaches in 2014 & 2015

* Super League general manager Blake Solly announced he was to leave his position in May to take over as chief executive of South Sydney Rabbitohs.

MAY
Black and White all over

Challenge Cup Round 6

Challenge Cup holders Leeds Rhinos made their exit from this year's competition when they were beaten at Huddersfield by 36-22 in a battle of Super League's bottom two clubs.

Nineteen-year-old Jordan Lilley gave the Rhinos an early advantage when his deceptive dummy pierced the Giants' defence on the halfway line before the exciting halfback offloaded to Brett Ferres, who passed for Jimmy Keinhorst to cross.

But once the Giants scored through Ukuma Ta'ai after 13 minutes, when he charged onto a Danny Brough inside pass and bulldozed his way over Josh Walters, the Giants, with Kyle Wood buzzing, were always in control. The manner of the next two tries was frustrating from a Leeds perspective, with Huddersfield going the full 100 metres for both scores. Leroy Cudjoe made 40 easy yards from a free play, which eventually culminated in Jermaine McGillvary superbly finishing a try from 15 metres out.

And it was McGillvary who created the next. With the line beckoning, former Giant Ferres lost possession of the ball. But despite suspicions of an illegal ball steal, the Giants were given the free play and McGillvary offloaded to Ryan Brierley, who finished with style as he raced 80 metres to score.

Ferres was sin-binned for his troubles after protesting Ben Thaler's decision to not give a penalty and, with Leeds down to twelve men, a scruffy Jake Connor field goal just before half-time gave Huddersfield a defining 19-6 lead at the break.

Huddersfield had tabled a bid to bring Gene Ormsby to the John Smith's Stadium on a permanent basis, after the Warrington winger had completed a month on loan with the Giants. But the Wolves turned down the offer and played Ormsby in the 70-10 Saturday Challenge Cup win at Oldham, playing this year in Stalybridge, in which he scored two tries.

Warrington were joint favourites at 5/2 against to win the Cup, along with Wigan, who the night before had won 54-4 at Dewsbury, with a brace of tries apiece for Josh Charnley, John Bateman and Oliver Gildart.

Hull FC ruthlessly dumped St Helens out at Langtree Park in the Sunday afternoon TV game with a 47-18 victory in their best performance of the season.

The were without two of their overseas stars, Frank Pritchard and Sika Manu, after the club had agreed to release both players for international duty to captain their respective countries, Samoa and Tonga, at Parramatta's Pirtek Stadium.

Hull were too powerful, too skilful and ultimately too good for their opponents on the warmest day so far of a cool spring. After Leon Pryce rolled back the years with a majestic sidestep to put Danny Houghton, who produced another stellar performance, over on 11 minutes, two more FC tries put them into a commanding lead.

The first came when Houghton turned provider as his pass set Scott Taylor off on a charging run to the line, before Marc Sneyd's delicate pass close to the line allowed FC captain Gareth Ellis to cross with relative ease.

Sneyd converted all three tries to put Hull 18-6 up, and Louie McCarthy-

Scarsbrook's try on 33 minutes was only temporary respite for the hosts. Hull's attacking prowess came to the fore again when fullback Jamie Shaul was able to exploit a quick play-the-ball from Mark Minichiello to dive in next to the posts. There was still time for Sneyd to tag on a field goal right on the half-time hooter and, at 25-12, Hull had nailed the game.

The last Hull try of a one-sided second half saw winger Fetuli Talanoa defy the laws of gravity to produce an incredible finish in the corner.

The Saturday TV game saw patched-up Castleford show spirit and skill to knock Salford out at the Mend-a-Hose Jungle by 32-18. The Tigers' squad had already been stretched in recent weeks and they suffered two major pre-match blows when Luke Gale and Luke Dorn pulled out in the build-up. Powell named hooker Paul McShane and prop Grant Millington as his starting halfback combination.

McShane in particular flourished in the role, scoring one try and creating two others as well as supplying an impressive kicking game throughout.

Dorn's withdrawal meant Danny Tickle made his debut for the Tigers. Tickle had not played since the previous September when he played for Widnes in the Qualifiers, before suffering a serious head injury in an off-field incident that seemed to have halted his career.

Salford winger Daniel Vidot finally made his Red Devils debut after missing the opening three months of the season following shoulder surgery.

Catalans cruised into the quarter-finals with a 40-4 televised defeat of Championship side Batley at the Fox's Biscuits Stadium on the Friday, with Vincent Duport in particular far too strong for the part-timers. Dave Taylor and Jason Baitieri each got a one-game ban on Early Guilty Pleas for dangerous throws.

Halifax took Widnes all the way at the Shay and were right in the mix until Jay Chapelhow's 74th-minute try ended the Sunday afternoon contest at 28-18.

And Wakefield were the other team in the hat after a hard-fought 40-22 win over impressive League 1 side Toulouse Olympique at Belle Vue. Tom Johnstone starred in the West Yorkshire heat as he scored four tries in another outstanding display.

The draw for the sixth round of the Ladbrokes Challenge Cup had been made in April live on BBC Radio 4's flagship news and current affairs programme Today and broadcast to three million listeners.

Round 14

Sam Tomkins finally made his second Wigan debut off the bench in the Friday game of round 14, the England international's first game in Super League since the 2013 Grand Final.

Tomkins was playing his first game since August 30th 2015, when he aggravated a knee problem while playing for New Zealand Warriors against Wests Tigers, and underwent knee ligament surgery.

There was no fairytale ending, despite Tomkins scoring in the 59th minute, as the Warriors were beaten 30-16 on home soil by Hull FC.

Hull came out and blitzed Wigan early, with their big pack taking command and their halfbacks Marc Sneyd and Leon Pryce dictating play. They scored three tries in the first 15 minutes and were looking comfortable at 18-0 but the Warriors gave themselves hope before the break with Oliver Gildart touching down to reduce the deficit to 18-4 at the interval.

Tries from John Bateman and Sam Tomkins saw Wigan reduce the gap to just two points with 20 minutes still left to play. With Hull spilling the ball through over-ambitious offloads the Warriors looked on course for a great comeback.

But then Jamie Shaul scored the try of the game from a brilliant Liam Watts offload deep in his own half. Shaul sidestepped Sam Tomkins superbly and then proved strong enough to be able to plant the ball down for a try in a Josh Charnley tackle. Fetuli Talanoa finished off the try-scoring with a trademark acrobatic effort in the corner.

St Helens leapt above Wigan and into the top four with a Friday night 34-20 home win over Salford. The entire Saints pack was superb, but Louie McCarthy-Scarsbrook was particularly outstanding, while Niall Evalds' hat-trick was a highlight for the Red Devils, who looked dangerous when they got the ball close to the line. But they ultimately spent too much time defending because of their handling errors in their own half and a number of penalties.

The night before, Luke Dorn was outstanding on his return to the Castleford side, scoring a hat-trick during Castleford's stunning 52-12 victory at Leeds, whose title defence was looking more and more like a pipedream.

Dorn, who announced after the game he would be retiring and heading back to Australia at the end of the season, made four of his side's 14 clean breaks as Luke Gale tormented the club that offloaded him as a junior.

It was a record defeat at home to Castleford for the Rhinos despite them opening the scoring with a Mitch Garbutt try on five minutes.

Catalans moved joint top of the table, level with Warrington and Hull FC with only points difference separating the sides, with a 16-14 home win over Huddersfield Giants on the Saturday.

The Dragons led by eight points before Jake Connor scored a superb try to narrow the lead to two points with fifteen minutes remaining, but the Catalans managed to hold on for a victory.

Huddersfield, joint bottom of the table with Leeds, went into the game without the talismanic Eorl Crabtree, who did not travel to Perpignan due to the birth of his son, but one positive for the Giants was the return to first-team action for Jamie Ellis after twelve weeks out with a shoulder injury.

The home side were without forward pair Dave Taylor and Jason Baitieri, both suspended for one game by the disciplinary panel on Tuesday evening, and they also lost Vincent Duport on the morning of the game to illness and had to cope further with Richie Myler leaving the field with an adductor injury.

On the Sunday afternoon, Wakefield confirmed themselves as serious top-eight contenders with a shock 36-28 home win over leaders Warrington.

Eight wins from nine - the only blip a home defeat to Hull FC - had the Wildcats now firmly lodged in mid-table. Leading 24-6 at the break after yet more eye-catching Rugby League, Wakefield showed both sides of their game either side of the break; the flair and panache needed to score points coupled with the grit and determination to see a game out.

Still without Chris Sandow, Warrington's halfback problems were worsened just before kick-off when Stefan Ratchford pulled out due to illness. Without another recognised halfback in their squad, Ben Currie filled the void at scrum-half. Young halfback Morgan Smith made his Super League debut off the bench after playing in the Cup-tie at Oldham.

Craig Hall scored two well-taken tries and created another, as the Wildcats proved too hot to handle for the patched-up Wolves side in the opening 40 minutes. It took only three minutes for Hall and Wakefield to score their first try, as the centre pounced on a glorious offload from fullback Max Jowitt before stepping around Kevin Penny to touch down.

Half-time didn't halt Wakefield's momentum. Within four minutes of the restart they were over for try number five, as Jacob Miller this time provided the inch-perfect pass for Matty Ashurst's second and a 30-6 lead. But, from there, Warrington began a fight back that looked set to stymie Wakefield, especially after they had Ben Jones Bishop, Anthony England and Danny Kirmond sin-binned.

A Joe Westerman break from deep looked to have put the Wolves in front but his pass to in-the-clear Daryl Clark was dropped cold. The Wildcats rallied and a smart grubber from boom rookie Jowitt allowed Jones-Bishop to pounce for the clinching score.

Hull Kingston Rovers paid tribute to their former player and coach Roger Millward MBE, who had died at the age of 68, with an emotional and poignant service before their 24-10 victory over Widnes.

Hundreds of floral tributes and pictures were brought to the KC Lightstream Stadium by supporters and the Robins officially retired the number six jersey Millward wore for the majority of his 406 appearances for the club, presenting it to his family on the field at the height of an emotional ceremony.

Shaun Lunt starred for Rovers as they moved to within three league points of eighth-placed Widnes.

Round 15 - Magic Weekend

The Magic Weekend, staged at St James' Park for the second year running, attracted a total weekend attendance of 68,276 to Newcastle, which was an all-time Magic Weekend record, surpassing the previous best of 67,788 that was set the previous year at the same venue.

The Saturday saw three games played in front of 39,331 fans while on Sunday 28,945 fans were in attendance.

In a weekend of shock results, Hull FC were the only team that went into the weekend in the top four to secure a victory, and after it they sat alone at the top of the table with 22 points from 15 matches, two points ahead of Warrington Wolves, Catalans Dragons and Wigan Warriors.

Hull FC's 28-16 victory over Hull Kingston Rovers came in the final match of the weekend. In what was Danny Houghton's 250th game for the club, Mahe Fonua bagged two tries to make it eight wins from their past nine Super League fixtures.

But they were made to work hard for it by their cross-city foes, as the Robins tied the game just after half-time at 10-10. A Graeme Horne try put Hull KR into the lead early in the second half, but the Black and Whites stormed home thanks to three further tries to Fonua, Jamie Shaul and Mark Minichiello.

In the game before that, St Helens missed an opportunity to move joint top of the table after being thrashed 48-20 by Huddersfield.

Danny Brough had Jamie Ellis back alongside him at halfback with Scott Grix at fullback, and all three played their parts in an accomplished win. Both hookers, Ryan Hinchcliffe and Kyle Wood, had big games, while out wide Leroy Cudjoe thrived again, providing three assists, including two for his prolific winger Jermaine McGillvary. Saints were without injured centre pairing Dom Peyroux and Mark Percival, so Welsh youngster Calvin Wellington made his debut.

Sam Rapira and Aaron Murphy's quick tries in the third quarter pulled the Giants clear of their opponents. The latter was one of the most bizarre tries of the season, as Jake Connor vollied a Brough pass high into the air, regathered and sent Murphy over out wide.

Wigan leapt above Saints into fourth, despite the loss of captain Sean O'Loughlin, who suffered a quad injury and was withdrawn during the first half of the game, with a Saturday evening 40-8 hammering of Leeds.

The Rhinos fell to their twelfth league defeat in 15 games and were clear bottom, though coach Brian McDermott said he was not giving up on making the Grand Final.

Despite the final scoreline it was close at the break. Willie Isa's two tries, to go with a solid defensive effort, had given Wigan the edge. But the contest was effectively over at the start of the second half, after two kicks in as many minutes exposed the luckless Ash Handley to put the outcome beyond doubt.

A similar late brace as Leeds further wilted, having played a man short for ten minutes after Zak Hardaker was sin-binned for a professional foul, inflated the final margin and the woes of the sinking champions.

After 31 minutes of Magic Weekend game two, Warrington looked on course to top the table, 14-0 up against Castleford and in complete control. But the Tigers somehow went from toothless to terrific in the blink of an eye. Not only did they fight back to beat the then league leaders 34-14, they did so in an utterly dazzling style.

Whether it was Junior Moors' utter dominance down the middle or Denny Solomona's trailblazing runs downfield, the Tigers put on one of the best attacking displays of 2016 from the moment Luke Dorn scored their first of the afternoon on 34 minutes from a move involving numerous Castleford players.

Another quickfire try before half-time by Grant Millington gave the Tigers the confidence to produce a stunning second half display.

Ryan Bailey finally made his long-awaited Warrington debut and returned from injury off the bench, after joining them at the end of 2015.

Game one saw Salford Red Devils edge Widnes 18-12, helped by two tries from Daniel Vidot, though Widnes had bossed much of the opening stanza, scoring twice themselves through Rhys Hanbury and Chris Bridge, who was returning from injury.

Despite having to briefly come off for a concussion assessment in the second half, Vidot scored after just four minutes and again twelve minutes from time, with Justin Carney further emphasising the threat the Red Devils now posed out wide by claiming their other try in between. The win was Salford's first since they were deducted six points for salary cap breaches which left them on eight league points.

Jacob Miller's jaw-dropping 50-metre field goal gave the Wildcats a thrilling 25-24 victory over the Catalans in the first game of Sunday. It was his first one-pointer since he came to Super League to join Hull FC in 2013.

Catalans had gone in front 14-0 early as they totally dominated, but the Wildcats came back twice in impressive fashion to pull off a famous victory.

Mickael Simon charged over against his former club to make it 24-all with Liam Finn's conversion. But then came the game's big moment. Simon turned from hero to villain after giving a penalty away for a ball steal. With Pat Richards' impeccable record from the boot over the years, it seemed certain he would put the Dragons back in front - but somehow, he cracked the ball against the posts.

And Trinity made them pay. Finn narrowly missed with a one-pointer before Miller, Wakefield's most creative influence all afternoon, slotted the ball between the posts from the most incredible of positions.

Round 16

In the week leading up to Magic Weekend, Salford owner Marwan Koukash had called on his fellow club chairmen to support a vote of no-confidence in the Rugby Football League, though few clubs showed any enthusiasm for a potential breakaway from the governing body.

One of the allegations made by Koukash against the RFL was that Catalans were getting preferential treatment when it came to applying the overseas player rules - prompting a war of words between Koukash and Catalans Chairman Bernard Guasch. The RFL confirmed that the Dragons did have nine overseas players, but only five of them were on the overseas quota and seven of them were non-Federation trained players, which was within the 2016 regulations. Louis Anderson (Tonga), Krisnan Inu (Samoa), Willie Mason (Samoa) and Pat Richards (Ireland) were all Kolpak players.

Salford's hopes of finishing in the top eight had in April been dealt a massive blow when they were deducted six points for salary cap breaches and their appeal was to be heard before the end of June by an independent tribunal.

The Red Devils were in fine form on the last Friday of May as they backed up their Magic Weekend success over Widnes Vikings and ended Wakefield's three-game unbeaten league run with a comprehensive 38-8 home success.

In an eventful opening 40 minutes, Salford, with powerhouse winger Justin Carney missing out after submitting an Early Guilty Plea for a dangerous throw on Chris Bridge, went in to the break 10-4 up thanks to tries from Niall Evalds and Ryan Lannon, Trinity ending the half with eleven men after having both Danny Kirmond and Ben Jones-Bishop sent to the sin bin. Salford scored three tries while Wakefield were undermanned. Three tries in the opening twelve minutes of the second half from Mark Flanagan, Lannon and Robert Lui put the Red Devils in full control and from then on they were in no danger of losing.

There were no complaints about the sin-binnings, and Kirmond subsequently received a one-game ban for tripping. But in the week Wakefield had been seething after being fined £1,000 for breaching RFL Operational Rules on the management of concussion, deemed to have failed in the win at Widnes in April to comply with an operational rule that said all players being treated for possible concussion must be removed from the field of play. Assessments could not be carried out on the field of play.

According to the RFL, Kirmond twice showed signs of concussion in the game but stayed on the field. 'I have a bee in my bonnet,' Wakefield Chairman Michael Carter told League Express. 'We have a guy on the field of play who is an A & E consultant specialist and two physios who are very highly qualified. They were confident that there was no risk of concussion.'

In the Friday TV game, Warrington racked up a record Super League score for the club against Leeds in a 52-18 hammering at Halliwell Jones Stadium. The return of Brad Dwyer and scrum-half Chris Sandow gave the Wolves - who had lost four of their previous six games - a multitude of additional attacking options. And with Stefan Ratchford thriving at fullback, Kurt Gidley immersed in the action from stand-off and centres Ryan Atkins and Rhys Evans both catching the eye, Tony Smith's side looked back on song.

Sandow was the standout returnee after a return from a seven-match absence with a hamstring injury, and there were two tries from Gene Ormsby, back from a loan spell at Huddersfield, and the excellent Daryl Clark. It was only 18-12 at half-time, but two tries in the opening ten minutes of the second half took the game away from Leeds, still two points adrift at the bottom of the table.

On the Sunday, Widnes, with Wests Tigers prop Jack Buchanan on debut, staged a dramatic comeback at home to Huddersfield to secure a 24-20 win, their first Super League win in over two months.

The Vikings, without a win in the league since mid-March and tumbling down the table at a rate of knots, seemed destined for a ninth consecutive defeat in the league, trailing Huddersfield 16-0 after half an hour. Tries to Nathan Mason, Danny Brough and Joe Wardle, two converted by Brough, saw the Giants seemingly on course for their fifth win of the season. But a try just before half-time from Corey Thompson kick-started a run of 24-unanswered points. Joe Mellor got two of the Vikings' four second-half tries before Jermaine McGillvary got Huddersfield back to within four points to set up a tense final ten minutes.

More bad news for the Giants was that new forward Sebastine Ikahihifo, who had only made his debut the week before in Newcastle, broke his jaw. Giants coach Paul Anderson revealed that Ikahihifo initially thought his painful jaw was caused by an aching wisdom tooth.

In the wake of the Hull KR's 34-16 defeat at Catalans Dragons on the Saturday, interim Robins head coach James Webster was full of praise for youngster Joe Wardill, who played two games in two days. Wardill started at centre for England Academy on the

Friday night in their 52-20 victory over France under-18s in Warrington. And the Beverley Braves product, who signed a four-year professional deal with Rovers after making his debut against Wigan Warriors on Easter Monday, arrived back in Hull at midnight before boarding a coach transfer at half past six in the morning to start on the wing in Perpignan.

Wardill scored a 63rd minute try at Gilbert Brutus but the chance of a Hull KR win was made all the more unlikely when they announced that Terry Campese would not travel to the south of France to protect his hamstring injury, with one eye on the fixture with Wakefield the following week. Two tries just before the interval for the Catalans effectively sealed the tie for the home side, with Glenn Stewart once again a stand-out and Tony Gigot scoring two tries.

Wigan backed up their Magic Weekend thrashing of Leeds with a 33-26 win at Castleford on the Thursday, ending the Tigers' three-match winning run and maintaining their spot inside the top four.

With Sean O'Loughlin absent, Wigan scrum-half Matty Smith organised his side to fine effect, landing six goals from seven attempts, including a couple from the touchline, and kicking the clinching field goal four minutes from the end.

Castleford coach Daryl Powell was highly critical of referee Ben Thaler after a game in which Jake Webster was sin-binned for dissent on the stroke of half-time. Powell was fined £500, half suspended until the end of 2017.

After 16 rounds of the competition Hull FC sat on top of the table with 24 points, two points clear of Warrington, Catalans and Wigan, after coming from behind at half-time to beat St Helens 32-24 at the KCOM Stadium on the Saturday.

After roaring into a 12-0 lead, Hull found themselves 18-14 behind until Carlos Tuimavave's try on 56 minutes. But, with Gareth Ellis outstanding, they produced a blistering finish for the third week running, Danny Washbrook's try three minutes from time making it five wins on the bounce and eleven from their last twelve matches.

St Helens could be considered unlucky not to have got anything out of the game. On the wrong end of a 12-2 penalty count and losing halfback Luke Walsh as early as the second minute, Keiron Cunningham's men played with a resilience and never-say-die attitude while giving their best performance for some weeks. Walsh had played in all Saints' 16 Super League games in 2016 but missed the next five matches.

FIRST UTILITY SUPER LEAGUE
Sunday 29th May

	P	W	D	L	F	A	D	Pts
Hull FC	16	12	0	4	441	347	94	24
Warrington Wolves	16	11	0	5	485	298	187	22
Catalans Dragons	16	11	0	5	456	331	125	22
Wigan Warriors	16	11	0	5	337	337	0	22
St Helens	16	9	0	7	392	397	-5	18
Wakefield Trinity Wildcats	16	8	0	8	353	426	-73	16
Castleford Tigers	16	7	1	8	409	448	-39	15
Widnes Vikings	16	7	0	9	362	339	23	14
Salford Red Devils *	16	8	0	8	422	397	25	10
Hull Kingston Rovers	16	4	1	11	330	431	-101	9
Huddersfield Giants	16	4	0	12	367	399	-32	8
Leeds Rhinos	16	3	0	13	268	472	-204	6

* Six points deducted for salary cap breaches in 2014 & 2015

JUNE
Wigan shrug off woes

Round 17

Hull Kingston Rovers ran out comfortable 54-16 winners at Wakefield in the Thursday night TV game, to keep their top-eight hopes alive, as James Webster's decision to rest Terry Campese for the trip to Catalans a week earlier ultimately paid off.

Campese and mercurial halfback partner Albert Kelly, along with hooker Shaun Lunt, controlled a game which the Robins had to win to have any chance of avoiding battling in the Middle Eights for the second year running. Kieran Dixon, who didn't find out he was playing until 24 hours before the trip to Belle Vue, registered a superb hat-trick on his return to the side as Rovers led 20-0 in as many minutes.

With Wakefield missing Ben Jones-Bishop, Ashley Gibson, Scott Moore, Anthony England and captain Danny Kirmond, they were well beaten and their mid-season bubble looked to have burst.

Leeds gave the Catalans a tight game at Headingley the night after but they ultimately fell by 24-12.

The first and last minutes of the game summed up the Rhinos' wretched season as they suffered their seventh successive loss. In the opening carry, as Willie Mason charged forward, Leeds lost Keith Galloway, a stinger on his shoulder causing him to lose feeling in his arm. And in the last minute, having had an intense ten minutes of pressure on the opposition line looking for what could have been a deserved, equalising score, Eloi Pelissier picked up a loose ball and scampered 60 metres on the final play to dash the blue and amber hopes.

The Dragons win was significant in coach Laurent Frayssinous' eyes as twelve of his squad of 17 were French, with Englishman Jodie Broughton also involved. 'We are the Catalans and we're proud of our French influence,' he said. 'Lucas Albert is 18, Fouad Yaha is 19 and there are other young French guys in the mix.'

Liam Sutcliffe played fullback, with Zak Hardaker having injured a shoulder in the defeat at Warrington the week before, and it was thought that the reigning Man of Steel had played his last game for the Rhinos. He was transfer-listed at £300,000 by the Rhinos, with a move to the NRL his desire. Leeds were rumoured to be keeping an eye on Dragons fullback Morgan Escaré, who was still under contract with the French side, but had only featured sporadically in 2016.

Huddersfield remained just two points ahead of Leeds in eleventh place. On a balmy Friday night at the John Smith's Stadium, a pair of tries each to Jake Webster and Denny Solomona was enough to see Castleford home 30-22.

The Tigers, with back-rower Junior Moors not for the first time in destructive form, took a six-point lead into the half-time break but shot ahead in the second half thanks to two tries in nine minutes. Huddersfield hit back in the final twelve minutes, with scores to Ryan Brierley and Jake Connor, but left their run too late.

In the week, star halfback Luke Gale spurned interest from the NRL to sign a five-year contract with the Tigers.

June

All the top four sides registered wins on the Friday night, with Warrington's win over St Helens at Langtree Park seeing fifth-placed Saints six points adrift of the play-off spots.

After the game Warrington coach Tony Smith revealed that his team had been suffering in the week leading up to the game, when training sessions were virtually impossible, and that some of his players should not have played in the 26-4 win.

Chris Sandow created the opening try for Ben Currie before scoring brilliantly himself with a superb sidestep around Atelea Vea. The injury absence of Luke Walsh was glaringly apparent throughout a first half in which St Helens dominated possession and territory and heaped pressure on the Warrington defence. But the Wolves rearguard stood firm to leave them pointless at half-time, while they scored three times themselves on their forays upfield.

The game was summed up in the space of 60 seconds just after the restart. Saints were attacking again when Matty Dawson's pass was intercepted by Sandow right on his own line. Moments later Daryl Clark was splitting the home defence up the middle and Stefan Ratchford supported to leave three defenders trailing in his wake for a brilliant breakaway try.

That week, St Helens halfback Travis Burns joined Championship side Leigh Centurions for the rest of the season, whilst Saints made a last-ditch effort to sign Manly forward Tom Symonds, who had agreed a move to Huddersfield.

Wigan had a close-run game at Salford before registering a 23-20 win. Wigan held a narrow 11-10 lead at the break after a pulsating 40 minutes. The Red Devils led 10-4 at one stage after a try double from Michael Dobson had cancelled out Josh Charnley's early score for the Warriors. Ryan Sutton's try saw the Warriors level it up before Matty Smith slotted over a field goal right on the siren.

Two further tries in the second half from Charnley saw the Warriors extend their advantage to 23-10, although tries from Josh Jones and Daniel Vidot set up a very tense finish as Wigan held on.

The 20-year-old front-rower Sutton was forced to play in the unfamiliar role of second row after Greg Burke was forced from the field after being knocked out in a head clash with team-mate Sam Powell. Sutton crossed for his first try of the season when he latched onto a neat kick from man of the match George Williams in the first half.

The Wigan club released a statement earlier in the week about an investigation into an incident outside a town centre gym less than 24 hours after their win over Castleford. Coach Shaun Wane was reluctant to add fuel to the fire around the future of John Bateman, who was not selected for the Salford game. It was understood that Bateman had been suspended for a month pending the investigation, while he had also been fined a month's wages.

Hull FC made it three weeks at the summit of Super League as they overwhelmed a struggling Widnes side in the second half to make it six league wins in a row.

The first half was high on errors and penalties and which ended with just one score apiece. But the Black and Whites once again showed their ability to go up the gears as they cut loose in the second half to register four tries in a devastating eleven-minute spell and record a 30-10 home win.

Round 18

The two clubs lying in the top two positions in the Super League table met in a highly anticipated Friday night TV game. And Hull FC maintained their two-point lead at the summit with a grinding 19-12 win at a humid Halliwell Jones Stadium.

Hull's tactics of targeting the Wolves' ball players worked a treat in an error-strewn 80 minutes. Warrington missed 30 tackles, with Daryl Clark missing over a quarter of that number according to the Opta stats. Kurt Gidley and Joe Westerman were forced to make 38 and 41 tackles respectively and Warrington didn't make a single clean break, compared to Hull making five.

Hull skipper Gareth Ellis took the battle to the Wolves up front throughout and came up with the contest's decisive try, breaking a half-hour deadlock to force his way over with 15 minutes left. Given that Warrington's only two tries had come directly from Hull mistakes - Gene Ormsby getting their first after Jamie Shaul collected and then lost a long Chris Sandow kick; and then Sandow sliding over after Benjamin Jullien charged down a Marc Sneyd kick - that was always likely to prove enough if Hull could hang on to the ball in the closing stages. They largely did before Sneyd slotted the field goal that sealed the points. Fetuli Talanoa and Mark Minichiello got the other two Hull tries in the first half.

The result meant the Wolves dropped to fourth by the end of the weekend after wins for Catalans and Wigan.

On the Friday night Wigan stole a late victory at Hull KR, Sam Tomkins scoring a try in the 78th minute and Matty Smith's conversion sealing a 20-18 win.

Wigan had stamped their authority on the game early on through two Dom Manfredi tries, but a resilient Hull KR, who were battling to keep their top-eight hopes alive, roared back to lead 18-8 heading into the final 15 minutes through tries to Albert Kelly, Thomas Minns and Mitch Allgood, all converted by Ken Sio. But Wigan's extra power and cohesion told late on, with Anthony Gelling and then Tomkins crossing.

Hull KR suffered another blow. Terry Campese, who had played only minutes of four previous league games, was expected to miss the rest of the season after suffering a serious hamstring injury in the 64th minute.

The Dragons beat St Helens 33-16 on the Saturday, with 17-year-old halfback Lucas Albert shining in front of a bumper home crowd. With Luke Walsh still out injured Saints' halfback woes continued as Jonny Lomax pulled out of the team in the warm-up with a tight adductor, while Theo Fages left the field at half-time with a knee injury.

Adam Swift's try five minutes into the second half had Saints back at 13-10 down but Jodie Broughton scored two more tries and in between those there was a beauty, reminiscent of the Dragons brand. Dave Taylor produced an offload and Albert's wide pass sent Fouad Yaha away down the left wing. The youngster drew the cover defence and passed inside to the supporting Morgan Escaré, who raced over to score.

Hull KR's defeat to Wigan left their task of making the Super 8s much harder as Widnes had produced a fine win at Castleford the night before and then on the Sunday Wakefield had ground out a 10-2 win at Huddersfield in the kind of wet conditions that had favoured the Giants and their kicking game in the past.

Danny Kirmond scored the only try of the game in the 69th minute and even then he looked to be slightly in front of Liam Finn's impromptu grubber to the line.

It was a four-pointer with the Giants now ten league points behind the Wildcats with five games to go before the split. Wakefield were level on points with fifth-placed St Helens and looking like a Super 8s team - after being involved in the Million Pound relegation game in 2015.

Both clubs had forwards arriving that week from the NRL to aid their end-of-season runs, Manly forward Tom Symonds Huddersfield bound and big prop David Fifita coming to Belle Vue.

The Giants looked all-but destined to join Leeds in the Qualifiers, nine months on from the night in which they were both fighting each other for the League Leaders Shield.

The Vikings held off a late fightback from Castleford to win 38-28 - Widnes were 38-12 ahead with eleven minutes left - at the Mend-A-Hose Jungle and moved five points clear of ninth-placed Hull KR.

Super League's top try-scorer Denny Solomona was switched from the wing to fullback when Luke Dorn had to withdraw. The Tigers badly missed Dorn's usual attacking contribution, while Solomona wasn't as effective at the rear.

Widnes hooker Lloyd White posed the Tigers problems from dummy-half throughout and netted two vital tries. The gamebreaker was Joe Mellor's try from a short kick-off on 65 minutes, scored simply by playing to the whistle, that gave the Vikings what proved to be an unassailable 26-point lead. The kick landed short of the ten-metre line as Mellor collected and raced unopposed to score, referee and former Royal Marine Jack Smith ruling the ball had crossed the line in the air before curling back.

Tigers' on-loan winger Paddy Flynn scored a hat-trick against his parent club.

Leeds ended their seven-match losing run with an 8-0 win over Salford Red Devils at Headingley on the Friday night. For 75 minutes, after Luke Briscoe's sole try and his first of the campaign, the tryline wasn't crossed and it wasn't until the 79th minute that Liam Sutcliffe's penalty made it a two-score lead.

Salford's hopes of making the top-eight looked dependent on their appeal against the salary cap points deduction scheduled for later in the month. Their captain Tommy Lee had been ruled out for the season following a knee operation. He hadn't featured since Salford's 44-26 victory over Hull KR at the end of April, which was his first appearance in over a month following a previous setback.

Round 19

Marc Sneyd's goalkicking secured a Sunday-afternoon victory for Hull at Castleford, as the Black and Whites recorded a 24-22 win, with Sneyd converting all four Hull tries, whilst Tigers goalkicker Danny Tickle could only convert one of Castleford's five tries.

Tickle's last effort, the conversion to Denny Solomona's spectacular 72nd-minute try, proved the most significant as it left the Airlie Birds with a two-point advantage that they held onto until the final whistle. The touchline conversion struck the post.

Hull had looked in control at half-time when they led 18-8 after going down 8-0 to Luke Dorn and Jake Webster tries. Frank Pritchard, Danny Houghton and Mahe Fonua all crossed for converted scores. But by the hour mark Paddy Flynn and Solomona had crossed and Tickle's one successful conversion had the Tigers on the march at 18-18

The architect of the game-winning try was 34-year-old halfback Leon Pryce, set to leave Hull at the end of the season. Having been sent on by Hull coach Lee Radford after starting on the bench, Pryce was tasked with dragging his team out of a hole in attack. Pryce stepped off his right foot before offloading to Jamie Shaul, who raced home and put Hull into what turned out to be an unassailable lead and an eighth straight league win that left them still two points clear at the top.

Wigan made it five wins on the bounce on a wet Thursday evening as they were pushed all the way in a 7-0 success against Widnes Vikings at the Select Security Stadium. The only try of the game came in the 48th minute from Josh Charnley, touching down following a slick passing move. That converted try and a Matty Smith field goal proved to be the difference as Wigan ground out a hard-fought win.

Widnes had a gilt-edged chance to get back in the game when Chris Dean broke through to race over 65 metres for what looked like an individual try. But he was unable to keep hold of the ball and knocked on just inches from the line in a last-ditch tackle by Charnley. Wigan halfback Jake Shorrocks picked up an injury on debut.

The Warriors confirmed they had re-signed winger Joe Burgess for the 2017 season as a replacement for rugby union bound Charnley. The 21-year-old was to return to his former club, after limited chances in the NRL with Sydney Roosters, on a three-year deal ahead of the new season.

In the week, Wigan confirmed that another Albert Goldthorpe Rookie of the Year, back-rower John Bateman, who won the award in 2012 while with Bradford Bulls, had been suspended by the club for eight weeks and fined £10,000 following an altercation with a teammate outside a local gym.

Warrington stayed in touch by beating Catalans 20-18 at home on the Friday.

The key moment in the game came thirteen minutes from the end, with the Dragons leading 18-16. With Warrington attacking, Kurt Gidley chipped to the corner. As the ball bounced, Todd Carney collected and raced clear before finding the supporting Morgan Escaré, who in turn found Jodie Broughton. The Catalans winger raced away and under the posts for a try, only for the video official to pull the play back for a late and high challenge by Eloi Pelissier on kicker Gidley. Gidley added the resulting penalty to level the scores.

Five minutes later Daryl Clark got over on the left, but video footage proved inconclusive and a penalty was awarded to the Wolves for Pelissier stealing the ball over the line. Up stepped Gidley to send the penalty sailing between the posts to give the home side the lead for the first time in the second half, and it proved enough.

The next day, Dragons president Bernard Guasch slammed Pelissier in the newspaper L'Indépendant, while expressing his pride that 13 players were French, including eighteen-year-old Jordan Dezaria, who made his debut from the bench.

On the same night, England winger Ryan Hall made a successful comeback against Wakefield, after being out for over three months with an ankle injury, in the Rhinos' 32-6 victory at Belle Vue - the first time the struggling Super League Champions had won away from Headingley in 2015.

Zak Hardaker also made a surprise return, on the wing, from a shoulder injury despite being transfer listed, the latest rumour that a swap deal was on the cards with Wests hooker Robbie Farah coming to Headingley and Hardaker going to the Tigers.

Liam Sutcliffe led the charge from fullback with a try and eight goals as the 2016 Rhinos claimed back-to-back wins for the first time. Leeds again proved masters of wet weather - the last three of their five victories had come in abysmal conditions - with their pack generally out-muscling a Wakefield middle shorn of the services of injured skipper Danny Kirmond and Nick Scruton, while demonstrating superior ball control.

Trinity were outplayed throughout, largely as a result of repeatedly coughing up possession and poor discipline. Twice the home side were reduced to twelve men by sin-binnings and, bearing in mind the massive territorial advantage savoured by the Rhinos and consequent amount of tackling the Wildcats were forced to do, they took some solace from restricting the Rhinos to just four tries. David Fifita made his Wakefield debut and spent ten minutes in the sin bin after throwing the ball at Jamie Jones-Buchanan.

Adam Swift bagged four tries as St Helens returned to winning ways with a second-half comeback and a 48-16 win against Hull KR at Langtree Park on the Friday night.

Saints were without a win in their last four Super League outings, and a fast start from Rovers looked to have the home side rocking as they raced into a 12-nil lead.

But a quick-fire double from Swift just before the break gave St Helens the momentum going into half-time, and when the winger completed his hat-trick six minutes into the second half, Saints were transformed.

The home side went on to control proceedings, racking up another six tries as they dominated the second half, much to the relief of under-fire coach Keiron Cunningham.

Huddersfield ended a traumatic week on the same night with a 31-30 win at Salford, the day after the sacking of head coach Paul Anderson and his assistant Kieron Purtill.

The club was already reeling with the death of Academy player Ronan Costello on the Tuesday following a serious injury in a match against Salford the previous Saturday.

The Giants, with Academy coach Andy Kelly in interim charge, responded with a gutsy performance and though they went behind early on they never lost the lead after a Ukuma Ta'ai try on 26 minutes. By the time Danny Brough kicked a field goal on 71 minutes they were 13 up, enough to absorb two late Salford tries.

But the game was overshadowed by the events of the week, with Ronan Costello's peers from the Academy and his junior club Brighouse Rangers leading the tributes.

FIRST UTILITY SUPER LEAGUE
Sunday 19th June

	P	W	D	L	F	A	D	Pts
Hull FC	19	15	0	4	514	391	123	30
Wigan Warriors	19	14	0	5	387	375	12	28
Warrington Wolves	19	13	0	6	543	339	204	26
Catalans Dragons	19	13	0	6	531	379	152	26
St Helens	19	10	0	9	460	472	-12	20
Wakefield Trinity Wildcats	19	9	0	10	385	514	-129	18
Castleford Tigers	19	8	1	10	489	532	-43	17
Widnes Vikings	19	8	0	11	410	404	6	16
Hull Kingston Rovers	19	5	1	13	418	515	-97	11
Salford Red Devils *	19	8	0	11	472	459	13	10
Huddersfield Giants	19	5	0	14	422	469	-47	10
Leeds Rhinos	19	5	0	14	320	502	-182	10

* *Six points deducted for salary cap breaches in 2014 & 2015*

June

Challenge Cup Quarter-finals

David Fifita played a starring role in the Thursday night game, scoring two tries - barging his way over to give the Wildcats the lead after less than two minutes - and earning the man of the match award as Wakefield registered a 28-16 victory at Huddersfield.

Wingers Ben Jones-Bishop and Tom Johnstone added further Wildcats tries, whilst Scott Grix, Jake Connor and Jermaine McGillvary (twice) replied for Huddersfield. Although the eight touchdowns were shared evenly, the Giants were unable to convert any from out wide, while Liam Finn improved all but one of Trinity's and added three penalties.

Wakefield's third victory over Huddersfield this season was perhaps all the more surprising as skipper Danny Kirmond (knee), experienced prop Nick Scruton (groin) and fellow forward Mickael Simon (concussion) were all ruled out beforehand.

Giants captain Danny Brough was sin-binned in the 13th minute for a high shot on Reece Lyne, who played no further part in the game. Brough was banned for a game the following Tuesday.

The following night, Warrington won a home game for the second week running thanks to a late Kurt Gidley penalty, this time knocking Widnes Vikings out of the Cup by 20-18.

Widnes led 12-10 at the break through converted tries from Joe Mellor and Matt Whitley, with Jack Hughes having opened the scoring on four minutes and Kevin Penny scoring for the hosts just before half-time.

Gidley levelled with a 55th minute penalty before hooker Brad Dwyer crossed to put Warrington back ahead but Charly Runciman levelled the scores off Brown's dunked pass at 18-18. Gidley's 73rd minute penalty settled the tie after the Vikings were pinged for offside after a Chris Sandow bomb was dropped.

Catalans coach Laurent Frayssinous launched a verbal attack on the heavily sanded KCOM Stadium pitch in the aftermath of his side's defeat to Hull FC on the Saturday.

The Dragons went down 22-8 to bring their participation in the 2016 Challenge Cup to an end and Hull's passage into the last four was as comfortable as the scoreline suggested as their pack, with prop Scott Taylor showing barnstorming form, got the better of their opponents.

Catalans handed a second debut to the versatile Benjamin Garcia, following his return to the club from Penrith Panthers earlier in the week and his try opened the scoring in the 13th minute.

Later that Saturday afternoon, Wigan booked their place in the semi-finals for the first time in three years with a comfortable home 26-12 win over Castleford Tigers.

The Warriors were clinical in the first-half as they led 22-0 at the break with a brace from Josh Charnley and scores from Dan Sarginson and Sam Tomkins putting them in full control.

The Warriors' defence was magnificent and had the Tigers' trademark wide plays taped, with some committed goal-line defence keeping their opponents scoreless. They again showed tenacity in defence in the second half, but the Tigers did manage to cross twice through Luke Gale and Ben Crooks, with those scores coming either side of a controversial Dom Manfredi try for the Warriors, given the green light by the video referee even though the winger had patently not grounded a kick into the in goal.

After the game, the Tigers announced they had re-signed former England halfback Rangi Chase, weeks after the player had announced his retirement from the game.

* On the Sunday afternoon, Batley Bulldogs and Dewsbury Rams paid tribute to Jo Cox, the former Labour MP for Batley and Spenborough, before their match at the Fox's Biscuits Stadium (Mount Pleasant). Cox tragically lost her life ten days earlier when she was attacked by a gun and knife-wielding local man in the centre of Birstall.

JULY
Champions deposed

Round 20

With three rounds to go before the split into three eights, reigning Champions and Challenge Cup holders Leeds Rhinos' hopes of avoiding the Qualifiers were finally dashed when they were downed 23-22 by Widnes at Headingley.

There were flashes of hope as the Rhinos twice established 12-point leads against a Widnes side who were more than playing a part in the contest, before frustration, inability to perform and a lack of ruthlessness took over. Joe Mellor struck the dramatic late field goal in the 79th minute that guaranteed the Vikings' place in the Super 8s.

Kallum Watkins, Ryan Hall and Joel Moon crossed for the Rhinos to open up a 16-10 lead at the break. But, after Mitch Garbutt's try, Patrick Ah Van and Rhys Hanbury levelled it at 22-22 before Mellor won the game.

The defeat came at the end of the week in which the Rhinos moved back into their Kirkstall training ground on the banks of the River Aire, after the completion of reinstatement works following the Boxing Day floods.

Huddersfield still had hopes of a miracle run into the top-eight after Jake Connor played a starring role from fullback during the Giants' 22-12 home Thursday-night win against leaders Hull FC, ending their ten-game winning streak. Connor had signed for the Airlie Birds for 2017, although Huddersfield were demanding a big transfer fee as Connor was still 21 and a 'homegrown' player.

In wet conditions, Hull looked void of ideas out wide without Jamie Shaul, while they didn't have the same bite down the middle without Liam Watts and Gareth Ellis.

The Giants, even though they were lacking the suspended Danny Brough, played the conditions much better, taking an 8-0 lead into half-time, Michael Lawrence getting the only try when he was first to a Jamie Ellis kick into the in-goal.

Danny Washbrook's converted try looked to have turned the tide but he went from hero to villain four minutes after his try as he failed to deal with a Kyle Wood kick in-goal, and the impressive Tom Symonds reacted quickest to score his first try in claret and gold.

With the eight-point advantage regained, the Giants went in for the kill. Hull's discipline evaded them again to send Huddersfield towards the line and, as a result Jermaine McGillvary scored in the corner, although the Giants were fortunate to be awarded the try after Jake Connor's pass appeared to be forward.

Then a majestic 40/20 from the imperious Connor put them in position, and Connor's pass put McGillvary in for his 150th career try. Mahe Fonua crashed over in the right corner two minutes from time to make the scoreline slightly more respectable.

Hull's shock defeat gave Wigan the chance to move level top and they proved to be the party spoilers in Perpignan as they ran out 26-6 winners over Catalans Dragons, celebrating their tenth year anniversary against their inaugural opponents.

With a club record of more than 11,800 inside the Stade Gilbert Brutus, the chief architect for the Warriors was England international Dan Sarginson. Sarginson scored the opening try, thanks to a fine miss-pass from the impressive Ryan Sutton that set Dom

Manfredi down the wing before he grubbered back to the in-goal, before creating a further two tries.

Three tries in ten first-half minutes effectively sealed the win for the Warriors, Sutton crashing over before the third try, a 40-metre stepping run from Oliver Gildart, proved a real heartbreaker for the home side, Matty Smith's 37th minute penalty giving the visitors a 20-2 lead at half-time.

Shortly after the interval, Justin Horo scored a superb solo effort in the left corner but the scoring was completed shortly after the hour, as Sarginson's deft grubber to the in-goal area allowed Manfredi to outmuscle Pat Richards down the touchline to get the crucial touch in the left corner.

Remarkably, both sides contained players who appeared in the first Catalans match in 2006 - Greg Mounis, Sean O'Loughlin and Richards all featuring in that historic game, with Richards making his debut for Wigan that night.

Warrington had dropped a further point behind Wigan the night before in east Hull as Iain Thornley's last-gasp try that Ben Cockayne goaled gave twelve-man Hull KR - Rovers prop James Green was dismissed for flooring former team-mate Jordan Cox late in the first half - a well-deserved 16-all draw against the in-form Wolves.

Having led 6-0 at the break through James Donaldson's effort, Thomas Minns added a second out wide for Hull KR after smart play from Albert Kelly to stretch the lead to 10-0.

But the Wolves struck three times, Matty Russell showing strength at the corner, Brad Dwyer touching down from dummy half and when Jack Hughes scored on the edge after Declan Patton's break and Stefan Ratchford converted, they looked to have won it.

But when a flying Kelly recovered Cockayne's short restart, the Robins had one last set. Kelly's cross-kick was palmed back by Joe Wardill for Thornley to cut inside and kick to the in-goal area. The ball deflected off Patton's boot and the centre reacted quickest, racing past three Wolves to get the touchdown, presenting Cockayne with the simple kick to give Rovers a point. Green received two-match ban for punching.

Catalans' defeat to Wigan gave St Helens a chance to keep the top four in sight, a chance they took with a 44-32 win at Wakefield, which also gave them a four-point lead over the sixth-placed Wildcats.

Kyle Amor was immense for Saints against his former club as they led for most of the final hour but, as the sides traded tries at regular intervals, they were never able to prevent tenacious Trinity, for whom Jacob Miller scored a hat-trick, snapping at their heels.

Four times the Lancashire club pulled 12 points clear, but it wasn't until the final play - a wonderful flowing break down the left, with Amor providing the final pass for Matty Fleming to race in - that they managed to put their hosts to bed.

Wakefield were not yet sure of a Super 8s place and the pressure was added to by the loss of Tom Johnstone, who injured his leg in the act of scoring, and a shoulder injury to Anthony England, who also picked up a two-match suspension for a shoulder charge on Jon Wilkin.

In his programme notes, Trinity chairman Michael Carter revealed he was in discussions with Dewsbury Rams about a ground-share for 2017 after talks to buy back Belle Vue stalled.

The exact composition of the Super 8s still depended in the outcome of Salford's appeal to an independent tribunal over the six points they had been deducted by the RFL for historical salary cap breaches, which was due that week. If successful, the Red Devils would move a point above Castleford after beating them at home by 22-18 on the Friday night, and level with Widnes and Wakefield, with a better points difference.

Gareth O'Brien held his nerve while others around him lost theirs in the closing stages. The fullback - who had been one of the success stories of the Super League season after his move from Warrington and from halfback to fullback - kicked three late penalties to go alongside a try and assist in an impressive all-round display.

Castleford coach Daryl Powell couldn't fault the effort of his injury-hit side, as they battled through the game while losing Joel Monaghan, Jake Webster and Mike McMeeken. It meant that Nathan Massey played 80 minutes and prop Larne Patrick ended up in the centres, but Powell still felt his side should have won after leading 18-10 midway through the second half.

* That week the government agreed to allocate funding of £15 million to back the RFL's bid to host the 2021 Rugby League World Cup, with a further £10 million towards improving Rugby League's infrastructure in its heartlands.

Round 21

Salford Red Devils' appeal to overturn their six-point deduction failed, the independent body Sports Resolutions finding that Tony Puletua had been paid through another company owned by Marwan Koukash and that there had been non-declaration of benefits to Lama Tasi and Theo Fages.

When the full transcript of the appeal hearing was published after the weekend it transpired the RFL had unsuccessfully tried to have the sanction increased to eight points, spread into the Qualifiers. The transcript made it clear that the sanction would have been greater if the tribunal had not been 'obviously impressed by Dr Koukash and the fact that he has learned much from his experience'.

Salford lost 40-14 at Warrington on the Thursday night as their place in the Qualifiers was confirmed just hours after the findings of the independent hearing were published.

Koukash was interviewed on TV pre-match casting doubt over whether he would remain at the club in 2017, promising to make a decision on his future at Salford at the end of the season.

His team showed tremendous commitment in the opening 35 minutes of the game, after which they led 6-4. But then double try scorers Ryan Atkins and Joe Westerman took charge for the Wolves, and, though the Red Devils stirred again after the break, a missed chance by former Warrington hooker Sean Kenny - Brad Dwyer dislodged the ball as he went over the line - proved crucial to their hopes of an unlikely comeback. Chris Sandow's terrific kicking game included two crucial second-half 40/20s.

James Roby made his 400th career appearance as Saints edged past Widnes 12-10 on the Friday, Mark Percival's 72nd minute penalty, for Matt Whitley's high tackle on Jonny Lomax, proving decisive in a game that could have gone either way. Prop Greg Burke starred off the bench for Widnes after joining the Vikings from Wigan just a few days before the game.

Hull KR were the only team outside the top eight that could avoid the Middle Eights. Rovers beat Huddersfield at home by 20-19 on the Friday night to stay alive and ensure the Giants would be in the Qualifiers, Ben Cockayne's penalty goal nine minutes from time winning the game after Hull KR rallied from 18-6 down at half-time and 19-6 early in the second half.

Adam Walker's miraculous offload from under a host of Giants to set up George Lawler's 52nd minute try turned the tide in Rovers' favour. The Giants threw everything they had at the Robins late on, but when Kyle Wood broke clear and found Ryan Brierley, the excellent Cockayne thumped him to the turf. The fullback stayed alert on the next play to bring Wood's chip to the in-goal area back into the field of play on the next tackle, ensuring his side held on for a huge win.

Hull KR's only realistic target was Wakefield, who almost overcame the odds at Wigan on the same night, as the Warriors gained a late come-from-behind 22-18 victory to go to the top of the Super League table after Hull FC went down 20-15 at home to Leeds Rhinos.

July

The match was won by Wigan thanks to two late tries by their young utility star Lewis Tierney, who was playing on the wing. Tierney scored in the 67th and 79th minutes and the club rewarded the 21-year-old son of their former hero Jason Robinson with a new contract to November 2019, with the option of a further year in the club's favour.

Wakefield were without three first-choice props and lost another a minute before half-time when Sean O'Loughlin was red carded for a high tackle on Chris Annakin, that ended the young prop's part in the game, and indeed the season as he injured his knee in the tackle. Wigan were well under strength too, with Kyle Shelford and Macauley Davies making debuts off the bench.

The first half was a fiery encounter, with Wigan coming from behind to lead at the break and having to cope with two players being sin-binned and one sent off. Max Jowitt put the Wildcats in front early on before Wigan hit back through tries from Olivier Gildart and Sam Powell, both set up by the brilliant George Williams, to lead 10-6 at the interval.

The half was marred by a surfeit of cheap shots and Wigan paid the penalty three times in total, with both Dom Manfredi and Josh Charnley spending time in the sin bin, while captain O'Loughlin was sent-off.

The Warriors refused to lie down, but it looked like they would come away with nothing as they headed into the final seconds two points behind. But more magic from Williams saw him put in a pinpoint kick for Tierney to touch down for his second try and win the game for Wigan.

The Rhinos stunned Hull on the same night as Kallum Watkins' two late tries earned Leeds an impressive 20-15 victory at KOCM Stadium.

Following a ten-game winning run that saw Hull FC open a gap at the top of the table, defeats to Leeds and Huddersfield, who both were set to finish in the bottom four, had seen them drop to second.

Hull were hit by injuries during the match. Already without Gareth Ellis and Frank Pritchard, they lost Carlos Tuimavave, Liam Watts and Mark Minichiello at various points in the game.

But Leeds, who gave a debut to impressive hooker James Segeyaro, who had come to Headingley from Penrith Panthers as part of a swap deal with Zak Hardaker, were beginning to look like the Rhinos of old. Ryan Hall and Liam Sutcliffe featured heavily in a last-ditch effort to hold Hull's Jamie Shaul up on the try line, preventing a matchwinner in the final minutes.

Castleford secured their spot in the Super 8s with a long-awaited home victory - they'd lost five home games in a row - a 38-24 success over the fading Catalans. Luke Dorn was at his very best all afternoon, with two well-taken tries part of an all-round marvellous performance. His second, converted by Luke Gale, on 55 minutes put the Tigers in a commanding position, 38-12 up.

Round 22

Hull FC ended their mini-slump in style with a Thursday-night 36-12 home victory over rivals Hull KR and the Airlie Birds moved back to the summit of the table after Wigan's defeat at Leeds the night after.

The defeat also confirmed that the Robins would enter the Qualifiers for the second successive year.

Coming into the game after suffering back-to-back defeats for the first time since March, Hull never looked in any danger as they physically dominated their opponents, completing three wins from three derbies in 2015 and extending their derby-winning run to five. They welcomed back inspirational skipper Gareth Ellis, who made a massive difference in the middle.

It was 18-0 by the break and 30-0 on 52 minutes as Marc Sneyd controlled with his kicking game and chimed in with some well-timed passes on the back of Danny

Houghton's continued excellence at dummy half. Mark Minichiello and Steve Michaels each finished with a couple of tries.

The rejuvenated Rhinos, with winger Tom Briscoe the latest player to return to the Rhinos' ranks after injuring his shoulder in April, ended the Warriors' eight-match winning run with an 18-16 win at Headingley.

James Segeyaro was an instant success on his 80-minute home debut, toughening the middle with 40 tackles and providing the range and speed of distribution that saw the likes of Kallum Watkins thrive.

Watkins held off numerous tackles to touch down for a converted try on 14 minutes, before Wigan's Josh Charnley soon reduced the gap and it remained 6-4 at half-time. Adam Cuthbertson and Brett Ferres tries made it 18-4 after 66 minutes

Wigan, who were without injured fullback Sam Tomkins and suspended-for-one-match captain Sean O'Loughlin, and gave a debut to New Zealand prop Frank-Paul Nuuausala, came back through tries from Jack Higginson and George Williams, but they couldn't repeat their last-second win of the week before against Wakefield.

The big talking point after the game was Taulima Tautai's cannonball tackle on Adam Cuthbertson. Tautai received a two-match ban, which was reduced to one game on appeal. Josh Charnley got two games for making contact with the match official.

On the Sunday, Warrington moved to within a point of the top of Super League with a convincing 42-26 victory at Castleford, remaining in third place but now on 31 league points, just one behind Hull FC and Wigan, thanks to a 26-point scoring spree after half-time.

Castleford, with Rangi Chase making his Super League return off the bench, led 18-16 at the break thanks to a Denny Solomona hat-trick but were blown off the park after the break by the rampant Wolves attack. Solomona finished with four tries in defeat, taking his tally to 30 in all competitions.

For the Wolves, Stefan Ratchford was brilliant in both attack and defence, scoring one try and stopping plenty, while Rhys Evans showed great pace for his two scores.

Wakefield had their top-eight finish rubber-stamped on the Thursday night after Hull FC defeated Hull KR, and went to Perpignan 48 hours later and beat Catalans 30-28 to cap off a great week for the club.

In the end the difference was a missed conversion, from Pat Richards in the 71st minute. Richards' attempt was ruled out by the officials, while the majority of the crowd appeared to think the ball passed over the posts and television replays seeming to suggest that the conversion was successful.

Max Jowitt crossed early on after good work by Craig Hall, but three quick tries by Tony Gigot, Dave Taylor and Justin Horo put the hosts in control.

Wakefield drew level at 18-18 at the break when Jonny Molloy powered over and Hall touched down. The Wildcats had regained the lead after an even first period when Bill Tupou made the most of some quick thinking by Hall to go over.

Catalans responded again when Morgan Escaré ran onto a Lucas Albert kick. Mikey Sio then crossed for the visitors and the reliable boot of Liam Finn made it 30-24, although Fouad Yaha then scored in the corner. Richards' missed conversion proved costly for Catalans.

The Catalans were now on a five-game losing streak as a last-minute dash down the touchline from Dave Taylor was not enough to edge the game. His attempted offload only found the touchline as Wakefield celebrated a famous win.

St Helens' 34-18 win, their fourth in succession, at Huddersfield the day after moved them level on points with fourth-placed Catalans.

Back-from-injury Luke Walsh was exceptional for Saints as the Giants' new coach, former Newcastle Knights coach Rick Stone, saw his side go in 22-12 down at the break thanks to Saints tries from Joe Greenwood, Jack Owens, Louie McCarthy-Scarsbrook and Jordan Turner.

July

Danny Brough and Tom Symonds responded for the Giants before the break, and Jermaine McGillvary's try, converted by Danny Brough, got them back to within four points on 46 minutes.

But Brough's last-tackle kick was intercepted by Swift on his own try-line, and he ran the full length of the pitch to score. Tom Symonds had a try ruled out for a forward pass, before Alex Walmsley's try wrapped up their fourth straight victory.

In the week, Saints utility Jordan Turner became the latest English player to head for the NRL as he announced he would be joining Canberra Raiders at the end of the season.

Mason Caton-Brown claimed his first hat-trick for Salford to complete their third win of the season over Widnes, a 32-24 success at the Select Security Stadium, boosting the Red Devils' chances of getting an additional home game in the forthcoming Qualifiers.

Caton-Brown, who had missed 16 weeks of the season with an ankle injury, started and finished the try scoring for a Salford side which was never behind, but was three times pulled back level and led by just two points before the former London Broncos winger's game-clinching strike two minutes from time.

Round 23

Ryan Hall's late try saw Leeds see off a resilient Hull KR side by 24-20 in the Thursday night game at the KC Lightstream Stadium to record their third win on the trot heading into the Super 8s Qualifiers.

The result secured the Rhinos the advantage of four home games in the make-or-break final phase of the season, while the Robins would face an extra match on the road as they looked to survive their second Middle 8s shootout in as many years.

For long periods there was little to separate the two sides in a nip-and-tuck affair, but when the excellent James Segeyaro crossed with 15 minutes to go, Leeds edged into a lead they would not relinquish. The contest was still hanging in the balance with two minutes remaining, but as Rovers chanced their arm from deep, Segeyaro's pressure saw a wayward Albert Kelly pass fumbled by Thomas Minns and Hall capitalised to score. There was still time for Kieran Dixon to race in for a consolation score for Rovers.

Friday night's games ended with Hull FC moving two points clear at the top of the table as St Helens won the derby at DW Stadium and Hull FC edged Salford.

Saints beat Wigan 23-4 in a blood and thunder match-up. It looked like these two would go into the interval all-square with two penalties from Mark Percival for the Saints either side of a try from Lewis Tierney, keeping them level at 4-4 in what was an even contest. But two tries from Percival and Morgan Knowles in the final ten minutes of the half saw St Helens take a 12-point lead into the break.

Wigan threw everything at St Helens in the second half but, not for the first time this season, their attack let them down as Saints, with Alex Walmsley immense, showed resolve. Luke Walsh sealed the game with a field goal before James Roby rubbed salt into the wound with a last-second try.

John Bateman was recalled to Wigan's starting line-up after a club-imposed eight-week suspension following an off-the-field incident, while Sam Tomkins and Sean O'Loughlin both returned after missing the defeat at Leeds through injury and suspension respectively.

Hull FC survived a second-half scare against Salford at the AJ Bell Stadium to emerge 28-20 winners. The Airlie Birds led 12-6 at the break through tries from Steve Michaels and Frank Pritchard, either side of a Michael Dobson score for Salford.

Second-half tries from Mason Caton-Brown, Niall Evalds and Rob Lui then put Salford ahead with ten minutes left, but further tries from Chris Green, Marc Sneyd and Mahe Fonua ensured the Black and Whites stayed top of the table.

Salford, meanwhile, were tooling up for the Qualifiers with the addition of Manly forwards Luke Burgess and Feleti Mateo. Burgess, who won the inaugural Albert Goldthorpe Rookie of the Year Medal in 2008, was making a return to Super League after five-and-a-half years in Australia with South Sydney and the Sea Eagles.

On the Saturday afternoon, Rick Stone's second game in charge of the Giants ended in defeat as they lost 34-30 at Warrington to have their position at the bottom of Super League rubber-stamped, the Wolves moving into second spot, just a point behind Hull.

Daryl Clark's late try sealed a see-saw clash between two well-matched sides. Ben Westwood was outstanding and he scored a crucial try just before half-time.

Winger Gene Ormsby finished with a hat-trick for the Giants after joining them permanently two weeks before, following a loan spell earlier in the season.

And on the Sunday, Castleford - with 14 players out - went into sixth spot after a 46-20 win at Wakefield, who moved down to eighth. The Wildcats, already suffering an injury crisis with a Cup semi-final to come the following week, ran out of troops in the second half after leading 16-10 at the break.

Wakefield led until the 58th minute when Luke Gale's try and goal, as centre Bill Tupou limped off in back play, put the Tigers in front for the first time. Four more tries followed with Gale and 2015 Albert Goldthorpe Rookie of the Year Andre Savelio, who had joined on loan from St Helens, running riot.

The Vikings finished the scheduled 23 rounds in seventh place after emerging with a comfortable 32-4 home victory over a disappointing, if injury weakened, Catalans side, whose once-so-promising season was suffering an alarming downward slide on a six-game losing run.

Joe Mellor celebrated his 100th Super League appearance by lighting up a damp and dull afternoon and his try on the hour was always likely to be enough against a Dragons side devoid of their usual sparkle in attack.

FIRST UTILITY SUPER LEAGUE
Sunday 24th July

	P	W	D	L	F	A	D	Pts
Hull FC	23	17	0	6	605	465	140	34
Warrington Wolves	23	16	1	6	675	425	250	33
Wigan Warriors	23	16	0	7	455	440	15	32
St Helens	23	14	0	9	573	536	37	28
Catalans Dragons	23	13	0	10	593	505	88	26
Castleford Tigers	23	10	1	12	617	640	-23	21
Widnes Vikings	23	10	0	13	499	474	25	20
Wakefield Trinity Wildcats	23	10	0	13	485	654	-169	20
Leeds Rhinos	23	8	0	15	404	576	-172	16
Salford Red Devils *	23	10	0	13	560	569	-9	14
Hull Kingston Rovers	23	6	2	15	486	610	-124	14
Huddersfield Giants	23	6	0	17	511	569	-58	12

* Six points deducted for salary cap breaches in 2014 & 2015

KINGSTONE PRESS CHAMPIONSHIP
Sunday 24th July

	P	W	D	L	F	A	D	Pts
Leigh Centurions	23	21	1	1	881	410	471	43
London Broncos	23	17	0	6	702	444	258	34
Batley Bulldogs	23	15	1	7	589	485	104	31
Featherstone Rovers	23	15	0	8	595	384	211	30
Bradford Bulls	23	13	2	8	717	446	271	28
Halifax	23	13	1	9	615	484	131	27
Sheffield Eagles	23	8	0	15	583	617	-34	16
Dewsbury Rams	23	8	0	15	486	603	-117	16
Swinton Lions	23	7	1	15	449	813	-364	15
Oldham	23	7	0	16	401	678	-277	14
Workington Town	23	5	1	17	455	756	-301	11
Whitehaven	23	5	1	17	367	720	-353	11

Challenge Cup Semi-finals

The top two sides in the Super League, Hull FC, at the top of the table after 23 rounds, and Warrington Wolves winning their semi-finals in contrasting style on the last weekend of July.

Hull beat Wigan 16-12 on the Friday night at the Keepmoat Stadium in Doncaster.

The game turned in four minutes in the second half, between the 47th and 51st minutes, when the Airlie Birds, trailing 8-2, scored two crucial tries, the first coming from Steve Michaels when Hull kept the ball alive for the winger to touch down in the corner.

And their second try came from a superb kick by Marc Sneyd that Dom Manfredi attempted to take with outstretched arms but failed to do so, with Fetuli Talanoa positioned to take advantage of the mistake to touch down.

Earlier in the 33rd minute, Wigan had been unlucky when Lewis Tierney had touched down, but the try was ruled out for a forward pass. If the try had been awarded Wigan would have gone two scores clear and it would have been a little more difficult for Hull to overhaul them.

It had been a tight and tense opening quarter until the 16th minute when Wigan stand-off George Williams produced the opening score of the semi-final. A high tackle by Liam Watts gave Wigan a penalty and, from that set, a quick play-the-ball by Ben Flower had the Hull defence scrambling, and Williams benefited with a trademark run to the line to score from close range. Matty Smith added the conversion.

As Hull's fearsome pack started to roll, a penalty under the sticks saw Sneyd take the two points. And they almost took the lead minutes later as Scott Taylor's pass put Gareth Ellis through a gap, but Sam Tomkins' brilliant tackle meant, in the eyes of the video referee, that Ellis didn't quite make the line.

Wigan started the better after the break, winning two penalties that allowed Smith to extend the lead with a penalty. Hull's levelling try in the 47th minute ended a superb passage of play that saw Carlos Tuimavave, Jamie Shaul and Ellis all get passes away, before the decisive pass from Frank Pritchard found Sika Manu, who gave it to Mahe Fonua and finally Michaels scored in the corner. Sneyd's touchline conversion levelled the game.

After Talanoa's try, Sneyd converted and then moved the distance between the teams to eight points with a penalty after Fonua had the ball stolen.

Wigan issued a response with nine minutes remaining, as another Williams pass sent Willie Isa to the line. Smith's missed conversion left four points between the teams. But the Airlie Birds hung on, sparking memorable scenes at the Keepmoat Stadium.

The following afternoon, it wasn't as close, as the Wolves hammered Wakefield 56-12 at Leigh Sports Village.

Wakefield started the game brilliantly, scoring a well-worked try on the left wing by Craig Hall, who was one of a number of top players to have signed for the Toronto Wolfpack, who were set to play in League One in 2017.

And they ended well, scoring a nicely constructed try by Max Jowitt on 66 minutes and then being very unlucky to have a second try by Hall disallowed on 74 minutes for a double movement. But by the time Jowitt scored his try Wakefield were losing 52-6.

Warrington scored their first try on 15 minutes by Jack Hughes, and their ninth by Ben Westwood on 64 minutes, scoring at a rate of just over a point a minute.

Warrington halfbacks Chris Sandow and Kurt Gidley controlled the game on the back of a dominant pack, with Daryl Clark in great form at dummy half.

Wakefield went into the game with a dozen players unavailable, including eleven injuries and promising youngster James Batchelor, who was away with England Academy in Australia. Coach Chris Chester was down to his final 16 players just hours before the game. Captain Danny Kirmond revealed he should not have played because of a knee injury but said he put his hand up to play due to his love for the club.

The prospect of a Hull-Warrington final was greeted with great anticipation.

* England Academy lost their two-match away series with the Combined High Schools in Australia, suffering a 50-26 defeat in Redcliffe, followed a week later by a 50-12 defeat at Shark Park, Cronulla.

Sunday 31st July 2016

COMBINED AUSTRALIAN HIGH SCHOOLS 50 ENGLAND ACADEMY 26
(at Redcliffe)

AUSTRALIA: Nic Cotric; Mawene Hiroti; Zac Lomax; Tiumavave Afualo; Campbell Graham; Lachlan Lam; Sean O'Sullivan; Pasami Saulo; Blake Brailey; Thomas Mikaele; Brodie Jones; Josh Curran; Sean Keppie. Subs: Dean Blore; Reece Robson; Payne Haas; Michael Tupou. **Tries:** Cotric, Hiroti 2, Lomax 2, Mikaele, Afualo, O'Sullivan, Jones; **Goals:** O'Sullivan 7.
ENGLAND: Lewis Heckford (Wigan Warriors); Liam Paisley (Wigan Warriors); Liam Walsh (Widnes Vikings); Joe Wardill (Hull Kingston Rovers); Matthew Costello (St Helens); Morgan Smith (Warrington Wolves); Rob Fairclough (St Helens); Matthew English (Huddersfield Giants); Josh Ganson (Wigan Warriors); Mikolaj Oledzki (Leeds Rhinos); James Batchelor (Wakefield Trinity Wildcats); Cameron Smith (Leeds Rhinos); Jack Wells (Wigan Warriors). Subs: Danny Walker (Widnes Vikings); Brad Walker (Widnes Vikings); Conor Fitzsimmons (Castleford Tigers); Caine Barnes (Wigan Warriors). **Tries:** Wardill, English, D Walker, Paisley, Heckford; **Goals:** Fairclough, Smith 2.

Sunday 6th August 2016

COMBINED AUSTRALIAN HIGH SCHOOLS 50 ENGLAND ACADEMY 12
(at Shark Park, Cronulla)

AUSTRALIA: Dean Blore; Mawene Hiroti; Zac Lomax; Nic Cotric; Campbell Graham; Lachlan Lam; Sean O'Sullivan; Pasami Saulo; Blake Brailey; Thomas Mikaele; Daniel Keir; Williams Burns; Sean Keppie. Subs: Tiumavave Afualo; Reece Robson; Payne Haas; Michael Tupou. **Tries:** Cotric 3, Lam 2, Lomax, Tupou, Blore, Afualo; **Goals:** O'Sullivan 7.
ENGLAND: Jez Litten (Hull FC); Craig Mullen (Wigan Warriors); Liam Walsh (Widnes Vikings); Joe Wardill (Hull Kingston Rovers); Will Oakes (Hull Kingston Rovers); Lewis Heckford (Wigan Warriors); Morgan Smith (Warrington Wolves); Matthew English (Huddersfield Giants); Josh Ganson (Wigan Warriors); Mikolaj Oledzki (Leeds Rhinos); James Batchelor (Wakefield Trinity Wildcats); Jack Wells (Wigan Warriors); Cameron Smith (Leeds Rhinos). Subs: Danny Walker (Widnes Vikings); Brad Walker (Widnes Vikings); Conor Fitzsimmons (Castleford Tigers); Owen Farnworth (Widnes Vikings). **Tries:** Ganson, Oledzki; **Goals:** M Smith 2.

AUGUST
The end of the hoodoo

Super League Super 8s - Round 1

In the Thursday night Super 8s kick-off, St Helens extended their winning run to six games with a 20-18 victory at the Halliwell Jones Stadium against Warrington to solidify their place in the top four.

The Wolves thought they had pinched it in the last minute. Trailing by two points, a move to the right culminated in Toby King putting Rhys Evans in at the corner. But the video referee ruled the winger's foot touched the whitewash, resulting in St Helens picking up two crucial points.

The Wolves' handling was far from precise and Saints led at half-time after Louie McCarthy-Scarsbrook and Daryl Clark swapped tries before Mark Percival's perfectly-timed pass allowed Adam Swift to sprint down the touchline ahead of Rhys Evans. In support was Jonny Lomax, who raced 25 metres to finish the move.

Warrington took to the field early ahead of the second half, going through some basic ball-handling drills after a sloppy display in the opening 40 minutes. Things didn't improve for them, though Saints weren't much better. Even so, there was plenty of drama and an exciting conclusion.

A frustrating 15 minutes late on culminated in the two teams exchanging blows in a confrontation, in which Jack Hughes was accused by some of attempting to gouge the eyes of McCarthy-Scarsbrook. He faced no charge after video review.

The next night Hull FC missed a chance to stay clear at the top when Castleford Tigers, whose play-off hopes were barely alive, produced a superb 30-16 win at KCOM Stadium.

Hull's form outside backs Fetuli Talanoa and Mahe Fonua both missed the game but there was no denying the Tigers' superiority, with Luke Gale at the centre of things, as he had been all season, as they led 24-0 until the hour mark. Makeshift winger Ryan Hampshire scored a couple of tries and Adam Milner sealed the win after the Airlie Birds had threatened a late comeback.

Wigan bounced back from their Cup semi-final exit with a 60-12 home annihilation of Wakefield.

It took the Warriors just five minutes to get the ball rolling with George Williams going over, and further tries from Sam Powell and Josh Charnley saw Wigan race into a 16-0 lead after 15 minutes. Sam Tomkins and Joe Arundel traded scores before John Bateman and Oliver Gildart gave the Warriors a 30-6 half-time lead.

After the break Wigan refused to take their foot off the pedal as they ran in a further five tries, with Williams and Tomkins adding to their first-half scores, while Dom Manfredi, Dan Sarginson and Matty Smith also got in on the act.

Wakefield's resources were almost exhausted and they gave debuts to Academy winger Judah Mazive and forward Frazer Morris. Mazive should have been in Australia with the England Academy side but had to fly home early from the tour following the death of his father.

August

They effectively had no chance of making the top-four play-off with six games to go, highlighting a fundamental weakness in the Super 8s structure, now in its second season and coming under intense scrutiny.

Widnes were in the same situation and went down 26-10 at Catalans on the Saturday night. Fouad Yaha scored three tries in eighteen second-half minutes to end a five-match losing run which had made the Dragons' own play-off chances remote.

Super 8s, The Qualifiers - Round 1

Luke Burgess and Feleti Mateo made debuts for Salford on the Sunday during their opening Qualifiers match against Huddersfield and the Red Devils won a 34-12 victory at the AJ Bell Stadium.

Mason Caton-Brown scored his second hat-trick in three games as halves Robert Lui and Michael Dobson ran the show. Salford were 24-0 up until the 55th minute and Caton-Brown's second try on the hour mark stemmed a Giants revival.

In the Saturday TV game, Leeds Rhinos, who had left their own form revival too late to make the top eight, ran away with a 62-6 win at Featherstone.

Rhinos coach Brian McDermott was able to name his strongest 17 of the year. Only Stevie Ward was unavailable through injury, having not appeared since the last game of the regular 2015 season. The result was a lopsided scoreline, fuelled by sparkling performances from Kallum Watkins and Liam Sutcliffe in particular, with the duo scoring 42 points between them, despite the Rhinos holding only an 18-6 lead at half-time.

Hull KR also made short work of Championship opponents, beating Batley Bulldogs 58-18 at KC Lightstream Stadium, Thomas Minns collecting a first-half hat-trick.

The Bulldogs posted the first points of the afternoon with a try from Alistair Leak just three minutes in, but the Super League side's extra quality and fitness told as they ran in six first-half scores to take a stranglehold on a game that they were never to lose. Albert Kelly was full of classy touches and dangerous plays as he guided the Robins to the big win.

Leigh Centurions opened their Qualifiers campaign with a 34-30 home win over fellow Championship side London Broncos, who had battled back from 34-8 down with eight minutes to go to lose by just four points.

Matty Dawson, signed from St Helens, and Mitch Brown, recruited from Cronulla and on debut, scored two tries each to help the Centurions to victory. Both players grabbed their second score after Reni Maitua went in for Leigh's third try after the break.

Martyn Ridyard kicked his seventh goal to put Leigh - Championship title winners for the third successive season - 26 points ahead. Then Broncos' Jamie Soward, who re-joined London in June from Penrith, and Leigh's Greg Worthington were sent-off for fighting in the 73rd minute, after Ireland World Cup centre Api Pewhairangi, playing stand-off, had scored what seemed a consolation try.

But Pewhairangi ran in another try, converted that and two more scores got the Broncos within four points, Andy Ackers and Daniel Harrison grabbing further tries when both sides were a man short.

Super League Super 8s - Round 2

Hull FC got back on the horse with a commanding 38-0 win at Widnes in the Thursday TV game, winger Fetuli Talanoa returning from injury and scoring a strong hat-trick against an injury-hit Vikings.

Rhys Hanbury, Stefan Marsh, Charly Runciman and Chris Dean were all missing from the previous week, with Denis Betts recalling youngsters Jay Chapelhow and Ed Chamberlain. Academy winger Ryan Ince was also handed his debut.

Hull's quick-fire brace of tries in the last ten minutes of the first half, from Carlos

64

Tuimavave and Talanoa, completely shattered the Vikings' resolve and ensured the two points were going back across the Pennines.

The Vikings became the first side to be ruled out of semi-final contention after St Helens' win against Catalans 24 hours later. It meant Widnes, who were at the top end of the table at Easter, were twelve points adrift of the four with ten left to play for.

St Helens were establishing themselves as the form side and they beat Catalans at home 39-16. Adam Swift's four tries, Luke Walsh's distribution and kicking game in midfield and some significant contributions from Jonny Lomax were the key ingredients in Saints' seventh successive win.

It put clear daylight between them and fifth-placed Catalans, whose star continued to wane despite a gutsy effort in what was an entertaining, if at times fractious clash.

Swift's hat-trick effort right on half-time, with Saints still down to twelve men - Walsh sin-binned for a dangerous tackle on Lucas Albert - took the initiative away from the Dragons.

Walsh was subsequently banned for two games, along with prop Luke Thompson, who had been put on report for a dangerous tackle on Justin Horo.

Australian international Willie Mason was given permission to leave the Dragons after having been ruled out for the rest of the season with an avulsion fracture (an injury to the bone in a location where a tendon or ligament attaches to the bone) and ankle ligament damage.

Wigan lost ground on Hull after a 36-22 defeat at on-song Castleford. A try three minutes from time by winger Ryan Hampshire, who was on a season-long loan from Wigan, helped the Tigers thwart a strong rally from 26-12 down to keep their lingering hopes of a place in the top-four play-offs alive.

The Warriors badly missed their captain Sean O'Loughlin, who pulled out the previous day with hamstring trouble. Apart from a spell midway through the second half they generally failed to fire. The Tigers, by contrast, had several outstanding figures, not least winger Denny Solomona. The leading try-scorer in Super League grabbed a scintillating hat-trick to take his season's tally to 31 tries.

Wigan winger Dom Manfredi suffered a season-ending anterior cruciate ligament injury.

Wakefield's play-off hopes were also officially ended on the Sunday by a 38-10 defeat at home to Warrington. The Wildcats were still in sight until Daryl Clark's try just before the hour mark helped the Wolves pull away and reclaim second spot.

Super 8s, The Qualifiers - Round 2

Leigh Centurions coach Neil Jukes urged his side to remain grounded after their 32-26 win over Super League Salford on the Saturday.

The Centurions weathered a considerable second-half storm to emerge winners and give the Qualifiers a much-needed boost after some one-sided scorelines on the opening weekend.

The Centurions became the first Championship club to defeat Super League opposition in this year's Qualifiers in a victory that was to prove pivotal in their quest for promotion. The previous year's failed Qualifiers berth was partly down to Leigh surrendering a 24-6 lead to Hull KR in the opening game of the competition, with the Centurions eventually finishing bottom of the table as they failed to overcome the setback.

Having taken a 20-10 lead against Salford, the Centurions were put under pressure by Ian Watson's side as the Red Devils cut the deficit to four points in the second half.

This year, however, Leigh absorbed the pressure and scored two tries through Matty Dawson and Adam Higson, who had had an inspired game in defence, to secure victory, earning them a vital two points, despite two late tries to Salford's Ben Murdoch-

Masila and Mason Caton-Brown.

Hull KR went down 22-18 at Leeds, with Rhinos hooker James Segeyaro scoring two late tries. As it had done at the Lightstream Stadium in the last of the regular season rounds, the ultimate difference proved to be the increasingly confident Liam Sutcliffe's goal kicking.

Huddersfield gained their first victory of the Super 8s qualifiers with a massive eleven-try 62-16 win over Featherstone at the John Smith's Stadium. Former Bradford junior Oliver Roberts gave an impressive attacking display that was rewarded with two tries.

London Broncos recorded a thumping 76-16 home victory against Batley Bulldogs. Andrew Henderson's team ran in 14 tries, with wingers Rhys Williams and Iliess Macani each waltzing over for a hat-trick of tries, whilst scrum-half Jamie Soward kicked ten goals.

The only negative for the Broncos saw Api Pewhairangi being stretchered off with a serious knee injury.

The Bulldogs players decided to pay for the club's fans' travel to the trip to Leigh the following week by way of an apology.

Super League Super 8s - Round 3

Hull FC guaranteed a play-off place and remained top of the table with a 44-nil hammering of Catalans on the Thursday night.

Hull rattled up a 22-point advantage by half-time, with tries from Dean Hadley, Mahe Fonua and Mark Minichiello. After the break, Fetuli Talanoa crossed and Fonua scored a second before Marc Sneyd added a try to his eight goals before Frank Pritchard grabbed a late seventh try

St Helens' winning run came to end with a bang on the Friday night. Saints, who had won their last seven Super League encounters and recently defeated the Warriors 23-4 at the DW Stadium, were unable to register a single point in a 25-0 reverse. Wigan centre Anthony Gelling was the match-winner with a hat-trick of tries.

Both teams had plenty of possession in the opening 40 minutes and ample opportunities to post points, but it was Wigan who led 12-0 thanks to a brace of tries from Gelling.

St Helens refused to give up, but they were second best all evening and further tries from Gelling and George Williams secured a comfortable victory for the Warriors.

Jack Hughes' last-minute try, after the Wolves had regained the kick-off from Luke Gale's seemingly match-winning field goal, both sealed Warrington's top-four place with a 14-11 home win and all but put an end to the Tigers' hopes.

It was harsh on a Castleford side that played their full part in a tense if often untidy clash. They had looked certain to take home the points and maintain their winning run in the Super 8s when Gale stepped forward, but it wasn't to be. Paul McShane didn't deserve to be on the losing side as he was a constant source of creativity and industry.

Widnes got their first win of the Super 8s against Wakefield on the Sunday, Patrick Ah Van getting two tries in a 40-8 home success.

The Vikings may not have had much to play for except pride, but they dominated the opening 40 minutes as Wakefield looked out of sorts and desperate for the season to come to an end. Three tries in the opening 20 minutes from Ah Van, Rhys Hanbury and Matt Whitley put the Vikings in full control, while Corey Thompson extended their advantage with their fourth try just before the break.

The Vikings took their foot off the gas a little in the second half, but still managed to cross for three tries through Stefan Marsh, Lloyd White and Ah Van. Craig Hall and Ben Jones-Bishop grabbed consolations for Trinity.

Super 8s, The Qualifiers - Round 3

Salford Red Devils were under pressure after Hull KR's 29-12 win in wet conditions at the AJ Bell Stadium on the Friday night. Not only had they lost two of their opening three games, including the previous week's fixture at Leigh, they would have to travel to face a rejuvenated Leeds side the week after Wembley without wingers Mason Caton-Brown and Justin Carney, both out for the remainder of the season through injury.

Against the Robins, Caton-Brown had grabbed his tenth try in five games before leaving the field with rib damage, while the blockbusting Carney had been recovering from a thigh problem since mid-July.

A string of desperate, last-gasp defensive efforts from Rovers denied the Red Devils on a number of occasions, while the men from east Hull found the extra quality to turn their opportunities into points.

The Robins' win was largely down to coming out of the blocks quickly, racing into a 12-point lead in as many minutes. First, Ben Cockayne's long pass allowed Josh Mantellato to finish brilliantly at the corner, then when Salford fumbled on the first tackle after a drop-out, Albert Kelly's lovely reverse kick was touched down by the impressive James Greenwood. Kelly's 67th minute field goal finally ended any chance of a Salford comeback.

Leeds' 42-28 victory at London on the Saturday afternoon was marked by three tries from winger Tom Briscoe in front of a record crowd for a Rugby League match at the Ealing Trailfinders venue of 1,845.

The Rhinos led 24-12 at the start of the second half and looked as though they were already taking control when Jamie Soward failed to find touch from a penalty and the Rhinos scored on the next set.

Danny McGuire was set to miss the rest of the season after suffering an ankle injury in the 32nd minute.

On the Sunday, Huddersfield moved up to third place in the Qualifiers table and took a step towards securing their Super League status for 2017 with a 58-28 victory over Batley at Mount Pleasant.

It was one-way traffic in the first half as the Giants ran in nine straight tries. Huddersfield were ruthless against their Championship opponents in the first 40 minutes and punished every error with impressive efficiency. But the Bulldogs bounced back in the second half to score 26 points. The Giants had seven different try-scorers, with Ryan Brierley grabbing a hat-trick and both Leroy Cudjoe and Tom Symonds finishing with doubles.

And down the road in Featherstone, Leigh Centurions edged closer to a return to Super League as they won 30-18 to maintain their perfect start to the Qualifiers. Reni Maitua and Mitch Brown crossed in the first half for a 12-8 lead, Josh Walters replying for Rovers.

Matty Dawson, Mickey Higham and Gareth Hock secured a 16th successive win for Leigh, although tries from Luke Briscoe and Jack Ormondroyd ensured a nervy finish until Hock's winner, which the officials took an age to award.

FIRST UTILITY SUPER LEAGUE - SUPER 8s
Sunday 21st August

	P	W	D	L	F	A	D	Pts
Hull FC	26	19	0	7	703	495	208	38
Warrington Wolves	26	18	1	7	745	466	279	37
Wigan Warriors	26	18	0	8	562	488	74	36
St Helens	26	16	0	10	632	595	37	32
Catalans Dragons	26	14	0	12	635	598	37	28
Castleford Tigers	26	12	1	13	694	692	2	25
Widnes Vikings	26	11	0	15	549	546	3	22
Wakefield Trinity Wildcats	26	10	0	16	515	792	-277	20

SUPER 8s - THE QUALIFIERS
Sunday 21st August

	P	W	D	L	F	A	D	Pts
Leeds Rhinos	3	3	0	0	126	52	74	6
Leigh Centurions	3	3	0	0	96	74	22	6
Huddersfield Giants	3	2	0	1	132	78	54	4
Hull Kingston Rovers	3	2	0	1	105	52	53	4
London Broncos	3	1	0	2	134	92	42	2
Salford Red Devils	3	1	0	2	72	73	-1	2
Featherstone Rovers	3	0	0	3	40	154	-114	0
Batley Bulldogs	3	0	0	3	62	192	-130	0

August

Challenge Cup Final

Gareth Ellis became the first man to lift the Challenge Cup at Wembley in a Hull FC shirt after leading his team to a nail-biting 12-10 win over Warrington Wolves.

Eight times Hull had been to Wembley before 2016, and eight times they had failed to win, the only anomaly in a run of defeats being the draw with Widnes in 1982.

It could have been so easily different, but for one of the most historic Challenge Cup moments. With Hull holding a slender two-point lead after having trailed by ten points going into the final quarter, Warrington were on the attack in the dying seconds and throwing everything at their defence.

HULL FC: 1 Jamie Shaul; 19 Steve Michaels; 2 Mahe Fonua; 24 Kirk Yeaman; 5 Fetuli Talanoa; 3 Carlos Tuimavave; 7 Marc Sneyd; 8 Scott Taylor; 9 Danny Houghton; 10 Liam Watts; 21 Sika Manu; 12 Mark Minichiello; 11 Gareth Ellis (C). Subs (all used): 22 Josh Bowden; 23 Frank Pritchard; 30 Danny Washbrook; 15 Chris Green.
Tries: Fonua (61), Shaul (73); **Goals:** Sneyd 2/2.
WOLVES: 6 Stefan Ratchford; 5 Matthew Russell; 24 Toby King; 4 Ryan Atkins; 3 Rhys Evans; 1 Kurt Gidley; 7 Chris Sandow; 8 Chris Hill (C); 9 Daryl Clark; 10 Ashton Sims; 11 Ben Currie; 12 Jack Hughes; 14 Joe Westerman. Subs (all used): 18 George King; 16 Brad Dwyer; 13 Ben Westwood; 33 Ryan Bailey.
Tries: Russell (34), Currie (54); **Goals:** Gidley 1/3.
Rugby Leaguer & League Express Men of the Match:
Hull FC: Danny Houghton; *Wolves:* Daryl Clark.
Penalty count: 3-3; **Half-time:** 0-6; **Referee:** Gareth Hewer; **Attendance:** 76,235 *(at Wembley Stadium)*.

The Wolves kept the ball alive, with Chris Sandow slinging the ball right and Ben Currie barging off Marc Sneyd and bustling away from Carlos Tuimavave. The line was inches away, as was the Challenge Cup for Warrington. A try seemed certain.

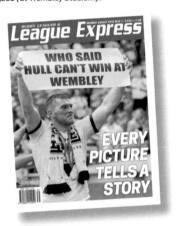

But somehow Hull hooker Danny Houghton shot across to cover to make one of the most remarkable tackles ever seen on the Wembley turf. Not only did he bring down Currie short of the line, the tackle dislodged the ball to win the Cup for the Airlie Birds. It was the 52nd tackle that Houghton had made.

Leading 10-0 after an hour, Warrington looked set to claim the Cup for the first time in four years, before being undone by a late Hull comeback orchestrated by Lance Todd Trophy winner Sneyd.

With 20 minutes left Hull FC's Wembley hoodoo looked certain to roll on for at least another twelve months. But Sneyd's magnificent 40/20 on the hour mark turned the game on its head, before Hull scored twelve unanswered points and Houghton produced his heroics.

Sneyd became only the second Hull FC player to win the Lance Todd Trophy (Tommy Harris achieved it whilst on the losing side against Wakefield Trinity in 1960). Two years before he had been unceremoniously hooked from the field after half an hour by his coach Daryl Powell as his Castleford side went down to Leeds.

The Wolves were not without their heroes. The likes of Chris Hill and Currie were tireless all afternoon, and Daryl Clark was their standout.

Clark was in great form and when he broke from midfield to set Currie up for the try that made it 10-0 on 54 minutes, it looked like the Wolves' name on the Challenge Cup, and probably his name on the Lance Todd Trophy.

An opening half filled with tension, big defensive plays and a feeling that Super League's best two sides were going to deliver a classic, yielded no points until the 34th minute, when Warrington broke the deadlock with a Matty Russell try.

It came after Chris Sandow pocketed a loose Frank Pritchard pass, dashing 80 metres downfield. But before he could get to the line, he was dragged down after an incredible track back from Jamie Shaul. Warrington kept their cool and Shaul and Mahe Fonua were

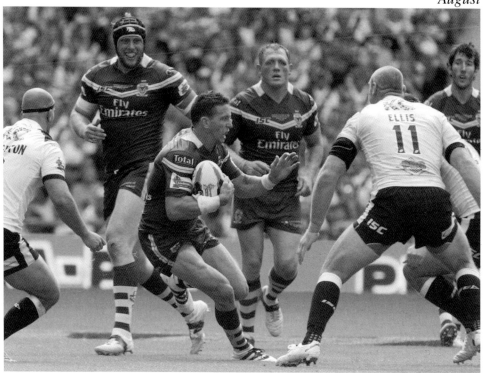

Warrington's Kurt Gidley closed down at Wembley by Hull FC's Gareth Ellis and Danny Houghton

powerless to prevent Russell diving over from dummy-half on the following play.

Kurt Gidley converted for a 6-0 half-time lead, and that should have been eight five minutes after the break when the Aussie missed a simple penalty, which was a crucial moment in the context of the game.

That looked like it may have let Hull off the hook, but, as the opening hour wore on, the Airlie Birds looked incapable of producing something to unlock a resolute Warrington defence. The frustration in the Hull end was palpable and their misery was compounded when Currie scampered over in the left corner after a wonderful break from Clark. Gidley again missed the goal, but a ten-point lead looked enormous, given Hull's insipid attacking play.

But then, as the hour mark approached, Sneyd caught Stefan Ratchford unaware and produced his sensational 40/20, and from that set, the halfback's towering kick to the corner towards Sandow was claimed by Fonua.

Sneyd converted for 10-6 and, with the final coming alive once again, it was now Hull applying all the pressure.

For a good ten minutes it looked like they wouldn't breach the Warrington line again, before the pinpoint kicking of Sneyd, and a move straight from the training ground, produced the goods. The halfback launched a kick in the air, Fonua patted back the ball back to him, and instinctively, by his side was Shaul, who raced round to dive in under the posts, bringing back memories of Paul Cooke in 2005 at Cardiff.

That finish gave Sneyd the simplest conversion to nudge Hull ahead.

But the drama wasn't over. As Warrington turned aggressors, they launched one last desperate attack, but Currie was denied by Houghton's Herculean effort.

That proved to be enough to keep Warrington at bay.

When the hooter sounded, delirium and pandemonium ensued among the 30,000 travelling Hull fans.

SEPTEMBER
Wolves top it off

Super League Super 8s - Round 4

Hull FC's Challenge Cup heroics halted their momentum in the Super 8s and the Friday after Wembley they were knocked off the top of the table at in-form St Helens, losing 31-10.

Winger Adam Swift's crucial contributions helped keep the race for Super League's summit wide open as well as securing St Helens' own play-off place. An intriguing contest was delicately poised at 18-10 just past the hour mark when the Black and Whites - who made seven changes from the Wembley triumph over Warrington - mounted an attack that could have set up a grandstand finale.

When Mahe Fonua offloaded to Steve Michaels by the right corner flag, it looked a score, until Swift reacted quickly to bundle the Hull man into touch. Moments later the Saints winger was producing a superb 60-metre break up the middle of the field to create the position for Atelea Vea's crucial second try and the home side eased to victory in the closing stages.

Leon Pryce, having played just once in the last eight weeks, captained Hull, 48 hours after his return to Bradford for 2017 was confirmed.

Wigan had already missed their chance to leapfrog Hull, having lost at home to Widnes the night before by 8-6. It was a magnificent defensive effort by the Vikings. Captain Kevin Brown played a crucial role as Widnes backed up their sensational 18-12 win at the DW Stadium in March.

Widnes deservedly led at half-time thanks to a brace of tries from right winger Corey Thompson and he also came up with some crucial tackles in the second half that set the platform for the win.

Wigan improved after the break, with a try from Liam Farrell reducing the deficit to two points. But, with their opponents having two players sin-binned, Jack Buchanan and Connor Farrell both for interference in the tackle, they were unable to take advantage.

There was no Wembley hangover for Warrington as they secured a vital two points with a 26-22 win at Catalans to take them top of the Super League table. Young halfback Declan Patton came into the team and scored two tries and five goals as the Wolves won for the second time in Perpignan in 2016. Seven days after he was denied a match-winning try by inches, Ben Currie scored the late try to seal the points.

Denny Solomona scored a first-half hat-trick as Castleford ran in eight tries to beat neighbours Wakefield for the third time in 2016. The winger went over before Rangi Chase extended the lead, and the hosts were 34-8 ahead at half-time thanks to Luke Dorn and Paul McShane's tries. Jake Webster touched down on his return from injury and Luke Gale capped another excellent display with a late try. Wakefield scored five tries through Tom Johnstone, who went over twice, Reece Lyne, Bill Tupou and Nick Scruton.

The Wildcats lacked the services of captain Danny Kirmond, Chris Annakin and Richard Owen, all of whom had sustained injuries in a motor accident seven days before. But they did give a debut to Warrington loanee Ben Harrison, playing his first game of the season.

Tigers front-rower Grant Millington was withdrawn and it was later revealed the Australian was suffering from a heart murmur, which would require minor surgery during the close season.

Castleford halfback Gale won the Albert Goldthorpe Medal for a second successive year, becoming only the second player to ever win the award in two consecutive seasons, following in the footsteps of Huddersfield halfback Danny Brough.

Super 8s, The Qualifiers - Round 4

Leigh Centurions captain Micky Higham said his side had 'one foot in Super League' following a Saturday TV win at Hull KR. The former Great Britain hooker was again pivotal as Leigh extended their perfect start to the Qualifiers, this time with a 25-18 victory against the Robins.

The Centurions produced a good second half in very wet conditions after Rovers had dominated the opening quarter to lead 12-0 with tries from Ken Sio and Josh Mantellato. 'Honestly I thought we were going to get mullered at that point,' said Leigh coach Neil Jukes.

Harrison Hansen came on when the Centurions trailed 12-0 and was inspirational, both in attack and defence. A try from Sam Hopkins put Leigh back in it. Andrew Dixon helped level the scores just after the break, before Matty Dawson crossed to give Leigh the lead. They scored their third try in seven minutes through Josh Drinkwater, though Matty Marsh's 65th minute set up a tense finale before Martyn Ridyard sealed it with a 78th-minute field goal.

Rovers named Maurice Blair at halfback alongside youngster Marsh after the surprise news of Albert Kelly's suspension by the club filtered through the terraces. The halfback had been granted permission to return to Australia for family reasons a fortnight before but reported back to the UK later than agreed.

Stevie Ward was handed a hero's reception by the Rhinos fans as he ended an 11-month lay-off in their 30-8 victory over Salford on the Friday. It was a poignant night of remembrance for former club President Harry Jepson, who had died in the week, as Leeds put one foot on the rung to Super League safety while Salford stood precariously on the precipice of the 'Million Pound Game' after their third consecutive defeat.

The difference again was prompter-in-chief James Segeyaro, who latched on to a Josh Griffin error for the game-turning try just before the hour – his fifth in as many games - with the Rhinos holding onto a narrow 12-8 lead, and had a part in the Rhinos' other four as well. When Griffin mishandled the ball in midfield, Segeyaro grubbered on twice and regathered to score to establish a two-score lead and wrest the initiative.

Danny Brough was the decisive force as Huddersfield Giants swept to their third successive victory over Championship opposition, beating London 40-4 at the John Smith's Stadium on the Friday night.

The Broncos more than held their own for much of the opening quarter but by half-time tries by Jermaine McGillvary and his right-flank partner Leroy Cudjoe had overhauled the 19th minute touchdown from the Championship's leading tryscorer Rhys Williams.

Within 13 minutes of the restart, further scores from Joe Wardle, Cudjoe and Michael Lawrence all but sealed the win.

The all-Championship game on the Sunday was a belter, with Batley beating Featherstone 11-10, a thrilling contest only split by Dominic Brambani's field goal right on half-time. Rovers led 10-7 up to the 69th minute when Wayne Reittie's won it for the Bulldogs.

Super League Super 8s - Round 5

It was a pivotal Friday night for the Super 8s as Warrington ended it three points clear at the top of the table with only two rounds left to play.

The Wolves produced a dominant first-half display to beat Widnes, for the fourth time in 2016, at home by 30-12, effectively securing the two points as they raced into a 20-0 lead at the break. Joe Philbin's try early in the second half took the score to 26-0 and effectively killed off any hope the Vikings had.

Kurt Gidley was back for the Wolves after recovering from the eye injury suffered at Wembley, but the stars of the show were Matt Russell and Stefan Ratchford.

Wigan defied all the odds to overturn an eight-point, half-time deficit to snatch victory from Hull's grasp in the closing stages at KCOM Stadium, the Warriors taking the lead when an inspired Taulima Tautai raced in under the posts in the 77th minute, ending 18-12 victors.

Having trailed 12-4 at half-time, with George Williams' 11th minute try cancelled out by Fetuli Talanoa and Mahe Fonua, Wigan dominated the scoring after the break. Sam Powell went in from dummy-half on the 65th minute to pull them within two points. Tautai then stretched out to turn the match late on and stun Hull.

Matty Smith's late penalty goal on the hooter rounded off a great win. John Bateman recovered from an early concussion scare and was magnificent for the Warriors.

On the same night, Wakefield had all the play in the second half at home to the Catalans but could only score one try through Craig Hall, Tony Gigot's 65th minute penalty sealing a 14-10 win for the Catalans.

On the Thursday night St Helens had made it mathematically impossible for the Dragons to catch them in fourth spot with a 40-16 home win over a patched up Castleford side that led 10-6 until the half-hour mark, by which time back-rower Junior Moors had joined the Tigers' casualty list with a knee injury.

With 13 players already sidelined, Andre Savelio unable to play against his parent club and Oliver Holmes pulling out on the day of the game through illness, Castleford coach Daryl Powell was forced to give a debut to Brandon Douglas, while winger Paddy Flynn played most of the game in the pack. It proved too much to fully test in-form Saints, who had excellent performances from Jonny Lomax and James Roby.

Kyle Amor, Luke Thompson and Morgan Knowles emerged from the bench just after the quarter mark to all touch down before half-time and take the impetus away from the Tigers.

Super 8s, The Qualifiers - Round 5

Leigh secured promotion to the top flight for the first time since 2005 with a 48-40 home victory against Huddersfield, their fifth win in succession in the Qualifiers, with Martyn Ridyard scoring two tries and eight goals for a personal tally of 24 points.

It was an amazing story. Local boy Ridyard, who had spent his entire career with the Centurions, was dropped from the team midway through the year, before returning to play a pivotal role throughout the Qualifiers.

Also key to victory along with Ridyard were mid-season signing Josh Drinkwater, who had signed a new contract to remain at the Leigh Sports Village until the end of 2019, hookers Micky Higham and Liam Hood, and winger Matty Dawson, who claimed a sparkling first-half hat-trick of tries. At one stage early in the second half, Leigh led 48-10.

Leeds received a double boost, not only mathematically securing their Super League status when they beat Batley 32-0 and Leigh triumphed over Huddersfield, but formally tying up the immediate future of boom hooker James Segeyaro on a deal until the end of 2018. The Papua New Guinean's initial deal had been until the end of the season.

On the Friday night Batley left the Headingley field to a chorus of acclaim from the South Stand as well as their loyal followers, enjoying a first visit in 33 years, in an astonishing crowd of over 15,000. The enthusiastic Bulldogs thwarted any score for more than a quarter hour of each half, conceding 16 points and three tries in each, the fitness difference between part and full-time only evident late on in the respective forty minutes.

Salford had to beat Featherstone at home to have any chance of avoiding the 4th v 5th play-off and they did so in style by 70-16.

A completely one-sided afternoon looked anything but possible following the opening minute, when Featherstone took the lead with a marvellous length-of-the-field try from Jordan Baldwinson, with Kyle Briggs converting for a 6-0 lead.

Incredibly, however, Featherstone would not complete a tackle in possession for the next 20 minutes. By the time they did, they were 20 points behind.

There was no Feleti Mateo in the home line-up. The 32-year-old Manly forward had lasted just 46 days at the Red Devils before leaving the club to head home, with family reasons cited as the reason.

It was an impressive show from Salford who had learned that week that director of rugby Tim Sheens was to move to Qualifiers rivals Hull KR as head coach at the end of the season. Sheens would step aside should the Million Pound Game be between his current employers and the side with whom he would take up a three-year contract for 2017, with the appointment going ahead even if the Robins were relegated to the Championship.

That looked less likely after Hull KR rose to third place in the Qualifiers, recording a 58-18 win at London Broncos, Thomas Minns grabbing a hat-trick.

The return of the influential Terry Campese from a serious hamstring injury – coupled with the comeback of football manager Jamie Peacock, who had come out of playing retirement – helped spark the Rovers, who had given Maurice Blair permission to return to Australia for his brother's funeral, and still not lifted Albert Kelly's internal suspension.

Super League Super 8s - Round 6

The League Leaders' Shield was on hand at the Halliwell Jones Stadium to be presented to the Wolves if they won their game with Wigan, and that outcome looked inevitable almost half way through the second half.

The Wolves were leading 28-14 after an hour and, when Wigan forward Ben Flower was sent off, it looked like a first piece of silverware since 2012 was heading the way of the Wolves.

But the Warriors produced a remarkable comeback with 12 men, scoring 21 unanswered points to win 35-28 after Flower had been dismissed for a late challenge on Wolves halfback Declan Patton as he made a kick. Within 15 minutes they were level, thanks to two tries from Josh Charnley and one from Lewis Tierney. Sam Tomkins lifted his game superbly when he needed to, scoring a vital try at the end of the first half, then demonstrating inspiring leadership after the dismissal of Flower to lead his side home.

Warrington suffered the blow of seeing Ben Currie damaging his ACL as he went over for the try that gave them what should have been a winning lead on 56 minutes.

The Wolves now had to avoid defeat at second-placed Hull the following Friday to claim first place.

Hull FC ended their Challenge Cup hangover with a first victory since Wembley, but had a close shave the night before in the Thursday TV game, when they recorded an 18-12 win at Wakefield, after trailing 8-0 just before half-time.

Mahe Fonua was the man who produced something special when Hull needed it most, galloping 50 metres upfield with eight minutes remaining as the Airlie Birds played hot potato in midfield on a 'free play', before scoring himself from dummy half on the next play.

September

St Helens made it ten wins from their last eleven to keep their impressive form going ahead of the play-offs with a 21-8 win in a fractious game at Widnes.

Adam Swift scored two early tries to put Saints in the box seat and the game was marred by an ugly brawl towards the end of the game, with two Widnes players shown red cards - captain Kevin Brown, in his 300th Super League appearance and winger Patrick Ah Van. Ah Van got sending off sufficient and Brown was banned for one game. Saints' second-rower Joe Greenwood was also charged and took and Early Guilty Plea to avoid suspension.

Denny Solomona scored two tries to set a new Super League try-scoring record as Castleford Tigers defeated Catalans 34-28 in Perpignan. Solomona levelled and then broke Lesley Vainikolo's twelve-year-old record of 36 tries in a regular season in the space of three first-half minutes. Luke Gale played a starring role for the visitors, who led 34-10 up to the hour mark as he created all but one of the Tigers' tries and added five conversions from six attempts. Paddy Flynn and Ben Crooks also scored try-braces.

Super 8s, The Qualifiers - Round 6

Over ten-and-a-half thousand people packed into Leigh Sports Village on the Sunday, taking advantage of owner Derek Beaumont's decision to make the game free as a celebration of Leigh's elevation to Super League, as the Centurions beat Batley 42-24.

The carnival atmosphere initially suited the visitors. Batley opened the scoring in the eighth minute when clever play from Pat Walker opened up the defence and David Scott turned on the afterburners to race away on the left. Walker converted and it was 6-0 to the visitors. But Leigh were in control by half-time, leading 24-6.

Willie Tonga's try on 63 minutes and subsequent conversion made it 36-12 and Leigh always looked likely to go on and claim victory.

There had been a stunning result the day before as London Broncos had a chance of making the promotion shoot-out following an outstanding 19-16 win at Salford. Any hopes the Red Devils had of avoiding the Million Pound game were ended as they suffered a shock defeat to Andrew Henderson's side, who could now take Salford's spot in the final game of the season if results went their way. They would need the Red Devils to slip up at Batley while they had to beat Featherstone on the last weekend.

Tries from William Barthau, Scott Leatherbarrow and Jamie Soward, plus Barthau's field goal, helped the Broncos into a 19-6 lead with 10 minutes left. But Josh Griffin crossed twice late on to set up a nervy finish. With only seconds remaining, Greg Johnson was bundled into touch by a wall of London defenders, crucially preventing a match-winning score.

Huddersfield survived a late scare to post a hugely important 22-14 home victory over Leeds in the battle to avoid the Million Pound Game.

The Giants were 20-0 ahead early in the second period but found themselves hanging on when the Rhinos, despite being ravaged by injuries, bounced back with a couple of tries.

The Giants recalled scrum-half Ryan Brierley - a notable absentee from the previous week's defeat at Leigh - while fullback Scott Grix and packman Tom Symonds also returned as Huddersfield faced what was close to a must-win game. Danny Brough tormented Leeds with an astute kicking game, forcing four goal-line drop-outs and kicking the five goals that ultimately separated the sides and ended Leeds' winning run at eight games.

Hull KR got the better of a spirited Featherstone to win 32-24 at Bigfellas Stadium to set up a huge game against Huddersfield the following weekend. The decisive period came just before half-time, when Shaun Lunt and Josh Mantellato grabbed quick-fire tries to send the Super League side into the break with the lead.

The Robins kicked on after the break, with a double from ex-Featherstone centre Thomas Minns and a James Greenwood effort swinging the contest firmly in their favour.

Super League Super 8s - Round 7

Former Hull winger Tom Lineham's two tries and two memorable try-saving tackles were vital in Warrington's 23-6 winner-takes-all victory at KCOM Stadium as they exerted revenge for their Wembley heartbreak to finally claim the League Leaders' Shield.

Wingers Lineham and Kevin Penny were both recalled after periods out of the first team and Lineham in particular was outstanding. Left out of the Challenge Cup Final and forced to ply his trade in the reserves for several weeks, Albert Goldthorpe Rookie of the Year in 2013 Lineham took his chance with both hands.

Warrington, who came into the game without Kurt Gidley, Chris Sandow, Ben Currie, Ben Westwood and Brad Dwyer and had a host of younger players in the starting thirteen and on the bench, led 10-0 at the interval.

But when Hull scored early in the second half from some smart footwork from Carlos Tuimavave the stage seemed set for a home comeback, with a big Hull crowd of over 17,000 urging them on. When Jamie Shaul made a great break on 51 minutes and passed to Scott Taylor for what looked a certain try, Lineham saved the day with a tremendous tackle from behind.

Halfback Declan Patton, who played with control and confidence throughout the game, kicked three straight penalty goals as Hull floundered from then on, and converted Lineham's second try before slotting a field goal ten minutes from time.

Wigan's 48-24 home win over Catalans on the same Friday night meant Hull ended in third spot and would have to travel to the DW Stadium for the following week's semi-final.

The Warriors were 36-0 up after 33 minutes against the Dragons, who had imploded at the latter end of the season amid rumours of poor of-field behaviour and an impending player clearout.

Wigan were in front after just two minutes as Anthony Gelling touched down, while a brace from George Williams and scores for John Bateman, Joe Bretherton and Josh Charnley saw the Warriors out of sight, leading 36-4 at the break.

Wigan captain Sean O'Loughlin was expected to return following five weeks out with a hamstring injury but he pulled out after the warm-up with a calf strain.

Shannon McDonnell grabbed a second-half hat-trick as form side St Helens made it 11 wins in their last 12 games with a 32-12 win over Wakefield. McDonnell, out of contract at the end of the season, moved onto the wing to cover for concussion victim Adam Swift and claimed his treble in a 23-minute spell which saw the home side stretch their lead from a fragile six points to three clear scores by the 71st minute.

Wigan's win meant Saints finished in fourth spot and had to travel to Warrington for the semi.

On the Sunday, Denny Solomona, with his seventh hat-trick of the season set a new Castleford club record of 42 tries in a season - eclipsing the total notched in 1993-94 of 40 by St John Ellis - in a 40-26 home win over Widnes and in the process also set a new overall record of Super League tries.

The Samoan ended the campaign with a total of 40 tries in Super League and 42 in all competitions, seeing him brush aside Danny McGuire and Lesley Vainikolo's 2004 record of 38 tries in a Super League campaign.

Castleford's retiring fullback Luke Dorn bowed out in real style, leading the team out as captain in his final game and scoring the Tigers' first try. It was a memorable occasion as the Tigers sealed a fifth-placed finish for the second time in as many seasons.

Super 8s, The Qualifiers - Round 7

Danny Brough kicked the winning field goal as Huddersfield beat Hull KR 23-22 at the KC Lightstream Stadium on the Saturday to finish third in the Qualifiers, avoiding the drama of the Million Pound Game at the expense of the Robins.

Tries from Leroy Cudjoe, Aaron Murphy and a double from the impressive Ryan Brierley had put the Giants into a commanding 22-4 lead at half-time. But Rovers, who were still without Albert Kelly, roared back to set up a grandstand finish. With the scores level going into the final ten minutes it was anyone's game, but good defensive pressure on Terry Campese forced a poor pass and a knock-on from James Donaldson. Huddersfield wasted little time in rolling into good field position for Brough to slot over a field goal to edge the Giants back into the lead, despite protestations from some in red and white that the kick had actually gone over the post.

The drama was still not finished though. Campese saw a 40-metre field goal attempt of his own hit the post, then in the final minute, the half-back's chip and chase resulted in Thomas Minns racing over. Rovers' jubilation was quickly replaced by the realisation that a push on Jake Connor by Campese was going to see the score disallowed by video referee Joe Cobb.

Salford Red Devils confirmed their place in the Million Pound Game as they ran eight tries past Batley in a 42-14 win at Mount Pleasant. Gareth O'Brien and Junior Sa'u sent Salford ahead before Batley's Wayne Reittie replied. But it was a polished show from Salford, who had to win to avoid automatic relegation, Weller Hauraki, twice, Greg Johnson and Josh Griffin all scoring before half-time. Reittie went over again for the hosts after the break.

The Red Devils scored twice more before full-time through Robert Lui and O'Brien with Chris Ulugia getting a Bulldogs consolation.

Leeds Rhinos finished top of the Qualifiers after a televised 37-12 home victory over second-placed Leigh on the Thursday night.

James Segeyaro's 36th minute try that made it 16-0 was a highlight, the Papuan blowing a kiss to pursuer Lee Smith on the hooker's 80-metre glory sprint to the line.

Jamie Jones-Buchanan copped a two-match suspension for dangerous contact on Leigh centre Greg Worthington.

London Broncos ended the season on a high with a nine-try, 46-6 rout against Featherstone Rovers, ultimately missing out on the Million Pound Game because of Salford's win at Batley.

Jamie Soward had a standout game despite missing three of his opening four attempts at goal. The Broncos halfback went on to kick five goals and assist a number of tries whilst winger Rhys Williams notched a terrific half-trick of touchdowns.

FIRST UTILITY SUPER LEAGUE - SUPER 8s
Final table - Sunday 25th September

	P	W	D	L	F	A	D	Pts
Warrington Wolves	30	21	1	8	852	541	311	43
Wigan Warriors	30	21	0	9	669	560	109	42
Hull FC	30	20	0	10	749	579	170	40
St Helens	30	20	0	10	756	641	115	40
Castleford Tigers	30	15	1	14	830	808	22	31
Catalans Dragons	30	15	0	15	723	716	7	30
Widnes Vikings	30	12	0	18	603	643	-40	24
Wakefield Trinity Wildcats	30	10	0	20	571	902	-331	20

SUPER 8s - THE QUALIFIERS
Final table - Sunday 25th September

	P	W	D	L	F	A	D	Pts
Leeds Rhinos	7	6	0	1	239	94	145	12
Leigh Centurions	7	6	0	1	223	193	30	12
Huddersfield Giants	7	5	0	2	257	166	91	10
Hull Kingston Rovers	7	4	0	3	235	142	93	8
Salford Red Devils	7	3	0	4	208	152	56	6
London Broncos	7	3	0	4	221	212	9	6
Batley Bulldogs	7	1	0	6	111	318	-207	2
Featherstone Rovers	7	0	0	7	96	313	-217	0

Super League Semi-finals

Warrington, still missing several of their key men, rose to the challenge superbly, winning 18-10 at home to St Helens to keep alive their dreams of a first Super League title, and their first Championship since 1955.

Both sides produced semi-final worthy performances. Saints led 10-8 after a tight first half but the game went away from them in a third quarter dominated by Warrington. At that stage, Stefan Ratchford stepped up to the plate, scoring one try and creating another to give the Wolves a two-score advantage that proved sufficient.

The sides were locked at 2-2 after half an hour with Declan Patton and Luke Walsh trading penalties - before the contest burst into life.

Warrington took the lead with the first of three disputed tries during the game as Gidley took Patton's flat pass and showed terrific bravery to burrow to the line - although replays raised questions over whether he grounded the ball.

Saints drew level with a try right out of the top drawer just before the break. Clever play from Jordan Turner on halfway released Swift down the left touchline, and he showed terrific pace and awareness to send Jonny Lomax to the line. Walsh added the simple extras and then kicked a penalty after the hooter had sounded to edge his side ahead.

But the lead lasted less than four minutes. Saints had shown some heroic defence to keep the Wolves at bay, but they could do nothing to stop Ratchford spotting a gap from dummy half and darting over from close range.

And the margin was two scores just after the hour mark. After the visitors coughed up possession on halfway with a poor last-tackle option, Ratchford's long pass put Tom Lineham in at the corner - although there were again questions about the finish, with Thaler awarding the try without video referral, which suggested Lineham had lost the ball.

Saints hurled everything they had at the Warrington defence and thought they had found a desperate late route back into the game through Dominic Peyroux.

But video ref Joe Cobb decided he didn't have the evidence to overturn Thaler's on-field decision that he hadn't grounded the ball, ending Saints' hopes and confirming the Wolves' first trip to Old Trafford since 2013.

Wigan had to come from behind to beat Hull FC 28-18 in a game they looked to be bossing to book their place in the Super League Grand Final for the fourth-successive season.

The Warriors dominated the opening period as they laid siege on Hull's line for the majority of the half to take a 14-0 advantage into the break.

Hull looked out of sorts and only troubled the Warriors with kicks to the corners as Wigan's forwards made sure they came out on top in any physical battle.

The Black and Whites, who were dreadful in the first half, looked a different side in the second period and managed to take the game by the scruff of the neck – with three unanswered tries giving them a sudden 18-16 lead going into the closing quarter.

Just when many thought Hull would go on and win the game from that position, it was Wigan who finished the stronger of the two sides, with two tries in the final 10 minutes to reach Old Trafford.

Lewis Tierney's regular spot in the side had been down to the season-ending injury suffered by Dom Manfredi in August, and he repaid his coach's faith with two smart tries.

Dan Sarginson, Liam Farrell and John Bateman - another try scorer in a dominant first-half display - stood up in the injury absence of Sam Tomkins and Sean O'Loughlin, notably when Hull began to find their foothold in the second half.

Matty Smith's goal-kicking looked as though it might have let the home side down when counterpart Marc Sneyd tacked on the extras to tries from Josh Bowden, Liam Watts and Steve Michaels.

But Sam Powell's effort in the 72nd minute proved to be the killer blow and Anthony Gelling's try in the closing minutes booked Wigan's place in the Grand Final.

OCTOBER
Warrior class

Million Pound Game

Salford secured their Super League status in a manner scarcely believable; scoring two tries in the final two minutes before Gareth O'Brien kicked a 45-metre field goal in the opening set of extra-time to consign Hull KR to relegation to the Championship.

Salford's relegation looked almost certain when, with the Robins leading 18-10 their captain Terry Campese kicked a 40/20 just after 63 minutes. If the Robins had scored in the next set of six, even one point for a field goal, that might have been the end of it. But instead they went for a power play and Maurice Blair was tackled on the sixth tackle.

Then on 73 minutes Robert Lui knocked on a simple pass 40 metres from his own line and a grubber from Matty Marsh won Rovers a goal-line drop-out just after 74 minutes. They couldn't score from that but Rovers looked secure when Josh Jones threw a mis-directed pass to his winger Greg Johnson and it went into touch.

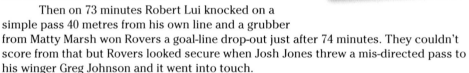

As the clock crept past the 78-minute mark, the Robins were still leading 18-10, but suddenly Josh Griffin - bound for Hull FC at the end of the season - took a hand, breaking down the left and giving a beautiful flicked pass to Niall Evalds, who went over in the corner. O'Brien missed the conversion and Hull KR kicked off again with less than a minute to go.

But again Josh Griffin stepped up to the mark, breaking down the left and putting Evalds into space again. The Rovers' defence stopped him, but the Red Devils swung the ball to the right and, as the final hooter sounded, they got the ball to Johnson on the wing and he touched down just inside the corner post to equalise the scores.

The Rovers fans couldn't believe it and they prayed for O'Brien to miss the conversion, which he did.

But then O'Brien kicked what must surely be the most memorable, and also the most valuable, field goal of all time from almost 50 metres and for the second week in a row Hull KR had lost by one point to a late score.

Amid scenes of Salford celebration and several on-field fights between supporters, Red Devils owner Marwan Koukash ended weeks of speculation by confirming he would be staying at the helm of the Red Devils.

Wigan's Dan Sarginson moves in to tackle Warrington's Ryan Atkins at Old Trafford

Super League Grand Final

Wigan won 12-6 at Old Trafford to be crowned Super League Champions at the expense of Warrington Wolves, who they also beat when they last won the title, in 2013.

Warriors coach Shaun Wane acclaimed the club's Grand Final triumph as his club's greatest achievement after a series of disruptions within his squad.

Injury was only one factor in Wigan's season but, as their casualty list showed no sign of easing in the run-up to the Grand Final, it looked like being critical.

The sight of knee-injury victims Sam Tomkins and Dom Manfredi on crutches joining the on-field celebrations at the end of the game told the story. Sam's brother Joel, Tony Clubb, Lee Mossop and Michael McIlorum had also been long-term absentees.

Captain Sean O'Loughlin played, though he was not named in the 19-man squad because of a torn calf picked up in the warm-up to the game against Catalans, which should have been his return from a series of hamstring complaints. He'd made a similar comeback ahead of the 2013 decider, that year leading his side to a 30-16 victory over the Wolves.

This year the skipper's emergence from the bench after 24 minutes was a crucial interjection, coming just after Declan Patton had given Warrington a 6-2 lead with his self-converted try after he dummied Matty Smith and rode John Bateman's tackle to score.

Another Wiganer born and bred, second-rower Liam Farrell, took the Harry Sunderland Trophy after a succession of line breaks and shuddering tackles. Farrell made the break and set up Oliver Gildart's equalising try on 55 minutes and then seven minutes later dislodged the ball from Tom Lineham to win the scrum that presaged Josh Charnley's winning try.

The Wolves played their hearts out and had their own injury problems. Ben Currie tore his ACL in the Super 8s defeat to Wigan. Ben Westwood suffered a pectoral injury in the Wembley defeat by Hull. Aussie prop Mitchell Dodds played only two games all year. Prop Ben Harrison missed all season until a short loan spell at the end of the Super 8s with Wakefield.

Chris Sandow had not appeared since sustaining a knee injury at Wembley and he was kept on the bench until the 53rd minute. His first touch was a huge bomb that Charnley spilled, setting the scene for Ryan Atkins to almost give the Wolves a two-score lead, building on the 6-2 advantage they had at half-time.

It took a breathtaking five-man tackle to prevent Atkins getting the ball down in the left corner, after Stefan Ratchford's pass out of a tackle allowed Jack Hughes to send Atkins to the line. Charnley, Dan Sarginson - both in their final games for the Warriors before heading of to rugby union and the Gold Coast Titans respectively - Anthony Gelling and Ben Flower were all involved, as was Smith, who seconds before had been involved in the tackle on Ratchford.

On another day Smith may have been man of the match. His second-half kicking game played a huge part in Wigan's win and he tackled like crazy. Then again, so did everybody else. This was the lowest scoring Grand Final since St Helens beat Bradford Bulls 8-6 in 1999.

Referee Robert Hicks thought Atkins had scored, but video evidence showed the centre had lost the ball.

Within a minute, instead of being eight or ten points behind, Wigan were level. George Williams sent Farrell racing through from 30 metres out and the man of the match drew Ratchford before feeding Gildart.

Smith couldn't add the goal from wide out and it was all square again, though Wigan had the upper hand. Warrington gave their all and attacked left and right. Sandow forced a goal-line drop out. But they couldn't find a way through a fanatical Warriors defence.

It took something special for Wigan to get their clinching try. Smith kicked downfield and, as Lineham returned the ball, Farrell's tackle managed to loosen his grip. In the set after the scrum the Warriors twice sent the ball right. They were closed down by onrushing wide defence the first time. But the second time, when Sarginson was closed down, he jinked inside before sliding a kick into the right corner. The ball bounced head high, but Charnley managed to catch it to score before he rolled over the dead-ball line.

Smith missed that conversion too, but when Joe Westerman was adjudged to have stripped the ball from O'Loughlin as he tried to get over the line, he sent the ball through the sticks into the Wigan supporters for the final score of the match.

With nine minutes to play it was by no means the end of it. If anything the excitement went up a notch. From the short kick-off the ball ended up with Sandow, who made ground. Atkins and Rhys Evans had tilts at the line but were stopped short.

Then the ball was moved left again, only for Matty Russell to be bundled over the corner flag by Charnley, Gelling and Smith. After Smith kicked out on the full with two minutes to go there was time for one last wave of Warrington attacks, with Westerman a scorer under the posts but for Sarginson's magnificent tackle.

Warrington had one play to go as Westerman played the ball and Kurt Gidley had the last charge. Smith and Gelling halted him inches from the line. It summed up the 2016 Grand Final in one play.

FIRST UTILITY SUPER LEAGUE - GRAND FINAL

Saturday 8th October 2016

WARRINGTON WOLVES 6 WIGAN WARRIORS 12

WOLVES: 6 Stefan Ratchford; 2 Tom Lineham; 3 Rhys Evans; 4 Ryan Atkins; 5 Matthew Russell; 1 Kurt Gidley; 26 Declan Patton; 8 Chris Hill (C); 9 Daryl Clark; 10 Ashton Sims; 27 Sam Wilde; 12 Jack Hughes; 14 Joe Westerman. Subs (all used): 24 Toby King; 18 George King; 7 Chris Sandow; 33 Ryan Bailey.
Try: Patton (21); **Goals:** Patton 1/1.
WARRIORS: 4 Dan Sarginson; 2 Josh Charnley; 3 Anthony Gelling; 20 Oliver Gildart; 22 Lewis Tierney; 6 George Williams; 7 Matty Smith; 24 Frank-Paul Nuuausala; 16 Sam Powell; 10 Ben Flower; 14 John Bateman; 12 Liam Farrell; 25 Willie Isa. Subs (all used): 8 Dominic Crosby; 19 Taulima Tautai; 21 Ryan Sutton; 13 Sean O'Loughlin (C).
Tries: Gildart (55), Charnley (63); **Goals:** Smith 2/4.
Rugby Leaguer & League Express Men of the Match: *Wolves:* Kurt Gidley; *Warriors:* Liam Farrell.
Penalty count: 4-6; **Half-time:** 6-2; **Referee:** Robert Hicks; **Attendance:** 70,202 *(at Old Trafford, Manchester).*

2
CHAMPIONSHIP
& LEAGUE 1 2016

CHAMPIONSHIP SEASON
Leigh shake it up

LEIGH CENTURIONS' ten-year hiatus from Super League finally came to an end, with a third consecutive year of dominance in the Championship being rewarded with promotion at the end of the season.

The Centurions had stormed through the regular season in 2015 but fell way short in the Qualifiers, finishing bottom following one win from seven matches.

Many doubted their promotion credentials in 2016, with naysayers more vocal following the shock resignation of head coach Paul Rowley ten days before the season and then the eventual departure of free-scoring halfback Ryan Brierley to Huddersfield Giants.

When Leigh, now being coached by Rowley's assistant Neil Jukes, lost their opening game of the season at Batley by 24-22, the Centurions appeared to be in danger of missing out on promotion again.

However, Jukes and his ever-changing squad; five permanent signings of experienced players were made while several others joined on loan, silenced all doubters over the remaining seven months of the season. They lost just two matches after defeat to the Bulldogs.

In league competition, they notched 22 straight victories to win the Championship at a canter, which prepared them perfectly for the start of the Qualifiers.

Naivety and a lack of game management had been the main criticisms aimed at Leigh following their unsuccessful 2015 Qualifiers run, and the same traits were being questioned after they almost surrendered a 34-8 lead in the opening Qualifiers game with London. Leigh eventually won the game 34-30, despite holding the 26-point advantage with seven minutes remaining.

However, Jukes' side proved that lessons had been learned from the year before as they put Super League on notice with a pivotal victory over Salford Red Devils.

What followed was nothing short of spectacular, as the Centurions went on to defeat Featherstone and Hull Kingston Rovers to move them within one victory of promotion.

Stood in their way were Huddersfield at Leigh Sports Village. And the Centurions once again put on an incredible display to rip apart the Giants, taking a 42-10 lead into half-time. Although Huddersfield mounted a fight back, the Centurions held on to secure a return to the Promised Land.

A celebration party at Leigh Sports Village followed a week later, with 10,556 people turning out for their victory over Batley, and although they ended the season with defeat at Leeds, it did nothing to overshadow what was an excellent year for Leigh.

Home-town hero Micky Higham was named the Championship's Player of the Year and another local, winger Adam Higson, had a great season, though they were both pipped at the club's awards' night by popular Aussie prop Dayne Weston.

Leigh start their Super League promotion party after defeating Huddersfield in the Qualifiers

LONDON BRONCOS entered 2016 like they did so many others, starting from scratch.

A disappointing 2015 campaign saw them fall short of a place in the top four in their first season back in the second tier, eventually losing in the Championship Shield Final.

However, 2016 proved to be an overwhelming success, with points difference the only thing costing them an unlikely place in the Million Pound Game and a shot at Super League.

A formidable backline featuring the Championship's top scorer Rhys Williams wreaked havoc all year, while French halfback William Barthau was instrumental in coach Andrew Henderson's offensive philosophy. The forwards also starred. Hooker James Cunningham was named Championship Young Player of the Year, while Eddie Battye and Daniel Harrison also impressed.

Henderson talked up his side from the outset, as he put together a squad that had a mix of Championship experience along with a number of impressive signings from overseas, with the likes of Mark Ioane and Nathan Stapleton joining the club.

In the end, the Broncos completely vindicated Henderson's optimism, as London surprised everyone to finish second in the Championship.

Despite winning five of their opening six league matches, few believed London would maintain their early season form. Consecutive defeats against Featherstone and Bradford did suggest things could go downhill, however, the Broncos responded emphatically, winning ten of their next 11 games to consolidate their place in the Qualifiers and a second-place finish in the Championship.

With no pressure on the players going into the Qualifiers, and with Aussie halfback Jamie Soward brought back for a second spell at the start of July, the Broncos gained plenty of admirers for their expansive and attractive brand of attacking rugby.

A narrow defeat to Leigh was followed by an emphatic 76-16 victory over Batley. They went on to earn praise in defeat to Leeds and Hull Kingston Rovers but, undoubtedly, the highlight came in the penultimate game of the season as they shocked Salford in a 19-16 victory that gave them a shot at progressing to the Million Pound Game.

Despite defeating Featherstone 46-6, Salford's victory over Batley killed London's hopes, but 2016 will go down as a huge success for the Broncos, and perhaps even the start of the club's rejuvenation.

Championship Season

BATLEY BULLDOGS enjoyed a superb season as they defied the odds to finish third in the Championship and secure a place in the Qualifiers.

The key to their success was an impressive recruitment drive leading up to the start of the season. Patch Walker, James Davey and Dominic Brambani all signed from Sheffield having helped the Eagles to years of success and their arrivals proved pivotal.

However, their long-standing forwards were equally as important, with Keegan Hirst, Alex Rowe and James Brown, in particular, earning high praise for their performances as Batley consistently won the battle in the forwards.

They made their mark on the opening day of the season, stunning the heavily tipped Leigh Centurions in a 24-22 victory. They followed that up with a string of victories and a draw at home to Bradford courtesy of a late Brambani penalty goal.

Although a run of four consecutive defeats threatened to ruin their top four hopes, a strong end to the season, winning nine of the final 11 games, secured a Qualifiers berth.

Recognition followed. John Kear, who announced that he would depart at the end of the season to take up a role at Wakefield as head of rugby, was named as the Championship's Coach of the Year. Meanwhile, Brambani was named on the three-man shortlist for the Championship Player of the Year alongside Misi Taulapapa and eventual winner Micky Higham.

Overall, it was a year for the underdogs and a perfect send-off for Kear.

FEATHERSTONE ROVERS made amends for missing out on the Qualifiers in 2015, as they secured the fourth and final spot thanks to an outstanding end to the regular season.

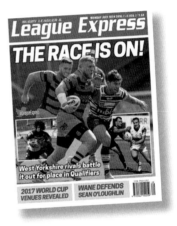

A 20-0 victory over Bradford Bulls in the final game of the Championship saw them leapfrog the Bulls in the table, ensuring a successful first full year at the helm for head coach Jon Sharp.

Their ability to defeat Batley, Halifax and Bradford on the bounce was an undoubted high for Rovers, who had struggled to defeat fellow top-six opponents in the lead up to their final three fixtures of the year. They had, in fact, won just two of eight matches against their top-six counterparts in league action before their victories in July.

A number of new signings had a big impact on their improvement. Misi Taulapapa, who joined from Sheffield, was named on the Championship Player of the Year shortlist, while John Davies, who also joined from Sheffield, won a number of awards at the club's end-of-season awards evening. Anthony Thackeray played a key role at halfback too after his arrival from Dewsbury while Michael Channing was impressive in the backline.

Rovers' strong relationship with Leeds Rhinos saw them take a number of players using dual-registration, with Jordan Baldwinson spending a second season at the club while Ash Handley, Ashton Goulding and Jordan Lilley also featured throughout the year.

BRADFORD BULLS endured a bitterly disappointing season as they failed to reach the top four.

Although the season ended with Bradford picking up their first silverware in a decade, victory in the Championship Shield did little to paper over the cracks at Odsal.

After coming agonisingly close to an immediate return to Super League in 2015, the Bulls were widely tipped to push for promotion once again.

However, an indifferent start to the season saw head coach James Lowes leave the club in April due to personal reasons, with Rohan Smith taking charge.

However, Smith failed to guide the club to the top four. Five defeats in Smith's first ten games in charge saw the Bulls consigned to the Championship Shield. They went into the final game of the season against Featherstone knowing victory would secure a place in the top four, but a 20-0 defeat meant they were short.

They went through the Championship Shield with relative ease, with just one defeat at the hands of relegated Workington, eventually defeating Sheffield in the final to end the season with a trophy.

Despite a disappointing year, the arrivals of fullback Kieren Moss and France international Dane Chisholm midway through the season offered promise moving forward, while the club's supporters were left pleased with the performances of centre Kris Welham, who scored 30 tries in as many appearances.

HALIFAX's pre-season optimism was left unfulfilled as they eventually finished sixth in the Championship.

After exceeding many people's expectations in 2015 by making the top four, many had tipped Richard Marshall's side to continue their progression with another run in the Qualifiers.

However, a lack of consistency proved to be Fax's downfall throughout the year. Although they ended the season with two victories over Bradford and Featherstone, defeats against Swinton and Sheffield, along with a draw at Whitehaven, ultimately proved to be costly.

Minimal changes were made to the club's squad in the off-season, with Fax instead investing part of the £780,000 windfall from the previous season on their infrastructure and a reserve-grade team.

The players that did come in failed to have the desired impact. Rehabilitation from a serious injury and personal problems restricted Simon Grix to just five appearances while Will Sharp failed to find the try-scoring form that saw him frequently top the charts at Featherstone.

After falling short of the top four, Halifax's season came to an ugly conclusion, as they managed just four wins in the Championship Shield before being knocked out in the play-off semi-final by Sheffield.

Adam Tangata was a shining star throughout the season and he swept the board at the club's end-of-season awards evening.

SHEFFIELD EAGLES ended a turbulent year by bowing out in the Championship Shield Final.

In what was their first year as a full-time club, the Eagles faced problems both on and off the field as their financial problems and issues with the council overshadowed action on the pitch.

After briefly flirting with relegation, the Eagles ended the regular season well to finish in sixth place, albeit, they a long way short of their third-place finish 12 months earlier.

A number of players who had played key roles in their recent successes left the club following their move to full time, with Sheffield replacing them with several young players such as Matty Fozard, George Tyson and Dave Hewitt, while experience was injected into the squad through Matt James and Scott Wheeldon.

Despite their disappointing season, Sheffield ended the regular season with victories against five of the top six, with Leigh the only team they failed to beat. The highlight came in the shape of a 46-28 victory at Bradford.

However, inconsistency proved costly, with home defeats to Whitehaven, Workington and Oldham particularly disappointing in an overall frustrating year.

Championship Season

DEWSBURY RAMS maintained their place in the middle of the Championship with a fifth consecutive mid-table finish.

Although the Rams couldn't quite mount a push for the Qualifiers as they had done the year before, the Rams still showed signs of promise throughout the year.

As has become the norm, Dewsbury were left trying to replace key players from the previous season, with Anthony Thackeray's move to Featherstone a particularly tough void to fill.

However, a number of young players, namely fullback Josh Guzdek and forward Jack Teanby, played superbly throughout the year to help bridge the financial gap between the Rams and many of their Championship counterparts.

Although the Rams did look relegation-threatened midway through the season, they steered way clear of the drop during the summer, with victory at Bradford a highlight for the season.

It was in many ways a year of ifs and buts for Dewsbury, who lost narrowly in five matches against teams above them in the league, and they felt aggrieved to have not come away with more in most of those outings.

Victory over Halifax in the Championship Shield helped them secure a spot in the Championship Shield play-offs, losing to eventual winners, Bradford, in the semi-final.

SWINTON LIONS consolidated their place in the Championship, safely avoiding relegation in their first year back in the second tier.

They earned recognition for their performances too. John Duffy's side became renowned for their exciting attacking style, which saw them pick up a number of impressive wins.

Back-to-back away victories at Halifax and Batley was a high point in the season and Duffy's side kept churning out results all year to ensure they had the bottom two at arm's length for the majority of the year.

Although their defensive record was disappointing, conceding 1,041 points at a rate of over 34 points a game, the Lions' ability to win tight encounters proved to be key to their survival.

Victory at the Summer Bash against rivals Oldham was a particularly pivotal result as they managed to overturn a 20-0 half-time deficit.

Chris Atkin and Macauley Hallett starred throughout the campaign and a number of the club's other youngsters flourished as the season developed, benefitting from the experience of Stuart Littler, among others, with the veteran centre celebrating his 500th career appearance during the season.

OLDHAM also survived in their maiden season back in the Championship, despite spending the year in the relegation scrap.

A 20-18 victory over Whitehaven in the penultimate round of Championship Shield fixtures confirmed their safety once and for all, as they defended heroically to ensure the Cumbrians would be relegated.

The Roughyeds enjoyed a number of memorable moments throughout the season, but none more so than their historic Challenge Cup victory over Super League side Hull Kingston Rovers at The Lightstream Stadium, when they beat James Webster's side 36-22.

Staggeringly, it was one of just three away victories for Scott Naylor's side all season, with their form on the road proving to be their biggest problem.

However, at home, they picked up some great victories, defeating Batley, Featherstone and Dewsbury at Bower Fold.

Among their key performers was Liam Thompson, who picked up two of the club's three major awards at the end-of-season presentation, while hooker Kenny Hughes was a fans' favourite.

WHITEHAVEN's four-year stay in the Championship came to an end as they suffered relegation to League 1.

The Cumbrians looked set to enjoy a good season after picking up three consecutive wins in March, defeating Swinton, Sheffield and Workington.

However, they managed just five further victories all season. Their lack of form eventually resulted in the departure of James Coyle midway through the Championship Shield campaign.

The outgoing head coach was replaced temporarily by the club's playing quartet of Craig Calvert, Carl Forster, Scott McAvoy and Dave Allen.

Although the new coaching staff had some success with victories over Workington and Dewsbury, a 20-18 defeat to Oldham condemned them to life in the third-tier.

Grant Gore was among the standout players for Haven, who will enter next season under the guidance of Forster, the game's youngest professional head coach at the age of 24.

WORKINGTON TOWN followed their Cumbrian rivals into League 1, with a disappointing year resulting in them finishing bottom of the Championship.

With Jarrod Sammut once again at their disposal many believed Workington would enjoy another year of safety in mid-table.

However, a small squad was riddled with injuries and that cost them dearly throughout the year. Their inability to field a full squad of players on more than one occasion highlighted their injury woe, with coach Phil Veivers managing to name just 14 players for their Championship Shield game against Halifax.

Despite some superb victories here and there, namely against Bradford in the Championship Shield, it was not enough for Town. In the past two seasons, the club had steered clear of safety with a string of victories, however that never materialised in 2016.

Sammut was, as expected, a shining light for Workington all season alongside winger Theerapol Ritson, but that wasn't enough to save them.

Three defeats to local rivals Whitehaven only added to the misery. A season to forget!

CHAMPIONSHIP AWARDS

PLAYER OF THE YEAR
Micky Higham
(Leigh Centurions)

YOUNG PLAYER OF THE YEAR
James Cunningham
(London Broncos)

COACH OF THE YEAR
John Kear
(Batley Bulldogs)

CLUB OF THE YEAR
Leigh Centurions

Micky Higham

LEAGUE 1 SEASON
Nothing Toulouse

TOULOUSE OLYMPIQUE earned promotion to the Championship at the first time of asking following a dominant season in League 1.

The French side ran riot all season, dropping just a single point in League 1 courtesy of a draw against Rochdale.

However, the Hornets proved to be a problem for Toulouse all year, none more so than in the Promotion Final as Rochdale ended their unbeaten run against League 1 opposition to threaten their hopes of promotion.

Thankfully for Toulouse, they were given a second opportunity through the regular play-off structure and duly took it as they defeated Barrow in the play-off final to secure a well-earned promotion.

Success was also found in the Challenge Cup, courtesy of a superb 10-8 triumph over Leigh Centurions before they bowed out at Wakefield in the next round.

Johnathon Ford was one of many players to stand out above the rest of his League 1 counterparts, the halfback having a huge impact on Toulouse's successful campaign. Sylvain Houles, backed by ambitious owners, has every right to be confident moving forward.

ROCHDALE HORNETS' first season under head coach Alan Kilshaw ended successfully, with the Hornets fulfilling their ambition of promotion to the Championship.

A shock victory in the Promotion Final against heavily tipped Toulouse secured Championship Rugby League at the first attempt, with tries through Jack Holmes, Lewis Galbraith, Chris Riley and Dave Cookson securing a 24-22 victory.

Meanwhile, it was a memorable season for long-serving stand-off Paul Crook, who wrote his name into Rochdale's history books by equalling the club's all-time scoring record with four crucial conversions in that victory over Toulouse.

And for Danny Yates, who was named League One Young player of the year.

Kilshaw's recruitment proved crucial in their success. The addition of forward Samir Tahraoui from Bradford proved to be an inspired move, forward Jono Smith also impressed after joining the club from North Wales while Chris Riley's arrival from Wakefield ended with him scoring 14 tries in 18 appearances.

A strong start to the year ensured the Hornets were in contention throughout, emphasised when they drew with Toulouse in April. It would be the only point the French side dropped all season.

Although a run of three defeats in five games during the end-of-season run-in threatened to ruin their season, they overcame the odds with that superb victory in France.

YORK CITY KNIGHTS enjoyed a solid season on the field. However, 2016 will sadly be remembered for the problems the club faced away from the pitch.

A difficult relationship with the City of York Council regarding the club's ability to use Bootham Crescent resulted in the club announcing they would fold, though that

Johnathon Ford, shown touching down against Hunslet, had an outstanding 2016 campaign for Toulouse Olympique

didn't happen as the club found new owners.

Sadly, the ongoing problems resulted in the RFL confirming the club would not be granted promotion should they earn it, and the Knights never recovered.

After winning five games on the bounce in June, the Knights then went on a run of seven defeats in their final nine matches that resulted in a fifth-placed finish in the Super 8s, and they were then defeated by Toulouse in the play-off semi-finals.

Away from league action, a late try resulted in the Knights suffering heartbreak in the iPro Sport Cup Final, losing to Keighley 22-18 in the Summer Bash opener at Bloomfield Road.

Kris Brining starred for the Knights throughout the season, which resulted in him earning a move to Salford.

DONCASTER fell just short of a shot at promotion, with their season ending in the play-off semi-finals at the expense of Barrow Raiders.

However, it was a bitterly disappointing end for the Dons, who were comfortably defeated 46-6 by the Raiders to emphatically crush their hopes of promotion.

The season had started well for Doncaster, having won five of their six opening matches, including a victory over the Cumbrians.

Impressive home form saw them eventually finish fourth, with an 80-18 victory over Hemel Stags one memorable match for the fans in 2016.

They ended the year with just three home league defeats, albeit, one of them was against Barrow, losing 40-12 in the opening Super 8s clash.

Fullback Tom Carr capped a fine season by cleaning up on all the end of season player of the year awards.

BARROW RAIDERS moved one step closer to promotion than the year before but fell short at the final hurdle.

The Raiders' play-off final defeat to Toulouse was somewhat expected after the French side's dominance over the year, however it was a disappointing end for the Raiders after a year of progression on and off the field.

An indifferent start to the year saw Barrow win just four of their opening eight matches while they were also knocked out of the Challenge Cup and iPro Sport Cup. A season of mediocrity looked set to follow.

However, a run of six wins in their final eight League 1 games saw them finish in fifth place, and earn a place in the Super 8s.

July saw the club hit top form. Six consecutive wins in the Super 8s saw the Raiders enter the play-offs full of momentum, which paid dividends when they defeated Doncaster 46-6 to reach the play-off final.

However, it wasn't meant to be for Paul Crarey's side, who went down 32-22 to Toulouse.

Ryan Fieldhouse starred in his first year at the club.

KEIGHLEY COUGARS picked up silverware in 2016, but it wasn't enough to save coach Paul March his job at the end of the season.

The Cougars picked up the first trophy of the season by winning the iPro Sport Cup with a 22-18 victory over York City Knights at Blackpool's Bloomfield Road.

However, a disappointing league campaign resulted in them finishing the regular season in sixth place, having flirted with the possibility of missing the out on the top eight before that.

Indifferent results prompted the club's chairman, Gary Fawcett, to publically confirm that March would lose his job if he couldn't guide Keighley to promotion.

Although they battled throughout the Super 8s, they missed out on the play-offs to Barrow by a single point, bringing an end to March's stay at the club.

HUNSLET HAWKS, like Keighley, parted ways with their manager at the end of the season after they failed to reach the play-offs.

Matt Bramald was given just one year at the helm after replacing Barry Eaton, and guided the club to a seventh-placed finish in their first year back in League One following relegation.

Three consecutive losses at the start of the season meant the Hawks were always playing catch up, and they rarely threatened to push for the play-offs.

One highlight of the year was their run in the Challenge Cup, with victories over Barrow and Doncaster resulting in a home tie against Salford, which they lost 14-50.

2016 will be remembered mainly as the year the club decided to remove the Hawks moniker from their name, changing to Hunslet RLFC and launching a new club logo.

LONDON SKOLARS enjoyed a superb season, becoming the only southern club to finish in the top eight.

Under the stewardship of Jermaine Coleman, the Skolars picked up four wins from their opening five league games to create a gap between themselves and the chasing pack.

Impressive victories on home soil proved pivotal to their success, as they knocked off some of the league's biggest clubs, including Keighley and Barrow.

As the regular season came to a conclusion, a pivotal 22-23 victory over Gloucestershire All Golds ensured they secured eighth place and a spot in the League 1 Super 8s.

Although the Skolars didn't pick up a victory in the Super 8s, it did little to overshadow the accomplishment of making the top eight.

NEWCASTLE THUNDER's start to life under new head coach Mike Mantelli was somewhat underwhelming, ending the season by missing the Super 8s.

Mantelli had expressed his fears before the season that the club might start the season slowly, and although they started well enough, their inability to beat teams above them meant they just missed out on a place in the top eight.

Thunder managed just one victory over top eight sides, a 26-46 win over London Skolars in May, and that ultimately cost them.

On the flip side, Thunder had impressed against lower league opponents, and they maintained that during the League 1 Shield campaign, winning all seven matches on their way to the Shield final. Prop Rhys Clarke and 17-try Thomas Reudiger were the standouts.

In the final, they met North Wales Crusaders, and they managed to pick up a trophy to end the season with a 31-26 victory.

NORTH WALES CRUSADERS endured a difficult year, which ended with defeat in the League 1 Shield final.

Off-field problems saw the club lose a number of players before and during the season, leaving head coach Anthony Murray with a number of problems early on in the season.

The financial issues surrounding the club had a detrimental effect on the start of their campaign too, losing four of their first five league matches.

Although the ship steadied thereafter, they fell well short of making the top eight. That resulted in a League 1 Shield run in which they won five of their seven games to make the final.

However, they couldn't pick up a trophy to end their season, as they lost to Newcastle Thunder.

The club's defence of the iPro Sport Cup was also disappointing, losing in the first round to Doncaster.

North Wales appointed Mike Grady as their new head coach, with Murray leaving following the season's conclusion.

COVENTRY BEARS' steady progression continued, improving on 2015 with an 11th placed finish.

The Bears picked up four victories in the regular season and went on to push a number of the big-hitters in the competition as the season developed.

A strong run in the League 1 Shield saw them hammer Oxford and pick up a superb victory over North Wales Crusaders.

As a result, Tom Tsang's side ended the season as the second highest southern based team in the league, with London Skolars the only club to finish above them.

Unfortunately for Coventry, they had little luck in either the Challenge Cup or iPro Sport Cup, falling at the first hurdle in both competitions.

GLOUCESTERSHIRE ALL GOLDS surrendered their stance as the top southern club in the league following their twelfth-placed finish, although Lee Greenwood, the All Golds head coach, can take credit from his policy to put faith in young, local players, as the club took a long-term outlook into its approach.

Unlike many of the other southern clubs, Gloucestershire played locally based players throughout the season, as they look to build stability within the club.

However, that did affect their league form, as they managed just three league wins, ending the season just two victories better off than bottom placed Hemel.

Defeat to Oxford followed in the Shield, although those losses were cushioned when they thrashed Hemel 74-18.

SOUTH WALES SCORPIONS ended the season by rebranding themselves as South Wales Ironmen.

They will be hoping that has a positive influence on results, as they ended the year with just one victory, which came over Oxford in a 38-20 triumph.

Their wait for another win spanned four months, when they eventually defeated Coventry Bears 18-14 in the Shield.

However, defeats to Hemel and Oxford meant they finished joint bottom of the Shield standings alongside Hemel.

Christiaan Roets was a standout star for the club during the season.

OXFORD's end of season improvement meant they avoided finishing bottom of the table at the end of the League 1 Shield.

Three wins in their final seven matches over Gloucestershire, Hemel and South Wales meant Tim Rumford's side ended the season on a high, and hopefully a sign of better things to come.

They had managed just two victories before that throughout the season, defeating Hemel in the Challenge Cup and league action.

They were one of several clubs to lose to amateur opponents in the Challenge Cup, being dumped out of the competition by Lock Lane in round three.

HEMEL STAGS finished bottom of the pile in League 1, picking up just two victories throughout the year.

A disappointing year saw the Stags lose in the first round of the iPro Sport Cup, get knocked out of the Challenge Cup by Cumbrian amateurs Kells and also finish at the foot of the table.

Troy Perkins' side first tasted success in April, when they defeated South Wales 30-14.

They defeated the same opposition a whole five months later, this time defeating the Welsh outfit 18-6.

Nevertheless, they still finished bottom, leaving them with plenty to work on going into the new season.

LEAGUE 1 AWARDS

PLAYER OF THE YEAR
Johnathon Ford
(Toulouse Olympique)

YOUNG PLAYER OF THE YEAR
Danny Yates
(Rochdale Hornets)

COACH OF THE YEAR
Sylvain Houles
(Toulouse Olympique)

CLUB OF THE YEAR
Toulouse Olympique

Sylvain Houles

LEAGUE 1 FINALS
Fun in the sun

Keighley's Paul Handforth stopped short of the York line during the iPRO Sport Cup Final

Charlie Martin's late winner ensured Keighley Cougars took home the first silverware of the season after a thrilling 22-18 iPro Sport Cup Final win over York in the first game of the Summer Bash weekend at Blackpool.

It looked set to be disappointment for the Cougars, who let their stranglehold of the game slip from their grasp and went behind to Ed Smith's try five minutes from time. But former Castleford junior Martin stole the show two minutes from time.

The opening try came from work-horse Knights forward Jack Aldous, who crashed over after Jonny Presley split the defence with a super flat pass.

However, Keighley regained their composure and hit the front with two tries in six minutes.

Both tries were scored by former Halifax players combining on the right wing. Paul White was the first to score, with the prolific winger racing to the corner following Liam Darville's cut-out pass, and just a few minutes later another venture up field saw Ritchie Hawkyard enter the Cougars attacking line, with Rikki Sheriffe the man benefitting as he dived over from close range.

The 10-4 advantage at the break was extended soon after. Keighley's forwards saw them surge up the field, with John Oakes delivering the final blow as he bumped off a defender to score from close-range.

Paul Handforth's kicking game proved too good for the Knights as they struggled to find an answer. However, in their moment of need, Presley came up with a piece of individual brilliance. A superb dummy dumbfounded the defence before he darted to the line just to the right of the sticks. Brett Turner's conversion cut the deficit to four points and the game was on.

Staggeringly, it appeared York were going to snatch victory. Ed Smith was the hero, with the centre leaping highest to came a cross-field kick from brother Pat Smith before superbly grounding the ball as the game reached its conclusion.

But Keighley weren't to be denied. They forced the initiative, with Handforth coming up with one last big play by stabbing a kick in goal and Martin pounced.

iPRO SPORT CUP FINAL

Saturday 28th May 2016

KEIGHLEY COUGARS 22 YORK CITY KNIGHTS 18

COUGARS: 22 Ritchie Hawkyard; 26 Vinny Finigan; 3 Rikki Sheriffe; 23 Charlie Martin; 5 Paul White; 24 Liam Darville; 7 Paul Handforth; 8 Scott Law; 9 James Feather; 12 Brendan Rawlins; 11 Josh Lynam; 17 John Oakes; 13 Ashley Lindsay. Subs (all used): 25 Darren Hawkyard; 19 Matthew Bailey; 35 Ross Peltier; 20 Aaron Ollett.
Tries: White (20), R Sheriffe (26), Oakes (44), Martin (78);
Goals: Handforth 3/4.
CITY KNIGHTS: 1 Ben Dent; 2 Brett Turner; 3 James Morland; 4 Ed Smith; 5 Austin Buchanan; 6 Jon Presley; 7 Danny Nicklas; 8 Brett Waller; 9 Pat Smith; 10 Jack Aldous; 11 Josh Tonks; 12 Mark Applegarth; 13 Mike Emmett. Subs (all used): 14 Kris Brining; 15 Russ Spiers; 16 Ross Osborne; 17 Brad Hey.
Tries: Aldous (10), Presley (57), E Smith (75); **Goals:** Turner 3/3.
Rugby Leaguer & League Express Men of the Match:
Cougars: Paul Handforth; *City Knights:* Brett Turner.
Penalty count: 8-5; **Half-time:** 10-6; **Referee:** Scott Mikalauskas.
(at Bloomfield Road, Blackpool).

Rochdale stunned League 1 runaway leaders Toulouse, winning the fight to earn automatic promotion to the Championship with a 24-22 win in the League 1 Promotion final at Stade Ernest Argelès.

The signs didn't look good for Rochdale following their previous visit a few weeks earlier, in which Toulouse inflicted a 40-point defeat but coach Alan Kilshaw's pride in his superb squad shone through as they upset the form book and nailed the unbeaten French team.

"I can't be more proud of the boys than what they have achieved this year," Kilshaw said.

"We were written off at the beginning of the year but we are champions."

The game was going to script as Toulouse shot into a 16-0 lead after tries from prop Bastien Canet, Rhys Curran and left centre Greg White, with the first two converted by Mark Kheirallah.

Winger Jack Holmes scored in the right corner to open the account for the visitors and Paul Crook added the goal and an easy penalty to make it 16-8 at half-time.

Rochdale's Josh Crowley on the charge against Toulouse during the League 1 Promotion Final

After Jono Smith was sin-binned for dissent, Hornets deservedly cut the lead again on 50 minutes with left centre Lewis Galbraith scoring in the corner and another superb touchline kick from man of the match Crook reduced the arrears to two points.

Hornets took the decisive lead with two tries around the 70-minute mark, Dave Cookson on hand from a spilled kick to score in the right corner and fullback Chris Riley wrong-footing Toulouse defenders from 15 metres out. Crook's conversion meant a Bastien Ader try in the right corner and excellent conversion from Kheirallah was too late to prevent the boys from Rochdale beginning their celebrations.

Toulouse were made to earn their promotion to the Championship with a battling but nervous 32-22 win in a League 1 Play-off final in which Barrow refused to lay down and surrender.

It was a long day for the visitors who had set off at five am to catch their flight only to be sat on the runway at Manchester Airport for 90 minutes, which delayed the start of the game. Nevertheless Barrow started well, taking an early lead through winger Eze Harper.

But just after the half-hour mark, Dan Toal received a yellow card for dangerous play and four minutes later fullback Fieldhouse was also given 10 minutes in the bin for a professional foul. The 11 men from Cumbria were unable to prevent Toulouse levelling the scores on 38 minutes through a Tony Maurel try.

After the break exciting young centre Gavin Marguerite went over to the right of the posts and Mark Kheirallah converted to set Toulouse on their way. Danny Hulme, Kuni Minga and Kheirallah, straight from a 20 metre tap, extended the lead to 26 points with only the final quarter to come.

Chris Fleming and Ryan Fieldhouse scored converted tries before Kheirallah coolly slotted over an easy penalty to ease home nerves, Fleming scoring his second try two minutes from time.

KINGSTONE PRESS LEAGUE 1 - PROMOTION FINAL

Saturday 17th September 2016

TOULOUSE OLYMPIQUE 22 ROCHDALE HORNETS 24

OLYMPIQUE: 1 Mark Kheirallah; 2 Tony Maurel; 3 Bastien Ader; 4 Gregory White; 5 Kuni Minga; 6 Johnathon Ford; 22 Danny Hulme; 8 Clement Boyer; 9 Kane Bentley; 16 Bastien Canet; 11 Sebastien Planas; 12 Rhys Curran; 26 Constantine Mika. Subs (all used): 14 Mourad Kriouache; 15 Maxime Puech; 17 Anthony Marion; 18 Tyla Hepi.
Tries: Canet (11), Curran (15), White (17), Ader (79); **Goals:** Kheirallah 3/4.
Sin bin: Kriouache (60) - dangerous challenge.
HORNETS: 1 Chris Riley; 2 Jack Holmes; 3 Dave Cookson; 4 Lewis Galbraith; 5 Dale Bloomfield; 6 Paul Crook; 7 Danny Yates; 8 Samir Tahraoui; 9 Ben Moores; 10 Warren Thompson; 11 Jono Smith; 12 Josh Crowley; 13 James Tilley. Subs (all used): 14 Ryan Maneely; 15 Jovili Taira; 16 Matty Hadden; 17 Mike Ratu.
Tries: Holmes (21), Galbraith (50), D Cookson (72), Riley (74);
Goals: Crook 4/5.
Sin bin: Smith (46) - dissent.
Rugby Leaguer & League Express Men of the Match:
Olympique: Kane Bentley; *Hornets:* Paul Crook.
Penalty count: 15-13; **Half-time:** 16-8;
Referee: Tom Crashley; **Attendance:** 3,513.

KINGSTONE PRESS LEAGUE 1 - PLAY-OFF FINAL

Saturday 1st October 2016

TOULOUSE OLYMPIQUE 32 BARROW RAIDERS 22

OLYMPIQUE: 1 Mark Kheirallah; 2 Tony Maurel; 21 Gavin Marguerite; 4 Gregory White; 5 Kuni Minga; 6 Johnathon Ford; 22 Danny Hulme; 8 Clement Boyer; 9 Kane Bentley; 16 Bastien Canet; 11 Sebastien Planas; 12 Rhys Curran; 17 Anthony Marion. Subs (all used): 14 Mourad Kriouache; 18 Tyla Hepi; 10 Samy Masselot; 26 Constantine Mika.
Tries: Maurel (38), Marguerite (48), Hulme (50), Minga (54), Kheirallah (60); **Goals:** Kheirallah 6/6.
RAIDERS: 1 Ryan Fieldhouse; 31 Eze Harper; 5 Cameron Pitman; 16 Max Wiper; 23 Chris Fleming; 3 Chris Hankinson; 28 Jamie Dallimore; 8 Joe Bullock; 29 Karl Ashall; 10 Oliver Wilkes; 11 Liam Harrison; 26 Danny Morrow; 13 Martin Aspinwall. Subs (all used): 9 Nathan Mossop; 12 Dan Toal; 17 Anthony Dawson; 19 Anthony Bate.
Tries: Harper (5), Fleming (69, 78), Fieldhouse (71); **Goals:** Hankinson 3/4.
Sin bin: D Toal (32) - high tackle; Fieldhouse (36) - professional foul.
Rugby Leaguer & League Express Men of the Match:
Olympique: Mark Kheirallah; *Raiders:* Martin Aspinwall.
Penalty count: 9-8; **Half-time:** 6-4;
Referee: Gareth Hewer; **Attendance:** 1,213.

3
INTERNATIONAL YEAR

INTERNATIONALS
World horizons

Anzac Test

Australia registered a 16-0 Anzac-Day win in Newcastle against a Kiwis line-up lacking most of their star names.

Roger Tuivasa-Sheck was out with a season-ending knee injury. Kieran Foran was missing from the game because of personal problems.

Issac Luke was overlooked because of poor form with his new club, the Warriors. Ben Matulino and Manu Vatuvei left out because of an off-pitch misdemeanour. Simon Mannering, Dean Whare and Jared Waerea-Hargreaves: the list went on and on.

The reshuffle put far too much pressure on former Golden Boot winner Shaun Johnson, who was the only recognised playmaker in the Kiwis' ranks.

Mal Meninga, in his first effort as Australia's coach, was disappointed at a few wasted opportunities, but was full of praise for his team's defence, which kept the Kiwis scoreless for the first time since 2007.

ANZAC TEST

Friday 6th May 2016

AUSTRALIA 16 NEW ZEALAND 0

AUSTRALIA: 1 Darius Boyd (Brisbane Broncos); 2 Semi Radradra (Parramatta Eels); 3 Greg Inglis (South Sydney Rabbitohs); 4 Josh Dugan (St George Illawarra Dragons); 5 Blake Ferguson (Sydney Roosters); 6 Johnathan Thurston (North Queensland Cowboys); 7 Cooper Cronk (Melbourne Storm); 8 Matt Scott (North Queensland Cowboys); 9 Cameron Smith (Melbourne Storm) (C); 10 Paul Gallen (Cronulla Sharks); 11 Josh Papalii (Canberra Raiders); 12 Matt Gillett (Brisbane Broncos); 13 Corey Parker (Brisbane Broncos). Subs (all used): 14 Josh McGuire (Brisbane Broncos); 15 Michael Morgan (North Queensland Cowboys); 16 James Tamou (North Queensland Cowboys); 17 Sam Thaiday (Brisbane Broncos). **Tries:** Boyd (14), Inglis (32), Ferguson (79); **Goals:** Thurston 1/3, Smith 1/2. **Sin bin:** Radradra (6) - professional foul.
NEW ZEALAND: 1 Jordan Kahu (Brisbane Broncos); 2 Jason Nightingale (St George Illawarra Dragons); 6 Tohu Harris (Melbourne Storm); 4 Gerard Beale (Cronulla Sharks); 5 Dallin Watene-Zelezniak (Penrith Panthers); 14 Kodi Nikorima (Brisbane Broncos); 7 Shaun Johnson (New Zealand Warriors); 8 Jesse Bromwich (Melbourne Storm) (C); 9 Lewis Brown (Manly Sea Eagles); 10 Adam Blair (Brisbane Broncos); 11 Kevin Proctor (Melbourne Storm); 12 Manu Ma'u (Parramatta Eels); 13 Jason Taumalolo (North Queensland Cowboys). Subs (all used): 15 Greg Eastwood (Canterbury Bulldogs); 16 Martin Taupau (Manly Sea Eagles); 17 Sam Moa (Sydney Roosters); 21 Kenny Bromwich (Melbourne Storm).
On report: Moa (44) - alleged late challenge; Blair (62) - alleged dangerous challenge.
Rugby Leaguer & League Express Men of the Match: *Australia:* Paul Gallen; *New Zealand:* Jesse Bromwich.
Half-time: 10-0; **Referee:** Gerard Sutton (Australia); **Attendance:** 27,724 *(at Hunter Stadium, Newcastle)*.

The Australians set up the win with a dominant opening 40 minutes. Nine minutes into the action, Aussie Test debutant Blake Ferguson lost control of the ball as he attempted to ground it in the right-hand corner. It mattered not though, and within a few minutes fullback Darius Boyd managed to plant the ball on the stripe.

Johnathan Thurston's conversion attempt drifted wide but a penalty goal midway through the half stretched the lead to 6-0. And in the shadow of half-time Greg Inglis pushed his way over, for the Australians to go to the break with a 10-0 lead.

It was a disjointed second half. Cameron Smith booted a penalty goal after Thurston was caught late by Sam Moa. It was the last score until Ferguson scored off a long pass from Boyd 50 seconds from full-time.

* Australia and New Zealand also met in a Four Nations warm-up played at Perth's nib Stadium in front of a 20,000-strong crowd. Two tries from Greg Inglis helped Australia see off an unadventurous Kiwis outfit 26-6.

2017 World Cup Qualifiers

Fourteen teams will contest the 15th Rugby League World Cup to be staged in Australia, New Zealand and Papua New Guinea in 2017, with the qualification process begun in 2015.

Seven of the eight quarter-finalists from the 2013 World Cup qualified automatically; hosts Australia and New Zealand, England, Fiji, France, Samoa and Scotland. The USA, who were also quarter-finalists, were denied automatic qualification after a long-running internal governance dispute saw their RLIF membership temporarily suspended in 2014. They were later accepted to take part in the qualification process and duly qualified in December 2015 by beating Canada and Jamaica in three-team qualifying tournament.

Papua New Guinea were to be involved in the qualifying competition but due to being selected as co-hosts of the tournament they also automatically qualified. The remaining six spots came from four different qualification zones; three from Europe, one from Asia/Pacific, one from the Americas and one from Middle East/Africa.

Tonga were the first team to qualify from the qualification stage after winning the Asia-Pacific play-off against Cook Islands in Sydney in October 2015. Lebanon joined them, winning the two-leg Middle East-Africa play-off with South Africa.

Wales, Ireland, Russia, Italy, Serbia and Spain played for the three Euro places, with Wales and Ireland qualifying by winning their groups and Italy securing the last spot with a 76-0 defeat of Russia at Leigh on the first Friday of November 2016.

2017 WORLD CUP QUALIFIERS

ASIA/PACIFIC
Saturday 17th October 2015
Tonga 28 Cook Islands 8
(at Campbelltown Stadium, Sydney)

MIDDLE EAST/AFRICA
Sunday 25th October 2015
South Africa 12 Lebanon 40
Saturday 31st October 2015
South Africa 16 Lebanon 50
(two legs, both at Brakpan, near Pretoria)

AMERICAS
Friday 4th December 2015
USA 20 Jamaica 14
(at Hodges Field, University of North Florida)
Tuesday 8th December 2015
Canada 18 Jamaica 18
(at Spec Martin Stadium, DeLand, Florida)
Saturday 12th December 2015
USA 34 Canada 24
(at Hodges Field, University of North Florida)

EUROPE

Pool A
Saturday 15th October 2016
Russia 40 Spain 6
(at Fily Stadium, Moscow)
Saturday 22nd October 2016
Spain 6 Ireland 46
(at Valencia)
Saturday 29th October 2016
Ireland 70 Russia 16
(at Carlisle Grounds, Bray)

Pool B
Saturday 15th October 2016
Wales 50 Serbia 0
(at Parc Stebonheath, Llanelli)
Saturday 22nd October 2016
Serbia 14 Italy 62
(at Makis Stadium, Belgrade)
Italy 14 Wales 20
(at Stadio Brianteo, Monza)

Play-off
Friday 4th November 2016
Italy 76 Russia 0
(at Leigh Sports Village)

TEST MATCH

Saturday 15th October 2016

AUSTRALIA 26 NEW ZEALAND 6

AUSTRALIA: 1 Darius Boyd (Brisbane Broncos); 2 Blake Ferguson (Sydney Roosters); 3 Greg Inglis (South Sydney Rabbitohs); 4 Josh Dugan (St George Illawarra Dragons); 5 Valentine Holmes (Cronulla Sharks); 6 Johnathan Thurston (North Queensland Cowboys); 7 Cooper Cronk (Melbourne Storm); 8 Matt Scott (North Queensland Cowboys); 9 Cameron Smith (Melbourne Storm) (C); 10 Shannon Boyd (Canberra Raiders); 11 Boyd Cordner (Sydney Roosters); 12 Matt Gillett (Brisbane Broncos); 13 Trent Merrin (Penrith Panthers). Subs (all used): 14 David Klemmer (Canterbury Bulldogs); 15 Michael Morgan (North Queensland Cowboys); 16 Tyson Frizell (St George Illawarra Dragons); 17 Sam Thaiday (Brisbane Broncos).
Tries: D Boyd (9), Inglis (15, 68), Holmes (43), Cordner (78);
Goals: Thurston 3/5.
NEW ZEALAND: 1 Jordan Kahu (Brisbane Broncos); 2 Jason Nightingale (St George Illawarra Dragons); 3 Solomone Kata (New Zealand Warriors); 4 Shaun Kenny-Dowall (Sydney Roosters); 5 Jordan Rapana (Canberra Raiders); 6 Thomas Leuluai (New Zealand Warriors); 7 Shaun Johnson (New Zealand Warriors); 8 Jesse Bromwich (Melbourne Storm) (C); 9 Issac Luke (New Zealand Warriors); 10 Jared Waerea-Hargreaves (Sydney Roosters); 11 Kevin Proctor (Melbourne Storm); 12 Tohu Harris (Melbourne Storm); 13 Jason Taumalolo (North Queensland Cowboys). Subs (all used): 14 Lewis Brown (Manly Sea Eagles); 15 Martin Taupau (Manly Sea Eagles); 16 Manu Ma'u (Parramatta Eels); 17 Adam Blair (Brisbane Broncos).
Try: Proctor (21); **Goals:** Luke 1/1.
Rugby Leaguer & League Express Men of the Match:
Australia: Greg Inglis; *New Zealand:* Solomone Kata.
Penalty count: 4-5; **Half-time:** 8-6; **Referee:** Matt Cecchin (Australia); **Attendance:** 20,283 *(at nib Stadium, Perth).*

OTHER INTERNATIONALS

European Championship C
Saturday 25th June 2016
Ukraine 46 Czech Republic 6
(at Rivne City Stadium)
Saturday 8th October 2016
Czech Republic 12 Ukraine 62
(at Havlichkuv Brod)

Nordic Cup
Saturday 16th July 2016
Sweden 24 Norway 40
(in Stockholm)

Friday 5th February 2016
Philippines 18 Serbia 12
(at Cabramatta, Sydney)

Saturday 7th May 2016
Tonga 6 Samoa 18
(at Parramatta Stadium, Sydney)

Saturday 7th May 2016
Papua New Guinea 24 Fiji 22
(at Parramatta Stadium, Sydney)

Sunday 8th May 2016
Cook Islands 30 Lebanon 20
(at Belmore Sports Ground, Sydney)

Sunday 12th June 2016
Italy 22 Lebanon 26
(in Catania, Sicily)

Sunday 12th June 2016
Chile 58 El Salvador 20
(at Henson Park, Sydney)

Americas Cup
Saturday 16th July 2016
Canada 38 Jamaica 2
(at Levittown, Pennsylvania)
Saturday 23rd July 2016
USA 54 Jamaica 4
(at AA Garthwaite Stadium, Conshohoken, PA)
Saturday 24th September 2016
Canada 8 USA 14
(at Lamport Stadium, Toronto, Canada)

Colonial Cup
Saturday 24th September 2016
Canada 8 USA 14
(at Lamport Stadium, Toronto, Canada)

Saturday 1st October 2016
USA 20 Canada 14
(at Eden Park, Wilmington, Delaware)

Saturday 6th August 2016
Germany 12 Belgium 26
(in Dusseldorf)

Saturday 13th August 2016
Netherlands 6 Germany 8
(in Rotterdam)

Saturday 20th August 2016
Samoa 40 Tonga 6
Canada 12 Fiji 26
(both at Aloha Stadium, Hawaii)

Saturday 3rd September 2016
Belgium 36 Netherlands 12
(at Brussels)

Saturday 24th September 2016
Czech Republic 12 Norway 6
(at Krupka Stadium, Teplice)
Spain 4 Serbia 64
(at Quatre Carreres, Valencia)

Saturday 8th October 2016
Ireland 58 Malta 10
(at Carlisle Grounds, Bray)
Samoa 18 Fiji 20
(at Park International Stadium, Apia)

Sunday 16th October 2016
Vanuatu 24
Solomon Islands 15
(at Port Vila Stadium, Vanuatu)
Ireland 16 Jamaica 68
(at Carlisle Grounds, Bray)

Friday 21st October 2016
Wales 16 Jamaica 17
(at Belle Vue, Wakefield)

Saturday 29th October 2016
South Africa 22 Niue 5
(in Pretoria)

SEASON DOWN UNDER
The curse is lifted

The long wait for Cronulla came to a dramatic conclusion in 2016. In their 50th year the Sharks won their first Premiership.

And even Cameron Smith, the disappointed captain of the beaten Melbourne Storm couldn't begrudge the Sharks players and their fans their moment of glory.

Cronulla prop Andrew Fifita snatched a 14-12 victory with a typically barnstorming try with just 11 minutes remaining in the Grand Final at Homebush.

However, in a gracious comment after the Storm's defeat, Smith noted: "I'm disappointed … very disappointed. But they [Cronulla Sharks] are a very special footy side. They deserve their win. They have been waiting for a long time. Everyone who loves Rugby League must be happy for the Sharks."

Talk about an understatement.

They joined the Premiership race in 1967 and, although they got close in 1973 and 1978 (and during the Super League split in 1997), the ultimate prize had until this season always eluded them. Now the trophy cupboard has a genuine prize. Not just one for a minor competition that no one can remember. This time it was the Provan Summons Trophy named after two of the greatest names in the game. And the two gentlemen of the game, Norm Provan and Arthur Summons, were there to present it to the Sharks captain Paul Gallen.

Gallen will treasure that moment until he dies. And with good reason. He ran some 160 metres and made 30 tackles to help ensure victory, although for a while late in the action he must have been worried.

What is it about recent Grand Finals?

Nothing given. Nothing accepted. The encounter started at a frenetic pace, and that continued for the whole of the night.

It was no holds barred from the moment Michael Ennis took Melbourne prop Jordan McLean high in the first set of six. Yes, he got penalised, but it didn't stop the ferocity of the Sharks' defence. In one of the early sets of tackles, Fifita managed to snare a penalty for a slow tackle by Cheyse Blair. Moments later Ennis put in a low kick but the Storm repelled the attack.

The first real chance came in the seventh minute when Melbourne winger Marika Koroibete was placed on report for a high tackle on Chad Townsend but that didn't worry the Fijian winger as he was off to rugby union after the Grand Final.

The Sharks took the option of taking the two points. In the long run it proved to have been a wise decision.

Luke Lewis was grassed millimetres short of the Melbourne line before Gallen slipped an inside pass from a clever scrum move to help Ben Barba grab the 100th try of his career. With the successful conversion the Sharks were ahead 8-0.

The action did not falter. Razzle, dazzle! It was incredible how each side kept up the frightening pace. The Sharks tried to go sideways, but to no avail. Right on half-time Cronulla winger Sosaia Feki went close, but was denied a try in the left hand corner. There had been a double knock-on in the lead-up.

Against the run of play the Storm struck back early in the second half when Kiwi Test captain Jesse Bromwich managed to plant the ball behind the tryline.

Even though players from each side were physically out on their feet the Storm seemed to dig a little deeper. Queensland Origin centre Will Chambers lifted. He spun through would-be defence to touch down and put Melbourne ahead for the first time all night.

Then there was a high Christian Welsh tackle on Townsend which gave the Sharks an extra incentive. Moments later Fifita charged to the line. He was caught but had the ability in a four-man tackle to reach out and plant the ball down under the black spot. The Sharks were back in front by two.

With a couple of minutes remaining the ball went through dozens of Storm hands. No try!

Then as then the siren was about to sound, there was another remarkable rally by the Storm. Again it was to no avail. Cronulla Sharks had survived and at long, long last had broken their Premiership duck.

The Storm could be considered unlucky. They had consistently been the best side in the season proper – largely thanks to their rock-like defence – and had taken out the Minor Premiership. And there was no questioning their defence in the Grand Final, especially that of captain Smith who made a remarkable 72 tackles.

But there was no denying the Sharks, with three of their pack making more than 150 metres in bullocking charges – Fifita (190), Matt Prior (165) and Gallen (160). Luke Lewis was a worthy winner of the Clive Churchill Medal as Man of the Match. He made a total of 140 metres in runs (with most of his charges very being vital) and 25 tackles. His was a performance to behold!

Here's how the clubs fared during the season:

CRONULLA SHARKS (Premiers)

Top pointscorer: James Maloney (219); *Top tryscorer:* Valentine Holmes (19)

What a transition for the Sharks! Two years ago Cronulla had the burden of the wooden spoon after being at the centre of a scandal involving the use of illegal dietary supplements, in which many of their players took the option of accepting suspensions rather that the more costly alternative of fighting the charges. Coach Shane Flanagan also had to stand aside. How the Sharks recovered is one of the great stories in NRL history.

In July they established a club record of 12 consecutive wins after coming back from an early 18-0 deficit to down Parramatta 34-24. The Sharks stretched the run to 15 with further wins, against the Roosters, Panthers and Knights. They fought out the Minor Premiership in the final round of the season proper, going down to Melbourne 26-6. However they strode to the Grand Final with successes against Canberra and North Queensland. Once there Cronulla turned the tables on the Storm.

They had a potent combination of hardened veterans and exciting youngsters. Hooker Michael Ennis was in his final season in the big league and directed play with aplomb. Paul Gallen was like the rock of Gibraltar in defence and an inspiration as captain. Andrew Fifita was probably Australia's best prop, but blotted his copybook during the year with some dubious lifestyle choices off the pitch. Matt Prior proved to be one of the most under-rated front-rowers and Wade Graham is ready to take over the leadership role from Gallen when he finally quits. Luke Lewis showed what a stayer he is – having won a Premiership with Penrith way back in 2003.

And what about the backline excitement? Stand-off James Maloney was arguably the best buy of the season. Centre Jack Bird is a superstar of the future. Fullback Ben Barba was greased lightning and winger Valentine Holmes was a real danger on the flank.

Season Down Under

MELBOURNE STORM (2nd/Minor Premiers)

Top pointscorer: Cameron Smith (194); *Top tryscorer:* Suliasi Vunivalu (23)

It was a sad finale to the season for the Melbourne Storm. Having been on top of the NRL Ladder for much of the season they beat the Sharks to take out the Minor Premiership in the last of the 26 regular rounds of rugby. Then, after beating last year's Premiers North Queensland and a resurgent Canberra Green Machine, they were hot favourites for the decider.

Their defence all year had been almost impenetrable, conceding only 12.5 points per match while making more tackles than any other club – a total of almost 9,000. Captain Cameron Smith was among the elite who made more than 1000, including 72 in the Grand Final. The tough resistance kept opposing sides to just 57 tries in 27 encounters with the Storm.

They completed more of their sets of six tackles than the other 15 sides – an incredible 82 per cent. This clinical approach meant they made fewer errors. Would you believe just eight per game?

Australia's scrum-half Cooper Cronk was always dangerous, especially when setting up team-mates for the chance to score. Without Billy Slater for the season, they were well covered by replacement Cameron Munster. Was there a more exciting duo on the wings – the Fijians Marika Koroibete and Suliasi Vunivalu? Vunivalu made his senior debut in April and went on to score 20 tries in 24 appearances, setting a Storm record for a season and another for an NRL debutant.

Cronk and Smith both played for Australia in the Anzac Test, the latter as captain. Prop Jesse Bromwich was skipper of the Kiwis and joined by his brother Kenny as well as Storm team-mate Tohu Harris.

CANBERRA RAIDERS (3rd)

Top pointscorer: Jarrod Croker (296); *Top tryscorer:* Jordan Rapana (23)

It was 'Back to the Future' for the 'Green Machine' – lean, mean and keen. The Raiders finished in the top two at the end of the normal season for the first time since 1995 and reached their first preliminary final in 19 years.

Their attack was phenomenal, scoring 688 points in their 26 regular rounds – the nearest to them trailed by more than 100 points. And only Minor Premiers Melbourne posted a larger points difference. Canberra's 10-match winning streak was just one short of the club record.

It was a close thing in the finals series, with their two losses, to Cronulla and Melbourne, by just two points. And their run was hampered by injuries to playmakers Josh Hodgson and Blake Austin.

The Raiders' improvement from 10th spot in 2015 was never more apparent than at the annual Dally M Awards gala night.

Skipper Jarrod Croker won three gongs – the Provan Summons Medal as the People's Choice Player of the Year, the Captain of the Year and the top pointscorer. His 296 points was an incredible 83 more than the next best figure, by the Sharks' James Maloney. Croker would have topped the 300-mark but for injuring a knee early in the preliminary final and handing over the goal-kicking duties to Aidan Sezer. Croker's final figure smashed Clinton Schifcofske's club record of 245 set in 2001.

Ricky Stuart was a stand-out Dally M Coach of the Year, and gracious in defeat when the Raiders were beaten in the penultimate weekend by the Storm.

Cook Islands World Cup winger Jordan Rapana was another record-breaker in 2016. His 23 tries broke the previous best by a Raider co-held by Noa Nadruku (1993), as well as Jason Croker and Brett Mullins (both 1994). It was enough to make the Kiwis Test squad at the of the season.

Canberra's England Test connection was dominant. Hodgson figured prominently in Dally M voting, and shared the Raiders' Player of the Year award (for the Mal Meninga Medal) with Josh Papalii. Second-rower Elliott Whitehead made the cynics sit up and take notice. Stuart is hoping for a similar impact in 2017 from the Green Machine's latest British recruit, utility Jordan Turner. While with his latest Super League club, St Helens, Turner played with another Raider who starred in 2016, Sia Sioliola.

Papalii played for Australia in the Anzac Test in 2016.

NORTH QUEENSLAND COWBOYS (4th)
Top pointscorer: Johnathan Thurston (201); *Top tryscorer:* Kyle Feldt (15)

For much of the season it seemed as if the Cowboys could reverse the trend of recent years when the reigning Premiers struggled to win back-to-back titles. It was so hard for opposition sides to break the North Queensland defensive line. Indeed, the Cowboys conceded the least points in their history – just 355 during the regular season. An average of fewer than 15 per match.

Much depended upon the inspirational co-captain and reigning Golden Boot Laureate Johnathan Thurston who helped pull many a match out of the fire. But there were many others including the free-striding loose forward Jason Taumalolo, who shared the Dally M Medal with Melbourne's Cooper Cronk, and Taumalolo's forward colleagues who made up one of the toughest packs in recent decades, each powering more than 100 metres per game.

Taumalolo made an average of 170 metres in each of his appearances, but the likes of co-captain Matt Scott, James Tamou, Ethan Lowe, Gavin Cooper, Scott Bolton, Ben Hannant and rookie Coen Hess were each equally as effective. Sadly for Cowboys' fans, Tamou is moving to Penrith next season.

The backs never disappointed, especially JT's partner in crime Michael Morgan, centres Justin O'Neill and Kane Linnett and the dancing winger Kyle Feldt.

Taumalolo played for the Kiwis in the Anzac Test against Cowboys team-mates Thurston, Scott, Morgan and Tamou.

BRISBANE BRONCOS (5th)
Top pointscorer: Jordan Kahu (144); *Top tryscorer:* Corey Oates (18)

Brisbane started like a house on fire early in 2016. The previous year's Grand Final losers looked likely to go one better this time around after winning seven of their first eight encounters. Then came a mid-season slump when the Broncos won just two of nine games and they slipped out of top-four contention with the vital second chance in the play-offs.

A late season rally in which they claimed the prize scalp of Melbourne Storm had them back focusing on the ultimate prize. But then came their final 2016 clash with the Cowboys. They had beaten North Queensland in 'golden point' extra time in a sensational encounter in March and again by one point two months later. It wasn't third time lucky, when the Cowboys got up through a converted try in extra time in the semi-finals. Another thriller!

Ben Hunt did not seem to have recovered from the trauma of his mistake that probably cost Brisbane success in the 2015 Grand Final. And new signing from the Titans, James Roberts, failed to fire. At the end of the season he was in rehabilitation trying to sort out personal problems.

England Test centre Jack Reed was forced into early retirement because of a chronic injury and the Broncos' Australian Test stalwart Corey Parker also called it a day at the end of 2016. They will be difficult to replace.

There are some positive signs. The ever-consistent David Mead has arrived from

103

the Gold Coast. And rookies, centre Tom Opacic and forwards Tevita Panagai Jr and Herman Ese'ese, have shown indications that they will be ready to step up to added responsibilities.

Darius Boyd, Matt Gillett, Parker, Josh McGuire and Sam Thaiday pulled on the green and gold for the Anzac Test, while Jordan Kahu and Adam Blair were in the Kiwis line-up.

PENRITH PANTHERS (6th)

Top pointscorer: Nathan Cleary (118); *Top tryscorer:* Josh Mansour (16)

Star Trek fans would be aware of the quote, 'to boldly go where no man has gone before'. One can only wonder if Penrith coach Anthony Griffin got his inspiration from the iconic television series. For in 2016 he went boldly on a course that a lesser person would never have taken.

Although he had lost Kiwi Test men Dean Whare and Peta Hiku as well as a future Kiwi in stand-off Te Maire Martin with season-ending injuries, he had no hesitation in axing the experienced trio of James Segeyaro, Jamie Soward and Elijah Taylor, the former two heading for Super League and Taylor to the Tigers.

The bold move paid off handsomely. Three youngsters, fullback and captain Matt Moylan, and halves Bryce Cartwright and Nathan Cleary were given their head and they responded brilliantly. The Panthers went on a late-season charge, winning seven of their last eight to grab a finals spot. One of those wins was particularly poignant. In Round 20 Penrith beat Brisbane 31-12. A satisfying result over the coach who took his job at the Broncos, Wayne Bennett.

Griffin was also not afraid to drop another talented young player Tyrone Peachey, giving a real wake-up call that shocked him out of a torpor. He finished the season firing on all cylinders.

So, too, did wizard winger Josh Mansour, who topped the Penrith try-scoring lists and the NRL charts for metres run per game (180) and was rewarded with a spot in the end of season Prime Minister's XIII that hammered the Kumuls. Moylan was also in that side.

The mix of young players of the future and a couple of clever old foxes, hooker Peter Wallace and prop Trent Merrin, was a formula for success. Merrin averaged 160 metres per game in bone-crushing charges, while Wallace was forever scheming and has found a new lease of life under Griffin's tutelage.

The arrival of James Tamou from North Queensland is a real plus for 2017, while the return of Hiku, Whare and Martin next season sets the scene for some fierce competition for backline spots.

CANTERBURY BULLDOGS (7th)

Top pointscorer: Moses Mbye (100); *Top tryscorer:* Sam Perrett (12)

It was a disappointing season for the Canterbury Bulldogs. They always looked secure in their run for a spot in the play-offs, especially with a run of seven wins in eight games midseason. But, despite the enthusiasm of inspirational captain, England Test prop James Graham, it was only on rare occasions that a vital top-four spot seemed possible.

Graham and fellow forward Josh Jackson looked right at home when taking it to the opposition. Will Hopoate at fullback was brilliant when on the pitch. But his Mormon beliefs meant he missed Sunday games. But it was in his contract!

Test man Brett Morris was a wizard when on the field, but he missed all the early season recovering from surgery. It is quite possible had he beeen available all season, the Bulldogs may have been much better placed when it came to finals time, when they disappeared from the scene in a lack-lustre performance, beaten 28-12 by the Panthers.

There is little to stir the fans' enthusiasm for 2017. The only exciting signing is Canberra winger Brenko Lee. And the halfback combinaton of Moses Mbye and Josh Reynolds must lift their games.

Mbye got a boost by his selection in the Prime Minister's XIII side that gave the Kumuls a hiding, with fellow Bulldogs Jackson and David Klemmer. Klemmer won the Dr George Peponis Medal as Canterbury's Player of the Year. Earlier in the season, Greg Eastwood had also been chosen in the Kiwis side for the Anzac Test.

GOLD COAST TITANS (8th)

Top pointscorer: Tyrone Roberts (120); *Top tryscorers:* Anthony Don & Ryan James (12)

There is little doubt that the Gold Coast Titans were the overachievers of 2016. Before a ball had been kicked they had been tipped to be among the sides fighting to avoid the wooden spoon. Not only did they escape from the group of cellar-dwellers but they snuck into the finals' group of eight in the last weekend. Once there they were denied success against the Broncos by what media critics suggested was an outrageously incompetent display by refereeing officials.

Much of the success in ending the Titans' finals drought can be credited to the young, off-season signing from the Brisbane Broncos, scrum-half Ash Taylor. Even though he had made his senior the previous year, the journalists from Rupert Murdoch's News Limited awarded him the Dally M Rookie of the Year award. But rarely has a youngster turned a club's fortunes around so dramatically. Take-no-prisoners forward Ryan James also played a major role, even though he earned many critics for some suspect tackles, including one that smashed the jaw of exciting Tigers fullback James Tedesco in the closing weeks of the season. Ryan James got a run with the Prime Minister's XIII against the Kumuls as the season drew to a close.

The Titans made headlines by signing Rugby League's prodigal son Jarryd Hayne on his return after defecting to American football. But after snatching a victory with a vital late field goal against Wests which set the foundations for the Titans' late run into the play-offs, he was switched from stand-off to fullback and disappointed in the closing rounds.

WESTS TIGERS (9th)

Top pointscorer: Mitchell Moses (113); *Top tryscorers:* David Nofoaluma & James Tedesco (14)

Any hopes of the Tigers making an impact on the race for the Premiership was shattered by the disgraceful on-going row between coach Jason Taylor and former captain Robbie Farah. The powers-that-be should have sorted it out at the start of the season, but did not have the common-sense to do so.

Despite this mismanagement, the club still managed to get within a whisker of making the play-offs, thanks to the brilliance of some of the young players such as halves Mitchell Moses and Luke Brooks, fullback James Tedesco and winger David Nofoaluma, and the maturity of new captain Aaron Woods who shouldered the responsibility thrust upon him with an understanding of people and the game well beyond his years.

The loss of Tedesco through injury at vital mid-season stages cost the Tigers dearly, but his form and that of Player of the Year Moses earned them representative kudos at the end of the year, together with Woods. They look to be shaping as the backbone of Test teams in the future. Tedesco was named as Fullback of the Year and Moses as Five-eighth (Stand-off) of the Year in the annual Dally M Awards, while Woods also polled well in the voting for the Dally M Medal.

The Taylor-Farah imbroglio came to and end when the hooker switched to the South Sydney Rabbitohs at the end of the season.

Season Down Under

NEW ZEALAND WARRIORS (10th)

Top pointscorer: Shaun Johnson (125); *Top tryscorer:* Solomone Kata (15)

The same old Warriors! For much of the season they looked to be one of the Premiership threats … but when the chips were down late in the year they disappointed. So much so that they were forced to bite the bullet and sign a new coach for 2017 – Kiwis Test mentor Stephen Kearney. Andrew McFadden wasn't shown the door, but he will only remain as one of Kearney's assistants in Auckland.

Player misbehaviour that saw five players dropped didn't help. Then there was Konrad Hurrell's mid-season departure to the Gold Coast. Marqee-signing Roger Tuivasa-Sheck suffered a season-ending injury, and the other new boy on the block Issac Luke took too long to get into the groove – a form slump that saw him dropped from the Kiwis Test squad. Indeed, scrum-half Shaun Johnson was the only Warrior to make the Test side for the Anzac Test against Australia.

However Kearney is optimistic, with some great rookies such as Jazz Tevaga – we resisted the temptation to make a pun on his great name – Nathaniel Roache, Bunty Afoa and Ata Hingano, who all stamped themselves as future Test hopefuls. Then there are the likely lads who debuted in 2016 and may be ready to star in the World Cup, Solomone Kata, David Fusitua and Sam Lisone.

But caution is needed. We've seen all this before.

ST GEORGE ILLAWARRA DRAGONS (11th)

Top pointscorer: Gareth Widdop (133); *Top tryscorer:* Kurt Mann (10)

The glory days of 'The Big Red V' are long gone. One simple statistic says it all. In 2016, the Dragons were second-worst attacking side in the NRL (only Newcastle who claimed the wooden-spoon scored fewer four-pointers).

You can't hope to challenge any side with just over 2.4 tries per game. A 36-point loss to the lowly Sydney Roosters when the Dragons still had a chance of making the play-offs said it all.

The halfback triumvirate Gareth Widdop, Benji Marshall and Mitch Rein got the blame. England Test stand-off Widdop lives to fight another day. But the other two did not have their contracts renewed for next season. Souths' scrum-half Cameron McInnes takes over from Rein and exciting rookie No 7 Drew Hutchison replaces the former Kiwis champion Marshall. Hutchison was given one match in the senior side as the 2016 season drew to a close to give him a taste for the big league.

The bookmakers suggest that coach Paul McGregor may also be shown the door as there has been little creative recruiting. The real bright spot was the form of former Wales forward Tyson Frizell, who made his State of Origin debut and was impressive for the Prime Minster's XIII against the Papua New Guinea Kumuls in the traditional end-of-season clash in Port Moresby.

Jason Nightingale turned out for the New Zealand Kiwis in the Anzac Day Test against Australia.

SOUTH SYDNEY RABBITOHS (12th)

Top pointscorer: Adam Reynolds (95); *Top tryscorer:* Alex Johnston (11)

No one could understand the unpredicable form of Souths early in the 2016 race for the Premiership. The balmy days of their 2014 title seem an era away. Many blamed big Sam Burgess, who early on seemed to be struggling with his return to Rugby League. Then there was the obvious animosity between the club owner, Hollywood superstar Russell Crowe and former 'darling' Luke Keary. At one stage Souths strung together nine straight losses and they were no chance of making the play-offs.

Granted there were injuries. And there were rumours about dissent in the ranks. At the very least, body language showed the players were far from happy. But, as the season came nearer to a close, everything seemed to change. South Sydney halted the New Zealand Warriors' charge to the finals' series and upset top-eight sides Cronulla and Canterbury.

In the end, the gloom had dissipated. They have signed former Test hooker Robbie Farah after 18-months of conflict with his Tigers coach Jason Taylor. It could prove to be the bargain buy for 2017 – as Farah's legs may have slowed, but he can still make his distinctive try-scoring darts from dummy half. His combination with scrum-half Adam Reynolds could prove decisive.

Greg Inglis captained the Prime Minister's XIII against the Papua New Guinea Kumuls, giving a clear indication he is seen as a future Australian Test skipper. He had earlier in the season been the only Rabbitoh to snare a place in the Anzac Test against the Kiwis. The Souths fans are looking forward to plenty of Inglis 'goanna crawls' in the future.

MANLY SEA EAGLES (13th)
Top pointscorer: Jamie Lyon (116); *Top tryscorer:* Jorge Taufua (12)

Manly Sea Eagles were another of the high-profile sides to disappoint their fans in 2016. There had been great expectations that new coach Trent Barrett would finish smiling in his first season as a senior NRL coach.

But everything went pear-shaped and the Sea Eagles couldn't take off. Unfortunately they lost their two experienced centres, Kiwis Test great Steve Matai and former Man of Steel Jamie Lyon, through injuries for much of the year. And the much-publicised recruits Nate Myles, Dylan Walker and (especially) Martin Taupau did not produce the goods. Scrum-half Daly Cherry-Evans had a very forgettable season, too.

The Sea Eagles sparked for a few weeks late in the year but could not continue through to claim a spot in the finals series, eventually beating only three other sides at home.

The one hope on the horizon is the arrival in 2016 of the brothers Tom and Jake Trbojevic. Twenty-year-old fullback Tom is a ready-made replacement for Brett Stewart, who has reached his use-by date. The former Junior Kangaroos prop Jake, 22, is already showing a maturity well beyond his years with his selection for the seond straight year in the Prime Minister's XIII to play the Papua New Guinea Kumuls before the season was over. And when Lyon was injured late in the year the youngster took over as Manly's captain. Jake Trbojevic was named Manly's Player of the Year.

Taupau got into the the Kiwis' line-up for the Anzac Test mainly on his former record. He was joined by utility Lewis Brown, who was press-ganged into the role of hooker.

It was a disappointing end to Lyon's grand career. In typical fashion, he announced he he was going to hang up his boots with no fanfare and certainly no regrets on his great contribution to the sport.

PARRAMATTA EELS (14th)
Top pointscorer: Michael Gordon (162); *Top tryscorer:* Bevan French (19)

Annus horribilis. The expression made famous by Queen Elizabeth II in 1992, marking the 40th anniversary of her succession to the throne could well have applied to Parramatta 24 years later.

The list of setbacks was almost endless. A salary-cap scandal and subsequent loss of 12 competition points, massive fine and forced shedding of key players. The atrocious conduct of the club's administrators. The many dramas and abrupt departure of stand-off Keiran Foran. Corey Norman's off-pitch indiscretions. The defection rumours involving Test winger Semi Radradra. Jarryd Hayne's snub on his return from American football.

Yet coach Brad Arthur was still able to rally his troops and the Eels' 13 victories would have normally been enough for them to make the play-offs. Now Arthur must build for the future with a side lacking in real depth.

Norman will be back. How vital he will be is shown that, had he not been stood down, he could very well have won the 2016 Dally M Medal. There is also the new excitement machine, 20-year-old winger/fullback Bevan French. In February, French starred in the Eels' Auckland Nines title win, scoring a record eight tries in the tournament. French made his NRL debut against the Knights in Round 12, scoring the first of 19 tries in just 13 appearances.

Second-rower Manu Ma'u, who won the Ken Thornett Medal as the Eels' Player of the Year, represented the Kiwis in the Anzac Test, with Radradra in the Australian lineup as well as the Prime Minister's XIII which thrashed the Papua New Guinea Kumuls by a record 58-0.

SYDNEY ROOSTERS (15th)

Top pointscorer: Latrell Mitchell (80); *Top tryscorer:* Latrell Mitchell (14)

What a dramatic turnaround for the Roosters! The Minor Premiers for three straight years, they were out of the mix after less than half the season, and at one stage fighting to avoid the wooden spoon.

A combination of off-pitch misbehaviour by playmaker Mitchell Pearce and injuries that kept the likes of Jared Waerea-Hargreaves and Boyd Cordner on the sidelines for half the season saw the Roosters behind the eight ball. They weren't helped by the departure at the end of the previous year of stars James Maloney (to the Sharks), Roger Tuivasa-Sheck (Warriors) and Michael Jennings (Eels). Just two wins in the first 11 rounds virtually killed off any finals hopes they may have had.

But on a positive note, a group of talented rookies stood up to be counted, including winger/fullback Latrell Mitchell, stand-off Connor Watson, utility Ryan Matterson and threequarter Joseph Manu. They helped in a late-season improvement in which they claimed the scalps of the Broncos and the Cowboys. And Parramatta fullback Michael Gordon and South Sydney stand-off Luke Keary are astute signings for 2017.

Blake Ferguson represented Australia in the Anzac Test, while Sam Moa was in the Kiwis' line-up. Pearce and Cordner finished the season in the Prime Minister's XIII that played Papua New Guinea in the traditional Port Moresby encounter. Hooker Jake Friend won the Jack Gibson Medal as the Roosters' Player of the Year.

NEWCASTLE KNIGHTS (16th)

Top pointscorer: Trent Hodkinson (99); *Top tryscorer:* Nathan Ross (9)

British Super League fans are well aware of the outstanding coaching credentials of Nathan Brown with his success at both Huddersfield and St Helens. But he could hardly have been expected to repeat the success with the Newcastle Knights, a club on its financial knees and with a dearth of talent. So it came as little surprise when they held on to the wooden spoon, with the worst record in the NRL side's history.

Newcastle became the first club since the Gold Coast Seagulls in 1993 to register just one win in a season. And the Knights' 18-game losing streak is the worst since Newtown managed 20 in 1977, when Brown was only four years old.

There is little light at the end of the tunnel. Veteran Kiwis Test stalwart Jeremy Smith has retired after 13 seasons in the NRL and the workaholic 26-year-old forward Robbie Rochow is headed to South Sydney after also being wooed by Cronulla.

Even before the 2016 season was over the bookmakers had the Knights as red-hot favourites to take out their third straight wooden spoon next year. Thankfully the fans haven't given up, with big attendances at home games throughout Newcastle's awful losing streak.

SEASON DOWN UNDER - ROUND-UP

NRL PREMIERSHIP FINALS SERIES

ELIMINATION FINALS
Friday 9th September 2016

Brisbane Broncos 44 .... Gold Coast Titans 28

Saturday 10th September 2016

Canberra Raiders 14 .... Cronulla Sharks 16

QUALIFYING FINALS
Saturday 10th September 2016

Melbourne Storm 16 .... North Queensland Cowboys 10

Sunday 11th September 2016

Penrith Panthers 28 .... Canterbury Bulldogs 12

SEMI-FINALS
Friday 16th September 2016

North Queensland Cowboys 26 .... Brisbane Broncos 20
(after extra-time)

Saturday 17th September 2016

Canberra Raiders 22 .... Penrith Panthers 12

PRELIMINARY FINALS
Friday 23rd September 2016

Cronulla Sharks 32 .... North Queensland Cowboys 20

Saturday 24th September 2016

Melbourne Storm 14 .... Canberra Raiders 12

NRL GRAND FINAL

Sunday 2nd October 2016

CRONULLA SHARKS 14 MELBOURNE STORM 12

SHARKS: 1 Ben Barba; **2** Sosaia Feki; **3** Jack Bird; **4** Ricky Leutele; **5** Valentine Holmes; **6** James Maloney; **7** Chad Townsend; **8** Andrew Fifita; **9** Michael Ennis; **10** Matt Prior; **11** Luke Lewis; **12** Wade Graham; **13** Paul Gallen (C). Subs (all used): **14** Gerard Beale; **15** Chris Heighington; **16** Sam Tagataese; **17** Jayson Bukuya.
Tries: Barba (14), Fifita (69); **Goals:** Maloney 3/3.
STORM: 1 Cameron Munster; **2** Suliasi Vunivalu; **3** Will Chambers; **4** Cheyse Blair; **5** Marika Koroibete; **6** Blake Green; **7** Cooper Cronk; **8** Jesse Bromwich; **9** Cameron Smith (C); **10** Jordan McLean; **11** Kevin Proctor; **12** Tohu Harris; **13** Dale Finucane. Subs (all used): **14** Kenny Bromwich; **15** Tim Glasby; **16** Christian Welch; **17** Ben Hampton.
Tries: J Bromwich (50), Chambers (64); **Goals:** Smith 2/2.
On report: Koroibete (7) - alleged high tackle on Townsend; Chambers (50) - alleged dangerous challenge.
Rugby Leaguer & League Express Men of the Match:
Sharks: Luke Lewis; *Storm:* Cameron Smith.
Half-time: 8-0; **Referees:** Matt Ceccin & Ben Cummins;
Attendance: 83,625 *(at ANZ Stadium, Sydney).*

NRL PREMIERSHIP - FINAL TABLE

	P	W	D	L	B	F	A	D	Pts
Melbourne Storm	24	19	0	5	2	563	302	261	42
Canberra Raiders	24	17	1	6	2	688	456	232	39
Cronulla Sharks	24	17	1	5	2	580	404	176	39
North Queensland Cowboys	24	15	0	9	2	584	355	229	34
Brisbane Broncos	24	15	0	9	2	554	434	120	34
Penrith Panthers	24	14	0	10	2	563	463	100	32
Canterbury Bulldogs	24	14	0	10	2	506	448	58	32
Gold Coast Titans	24	11	1	12	2	508	497	11	27
Wests Tigers	24	11	0	13	2	499	607	-108	26
New Zealand Warriors	24	10	0	14	2	513	601	-88	24
St George Illawarra Dragons	24	10	0	14	2	341	538	-197	24
South Sydney Rabbitohs	24	9	0	15	2	473	549	-76	22
Manly Sea Eagles	24	8	0	16	2	454	563	-109	20
Parramatta Eels *	24	13	0	11	2	298	324	-26	18
Sydney Roosters	24	6	0	18	2	443	576	-133	16
Newcastle Knights	24	1	1	22	2	305	800	-495	7

* 12 points deducted and points-difference adjusted for salary cap offences

LEADING POINTSCORERS

Jarrod Croker	Canberra Raiders	296
James Maloney	Cronulla Sharks	219
Johnathan Thurston	North Queensland Cowboys	201
Cameron Smith	Melbourne Storm	194
Michael Gordon	Parramatta Eels	162

LEADING TRYSCORERS

Jordan Rapana	Canberra Raiders	23
Suliasi Vunivalu	Melbourne Storm	23
Valentine Holmes	Cronulla Sharks	19
Bevan French	Parramatta Eels	19
Corey Oates	Brisbane Broncos	18
Jarrod Croker	Canberra Raiders	18

DALLY M AWARDS

Dally M Medal (Players of the Year):
Cooper Cronk (Melbourne Storm)
& Jason Taumalolo (North Queensland Cowboys)
Provan Summons Medal (People's Choice):
Jarrod Croker (Canberra Raiders)
Coach of the Year: Ricky Stuart (Canberra Raiders)
Captain of the Year: Jarrod Croker (Canberra Raiders)
Representative Player of the Year: Cameron Smith (Melbourne Storm)
Rookie of the Year: Ash Taylor (Gold Coast Titans)
Holden Cup (Under-20s) Player of the Year:
Jaiden Brailey (Cronulla Sharks)
Female Player of the Year: Kezie Apps

STATE OF ORIGIN

Queensland wrapped up the State of Origin series with a solid 26-16 victory in the second encounter at Brisbane's Lang Park complex. It was the Maroons' tenth series success in the past twelve seasons.

But the NSW Blues lifted to avoid a whitewash in the final clash at Homebush on July 13th. The Blues could still hold their heads high.

In the lead-up to the game, the media kept reminding fans it was "a dead rubber". Some Rugby League reporters even claimed that the Sydney Swans Australian rules match against the Premiers Hawthorn the following night was the most important football clash of the week.

No wonder that there were only 61,267 fans in the stadium, which can hold around 83,000. But none of those present would regret their decision to venture out on the icy winter's night and be in the stands, witnessing one of the most incredibly exciting finishes in the history of the interstate clashes, with NSW centre Michael Jennings snatching victory with just 78 seconds left on the clock.

To add to the significance of the moment, long-serving Blues captain Paul Gallen then proceeded to boot the conversion in the final effort of his illustrious Origin career.

Queensland captain Cameron Smith was awarded the Wally Lewis Medal as Man of the Series. It was fourth time Smith had been so honoured – winning previously in 2007, 2011 and 2013. No other player in the medal's 13-year history has won it more than once.

NSW State of Origin coach Laurie Daley had one word of advice to his players before kick-off in the first clash with the Maroons at Homebush.

"Get out there and enjoy the moment." And for the media he added the comment: "We bleed blue!"

Sadly neither Daley nor his players enjoyed the moment, as Queensland won a dour encounter 6-4.

And, in a game in which defence was utmost in the mindset of all those on the pitch, in the entire second half not a single point was scored by either side. According to Daley, there should have been points scored – a try to NSW centre Josh Morris in the 66th minute. Morris had stormed over Queensland centre Greg Inglis and thought he had managed to plant the ball over the line.

On the advice of the experienced touch judge, Jeff Younis, referee Gerard Sutton initially ruled it to be a try. However, to be on the safe side, he sent the decision to the video bunker where the senior review official Bernard Sutton ruled otherwise.

Even though he knew it would never happen, Daley called for both on-field referees, Gerard Sutton and Ben Cummins, to be axed for Origin II.

The loss meant the Blues would face an uphill (but not impossible) battle to square the series at the Lang Park complex in Brisbane on June 22nd.

It was a torrid opening in slippery conditions at the former Olympic stadium.

Some 13 minutes into the action Australian Test back-rower Matt Gillett was grassed a metre or so short of the stripe before Queensland captain Cameron Smith, realising that every point could count, decided to break the deadlock by giving Johnathan Thurston an easy attempt at a penalty goal.

Eventually NSW second-rower Boyd Cordner, arguably his side's best on the night, broke the Maroons' defensive line when stand-off James Maloney handed him a sniff of the tryline. Cordner danced past Cooper Conk to score.

It prompted the critics in the press box to wonder whether the Storm's scrum-half was truly fit after only passing a fitness test at the eleventh hour.

Just before half-time the Maroons looked dangerous and everyone expected them to kick high on the sixth tackle.

Instead they ran the ball, and winger Dane Gagai scored in the right-hand corner off a pass from Thurston that was flung on by Darius Boyd.

JT's conversion attempt went wide for the Maroons to go to the break with a slim (but eventually … winning) two-point lead.

Soon after the resumption for the second half, Gagai sped for the whitewash again.

But Maloney and Cordner smashed him into touch a metre short of the line.

It was a tough, no holds-barred match.

STATE OF ORIGIN - GAME I

Wednesday 1st June 2016

NEW SOUTH WALES 4 QUEENSLAND 6

NEW SOUTH WALES: 1 Matt Moylan (Penrith Panthers); 2 Blake Ferguson (Sydney Roosters); 3 Michael Jennings (Parramatta Eels); 18 Josh Morris (Canterbury Bulldogs); 5 Josh Mansour (Penrith Panthers); 6 James Maloney (Cronulla Sharks); 7 Adam Reynolds (South Sydney Rabbitohs); 8 Aaron Woods (Wests Tigers); 9 Robbie Farah (Wests Tigers); 15 James Tamou (North Queensland Cowboys); 11 Boyd Cordner (Sydney Roosters); 12 Josh Jackson (Canterbury Bulldogs); 10 Paul Gallen (Cronulla Sharks) (C). Subs (all used): 13 Greg Bird (Gold Coast Titans); 14 Dylan Walker (Manly Sea Eagles); 16 David Klemmer (Canterbury Bulldogs); 17 Andrew Fifita (Cronulla Sharks).
Try: Cordner (25); **Goals:** Reynolds 0/1.
QUEENSLAND: 1 Darius Boyd (Brisbane Broncos); 2 Corey Oates (Brisbane Broncos); 3 Greg Inglis (South Sydney Rabbitohs); 4 Justin O'Neill (North Queensland Cowboys); 5 Dane Gagai (Newcastle Knights); 6 Johnathan Thurston (North Queensland Cowboys); 7 Cooper Cronk (Melbourne Storm); 8 Matt Scott (North Queensland Cowboys); 9 Cameron Smith (Melbourne Storm) (C); 10 Nate Myles (Manly Sea Eagles); 11 Matt Gillett (Brisbane Broncos); 12 Sam Thaiday (Brisbane Broncos); 13 Corey Parker (Brisbane Broncos). Subs (all used): 14 Michael Morgan (North Queensland Cowboys); 15 Josh McGuire (Brisbane Broncos); 16 Aidan Guerra (Sydney Roosters); 17 Josh Papalii (Canberra Raiders).
Try: Gagai (37); **Goals:** Thurston 1/2.
Rugby Leaguer & League Express Men of the Match:
New South Wales: Boyd Cordner; *Queensland:* Darius Boyd.
Half-time: 4-6; **Referees:** Gerard Sutton & Ben Cummins;
Attendance: 80,251 *(at ANZ Stadium, Sydney).*

Queensland wrapped up the State of Origin series with a solid 26-16 victory in the second encounter at Brisbane's Lang Park complex.

The Maroons will be without long-serving stalwart Corey Parker next season. Just 48 hours before kick-off in Brisbane, Parker surprised the fans and his Queensland team-mates by announcing he would hang up his boots at the end of this year.

His announcement gave the Queenslanders added incentive to win the match, given that it was Parker's final Origin appearance at the arena known colloquially as 'The Cauldron'.

And Parker, who the previous year won the Wally Lewis Medal as Origin Man of the Series, turned in one of his greatest displays. He made 18 storming runs, pulled off 30 tackles and made one of his great offloads at a vital stage midway through the second half that almost resulted in a try to fullback Darius Boyd.

STATE OF ORIGIN - GAME II

Wednesday 22nd June 2016

QUEENSLAND 26 NEW SOUTH WALES 16

QUEENSLAND: 1 Darius Boyd (Brisbane Broncos); 2 Corey Oates (Brisbane Broncos); 3 Greg Inglis (South Sydney Rabbitohs); 4 Justin O'Neill (North Queensland Cowboys); 5 Dane Gagai (Newcastle Knights); 6 Johnathan Thurston (North Queensland Cowboys); 7 Cooper Cronk (Melbourne Storm); 8 Matt Scott (North Queensland Cowboys); 9 Cameron Smith (Melbourne Storm) (C); 10 Josh McGuire (Brisbane Broncos); 11 Matt Gillett (Brisbane Broncos); 12 Sam Thaiday (Brisbane Broncos); 13 Corey Parker (Brisbane Broncos). Subs (all used): 14 Michael Morgan (North Queensland Cowboys); 15 Jacob Lillyman (New Zealand Warriors); 16 Aidan Guerra (Sydney Roosters); 17 Josh Papalii (Canberra Raiders). **Tries:** Gagai (32, 47, 63), Oates (72); **Goals:** Thurston 5/6. **On report:** Thaiday (13) - alleged dangerous challenge on Gallen.
NEW SOUTH WALES: 1 Matt Moylan (Penrith Panthers); 2 Blake Ferguson (Sydney Roosters); 3 Michael Jennings (Parramatta Eels); 14 Dylan Walker (Manly Sea Eagles); 5 Josh Mansour (Penrith Panthers); 6 James Maloney (Cronulla Sharks); 7 Adam Reynolds (South Sydney Rabbitohs); 8 Aaron Woods (Wests Tigers); 9 Robbie Farah (Wests Tigers); 10 James Tamou (North Queensland Cowboys); 15 Tyson Frizell (St George Illawarra Dragons); 12 Josh Jackson (Canterbury Bulldogs); 13 Paul Gallen (Cronulla Sharks) (C). Subs (all used): 11 Greg Bird (Gold Coast Titans); 16 David Klemmer (Canterbury Bulldogs); 17 Andrew Fifita (Cronulla Sharks); 18 Jack Bird (Cronulla Sharks).
Tries: Frizell (56), Maloney (66); **Goals:** Reynolds 3/3, Maloney 1/1. **Rugby Leaguer & League Express Men of the Match:** *Queensland:* Johnathan Thurston; *New South Wales:* Josh Jackson. **Half-time:** 10-4; **Referees:** Gerard Sutton & Ben Cummins; **Attendance:** 52,293 *(at Suncorp Stadium, Brisbane).*

Even though the Maroons started on fire with a wonderful break by Cameron Smith and a superb tactical kick along the turf by Johnathan Thurston, they accepted an easy two points from a Thurston penalty goal to take the lead after six minutes.

New South Wales equalised with a goal from Adam Reynolds four minutes later. They stretched the lead after Sam Thaiday was placed on report for a spear tackle on Paul Gallen. Thaiday was charged by the judiciary and received a two-match ban for his early guilty plea.

When James Maloney held down Cooper Cronk in a tackle, Thurston was able to level the scores. The Queenslanders were under heavy assault.

However as half-time approached, and against the run of play, Queensland winger Dane Gagai changed the momentum with a try after an 80-metre sprint down the right flank in which he outpaced Origin debutant and former Wales World Cup back-rower Tyson Frizell.

Thurston booted a remarkable conversion from the sideline and there was no looking back. Gagai was to score two more tries in the second spell to post what was a rare Origin hat-trick.

Behind 20-16, the Blues went close to reaching the lead again. Maloney booted the ball over the tryline. Frizell and New South Wales' centre Michael Jennings gave chase. The former grounded the ball, but video replays showed Jennings had ever so gently flicked the ball forward moments earlier.

Corey Oates sealed the victory with a late Queensland try.

The third State of Origin encounter at Sydney's former Olympic stadium produced one of the most incredibly exciting finishes in the history of the interstate clashes, with NSW centre Michael Jennings snatching an 18-14 victory with just 78 seconds left on the clock.

Paul Gallen then proceeded to boot the conversion in the final effort of his illustrious Origin career.

The Queenslanders looked headed for a three-nil success in the 2016 series when fullback Darius Boyd scored six minutes before full time for the Maroons to lead 14-12. However the NSW players were not yet ready to throw in the towel.

The Blues' debutant fullback James Tedesco looked like scoring a spectacular solo try as the crowd waited for the final siren. But he was dragged down a metre from the try-line in a wonderful tackle by Test scrum-half Cooper Cronk.

A quick play-the-ball and Jennings darted past three would-be Queensland defenders before pushing his way over a couple more to plant the ball down for the winning try.

It was typical Origin rugby from the kick-off. Fire and brimstone! No quarter either expected or given! A desperation tackle kept Queensland winger Corey Oates from scoring soon after the start.

But four-and-a-half minutes into the action some fine work by Johnathan Thurston and Darius Boyd set up Maroons centre Greg Inglis to score in the left-hand corner. This extended Inglis' Origin try-scoring record to 18. Eventually NSW loose-forward Tyson Frizell charged across the stripe to level the scores.

The Maroons were forced into a lot of defence, largely because of a lopsided penalty count. This favoured the Blues 9-1 at half-time and 12-3 in the entire game.

Queensland suffered a tough call when Cronk was dispatched to the sin bin for a professional foul with nine minutes of the first half remaining. Moments later, Dane Gagai touched the ball before it bounced over the dead-ball line giving the New South Welshmen another sniff from a Queensland goal-line drop-out.

It was to no avail. As Thurston warned as he came from the pitch at the break, with Queensland ahead 6-4: "We gave them too much ball. It will be different in the second half."

Less than a minute after resumption of play, Sharks hardman Andrew Fifita scored a controversial try off a kick. Jennings was in front of the kicker, Wade Graham. But the referees ruled he did not affect the ultimate result - even though a different interpretation had been taken in other matches this season.

Minutes later Inglis was penalised for a shoulder charge on Josh Dugan. It resulted in Dugan undergoing surgery 48 hours later for a broken jaw, and Inglis suspended for three matches.

What followed was a bizarre scenario when Maroons debutant Gavin Cooper scored for Queensland.

Fifita raced in to disrupt the Queensland players celebrating the try. It was a case of 10 minutes in the sin-bin, an angry frown from his club and Origin captain Gallen, and a one-match suspension.

Then came the countdown to the nail-biting finish.

STATE OF ORIGIN - GAME III

Wednesday 13th July 2016

NEW SOUTH WALES 18 QUEENSLAND 14

NEW SOUTH WALES: 1 James Tedesco (Wests Tigers); 2 Blake Ferguson (Sydney Roosters); 3 Michael Jennings (Parramatta Eels); 4 Josh Dugan (St George Illawarra Dragons); 5 Josh Mansour (Penrith Panthers); 14 Matt Moylan (Penrith Panthers); 7 James Maloney (Cronulla Sharks); 8 Aaron Woods (Wests Tigers); 9 Robbie Farah (Wests Tigers); 10 Paul Gallen (Cronulla Sharks) (C); 11 Wade Graham (Cronulla Sharks); 12 Josh Jackson (Canterbury Bulldogs); 13 Tyson Frizell (St George Illawarra Dragons). Subs (all used): 6 Jack Bird (Cronulla Sharks); 15 James Tamou (North Queensland Cowboys); 16 David Klemmer (Canterbury Bulldogs); 17 Andrew Fifita (Cronulla Sharks).
Tries: Frizell (22), Fifita (41), Jennings (79); **Goals:** Maloney 2/2, Gallen 1/1. **Sin bin:** Fifita (51) - fighting.
QUEENSLAND: 1 Darius Boyd (Brisbane Broncos); 2 Corey Oates (Brisbane Broncos); 3 Greg Inglis (South Sydney Rabbitohs); 4 Justin O'Neill (North Queensland Cowboys); 5 Dane Gagai (Newcastle Knights); 6 Johnathan Thurston (North Queensland Cowboys); 7 Cooper Cronk (Melbourne Storm); 8 Matt Scott (North Queensland Cowboys); 9 Cameron Smith (Melbourne Storm) (C); 10 Nate Myles (Manly Sea Eagles); 11 Matt Gillett (Brisbane Broncos); 12 Sam Thaiday (Brisbane Broncos); 13 Corey Parker (Brisbane Broncos). Subs (all used): 14 Gavin Cooper (North Queensland Cowboys); 15 Josh McGuire (Brisbane Broncos); 16 Aidan Guerra (Sydney Roosters); 17 Jacob Lillyman (New Zealand Warriors).
Tries: Inglis (5), Cooper (51), Boyd (74); **Goals:** Thurston 1/3. **Sin bin:** Cronk (31) - professional foul.
Rugby Leaguer & League Express Men of the Match:
New South Wales: James Tedesco; *Queensland:* Corey Parker.
Half-time: 6-4, **Referees:** Gerard Sutton & Ben Cummins; **Attendance:** 61,267 *(at ANZ Stadium, Sydney).*

Wally Lewis Medal (Man of the Series): Cameron Smith (Queensland).

PERSONALITIES OF 2016

Mike 'Stevo' Stephenson

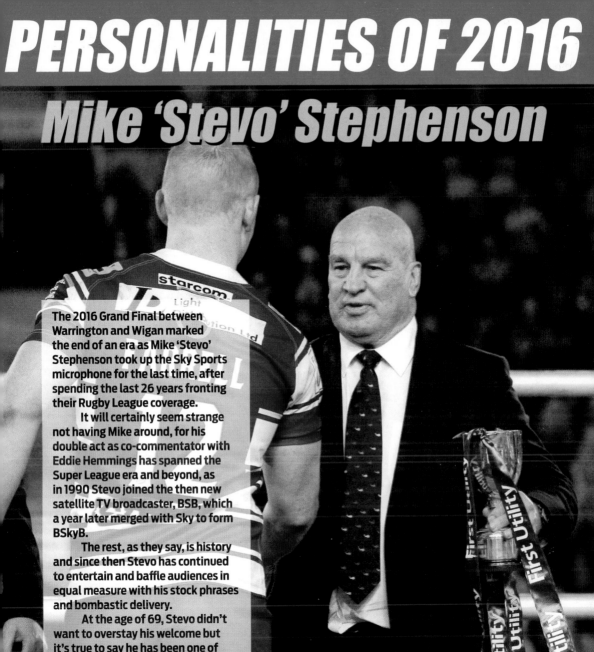

The 2016 Grand Final between Warrington and Wigan marked the end of an era as Mike 'Stevo' Stephenson took up the Sky Sports microphone for the last time, after spending the last 26 years fronting their Rugby League coverage.

It will certainly seem strange not having Mike around, for his double act as co-commentator with Eddie Hemmings has spanned the Super League era and beyond, as in 1990 Stevo joined the then new satellite TV broadcaster, BSB, which a year later merged with Sky to form BSkyB.

The rest, as they say, is history and since then Stevo has continued to entertain and baffle audiences in equal measure with his stock phrases and bombastic delivery.

At the age of 69, Stevo didn't want to overstay his welcome but it's true to say he has been one of the most recognised faces in British Rugby League for the past quarter of a century. His credentials couldn't have been stronger, as a World Cup winner in 1972 and a star player on both sides of the world. He has also been responsible for preserving the history of the game, which manifested itself with him opening the Rugby League museum in the George Hotel, in Huddersfield, now set to find a permanent home in 2020 in Bradford. He'll be missed.

Tom Johnstone
Wakefield Trinity Wildcats

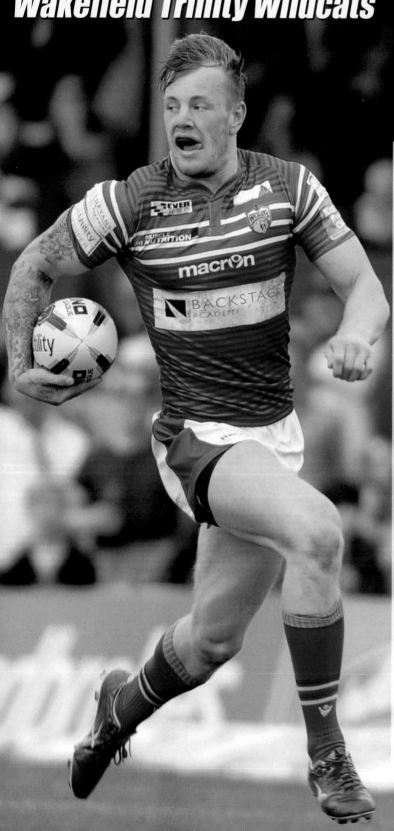

There were some strong contenders for the Super League Young Player of the Year award in 2016 but there weren't any as exciting as Wakefield Trinity Wildcats speedster Tom Johnstone.

The rangy winger, born in Germany where his serviceman father was stationed, marked himself down as one of the game's brightest prospects with some accomplished finishes on the left flank as the Wildcats defied pre-season predictions, a mid-season wonder-run securing them a place in the top-eight and the Super 8s.

Johnstone, who came through the junior ranks at Leeds club Stanningley, scored 20 tries in 2016, much to the delight of the Trinity faithful, grateful to see not only one, but two home-produced talents picking up awards at the end of the season, with fullback Max Jowitt named the Albert Goldthorpe Rookie of the Year. The pair didn't just benefit from Wakefield's better season, they were major players in it.

The public first got sight of a raw-boned 18-year-old Tom Johnstone holding his own in the Boxing Day friendly at Headingley in 2013 though he had to wait until round 7 of 2015 until his first-grade debut at Wigan. His first year was good enough to see him tied up on a three-year contract but, after a stellar 2016, the 21-year-old signed a new four-year deal at Belle Vue. It would take a lot to see Wakefield give up the burgeoning talent of Tom Johnstone.

Danny Houghton
Hull F.C.

2016 was a heady year for Hull FC, if only for the fact that the famous old club won at Wembley for the first time in its 150-year history.

The Airlie Birds had previously won the Challenge Cup three times in 16 finals - but never at Wembley.

But in 2016 that all changed, a thrilling 12-10 win over Warrington ending their hoodoo at the ninth attempt. And if one single incident summed the spirit that took Hull FC home it was the 52nd tackle of the game that hooker Danny Houghton made to deny Wolves back-rower Ben Currie the winning try and a place in history, seconds from the end of one of the most exciting finals of all time.

It was a great year for Hull and fitting on the Monday before the Grand Final that Danny Houghton won the Steve Prescott Man of Steel. His teammate and captain Gareth Ellis was also nominated on the three-man shortlist and Hull FC were named Club of the Year.

Since making his debut in a 20-8 home win over Harlequins in July 2007, in a side, incidentally, captained by his current coach Lee Radford, Houghton has been a bedrock of Hull sides, quickly developing into a true leader. He is certainly durable and was an ever-present in 2016, scoring seven tries and making a staggering 1,289 tackles in the 30 rounds of Super League XXI.

Leigh Centurions managed to break the mould in 2016, winning promotion back into Super League for the first time since their miserable single Super League season in the top flight in 2005.

And they did it in style, at the end of a campaign that had seen the departure of coach Paul Rowley only days before the season began. New coach Neil Jukes and club chairman Derek Beaumont certainly played a clever hand in assembling a side that was good enough to beat three of the four Super League teams in the Qualifiers but their smartest signing had arguably been made in May of 2015, when the Centurions paid a sizeable sum to bring Micky Higham back home from Warrington.

It had been a long time away for the former Great Britain hooker who had signed for St Helens from Leigh in November 2000. He went on to win a Super League title with Saints and two Challenge Cups with the Wolves but the 36-year-old put skippering the Centurions to promotion in 2016 right up there with any of his previous illustrious achievements.

Micky Higham
Leigh Centurions

Super League had a new record try-scorer by the end of 2016. Denny Solomona crowned his second season at Castleford Tigers by scoring his seventh hat-trick of the season in a round-30 home win over Widnes, taking his Super League total to 40 for the season, two clear of the previous record of 38, set in 2004 by both Danny McGuire and Lesley Vainikolo.

The illustrious duo scored some pretty good tries between them that year but very few were as spectacular as some of the ones scored by Solomona in 2016.

Freakish was a word often used to describe the fullback turned winger's ability to score tries in the left corner, either by hanging in the air before somehow planting the ball down, or rising majestically above opponents to grab the ball out of sky for another four-pointer.

Auckland-born, of Samoan descent Solomona first came to England to join London Broncos in 2014, having come through the junior system at Melbourne Storm and finding his way blocked by the great Billy Slater. His speed and talent was undeniable - Wayne Bennett picked out him and Jason Taumalolo as the best juniors of their generation in 2011. But it took a move to the Tigers for 2015 and the strong guidance of coach Daryl Powell to give him the motivation to get the best out of himself.

Denny Solomona
Castleford Tigers

2016 SEASON REVIEW

LEFT: Matt Scott tries to shake off the attention of Brett Ferres and Liam Sutcliffe during the World Club Challenge

BELOW: Kallum Watkins fights for a loose ball under pressure from Johnathan Thurston

DACIA
RUGBY LEAGUE
WORLD CLUB SERIES

RIGHT: Daniel Tupou leaves St Helens' Tom Makinson behind on the way to a Sydney Roosters try

ABOVE: Brisbane's Greg Eden races away from Wigan's Oliver Gildart

LEFT: Wakefield's Jacob Miller lands a long-distance field goal to earn victory against Catalans Dragons

LEFT: Salford's Junior Sa'u chased down by Widnes' Manase Manuokafoa

RIGHT: Castleford's Luke Dorn mobbed after scoring against Warrington

BELOW: Fans enjoy the Magic Weekend inside Newcastle's St James' Park

DACIA MAGIC WEEKEND

SUPER LEAGUE AWARDS

STEVE PRESCOTT MBE MAN OF STEEL
Danny Houghton (Hull FC)

YOUNG PLAYER OF THE YEAR
Tom Johnstone (Wakefield Trinity Wildcats)

COACH OF THE YEAR
Lee Radford (Hull FC)

CLUB OF THE YEAR
Hull FC

TOP TRY SCORER
Denny Solomona (Castleford Tigers) (40)

TOP METRE MAKER
Chris Hill (Warrington Wolves) (3983)

TOP TACKLER
Danny Houghton (Hull FC) (1289)

(totals include regular season & Super 8s only)

SUPER LEAGUE DREAM TEAM
(previous selections in italics)

1 Jamie Shaul (Hull FC) *Debut*
2 Denny Solomona (Castleford Tigers) *Debut*
3 Ryan Atkins (Warrington Wolves) *2012*
4 Mahe Fonua (Hull FC) *Debut*
5 Dominic Manfredi (Wigan Warriors) *Debut*
6 Kurt Gidley (Warrington Wolves) *Debut*
7 Luke Gale (Castleford Tigers) *2015*
8 Chris Hill (Warrington Wolves) *2012, 2014*
9 Danny Houghton (Hull FC) *Debut*
10 Scott Taylor (Hull FC) *Debut*
11 Ben Currie (Warrington Wolves) *Debut*
12 Mark Minichiello (Hull FC) *Debut*
13 Gareth Ellis (Hull FC) *2003, 2006, 2007, 2008*

ALBERT GOLDTHORPE MEDAL
Luke Gale (Castleford Tigers)

ALBERT GOLDTHORPE ROOKIE OF THE YEAR
Max Jowitt (Wakefield Trinity Wildcats)

BELOW LEFT: Danny Houghton - 2016 Man of Steel
BELOW RIGHT: Tom Johnstone - 2016 Young Player of the Year

BELOW: The 2016 Super League Dream Team *(Not pictured: Denny Solomona)*

LEFT: Wigan's Liam Farrell drives Widnes' Corey Thompson backwards

LEFT: Warrington's Joe Westerman and Daryl Clark show off the League Leaders' Shield

LEFT: Catalans Dragons' Glenn Stewart looks for support against Castleford

LEFT: Wigan's John Bateman halted by Hull FC's Liam Watts and Danny Washbrook

RIGHT: Warrington duo Chris Hill and Kurt Gidley combine to bring down St Helens' Jonny Lomax

First Utility SUPER LEAGUE SUPER8s

First Utility SUPER LEAGUE PLAY-OFFS

HULL FC....................................12
WARRINGTON WOLVES.......................10

BELOW: Mahe Fonua crashes past Chris Sandow and Ryan Atkins to score Hull FC's 61st minute try

Ladbrokes
CHALLENGE CUP

LEFT: Coach Lee Radford and hooker Danny Houghton celebrate their sides' first-ever Wembley win

BELOW: Fetuli Talanoa takes on Daryl Clark and George King

WARRINGTON WOLVES...................... 6
WIGAN WARRIORS 12

RIGHT: Ryan Sutton leads the celebratory charge from the Wigan bench at the final hooter

First Utility
SUPER LEAGUE
GRAND FINAL

RIGHT: Warriors captain Sean O'Loughlin, coach Shaun Wane and Harry Sunderland Trophy winner Liam Farrell show off the Super League trophy

BELOW: Chris Sandow looks to fend off George Williams, as Dominic Crosby closes in

ABOVE: Leigh Centurions celebrate promotion to Super League with their fans

BELOW: London Broncos' Kameron Pearce-Paul knocks the ball dead under pressure from Salford's Josh Griffin

SUPER8s THE QUALIFIERS

RIGHT: Leeds' Joel Moon breaks through against Featherstone

BELOW: Huddersfield's Ukuma Ta'ai, Danny Brough and Ryan Hinchcliffe wrap up Hull KR's Josh Mantellato

LEFT: Batley's Dominic Brambani grabbed by Featherstone's Steve Snitch

ABOVE: Jubilation for Salford players and fans following Gareth O'Brien's golden point field goal

£1M GAME

LEFT: Red Devils owner Marwan Koukash celebrates with fans

RIGHT: Jamie Peacock, out of retirement, looks for a way past Mark Flanagan

RIGHT: Featherstone's Anthony Thackeray looks to break free from the clutches of Bradford's Dale Ferguson in a shootout for a Super 8s place

LEFT: Batley's Wayne Reittie in action against Dewsbury at the Summer Bash in Blackpool

Kingstone Press
CHAMPIONSHIP

BELOW: The Halifax defence can't stop Leigh's Micky Higham from scoring in an early season clash at The Shay

ABOVE: Bradford celebrate their Championship Shield Final victory against Sheffield

LEFT: Newcastle Thunder picked up the inaugural League 1 Shield after defeating North Wales Crusaders

BELOW: Delight for Ben Moores as Rochdale pull off a stunning win at previously unbeaten Toulouse to earn the first League 1 promotion place

LEFT: Barrow's Martin Aspinwall tackled by the Toulouse defence as Olympique earn promotion from League 1

BELOW: Keighley's Ash Lindsay, Paul Handforth, coach Paul March and Paul White after League 1 Cup success against York

BELOW: Cronulla captain Paul Gallen lifts the Provan-Summons Trophy following the Sharks' first-ever Grand Final victory

LEFT: Cooper Cronk gets a kick away under pressure

BELOW: Andrew Fifita looks to break free as Blake Green watches on

NRL
TELSTRA
PREMIERSHIP

GRAND FINAL
SYDNEY 2016

5
STATISTICAL REVIEW

SUPER LEAGUE PLAYERS
1996-2016

Super League Players 1996-2016

PLAYER	CLUB	YEAR	APP	TRIES	GOALS	FG	PTS
Jordan Abdull	Hull	2014-16	22(12)	5	7	0	34
Carl Ablett	Leeds	2004,					
		2006-16	205(33)	60	0	0	240
	London	2005	3(2)	0	0	0	0
Darren Abram	Oldham	1996-97	25(2)	11	0	0	44
Mitch Achurch	Leeds	2013-16	25(50)	14	0	0	56
Brad Adams	Bradford	2014	1(1)	0	0	0	0
Darren Adams	Paris	1996	9(1)	1	0	0	4
Guy Adams	Huddersfield	1998	1(2)	0	0	0	0
Luke Adamson	Salford	2006-07,					
		2009-12	73(39)	11	1	0	46
Matt Adamson	Leeds	2002-04	54(8)	9	0	0	36
Phil Adamson	St Helens	1999	(1)	0	0	0	0
Toby Adamson	Salford	2010	(1)	0	0	0	0
Danny Addy	Bradford	2010-14	49(42)	13	7	0	66
Ade Adebisi	London	2004	(1)	0	0	0	0
Patrick Ah Van	Widnes	2012-16	84	62	54	0	356
	Bradford	2011	26	9	87	0	210
Jamie Ainscough	Wigan	2002-03	30(2)	18	0	0	72
Shaun Ainscough	Bradford	2011-12	27	15	0	0	60
	Wigan	2009-10	12	13	0	0	52
	Castleford	2010	7	4	0	0	16
Glen Air	London	1998-2001	57(13)	27	0	1	109
Paul Aiton	Catalans	2016	6(6)	2	0	0	8
	Leeds	2014-15	36(6)	2	0	0	8
	Wakefield	2012-13	43(2)	7	0	0	28
Makali Aizue	Hull KR	2007-09	18(32)	4	0	0	16
Darren Albert	St Helens	2002-05	105	77	0	0	308
Lucas Albert	Catalans	2015-16	12	3	2	0	16
Paul Alcock	Widnes	2003, 2005	1(7)	1	0	0	4
Neil Alexander	Salford	1998	(1)	0	0	0	0
Malcolm Alker	Salford	1997-2002, 2004-07, 2009-10	271(2)	40	0	1	161
Danny Allan	Leeds	2008-09	2(5)	0	0	0	0
Chris Allen	Castleford	1996	(1)	0	0	0	0
Dave Allen	Widnes	2012-14	50(13)	5	0	0	20
	Wigan	2003, 2005	6(15)	2	0	0	8
Gavin Allen	London	1996	10	0	0	0	0
John Allen	Workington	1996	20(1)	6	0	0	24
Ray Allen	London	1996	5(3)	3	0	0	12
Mitchell Allgood	Hull KR	2015-16	27(2)	5	0	0	20
Richard Allwood	Gateshead	1999	(4)	0	0	0	0
Sean Allwood	Gateshead	1999	3(17)	1	0	0	4
David Alstead	Warrington	2000-02	23(10)	3	0	0	12
Luke Ambler	Harlequins	2011	5(17)	1	0	0	4
	Leeds	2010	1(8)	1	0	0	4
Asa Amone	Halifax	1996-97	32(7)	10	0	0	40
Kyle Amor	St Helens	2014-16	60(16)	12	0	0	48
	Wakefield	2011-13	51(23)	9	0	0	36
	Leeds	2010	(3)	0	0	0	0
Thibaut Ancely	Catalans	2011	(2)	0	0	0	0
Grant Anderson	Castleford	1996-97	15(6)	3	0	0	12
Louis Anderson	Catalans	2012-16	72(23)	26	0	0	104
	Warrington	2008-11	92	18	0	0	72
Paul Anderson	St Helens	2005-06	48(5)	7	1	0	30
	Bradford	1997-2004	74(104)	30	0	0	120
	Halifax	1996	5(1)	1	0	0	4
Paul Anderson	Sheffield	1999	3(7)	1	0	0	4
	St Helens	1996-98	2(28)	4	1	0	18
Scott Anderson	Wakefield	2014-16	25(18)	2	0	0	8
Vinnie Anderson	Salford	2011-12	33(3)	14	0	0	56
	Warrington	2007-10	57(19)	22	0	0	88
	St Helens	2005-06	28(14)	17	0	0	68
Phil Anderton	St Helens	2004	1	0	0	0	0
Chris Annakin	Wakefield	2013-16	3(36)	1	0	0	4
Eric Anselme	Leeds	2008	2(2)	2	0	0	8
	Halifax	1997	(2)	0	0	0	0
Mark Applegarth	Wakefield	2004-07	20(5)	3	0	0	12
Graham Appo	Warrington	2002-05	60(13)	35	80	0	300
	Huddersfield	2001	7	4	0	0	16
Anthony Armour	London	2005	11(7)	1	0	0	4
Colin Armstrong	Workington	1996	11(2)	1	0	0	4
Tom Armstrong	St Helens	2009-11	10(5)	9	0	0	36
Richard Armswood	Workington	1996	5(1)	1	0	0	4
Danny Arnold	Salford	2001-02	26(13)	13	0	0	52
	Huddersfield	1998-2000	55(7)	26	0	0	104
	Castleford	2000	(4)	0	0	0	0
	St Helens	1996-97	40(1)	33	0	0	132
Tinirau Arona	Wakefield	2016	15(13)	0	0	0	0
Joe Arundel	Wakefield	2015-16	36(4)	8	4	0	40
	Bradford	2014	9(3)	5	0	0	20
	Hull	2013-14	16	7	1	0	30
	Castleford	2008, 2010-12	35(4)	14	2	0	60
Craig Ashall	St Helens	2006	1	1	0	0	4
Nathan Ashe	St Helens	2011-13	6(4)	0	0	0	0
Chris Ashton	Wigan	2005-07	44(2)	25	2	0	104
Matty Ashurst	Wakefield	2015-16	27(3)	7	0	0	28
	Salford	2012-14	65(7)	11	0	0	44
	St Helens	2009-11	12(39)	8	0	0	32
Jack Ashworth	St Helens	2015-16	4(3)	2	0	0	8
Roy Asotasi	Warrington	2014-15	16(37)	5	1	0	22
Peter Aspinall	Huddersfield	2013	1(1)	0	0	0	0
Martin Aspinwall	Hull	2012	12(15)	0	0	0	0
	Castleford	2011	12(6)	2	0	0	8
	Huddersfield	2006-10	72(8)	22	0	0	88
	Wigan	2001-05	85(13)	27	0	0	108
Mark Aston	Sheffield	1996-99	67(6)	6	243	6	516
Paul Atcheson	Widnes	2002-04	16(35)	4	0	0	16
	St Helens	1998-2000	58(4)	18	0	0	72
	Oldham	1996-97	40	21	0	0	84
David Atkins	Huddersfield	2001	26(1)	4	0	0	16
Jordan Atkins	London	2014	13(1)	4	0	0	16
Ryan Atkins	Warrington	2010-16	186(1)	116	0	0	464
	Wakefield	2006-09	86(2)	45	0	0	180
Josh Atkinson	Castleford	2012	2	0	0	0	0
Brad Attwood	Halifax	2003	(3)	0	0	0	0
Warren Ayres	Salford	1999	2(9)	1	2	0	8
Jerome Azema	Paris	1997	(1)	0	0	0	0
Marcus Bai	Bradford	2006	24	9	0	0	36
	Leeds	2004-05	57	42	0	0	168
David Baildon	Hull	1998-99	26(2)	4	0	0	16
Jean-Philippe Baile							
	Catalans	2008-14	62(16)	23	0	0	92
Andy Bailey	Hull	2004-05	2(8)	1	0	0	4
Chris Bailey	Huddersfield	2014-15	17(17)	5	0	0	20
	London	2012-13	41	14	0	0	56
	Harlequins	2011	24	3	0	0	12
Julian Bailey	Huddersfield	2003-04	47	13	0	0	52
Phil Bailey	Wigan	2007-10	84(4)	13	0	0	52
Ricky Bailey	St Helens	2015	1	0	0	0	0
Ryan Bailey	Warrington	2016	1(11)	0	0	0	0
	Castleford	2015	3(2)	0	0	0	0
	Hull KR	2015	(1)	1	0	0	4
	Leeds	2002-14	171(102)	17	0	0	68
Jason Baitieri	Catalans	2011-16	114(29)	17	0	0	68
Simon Baldwin	Salford	2004-06	20(29)	3	0	0	12
	Sheffield	1999	7(15)	2	0	0	8
	Halifax	1996-98	41(15)	16	0	1	65
Jordan Baldwinson	Leeds	2013, 2016	(3)	0	0	0	0
	Bradford	2014	2(4)	0	0	0	0
Rob Ball	Wigan	1998-2000	3(4)	0	0	0	0
Paul Ballard	Celtic	2009	2	0	0	0	0
	Widnes	2005	3(1)	2	0	0	8
Darren Bamford	Salford	2005	2(1)	0	0	0	0
Michael Banks	Bradford	1998	(1)	0	0	0	0
Steve Bannister	Harlequins	2007	(6)	0	0	0	0
	St Helens	2006-07	(3)	0	0	0	0
Frederic Banquet	Paris	1996	16(2)	7	4	0	36
Lee Bardauskas	Castleford	1996-97	(2)	0	0	0	0
Craig Barker	Workington	1996	(2)	0	0	0	0
Dwayne Barker	Harlequins	2008	5(5)	1	0	0	4
	London	2004	3	1	0	0	4
	Hull	2003	(1)	0	0	0	0
Mark Barlow	Wakefield	2002	(1)	0	0	0	0
Danny Barnes	Halifax	1999	2	0	0	0	0
Richie Barnett	Salford	2007	7	4	0	0	16
	Warrington	2006-07	26(10)	15	0	0	60
	Hull	2004-05	21(5)	21	0	0	84
	Widnes	2005	4	2	0	0	8
Richie Barnett	Hull	2003-04	31(1)	17	0	0	68
	London	2001-02	31(4)	13	0	0	52
David Barnhill	Leeds	2000	20(8)	5	0	0	20
Trent Barrett	Wigan	2007-08	53(1)	22	0	4	92
Paul Barrow	Warrington	1996-97	1(10)	1	0	0	4
Scott Barrow	St Helens	1997-2000	9(13)	1	0	0	4
Steve Barrow	London	2000	2	0	0	0	0
	Hull	1998-99	4(17)	1	0	0	4
	Wigan	1996	(8)	3	0	0	12
William Barthau	Catalans	2010, 2012-14	13(3)	2	15	0	38
Ben Barton	Huddersfield	1998	1(6)	1	0	0	4
Danny Barton	Salford	2001	1	0	0	0	0
Wayne Bartrim	Castleford	2002-03	41(2)	9	157	0	350
Greg Barwick	London	1996-97	30(4)	21	110	2	306
David Bastian	Halifax	1996	(2)	0	0	0	0
James Batchelor	Wakefield	2016	(3)	0	0	0	0
Ashley Bateman	Celtic	2009	1	0	0	0	0
John Bateman	Wigan	2014-16	71(8)	24	0	0	96
	Bradford	2011-13	25(5)	7	0	0	28
David Bates	Castleford	2001-02	(4)	0	0	0	0
	Warrington	2001	1(2)	0	0	0	0

Super League Players 1996-2016

PLAYER	CLUB	YEAR	APP	TRIES	GOALS	FG	PTS
Sam Bates	Bradford	2014	(2)	0	0	0	0
Nathan Batty	Wakefield	2001	1(1)	0	0	0	0
Andreas Bauer	Hull KR	2007	10(2)	5	0	0	20
Russell Bawden	London	1996-97, 2002-04	50(49)	15	0	0	60
Neil Baxter	Salford	2001	1	0	0	0	0
Neil Baynes	Salford	1999-2002, 2004	84(19)	10	0	0	40
	Wigan	1996-98	(10)	1	0	0	4
Chris Beasley	Celtic	2009	15(5)	2	0	0	8
Chris Beattie	Catalans	2006	22(5)	3	0	0	12
Richard Beaumont	Hull KR	2011-13	1(16)	1	0	0	4
Robbie Beazley	London	1997-99	48(15)	13	0	0	52
Robbie Beckett	Halifax	2002	27	15	0	0	60
Matty Beharrell	Hull KR	2013	1	0	0	0	0
Dean Bell	Leeds	1996	1	1	0	0	4
Ian Bell	Hull	2003	(1)	0	0	0	0
Mark Bell	Wigan	1998	22	12	0	0	48
Paul Bell	Leeds	2000	1	0	0	0	0
Steven Bell	Catalans	2009-10	43	14	0	0	56
Troy Bellamy	Paris	1997	5(10)	0	0	0	0
Adrian Belle	Huddersfield	1998	10(2)	0	0	0	0
	Oldham	1996	19	8	0	0	32
Jamie Benn	Castleford	1998, 2000	3(8)	1	15	0	34
Andy Bennett	Warrington	1996	6(5)	1	0	0	4
Mike Bennett	St Helens	2000-08	74(70)	15	0	0	60
Andrew Bentley	Catalans	2007-10	9(15)	1	0	0	4
John Bentley	Huddersfield	1999	13(4)	3	0	0	12
	Halifax	1996, 1998	22(3)	24	0	0	96
Kane Bentley	Catalans	2007-10	11(19)	5	0	0	20
Phil Bergman	Paris	1997	20(1)	14	0	0	56
Shaun Berrigan	Hull	2008-10	60(8)	12	0	0	48
Joe Berry	Huddersfield	1998-99	25(14)	3	0	0	12
David Berthezene	Salford	2007	9(1)	0	0	0	0
	Catalans	2006-07	5(14)	0	0	0	0
Colin Best	Hull	2003-04	57	34	0	0	136
Roger Best	London	1997-98	1(5)	1	0	0	4
Bob Beswick	Wigan	2004-05	5(14)	2	0	0	8
Monty Betham	Wakefield	2006	26	2	0	0	8
Mike Bethwaite	Workington	1996	17(3)	1	0	0	4
Denis Betts	Wigan	1998-2001	82(24)	33	0	0	132
Cliff Beverley	Salford	2004-05	47(1)	14	0	0	56
Kyle Bibb	Wakefield	2008-10	1(24)	0	0	0	0
	Harlequins	2010	(2)	0	0	0	0
	Hull KR	2009	(2)	0	0	0	0
Jake Bibby	Salford	2016	3(2)	0	0	0	0
Adam Bibey	Widnes	2004	(1)	0	0	0	0
Ricky Bibey	Wakefield	2007-09	32(25)	1	0	0	4
	St Helens	2004	4(14)	0	0	0	0
	Wigan	2001-03	5(29)	0	0	0	0
Chris Birchall	Halifax	2002-03	24(22)	4	0	0	16
	Bradford	2000	(1)	0	0	0	0
Deon Bird	Castleford	2006	17(6)	5	0	0	20
	Widnes	2003-04	39(6)	9	0	0	36
	Wakefield	2002	10(1)	1	0	0	4
	Hull	2000-02	37(22)	20	0	0	80
	Gateshead	1999	19(3)	13	0	0	52
	Paris	1996-97	30	12	2	0	52
Greg Bird	Catalans	2009	20(2)	5	3	0	26
Mike Bishay	London	2013-14	7(11)	2	2	0	12
Nathan Blacklock	Hull	2005-06	44(3)	33	0	0	132
Ben Blackmore	Huddersfield	2013-14	3	4	0	0	16
	Castleford	2012	1	0	0	0	0
Richie Blackmore	Leeds	1997-2000	63	25	0	0	100
Anthony Blackwood	Crusaders	2010	1	0	0	0	0
	Celtic	2009	25	5	0	0	20
Jack Blagbrough	Huddersfield	2013	(1)	0	0	0	0
Maurice Blair	Hull KR	2015-16	41(2)	9	1	0	38
Luke Blake	Wakefield	2009	(2)	0	0	0	0
Matthew Blake	Castleford	2003-04	1(5)	0	0	0	0
Steve Blakeley	Salford	1997-2002	103(5)	26	241	2	588
	Warrington	2000	4(3)	1	9	0	22
Richard Blakeway	Castleford	2002-04	1(14)	0	0	0	0
Damien Blanch	Catalans	2011-13	70	42	0	0	168
	Wakefield	2008-10	44(3)	31	0	0	124
	Castleford	2006	3(2)	0	0	0	0
Matt Blaymire	Wakefield	2007-11	96(3)	26	0	1	105
Ian Blease	Salford	1997	(1)	0	0	0	0
Jamie Bloem	Huddersfield	2003	18(4)	3	11	0	34
	Halifax	1998-2002	82(25)	25	100	2	302
Vea Bloomfield	Paris	1996	4(14)	3	0	0	12
Matty Blythe	Bradford	2013-14	24(6)	8	0	0	32
	Warrington	2007-12	28(27)	12	0	0	48
Ben Bolger	London	2012	2(7)	1	0	0	4
	Harlequins	2010-11	4(15)	0	0	0	0
Pascal Bomati	Paris	1996	17(1)	10	0	0	40
Simon Booth	Hull	1998-99	15(9)	2	0	0	8
	St Helens	1996-97	10(4)	1	0	0	4
Steve Booth	Huddersfield	1998-99	16(4)	2	3	0	14
Alan Boothroyd	Halifax	1997	2(3)	0	0	0	0
Thomas Bosc	Catalans	2006-16	193(16)	47	483	12	1166
John Boslem	Paris	1996	(5)	0	0	0	0
Liam Bostock	St Helens	2004	1	0	0	0	0
Liam Botham	Wigan	2005	5	0	0	0	0
	Leeds	2003-05	2(11)	4	0	0	16
	London	2004	6(2)	3	7	0	26
Frano Botica	Castleford	1996	21	5	84	2	190
Matthew Bottom	Leigh	2005	(1)	0	0	0	0
Hadj Boudebza	Paris	1996	(2)	0	0	0	0
John Boudebza	Hull KR	2015-16	13(17)	2	0	0	8
David Boughton	Huddersfield	1999	26(1)	4	0	0	16
Julian Bousquet	Catalans	2012-16	29(59)	7	0	0	28
David Bouveng	Halifax	1997-99	66(2)	19	0	0	76
Josh Bowden	Hull	2012-16	31(53)	9	0	0	36
Matt Bowen	Wigan	2014-15	43	21	31	0	146
Tony Bowes	Huddersfield	1998	3(2)	0	0	0	0
Radney Bowker	London	2004	3	1	0	0	4
	St Helens	2001	(1)	0	0	0	0
David Boyle	Bradford	1999-2000	36(13)	15	0	1	61
Ryan Boyle	Castleford	2006, 2008-09, 2013-16	12(60)	5	0	0	20
	Salford	2010-13	57(14)	3	0	0	12
Andy Bracek	Crusaders	2011	(2)	0	0	0	0
	Warrington	2005-08	7(49)	7	0	0	28
	St Helens	2004	(1)	0	0	0	0
David Bradbury	Hudds-Sheff	2000	21(2)	1	0	0	4
	Salford	1997-99	23(10)	6	0	0	24
	Oldham	1996-97	19(6)	9	0	0	36
John Braddish	St Helens	2001-02	1(1)	0	3	0	6
Graeme Bradley	Bradford	1996-98	62(1)	29	0	0	116
Nick Bradley-Qalilawa	Harlequins	2006	27	6	0	0	24
	London	2005	28	19	0	0	76
Darren Bradstreet	London	1999-2000	1(3)	0	0	0	0
Dominic Brambani	Castleford	2004	2(2)	0	0	0	0
Joe Bretherton	Wigan	2016	2(9)	1	0	0	4
Liam Bretherton	Wigan	1999	(5)	2	0	0	8
	Warrington	1997	(2)	0	0	0	0
Johnny Brewer	Halifax	1996	4(2)	2	0	0	8
Chris Bridge	Widnes	2016	13	2	4	0	16
	Warrington	2005-15	186(17)	89	248	1	853
	Bradford	2003-04	2(14)	4	6	0	28
Danny Bridge	Bradford	2014	4(4)	0	0	0	0
	Warrington	2013	(2)	0	0	0	0
Ryan Brierley	Huddersfield	2016	13(1)	5	0	0	20
Lee Briers	Warrington	1997-2013	365(12)	130	810	70	2210
	St Helens	1997	3	0	11	0	22
Carl Briggs	Salford	1999	8(5)	3	0	1	13
	Halifax	1996	5(3)	1	0	0	4
Kyle Briggs	Bradford	2011	6	4	0	0	16
	Harlequins	2011	3	0	0	0	0
Mike Briggs	Widnes	2002	1(2)	1	0	0	4
Luke Briscoe	Leeds	2014, 2016	5(4)	2	0	0	8
	Wakefield	2014	2	0	0	0	0
Shaun Briscoe	Widnes	2012-13	11(2)	4	0	0	16
	Hull KR	2008-11	92	27	0	0	108
	Hull	2004-07	83(9)	50	0	0	200
	Wigan	2002-03	23(5)	11	0	0	44
Tom Briscoe	Leeds	2014-16	47	22	0	0	88
	Hull	2008-13	131(3)	83	0	0	332
Darren Britt	St Helens	2002-03	41	3	0	0	12
Gary Broadbent	Salford	1997-2002	117(2)	22	0	0	88
Paul Broadbent	Wakefield	2002	16(5)	0	0	0	0
	Hull	2000-01	40(9)	3	0	0	12
	Halifax	1999	26(1)	2	0	0	8
	Sheffield	1996-98	63(1)	6	0	0	24
Andrew Brocklehurst	Salford	2004-07	34(23)	5	0	0	20
	London	2004	12(6)	2	0	0	8
	Halifax	2001-03	37(8)	2	0	0	8
Justin Brooker	Wakefield	2001	25	9	0	0	36
	Bradford	2000	17(4)	11	0	0	44
Sam Brooks	Widnes	2016	(2)	0	0	0	0
Danny Brough	Huddersfield	2010-16	171(4)	40	598	15	1371
	Wakefield	2008-10	50(1)	14	174	4	408
	Castleford	2006	10	1	31	2	68
	Hull	2005-06	25(12)	3	85	1	183
Jodie Broughton	Catalans	2016	26	19	0	0	76
	Huddersfield	2014-15	30	16	0	0	64
	Salford	2010-13	93	53	0	0	212
	Hull	2008-09	9(3)	6	0	0	24

Super League Players 1996-2016

PLAYER	CLUB	YEAR	APP	TRIES	GOALS	FG	PTS
Alex Brown	Hull KR	2013	16	9	0	0	36
	Huddersfield	2009	1	0	0	0	0
Darren Brown	Salford	1999-2001	47(9)	11	6	0	56
Gavin Brown	Leeds	1996-97	5(2)	1	2	0	8
Kevin Brown	Widnes	2013-16	80	37	1	1	151
	Huddersfield	2006-12	156	43	0	1	173
	Wigan	2003-06	46(18)	27	0	0	108
Lee Brown	Hull	1999	(1)	0	0	0	0
Michael Brown	Huddersfield	2008	(1)	0	0	0	0
Michael Brown	London	1996	(2)	0	0	0	0
Todd Brown	Paris	1996	8(1)	2	0	0	8
Adrian Brunker	Wakefield	1999	17	6	0	0	24
Lamont Bryan	Harlequins	2008-11	9(22)	2	0	0	8
Justin Bryant	Paris	1996	4(1)	0	0	0	0
	London	1996	7(8)	1	0	0	4
Mark Bryant	London	2012-13	16(36)	3	1	0	14
	Crusaders	2010-11	42(8)	1	0	0	4
	Celtic	2009	23(3)	0	0	0	0
Austin Buchanan	Wakefield	2005-06	6	2	0	0	8
	London	2003	3(1)	2	0	0	8
Jack Buchanan	Widnes	2016	12(2)	0	0	0	0
Danny Buderus	Leeds	2009-11	57(14)	14	0	0	56
Neil Budworth	Celtic	2009	8(19)	0	0	0	0
	Harlequins	2006	2(19)	0	0	0	0
	London	2002-05	59(11)	4	1	0	18
James Bunyan	Huddersfield	1998-99	8(7)	2	0	0	8
Andy Burgess	Salford	1997	3(12)	0	0	0	0
Joe Burgess	Wigan	2013-15	52	45	0	0	180
Luke Burgess	Leeds	2008-11	10(63)	6	0	0	24
	Harlequins	2007	(3)	0	0	0	0
Sam Burgess	Bradford	2006-09	46(34)	14	5	0	66
Tom Burgess	Bradford	2011-12	1(41)	3	0	0	12
Greg Burke	Widnes	2016	8(1)	0	0	0	0
	Wigan	2013-14, 2016	13(26)	1	0	0	4
	Hull KR	2015	9(5)	0	0	0	0
	Bradford	2014	(1)	0	0	0	0
Joe Burke	Crusaders	2011	(1)	0	0	0	0
Mike Burnett	Harlequins	2011	16(4)	1	0	0	4
	Hull	2008-10	13(21)	3	0	0	12
Darren Burns	Warrington	2002-04	66(6)	19	0	0	76
Gary Burns	Oldham	1996	6	1	0	0	4
Paul Burns	Workington	1996	5(2)	1	0	0	4
Travis Burns	St Helens	2015-16	27(2)	4	28	0	72
	Hull KR	2013-14	46	8	81	2	196
Rob Burrow	Leeds	2001-16	304(103)				
				163	126	5	909
Dean Busby	Warrington	1999-2002	34(34)	7	0	0	28
	Hull	1998	8(6)	0	0	0	0
	St Helens	1996-98	1(7)	0	0	0	0
Tom Bush	Leeds	2010	3(1)	1	0	0	4
Ikram Butt	London	1996	5(1)	0	0	0	0
Shane Byrne	Huddersfield	1998-99	1(5)	0	0	0	0
Todd Byrne	Hull	2008-09	20	4	0	0	16
Didier Cabestany	Paris	1996-97	20(6)	2	0	0	8
Hep Cahill	Widnes	2012-16	89(4)	3	0	0	12
	Crusaders	2011	16	2	0	0	8
Joel Caine	Salford	2004	24	8	13	0	58
	London	2003	6	4	1	0	18
Mark Calderwood	Harlequins	2011	13	2	0	0	8
	Hull	2009-10	23	6	0	0	24
	Wigan	2006-08	64	23	0	0	92
	Leeds	2001-05	117(9)	88	0	0	352
Mike Callan	Warrington	2002	(4)	0	0	0	0
Matt Calland	Huddersfield	2003	2	0	0	0	0
	Hull	1999	1	0	0	0	0
	Bradford	1996-98	44(5)	24	0	0	96
Dean Callaway	London	1999-2000	26(24)	12	0	0	48
Laurent Cambres	Paris	1996	(1)	0	0	0	0
Chris Campbell	Warrington	2000	7(1)	2	0	0	8
Liam Campbell	Wakefield	2005	(1)	0	0	0	0
Logan Campbell	Hull	1998-99, 2001	70(13)	14	0	0	56
	Castleford	2000	14(2)	3	0	0	12
	Workington	1996	7(1)	1	0	0	4
Terry Campese	Hull KR	2015-16	19(1)	2	4	0	16
Blake Cannova	Widnes	2002	(1)	0	0	0	0
Phil Cantillon	Widnes	2002-03	27(21)	18	0	0	72
	Leeds	1997	(1)	0	0	0	0
Liam Carberry	Widnes	2014-15	2(5)	0	0	0	0
Damien Cardace	Catalans	2012, 2014-15	23	14	0	0	56
Daryl Cardiss	Warrington	2003-04	23(2)	3	4	0	20
	Halifax	1999-2003	91(8)	39	4	0	164
	Wigan	1996-98	12(6)	4	0	0	16
Dale Cardoza	Warrington	2002	5	1	0	0	4
	Halifax	2001	3	1	0	0	4
	Huddersfield	2000-01	20(9)	11	0	0	44
	Sheffield	1998-99	11(7)	3	0	0	12
Paul Carige	Salford	1999	24(1)	7	0	0	28
Dane Carlaw	Catalans	2008-10	58(15)	9	0	0	36
Keal Carlile	Hull KR	2012-15	6(28)	1	0	0	4
	Huddersfield	2009, 2011	2(1)	1	0	0	4
	Bradford	2008	(1)	0	0	0	0
Jim Carlton	Huddersfield	1999	3(11)	2	0	0	8
George Carmont	Wigan	2008-12	136	71	0	0	284
Brian Carney	Warrington	2009	4	2	0	0	8
	Wigan	2001-05	91(10)	42	1	0	170
	Hull	2000	13(3)	7	0	0	28
	Gateshead	1999	3(2)	2	0	0	8
Justin Carney	Salford	2016	19	9	0	0	36
	Castleford	2013-15	58	56	0	0	224
Martin Carney	Warrington	1997	(1)	0	0	0	0
Todd Carney	Catalans	2015-16	32	9	4	1	45
Omari Caro	Hull KR	2013-14	21	20	0	0	80
	London	2012	11	4	0	0	16
Paul Carr	Sheffield	1996-98	45(5)	15	0	0	60
Bernard Carroll	London	1996	2(1)	1	0	0	4
Mark Carroll	London	1998	15(3)	1	0	0	4
Tonie Carroll	Leeds	2001-02	42(2)	30	0	0	120
Darren Carter	Workington	1996	10(3)	0	1	0	2
Steve Carter	Widnes	2002	14(7)	4	0	0	16
John Cartwright	Salford	1997	9	0	0	0	0
Garreth Carvell	Castleford	2014	1(4)	1	0	0	4
	Hull	2001-08, 2014	75(84)	22	0	0	88
	Warrington	2009-13	77(40)	13	0	0	52
	Leeds	1997-2000	(4)	0	0	0	0
	Gateshead	1999	4(4)	1	0	0	4
Garen Casey	Salford	1999	13(5)	3	23	0	58
Ray Cashmere	Salford	2009-11	63(3)	5	0	0	20
Mick Cassidy	Widnes	2005	24	0	0	0	0
	Wigan	1996-2004	184(36)	30	0	0	120
Remi Casty	Catalans	2006-13, 2015-16	124(91)	21	0	0	84
Ned Catic	Castleford	2008	7(7)	3	0	0	12
	Wakefield	2006-07	17(29)	4	0	0	16
Mason Caton-Brown	Salford	2014-16	28	10	0	0	40
	London	2013-14	19	15	0	0	60
Joe Cator	Hull KR	2016	(2)	0	0	0	0
Chris Causey	Warrington	1997-99	(18)	1	0	0	4
Jason Cayless	St Helens	2006-09	62(9)	7	0	0	28
Arnaud Cervello	Paris	1996	4	4	0	0	16
Marshall Chalk	Celtic	2009	13	4	0	0	16
Ed Chamberlain	Widnes	2016	3(1)	0	0	0	0
Gary Chambers	Warrington	1996-2000	65(28)	2	0	0	8
Pierre Chamorin	Paris	1996-97	27(3)	8	3	0	38
Alex Chan	Catalans	2006-08	59(19)	11	0	0	44
Jason Chan	Hull KR	2014	5(1)	3	0	0	12
	Huddersfield	2012-14	46(12)	9	0	0	36
	Crusaders	2010-11	48(1)	10	0	0	40
	Celtic	2009	17(6)	3	0	0	12
Joe Chandler	Leeds	2008	(1)	0	0	0	0
Michael Channing	Castleford	2013-15	27(2)	8	0	0	32
	London	2012-13	15(3)	2	0	0	8
Jay Chapelhow	Widnes	2016	1(6)	0	0	0	0
Ted Chapelhow	Widnes	2016	(1)	0	0	0	0
Chris Chapman	Leeds	1999	(1)	0	0	0	0
Damien Chapman	London	1998	6(2)	3	4	1	21
David Chapman	Castleford	1996-98	24(6)	8	0	0	32
Jaymes Chapman	Halifax	2002-03	5(8)	1	0	0	4
Richard Chapman	Sheffield	1996	1	2	0	0	8
Chris Charles	Salford	2004-06	59(16)	6	140	0	304
	Castleford	2001	1(4)	1	0	0	4
Olivier Charles	Catalans	2007	2	2	0	0	8
Josh Charnley	Wigan	2010-16	151(2)	141	77	0	718
	Hull KR	2010	5	5	0	0	20
Lewis Charnock	St Helens	2013, 2015	4(1)	2	6	0	20
Rangi Chase	Castleford	2009-13, 2016	119(7)	39	0	3	159
	Salford	2014-15	37	10	13	2	68
Andy Cheetham	Huddersfield	1998-99	30	11	0	0	44
Kris Chesney	London	1998	1(2)	0	0	0	0
Chris Chester	Hull KR	2007-08	28(6)	4	0	0	16
	Hull	2002-06	67(25)	13	0	0	52
	Wigan	1999-2001	21(22)	5	0	0	20
	Halifax	1996-99	47(14)	16	15	1	95
Lee Chilton	Workington	1996	10(3)	6	0	0	24
Dane Chisholm	Hull KR	2015	1	0	0	0	0
Gary Christie	Bradford	1996-97	4(7)	1	0	0	4
James Clare	Castleford	2012-15	33	21	0	0	84
Daryl Clark	Warrington	2015-16	50(7)	15	0	0	60
	Castleford	2011-14	34(51)	31	0	0	124
Dean Clark	Leeds	1996	11(2)	3	0	0	12

PLAYER	CLUB	YEAR	APP	TRIES	GOALS	FG	PTS
Des Clark	St Helens	1999	4	0	0	0	0
	Halifax	1998-99	35(13)	6	0	0	24
Greg Clarke	Halifax	1997	1(1)	0	0	0	0
John Clarke	Oldham	1996-97	27(4)	5	0	0	20
Jon Clarke	Widnes	2012-14	59(1)	5	0	0	20
	Warrington	2001-11	217(25)	56	2	0	228
	London	2000-01	19(11)	2	0	0	8
	Wigan	1997-99	13(10)	3	0	0	12
Chris Clarkson	Hull KR	2016	20	1	0	0	4
	Widnes	2015	17(1)	4	0	0	16
	Leeds	2010-14	61(39)	9	0	0	36
Adam Clay	Salford	2011	2	3	0	0	12
Ryan Clayton	Castleford	2004, 2008-10	36(24)	5	0	0	20
	Salford	2006	3(8)	2	0	0	8
	Huddersfield	2005	4(6)	0	0	0	0
	Halifax	2000, 2002-03	28(12)	6	0	0	24
Gavin Clinch	Salford	2004	21(1)	1	0	1	5
	Halifax	1998-99, 2001-02	88(2)	26	45	5	199
	Hudds-Sheff	2000	18(2)	5	0	1	21
	Wigan	1999	10(2)	4	12	0	40
Joel Clinton	Hull KR	2010-12	42(14)	2	0	0	8
John Clough	Salford	2004-06	1(16)	0	0	0	0
Paul Clough	Widnes	2014	4(8)	1	0	0	4
	St Helens	2005-13	53(113)	16	0	0	64
Tony Clubb	Wigan	2014-16	21(39)	10	0	0	40
	London	2012-13	24(8)	7	0	0	28
	Harlequins	2006-11	100(11)	29	0	0	116
Bradley Clyde	Leeds	2001	7(5)	1	0	0	4
Michael Coady	Leeds	2010	1	0	0	0	0
Evan Cochrane	London	1996	5(1)	1	0	0	4
Ben Cockayne	Hull KR	2007-11, 2014-16	125(30)	38	18	0	188
	Wakefield	2012-13	54	28	2	0	116
Liam Colbon	Hull	2014	8	1	0	0	4
	London	2012-13	22	5	0	0	20
	Hull KR	2009-11	51	20	0	0	80
	Wigan	2004-05, 2007-08	37(14)	15	0	0	60
Anthony Colella	Huddersfield	2003	5(1)	2	0	0	8
Liam Coleman	Leigh	2005	1(4)	0	0	0	0
Andy Coley	Wigan	2008-11	100(10)	8	0	0	32
	Salford	2001-02, 2004-07	112(34)	34	0	0	136
Richard Colley	Bradford	2004	1	0	0	0	0
Steve Collins	Hull	2000	28	17	0	0	68
	Gateshead	1999	20(4)	13	0	0	52
Wayne Collins	Leeds	1997	21	3	0	0	12
Dean Collis	Wakefield	2012-15	64	28	0	0	112
Aurelien Cologni	Catalans	2006	4(1)	3	0	0	12
Gary Connolly	Widnes	2005	20	4	1	0	18
	Wigan	1996-2002, 2004	168(10)	70	5	0	290
	Leeds	2003-04	27	6	0	0	24
Jake Connor	Huddersfield	2013-16	47(1)	21	2	0	88
Nathan Conroy	Bradford	2013-14	(4)	0	0	0	0
Matt Cook	Castleford	2008, 2015-16	13(34)	4	0	0	16
	London	2012-14	50(7)	8	0	0	32
	Hull KR	2010-11	9(16)	7	0	0	28
	Bradford	2005-09	11(52)	4	0	0	16
Mick Cook	Sheffield	1996	9(10)	2	0	0	8
Paul Cook	Huddersfield	1998-99	11(6)	2	13	0	34
	Bradford	1996-97	14(8)	7	38	1	105
Peter Cook	St Helens	2004	(1)	0	0	0	0
Paul Cooke	Wakefield	2010	16(1)	3	36	1	85
	Hull KR	2007-10	54(5)	8	76	2	186
	Hull	1999-2007	177(27)	32	333	4	798
Ben Cooper	Leigh	2005	25(1)	5	0	0	20
	Huddersfield	2000-01, 2003-04	28(12)	3	0	0	12
Michael Cooper	Warrington	2006-13	29(87)	6	0	0	24
	Castleford	2010	1(5)	2	0	0	8
Ged Corcoran	Halifax	2003	1(11)	0	0	0	0
Wayne Corcoran	Halifax	2003	4(2)	0	0	0	0
Jamie Cording	Huddersfield	2011-13	4(21)	5	0	0	20
Josh Cordoba	Hull	2009	8	1	0	0	4
Mark Corvo	Salford	2002	7(5)	0	0	0	0
Neville Costigan	Hull KR	2014	24	3	0	0	12
Brandon Costin	Huddersfield	2001, 2003-04	69	42	93	3	357
	Bradford	2002	20(1)	8	0	0	32
Wes Cotton	London	1997-98	12	3	0	0	12
Phil Coussons	Salford	1997	7(2)	3	0	0	12
Alex Couttet	Paris	1997	1	0	0	0	0
Nick Couttet	Paris	1997	1	0	0	0	0
Jamie Coventry	Castleford	1996	1	0	0	0	0
Jimmy Cowan	Oldham	1996-97	2(8)	0	0	0	0
Will Cowell	Warrington	1998-2000	6(8)	1	0	0	4
Neil Cowie	Wigan	1996-2001	116(27)	10	0	1	41
Danny Cowling	Wakefield	2012-13	2	0	0	0	0
Jordan Cox	Warrington	2016	(16)	0	0	0	0
	Hull KR	2011-15	17(44)	4	0	0	16
	Huddersfield	2015	(2)	0	0	0	0
Mark Cox	London	2003	(3)	0	0	0	0
James Coyle	Wigan	2005	2(3)	1	0	0	4
Thomas Coyle	Wigan	2008	2(1)	0	0	0	0
Eorl Crabtree	Huddersfield	2001, 2003-16	180(167)	52	0	0	208
Andy Craig	Halifax	1999	13(7)	1	3	0	10
	Wigan	1996	5(5)	2	0	0	8
Owen Craigie	Widnes	2005	15	7	0	2	30
Scott Cram	London	1999-2002	65(7)	4	0	0	16
Danny Craven	Widnes	2012-15	27(14)	5	3	2	28
Steve Craven	Hull	1998-2003	53(42)	4	0	0	16
Nicky Crellin	Workington	1996	(2)	0	0	0	0
Jason Critchley	Wakefield	2000	7(1)	4	0	0	16
	Castleford	1997-98	27(3)	11	0	0	44
Jason Croker	Catalans	2007-09	56(2)	11	0	1	45
Martin Crompton	Salford	1998-2000	30(6)	11	6	2	58
	Oldham	1996-97	36(1)	16	0	3	67
Paul Crook	Widnes	2005	2(2)	0	5	1	11
Paul Crook	Oldham	1996	4(9)	0	3	0	6
Jason Crookes	Hull	2013-14	15(1)	5	0	0	20
	Bradford	2009-12	25(1)	7	0	0	28
Ben Crooks	Castleford	2016	24(2)	5	1	0	22
	Hull	2012-14	42(3)	30	23	0	166
Lee Crooks	Castleford	1996-97	27(2)	2	14	0	36
Dominic Crosby	Wigan	2012-16	57(35)	6	0	0	24
Alan Cross	St Helens	1997	(2)	0	0	0	0
Ben Cross	Widnes	2012-13	27(1)	2	0	0	8
	Wigan	2011	(4)	0	0	0	0
	Leeds	2011	1(9)	0	0	0	0
Steve Crossley	Castleford	2015	(6)	0	0	0	0
	Bradford	2010-11	(9)	1	0	0	4
Garret Crossman	Hull KR	2008	8(18)	0	0	0	0
Steve Crouch	Castleford	2004	4(1)	2	0	0	8
Kevin Crouthers	Warrington	2001-03	12(1)	4	0	0	16
	London	2000	6(4)	1	0	0	4
	Wakefield	1999	4(4)	1	0	0	4
	Bradford	1997-98	3(9)	2	0	0	8
Jordan Crowther	Wakefield	2014-16	3(9)	1	0	0	4
Matt Crowther	Hull	2001-03	48	20	166	0	412
	Hudds-Sheff	2000	10(4)	5	22	0	64
	Sheffield	1996-99	43(4)	22	10	0	108
Heath Cruckshank	Halifax	2003	19(1)	0	0	0	0
	St Helens	2001	1(12)	0	0	0	0
Leroy Cudjoe	Huddersfield	2008-16	221(1)	92	57	1	483
Paul Cullen	Warrington	1996	19	3	0	0	12
Francis Cummins	Leeds	1996-2005	217(13)	120	26	2	534
James Cunningham	Hull	2012, 2014-15	(9)	0	0	0	0
	London	2014	10(7)	2	0	0	8
Keiron Cunningham	St Helens	1996-2010	357(24)	138	0	0	552
Liam Cunningham	Hull	2010	(1)	0	0	0	0
Ben Currie	Warrington	2012-16	76(29)	48	0	0	192
Andy Currier	Warrington	1996-97	(2)	1	0	0	4
Peter Cusack	Hull	2008-10	34(22)	3	0	0	12
Adam Cuthbertson	Leeds	2015-16	37(12)	10	0	0	40
Alrix Da Costa	Catalans	2016	4(3)	0	0	0	0
Joe Dakuitoga	Sheffield	1996	6(3)	0	0	0	0
Matty Dale	Hull	2006, 2008	(7)	1	0	0	4
	Wakefield	2008	1(1)	0	0	0	0
Brett Dallas	Wigan	2000-06	156	89	0	0	356
Mark Dalle Cort	Celtic	2009	23	4	0	0	16
Paul Darbyshire	Warrington	1997	(6)	0	0	0	0
James Davey	Wakefield	2009-11	3(14)	1	0	0	4
Maea David	Hull	1998	1	0	0	0	0
Alex Davidson	Salford	2011, 2013	(3)	0	0	0	0
Paul Davidson	Halifax	2001-03	22(30)	10	0	0	40
	London	2000	6(10)	4	0	0	16
	St Helens	1998-99	27(16)	7	0	0	28
	Oldham	1996-97	17(18)	14	0	1	57
Ben Davies	Castleford	2011, 2013	3(4)	2	0	0	8
	Widnes	2012-13	10(15)	3	0	0	12
	Wigan	2010		0	0	0	0
Gareth Davies	Warrington	1996-97	1(6)	0	0	0	0
Geraint Davies	Celtic	2009	(7)	0	0	0	0
John Davies	Castleford	2010-12	1(6)	1	0	0	4

Super League Players 1996-2016

PLAYER	CLUB	YEAR	APP	TRIES	GOALS	FG	PTS
Jordan Davies	Salford	2013	2(3)	0	0	0	0
Macauley Davies	Wigan	2016	(1)	0	0	0	0
Olly Davies	St Helens	2016	(1)	0	0	0	0
Wes Davies	Wigan	1998-2001	22(22)	11	0	0	44
Brad Davis	Castleford	1997-2000, 2004,2006	102(3)	31	43	10	220
	Wakefield	2001-03	51(12)	15	22	5	109
Matty Dawson	St Helens	2014-16	46(1)	15	0	0	60
	Huddersfield	2012-13	4	0	0	0	0
Brad Day	Castleford	2014	(1)	0	0	0	0
Matt Daylight	Hull	2000	17(1)	7	0	0	28
	Gateshead	1999	30	25	0	0	100
Michael De Vere	Huddersfield	2005-06	36	6	74	0	172
Paul Deacon	Wigan	2010-11	32(11)	4	14	0	44
	Bradford	1998-2009	258(43)	72	1029	23	2369
	Oldham	1997	(2)	0	0	0	0
Chris Dean	Widnes	2012-16	101(5)	20	0	0	80
	Wakefield	2011	20	8	0	0	32
	St Helens	2007-10	18(3)	9	0	0	36
Craig Dean	Halifax	1996-97	25(11)	12	1	1	51
Gareth Dean	London	2002	(4)	0	0	0	0
Yacine Dekkiche	Hudds-Sheff	2000	11(3)	3	0	0	12
Brett Delaney	Leeds	2010-16	133(16)	23	0	0	92
Jason Demetriou	Wakefield	2004-10	174(3)	50	2	0	204
	Widnes	2002-03	47(1)	15	1	0	62
Martin Dermott	Warrington	1997	1	0	0	0	0
David Despin	Paris	1996	(1)	0	0	0	0
Fabien Devecchi	Paris	1996-97	17(10)	2	0	0	8
Paul Devlin	Widnes	2002-04	32	16	0	0	64
Jordan Dezaria	Catalans	2016	(1)	0	0	0	0
Stuart Dickens	Salford	2005	4(5)	0	4	0	8
Tyler Dickinson	Huddersfield	2016	(1)	0	0	0	0
Matt Diskin	Bradford	2011-14	64(16)	11	0	0	44
	Leeds	2001-10	195(37)	40	0	0	160
Andrew Dixon	Salford	2013-14	34(2)	8	0	0	32
	St Helens	2009-12	19(41)	12	0	0	48
Kieran Dixon	Hull KR	2015-16	23(4)	21	9	0	102
	London	2012-14	49(1)	32	2	0	132
Kirk Dixon	Castleford	2008-14	143(2)	63	267	0	786
	Hull	2004-06	13(4)	7	4	0	36
Paul Dixon	Sheffield	1996-97	5(9)	1	0	0	4
Gareth Dobson	Castleford	1998-2000	(10)	0	0	0	0
Michael Dobson	Salford	2015-16	36(1)	8	31	1	95
	Hull KR	2008-13	142	51	500	11	1215
	Wigan	2006	14	5	61	0	142
	Catalans	2006	10	4	31	1	79
Michael Docherty	Hull	2000-01	(6)	0	0	0	0
Mitchell Dodds	Warrington	2016	(2)	0	0	0	0
Erjon Dollapi	London	2013-14	(18)	4	0	0	16
Sid Domic	Hull	2006-07	39(4)	15	0	0	60
	Wakefield	2004-05	48	30	0	0	120
	Warrington	2002-03	41(4)	17	0	0	68
Scott Donald	Leeds	2006-10	131	77	0	0	308
James Donaldson	Hull KR	2015-16	8(19)	2	0	0	8
	Bradford	2009-14	38(35)	4	0	0	16
Glen Donkin	Hull	2002-03	(10)	1	0	0	4
Stuart Donlan	Castleford	2008	20	8	0	0	32
	Huddersfield	2004-06	59(3)	15	0	0	60
	Halifax	2001-03	65(2)	22	0	0	88
Jason Donohue	Bradford	1996	(4)	0	0	0	0
Jeremy Donougher	Bradford	1996-99	40(21)	13	0	0	52
Justin Dooley	London	2000-01	37(18)	2	0	0	8
Dane Dorahy	Halifax	2003	20	7	45	0	118
	Wakefield	2000-01	16(2)	4	19	1	55
Jamie Doran	Wigan	2014	(2)	0	0	0	0
Luke Dorn	Castleford	2008, 2014-16	78(2)	60	0	0	240
	London	2005, 2012-13	58(8)	42	0	0	168
	Harlequins	2006, 2009-11	83(1)	57	0	0	228
	Salford	2007	19(8)	11	0	0	44
Brandon Douglas	Castleford	2016	(1)	0	0	0	0
Ewan Dowes	Hull	2003-11	169(51)	10	0	0	40
	Leeds	2001-03	1(9)	0	0	0	0
Jack Downs	Hull	2015-16	2(5)	0	0	0	0
Adam Doyle	Warrington	1998	9(3)	4	0	0	16
Rod Doyle	Sheffield	1997-99	52(10)	10	0	0	40
Brad Drew	Huddersfield	2005-07, 2010	78(13)	18	13	1	99
	Wakefield	2008-09	27(9)	7	14	1	57
Josh Drinkwater	London	2014	23(1)	5	54	0	128
Damien Driscoll	Salford	2001	23(1)	1	0	0	4
James Duckworth	London	2014	3	0	0	0	0
	Leeds	2013	2	1	0	0	4
Gil Dudson	Widnes	2015-16	33(9)	1	0	0	4
	Wigan	2012-14	26(16)	2	0	0	8
	Crusaders	2011	3(7)	0	0	0	0
	Celtic	2009	(1)	0	0	0	0
Jason Duffy	Leigh	2005	3(1)	0	0	0	0
John Duffy	Leigh	2005	21	6	0	0	24
	Salford	2000	3(11)	0	1	1	3
	Warrington	1997-99	12(12)	0	0	0	0
Tony Duggan	Celtic	2009	4	3	0	0	12
Andrew Duncan	London	1997	2(4)	2	0	0	8
	Warrington	1997	(1)	0	0	0	0
Andrew Dunemann	Salford	2006	25	1	0	2	6
	Leeds	2003-05	76(4)	11	0	2	46
	Halifax	1999-2002	68	19	0	1	77
Matt Dunford	London	1997-98	18(20)	3	0	1	13
Vincent Duport	Catalans	2007-09, 2011-16	133(14)	63	0	0	252
Jamie Durbin	Widnes	2005	1	0	0	0	0
	Warrington	2003	(1)	0	0	0	0
Scott Dureau	Catalans	2011-15	88(1)	29	315	10	756
James Durkin	Paris	1997	(5)	0	0	0	0
Bernard Dwyer	Bradford	1996-2000	65(10)	14	0	0	56
Brad Dwyer	Warrington	2012-16	6(50)	9	0	0	36
	Huddersfield	2013	(6)	0	0	0	0
Luke Dyer	Crusaders	2010	23(1)	5	0	0	20
	Celtic	2009	21	6	0	0	24
	Hull KR	2007	26	13	0	0	52
	Castleford	2006	17(2)	5	0	0	20
Adam Dykes	Hull	2008	12	1	0	2	6
Jim Dymock	London	2001-04	94(1)	15	0	1	61
Leo Dynevor	London	1996	8(11)	5	7	0	34
Jason Eade	Paris	1997	9	4	0	0	16
Michael Eagar	Hull	2004-05	12	4	0	0	16
	Castleford	1999-2003	130(2)	60	0	0	240
	Warrington	1998	21	6	0	0	24
Kyle Eastmond	St Helens	2007-11	46(20)	35	117	3	377
Greg Eastwood	Leeds	2010	5(12)	1	0	0	4
Barry Eaton	Widnes	2002	25	2	49	4	110
	Castleford	2000	1(4)	0	3	0	6
Greg Ebrill	Salford	2002	15(6)	1	0	0	4
Cliff Eccles	Salford	1997-98	30(5)	1	0	0	4
Chris Eckersley	Warrington	1996	1	0	0	0	0
Greg Eden	Hull KR	2013-14	37	23	0	0	92
	Salford	2014	4	1	0	0	4
	Huddersfield	2012	24	8	0	0	32
	Castleford	2011	2	1	0	0	4
Steve Edmed	Sheffield	1997	15(1)	0	0	0	0
Mark Edmondson	Salford	2007	10(2)	0	0	0	0
	St Helens	1999-2005	27(75)	10	0	0	40
Diccon Edwards	Castleford	1996-97	10(5)	1	0	0	4
Grant Edwards	Castleford	2006	(2)	0	0	0	0
Max Edwards	Harlequins	2010	1	0	0	0	0
Peter Edwards	Salford	1997-98	35(2)	4	0	0	16
Shaun Edwards	London	1997-2000	32(8)	16	1	0	66
	Bradford	1998	8(2)	4	0	0	16
	Wigan	1996	17(3)	12	1	0	50
Danny Ekis	Halifax	2001	(1)	0	0	0	0
Abi Ekoku	Bradford	1997-98	21(4)	6	0	0	24
	Halifax	1996	15(1)	5	0	0	20
Shane Elford	Huddersfield	2007-08	26(1)	7	0	0	28
Olivier Elima	Catalans	2008-10, 2013-16	99(35)	34	0	0	136
	Bradford	2011-12	37(3)	12	0	0	48
	Wakefield	2003-07	40(47)	13	0	0	52
	Castleford	2002	(1)	1	0	0	4
Abderazak Elkhalouki	Paris	1997	(1)	0	0	0	0
George Elliott	Leeds	2011	1	0	0	0	0
Andy Ellis	Wakefield	2012	10	0	0	0	0
	Harlequins	2010-11	26(11)	8	0	0	32
Gareth Ellis	Hull	2013-16	69(2)	16	0	0	64
	Leeds	2005-08	109	24	1	0	98
	Wakefield	1999-2004	86(17)	21	2	0	88
Jamie Ellis	Huddersfield	2015-16	37(3)	14	31	3	121
	Castleford	2012-14	36(8)	10	80	1	201
	Hull	2012	4(5)	1	0	0	4
	St Helens	2009	1(2)	0	1	0	2
Danny Ellison	Castleford	1998-99	7(16)	6	0	0	24
	Wigan	1996-97	15(1)	13	0	0	52
Andrew Emelio	Widnes	2005	22(2)	8	0	0	32
Jake Emmitt	Salford	2013	5(10)	0	0	0	0
	Castleford	2011-13	32(17)	0	0	0	0
	St Helens	2008-10	1(16)	1	0	0	4
Anthony England	Wakefield	2016	15(1)	0	0	0	0
	Warrington	2014-15	12(21)	3	0	0	12
Patrick Entat	Paris	1996	22	2	0	0	8
Jason Erba	Sheffield	1997	1(4)	0	0	0	0
Morgan Escare	Catalans	2013-16	83	58	1	2	236
Ryan Esders	Harlequins	2009-10	9(11)	3	0	0	12
	Hull KR	2009	(1)	0	0	0	0

PLAYER	CLUB	YEAR	APP	TRIES	GOALS	FG	PTS
Sonny Esslemont	Hull KR	2014-15	(5)	0	0	0	0
Niall Evalds	Salford	2013-16	40(10)	33	0	0	132
Ben Evans	Warrington	2014-15	3(16)	2	0	0	8
	Bradford	2013	3(12)	1	0	0	4
James Evans	Castleford	2009-10	26(1)	13	0	0	52
	Bradford	2007-08	43(5)	20	0	0	80
	Wakefield	2006	6	3	0	0	12
	Huddersfield	2004-06	51	22	0	0	88
Paul Evans	Paris	1997	18	8	0	0	32
Rhys Evans	Warrington	2010-16	77(4)	33	0	0	132
Wayne Evans	London	2002	11(6)	2	0	0	8
Toby Everett	London	2014	(2)	0	0	0	0
Richie Eyres	Warrington	1997	2(5)	0	0	0	0
	Sheffield	1997	2(3)	0	0	0	0
Henry Fa'afili	Warrington	2004-07	90(1)	70	0	0	280
David Fa'alogo	Huddersfield	2010-12	38(16)	13	0	0	52
Sala Fa'alogo	Widnes	2004-05	8(15)	2	0	0	8
Richard Fa'aoso	Castleford	2006	10(15)	5	0	0	20
Maurie Fa'asavalu	St Helens	2004-10	5(137)	29	0	0	116
Bolouagi Fagborun	Huddersfield	2004-06	4(2)	1	0	0	4
Theo Fages	St Helens	2016	14(3)	7	0	0	28
	Salford	2013-15	57(5)	18	4	0	80
Esene Faimalo	Salford	1997-99	23(25)	2	0	0	8
	Leeds	1996	3(3)	0	0	0	0
Joe Faimalo	Salford	1998-2000	23(47)	7	0	0	28
	Oldham	1996-97	37(5)	7	0	0	28
Jacob Fairbank	Huddersfield	2011-15	12(3)	0	0	0	0
	Wakefield	2014	1(3)	0	0	0	0
	London	2013	4(1)	1	0	0	4
	Bradford	2013	(2)	0	0	0	0
Karl Fairbank	Bradford	1996	17(2)	4	0	0	16
David Fairleigh	St Helens	2001	26(1)	8	0	0	32
David Faiumu	Huddersfield	2008-14	38(108)	13	0	0	52
Jamal Fakir	Bradford	2014	5(8)	1	0	0	4
	Catalans	2006-14	55(100)	13	0	0	52
Jim Fallon	Leeds	1996	10	5	0	0	20
Beau Falloon	Leeds	2016	8(2)	0	0	0	0
Ben Farrar	London	2014	22	1	0	0	4
	Catalans	2011	13	3	0	0	12
Danny Farrar	Warrington	1998-2000	76	13	0	0	52
Andy Farrell	Wigan	1996-2004	230	77	1026	16	2376
Anthony Farrell	Widnes	2002-03	24(22)	4	1	0	18
	Leeds	1997-2001	99(23)	18	0	0	72
	Sheffield	1996	14(5)	5	0	0	20
Connor Farrell	Widnes	2016	3(9)	3	0	0	12
	Wigan	2014-15	1(8)	1	0	0	4
Craig Farrell	Hull	2000-01	1(3)	0	0	0	0
Liam Farrell	Wigan	2010-16	114(47)	66	0	0	264
Brad Fash	Hull	2015	(7)	0	0	0	0
Abraham Fatnowna							
	London	1997-98	7(2)	2	0	0	8
	Workington	1996	5	2	0	0	8
	Hull	2005	3	1	0	0	4
Vince Fawcett	Wakefield	1999	13(1)	2	0	0	8
	Warrington	1998	4(7)	1	0	0	4
	Oldham	1997	5	3	0	0	12
Danny Fearon	Huddersfield	2001	(1)	0	0	0	0
	Halifax	1999-2000	5(6)	0	0	0	0
Chris Feather	Castleford	2009	1(23)	0	0	0	0
	Bradford	2007-08	7(20)	1	0	0	4
	Leeds	2003-04, 2006	16(35)	6	0	0	24
	Wakefield	2001-02, 2004-05	29(32)	9	0	0	36
Dom Feaunati	Leigh	2005	4	1	0	0	4
	St Helens	2004	10(7)	7	0	0	28
Adel Fellous	Hull	2008	1(2)	0	0	0	0
	Catalans	2006-07	16(22)	4	0	0	16
Luke Felsch	Hull	2000-01	46(6)	7	0	0	28
	Gateshead	1999	28(1)	2	0	0	8
Leon Felton	Warrington	2002	4(2)	0	0	0	0
	St Helens	2001	1(1)	0	0	0	0
Dale Ferguson	Bradford	2014	3(3)	0	0	0	0
	Huddersfield	2011-13	34(18)	13	0	0	52
	Hull KR	2013	3(1)	1	0	0	4
	Wakefield	2007-11	40(14)	12	0	0	48
Brett Ferres	Leeds	2016	15(2)	4	0	0	16
	Huddersfield	2012-15	72	27	0	0	108
	Castleford	2009-12	78(5)	26	0	0	104
	Wakefield	2007-08	36(2)	6	5	0	34
	Bradford	2005-06	18(17)	11	2	0	48
David Ferriol	Catalans	2007-12	72(55)	8	0	0	32
Jason Ferris	Leigh	2005	4	1	0	0	4
Jamie Field	Wakefield	1999-2006	133(59)	19	0	0	76
	Huddersfield	1998	15(5)	0	0	0	0
	Leeds	1996-97	3(11)	0	0	0	0
Mark Field	Wakefield	2003-07	28(7)	3	0	0	12
Jamie Fielden	London	2003	(1)	0	0	0	0
	Huddersfield	1998-2000	4(8)	0	0	0	0
Stuart Fielden	Huddersfield	2013	8(1)	0	0	0	0
	Wigan	2006-12	105(24)	2	0	0	8
	Bradford	1998-2006	142(78)	41	0	0	164
David Fifita	Wakefield	2016	5(6)	0	0	0	0
Lafaele Filipo	Workington	1996	15(4)	3	0	0	12
Salesi Finau	Warrington	1996-97	16(15)	8	0	0	32
Brett Finch	Wigan	2011-12	49(3)	16	0	0	64
Vinny Finigan	Bradford	2010	4(1)	4	0	0	16
Liam Finn	Wakefield	2004, 2016	31(1)	2	84	0	176
	Castleford	2014-15	45(2)	8	5	2	44
	Halifax	2002-03	16(5)	2	30	1	69
Lee Finnerty	Halifax	2003	18(2)	5	2	0	24
Phil Finney	Warrington	1998	1	0	0	0	0
Simon Finnigan	Widnes	2003-05, 2012	56(24)	21	0	0	84
	Huddersfield	2009-10	22(5)	6	0	0	24
	Bradford	2008	14(13)	8	0	0	32
	Salford	2006-07	50	17	0	0	68
Matt Firth	Halifax	2000-01	12(2)	0	0	0	0
Andy Fisher	Wakefield	1999-2000	31(8)	4	0	0	16
Ben Fisher	London	2013	8(12)	1	0	0	4
	Catalans	2012	9(5)	1	0	0	4
	Hull KR	2007-11	78(46)	18	0	0	72
Craig Fitzgibbon	Hull	2010-11	42(1)	9	8	0	52
Daniel Fitzhenry	Hull KR	2008-09	36(11)	14	0	0	56
Karl Fitzpatrick	Salford	2004-07, 2009-10	89(11)	33	2	0	136
Conor Fitzsimmons	Castleford	2016	(2)	0	0	0	0
Mark Flanagan	Salford	2016	19(3)	3	0	0	12
	St Helens	2012-15	40(39)	9	0	0	36
	Wigan	2009	3(7)	1	0	0	4
Chris Flannery	St Helens	2007-12	108(11)	32	0	0	128
Darren Fleary	Leigh	2005	24	1	0	0	4
	Huddersfield	2003-04	43(8)	4	0	0	16
	Leeds	1997-2002	98(9)	3	0	0	12
Daniel Fleming	Castleford	2013-14	(15)	1	0	0	4
Greg Fleming	London	1999-2000	64(1)	40	2	0	164
Matty Fleming	St Helens	2015-16	15	6	0	0	24
Adam Fletcher	Castleford	2006, 2008	16(7)	11	0	0	44
Bryan Fletcher	Wigan	2006-07	47(2)	14	0	0	56
Richard Fletcher	Castleford	2006	13(5)	3	4	0	20
	Hull	1999-2004	11(56)	5	0	0	20
Greg Florimo	Halifax	2000	26	6	4	0	32
	Wigan	1999	18(2)	7	1	0	30
Ben Flower	Wigan	2012-16	80(24)	16	0	0	64
	Crusaders	2010-11	10(23)	2	0	0	8
	Celtic	2009	2(15)	0	0	0	0
Jason Flowers	Salford	2004	6(1)	0	0	0	0
	Halifax	2002	24(4)	4	0	0	16
	Castleford	1996-2001	119(19)	33	0	1	133
Stuart Flowers	Castleford	1996	(3)	0	0	0	0
Adrian Flynn	Castleford	1996-97	19(2)	10	0	0	40
Paddy Flynn	Castleford	2016	9(1)	6	0	0	24
	Widnes	2012-15	72	41	0	0	164
Wayne Flynn	Sheffield	1997	3(5)	0	0	0	0
Adam Fogerty	Warrington	1998	4	0	0	0	0
	St Helens	1996	13	1	0	0	4
Mahe Fonua	Hull	2016	24	13	0	0	52
Liam Foran	Salford	2013	10(3)	1	0	0	4
Carl Forber	Leigh	2005	4	1	0	0	4
	St Helens	2004	1(1)	0	6	0	12
Paul Forber	Salford	1997-98	19(12)	4	0	0	16
Byron Ford	Hull KR	2007	13	6	0	0	24
James Ford	Castleford	2009	3(5)	1	0	0	4
Mike Ford	Castleford	1997-98	25(12)	5	0	3	23
	Warrington	1996	3	0	0	0	0
Jim Forshaw	Salford	1999	(1)	0	0	0	0
Mike Forshaw	Warrington	2004	20(1)	5	0	0	20
	Bradford	1997-2003	162(7)	32	0	0	128
	Leeds	1996	11(3)	5	0	0	20
Carl Forster	Salford	2015-16	5(7)	1	0	0	4
	St Helens	2011-12, 2014	(4)	0	0	0	0
	London	2014	2(3)	0	0	0	0
Mark Forster	Warrington	1996-2000	102(1)	40	0	0	160
Alex Foster	London	2014	20	3	0	0	12
	Leeds	2013	(8)	1	0	0	4
David Foster	Halifax	2000-01	4(9)	0	0	0	0
Jamie Foster	Huddersfield	2016	3	2	5	0	18
	Bradford	2013-14	32	12	111	0	270
	Hull	2012	9	5	45	0	110
	St Helens	2010-12	44(3)	30	201	0	522
Peter Fox	Wakefield	2007, 2012-14	85	44	0	0	176
	Hull KR	2008-11	95	52	0	0	208

Super League Players 1996-2016

PLAYER	CLUB	YEAR	APP	TRIES	GOALS	FG	PTS
Matty Fozzard	St Helens	2014	1	0	0	0	0
Nick Fozzard	Castleford	2011	7(10)	0	0	0	0
	St Helens	2004-08, 2010	100(25)	7	0	0	28
	Hull KR	2009	18(4)	1	0	0	4
	Warrington	2002-03	43(11)	2	0	0	8
	Huddersfield	1998-2000	24(8)	2	0	0	8
	Leeds	1996-97	6(16)	3	0	0	12
David Fraisse	Workington	1996	8	0	0	0	0
Daniel Frame	Widnes	2002-05	100(6)	24	0	0	96
Paul Franze	Castleford	2006	2(1)	0	0	0	0
Laurent Frayssinous	Catalans	2006	14(2)	3	32	0	76
Andrew Frew	Halifax	2003	17	5	0	0	20
	Wakefield	2002	21	8	0	0	32
	Huddersfield	2001	26	15	0	0	60
Dale Fritz	Castleford	1999-2003	120(4)	9	0	0	36
Gareth Frodsham	St Helens	2008-09	1(9)	0	0	0	0
Liam Fulton	Huddersfield	2009	12(3)	4	0	0	16
David Furner	Leeds	2003-04	45	8	23	0	78
	Wigan	2001-02	51(2)	21	13	0	110
David Furness	Castleford	1996	(1)	0	0	0	0
Matt Gafa	Harlequins	2006-09	81	26	16	0	136
Luke Gale	Castleford	2015-16	57	17	219	3	509
	Bradford	2012-14	56(2)	13	108	4	272
	Harlequins	2009-11	56(12)	18	86	3	247
Ben Galea	Hull	2013	12(2)	3	0	0	12
	Hull KR	2008-12	115(2)	33	0	0	132
Danny Galea	Widnes	2014-15	38(4)	5	0	0	20
Tommy Gallagher	Hull KR	2007	1(7)	0	0	0	0
	Widnes	2004	(6)	0	0	0	0
	London	2003	1(9)	1	0	0	4
Keith Galloway	Leeds	2016	21(1)	1	0	0	4
Mark Gamson	Sheffield	1996	3	0	0	0	0
Jim Gannon	Hull KR	2007	7(16)	1	0	0	4
	Huddersfield	2003-06	79(14)	11	0	0	44
	Halifax	1999-2002	83(4)	14	0	0	56
Mitch Garbutt	Leeds	2015-16	17(12)	3	0	0	12
Steve Garces	Salford	2001	(1)	0	0	0	0
Benjamin Garcia	Catalans	2013-16	17(40)	11	0	0	44
Jean-Marc Garcia	Sheffield	1996-97	35(3)	22	0	0	88
Ade Gardner	Hull KR	2014	18	7	0	0	28
	St Helens	2002-13	236(12)	146	0	0	584
Matt Gardner	Harlequins	2009	6(3)	2	0	0	8
	Huddersfield	2006-07	22(3)	7	0	0	28
	Castleford	2004	1	1	0	0	4
Steve Gartland	Oldham	1996	1(1)	0	1	0	2
Daniel Gartner	Bradford	2001-03	74(1)	26	0	0	104
Dean Gaskell	Warrington	2002-05	58(1)	10	0	0	40
Lee Gaskell	Bradford	2014	21	5	0	0	20
	Salford	2013	17	8	2	0	36
	St Helens	2010-13	33(9)	14	12	1	81
George Gatis	Huddersfield	2008	5(5)	1	0	0	4
Richard Gay	Castleford	1996-2002	94(16)	39	0	0	156
Andrew Gee	Warrington	2000-01	33(1)	4	0	0	16
Matty Gee	Salford	2015	(2)	0	0	0	0
Anthony Gelling	Wigan	2012-16	81(1)	44	0	0	176
Stanley Gene	Hull KR	2007-09	37(17)	9	0	0	36
	Bradford	2006	5(16)	8	0	0	32
	Huddersfield	2001, 2003-05	70(6)	27	0	0	108
	Hull	2000-01	5(23)	6	0	0	24
Steve Georgallis	Warrington	2001	5(1)	2	0	0	8
Luke George	Bradford	2014	9(1)	3	0	0	12
	Huddersfield	2012-13	28(2)	18	0	0	72
	Hull KR	2013	4	2	0	0	8
	Wakefield	2007-11	38(3)	24	0	0	96
Shaun Geritas	Warrington	1997	(5)	1	0	0	4
Alex Gerrard	Widnes	2012-16	38(31)	3	0	0	12
Anthony Gibbons	Leeds	1996	9(4)	2	0	1	9
David Gibbons	Leeds	1996	3(4)	2	0	0	8
Scott Gibbs	St Helens	1996	9	3	0	0	12
Ashley Gibson	Wakefield	2016	5	3	0	0	12
	Castleford	2014-15	27	9	0	0	36
	Salford	2010-13	77(4)	41	0	0	164
	Leeds	2005-09	25(7)	13	9	0	70
Damian Gibson	Castleford	2003-04	40(3)	5	0	0	20
	Salford	2002	28	3	0	0	12
	Halifax	1998-2001	104(1)	39	0	0	156
	Leeds	1997	18	3	0	0	12
Kurt Gidley	Warrington	2016	26	8	87	0	206
Matt Gidley	St Helens	2007-10	105	40	6	0	172
Tony Gigot	Catalans	2010-11, 2015-16	54(13)	21	16	0	116
	London	2014	2	0	4	0	8
Ian Gildart	Oldham	1996-97	31(7)	0	0	0	0
Oliver Gildart	Wigan	2015-16	31(2)	14	0	0	56
	Salford	2015	3	1	0	0	4
Chris Giles	Widnes	2003-04	35	12	0	0	48
	St Helens	2002	(1)	0	0	0	0
Peter Gill	London	1996-99	75(6)	20	0	0	80
Carl Gillespie	Halifax	1996-99	47(36)	13	0	0	52
Michael Gillett	London	2001-02	23(21)	12	2	0	52
Simon Gillies	Warrington	1999	28	6	0	0	24
Tom Gilmore	Widnes	2012-16	17(1)	6	3	2	32
Lee Gilmour	Wakefield	2014	10(3)	2	0	0	8
	Castleford	2013	10(2)	0	0	0	0
	Huddersfield	2010-12	71(1)	17	0	0	68
	St Helens	2004-09	149(3)	41	0	0	164
	Bradford	2001-03	44(31)	20	0	0	80
	Wigan	1997-2000	44(39)	22	0	0	88
Marc Glanville	Leeds	1998-99	43(3)	5	0	0	20
Eddie Glaze	Castleford	1996	1	0	0	0	0
Paul Gleadhill	Leeds	1996	4	0	0	0	0
Ben Gledhill	Salford	2012-13	3(10)	1	0	0	4
	Wakefield	2010-11	(16)	0	0	0	0
Mark Gleeson	Warrington	2000-08	38(102)	12	0	0	48
Martin Gleeson	Salford	2013-14	26(1)	4	0	0	16
	Hull	2011	6	4	0	0	16
	Wigan	2009-11	46(1)	19	0	0	76
	Warrington	2005-09	110(1)	44	0	0	176
	St Helens	2002-04	56(1)	25	0	0	100
	Huddersfield	1999-2001	47(9)	18	0	0	72
Sean Gleeson	Hull KR	2013	6	0	0	0	0
	Salford	2011-12	35	14	0	0	56
	Wakefield	2007-10	67(6)	20	0	0	80
	Wigan	2005-06	3(3)	0	0	0	0
Jon Goddard	Hull KR	2007	20	2	0	0	8
	Castleford	2000-01	(2)	0	0	0	0
Richard Goddard	Castleford	1996-97	11(3)	2	10	0	28
Brad Godden	Leeds	1998-99	47	15	0	0	60
Pita Godinet	Wakefield	2014-15	18(19)	10	0	0	40
Wayne Godwin	Salford	2011-13, 2015	43(8)	6	0	0	24
	Bradford	2008-10	16(44)	9	0	0	36
	Hull	2007	3(13)	1	0	0	4
	Wigan	2005-06	9(38)	6	0	0	24
	Castleford	2001-04	30(33)	18	56	0	184
Jason Golden	London	2012	7(2)	1	0	0	4
	Harlequins	2009-11	34(12)	3	0	0	12
	Wakefield	2007-08	26(5)	1	0	0	4
Marvin Golden	Widnes	2003	4	1	0	0	4
	London	2001	17(2)	1	0	0	4
	Halifax	2000	20(2)	5	0	0	20
	Leeds	1996-99	43(11)	19	0	0	76
Ashton Golding	Leeds	2014-16	10(4)	2	0	0	8
Brett Goldspink	Halifax	2000-02	64(5)	2	0	0	8
	Wigan	1999	6(16)	1	0	0	4
	St Helens	1998	19(4)	2	0	0	8
	Oldham	1997	13(2)	0	0	0	0
Lee Gomersall	Hull KR	2008	1	0	0	0	0
Luke Goodwin	London	1998	9(2)	3	1	1	15
	Oldham	1997	16(4)	10	17	2	76
Grant Gore	Widnes	2012-15	6(11)	1	0	0	4
Aaron Gorrell	Catalans	2007-08	23	6	14	0	52
Andy Gorski	Salford	2001-02	(2)	0	0	0	0
Cyrille Gossard	Catalans	2006-12	54(30)	5	0	0	20
Bobbie Goulding	Salford	2001-02	31(1)	2	56	4	124
	Wakefield	2000	12	3	25	3	65
	Huddersfield	1998-99	27(1)	3	65	4	146
	St Helens	1996-98	42(2)	9	210	4	460
Bobbie Goulding (Jnr)	Wakefield	2013	1(2)	0	1	0	2
Darrell Goulding	Hull KR	2015	8	1	0	0	4
	Wigan	2005-14	129(24)	68	0	0	272
	Salford	2009	9	5	0	0	20
Mick Govin	Leigh	2005	5(6)	4	0	0	16
Craig Gower	London	2012-13	40	7	24	0	76
David Gower	Salford	2006-07	(16)	0	0	0	0
Shane Grady	London	2013	5(4)	1	2	0	8
James Graham	St Helens	2003-11	132(63)	47	0	0	188
Nathan Graham	Bradford	1996-98	17(28)	4	0	1	17
Nick Graham	Wigan	2003	13(1)	2	0	0	8
Dalton Grant	Crusaders	2011	(1)	0	0	0	0
Jon Grayshon	Harlequins	2007-09	10(32)	4	0	0	16
	Huddersfield	2003-06	7(43)	5	0	0	20
Blake Green	Wigan	2013-14	42(1)	15	0	0	60
	Hull KR	2011-12	35	14	0	0	56
Brett Green	Gateshead	1999	10(2)	0	0	0	0
Chris Green	Hull	2012-16	14(64)	6	0	0	24
James Green	Hull KR	2012-16	8(64)	3	0	0	12
Toby Green	Huddersfield	2001	3(1)	1	0	0	4
Craig Greenhill	Castleford	2004	21(4)	1	0	0	4
	Hull	2002-03	56	3	2	0	16

PLAYER	CLUB	YEAR	APP	TRIES	GOALS	FG	PTS
Clint Greenshields	Catalans	2007-12	137	81	0	0	324
Brandon Greenwood							
	Halifax	1996	1	0	0	0	0
Gareth Greenwood	Huddersfield	2003	(1)	0	0	0	0
	Halifax	2002	1	0	0	0	0
James Greenwood	Hull KR	2015-16	13(13)	4	0	0	16
	Salford	2015	1(1)	1	0	0	4
	Wigan	2013, 2015	(2)	0	0	0	0
	London	2014	10(5)	3	0	0	12
Joe Greenwood	St Helens	2012-16	39(28)	26	0	0	104
Lee Greenwood	Huddersfield	2005	7	3	0	0	12
	London	2004-05	30(2)	19	0	0	76
	Halifax	2000-03	38(2)	17	0	0	68
	Sheffield	1999	1(1)	0	0	0	0
Nick Gregson	Wigan	2016	5(4)	1	0	0	4
James Grehan	Castleford	2012	2(2)	0	0	0	0
Maxime Greseque	Wakefield	2007	2(1)	0	0	0	0
Mathieu Griffi	Catalans	2006-08	1(25)	0	0	0	0
Darrell Griffin	Salford	2013-15	31(27)	1	0	0	4
	Leeds	2012	8(19)	2	0	0	8
	Huddersfield	2007-11	65(60)	13	0	0	52
	Wakefield	2003-06	55(37)	9	3	0	42
George Griffin	Salford	2015-16	32(4)	5	0	0	20
	Wakefield	2015	5	0	0	0	0
	London	2014	(19)	1	0	0	4
	Hull KR	2012-13	11(7)	0	0	0	0
Josh Griffin	Salford	2014-16	42	23	77	0	246
	Castleford	2012	20	13	1	0	54
	Wakefield	2011	17	5	21	0	62
	Huddersfield	2009	2	0	0	0	0
Jonathan Griffiths	Paris	1996	(4)	1	0	0	4
Andrew Grima	Workington	1996	2(9)	2	0	0	8
Tony Grimaldi	Hull	2000-01	56(1)	14	0	0	56
	Gateshead	1999	27(2)	10	0	0	40
Danny Grimley	Sheffield	1996	4(1)	1	0	0	4
Scott Grix	Huddersfield	2010-16	137(11)	52	32	0	272
	Wakefield	2008-09	39(3)	18	0	0	72
Simon Grix	Warrington	2006-14	133(25)	42	0	0	168
	Halifax	2003	2(4)	0	0	0	0
Brett Grogan	Gateshead	1999	14(7)	3	0	0	12
Brent Grose	Warrington	2003-07	134(1)	55	0	0	220
David Guasch	Catalans	2010	1	0	0	0	0
Joan Guasch	Catalans	2014-15	(6)	0	0	0	0
Renaud Guigue	Catalans	2006	14(4)	3	0	0	12
Jerome Guisset	Catalans	2006-10	102(23)	9	0	0	36
	Wigan	2005	20(2)	3	0	0	12
	Warrington	2000-04	59(65)	21	0	0	84
Awen Guttenbeil	Castleford	2008	19	0	0	0	0
Reece Guy	Oldham	1996	3(4)	0	0	0	0
Josh Guzdek	Hull KR	2013, 2015	2	1	0	0	4
Tom Haberecht	Castleford	2008	2(2)	1	0	0	4
Dean Hadley	Hull	2013-16	27(19)	6	0	0	24
Gareth Haggerty	Harlequins	2008-09	8(28)	6	0	0	24
	Salford	2004-07	1(93)	15	0	0	60
	Widnes	2002	1(2)	1	0	0	4
Kurt Haggerty	Widnes	2012	6(8)	2	0	0	8
Andy Haigh	St Helens	1996-98	20(16)	11	0	0	44
Scott Hale	St Helens	2011	(3)	1	0	0	4
Michael Haley	Leeds	2008	(1)	0	0	0	0
Carl Hall	Leeds	1996	7(2)	3	0	0	12
Craig Hall	Wakefield	2015-16	35	14	30	0	116
	Hull KR	2011-14	74(3)	38	41	2	236
	Hull	2007-10	59(9)	39	11	0	178
Glenn Hall	Bradford	2010	7(18)	2	0	0	8
Martin Hall	Halifax	1998	2(10)	0	0	0	0
	Hull	1999	7	0	0	0	0
	Castleford	1998	4	0	0	0	0
	Wigan	1996-97	31(5)	7	6	0	40
Ryan Hall	Leeds	2007-16	228(3)	177	0	0	708
Steve Hall	Widnes	2004	1	0	0	0	0
	London	2002-03	35(3)	10	0	0	40
	St Helens	1999-2001	36(22)	19	0	0	76
Graeme Hallas	Huddersfield	2001	1	0	0	0	0
	Hull	1998-99	30(10)	8	39	1	103
	Halifax	1996	11(4)	5	0	0	20
Sam Hallas	Leeds	2016	(2)	0	0	0	0
Macauley Hallett	Hull KR	2014	2	3	0	0	12
Dave Halley	Bradford	2007-10	63(12)	20	0	0	80
	Wakefield	2009	5	4	0	0	16
Danny Halliwell	Salford	2007	2(3)	0	0	0	0
	Leigh	2005	5	3	0	0	12
	Halifax	2000-03	17(8)	4	0	0	16
	Warrington	2002	9(1)	8	0	0	32
	Wakefield	2002	3	0	0	0	0
Colum Halpenny	Wakefield	2003-06	103(1)	36	0	0	144
	Halifax	2002	22	12	0	0	48
Jon Hamer	Bradford	1996	(1)	0	0	0	0
Andrew Hamilton	London	1997, 2003	1(20)	3	0	0	12
John Hamilton	St Helens	1998	3	0	0	0	0
Karle Hammond	Halifax	2002	10(2)	2	14	0	36
	Salford	2001	2(3)	1	0	0	4
	London	1999-2000	47	23	2	3	99
	St Helens	1996-98	58(8)	28	0	4	116
Ryan Hampshire	Castleford	2016	19(2)	8	0	0	32
	Wigan	2013-15	20(5)	8	24	0	80
Rhys Hanbury	Widnes	2012-16	122	62	89	1	427
	Crusaders	2010-11	26(1)	14	0	0	56
Anthony Hancock	Paris	1997	8(6)	1	0	0	4
Michael Hancock	Salford	2001-02	12(24)	7	0	0	28
Jordan Hand	Wakefield	2015	(2)	0	0	0	0
	St Helens	2013-14	(3)	0	0	0	0
Gareth Handford	Castleford	2001	7(2)	0	0	0	0
	Bradford	2000	1(1)	0	0	0	0
Paul Handforth	Castleford	2006	2(15)	2	1	0	10
	Wakefield	2000-04	17(44)	10	13	0	66
Ash Handley	Leeds	2014-16	36	17	0	0	68
Paddy Handley	Leeds	1996	1(1)	2	0	0	8
Dean Hanger	Warrington	1999	7(11)	3	0	0	12
	Huddersfield	1998	20(1)	5	0	0	20
Josh Hannay	Celtic	2009	17	2	24	0	56
Harrison Hansen	Salford	2014-15	41(2)	7	0	0	28
	Wigan	2004-13	155(62)	39	0	0	156
Lee Hansen	Wigan	1997	10(5)	0	0	0	0
Shontayne Hape	Bradford	2003-08	123(2)	79	0	0	316
Lionel Harbin	Wakefield	2001	(1)	0	0	0	0
Zak Hardaker	Leeds	2011-16	135	57	43	1	315
Ian Hardman	Hull KR	2007	18	4	0	0	16
	St Helens	2003-07	32(11)	9	5	0	46
Jeff Hardy	Hudds-Sheff	2000	20(5)	6	0	1	25
	Sheffield	1999	22(4)	7	0	0	28
Spencer Hargrave	Castleford	1996-99	(6)	0	0	0	0
Bryn Hargreaves	Bradford	2011-12	45(5)	1	0	0	4
	St Helens	2007-10	53(44)	7	0	0	28
	Wigan	2004-06	16(12)	1	0	0	4
Lee Harland	Castleford	1996-2004	148(35)	20	0	0	80
Neil Harmon	Halifax	2003	13(3)	0	0	0	0
	Salford	2001	6(5)	0	0	0	0
	Bradford	1998-2000	15(13)	2	0	0	8
	Huddersfield	1998	12	1	0	0	4
	Leeds	1996	10	1	0	0	4
Ben Harris	Bradford	2005-07	70(4)	24	0	0	96
Iestyn Harris	Bradford	2004-08	109(11)	35	87	2	316
	Leeds	1997-2001	111(7)	57	490	6	1214
	Warrington	1996	16	4	63	2	144
Ben Harrison	Wakefield	2016	3	0	0	0	0
	Warrington	2007-15	125(59)	14	0	0	56
Karl Harrison	Hull	1999	26	2	0	0	8
	Halifax	1996-98	60(2)	2	0	0	8
Andrew Hart	London	2004	12(1)	2	0	0	8
Tim Hartley	Harlequins	2006	2	1	0	0	4
	Salford	2004-05	6(7)	5	0	0	20
Carlos Hassan	Bradford	1996	6(4)	2	0	0	8
Phil Hassan	Wakefield	2002	9(1)	0	0	0	0
	Halifax	2000-01	25(4)	3	0	0	12
	Salford	1998	15	2	0	0	8
	Leeds	1996-97	38(4)	12	0	0	48
Tom Haughey	Castleford	2006	1(3)	1	0	0	4
	London	2003-04	10(8)	1	0	0	4
	Wakefield	2001-02	5(11)	0	0	0	0
Simon Haughton	Wigan	1996-2002	63(46)	32	0	0	128
Solomon Haumono							
	Harlequins	2006	10(9)	6	0	0	24
	London	2005	24(5)	8	0	0	32
Weller Hauraki	Salford	2015-16	20(8)	4	0	0	16
	Castleford	2013-14	9	9	0	0	36
	Leeds	2011-12	18(17)	6	0	0	24
	Crusaders	2010	26(1)	11	0	0	44
Richie Hawkyard	Bradford	2007	1(2)	1	0	0	4
Andy Hay	Widnes	2003-04	50(2)	7	0	0	28
	Leeds	1997-2002	112(27)	43	0	0	172
	Sheffield	1996-97	17(3)	5	0	0	20
Adam Hayes	Hudds-Sheff	2000	2(1)	0	0	0	0
Joey Hayes	Salford	1999	2	0	0	0	0
	St Helens	1996-98	11(6)	7	0	0	28
James Haynes	Hull KR	2009	1	0	0	0	0
Mathew Head	Hull	2007	9(1)	1	0	1	5
Mitch Healey	Castleford	2001-03	68(1)	10	16	0	72
Daniel Heckenberg	Harlequins	2006-09	31(39)	4	0	0	16
Chris Heil	Hull KR	2012-13	4	2	0	0	8
Ricky Helliwell	Salford	1997-99	(2)	0	0	0	0
Tom Hemingway	Huddersfield	2005-09	7(7)	1	17	0	38
Bryan Henare	St Helens	2000-01	4(12)	1	0	0	4

Super League Players 1996-2016

PLAYER	CLUB	YEAR	APP	TRIES	GOALS	FG	PTS
Richard Henare	Warrington	1996-97	28(2)	24	0	0	96
Andrew Henderson							
	Castleford	2006, 2008	44(11)	4	0	0	16
Ian Henderson	Catalans	2011-15	118(9)	12	0	0	48
	Bradford	2005-07	33(37)	13	0	0	52
Kevin Henderson	Wakefield	2005-11	52(68)	9	0	0	36
	Leigh	2005	(1)	0	0	0	0
Adam Henry	Bradford	2014	23(1)	5	0	0	20
Mark Henry	Salford	2009-11	67	22	0	0	88
Brad Hepi	Castleford	1999, 2001	9(21)	3	0	0	12
	Salford	2000	3(5)	0	0	0	0
	Hull	1998	15(1)	3	0	0	12
Tyla Hepi	Hull KR	2013	(4)	0	0	0	0
Jon Hepworth	Castleford	2003-04	19(23)	7	8	0	44
	Leeds	2003	(1)	0	0	0	0
	London	2002	(2)	0	0	0	0
Marc Herbert	Bradford	2011	20	4	2	0	20
Aaron Heremaia	Widnes	2015-16	16(33)	4	0	0	16
	Hull	2012-14	27(37)	12	0	0	48
Maxime Herold	London	2014	(2)	0	0	0	0
Ian Herron	Hull	2000	9	1	17	0	38
	Gateshead	1999	25	4	105	0	226
Jason Hetherington							
	London	2001-02	37	9	0	0	36
Gareth Hewitt	Salford	1999	2(1)	0	0	0	0
Andrew Hick	Hull	2000	9(9)	1	0	4	4
	Gateshead	1999	12(5)	2	0	0	8
Jarrad Hickey	Wakefield	2011	(8)	2	0	0	8
Chris Hicks	Warrington	2008-10	72	56	119	0	462
Paul Hicks	Wakefield	1999	(1)	0	0	0	0
Darren Higgins	London	1998	5(6)	2	0	0	8
Iain Higgins	London	1997-98	1(7)	2	0	0	8
Liam Higgins	Wakefield	2011	4(12)	0	0	0	0
	Castleford	2008-10	42(32)	2	0	0	8
	Hull	2003-06	1(34)	0	0	0	0
Jack Higginson	Wigan	2016	2(1)	1	0	0	4
Mick Higham	Warrington	2009-15	73(78)	34	0	0	136
	Wigan	2006-08	61(28)	13	0	0	52
	St Helens	2001-05	43(56)	32	0	0	128
Chris Highton	Warrington	1997	1(1)	0	0	0	0
David Highton	London	2004-05	21(24)	2	0	0	8
	Salford	2002	4(5)	2	0	0	8
	Warrington	1998-2001	18(14)	2	0	0	8
Paul Highton	Salford	1998-2002, 2004-07	114(80)	14	0	0	56
	Halifax	1996-97	12(18)	2	0	0	8
Andy Hill	Huddersfield	1999	(4)	0	0	0	0
	Castleford	1999	4(4)	0	0	0	0
Chris Hill	Warrington	2012-16	138(10)	19	0	0	76
	Leigh	2005	(1)	0	0	0	0
Danny Hill	Wigan	2006-07	1(10)	0	0	0	0
	Hull KR	2007	2	0	0	0	0
	Hull	2004-06	4(6)	0	0	0	0
Howard Hill	Oldham	1996-97	22(12)	4	0	0	16
John Hill	St Helens	2003	(1)	0	0	0	0
	Halifax	2003	1(2)	0	0	0	0
	Warrington	2001-02	(4)	0	0	0	0
Scott Hill	Harlequins	2007-08	41(2)	13	0	0	52
Mark Hilton	Warrington	1996-2000, 2002-06	141(40)	7	0	0	28
Ryan Hinchcliffe	Huddersfield	2016	21(1)	1	0	0	4
Ian Hindmarsh	Catalans	2006	25	3	0	0	12
Jy Hitchcox	Castleford	2016	8	7	0	0	28
Brendan Hlad	Castleford	2008	(3)	0	0	0	0
Andy Hobson	Widnes	2004	5(13)	0	0	0	0
	Halifax	1998-2003	51(85)	8	0	0	32
Gareth Hock	Salford	2014-15	15(1)	4	0	0	16
	Widnes	2013	15(2)	9	1	0	38
	Wigan	2003-09, 2011-12	126(43)	38	0	0	152
Tommy Hodgkinson							
	St Helens	2006	(1)	0	0	0	0
Andy Hodgson	Wakefield	1999	14(2)	2	1	0	10
	Bradford	1997-98	8(2)	4	0	0	16
Brett Hodgson	Warrington	2011-13	66	33	268	1	669
	Huddersfield	2009-10	45	13	166	0	384
David Hodgson	Hull KR	2012-14	51	31	0	0	124
	Huddersfield	2008-11	84	59	0	0	236
	Salford	2005-07	81	30	47	0	214
	Wigan	2000-04	90(19)	43	0	0	172
	Halifax	1999	10(3)	5	0	0	20
Elliot Hodgson	Huddersfield	2009	1	0	0	0	0
Josh Hodgson	Hull KR	2010-14	98(29)	35	0	0	140
	Hull	2009	(2)	0	0	0	0
Ryan Hoffman	Wigan	2011	28(1)	11	0	0	44
Darren Hogg	London	1996	(1)	0	0	0	0

PLAYER	CLUB	YEAR	APP	TRIES	GOALS	FG	PTS
Michael Hogue	Paris	1997	5(7)	0	0	0	0
Lance Hohaia	St Helens	2012-15	67(9)	21	0	1	85
Chris Holden	Warrington	1996-97	2(1)	0	0	0	0
Daniel Holdsworth	Hull	2013	19	2	28	2	66
	Salford	2010-12	71	18	183	1	439
Stephen Holgate	Halifax	2000	1(10)	0	0	0	0
	Hull	1999	1	0	0	0	0
	Wigan	1997-98	11(26)	2	0	0	8
	Workington	1996	19	3	0	0	12
Stephen Holker	Hull KR	2015-16	(4)	0	0	0	0
Martyn Holland	Wakefield	2000-03	52(3)	6	0	0	24
Oliver Holmes	Castleford	2010-16	113(20)	22	0	0	88
Tim Holmes	Widnes	2004-05	15(4)	0	0	0	0
Tom Holmes	Castleford	2015-16	4(4)	1	0	0	4
Graham Holroyd	Huddersfield	2003	3(5)	0	0	0	0
	Salford	2000-02	40(11)	8	75	5	187
	Halifax	1999	24(2)	3	74	5	165
	Leeds	1996-98	40(26)	22	101	8	298
Dallas Hood	Wakefield	2003-04	18(9)	1	0	0	4
Liam Hood	Salford	2015	2(15)	0	0	0	0
	Leeds	2012	1(4)	3	0	0	12
Jason Hooper	St Helens	2003-07	89(6)	35	30	0	200
Will Hope	Salford	2013	1(2)	0	0	0	0
Lee Hopkins	Harlequins	2006-07	44(3)	11	0	0	44
	London	2005	29	6	0	0	24
Sean Hoppe	St Helens	1999-2002	69(16)	32	0	0	128
Graeme Horne	Hull KR	2012-16	81(18)	21	0	0	84
	Huddersfield	2010-11	23(17)	11	0	0	44
	Hull	2003-09	49(74)	24	0	0	96
Richard Horne	Hull	1999-2014	341(16)	115	12	6	490
Justin Horo	Catalans	2016	23(1)	9	0	0	36
John Hough	Warrington	1996-97	9	2	0	0	8
Danny Houghton	Hull	2007-16	199(47)	33	0	0	132
Sylvain Houles	Wakefield	2003, 2005	8(1)	1	0	0	4
	London	2001-02	17(10)	11	0	0	44
	Hudds-Sheff	2000	5(2)	1	0	0	4
Chris Houston	Widnes	2016	26(1)	1	0	0	4
Harvey Howard	Wigan	2001-02	25(27)	1	0	0	4
	Bradford	1998	4(2)	1	0	0	4
	Leeds	1996	8	0	0	0	0
Kim Howard	London	1997	4(5)	0	0	0	0
Stuart Howarth	Wakefield	2011, 2015-16	30(5)	4	0	0	16
	Hull	2015	2(3)	0	0	0	0
	Salford	2012-14	25(12)	1	0	0	4
	St Helens	2013	14(1)	0	0	0	0
Stuart Howarth	Workington	1996	(2)	0	0	0	0
David Howell	London	2012-13	24	5	0	0	20
	Harlequins	2008-11	76	26	0	0	104
Phil Howlett	Bradford	1999	5(1)	2	0	0	8
Craig Huby	Huddersfield	2015-16	37(2)	2	0	0	8
	Castleford	2003-04, 2006, 2008-14	130(57)	27	41	0	190
Ryan Hudson	Castleford	2002-04, 2009-12	138(12)	31	0	0	124
	Huddersfield	1998-99, 2007-08	51(22)	10	0	0	40
	Wakefield	2000-01	42(9)	11	0	1	45
Adam Hughes	Widnes	2002-05	89(2)	45	51	0	282
	Halifax	2001	8(8)	8	0	0	32
	Wakefield	1999-2000	43(3)	21	34	0	152
	Leeds	1996-97	4(5)	4	0	0	16
Ian Hughes	Sheffield	1996	9(8)	4	0	0	16
Jack Hughes	Warrington	2016	27	4	0	0	16
	Huddersfield	2015	30(1)	5	0	0	20
	Wigan	2011-14	31(33)	9	0	0	36
Mark Hughes	Catalans	2006	23	9	0	0	36
Steffan Hughes	London	1999-2001	1(13)	1	0	0	4
David Hulme	Salford	1997-99	53(1)	5	0	0	20
	Leeds	1996	8(1)	2	0	0	8
Declan Hulme	Widnes	2013-15	5	2	0	0	8
Paul Hulme	Warrington	1996-97	23(1)	2	0	0	8
Gary Hulse	Widnes	2005	12(5)	2	0	0	8
	Warrington	2001-04	20(28)	8	0	1	33
Alan Hunte	Salford	2002	19(2)	9	0	0	36
	Warrington	1999-2001	83	49	0	0	196
	Hull	1998	21	7	0	0	28
	St Helens	1996-97	30(2)	28	0	0	112
Alex Hurst	London	2013	8(2)	2	0	0	8
Kieran Hyde	Wakefield	2010-11	11	4	4	0	24
Nick Hyde	Paris	1997	5(5)	1	0	0	4
Chaz I'Anson	Hull KR	2007-10	17(13)	3	0	0	12
Sebastine Ikahihifo							
	Huddersfield	2016	1(3)	0	0	0	0
Ryan Ince	Widnes	2016	1	0	0	0	0
Krisnan Inu	Catalans	2015-16	21	8	3	0	38

Super League Players 1996-2016

PLAYER	CLUB	YEAR	APP	TRIES	GOALS	FG	PTS
Andy Ireland	Hull	1998-99	22(15)	0	0	0	0
	Bradford	1996	1	0	0	0	0
Kevin Iro	St Helens	1999-2001	76	39	0	0	156
	Leeds	1996	16	9	0	0	36
Willie Isa	Wigan	2016	25(1)	2	0	0	8
	Widnes	2012-15	44(33)	3	0	0	12
	Castleford	2011	7(2)	6	0	0	24
Andrew Isherwood	Wigan	1998-99	(5)	0	0	0	0
Olu Iwenofu	London	2000-01	2(1)	0	0	0	0
Chico Jackson	Hull	1999	(4)	0	0	0	0
Lee Jackson	Hull	2001-02	37(9)	12	1	0	50
	Leeds	1999-2000	28(24)	7	0	0	28
Michael Jackson	Sheffield	1998-99	17(17)	2	0	0	8
	Halifax	1996-97	27(6)	11	0	0	44
Paul Jackson	Castleford	2003-04, 2010-12	44(30)	5	0	0	20
	Huddersfield	1998, 2005-09	50(73)	4	0	0	16
	Wakefield	1999-2002	57(42)	2	0	0	8
Rob Jackson	Leigh	2005	20(3)	5	0	0	20
	London	2002-04	26(14)	9	0	0	36
Wayne Jackson	Halifax	1996-97	17(5)	2	0	0	8
Aled James	Crusaders	2011	1	0	0	0	0
	Celtic	2009	3(3)	0	0	0	0
	Widnes	2003	3	0	0	0	0
Andy James	Halifax	1996	(4)	0	0	0	0
Jordan James	Wigan	2006, 2014	3(18)	4	0	0	16
	Salford	2012-13	1(40)	6	0	0	24
	Crusaders	2010-11	5(24)	3	0	0	12
	Celtic	2009	17(4)	1	0	0	4
Matt James	Wakefield	2012	(4)	0	0	0	0
	Harlequins	2010	(2)	0	0	0	0
	Bradford	2006-09	1(23)	0	0	0	0
Pascal Jampy	Catalans	2006	4(7)	0	0	0	0
	Paris	1996-97	3(2)	0	0	0	0
Adam Janowski	Harlequins	2008	(1)	0	0	0	0
Ben Jeffries	Bradford	2008-09, 2011-12	76(3)	20	0	0	80
	Wakefield	2003-07, 2010-11	151(10)	70	20	6	326
Mick Jenkins	Hull	2000	24	2	0	0	8
	Gateshead	1999	16	3	0	0	12
Ed Jennings	London	1998-99	1(2)	0	0	0	0
Rod Jensen	Huddersfield	2007-08	26(3)	13	0	0	52
Anthony Jerram	Warrington	2007	(2)	0	0	0	0
Lee Jewitt	Castleford	2014-16	22(12)	0	0	0	0
	Salford	2007, 2009-13	32(62)	4	0	0	16
	Wigan	2005	(2)	0	0	0	0
Isaac John	Wakefield	2012	13	1	19	0	42
Andrew Johns	Warrington	2005	3	1	12	1	29
Matthew Johns	Wigan	2001	24	3	0	1	13
Andy Johnson	Salford	2004-05	8(26)	7	0	0	28
	Castleford	2002-03	32(16)	11	0	0	44
	London	2000-01	24(21)	12	0	0	48
	Huddersfield	1999	5	1	0	0	4
	Wigan	1996-99	24(20)	19	0	0	76
Bruce Johnson	Widnes	2004-05	(4)	0	0	0	0
Dallas Johnson	Catalans	2010	26	1	0	0	4
Greg Johnson	Salford	2014-16	48	20	1	0	82
	Wakefield	2011	12	2	0	0	8
Jack Johnson	Warrington	2015-16	7	3	0	0	12
Jason Johnson	St Helens	1997-99	2	0	0	0	0
Josh Johnson	Huddersfield	2013-16	14(17)	0	0	0	0
Mark Johnson	Salford	1999-2000	22(9)	16	0	0	64
	Hull	1998	10(1)	4	0	0	16
	Workington	1996	12	4	0	0	16
Nick Johnson	Hull KR	2012	1	0	0	0	0
Nick Johnson	London	2003	(1)	0	0	0	0
Paul Johnson	Crusaders	2011	6(4)	0	0	0	0
	Wakefield	2010	12(3)	4	0	0	16
	Warrington	2007-09	37(9)	17	0	0	68
	Bradford	2004-06	46(8)	19	0	0	76
	Wigan	1996-2003	74(46)	54	0	0	216
Paul Johnson	Widnes	2014	5(11)	0	0	0	0
	Hull	2013	3(16)	0	0	0	0
	Wakefield	2011-12	25(21)	6	0	0	24
	St Helens	2010	(2)	0	0	0	0
Richard Johnson	Bradford	2008	(2)	0	0	0	0
Ben Johnston	Castleford	2012	2	0	0	0	0
Jordan Johnstone	Widnes	2016	(2)	0	0	0	0
Tom Johnstone	Wakefield	2015-16	32	23	0	0	92
Ben Jones	Harlequins	2010	(2)	0	0	0	0
Chris Jones	Leigh	2005	1(1)	0	0	0	0
Danny Jones	Halifax	2003	1	0	0	0	0
David Jones	Oldham	1997	14(1)	5	0	0	20
Josh Jones	Salford	2016	23	6	0	0	24
	St Helens	2012-15	88(9)	22	0	0	88
Mark Jones	Warrington	1996	8(11)	2	0	0	8
Phil Jones	Leigh	2005	16	8	31	0	94
	Wigan	1999-2001	14(7)	6	25	0	74
Stacey Jones	Catalans	2006-07	39	11	43	3	133
Stephen Jones	Huddersfield	2005	(1)	0	0	0	0
Stuart Jones	Castleford	2009-12	69(27)	14	0	0	56
	Huddersfield	2004-08	96(22)	17	0	0	68
	St Helens	2003	(18)	2	0	0	8
	Wigan	2002	5(3)	1	0	0	4
Ben Jones-Bishop	Wakefield	2016	19	10	0	0	40
	Salford	2015	17	12	0	0	48
	Leeds	2008-09, 2011-14	70(2)	46	0	0	184
	Harlequins	2010	17	10	0	0	40
Jamie Jones-Buchanan	Leeds	1999-2016	249(68)	64	0	0	256
Tim Jonkers	Wigan	2006	3(1)	0	0	0	0
	Salford	2004-06	5(11)	0	0	0	0
	St Helens	1999-2004	41(64)	12	0	0	48
Darren Jordan	Wakefield	2003	(1)	0	0	0	0
Phil Joseph	Salford	2016	(12)	0	0	0	0
	Widnes	2013-15	11(38)	1	0	0	4
	Bradford	2012	(6)	0	0	0	0
	Huddersfield	2004	7(6)	0	0	0	0
Max Jowitt	Wakefield	2014-16	22(1)	5	0	0	20
Warren Jowitt	Hull	2003	(2)	0	0	0	0
	Salford	2001-02	17(4)	2	0	0	8
	Wakefield	2000	19(3)	8	0	0	32
	Bradford	1996-99	13(25)	5	0	0	20
Chris Joynt	St Helens	1996-2004	201(14)	68	0	0	272
Benjamin Jullien	Warrington	2016	4(7)	1	0	0	4
Gregory Kacala	Paris	1996	7	1	0	0	4
Andy Kain	Castleford	2004, 2006	9(7)	3	10	0	32
Antonio Kaufusi	Huddersfield	2014	15(2)	1	0	0	4
	Bradford	2014	4	0	0	0	0
	London	2012-13	44(5)	5	0	0	20
Mal Kaufusi	London	2004	1(3)	0	0	0	0
Ben Kavanagh	Wakefield	2015	6(3)	0	0	0	0
	Widnes	2012-15	18(33)	0	0	0	0
Liam Kay	Wakefield	2012-13	4	4	0	0	16
Ben Kaye	Harlequins	2009-10	2(13)	0	0	0	0
	Leeds	2008	2(2)	1	0	0	4
Elliot Kear	Bradford	2012-14	53(2)	17	0	0	68
	Crusaders	2010-11	16(1)	4	0	0	16
	Celtic	2009	3	0	0	0	0
Brett Kearney	Bradford	2010-14	107	55	0	0	220
Stephen Kearney	Hull	2005	22(2)	5	0	0	20
Damon Keating	Wakefield	2002	7(17)	1	0	0	4
Kris Keating	Hull KR	2014	23	5	0	0	20
Shaun Keating	London	1996	1(3)	0	0	0	0
Mark Keenan	Workington	1996	3(4)	1	0	0	4
Jimmy Keinhorst	Leeds	2012-16	31(18)	18	0	0	72
	Wakefield	2014	7	1	0	0	4
Albert Kelly	Hull KR	2015-16	37	21	3	0	90
Tony Kemp	Wakefield	1999-2000	15(5)	2	0	1	9
	Leeds	1996-98	23(2)	5	0	1	22
Damien Kennedy	London	2003	5(11)	1	0	0	4
Ian Kenny	St Helens	2004	(1)	0	0	0	0
Sean Kenny	Salford	2016	(4)	0	0	0	0
Jason Kent	Leigh	2005	23	1	0	0	4
Liam Kent	Hull	2012-13	1(5)	0	0	0	0
Shane Kenward	Wakefield	1999	28	6	0	0	24
	Salford	1998	1	0	0	0	0
Jason Keough	Paris	1997	2	1	0	0	4
Keiran Kerr	Widnes	2005	6	2	0	0	8
Martin Ketteridge	Halifax	1996	7(5)	0	0	0	0
Ronnie Kettlewell	Warrington	1996	(1)	0	0	0	0
Joe Keyes	London	2014	7	5	0	0	20
Younes Khattabi	Catalans	2006-08	24(4)	10	0	0	40
David Kidwell	Warrington	2001-02	14(12)	9	0	0	36
Andrew King	London	2003	23(1)	15	0	0	60
Dave King	Huddersfield	1998-99	11(17)	2	0	0	8
George King	Warrington	2014-16	6(43)	1	0	0	4
James King	Leigh	2005	5(7)	0	0	0	0
Kevin King	Wakefield	2005	8(1)	2	0	0	8
	Castleford	2004	(1)	0	0	0	0
Matt King	Warrington	2008-11	91	58	0	0	232
Paul King	Wakefield	2010-11	10(19)	0	0	1	1
	Hull	1999-2009	136(93)	20	0	1	81
Toby King	Warrington	2014-16	16(6)	3	0	0	12
Andy Kirk	Wakefield	2005	6(3)	1	0	0	4
	Salford	2004	20	5	0	0	20
	Leeds	2001-02	4(4)	0	0	0	0
Ian Kirke	Wakefield	2015	2(2)	1	0	0	4
	Leeds	2006-14	52(132)	10	0	0	40

Super League Players 1996-2016

PLAYER	CLUB	YEAR	APP	TRIES	GOALS	FG	PTS
John Kirkpatrick	London	2004-05	18(1)	5	0	0	20
	St Helens	2001-03	10(11)	10	0	0	40
	Halifax	2003	4	1	0	0	4
Danny Kirmond	Wakefield	2010, 2012-16	104(4)	36	0	0	144
	Huddersfield	2008-11	18(31)	9	0	0	36
Wayne Kitchin	Workington	1996	11(6)	3	17	1	47
Sione Kite	Widnes	2012	6(8)	1	0	0	4
Ian Knott	Leigh	2005	8(1)	2	0	0	8
	Wakefield	2002-03	34(5)	7	79	0	186
	Warrington	1996-2001	68(41)	24	18	0	132
Matt Knowles	Wigan	1996	(3)	0	0	0	0
Michael Knowles	Castleford	2006	(1)	0	0	0	0
Morgan Knowles	St Helens	2016	5(17)	4	0	0	16
Phil Knowles	Salford	1997	1	0	0	0	0
Simon Knox	Halifax	1999	(6)	0	0	0	0
	Salford	1998	1(1)	0	0	0	0
	Bradford	1996-98	9(19)	7	0	0	28
Toa Kohe-Love	Warrington	1996-2001, 2005-06	166(3)	90	0	0	360
	Bradford	2004	1(1)	0	0	0	0
	Hull	2002-03	42	19	0	0	76
Paul Koloi	Wigan	1997	1(2)	1	0	0	4
Craig Kopczak	Salford	2016	22	5	0	0	20
	Huddersfield	2013-15	48(37)	6	0	0	24
	Bradford	2006-12	32(83)	10	0	0	40
Michael Korkidas	Wakefield	2003-06, 2009-11	133(36)	15	0	0	60
	Huddersfield	2009	4(1)	1	0	0	4
	Castleford	2008	15(6)	1	0	0	4
	Salford	2007	26(1)	1	0	0	4
Nick Kouparitsas	Harlequins	2011	2(13)	1	0	0	4
Olsi Krasniqi	Salford	2015-16	(13)	0	0	0	0
	London	2012-14	28(34)	3	0	0	12
	Harlequins	2010-11	3(20)	1	0	0	4
David Krause	London	1996-97	22(1)	7	0	0	28
Ben Kusto	Huddersfield	2001	21(4)	9	0	1	37
Anthony Laffranchi	St Helens	2012-14	50(18)	19	0	0	76
James Laithwaite	Warrington	2013-15	23(22)	1	0	0	4
	Hull KR	2012	1(2)	1	0	0	4
Adrian Lam	Wigan	2001-04	105(2)	40	1	9	171
Callum Lancaster	Hull	2014-16	7	9	0	0	36
Mark Lane	Paris	1996	(2)	0	0	0	0
Allan Langer	Warrington	2000-01	47	13	4	0	60
Kevin Langer	London	1996	12(4)	2	0	0	8
Junior Langi	Salford	2005-06	27(7)	7	0	0	28
Chris Langley	Huddersfield	2000-01	18(1)	3	0	0	12
Gareth Langley	St Helens	2006	1	1	3	0	10
Jamie Langley	Hull KR	2014	6(5)	1	0	0	4
	Bradford	2002-13	182(57)	36	0	0	144
Ryan Lannon	Salford	2015-16	4(9)	2	0	0	8
Kevin Larroyer	Hull KR	2014-16	34(13)	9	0	0	36
	Catalans	2012-13	9(10)	6	0	0	24
Andy Last	Hull	1999-2005	16(10)	4	0	0	16
Sam Latus	Hull KR	2010-13	34(3)	13	0	0	52
Epalahame Lauaki	Wigan	2012-13	14(16)	2	0	0	8
	Hull	2009-11	3(50)	4	0	0	16
Dale Laughton	Warrington	2002	15(1)	0	0	0	0
	Huddersfield	2000-01	36(2)	4	0	0	16
	Sheffield	1996-99	48(22)	5	0	0	20
Ali Lauitiiti	Wakefield	2012-15	46(31)	16	0	0	64
	Leeds	2004-11	64(117)	58	0	0	232
Jason Laurence	Salford	1997	1	0	0	0	0
Graham Law	Wakefield	1999-2002	34(30)	6	40	0	104
Neil Law	Wakefield	1999-2002	83	39	0	0	156
	Sheffield	1998	1(1)	1	0	0	4
Dean Lawford	Widnes	2003-04	17(1)	5	2	4	28
	Halifax	2001	1(1)	0	0	0	0
	Leeds	1997-2000	15(8)	2	3	0	14
	Huddersfield	1999	6(1)	0	6	1	13
	Sheffield	1996	9(5)	2	1	1	11
George Lawler	Hull KR	2016	12(5)	1	0	0	4
Johnny Lawless	Halifax	2001-03	73(1)	10	0	0	40
	Hudds-Sheff	2000	19(6)	3	0	0	12
	Sheffield	1996-99	76(4)	11	0	0	44
Michael Lawrence	Huddersfield	2007-16	169(33)	44	0	0	176
Adam Lawton	Widnes	2013-14	2(10)	5	0	0	20
Charlie Leaeno	Wakefield	2010	7(3)	2	0	0	8
Mark Leafa	Castleford	2008	5(9)	1	0	0	4
	Leigh	2005	28	2	0	0	8
Leroy Leapai	London	1996	2	0	0	0	0
Jim Leatham	Hull	1998-99	20(18)	4	0	0	16
	Leeds	1997	(1)	0	0	0	0
Andy Leathem	Warrington	1999	2(8)	0	0	0	0
	St Helens	1996-98	20(1)	1	0	0	4
Danny Lee	Gateshead	1999	16(2)	0	0	0	0
Jason Lee	Halifax	2001	10(1)	2	0	0	8
Mark Lee	Salford	1997-2000	25(11)	1	0	4	8
Robert Lee	Hull	1999	4(3)	0	0	0	0
Tommy Lee	Salford	2014-16	37(5)	4	0	0	16
	London	2013	16(4)	2	0	0	8
	Huddersfield	2012	11(7)	3	0	0	12
	Wakefield	2011	25	6	0	0	24
	Crusaders	2010	3(9)	0	0	0	0
	Hull	2005-09	44(27)	6	0	0	24
Kruise Leeming	Huddersfield	2013-16	6(30)	3	0	0	12
Matthew Leigh	Salford	2000	(6)	0	0	0	0
Chris Leikvoll	Warrington	2004-07	72(18)	4	0	0	16
Jim Lenihan	Huddersfield	1999	19(1)	10	0	0	40
Mark Lennon	Celtic	2009	10(3)	1	8	0	20
	Hull KR	2007	11(4)	5	7	0	34
	Castleford	2001-03	30(21)	10	21	0	82
Tevita Leo-Latu	Wakefield	2006-10	28(49)	10	0	0	40
Gary Lester	Hull	1998-99	46	17	0	0	68
Stuart Lester	Wigan	1997	1(3)	0	0	0	0
Heath L'Estrange	Bradford	2010-13	56(35)	7	0	0	28
Afi Leuila	Oldham	1996-97	17(3)	2	0	0	8
Kylie Leuluai	Leeds	2007-15	182(45)	20	0	0	80
Macgraff Leuluai	Widnes	2012-16	48(47)	5	0	0	20
Phil Leuluai	Salford	2007, 2009-10	7(47)	3	0	0	12
Thomas Leuluai	Wigan	2007-12	167(1)	51	0	0	204
	Harlequins	2006	15(2)	6	0	0	24
	London	2005	20	13	0	0	52
Simon Lewis	Castleford	2001	4	3	0	0	12
Paul Leyland	St Helens	2006	1	0	0	0	0
Jon Liddell	Leeds	2001	1	0	0	0	0
Jason Lidden	Castleford	1997	15(1)	7	0	0	28
Jordan Lilley	Leeds	2015-16	15(7)	2	28	0	64
Danny Lima	Wakefield	2007	(3)	0	0	0	0
	Salford	2006	7(2)	0	0	0	0
	Warrington	2004-06	15(47)	9	0	0	36
Jeff Lima	Catalans	2014-15	37(7)	3	1	0	14
	Wigan	2011-12	24(29)	4	0	0	16
Tom Lineham	Warrington	2016	21	15	0	0	60
	Hull	2012-15	61(1)	50	0	0	200
Harry Little	London	2013	2	0	0	0	0
Craig Littler	St Helens	2006	1	1	0	0	4
Stuart Littler	Salford	1998-2002, 2004-07, 2009-10	217(30)	65	0	0	260
Peter Livett	Workington	1996	3(1)	0	0	0	0
Rhodri Lloyd	Wigan	2012-13, 2015	3(4)	0	0	0	0
	Widnes	2014	(4)	0	0	0	0
	London	2013	2	0	0	0	0
Kevin Locke	Wakefield	2015	3	0	0	0	0
	Salford	2014-15	13	6	11	0	46
Jack Logan	Hull	2014-16	21	9	0	0	36
Scott Logan	Wigan	2006	10(11)	0	0	0	0
	Hull	2001-03	27(20)	5	0	0	20
Jamahl Lolesi	Huddersfield	2007-10	75(9)	27	0	0	108
Filimone Lolohea	Harlequins	2006	3(6)	0	0	0	0
	London	2005	8(15)	0	0	0	0
David Lomax	Huddersfield	2000-01	45(9)	4	0	0	16
	Paris	1997	19(2)	1	0	0	4
Jonny Lomax	St Helens	2009-16	126(2)	58	84	2	402
Dave Long	London	1999	(1)	0	0	0	0
Karl Long	London	2003	(1)	0	0	0	0
	Widnes	2002	4	1	0	0	4
Sean Long	Hull	2010-11	22	6	0	0	24
	St Helens	1997-2009	263(8)	126	826	20	2176
	Wigan	1996-97	1(5)	0	0	0	0
Davide Longo	Bradford	1996	1(3)	0	0	0	0
Gary Lord	Oldham	1996-97	28(12)	3	0	0	12
Paul Loughlin	Huddersfield	1998-99	34(2)	4	4	0	24
	Bradford	1996-97	36(4)	15	8	0	76
Rhys Lovegrove	Hull KR	2007-14	75(74)	19	0	0	76
Karl Lovell	Hudds-Sheff	2000	14	5	0	0	20
	Sheffield	1999	22(4)	8	0	0	32
Will Lovell	London	2012-14	16(16)	4	0	0	16
James Lowes	Bradford	1996-2003	205	84	2	2	342
Laurent Lucchese	Paris	1996	13(5)	2	0	0	8
Robert Lui	Salford	2016	19	8	1	0	34
Zebastian Luisi	Harlequins	2006-07	23(2)	4	0	0	16
	London	2004-05	21(1)	7	0	0	28
Keith Lulia	Bradford	2012-13	50	19	0	0	76
Shaun Lunt	Hull KR	2015-16	20(5)	10	0	0	40
	Huddersfield	2009-15	73(39)	60	0	0	240
	Leeds	2012	10(9)	7	0	0	28
Peter Lupton	Crusaders	2010-11	37(9)	10	0	0	40
	Celtic	2009	16(4)	4	0	0	16
	Castleford	2006, 2008	40	11	0	0	44
	Hull	2003-06	19(26)	10	3	0	46
	London	2000-02	10(15)	2	2	0	12

PLAYER	CLUB	YEAR	APP	TRIES	GOALS	FG	PTS
Andy Lynch	Castleford	1999-2004,					
		2014-16	143(49)	17	0	0	68
	Hull	2012-13	39(14)	3	0	0	12
	Bradford	2005-11	159(29)	46	0	0	184
Reece Lyne	Wakefield	2013-16	75	24	0	0	96
	Hull	2010-11	11(1)	2	0	0	8
Jamie Lyon	St Helens	2005-06	54(1)	39	172	0	500
Iliess Macani	London	2013-14	12(3)	4	0	0	16
Duncan MacGillivray							
	Wakefield	2004-08	75(18)	6	0	0	24
Brad Mackay	Bradford	2000	24(2)	8	0	0	32
Graham Mackay	Hull	2002	27	18	24	0	120
	Bradford	2001	16(3)	12	1	0	50
	Leeds	2000	12(8)	10	2	0	44
Keiron Maddocks	Leigh	2005	1(3)	0	0	0	0
Steve Maden	Leigh	2005	23	9	0	0	36
	Warrington	2002	3	0	0	0	0
Mateaki Mafi	Warrington	1996-97	7(8)	7	0	0	28
Shaun Magennis	St Helens	2010-12	7(19)	3	0	0	12
Brendan Magnus	London	2000	3	1	0	0	4
Mark Maguire	London	1996-97	11(4)	7	13	0	54
Adam Maher	Hull	2000-03	88(4)	24	0	0	96
	Gateshead	1999	21(5)	3	0	0	12
Lee Maher	Leeds	1996	4(1)	0	0	0	0
Will Maher	Castleford	2014-16	1(23)	1	0	0	4
Shaun Mahony	Paris	1997	5	0	0	0	0
Hutch Maiava	Hull	2007	(19)	1	0	0	4
David Maiden	Hull	2000-01	32(10)	11	0	0	44
	Gateshead	1999	5(16)	8	0	0	32
Craig Makin	Salford	1999-2001	24(20)	2	0	0	8
Tom Makinson	St Helens	2011-16	120(5)	80	94	0	508
Brady Malam	Wigan	2000	5(20)	1	0	0	4
Dominic Maloney	Hull	2009	(7)	0	0	0	0
Francis Maloney	Castleford	1998-99,					
		2003-04	71(7)	24	33	3	165
	Salford	2001-02	45(1)	26	5	0	114
	Wakefield	2000	11	1	1	0	6
	Oldham	1996-97	39(2)	12	91	2	232
Dominic Manfredi	Wigan	2013-16	52	47	0	0	188
	Salford	2014	1	2	0	0	8
George Mann	Warrington	1997	14(5)	1	0	0	4
	Leeds	1996	11(4)	2	0	0	8
Dane Manning	Leeds	2009	(1)	0	0	0	0
Josh Mantellato	Hull KR	2015-16	26	16	88	0	240
Misili Manu	Widnes	2005	1	0	0	0	0
Sika Manu	Hull	2016	25(1)	4	0	0	16
Willie Manu	St Helens	2013-14	35(11)	9	0	0	36
	Hull	2007-12	133(18)	33	0	0	132
	Castleford	2006	19(4)	9	0	0	36
Manase Manuokafoa							
	Widnes	2015-16	3(45)	3	0	0	12
	Bradford	2012-14	49(21)	3	0	0	12
Darren Mapp	Celtic	2009	9(2)	1	0	0	4
David March	Wakefield	1999-2007	164(23)	34	126	0	388
Paul March	Wakefield	1999-2001,					
		2007	42(31)	17	23	0	114
	Huddersfield	2003-06	71(19)	17	36	1	141
Nick Mardon	London	1997-98	14	2	0	0	8
Thibaut Margalet	Catalans	2013-16	(6)	0	0	0	0
Remy Marginet	Catalans	2011	2	0	9	0	18
Antoni Maria	Catalans	2012-16	4(33)	0	0	0	0
Frankie Mariano	Castleford	2014-16	14(21)	8	0	0	32
	Wakefield	2011-13	41(12)	20	0	0	80
	Hull KR	2010	(3)	0	0	0	0
Oliver Marns	Halifax	1996-2002	54(19)	23	0	0	92
Paul Marquet	Warrington	2002	23(2)	0	0	0	0
Callum Marriott	Salford	2011	(1)	0	0	0	0
Iain Marsh	Salford	1998-2001	1(4)	0	0	0	0
Lee Marsh	Salford	2001-02	3(4)	0	0	0	0
Matthew Marsh	Hull KR	2015-16	13(2)	3	0	0	12
Stefan Marsh	Widnes	2012-16	90	49	14	0	224
	Wigan	2010-11	12	3	0	0	12
Richard Marshall	Leigh	2005	4(16)	0	0	0	0
	London	2002-03	33(11)	1	0	0	4
	Huddersfield	2000-01	35(14)	1	0	0	4
	Halifax	1996-99	38(34)	2	0	0	8
Charlie Martin	Castleford	2013	(6)	0	0	0	0
Jason Martin	Paris	1997	15(2)	3	0	0	12
Scott Martin	Salford	1997-99	32(18)	8	0	0	32
Tony Martin	Hull	2012	10	1	0	0	4
	Crusaders	2010-11	40(1)	14	1	0	58
	Wakefield	2008-09	33	10	33	0	106
	London	1996-97,					
		2001-03	97(1)	36	170	1	485
Mick Martindale	Halifax	1996	(4)	0	0	0	0
Sebastien Martins	Catalans	2006,					
		2009-11	(21)	2	0	0	8
Tommy Martyn	St Helens	1996-2003	125(20)	87	63	12	486
Dean Marwood	Workington	1996	9(6)	0	22	0	44
Martin Masella	Warrington	2001	10(14)	5	0	0	20
	Wakefield	2000	14(8)	4	0	0	16
	Leeds	1997-1999	59(5)	1	0	0	4
Colin Maskill	Castleford	1996	8	1	1	0	6
Mose Masoe	St Helens	2014-15	17(39)	10	0	0	40
Keith Mason	Castleford	2006, 2013	11(6)	0	0	0	0
	Huddersfield	2006-12	118(14)	4	0	0	16
	St Helens	2003-05	33(23)	4	0	0	16
	Wakefield	2000-01	5(17)	0	0	0	0
Nathan Mason	Huddersfield	2013, 2015-16	3(18)	3	0	0	12
Willie Mason	Catalans	2016	6(8)	1	0	0	4
	Hull KR	2011	6	1	0	0	4
Samy Masselot	Wakefield	2011	(1)	0	0	0	0
Nathan Massey	Castleford	2008-16	79(53)	8	0	0	32
Nesiasi Mataitonga							
	London	2014	11(1)	1	0	0	4
Vila Matautia	St Helens	1996-2001	31(68)	9	0	0	36
Feleti Mateo	London	2005	4(10)	1	0	0	4
Barrie-Jon Mather	Castleford	1998,					
		2000-02	50(12)	21	0	0	84
Richard Mathers	Wakefield	2012-14	71	24	0	0	96
	Castleford	2011	21(1)	7	0	0	28
	Warrington	2002,					
		2009-10	42(3)	11	0	0	44
	Wigan	2008-09	23(1)	2	0	0	8
	Leeds	2002-06	85(2)	26	0	0	104
Jamie Mathiou	Leeds	1997-2001	31(82)	3	0	0	12
Masi Matongo	Hull	2015	(1)	0	0	0	0
Terry Matterson	London	1996-98	46	15	90	6	246
Vic Mauro	Salford	2013	1(7)	1	0	0	4
Luke May	Harlequins	2009-10	(3)	0	0	0	0
Casey Mayberry	Halifax	2000	1(1)	0	0	0	0
Chris Maye	Halifax	2003	3(4)	0	0	0	0
Judah Mazive	Wakefield	2016	2	1	0	0	4
Joe Mbu	Harlequins	2006-09	33(20)	3	0	0	12
	London	2003-05	29(19)	4	0	0	16
Danny McAllister	Gateshead	1999	3(3)	1	0	0	4
	Sheffield	1996-97	33(7)	10	0	0	40
John McAtee	St Helens	1996	2(1)	0	0	0	0
Nathan McAvoy	Bradford	1998-2002,					
		2007	83(31)	46	0	0	184
	Wigan	2006	15(2)	5	0	0	20
	Salford	1997-98,					
		2004-05	57(4)	18	0	0	72
Tyrone McCarthy	Hull KR	2015	20(1)	4	0	0	16
	Warrington	2009-13	12(24)	2	0	0	8
	Wakefield	2011	2(5)	1	0	0	4
Louie McCarthy-Scarsbrook							
	St Helens	2011-16	108(62)	35	0	0	140
	Harlequins	2006-10	41(50)	17	0	0	68
Dave McConnell	London	2003	(4)	0	0	0	0
	St Helens	2001-02	3(2)	4	0	0	16
Robbie McCormack							
	Wigan	1998	24	2	0	0	8
Steve McCurrie	Leigh	2005	7(3)	1	0	0	4
	Widnes	2002-04	55(22)	10	0	0	40
	Warrington	1998-2001	69(26)	31	0	0	124
Barrie McDermott	Leeds	1996-2005	163(69)	28	0	0	112
Brian McDermott	Bradford	1996-2002	138(32)	33	0	0	132
Ryan McDonald	Widnes	2002-03	6(4)	0	0	0	4
Wayne McDonald	Huddersfield	2005-06	11(23)	1	0	0	4
	Wigan	2005	(4)	0	0	0	0
	Leeds	2002-05	34(47)	14	0	0	56
	St Helens	2001	7(11)	4	0	0	16
	Hull	2000	5(8)	4	0	0	16
	Wakefield	1999	9(17)	8	0	0	32
Shannon McDonnell							
	St Helens	2014-16	28	15	0	0	60
	Hull	2013	19	2	0	0	8
	Hull KR	2012	21	6	0	0	24
Craig McDowell	Huddersfield	2003	(1)	0	0	0	0
	Warrington	2002	(1)	0	0	0	0
	Bradford	2000	(1)	0	0	0	0
Wes McGibbon	Halifax	1999	1	0	0	0	0
Jermaine McGillvary							
	Huddersfield	2010-16	160	114	0	0	456
Dean McGilvray	Salford	2009-10	14	4	0	0	16
	St Helens	2006-08	5(1)	1	0	0	4
Billy McGinty	Workington	1996	1	0	0	0	0
Ryan McGoldrick	Salford	2013	19(1)	3	0	1	13
	Hull	2012	8	1	0	0	4
	Castleford	2006,					
		2008-12	129(5)	24	11	0	118
Kevin McGuinness	Salford	2004-07	63(3)	11	0	0	44

Super League Players 1996-2016

PLAYER	CLUB	YEAR	APP	TRIES	GOALS	FG	PTS
Casey McGuire	Catalans	2007-10	87(4)	27	0	0	108
Danny McGuire	Leeds	2001-16	304(38)	230	0	4	924
Gary McGuirk	Workington	1996	(4)	0	0	0	0
Michael McIlorum	Wigan	2007-16	138(52)	21	0	0	84
Richard McKell	Castleford	1997-98	22(7)	2	0	0	8
Chris McKenna	Bradford	2006-07	40(7)	7	0	0	28
	Leeds	2003-05	65(4)	18	0	0	72
Phil McKenzie	Workington	1996	4	0	0	0	0
Chris McKinney	Oldham	1996-97	4(9)	2	0	0	8
Wade McKinnon	Hull	2012	10	4	0	0	16
Mark McLinden	Harlequins	2006-08	46(1)	20	0	1	81
	London	2005	22(3)	8	0	0	32
Mike McMeeken	Castleford	2015-16	33(7)	6	0	0	24
	London	2012-14	25(9)	5	0	0	20
Shayne McMenemy							
	Hull	2003-07	80(8)	12	0	0	48
	Halifax	2001-03	63	11	0	0	44
Andy McNally	London	2004	5(3)	0	0	0	0
	Castleford	2001, 2003	2(5)	1	0	0	4
Gregg McNally	Huddersfield	2011	1	0	6	0	12
Steve McNamara	Huddersfield	2001, 2003	41(9)	3	134	1	281
	Wakefield	2000	15(2)	2	32	0	72
	Bradford	1996-99	90(3)	14	348	7	759
Paul McNicholas	Hull	2004-05	28(12)	4	0	0	16
Neil McPherson	Salford	1997	(1)	0	0	0	0
Shannan McPherson							
	Salford	2012-14	20(11)	0	0	0	0
Duncan McRae	London	1996	11(2)	3	0	1	13
Paul McShane	Castleford	2015-16	17(19)	6	0	0	24
	Wakefield	2014-15	39(9)	5	0	0	20
	Leeds	2009-13	17(38)	12	0	0	48
	Widnes	2012	6(5)	3	4	0	20
	Hull	2010	(4)	0	0	0	0
Derek McVey	St Helens	1996-97	28(4)	6	1	0	26
Dallas Mead	Warrington	1997	2	0	0	0	0
Robbie Mears	Leigh	2005	8(6)	0	0	0	0
	Leeds	2001	23	6	0	0	24
Paul Medley	Bradford	1996-98	6(35)	9	0	0	36
Francis Meli	Salford	2014	16	11	0	0	44
	St Helens	2006-13	194(1)	122	0	0	488
Vince Mellars	Wakefield	2012-13	21(5)	4	0	0	16
	Crusaders	2010-11	46	17	0	0	68
Chris Melling	London	2012-13	25(12)	5	2	0	24
	Harlequins	2007-11	100(11)	33	6	0	144
	Wigan	2004-05	8(2)	1	3	0	10
Alex Mellor	Bradford	2013-14	(10)	0	0	0	0
Joe Mellor	Widnes	2012-16	104	39	0	1	157
	Wigan	2012	1(1)	1	0	0	4
	Harlequins	2011	(1)	0	0	0	0
Paul Mellor	Castleford	2003-04	36(3)	18	0	0	72
James Mendeika	London	2013	4(2)	2	0	0	8
Craig Menkins	Paris	1997	4(5)	0	0	0	0
Luke Menzies	Hull KR	2008	(1)	0	0	0	0
Steve Menzies	Catalans	2011-13	61(6)	30	0	0	120
	Bradford	2009-10	52(1)	24	1	0	98
Gary Mercer	Castleford	2002	(1)	0	0	0	0
	Leeds	1996-97, 2001	40(2)	9	0	0	36
	Warrington	2001	18	2	0	0	8
	Halifax	1998-2001	73(2)	16	0	0	64
Tony Mestrov	London	1996-97, 2001	59(8)	4	0	0	16
	Wigan	1998-2000	39(39)	3	0	0	12
Keiran Meyer	London	1996	4	1	0	0	4
Brad Meyers	Bradford	2005-06	40(11)	13	0	0	52
Steve Michaels	Hull	2015-16	49	19	0	0	76
Gary Middlehurst	Widnes	2004	(2)	0	0	0	0
Simon Middleton	Castleford	1996-97	19(3)	8	0	0	32
Constantine Mika	Hull KR	2012-13	45(4)	9	0	0	36
Daryl Millard	Catalans	2011-14	91	38	1	0	154
	Wakefield	2010-11	21(1)	11	0	0	44
Shane Millard	Wigan	2007	19(6)	3	0	0	12
	Leeds	2006	6(21)	3	0	0	12
	Widnes	2003-05	69	23	0	0	92
	London	1998-2001	72(14)	11	1	0	46
Jack Miller	Huddersfield	2013	1	0	1	0	2
Jacob Miller	Wakefield	2015-16	48	19	17	1	111
	Hull	2013-14	20	6	9	0	42
Grant Millington	Castleford	2012-16	88(35)	18	0	0	72
David Mills	Harlequins	2006-07, 2010	25(32)	2	0	0	8
	Hull KR	2008-09	20(11)	1	0	0	4
	Widnes	2002-05	17(77)	8	0	0	32
Lewis Mills	Celtic	2009	(4)	0	0	0	0
Adam Milner	Castleford	2010-16	102(44)	24	0	0	96
Lee Milner	Halifax	1999	(1)	0	0	0	0
Elliot Minchella	Leeds	2013-14	(6)	1	0	0	4
Mark Minichiello	Hull	2015-16	48(3)	14	0	0	56
Greg Minikin	Castleford	2016	15(1)	6	0	0	24
Thomas Minns	Hull KR	2016	14(1)	10	0	0	40
	London	2014	23	6	0	0	24
	Leeds	2013	2(1)	1	0	0	4
John Minto	London	1996	13	4	0	0	16
Lee Mitchell	Castleford	2012	13(10)	2	0	0	8
	Warrington	2007-11	8(27)	4	0	0	16
	Harlequins	2011	11(1)	1	0	0	4
Sam Moa	Hull	2009-12	29(44)	6	0	0	24
Martin Moana	Salford	2004	6(3)	1	0	0	4
	Halifax	1996-2001, 2003	126(22)	62	0	1	249
	Wakefield	2002	19(2)	10	0	0	40
	Huddersfield	2001	3(3)	2	0	0	8
Adam Mogg	Catalans	2007-10	74	19	0	1	77
Jon Molloy	Wakefield	2013-16	25(18)	5	0	0	20
	Huddersfield	2011-12	2(1)	0	0	0	0
Steve Molloy	Huddersfield	2000-01	26(20)	3	0	0	12
	Sheffield	1998-99	32(17)	3	0	0	12
Chris Molyneux	Huddersfield	2000-01	1(18)	0	0	0	0
	Sheffield	1999	1(2)	0	0	0	0
Joel Monaghan	Castleford	2016	16	5	0	0	20
	Warrington	2011-15	127	125	2	0	504
Michael Monaghan							
	Warrington	2008-14	143(28)	31	0	4	128
Joel Moon	Leeds	2013-16	91	41	0	0	164
	Salford	2012	17	9	0	0	36
Adrian Moore	Huddersfield	1998-99	1(4)	0	0	0	0
Danny Moore	London	2000	7	0	0	0	0
	Wigan	1998-99	49(3)	18	0	0	72
Gareth Moore	Wakefield	2011	5	1	14	1	33
Jason Moore	Workington	1996	(5)	0	0	0	0
Richard Moore	Wakefield	2007-10, 2014	52(57)	10	0	0	40
	Leeds	2012-13	3(27)	1	0	0	4
	Crusaders	2011	11(10)	1	0	0	4
	Leigh	2005					
	Bradford	2002-04	1(26)	0	0	0	0
	London	2002, 2004	5(9)	2	0	0	8
Scott Moore	Wakefield	2015-16	12(2)	0	0	0	0
	Castleford	2008, 2015	24(6)	2	0	0	8
	London	2014	26	3	0	0	12
	Huddersfield	2009, 2012	29(7)	9	0	0	36
	Widnes	2012	3(3)	0	0	0	0
	St Helens	2004-07, 2010-11	29(37)	9	0	0	36
Junior Moors	Castleford	2015-16	29(15)	5	0	0	20
Dennis Moran	Wigan	2005-06	39	17	1	1	71
	London	2001-04	107(2)	74	2	5	305
Kieran Moran	Hull KR	2016	(5)	0	0	0	0
Willie Morganson	Sheffield	1997-98	18(12)	5	3	0	26
Paul Moriarty	Halifax	1996	3(2)	0	0	0	0
Adrian Morley	Salford	2014-15	31(14)	2	0	0	8
	Warrington	2007-13	135(21)	8	0	0	32
	Bradford	2005	2(4)	0	0	0	0
	Leeds	1996-2000	95(14)	25	0	0	100
Chris Morley	Salford	1999	3(5)	0	0	0	0
	Warrington	1998	2(8)	0	0	0	0
	St Helens	1996-97	21(16)	4	0	0	16
Frazer Morris	Wakefield	2016	(1)	0	0	0	0
Glenn Morrison	Wakefield	2010-11	43(1)	9	0	0	36
	Bradford	2007-09	48(2)	19	0	0	76
Iain Morrison	Hull KR	2007	5(6)	1	0	0	4
	Huddersfield	2003-05	11(23)	0	0	0	0
	London	2001	(1)	0	0	0	0
Dale Morton	Wakefield	2009-11	22(3)	8	5	0	42
Gareth Morton	Hull KR	2007	7(4)	3	23	0	58
	Leeds	2001-02	1(1)	0	0	0	0
Lee Mossop	Wigan	2008-13, 2015-16	80(65)	11	0	0	44
	Huddersfield	2009	1(4)	1	0	0	4
Aaron Moule	Salford	2006-07	45	17	0	0	68
	Widnes	2004-05	29	12	0	0	48
Bradley Moules	Wakefield	2016	(1)	0	0	0	0
Wilfried Moulinec	Paris	1996	1	0	0	0	0
Gregory Mounis	Catalans	2006-16	149(105)	27	19	0	146
Mark Moxon	Huddersfield	1998-2001	20(5)	1	0	1	5
Rob Mulhern	Hull KR	2016	8(11)	1	0	0	4
	Leeds	2014-15	(5)	0	0	0	0
Anthony Mullally	Leeds	2016	(14)	1	0	0	4
	Wakefield	2015	(2)	0	0	0	0
	Huddersfield	2013-15	12(24)	5	0	0	20
	Bradford	2014	1(5)	0	0	0	0
	Widnes	2012	(9)	0	0	0	0

PLAYER	CLUB	YEAR	APP	TRIES	GOALS	FG	PTS
Jake Mullaney	Salford	2014	12	2	24	0	56
Brett Mullins	Leeds	2001	5(3)	1	0	0	4
Damian Munro	Widnes	2002	8(2)	1	0	0	4
	Halifax	1996-97	9(6)	8	0	0	32
Matt Munro	Oldham	1996-97	26(5)	8	0	0	32
Ben Murdoch-Masila	Salford	2016	23	1	0	0	4
Craig Murdock	Salford	2000	(2)	0	0	0	0
	Hull	1998-99	21(6)	8	0	2	34
	Wigan	1996-98	18(17)	14	0	0	56
Aaron Murphy	Huddersfield	2012-16	108	57	0	0	228
	Wakefield	2008-11	57(2)	12	0	0	48
Jack Murphy	Wigan	2012, 2014	3	1	0	0	4
	Salford	2013	10	3	1	0	14
Jamie Murphy	Crusaders	2011	(2)	0	0	0	0
Jobe Murphy	Bradford	2013	(4)	0	0	0	0
Justin Murphy	Catalans	2006-08	59	49	0	0	196
	Widnes	2004	5	1	0	0	4
Doc Murray	Warrington	1997	(2)	0	0	0	0
	Wigan	1997	6(2)	0	0	0	0
Scott Murrell	Hull KR	2007-12	114(24)	24	26	1	149
	Leeds	2005	(1)	0	0	0	0
	London	2004	3(3)	2	0	0	8
David Mycoe	Sheffield	1996-97	12(13)	1	0	0	4
Richard Myler	Catalans	2016	18	10	2	0	44
	Warrington	2010-15	127(4)	69	1	1	279
	Salford	2009	18	11	0	0	44
Rob Myler	Oldham	1996-97	19(2)	6	0	0	24
Stephen Myler	Salford	2006	4(8)	1	15	0	34
	Widnes	2003-05	35(14)	8	74	0	180
Vinny Myler	Salford	2004	(4)	0	0	0	0
	Bradford	2003	(1)	0	0	0	0
Matt Nable	London	1997	2(2)	1	0	0	4
Brad Nairn	Workington	1996	14	4	0	0	16
Frank Napoli	London	2000	14(6)	2	0	0	8
Carlo Napolitano	Salford	2000	(3)	1	0	0	4
Stephen Nash	Castleford	2012	3(4)	0	0	0	0
	Salford	2007, 2009	2(18)	1	0	0	4
	Widnes	2005	4(1)	0	0	0	0
Curtis Naughton	Hull	2015-16	26	13	1	0	54
	Bradford	2013	1	0	0	0	0
Romain Navarrete	Catalans	2016	(11)	0	0	0	0
Jim Naylor	Halifax	2000	7(6)	2	0	0	8
Scott Naylor	Salford	1997-98, 2004	30(1)	9	0	0	36
	Bradford	1999-2003	127(1)	51	0	0	204
Adam Neal	Salford	2010-13	17(28)	0	0	0	0
Mike Neal	Salford	1998	(1)	0	0	0	0
	Oldham	1996-97	6(4)	3	0	0	12
Jonathan Neill	Huddersfield	1998-99	20(11)	0	0	0	0
	St Helens	1996	1	0	0	0	0
Chris Nero	Salford	2011-13	31(16)	7	0	0	28
	Bradford	2008-10	65(5)	24	0	0	96
	Huddersfield	2004-07	97(8)	38	0	0	152
Jason Netherton	Hull KR	2007-14	60(74)	4	0	0	16
	London	2003-04	6	0	0	0	0
	Halifax	2002	2(3)	0	0	0	0
	Leeds	2001	(3)	0	0	0	0
Kirk Netherton	Castleford	2009-10	5(23)	3	0	0	12
	Hull KR	2007-08	9(15)	2	0	0	8
Paul Newlove	Castleford	2004	5	1	0	0	4
	St Helens	1996-2003	162	106	0	0	424
Richard Newlove	Wakefield	2003	17(5)	8	0	0	32
Clint Newton	Hull KR	2008-11	90(3)	37	0	0	148
Terry Newton	Wakefield	2010	(2)	0	0	0	0
	Bradford	2006-09	83(6)	26	0	0	104
	Wigan	2000-05	157(9)	62	0	0	248
	Leeds	1996-1999	55(14)	4	0	0	16
Gene Ngamu	Huddersfield	1999-2000	29(2)	9	67	0	170
Danny Nicklas	Hull	2010, 2012	2(8)	0	0	0	0
Sonny Nickle	St Helens	1999-2002	86(18)	14	0	0	56
	Bradford	1996-98	25(16)	9	0	0	36
Jason Nicol	Salford	2000-02	52(7)	11	0	0	44
Tawera Nikau	Warrington	2000-01	51	7	0	0	28
Rob Nolan	Hull	1998-99	20(11)	6	0	0	24
Paul Noone	Harlequins	2006	5(2)	0	0	0	0
	Warrington	2000-06	60(59)	12	20	0	88
Chris Norman	Halifax	2003	13(3)	2	0	0	8
Paul Norman	Oldham	1996	(1)	0	0	0	0
Andy Northey	St Helens	1996-97	8(17)	2	0	0	8
Danny Nutley	Castleford	2006	28	3	0	0	12
	Warrington	1998-2001	94(1)	3	0	0	12
Tony Nuttall	Oldham	1996-97	1(7)	0	0	0	0
Frank-Paul Nuuausala	Wigan	2016	5(6)	0	0	0	0
Will Oakes	Hull KR	2016	1	0	0	0	0

PLAYER	CLUB	YEAR	APP	TRIES	GOALS	FG	PTS
Adam O'Brien	Bradford	2011-14	12(29)	6	0	0	24
Clinton O'Brien	Wakefield	2003	(2)	0	0	0	0
Gareth O'Brien	Salford	2016	22	3	51	0	114
	Warrington	2011-15	48(3)	16	69	3	205
	St Helens	2013	7	0	25	0	50
	Castleford	2013	2	0	0	1	1
	Widnes	2012	4	0	15	0	30
Sam Obst	Hull	2011	17(6)	6	0	0	24
	Wakefield	2005-11	100(28)	40	7	0	174
Jamie O'Callaghan	London	2012-14	44(2)	4	0	0	16
	Harlequins	2008-11	54(3)	12	0	0	48
Eamon O'Carroll	Widnes	2012-16	58(5)	3	0	0	12
	Hull	2012	1(9)	0	0	0	0
	Wigan	2006-11	2(59)	3	0	0	12
Matt O'Connor	Paris	1997	11(4)	1	26	2	58
Terry O'Connor	Widnes	2005	25	2	0	0	8
	Wigan	1996-2004	177(45)	9	0	0	36
Jarrod O'Doherty	Huddersfield	2003	26	3	0	0	12
David O'Donnell	Paris	1997	21	3	0	0	12
Luke O'Donnell	Huddersfield	2011-13	22(2)	2	0	0	8
Martin Offiah	Salford	2000-01	41	20	0	2	82
	London	1996-99	29(3)	21	0	0	84
	Wigan	1996	8	7	0	0	28
Mark O'Halloran	London	2004-05	34(3)	10	0	0	40
Ryan O'Hara	Hull KR	2012	8(7)	1	0	0	4
	Crusaders	2010-11	41(8)	3	0	0	12
	Celtic	2009	27	3	0	0	12
Hefin O'Hare	Huddersfield	2001, 2003-05	72(10)	27	0	0	108
Edwin Okanga-Ajwang	Salford	2013	2	0	0	0	0
Hitro Okesene	Hull	1998	21(1)	0	0	0	0
Anderson Okiwe	Sheffield	1997	1	0	0	0	0
Tom Olbison	Bradford	2009-14	55(26)	11	0	0	44
Michael Oldfield	Catalans	2014-15	41	28	0	0	112
Jamie Olejnik	Paris	1997	11	8	0	0	32
Aaron Ollett	Hull KR	2013-15	5(16)	1	0	0	4
Kevin O'Loughlin	Halifax	1997-98	2(4)	0	0	0	0
	St Helens	1997	(3)	0	0	0	0
Sean O'Loughlin	Wigan	2002-16	314(22)	66	3	2	272
Mark O'Meley	Hull	2010-13	70(13)	13	0	0	52
Jules O'Neill	Widnes	2003-05	57(3)	14	158	7	379
	Wakefield	2005	10(2)	2	4	0	16
	Wigan	2002-03	29(1)	12	72	0	192
Julian O'Neill	Widnes	2002-05	57(39)	3	0	0	12
	Wakefield	2001	24(1)	2	0	0	8
	St Helens	1997-2000	95(8)	5	0	0	20
Mark O'Neill	Hull KR	2007	17	5	0	0	20
	Leeds	2006	1(8)	0	0	0	0
Steve O'Neill	Gateshead	1999	1(1)	0	0	0	0
Tom O'Reilly	Warrington	2001-02	8(6)	1	0	0	4
Matt Orford	Bradford	2010	12	3	31	2	76
Gene Ormsby	Huddersfield	2016	4	4	0	0	16
	Warrington	2014-16	37	26	0	0	104
Chris Orr	Huddersfield	1998	19(3)	2	0	0	8
Danny Orr	Castleford	1997-2003, 2011-12	197(23)	75	308	3	919
	Harlequins	2007-10	90(4)	13	96	0	244
	Wigan	2004-06	66(2)	18	12	0	96
Gareth Owen	Salford	2010, 2012-13	4(32)	6	0	0	24
Nick Owen	Leigh	2005	8(1)	1	11	0	26
Richard Owen	Wakefield	2014-15	29(1)	9	0	0	36
	Castleford	2008-14	109(3)	57	0	0	228
Jack Owens	St Helens	2016	26	6	14	0	52
	Widnes	2012-15	53(1)	26	103	0	310
Lopini Paea	Wakefield	2015	1(3)	0	0	0	0
	Catalans	2011-14	41(41)	9	0	0	36
Mickey Paea	Hull	2014-15	44(5)	3	0	0	12
	Hull KR	2012-13	34(17)	5	0	0	20
Mathias Pala	Catalans	2011-15	28(1)	4	0	0	16
Iafeta Palea'aesina	Hull	2014-16	(47)	1	0	0	4
	Salford	2011-12	4(37)	3	0	0	12
	Wigan	2006-10	55(77)	16	0	0	64
Jason Palmada	Workington	1996	12	2	0	0	8
Junior Paramore	Castleford	1996	5(5)	3	0	0	12
Paul Parker	Hull	1999-2002	23(18)	9	0	0	36
Rob Parker	Castleford	2011	4(2)	2	0	0	8
	Salford	2009-11	23(14)	4	0	0	16
	Warrington	2006-08	10(56)	6	0	0	24
	Bradford	2000, 2002-05	19(76)	14	0	0	56
	London	2001	9	1	0	0	4
Wayne Parker	Halifax	1996-97	12(1)	0	0	0	0
Ian Parry	Warrington	2001	(1)	0	0	0	0
Jules Parry	Paris	1996	10(2)	0	0	0	0

Super League Players 1996-2016

PLAYER	CLUB	YEAR	APP	TRIES	GOALS	FG	PTS
Regis Pastre-Courtine	Paris	1996	4(3)	4	0	0	16
Cory Paterson	Salford	2015	14(1)	7	6	0	40
	Hull KR	2013	15	7	0	0	28
Andrew Patmore	Oldham	1996	8(5)	3	0	0	12
Larne Patrick	Castleford	2016	14(1)	1	0	0	4
	Huddersfield	2009-14, 2016	30(107)	30	0	0	120
	Wigan	2015	7(20)	4	0	0	16
Luke Patten	Salford	2011-12	53	16	0	0	64
Declan Patton	Warrington	2015-16	16(1)	4	24	2	66
Henry Paul	Harlequins	2006-08	60(1)	8	94	2	222
	Bradford	1999-2001	81(5)	29	350	6	822
	Wigan	1996-98	60	37	23	0	194
Junior Paul	London	1996	3	1	0	0	4
Robbie Paul	Salford	2009	2(24)	2	0	0	8
	Huddersfield	2006-07	44(8)	7	0	0	28
	Bradford	1996-2005	198(31)	121	3	0	490
Jason Payne	Castleford	2006	1(1)	0	0	0	0
Danny Peacock	Bradford	1997-99	32(2)	15	0	0	60
Jamie Peacock	Leeds	2006-15	234(16)	24	0	0	96
	Bradford	1999-2005	163(25)	38	0	0	152
Martin Pearson	Wakefield	2001	21(1)	3	60	3	135
	Halifax	1997-98, 2000	55(6)	24	181	0	458
	Sheffield	1999	17(6)	9	36	2	110
Jacques Pech	Paris	1996	16	0	0	0	0
Mike Pechey	Warrington	1998	6(3)	2	0	0	8
Bill Peden	London	2003	21(3)	7	0	0	28
Adam Peek	Crusaders	2010-11	5(22)	1	0	0	4
	Celtic	2009	5(12)	3	0	0	12
Eloi Pelissier	Catalans	2011-16	38(104)	23	0	1	93
Dimitri Pelo	Catalans	2007-10	79	37	0	0	148
Sean Penkywicz	Huddersfield	2004-05	21(11)	7	0	0	28
	Halifax	2000-03	29(27)	8	0	0	32
Julian Penni	Salford	1998-99	4	0	0	0	0
Kevin Penny	Warrington	2006-09, 2014-16	79(1)	52	0	0	208
	Wakefield	2011	5	1	0	0	4
	Harlequins	2010	5	3	0	0	12
Lee Penny	Warrington	1996-2003	140(5)	54	0	0	216
Paul Penrice	Workington	1996	11(2)	2	0	0	8
Chris Percival	Widnes	2002-03	26	6	0	0	24
Mark Percival	St Helens	2013-16	62(2)	28	109	0	330
Apollo Perelini	St Helens	1996-2000	103(16)	27	0	0	108
Ugo Perez	Catalans	2015	(2)	0	0	0	0
Mark Perrett	Halifax	1996-97	15(4)	4	0	0	16
Josh Perry	St Helens	2011-13	32(9)	2	0	0	8
Shane Perry	Catalans	2009	8(8)	1	0	0	4
Adam Peters	Paris	1997	16(3)	0	0	0	0
Dominic Peters	London	1998-2003	58(11)	12	0	0	48
Mike Peters	Warrington	2000	2(12)	1	0	0	4
	Halifax	2000	1	0	0	0	0
Willie Peters	Widnes	2004	9	3	0	2	14
	Wigan	2000	29	15	5	6	76
	Gateshead	1999	27	11	1	6	52
Dave Petersen	Hull KR	2012	2(2)	1	0	0	4
Matt Petersen	Wakefield	2008-09	14	3	0	0	12
Adrian Petrie	Workington	1996	(1)	0	0	0	0
Eddy Pettybourne	Wigan	2014	1(15)	0	0	0	0
Dominique Peyroux	St Helens	2016	20	2	0	0	8
Cameron Phelps	Widnes	2012-15	66(1)	23	2	0	96
	Hull	2011	19	2	0	0	8
	Wigan	2008-10	43(1)	14	4	0	64
Joe Philbin	Warrington	2014-16	6(18)	4	0	0	16
Rowland Phillips	Workington	1996	22	1	0	0	4
Nathan Picchi	Leeds	1996	(1)	0	0	0	0
Ian Pickavance	Hull	1999	4(2)	2	0	0	8
	Huddersfield	1999	3(14)	0	0	0	0
	St Helens	1996-98	12(44)	6	0	0	24
James Pickering	Castleford	1999	1(19)	0	0	0	0
Steve Pickersgill	Widnes	2012-13	27(8)	1	0	0	4
	Warrington	2005-09	1(36)	0	0	0	0
Nick Pinkney	Salford	2000-02	64	29	0	0	116
	Halifax	1999	26(2)	13	0	0	52
	Sheffield	1997-98	33	10	0	0	40
Mikhail Piskunov	Paris	1996	1(1)	1	0	0	4
Darryl Pitt	London	1996	2(16)	4	0	1	17
Jay Pitts	Bradford	2014	15(1)	3	0	0	12
	Hull	2012-14	18(30)	1	0	0	4
	Leeds	2009-12	10(15)	2	0	0	8
	Wakefield	2008-09	9(8)	2	0	0	8
Andy Platt	Salford	1997-98	20(3)	1	0	0	4
Michael Platt	Salford	2001-02, 2014	4(1)	1	0	0	4
	Bradford	2007-13	121(6)	44	0	0	176
	Castleford	2006	26	7	0	0	28
Willie Poching	Leeds	2002-06	58(73)	44	0	0	176
	Wakefield	1999-2001	65(4)	20	0	0	80
Ben Pomeroy	Catalans	2014-15	44	10	0	0	40
Quentin Pongia	Wigan	2003-04	15(10)	0	0	0	0
Justin Poore	Hull KR	2014	7	0	0	0	0
	Wakefield	2013	23	1	0	0	4
Dan Potter	Widnes	2002-03	34(2)	6	0	0	24
	London	2001	1(3)	1	0	0	4
Craig Poucher	Hull	1999-2002	31(5)	5	0	0	20
Andy Powell	Wigan	2013	2(3)	1	0	0	4
Bryn Powell	Salford	2004	1(1)	0	0	0	0
Daio Powell	Sheffield	1999	13(1)	2	0	0	8
	Halifax	1997-98	30(3)	17	0	0	68
Daryl Powell	Leeds	1998-2000	49(30)	12	0	2	50
Sam Powell	Wigan	2012-16	58(32)	15	0	2	62
Karl Pratt	Bradford	2003-05	35(19)	18	0	0	72
	Leeds	1999-2002	62(12)	33	0	0	132
Paul Prescott	Wigan	2004-13	49(75)	4	0	0	16
Steve Prescott	Hull	1998-99, 2001-03	99	46	191	3	569
	Wakefield	2000	22(1)	3	13	0	38
	St Helens	1996-97	32	15	17	0	94
Lee Prest	Workington	1996	(1)	0	0	0	0
Gareth Price	Salford	2002	(2)	0	0	0	0
	London	2002	2(2)	3	0	0	12
	St Helens	1999	(11)	2	0	0	8
Gary Price	Wakefield	1999-2001	55(13)	11	0	0	44
Richard Price	Sheffield	1996	1(2)	0	0	0	0
Tony Priddle	Paris	1997	11(7)	3	0	0	12
Frank Pritchard	Hull	2016	10(13)	4	0	0	16
Karl Pryce	Bradford	2003-06, 2012	47(19)	46	1	0	186
	Harlequins	2011	11(7)	12	0	0	48
	Wigan	2009-10	11(2)	12	0	0	48
Leon Pryce	Hull	2015-16	32(2)	8	0	0	32
	Catalans	2012-14	72(2)	15	0	0	60
	St Helens	2006-11	133(3)	64	0	0	256
	Bradford	1998-2005	159(29)	86	0	0	344
Waine Pryce	Wakefield	2007	10(2)	4	0	0	16
	Castleford	2000-06	97(12)	49	0	0	196
Tony Puletua	Hull KR	2015	7	0	0	0	0
	Salford	2014	16(9)	3	0	0	12
	St Helens	2009-13	108(18)	39	0	0	156
Andrew Purcell	Castleford	2000	15(5)	3	0	0	12
	Hull	1999	27	4	0	0	16
Rob Purdham	Harlequins	2006-11	112(3)	18	131	1	335
	London	2002-05	53(15)	16	2	1	69
Adrian Purtell	Bradford	2012-14	45(1)	16	0	0	64
Luke Quigley	Catalans	2007	16(1)	1	0	0	4
Adam Quinlan	St Helens	2015	11	6	0	0	24
Damien Quinn	Celtic	2009	20(1)	4	12	0	40
Scott Quinnell	Wigan	1996	6(3)	1	0	0	4
Florian Quintilla	Catalans	2008-09	1(4)	0	0	0	0
Lee Radford	Hull	1998, 2006-12	138(30)	23	1	0	94
	Bradford	1999-2005	79(65)	18	12	0	96
Kris Radlinski	Wigan	1996-2006	236(1)	134	1	0	538
Sebastien Raguin	Catalans	2007-12	103(22)	28	0	0	112
Adrian Rainey	Castleford	2002	4(7)	1	0	0	4
Andy Raleigh	Wakefield	2012-14	42(21)	9	0	0	36
	Huddersfield	2006-11	74(46)	13	0	0	52
Jean-Luc Ramondou	Paris	1996	1(1)	1	0	0	4
Chad Randall	London	2012-13	29(9)	4	0	0	16
	Harlequins	2006-11	141(2)	37	0	1	149
Craig Randall	Halifax	1999	8(11)	4	0	0	16
	Salford	1997-98	12(18)	4	0	0	16
Jordan Rankin	Hull	2014-15	41(6)	20	43	0	166
Scott Ranson	Oldham	1996-97	19(2)	7	0	0	28
Aaron Raper	Castleford	1999-2001	48(4)	4	2	1	21
Sam Rapira	Huddersfield	2016	15(8)	2	0	0	8
Steve Rapira	Salford	2014	5(13)	0	0	0	0
Stefan Ratchford	Warrington	2012-16	127(10)	51	146	2	498
	Salford	2007, 2009-11	65(5)	23	20	0	132
Mike Ratu	Hull KR	2010	5	1	0	0	4
	Leeds	2007, 2009	1(5)	1	0	0	4
Paul Rauhihi	Warrington	2006-09	67(20)	10	0	0	40
Ben Rauter	Wakefield	2001	15(6)	4	0	0	16
Gareth Raynor	Bradford	2011	18	4	0	0	16
	Crusaders	2010	7	4	0	0	16
	Hull	2001-09	186	102	0	0	408
	Leeds	2000	(3)	0	0	0	0
Tony Rea	London	1996	22	4	0	0	16

PLAYER	CLUB	YEAR	APP	TRIES	GOALS	FG	PTS
Stuart Reardon	Crusaders	2011	25	11	0	0	44
	Bradford	2003-05, 2010	78(11)	37	0	0	148
	Warrington	2006-08	48	12	0	0	48
	Salford	2002	7(1)	3	0	0	12
Mark Reber	Wigan	1999-2000	9(9)	5	0	0	20
Alan Reddicliffe	Warrington	2001	1	0	0	0	0
Tahi Reihana	Bradford	1997-98	17(21)	0	0	0	0
Paul Reilly	Wakefield	2008	5(2)	1	0	0	4
	Huddersfield	1999-2001, 2003-07	150(8)	35	1	0	142
Robert Relf	Widnes	2002-04	68(2)	5	0	0	20
Steve Renouf	Wigan	2000-01	55	40	0	0	160
Steele Retchless	London	1998-2004	177(6)	13	0	0	52
Ben Reynolds	Castleford	2013-14	1(3)	0	0	0	0
Scott Rhodes	Hull	2000	2	0	0	0	0
Phillipe Ricard	Paris	1996-97	2	0	0	0	0
Andy Rice	Huddersfield	2000-01	2(13)	1	0	0	4
Basil Richards	Huddersfield	1998-99	28(17)	1	0	0	4
Craig Richards	Oldham	1996	1	0	0	0	0
Greg Richards	St Helens	2013-16	18(48)	1	0	0	4
Pat Richards	Catalans	2016	19	8	69	0	174
	Wigan	2006-13	199	147	759	4	2110
Andy Richardson	Hudds-Sheff	2000	(2)	0	0	0	0
Sean Richardson	Widnes	2002	2(18)	1	0	0	4
	Wakefield	1999	5(1)	0	0	0	0
	Castleford	1996-97	3(8)	1	0	0	4
Mark Riddell	Wigan	2009-10	45(11)	5	2	0	24
Neil Rigby	St Helens	2006	(1)	0	0	0	0
Shane Rigon	Bradford	2001	14(11)	12	0	0	48
Craig Rika	Halifax	1996	2	0	0	0	0
Chris Riley	Wakefield	2014-15	44	16	0	0	64
	Warrington	2005-14	146(10)	102	0	0	408
	Harlequins	2011	3	2	0	0	8
Glenn Riley	Warrington	2013-14	(15)	0	0	0	0
Peter Riley	Workington	1996	7(5)	0	0	0	0
Julien Rinaldi	London	2012	4(16)	1	0	0	4
	Wakefield	2002, 2010-11	27(9)	6	0	0	24
	Bradford	2009	(7)	1	0	0	4
	Harlequins	2007-08	4(43)	9	0	0	36
	Catalans	2006	16(6)	3	1	0	14
Dean Ripley	Castleford	2004	3(4)	1	0	0	4
Leroy Rivett	Warrington	2002	9	1	0	0	4
	Hudds-Sheff	2000	5(1)	1	0	0	4
	Leeds	1996-2000	39(15)	21	0	0	84
Jason Roach	Warrington	1998-99	29(7)	15	0	0	60
	Castleford	1997	7	4	0	0	16
Ben Roarty	Castleford	2006	11(6)	2	0	0	8
	Huddersfield	2003-05	52	5	0	0	20
Amos Roberts	Wigan	2009-11	47(2)	27	5	0	118
Ben Roberts	Castleford	2015-16	22(8)	10	0	2	42
Mark Roberts	Wigan	2003	(3)	0	0	0	0
Oliver Roberts	Huddersfield	2016	4(18)	0	0	0	0
	Bradford	2013-14	(5)	0	0	0	0
Robert Roberts	Huddersfield	2001	(1)	0	0	0	0
	Halifax	2000	(3)	0	0	0	0
	Hull	1999	24(2)	4	13	4	46
Michael Robertson	London	2012-13	35	17	0	0	68
Stan Robin	Catalans	2015-16	5(2)	1	0	0	4
Chad Robinson	Harlequins	2009	13(1)	2	0	0	8
Connor Robinson	Hull KR	2014-15	(2)	0	0	0	0
Craig Robinson	Wakefield	2005	(1)	0	0	0	0
Jason Robinson	Wigan	1996-2000	126(1)	87	0	1	349
Jeremy Robinson	Paris	1997	10(3)	1	21	0	46
John Robinson	Widnes	2003-04	7	1	0	0	4
Luke Robinson	Huddersfield	2008-15	191(18)	45	4	0	188
	Salford	2005-07	79	28	10	2	134
	Wigan	2002-04	17(25)	9	6	1	49
	Castleford	2004	9	4	3	0	22
Will Robinson	Hull	2000	22	4	0	0	16
	Gateshead	1999	28	9	0	0	36
Ash Robson	Castleford	2015	3	1	0	0	4
James Roby	St Helens	2004-16	217(118)	82	1	0	330
Mike Roby	St Helens	2004	(1)	0	0	0	0
Carl Roden	Warrington	1997	1	0	0	0	0
Shane Rodney	London	2012-13	28	3	12	0	36
Matt Rodwell	Warrington	2002	10	3	0	0	12
Darren Rogers	Castleford	1999-2004	162(1)	81	0	0	324
	Salford	1997-98	42	16	0	0	64
Jamie Rooney	Wakefield	2003-09	113(7)	60	321	21	903
	Castleford	2001	2(1)	0	6	0	12
Jonathan Roper	Castleford	2001	13	7	12	0	52
	Salford	2000	1(4)	1	3	0	10
	London	2000	4	0	0	0	0
	Warrington	1996-2000	75(8)	33	71	0	274
Scott Roskell	London	1996-97	30(2)	16	0	0	64
Steve Rosolen	London	1996-98	25(9)	10	0	0	40
Adam Ross	London	1996	(1)	0	0	0	0
Paul Round	Castleford	1996	(3)	0	0	0	0
Steve Rowlands	Widnes	2004-05	18(3)	2	15	0	38
	St Helens	2003	(1)	0	0	0	0
Paul Rowley	Leigh	2005	15(7)	3	0	0	12
	Huddersfield	2001	24	3	0	0	12
	Halifax	1996-2000	107(3)	27	1	3	113
Nigel Roy	London	2001-04	100	39	0	0	156
Nicky Royle	Widnes	2004	13	7	0	0	28
Shad Royston	Bradford	2011	17(1)	10	0	0	40
Chris Rudd	Warrington	1996-98	31(17)	10	16	0	72
Sean Rudder	Catalans	2006	22(1)	6	0	0	24
	Castleford	2004	9(3)	2	0	0	8
Charly Runciman	Widnes	2016	25	4	0	0	16
James Rushforth	Halifax	1997	(4)	0	0	0	0
Danny Russell	Huddersfield	1998-2000	50(13)	8	0	0	32
Ian Russell	Oldham	1997	1(3)	1	0	0	4
	Paris	1996	3	0	0	0	0
Matthew Russell	Warrington	2014-16	59(4)	16	0	0	64
	Hull	2012	6	0	0	0	0
	Wigan	2012	2	3	0	0	12
Richard Russell	Castleford	1996-98	37(4)	2	0	0	8
Robert Russell	Salford	1998-99	2(1)	0	1	0	2
Sean Rutgerson	Salford	2004-06	60(9)	4	0	0	16
Chris Ryan	London	1998-99	44(3)	17	10	0	88
Matt Ryan	Wakefield	2014-15	28(12)	7	0	0	28
Sean Ryan	Castleford	2004	11(5)	2	0	0	8
	Hull	2002-03	53	8	0	0	32
Justin Ryder	Wakefield	2004	19(3)	11	0	0	44
Jason Ryles	Catalans	2009	19(2)	2	0	0	8
Setaimata Sa	Widnes	2016	7(5)	3	0	0	12
	Hull	2014-15	18(6)	6	0	0	24
	Catalans	2010-12	58(5)	21	0	0	84
Teddy Sadaoui	Catalans	2006	7	0	0	0	0
Liam Salter	Hull KR	2012-16	71	16	0	0	64
Matt Salter	London	1997-99	14(34)	0	0	0	0
Ben Sammut	Hull	2000	20	4	67	0	150
	Gateshead	1999	26(2)	6	17	0	58
Jarrod Sammut	Wakefield	2014-15	19(1)	9	52	0	140
	Bradford	2012-13	35(3)	28	47	1	207
	Crusaders	2010-11	17(16)	17	0	0	68
Dean Sampson	Castleford	1996-2003	124(28)	24	0	0	96
Paul Sampson	London	2004	1(2)	1	0	0	4
	Wakefield	2000	17	8	0	0	32
Lee Sanderson	London	2004	1(5)	1	7	0	18
Chris Sandow	Warrington	2015-16	27(1)	11	26	1	97
Jason Sands	Paris	1996-97	28	0	0	0	0
Mitchell Sargent	Castleford	2008-10	37(21)	6	0	0	24
Dan Sarginson	Wigan	2014-16	71(1)	21	0	0	84
	London	2012-13	35(1)	10	0	0	40
	Harlequins	2011	8	5	0	0	20
Matt Sarsfield	Salford	2016	2(2)	1	0	0	4
Junior Sa'u	Salford	2014-16	64	29	0	0	116
Andre Savelio	Castleford	2016	6(1)	1	0	0	4
	St Helens	2014-16	12(25)	2	0	0	8
Lokeni Savelio	Halifax	2000	2(11)	0	0	0	0
	Salford	1997-98	18(20)	0	0	0	0
Tom Saxton	Salford	2007	5	0	0	0	0
	Wakefield	2006	9(6)	2	0	0	8
	Hull	2005	19(8)	3	0	0	12
	Castleford	2002-04	37(12)	11	0	0	44
Jonathan Scales	Halifax	2000	1	0	0	0	0
	Bradford	1996-98	46(4)	24	0	0	96
Andrew Schick	Castleford	1996-98	45(13)	10	0	0	40
Clinton Schifcofske	Crusaders	2010-11	44	5	115	0	250
Garry Schofield	Huddersfield	1998	(2)	0	0	0	0
Gary Schubert	Workington	1996	(1)	0	0	0	0
Matt Schultz	Hull	1998-99	23(9)	2	0	0	8
	Leeds	1996	2(4)	0	0	0	0
John Schuster	Halifax	1996-97	31	9	127	3	293
Nick Scruton	Wakefield	2014-16	62(3)	9	0	0	36
	Bradford	2009-14	70(27)	5	0	0	20
	Leeds	2002, 2004-08	11(53)	3	0	0	12
	Hull	2004	2(16)	3	0	0	12
Danny Sculthorpe	Huddersfield	2009	5(8)	0	0	0	0
	Wakefield	2007-09	14(28)	1	0	0	4
	Castleford	2006	18(1)	4	0	1	17
	Wigan	2002-05	13(49)	7	0	0	28
Paul Sculthorpe	St Helens	1998-2008	223(4)	94	356	7	1095
	Warrington	1996-97	40	6	0	0	24
Mick Seaby	London	1997	3(2)	1	0	0	4
Danny Seal	Halifax	1996-99	8(17)	3	0	0	12
Matt Seers	Wakefield	2003	11(1)	2	0	0	8

147

Super League Players 1996-2016

PLAYER	CLUB	YEAR	APP	TRIES	GOALS	FG	PTS
James Segeyaro	Leeds	2016	3	1	0	0	4
Paul Seguier	Catalans	2016	(3)	0	0	0	0
Anthony Seibold	London	1999-2000	33(19)	5	0	0	20
Keith Senior	Leeds	1999-2011	319(2)	159	0	0	636
	Sheffield	1996-99	90(2)	40	0	0	160
Fili Seru	Hull	1998-99	37(1)	13	0	0	52
Anthony Seuseu	Halifax	2003	1(11)	1	0	0	4
Jerry Seuseu	Wigan	2005-06	29(9)	1	0	0	4
Brett Seymour	Hull	2012-13	26(1)	7	0	0	28
Will Sharp	Hull	2011-12	27(8)	10	0	0	40
	Harlequins	2008-10	65(1)	19	0	0	76
Jamie Shaul	Hull	2013-16	75	45	0	0	180
Darren Shaw	Salford	2002	5(9)	1	0	0	4
	London	1996, 2002	22(8)	3	0	0	12
	Castleford	2000-01	50(6)	1	0	0	4
	Sheffield	1998-99	51(1)	3	0	1	13
Mick Shaw	Halifax	1999	5	1	0	0	4
	Leeds	1996	12(2)	7	0	0	28
Ryan Shaw	Hull KR	2016	6(1)	4	6	0	28
	London	2013	2	1	2	0	8
Phil Shead	Paris	1996	3(2)	0	0	0	0
Richard Sheil	St Helens	1997	(1)	0	0	0	0
Kelly Shelford	Warrington	1996-97	25(3)	4	0	2	18
Kyle Shelford	Wigan	2016	(1)	0	0	0	0
Michael Shenton	Castleford	2004, 2006, 2008-10, 2013-16	178(2)	83	0	0	332
	St Helens	2011-12	51	15	0	0	60
Ryan Sheridan	Castleford	2004	2	0	0	0	0
	Widnes	2003	14(3)	2	0	0	8
	Leeds	1997-2002	123(7)	46	0	1	185
	Sheffield	1996	9(3)	5	0	1	21
Louis Sheriff	Hull KR	2011-12	8	3	0	0	12
Rikki Sheriffe	Bradford	2009-10	51	14	0	0	56
	Harlequins	2006-08	35(1)	16	0	0	64
	Halifax	2003	6(1)	3	0	0	12
Ian Sherratt	Oldham	1996	5(3)	1	0	0	4
Brent Sherwin	Catalans	2010	12	1	0	1	5
	Castleford	2008-10	48(1)	4	0	3	19
Peter Shiels	St Helens	2001-02	44(3)	11	0	0	44
Gary Shillabeer	Huddersfield	1999	(2)	0	0	0	0
Mark Shipway	Salford	2004-05	30(12)	3	0	0	12
Jake Shorrocks	Wigan	2016	2(10)	0	8	0	16
Ian Sibbit	Bradford	2011-12	11(7)	0	0	0	0
	Salford	2005-07, 2009-10	64(17)	11	0	0	44
	Warrington	1999-2001, 2003-04	63(18)	24	0	0	96
Mark Sibson	Huddersfield	1999	2	2	0	0	8
Adam Sidlow	Bradford	2013-14	20(22)	8	0	0	32
	Salford	2009-12	34(44)	14	0	0	56
Harry Siejka	Wakefield	2014	6(3)	1	0	0	4
Jordan Sigismeau	Catalans	2015-16	11	3	0	0	12
Jon Simms	St Helens	2002	(1)	0	0	0	0
Craig Simon	Hull	2000	23(2)	8	0	0	32
	Gateshead	1999	25(4)	6	0	0	24
Mickael Simon	Wakefield	2015-16	15(22)	3	0	0	12
	Catalans	2010-14	25(40)	2	0	0	8
Darren Simpson	Huddersfield	1998-99	17(1)	5	0	0	20
Jamie Simpson	Huddersfield	2011	8(1)	0	0	0	0
Jared Simpson	Huddersfield	2015-16	6	2	0	0	8
Robbie Simpson	London	1999	6(7)	0	0	0	0
Ashton Sims	Warrington	2015-16	54(4)	4	0	0	16
Kevin Sinfield	Leeds	1997-2015	425(29)	70	1566	31	3443
Matt Sing	Hull	2007-08	41	14	0	0	56
Wayne Sing	Paris	1997	18(1)	2	0	0	8
Brad Singleton	Leeds	2011-16	45(44)	13	0	0	52
	Wakefield	2013	(1)	0	0	0	0
Fata Sini	Salford	1997	22	7	0	0	28
Ken Sio	Hull KR	2015-16	42	23	13	0	118
Michael Sio	Wakefield	2015-16	20(12)	6	0	0	24
John Skandalis	Huddersfield	2007-08	37(5)	4	0	0	16
Dylan Skee	Harlequins	2008-09	(3)	0	0	0	0
Ben Skerrett	Castleford	2003	(1)	0	0	0	0
Kelvin Skerrett	Halifax	1997-99	31(6)	2	0	0	8
	Wigan	1996	1(8)	0	0	0	0
Troy Slattery	Wakefield	2002-03	33(5)	4	0	0	16
	Huddersfield	1999	3	1	0	0	4
Mick Slicker	Huddersfield	2001, 2003-05	17(48)	2	0	0	8
	Sheffield	1999	(3)	1	0	0	4
	Halifax	1997	2(5)	0	0	0	0
Nick Slyney	London	2014	20(4)	3	0	0	12
Ian Smales	Castleford	1996-97	10(8)	5	0	0	20
Aaron Smith	Castleford	2006	(2)	0	0	0	0
	Bradford	2003-04	12(1)	3	0	0	12
Andy Smith	Harlequins	2007	6(3)	3	0	0	12
	Bradford	2004-06	9(9)	4	0	0	16
	Salford	2005	4	1	0	0	4
Byron Smith	Castleford	2004	(9)	0	0	0	0
	Halifax	2003	6(1)	0	0	0	0
Cameron Smith	Leeds	2016	(1)	0	0	0	0
Chris Smith	Hull	2001-02	12	3	0	0	12
	St Helens	1998-2000	62(9)	26	0	0	104
	Castleford	1996-97	36(1)	12	0	0	48
Craig Smith	Wigan	2002-04	77(3)	10	0	0	40
Damien Smith	St Helens	1998	21(1)	8	0	0	32
Daniel Smith	Huddersfield	2015-16	2(11)	1	0	0	4
	Wakefield	2014-15	21(15)	6	0	0	24
Danny Smith	Paris	1996	10(2)	1	15	0	34
	London	1996	2(1)	1	0	0	4
Darren Smith	St Helens	2003	25(1)	14	0	0	56
Gary Smith	Castleford	2001	(1)	0	0	0	0
Hudson Smith	Bradford	2000	8(22)	2	0	0	8
	Salford	1999	23(2)	5	0	0	20
James Smith	Salford	2000	23(3)	6	0	0	24
Jamie Smith	Hull	1998-99	24(6)	6	12	0	48
	Workington	1996	5(3)	0	1	0	2
Jason Smith	Hull	2001-04	61(3)	17	0	1	69
Jeremy Smith	Wakefield	2011	9(1)	1	0	0	4
	Salford	2009-10	27(17)	2	0	0	8
Kris Smith	London	2001	(1)	0	0	0	0
	Halifax	2001	(1)	0	0	0	0
Lee Smith	Wakefield	2012-13, 2015	30(4)	16	54	2	174
	Leeds	2005-12	125(10)	60	34	1	309
Leigh Smith	Workington	1996	9	4	0	0	16
Mark Smith	Widnes	2005	12(15)	4	0	0	16
	Wigan	1999-2004	35(77)	8	0	0	32
Martyn Smith	Harlequins	2010	(2)	0	0	0	0
Matty Smith	Wigan	2012-16	122(3)	17	279	25	651
	Salford	2010-12	67(4)	13	6	1	65
	St Helens	2006-08, 2010	17(2)	3	10	1	33
	Celtic	2009	15(1)	3	2	1	17
Michael Smith	Hull KR	2007	(3)	1	0	0	4
	Castleford	1998, 2001-04	86(33)	32	0	0	128
	Hull	1999	12(6)	3	0	0	12
Morgan Smith	Warrington	2016	(6)	1	1	0	6
Paul Smith	Huddersfield	2004-06	52(17)	13	0	0	52
Paul Smith	Warrington	2001	(1)	0	0	0	0
	Castleford	1997-2000	6(37)	3	0	0	12
Paul Smith	London	1997	7(1)	2	0	0	8
Peter Smith	Oldham	1996	2	0	0	0	0
Richard Smith	Wakefield	2001	8(1)	1	0	0	4
	Salford	1997	(1)	1	0	0	4
Tim Smith	Wakefield	2012-15	79	11	0	0	44
	Salford	2014	12	2	7	0	22
	Wigan	2008-09	13(8)	2	0	0	8
Tony Smith	Hull	2001-03	43(5)	26	0	0	104
	Wigan	1997-2000	66(5)	46	0	0	184
	Castleford	1996-97	18(2)	10	0	0	40
Tony Smith	Workington	1996	9	1	0	0	4
Tyrone Smith	Harlequins	2006-07	49(3)	13	0	0	52
	London	2005	20(4)	11	0	0	44
Rob Smyth	Leigh	2005	15(1)	4	0	0	16
	Warrington	2000-03	65	35	20	0	180
	London	1998-2000	32(2)	9	15	0	66
	Wigan	1996	11(5)	16	0	0	64
Marc Sneyd	Hull	2015-16	55	7	182	11	403
	Castleford	2014	25(1)	6	100	2	226
	Salford	2010-13	33(12)	4	61	3	141
Steve Snitch	Castleford	2010-12	38(18)	10	0	0	40
	Wakefield	2002-05, 2009	33(55)	9	0	0	36
	Huddersfield	2006-08	24(35)	12	0	0	48
Bright Sodje	Wakefield	2000	15	4	0	0	16
	Sheffield	1996-99	54	34	0	0	136
Iosia Soliola	St Helens	2010-14	83(24)	27	0	0	108
David Solomona	Warrington	2010-12	8(49)	16	1	0	66
	Bradford	2007-09	44(9)	19	0	0	76
	Wakefield	2004-06	73(3)	26	0	0	104
Denny Solomona	Castleford	2015-16	42	58	0	0	232
	London	2014	19(1)	8	0	0	32
Alfred Songoro	Wakefield	1999	8(5)	4	0	0	16
Romain Sort	Paris	1997	(1)	0	0	0	0
Paul Southern	Salford	1997-2002	79(33)	6	13	0	50
	St Helens	2002	1(1)	0	0	0	0
Steve Southern	Wakefield	2012	7(8)	3	0	0	12
Cain Southernwood	Bradford	2010	2	0	0	0	0

PLAYER	CLUB	YEAR	APP	TRIES	GOALS	FG	PTS
Roy Southernwood							
	Wakefield	1999	1	0	0	0	0
	Halifax	1996	2	0	0	0	0
Jason Southwell	Huddersfield	2004	(1)	0	0	0	0
Waisale Sovatabua							
	Wakefield	2001-03	44(3)	19	0	0	76
	Hudds-Sheff	2000	23(1)	8	0	0	32
	Sheffield	1996-99	56(17)	19	0	1	77
Jamie Soward	London	2013	6(1)	4	21	0	58
Yusef Sozi	London	2000-01	(5)	0	0	0	0
Scott Spaven	Hull KR	2010	(2)	0	0	0	0
Andy Speak	Castleford	2001	4(4)	0	0	0	0
	Wakefield	2000	6(5)	2	0	0	8
	Leeds	1999	4	1	0	0	4
Dom Speakman	St Helens	2013	(1)	0	0	0	0
Tim Spears	Castleford	2003	(3)	0	0	0	0
Jake Spedding	St Helens	2016	2	0	0	0	0
Ady Spencer	London	1996-99	8(36)	5	0	0	20
Jack Spencer	Salford	2009-11	(7)	0	0	0	0
Tom Spencer	Wigan	2012-13	(7)	0	0	0	0
Rob Spicer	Wakefield	2002-05	28(18)	4	0	0	16
Russ Spiers	Wakefield	2011	(2)	0	0	0	0
Gadwin Springer	Castleford	2015-16	8(22)	2	0	0	8
	Catalans	2014-15	(3)	1	0	0	4
Stuart Spruce	Widnes	2002-03	45(4)	19	0	0	76
	Bradford	1996-2001	107(2)	57	0	0	228
Lee St Hilaire	Castleford	1997	4(2)	0	0	0	0
Marcus St Hilaire	Bradford	2006-07	34(1)	12	0	0	48
	Huddersfield	2003-05	72(2)	30	0	0	120
	Leeds	1996-2002	59(33)	31	0	0	124
Cyril Stacul	Catalans	2007-12	61(1)	18	0	0	72
Dylan Stainton	Workington	1996	2(3)	0	0	0	0
Mark Stamper	Workington	1996	(1)	0	0	0	0
John Stankevitch	Widnes	2005	17(5)	0	0	0	0
	St Helens	2000-04	74(40)	25	0	0	100
Gareth Stanley	Bradford	2000	1	1	0	0	4
Craig Stapleton	Salford	2009	24	2	0	0	8
	Leigh	2005	27(1)	4	0	0	16
Graham Steadman	Castleford	1996-97	11(17)	5	0	0	20
Jon Steel	Hull KR	2007-08	18	6	0	0	24
Jamie Stenhouse	Warrington	2000-01	9(3)	3	0	0	12
Gareth Stephens	Sheffield	1997-99	23(6)	2	0	0	8
David Stephenson	Hull	1998	11(7)	3	0	0	12
	Oldham	1997	10(8)	2	0	0	8
Francis Stephenson							
	London	2002-05	42(34)	5	0	0	20
	Wigan	2001	2(9)	0	0	0	0
	Wakefield	1999-2000	50(1)	6	0	0	24
Paul Sterling	Leeds	1997-2000	79(12)	50	0	0	200
Paul Stevens	Oldham	1996	2(1)	0	0	0	0
	London	1996	(1)	0	0	0	0
Warren Stevens	Leigh	2005	4(14)	1	0	0	4
	Warrington	1996-99, 2002-05	17(66)	1	0	0	4
	Salford	2001	(8)	0	0	0	0
Anthony Stewart	Harlequins	2006	4	0	0	0	0
	Salford	2004-06	51(2)	15	0	0	60
	St Helens	1997-2003	93(23)	44	0	0	176
Glenn Stewart	Catalans	2016	28	3	0	0	12
Troy Stone	Widnes	2002	18(6)	1	0	0	4
	Huddersfield	2001	12(1)	1	0	0	4
James Stosic	Wakefield	2009	8(10)	1	0	0	4
Lynton Stott	Wakefield	1999	21	4	6	1	29
	Sheffield	1996-98	40(4)	15	0	0	60
Mitchell Stringer	Salford	2005-06	12(4)	0	0	0	0
	London	2004-05	10(19)	0	0	0	0
Graham Strutton	London	1996	9(1)	2	0	0	8
Matt Sturm	Leigh	2005	8(19)	3	0	0	12
	Warrington	2002-04	1(18)	0	0	0	0
	Huddersfield	1998-99	46	8	0	0	32
Anthony Sullivan	St Helens	1996-2001	137(2)	105	0	0	420
Michael Sullivan	Warrington	2006-07	21(16)	8	1	0	34
Phil Sumner	Warrington	1996	(5)	0	0	0	0
Liam Sutcliffe	Leeds	2013-16	53(23)	28	66	0	244
	Bradford	2014	3(1)	1	0	0	4
Ryan Sutton	Wigan	2014-16	21(33)	3	0	0	12
Simon Svabic	Salford	1998-2000	13(5)	3	19	0	50
Luke Swain	Salford	2009-10	54	3	0	0	12
Richard Swain	Hull	2004-07	89	5	0	0	20
Anthony Swann	Warrington	2001	3	1	0	0	4
Logan Swann	Warrington	2005-06	49(1)	17	0	0	68
	Bradford	2004	25	6	0	0	24
Willie Swann	Warrington	1996-97	25(2)	6	0	0	24
Adam Swift	St Helens	2012-16	85	63	0	0	252
Nathan Sykes	Castleford	1996-2004	158(52)	3	0	0	12

PLAYER	CLUB	YEAR	APP	TRIES	GOALS	FG	PTS
Paul Sykes	Wakefield	2012-14	59(1)	12	135	6	324
	Bradford	1999-2002, 2008-12	99(4)	35	64	2	270
	Harlequins	2006-07	31(2)	15	47	1	155
	London	2001-05	95(1)	26	219	3	545
Wayne Sykes	London	1999	(2)	0	0	0	0
Tom Symonds	Huddersfield	2016	4	2	0	0	8
Ukuma Ta'ai	Huddersfield	2013-16	63(38)	30	0	0	120
Semi Tadulala	Wakefield	2004-07, 2011	92	37	0	0	148
	Bradford	2008-09	49	30	0	0	120
Whetu Taewa	Sheffield	1997-98	33(7)	8	0	0	32
Zeb Taia	Catalans	2013-15	75	35	0	0	140
Alan Tait	Leeds	1996	3(3)	1	0	0	4
Fetuli Talanoa	Hull	2014-16	74(1)	34	0	0	136
Willie Talau	Salford	2009-10	22	4	0	0	16
	St Helens	2003-08	130(1)	50	0	0	200
Ian Talbot	Wakefield	1999	9(5)	2	31	0	70
	Wigan	1997	3	1	0	0	4
Albert Talipeau	Wakefield	2004	2(3)	0	0	0	0
Gael Tallec	Halifax	2000	5(19)	3	0	0	12
	Castleford	1998-99	19(21)	3	0	0	12
	Wigan	1996-97	8(12)	3	0	0	12
Joe Tamani	Bradford	1996	11(3)	4	0	0	16
Ryan Tandy	Hull KR	2007	8(4)	2	0	0	8
Andrew Tangata-Toa							
	Huddersfield	1999	15	2	0	0	8
David Tangata-Toa	Celtic	2009	1(18)	4	0	0	16
	Hull KR	2007	(17)	3	0	0	12
Jordan Tansey	Huddersfield	2016	2	1	1	0	6
	Wakefield	2015	4	1	0	0	4
	Castleford	2013-15	44(1)	15	0	0	60
	Crusaders	2011	14(4)	5	0	0	20
	Hull	2009-10	30	9	0	0	36
	Leeds	2006-08	18(32)	19	3	0	82
Lama Tasi	St Helens	2016	9(8)	0	0	0	0
	Salford	2014-15	27(11)	2	0	0	8
Kris Tassell	Wakefield	2002	24	10	0	0	40
	Salford	2000-01	35(10)	12	0	0	48
Shern Tatupu	Wigan	1996	(3)	0	0	0	0
Tony Tatupu	Wakefield	2000-01	20	2	0	0	8
	Warrington	1997	21(1)	6	0	0	24
Taulima Tautai	Wigan	2015-16	6(50)	2	0	0	8
	Wakefield	2013-14	6(19)	2	0	0	8
Dave Taylor	Catalans	2016	20(4)	8	0	0	32
James Taylor	Leigh	2005	(4)	0	0	0	0
Joe Taylor	Paris	1997	9(5)	2	0	0	8
Lawrence Taylor	Sheffield	1996	(1)	0	0	0	0
Scott Taylor	Hull	2016	28(2)	3	0	0	12
	Salford	2015	23	5	0	0	20
	Wigan	2013-14	18(29)	6	0	0	24
	Hull KR	2009-12	21(29)	8	0	0	32
Frederic Teixido	Sheffield	1999	(4)	0	0	0	0
	Paris	1996-97	2(3)	1	0	0	4
Lionel Teixido	Catalans	2006-07	11(13)	3	0	0	12
Karl Temata	London	2005, 2012	1(8)	1	0	0	4
	Harlequins	2006-11	94(22)	7	0	0	28
Jason Temu	Hull	1998	13(2)	1	0	0	4
	Oldham	1996-97	25(3)	1	0	0	4
Paul Terry	London	1997	(1)	0	0	0	0
Anthony Thackeray							
	Castleford	2008	3(6)	0	0	0	0
	Hull	2007	2	0	0	0	0
Jamie Thackray	Crusaders	2010	1(16)	2	0	0	8
	Hull	2005-06, 2008-09	37(45)	6	0	0	24
	Leeds	2006-07	5(27)	7	0	0	28
	Castleford	2003-04	7(11)	3	0	0	12
	Halifax	2000-02	10(38)	3	0	0	12
Adam Thaler	Castleford	2002	(1)	0	0	0	0
Gareth Thomas	Crusaders	2010-11	27(1)	6	0	0	24
Giles Thomas	London	1997-99	1(2)	0	0	0	0
Oscar Thomas	London	2014	4(2)	0	1	0	2
Rob Thomas	Harlequins	2011	(2)	0	0	0	0
Steve Thomas	London	2004	4(2)	0	0	0	0
	Warrington	2001	2	0	0	0	0
Alex Thompson	Warrington	2009	(1)	1	0	0	4
Alex Thompson	Sheffield	1997	4(11)	0	0	0	0
Bobby Thompson	Salford	1999	28	5	2	0	24
Corey Thompson	Widnes	2016	30	27	6	0	120
David Thompson	Hull KR	2016	1	0	0	0	0
Jordan Thompson	Hull	2014-16	14(56)	11	0	0	44
	Castleford	2009-13	47(24)	25	0	0	100
Luke Thompson	St Helens	2013-16	22(45)	9	0	0	36
Sam Thompson	Harlequins	2009	(2)	0	0	0	0
	St Helens	2008	(5)	0	0	0	0

Super League Players 1996-2016

PLAYER	CLUB	YEAR	APP	TRIES	GOALS	FG	PTS
Chris Thorman	Hull	2009	19(2)	1	0	0	4
	Huddersfield	2000-01, 2005-08	126(20)	51	320	3	847
	London	2003	26(1)	7	81	1	191
	Sheffield	1999	5(13)	2	8	1	25
Tony Thorniley	Warrington	1997	(5)	0	0	0	0
Andy Thornley	Salford	2009	(1)	1	0	0	4
Iain Thornley	Hull KR	2016	21	10	0	0	40
	Wigan	2012-14	40	25	0	0	100
Danny Tickle	Castleford	2016	6(3)	0	1	0	2
	Widnes	2014-15	33(1)	3	88	0	188
	Hull	2007-13	159(5)	45	528	1	1237
	Wigan	2002-06	94(36)	34	200	2	538
	Halifax	2000-02	25(17)	10	91	2	224
Kris Tickle	Warrington	2001	(1)	0	0	0	0
Lewis Tierney	Wigan	2013-16	25	11	0	0	44
James Tilley	St Helens	2013-14	(3)	0	0	0	0
Dane Tilse	Hull KR	2015-16	29(1)	1	0	0	4
John Timu	London	1998-2000	57(3)	11	0	0	44
Kerrod Toby	London	1997	2(2)	0	0	0	0
Tulsen Tollett	London	1996-2001	105(5)	38	49	1	251
Joel Tomkins	Wigan	2005-11, 2014-16	141(40)	56	0	0	224
Logan Tomkins	Salford	2014-16	31(17)	4	0	0	16
	Wigan	2012-15	9(32)	1	0	0	4
Sam Tomkins	Wigan	2009-13, 2016	137(6)	113	28	1	509
Glen Tomlinson	Wakefield	1999-2000	41(5)	8	0	0	32
	Hull	1998	5	1	0	0	4
	Bradford	1996-97	27(13)	12	0	0	48
Willie Tonga	Catalans	2015	18	6	0	0	24
Ryan Tongia	Wakefield	2011	4	2	0	0	8
Ian Tonks	Castleford	1996-2001	32(50)	11	13	0	70
Tony Tonks	Huddersfield	2012	(1)	0	0	0	0
Motu Tony	Wakefield	2011-12	7(3)	1	0	0	4
	Hull	2005-09	76(20)	25	0	0	100
	Castleford	2004	8(1)	1	0	0	4
Mark Tookey	Harlequins	2006	12(14)	1	0	0	4
	London	2005	13(14)	5	0	0	20
	Castleford	2004	2(8)	1	0	0	4
Clinton Toopi	Leeds	2006-08	40(3)	9	0	0	36
David Tootill	Harlequins	2008	(4)	0	0	0	0
Paul Topping	Oldham	1996-97	23(10)	1	19	0	42
Patrick Torreilles	Paris	1996	9(1)	1	25	0	54
Albert Torrens	Huddersfield	2006	7	5	0	0	20
Mat Toshack	London	1998-2004	120(21)	24	0	0	96
Julien Touxagas	Catalans	2006-11	14(45)	4	0	0	16
Darren Treacy	Salford	2002	24(1)	6	1	0	26
Dean Treister	Hull	2003	16(1)	3	0	0	12
Rocky Trimarchi	Crusaders	2010	16(8)	0	0	0	0
Steve Trindall	London	2003-05	40(20)	3	0	0	12
Shane Tronc	Wakefield	2010	8(3)	2	0	0	8
Kyle Trout	Wakefield	2012-15	6(17)	3	0	0	12
George Truelove	Wakefield	2002	2	1	0	0	4
	London	2000	5	1	0	0	4
Va'aiga Tuigamala	Wigan	1996	21	10	3	0	46
Fereti Tuilagi	St Helens	1999-2000	43(15)	21	0	0	84
	Halifax	1996-98	55(3)	27	0	0	108
Carlos Tuimavave	Hull	2016	21(1)	7	0	0	28
Evarn Tuimavave	Hull KR	2013	11(12)	2	0	0	8
Sateki Tuipulotu	Leeds	1996	6(3)	1	2	0	8
Anthony Tupou	Wakefield	2016	12(9)	4	0	0	16
Bill Tupou	Wakefield	2015-16	17(1)	3	0	0	12
Tame Tupou	Bradford	2007-08	10(7)	8	0	0	32
Jansin Turgut	Hull	2015-16	(5)	0	0	0	0
Neil Turley	Leigh	2005	6(3)	2	20	1	49
Darren Turner	Huddersfield	2000-01, 2003-04	42(13)	13	0	0	52
	Sheffield	1996-99	41(29)	15	0	0	60
Ian Turner	Paris	1996	1(1)	1	0	0	4
Jordan Turner	St Helens	2013-16	106(4)	44	13	3	205
	Hull	2010-12	62(5)	28	0	0	112
	Salford	2006-07, 2009	22(10)	4	1	0	18
Chris Tuson	Hull	2014	10(1)	0	0	0	0
	Wigan	2008, 2010-13	24(49)	13	0	0	52
	Castleford	2010	3(5)	0	0	0	0
Gregory Tutard	Paris	1996	1(1)	0	0	0	0
Brendon Tuuta	Warrington	1998	18(2)	4	0	0	16
	Castleford	1996-97	41(1)	3	0	0	12
Steve Tyrer	Salford	2010	20	6	9	0	42
	Celtic	2009	8	2	5	0	18
	St Helens	2006-08	17(3)	12	42	0	132
Bobby Tyson-Wilson	Hull	2015	(1)	0	0	0	0
Harry Tyson-Wilson	Hull	2014	(1)	0	0	0	0
Wayne Ulugia	Hull KR	2014	3	1	0	0	4
Mike Umaga	Halifax	1996-97	38(1)	16	5	0	74
Kava Utoikamanu	Paris	1996	6(3)	0	0	0	0
Frederic Vaccari	Catalans	2010-11, 2013-14	50	26	0	0	104
David Vaealiki	Wigan	2005-07	67(1)	17	0	0	68
Joe Vagana	Bradford	2001-08	176(44)	17	0	0	68
Nigel Vagana	Warrington	1997	20	17	0	0	68
Tevita Vaikona	Bradford	1998-2004	145(2)	89	0	0	356
Lesley Vainikolo	Bradford	2002-07	132(4)	136	1	0	546
Eric Van Brussel	Paris	1996	2	0	0	0	0
Jace Van Dijk	Celtic	2009	19	1	1	0	6
Richard Varkulis	Warrington	2004	4(1)	3	0	0	12
Marcus Vassilakopoulos	Sheffield	1997-99	15(11)	3	10	2	34
	Leeds	1996-97	1(3)	0	0	0	0
Atelea Vea	St Helens	2015-16	19(17)	10	0	0	40
	London	2014	19(3)	2	0	0	8
Josh Veivers	Salford	2012	5	2	0	0	8
	Wakefield	2011	10(2)	2	22	0	52
Phil Veivers	Huddersfield	1998	7(6)	1	0	0	4
	St Helens	1996	(1)	1	0	0	4
Michael Vella	Hull KR	2007-11	111(5)	13	0	0	52
Bruno Verges	Catalans	2006	25	6	0	0	24
Eric Vergniol	Paris	1996	14(1)	6	0	0	24
Gray Viane	Salford	2007	9	2	0	0	8
	Castleford	2006	20(7)	14	0	0	56
	Widnes	2005	20	13	0	0	52
	St Helens	2004	4	1	0	0	4
Joe Vickery	Leeds	2013	9	1	0	0	4
Daniel Vidot	Salford	2016	5(1)	5	0	0	20
Adrian Vowles	Castleford	1997-2001, 2003	125(1)	29	1	1	119
	Wakefield	2002-03	24(3)	6	1	0	26
	Leeds	2002	14(3)	2	0	0	8
Michael Wainwright	Castleford	2008-10	70	22	0	0	88
	Wakefield	2004-05	21(10)	8	0	0	32
Mike Wainwright	Salford	2000-02, 2007	75(3)	9	0	0	36
	Warrington	1996-99, 2003-07	168(14)	23	0	0	92
Adam Walker	Hull KR	2013-16	60(27)	6	0	0	24
	Huddersfield	2010-12	1(5)	0	0	0	0
Alex Walker	London	2014	1	0	0	0	0
Anthony Walker	Wakefield	2015-16	1(7)	1	0	0	4
	St Helens	2013-14	9(7)	2	0	0	8
Ben Walker	Leeds	2002	23(1)	8	100	0	232
Brad Walker	Widnes	2016	(1)	0	0	0	0
Chev Walker	Bradford	2011-14	44(22)	5	0	0	20
	Hull KR	2008-09	24(7)	5	0	0	20
	Leeds	1999-2006	142(19)	77	0	0	308
Chris Walker	Catalans	2010	11	6	2	0	28
Jonathan Walker	Hull KR	2014	2(6)	0	0	0	0
	Castleford	2010-13	17(31)	4	0	0	16
Jonny Walker	Wigan	2016	(1)	0	0	0	0
Matt Walker	Huddersfield	2001	3(6)	0	0	0	0
Anthony Wall	Paris	1997	9	3	3	0	18
Jon Wallace	London	2014	4(12)	0	0	0	0
Mark Wallace	Workington	1996	14(1)	3	0	0	12
Alex Walmsley	St Helens	2013-16	58(50)	12	0	0	48
Adam Walne	Salford	2012-16	7(42)	2	0	0	8
Jordan Walne	Salford	2013-16	20(28)	3	0	0	12
Joe Walsh	Huddersfield	2009	1(1)	1	0	0	4
	Harlequins	2007-08	1(4)	0	0	0	0
Luke Walsh	St Helens	2014-16	56(2)	14	188	9	441
Lucas Walshaw	Wakefield	2011-14	15(6)	3	0	0	12
Josh Walters	Leeds	2014-16	9(19)	7	0	0	28
Kerrod Walters	Gateshead	1999	10(12)	2	1	0	10
Kevin Walters	Warrington	2001	1	0	0	0	0
Jason Walton	Wakefield	2016	7(8)	0	0	0	0
	Salford	2009, 2014-15	7(19)	1	0	0	4
Barry Ward	St Helens	2002-03	20(30)	4	0	0	16
Danny Ward	Harlequins	2008-11	89(7)	4	0	0	16
	Hull KR	2007	11(9)	0	0	0	0
	Castleford	2006	18(7)	2	0	0	8
	Leeds	1999-2005	70(48)	9	0	1	37
Robbie Ward	Leeds	2014-15	5(3)	1	0	0	4
Stevie Ward	Leeds	2012-15	50(23)	10	0	0	40
Joe Wardill	Hull KR	2016	6(1)	1	0	0	4
Joe Wardle	Huddersfield	2011-16	125	58	0	0	232
	Bradford	2010	1(1)	0	0	0	0
Phil Waring	Salford	1997-99	6(8)	2	0	0	8

PLAYER	CLUB	YEAR	APP	TRIES	GOALS	FG	PTS
Brett Warton	London	1999-2001	49(7)	14	133	0	322
Kyle Warren	Castleford	2002	13(14)	3	0	0	12
Danny Washbrook	Hull	2005-11, 2016	101(47)	15	0	0	60
	Wakefield	2012-15	93(8)	12	0	0	48
Adam Watene	Wakefield	2006-08	45(8)	5	0	0	20
	Bradford	2006	(4)	0	0	0	0
Frank Watene	Wakefield	1999-2001	24(37)	6	0	0	24
Trent Waterhouse	Warrington	2012-14	65(5)	15	0	0	60
Luke Waterworth	Wigan	2016	1	0	0	0	0
Kallum Watkins	Leeds	2008-16	155(7)	89	0	0	356
Dave Watson	Sheffield	1998-99	41(4)	4	0	0	16
Ian Watson	Salford	1997, 2002	24(17)	8	3	5	43
	Workington	1996	4(1)	1	15	0	34
Kris Watson	Warrington	1996	11(2)	2	0	0	8
Anthony Watts	Widnes	2012	(1)	0	0	0	0
Brad Watts	Widnes	2005	6	3	0	0	12
Liam Watts	Hull	2012-16	92(16)	7	0	0	28
	Hull KR	2008, 2010-12	31(26)	6	0	0	24
Michael Watts	Warrington	2002	3	0	0	0	0
Brent Webb	Catalans	2013-14	10	2	0	0	8
	Leeds	2007-12	137(1)	73	0	0	292
Jason Webber	Salford	2000	25(1)	10	0	0	40
Ian Webster	St Helens	2006	1	0	0	0	0
Jake Webster	Castleford	2013-16	56(9)	26	0	0	104
	Hull KR	2008-12	95(1)	34	7	0	150
James Webster	Hull	2008	1	0	0	0	0
	Hull KR	2007-08	36	2	0	2	10
Pat Weisner	Hull KR	2007	(2)	0	0	0	0
	Harlequins	2006	10(6)	3	0	0	12
Taylor Welch	Warrington	2008	1	0	0	0	0
Kris Welham	Hull KR	2007-15	164(2)	90	1	0	362
Paul Wellens	St Helens	1998-2015	399(40)	199	34	1	865
Calvin Wellington	St Helens	2016	1	0	0	0	0
Jack Wells	Wigan	2016	(3)	0	0	0	0
Jon Wells	Harlequins	2006-09	66	10	0	0	40
	London	2004-05	42(2)	19	0	0	76
	Wakefield	2003	22(1)	1	0	0	4
	Castleford	1996-2002	114(14)	49	0	0	196
Dwayne West	St Helens	2000-02	8(16)	6	0	0	24
	Wigan	1999	1(1)	0	0	0	0
Joe Westerman	Warrington	2016	29(1)	10	0	0	40
	Hull	2011-15	110(10)	26	52	1	209
	Castleford	2008-10	68(7)	29	151	0	418
Craig Weston	Widnes	2002, 2004	23(9)	2	1	2	12
	Huddersfield	1998-99	46(1)	15	15	0	90
Ben Westwood	Warrington	2002-16	325(19)	111	63	0	570
	Wakefield	1999-2002	31(7)	8	1	0	34
Michael Weyman	Hull KR	2014	22(1)	7	0	0	28
Andrew Whalley	Workington	1996	(2)	0	0	0	0
Paul Whatuira	Huddersfield	2008-10	59	23	0	0	92
Scott Wheeldon	Castleford	2014-15	14(23)	5	0	0	20
	London	2012-13	27(4)	3	0	0	12
	Hull KR	2009-12	30(42)	4	0	0	16
	Hull	2006-08	2(60)	4	0	0	16
Gary Wheeler	Warrington	2015-16	6(4)	4	0	0	16
	St Helens	2008-14	48(10)	17	13	0	94
Matt Whitaker	Castleford	2006	8(2)	0	0	0	0
	Widnes	2004-05	10(20)	9	0	0	36
	Huddersfield	2003-04	3(14)	0	0	0	0
Ben White	Leeds	2014	1	0	0	0	0
David White	Wakefield	2000	(1)	0	0	0	0
Josh White	Salford	1998	18(3)	5	5	1	31
	London	1997	14(2)	8	0	1	33
Lloyd White	Widnes	2012-16	60(40)	23	20	1	133
	Crusaders	2010-11	13(11)	8	0	0	32
	Celtic	2009	6	1	0	0	4
Paul White	Salford	2009	1	1	0	0	4
	Wakefield	2006-07	24(12)	12	0	0	48
	Huddersfield	2003-05	11(32)	17	16	0	100
Elliott Whitehead	Catalans	2013-15	64(1)	30	0	0	120
	Bradford	2009-13	90(10)	30	0	0	120
Richard Whiting	Hull	2004-15	163(72)	69	19	2	316
Matt Whitley	Widnes	2015-16	14(22)	8	0	0	32
Emmerson Whittel	Bradford	2014	(1)	0	0	0	0
Danny Whittle	Warrington	1998	(2)	0	0	0	0
David Whittle	St Helens	2002	1(2)	0	0	0	0
	Warrington	2001	1(2)	0	0	0	0
Jon Whittle	Wakefield	2006	8(2)	3	0	0	12
	Widnes	2005	13	2	0	0	8
	Wigan	2003	1	0	0	0	0
Joel Wicks	London	2013-14	3(10)	0	0	0	0
Dean Widders	Castleford	2009-11	25(32)	23	0	0	92
Stephen Wild	Salford	2011-13	71	4	0	0	16
	Huddersfield	2006-10	116(2)	33	0	0	132
	Wigan	2001-05	67(20)	24	0	0	96
Sam Wilde	Warrington	2015-16	3(13)	1	0	0	4
Matty Wildie	Wakefield	2010-14	13(26)	3	0	0	12
Oliver Wilkes	Wakefield	2008-09, 2012-13	55(47)	10	0	0	40
	Harlequins	2010-11	39(13)	4	0	0	16
	Wigan	2006	1(5)	0	0	0	0
	Leigh	2005	13(1)	1	0	0	4
	Huddersfield	2000-01	1(6)	0	0	0	0
	Sheffield	1998	(1)	0	0	0	0
Jon Wilkin	St Helens	2003-16	295(28)	77	0	2	310
Alex Wilkinson	Hull	2003-04	11(4)	1	0	0	4
	Huddersfield	2003	8	4	0	0	16
	London	2002	5(1)	0	0	0	0
	Bradford	2000-01	3(3)	1	0	0	4
Bart Williams	London	1998	5(3)	1	0	0	4
Connor Williams	Salford	2016	(1)	0	0	0	0
Daley Williams	Salford	2006-07	9(2)	4	0	0	16
Danny Williams	Harlequins	2006	9(13)	4	0	0	16
	London	2005	1(16)	0	0	0	0
Danny Williams	Bradford	2014	7	2	0	0	8
	Salford	2011-14	54	31	0	0	124
	Leeds	2006, 2008	13(2)	7	0	0	28
	Hull	2008	3	0	0	0	0
Dave Williams	Harlequins	2008-11	1(17)	0	0	0	0
Desi Williams	Wigan	2004	2	0	0	0	0
George Williams	Wigan	2013-16	62(13)	23	8	0	108
Jonny Williams	London	2004	(4)	0	0	0	0
Lee Williams	Crusaders	2011	1(7)	0	0	0	0
Rhys Williams	Warrington	2010-13	23(1)	15	0	0	60
	Salford	2013	4	0	0	0	0
	Castleford	2012	8	4	0	0	16
	Crusaders	2011	6	3	0	0	12
Sam Williams	Catalans	2014	11(1)	4	21	0	58
Luke Williamson	Harlequins	2009-10	39	6	0	0	24
John Wilshere	Salford	2006-07, 2009	72(2)	32	142	0	412
	Leigh	2005	26	8	6	0	44
	Warrington	2004	5	2	0	0	8
Craig Wilson	Hull	2000	2(16)	1	0	1	5
	Gateshead	1999	17(11)	5	0	1	21
George Wilson	Paris	1996	7(2)	3	0	0	12
John Wilson	Catalans	2006-08	69	23	0	0	92
Richard Wilson	Hull	1998-99	(13)	0	0	0	0
Scott Wilson	Warrington	1998-99	23(2)	6	0	0	24
Johan Windley	Hull	1999	2(2)	1	0	0	4
Paul Wingfield	Warrington	1997	5(3)	6	1	0	26
Frank Winterstein	Widnes	2012-13	37(9)	16	0	0	64
	Crusaders	2010-11	26(19)	4	0	0	16
	Wakefield	2009	(5)	0	0	0	0
Lincoln Withers	Hull KR	2012-13	18(22)	10	0	0	40
	Crusaders	2010-11	47	4	0	0	16
	Celtic	2009	21	6	0	0	24
Michael Withers	Wigan	2007	6(1)	1	0	0	4
	Bradford	1999-2006	156(6)	94	15	4	410
Michael Witt	London	2012-13	37	10	89	1	219
	Crusaders	2010-11	39	13	47	4	150
Jeff Wittenberg	Huddersfield	1998	18(1)	1	0	0	4
	Bradford	1997	8(9)	4	0	0	16
Josh Wood	Salford	2015-16	3(2)	0	0	0	0
Kyle Wood	Huddersfield	2011, 2013-16	39(33)	7	0	0	28
	Wakefield	2012-13	5(37)	9	0	0	36
	Castleford	2010	1(4)	0	0	0	0
Martin Wood	Sheffield	1997-98	24(11)	4	18	2	54
Mikey Wood	Huddersfield	2016	(1)	0	0	0	0
Nathan Wood	Warrington	2002-05	90	38	0	3	155
	Wakefield	2002	11	2	0	0	8
Paul Wood	Warrington	2000-14	138(171)	40	0	0	160
Phil Wood	Widnes	2004	2(1)	0	0	0	0
Sam Wood	Bradford	2013-14	7(1)	0	0	0	0
Sam Wood	Huddersfield	2016	4	0	0	0	0
James Woodburn-Hall	London	2013-14	9(4)	2	0	0	8
Darren Woods	Widnes	2005	(1)	0	0	0	0
David Woods	Halifax	2002	18(2)	8	0	0	32
Simon Worrall	Leeds	2008-09	5(16)	1	0	0	4
Michael Worrincy	Bradford	2009-10	12(34)	12	0	0	48
	Harlequins	2006-08	20(12)	10	0	0	40
Rob Worrincy	Castleford	2004	1	0	0	0	0
Troy Wozniak	Widnes	2004	13(7)	1	0	0	4
Matthew Wray	Wakefield	2002-03	13(3)	2	0	0	8
David Wrench	Wakefield	2002-06	28(52)	6	0	0	24
	Leeds	1999-2001	7(17)	0	0	0	0
Callum Wright	Wigan	2014	(2)	0	0	0	0
Craig Wright	Castleford	2000	1(9)	0	0	0	0
Nigel Wright	Huddersfield	1999	4(6)	1	0	0	4
	Wigan	1996-97	5(5)	2	0	1	9

Super League Players 1996-2016

PLAYER	CLUB	YEAR	APP	TRIES	GOALS	FG	PTS
Ricky Wright	Sheffield	1997-99	2(13)	0	0	0	0
Vincent Wulf	Paris	1996	13(4)	4	0	0	16
Andrew Wynyard	London	1999-2000	34(6)	4	0	0	16
Bagdad Yaha	Paris	1996	4(4)	2	4	0	16
Fouad Yaha	Catalans	2015-16	24	11	0	0	44
Malakai Yasa	Sheffield	1996	1(3)	0	0	0	0
Andy Yates	Wakefield	2016	(7)	0	0	0	0
	Leeds	2015	(9)	1	0	0	4
Kirk Yeaman	Hull	2001-16	321(18)	159	0	0	636
Grant Young	London	1998-99	22(2)	2	0	0	8
Nick Youngquest	Castleford	2011-12	37	28	0	0	112
	Crusaders	2010	26(1)	9	0	0	36
Ronel Zenon	Paris	1996	(4)	0	0	0	0
Nick Zisti	Bradford	1999	6(1)	0	0	0	0
Freddie Zitter	Catalans	2006	1	0	0	0	0

OLD FACES - Players making their Super League debuts for new clubs in 2016

PLAYER	CLUB	DEBUT vs	ROUND	DATE
Paul Aiton	Catalans	Wigan (a)	1	5/2/16
Ryan Bailey	Warrington	Castleford (MW)	15	21/5/16
Jordan Baldwinson	Leeds	Salford (a) (D2)	10	9/4/16
Chris Bridge	Widnes	Wakefield (a)	1	7/2/16
Jodie Broughton	Catalans	Leeds (h)	3	27/2/16
Greg Burke	Widnes	St Helens (a)	21	8/7/16
Greg Burke	Wigan	Huddersfield (a) (D2)	2	12/2/16
Justin Carney	Salford	Hull (a)	1	5/2/16
Rangi Chase	Castleford	Warrington (h) (D2)	22	17/7/16
Chris Clarkson	Hull KR	Castleford (h)	1	7/2/16
Jordan Cox	Warrington	Leeds (a)	1	4/2/16
Ben Crooks	Castleford	Hull KR (a)	1	7/2/16
Anthony England	Wakefield	Widnes (h)	1	7/2/16
Theo Fages	St Helens	Salford (a)	2	11/2/16
Connor Farrell	Widnes	Wakefield (a)	1	7/2/16
Brett Ferres	Leeds	Warrington (h)	1	4/2/16
Liam Finn	Wakefield	Widnes (h) (D2)	1	7/2/16
Mark Flanagan	Salford	Hull (a)	1	5/2/16
Paddy Flynn	Castleford	Leeds (a)	14	12/5/16
Jamie Foster	Huddersfield	Wigan (h)	2	12/2/16
Ashley Gibson	Wakefield	Castleford (a)	2	14/2/16
Ryan Hampshire	Castleford	Salford (h)	5	13/3/16
Ben Harrison	Wakefield	Castleford (a)	S84	2/9/16
Jack Hughes	Warrington	Leeds (a)	1	4/2/16
Willie Isa	Wigan	Catalans (h)	1	5/2/16
Josh Jones	Salford	Hull (a)	1	5/2/16
Ben Jones-Bishop	Wakefield	Widnes (h)	1	7/2/16
Phil Joseph	Salford	Hull (a)	1	5/2/16
Craig Kopczak	Salford	Hull (a)	1	5/2/16
Tom Lineham	Warrington	Leeds (a)	1	4/2/16
Willie Mason	Catalans	Leeds (h)	3	27/2/16
Thomas Minns	Hull KR	Castleford (h)	1	7/2/16
Joel Monaghan	Castleford	Hull KR (a)	1	7/2/16
Rob Mulhern	Hull KR	Castleford (h)	1	7/2/16
Anthony Mullally	Leeds	Catalans (a)	3	27/2/16
(club debut: North Queensland (h), WCC, 21/2/16)				
Richard Myler	Catalans	Wigan (a)	1	5/2/16
Gareth O'Brien	Salford	Hull (a)	1	5/2/16
Gene Ormsby	Huddersfield	Hull (a)	10	8/4/16
Gene Ormsby	Huddersfield	St Helens (h) (D2)	22	17/7/16
Jack Owens	St Helens	Huddersfield (h)	1	5/2/16
Larne Patrick	Castleford	Hull KR (h)	12	24/4/16
Larne Patrick	Huddersfield	St Helens (a) (D2)	1	5/2/16
Pat Richards	Catalans	Wigan (a)	1	5/2/16
Oliver Roberts	Huddersfield	St Helens (a)	1	5/2/16
Setaimata Sa	Widnes	Wakefield (a)	1	7/2/16
Andre Savelio	Castleford	Wakefield (a)	23	24/7/16
Ryan Shaw	Hull KR	Wakefield (h)	11	21/2/16
Jordan Tansey	Huddersfield	Hull KR (h)	5	13/3/16
Lama Tasi	St Helens	Huddersfield (h)	1	5/2/16
Scott Taylor	Hull	Salford (h)	1	5/2/16
Iain Thornley	Hull KR	Castleford (h)	1	7/2/16
Danny Tickle	Castleford	Leeds (a)	14	12/5/16
(club debut: Salford (h), CCR6, 7/5/16)				
Sam Tomkins	Wigan	Hull (h) (D2)	14	13/5/16
Jason Walton	Wakefield	Castleford (a)	2	14/2/16
Danny Washbrook	Hull	Salford (h) (D2)	1	5/2/16
Joe Westerman	Warrington	Leeds (a)	1	4/2/16
Andy Yates	Wakefield	Leeds (a)	8	28/3/16
(club debut: Halifax (h), S8-QR6, 19/9/15)				

Players making their club debuts in other competitions in 2016

PLAYER	CLUB	DEBUT vs	ROUND	DATE
Luke Burgess	Salford	Huddersfield (h)	S8-QR1	7/8/16
Matthew Haggarty	Salford	Hunslet (a)	CCR5	17/4/16
Josh Jordan-Roberts	Leeds	Leigh (h)	S8-QR1	22/9/16
Will Jubb	Hull KR	London Broncos (a)	S8-QR5	11/9/16
Feleti Mateo	Salford	Huddersfield (h)	S8-QR1	7/8/16
Jamie Peacock	Hull KR	London Broncos (a)	S8-QR5	11/9/16

NEW FACES - Players making their Super League debuts in 2016

PLAYER	CLUB	DEBUT vs	ROUND	DATE
Tinirau Arona	Wakefield	Widnes (h)	1	7/2/16
James Batchelor	Wakefield	Warrington (h)	S82	14/8/16
Jake Bibby	Salford	Widnes (MW)	15	21/5/16
(club debut: Hull KR (a), S8-QR7, 27/9/15)				
Joe Bretherton	Wigan	Wakefield (a)	10	10/4/16
Ryan Brierley	Huddersfield	Wakefield (a)	7	25/3/16
Sam Brooks	Widnes	Catalans (a)	9	2/4/16
Jack Buchanan	Widnes	Huddersfield (h)	16	29/5/16
Joe Cator	Hull KR	Wigan (a)	8	28/3/16
Ed Chamberlain	Widnes	St Helens (h)	8	28/3/16
Jay Chapelhow	Widnes	Castleford (h)	18	9/6/16
(club debut: Leigh (h), S8-QR7, 27/9/15)				
Ted Chapelhow	Widnes	Castleford (h)	S87	25/9/16
Alrix Da Costa	Catalans	St Helens (h)	11	14/4/16
Macauley Davies	Wigan	Wakefield (h)	21	8/7/16
Olly Davies	St Helens	Wakefield (h)	S87	23/9/16
(club debut: York (h), CCR6, 15/5/15)				
Jordan Dezaria	Catalans	Warrington (a)	19	17/6/16
Tyler Dickinson	Huddersfield	Leeds (a)	4	4/3/16
Mitchell Dodds	Warrington	Salford (a)	4	3/3/16
Brandon Douglas	Castleford	St Helens (a)	S85	8/9/16
Beau Falloon	Leeds	Wigan (a)	5	11/3/16
David Fifita	Wakefield	Leeds (h)	19	17/6/16
Conor Fitzsimmons	Castleford	St Helens (h)	13	1/5/16
Mahe Fonua	Hull	Salford (h)	1	5/2/16
Keith Galloway	Leeds	Warrington (h)	1	4/2/16
Kurt Gidley	Warrington	Leeds (a)	1	4/2/16
Nick Gregson	Wigan	Leeds (h)	5	11/3/16
Sam Hallas	Leeds	Wigan (MW)	15	21/5/16
Jack Higginson	Wigan	Warrington (h)	9	1/4/16
Ryan Hinchcliffe	Huddersfield	St Helens (h)	1	5/2/16
Jy Hitchcox	Castleford	Hull (a)	3	25/2/16
Justin Horo	Catalans	Wigan (a)	1	5/2/16
Chris Houston	Widnes	Wakefield (a)	1	7/2/16
Sebastine Ikahihifo	Huddersfield	St Helens (MW)	15	22/5/16
Ryan Ince	Widnes	Hull (h)	S82	11/8/16
Jordan Johnstone	Widnes	Catalans (a)	9	2/4/16
Benjamin Jullien	Warrington	Leeds (a)	1	4/2/16
Sean Kenny	Salford	Castleford (h)	20	1/7/16
Morgan Knowles	St Helens	Salford (a)	2	11/2/16
(club debut: York (h), CCR6, 15/5/15)				
George Lawler	Hull KR	Castleford (h)	1	5/2/16
(club debut: Widnes (a), S8-QR3, 23/8/15)				
Robert Lui	Salford	Hull (a)	1	5/2/16
Sika Manu	Hull	Salford (h)	1	5/2/16
Judah Mazive	Wakefield	Wigan (a)	S81	5/8/16
Greg Minikin	Castleford	Leeds (h)	7	24/3/16
Kieran Moran	Hull KR	Widnes (a)	4	3/3/16
Frazer Morris	Wakefield	Wigan (a)	S81	5/8/16
Bradley Moules	Wakefield	Castleford (h)	23	24/7/16
Ben Murdoch-Masila	Salford	Hull (a)	1	5/2/16
Romain Navarrete	Catalans	Huddersfield (h)	14	14/5/16
Frank-Paul Nuuausala	Wigan	Leeds (a)	22	15/7/16
Will Oakes	Hull KR	Wigan (a)	8	28/3/16
Dominique Peyroux	St Helens	Huddersfield (h)	1	5/2/16
Frank Pritchard	Hull	Salford (h)	1	5/2/16
Sam Rapira	Huddersfield	St Helens (a)	1	5/2/16
Charly Runciman	Widnes	Wakefield (a)	1	7/2/16
(club debut: Halifax (a), S8-QR1, 9/8/15)				
Matt Sarsfield	Salford	Hull (a)	1	5/2/16
James Segeyaro	Leeds	Hull (a)	21	8/7/16
Paul Seguier	Catalans	Wakefield (a)	S85	9/9/16
Kyle Shelford	Wigan	Wakefield (h)	21	8/7/16
Jake Shorrocks	Wigan	Widnes (a)	19	16/6/16
Cameron Smith	Leeds	Huddersfield (a)	13	29/4/16
Morgan Smith	Warrington	Wakefield (a)	14	15/5/16
(club debut: Oldham (a), CCR6, 7/5/16)				
Jake Spedding	St Helens	Warrington (a)	10	8/4/16
Glenn Stewart	Catalans	Wigan (a)	1	5/2/16
Tom Symonds	Huddersfield	Salford (a)	19	17/6/16
Dave Taylor	Catalans	Wigan (a)	1	5/2/16
Corey Thompson	Widnes	Wakefield (a)	1	7/2/16
David Thompson	Hull KR	Huddersfield (a)	21	8/7/16
Carlos Tuimavave	Hull	Salford (h)	1	5/2/16
Anthony Tupou	Wakefield	Widnes (h)	1	7/2/16
Daniel Vidot	Salford	St Helens (a)	14	13/5/16
(club debut: Castleford (a), CCR6, 7/5/16)				
Brad Walker	Widnes	Castleford (a)	18	9/6/16
Joe Wardill	Hull KR	Castleford (a)	8	28/3/16
Luke Waterworth	Wigan	Hull KR (h)	8	28/3/16
Calvin Wellington	St Helens	Huddersfield (MW)	15	22/5/16
Jack Wells	Wigan	Wakefield (a)	10	10/4/16
Connor Williams	Salford	Wigan (h)	17	3/6/16
Mikey Wood	Huddersfield	Castleford (a)	9	3/4/16
Sam Wood	Huddersfield	Wigan (h)	2	12/2/16

All totals in 'Super League Players 1996-2016' include play-off games & Super League Super 8s from 2015. 2015-2016 Super 8s (Qualifiers) not included.

SUPER LEAGUE XXI
Club by Club

21 October 2015 - scrum-half Liam Finn signs for Wakefield.

27 October 2015 - Joel Monaghan, released by Warrington, joins on two-year deal.

29 October 2015 - centre Greg Minikin signs from York City Knights on two-year deal.

19 November 2015 - Mike McMeeken signs two-year contract extension to end of 2018.

20 November 2015 - Matt Cook signs one-year contract extension to end of 2017.

21 November 2015 - winger Denny Solomona signs new contract to end of 2018.

27 December 2015 - 42-28 home festive friendly win over Featherstone.

7 February 2016 - last-minute converted try by Josh Mantellato means 16-all draw at Hull KR in round one. Captain Michael Shenton leaves field injured on 23 minutes.

8 February 2016 - Michael Shenton ruled out for season with ACL injury. Hull KR hooker John Boudebza gets four-match ban.

9 February 2016 - hooker Adam Milner signs two-year contract extension to end of 2018 season.

10 February 2016 - back-rower Oliver Holmes signs new two-year contract to end of 2018.

11 February 2016 - Andy Lynch agrees one-year contract extension to end of 2017.

14 February 2016 - Denny Solomona produces two spectacular finishes in 40-6 round-two home hammering of Wakefield.

26 February 2016 - debutant Jy Hitchcox scores two tries and Denny Solomona gets hat-trick in 31-24 win at Hull FC.

4 March 2016 - Junior Moors, Ben Roberts and Grant Millington injured in first defeat of season, by 28-22 at St Helens in round 4.

8 March 2016 - Junior Moors has surgery on hand and faces six weeks out.

9 March 2016 - Ben Roberts' two-year contract due to run out at end of season extended to end of 2019.

13 March 2016 - Justin Carney, on loan from Tigers, scores two tries in 32-16 home defeat by Salford.

18 March 2016 - 56-12 thrashing at table-topping Warrington. Matt Cook gets two-match ban for dangerous contact on Brad Dwyer.

24 March 2016 - late Jake Webster try earns 18-14 Easter Thursday home win over Leeds and ends three-match losing streak.

28 March 2016 - 41-22 Easter Monday defeat at Catalans.

3 April 2016 - Jy Hitchcox scores hat-trick in 38-34 home win over Huddersfield.

6 April 2016 - Lee Jewitt to leave at end of season to join Townsville Blackhawks.

7 April 2016 - Jake Webster agrees one-year contract extension to end of 2017.

10 April 2016 - Denny Solomona hat-trick helps secure 34-24 win at Widnes Vikings.

16 April 2016 - 26-12 defeat at Wigan.

21 April 2016 - Huddersfield forward Larne Patrick joins on loan until end of season.

24 April 2016 - 58-16 home defeat to Hull KR.

KEY DATES

25 April 2016 - on-loan Justin Carney signs permanent deal with Salford.

26 April 2016 - Danny Tickle joins from Widnes on loan to end of season.

1 May 2016 - Andy Lynch breaks fibula in 30-20 home defeat to St Helens.

3 May 2016 - Paddy Flynn signs from Widnes on loan to end of season.

7 May 2016 - Paul McShane stars at scrum-half in 32-18 Challenge Cup win over Salford.

12 May 2016 - Luke Dorn scores hat-trick in 52-12 defeat of Leeds at Headingley.

13 May 2016 - Luke Dorn announces retirement at end of season.

21 May 2016 - 34-14 win over Warrington at Magic Weekend after trailing 14-0. Ben Roberts aggravates foot injury.

24 May 2016 - Ben Roberts ruled out for season with foot injury.

27 May 2016 - 33-26 home defeat to Wigan.

3 June 2016 - Luke Gale signs new five-year contract to end of 2021.

4 June 2016 - 30-22 win at Huddersfield.

8 June 2016 - on-loan Larne Patrick signs permanent three-year deal.

10 June 2016 - Paddy Flynn scores hat-trick in 38-28 home defeat by Widnes.

13 June 2016 - Greg Eden re-signs from Brisbane on two-year contract from 2017.

19 June 2016 - Danny Tickle's late touchline conversion bounces back off post in 24-22 home defeat to league leaders Hull FC.

24 June 2016 - young stand-off Kieron Gill joins Oldham on loan.

25 June 2016 - 26-12 Challenge Cup quarter-final defeat at Wigan.

1 July 2016 - Mike McMeeken breaks fibula and Joel Monaghan dislocates elbow in 22-18 loss at Salford, a fourth successive defeat.

2 July 2016 - Rangi Chase returns on contract to end of season.

10 July 2016 - top-eight place secured with 38-24 home win over Catalans.

17 July 2016 - Rangi Chase makes second debut as Denny Solomona scores four tries in 42-26 home defeat by Warrington.

20 July 2016 - Andre Savelio joins from St Helens on loan until the end of season.

24 July 2016 - 30 points in last 23 minutes secures 46-20 win at Wakefield.

5 August 2016 - 30-16 opening Super 8s win at leaders Hull FC.

12 August 2016 - Denny Solomona scores hat-trick as 36-22 home win over Wigan boosts play-off hopes.

20 August 2016 - last-second Jack Hughes try means 14-11 defeat at Warrington.

1 September 2016 - injury-plagued Frankie Mariano not offered new contract.

2 September 2016 - Denny Solomona crosses for hat-trick in 46-22 home win over Wakefield.

8 September 2016 - 40-16 defeat at St Helens ends play-off chances.

17 September 2016 - Denny Solomona scores two tries to break Lesley Vainikolo's 12-year Super League record of 36 in a season in 34-28 win in Perpignan.

25 September 2016 - Denny Solomona scores hat-trick in 40-26 home win over Widnes to set new Super League tries-in-season record of 40.

28 September 2016 - Rangi Chase signs 12-month contract.

4 October 2016 - Matt Cook extends contract by 12 months to end of 2018.

CLUB RECORDS
Highest score: 106-0 v Rochdale, 9/9/2007 **Highest score against:** 12-76 v Leeds, 14/8/2009 **Record attendance:** 25,449 v Hunslet, 9/3/35

MATCH RECORDS
Tries: 5 Derek Foster v Hunslet, 10/11/72 John Joyner v Millom, 16/9/73 Steve Fenton v Dewsbury, 27/1/78 Ian French v Hunslet, 9/2/86 St John Ellis v Whitehaven, 10/12/89 **Goals:** 17 Sammy Lloyd v Millom, 16/9/73 **Points:** 43 Sammy Lloyd v Millom, 16/9/73

SEASON RECORDS
Tries: 42 Denny Solomona 2016 **Goals:** 158 Sammy Lloyd 1976-77 **Points:** 334 Bob Beardmore 1983-84

CAREER RECORDS
Tries: 206 Alan Hardisty 1958-71 **Goals:** 875 Albert Lunn 1951-63 **Points:** 1,870 Albert Lunn 1951-63 **Appearances:** 613 John Joyner 1973-92

CASTLEFORD TIGERS

DATE	FIXTURE	RESULT	SCORERS	LGE	ATT
7/2/16	Hull KR (a)	D16-16	t:Solomona,Webster(2) g:Gale(2)	6th	11,011
14/2/16	Wakefield (h)	W40-6	t:Solomona(2),Roberts,Dorn,O Holmes(2),Milner g:Gale(6)	5th	9,761
25/2/16	Hull FC (a)	W24-31	t:Hitchcox(2),Solomona(3) g:Gale(5) fg:Gale	4th	10,247
4/3/16	St Helens (a)	L28-22	t:Millington,McMeeken,Milner g:Gale(4),Crooks	5th	11,298
13/3/16	Salford (h)	L16-32	t:Solomona(3) g:Gale(2)	6th	8,151
18/3/16	Warrington (a)	L56-12	t:Monaghan,Springer g:Gale(2)	8th	10,940
24/3/16	Leeds (h)	W18-14	t:Lynch,Webster(2) g:Gale(3)	7th	11,426
28/3/16	Catalans Dragons (a)	L41-22	t:Minikin(2),Monaghan(2) g:Gale(3)	8th	10,351
3/4/16	Huddersfield (h)	W38-34	t:McMeeken(2),Minikin,Hitchcox(3),Webster g:Gale(5)	7th	6,631
10/4/16	Widnes (a)	W24-34	t:Solomona(3),Boyle,Gale,McShane g:Gale(5)	7th	5,081
15/4/16	Wigan (a)	L26-12	t:Solomona,Millington g:Gale(2)	7th	11,849
24/4/16	Hull KR (h)	L16-58	t:Webster,Hampshire,Hitchcox g:Gale(2)	7th	7,106
1/5/16	St Helens (h)	L20-30	t:Monaghan,Solomona,McMeeken,Hitchcox g:Gale(2)	8th	6,658
7/5/16	Salford (h) (CCR6)	W32-18	t:McMeeken(2),Webster,Solomona(2),McShane g:McShane(4)	N/A	3,317
12/5/16	Leeds (a)	W12-52	t:Dorn(3),Solomona(2),Monaghan,Springer,Crooks,Millington g:Gale(8)	7th	17,213
21/5/16	Warrington (MW) ●	W34-14	t:Dorn(2),Millington,Solomona(2),McMeeken g:Gale(5)	7th	N/A
26/5/16	Wigan (h)	L26-33	t:McShane,Solomona(2) g:Gale(5)	7th	5,558
3/6/16	Huddersfield (a)	W22-30	t:Solomona(2),Webster(2),Gale g:Gale(5)	6th	5,741
9/6/16	Widnes (h)	L28-38	t:Flynn(3),Patrick,Gale g:Gale(4)	7th	4,968
19/6/16	Hull FC (h)	L22-24	t:Dorn,Webster,Flynn,Solomona(2) g:Tickle	7th	10,790
25/6/16	Wigan (a) (CCQF)	L26-12	t:Gale,Crooks g:Gale(2)	N/A	8,010
1/7/16	Salford (a)	L22-18	t:Webster(2),Dorn g:Gale(3)	8th	2,275
10/7/16	Catalans Dragons (h)	W38-24	t:Hampshire(2),Mariano,McShane,Dorn(2),O Holmes g:Gale(5)	6th	5,586
17/7/16	Warrington (h)	L26-42	t:Mariano,Solomona(4),Crooks g:Gale	7th	8,060
24/7/16	Wakefield (a)	W20-46	t:Minikin(2),O Holmes,Savelio,Gale,Moors,T Holmes,Hampshire g:Gale(7)	6th	6,855
5/8/16	Hull FC (a) (S8)	W16-30	t:Minikin,Hampshire(2),Gale,Dorn,Milner g:Gale(3)	6th	9,936
12/8/16	Wigan (h) (S8)	W36-22	t:Solomona(3),McShane,Hampshire,O Holmes g:Gale(6)	6th	6,325
20/8/16	Warrington (a) (S8)	L14-11	t:Solomona g:Gale(3) fg:Gale	6th	9,228
2/9/16	Wakefield (h) (S8)	W46-22	t:Solomona(3),Chase,Dorn,McShane,Webster,Gale g:Gale(7)	6th	6,283
8/9/16	St Helens (a) (S8)	L40-16	t:Dorn,Hampshire,Maher g:Gale(2)	6th	9,448
17/9/16	Catalans Dragons (a) (S8)	W28-34	t:Flynn(2),Solomona(2),Crooks(2) g:Gale(5)	6th	7,802
25/9/16	Widnes (h) (S8)	W40-26	t:Dorn,Solomona(3),Crooks,Cook,McShane g:Gale(6)	5th	7,103

● Played at St James' Park, Newcastle

		APP		TRIES		GOALS		FG		PTS	
	D.O.B.	ALL	SL	ALL	SL	ALL	SL	ALL	SL	ALL	SL
Ryan Boyle	17/10/87	2(4)	2(4)	1	1	0	0	0	0	4	4
Rangi Chase	11/4/86	5(2)	5(2)	1	1	0	0	0	0	4	4
Matt Cook	14/11/86	7(22)	7(20)	1	1	0	0	0	0	4	4
Ben Crooks	15/6/93	26(2)	24(2)	6	5	1	1	0	0	26	22
Luke Dorn	2/7/82	21	20	14	14	0	0	0	0	56	56
Brandon Douglas	17/8/97	(1)	(1)	0	0	0	0	0	0	0	0
Conor Fitzsimmons	7/5/98	(2)	(2)	0	0	0	0	0	0	0	0
Paddy Flynn	11/12/87	9(1)	9(1)	6	6	0	0	0	0	24	24
Luke Gale	22/6/88	30	29	7	6	120	118	2	2	270	262
Ryan Hampshire	29/12/94	20(2)	19(2)	8	8	0	0	0	0	32	32
Jy Hitchcox	18/8/89	8(1)	8	7	7	0	0	0	0	28	28
Oliver Holmes	7/8/92	13(2)	13(1)	5	5	0	0	0	0	20	20
Tom Holmes	2/3/96	4(3)	4(3)	1	1	0	0	0	0	4	4
Lee Jewitt	14/2/87	16(2)	14(2)	0	0	0	0	0	0	0	0
Andy Lynch	20/10/79	12	12	1	1	0	0	0	0	4	4
Will Maher	4/11/95	1(14)	1(14)	1	1	0	0	0	0	4	4
Frankie Mariano	10/5/87	2(3)	2(3)	2	2	0	0	0	0	8	8
Nathan Massey	11/7/89	18(3)	16(3)	0	0	0	0	0	0	0	0
Mike McMeeken	10/5/94	21(2)	19(2)	7	5	0	0	0	0	28	20
Paul McShane	19/11/89	18(14)	16(14)	7	6	4	0	0	0	36	24
Grant Millington	1/11/86	15(12)	13(12)	4	4	0	0	0	0	16	16
Adam Milner	19/12/91	26(6)	25(5)	3	3	0	0	0	0	12	12
Greg Minikin	29/3/95	16(1)	15(1)	6	6	0	0	0	0	24	24
Joel Monaghan	22/4/82	18	16	5	5	0	0	0	0	20	20
Junior Moors	30/7/86	18(4)	16(4)	1	1	0	0	0	0	4	4
Larne Patrick	3/11/88	16(1)	14(1)	1	1	0	0	0	0	4	4
Ben Roberts	8/7/85	5	5	1	1	0	0	0	0	4	4
Andre Savelio	21/3/95	6(1)	6(1)	1	1	0	0	0	0	4	4
Michael Shenton	22/7/86	1	1	0	0	0	0	0	0	0	0
Denny Solomona	27/10/93	29	27	42	40	0	0	0	0	168	160
Gadwin Springer	4/4/93	6(15)	6(14)	2	2	0	0	0	0	8	8
Danny Tickle	10/3/83	6(5)	6(3)	0	0	1	1	0	0	2	2
Jake Webster	29/10/83	21(2)	20(2)	14	13	0	0	0	0	56	52

Denny Solomona

LEAGUE RECORD
P30-W15-D1-L14
(5th, SL)
F830, A808, Diff+22
31 points.

CHALLENGE CUP
Quarter Finalists

ATTENDANCES
Best - v Leeds (SL - 11,426)
Worst - v Salford (CC - 3,317)
Total (SL/S8s only) - 104,406
Average (SL/S8s only) - 7,458
(Up by 361 on 2015)

'SL' totals include Super 8s; 'All' totals also include Challenge Cup

18 November 2015 - Dragons hold talks with Australian forward Willie Mason.

7 December 2015 - Willie Tonga released from contract with a year to go to join Leigh.

23 January 2016 - 26-16 friendly defeat at Huddersfield.

27 January 2016 - Remi Casty named club captain for 2016 season.

4 February 2016 - Paul Aiton and Louis Anderson injured early in first half of 12-6 round-one defeat at boggy Wigan.

8 February 2016 - Paul Aiton out for six weeks with torn pectoral.

13 February 2016 - 38-10 round-two home defeat by Hull FC.

15 February 2016 - Willie Mason signs on one-year contract.

27 February 2016 - Willie Mason makes debut in first win of season, by 32-28 at home to Leeds.

6 March 2016 - 42-28 win at Wakefield in round 4 after leading 26-0 after 25 minutes.

12 March 2016 - 30-20 home defeat to Warrington.

20 March 2016 - Jodie Broughton scores hat-trick in 46-26 win at Huddersfield. Krisnan Inu gets three-match ban for dangerous tackle on Eorl Crabtree.

25 March 2016 - Dave Taylor double helps secure 26-12 Good Friday win at Salford.

25 March 2016 - Morgan Escaré scores two tries in seasonal debut in 41-22 home Easter Monday win over Castleford. Remi Casty suffers rib injury.

2 April 2016 - hard 21-8 home win over Widnes is fourth straight win.

7 April 2016 - Jodie Broughton scores two tries in 40-nil away TV hammering of Hull KR. Eloi Pelissier banned for two games for dangerous contact on Adam Walker.

14 April 2016 - Jodie Broughton scores four tries in televised 30-12 win at St Helens.

16 April 2016 - reserve team Saint-Esteve XIII Catalan win Coupe de France with 33-16 win over Limoux in Carcassonne.

23 April 2016 - Krisnan Inu suffers season-ending knee injury in 42-32 home win over Salford.

29 April 2016 - 28-26 defeat at Hull FC ends seven-match winning run.

6 May 2016 - 40-4 win at Batley ensures passage into Challenge Cup quarter-finals.

10 May 2016 - Dave Taylor and Jason Baitieri get one-match bans on EGPs for dangerous throws in Batley game.

14 May 2016 - Richie Myler suffers groin injury in early stages of 16-14 home win over Huddersfield.

22 May 2016 - late field goal means 25-24 defeat to Wakefield at Magic Weekend.

26 May 2016 - back-rower Ugo Perez joins Championship side Whitehaven on loan until end of season.

28 May 2016 - 34-16 home win over Hull KR.

3 June 2016 - 12 home-grown players record 24-12 win at Leeds.

11 June 2016 - 33-16 home win over St Helens.

KEY DATES

14 June 2016 - Justin Horo takes EGP and avoids suspension for dangerous tackle on Adam Swift.

17 June 2016 - late Kurt Gidley penalty goal means 20-18 defeat at Warrington.

22 June 2016 - Tony Gigot gets one match for dangerous tackle on Ryan Atkins.

25 June 2016 - 22-8 defeat Hull FC in Challenge Cup quarter-final.

28 June 2016 - Eloi Pelissier escapes suspension but gets fine for tripping.

2 July 2016 - record crowd celebrates ten-year anniversary before 26-6 home defeat to Wigan.

10 July 2016 - 38-24 defeat at Castleford is fourth in a row.

16 July 2016 - Pat Richards misses conversion to Fouad Yaha's late try in 30-28 home defeat by Wakefield. Richards and Willie Mason out for season with ankle injuries.

18 July 2016 - Antoni Maria to leave at the end of season to join Leigh Centurions

21 July 2016 - Pat Richards to retire at end of season.

24 July 2016 - 32-4 defeat at Widnes means fifth-spot regular season finish. Antoni Maria out for season with ankle injury

28 July 2016 - winger Jodie Broughton signs new two-year deal until 2019.

2 August 2016 - centre Vincent Duport signs new two year contract to end of 2018.

6 August 2016 - Fouad Yaha scores 17-minute second-half hat-trick as 26-10 home win over Widnes ends run of five straight defeats.

9 August 2016 - Krisnan Inu signs new two-year contract to end of 2018.

10 August 2016 - Willie Mason and club agree immediate release.

12 August 2016 - Todd Carney out for season with knee ligament damage in 39-16 defeat at St Helens.

18 August 2016 - 44-0 defeat at Hull FC.

30 August 2016 - Dave Taylor suspended for two games for dangerous throw against Hull FC. And found not guilty of gouging Jonny Lomax in defeat at St Helens.

3 September 2016 - late Ben Currie try secures Warrington 26-22 win in Perpignan.

6 September 2016 - young prop Romain Navarrete suspended for two games for raising knee in tackle. Julian Bousquet (raising knee in tackle) and Richie Myler (tripping) avoid bans with EGPs.

9 September 2016 - 14-10 win at Wakefield ends three-match losing run.

12 September 2016 - Olivier Elima to leave at end of season.

13 September 2016 - halfback Stan Robin to join Toulouse at end of season.

13 September 2016 - Jason Baitieri suffers season-ending ankle injury in training.

13 September 2016 - Greg Mounis to retire at end of season.

15 September 2016 - Fouad Yaha suffers season-ending ankle injury in training.

15 September 2016 - Thomas Bosc signs new one year contract extension to end of 2017.

16 September 2016 - Glenn Stewart released for family reasons.

17 September 2016 - 34-28 home defeat by Castleford.

22 September 2016 - hooker Eloi Pelissier to leave the club at end of season.

23 September 2016 - season ends with 48-24 defeat at Wigan.

5 October 2016 - young prop Romain Navarrete signs for Wigan.

11 October 2016 - former prop Alex Chan to return as general manager on three-year contract.

12 October 2016 - former forward Greg Bird signs five-year contract, three years as player and two as assistant coach.

18 October 2016 - Todd Carney, Morgan Escaré and Dave Taylor released from remainder of contract by mutual agreement. Escaré joins Wigan.

18 October 2016 - Luke Burgess signs from Manly on two-year contract.

CLUB RECORDS

Highest score: 92-8 v York, 12/5/2013
Highest score against:
12-60 v Leeds, 15/9/2006
16-60 v Huddersfield, 28/6/2013
Record attendance: 18,150 v Warrington, 20/6/2009 *(Barcelona)*
11,856 v Wigan, 2/7/2016 *(Stade Gilbert Brutus)*

MATCH RECORDS

Tries:
4 Justin Murphy v Warrington, 13/9/2008
Damien Cardace v Widnes, 31/3/2012
Kevin Larroyer v York, 12/5/2012
Jodie Broughton v St Helens, 14/4/2016
Goals:
11 Thomas Bosc v Featherstone, 31/3/2007
Thomas Bosc v Batley, 29/5/2010
Scott Dureau v Widnes, 31/3/2012
Points:
26 Thomas Bosc v Featherstone, 31/3/2007

SEASON RECORDS

Tries: 29 Morgan Escare 2014
Goals: 134 Scott Dureau 2012
Points: 319 Scott Dureau 2012

CAREER RECORDS

Tries: 86 Clint Greenshields 2007-2012
Goals:
579 *(inc 14fg)* Thomas Bosc 2006-2016
Points: 1,376 Thomas Bosc 2006-2016
Appearances:
273 Gregory Mounis 2006-2016

CATALANS DRAGONS

DATE	FIXTURE	RESULT	SCORERS	LGE	ATT
5/2/16	Wigan (a)	L12-6	t:Horo g:Richards	9th	13,436
13/2/16	Hull FC (h)	L10-38	t:Richards(2) g:Richards	10th	10,234
27/2/16	Leeds (h)	W32-28	t:Taylor(2),Myler,Inu,Gigot g:Richards(6)	8th	8,172
6/3/16	Wakefield (a)	W28-42	t:Broughton,Duport,Richards,Baitieri,Stewart,Myler,Gigot(2) g:Richards(5)	8th	4,442
12/3/16	Warrington (h)	L20-30	t:Carney,Richards,Duport g:Richards(4)	8th	8,859
20/3/16	Huddersfield (a)	W26-46	t:Anderson,Stewart,Broughton(3),Aiton,Bousquet,Myler g:Richards(7)	7th	4,607
25/3/16	Salford (a)	W12-26	t:Gigot,Pelissier,Taylor(2) g:Richards(5)	6th	3,485
28/3/16	Castleford (h)	W41-22	t:Broughton,Anderson,Carney(2),Escare(2),Aiton g:Bosc(6) fg:Escare	4th	10,351
2/4/16	Widnes (h)	W21-8	t:Richards,Duport,Taylor,Pelissier g:Richards(2) fg:Bosc	4th	8,642
7/4/16	Hull KR (a)	W0-40	t:Broughton(2),Duport,Inu,Mounis,Myler,Mason g:Richards(5),Bosc	2nd	6,764
14/4/16	St Helens (a)	W12-30	t:Broughton(4),Myler,Richards g:Richards(3)	2nd	9,362
23/4/16	Salford (h)	W42-32	t:Broughton(2),Escare,Duport,Myler(2),Richards g:Richards(6),Bosc	2nd	9,686
29/4/16	Hull FC (a)	L28-26	t:Anderson,Richards(2),Baitieri,Pelissier g:Richards(3)	2nd	11,374
6/5/16	Batley (a) (CCR6)	W4-40	t:Yaha,Duport(2),Myler,Taylor,Gigot(2) g:Richards(6)	N/A	1,249
14/5/16	Huddersfield (h)	W16-14	t:Anderson,Horo,Gigot g:Richards(2)	2nd	10,387
22/5/16	Wakefield (MW) ●	L24-25	t:Horo,Broughton(2),Gigot,Duport g:Richards(2)	3rd	N/A
28/5/16	Hull KR (h)	W34-16	t:Broughton,Carney,Albert,Anderson,Gigot(2) g:Richards(5)	3rd	9,859
3/6/16	Leeds (a)	W12-24	t:Horo,Yaha,Baitieri,Pelissier g:Carney(4)	3rd	14,016
11/6/16	St Helens (h)	W33-16	t:Yaha,Albert,Broughton(2),Escare,Gigot g:Richards(2),Bosc(2) fg:Carney	2nd	10,789
17/6/16	Warrington (a)	L20-18	t:Bousquet,Yaha g:Richards(5)	4th	9,259
25/6/16	Hull FC (a) (CCQF)	L22-8	t:Garcia,Yaha	N/A	9,639
2/7/16	Wigan (h)	L6-26	t:Horo g:Richards	4th	11,856
10/7/16	Castleford (a)	L38-24	t:Horo,Yaha,Casty,Bousquet g:Bosc(3),Gigot	4th	5,586
16/7/16	Wakefield (h)	L28-30	t:Gigot,Taylor,Horo,Escare,Yaha g:Richards(4)	4th	8,562
24/7/16	Widnes (a)	L32-4	t:Taylor	5th	4,195
6/8/16	Widnes (h) (S8)	W26-10	t:Broughton,Horo,Yaha(3) g:Bosc(3)	5th	8,562
12/8/16	St Helens (a) (S8)	L39-16	t:Taylor,Baitieri,Duport g:Albert(2)	5th	9,440
18/8/16	Hull FC (a) (S8)	L44-0		5th	10,494
3/9/16	Warrington (h) (S8)	L22-26	t:Duport,Myler,Garcia g:Gigot(5)	5th	7,108
9/9/16	Wakefield (a) (S8)	W10-14	t:Baitieri,Bousquet g:Gigot(3)	5th	2,612
17/9/16	Castleford (h) (S8)	L28-34	t:Elima,Stewart,Pelissier,Anderson,Myler g:Gigot(4)	5th	7,802
23/9/16	Wigan (a) (S8)	L48-24	t:Duport,Horo,Albert,Myler,Sigismeau g:Myler(2)	6th	16,140

● Played at St James' Park, Newcastle

	D.O.B.	APP ALL	SL	TRIES ALL	SL	GOALS ALL	SL	FG ALL	SL	PTS ALL	SL
Paul Aiton	29/5/85	6(6)	6(6)	2	2	0	0	0	0	8	8
Lucas Albert	4/7/98	12	10	3	3	2	2	0	0	16	16
Louis Anderson	27/6/85	18(3)	17(3)	6	6	0	0	0	0	24	24
Jason Baitieri	2/7/89	25(2)	23(2)	5	5	0	0	0	0	20	20
Thomas Bosc	5/8/83	7(13)	7(11)	0	0	16	16	1	1	33	33
Julian Bousquet	18/7/91	12(20)	12(18)	4	4	0	0	0	0	16	16
Jodie Broughton	9/1/88	27	26	19	19	0	0	0	0	76	76
Todd Carney	2/6/86	21	20	4	4	4	4	1	1	25	25
Remi Casty	5/2/85	20(7)	18(7)	1	1	0	0	0	0	4	4
Alrix Da Costa	2/10/97	4(3)	4(3)	0	0	0	0	0	0	0	0
Jordan Dezaria	6/11/96	(1)	(1)	0	0	0	0	0	0	0	0
Vincent Duport	15/12/87	28	27	11	9	0	0	0	0	44	36
Olivier Elima	19/5/83	3(6)	3(6)	1	1	0	0	0	0	4	4
Morgan Escare	18/10/91	10	9	5	5	0	0	1	1	21	21
Benjamin Garcia	5/4/93	12	11	2	1	0	0	0	0	8	4
Tony Gigot	27/12/90	30	29	12	10	13	13	0	0	74	66
Justin Horo	7/9/86	25(1)	23(1)	9	9	0	0	0	0	36	36
Krisnan Inu	17/3/87	9	9	2	2	0	0	0	0	8	8
Thibaut Margalet	3/1/93	(1)	(1)	0	0	0	0	0	0	0	0
Antoni Maria	21/3/87	3(9)	3(9)	0	0	0	0	0	0	0	0
Willie Mason	15/4/80	7(9)	6(8)	1	1	0	0	0	0	4	4
Gregory Mounis	18/1/85	4(18)	4(16)	1	1	0	0	0	0	4	4
Richard Myler	21/5/90	19	18	11	10	2	2	0	0	48	44
Romain Navarrete	30/6/94	(11)	(11)	0	0	0	0	0	0	0	0
Eloi Pelissier	18/6/91	22(7)	20(7)	5	5	0	0	0	0	20	20
Pat Richards	27/2/82	21	19	9	9	75	69	0	0	186	174
Stan Robin	21/10/90	(1)	(1)	0	0	0	0	0	0	0	0
Paul Seguier	8/9/97	(3)	(3)	0	0	0	0	0	0	0	0
Jordan Sigismeau	22/12/92	3	3	1	1	0	0	0	0	4	4
Glenn Stewart	11/1/84	30	28	3	3	0	0	0	0	12	12
Dave Taylor	7/8/88	21(5)	20(4)	9	8	0	0	0	0	36	32
Fouad Yaha	19/8/96	17	15	10	8	0	0	0	0	40	32

'SL' totals include Super 8s; 'All' totals also include Challenge Cup

Jodie Broughton

LEAGUE RECORD
P30-W15-D0-L15
(6th, SL)
F723, A716, Diff+7
30 points.

CHALLENGE CUP
Quarter Finalists

ATTENDANCES
Best - v Wigan (SL - 11,856)
Worst - v Warrington (S8 - 7,108)
Total (SL/S8s only) - 130,869
Average (SL/S8s only) - 9,348
(Up by 713 on 2015)

KEY DATES

9 October 2015 - Giants fined £1,000 for breaching RFL Operational Rules surrounding management of concussion in previous season's game with Castleford.

21 October 2015 - Jacob Wardle, brother of Joe, promoted to first team squad.

15 December 2015 - England forward Brett Ferres transfer listed following investigation into 'conduct away from the field'.

4 January 2016 - Brett Ferres signs for Leeds.

6 January 2016 - Craig Huby breaks wrist in training and will miss start of season.

17 January 2016 - 38-6 victory at Hull KR in David Hodgson's Testimonial.

23 January 2016 - 26-16 home friendly win over Catalans.

5 February 2016 - captain Danny Brough withdrawn at half-time and Scott Grix dislocates shoulder in 30-16 round-one defeat at St Helens.

8 February 2016 - former St Helens and Bradford winger Jamie Foster arrives on trial.

9 February 2016 - Luke Robinson, aged 31, forced to retire with hip injury.

12 February 2016 - late Josh Charnley try means 18-13 round-two home defeat for injury-hit Giants.

20 February 2016 - Michael Lawrence signs contract extension to end of 2019.

28 February 2016 - Jamie Ellis injures shoulder in first half of 36-18 home defeat by Widnes and faces 12 weeks out.

4 March 2016 - Danny Brough returns in 20-16 defeat at Leeds.

9 March 2016 - Jordan Tansey joins from Wakefield on one-month loan.

13 March 2016 - Jermaine McGillvary scores 100th Super League try in first win of season, by 38-6 over Hull KR at home.

20 March 2016 - Joe Wardle gets two-match ban for high tackle on Remi Casty following 46-26 home defeat by Catalans.

21 March 2016 - Leigh stand-off Ryan Brierley signs on four-and-a-half year contract.

25 March 2016 - Ryan Brierley makes debut in 36-22 Good Friday defeat at Wakefield.

28 March 2016 - 26-24 home Easter Monday defeat to Salford.

3 April 2016 - Jermaine McGillvary scores hat-trick in 38-34 defeat at Castleford to make it eight defeats from nine games.

5 April 2016 - winger Gene Ormsby joins on month's loan from Warrington.

9 April 2016 - captain Danny Brough's sin-binning crucial in 37-20 defeat at in-form Hull FC.

16 April 2016 - Danny Brough masterminds rain-soaked 11-0 home win over league leaders Warrington.

21 April 2016 - Larne Patrick joins Castleford on loan to end of season.

21 April 2016 - Ryan Brierley scores hat-trick in 26-19 defeat at Wigan. Craig Huby tears pectoral.

29 April 2016 - Giants move off bottom of table with 28-20 home win over Leeds.

2 May 2016 - coach Paul Anderson fined £500, half suspended, following comments about referee following Round 12 defeat at Wigan.

6 May 2016 - 36-22 home Challenge Cup win over Leeds.

15 May 2016 - St George Illawarra back-rower Sebastine Ikahihifo joins on two-and-a-half year deal.

21 May 2016 - halfback Jamie Ellis signs new contract to end of 2019.

22 May 2016 - 48-20 win over St Helens at Magic Weekend.

25 May 2016 - assistant coach Kieron Purtill to leave for Leigh at end of season.

26 May 2016 - young prop Nathan Mason extends contract to end of 2018.

29 May 2016 - Sebastine Ikahihifo breaks jaw in 24-20 defeat at Widnes.

4 June 2016 - 30-22 home defeat by Castleford.

8 June 2016 - on-loan Larne Patrick signs permanent three-year deal with Castleford.

12 June 2016 - 10-2 home defeat to Wakefield.

14 June 2016 - young player Ronan Costello dies after serious injury in Academy game with Salford the previous Saturday.

15 June 2016 - Manly back-rower Tom Symonds joins on three-and-a-half-year contract.

16 June 2016 - head coach Paul Anderson and assistant Kieron Purtill sacked. Head of youth Andy Kelly takes charge.

18 June 2016 - Jake Connor set to move to Hull FC at season end. Giants demand transfer fee.

23 June 2016 - 28-16 home Challenge Cup defeat to Wakefield.

28 June 2016 - Danny Brough suspended for one game for high tackle on Reece Lyne.

30 June 2016 - Jake Connor stars in 22-12 home win over league leaders Hull FC.

8 July 2016 - 19-6 lead at Hull KR ends in 20-19 defeat.

11 July 2016 - former Newcastle Knights coach Rick Stone appointed head coach until end of 2018 season.

14 July 2016 - Warrington winger Gene Ormsby joins with immediate effect after agreeing to join Giants for 2017 season.

17 July 2016 - 34-18 home defeat by St Helens in Rick Stone's first game in charge.

23 July 2016 - Gene Ormsby scores hat-trick in 34-30 last-regular round defeat at Warrington.

7 August 2016 - 34-12 defeat at Salford in first Middle Eights game.

9 August 2016 - Danny Brough gets two-match ban for striking with elbow.

14 August 2016 - Rick Stone gets first win with 62-16 home Qualifiers Super 8s victory over Featherstone.

21 August 2016 - Ryan Brierley scores hat-trick of tries in comfortable 58-28 win at Batley.

3 September 2016 - 40-4 home win over London Broncos.

10 September 2016 - 48-40 defeat at Leigh after trailing 48-10.

18 September 2016 - 22-14 home win ends Leeds Rhinos' eight-match winning run.

24 September 2016 - Danny Brough field goal seven minutes from time secures Super League status with 23-22 win at Hull KR.

26 September 2016 - Scott Grix re-signs for Wakefield.

CLUB RECORDS

Highest score:
142-4 v Blackpool G, 26/11/94
Highest score against:
12-94 v Castleford, 18/9/88
Record attendance:
32,912 v Wigan, 4/3/50 *(Fartown)*
15,629 v Leeds, 10/2/2008
(McAlpine/Galpharm/John Smith's Stadium)

MATCH RECORDS

Tries:
10 Lionel Cooper v Keighley, 17/11/51
Goals: 18 Major Holland
v Swinton Park, 28/2/1914
Points: 39 Major Holland
v Swinton Park, 28/2/1914

SEASON RECORDS

Tries: 80 Albert Rosenfeld 1913-14
Goals: 156 *(inc 2fg)* Danny Brough 2013
Points: 346 Danny Brough 2013

CAREER RECORDS

Tries: 420 Lionel Cooper 1947-55
Goals: 958 Frank Dyson 1949-63
Points: 2,072 Frank Dyson 1949-63
Appearances: 485 Douglas Clark 1909-29

HUDDERSFIELD GIANTS

DATE	FIXTURE	RESULT	SCORERS	LGE	ATT
5/2/16	St Helens (a)	L30-16	t:Murphy,Ta'ai,Connor g:Ellis(2)	11th	10,408
12/2/16	Wigan (h)	L13-18	t:McGillvary,Foster g:Ellis(2) fg:Ellis	9th	5,912
28/2/16	Widnes (h)	L18-36	t:Lawrence,Patrick,Foster g:Foster(3)	11th	5,183
4/3/16	Leeds (a)	L20-16	t:Brough,McGillvary,Lawrence g:Foster(2)	12th	14,692
13/3/16	Hull KR (h)	W38-6	t:Tansey,Lawrence,Murphy,McGillvary,Patrick,Ta'ai g:Brough(7)	9th	5,610
20/3/16	Catalans Dragons (h)	L26-46	t:Connor,McGillvary,Patrick,Cudjoe,Leeming g:Brough(2),Tansey	11th	4,607
25/3/16	Wakefield (a)	L36-22	t:McGillvary,Connor(2),Murphy g:Brough(3)	12th	4,989
28/3/16	Salford (h)	L24-26	t:Ta'ai(2),Connor,McGillvary g:Brough(4)	12th	4,885
3/4/16	Castleford (a)	L38-34	t:Cudjoe(2),McGillvary(3),Rapira g:Brough(5)	12th	6,631
8/4/16	Hull FC (a)	L37-20	t:Wardle,Murphy,Brough,McGillvary g:Brough(2)	12th	10,557
15/4/16	Warrington (h)	W11-0	t:Murphy,Cudjoe g:Brough fg:Brough	12th	5,427
21/4/16	Wigan (a)	L26-19	t:Brierley(3) g:Brough(3) fg:Brough	12th	10,914
29/4/16	Leeds (h)	W28-20	t:Ta'ai,Ormsby,McGillvary,Connor,Crabtree g:Brough(4)	11th	7,536
6/5/16	Leeds (h) (CCR6)	W36-22	t:Ta'ai,McGillvary,Brierley,K Wood,Brough g:Brough(6) fg:Connor,Brough(3)	N/A	4,979
14/5/16	Catalans Dragons (a)	L16-14	t:Mason,Connor g:Brough(3)	11th	10,387
22/5/16	St Helens (MW) ●	W48-20	t:McGillvary(2),Ta'ai,Murphy,Hinchcliffe,K Wood g:Brough(8)	11th	N/A
29/5/16	Widnes (a)	L24-20	t:Mason,Brough,Wardle,McGillvary g:Brough(2)	11th	4,683
3/6/16	Castleford (h)	L22-30	t:Ellis,Cudjoe,Brierley,Connor g:Ellis(3)	11th	5,741
12/6/16	Wakefield (h)	L2-10	g:Brough	11th	5,077
17/6/16	Salford (a)	W30-31	t:Connor,Ta'ai,Cudjoe,Crabtree,Wardle g:Brough(5) fg:Brough	11th	1,958
23/6/16	Wakefield (h) (CCQF)	L16-28	t:Grix,Connor,McGillvary(2)	N/A	3,289
30/6/16	Hull FC (h)	W22-12	t:Lawrence,Symonds,McGillvary(2) g:Ellis(3)	10th	4,143
8/7/16	Hull KR (a)	L20-19	t:Brierley,Connor,Ellis g:Ellis(3) fg:Brough	11th	6,434
17/7/16	St Helens (h)	L18-34	t:Brough,Symonds,McGillvary g:Brough(3)	12th	5,526
23/7/16	Warrington (a)	L34-30	t:Ormsby(3),Murphy,Mason,Huby g:Brough(3)	12th	9,829
7/8/16	Salford (a) (S8-Q)	L34-12	t:Mason,Roberts g:Brough(2)	6th(S8-Q)	2,184
14/8/16	Featherstone (h) (S8-Q)	W62-16	t:Lawrence,Roberts(2),Ormsby,Brierley(2),Ta'ai(2),K Wood(2),Hinchcliffe g:Ellis(9)	5th(S8-Q)	3,690
21/8/16	Batley (a) (S8-Q)	W28-58	t:Cudjoe(2),Ormsby,Crabtree,Symonds(2),Connor,Wardle,Brierley(3) g:Ellis(7)	3rd(S8-Q)	2,201
2/9/16	London Broncos (h) (S8-Q)	W40-4	t:McGillvary,Cudjoe(2),Wardle,Lawrence,Brough,Murphy g:Brough(6)	3rd(S8-Q)	3,794
10/9/16	Leigh (a) (S8-Q)	L48-40	t:Lawrence,Murphy,Connor,Cudjoe(2),Ellis(2) g:Brough(6)	4th(S8-Q)	5,934
18/9/16	Leeds (h) (S8-Q)	W22-14	t:Cudjoe,Brierley,Brough g:Brough(5)	4th(S8-Q)	6,666
24/9/16	Hull KR (a) (S8-Q)	W22-23	t:Brierley(2),Cudjoe,Murphy g:Brough(3) fg:Brough	3rd(S8-Q)	8,024

● *Played at St James' Park, Newcastle*

		APP		TRIES		GOALS		FG		PTS	
	D.O.B.	ALL	SL	ALL	SL	ALL	SL	ALL	SL	ALL	SL
Ryan Brierley	12/3/92	18(1)	13(1)	14	5	0	0	0	0	56	20
Danny Brough	15/1/83	25(1)	18(1)	7	4	84	56	8	4	204	132
Jake Connor	18/10/94	30(1)	21(1)	13	10	0	0	1	0	53	40
Eorl Crabtree	2/10/82	14(8)	9(7)	3	2	0	0	0	0	12	8
Leroy Cudjoe	7/4/88	32	23	14	6	0	0	0	0	56	24
Tyler Dickinson	18/8/96	(1)	(1)	0	0	0	0	0	0	0	0
Jamie Ellis	4/10/89	17(1)	11(1)	5	3	29	13	1	1	79	39
Jamie Foster	27/7/90	3	3	2	2	5	5	0	0	18	18
Scott Grix	1/5/84	9	5	1	0	0	0	0	0	4	0
Ryan Hinchcliffe	7/10/84	30(1)	21(1)	2	1	0	0	0	0	8	4
Craig Huby	21/5/86	15	8	1	1	0	0	0	0	4	4
Sebastine Ikahihifo	27/1/91	4(7)	1(3)	0	0	0	0	0	0	0	0
Josh Johnson	25/7/94	8(9)	7(7)	0	0	0	0	0	0	0	0
Michael Lawrence	12/4/90	32	23	7	4	0	0	0	0	28	16
Kruise Leeming	7/9/95	3(14)	3(12)	1	1	0	0	0	0	4	4
Nathan Mason	8/9/93	3(22)	3(15)	4	3	0	0	0	0	16	12
Jermaine McGillvary	16/5/88	28	22	21	17	0	0	0	0	84	68
Aaron Murphy	26/11/88	30(1)	22	10	7	0	0	0	0	40	28
Gene Ormsby	12/9/92	7	4	6	4	0	0	0	0	24	16
Larne Patrick	3/11/88	5(5)	5(5)	3	3	0	0	0	0	12	12
Sam Rapira	8/4/87	17(13)	15(8)	2	2	0	0	0	0	8	8
Oliver Roberts	24/12/94	5(25)	4(18)	3	0	0	0	0	0	12	0
Jared Simpson	4/1/96	1	1	0	0	0	0	0	0	0	0
Daniel Smith	20/3/93	1(3)	1(3)	0	0	0	0	0	0	0	0
Tom Symonds	17/2/89	9	4	4	2	0	0	0	0	16	8
Ukuma Ta'ai	17/1/87	32	23	10	7	0	0	0	0	40	28
Jordan Tansey	9/9/86	2	2	1	1	1	1	0	0	6	6
Joe Wardle	22/9/91	21	13	5	3	0	0	0	0	20	12
Kyle Wood	18/6/89	11(12)	10(6)	4	1	0	0	0	0	16	4
Mikey Wood	18/4/96	(1)	(1)	0	0	0	0	0	0	0	0
Sam Wood	11/6/97	4(1)	4	0	0	0	0	0	0	0	0

'SL' totals include regular season only; 'All' totals also include Super 8s (Qualifiers) & Challenge Cup

Ukuma Ta'ai

LEAGUE RECORD
SL: P23-W6-D0-L17 (12th)
F511, A569, Diff-58, 12 points.

S8-Q: P7-W5-D0-L2 (3rd)
F257, A166, Diff+91, 10 points.

CHALLENGE CUP
Quarter Finalists

ATTENDANCES
Best - v Leeds (SL - 7,536)
Worst - v Wakefield (CC - 3,289)
Total (SL/S8s only) - 73,797
Average (SL/S8s only) - 5,271
(Down by 671 on 2015)

20 October 2015 - Warrington Wolves pay transfer fee of 150,000 pounds to sign Joe Westerman.

12 November 2015 - new signing Frank Pritchard rejects last-minute offers to keep him in NRL.

30 November 2015 - former Leeds player Lee Smith arrives on trial.

13 January 2016 - Iafeta Palea'aesina appointed new player welfare officer which will combine with playing role.

24 January 2016 - 60-20 home thrashing of Hull Kingston Rovers to win Clive Sullivan Trophy.

28 January 2016 - Australian forward Mark Minichiello agrees contract extension to end of 2017 season.

30 January 2016 - Gareth Ellis to remain as captain for 2016.

5 February 2016 - Carlos Tuimavave and Mahe Fonua score debut tries in comfortable 42-20 round-one home win over Salford.

11 February 2016 - Mahe Fonua to undergo surgery on knee injured in round one. Proposed loan move to Huddersfield of Curtis Naughton called off.

13 February 2016 - Jamie Shaul misses birth of first child and stars in 38-10 round-two victory at Catalans.

18 February 2016 - Richard Whiting goes to Leigh on two-months' loan.

25 February 2016 - Jamie Shaul scores two tries in first defeat of season, by 31-24 at home to Castleford.

4 March 2016 - two late Matty Smith field goals earn Wigan 26-25 win at KC Stadium.

10 March 2016 - 46-6 televised defeat at Widnes after leading 6-0.

18 March 2016 - 22-4 home win over Wakefield ends three-match losing run.

25 March 2016 - 22-20 Good Friday victory at Hull KR after trailing 20-0 with less than 20 minutes to play.

28 March 2016 - Curtis Naughton's second try five minutes from time produces dramatic 26-24 home Easter Monday win that ends Warrington's 100 per cent start to season.

2 April 2016 - Marc Sneyd 45-metre field goal four minutes from time secures fourth consecutive win, 17-16 victory over St Helens at Langtree Park.

8 April 2016 - Jamie Shaul scores two tries in 37-20 home win over Huddersfield.

14 April 2016 - Richard Whiting joins Leigh on permanent deal.

15 April 2016 - 20-18 rain-soaked defeat at Leeds ends five-match winning run.

24 April 2016 - Fetuli Talanoa scores four tries in 46-28 victory at in-form Wakefield.

29 April 2016 - Josh Bowden, Dean Hadley and Chris Green agree new deals to end of 2019. Jordan Abdull joins Featherstone on loan.

29 April 2016 - head coach Lee Radford signs new three-year deal until end of 2019 season.

29 April 2016 - 28-26 home win over Catalans ends Dragons' seven-match winning run.

HULL F.C.

Est. 1865

KEY DATES

8 May 2016 - Brad Fash joins Leigh on month's loan.

8 May 2016 - 47-18 Challenge Cup win at St Helens. Frank Pritchard and Sika Manu absent on international duty.

13 May 2016 - 30-16 win at Wigan moves Hull into second spot. Frank Pritchard misses game after getting one-game ban for high tackle in Samoa's 18-6 win over Tonga.

22 May 2016 - 28-16 Magic Weekend win over Hull KR secures top spot.

28 May 2016 - 32-24 home win over St Helens is sixth league win in a row.

1 June 2016 - Salford centre Josh Griffin signs three-year contract from 2017.

4 June 2016 - 30-10 home win over Widnes.

10 June 2016 - 19-12 win at second-placed Warrington.

18 June 2016 - Huddersfield centre Jake Connor signs two-year contract from 2017.

19 June 2016 - 24-22 win at Castleford.

25 June 2016 - 22-8 home Challenge Cup quarter-final win over Catalans.

28 June 2016 - young Halifax centre Nick Rawsthorne signs for 2017 on one-year deal with club having further option.

30 June 2016 - 22-12 defeat at Huddersfield ends ten-match winning run.

8 July 2016 - 71st-minute 15-8 lead ends in 20-15 home defeat by bottom club Leeds.

14 July 2016 - 36-12 home derby win regains top spot and condemns Rovers to Middle Eights.

23 July 2016 - 28-20 last regular round win at Salford moves Hull two points clear.

29 July 2016 - come-from-behind 16-12 win over Wigan in Challenge Cup semi-final at Doncaster.

6 August 2016 - 30-16 home defeat to Castleford in Super 8s opener.

11 August 2016 - Fetuli Talanoa scores hat-trick in 38-0 victory at Widnes.

18 August 2016 - 44-0 home win over Catalans secures Super 8s semi-finals place.

27 August 2016 - comeback 12-10 Challenge Cup final win over Warrington secures first ever win at Wembley.

30 August 2016 - winger Steve Michaels not offered new contract.

2 September 2016 - 31-10 defeat at St Helens.

9 September 2016 - 12-4 lead after an hour ends in last minute 18-12 home defeat by Wigan.

15 September 2016 - late Mahe Fonua try earns 18-12 win at Wakefield.

22 September 2016 - Kirk Yeaman announces he will retire at end of season.

23 September 2016 - 23-6 home defeat by Warrington means third-placed finish and away semi-final at Wigan.

30 September 2016 - 28-18 semi-final defeat at Wigan.

3 October 2016 - Danny Houghton announced Steve Prescott Man of Steel.

CLUB RECORDS

Highest score: 88-0 v Sheffield, 2/3/2003
Highest score against:
18-76 v Huddersfield, 19/9/2013
Record attendance:
28,798 v Leeds, 7/3/36 *(The Boulevard)*
23,004 v Hull KR, 2/9/2007 *(KC Stadium)*

MATCH RECORDS

Tries: 7 Clive Sullivan v Doncaster, 15/4/68
Goals: 14 Jim Kennedy v Rochdale, 7/4/21
Sammy Lloyd v Oldham, 10/9/78
Matt Crowther v Sheffield, 2/3/2003
Points: 36 Jim Kennedy v Keighley, 29/1/21

SEASON RECORDS

Tries: 52 Jack Harrison 1914-15
Goals: 170 Sammy Lloyd 1978-79
Points: 369 Sammy Lloyd 1978-79

CAREER RECORDS

Tries: 250 Clive Sullivan 1961-74; 1981-85
Goals: 687 Joe Oliver 1928-37; 1943-45
Points: 1,842 Joe Oliver 1928-37; 1943-45
Appearances: 500 Edward Rogers 1906-25

HULL F.C.

HULL F.C.

DATE	FIXTURE	RESULT	SCORERS	LGE	ATT
5/2/16	Salford (h)	W42-20	t:Pryce,Fonua,Thompson,Talanoa,Tuimavave,Bowden,Logan,Shaul g:Sneyd(5)	1st	12,265
13/2/16	Catalans Dragons (a)	W10-38	t:Talanoa(2),Manu,Bowden,Logan,Ellis,Shaul g:Sneyd(5)	2nd	10,234
25/2/16	Castleford (h)	L24-31	t:Thompson,Michaels,Shaul(2) g:Sneyd(4)	5th	10,247
4/3/16	Wigan (h)	L25-26	t:Michaels(2),Pryce,Manu g:Sneyd(4) fg:Sneyd	6th	10,660
10/3/16	Widnes (a)	L46-6	t:Pritchard g:Sneyd	7th	4,753
18/3/16	Wakefield (h)	W22-4	t:Minichiello(2),Naughton,Tuimavave g:Sneyd(3)	5th	9,600
25/3/16	Hull KR (a)	W20-22	t:Shaul,Houghton,Fonua,Michaels g:Sneyd(3)	4th	11,050
28/3/16	Warrington (h)	W26-24	t:Sneyd,Shaul,Naughton(2),Yeaman g:Sneyd(3)	5th	9,967
1/4/16	St Helens (a)	W16-17	t:Houghton,Naughton,Yeaman g:Sneyd(2) fg:Sneyd	5th	10,230
8/4/16	Huddersfield (h)	W37-20	t:Bowden,Watts,Shaul(2),Houghton,Naughton g:Sneyd(6) fg:Sneyd	3rd	10,557
15/4/16	Leeds (a)	L20-18	t:Green,Yeaman,Houghton g:Sneyd(3)	4th	15,888
24/4/16	Wakefield (a)	W28-46	t:Ellis,Talanoa(4),Bowden,Yeaman,Shaul g:Sneyd(7)	4th	6,701
29/4/16	Catalans Dragons (h)	W28-26	t:Talanoa,Naughton,Manu,Taylor g:Sneyd(6)	3rd	11,374
8/5/16	St Helens (a) (CCR6)	W18-47	t:Houghton,Taylor(2),Ellis,Shaul,Naughton,Yeaman,Talanoa g:Sneyd(7) fg:Sneyd	N/A	7,094
13/5/16	Wigan (a)	W16-30	t:Sneyd,Michaels,Taylor,Shaul,Talanoa g:Sneyd(5)	3rd	15,083
22/5/16	Hull KR (MW) ●	W28-16	t:Fonua(2),Naughton,Shaul,Minichiello g:Sneyd(4)	1st	N/A
28/5/16	St Helens (h)	W32-24	t:Ellis,Fonua,Tuimavave,Taylor,Washbrook g:Sneyd(6)	1st	11,247
3/6/16	Widnes (h)	W30-10	t:Tuimavave,Yeaman,Bowden,Houghton,Shaul g:Sneyd(5)	1st	10,259
10/6/16	Warrington (a)	W12-19	t:Talanoa,Minichiello,Ellis g:Sneyd(3) fg:Sneyd	1st	10,513
19/6/16	Castleford (a)	W22-24	t:Pritchard,Houghton,Fonua,Shaul g:Sneyd(4)	1st	10,790
25/6/16	Catalans Dragons (h) (CCQF)	W22-8	t:Michaels,Pritchard,Houghton g:Sneyd(5)	N/A	9,639
30/6/16	Huddersfield (a)	L22-12	t:Washbrook,Fonua g:Sneyd(2)	1st	4,143
8/7/16	Leeds (h)	L15-20	t:Tuimavave,Yeaman g:Sneyd(3) fg:Sneyd	2nd	10,618
14/7/16	Hull KR (h)	W36-12	t:Watts,Houghton,Minichiello(2),Michaels(2) g:Sneyd(6)	1st	17,481
22/7/16	Salford (a)	W20-28	t:Michaels,Pritchard,Green,Sneyd,Fonua g:Sneyd(4)	1st	3,225
29/7/16	Wigan (CCSF) ●●	W16-12	t:Michaels,Talanoa g:Sneyd(4)	N/A	10,488
5/8/16	Castleford (h) (S8)	L16-30	t:Michaels,Washbrook,Shaul g:Sneyd(2)	1st	9,936
11/8/16	Widnes (a) (S8)	W0-38	t:Abdull,Talanoa(3),Tuimavave,Michaels,Hadley g:Abdull(5)	1st	4,359
18/8/16	Catalans Dragons (h) (S8)	W44-0	t:Hadley,Fonua(2),Minichiello,Talanoa,Sneyd,Pritchard g:Sneyd(8)	1st	10,494
27/8/16	Warrington (CCF) ●●●	W12-10	t:Fonua,Shaul g:Sneyd(2)	N/A	76,235
2/9/16	St Helens (a) (S8)	L31-10	t:Fonua,Manu g:Naughton	2nd	10,086
9/9/16	Wigan (h) (S8)	L12-18	t:Talanoa,Fonua g:Sneyd(2)	2nd	11,686
15/9/16	Wakefield (a) (S8)	W12-18	t:Washbrook,Thompson,Fonua g:Sneyd(3)	2nd	3,413
23/9/16	Warrington (h) (S8)	L6-23	t:Tuimavave g:Sneyd	3rd	17,453
30/9/16	Wigan (a) (SF)	L28-18	t:Bowden,Watts,Michaels g:Sneyd(3)	N/A	10,013

● Played at St James' Park, Newcastle
●● Played at Keepmoat Stadium, Doncaster
●●● Played at Wembley Stadium

		APP		TRIES		GOALS		FG		PTS	
	D.O.B.	ALL	SL	ALL	SL	ALL	SL	ALL	SL	ALL	SL
Jordan Abdull	5/2/96	7(2)	7(2)	1	1	5	5	0	0	14	14
Josh Bowden	14/1/92	10(23)	10(20)	6	6	0	0	0	0	24	24
Jack Downs	10/11/95	(2)	(2)	0	0	0	0	0	0	0	0
Gareth Ellis	3/5/81	23(2)	19(2)	5	4	0	0	0	0	20	16
Mahe Fonua	24/12/92	28	24	14	13	0	0	0	0	56	52
Chris Green	3/1/90	2(23)	2(19)	2	2	0	0	0	0	8	8
Dean Hadley	5/8/92	5(11)	5(10)	2	2	0	0	0	0	8	8
Danny Houghton	25/9/88	34	30	9	7	0	0	0	0	36	28
Callum Lancaster	13/10/96	1	1	0	0	0	0	0	0	0	0
Jack Logan	8/9/95	6	6	2	2	0	0	0	0	8	8
Sika Manu	22/1/87	28(1)	25(1)	4	4	0	0	0	0	16	16
Steve Michaels	13/1/87	29	26	13	11	0	0	0	0	52	44
Mark Minichiello	30/1/82	25(3)	21(3)	7	7	0	0	0	0	28	28
Curtis Naughton	25/2/95	16	15	8	7	1	1	0	0	34	30
Iafeta Palea'aesina	10/2/82	(6)	(6)	0	0	0	0	0	0	0	0
Frank Pritchard	3/11/83	10(16)	10(13)	5	4	0	0	0	0	20	16
Leon Pryce	9/10/81	11(2)	10(2)	2	2	0	0	0	0	8	8
Jamie Shaul	1/7/92	32	28	16	14	0	0	0	0	64	56
Marc Sneyd	9/2/91	33	29	4	4	131	113	6	5	284	247
Fetuli Talanoa	23/11/87	28(1)	24(1)	17	15	0	0	0	0	68	60
Scott Taylor	27/2/91	32(2)	28(2)	5	3	0	0	0	0	20	12
Jordan Thompson	4/9/91	5(21)	5(19)	3	3	0	0	0	0	12	12
Carlos Tuimavave	10/1/92	24(1)	21(1)	7	7	0	0	0	0	28	28
Jansin Turgut	8/3/96	(1)	(1)	0	0	0	0	0	0	0	0
Danny Washbrook	18/9/85	10(20)	9(17)	4	4	0	0	0	0	16	16
Liam Watts	8/7/90	28(3)	24(3)	3	3	0	0	0	0	12	12
Kirk Yeaman	15/9/83	28	24	7	6	0	0	0	0	28	24

'SL' totals include Super 8s & semi-final; 'All' totals also include Challenge Cup

Marc Sneyd

LEAGUE RECORD
P30-W20-D0-L10
(3rd, SL/Semi-Finalists)
F749, A579, Diff+170
40 points.

CHALLENGE CUP
Winners

ATTENDANCES
Best - v Hull KR (SL - 17,481)
Worst - v Wakefield (SL - 9,600)
Total (SL/S8s only) - 173,844
Average (SL/S8s only) - 11,590
(Up by 417 on 2015)

21 October 2015 - Academy back-rower George Lawler signs two-year full-time contract.

18 November 2015 - Jordan Cox released to join Warrington on 12-month contract.

4 December 2015 - young Leeds prop Rob Mulhern joins on two-year contract.

17 January 2016 - 38-6 home defeat by Huddersfield in David Hodgson's Testimonial.

24 January 2016 - 60-20 thrashing at Hull FC in Clive Sullivan Trophy friendly.

7 February 2016 - last-minute converted touchline try by Josh Mantellato earns 16-all home, round-one draw with Castleford.

9 February 2016 - hooker John Boudebza banned for four matches for dangerous tackle on Michael Shenton. Appeal fails.

14 February 2016 - James Donaldson ruled out for ten weeks with dislocated wrist after 38-8 defeat at Warrington.

21 February 2016 - 14-12 home defeat by Wakefield in brought-forward round 11 game.

24 February 2016 - coach Chris Chester departs by mutual consent. Assistant Willie Poching takes temporary charge.

26 February 2016 - Albert Kelly injured in first half in 31-22 home defeat by St Helens, after leading 16-10 at half-time.

1 March 2016 - prop James Green banned for one match after sin-binning for fighting with Travis Burns.

2 March 2016 - boom rookie George Lawler signs new four-year contract.

4 March 2016 - Liam Salter suffers shoulder injury which requires surgery in 30-16 round 5 defeat at Widnes.

5 March 2016 - New head coach is 'identified'. James Webster takes over until end of 2016 season.

13 March 2016 - Terry Campese comes back from knee reconstruction after eight months in 38-6 defeat at win-less Huddersfield and tears hamstring.

20 March 2016 - 44-30 round six home win, first of season, after leading 30-6 at half-time, over Salford in interim head coach James Webster's first home game.

25 March 2016 - Josh Mantellato breaks arm in 22-20 Good Friday home defeat to Hull FC, after leading 20-0 with less than 20 minutes to play.

28 March 2016 - teenagers Will Oakes, Joe Cator and Joe Wardill make debuts in battling 30-16 Easter Monday defeat at Wigan. Ryan Shaw's season ended with ACL injury.

1 April 2016 - Shaun Lunt scores two tries in 30-10 victory over Leeds at Headingley. Terry Campese leaves field after 15 minutes with aggravated hamstring injury.

7 April 2016 - 40-nil home TV hammering by Catalans.

13 April 2016 - Academy products Matty Marsh, to end of 2018 with option for further 12 months, Kieran Moran, three years and Joe Wardill, four years, sign long-term contracts.

16 April 2016 - 36-22 home defeat to Championship Oldham Roughyeds is shock of round and means Challenge Cup elimination at first hurdle.

KEY DATES

24 April 2016 - Thomas Minns scores hat-trick in 58-16 away win at Castleford.

30 April 2016 - 44-26 defeat at Salford.

3 May 2016 - playing and coaching legend Roger Millward passes away aged 68.

15 May 2016 - tribute paid to Roger Millward before 24-10 home victory over Widnes.

22 May 2016 - 28-16 defeat to Hull FC at Magic Weekend.

28 May 2016 - Terry Campese left at home for trip to Perpignan and 34-16 defeat to Catalans.

2 June 2016 - Campese returns and Kieran Dixon scores hat-trick in 54-16 win at Wakefield.

10 June 2016 - last-minute Matty Smith conversion snatches Wigan 20-18 win at KC Lightstream Stadium. Terry Campese sustains hamstring injury.

17 June 2016 - 48-16 hammering at St Helens after leading 12-0.

20 June 2016 - Terry Campese ruled out for season with hamstring injury.

2 July 2016 - James Green sent off just before half-time for punching Jordan Cox but late Iain Thornley try and Ben Cockayne conversion secure 16-all home draw with Warrington.

3 July 2016 - threequarter David Thompson joins on loan to season end from Warrington.

5 July 2016 - assistant coach Willie Poching to leave at end of season.

9 July 2016 - Ben Cockayne kicks late penalty to secure 20-19 comeback win over Huddersfield to keep Super 8s hopes alive.

14 July 2016 - 36-12 defeat at Hull FC guarantees Middle Eights for Robins.

21 July 2016 - 24-20 home defeat to Leeds means 11th-place finish. prop James Green out for season with dislocated shoulder.

7 August 2016 - Thomas Minns scores hat-trick in 58-18 home win over Batley in opening Qualifiers Super 8s fixture.

12 August 2016 - 22-18 defeat at Leeds.

19 August 2016 - Josh Mantellato scores 16-points in 29-12 victory at Salford.

3 September 2016 - Albert Kelly suspended after returning from Australia later than agreed.

3 September 2016 - 12-0 lead ends in 25-18 home defeat by Leigh. George Lawler breaks vertebrae but plays on.

5 September 2016 - Maurice Blair returns home to attend brother's funeral.

5 September 2016 - Director of Rugby Jamie Peacock announces he will come out of retirement.

9 September 2016 - former Australia coach Tim Sheens to take up role as head coach at end of season on three-year contract, regardless of outcome of Qualifiers. James Webster to stay on as assistant.

11 September 2016 - Jamie Peacock makes debut and Terry Campese returns in 58-18 win at London Broncos.

18 September 2016 - 32-24 win at Featherstone.

24 September 2016 - Danny Brough field goal seven minutes from time means 23-22 home defeat to Huddersfield and place in Million Pound Game.

1 October 2016 - 45-metre golden-point Gareth O'Brien field goal earns Salford 19-18 win at KC Lightstream Stadium and relegation for Rovers.

6 October 2016 - hooker Shaun Lunt to honour remaining three years of contract. James Green leaves for Leigh.

10 October 2016 - Maurice Blair, the club's Player of the Year for 2016, agrees one-year extension contract to end of 2018.

11 October 2016 - centre Thomas Minns to honour remaining two-years of contract.

12 October 2016 - prop Nick Scruton signs from Wakefield for 2017 season.

17 October 2016 - Adam Walker leaves for St Helens, Iain Thornley signs for Catalans.

18 October 2016 - Mitch Clark and Danny Addy sign from Bradford on one-year contracts with options for further two-years.

CLUB RECORDS

Highest score:
100-6 v Nottingham City, 19/8/90
Highest score against:
6-84 v Wigan, 1/4/2013
Record attendance:
27,670 v Hull FC, 3/4/53 *(Boothferry Park)*
11,811 v Leeds, 8/2/2015 *(Craven Park)*

MATCH RECORDS

Tries: 11 George West
v Brooklands Rovers, 4/3/1905
Goals:
14 Alf Carmichael v Merthyr, 8/10/1910
Mike Fletcher v Whitehaven, 18/3/90
Colin Armstrong v Nottingham City, 19/8/90
Damien Couturier v Halifax, 23/4/2006
Points: 53 George West
v Brooklands Rovers, 4/3/1905

SEASON RECORDS

Tries: 45 Gary Prohm 1984-85
Goals: 199 Mike Fletcher 1989-90
Points: 450 Mike Fletcher 1989-90

CAREER RECORDS

Tries: 207 Roger Millward 1966-80
Goals: 1,268 Mike Fletcher 1987-98
Points: 2,760 Mike Fletcher 1987-98
Appearances: 489 Mike Smith 1975-91

HULL KINGSTON ROVERS

DATE	FIXTURE	RESULT	SCORERS	LGE	ATT
7/2/16	Castleford (h)	D16-16	t:Donaldson,Mantellato(2) g:Mantellato(2)	6th	11,011
14/2/16	Warrington (a)	L38-8	t:Thornley,Dixon	8th	11,037
21/2/16	Wakefield (h)	L12-14	t:Dixon,Walker,Sio	9th	7,207
26/2/16	St Helens (h)	L22-31	t:Cockayne,Blair,Green,Shaw g:Shaw(3)	10th	6,517
4/3/16	Widnes (a)	L30-16	t:Blair,Minns,Shaw g:Shaw(2)	11th	5,013
13/3/16	Huddersfield (a)	L38-6	t:Minns g:Shaw	12th	5,610
20/3/16	Salford (h)	W44-30	t:Blair,Thornley,Horne,Sio,Greenwood,Shaw,Marsh g:Mantellato(8)	10th	6,593
25/3/16	Hull FC (h)	L20-22	t:Shaw,Sio,Thornley g:Mantellato(4)	11th	11,050
28/3/16	Wigan (a)	L30-16	t:Horne,Thornley(2) g:Dixon(2)	11th	11,268
1/4/16	Leeds (a)	W10-30	t:Lunt(2),Dixon,Cockayne,Allgood,Mulhern g:Dixon(2),Cockayne	10th	15,384
7/4/16	Catalans Dragons (h)	L0-40		10th	6,764
16/4/16	Oldham (h) (CCR5)	L22-36	t:Tilse(2),Lunt,Blair,Wardill g:Cockayne	N/A	3,056
24/4/16	Castleford (a)	W16-58	t:Blair,Minns(3),Kelly,Horne,Thornley(2),Allgood,Sio(2) g:Cockayne(7)	10th	7,106
30/4/16	Salford (a)	L44-26	t:Blair,Thornley,Sio,Minns(2) g:Sio(2),Blair	9th	3,048
15/5/16	Widnes (h)	W24-10	t:Lunt,Sio,Greenwood,Kelly g:Cockayne(4)	9th	7,506
22/5/16	Hull FC (MW) ●	L28-16	t:Lunt,Horne g:Campese(4)	9th	N/A
28/5/16	Catalans Dragons (a)	L34-16	t:Larroyer,Wardill,Sio,Kelly	10th	9,859
2/6/16	Wakefield (a)	W16-54	t:Dixon(3),Kelly(2),Greenwood(2),Lunt,Green,Blair g:Sio(7)	9th	5,082
10/6/16	Wigan (h)	L18-20	t:Kelly,Minns,Allgood g:Sio(3)	9th	7,507
17/6/16	St Helens (a)	L48-16	t:Lunt,Clarkson,Minns g:Dixon(2)	9th	9,488
1/7/16	Warrington (h)	D16-16	t:Donaldson,Minns,Thornley g:Cockayne(2)	11th	6,827
8/7/16	Huddersfield (h)	W20-19	t:Marsh,Kelly,Lawler g:Cockayne(4)	9th	6,434
14/7/16	Hull FC (a)	L36-12	t:Walker,Thornley g:Mantellato(2)	10th	17,481
21/7/16	Leeds (h)	L20-24	t:Marsh,Blair,Sio,Dixon g:Mantellato(2)	11th	8,109
7/8/16	Batley (h) (S8-Q)	W58-18	t:Thornley,Minns(3),Marsh,Greenwood(2),Cockayne,Blair,Mantellato g:Mantellato(9)	2nd(S8-Q)	6,684
12/8/16	Leeds (a) (S8-Q)	L22-18	t:Greenwood,Donaldson,Lawler g:Mantellato(3)	4th(S8-Q)	14,180
19/8/16	Salford (a) (S8-Q)	W12-29	t:Mantellato,Greenwood,Sio,Minns g:Mantellato(6) fg:Kelly	4th(S8-Q)	2,074
3/9/16	Leigh (h) (S8-Q)	L18-25	t:Sio,Mantellato,Marsh g:Mantellato(3)	4th(S8-Q)	7,363
11/9/16	London Broncos (a) (S8-Q)	W18-58	t:Minns(3),Cockayne,Dixon,Greenwood,Marsh(2),Donaldson,Jubb g:Mantellato(9)	3rd(S8-Q)	1,215
18/9/16	Featherstone (a) (S8-Q)	W24-32	t:Mantellato(2),Lunt,Minns(2),Greenwood g:Mantellato(4)	3rd(S8-Q)	4,034
24/9/16	Huddersfield (h) (S8-Q)	L22-23	t:Blair,Sio,Allgood,Thornley g:Mantellato(3)	4th(S8-Q)	8,024
1/10/16	Salford (h) (MPG)	L18-19 *(aet)*	t:Walker,Mantellato,Minns g:Mantellato(3)	N/A	6,562

● *Played at St James' Park, Newcastle*

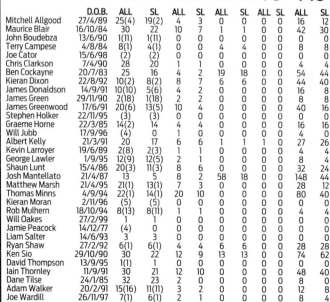

	D.O.B.	APP		TRIES		GOALS		FG		PTS	
		ALL	SL	ALL	SL	ALL	SL	ALL	SL	ALL	SL
Mitchell Allgood	27/4/89	25(4)	19(2)	4	3	0	0	0	0	16	12
Maurice Blair	16/10/84	30	22	10	7	1	1	0	0	42	30
John Boudebza	13/6/90	1(11)	1(11)	0	0	0	0	0	0	0	0
Terry Campese	4/8/84	8(1)	4(1)	0	0	4	4	0	0	8	8
Joe Cator	15/6/98	(2)	(2)	0	0	0	0	0	0	0	0
Chris Clarkson	7/4/90	28	20	1	1	0	0	0	0	4	4
Ben Cockayne	20/7/83	25	16	4	2	19	18	0	0	54	44
Kieran Dixon	22/8/92	10(2)	8(2)	8	7	6	6	0	0	44	40
James Donaldson	14/9/91	10(10)	5(6)	4	2	0	0	0	0	16	8
James Green	29/11/90	2(18)	1(18)	2	2	0	0	0	0	8	8
James Greenwood	17/6/91	20(6)	13(5)	10	4	0	0	0	0	40	16
Stephen Holker	22/11/95	(3)	(3)	0	0	0	0	0	0	0	0
Graeme Horne	22/3/85	14(2)	14	4	4	0	0	0	0	16	16
Will Jubb	17/9/96	(4)	0	1	0	0	0	0	0	4	0
Albert Kelly	21/3/91	20	17	6	6	1	1	1	0	27	26
Kevin Larroyer	19/6/89	2(8)	2(3)	1	1	0	0	0	0	4	4
George Lawler	1/9/95	12(9)	12(5)	2	1	0	0	0	0	8	4
Shaun Lunt	15/4/86	20(3)	11(3)	8	6	0	0	0	0	32	24
Josh Mantellato	21/4/87	13	5	8	2	58	18	0	0	148	44
Matthew Marsh	21/4/95	21(1)	13(1)	7	3	0	0	0	0	28	12
Thomas Minns	4/9/94	22(1)	14(1)	20	10	0	0	0	0	80	40
Kieran Moran	2/11/96	(5)	(5)	0	0	0	0	0	0	0	0
Rob Mulhern	18/10/94	8(13)	8(11)	1	1	0	0	0	0	4	4
Will Oakes	27/2/99	1	1	0	0	0	0	0	0	0	0
Jamie Peacock	14/12/77	(4)	0	0	0	0	0	0	0	0	0
Liam Salter	14/6/93	3	3	0	0	0	0	0	0	0	0
Ryan Shaw	27/2/92	6(1)	6(1)	4	4	6	6	0	0	28	28
Ken Sio	29/10/90	30	22	12	9	13	13	0	0	74	62
David Thompson	13/9/95	1(1)	1	0	0	0	0	0	0	0	0
Iain Thornley	11/9/91	30	21	12	10	0	0	0	0	48	40
Dane Tilse	24/1/85	32	23	2	0	0	0	0	0	8	0
Adam Walker	20/2/91	15(16)	11(11)	3	2	0	0	0	0	12	8
Joe Wardill	26/11/97	7(1)	6(1)	2	1	0	0	0	0	8	4

'SL' totals include regular season only; 'All' totals also include Super 8s (Qualifiers) & Challenge Cup

Thomas Minns

LEAGUE RECORD
SL: P23-W6-D2-L15 (11th)
F486, A610, Diff-124, 14 points.

S8-Q: P7-W4-D0-L3 (4th)
F235, A142, Diff+93, 8 points.
(Losers, Million Pound Game)

CHALLENGE CUP
Round Five

ATTENDANCES
Best - v Hull FC (SL - 11,050)
Worst - v Oldham (CC - 3,056)
Total (SL/S8s only) - 114,158
Average (SL/S8s only) - 7,610
(Down by 174 on 2015)

KEY DATES

15 April 2016 - 20-18 victory over Hull at rain-soaked Headingley Carnegie ends four-game losing run.

22 April 2016 - Zak Hardaker suffers head injury in 38-34 defeat at St Helens.

30 April 2016 - Academy loose forward Cameron Smith makes debut off bench in 28-20 defeat at Huddersfield that sinks Rhinos to bottom of table.

6 May 2016 - 36-22 Challenge Cup defeat at Huddersfield.

12 May 2016 - 52-12 home hammering by Castleford.

21 May 2016 - 40-8 defeat by Wigan at Magic Weekend.

27 May 2016 - 52-18 defeat at Warrington.

4 June 2016 - 24-12 home defeat by Catalans.

4 June 2016 - Zak Hardaker transfer listed at £300,000.

10 June 2016 - Luke Briscoe scores game's only try in sixth minute of 8-0 home win over Salford that ends seven-game losing run.

18 June 2016 - Liam Sutcliffe scores 20 points in 32-6 win at Wakefield.

22 June 2016 - Penrith's PNG international hooker James Segeyaro and Zak Hardaker in immediate swap deal for remainder of season with view to long-term arrangement.

1 July 2016 - Kirkstall training base re-opened for first time since Boxing Day floods.

3 July 2016 - late Joe Mellor field goal secures 23-22 Widnes win at Headingley and ends chances of Super 8s.

3 July 2016 - hooker Beau Falloon's 12 month contract terminated after arrival of James Segeyaro.

8 July 2016 - Academy prop Mikolaj Oledzki signs five-year contract.

9 July 2016 - James Segeyaro makes debut as two Kallum Watkins tries in last ten minutes secures 20-15 win at leaders Hull FC.

16 July 2016 - 18-16 home win over Wigan.

21 July 2016 - Jordan Baldwinson, Josh Walters and Luke Briscoe go on loan to Featherstone for rest of season.

21 July 2016 - 24-20 win at Hull KR means ninth-placed finish.

28 July 2016 - Brett Ferres signs three-year deal to end of 2019.

6 August 2016 - 62-6 victory at Featherstone in Qualifiers Super 8s opener.

12 August 2016 - James Segeyaro scores two tries in hard-fought 22-18 home win over Hull KR.

20 August 2016 - Tom Briscoe hat-trick in 42-28 win at London Broncos.

23 October 2015 - Gold Coast hooker Beau Falloon signs 12-month contract for 2016.

18 November 2015 - Jimmy Keinhorst signs new three-year contract.

20 November 2015 - Mitch Garbutt signs new four-year contract to end of 2019.

26 December 2015 - 14-6 home, Boxing Day defeat to Wakefield.

26 December 2015 - Kirkstall training base badly damaged in flooding.

4 January 2016 - Brett Ferres signs from Huddersfield on initial 12-month deal for undisclosed fee.

15 January 2016 - Danny McGuire named new club captain.

5 February 2016 - Danny McGuire withdrawn in first half with knee injury in opening night 12-10 home defeat to Warrington.

14 February 2016 - Tom Briscoe, Carl Ablett and Ashton Golding withdrawn with ankle injuries in 56-12 round-two thrashing at Widnes.

21 February 2016 - 38-4 defeat by North Queensland Cowboys in World Club Challenge at Headingley. Mitch Garbutt sent off for punch on James Tamou.

22 February 2016 - Mitch Garbutt gets two-match ban.

4 March 2016 - 20-16 home win over Huddersfield secures first league points.

11 March 2016 - last-minute Zak Hardaker try avoids first nilling since 1998 in 28-6 defeat at Wigan.

18 March 2016 - 30-18 home win over St Helens after leading 16-0 inside 11 minutes. Jamie Jones-Buchanan makes 300th Super League appearance. Ryan Hall suffers leg injury.

24 March 2016 - late Jake Webster try means 18-14 Easter Thursday defeat at Castleford.

28 March 2016 - late Craig Hall breakaway try means 20-16 Easter Monday home defeat to Wakefield.

1 April 2016 - former hooker Shaun Lunt inspires 30-10 victory by Hull KR at Headingley, despite return of captain Danny McGuire from knee injury sustained in round one.

10 April 2016 - 14-10 defeat at Salford.

24 August 2016 - Kevin Sinfield appointed RFL Rugby Director.

29 August 2016 - club president Harry Jepson OBE dies aged 96.

2 September 2016 - Stevie Ward plays first game of season in 30-8 home win over Salford.

9 September 2016 - James Segeyaro agrees new two-year contract.

9 September 2016 - Super League life secured with 32-0 home win over Batley.

18 September 2016 - eight-match winning run ended with 22-14 defeat at Huddersfield.

22 September 2016 - 37-12 home win over Leigh means top spot in Qualifiers.

7 October 2016 - Featherstone prop Jack Ormondroyd joins on three-year contract.

CLUB RECORDS
Highest score: 106-10 v Swinton, 11/2/2001   **Highest score against:** 6-74 v Wigan, 20/5/92   **Record attendance:** 40,175 v Bradford, 21/5/47

MATCH RECORDS
Tries: 8 Fred Webster v Coventry, 12/4/1913   Eric Harris v Bradford, 14/9/31   **Goals:**   17 Iestyn Harris v Swinton, 11/2/2001   **Points:**   42 Iestyn Harris v Huddersfield, 16/7/99

SEASON RECORDS
Tries: 63 Eric Harris 1935-36   **Goals:** 173 *(inc 5fg)* Kevin Sinfield 2012   **Points:** 431 Lewis Jones 1956-57

CAREER RECORDS
Tries: 391 Eric Harris 1930-39   **Goals:**   1,831 *(inc 39fg)* Kevin Sinfield 1997-2015   **Points:** 3,967 Kevin Sinfield 1997-2015   **Appearances:** 625 John Holmes 1968-89

LEEDS RHINOS

DATE	FIXTURE	RESULT	SCORERS	LGE	ATT
4/2/16	Warrington (h)	L10-12	t:Singleton,Hall g:Hardaker	8th	16,168
14/2/16	Widnes (a)	L56-12	t:Watkins,Burrow g:Lilley(2)	12th	6,596
21/2/16	North Queensland (h) (WCC)	L4-38	t:Burrow	N/A	19,778
27/2/16	Catalans Dragons (a)	L32-28	t:Watkins(2),Sutcliffe,Hall,Handley g:Lilley(4)	12th	8,172
4/3/16	Huddersfield (h)	W20-16	t:Moon,Sutcliffe,Keinhorst g:Lilley(4)	9th	14,692
11/3/16	Wigan (a)	L28-6	t:Hardaker g:Hardaker	10th	14,425
18/3/16	St Helens (h)	W30-18	t:Jones-Buchanan,Cuthbertson,Sutcliffe,Ablett,Handley g:Sutcliffe(5)	9th	17,131
24/3/16	Castleford (a)	L18-14	t:Moon,Watkins,T Briscoe g:Sutcliffe	9th	11,426
28/3/16	Wakefield (h)	L16-20	t:Moon,T Briscoe,Achurch g:Sutcliffe(2)	10th	16,314
1/4/16	Hull KR (h)	L10-30	t:Jones-Buchanan,Ablett g:Hardaker	11th	15,384
9/4/16	Salford (a)	L14-10	t:Galloway,Golding g:Hardaker	11th	4,912
15/4/16	Hull FC (h)	W20-18	t:Keinhorst,Lilley,Jones-Buchanan g:Lilley(4)	10th	15,888
22/4/16	St Helens (a)	L38-34	t:Golding,Burrow,Keinhorst(2),Handley,Mullally g:Lilley(5)	11th	11,271
29/4/16	Huddersfield (a)	L28-20	t:Lilley,Walters,Burrow g:Lilley(4)	12th	7,536
6/5/16	Huddersfield (a) (CCR6)	L36-22	t:Keinhorst(2),Sutcliffe,Mullally g:Lilley(3)	N/A	4,979
12/5/16	Castleford (h)	L12-52	t:Garbutt,Handley g:Lilley(2)	12th	17,213
21/5/16	Wigan (MW) ●	L8-40	t:Watkins,Achurch	12th	N/A
27/5/16	Warrington (a)	L52-18	t:Keinhorst,Ferres(2) g:Sutcliffe(3)	12th	10,317
3/6/16	Catalans Dragons (h)	L12-24	t:Ferres,Walters g:Lilley(2)	12th	14,016
10/6/16	Salford (h)	W8-0	t:L Briscoe g:Sutcliffe(2)	12th	14,462
17/6/16	Wakefield (a)	W6-32	t:Achurch,Singleton(2),Sutcliffe g:Sutcliffe(8)	12th	7,161
3/7/16	Widnes (h)	L22-23	t:Watkins,Hall,Moon,Garbutt g:Sutcliffe(3)	12th	16,130
8/7/16	Hull FC (a)	W15-20	t:Sutcliffe,Moon,Watkins(2) g:Sutcliffe(2)	12th	10,618
15/7/16	Wigan (h)	W18-16	t:Watkins,Cuthbertson,Ferres g:Sutcliffe(3)	11th	16,712
21/7/16	Hull KR (a)	W20-24	t:Keinhorst,Burrow,Segeyaro,Hall g:Sutcliffe(4)	9th	8,109
6/8/16	Featherstone (a) (S8-Q)	W6-62	t:Watkins(4),Sutcliffe(2),Moon(2),Achurch,Ablett,T Briscoe g:Sutcliffe(9)	1st(S8-Q)	6,671
12/8/16	Hull KR (h) (S8-Q)	W22-18	t:Watkins,Segeyaro(2) g:Sutcliffe(5)	1st(S8-Q)	14,180
20/8/16	London Broncos (a) (S8-Q)	W28-42	t:T Briscoe(3),Sutcliffe,Segeyaro,Lilley,Achurch,Watkins g:Sutcliffe(5)	1st(S8-Q)	1,845
2/9/16	Salford (h) (S8-Q)	W30-8	t:Jones-Buchanan,Watkins,Segeyaro,Ablett,Cuthbertson g:Sutcliffe,Lilley(4)	1st(S8-Q)	13,996
9/9/16	Batley (h) (S8-Q)	W32-0	t:T Briscoe,Watkins(2),Hall(2),Burrow g:Lilley(4)	1st(S8-Q)	15,135
18/9/16	Huddersfield (a) (S8-Q)	L22-14	t:Cuthbertson,T Briscoe,Handley g:Sutcliffe	2nd(S8-Q)	6,666
22/9/16	Leigh (h) (S8-Q)	W37-12	t:Ferres,Keinhorst(2),Segeyaro,Golding,Moon,T Briscoe g:Watkins(4) fg:Moon	1st(S8-Q)	14,747

● *Played at St James' Park, Newcastle*

	D.O.B.	APP ALL	SL	TRIES ALL	SL	GOALS ALL	SL	FG ALL	SL	PTS ALL	SL
Carl Ablett	19/12/85	17(1)	11(1)	4	2	0	0	0	0	16	8
Mitch Achurch	14/7/88	9(12)	9(8)	5	3	0	0	0	0	20	12
Jordan Baldwinson	10/11/94	(1)	(1)	0	0	0	0	0	0	0	0
Luke Briscoe	11/3/94	5(2)	5(1)	1	1	0	0	0	0	4	4
Tom Briscoe	19/3/90	13	6	9	2	0	0	0	0	36	8
Rob Burrow	26/9/82	27(1)	20(1)	6	4	0	0	0	0	24	16
Adam Cuthbertson	24/2/85	13(13)	11(7)	4	2	0	0	0	0	16	8
Brett Delaney	26/10/85	8(5)	7(4)	0	0	0	0	0	0	0	0
Beau Falloon	21/5/87	8(2)	8(2)	0	0	0	0	0	0	0	0
Brett Ferres	17/4/86	24(2)	15(2)	5	4	0	0	0	0	20	16
Mitch Garbutt	18/4/89	12(11)	10(7)	2	2	0	0	0	0	8	8
Keith Galloway	2/9/85	28(2)	21(1)	1	1	0	0	0	0	4	4
Ashton Golding	4/9/96	9(4)	7(2)	3	2	0	0	0	0	12	8
Ryan Hall	27/11/87	17(1)	10(1)	6	4	0	0	0	0	24	16
Sam Hallas	18/10/96	(3)	(2)	0	0	0	0	0	0	0	0
Ash Handley	16/2/96	20(1)	17	5	4	0	0	0	0	20	16
Zak Hardaker	17/10/91	18	16	1	1	4	4	0	0	12	12
Jamie Jones-Buchanan	1/8/81	24(3)	16(3)	4	3	0	0	0	0	16	12
Josh Jordan-Roberts	26/8/98	(1)	0	0	0	0	0	0	0	0	0
Jimmy Keinhorst	14/7/90	16(12)	10(9)	10	6	0	0	0	0	40	24
Jordan Lilley	4/9/96	18(6)	14(4)	3	2	38	27	0	0	88	62
Danny McGuire	6/12/82	13	10	0	0	0	0	0	0	0	0
Joel Moon	20/5/88	20(1)	14	8	5	0	0	1	0	33	20
Anthony Mullally	28/6/91	(18)	(14)	2	1	0	0	0	0	8	4
James Segeyaro	11/7/90	10	3	6	1	0	0	0	0	24	4
Brad Singleton	29/10/92	20(6)	13(6)	3	3	0	0	0	0	12	12
Cameron Smith	7/11/98	(2)	(1)	0	0	0	0	0	0	0	0
Liam Sutcliffe	25/11/94	29(2)	20(2)	9	5	54	33	0	0	144	86
Josh Walters	23/12/94	4(9)	3(8)	2	2	0	0	0	0	8	8
Stevie Ward	17/11/93	2(2)	0	0	0	0	0	0	0	0	0
Kallum Watkins	12/3/91	32	23	18	9	4	0	0	0	80	36

Kallum Watkins

LEAGUE RECORD
SL: P23-W8-D0-L15 (9th)
F404, A576, Diff-172, 16 points.

S8-Q: P7-W6-D0-L1 (1st)
F239, A94, Diff+145, 12 points.

CHALLENGE CUP
Round Six

ATTENDANCES
Best - v North Queensland
(WCC - 19,778)
Worst - v Salford (S8 - 13,996)
Total (SL/S8s only) - 232,168
Average (SL/S8s only) - 15,478
(Down by 246 on 2015)

'SL' totals include regular season only; 'All' totals also include Super 8s (Qualifiers), Challenge Cup & World Club Challenge

3 October 2015 - St Helens forward Mark Flanagan, Widnes prop Phil Joseph, Huddersfield prop Craig Kopczak, Warrington halfback Gareth O'Brien, North Queensland stand-off Robert Lui and Penrith Panthers prop Ben Murdoch-Masila all signed. Prop Olsi Krasniqi agrees two-year deal after joining in June.

27 October 2015 - prop Matthew Haggarty signs on season-long loan from St Helens.

3 November 2015 - Castleford Tigers winger Justin Carney joins on year-long loan deal.

5 November 2015 - Ben Jones-Bishop, 12 months into three-year contract, signs for Wakefield on free transfer.

10 November 2015 - winger Daniel Vidot signs from Brisbane Broncos on two-year contract. Darrell Griffin released from last year of contract to join Featherstone.

19 November 2015 - hooker Liam Hood and prop Luke Menzies released.

25 November 2015 - Wigan hooker Logan Tomkins, after two loan spells, signs permanent 12-month contract.

6 December 2015 - second-rower Matt Sarsfield signs from Leigh.

7 January 2016 - Daniel Vidot likely to miss half the 2016 season after sustaining shoulder injury in training.

7 January 2016 - Marwan Koukash confirms takeover as club's chief executive following departure of Martin Vickers.

14 January 2016 - former St Helens centre Josh Jones signs for two years, with option for further year, after aborted spell at rugby union club Exeter.

25 January 2016 - 32-16 home friendly win over Wigan.

5 February 2016 - 42-22 defeat at Hull FC in round one.

10 February 2016 - Academy product, forward Ryan Lannon signs new three-year contract to end of 2018 season.

11 February 2016 - Robert Lui and Niall Evalds each score braces in 44-10 home hammering of St Helens.

21 February 2016 - 28-20 home victory ends Widnes's 100 per cent start to season in brought-forward round 11 game.

3 March 2016 - last-second Chris Sandow field goal gives Warrington 31-30 Thursday TV win at AJ Bell Stadium.

4 March 2016 - Red Devils charged with breaches of salary cap in 2014 and 2015.

13 March 2016 - Justin Carney scores two tries on return to Castleford in 32-16 victory. Robert Lui picks up knee injury.

20 March 2016 - 44-30 defeat at win-less Hull KR after trailing 30-6 at half-time.

25 March 2016 - 26-12 home Good Friday defeat to Catalans.

28 March 2016 - 26-24 Easter Monday win at Huddersfield sees Justin Carney and Junior Sa'u involved in crowd trouble after final whistle.

2 April 2016 - Justin Carney sustains ankle injury in 32-18 defeat at Wakefield.

9 April 2016 - Robert Lui returns from knee injury in 14-10 home win over Leeds.

17 April 2016 - Josh Griffin scores hat-trick in 50-14 Challenge Cup victory at League One Hunslet.

KEY DATES

25 April 2016 - Castleford loanee Justin Carney signs permanent deal until end of 2019 despite interest from Wigan.

25 April 2016 - Salford found guilty of salary cap breaches in 2014 and 2015 and deducted six league points with immediate effect.

30 April 2016 - Junior Sa'u scores hat-trick in 44-26 home victory over Hull KR.

3 May 2016 - Logan Tomkins banned for one match for dangerous contact on Albert Kelly.

7 May 2016 - Daniel Vidot scores two tries on debut in 32-18 Challenge Cup defeat at Castleford.

14 May 2016 - Niall Evalds scores hat-trick in 34-20 defeat at St Helens.

17 May 2016 - Niall Evalds takes one-match EGP ban for dangerous contact.

21 May 2016 - Daniel Vidot scores two tries in 18-12 Magic Weekend win over Widnes.

27 May 2016 - 38-8 home win over Wakefield.

1 June 2016 - Josh Griffin signs for Hull FC for 2017.

4 June 2016 - 23-20 home defeat to Wigan.

7 June 2016 - young prop Daniel Murray signs from Warrington on two-year contract.

13 June 2016 - Red Devils charged following crowd trouble at Huddersfield on 28 March.

18 June 2016 - late comeback too late in 31-30 home defeat by Huddersfield.

24 June 2016 - Warrington hooker Sean Kenny signs with immediate effect for nominal fee.

2 July 2016 - 22-18 home win over Castleford keeps top-eight hopes alive.

7 July 2016 - independent body Sports Resolutions upholds RFL decision to find Salford Red Devils guilty of breaching salary cap in 2014 and 2015 season.

7 July 2016 - 40-14 defeat at Warrington ends Super 8s hopes.

16 July 2016 - Mason Caton-Brown scores hat-trick in 32-24 win at Widnes.

22 July 2016 - prop Luke Burgess and Manly teammate Feleti Mateo sign for Middle Eights campaign.

22 July 2016 - 28-20 home defeat by Hull FC means 10th-placed finish.

7 August 2016 - Mason Caton-Brown scores hat-trick in 34-12 home win over Huddersfield in first Middle Eights game. Luke Burgess and Feleti Mateo make debuts.

13 August 2016 - Mason Caton-Brown scores twice in 32-26 defeat at Leigh.

19 August 2016 - 29-12 home defeat by Hull KR.

2 September 2016 - 30-8 defeat at Leeds rules out top-three finish in Middle Eights.

6 September 2016 - Feleti Mateo returns to Australia for family reasons.

9 September 2016 - Mason Caton-Brown signs for Wakefield.

11 September 2016 - 70-16 home mauling of Featherstone Rovers.

17 September 2016 - shock 19-16 home defeat by London Broncos.

25 September 2016 - 42-14 rout at part-timers Batley Bulldogs earns place in 4th v 5th play-off.

1 October 2016 - 45-metre golden-point Gareth O'Brien field goal earns 19-18 Million Pound Game win at Hull KR, after trailing 18-10 with two minutes to full-time.

18 October 2016 - prop Lama Tasi re-signs from St Helens on one-year deal. hooker Kris Brining signs from York.

19 October 2016 - Tommy Lee signs for St Helens.

CLUB RECORDS

Highest score:
100-12 v Gateshead, 23/3/2003
Highest score against:
16-96 v Bradford, 25/6/2000
Record attendance:
26,470 v Warrington, 13/2/37
(The Willows)
7,102 v Wakefield, 16/2/2014
(AJ Bell Stadium)

MATCH RECORDS

Tries:
6 Frank Miles v Lees, 5/3/1898
Ernest Bone v Goole, 29/3/1902
Jack Hilton v Leigh, 7/10/39
Goals:
14 Steve Blakeley v Gateshead, 23/3/2003
Points:
39 Jim Lomas v Liverpool City, 2/2/1907

SEASON RECORDS

Tries: 46 Keith Fielding 1973-74
Goals: 221 David Watkins 1972-73
Points: 493 David Watkins 1972-73

CAREER RECORDS

Tries: 297 Maurice Richards 1969-83
Goals: 1,241 David Watkins 1967-79
Points: 2,907 David Watkins 1967-79
Appearances:
498 Maurice Richards 1969-83

SALFORD RED DEVILS

DATE	FIXTURE	RESULT	SCORERS	LGE	ATT
5/2/16	Hull FC (a)	L42-20	t:J Griffin,Sa'u(2),Evalds g:J Griffin,Dobson	12th	12,265
11/2/16	St Helens (h)	W44-10	t:Johnson,Kopczak,Lui(2),Evalds(2),A Walne,Dobson g:J Griffin(2),Dobson(4)	6th	4,386
21/2/16	Widnes (h)	W28-20	t:Carney,Flanagan(2),Johnson,J Griffin g:Dobson(3),O'Brien	4th	5,098
25/2/16	Wigan (a)	L20-16	t:Sa'u,J Griffin,Murdoch-Masila g:O'Brien,J Griffin	6th	10,897
3/3/16	Warrington (h)	L30-31	t:Sa'u(2),Jones,Johnson,J Griffin g:Dobson,O'Brien(4)	7th	4,381
13/3/16	Castleford (h)	W16-32	t:Johnson,J Griffin(2),Carney(2) g:O'Brien(6)	5th	8,151
20/3/16	Hull KR (a)	L44-30	t:Kopczak(2),G Griffin(2),Johnson g:O'Brien(5)	6th	6,593
25/3/16	Catalans Dragons (h)	L12-26	t:J Griffin,Johnson(2)	8th	3,485
28/3/16	Huddersfield (a)	W24-26	t:Kopczak,O'Brien,J Griffin,Carney,Evalds g:Dobson(3)	7th	4,885
2/4/16	Wakefield (a)	L32-18	t:O'Brien,Sarsfield,Carney g:O'Brien(2),Dobson	8th	4,048
9/4/16	Leeds (h)	W14-10	t:Tomkins,Lui g:O'Brien,Dobson(2)	8th	4,912
17/4/16	Hunslet (a) (CCR5)	W14-50	t:Lannon,Bibby(2),J Griffin(3),Wood,Lui(2) g:Dobson(3),O'Brien(4)	N/A	834
23/4/16	Catalans Dragons (a)	L42-32	t:Evalds(2),Carney,Sa'u(3) g:O'Brien(2),Dobson(2)	8th	9,686
30/4/16	Hull KR (h)	W44-26	t:Sa'u(3),Lui(2),Evalds,G Griffin,Jones g:Dobson(2),O'Brien(4)	10th	3,048
7/5/16	Castleford (a) (CCR6)	L32-18	t:Sa'u(2),Lui g:O'Brien(3)	N/A	3,317
13/5/16	St Helens (a)	L34-20	t:Evalds(3),Carney g:O'Brien,Dobson	10th	9,299
21/5/16	Widnes (MW) ●	W18-12	t:Vidot(2),Carney g:O'Brien(2),Dobson	10th	N/A
27/5/16	Wakefield (h)	W38-8	t:Evalds,Lannon(2),Flanagan,Lui,G Griffin,Sa'u g:O'Brien(4),Dobson	9th	3,022
3/6/16	Wigan (h)	L20-23	t:Dobson(2),Jones,Vidot g:Dobson,Lui	10th	4,096
10/6/16	Leeds (a)	L8-0		10th	14,462
17/6/16	Huddersfield (h)	L30-31	t:Kopczak,Vidot(2),Jones(2) g:O'Brien(5)	10th	1,958
1/7/16	Castleford (h)	W22-18	t:O'Brien,Dobson,Caton-Brown g:O'Brien(5)	9th	2,275
7/7/16	Warrington (a)	L40-14	t:Sa'u,J Griffin,Lui g:O'Brien	10th	9,024
15/7/16	Widnes (a)	W24-32	t:Caton-Brown(3),Carney,Jones g:O'Brien(5),Dobson	9th	4,636
22/7/16	Hull FC (h)	L20-28	t:Dobson,Caton-Brown,Evalds,Lui g:O'Brien(2)	10th	3,225
7/8/16	Huddersfield (h) (S8-Q)	W34-12	t:G Griffin,Caton-Brown(3),Hauraki,Murdoch-Masila g:O'Brien(5)	3rd(S8-Q)	2,184
13/8/16	Leigh (a) (S8-Q)	L32-26	t:Caton-Brown(2),Evalds,Lui,Murdoch-Masila g:O'Brien(3)	6th(S8-Q)	4,547
19/8/16	Hull KR (h) (S8-Q)	L12-29	t:Caton-Brown,O'Brien g:O'Brien(2)	6th(S8-Q)	2,074
2/9/16	Leeds (a) (S8-Q)	L30-8	t:G Griffin g:O'Brien(2)	6th(S8-Q)	13,996
11/9/16	Featherstone (h) (S8-Q)	W70-16	t:Hauraki(2),Sa'u(2),Jones(2),Vidot,Evalds,Murdoch-Masila(2),Tomkins, Krasniqi,Dobson g:O'Brien(9)	5th(S8-Q)	1,759
17/9/16	London Broncos (h) (S8-Q)	L16-19	t:G Griffin,J Griffin(2) g:O'Brien(2)	5th(S8-Q)	2,521
25/9/16	Batley (a) (S8-Q)	W14-42	t:O'Brien,Sa'u,Hauraki(2),Johnson,J Griffin,Lui g:O'Brien(5)	5th(S8-Q)	1,520
1/10/16	Hull KR (a) (MPG)	W18-19 (aet)	t:Murdoch-Masila,Evalds(2),Johnson g:O'Brien fg:O'Brien	N/A	6,562

● *Played at St James' Park, Newcastle*

	D.O.B.	APP		TRIES		GOALS		FG		PTS	
		ALL	SL	ALL	SL	ALL	SL	ALL	SL	ALL	SL
Jake Bibby	17/6/96	4(2)	3(2)	2	0	0	0	0	0	8	0
Luke Burgess	20/2/87	6(2)	0	0	0	0	0	0	0	0	0
Justin Carney	16/6/88	21	19	9	9	0	0	0	0	36	36
Mason Caton-Brown	24/5/93	8	5	11	5	0	0	0	0	44	20
Michael Dobson	29/5/86	33	23	6	5	27	24	0	0	78	68
Niall Evalds	26/8/93	12(9)	7(7)	16	12	0	0	0	0	64	48
Mark Flanagan	4/12/87	28(3)	19(3)	3	3	0	0	0	0	12	12
Carl Forster	4/6/92	2(1)	2(1)	0	0	0	0	0	0	0	0
George Griffin	26/6/92	32	23	7	4	0	0	0	0	28	16
Josh Griffin	9/5/90	26	17	15	9	4	4	0	0	68	44
Matthew Haggarty	8/1/91	(1)	0	0	0	0	0	0	0	0	0
Weller Hauraki	18/2/85	10(12)	4(8)	5	0	0	0	0	0	20	0
Greg Johnson	20/2/90	13	9	9	7	0	0	0	0	36	28
Josh Jones	12/5/93	30(1)	23	8	6	0	0	0	0	32	24
Phil Joseph	10/1/85	2(12)	(12)	0	0	0	0	0	0	0	0
Sean Kenny	21/10/94	(9)	(4)	0	0	0	0	0	0	0	0
Craig Kopczak	20/12/86	25(5)	22	5	5	0	0	0	0	20	20
Olsi Krasniqi	26/6/92	(19)	(10)	1	0	0	0	0	0	4	0
Ryan Lannon	11/1/96	5(6)	4(5)	3	2	0	0	0	0	12	8
Tommy Lee	1/2/88	8(1)	8(1)	0	0	0	0	0	0	0	0
Robert Lui	23/2/90	26(3)	19	13	8	1	1	0	0	54	34
Feleti Mateo	2/5/85	2(1)	0	0	0	0	0	0	0	0	0
Ben Murdoch-Masila	7/2/91	32	23	6	1	0	0	0	0	24	4
Gareth O'Brien	31/10/91	32	22	6	3	87	51	1	0	199	114
Junior Sa'u	18/4/87	32	22	18	13	0	0	0	0	72	52
Matt Sarsfield	10/9/91	3(2)	2(2)	1	1	0	0	0	0	4	4
Logan Tomkins	1/8/91	24(7)	16(7)	2	1	0	0	0	0	8	4
Daniel Vidot	8/2/90	8(2)	5(1)	6	5	0	0	0	0	24	20
Adam Walne	3/10/92	1(23)	(19)	1	1	0	0	0	0	4	4
Jordan Walne	28/12/92	1(8)	(7)	0	0	0	0	0	0	0	0
Connor Williams	29/8/98	(1)	(1)	0	0	0	0	0	0	0	0
Josh Wood	15/11/95	3(2)	2(2)	1	0	0	0	0	0	4	0

'SL' totals include regular season only; 'All' totals also include Super 8s (Qualifiers) & Challenge Cup

Gareth O'Brien

LEAGUE RECORD
SL: P23-W10-D0-L13 (10th)
F560, A569, Diff-9, 14 points.
(6 points deducted for salary cap breaches in 2014 & 2015)

S8-Q: P7-W3-D0-L4 (5th)
F208, A152, Diff+56, 6 points.
(Winners, Million Pound Game)

CHALLENGE CUP
Round Six

ATTENDANCES
Best - v Widnes (SL - 5,098)
Worst - v Featherstone (S8 - 1,759)
Total (SL/S8s only) - 48,424
Average (SL/S8s only) - 3,228
(Down by 878 on 2015)

2 September 2015 - Mark Flanagan moves to Salford.

27 October 2015 - prop Matthew Haggarty signs season-long loan deal at Salford.

5 November 2015 - Jack Owens signs from Widnes on two-year contract.

14 January 2016 - Josh Jones signs for Salford after aborted spell at rugby union club Exeter.

24 January 2016 - 30-16 home Karalius Cup defeat to Widnes.

27 January 2016 - head coach Keiron Cunningham signs contract until end of 2018.

3 February 2016 - Latvian dual-code international Mikus Ozols arrives on trial.

5 February 2016 - James Roby suffers shoulder injury in 30-16 round-one home win over Huddersfield.

11 February 2016 - James Roby and Dominique Peyroux missing and Mark Percival suffers knee injury in 44-10 televised hammering at Salford.

15 February 2016 - Mark Percival injury confirmed as ruptured medial ligaments.

19 February 2016 - Dominique Peyroux scores first two tries for club in disappointing 38-12 World Series home defeat by Sydney Roosters.

27 February 2016 - 31-22 win at Hull KR ends eight-year drought in east Hull as James Roby returns to inspire second-half comeback.

1 March 2016 - Travis Burns banned for one match after sin-binning for fighting with Hull KR prop James Green.

4 March 2016 - Matty Dawson scores two tries as 28-22 home victory ends Castleford's unbeaten run.

11 March 2016 - Adam Swift suffers ankle injury in 44-4 home defeat of Wakefield. Wildcats prop Tinirau Arona gets two match ban for dangerous contact.

18 March 2016 - 30-18 defeat at Leeds.

25 March 2016 - 24-12 home Good Friday defeat to Wigan is first home loss of season.

28 March 2016 - winger Tommy Makinson set to miss rest of season after sustaining knee injury in 20-12 Easter Monday win at Widnes.

2 April 2016 - Marc Sneyd 45-metre field goal four minutes from time means 17-16 home defeat to Hull FC.

9 April 2016 - Theo Fages inspires 25-22 win at league leaders Warrington.

14 April 2016 - 30-12 home defeat to Catalans.

22 April 2016 - Jonny Lomax returns after over year out with knee injury and scores two tries in thrilling 38-34 home victory over Leeds. Mark Percival also back after two months out.

1 May 2016 - Saints come from behind twice to win 30-20 at Castleford.

8 May 2016 - 47-18 Challenge Cup home defeat to Hull FC.

14 May 2016 - 34-20 home win over Salford.

22 May 2016 - 48-20 win defeat by Huddersfield at Magic Weekend.

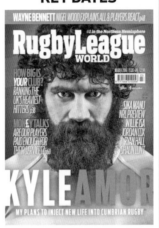

KEY DATES

28 May 2016 - Luke Walsh limps off with lower leg injury after two minutes of 32-24 defeat at Hull FC.

2 June 2016 - Travis Burns joins Leigh on loan to end of season.

4 June 2016 - 26-4 reverse at Warrington is third successive defeat.

7 June 2016 - Lewis Charnock joins Bradford on month's loan.

18 June 2016 - Adam Swift gets four tries in 48-16 home win over Hull KR.

3 July 2016 - late tries to Jordan Turner and Matty Fleming secure 44-32 win at Wakefield.

9 July 2016 - late penalty from Mark Percival secures 12-10 home win over Widnes.

14 July 2016 - Jordan Turner set to move to Canberra Raiders at end of season.

17 July 2016 - Saints move level on points with fourth-placed Catalans after 34-18 win at Huddersfield.

20 July 2016 - Andre Savelio joins Castleford on loan to end of season.

21 July 2016 - Matty Dawson transferred to Leigh.

22 July 2016 - 23-4 win at Wigan secures regular-season, top-four finish.

4 August 2016 - 20-18 win at Warrington in Super 8s' opener.

11 August 2016 - Louie McCarthy-Scarsbrook signs two-year contract extension.

12 August 2016 - Adam Swift scores four tries in 39-16 home win over Catalans. Luke Walsh banned for two games for dangerous throw on Lucas Albert. Luke Thompson banned for two games for shoulder charge on Justin Horo.

15 August 2016 - juniors Calvin Wellington, Regan Grace, Ricky Bailey and Jake Spedding sign to end of 2017.

16 August 2016 - Morgan Knowles signs three-year contract. Matty Fleming signs to end of 2017

19 August 2016 - 25-0 defeat at Wigan ends winning run at seven games.

22 August 2016 - Ryan Morgan signs from Melbourne on three-year contract.

30 August 2016 - on-loan-at-Leigh Travis Burns to join the Wynnum Manly Seagulls at end of season.

2 September 2016 - Jack Owens scores two tries and five goals in 31-10 home win over Hull FC.

8 September 2016 - play-off spot confirmed with 40-16 home win over Castleford.

18 September 2016 - Adam Swift scores two tries in 21-8 victory at Widnes.

23 September 2016 - 32-12 home win over Wakefield secures third spot and semi-final at Warrington.

26 September 2016 - sudden-death 22-20 win over Wigan in 2016 Academy Grand Final maintains season's 22-match unbeaten run.

28 September 2016 - Scotland prop Luke Douglas signs from Gold Coast on three-year contract.

29 September 2016 - 18-10 semi-final defeat at Warrington.

5 October 2016 - Atelea Vea signs for Leigh.

11 October 2016 - Matty Smith re-signs from Wigan on three-year contract.

17 October 2016 - prop Adam Walker signs from Hull KR on two-year contract.

18 October 2016 - prop Andre Savelio joins Warrington Wolves.

CLUB RECORDS

Highest score:
112-0 v Carlisle, 14/9/86
Highest score against:
6-78 v Warrington, 12/4/1909
Record attendance:
35,695 v Wigan, 26/12/49 *(Knowsley Road)*
17,980 v Wigan, 6/4/2012
v Wigan, 18/4/2014
v South Sydney, 22/2/2015 *(Langtree Park)*

MATCH RECORDS

Tries: 6 Alf Ellaby v Barrow, 5/3/32
Steve Llewellyn v Castleford, 3/3/56
Steve Llewellyn v Liverpool, 20/8/56
Tom van Vollenhoven v Wakefield, 21/12/57
Tom van Vollenhoven v Blackpool, 23/4/62
Frank Myler v Maryport, 1/9/69
Shane Cooper v Hull, 17/2/88
Goals: 16 Paul Loughlin v Carlisle, 14/9/86
Points:
40 Paul Loughlin v Carlisle, 14/9/86

SEASON RECORDS

Tries: 62 Tom van Vollenhoven 1958-59
Goals: 214 Kel Coslett 1971-72
Points: 452 Kel Coslett 1971-72

CAREER RECORDS

Tries: 392 Tom van Vollenhoven 1957-68
Goals: 1,639 Kel Coslett 1962-76
Points: 3,413 Kel Coslett 1962-76
Appearances: 531 Kel Coslett 1962-76

ST HELENS

DATE	FIXTURE	RESULT	SCORERS	LGE	ATT
5/2/16	Huddersfield (h)	W30-16	t:Percival(2),Vea,Turner,Thompson g:Walsh(5)	2nd	10,408
11/2/16	Salford (a)	L44-10	t:Walmsley,Swift g:Walsh	7th	4,386
19/2/16	Sydney Roosters (h) (WCS)	L12-38	t:Peyroux(2) g:Walsh(2)	N/A	14,008
26/2/16	Hull KR (a)	W22-31	t:McDonnell,Makinson,Dawson,Wilkin,Vea g:Walsh(5) fg:Walsh	7th	6,517
4/3/16	Castleford (h)	W28-22	t:Swift,Vea,Dawson(2),McCarthy-Scarsbrook g:Walsh(4)	4th	11,298
11/3/16	Wakefield (h)	W44-4	t:Greenwood(2),Wilkin,Roby(2),Makinson(2),Dawson g:Walsh(6)	4th	10,008
18/3/16	Leeds (a)	L30-18	t:Amor,Walsh,McCarthy-Scarsbrook g:Walsh(3)	4th	17,131
25/3/16	Wigan (h)	L12-24	t:Greenwood,Fages g:Walsh(2)	5th	17,890
28/3/16	Widnes (a)	W12-20	t:Greenwood,McCarthy-Scarsbrook,Makinson g:Walsh(4)	6th	9,076
1/4/16	Hull FC (h)	L16-17	t:Greenwood,Dawson,Turner g:Walsh,Owens	6th	10,230
8/4/16	Warrington (a)	W22-25	t:Amor,Ashworth,Dawson,Knowles g:Walsh(4) fg:Walsh	6th	13,678
14/4/16	Catalans Dragons (h)	L12-30	t:Fages,Walsh g:Walsh(2)	6th	9,362
22/4/16	Leeds (h)	W38-34	t:Lomax(2),Greenwood(2),Amor,Fages(2) g:Walsh(5)	5th	11,271
1/5/16	Castleford (a)	W20-30	t:Greenwood(2),McDonnell,Amor,Lomax g:Walsh(5)	5th	6,658
8/5/16	Hull FC (h) (CCR6)	L18-47	t:Percival,McCarthy-Scarsbrook,Walsh g:Walsh(3)	N/A	7,094
13/5/16	Salford (h)	W34-20	t:McCarthy-Scarsbrook,Percival,Peyroux,Lomax,Fages,Amor g:Walsh(5)	4th	9,299
22/5/16	Huddersfield (MW) ●	L48-20	t:Dawson,Owens,Fages,Swift g:Walsh(2)	5th	N/A
28/5/16	Hull FC (a)	L32-24	t:Swift,Lomax,Vea,Ashworth g:Owens(4)	5th	11,247
3/6/16	Warrington (h)	L4-26	t:Lomax	5th	11,353
11/6/16	Catalans Dragons (a)	L33-16	t:McCarthy-Scarsbrook,Swift,McDonnell g:Owens(2)	5th	10,789
17/6/16	Hull KR (h)	W48-16	t:Swift(4),McDonnell,Percival,McCarthy-Scarsbrook,Peyroux,Walmsley g:Percival(6)	5th	9,488
3/7/16	Wakefield (a)	W32-44	t:Percival,Richards,Lomax(2),Knowles,Roby,Turner,Fleming g:Percival(6)	5th	4,859
8/7/16	Widnes (h)	W12-10	t:Turner,Fleming g:Percival(2)	5th	11,566
17/7/16	Huddersfield (a)	W18-34	t:Greenwood,Owens,McCarthy-Scarsbrook,Turner,Swift,Walmsley g:Percival(5)	5th	5,526
22/7/16	Wigan (a)	W4-23	t:Percival,Knowles,Roby g:Percival(5) fg:Walsh	4th	20,049
4/8/16	Warrington (a) (S8)	W18-20	t:McCarthy-Scarsbrook,Lomax,Turner g:Percival(4)	4th	10,759
12/8/16	Catalans Dragons (h) (S8)	W39-16	t:Swift(4),Owens,Greenwood g:Walsh(6),Owens fg:Walsh	4th	9,440
19/8/16	Wigan (a) (S8)	L25-0		4th	15,265
2/9/16	Hull FC (h) (S8)	W31-10	t:Owens(2),Fleming,Vea(2) g:Owens(5) fg:Turner	4th	10,086
8/9/16	Castleford (h) (S8)	W40-16	t:Fleming,Knowles,Amor,Thompson,McCarthy-Scarsbrook,Swift,Walmsley g:Walsh(5),Owens	4th	9,448
18/9/16	Widnes (a) (S8)	W8-21	t:Swift(2),Fleming,Vea g:Walsh(2) fg:Walsh	4th	6,128
23/9/16	Wakefield (h) (S8)	W32-12	t:McCarthy-Scarsbrook,Owens,McDonnell(3),Fages g:Walsh(4)	4th	9,516
29/9/16	Warrington (a) (SF)	L18-10	t:Lomax g:Walsh(3)	N/A	12,036

● *Played at St James' Park, Newcastle*

	D.O.B.	APP ALL	APP SL	TRIES ALL	TRIES SL	GOALS ALL	GOALS SL	FG ALL	FG SL	PTS ALL	PTS SL
Kyle Amor	26/5/87	17(16)	16(15)	6	6	0	0	0	0	24	24
Jack Ashworth	3/7/95	3(3)	3(3)	2	2	0	0	0	0	8	8
Travis Burns	6/2/84	3(2)	2(2)	0	0	0	0	0	0	0	0
Olly Davies	30/11/95	(1)	(1)	0	0	0	0	0	0	0	0
Matty Dawson	2/10/90	16	15	7	7	0	0	0	0	28	28
Theo Fages	23/8/94	15(3)	14(3)	7	7	0	0	0	0	28	28
Matty Fleming	13/1/96	9	9	5	5	0	0	0	0	20	20
Joe Greenwood	2/4/93	22(2)	20(2)	11	11	0	0	0	0	44	44
Morgan Knowles	5/11/96	5(19)	5(17)	4	4	0	0	0	0	16	16
Jonny Lomax	4/9/90	18	17	10	10	0	0	0	0	40	40
Tom Makinson	10/10/91	9	8	4	4	0	0	0	0	16	16
Louie McCarthy-Scarsbrook	14/1/86	28(5)	27(4)	11	10	0	0	0	0	44	40
Shannon McDonnell	5/8/87	18	18	7	7	0	0	0	0	28	28
Jack Owens	3/6/94	28	26	6	6	14	14	0	0	52	52
Mark Percival	29/5/94	16	15	7	6	28	28	0	0	84	80
Dominique Peyroux	21/1/89	22	20	4	2	0	0	0	0	16	8
Greg Richards	12/7/95	11(15)	11(14)	1	1	0	0	0	0	4	4
James Roby	22/11/85	28(2)	27(2)	4	4	0	0	0	0	16	16
Andre Savelio	21/3/95	6(4)	5(4)	0	0	0	0	0	0	0	0
Jake Spedding	26/9/96	2	2	0	0	0	0	0	0	0	0
Adam Swift	20/2/93	22	21	17	17	0	0	0	0	68	68
Lama Tasi	3/5/90	9(10)	9(8)	0	0	0	0	0	0	0	0
Luke Thompson	27/4/95	3(21)	3(20)	2	2	0	0	0	0	8	8
Jordan Turner	9/1/89	26(2)	25(2)	6	6	0	0	1	1	25	25
Atelea Vea	27/11/86	13(14)	11(14)	7	7	0	0	0	0	28	28
Alex Walmsley	10/4/90	21(12)	19(12)	4	4	0	0	0	0	16	16
Luke Walsh	12/5/87	26	24	3	2	79	74	5	5	175	161
Calvin Wellington	10/12/95	1	1	0	0	0	0	0	0	0	0
Jon Wilkin	11/1/83	32(1)	30(1)	2	2	0	0	0	0	8	8

'SL' totals include Super 8s & semi-final; 'All' totals also include Challenge Cup & World Club Series

Kyle Amor

LEAGUE RECORD
P30-W20-D0-L10
(4th, SL/Semi-Finalists)
F756, A641, Diff+115
40 points.

CHALLENGE CUP
Round Six

ATTENDANCES
Best - v Wigan (SL - 17,890)
Worst - v Hull FC (CC - 7,094)
Total (SL/S8s only) - 160,663
Average (SL/S8s only) - 10,711
(Down by 1,152 on 2015)

20 October 2015 - centre Bill Tupou re-signs for 2016.

23 October 2015 - centre Ashley Gibson signs on two-year deal.

27 October 2015 - back-row forward Jon Molloy signs new two-year deal to end of 2017.

28 October 2015 - centre Joe Arundel signs new two-year contract to end of 2017.

2 November 2015 - Cronulla's former Kangaroo forward Anthony Tupou signs on two-year deal.

5 November 2015 - Cronulla and Cook Islands prop Tinirau Arona joins on 12-month deal.

5 November 2015 - Ben Jones-Bishop joins from Salford Red Devils on 12-month deal after free transfer.

9 November 2015 - hooker Scott Moore signs two-year contract.

16 December 2015 - Tom Johnstone signs new four-year contract to end of 2019.

26 December 2015 - 14-6 Boxing Day win over Leeds at Headingley.

7 February 2016 - 24-16 round-one home defeat to Widnes.

11 February 2016 - Wildcats fined 2,000 pounds, half suspended, for racist chanting at Bradford Qualifier game in October.

14 February 2016 - 40-6 round-two hammering at Castleford.

21 February 2016 - Liam Finn's three goals the difference in first win of season, by 14-12 at Hull KR in brought-forward round 11 game.

29 February 2016 - Richard Owen goes to Leigh on loan, Jordan Crowther to York, both for one-month.

6 March 2016 - 42-28 round-four home defeat by Catalans.

7 March 2016 - head coach Brian Smith resigns. Assistant Stuart Dickens takes over as caretaker.

9 March 2016 - Jordan Tansey joins Huddersfield on month's loan.

11 March 2016 - prop Tinirau Arona gets two-game ban for dangerous contact on Adam Swift during 44-4 defeat at St Helens.

16 March 2016 - Chris Chester appointed head coach weeks after leaving Hull KR. John Kear to join as head of rugby from 2017.

25 March 2016 - Tom Johnstone length-of-the-field try seals 36-22 home Good Friday win over Huddersfield in Chris Chester's first game in charge.

28 March 2016 - Craig Hall scores length-of-field try two minutes from time to secure 20-16 win at Leeds, a first victory at Headingley since 2007.

2 April 2016 - Tom Johnstone scores hat-trick in televised 32-18 home victory over Salford.

10 April 2016 - Jacob Miller scores hat-trick in sensational 62-0 home win over third-placed Wigan. Nick Scruton found not guilty of dangerous contact on Tony Clubb.

19 April 2016 - Chris Annakin signs new contract to end of 2017.

22 April 2016 - Mickael Simon signs new contract to end of 2018.

KEY DATES

24 April 2016 - Reece Lyne suffers hamstring injury in 46-28 home defeat to Hull FC that ends five-match winning run.

25 April 2016 - Bill Tupou signs new contract to end of 2018.

27 April 2016 - Michael Sio signs new contract to end of 2018.

29 April 2016 - Scott Moore sent off for punching before Craig Hall scores last minute try, converted by Liam Finn to secure 18-16 win at Widnes. Ashley Gibson dislocates shoulder in dangerous throw by Patrick Ah Van.

3 May 2016 - Scott Moore banned for two games for high tackle on Patrick Ah Van.

6 May 2016 - Tinirau Arona, on 12-month deal, signs new one-year contract with option for further year.

15 May 2016 - 36-28 home win over Warrington after leading 30-6 just after half-time.

17 May 2016 - Scott Moore banned for further four games for gouging during fight in win at Widnes. Anthony England gets one game for punching in Warrington win.

19 May 2016 - Danny Kirmond signs new two-year contract to end of 2018.

22 May 2016 - Jacob Miller kicks 50-metre field goal to beat Catalans 25-24 at Magic Weekend.

25 May 2016 - Wildcats fined £1,000 for breaching concussion guidelines in defeat at Widnes.

26 May 2016 - prop Anthony Walker goes to Whitehaven on loan.

31 May 2016 - Danny Kirmond takes one-game EGP ban for tripping.

10 June 2016 - Cronulla prop David Fifita signs to end of season with option for 2017.

12 June 2016 - Danny Kirmond scores only try of 10-2 wet-weather win at Huddersfield.

18 June 2016 - David Fifita sin-binned on debut, in 32-6 home defeat by Leeds.

23 June 2016 - Stuart Howarth joins Bradford on month's loan.

23 June 2016 - David Fifita scores two tries in 28-16 Challenge Cup win at Huddersfield.

3 July 2016 - groundsharing talks with Dewsbury announced after lack of progress in buying Belle Vue back from bank.

3 July 2016 - Tom Johnstone picks up leg injury in act of scoring as two late tries ensure home defeat to St Helens by 44-32.

5 July 2016 - Academy starlets Frazer Morris and Bradley Moules sign one-year deals to end of 2017.

9 July 2016 - last-second try leads to 22-18 defeat at Wigan.

16 July 2016 - Wildcats move into sixth place with 30-28 win at Catalans Dragons and secure Super 8s place. Scott Moore banned for one game for high tackle on Morgan Escaré.

22 July 2016 - prop Ben Harrison joins on loan from Warrington to end of season.

24 July 2016 - 30 points conceded in last 23 minutes means 46-20 last regular round home defeat to Castleford. Matt Ashurst breaks jaw.

27 July 2016 - Ben Jones-Bishop takes up contract option to end of 2017.

29 July 2016 - Tom Johnstone signs new four-and-a-half year deal to end of 2020.

30 July 2016 - 56-12 Challenge Cup semi-final defeat by Warrington at Leigh.

11 August 2016 - Batley prop Keegan Hirst signs one-year deal with option of further 12 months.

26 August 2016 - Jordan Tansey agrees mutual release from contract with immediate effect.

26 August 2016 - Chris Annakin, Danny Kirmond, and Richard Owen hospitalised after road traffic accident on Heath Common.

2 September 2016 - Jason Walton to move to Bradford at end of season.

8 September 2016 - prop Scott Anderson to retire at end of season.

9 September 2016 - winger/centre Mason Caton-Brown to join from Salford on two-year deal.

23 September 2016 - 32-12 defeat at St Helens ends point-less Super 8s campaign.

26 September 2016 - Scott Grix re-joins from Huddersfield on two-year deal.

29 September 2016 - Canberra Raiders halfback Sam Williams joins one one-year deal for 2017.

4 October 2016 - David Fifita banned for two games for dangerous contact in last-round defeat at St Helens.

CLUB RECORDS

Highest score:
90-12 v Highfield, 27/10/92
Highest score against:
0-86 v Castleford, 17/4/95
Record attendance:
30,676 v Huddersfield, 26/2/21

MATCH RECORDS

Tries:
7 Fred Smith v Keighley, 25/4/59
Keith Slater v Hunslet, 6/2/71
Goals:
13 Mark Conway v Highfield, 27/10/92
Points:
36 Jamie Rooney v Chorley, 27/2/2004

SEASON RECORDS

Tries: 38 Fred Smith 1959-60
David Smith 1973-74
Goals: 163 Neil Fox 1961-62
Points: 407 Neil Fox 1961-62

CAREER RECORDS

Tries: 272 Neil Fox 1956-74
Goals: 1,836 Neil Fox 1956-74
Points: 4,488 Neil Fox 1956-74
Appearances:
605 Harry Wilkinson 1930-49

WAKEFIELD T WILDCATS

DATE	FIXTURE	RESULT	SCORERS	LGE	ATT
7/2/16	Widnes (h)	L16-24	t:Howarth,Lyne,Sio g:Finn(2)	10th	5,240
14/2/16	Castleford (a)	L40-6	t:Howarth g:Finn	11th	9,761
21/2/16	Hull KR (a)	W12-14	t:Simon,Howarth g:Finn(3)	8th	7,207
26/2/16	Warrington (a)	L34-16	t:Hall,A Tupou,Molloy g:Finn(2)	9th	10,631
6/3/16	Catalans Dragons (h)	L28-42	t:A Tupou,Arundel,Lyne,Johnstone,Simon g:Finn(4)	10th	4,442
11/3/16	St Helens (a)	L44-4	t:Jones-Bishop	11th	10,008
18/3/16	Hull FC (a)	L22-4	t:Arundel	12th	9,600
25/3/16	Huddersfield (h)	W36-22	t:Johnstone(2),Sio,Lyne,Jowitt,Scruton g:Finn(6)	10th	4,989
28/3/16	Leeds (a)	W16-20	t:Ashurst,Miller,Hall g:Finn(4)	9th	16,314
2/4/16	Salford (h)	W32-18	t:Miller,Sio,Johnstone(3),Lyne g:Finn(4)	9th	4,048
10/4/16	Wigan (h)	W62-0	t:Scruton(2),Miller(3),Johnstone,Finn,Kirmond(2),Jones-Bishop,Jowitt g:Finn(9)	9th	5,751
15/4/16	Sheffield (h) (CCR5)	W44-10	t:Finn(2),Johnstone,Jones-Bishop,Arona,Simon(2),Sio g:Finn(6)	N/A	2,257
24/4/16	Hull FC (h)	L28-46	t:Gibson(3),Johnstone,Kirmond g:Finn(4)	9th	6,701
29/4/16	Widnes (h)	W16-18	t:A Tupou,Hall g:Finn(5)	7th	4,398
8/5/16	Toulouse (h) (CCR6)	W40-22	t:Johnstone(4),Miller,Hall,Ashurst g:Finn(6)	N/A	2,539
15/5/16	Warrington (h)	W36-28	t:Hall(2),Ashurst(2),Johnstone,Jones-Bishop g:Finn(6)	6th	5,180
22/5/16	Catalans Dragons (MW) ●	W24-25	t:Jones-Bishop(2),Sio,Simon g:Finn(4) fg:Miller	6th	N/A
27/5/16	Salford (a)	L38-8	t:A Tupou,Jones-Bishop	6th	3,022
2/6/16	Hull KR (h)	L16-54	t:B Tupou,Sio,Hall g:Finn(2)	7th	5,082
12/6/16	Huddersfield (a)	W2-10	t:Kirmond g:Finn(3)	6th	5,077
17/6/16	Leeds (h)	L6-32	t:Jones-Bishop g:Finn	6th	7,161
23/6/16	Huddersfield (a) (CCQF)	W16-28	t:Fifita(2),Jones-Bishop,Johnstone g:Finn(6)	N/A	3,289
3/7/16	St Helens (h)	L32-44	t:Miller(3),Johnstone,Finn,Jones-Bishop g:Finn(4)	7th	4,859
8/7/16	Wigan (a)	L22-18	t:Jowitt,Lyne,Jones-Bishop g:Finn(3)	8th	11,121
16/7/16	Catalans Dragons (a)	W28-30	t:Jowitt,Molloy,Hall,B Tupou,Sio g:Finn(5)	6th	8,562
24/7/16	Castleford (h)	L20-46	t:Miller,Arundel(2),Lyne g:Finn(2)	8th	6,855
30/7/16	Warrington (CCSF) ●●	L12-56	t:Hall,Jowitt g:Finn(2)	N/A	10,358
5/8/16	Wigan (a) (S8)	L60-12	t:Arundel,Hall g:Finn(2)	8th	10,593
14/8/16	Warrington (h) (S8)	L10-38	t:Molloy,Mazive g:Finn	8th	3,552
21/8/16	Widnes (a) (S8)	L40-8	t:Hall,Jones-Bishop	8th	4,010
2/9/16	Castleford (a) (S8)	L46-22	t:Lyne,Johnstone(2),B Tupou,Scruton g:Finn	8th	6,283
9/9/16	Catalans Dragons (h) (S8)	L10-14	t:Jowitt,Hall g:Finn	8th	2,612
15/9/16	Hull FC (h) (S8)	L12-18	t:Arundel,Johnstone g:Finn(2)	8th	3,413
23/9/16	St Helens (a) (S8)	L32-12	t:Hall,Johnstone g:Finn(2)	8th	9,516

● Played at St James' Park, Newcastle   ●● Played at Leigh Sports Village

		APP		TRIES		GOALS		FG		PTS	
	D.O.B.	ALL	SL	ALL	SL	ALL	SL	ALL	SL	ALL	SL
Scott Anderson	8/1/86	3(13)	3(11)	0	0	0	0	0	0	0	0
Chris Annakin	30/1/91	(14)	(12)	0	0	0	0	0	0	0	0
Tinirau Arona	8/5/89	17(15)	15(13)	1	0	0	0	0	0	4	0
Joe Arundel	22/8/91	23(4)	21(4)	6	6	0	0	0	0	24	24
Matty Ashurst	1/11/89	25(3)	22(3)	4	3	0	0	0	0	16	12
James Batchelor	9/4/98	(3)	(3)	0	0	0	0	0	0	0	0
Jordan Crowther	19/2/97	2(4)	2(2)	0	0	0	0	0	0	0	0
Anthony England	19/10/86	18(1)	15(1)	0	0	0	0	0	0	0	0
David Fifita	28/6/89	7(6)	5(6)	2	0	0	0	0	0	8	0
Liam Finn	2/11/83	34	30	4	2	103	83	0	0	222	174
Ashley Gibson	25/9/86	6	5	3	3	0	0	0	0	12	12
Craig Hall	21/2/88	23	20	13	11	0	0	0	0	52	44
Ben Harrison	24/2/88	3	3	0	0	0	0	0	0	0	0
Stuart Howarth	25/1/90	11(3)	9(3)	3	3	0	0	0	0	12	12
Tom Johnstone	13/8/95	25	22	20	14	0	0	0	0	80	56
Ben Jones-Bishop	24/8/88	23	19	12	10	0	0	0	0	48	40
Max Jowitt	6/5/97	23(1)	20(1)	6	5	0	0	0	0	24	20
Danny Kirmond	11/11/85	13(1)	12	4	4	0	0	0	0	16	16
Reece Lyne	2/12/92	27	25	7	7	0	0	0	0	28	28
Judah Mazive	2/1/98	2	2	1	1	0	0	0	0	4	4
Jacob Miller	22/8/92	32	28	10	9	0	0	1	1	41	37
Jon Molloy	23/3/91	17(5)	16(5)	3	3	0	0	0	0	12	12
Scott Moore	23/1/88	14(1)	12(1)	0	0	0	0	0	0	0	0
Frazer Morris	22/2/97	(1)	(1)	0	0	0	0	0	0	0	0
Bradley Moules	23/11/96	(1)	(1)	0	0	0	0	0	0	0	0
Nick Scruton	24/12/84	23(2)	22(2)	4	4	0	0	0	0	16	16
Mickael Simon	2/4/87	9(14)	9(12)	5	3	0	0	0	0	20	12
Michael Sio	16/5/93	22(10)	18(10)	7	6	0	0	0	0	28	24
Anthony Tupou	1/3/83	14(9)	12(9)	4	4	0	0	0	0	16	16
Bill Tupou	2/7/90	17(1)	16(1)	3	3	0	0	0	0	12	12
Anthony Walker	28/12/91	(4)	(4)	0	0	0	0	0	0	0	0
Jason Walton	13/6/90	9(10)	7(8)	0	0	0	0	0	0	0	0
Andy Yates	23/2/90	(10)	(7)	0	0	0	0	0	0	0	0

Liam Finn

LEAGUE RECORD
P30-W10-D0-L20
(8th, SL)
F571, A902, Diff-331
20 points.

CHALLENGE CUP
Semi-Finalists

ATTENDANCES
Best - v Leeds (SL - 7,161)
Worst - v Sheffield (CC - 2,257)
Total (SL/S8s only) - 69,885
Average (SL/S8s only) - 4,992
(Up by 889 on 2015)

'SL' totals include Super 8s; 'All' totals also include Challenge Cup

27 October 2015 - Ashton Sims extends two-year contract by a year to end of 2017.

5 November 2015 - forward Ben Harrison undergoes knee, wrist and ankle surgery and could miss most of 2016 season.

18 November 2015 - Hull KR release forward Jordan Cox to enable him to move to Wolves on 12-month contract.

24 November 2015 - prop Ryan Bailey joins on 12-month deal but needs ankle surgery.

27 December 2015 - 40-0 festive friendly win at Widnes.

11 January 2016 - Chris Hill appointed club captain.

5 February 2016 - Stefan Ratchford and Mitchell Dodds missing after off-season wrist surgery as Wolves win round-one game at Leeds 12-10.

14 February 2016 - Tom Lineham scores hat-trick in 38-8 round-two home win over Hull KR.

16 February 2016 - Ben Westwood banned for one match for dangerous contact on Albert Kelly.

26 February 2016 - Ben Currie and Chris Sandow score twice as 34-16 home win over Wakefield maintains 100 per-cent record.

3 March 2016 - last second 40-metre Chris Sandow field goal earns 31-30 win at Salford, despite trailing 30-12 on 50 minutes. Mitchell Dodds makes debut off bench.

12 March 2016 - in his second appearance, Mitchell Dodds breaks tibia and fibula during 30-20 win at Catalans.

18 March 2016 - Chris Sandow stars as 100 per-cent start maintained with 56-12 home thrashing of Castleford.

25 March 2016 - Wolves leapfrog Widnes to top table with a 28-10 home Good Friday victory over the Vikings, after trailing 10-0 after 24 minutes.

28 March 2016 - Curtis Naughton try five minutes from time means dramatic 26-24 round eight Easter Monday defeat at Hull FC that ends 100 per cent start to season.

1 April 2016 - 28-16 win at Wigan despite first-half loss of Chris Sandow to hamstring injury and Rhys Evans to shoulder injury. Wolves move two points clear at top of table.

5 April 2016 - Gene Ormsby joins Huddersfield on month's loan.

8 April 2016 - 25-22 home defeat to St Helens.

15 April 2016 - 11-0 defeat at Huddersfield.

22 April 2016 - 48-16 win at Widnes ends two-match losing run.

26 April 2016 - Tony Smith signs new contract to end of 2018.

27 April 2016 - Kurt Gidley extends contract to end of 2017.

28 April 2016 - 40-10 win at Wigan creates two-point gap at top of table. Jack Hughes plays most of game with broken hand and ruled out for six weeks.

15 May 2016 - 36-28 defeat at Wakefield after trailing 30-6 just after half-time.

18 May 2016 - Ben Westwood signs new contract for 2017.

21 May 2016 - 34-14 defeat by Castleford at Magic Weekend after leading 14-0.

KEY DATES

27 May 2016 - Kurt Gidley scores 20 points as Chris Sandow returns from hamstring injury in 52-18 home win over Leeds.

1 June 2016 - Ben Evans joins Leigh on month's loan.

4 June 2016 - 26-4 win at St Helens.

7 June 2016 - young prop Daniel Murray signs for Salford.

9 June 2016 - St George Illawarra prop Mike Cooper signs three-year deal and will return from 2017.

10 June 2016 - 19-12 home defeat by league leaders Hull FC.

18 June 2016 - late Kurt Gidley penalty earns 20-18 home victory over Catalans.

22 June 2016 - Ashton Sims suspended for two games for high tackle.

24 June 2016 - reserve hooker Sean Kenny signs for Salford with immediate effect.

24 June 2016 - late Kurt Gidley penalty earns 20-18 home Challenge Cup quarter-final victory over Widnes.

28 June 2016 - Ryan Atkins banned for one game for dangerous contact.

2 July 2016 - 16-all draw at Hull KR.

3 July 2016 - threequarter David Thompson joins Hull KR on loan to season end.

7 July 2016 - Ryan Atkins and Joe Westerman score try-braces in 40-14 home win over Salford.

14 July 2016 - Gene Ormsby released to join Huddersfield on permanent basis.

17 July 2016 - Rhys Evans scores double in 42-26 win at Castleford.

22 July 2016 - Ben Harrison joins Wakefield on loan to end of season.

23 July 2016 - Daryl Clark scores late try to secure 34-30 home win over Huddersfield.

26 July 2016 - James Laithwaite and Gary Wheeler sign for Toronto Wolfpack for 2017.

30 July 2016 - 56-12 Challenge Cup semi-final win over Wakefield at Leigh.

4 August 2016 - late Rhys Evans try disallowed as Super 8s opener ends in 20-18 home defeat by St Helens.

13 August 2016 - 38-10 win at Wakefield.

19 August 2016 - Matty Blythe to return from Bradford on one-year deal.

20 August 2016 - play-off place secured as last-second Jack Hughes try secures 14-11 home win over Castleford.

27 August 2016 - 12-10 Challenge Cup final defeat by Hull FC. Kurt Gidley suffers eye-socket injury. Chris Sandow injures knee. Ben Westwood tears pectoral.

3 September 2016 - 26-22 win at Catalans moves Wolves to top of table.

10 September 2016 - 30-12 home win over Widnes maintains top spot.

16 September 2016 - 35-28 home defeat by Wigan denies Wolves League Leaders trophy presentation. Ben Currie suffers season-ending ACL injury.

23 September 2016 - 23-6 win at Hull FC clinches League Leaders Shield.

24 September 2016 - prop Ben Evans to leave the club at end of season.

29 September 2016 - 18-10 home semi-final win over St Helens.

4 October 2016 - reserve winger Dave Thompson joins Leigh.

8 October 2016 - 12-6 defeat to Wigan in Grand Final.

12 October 2016 - Ryan Bailey, Jordan Cox and Mitchell Dodds to leave club.

13 October 2016 - chief executive Roger Draper leaves to join Super League.

18 October 2016 - Wigan prop Dom Crosby joins on two-year contract; St Helens prop Andre Savelio on one-year deal.

CLUB RECORDS

Highest score:
112-0 v Swinton, 20/5/2011
Highest score against:
12-84 v Bradford, 9/9/2001
Record attendance:
34,404 v Wigan, 22/1/49 *(Wilderspool)*
15,008 v Widnes, 25/3/2016
(Halliwell Jones Stadium)

MATCH RECORDS

Tries:
7 Brian Bevan v Leigh, 29/3/48
Brian Bevan v Bramley, 22/4/53
Goals:
16 Lee Briers v Swinton, 20/5/2011
Points:
44 Lee Briers v Swinton, 20/5/2011

SEASON RECORDS

Tries: 66 Brian Bevan 1952-53
Goals: 170 Steve Hesford 1978-79
Points: 363 Harry Bath 1952-53

CAREER RECORDS

Tries: 740 Brian Bevan 1945-62
Goals: 1,159 Steve Hesford 1975-85
Points: 2,586 Lee Briers 1997-2013
Appearances: 620 Brian Bevan 1945-62

WARRINGTON WOLVES

DATE	FIXTURE	RESULT	SCORERS	LGE	ATT
4/2/16	Leeds (a)	W10-12	t:Sandow,Penny g:Gidley(2)	5th	16,168
14/2/16	Hull KR (h)	W38-8	t:Currie,Westerman,Lineham(3),Clark g:Gidley(7)	3rd	11,037
26/2/16	Wakefield (h)	W34-16	t:Currie(2),Penny,Gidley,Sandow(2) g:Gidley(5)	2nd	10,631
3/3/16	Salford (a)	W30-31	t:Hughes,Currie,Atkins(2),Sims g:Sandow(5) fg:Sandow	2nd	4,381
12/3/16	Catalans Dragons (a)	W20-30	t:R Evans(2),Currie,G King,Sandow g:Gidley(5)	2nd	8,859
18/3/16	Castleford (h)	W56-12	t:Sandow(2),Penny,Lineham(2),Russell(2),Atkins,Currie(2),Dwyer g:Gidley(6)	2nd	10,940
25/3/16	Widnes (h)	W28-10	t:Sandow,Lineham,Gidley,Atkins,Currie g:Gidley(4)	1st	15,008
28/3/16	Hull FC (a)	L26-24	t:Atkins,Lineham(2),Penny,Sandow g:Sandow,Ratchford	1st	9,967
1/4/16	Wigan (a)	W16-28	t:Currie,Lineham,Penny,Ratchford,Atkins g:Ratchford,Gidley(3)	1st	17,480
8/4/16	St Helens (h)	L22-25	t:Penny(2),Atkins,Currie,Lineham g:Westwood	1st	13,678
15/4/16	Huddersfield (a)	L11-0		1st	5,427
22/4/16	Widnes (a)	W16-48	t:Gidley,Penny(2),Westerman(2),Westwood,Ratchford(2) g:Gidley(7),Ratchford	1st	7,441
28/4/16	Wigan (h)	W40-10	t:Clark,Westwood(2),Penny,Atkins(2),Jullien g:Gidley(5),Ratchford	1st	11,724
7/5/16	Oldham (a) (CCR6)	W10-70	t:Hill,Jullien(2),Currie(2),R Evans,G King(3),Lineham,Ormsby(2),Smith g:Gidley(6),Ratchford(3)	N/A	2,394
15/5/16	Wakefield (a)	L36-28	t:Westerman(2),Clark,Gidley,Russell g:Gidley(3),Smith	1st	5,180
21/5/16	Castleford (MW) ●	L34-14	t:Ratchford,Gidley,Currie g:Gidley	2nd	N/A
27/5/16	Leeds (h)	W52-18	t:Ormsby(2),Lineham,Dwyer,Atkins,Ratchford,Gidley,Clark(2) g:Gidley(8)	2nd	10,317
3/6/16	St Helens (a)	W4-26	t:Currie,Sandow,Atkins,Ratchford,R Evans g:Gidley(3)	2nd	11,353
10/6/16	Hull FC (h)	L12-19	t:Ormsby,Sandow g:Gidley(2)	4th	10,513
17/6/16	Catalans Dragons (h)	W20-18	t:Atkins,Penny,Dwyer g:Gidley(4)	3rd	9,259
24/6/16	Widnes (h) (CCQF)	W20-18	t:Hughes,Penny,Dwyer g:Gidley(4)	N/A	7,773
1/7/16	Hull KR (a)	D16-16	t:Russell,Dwyer,Hughes g:Ratchford(2)	3rd	6,827
7/7/16	Salford (h)	W40-14	t:Westerman(2),Atkins(2),Lineham,Patton,Russell g:Ratchford,Patton(5)	3rd	9,024
17/7/16	Castleford (a)	W26-42	t:R Evans(2),Ratchford,Dwyer,Currie,T King,Clark g:Sandow(4),Gidley(3)	3rd	8,060
23/7/16	Huddersfield (h)	W34-30	t:Ratchford,Currie,Westwood,Sandow,Atkins,Clark g:Gidley(5)	2nd	9,829
30/7/16	Wakefield (CCSF) ●●	W12-56	t:Hughes,Clark,R Evans,Gidley,Sandow,Ratchford,Currie,T King(2),Westwood g:Gidley(7),Ratchford	N/A	10,358
4/8/16	St Helens (h) (S8)	L18-20	t:Clark,Hughes,Atkins g:Gidley(3)	3rd	10,759
14/8/16	Wakefield (a) (S8)	W10-38	t:Currie,Hill,Atkins,Russell(2),Clark,Westerman g:Gidley(5)	2nd	3,552
20/8/16	Castleford (h) (S8)	W14-11	t:Westerman,R Evans,Hughes g:Gidley	2nd	9,228
27/8/16	Hull FC (CCF) ●●●	L12-10	t:Russell,Currie g:Gidley	N/A	76,235
3/9/16	Catalans Dragons (a) (S8)	W22-26	t:Patton(2),Penny,Currie g:Patton(5)	1st	7,108
9/9/16	Widnes (h) (S8)	W30-12	t:Hill,Sims,Smith,Philbin,Russell g:Gidley(5)	1st	10,488
16/9/16	Wigan (h) (S8)	L28-35	t:Russell,Gidley,Hill,Westerman,Currie g:Patton(4)	1st	13,044
23/9/16	Hull FC (a) (S8)	W6-23	t:Lineham(2),Penny g:Patton(5) fg:Patton	1st	17,453
29/9/16	St Helens (SF)	W18-10	t:Gidley,Ratchford,Lineham g:Patton(3)	N/A	12,036
8/10/16	Widnes (GF) ●●●●	L6-12	t:Patton g:Patton	N/A	70,202

● *Played at St James' Park, Newcastle* ●● *Played at Leigh Sports Village* ●●● *Played at Wembley Stadium* ●●●● *Played at Old Trafford, Manchester*

		APP		TRIES		GOALS		FG		PTS	
	D.O.B.	ALL	SL	ALL	SL	ALL	SL	ALL	SL	ALL	SL
Ryan Atkins	7/10/85	31(1)	28(1)	17	17	0	0	0	0	68	68
Ryan Bailey	11/11/83	1(14)	1(11)	0	0	0	0	0	0	0	0
Daryl Clark	10/2/93	31(1)	27(1)	10	9	0	0	0	0	40	36
Jordan Cox	27/5/92	(18)	(16)	0	0	0	0	0	0	0	0
Ben Currie	15/7/94	33	29	21	17	0	0	0	0	84	68
Mitchell Dodds	3/7/89	(2)	(2)	0	0	0	0	0	0	0	0
Brad Dwyer	28/4/93	5(18)	5(15)	6	5	0	0	0	0	24	20
Rhys Evans	30/10/92	33(1)	29(1)	8	6	0	0	0	0	32	24
Kurt Gidley	7/6/82	30	26	9	8	105	87	0	0	246	206
Chris Hill	3/11/87	36	32	4	3	0	0	0	0	16	12
Jack Hughes	4/1/92	30	27	6	4	0	0	0	0	24	16
Jack Johnson	25/4/96	3	3	0	0	0	0	0	0	0	0
Benjamin Jullien	1/3/95	5(7)	4(7)	3	1	0	0	0	0	12	4
George King	24/2/95	2(32)	2(28)	4	1	0	0	0	0	16	4
Toby King	9/7/96	11(5)	9(5)	3	1	0	0	0	0	12	4
Tom Lineham	21/9/91	22	21	16	15	0	0	0	0	64	60
Gene Ormsby	12/9/92	5	4	5	3	0	0	0	0	20	12
Declan Patton	23/5/95	8(1)	8(1)	4	4	23	23	1	1	63	63
Kevin Penny	3/10/87	20	18	14	13	0	0	0	0	56	52
Joe Philbin	16/11/94	1(7)	(7)	1	1	0	0	0	0	4	4
Stefan Ratchford	19/7/88	28(4)	24(4)	10	9	11	7	0	0	62	50
Matthew Russell	6/6/93	31	28	10	9	0	0	0	0	40	36
Chris Sandow	9/1/89	23(1)	20(1)	12	11	10	10	1	1	69	65
Ashton Sims	26/2/85	33	30	2	2	0	0	0	0	8	8
Morgan Smith	30/4/98	(7)	(6)	2	1	1	1	0	0	10	6
Joe Westerman	15/11/89	33(1)	29(1)	10	10	0	0	0	0	40	40
Ben Westwood	25/7/81	10(13)	9(11)	5	4	1	1	0	0	22	18
Gary Wheeler	30/9/89	(1)	(1)	0	0	0	0	0	0	0	0
Sam Wilde	8/9/95	3(8)	3(7)	0	0	0	0	0	0	0	0

'SL' totals include Super 8s, semi-final & Grand Final; 'All' totals also include Challenge Cup

Ben Currie

LEAGUE RECORD
P30-W21-D1-L8
(1st, SL/Grand Final Runners-Up)
F852, A541, Diff+311
43 points.

CHALLENGE CUP
Runners-Up

ATTENDANCES
Best - v Widnes (SL - 15,008)
Worst - v Widnes (CC - 7,773)
Total (SL/S8s/SF only) - 177,515
Average (SL/S8s/SF only) - 11,095
(Up by 1,637 on 2015)

28 October 2015 - goal-kicking winger or fullback Jack Owens released and joins St Helens.

1 November 2015 - Danny Tickle hospitalised following assault outside a Wigan nightclub.

19 November 2015 - Aussie forward Danny Galea retires from playing at age 32.

26 November 2015 - Danny Craven goes on season-long loan to Featherstone for 2016.

1 December 2015 - forward Chris Houston signs from Newcastle Knights on two-year deal.

4 December 2015 - Aaron Heremaia signs one-year contract extension to end of 2017.

6 December 2015 - forward Ben Kavanagh released.

13 January 2016 - prop Connor Farrell signs from Wigan on season-long loan deal.

16 January 2016 - Lloyd White signs two-year contract extension to end of 2018.

22 January 2016 - Scotland international prop Sam Brooks signs from Whitehaven on two-year contract.

24 January 2016 - 30-16 win at St Helens retains Karalius Cup.

7 February 2016 - debutant Setaimata Sa scores two tries in 24-16 round-one win at Wakefield.

14 February 2016 - Corey Thompson scores hat-trick in 56-12 home thrashing of champions Leeds as Vikings top the table after two rounds.

21 February 2016 - 28-20 defeat at Salford ends 100 per cent start to season in brought-forward round 11 game.

28 February 2016 - first-ever Super League away win at Huddersfield, by 36-18.

4 March 2016 - star performer Joe Mellor and Corey Thompson each score twice in 30-16 home win over Hull KR.

10 March 2016 - Stefan Marsh scores hat-trick and Corey Thompson scores two tries to take tally to 10 in six appearances, in televised 46-6 home victory over Hull FC.

17 March 2016 - Vikings overturn 8-0 half-time deficit to secure 18-12 win at unbeaten Wigan and open up two-point lead at top of table.

23 March 2016 - Danny Tickle is released by mutual consent.

23 March 2016 - Charly Runciman signs two-year contract extension to end of 2018.

25 March 2016 - Warrington leapfrog Vikings, lacking Kevin Brown, to top of table after 28-10 home Good Friday victory.

30 March 2016 - scrum-half Joe Mellor signs new three-year contract to end of 2019.

31 March 2016 - prop Eamon O'Carroll signs two-year contract extension to end of 2018.

2 April 2016 - Jordan Johnstone and Sam Brooks make debuts as injury hit side loses 21-8 at Catalans.

4 April 2016 - Chris Dean signs new two-year deal to end of 2018.

4 April 2016 - Stefan Marsh signs two-year contract extension to end of 2018.

7 April 2016 - Rhys Hanbury signs three-year extension to end of 2019.

WIDNES VIKINGS
KEY DATES

10 April 2016 - 34-24 home defeat to Castleford after leading 18-0 at end of first quarter.

12 April 2016 - Patrick Ah Van signs two-year extension to end of 2018.

17 April 2016 - 62-6 Challenge Cup win at Rochdale.

22 April 2016 - Jordan Johnstone signs two-year senior contract.

22 April 2016 - Kevin Brown and Chris Bridge injured in 48-16 home defeat by Warrington.

28 April 2016 - Denis Betts appointed England assistant coach.

29 April 2016 - Aaron Heremaia sent off for punching; Patrick Ah Van, Stefan Marsh and Lloyd White sin-binned in 18-16 home defeat by Wakefield.

3 May 2016 - Patrick Ah Van pleads guilty to dangerous throw on Ashley Gibson and gets five-match ban. Stefan Marsh take EGP for tripping and gets two matches.

3 May 2016 - Paddy Flynn joins Castleford on loan for season.

8 May 2016 - 28-18 win at Halifax takes Vikings into Challenge Cup quarter-finals.

11 May 2016 - prop Jack Buchanan joins from Wests Tigers on an 18-month deal.

15 May 2016 - 24-10 defeat at Hull KR is seventh league loss in a row.

18 May 2016 - Vikings fined £2,500 for fielding 14 players on two occasions in win over Hull FC in round 5.

29 May 2016 - 24-20 home win over Huddersfield, after trailing 16-0, ends eight-match losing league run.

4 June 2016 - 30-10 defeat at Hull FC.

9 June 2016 - Macgraff Leuluai signs two-year contract extension.

10 June 2016 - Tom Gilmore signs new contract to end of 2018.

16 June 2016 - wet-weather 7-0 home defeat to Wigan.

24 June 2016 - late Kurt Gidley penalty means 20-18 Challenge Cup quarter-final defeat at Warrington.

3 July 2016 - late Joe Mellor field goal ensures 23-22 win at Leeds, the first since 2002.

5 July 2016 - Wigan prop Greg Burke signs two-and-a-half year deal with immediate effect.

24 July 2016 - Joe Mellor stars in 100th Super League appearance, a 32-4 round-23 home win over Catalans.

4 August 2016 - Hep Cahill activates contract option to sign for sixth year in 2017.

5 August 2016 - Corey Thompson extends two-year contract by one year to end of 2018.

6 August 2016 - 26-10 defeat at Catalans in Super 8s opener.

11 August 2016 - 38-0 home hammering by top of the table Hull FC.

21 August 2016 - 40-8 home win over Wakefield moves Vikings into sixth spot.

1 September 2016 - Corey Thompson scores two tries in 8-6 win at Wigan, despite a 20-8 penalty count against and two sin-binnings. Stefan Marsh's season ended with knee injury.

10 September 2016 - 30-12 defeat at Warrington.

18 September 2016 - Kevin Brown and Patrick Ah Van sent off three minutes from end of 21-8 home defeat by St Helens.

20 September 2016 - Kevin Brown gets one-game ban for fighting. Patrick Ah Van gets sending off sufficient.

25 September 2016 - 40-26 defeat at Castleford ends season.

CLUB RECORDS
Highest score: 90-4 v Doncaster, 10/6/2007 **Highest score against:** 6-76 v Catalan Dragons, 31/3/2012 **Record attendance:** 24,205 v St Helens, 16/2/61
MATCH RECORDS
Tries: 7 Phil Cantillon v York, 18/2/2001 **Goals:** 14 Mark Hewitt v Oldham, 25/7/99 Tim Hartley v Saddleworth, 7/3/2009 **Points:** 38 Gavin Dodd v Doncaster, 10/6/2007
SEASON RECORDS
Tries: 58 Martin Offiah 1988-89 **Goals:** 161 Mick Nanyn 2007 **Points:** 434 Mick Nanyn 2007
CAREER RECORDS
Tries: 234 Mal Aspey 1964-80 **Goals:** 1,083 Ray Dutton 1966-78 **Points:** 2,195 Ray Dutton 1966-78 **Appearances:** 591 Keith Elwell 1970-86

WIDNES VIKINGS

WIDNES VIKINGS

DATE	FIXTURE	RESULT	SCORERS	LGE	ATT
7/2/16	Wakefield (a)	W16-24	t:Sa(2),Hanbury,White g:Hanbury(4)	3rd	5,240
14/2/16	Leeds (h)	W56-12	t:Marsh(2),Sa,Thompson(3),White,Runciman,Mellor,Farrell g:Hanbury(8)	1st	6,596
21/2/16	Salford (a)	L28-20	t:Hanbury,Houston,Marsh,Thompson g:Hanbury(2)	2nd	5,098
28/2/16	Huddersfield (a)	W18-36	t:Dean,Marsh(2),Runciman,Leuluai,Thompson(2) g:Hanbury(4)	1st	5,183
4/3/16	Hull KR (h)	W30-16	t:Hanbury,Mellor(2),Thompson(2) g:Hanbury(5)	1st	5,013
10/3/16	Hull FC (h)	W46-6	t:Mellor,Thompson(2),Marsh(3),Hanbury,Brown,Whitley g:Hanbury(5)	1st	4,753
17/3/16	Wigan (a)	W12-18	t:Whitley,Marsh,Runciman g:Hanbury(3)	1st	11,733
25/3/16	Warrington (a)	L28-10	t:Gilmore,Hanbury g:Hanbury	2nd	15,008
28/3/16	St Helens (h)	L12-20	t:Hanbury(2) g:Hanbury(2)	3rd	9,076
2/4/16	Catalans Dragons (a)	L21-8	t:Thompson g:Hanbury(2)	4th	8,642
10/4/16	Castleford (h)	L24-34	t:Ah Van,Leuluai,Thompson,White g:Bridge(4)	5th	5,081
17/4/16	Rochdale (a) (CCR5)	W6-62	t:Bridge(3),Johnstone,Brown(3),Dean,Thompson,Marsh,Manuokafoa, White g:Bridge(7)	N/A	1,242
22/4/16	Warrington (h)	L16-48	t:Mellor,Thompson,Marsh g:Hanbury(2)	6th	7,441
29/4/16	Wakefield (h)	L16-18	t:Runciman,O'Carroll,Hanbury g:Hanbury(2)	6th	4,398
8/5/16	Halifax (a) (CCR6)	W18-28	t:Heremaia,White,Houston,Runciman,J Chapelhow g:Hanbury(4)	N/A	2,032
15/5/16	Hull KR (a)	L24-10	t:Dudson,Thompson g:Hanbury	8th	7,506
21/5/16	Salford (MW) ●	L18-12	t:Hanbury,Bridge g:Hanbury(2)	8th	N/A
29/5/16	Huddersfield (h)	W24-20	t:Thompson(2),Mellor(2),Marsh g:Hanbury(2)	8th	4,683
3/6/16	Hull FC (a)	L30-10	t:Hanbury,Dean g:Hanbury	8th	10,259
9/6/16	Castleford (a)	W28-38	t:Leuluai,Ah Van(2),Bridge,White(2),Mellor g:Hanbury(5)	8th	4,968
16/6/16	Wigan (h)	L0-7		8th	6,219
24/6/16	Warrington (a) (CCQF)	L20-18	t:Mellor,Whitley,Runciman g:Hanbury(3)	N/A	7,773
3/7/16	Leeds (a)	W22-23	t:Thompson,Mellor,Ah Van,Hanbury g:Hanbury(3) fg:Mellor	6th	16,130
8/7/16	St Helens (a)	L12-10	t:Thompson,Ah Van g:Hanbury	7th	11,566
15/7/16	Salford (h)	L24-32	t:Whitley(2),Ah Van,Thompson g:White(3),Thompson	8th	4,636
24/7/16	Catalans Dragons (h)	W32-4	t:Thompson,Ah Van,Mellor,Heremaia,Marsh g:Thompson(3),Marsh(3)	7th	4,195
6/8/16	Catalans Dragons (a) (S8)	L26-10	t:Whitley,Ah Van g:White	7th	8,562
11/8/16	Hull FC (h) (S8)	L0-38		7th	4,359
21/8/16	Wakefield (h) (S8)	W40-8	t:Ah Van(2),Hanbury,Whitley,Thompson,Marsh,White g:White(5),Thompson	7th	4,010
1/9/16	Wigan (a) (S8)	W6-8	t:Thompson(2)	7th	11,495
9/9/16	Warrington (a) (S8)	L30-12	t:Mellor,Thompson g:Thompson,White	7th	10,488
18/9/16	St Helens (h) (S8)	L8-21	t:Ah Van,Thompson	7th	6,128
25/9/16	Castleford (a) (S8)	L40-26	t:Farrell(2),Thompson(2),Ah Van g:White(3)	7th	7,103

● *Played at St James' Park, Newcastle*

		APP		TRIES		GOALS		FG		PTS	
	D.O.B.	ALL	SL	ALL	SL	ALL	SL	ALL	SL	ALL	SL
Patrick Ah Van	17/3/88	19	18	12	12	0	0	0	0	48	48
Chris Bridge	5/7/84	15	13	5	2	11	4	0	0	42	16
Sam Brooks	29/9/93	(3)	(2)	0	0	0	0	0	0	0	0
Kevin Brown	2/10/84	26	24	4	1	0	0	0	0	16	4
Jack Buchanan	10/4/92	13(2)	12(2)	0	0	0	0	0	0	0	0
Greg Burke	12/2/93	8(1)	8(1)	0	0	0	0	0	0	0	0
Hep Cahill	15/10/86	26(3)	24(2)	0	0	0	0	0	0	0	0
Ed Chamberlain	8/2/96	5(1)	3(1)	0	0	0	0	0	0	0	0
Jay Chapelhow	21/9/95	1(8)	1(6)	1	0	0	0	0	0	4	0
Ted Chapelhow	21/9/95	(1)	(1)	0	0	0	0	0	0	0	0
Chris Dean	17/1/88	29(2)	26(2)	3	2	0	0	0	0	12	8
Gil Dudson	16/6/90	19(7)	17(6)	1	1	0	0	0	0	4	4
Connor Farrell	6/11/93	3(9)	3(9)	3	3	0	0	0	0	12	12
Paddy Flynn	11/12/87	1	0	0	0	0	0	0	0	0	0
Alex Gerrard	5/11/91	(5)	(5)	0	0	0	0	0	0	0	0
Tom Gilmore	2/2/94	5	4	1	1	0	0	0	0	4	4
Rhys Hanbury	27/8/85	30	28	12	12	62	55	0	0	172	158
Aaron Heremaia	19/9/82	8(20)	7(19)	2	1	0	0	0	0	8	4
Chris Houston	15/2/85	28(1)	26(1)	2	1	0	0	0	0	8	4
Ryan Ince	16/9/96	1	1	0	0	0	0	0	0	0	0
Jordan Johnstone	24/5/97	(4)	(2)	1	0	0	0	0	0	4	0
Macgraff Leuluai	9/2/90	13(14)	10(14)	3	3	0	0	0	0	12	12
Manase Manuokafoa	24/3/85	2(27)	1(25)	1	0	0	0	0	0	4	0
Stefan Marsh	3/9/90	20	19	14	13	3	3	0	0	62	58
Joe Mellor	28/11/90	32	30	12	11	0	0	1	1	49	45
Eamon O'Carroll	13/6/87	15	15	1	1	0	0	0	0	4	4
Charly Runciman	22/7/93	27	25	6	4	0	0	0	0	24	16
Setaimata Sa	14/9/87	8(5)	7(5)	3	3	0	0	0	0	12	12
Corey Thompson	15/5/90	33	30	28	27	6	6	0	0	124	120
Brad Walker	30/1/98	(1)	(1)	0	0	0	0	0	0	0	0
Lloyd White	9/8/88	29(1)	26(1)	7	6	13	13	0	0	54	50
Matt Whitley	20/1/96	13(16)	12(14)	8	6	0	0	0	0	32	24

'SL' totals include Super 8s; 'All' totals also include Challenge Cup

Corey Thompson

LEAGUE RECORD
P30-W12-D0-L18
(7th, SL)
F603, A643, Diff-40
24 points.

CHALLENGE CUP
Quarter Finalists

ATTENDANCES
Best - v St Helens (SL - 9,076)
Worst - v Wakefield (S8 - 4,010)
Total (SL/S8s only) - 76,588
Average (SL/S8s only) - 5,471
(Down by 505 on 2015)

175

10 November 2015 - Sam Tomkins undergoes knee surgery and out until Easter.

10 November 2015 - Ryan Hampshire signs three-year contract extension until end of 2018 and moves to Castleford on loan for 2016 season.

25 November 2015 - Logan Tomkins released and joins Salford.

18 December 2015 - Darrell Goulding takes up position of Youth Development Coach.

22 December 2015 - Michael McIlorum has bone graft on previous broken arm that hadn't healed properly.

13 January 2016 - prop Connor Farrell signs for Widnes on season-long loan deal after signing contract extension until end of 2018.

25 January 2016 - 32-16 friendly defeat at Salford.

5 February 2016 - two early Michael McIlorum tries help grind out opening-round 12-6 home win over Catalans in mudbath.

12 February 2016 - Josh Charnley crosses with four minutes left to secure 18-13 victory at injury-hit Huddersfield Giants.

14 February 2016 - Rhodri Lloyd moves on a permanent deal to Swinton.

16 February 2016 - prop Ben Flower signs new four-year deal until end of 2020 season.

20 February 2016 - Michael McIlorum to undergo surgery after breaking and dislocating ankle in 42-12 defeat by Brisbane Broncos in the World Club Series. Willie Isa out for six weeks with knee injury.

25 February 2016 - late Dom Manfredi try secures 20-16 home win over Salford.

4 March 2016 - two late Matty Smith field goals earn Wigan 26-25 win at KC Stadium.

11 March 2016 - 28-6 round-five home win over Leeds.

17 March 2016 - 18-12 home defeat by Widnes win ends 100 per cent league record in 2016 in first home Super League loss for 21 months.

25 March 2016 - 24-12 Good Friday win at St Helens.

30 March 2016 - Josh Charnley, to Sale rugby union and Dan Sarginson, to Gold Coast Titans, to leave at season end.

1 April 2016 - 28-16 home defeat by Warrington. Liam Farrell gets one-match ban on early guilty plea for use of knees on try-scoring Stefan Ratchford.

10 April 2016 - injury hit side crashes 62-0 at in-form Wakefield.

15 April 2016 - two tries from John Bateman helps secure 26-12 home victory over Castleford.

21 April 2016 - Dan Sarginson scores last-minute try to secure 26-19 home win over Huddersfield.

8 May 2016 - Josh Charnley scores 22 points in 54-4 Challenge Cup win at Dewsbury.

13 May 2016 - 30-16 home defeat by Hull FC sees Warriors drop out of top four. Sam Tomkins scores try on return.

21 May 2016 - 40-8 win over Leeds at Magic Weekend.

26 May 2016 - 33-26 win at Castleford moves Warriors back to joint top of table.

KEY DATES

ALSO INSIDE GALE EYEING ENGLAND SPOT | VIKINGS REFUSE TO SPEND BIG

RUGBY LEAGUER &
League Express
SEVEN UP

Dominant derby display sees Wigan dispose of fierce rivals St Helens for the seventh Good Friday in a row

WIGAN WINGER

PLUS EVERY SUPER LEAGUE, CHAMPIONSHIP, LEAGUE 1 & NRL REPORT

3 June 2016 - Josh Charnley scores hat-trick in 23-20 win at Salford.

10 June 2016 - Sam Tomkins scores last-gasp try and Matty Smith seals 20-18 win at Hull KR.

15 June 2016 - John Bateman fined £10,000 by club and banned for eight games after a fight with a teammate on May 27.

16 June 2016 - Josh Charnley scores only try in 7-0 win at Widnes. Ben Flower gets one-match ban for dangerous throw.

17 June 2016 - Joe Burgess to re-join on three-year deal after one season with Sydney Roosters.

23 June 2016 - Frank Paul Nuuausala signs immediately from Canberra Raiders on three-and-a-half-year deal.

26 June 2016 - 26-12 home win over Castleford in Challenge Cup quarter-final.

2 July 2016 - 26-6 win at Catalans spoils Dragons tenth anniversary party.

3 July 2016 - Thomas Leuluai re-signs for 2017 and will then take up coaching role.

5 July 2016 - prop Greg Burke joins Widnes with immediate effect.

8 July 2016 - Sean O'Loughlin sent off for high tackle on Chris Annakin as Lewis Tierney scores last-second try to secured 22-18 home win over Wakefield.

10 July 2016 - Lewis Tierney signs contract extension to end of 2019 with option for further year in club's favour.

12 July 2016 - Sean O'Loughlin banned for one game.

16 July 2016 - Frank-Paul Nuuausala makes debut in 18-16 defeat at Leeds. Josh Charnley banned for two games for contact with match official. Taulima Tautai gets two games for dangerous contact on Adam Cuthbertson.

20 July 2016 - Taulima Tautai ban reduced to one game on appeal. Josh Charnley's appeal rejected.

22 July 2016 - 23-4 home defeat by St Helens. Frank-Paul Nuuausala gets one-game ban for punch on Louie McCarthy-Scarsbrook.

29 July 2016 - 16-12 Challenge Cup semi-final defeat by Hull FC at Doncaster.

5 August 2016 - Sam Tomkins scores 150th Wigan try in 60-12 home Super 8s win over Wakefield as Warriors draw level with Hull FC at top.

12 August 2016 - Dom Manfredi's season ended with ACL damage in 36-22 defeat at Castleford.

19 August 2016 - Anthony Gelling scores hat-trick in 25-0 home win over St Helens.

1 September 2016 - 8-6 home defeat by Widnes.

9 September 2016 - late Taulima Tautai try seals comeback 18-12 win at Hull FC.

16 September 2016 - dramatic 35-28 comeback win at Warrington despite trailing 28-14 before dismissal of Ben Flower on 56 minutes. Sam Tomkins' season ended with foot injury.

20 September 2016 - Ben Flower banned for two matches for elbow on Declan Patton.

23 September 2016 - 48-24 home win over Catalans to set up home semi-final against Hull FC. Sean O'Loughlin injures calf in warm-up after five weeks out with hamstring problem.

30 September 2016 - 18-10 home semi-final win over Hull FC.

5 October 2016 - Catalans prop Romain Navarrete joins on two-year deal.

8 October 2016 - Liam Farrell wins Harry Sunderland Trophy in 12-6 Grand Final win.

11 October 2016 - Matty Smith re-joins St Helens.

11 October 2016 - former Academy winger Liam Forsyth re-joins from Bath rugby union on two-year contract.

11 October 2016 - Morgan Escaré joins on initial one-year deal.

CLUB RECORDS

Highest score:
116-0 v Flimby & Fothergill, 14/2/25
Highest score against:
0-75 v St Helens, 26/6/2005
Record attendance:
47,747 v St Helens, 27/3/59 *(Central Park)*
25,004 v St Helens, 25/3/2005
(JJB/DW Stadium)

MATCH RECORDS

Tries: 10 Martin Offiah v Leeds, 10/5/92
Shaun Edwards v Swinton, 29/9/92
Goals: 22 Jim Sullivan
v Flimby & Fothergill, 14/2/25
Points: 44 Jim Sullivan
v Flimby & Fothergill, 14/2/25

SEASON RECORDS

Tries: 62 Johnny Ring 1925-26
Goals: 186 Frano Botica 1994-95
Points: 462 Pat Richards 2010

CAREER RECORDS

Tries: 478 Billy Boston 1953-68
Goals: 2,317 Jim Sullivan 1921-46
Points: 4,883 Jim Sullivan 1921-46
Appearances: 774 Jim Sullivan 1921-46

WIGAN WARRIORS

DATE	FIXTURE	RESULT	SCORERS	LGE	ATT
5/2/16	Catalans Dragons (h)	W12-6	t:McIlorum(2) g:Smith(2)	4th	13,436
12/2/16	Huddersfield (a)	W13-18	t:Farrell,Manfredi,Charnley g:Smith(3)	4th	5,912
20/2/16	Brisbane (h) (WCS)	L12-42	t:Sarginson,Williams g:Smith,Powell	N/A	19,103
25/2/16	Salford (h)	W20-16	t:Gildart(2),Gelling,Manfredi g:Smith(2)	3rd	10,897
4/3/16	Hull FC (a)	W25-26	t:Flower,Williams,Bateman,Charnley g:Smith(4) fg:Smith(2)	3rd	10,660
11/3/16	Leeds (h)	W28-6	t:Bateman,Gildart,Manfredi,Clubb,Gelling g:Smith(4)	3rd	14,425
17/3/16	Widnes (h)	L12-18	t:Farrell,Charnley(2)	3rd	11,733
25/3/16	St Helens (a)	W12-24	t:Manfredi,Powell,J Tomkins,Smith g:Smith(4)	3rd	17,890
28/3/16	Hull KR (h)	W30-16	t:Tierney,Charnley(3),Manfredi,Gildart g:Charnley(3)	2nd	11,268
1/4/16	Warrington (h)	L16-28	t:Manfredi(3) g:Charnley(2)	2nd	17,480
10/4/16	Wakefield (a)	L62-0		4th	5,751
15/4/16	Castleford (h)	W26-12	t:Tierney,Bateman(2),Gregson g:Smith(5)	3rd	11,849
21/4/16	Huddersfield (h)	W26-19	t:Gelling,Bateman,Smith,Sarginson g:Smith(4) fg:Smith(2)	3rd	10,914
28/4/16	Warrington (a)	L40-10	t:Charnley,Bateman g:Smith	4th	11,724
8/5/16	Dewsbury (a) (CCR6)	W4-54	t:Charnley(2),Williams,Gildart(2),Sarginson,Bateman(2),Sutton,Tierney g:Charnley(7)	N/A	3,102
13/5/16	Hull FC (h)	L16-30	t:Gildart,Bateman,S Tomkins g:Smith(2)	5th	15,083
21/5/16	Leeds (MW) ●	W8-40	t:Isa(2),Williams,Manfredi,Flower,Gildart,Sarginson g:Smith(6)	4th	N/A
26/5/16	Castleford (a)	W26-33	t:Charnley(2),S Tomkins,Manfredi,Powell g:Smith(6) fg:Smith	4th	5,558
3/6/16	Salford (a)	W20-23	t:Charnley(3),Sutton g:Smith(3) fg:Smith	4th	4,096
10/6/16	Hull KR (a)	W18-20	t:Manfredi(2),Gelling,S Tomkins g:Smith(2)	3rd	7,507
16/6/16	Widnes (h)	W0-7	t:Charnley g:Smith fg:Smith	2nd	6,219
25/6/16	Castleford (h) (CCQF)	W26-12	t:Sarginson,S Tomkins,Charnley(2),Manfredi g:Smith(3)	N/A	8,010
2/7/16	Catalans Dragons (a)	W6-26	t:Sarginson,Sutton,Gildart,Manfredi g:Smith(5)	2nd	11,856
8/7/16	Wakefield (h)	W22-18	t:Gildart,Powell,Tierney(2) g:Smith(3)	1st	11,121
15/7/16	Leeds (a)	L18-16	t:Charnley,Higginson,Williams g:Smith(2)	2nd	16,712
22/7/16	St Helens (h)	L4-23	t:Tierney	3rd	20,049
29/7/16	Hull FC (CCSF) ●●	L16-12	t:Williams,Isa g:Smith(2)	N/A	10,488
5/8/16	Wakefield (h) (S8)	W60-12	t:Williams(2),Powell,Charnley,S Tomkins(2),Bateman,Gildart,Manfredi, Sarginson,Smith g:Smith(3),Shorrocks(5)	2nd	10,593
12/8/16	Castleford (a) (S8)	L36-22	t:Powell,Flower,Bateman,Mossop g:Smith(3)	3rd	6,325
19/8/16	St Helens (h) (S8)	W25-0	t:Gelling(3),Williams g:Smith(4) fg:Smith	3rd	15,265
1/9/16	Widnes (h) (S8)	L6-8	t:Farrell g:Shorrocks	3rd	11,495
9/9/16	Hull FC (a) (S8)	W12-18	t:Williams,Powell,Tautai g:Smith(3)	3rd	11,686
16/9/16	Warrington (a) (S8)	W28-35	t:Tierney(2),S Tomkins,Charnley(2),Gelling g:Smith(3),Shorrocks(2) fg:Smith	3rd	13,044
23/9/16	Catalans Dragons (h) (S8)	W48-24	t:Gelling,Williams(2),Bateman,Bretherton,Charnley,Smith(2) g:Smith(8)	2nd	16,140
30/9/16	Hull FC (h) (SF)	W28-18	t:Tierney(2),Bateman,Powell,Gelling g:Smith(4)	N/A	10,013
8/10/16	Warrington (GF) ●●●	W6-12	t:Gildart,Charnley g:Smith(2)	N/A	70,202

● Played at St James' Park, Newcastle ●● Played at Keepmoat Stadium, Doncaster ●●● Played at Old Trafford, Manchester

		APP		TRIES		GOALS		FG		PTS	
	D.O.B.	ALL	SL	ALL	SL	ALL	SL	ALL	SL	ALL	SL
John Bateman	30/9/93	27	24	13	11	0	0	0	0	52	44
Joe Bretherton	5/10/95	2(11)	2(9)	1	1	0	0	0	0	4	4
Greg Burke	12/2/93	4(15)	4(13)	0	0	0	0	0	0	0	0
Josh Charnley	26/6/91	32	30	24	20	12	5	0	0	120	90
Tony Clubb	12/6/87	8(7)	8(6)	1	1	0	0	0	0	4	4
Dominic Crosby	11/12/90	12(6)	11(5)	0	0	0	0	0	0	0	0
Macauley Davies	4/9/96	(1)	(1)	0	0	0	0	0	0	0	0
Liam Farrell	2/7/90	15(1)	14(1)	3	3	0	0	0	0	12	12
Ben Flower	19/10/87	27	24	3	3	0	0	0	0	12	12
Anthony Gelling	18/10/92	22	20	10	10	0	0	0	0	40	40
Oliver Gildart	6/8/96	28(2)	24(2)	12	10	0	0	0	0	48	40
Nick Gregson	17/12/95	5(4)	5(4)	1	0	0	0	0	0	4	4
Jack Higginson	4/4/97	2(1)	2(1)	1	1	0	0	0	0	4	4
Willie Isa	1/1/89	29(1)	25(1)	3	2	0	0	0	0	12	8
Dominic Manfredi	1/10/93	25	21	15	14	0	0	0	0	60	56
Michael McIlorum	10/1/88	3	2	2	2	0	0	0	0	8	8
Lee Mossop	17/1/89	12(13)	10(12)	1	1	0	0	0	0	4	4
Frank-Paul Nuuausala	13/2/87	5(6)	5(6)	0	0	0	0	0	0	0	0
Sean O'Loughlin	24/11/82	18(1)	14(1)	0	0	0	0	0	0	0	0
Sam Powell	3/7/92	33(3)	30(2)	7	7	1	0	0	0	30	28
Dan Sarginson	26/5/93	32(1)	28(1)	7	4	0	0	0	0	28	16
Kyle Shelford	13/9/96	(1)	(1)	0	0	0	0	0	0	0	0
Jake Shorrocks	26/10/95	2(10)	2(10)	0	0	8	8	0	0	16	16
Matty Smith	23/7/87	35	31	5	5	95	89	9	9	219	207
Ryan Sutton	2/8/95	17(18)	15(16)	3	2	0	0	0	0	12	8
Taulima Tautai	3/4/88	1(34)	1(30)	1	1	0	0	0	0	4	4
Lewis Tierney	20/10/94	22(1)	20	10	9	0	0	0	0	40	36
Joel Tomkins	21/3/87	9(1)	9	1	1	0	0	0	0	4	4
Sam Tomkins	23/3/89	15(1)	13(1)	7	6	0	0	0	0	28	24
Luke Waterworth	20/6/96	1	1	0	0	0	0	0	0	0	0
Jack Wells	21/9/97	(3)	(3)	0	0	0	0	0	0	0	0
George Williams	31/10/94	25(1)	21(1)	12	9	0	0	0	0	48	36

'SL' totals include Super 8s, semi-final & Grand Final; 'All' totals also include Challenge Cup & World Club Series

Sam Powell

LEAGUE RECORD
P30-W21-D0-L9
(2nd, SL/Grand Final Winners,
Champions)
F669, A560, Diff+109
42 points.

CHALLENGE CUP
Semi-Finalists

ATTENDANCES
Best - v St Helens (SL - 20,049)
Worst - v Castleford (CC - 8,010)
Total (SL/S8s/SF only) - 211,761
Average (SL/S8s/SF only) - 13,235
(Up by 84 on 2015)

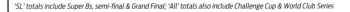

177

SUPER LEAGUE XXI
Round by Round

ROUND 1

Thursday 4th February 2016

LEEDS RHINOS 10 WARRINGTON WOLVES 12

RHINOS: 1 Zak Hardaker; 2 Tom Briscoe; 3 Kallum Watkins; 4 Joel Moon; 5 Ryan Hall; 14 Liam Sutcliffe; 6 Danny McGuire (C); 8 Keith Galloway (D); 7 Rob Burrow; 10 Adam Cuthbertson; 26 Brett Ferres (D); 12 Carl Ablett; 15 Brett Delaney. Subs (all used): 17 Mitch Garbutt; 16 Brad Singleton; 25 Jordan Lilley; 18 Jimmy Keinhorst.
Tries: Singleton (47), Hall (54); **Goals:** Hardaker 1/3.
WOLVES: 5 Matthew Russell; 20 Kevin Penny; 3 Rhys Evans; 11 Ben Currie; 2 Tom Lineham (D); 1 Kurt Gidley (D); 7 Chris Sandow; 8 Chris Hill (C); 9 Daryl Clark; 10 Ashton Sims; 13 Ben Westwood; 12 Jack Hughes (D); 14 Joe Westerman (D). Subs (all used): 32 Jordan Cox (D); 16 Brad Dwyer; 18 George King; 29 Benjamin Jullien (D).
Tries: Sandow (36), Penny (67); **Goals:** Gidley 2/2.
Rugby Leaguer & League Express Men of the Match: *Rhinos:* Ryan Hall; *Wolves:* Ben Currie.
Penalty count: 10-5; **Half-time:** 0-6;
Referee: James Child; **Attendance:** 16,168.

Friday 5th February 2016

HULL FC 42 SALFORD RED DEVILS 20

HULL FC: 1 Jamie Shaul; 2 Mahe Fonua (D); 4 Jack Logan; 3 Carlos Tuimavave (D); 5 Fetuli Talanoa; 6 Leon Pryce; 7 Marc Sneyd; 8 Scott Taylor (D); 9 Danny Houghton (C); 10 Liam Watts; 12 Mark Minichiello; 21 Sika Manu (D); 16 Jordan Thompson. Subs (all used): 30 Danny Washbrook (D2); 15 Chris Green; 23 Frank Pritchard (D); 22 Josh Bowden.
Tries: Pryce (4), Fonua (19), Thompson (27), Talanoa (31), Tuimavave (34), Bowden (44), Logan (47), Shaul (53); **Goals:** Sneyd 5/8.
RED DEVILS: 14 Gareth O'Brien (D); 2 Justin Carney (D); 33 Josh Jones (D); 4 Junior Sa'u; 3 Josh Griffin; 6 Robert Lui (D); 7 Michael Dobson; 8 Craig Kopczak (D); 9 Tommy Lee (C); 10 George Griffin; 11 Ben Murdoch-Masila (D); 22 Matt Sarsfield (D); 13 Mark Flanagan (D). Subs (all used): 1 Niall Evalds; 16 Olsi Krasniqi; 17 Phil Joseph (D); 19 Logan Tomkins.
Tries: J Griffin (11), Sa'u (58, 72), Evalds (70);
Goals: J Griffin 1/2, Dobson 1/2.
Sin bin: Lee (66) - punching.
Rugby Leaguer & League Express Men of the Match: *Hull FC:* Danny Houghton; *Red Devils:* Ben Murdoch-Masila.
Penalty count: 8-7; **Half-time:** 26-6;
Referee: Chris Kendall; **Attendance:** 12,265.

ST HELENS 30 HUDDERSFIELD GIANTS 16

SAINTS: 22 Jack Owens (D); 2 Tom Makinson; 18 Dominique Peyroux (D); 4 Mark Percival; 5 Adam Swift; 3 Jordan Turner; 7 Luke Walsh; 10 Kyle Amor; 9 James Roby; 14 Lama Tasi (D); 12 Jon Wilkin (C); 11 Atelea Vea; 13 Louie McCarthy-Scarsbrook. Subs (all used): 8 Alex Walmsley; 15 Greg Richards; 16 Andre Savelio; 17 Luke Thompson.
Tries: Percival (7, 36), Vea (25), Turner (47), Thompson (60); **Goals:** Walsh 5/6.
GIANTS: 1 Scott Grix; 2 Jermaine McGillvary; 3 Leroy Cudjoe; 18 Jake Connor; 5 Aaron Murphy; 6 Danny Brough (C); 7 Jamie Ellis; 16 Sam Rapira (D); 9 Ryan Hinchcliffe (D); 8 Eorl Crabtree; 17 Ukuma Ta'ai; 12 Michael Lawrence; 13 Larne Patrick (D2). Subs (all used): 14 Daniel Smith; 19 Josh Johnson; 20 Kruise Leeming; 22 Oliver Roberts (D).
Tries: Murphy (12), Ta'ai (57), Connor (69);
Goals: Brough 0/1, Ellis 2/2.
Rugby Leaguer & League Express Men of the Match: Saints: Luke Walsh; Giants: Jamie Ellis.
Penalty count: 9-7; **Half-time:** 16-4;
Referee: Robert Hicks; **Attendance:** 10,408.

WIGAN WARRIORS 12 CATALANS DRAGONS 6

WARRIORS: 22 Lewis Tierney; 2 Josh Charnley; 3 Anthony Gelling; 4 Dan Sarginson; 5 Dominic Manfredi; 6 George Williams; 7 Matty Smith; 10 Ben Flower; 9 Michael McIlorum; 13 Sean O'Loughlin (C); 25 Willie Isa (D); 12 Liam Farrell; 14 John Bateman. Subs (all used): 15 Tony Clubb; 16 Sam Powell; 19 Taulima Tautai; 21 Ryan Sutton.
Tries: McIlorum (14, 18); **Goals:** Smith 2/3.
DRAGONS: 1 Tony Gigot; 20 Fouad Yaha; 3 Krisnan Inu; 4 Vincent Duport; 5 Pat Richards (D); 6 Todd Carney; 7 Richard Myler (D); 15 Julian Bousquet; 9 Paul Aiton (D); 8 Louis Anderson; 11 Glenn Stewart (D); 12 Justin Horo (D); 13 Jason Baitieri (C). Subs (all used): 14 Dave Taylor (D); 17 Gregory Mounis; 19 Olivier Elima; 16 Eloi Pelissier.
Try: Horo (42); **Goals:** Richards 1/1.
Rugby Leaguer & League Express Men of the Match: *Warriors:* Michael McIlorum; *Dragons:* Dave Taylor.
Penalty count: 6-8; **Half-time:** 10-0;
Referee: Ben Thaler; **Attendance:** 13,436.

Sunday 7th February 2016

HULL KINGSTON ROVERS 16 CASTLEFORD TIGERS 16

ROVERS: 18 Ben Cockayne; 1 Ken Sio; 21 Thomas Minns (D); 4 Iain Thornley (D); 2 Josh Mantellato; 11 Maurice Blair; 7 Albert Kelly; 17 Dane Tilse; 24 George Lawler; 10 Mitchell Allgood; 12 Graeme Horne (C); 13 Chris Clarkson (D); 20 James Greenwood. Subs (all used): 26 Rob Mulhern (D); 15 James Donaldson; 16 James Green; 19 John Boudebza.
Tries: Donaldson (39), Mantellato (58, 78);
Goals: Mantellato 2/3.
Sin bin: Allgood (24) - fighting.
TIGERS: 1 Luke Dorn; 2 Joel Monaghan (D); 19 Ben Crooks (D); 4 Michael Shenton (C); 5 Denny Solomona; 6 Ben Roberts; 7 Luke Gale; 10 Grant Millington; 15 Paul McShane; 16 Matt Cook; 11 Oliver Holmes; 12 Mike McMeeken; 14 Lee Jewitt. Subs (all used): 21 Ryan Boyle; 9 Adam Milner; 17 Junior Moors; 3 Jake Webster.
Tries: Solomona (17), Webster (49, 62); **Goals:** Gale 2/3.
Sin bin: Jewitt (24) - fighting.
Rugby Leaguer & League Express Men of the Match: *Rovers:* Ben Cockayne; *Tigers:* Denny Solomona.
Penalty count: 7-6; **Half-time:** 6-6;
Referee: Richard Silverwood; **Attendance:** 11,011.

WAKEFIELD TRINITY WILDCATS 16 WIDNES VIKINGS 24

WILDCATS: 1 Ben Jones-Bishop (D); 2 Tom Johnstone; 3 Bill Tupou; 18 Joe Arundel; 14 Reece Lyne; 6 Jacob Miller; 7 Liam Finn (D2); 8 Nick Scruton; 24 Stuart Howarth; 10 Anthony England (D); 17 Matty Ashurst; 12 Danny Kirmond (C); 16 Tinirau Arona (D). Subs (all used): 20 Michael Sio; 23 Scott Anderson; 13 Anthony Tupou (D); 19 Jon Molloy.
Tries: Howarth (7), Lyne (44), Sio (67); **Goals:** Finn 2/3.
VIKINGS: 1 Rhys Hanbury; 2 Corey Thompson (D); 3 Chris Bridge (D); 4 Charly Runciman; 5 Patrick Ah Van; 6 Kevin Brown (C); 7 Joe Mellor; 8 Eamon O'Carroll; 9 Lloyd White; 18 Gil Dudson; 15 Setaimata Sa (D); 32 Connor Farrell (D); 13 Hep Cahill. Subs (all used): 14 Chris Dean; 10 Manase Manuokafoa; 11 Chris Houston (D); 33 Aaron Heremaia.
Tries: Sa (19, 36), Hanbury (34), White (50);
Goals: Hanbury 4/4.
Rugby Leaguer & League Express Men of the Match: *Wildcats:* Anthony Tupou; *Vikings:* Rhys Hanbury.
Penalty count: 11-6; **Half-time:** 4-18;
Referee: Phil Bentham; **Attendance:** 5,240.

ROUND 2

Thursday 11th February 2016

SALFORD RED DEVILS 44 ST HELENS 10

RED DEVILS: 14 Gareth O'Brien; 2 Justin Carney; 33 Josh Jones; 3 Josh Griffin; 18 Greg Johnson; 6 Robert Lui; 7 Michael Dobson; 8 Craig Kopczak; 9 Tommy Lee (C); 10 George Griffin; 11 Ben Murdoch-Masila; 13 Mark Flanagan; 21 Ryan Lannon. Subs (all used): 1 Niall Evalds; 15 Adam Walne; 17 Phil Joseph; 19 Logan Tomkins.
Tries: Johnson (3), Kopczak (8), Lui (12, 38), Evalds (35, 77), A Walne (42), Dobson (55);
Goals: J Griffin 2/3, Dobson 4/6.
SAINTS: 22 Jack Owens; 2 Tom Makinson; 13 Louie McCarthy-Scarsbrook; 4 Mark Percival; 5 Adam Swift; 3 Jordan Turner; 7 Luke Walsh; 10 Kyle Amor; 28 Morgan Knowles; 14 Lama Tasi; 11 Atelea Vea; 12 Jon Wilkin (C); 17 Luke Thompson. Subs (all used): 8 Alex Walmsley; 15 Greg Richards; 16 Andre Savelio; 19 Theo Fages (D).
Tries: Walmsley (16), Swift (62); **Goals:** Walsh 1/2.
Sin bin: Walsh (30) - professional foul.
Rugby Leaguer & League Express Men of the Match: *Red Devils:* Robert Lui; *Saints:* Alex Walmsley.
Penalty count: 8-7; **Half-time:** 32-6;
Referee: Richard Silverwood; **Attendance:** 4,386.

Friday 12th February 2016

HUDDERSFIELD GIANTS 13 WIGAN WARRIORS 18

GIANTS: 5 Aaron Murphy; 2 Jermaine McGillvary; 3 Leroy Cudjoe; 31 Sam Wood (D); 29 Jamie Foster (D); 18 Jake Connor; 7 Jamie Ellis; 16 Sam Rapira; 9 Ryan Hinchcliffe (C); 19 Josh Johnson; 17 Ukuma Ta'ai; 12 Michael Lawrence; 13 Larne Patrick. Subs (all used): 14 Daniel Smith; 20 Kruise Leeming; 21 Nathan Mason; 22 Oliver Roberts.
Tries: McGillvary (24), Foster (65); **Goals:** Ellis 2/3;
Field goal: Ellis (70).
WARRIORS: 22 Lewis Tierney; 2 Josh Charnley; 3 Anthony Gelling; 4 Dan Sarginson; 5 Dominic Manfredi; 16 Sam Powell; 7 Matty Smith; 10 Ben Flower; 9 Michael McIlorum; 13 Sean O'Loughlin (C); 12 Liam Farrell; 25 Willie Isa; 14 John Bateman. Subs (all used): 15 Tony Clubb; 19 Taulima Tautai; 21 Ryan Sutton; 26 Greg Burke (D2).
Tries: Farrell (43), Manfredi (58), Charnley (77);
Goals: Smith 3/3.
Rugby Leaguer & League Express Men of the Match: *Giants:* Jamie Ellis; *Warriors:* John Bateman.
Penalty count: 11-10; **Half-time:** 6-0;
Referee: Phil Bentham; **Attendance:** 5,912.

Saturday 13th February 2016

CATALANS DRAGONS 10 HULL FC 38

DRAGONS: 1 Tony Gigot; 20 Fouad Yaha; 3 Krisnan Inu; 4 Vincent Duport; 5 Pat Richards; 6 Todd Carney; 7 Richard Myler; 8 Louis Anderson; 16 Eloi Pelissier; 15 Julian Bousquet; 11 Glenn Stewart; 12 Justin Horo; 13 Jason Baitieri (C). Subs (all used): 14 Dave Taylor; 17 Gregory Mounis; 18 Thomas Bosc; 19 Olivier Elima.
Tries: Richards (13, 22); **Goals:** Richards 1/2.
HULL FC: 1 Jamie Shaul; 19 Steve Michaels; 4 Jack Logan; 3 Carlos Tuimavave; 5 Fetuli Talanoa; 6 Leon Pryce; 7 Marc Sneyd; 8 Scott Taylor; 9 Danny Houghton; 10 Liam Watts; 21 Sika Manu; 12 Mark Minichiello; 16 Jordan Thompson. Subs (all used): 11 Gareth Ellis (C); 22 Josh Bowden; 23 Frank Pritchard; 30 Danny Washbrook.
Tries: Talanoa (8, 62), Manu (16), Bowden (26), Logan (31), Ellis (59), Shaul (66); **Goals:** Sneyd 5/8.
Sin bin: Pryce (51) - off the ball challenge.
Rugby Leaguer & League Express Men of the Match: *Dragons:* Glenn Stewart; *Hull FC:* Jamie Shaul.
Penalty count: 6-10; **Half-time:** 10-22;
Referee: Robert Hicks; **Attendance:** 10,234.

Sunday 14th February 2016

WARRINGTON WOLVES 38 HULL KINGSTON ROVERS 8

WOLVES: 5 Matthew Russell; 20 Kevin Penny; 3 Rhys Evans; 11 Ben Currie; 2 Tom Lineham; 1 Kurt Gidley; 7 Chris Sandow; 8 Chris Hill (C); 9 Daryl Clark; 10 Ashton Sims; 13 Ben Westwood; 12 Jack Hughes; 14 Joe Westerman. Subs (all used): 4 Ryan Atkins; 16 Brad Dwyer; 18 George King; 32 Jordan Cox.
Tries: Currie (4), Westerman (18), Lineham (44, 67, 73), Clark (75); **Goals:** Gidley 7/7.
Sin bin: Gidley (38) - professional foul.
ROVERS: 18 Ben Cockayne; 5 Kieran Dixon; 4 Iain Thornley; 21 Thomas Minns; 1 Ken Sio; 11 Maurice Blair; 7 Albert Kelly; 16 James Green; 24 George Lawler; 17 Dane Tilse; 12 Graeme Horne (C); 13 Chris Clarkson; 10 Mitchell Allgood. Subs (all used): 8 Adam Walker; 15 James Donaldson; 25 Stephen Holker; 26 Rob Mulhern.
Tries: Thornley (50), Dixon (70);
Goals: Dixon 0/1, Kelly 0/1.
Rugby Leaguer & League Express Men of the Match: *Wolves:* Chris Hill; *Rovers:* George Lawler.
Penalty count: 10-7; **Half-time:** 12-0;
Referee: Ben Thaler; **Attendance:** 11,037.

WIDNES VIKINGS 56 LEEDS RHINOS 12

VIKINGS: 1 Rhys Hanbury; 2 Corey Thompson; 3 Chris Bridge; 4 Charly Runciman; 17 Stefan Marsh; 6 Kevin Brown (C); 7 Joe Mellor; 8 Eamon O'Carroll; 9 Lloyd White; 18 Gil Dudson; 15 Setaimata Sa; 32 Connor Farrell; 11 Chris Houston. Subs (all used): 14 Chris Dean; 33 Aaron Heremaia; 10 Manase Manuokafoa; 13 Hep Cahill.
Tries: Marsh (5, 69), Sa (9), Thompson (12, 47, 61), White (27), Runciman (36), Mellor (49), Farrell (66);
Goals: Hanbury 8/10.
RHINOS: 1 Zak Hardaker; 2 Tom Briscoe; 3 Kallum Watkins; 4 Joel Moon; 5 Ryan Hall; 14 Liam Sutcliffe; 25 Jordan Lilley; 8 Keith Galloway; 7 Rob Burrow (C); 10 Adam Cuthbertson; 26 Brett Ferres; 12 Carl Ablett; 15 Brett Delaney. Subs (all used): 17 Mitch Garbutt; 16 Brad Singleton; 18 Jimmy Keinhorst; 23 Ashton Golding.
Tries: Watkins (40), Burrow (73); **Goals:** Lilley 2/2.
Rugby Leaguer & League Express Men of the Match: *Vikings:* Rhys Hanbury; *Rhinos:* Rob Burrow.
Penalty count: 7-11; **Half-time:** 28-6;
Referee: George Stokes; **Attendance:** 6,596.

CASTLEFORD TIGERS 40 WAKEFIELD TRINITY WILDCATS 6

TIGERS: 1 Luke Dorn; 2 Joel Monaghan; 19 Ben Crooks; 3 Jake Webster; 5 Denny Solomona; 6 Ben Roberts; 7 Luke Gale (C); 8 Andy Lynch; 15 Paul McShane; 10 Grant Millington; 11 Oliver Holmes; 12 Mike McMeeken; 14 Lee Jewitt. Subs (all used): 9 Adam Milner; 17 Junior Moors; 13 Nathan Massey; 16 Matt Cook.
Tries: Solomona (13, 57), Roberts (24), Dorn (36), O Holmes (42, 64), Milner (50); **Goals:** Gale 6/7.
WILDCATS: 1 Ben Jones-Bishop; 14 Reece Lyne; 4 Ashley Gibson (D); 18 Joe Arundel; 3 Bill Tupou; 6 Jacob Miller; 7 Liam Finn; 8 Nick Scruton; 24 Stuart Howarth; 10 Anthony England; 12 Danny Kirmond (C); 17 Matty Ashurst; 16 Tinirau Arona. Subs (all used): 13 Anthony Tupou; 20 Michael Sio; 23 Scott Anderson; 31 Jason Walton (D).
Try: Howarth (6); **Goals:** Finn 1/1.

Rugby Leaguer & League Express Men of the Match: *Tigers:* Luke Gale; *Wildcats:* Stuart Howarth.
Penalty count: 12-6; **Half-time:** 18-6;
Referee: James Child; **Attendance:** 9,761.

ROUND 11

Sunday 21st February 2016

HULL KINGSTON ROVERS 12
WAKEFIELD TRINITY WILDCATS 14

ROVERS: 18 Ben Cockayne; 1 Ken Sio; 3 Liam Salter; 4 Iain Thornley; 5 Kieran Dixon; 11 Maurice Blair; 7 Albert Kelly; 8 Adam Walker; 24 George Lawler; 17 Dane Tilse; 13 Chris Clarkson; 12 Graeme Horne (C); 10 Mitchell Allgood. Subs (all used): 26 Rob Mulhern; 23 Ryan Shaw (D); 20 James Greenwood; 16 James Green.
Tries: Dixon (4), Walker (34), Sio (62);
Goals: Dixon 0/2, Shaw 0/1.
Sin bin: Blair (54) - obstruction.
WILDCATS: 1 Ben Jones-Bishop; 2 Tom Johnstone; 3 Bill Tupou; 18 Joe Arundel; 14 Reece Lyne; 6 Jacob Miller; 7 Liam Finn (C); 11 Mickael Simon; 24 Stuart Howarth; 10 Anthony England; 19 Jon Molloy; 13 Anthony Tupou; 16 Tinirau Arona. Subs (all used): 20 Michael Sio; 23 Scott Anderson; 31 Jason Walton; 26 Chris Annakin.
Tries: Simon (6), Howarth (23); **Goals:** Finn 3/3.
Rugby Leaguer & League Express Men of the Match: *Rovers:* Maurice Blair; *Wildcats:* Liam Finn.
Penalty count: 15-11; **Half-time:** 8-12;
Referee: Robert Hicks; **Attendance:** 7,207.

SALFORD RED DEVILS 28 WIDNES VIKINGS 20

RED DEVILS: 14 Gareth O'Brien; 2 Justin Carney; 4 Junior Sa'u; 3 Josh Griffin; 18 Greg Johnson; 6 Robert Lui; 7 Michael Dobson; 8 Craig Kopczak; 9 Tommy Lee (C); 10 George Griffin; 11 Ben Murdoch-Masila; 33 Josh Jones; 13 Mark Flanagan. Subs (all used): 19 Logan Tomkins; 15 Adam Walne; 21 Ryan Lannon; 17 Phil Joseph.
Tries: Carney (3), Flanagan (6, 76), Johnson (25), J Griffin (32); **Goals:** Dobson 3/3, J Griffin 0/1, O'Brien 1/1.
Sin bin: O'Brien (20) - holding down.
VIKINGS: 1 Rhys Hanbury; 2 Corey Thompson; 3 Chris Bridge; 4 Charly Runciman; 17 Stefan Marsh; 7 Joe Mellor; 6 Kevin Brown (C); 8 Eamon O'Carroll; 9 Lloyd White; 18 Gil Dudson; 15 Setaimata Sa; 11 Chris Houston; 13 Hep Cahill. Subs (all used): 32 Connor Farrell; 10 Manase Manuokafoa; 19 Macgraff Leuluai; 33 Aaron Heremaia.
Tries: Hanbury (36), Houston (38), Marsh (49), Thompson (69); **Goals:** Hanbury 2/4.
Rugby Leaguer & League Express Men of the Match: *Red Devils:* Tommy Lee; *Vikings:* Rhys Hanbury.
Penalty count: 11-9; **Half-time:** 22-10;
Referee: Phil Bentham; **Attendance:** 5,098.

ROUND 3

Thursday 25th February 2016

HULL FC 24 CASTLEFORD TIGERS 31

HULL FC: 1 Jamie Shaul; 19 Steve Michaels; 4 Jack Logan; 3 Carlos Tuimavave; 5 Fetuli Talanoa; 6 Leon Pryce; 7 Marc Sneyd; 8 Scott Taylor; 9 Danny Houghton; 10 Liam Watts; 12 Mark Minichiello; 21 Sika Manu; 16 Jordan Thompson. Subs (all used): 30 Danny Washbrook; 11 Gareth Ellis (C); 23 Frank Pritchard; 22 Josh Bowden.
Tries: Thompson (15), Michaels (34), Shaul (38, 58);
Goals: Sneyd 4/4.
TIGERS: 1 Luke Dorn; 25 Jy Hitchcox (D); 19 Ben Crooks; 3 Jake Webster; 5 Denny Solomona; 6 Ben Roberts; 7 Luke Gale (C); 8 Andy Lynch; 15 Paul McShane; 10 Grant Millington; 11 Oliver Holmes; 12 Mike McMeeken; 14 Lee Jewitt. Subs (all used): 9 Adam Milner; 13 Nathan Massey; 16 Matt Cook; 17 Junior Moors.
Tries: Hitchcox (2, 28), Solomona (8, 55, 80);
Goals: Gale 5/6; **Field goal:** Gale (74).
Rugby Leaguer & League Express Men of the Match: *Hull FC:* Jamie Shaul; *Tigers:* Luke Gale.
Penalty count: 9-7; **Half-time:** 18-18;
Referee: Robert Hicks; **Attendance:** 10,247.

WIGAN WARRIORS 20 SALFORD RED DEVILS 16

WARRIORS: 22 Lewis Tierney; 20 Oliver Gildart; 3 Anthony Gelling; 4 Dan Sarginson; 5 Dominic Manfredi; 6 George Williams; 7 Matty Smith; 21 Ryan Sutton; 16 Sam Powell; 10 Ben Flower; 14 John Bateman; 12 Liam Farrell; 13 Sean O'Loughlin (C). Subs (all used): 15 Tony Clubb; 17 Lee Mossop; 19 Taulima Tautai; 26 Greg Burke.
Tries: Gildart (8, 22), Gelling (44), Manfredi (77);
Goals: Smith 2/4.
RED DEVILS: 14 Gareth O'Brien; 2 Justin Carney; 4 Junior Sa'u; 3 Josh Griffin; 18 Greg Johnson; 6 Robert Lui; 7 Michael Dobson; 8 Craig Kopczak; 9 Tommy Lee (C); 10 George Griffin; 11 Ben Murdoch-Masila; 33 Josh Jones; 13 Mark Flanagan. Subs (all used): 1 Niall Evalds; 20 Jordan Walne; 19 Logan Tomkins; 16 Olsi Krasniqi.
Tries: Sa'u (57), J Griffin (67), Murdoch-Masila (73);
Goals: O'Brien 1/3, J Griffin 1/1.
Rugby Leaguer & League Express Men of the Match: *Warriors:* Oliver Gildart; *Red Devils:* Robert Lui.
Penalty count: 8-10; **Half-time:** 10-2;
Referee: George Stokes; **Attendance:** 10,897.

Friday 26th February 2016

HULL KINGSTON ROVERS 22 ST HELENS 31

ROVERS: 18 Ben Cockayne; 1 Ken Sio; 3 Liam Salter; 4 Iain Thornley; 23 Ryan Shaw; 11 Maurice Blair; 7 Albert Kelly; 8 Adam Walker; 24 George Lawler; 17 Dane Tilse; 12 Graeme Horne (C); 13 Chris Clarkson; 10 Mitchell Allgood. Subs (all used): 25 Stephen Holker; 16 James Green; 20 James Greenwood; 26 Rob Mulhern.
Tries: Cockayne (10), Blair (17), Green (29), Shaw (80);
Goals: Shaw 3/4.
Sin bin: Green (31) - fighting.
SAINTS: 23 Shannon McDonnell; 2 Tom Makinson; 18 Dominique Peyroux; 21 Matty Dawson; 5 Adam Swift; 3 Jordan Turner; 7 Luke Walsh; 8 Alex Walmsley; 6 Travis Burns; 16 Andre Savelio; 11 Atelea Vea; 12 Jon Wilkin (C); 13 Louie McCarthy-Scarsbrook. Subs (all used): 9 James Roby; 10 Kyle Amor; 14 Lama Tasi; 17 Luke Thompson.
Tries: McDonnell (4), Makinson (27), Dawson (48), Wilkin (59), Vea (67); **Goals:** Walsh 5/7;
Field goal: Walsh (77).
Sin bin: Burns (31) - fighting.
Rugby Leaguer & League Express Men of the Match: *Rovers:* Dane Tilse; *Saints:* Tom Makinson.
Penalty count: 7-7; **Half-time:** 16-10;
Referee: Phil Bentham; **Attendance:** 6,517.

WARRINGTON WOLVES 34
WAKEFIELD TRINITY WILDCATS 16

WOLVES: 5 Matthew Russell; 20 Kevin Penny; 3 Rhys Evans; 4 Ryan Atkins; 2 Tom Lineham; 1 Kurt Gidley; 7 Chris Sandow; 8 Chris Hill (C); 9 Daryl Clark; 10 Ashton Sims; 11 Ben Currie; 12 Jack Hughes; 14 Joe Westerman. Subs (all used): 16 Brad Dwyer; 18 George King; 29 Benjamin Jullien; 32 Jordan Cox.
Tries: Currie (2, 56), Penny (10), Gidley (23), Sandow (37, 53); **Goals:** Gidley 5/6.
WILDCATS: 25 Craig Hall; 14 Reece Lyne; 18 Joe Arundel; 31 Jason Walton; 2 Tom Johnstone; 6 Jacob Miller; 7 Liam Finn; 8 Nick Scruton (C); 24 Stuart Howarth; 10 Anthony England; 19 Jon Molloy; 17 Matty Ashurst; 11 Mickael Simon. Subs (all used): 20 Michael Sio; 13 Anthony Tupou; 16 Tinirau Arona; 26 Chris Annakin.
Tries: Hall (14), A Tupou (48), Molloy (77); **Goals:** Finn 2/3.
Rugby Leaguer & League Express Men of the Match: *Wolves:* Chris Sandow; *Wildcats:* Jacob Miller.
Penalty count: 10-9; **Half-time:** 24-6;
Referee: Richard Silverwood; **Attendance:** 10,631.

Saturday 27th February 2016

CATALANS DRAGONS 32 LEEDS RHINOS 28

DRAGONS: 1 Tony Gigot; 2 Jodie Broughton (D); 3 Krisnan Inu; 4 Vincent Duport; 5 Pat Richards; 6 Todd Carney; 7 Richard Myler; 14 Dave Taylor; 16 Eloi Pelissier; 15 Julian Bousquet; 11 Glenn Stewart; 12 Justin Horo; 13 Jason Baitieri (C). Subs (all used): 17 Gregory Mounis; 18 Thomas Bosc; 19 Olivier Elima; 29 Willie Mason (D).
Tries: Taylor (6, 61), Myler (35), Inu (42), Gigot (45);
Goals: Richards 6/6.
RHINOS: 1 Zak Hardaker; 22 Ash Handley; 3 Kallum Watkins; 4 Joel Moon; 5 Ryan Hall; 14 Liam Sutcliffe; 25 Jordan Lilley; 8 Keith Galloway; 7 Rob Burrow (C); 16 Brad Singleton; 26 Brett Ferres; 18 Jimmy Keinhorst; 15 Brett Delaney. Subs (all used): 10 Adam Cuthbertson; 19 Mitch Achurch; 20 Anthony Mullally; 21 Josh Walters.
Tries: Watkins (22, 77), Sutcliffe (49), Hall (54), Handley (69); **Goals:** Lilley 4/6.
Rugby Leaguer & League Express Men of the Match: *Dragons:* Dave Taylor; *Rhinos:* Liam Sutcliffe.
Penalty count: 7-8; **Half-time:** 12-8;
Referee: Ben Thaler; **Attendance:** 8,172.

Sunday 28th February 2016

HUDDERSFIELD GIANTS 18 WIDNES VIKINGS 36

GIANTS: 5 Aaron Murphy; 2 Jermaine McGillvary; 3 Leroy Cudjoe; 31 Sam Wood; 29 Jamie Foster; 18 Jake Connor; 7 Jamie Ellis; 16 Sam Rapira; 9 Ryan Hinchcliffe (C); 19 Josh Johnson; 17 Ukuma Ta'ai; 12 Michael Lawrence; 13 Larne Patrick. Subs (all used): 14 Daniel Smith; 20 Kruise Lemming; 21 Nathan Mason; 22 Oliver Roberts.
Tries: Lawrence (32), Patrick (53), Foster (77);
Goals: Foster 3/3.
Sin bin: Mason (38) - repeated team offences.
VIKINGS: 1 Rhys Hanbury; 2 Corey Thompson; 3 Chris Bridge; 4 Charly Runciman; 17 Stefan Marsh; 7 Joe Mellor; 6 Kevin Brown (C); 8 Eamon O'Carroll; 9 Lloyd White; 18 Gil Dudson; 14 Chris Dean; 11 Chris Houston; 13 Hep Cahill. Subs (all used): 22 Matt Whitley; 10 Manase Manuokafoa; 19 Macgraff Leuluai; 33 Aaron Heremaia.
Tries: Dean (12), Marsh (17, 42), Runciman (19), Leuluai (38), Thompson (48, 65); **Goals:** Hanbury 4/7.
Rugby Leaguer & League Express Men of the Match: *Giants:* Michael Lawrence; *Vikings:* Lloyd White.
Penalty count: 9-12; **Half-time:** 6-22;
Referee: James Child; **Attendance:** 5,183.

ROUND 4

Thursday 3rd March 2016

SALFORD RED DEVILS 30 WARRINGTON WOLVES 31

RED DEVILS: 14 Gareth O'Brien; 2 Justin Carney; 4 Junior Sa'u; 3 Josh Griffin; 18 Greg Johnson; 6 Robert Lui; 7 Michael Dobson; 8 Craig Kopczak; 9 Tommy Lee (C); 10 George Griffin; 11 Ben Murdoch-Masila; 33 Josh Jones; 13 Mark Flanagan. Subs (all used): 1 Niall Evalds; 15 Adam Walne; 19 Logan Tomkins; 20 Jordan Walne.
Tries: Sa'u (3, 28), Jones (16), Johnson (24), J Griffin (33);
Goals: Dobson 1/1, O'Brien 4/5.
Sin bin: Carney (53) - punching.
WOLVES: 5 Matthew Russell; 20 Kevin Penny; 3 Rhys Evans; 4 Ryan Atkins; 2 Tom Lineham; 6 Stefan Ratchford; 7 Chris Sandow; 8 Chris Hill (C); 16 Brad Dwyer; 10 Ashton Sims; 11 Ben Currie; 12 Jack Hughes; 14 Joe Westerman. Subs: 15 Mitchell Dodds (D); 18 George King; 29 Benjamin Jullien (not used); 23 Gary Wheeler.
Tries: Hughes (8), Currie (11), Atkins (60, 63), Sims (66);
Goals: Sandow 5/6; **Field goal:** Sandow (80).
Sin bin: Currie (53) - retaliation.
Rugby Leaguer & League Express Men of the Match: *Red Devils:* Junior Sa'u; *Wolves:* Chris Sandow.
Penalty count: 12-9; **Half-time:** 28-12;
Referee: Robert Hicks; **Attendance:** 4,381.

Friday 4th March 2016

HULL FC 25 WIGAN WARRIORS 26

HULL FC: 1 Jamie Shaul; 19 Steve Michaels; 4 Jack Logan; 3 Carlos Tuimavave; 5 Fetuli Talanoa; 6 Leon Pryce; 7 Marc Sneyd; 8 Scott Taylor; 9 Danny Houghton; 10 Liam Watts; 12 Mark Minichiello; 21 Sika Manu; 11 Gareth Ellis (C). Subs (all used): 15 Chris Green; 16 Jordan Thompson; 22 Josh Bowden; 30 Danny Washbrook.
Tries: Michaels (18, 68), Pryce (59), Manu (64);
Goals: Sneyd 4/4; **Field goal:** Sneyd (77).
WARRIORS: 22 Lewis Tierney; 2 Josh Charnley; 3 Anthony Gelling; 4 Dan Sarginson; 5 Dominic Manfredi; 6 George Williams; 7 Matty Smith; 10 Ben Flower; 16 Sam Powell; 21 Ryan Sutton; 12 Liam Farrell (C); 14 John Bateman; 26 Greg Burke. Subs (all used): 15 Tony Clubb; 17 Lee Mossop; 19 Taulima Tautai; 20 Oliver Gildart.
Tries: Flower (2), Williams (23), Bateman (54), Charnley (73); **Goals:** Smith 4/5;
Field goals: Smith (75, 79).
Rugby Leaguer & League Express Men of the Match: *Hull FC:* Marc Sneyd; *Warriors:* Anthony Gelling.
Penalty count: 11-8; **Half-time:** 6-14;
Referee: Ben Thaler; **Attendance:** 10,660.

LEEDS RHINOS 20 HUDDERSFIELD GIANTS 16

RHINOS: 1 Zak Hardaker; 22 Ash Handley; 3 Kallum Watkins; 4 Joel Moon; 5 Ryan Hall; 14 Liam Sutcliffe; 25 Jordan Lilley; 8 Keith Galloway; 7 Rob Burrow (C); 10 Adam Cuthbertson; 15 Brett Delaney; 26 Brett Ferres; 16 Brad Singleton. Subs: 21 Josh Walters; 20 Anthony Mullally; 18 Jimmy Keinhorst; 24 Jordan Baldwinson (not used).
Tries: Moon (8), Sutcliffe (58), Keinhorst (68);
Goals: Lilley 4/4.
GIANTS: 5 Aaron Murphy; 2 Jermaine McGillvary; 3 Leroy Cudjoe; 12 Michael Lawrence; 29 Jamie Foster; 18 Jake Connor; 6 Danny Brough; 16 Sam Rapira; 9 Ryan Hinchcliffe (C); 14 Daniel Smith; 17 Ukuma Ta'ai; 22 Oliver Roberts; 13 Larne Patrick. Subs (all used): 19 Josh Johnson; 20 Kruise Leeming; 21 Nathan Mason; 25 Tyler Dickinson (D).
Tries: Brough (14), McGillvary (30), Lawrence (64);
Goals: Foster 2/3.
Rugby Leaguer & League Express Men of the Match: *Rhinos:* Brad Singleton; *Giants:* Ryan Hinchcliffe.
Penalty count: 13-8; **Half-time:** 6-12;
Referee: Richard Silverwood; **Attendance:** 14,692.

ST HELENS 28 CASTLEFORD TIGERS 22

SAINTS: 23 Shannon McDonnell; 2 Tom Makinson; 18 Dominique Peyroux; 21 Matty Dawson; 5 Adam Swift; 3 Jordan Turner; 7 Luke Walsh; 8 Alex Walmsley; 9 James Roby; 10 Kyle Amor; 11 Atelea Vea; 12 Jon Wilkin (C); 13 Louie McCarthy-Scarsbrook. Subs (all used): 14 Lama Tasi; 15 Greg Richards; 17 Luke Thompson; 19 Theo Fages.
Tries: Swift (19), Vea (28), Dawson (33, 68), McCarthy-Scarsbrook (59); **Goals:** Walsh 4/5.
TIGERS: 1 Luke Dorn; 25 Jy Hitchcox; 19 Ben Crooks; 3 Jake Webster; 5 Denny Solomona; 6 Ben Roberts; 7 Luke Gale (C); 8 Andy Lynch; 15 Paul McShane; 10 Grant Millington; 17 Junior Moors; 12 Mike McMeeken; 14 Lee Jewitt. Subs (all used): 9 Adam Milner; 13 Nathan Massey; 16 Matt Cook; 23 Will Maher.
Tries: Millington (10), McMeeken (22), Milner (73); **Goals:** Gale 4/4, Crooks 1/1.
Rugby Leaguer & League Express Men of the Match: *Saints:* Atelea Vea; *Tigers:* Mike McMeeken.
Penalty count: 5-10; **Half-time:** 16-14;
Referee: James Child; **Attendance:** 11,298.

WIDNES VIKINGS 30 HULL KINGSTON ROVERS 16

VIKINGS: 1 Rhys Hanbury; 2 Corey Thompson; 3 Chris Bridge; 4 Charly Runciman; 17 Stefan Marsh; 6 Kevin Brown (C); 7 Joe Mellor; 8 Eamon O'Carroll; 9 Lloyd White; 18 Gil Dudson; 14 Chris Dean; 11 Chris Houston; 13 Hep Cahill. Subs (all used): 32 Connor Farrell; 19 Macgraff Leuluai; 10 Manase Manuokafoa; 22 Matt Whitley.
Tries: Hanbury (15), Mellor (23, 34), Thompson (36, 47); **Goals:** Hanbury 5/6.
ROVERS: 18 Ben Cockayne; 1 Ken Sio; 3 Liam Salter; 4 Iain Thornley; 23 Ryan Shaw; 22 Matthew Marsh; 11 Maurice Blair (C); 8 Adam Walker; 24 George Lawler; 17 Dane Tilse; 13 Chris Clarkson; 20 James Greenwood; 10 Mitchell Allgood. Subs (all used): 25 Stephen Holker; 26 Rob Mulhern; 21 Thomas Minns; 28 Kieran Moran (D).
Tries: Blair (5), Minns (28), Shaw (62); **Goals:** Shaw 2/3.
Rugby Leaguer & League Express Men of the Match: *Vikings:* Joe Mellor; *Rovers:* Dane Tilse.
Penalty count: 10-8; **Half-time:** 22-12;
Referee: Gareth Hewer; **Attendance:** 5,013.

Sunday 6th March 2016

WAKEFIELD TRINITY WILDCATS 28 CATALANS DRAGONS 42

WILDCATS: 1 Ben Jones-Bishop; 14 Reece Lyne; 18 Joe Arundel; 25 Craig Hall; 2 Tom Johnstone; 6 Jacob Miller; 7 Liam Finn; 8 Nick Scruton (C); 24 Stuart Howarth; 10 Anthony England; 19 Jon Molloy; 17 Matty Ashurst; 11 Mickael Simon. Subs (all used): 13 Anthony Tupou; 16 Tinirau Arona; 20 Michael Sio; 23 Scott Anderson.
Tries: A Tupou (32), Arundel (35), Lyne (44), Johnstone (50), Simon (78); **Goals:** Finn 4/5.
DRAGONS: 1 Tony Gigot; 2 Jodie Broughton; 3 Krisnan Inu; 4 Vincent Duport; 5 Pat Richards; 6 Todd Carney; 7 Richard Myler; 8 Louis Anderson; 16 Eloi Pelissier; 14 Dave Taylor; 11 Glenn Stewart; 12 Justin Horo; 13 Jason Baitieri. Subs (all used): 10 Remi Casty (C); 15 Julian Bousquet; 18 Thomas Bosc; 29 Willie Mason.
Tries: Broughton (6), Duport (14), Richards (16), Baitieri (20), Stewart (27), Myler (54), Gigot (58, 68); **Goals:** Richards 5/8.
Rugby Leaguer & League Express Men of the Match: *Wildcats:* Tom Johnstone; *Dragons:* Dave Taylor.
Penalty count: 14-7; **Half-time:** 10-26;
Referee: Phil Bentham; **Attendance:** 4,442.

ROUND 5

Thursday 10th March 2016

WIDNES VIKINGS 46 HULL FC 6

VIKINGS: 1 Rhys Hanbury; 2 Corey Thompson; 3 Chris Bridge; 4 Charly Runciman; 17 Stefan Marsh; 6 Kevin Brown (C); 7 Joe Mellor; 8 Eamon O'Carroll; 9 Lloyd White; 10 Manase Manuokafoa; 14 Chris Dean; 11 Chris Houston; 13 Hep Cahill. Subs (all used): 19 Macgraff Leuluai; 20 Alex Gerrard; 22 Matt Whitley; 33 Aaron Heremaia.
Tries: Mellor (14), Thompson (19, 27), Marsh (31, 52, 66), Hanbury (38), Brown (46), Whitley (57); **Goals:** Hanbury 5/9.
HULL FC: 1 Jamie Shaul; 19 Steve Michaels; 4 Jack Logan; 3 Carlos Tuimavave; 5 Fetuli Talanoa; 13 Jordan Abdull; 7 Marc Sneyd; 8 Scott Taylor; 9 Danny Houghton; 22 Josh Bowden; 21 Sika Manu; 23 Frank Pritchard; 11 Gareth Ellis (C). Subs (all used): 16 Jordan Thompson; 12 Mark Minichiello; 30 Danny Washbrook; 10 Liam Watts.
Try: Pritchard (7); **Goals:** Sneyd 1/1.
Rugby Leaguer & League Express Men of the Match: *Vikings:* Joe Mellor; *Hull FC:* Gareth Ellis.
Penalty count: 9-9; **Half-time:** 24-6;
Referee: Richard Silverwood; **Attendance:** 4,753.

Friday 11th March 2016

ST HELENS 44 WAKEFIELD TRINITY WILDCATS 4

SAINTS: 23 Shannon McDonnell; 2 Tom Makinson; 18 Dominique Peyroux; 21 Matty Dawson; 5 Adam Swift; 3 Jordan Turner; 7 Luke Walsh; 8 Alex Walmsley; 9 James Roby; 10 Kyle Amor; 11 Atelea Vea; 20 Joe Greenwood; 12 Jon Wilkin (C). Subs (all used): 13 Louie McCarthy-Scarsbrook; 14 Lama Tasi; 15 Greg Richards; 17 Luke Thompson.
Tries: Greenwood (3, 8), Wilkin (17), Roby (25, 53), Makinson (29, 62), Dawson (68); **Goals:** Walsh 6/8.
WILDCATS: 1 Ben Jones-Bishop; 14 Reece Lyne; 31 Jason Walton; 25 Craig Hall; 2 Tom Johnstone; 6 Jacob Miller; 7 Liam Finn; 8 Nick Scruton (C); 24 Stuart Howarth; 10 Anthony England; 13 Anthony Tupou; 17 Matty Ashurst; 16 Tinirau Arona. Subs (all used): 11 Mickael Simon; 20 Michael Sio; 23 Scott Anderson; 27 Anthony Walker.
Try: Jones-Bishop (42); **Goals:** Finn 0/1.
Rugby Leaguer & League Express Men of the Match: *Saints:* Kyle Amor; *Wildcats:* Craig Hall.
Penalty count: 11-6; **Half-time:** 30-0;
Referee: Gareth Hewer; **Attendance:** 10,008.

WIGAN WARRIORS 28 LEEDS RHINOS 6

WARRIORS: 4 Dan Sarginson; 2 Josh Charnley; 3 Anthony Gelling; 20 Oliver Gildart; 5 Dominic Manfredi; 13 Sean O'Loughlin (C); 7 Matty Smith; 15 Tony Clubb; 16 Sam Powell; 10 Ben Flower; 14 John Bateman; 12 Liam Farrell; 26 Greg Burke. Subs (all used): 17 Lee Mossop; 19 Taulima Tautai; 21 Ryan Sutton; 27 Nick Gregson (D).
Tries: Bateman (27), Gildart (56), Manfredi (60), Clubb (66), Gelling (68); **Goals:** Smith 4/5.
RHINOS: 1 Zak Hardaker; 22 Ash Handley; 3 Kallum Watkins; 18 Jimmy Keinhorst; 5 Ryan Hall; 14 Liam Sutcliffe; 25 Jordan Lilley; 8 Keith Galloway; 7 Rob Burrow (C); 10 Adam Cuthbertson; 19 Mitch Achurch; 26 Brett Ferres; 16 Brad Singleton. Subs (all used): 9 Beau Falloon (D); 11 Jamie Jones-Buchanan; 17 Mitch Garbutt; 20 Anthony Mullally.
Try: Hardaker (80); **Goals:** Hardaker 1/1.
Rugby Leaguer & League Express Men of the Match: *Warriors:* Sean O'Loughlin; *Rhinos:* Beau Falloon.
Penalty count: 9-7; **Half-time:** 6-0;
Referee: Ben Thaler; **Attendance:** 14,425.

Saturday 12th March 2016

CATALANS DRAGONS 20 WARRINGTON WOLVES 30

DRAGONS: 1 Tony Gigot; 2 Jodie Broughton; 3 Krisnan Inu; 4 Vincent Duport; 5 Pat Richards; 6 Todd Carney; 7 Richard Myler; 14 Dave Taylor; 16 Eloi Pelissier; 29 Willie Mason; 11 Glenn Stewart; 12 Justin Horo; 8 Louis Anderson. Subs: 10 Remi Casty (C); 13 Jason Baitieri; 15 Julian Bousquet; 18 Thomas Bosc (not used).
Tries: Carney (9), Richards (23), Duport (44); **Goals:** Richards 4/4.
WOLVES: 5 Matthew Russell; 20 Kevin Penny; 3 Rhys Evans; 4 Ryan Atkins; 2 Tom Lineham; 1 Kurt Gidley; 7 Chris Sandow; 8 Chris Hill (C); 16 Brad Dwyer; 10 Ashton Sims; 11 Ben Currie; 12 Jack Hughes; 14 Joe Westerman. Subs (all used): 6 Stefan Ratchford; 15 Mitchell Dodds; 18 George King; 32 Jordan Cox.
Tries: R Evans (11, 60), Currie (30), G King (77), Sandow (80); **Goals:** Gidley 5/5.
On report: Hill (36) - alleged shoulder charge on Myler.
Rugby Leaguer & League Express Men of the Match: *Dragons:* Glenn Stewart; *Wolves:* Matthew Russell.
Penalty count: 7-11; **Half-time:** 14-12;
Referee: James Child; **Attendance:** 8,859.

Sunday 13th March 2016

HUDDERSFIELD GIANTS 38 HULL KINGSTON ROVERS 6

GIANTS: 32 Jordan Tansey (D); 2 Jermaine McGillvary; 3 Leroy Cudjoe; 18 Jake Connor; 5 Aaron Murphy; 6 Danny Brough; 15 Kyle Wood; 8 Eorl Crabtree; 9 Ryan Hinchcliffe (C); 16 Sam Rapira; 4 Joe Wardle; 12 Michael Lawrence; 17 Ukuma Ta'ai. Subs (all used): 13 Larne Patrick; 19 Josh Johnson; 20 Kruise Leeming; 22 Oliver Roberts.
Tries: Tansey (4), Lawrence (10), Murphy (50), McGillvary (67), Patrick (72), Ta'ai (76); **Goals:** Brough 7/7.
ROVERS: 18 Ben Cockayne; 23 Ryan Shaw; 4 Iain Thornley; 21 Thomas Minns; 1 Ken Sio; 11 Maurice Blair; 22 Matthew Marsh; 8 Adam Walker; 9 Shaun Lunt; 17 Dane Tilse; 13 Chris Clarkson; 12 Graeme Horne; 10 Mitchell Allgood. Subs (all used): 16 James Green; 20 James Greenwood; 6 Terry Campese (C); 19 John Boudebza.
Try: Minns (44); **Goals:** Shaw 1/1.
Rugby Leaguer & League Express Men of the Match: *Giants:* Danny Brough; *Rovers:* Iain Thornley.
Penalty count: 7-9; **Half-time:** 12-0;
Referee: Robert Hicks; **Attendance:** 5,610.

CASTLEFORD TIGERS 16 SALFORD RED DEVILS 32

TIGERS: 1 Luke Dorn; 2 Joel Monaghan; 19 Ben Crooks; 3 Jake Webster; 5 Denny Solomona; 18 Ryan Hampshire (D); 7 Luke Gale (C); 8 Andy Lynch; 9 Adam Milner; 14 Lee Jewitt; 12 Mike McMeeken; 16 Matt Cook; 13 Nathan Massey. Subs (all used): 15 Paul McShane; 21 Ryan Boyle; 22 Gadwin Springer; 23 Will Maher.
Tries: Solomona (38, 62, 73); **Goals:** Gale 2/4.
RED DEVILS: 14 Gareth O'Brien; 2 Justin Carney; 4 Junior Sa'u; 3 Josh Griffin; 18 Greg Johnson; 6 Robert Lui; 7 Michael Dobson; 8 Craig Kopczak; 9 Tommy Lee (C); 10 George Griffin; 11 Ben Murdoch-Masila; 33 Josh Jones; 21 Ryan Lannon. Subs (all used): 13 Mark Flanagan; 15 Adam Walne; 19 Logan Tomkins; 17 Phil Joseph.
Tries: Johnson (30), J Griffin (50, 76), Carney (57, 79); **Goals:** O'Brien 6/6.
Sin bin: Carney (4) - punching Massey.
Rugby Leaguer & League Express Men of the Match: *Tigers:* Denny Solomona; *Red Devils:* Gareth O'Brien.
Penalty count: 8-6; **Half-time:** 6-8;
Referee: Phil Bentham; **Attendance:** 8,151.

ROUND 6

Thursday 17th March 2016

WIGAN WARRIORS 12 WIDNES VIKINGS 18

WARRIORS: 4 Dan Sarginson; 2 Josh Charnley; 3 Anthony Gelling; 20 Oliver Gildart; 5 Dominic Manfredi; 13 Sean O'Loughlin (C); 7 Matty Smith; 15 Tony Clubb; 16 Sam Powell; 10 Ben Flower; 14 John Bateman; 12 Liam Farrell; 19 Taulima Tautai. Subs: 17 Lee Mossop; 21 Ryan Sutton; 26 Greg Burke; 27 Nick Gregson (not used).
Tries: Farrell (17), Charnley (35, 54); **Goals:** Smith 0/3.
VIKINGS: 1 Rhys Hanbury; 2 Corey Thompson; 14 Chris Dean; 4 Charly Runciman; 17 Stefan Marsh; 7 Joe Mellor; 6 Kevin Brown (C); 8 Eamon O'Carroll; 33 Aaron Heremaia; 18 Gil Dudson; 15 Setaimata Sa; 11 Chris Houston; 13 Hep Cahill. Subs (all used): 10 Manase Manuokafoa; 19 Macgraff Leuluai; 20 Alex Gerrard; 22 Matt Whitley.
Tries: Whitley (46), Marsh (60), Runciman (62); **Goals:** Hanbury 3/4.
Rugby Leaguer & League Express Men of the Match: *Warriors:* Sean O'Loughlin; *Vikings:* Rhys Hanbury.
Penalty count: 9-8; **Half-time:** 8-0;
Referee: Richard Silverwood; **Attendance:** 11,733.

Friday 18th March 2016

HULL FC 22 WAKEFIELD TRINITY WILDCATS 4

HULL FC: 1 Jamie Shaul; 19 Steve Michaels; 4 Jack Logan; 24 Kirk Yeaman; 20 Curtis Naughton; 3 Carlos Tuimavave; 7 Marc Sneyd; 8 Scott Taylor; 9 Danny Houghton; 22 Josh Bowden; 21 Sika Manu; 12 Mark Minichiello; 11 Gareth Ellis (C). Subs (all used): 10 Liam Watts; 15 Chris Green; 23 Frank Pritchard; 30 Danny Washbrook.
Tries: Minichiello (15, 28), Naughton (33), Tuimavave (50); **Goals:** Sneyd 3/4.
WILDCATS: 25 Craig Hall; 21 Max Jowitt; 4 Ashley Gibson; 18 Joe Arundel; 2 Tom Johnstone; 6 Jacob Miller; 7 Liam Finn; 8 Nick Scruton (C); 24 Stuart Howarth; 10 Anthony England; 19 Jon Molloy; 17 Matty Ashurst; 13 Anthony Tupou. Subs (all used): 20 Michael Sio; 11 Mickael Simon; 26 Chris Annakin; 27 Anthony Walker.
Try: Arundel (23); **Goals:** Finn 0/1.
Rugby Leaguer & League Express Men of the Match: *Hull FC:* Mark Minichiello; *Wildcats:* Mickael Simon.
Penalty count: 7-10; **Half-time:** 16-4;
Referee: James Child; **Attendance:** 9,600.

LEEDS RHINOS 30 ST HELENS 18

RHINOS: 1 Zak Hardaker; 22 Ash Handley; 3 Kallum Watkins; 4 Joel Moon; 5 Ryan Hall; 14 Liam Sutcliffe; 7 Rob Burrow (C); 8 Keith Galloway; 9 Beau Falloon; 10 Adam Cuthbertson; 12 Carl Ablett; 26 Brett Ferres; 11 Jamie Jones-Buchanan. Subs (all used): 20 Anthony Mullally; 15 Brett Delaney; 21 Josh Walters; 25 Jordan Lilley.
Tries: Jones-Buchanan (3), Cuthbertson (5), Sutcliffe (10), Ablett (39), Handley (55); **Goals:** Sutcliffe 5/6.
SAINTS: 23 Shannon McDonnell; 2 Tom Makinson; 18 Dominique Peyroux; 21 Matty Dawson; 22 Jack Owens; 3 Jordan Turner; 7 Luke Walsh; 8 Alex Walmsley; 9 James Roby; 10 Kyle Amor; 11 Atelea Vea; 20 Joe Greenwood; 12 Jon Wilkin (C). Subs (all used): 14 Lama Tasi; 15 Greg Richards; 13 Louie McCarthy-Scarsbrook; 17 Luke Thompson.
Tries: Amor (17), Walsh (21), McCarthy-Scarsbrook (36); **Goals:** Walsh 3/3.
Sin bin: McCarthy-Scarsbrook (79) - professional foul.
On report:
Peyroux (34) - alleged shoulder charge on Hardaker.
Rugby Leaguer & League Express Men of the Match: *Rhinos:* Ash Handley; *Saints:* Luke Walsh.
Penalty count: 9-7; **Half-time:** 22-18;
Referee: Ben Thaler; **Attendance:** 17,131.

WARRINGTON WOLVES 56 CASTLEFORD TIGERS 12

WOLVES: 5 Matthew Russell; 20 Kevin Penny; 3 Rhys Evans; 4 Ryan Atkins; 2 Tom Lineham; 1 Kurt Gidley; 7 Chris Sandow; 8 Chris Hill (C); 16 Brad Dwyer; 10 Ashton Sims; 11 Ben Currie; 12 Jack Hughes; 14 Joe Westerman. Subs (all used): 6 Stefan Ratchford; 9 Daryl Clark; 18 George King; 32 Jordan Cox.
Tries: Sandow (3, 42), Penny (10), Lineham (17, 67), Russell (23, 30), Atkins (35), Currie (36, 80), Dwyer (65); **Goals:** Gidley 6/9, Sandow 0/1.
Sin bin: Ratchford (75) - high tackle.
TIGERS: 25 Jy Hitchcox; 2 Joel Monaghan; 19 Ben Crooks; 3 Jake Webster; 5 Denny Solomona; 18 Ryan Hampshire; 7 Luke Gale (C); 8 Andy Lynch; 9 Adam Milner; 23 Will Maher; 10 Grant Millington; 12 Mike McMeeken; 13 Nathan Massey. Subs (all used): 15 Paul McShane; 16 Matt Cook; 20 Frankie Mariano; 22 Gadwin Springer.
Tries: Monaghan (46), Springer (57); **Goals:** Gale 2/2.
Rugby Leaguer & League Express Men of the Match: *Wolves:* Chris Sandow; *Tigers:* Luke Gale.
Penalty count: 5-6; **Half-time:** 38-0;
Referee: Robert Hicks; **Attendance:** 10,940.

Sunday 20th March 2016

HUDDERSFIELD GIANTS 26 CATALANS DRAGONS 46

GIANTS: 32 Jordan Tansey; 2 Jermaine McGillvary; 3 Leroy Cudjoe; 18 Jake Connor; 5 Aaron Murphy; 6 Danny Brough; 15 Kyle Wood; 8 Eorl Crabtree; 9 Ryan Hinchcliffe (C); 16 Sam Rapira; 4 Joe Wardle; 12 Michael Lawrence; 17 Ukuma Ta'ai. Subs (all used): 13 Larne Patrick; 20 Kruise Leeming; 21 Nathan Mason; 22 Oliver Roberts.
Tries: Connor (19), McGillvary (22), Patrick (26), Cudjoe (37), Leeming (70); **Goals:** Brough 2/4, Tansey 1/1.
Dismissal: Wardle (49) - high tackle on Casty.
DRAGONS: 1 Tony Gigot; 2 Jodie Broughton; 3 Krisnan Inu; 4 Vincent Duport; 5 Pat Richards; 6 Todd Carney; 7 Richard Myler; 14 Dave Taylor; 16 Eloi Pelissier; 15 Julian Bousquet; 8 Louis Anderson; 11 Glenn Stewart; 13 Jason Baitieri. Subs (all used): 9 Paul Aiton; 10 Remi Casty (C); 17 Gregory Mounis; 29 Willie Mason.
Tries: Anderson (8), Stewart (13), Broughton (42, 47, 53), Aiton (57), Bousquet (63), Myler (73); **Goals:** Richards 7/8.
Sin bin: Inu (21) - dangerous challenge on Crabtree.
Rugby Leaguer & League Express Men of the Match: *Giants:* Jermaine McGillvary; *Dragons:* Jodie Broughton.
Penalty count: 6-9; **Half-time:** 20-12;
Referee: Ben Thaler; **Attendance:** 4,607.

HULL KINGSTON ROVERS 44 SALFORD RED DEVILS 30

ROVERS: 18 Ben Cockayne; 1 Ken Sio; 23 Ryan Shaw; 4 Iain Thornley; 2 Josh Mantellato; 11 Maurice Blair; 22 Matthew Marsh; 8 Adam Walker; 24 George Lawler; 17 Dane Tilse; 13 Chris Clarkson; 12 Graeme Horne (C); 10 Mitchell Allgood. Subs (all used): 20 James Greenwood; 16 James Green; 19 John Boudebza; 26 Rob Mulhern.
Tries: Blair (15), Thornley (17), Horne (21), Sio (34), Greenwood (39), Shaw (67), Marsh (80);
Goals: Mantellato 8/10.
RED DEVILS: 1 Niall Evalds; 2 Justin Carney; 4 Junior Sa'u; 3 Josh Griffin; 18 Greg Johnson; 14 Gareth O'Brien; 7 Michael Dobson; 8 Craig Kopczak; 9 Tommy Lee (C); 10 George Griffin; 11 Ben Murdoch-Masila; 33 Josh Jones; 21 Ryan Lannon. Subs (all used): 13 Mark Flanagan; 15 Adam Walne; 19 Logan Tomkins; 17 Phil Joseph.
Tries: Kopczak (4, 75), G Griffin (44, 48), Johnson (64);
Goals: O'Brien 5/5.
Rugby Leaguer & League Express Men of the Match: *Rovers:* Maurice Blair; *Red Devils:* Craig Kopczak.
Penalty count: 8-6; **Half-time:** 30-6;
Referee: Gareth Hewer; **Attendance:** 6,593.

ROUND 7

Thursday 24th March 2016

CASTLEFORD TIGERS 18 LEEDS RHINOS 14

TIGERS: 5 Denny Solomona; 2 Joel Monaghan; 19 Ben Crooks; 3 Jake Webster; 25 Jy Hitchcox; 18 Ryan Hampshire; 7 Luke Gale (C); 8 Andy Lynch; 9 Adam Milner; 21 Ryan Boyle; 10 Grant Millington; 12 Mike McMeeken; 13 Nathan Massey. Subs (all used): 15 Paul McShane; 22 Gadwin Springer; 23 Will Maher; 24 Greg Minikin (D).
Tries: Lynch (10), Webster (13, 74); **Goals:** Gale 3/3.
RHINOS: 1 Zak Hardaker; 2 Tom Briscoe; 3 Kallum Watkins; 4 Joel Moon; 22 Ash Handley; 14 Liam Sutcliffe; 7 Rob Burrow (C); 8 Keith Galloway; 9 Beau Falloon; 10 Adam Cuthbertson; 12 Carl Ablett; 26 Brett Ferres; 11 Jamie Jones-Buchanan. Subs: 25 Jordan Lilley (not used); 20 Anthony Mullally; 21 Josh Walters; 18 Jimmy Keinhorst.
Tries: Moon (20), Watkins (24), T Briscoe (35);
Goals: Sutcliffe 1/3.
Rugby Leaguer & League Express Men of the Match: *Tigers:* Jake Webster; *Rhinos:* Brett Ferres.
Penalty count: 9-9; **Half-time:** 12-14;
Referee: James Child; **Attendance:** 11,426.

Friday 25th March 2016

HULL KINGSTON ROVERS 20 HULL FC 22

ROVERS: 18 Ben Cockayne; 1 Ken Sio; 23 Ryan Shaw; 4 Iain Thornley; 2 Josh Mantellato; 11 Maurice Blair; 7 Albert Kelly; 8 Adam Walker; 24 George Lawler; 17 Dane Tilse; 13 Chris Clarkson; 12 Graeme Horne (C); 10 Mitchell Allgood. Subs (all used): 16 James Green; 20 James Greenwood; 26 Rob Mulhern; 19 John Boudebza.
Tries: Shaw (14), Sio (29), Thornley (51);
Goals: Mantellato 4/5.
HULL FC: 1 Jamie Shaul; 19 Steve Michaels; 24 Kirk Yeaman; 2 Mahe Fonua; 20 Curtis Naughton; 3 Carlos Tuimavave; 7 Marc Sneyd; 8 Scott Taylor; 9 Danny Houghton; 10 Liam Watts; 23 Frank Pritchard; 12 Mark Minichiello; 11 Gareth Ellis (C). Subs (all used): 14 Iafeta Palea'aesina; 15 Chris Green; 30 Danny Washbrook; 22 Josh Bowden.
Tries: Shaul (59), Houghton (64), Fonua (71), Michaels (75); **Goals:** Sneyd 3/4.
Rugby Leaguer & League Express Men of the Match: *Rovers:* Maurice Blair; *Hull FC:* Gareth Ellis.
Penalty count: 9-8; **Half-time:** 12-0;
Referee: Phil Bentham; **Attendance:** 11,050.

SALFORD RED DEVILS 12 CATALANS DRAGONS 26

RED DEVILS: 14 Gareth O'Brien; 2 Justin Carney; 4 Junior Sa'u; 3 Josh Griffin; 18 Greg Johnson; 9 Tommy Lee (C); 7 Michael Dobson; 8 Craig Kopczak; 19 Logan Tomkins; 10 George Griffin; 11 Ben Murdoch-Masila; 33 Josh Jones; 23 Carl Forster. Subs (all used): 13 Mark Flanagan; 15 Adam Walne; 22 Matt Sarsfield; 17 Phil Joseph.
Tries: J Griffin (16), Johnson (59, 66); **Goals:** O'Brien 0/3.
DRAGONS: 1 Tony Gigot; 2 Jodie Broughton; 12 Justin Horo; 4 Vincent Duport; 5 Pat Richards; 6 Todd Carney; 7 Richard Myler; 14 Dave Taylor; 16 Eloi Pelissier; 15 Julian Bousquet; 8 Louis Anderson; 11 Glenn Stewart; 17 Gregory Mounis. Subs (all used): 9 Paul Aiton; 10 Remi Casty (C); 22 Antoni Maria; 29 Willie Mason.
Tries: Gigot (3), Pelissier (27), Taylor (52, 78);
Goals: Richards 5/6.
Rugby Leaguer & League Express Men of the Match: *Red Devils:* Justin Carney; *Dragons:* Todd Carney.
Penalty count: 14-10; **Half-time:** 4-12;
Referee: Richard Silverwood; **Attendance:** 3,485.

WAKEFIELD TRINITY WILDCATS 36 HUDDERSFIELD GIANTS 22

WILDCATS: 21 Max Jowitt; 14 Reece Lyne; 18 Joe Arundel; 4 Ashley Gibson; 2 Tom Johnstone; 6 Jacob Miller; 7 Liam Finn; 8 Nick Scruton; 9 Scott Moore; 10 Anthony England; 12 Danny Kirmond (C); 17 Matty Ashurst; 20 Michael Sio. Subs (all used): 11 Mickael Simon; 26 Chris Annakin; 24 Stuart Howarth; 19 Jon Molloy.
Tries: Johnstone (14, 72), Sio (26), Lyne (34), Jowitt (60), Scruton (78); **Goals:** Finn 6/6.
Sin bin: Simon (63) - fighting.
GIANTS: 24 Jared Simpson; 2 Jermaine McGillvary; 3 Leroy Cudjoe; 18 Jake Connor; 5 Aaron Murphy; 6 Danny Brough; 34 Ryan Brierley (D); 10 Craig Huby; 15 Kyle Wood; 16 Sam Rapira; 17 Ukuma Ta'ai; 12 Michael Lawrence; 9 Ryan Hinchcliffe (C). Subs (all used): 13 Larne Patrick; 19 Josh Johnson; 20 Kruise Leeming; 21 Nathan Mason.
Tries: McGillvary (9), Connor (36, 42), Murphy (66);
Goals: Brough 3/5.
Sin bin: Patrick (63) - fighting.
Rugby Leaguer & League Express Men of the Match: *Wildcats:* Max Jowitt; *Giants:* Jake Connor.
Penalty count: 9-8; **Half-time:** 18-14;
Referee: Gareth Hewer; **Attendance:** 4,989.

WARRINGTON WOLVES 28 WIDNES VIKINGS 10

WOLVES: 5 Matthew Russell; 20 Kevin Penny; 3 Rhys Evans; 4 Ryan Atkins; 2 Tom Lineham; 1 Kurt Gidley; 7 Chris Sandow; 8 Chris Hill (C); 9 Daryl Clark; 10 Ashton Sims; 11 Ben Currie; 12 Jack Hughes; 14 Joe Westerman. Subs (all used): 6 Stefan Ratchford; 13 Ben Westwood; 18 George King; 32 Jordan Cox.
Tries: Sandow (25), Lineham (28), Gidley (51), Atkins (68), Currie (74); **Goals:** Gidley 4/6.
VIKINGS: 1 Rhys Hanbury; 2 Corey Thompson; 14 Chris Dean; 17 Stefan Marsh; 5 Patrick Ah Van; 7 Joe Mellor (C); 21 Tom Gilmore; 8 Eamon O'Carroll; 9 Lloyd White; 18 Gil Dudson; 15 Setaimata Sa; 11 Chris Houston; 19 Macgraff Leuluai. Subs (all used): 10 Manase Manuokafoa; 20 Alex Gerrard; 33 Aaron Heremaia; 22 Matt Whitley.
Tries: Gilmore (5), Hanbury (22); **Goals:** Hanbury 1/2.
Rugby Leaguer & League Express Men of the Match: *Wolves:* Kurt Gidley; *Vikings:* Rhys Hanbury.
Penalty count: 3-2; **Half-time:** 10-10;
Referee: Ben Thaler; **Attendance:** 15,008.

ST HELENS 12 WIGAN WARRIORS 24

SAINTS: 23 Shannon McDonnell; 2 Tom Makinson; 18 Dominique Peyroux; 21 Matty Dawson; 22 Jack Owens; 19 Theo Fages; 7 Luke Walsh; 14 Lama Tasi; 6 Travis Burns; 10 Kyle Amor; 12 Jon Wilkin (C); 20 Joe Greenwood; 13 Louie McCarthy-Scarsbrook. Subs (all used): 8 Alex Walmsley; 9 James Roby; 15 Greg Richards; 17 Luke Thompson.
Tries: Greenwood (61), Fages (71); **Goals:** Walsh 2/2.
WARRIORS: 4 Dan Sarginson; 5 Dominic Manfredi; 3 Anthony Gelling; 20 Oliver Gildart; 2 Josh Charnley; 13 Sean O'Loughlin (C); 7 Matty Smith; 10 Ben Flower; 16 Sam Powell; 15 Tony Clubb; 11 Joel Tomkins; 14 John Bateman; 26 Greg Burke. Subs (all used): 17 Lee Mossop; 19 Taulima Tautai; 21 Ryan Sutton; 27 Nick Gregson.
Tries: Manfredi (21), Powell (26), J Tomkins (31), Smith (69); **Goals:** Smith 4/5.
Rugby Leaguer & League Express Men of the Match: *Saints:* Theo Fages; *Warriors:* Dominic Manfredi.
Penalty count: 10-10; **Half-time:** 0-16;
Referee: Robert Hicks; **Attendance:** 17,890.

ROUND 8

Monday 28th March 2016

HUDDERSFIELD GIANTS 24 SALFORD RED DEVILS 26

GIANTS: 34 Ryan Brierley; 2 Jermaine McGillvary; 3 Leroy Cudjoe; 18 Jake Connor; 5 Aaron Murphy; 6 Danny Brough; 15 Kyle Wood; 8 Eorl Crabtree; 9 Ryan Hinchcliffe (C); 10 Craig Huby; 13 Larne Patrick; 12 Michael Lawrence; 17 Ukuma Ta'ai. Subs (all used): 16 Sam Rapira; 19 Josh Johnson; 20 Kruise Leeming; 22 Oliver Roberts.
Tries: Ta'ai (27, 61), Connor (35), McGillvary (58);
Goals: Brough 4/4.
RED DEVILS: 14 Gareth O'Brien; 2 Justin Carney; 4 Junior Sa'u; 3 Josh Griffin; 24 Mason Caton-Brown; 26 Josh Wood; 7 Michael Dobson (C); 8 Craig Kopczak; 19 Logan Tomkins; 10 George Griffin; 11 Ben Murdoch-Masila; 33 Josh Jones; 13 Mark Flanagan. Subs (all used): 1 Niall Evalds; 15 Adam Walne; 22 Matt Sarsfield; 23 Carl Forster.
Tries: Kopczak (17), O'Brien (31), J Griffin (44), Carney (68), Evalds (71); **Goals:** Dobson 3/4, O'Brien 0/2.
Rugby Leaguer & League Express Men of the Match: *Giants:* Ukuma Ta'ai; *Red Devils:* Craig Kopczak.
Penalty count: 6-7; **Half-time:** 12-10;
Referee: Joe Cobb; **Attendance:** 4,885.

HULL FC 26 WARRINGTON WOLVES 24

HULL FC: 1 Jamie Shaul; 31 Callum Lancaster; 19 Steve Michaels; 24 Kirk Yeaman; 20 Curtis Naughton; 13 Jordan Abdull; 7 Marc Sneyd; 10 Liam Watts; 9 Danny Houghton; 22 Josh Bowden; 11 Gareth Ellis (C); 17 Dean Hadley; 30 Danny Washbrook. Subs (all used): 8 Scott Taylor; 14 Iafeta Palea'aesina; 15 Chris Green; 25 Jansin Turgut.
Tries: Sneyd (7), Shaul (28), Naughton (56, 75), Yeaman (59); **Goals:** Sneyd 3/5.
WOLVES: 28 Jack Johnson; 2 Tom Lineham; 3 Rhys Evans; 4 Ryan Atkins; 20 Kevin Penny; 6 Stefan Ratchford; 7 Chris Sandow; 8 Chris Hill (C); 9 Daryl Clark; 10 Ashton Sims; 12 Jack Hughes; 11 Ben Currie; 14 Joe Westerman. Subs (all used): 13 Ben Westwood; 18 George King; 26 Declan Patton; 32 Jordan Cox.
Tries: Atkins (19), Lineham (23, 68), Penny (36), Sandow (39); **Goals:** Sandow 1/3, Ratchford 1/2.
Rugby Leaguer & League Express Men of the Match: *Hull FC:* Marc Sneyd; *Wolves:* Chris Sandow.
Penalty count: 6-5; **Half-time:** 10-20;
Referee: Robert Hicks; **Attendance:** 9,967.

LEEDS RHINOS 16 WAKEFIELD TRINITY WILDCATS 20

RHINOS: 1 Zak Hardaker; 2 Tom Briscoe; 3 Kallum Watkins; 4 Joel Moon; 22 Ash Handley; 14 Liam Sutcliffe; 25 Jordan Lilley; 16 Brad Singleton; 9 Beau Falloon; 10 Adam Cuthbertson; 18 Jimmy Keinhorst; 21 Josh Walters; 11 Jamie Jones-Buchanan. Subs (all used): 7 Rob Burrow (C); 17 Mitch Garbutt; 19 Mitch Achurch; 20 Anthony Mullally.
Tries: Moon (32), T Briscoe (51), Achurch (70);
Goals: Sutcliffe 2/4.
WILDCATS: 25 Craig Hall; 2 Tom Johnstone; 18 Joe Arundel; 14 Reece Lyne; 1 Ben Jones-Bishop; 7 Liam Finn; 6 Jacob Miller; 8 Nick Scruton; 9 Scott Moore; 11 Mickael Simon; 12 Danny Kirmond (C); 17 Matty Ashurst; 19 Jon Molloy. Subs (all used): 20 Michael Sio; 16 Tinirau Arona; 28 Andy Yates; 31 Jason Walton.
Tries: Ashurst (15), Miller (47), Hall (80); **Goals:** Finn 4/5.
Sin bin: Moore (62) - professional foul.

Rugby Leaguer & League Express Men of the Match:
Rhinos: Adam Cuthbertson; *Wildcats:* Tom Johnstone.
Penalty count: 14-5; **Half-time:** 6-8;
Referee: Phil Bentham; **Attendance:** 16,314.

WIDNES VIKINGS 12 ST HELENS 20

VIKINGS: 1 Rhys Hanbury; 2 Corey Thompson; 14 Chris Dean; 25 Ed Chamberlain (D); 5 Patrick Ah Van; 7 Joe Mellor (C); 21 Tom Gilmore; 8 Eamon O'Carroll; 33 Aaron Heremaia; 18 Gil Dudson; 15 Setaimata Sa; 11 Chris Houston; 13 Hep Cahill. Subs (all used): 10 Manase Manuokafoa; 20 Alex Gerrard; 19 Macgraff Leuluai; 22 Matt Whitley.
Tries: Hanbury (12, 70); **Goals:** Hanbury 2/2.
SAINTS: 23 Shannon McDonnell; 2 Tom Makinson; 18 Dominique Peyroux; 21 Matty Dawson; 22 Jack Owens; 19 Theo Fages; 7 Luke Walsh; 8 Alex Walmsley; 9 James Roby; 16 Andre Savelio; 20 Joe Greenwood; 13 Louie McCarthy-Scarsbrook; 12 Jon Wilkin (C). Subs (all used): 6 Travis Burns; 10 Kyle Amor; 3 Jordan Turner; 17 Luke Thompson.
Tries: Greenwood (5), McCarthy-Scarsbrook (16), Makinson (21); **Goals:** Walsh 4/5.
Rugby Leaguer & League Express Men of the Match:
Vikings: Rhys Hanbury; *Saints:* Luke Walsh.
Penalty count: 11-11; **Half-time:** 6-16;
Referee: Richard Silverwood; **Attendance:** 9,076.

CATALANS DRAGONS 41 CASTLEFORD TIGERS 22

DRAGONS: 21 Morgan Escare; 2 Jodie Broughton; 1 Tony Gigot; 4 Vincent Duport; 20 Fouad Yaha; 6 Todd Carney; 18 Thomas Bosc; 14 Dave Taylor; 16 Eloi Pelissier; 15 Julian Bousquet; 8 Louis Anderson; 11 Glenn Stewart; 17 Gregory Mounis. Subs (all used): 9 Paul Aiton; 10 Remi Casty (C); 13 Jason Baitieri; 29 Willie Mason.
Tries: Broughton (4), Anderson (19), Carney (24, 57), Escare (40, 49), Aiton (65); **Goals:** Bosc 6/7;
Field goal: Escare (77).
TIGERS: 5 Denny Solomona; 2 Joel Monaghan; 19 Ben Crooks; 24 Greg Minikin; 25 Jy Hitchcox; 18 Ryan Hampshire; 7 Luke Gale (C); 8 Andy Lynch; 9 Adam Milner; 21 Ryan Boyle; 3 Jake Webster; 12 Mike McMeeken; 13 Nathan Massey. Subs (all used): 10 Grant Millington; 15 Paul McShane; 23 Will Maher; 27 Tom Holmes.
Tries: Minikin (14, 35), Monaghan (30, 69);
Goals: Gale 3/4.
Rugby Leaguer & League Express Men of the Match:
Dragons: Todd Carney; *Tigers:* Greg Minikin.
Penalty count: 9-5; **Half-time:** 22-16;
Referee: Ben Thaler; **Attendance:** 10,351.

WIGAN WARRIORS 30 HULL KINGSTON ROVERS 16

WARRIORS: 22 Lewis Tierney; 5 Dominic Manfredi; 3 Anthony Gelling; 20 Oliver Gildart; 2 Josh Charnley; 13 Sean O'Loughlin (C); 7 Matty Smith; 17 Lee Mossop; 32 Luke Waterworth (D); 15 Tony Clubb; 11 Joel Tomkins; 27 Nick Gregson; 14 John Bateman. Subs (all used): 4 Dan Sarginson; 16 Sam Powell; 19 Taulima Tautai; 21 Ryan Sutton.
Tries: Tierney (25), Charnley (45, 49, 77), Manfredi (66), Gildart (69); **Goals:** Charnley 3/6.
ROVERS: 5 Kieran Dixon; 27 Will Oakes (D); 4 Iain Thornley; 1 Ken Sio; 23 Ryan Shaw; 22 Matthew Marsh; 11 Maurice Blair; 26 Rob Mulhern; 24 George Lawler; 17 Dane Tilse; 20 James Greenwood; 12 Graeme Horne (C); 10 Mitchell Allgood. Subs (all used): 8 Adam Walker; 28 Kieran Moran; 30 Joe Cator (D); 29 Joe Wardill (D).
Tries: Horne (37), Thornley (39, 51); **Goals:** Dixon 2/3.
Rugby Leaguer & League Express Men of the Match:
Warriors: Josh Charnley; *Rovers:* Iain Thornley.
Penalty count: 9-7; **Half-time:** 4-10;
Referee: Chris Kendall; **Attendance:** 11,268.

ROUND 9

Friday 1st April 2016

LEEDS RHINOS 10 HULL KINGSTON ROVERS 30

RHINOS: 1 Zak Hardaker; 22 Ash Handley; 3 Kallum Watkins; 4 Joel Moon; 14 Liam Sutcliffe; 6 Danny McGuire (C); 7 Rob Burrow; 8 Keith Galloway; 9 Beau Falloon; 10 Adam Cuthbertson; 19 Mitch Achurch; 12 Carl Ablett; 11 Jamie Jones-Buchanan. Subs (all used): 20 Anthony Mullally; 17 Mitch Garbutt; 21 Josh Walters; 16 Brad Singleton.
Tries: Jones-Buchanan (61), Ablett (67);
Goals: Hardaker 1/2.
ROVERS: 18 Ben Cockayne; 1 Ken Sio; 12 Graeme Horne; 4 Iain Thornley; 5 Kieran Dixon; 6 Terry Campese (C); 22 Matthew Marsh; 17 Dane Tilse; 13 Chris Clarkson; 26 Rob Mulhern; 11 Maurice Blair; 20 James Greenwood; 10 Mitchell Allgood. Subs (all used): 8 Adam Walker; 9 Shaun Lunt; 16 James Green; 28 Kieran Moran.
Tries: Lunt (19, 33), Dixon (43), Cockayne (54), Allgood (72), Mulhern (76); **Goals:** Dixon 2/5, Cockayne 1/1.
Rugby Leaguer & League Express Men of the Match:
Rhinos: Jamie Jones-Buchanan; *Rovers:* Shaun Lunt.
Penalty count: 4-4; **Half time:** 0-10;
Referee: Richard Silverwood; **Attendance:** 15,384.

ST HELENS 16 HULL FC 17

SAINTS: 23 Shannon McDonnell; 22 Jack Owens; 18 Dominique Peyroux; 3 Jordan Turner; 21 Matty Dawson; 19 Theo Fages; 7 Luke Walsh; 8 Alex Walmsley; 9 James Roby; 16 Andre Savelio; 20 Joe Greenwood; 13 Louie McCarthy-Scarsbrook; 12 Jon Wilkin (C). Subs (all used): 6 Travis Burns; 10 Kyle Amor; 15 Greg Richards; 17 Luke Thompson.
Tries: Greenwood (4), Dawson (27), Turner (33);
Goals: Walsh 1/1, Owens 1/3.
HULL FC: 1 Jamie Shaul; 19 Steve Michaels; 2 Mahe Fonua; 24 Kirk Yeaman; 20 Curtis Naughton; 3 Carlos Tuimavave; 7 Marc Sneyd; 8 Scott Taylor; 9 Danny Houghton; 10 Liam Watts; 12 Mark Minichiello; 21 Sika Manu; 11 Gareth Ellis (C). Subs (all used): 16 Jordan Thompson; 17 Dean Hadley; 22 Josh Bowden; 23 Frank Pritchard.
Tries: Houghton (21), Naughton (38), Yeaman (60);
Goals: Sneyd 2/3; **Field goal:** Sneyd (76).
Rugby Leaguer & League Express Men of the Match:
Saints: Alex Walmsley; *Hull FC:* Marc Sneyd.
Penalty count: 8-6; **Half-time:** 16-10;
Referee: James Child; **Attendance:** 10,230.

WIGAN WARRIORS 16 WARRINGTON WOLVES 28

WARRIORS: 4 Dan Sarginson; 5 Dominic Manfredi; 30 Jack Higginson (D); 20 Oliver Gildart; 2 Josh Charnley; 13 Sean O'Loughlin (C); 7 Matty Smith; 17 Lee Mossop; 16 Sam Powell; 15 Tony Clubb; 11 Joel Tomkins; 12 Liam Farrell; 25 Willie Isa. Subs (all used): 19 Taulima Tautai; 21 Ryan Sutton; 26 Greg Burke; 27 Nick Gregson.
Tries: Manfredi (33, 49, 61); **Goals:** Smith 0/1, Charnley 2/2.
Sin bin: Farrell (14) - holding down.
WOLVES: 5 Matthew Russell; 20 Kevin Penny; 3 Rhys Evans; 4 Ryan Atkins; 2 Tom Lineham; 1 Kurt Gidley; 7 Chris Sandow; 8 Chris Hill (C); 9 Daryl Clark; 10 Ashton Sims; 11 Ben Currie; 12 Jack Hughes; 13 Ben Westwood. Subs (all used): 6 Stefan Ratchford; 14 Joe Westerman; 18 George King; 32 Jordan Cox.
Tries: Currie (12), Lineham (15), Penny (19), Ratchford (36), Atkins (43); **Goals:** Sandow 0/3, Ratchford 1/1, Gidley 3/3, Westerman 0/1.
Rugby Leaguer & League Express Men of the Match:
Warriors: Dominic Manfredi; *Wolves:* Daryl Clark.
Penalty count: 6-10; **Half-time:** 4-22;
Referee: Robert Hicks; **Attendance:** 17,480.

Saturday 2nd April 2016

**WAKEFIELD TRINITY WILDCATS 32
SALFORD RED DEVILS 18**

WILDCATS: 21 Max Jowitt; 1 Ben Jones-Bishop; 18 Joe Arundel; 14 Reece Lyne; 2 Tom Johnstone; 6 Jacob Miller; 7 Liam Finn; 8 Nick Scruton; 9 Scott Moore; 10 Anthony England; 12 Danny Kirmond (C); 17 Matty Ashurst; 20 Michael Sio. Subs (all used): 11 Mickael Simon; 16 Tinirau Arona; 19 Jon Molloy; 31 Jason Walton.
Tries: Miller (2), Sio (6), Johnstone (37, 47, 77), Lyne (74);
Goals: Finn 4/6.
RED DEVILS: 14 Gareth O'Brien; 2 Justin Carney; 4 Junior Sa'u; 33 Josh Jones; 3 Josh Griffin; 26 Josh Wood; 7 Michael Dobson (C); 23 Carl Forster; 19 Logan Tomkins; 10 George Griffin; 11 Ben Murdoch-Masila; 22 Matt Sarsfield; 13 Mark Flanagan. Subs (all used): 1 Niall Evalds; 15 Adam Walne; 16 Olsi Krasniqi; 20 Jordan Walne.
Tries: O'Brien (15), Sarsfield (34), Carney (61);
Goals: O'Brien 2/2, Dobson 1/1.
Rugby Leaguer & League Express Men of the Match:
Wildcats: Tom Johnstone; *Red Devils:* Gareth O'Brien.
Penalty count: 4-5; **Half-time:** 16-12;
Referee: Joe Cobb; **Attendance:** 4,048.

CATALANS DRAGONS 21 WIDNES VIKINGS 8

DRAGONS: 21 Morgan Escare; 2 Jodie Broughton; 1 Tony Gigot; 4 Vincent Duport; 5 Pat Richards; 18 Thomas Bosc; 7 Richard Myler; 15 Julian Bousquet; 16 Eloi Pelissier; 29 Willie Mason; 11 Glenn Stewart; 14 Dave Taylor; 13 Jason Baitieri (C). Subs (all used): 9 Paul Aiton; 17 Gregory Mounis; 19 Olivier Elima; 22 Antoni Maria.
Tries: Richards (4), Duport (43), Taylor (68), Pelissier (77); **Goals:** Richards 2/4; **Field goal:** Bosc (73).
VIKINGS: 1 Rhys Hanbury; 2 Corey Thompson; 14 Chris Dean; 4 Charly Runciman; 5 Patrick Ah Van; 7 Joe Mellor (C); 21 Tom Gilmore; 8 Eamon O'Carroll; 33 Aaron Heremaia; 18 Gil Dudson; 22 Matt Whitley; 11 Chris Houston; 19 Macgraff Leuluai. Subs (all used): 10 Manase Manuokafoa; 25 Ed Chamberlain; 34 Sam Brooks (D); 35 Jordan Johnstone (D).
Try: Thompson (53); **Goals:** Hanbury 2/2.
Rugby Leaguer & League Express Men of the Match:
Dragons: Dave Taylor; *Vikings:* Joe Mellor.
Penalty count: 7-10; **Half-time:** 4-0;
Referee: Gareth Hewer; **Attendance:** 8,642.

Sunday 3rd April 2016

CASTLEFORD TIGERS 38 HUDDERSFIELD GIANTS 34

TIGERS: 18 Ryan Hampshire; 24 Greg Minikin; 19 Ben Crooks; 3 Jake Webster; 25 Jy Hitchcox; 27 Tom Holmes; 7 Luke Gale (C); 8 Andy Lynch; 9 Adam Milner; 14 Lee Jewitt; 12 Mike McMeeken; 10 Grant Millington; 13 Nathan Massey. Subs (all used): 16 Matt Cook; 15 Paul McShane; 23 Will Maher; 21 Ryan Boyle.
Tries: McMeeken (18, 48), Minikin (29), Hitchcox (40, 69, 75), Webster (71); **Goals:** Gale 5/7.
GIANTS: 34 Ryan Brierley; 2 Jermaine McGillvary; 3 Leroy Cudjoe; 4 Joe Wardle; 5 Aaron Murphy; 6 Danny Brough; 18 Jake Connor; 16 Sam Rapira; 9 Ryan Hinchcliffe (C); 10 Craig Huby; 12 Michael Lawrence; 17 Ukuma Ta'ai; 22 Oliver Roberts. Subs (all used): 8 Eorl Crabtree; 13 Larne Patrick; 21 Nathan Mason; 27 Mikey Wood (D).
Tries: Cudjoe (10, 50), McGillvary (36, 45, 77), Rapira (61);
Goals: Brough 5/6.
Rugby Leaguer & League Express Men of the Match:
Tigers: Mike McMeeken; *Giants:* Jermaine McGillvary.
Penalty count: 8-8; **Half-time:** 16-12;
Referee: Phil Bentham; **Attendance:** 6,631.

ROUND 10

Thursday 7th April 2016

HULL KINGSTON ROVERS 0 CATALANS DRAGONS 40

ROVERS: 18 Ben Cockayne; 1 Ken Sio; 21 Thomas Minns; 4 Iain Thornley; 5 Kieran Dixon; 11 Maurice Blair; 22 Matthew Marsh; 26 Rob Mulhern; 24 George Lawler; 17 Dane Tilse; 13 Chris Clarkson (C); 20 James Greenwood; 10 Mitchell Allgood. Subs (all used): 8 Adam Walker; 9 Shaun Lunt; 16 James Green; 28 Kieran Moran.
Sin bin: Cockayne (52) - professional foul.
DRAGONS: 1 Tony Gigot; 2 Jodie Broughton; 3 Krisnan Inu; 4 Vincent Duport; 5 Pat Richards; 18 Thomas Bosc; 7 Richard Myler; 14 Dave Taylor; 16 Eloi Pelissier; 29 Willie Mason; 11 Glenn Stewart; 8 Louis Anderson; 13 Jason Baitieri (C). Subs (all used): 15 Julian Bousquet; 17 Gregory Mounis; 19 Olivier Elima; 23 Stan Robin.
Tries: Broughton (2, 22), Duport (5), Inu (28), Mounis (35), Myler (49), Mason (54);
Goals: Richards 5/6, Bosc 1/1.
Rugby Leaguer & League Express Men of the Match:
Rovers: James Green; *Dragons:* Richard Myler.
Penalty count: 10-9; **Half-time:** 0-28;
Referee: Richard Silverwood; **Attendance:** 6,764.

Friday 8th April 2016

HULL FC 37 HUDDERSFIELD GIANTS 20

HULL FC: 1 Jamie Shaul; 19 Steve Michaels; 2 Mahe Fonua; 24 Kirk Yeaman; 20 Curtis Naughton; 17 Dean Hadley; 7 Marc Sneyd; 8 Scott Taylor; 9 Danny Houghton (C); 10 Liam Watts; 21 Sika Manu; 23 Frank Pritchard; 22 Josh Bowden. Subs (all used): 5 Fetuli Talanoa; 14 Iafeta Palea'aesina; 15 Chris Green; 16 Jordan Thompson.
Tries: Bowden (6), Watts (21), Shaul (32, 61), Houghton (55), Naughton (64); **Goals:** Sneyd 6/6;
Field goal: Sneyd (80).
GIANTS: 34 Ryan Brierley; 2 Jermaine McGillvary; 3 Leroy Cudjoe; 5 Aaron Murphy; 35 Gene Ormsby (D); 6 Danny Brough; 18 Jake Connor; 16 Sam Rapira; 9 Ryan Hinchcliffe (C); 10 Craig Huby; 4 Joe Wardle; 17 Ukuma Ta'ai; 12 Michael Lawrence. Subs (all used): 8 Eorl Crabtree; 13 Larne Patrick; 20 Kruise Leeming; 22 Oliver Roberts.
Tries: Wardle (12), Murphy (17), Brough (36), McGillvary (71); **Goals:** Brough 2/4.
Sin bin: Brough (55) - dissent.
Rugby Leaguer & League Express Men of the Match:
Hull FC: Marc Sneyd; *Giants:* Leroy Cudjoe.
Penalty count: 7-6; **Half-time:** 18-16;
Referee: Robert Hicks; **Attendance:** 10,557.

WARRINGTON WOLVES 22 ST HELENS 25

WOLVES: 5 Matthew Russell; 2 Tom Lineham; 11 Ben Currie; 4 Ryan Atkins; 20 Kevin Penny; 1 Kurt Gidley; 6 Stefan Ratchford; 8 Chris Hill (C); 9 Daryl Clark; 10 Ashton Sims; 13 Ben Westwood; 12 Jack Hughes; 14 Joe Westerman. Subs (all used): 3 Rhys Evans; 18 George King; 25 Joe Philbin; 29 Benjamin Jullien.
Tries: Penny (7, 74), Atkins (12), Currie (40), Lineham (79);
Goals: Westwood 1/3, Gidley 0/1
(last conversion attempt declined).
On report:
Atkins (64) - alleged dangerous contact on Wilkin.
SAINTS: 23 Shannon McDonnell; 22 Jack Owens; 3 Jordan Turner; 21 Matty Dawson; 33 Jake Spedding (D); 19 Theo Fages; 7 Luke Walsh; 8 Alex Walmsley; 9 James Roby; 16 Andre Savelio; 13 Louie McCarthy-Scarsbrook; 27 Jack

Ashworth; 12 Jon Wilkin (C). Subs (all used): 10 Kyle Amor; 15 Greg Richards; 17 Luke Thompson; 28 Morgan Knowles.
Tries: Amor (16), Ashworth (20), Dawson (46), Knowles (70); **Goals:** Walsh 4/5; **Field goal:** Walsh (72).
Rugby Leaguer & League Express Men of the Match: *Wolves:* Stefan Ratchford; *Saints:* Theo Fages.
Penalty count: 8-3; **Half-time:** 14-12;
Referee: Ben Thaler; **Attendance:** 13,678.

Saturday 9th April 2016

SALFORD RED DEVILS 14 LEEDS RHINOS 10

RED DEVILS: 14 Gareth O'Brien; 2 Justin Carney; 4 Junior Sa'u; 3 Josh Griffin; 1 Niall Evalds; 6 Robert Lui; 7 Michael Dobson (C); 8 Craig Kopczak; 19 Logan Tomkins; 10 George Griffin; 11 Ben Murdoch-Masila; 33 Josh Jones; 13 Mark Flanagan. Subs (all used): 15 Adam Walne; 16 Olsi Krasniqi; 20 Jordan Walne; 26 Josh Wood.
Tries: Tomkins (22), Lui (45);
Goals: O'Brien 1/1, Dobson 2/2.
RHINOS: 1 Zak Hardaker; 23 Ashton Golding; 3 Kallum Watkins; 14 Liam Sutcliffe; 22 Ash Handley; 6 Danny McGuire (C); 7 Rob Burrow; 16 Brad Singleton; 9 Beau Falloon; 19 Mitch Achurch; 17 Mitch Garbutt; 12 Carl Ablett; 11 Jamie Jones-Buchanan. Subs (all used): 8 Keith Galloway; 20 Anthony Mullally; 24 Jordan Baldwinson (D2); 25 Jordan Lilley.
Tries: Galloway (73), Golding (76); **Goals:** Hardaker 1/2.
Rugby Leaguer & League Express Men of the Match: *Red Devils:* Robert Lui; *Rhinos:* Jamie Jones-Buchanan.
Penalty count: 4-6; **Half-time:** 8-0;
Referee: Phil Bentham; **Attendance:** 4,912.

Sunday 10th April 2016

WAKEFIELD TRINITY WILDCATS 62 WIGAN WARRIORS 0

WILDCATS: 21 Max Jowitt; 2 Tom Johnstone; 18 Joe Arundel; 14 Reece Lyne; 1 Ben Jones-Bishop; 6 Jacob Miller; 7 Liam Finn; 8 Nick Scruton; 9 Scott Moore; 10 Anthony England; 13 Anthony Tupou; 12 Danny Kirmond (C); 20 Michael Sio. Subs (all used): 11 Mickael Simon; 16 Tinirau Arona; 17 Matty Ashurst; 19 Jon Molloy.
Tries: Scruton (11, 73), Miller (24, 35, 52), Johnstone (28), Finn (48), Kirmond (58, 65), Jones-Bishop (68), Jowitt (71); **Goals:** Finn 9/11.
WARRIORS: 4 Dan Sarginson; 2 Josh Charnley; 30 Jack Higginson; 20 Oliver Gildart; 22 Lewis Tierney; 27 Nick Gregson; 7 Matty Smith (C); 15 Tony Clubb; 16 Sam Powell; 17 Lee Mossop; 11 Joel Tomkins; 25 Willie Isa; 21 Ryan Sutton. Subs (all used): 19 Taulima Tautai; 26 Greg Burke; 29 Joe Bretherton (D); 34 Jack Wells (D).
Rugby Leaguer & League Express Men of the Match: *Wildcats:* Jacob Miller; *Warriors:* Greg Burke.
Penalty count: 8-12; **Half-time:** 22-0;
Referee: Gareth Hewer; **Attendance:** 5,751.

WIDNES VIKINGS 24 CASTLEFORD TIGERS 34

VIKINGS: 1 Rhys Hanbury; 2 Corey Thompson; 3 Chris Bridge; 14 Chris Dean; 5 Patrick Ah Van; 6 Kevin Brown (C); 7 Joe Mellor; 8 Eamon O'Carroll; 33 Aaron Heremaia; 18 Gil Dudson; 15 Setaimata Sa; 11 Chris Houston; 19 Macgraff Leuluai. Subs (all used): 9 Lloyd White; 20 Alex Gerrard; 22 Matt Whitley; 34 Sam Brooks.
Tries: Ah Van (2), Leuluai (8), Thompson (18), White (72); **Goals:** Bridge 4/4.
TIGERS: 18 Ryan Hampshire; 2 Joel Monaghan; 24 Greg Minikin; 3 Jake Webster; 5 Denny Solomona; 27 Tom Holmes; 7 Luke Gale (C); 8 Andy Lynch; 9 Adam Milner; 14 Lee Jewitt; 16 Matt Cook; 12 Mike McMeeken; 13 Nathan Massey. Subs (all used): 15 Paul McShane; 23 Will Maher; 22 Gadwin Springer; 21 Ryan Boyle.
Tries: Solomona (25, 28, 43), Boyle (52), Gale (63), McShane (78); **Goals:** Gale 5/6.
Rugby Leaguer & League Express Men of the Match: *Vikings:* Macgraff Leuluai; *Tigers:* Luke Gale.
Penalty count: 7-9; **Half-time:** 18-10;
Referee: Joe Cobb; **Attendance:** 5,081.

ROUND 11

Thursday 14th April 2016

ST HELENS 12 CATALANS DRAGONS 30

SAINTS: 23 Shannon McDonnell; 22 Jack Owens; 3 Jordan Turner; 21 Matty Dawson; 33 Jake Spedding; 19 Theo Fages; 7 Luke Walsh; 8 Alex Walmsley; 9 James Roby; 16 Andre Savelio; 13 Louie McCarthy-Scarsbrook; 27 Jack Ashworth; 12 Jon Wilkin (C). Subs (all used): 10 Kyle Amor; 14 Lama Tasi; 15 Greg Richards; 28 Morgan Knowles.
Tries: Fages (27), Walsh (38); **Goals:** Walsh 2/2.

DRAGONS: 1 Tony Gigot; 2 Jodie Broughton; 3 Krisnan Inu; 4 Vincent Duport; 5 Pat Richards; 6 Todd Carney; 7 Richard Myler; 14 Dave Taylor; 28 Alrix Da Costa (D); 15 Julian Bousquet; 11 Glenn Stewart; 8 Louis Anderson; 13 Jason Baitieri. Subs (all used): 10 Remi Casty (C); 12 Justin Horo; 17 Gregory Mounis; 18 Thomas Bosc.
Tries: Broughton (7, 14, 33, 64), Myler (46), Richards (49); **Goals:** Richards 3/7.
On report:
Mounis (22) - alleged dangerous challenge on Savelio.
Rugby Leaguer & League Express Men of the Match: *Saints:* Louie McCarthy-Scarsbrook;
Dragons: Jodie Broughton.
Penalty count: 6-4; **Half-time:** 12-14;
Referee: Robert Hicks; **Attendance:** 9,362.

Friday 15th April 2016

HUDDERSFIELD GIANTS 11 WARRINGTON WOLVES 0

GIANTS: 34 Ryan Brierley; 2 Jermaine McGillvary; 3 Leroy Cudjoe; 18 Jake Connor; 5 Aaron Murphy; 6 Danny Brough; 15 Kyle Wood; 19 Josh Johnson; 9 Ryan Hinchcliffe (C); 10 Craig Huby; 4 Joe Wardle; 17 Ukuma Ta'ai; 12 Michael Lawrence. Subs (all used): 16 Sam Rapira; 20 Kruise Leeming; 21 Nathan Mason; 22 Oliver Roberts.
Tries: Murphy (35), Cudjoe (70); **Goals:** Brough 1/3;
Field goal: Brough (65).
WOLVES: 5 Matthew Russell; 20 Kevin Penny; 12 Jack Hughes; 4 Ryan Atkins; 3 Rhys Evans; 1 Kurt Gidley; 6 Stefan Ratchford; 8 Chris Hill (C); 9 Daryl Clark; 10 Ashton Sims; 13 Ben Westwood; 11 Ben Currie; 14 Joe Westerman. Subs (all used): 18 George King; 25 Joe Philbin; 29 Benjamin Jullien; 27 Sam Wilde.
Rugby Leaguer & League Express Men of the Match: *Giants:* Danny Brough; *Wolves:* Daryl Clark.
Penalty count: 5-6; **Half-time:** 4-0;
Referee: Richard Silverwood; **Attendance:** 5,427.

LEEDS RHINOS 20 HULL FC 18

RHINOS: 1 Zak Hardaker; 23 Ashton Golding; 3 Kallum Watkins; 18 Jimmy Keinhorst; 22 Ash Handley; 14 Liam Sutcliffe; 25 Jordan Lilley; 8 Keith Galloway; 7 Rob Burrow (C); 17 Mitch Garbutt; 12 Carl Ablett; 19 Mitch Achurch; 11 Jamie Jones-Buchanan. Subs: 9 Beau Falloon (not used); 15 Brett Delaney; 16 Brad Singleton; 20 Anthony Mullally.
Tries: Keinhorst (16), Lilley (60), Jones-Buchanan (73);
Goals: Lilley 4/4.
HULL FC: 20 Curtis Naughton; 19 Steve Michaels; 2 Mahe Fonua; 24 Kirk Yeaman; 5 Fetuli Talanoa; 30 Danny Washbrook; 7 Marc Sneyd; 8 Scott Taylor; 9 Danny Houghton (C); 10 Liam Watts; 23 Frank Pritchard; 21 Sika Manu; 22 Josh Bowden. Subs (all used): 15 Chris Green; 16 Jordan Thompson; 14 Iafeta Palea'aesina; 17 Dean Hadley.
Tries: Green (31), Yeaman (42), Houghton (76);
Goals: Sneyd 3/3.
Rugby Leaguer & League Express Men of the Match: *Rhinos:* Jamie Jones-Buchanan; *Hull FC:* Frank Pritchard.
Penalty count: 9-5; **Half-time:** 8-6;
Referee: Joe Cobb; **Attendance:** 15,888.

WIGAN WARRIORS 26 CASTLEFORD TIGERS 12

WARRIORS: 4 Dan Sarginson; 2 Josh Charnley; 14 John Bateman; 20 Oliver Gildart; 22 Lewis Tierney; 27 Nick Gregson; 7 Matty Smith; 15 Tony Clubb; 16 Sam Powell; 17 Lee Mossop; 11 Joel Tomkins (C); 25 Willie Isa; 21 Ryan Sutton. Subs (all used): 8 Dominic Crosby; 19 Taulima Tautai; 26 Greg Burke; 29 Joe Bretherton.
Tries: Tierney (11), Bateman (60, 79), Gregson (70);
Goals: Smith 5/5.
TIGERS: 18 Ryan Hampshire; 2 Joel Monaghan; 24 Greg Minikin; 3 Jake Webster; 5 Denny Solomona; 27 Tom Holmes; 7 Luke Gale (C); 8 Andy Lynch; 9 Adam Miller; 14 Lee Jewitt; 11 Oliver Holmes; 12 Mike McMeeken; 13 Nathan Massey. Subs (all used): 10 Grant Millington; 15 Paul McShane; 16 Matt Cook; 23 Will Maher.
Tries: Solomona (8), Millington (46); **Goals:** Gale 2/2.
Sin bin: Gale (11) - dissent.
Rugby Leaguer & League Express Men of the Match: *Warriors:* John Bateman; *Tigers:* Luke Gale.
Penalty count: 7-7; **Half-time:** 8-6;
Referee: Phil Bentham; **Attendance:** 11,849.

ROUND 12

Thursday 21st April 2016

WIGAN WARRIORS 26 HUDDERSFIELD GIANTS 19

WARRIORS: 4 Dan Sarginson; 2 Josh Charnley; 3 Anthony Gelling; 20 Oliver Gildart; 22 Lewis Tierney; 27 Nick Gregson; 7 Matty Smith; 10 Ben Flower; 16 Sam Powell; 17 Lee Mossop; 14 John Bateman (C); 25 Willie Isa; 21 Ryan Sutton. Subs (all used): 15 Tony Clubb; 19 Taulima Tautai; 26 Greg Burke; 34 Jack Wells.
Tries: Gelling (6), Bateman (55), Smith (69), Sarginson (79); **Goals:** Smith 4/4;
Field goals: Smith (70, 78).

GIANTS: 34 Ryan Brierley; 2 Jermaine McGillvary; 3 Leroy Cudjoe; 18 Jake Connor; 5 Aaron Murphy; 6 Danny Brough; 15 Kyle Wood; 19 Josh Johnson; 9 Ryan Hinchcliffe (C); 10 Craig Huby; 4 Joe Wardle; 17 Ukuma Ta'ai; 12 Michael Lawrence. Subs (all used): 16 Sam Rapira; 20 Kruise Leeming; 21 Nathan Mason; 22 Oliver Roberts.
Tries: Brierley (13, 33, 59); **Goals:** Brough 3/3;
Field goal: Brough (74).
Sin bin: Mason (55) - interference;
Murphy (71) - holding down.
Rugby Leaguer & League Express Men of the Match: *Warriors:* Anthony Gelling; *Giants:* Ryan Brierley.
Penalty count: 10-5; **Half-time:** 6-12;
Referee: Joe Cobb; **Attendance:** 10,914.

Friday 22nd April 2016

ST HELENS 38 LEEDS RHINOS 34

SAINTS: 23 Shannon McDonnell; 1 Jonny Lomax; 21 Matty Dawson; 4 Mark Percival; 22 Jack Owens; 19 Theo Fages; 7 Luke Walsh; 14 Lama Tasi; 9 James Roby; 10 Kyle Amor; 13 Louie McCarthy-Scarsbrook; 20 Joe Greenwood; 12 Jon Wilkin (C). Subs (all used): 8 Alex Walmsley; 11 Atelea Vea; 15 Greg Richards; 28 Morgan Knowles.
Tries: Lomax (5, 38), Greenwood (7, 53), Amor (47), Fages (58, 70); **Goals:** Walsh 5/7.
RHINOS: 1 Zak Hardaker; 23 Ashton Golding; 3 Kallum Watkins; 18 Jimmy Keinhorst; 22 Ash Handley; 25 Jordan Lilley; 7 Rob Burrow (C); 8 Keith Galloway; 9 Beau Falloon; 17 Mitch Garbutt; 15 Brett Delaney; 12 Carl Ablett; 11 Jamie Jones-Buchanan. Subs (all used): 14 Liam Sutcliffe; 16 Brad Singleton; 19 Mitch Achurch; 20 Anthony Mullally.
Tries: Golding (23), Burrow (29), Keinhorst (34, 74), Handley (49), Mullally (67); **Goals:** Lilley 5/6.
Rugby Leaguer & League Express Men of the Match: *Saints:* Jonny Lomax; *Rhinos:* Rob Burrow.
Penalty count: 4-4; **Half-time:** 16-16;
Referee: Phil Bentham; **Attendance:** 11,271.

WIDNES VIKINGS 16 WARRINGTON WOLVES 48

VIKINGS: 1 Rhys Hanbury; 2 Corey Thompson; 3 Chris Bridge; 4 Charly Runciman; 17 Stefan Marsh; 7 Joe Mellor; 6 Kevin Brown (C); 8 Eamon O'Carroll; 9 Lloyd White; 18 Gil Dudson; 14 Chris Dean; 11 Chris Houston; 13 Hep Cahill. Subs (all used): 33 Aaron Heremaia; 10 Manase Manuokafoa; 15 Setaimata Sa; 19 Macgraff Leuluai.
Tries: Mellor (14), Thompson (46), Marsh (66);
Goals: Hanbury 2/3.
WOLVES: 5 Matthew Russell; 20 Kevin Penny; 3 Rhys Evans; 4 Ryan Atkins; 28 Jack Johnson; 1 Kurt Gidley; 6 Stefan Ratchford; 8 Chris Hill (C); 9 Daryl Clark; 10 Ashton Sims; 12 Jack Hughes; 11 Ben Currie; 14 Joe Westerman. Subs (all used): 13 Ben Westwood; 18 George King; 29 Benjamin Jullien; 32 Jordan Cox.
Tries: Gidley (6), Penny (11, 57), Westerman (18, 39), Westwood (34), Ratchford (63, 77);
Goals: Gidley 7/7, Ratchford 1/1.
Rugby Leaguer & League Express Men of the Match: *Vikings:* Chris Houston; *Wolves:* Kurt Gidley.
Penalty count: 3-7; **Half-time:** 6-30;
Referee: Robert Hicks; **Attendance:** 7,441.

Saturday 23rd April 2016

CATALANS DRAGONS 42 SALFORD RED DEVILS 32

DRAGONS: 21 Morgan Escare; 2 Jodie Broughton; 3 Krisnan Inu; 4 Vincent Duport; 5 Pat Richards; 6 Todd Carney; 7 Richard Myler; 14 Dave Taylor; 28 Alrix Da Costa; 8 Louis Anderson; 11 Glenn Stewart; 12 Justin Horo; 13 Jason Baitieri. Subs (all used): 10 Remi Casty (C); 15 Julian Bousquet; 18 Thomas Bosc; 29 Willie Mason.
Tries: Broughton (5, 54), Escare (21), Duport (34), Myler (52, 57), Richards (75); **Goals:** Richards 6/8, Bosc 1/1.
RED DEVILS: 14 Gareth O'Brien; 2 Justin Carney; 4 Junior Sa'u; 3 Josh Griffin; 1 Niall Evalds; 6 Robert Lui; 7 Michael Dobson (C); 8 Craig Kopczak; 19 Logan Tomkins; 10 George Griffin; 11 Ben Murdoch-Masila; 33 Josh Jones; 13 Mark Flanagan. Subs (all used): 12 Weller Hauraki; 15 Adam Walne; 16 Olsi Krasniqi; 26 Josh Wood.
Tries: Evalds (3, 66), Carney (10), Sa'u (24, 50, 62);
Goals: O'Brien 2/4, Dobson 2/3.
Rugby Leaguer & League Express Men of the Match: *Dragons:* Todd Carney; *Red Devils:* Robert Lui.
Penalty count: 9-7; **Half-time:** 16-14;
Referee: Gareth Hewer; **Attendance:** 9,686.

Sunday 24th April 2016

WAKEFIELD TRINITY WILDCATS 28 HULL FC 46

WILDCATS: 21 Max Jowitt; 1 Ben Jones-Bishop; 4 Ashley Gibson; 14 Reece Lyne; 2 Tom Johnstone; 6 Jacob Miller; 7 Liam Finn; 10 Anthony England; 9 Scott Moore; 8 Nick

Hull FC's Marc Sneyd kicks the ball past Catalans Dragons duo Gregory Mounis and Tony Gigot

Scruton; 13 Anthony Tupou; 12 Danny Kirmond (C); 20 Michael Sio. Subs (all used): 11 Mickael Simon; 17 Matty Ashurst; 19 Jon Molloy; 16 Tinirau Arona.
Tries: Gibson (7, 33, 37), Johnstone (29), Kirmond (45);
Goals: Finn 4/6.
HULL FC: 1 Jamie Shaul; 20 Curtis Naughton; 2 Mahe Fonua; 24 Kirk Yeaman; 5 Fetuli Talanoa; 6 Leon Pryce; 7 Marc Sneyd; 10 Liam Watts; 9 Danny Houghton; 22 Josh Bowden; 21 Sika Manu; 23 Frank Pritchard; 11 Gareth Ellis (C). Subs (all used): 12 Mark Minichiello; 15 Chris Green; 30 Danny Washbrook; 8 Scott Taylor.
Tries: Ellis (13), Talanoa (19, 24, 48, 74), Bowden (21), Yeaman (55), Shaul (76); **Goals:** Sneyd 7/8.
On report:
Ellis (12) - alleged dangerous challenge on Simon.
Rugby Leaguer & League Express Men of the Match:
Wildcats: Michael Sio; *Hull FC:* Fetuli Talanoa.
Penalty count: 7-7; **Half-time:** 24-24;
Referee: Richard Silverwood; **Attendance:** 6,701.

CASTLEFORD TIGERS 16 HULL KINGSTON ROVERS 58

TIGERS: 5 Denny Solomona; 2 Joel Monaghan; 24 Greg Minikin; 3 Jake Webster; 25 Jy Hitchcox; 18 Ryan Hampshire; 7 Luke Gale (C); 8 Andy Lynch; 9 Adam Milner; 14 Lee Jewitt; 10 Grant Millington; 12 Mike McMeeken; 13 Nathan Massey. Subs (all used): 15 Paul McShane; 32 Larne Patrick (D); 16 Matt Cook; 17 Junior Moors.
Tries: Webster (14), Hampshire (18), Hitchcox (36);
Goals: Gale 2/3.
Sin bin: McShane (63) - fighting.
ROVERS: 18 Ben Cockayne; 1 Ken Sio; 21 Thomas Minns; 4 Iain Thornley; 29 Joe Wardill; 11 Maurice Blair; 7 Albert Kelly; 17 Dane Tilse; 9 Shaun Lunt; 26 Rob Mulhern; 13 Chris Clarkson; 12 Graeme Horne (C); 10 Mitchell Allgood. Subs (all used): 19 John Boudebza; 15 James Donaldson; 16 James Green; 8 Adam Walker.
Tries: Blair (2), Minns (20, 41, 78), Kelly (27), Horne (30), Thornley (53, 80), Allgood (58), Sio (64, 76);
Goals: Cockayne 7/12.
Sin bin: Lunt (63) - fighting.
Rugby Leaguer & League Express Men of the Match:
Tigers: Luke Gale; *Rovers:* Albert Kelly.
Penalty count: 9-9; **Half-time:** 16-20;
Referee: Ben Thaler; **Attendance:** 7,106.

ROUND 13

Thursday 28th April 2016

WARRINGTON WOLVES 40 WIGAN WARRIORS 10

WOLVES: 5 Matthew Russell; 20 Kevin Penny; 3 Rhys Evans; 4 Ryan Atkins; 2 Tom Lineham; 1 Kurt Gidley; 6 Stefan Ratchford; 8 Chris Hill (C); 9 Daryl Clark; 10 Ashton Sims; 12 Jack Hughes; 11 Ben Currie; 14 Joe Westerman. Subs (all used): 13 Ben Westwood; 18 George King; 29 Benjamin Jullien; 32 Jordan Cox.
Tries: Clark (23), Westwood (29, 79), Penny (39), Atkins (48, 58), Jullien (64);
Goals: Gidley 5/6, Ratchford 1/1.
WARRIORS: 4 Dan Sarginson; 2 Josh Charnley; 3 Anthony Gelling; 20 Oliver Gildart; 22 Lewis Tierney; 27 Nick Gregson; 7 Matty Smith; 15 Tony Clubb; 16 Sam Powell; 17 Lee Mossop; 14 John Bateman (C); 25 Willie Isa; 21 Ryan Sutton. Subs (all used): 6 George Williams; 19 Taulima Tautai; 26 Greg Burke; 34 Jack Wells.
Tries: Charnley (17), Bateman (69); **Goals:** Smith 1/2.
Rugby Leaguer & League Express Men of the Match:
Wolves: Daryl Clark; *Warriors:* John Bateman.
Penalty count: 8-8; **Half-time:** 18-4;
Referee: Phil Bentham; **Attendance:** 11,724.

Friday 29th April 2016

HUDDERSFIELD GIANTS 28 LEEDS RHINOS 20

GIANTS: 34 Ryan Brierley; 2 Jermaine McGillvary; 3 Leroy Cudjoe; 5 Aaron Murphy; 35 Gene Ormsby; 6 Danny Brough; 15 Kyle Wood; 8 Eorl Crabtree; 9 Ryan Hinchcliffe (C); 19 Josh Johnson; 4 Joe Wardle; 17 Ukuma Ta'ai; 12 Michael Lawrence. Subs (all used): 16 Sam Rapira; 18 Jake Connor; 21 Nathan Mason; 22 Oliver Roberts.
Tries: Ta'ai (5), Ormsby (44), McGillvary (61), Connor (73), Crabtree (79); **Goals:** Brough 4/5.
RHINOS: 23 Ashton Golding; 29 Luke Briscoe; 3 Kallum Watkins; 18 Jimmy Keinhorst; 22 Ash Handley; 14 Liam Sutcliffe; 25 Jordan Lilley; 8 Keith Galloway; 7 Rob Burrow (C); 17 Mitch Garbutt; 19 Mitch Achurch; 26 Brett Ferres; 11 Jamie Jones-Buchanan. Subs (all used): 16 Brad Singleton; 20 Anthony Mullally; 21 Josh Walters; 28 Cameron Smith (D).
Tries: Lilley (25), Walters (49), Burrow (68);
Goals: Lilley 4/4.

Rugby Leaguer & League Express Men of the Match:
Giants: Danny Brough; *Rhinos:* Rob Burrow.
Penalty count: 7-8; **Half-time:** 4-8;
Referee: Robert Hicks; **Attendance:** 7,536.

HULL FC 28 CATALANS DRAGONS 26

HULL FC: 1 Jamie Shaul; 20 Curtis Naughton; 2 Mahe Fonua; 24 Kirk Yeaman; 5 Fetuli Talanoa; 6 Leon Pryce; 7 Marc Sneyd; 8 Scott Taylor; 9 Danny Houghton (C); 10 Liam Watts; 21 Sika Manu; 23 Frank Pritchard; 30 Danny Washbrook. Subs (all used): 16 Jordan Thompson; 15 Chris Green; 17 Dean Hadley; 22 Josh Bowden.
Tries: Talanoa (5), Naughton (9), Manu (18), Taylor (56);
Goals: Sneyd 6/7.
DRAGONS: 1 Tony Gigot; 2 Jodie Broughton; 12 Justin Horo; 4 Vincent Duport; 5 Pat Richards; 18 Thomas Bosc; 7 Richard Myler; 10 Remi Casty (C); 28 Alrix Da Costa; 29 Willie Mason; 11 Glenn Stewart; 8 Louis Anderson; 13 Jason Baitieri. Subs (all used): 15 Julian Bousquet; 16 Eloi Pelissier; 17 Gregory Mounis; 22 Antoni Maria.
Tries: Anderson (13), Richards (25, 35), Baitieri (65), Pelissier (72); **Goals:** Richards 3/5.
Sin bin: Casty (56) - interference.
Rugby Leaguer & League Express Men of the Match:
Hull FC: Danny Houghton; *Dragons:* Richard Myler.
Penalty count: 14-9; **Half-time:** 20-14;
Referee: Ben Thaler; **Attendance:** 11,374.

WIDNES VIKINGS 16 WAKEFIELD TRINITY WILDCATS 18

VIKINGS: 1 Rhys Hanbury; 2 Corey Thompson; 5 Patrick Ah Van; 4 Charly Runciman; 17 Stefan Marsh; 7 Joe Mellor (C); 33 Aaron Heremaia; 18 Gil Dudson; 9 Lloyd White; 8 Eamon O'Carroll; 14 Chris Dean; 11 Chris Houston; 13 Hep Cahill. Subs (all used): 10 Manase Manuokafoa; 15 Setaimata Sa; 19 Macgraff Leuluai; 22 Matt Whitley.
Tries: Runciman (43), O'Carroll (52), Hanbury (62);
Goals: Hanbury 2/3.
Dismissal: Heremaia (20) - fighting.
Sin bin: Ah Van (9) - dangerous challenge on Gibson; White (60) - professional foul; Marsh (78) - tripping Miller.
WILDCATS: 21 Max Jowitt; 1 Ben Jones-Bishop; 4 Ashley Gibson; 25 Craig Hall; 2 Tom Johnstone; 6 Jacob Miller; 7 Liam Finn; 8 Nick Scruton; 9 Scott Moore; 16 Tinirau Arona; 12 Danny Kirmond; 17 Matty Ashurst; 13 Anthony Tupou. Subs (all used): 11 Mickael Simon; 24 Stuart Howarth; 26 Chris Annakin; 28 Andy Yates.

Tries: A Tupou (35), Hall (79); **Goals:** Finn 5/5.
Dismissal: Moore (20) - fighting.
Rugby Leaguer & League Express Men of the Match:
Vikings: Joe Mellor; *Wildcats:* Jacob Miller.
Penalty count: 10-16; **Half-time:** 0-8;
Referee: Joe Cobb; **Attendance:** 4,398.

Saturday 30th April 2016

SALFORD RED DEVILS 44 HULL KINGSTON ROVERS 26

RED DEVILS: 14 Gareth O'Brien; 2 Justin Carney; 4 Junior Sa'u; 3 Josh Griffin; 1 Niall Evalds; 6 Robert Lui; 7 Michael Dobson; 8 Craig Kopczak; 19 Logan Tomkins; 10 George Griffin; 11 Ben Murdoch-Masila; 33 Josh Jones; 13 Mark Flanagan. Subs (all used): 9 Tommy Lee (C); 12 Weller Hauraki; 15 Adam Walne; 16 Olsi Krasniqi.
Tries: Sa'u (8, 59, 71), Lui (11, 76), Evalds (16), G Griffin (37), Jones (40); **Goals:** Dobson 2/4, O'Brien 4/4.
Sin bin: Tomkins (64) - dangerous challenge on Kelly.
ROVERS: 22 Matthew Marsh; 1 Ken Sio; 21 Thomas Minns; 4 Iain Thornley; 29 Joe Wardill; 11 Maurice Blair; 7 Albert Kelly; 17 Dane Tilse; 9 Shaun Lunt; 26 Rob Mulhern; 13 Chris Clarkson; 12 Graeme Horne (C); 10 Mitchell Allgood. Subs (all used): 19 John Boudebza; 15 James Donaldson; 16 James Green; 8 Adam Walker.
Tries: Blair (22), Thornley (48), Sio (61), Minns (65, 73);
Goals: Sio 2/2, Blair 1/3.
On report: Allgood (58) - alleged late challenge.
Rugby Leaguer & League Express Men of the Match:
Red Devils: Gareth O'Brien; *Rovers:* Shaun Lunt.
Penalty count: 6-6; **Half-time:** 28-6;
Referee: Richard Silverwood; **Attendance:** 3,048.

Sunday 1st May 2016

CASTLEFORD TIGERS 20 ST HELENS 30

TIGERS: 18 Ryan Hampshire; 25 Jy Hitchcox; 19 Ben Crooks; 2 Joel Monaghan; 5 Denny Solomona; 10 Grant Millington; 7 Luke Gale (C); 8 Andy Lynch; 9 Adam Milner; 14 Lee Jewitt; 16 Matt Cook; 12 Mike McMeeken; 13 Nathan Massey. Subs (all used): 15 Paul McShane; 23 Will Maher; 22 Gadwin Springer; 31 Conor Fitzsimmons (D).
Tries: Monaghan (12), Solomona (27), McMeeken (48), Hitchcox (53); **Goals:** Gale 2/4.
SAINTS: 23 Shannon McDonnell; 1 Jonny Lomax; 18 Dominique Peyroux; 4 Mark Percival; 22 Jack Owens; 19 Theo Fages; 7 Luke Walsh; 8 Alex Walmsley; 9 James Roby; 10 Kyle Amor; 11 Atelea Vea; 20 Joe Greenwood; 12 Jon Wilkin (C). Subs (all used): 13 Louie McCarthy-Scarsbrook; 14 Lama Tasi; 15 Greg Richards; 28 Morgan Knowles.
Tries: Greenwood (18, 64), McDonnell (45), Amor (62), Lomax (75); **Goals:** Walsh 5/5.
Rugby Leaguer & League Express Men of the Match:
Tigers: Mike McMeeken; *Saints:* Joe Greenwood.
Penalty count: 7-6; **Half-time:** 10-6;
Referee: Gareth Hewer; **Attendance:** 6,658.

ROUND 14

Thursday 12th May 2016

LEEDS RHINOS 12 CASTLEFORD TIGERS 52

RHINOS: 23 Ashton Golding; 22 Ash Handley; 3 Kallum Watkins; 18 Jimmy Keinhorst; 1 Zak Hardaker; 6 Danny McGuire (C); 25 Jordan Lilley; 8 Keith Galloway; 7 Rob Burrow; 17 Mitch Garbutt; 11 Jamie Jones-Buchanan; 26 Brett Ferres; 10 Adam Cuthbertson. Subs (all used): 14 Liam Sutcliffe; 19 Mitch Achurch; 20 Anthony Mullally; 21 Josh Walters.
Tries: Garbutt (5), Handley (52); **Goals:** Lilley 2/2.
TIGERS: 1 Luke Dorn; 34 Paddy Flynn (D); 19 Ben Crooks; 2 Joel Monaghan; 5 Denny Solomona; 15 Paul McShane; 7 Luke Gale (C); 32 Larne Patrick; 9 Adam Milner; 14 Lee Jewitt; 12 Mike McMeeken; 17 Junior Moors; 13 Nathan Massey. Subs (all used): 16 Matt Cook; 10 Grant Millington; 22 Gadwin Springer; 33 Danny Tickle.
Tries: Dorn (9, 28, 33), Solomona (16, 42), Monaghan (39), Springer (44), Crooks (57), Millington (74); **Goals:** Gale 8/9.
Rugby Leaguer & League Express Men of the Match:
Rhinos: Keith Galloway; *Tigers:* Luke Gale.
Penalty count: 7-6; **Half-time:** 6-30;
Referee: Richard Silverwood; **Attendance:** 17,213.

Friday 13th May 2016

ST HELENS 34 SALFORD RED DEVILS 20

SAINTS: 1 Jonny Lomax; 5 Adam Swift; 21 Matty Dawson; 4 Mark Percival; 22 Jack Owens; 19 Theo Fages; 7 Luke Walsh; 14 Lama Tasi; 9 James Roby; 10 Kyle Amor; 18 Dominique Peyroux; 12 Jon Wilkin (C); 13 Louie McCarthy-Scarsbrook. Subs (all used): 8 Alex Walmsley; 11 Atelea Vea; 16 Andre Savelio; 28 Morgan Knowles.
Tries: McCarthy-Scarsbrook (11), Percival (19), Peyroux (37), Lomax (48), Fages (65), Amor (75);
Goals: Walsh 5/6.
RED DEVILS: 14 Gareth O'Brien; 2 Justin Carney; 4 Junior Sa'u; 1 Niall Evalds; 5 Daniel Vidot; 6 Robert Lui; 7 Michael Dobson (C); 8 Craig Kopczak; 19 Logan Tomkins; 10 George Griffin; 11 Ben Murdoch-Masila; 33 Josh Jones; 21 Ryan Lannon. Subs (all used): 12 Weller Hauraki; 15 Adam Walne; 16 Olsi Krasniqi; 17 Phil Joseph.
Tries: Evalds (5, 40, 54), Carney (50);
Goals: O'Brien 1/3, Dobson 1/1.
Rugby Leaguer & League Express Men of the Match:
Saints: Louie McCarthy-Scarsbrook; *Red Devils:* Niall Evalds.
Penalty count: 11-9; **Half-time:** 16-8;
Referee: Chris Kendall; **Attendance:** 9,299.

WIGAN WARRIORS 16 HULL FC 30

WARRIORS: 4 Dan Sarginson; 2 Josh Charnley; 20 Oliver Gildart; 14 John Bateman; 5 Dominic Manfredi; 6 George Williams; 7 Matty Smith; 8 Dominic Crosby; 16 Sam Powell; 17 Lee Mossop; 11 Joel Tomkins; 25 Willie Isa; 13 Sean O'Loughlin (C). Subs (all used): 1 Sam Tomkins (D2); 15 Tony Clubb; 19 Taulima Tautai; 21 Ryan Sutton.
Tries: Gildart (26), Bateman (54), S Tomkins (59);
Goals: Smith 2/3.
HULL FC: 1 Jamie Shaul; 19 Steve Michaels; 2 Mahe Fonua; 24 Kirk Yeaman; 5 Fetuli Talanoa; 6 Leon Pryce; 7 Marc Sneyd; 8 Scott Taylor; 9 Danny Houghton; 10 Liam Watts; 30 Danny Washbrook; 12 Mark Minichiello; 11 Gareth Ellis (C). Subs (all used): 15 Chris Green; 16 Jordan Thompson; 21 Sika Manu; 22 Josh Bowden.
Tries: Sneyd (3), Michaels (10), Taylor (15), Shaul (65), Talanoa (68); **Goals:** Sneyd 5/7.
Rugby Leaguer & League Express Men of the Match:
Warriors: John Bateman; *Hull FC:* Leon Pryce.
Penalty count: 9-10; **Half-time:** 4-18;
Referee: Ben Thaler; **Attendance:** 15,083.

Saturday 14th May 2016

CATALANS DRAGONS 16 HUDDERSFIELD GIANTS 14

DRAGONS: 1 Tony Gigot; 2 Jodie Broughton; 12 Justin Horo; 5 Pat Richards; 20 Fouad Yaha; 6 Todd Carney; 7 Richard Myler; 29 Willie Mason; 16 Eloi Pelissier; 10 Remi Casty (C); 8 Louis Anderson; 11 Glenn Stewart; 17 Gregory Mounis. Subs (all used): 15 Julian Bousquet; 18 Thomas Bosc; 22 Antoni Maria; 30 Romain Navarrete (D).
Tries: Anderson (32), Horo (52), Gigot (56);
Goals: Richards 2/3.
GIANTS: 34 Ryan Brierley; 2 Jermaine McGillvary; 3 Leroy Cudjoe; 18 Jake Connor; 5 Aaron Murphy; 6 Danny Brough; 15 Kyle Wood; 17 Ukuma Ta'ai; 9 Ryan Hinchcliffe (C); 19 Josh Johnson; 4 Joe Wardle; 22 Oliver Roberts; 12 Michael Lawrence. Subs: 7 Jamie Ellis; 16 Sam Rapira; 21 Nathan Mason; 25 Tyler Dickinson (not used).
Tries: Mason (26), Connor (65); **Goals:** Brough 3/3.
Rugby Leaguer & League Express Men of the Match:
Dragons: Louis Anderson; *Giants:* Michael Lawrence.
Penalty count: 10-8; **Half-time:** 6-8;
Referee: Gareth Hewer; **Attendance:** 10,387.

Sunday 15th May 2016

HULL KINGSTON ROVERS 24 WIDNES VIKINGS 10

ROVERS: 18 Ben Cockayne; 1 Ken Sio; 21 Thomas Minns; 12 Graeme Horne (C); 29 Joe Wardill; 11 Maurice Blair; 7 Albert Kelly; 17 Dane Tilse; 9 Shaun Lunt; 8 Adam Walker; 20 James Greenwood; 15 James Donaldson; 10 Mitchell Allgood. Subs (all used): 28 Kieran Moran; 19 John Boudebza; 24 George Lawler; 16 James Green.
Tries: Lunt (4), Sio (42), Greenwood (63), Kelly (75);
Goals: Cockayne 4/4.
VIKINGS: 1 Rhys Hanbury; 2 Corey Thompson; 4 Charly Runciman; 14 Chris Dean; 25 Ed Chamberlain; 7 Joe Mellor (C); 33 Aaron Heremaia; 8 Eamon O'Carroll; 9 Lloyd White; 18 Gil Dudson; 11 Chris Houston; 22 Matt Whitley; 13 Hep Cahill. Subs (all used): 35 Jordan Johnstone; 10 Manase Manuokafoa; 15 Setaimata Sa; 19 Macgraff Leuluai.
Tries: Dudson (58), Thompson (67); **Goals:** Hanbury 1/2.
Rugby Leaguer & League Express Men of the Match:
Rovers: Shaun Lunt; *Vikings:* Joe Mellor.
Penalty count: 7-8; **Half-time:** 6-0;
Referee: Robert Hicks; **Attendance:** 7,506.

WAKEFIELD TRINITY WILDCATS 36 WARRINGTON WOLVES 28

WILDCATS: 21 Max Jowitt; 1 Ben Jones-Bishop; 25 Craig Hall; 18 Joe Arundel; 2 Tom Johnstone; 6 Jacob Miller; 7 Liam Finn; 8 Nick Scruton; 20 Michael Sio; 11 Mickael Simon; 12 Danny Kirmond (C); 17 Matty Ashurst; 16 Tinirau Arona. Subs (all used): 23 Scott Anderson; 26 Chris Annakin; 10 Anthony England; 13 Anthony Tupou.
Tries: Hall (3, 20), Ashurst (7, 44), Johnstone (33), Jones-Bishop (78); **Goals:** Finn 6/7.
Sin bin: Jones-Bishop (53) - professional foul; England (68) - fighting; Kirmond (75) - tripping Smith.
WOLVES: 5 Matthew Russell; 20 Kevin Penny; 3 Rhys Evans; 4 Ryan Atkins; 2 Tom Lineham; 1 Kurt Gidley; 11 Ben Currie; 8 Chris Hill (C); 9 Daryl Clark; 10 Ashton Sims; 29 Benjamin Jullien; 13 Ben Westwood; 14 Joe Westerman. Subs (all used): 32 Jordan Cox; 25 Joe Philbin; 18 George King; 31 Morgan Smith.
Tries: Westerman (14, 70), Clark (48), Gidley (51), Russell (54); **Goals:** Gidley 3/4, Smith 1/1.
Sin bin: Gidley (68) - fighting.
Rugby Leaguer & League Express Men of the Match:
Wildcats: Jacob Miller; *Wolves:* Joe Westerman.
Penalty count: 6-7; **Half-time:** 24-6;
Referee: Chris Campbell; **Attendance:** 5,180.

ROUND 15 - MAGIC WEEKEND

Saturday 21st May 2016

SALFORD RED DEVILS 18 WIDNES VIKINGS 12

RED DEVILS: 14 Gareth O'Brien; 2 Justin Carney; 4 Junior Sa'u; 25 Jake Bibby; 5 Daniel Vidot; 6 Robert Lui; 7 Michael Dobson (C); 8 Craig Kopczak; 19 Logan Tomkins; 10 George Griffin; 11 Ben Murdoch-Masila; 33 Josh Jones; 13 Mark Flanagan. Subs (all used): 12 Weller Hauraki; 15 Adam Walne; 17 Phil Joseph; 21 Ryan Lannon.
Tries: Vidot (4, 68), Carney (55);
Goals: O'Brien 2/3, Dobson 1/1.
VIKINGS: 1 Rhys Hanbury; 2 Corey Thompson; 4 Charly Runciman; 3 Chris Bridge; 17 Stefan Marsh; 7 Joe Mellor; 6 Kevin Brown (C); 8 Eamon O'Carroll; 9 Lloyd White; 18 Gil Dudson; 11 Chris Houston; 14 Chris Dean; 13 Hep Cahill. Subs (all used): 33 Aaron Heremaia; 10 Manase Manuokafoa; 22 Matt Whitley; 19 Macgraff Leuluai.
Tries: Hanbury (9), Bridge (30); **Goals:** Hanbury 2/3.
Rugby Leaguer & League Express Men of the Match:
Red Devils: Michael Dobson; *Vikings:* Rhys Hanbury.
Penalty count: 5-9; **Half-time:** 4-12;
Referee: James Child.

CASTLEFORD TIGERS 34 WARRINGTON WOLVES 14

TIGERS: 1 Luke Dorn; 34 Paddy Flynn; 19 Ben Crooks; 2 Joel Monaghan; 5 Denny Solomona; 6 Ben Roberts; 7 Luke Gale (C); 33 Danny Tickle; 9 Adam Milner; 10 Grant Millington; 17 Junior Moors; 12 Mike McMeeken; 13 Nathan Massey. Subs (all used): 15 Paul McShane; 22 Gadwin Springer; 3 Jake Webster; 16 Matt Cook.
Tries: Dorn (34, 66), Millington (39), Solomona (47, 56), McMeeken (50); **Goals:** Gale 5/7.
WOLVES: 5 Matthew Russell; 22 Gene Ormsby; 24 Toby King; 29 Benjamin Jullien; 2 Tom Lineham; 1 Kurt Gidley; 6 Stefan Ratchford; 8 Chris Hill (C); 9 Daryl Clark; 10 Ashton Sims; 11 Ben Currie; 13 Ben Westwood; 14 Joe Westerman. Subs (all used): 32 Jordan Cox; 33 Ryan Bailey (D); 18 George King; 31 Morgan Smith.
Tries: Ratchford (4), Gidley (8), Currie (31);
Goals: Gidley 1/3.
Rugby Leaguer & League Express Men of the Match:
Tigers: Junior Moors; *Wolves:* Stefan Ratchford.
Penalty count: 8-6; **Half-time:** 12-14;
Referee: Gareth Hewer.

LEEDS RHINOS 8 WIGAN WARRIORS 40

RHINOS: 1 Zak Hardaker; 22 Ash Handley; 3 Kallum Watkins; 18 Jimmy Keinhorst; 23 Ashton Golding; 6 Danny McGuire (C); 25 Jordan Lilley; 8 Keith Galloway; 11 Jamie Jones-Buchanan; 16 Brad Singleton; 26 Brett Ferres; 10 Adam Cuthbertson; 21 Josh Walters. Subs (all used): 19 Mitch Achurch; 20 Anthony Mullally; 27 Sam Hallas (D); 29 Luke Briscoe.
Tries: Watkins (8), Achurch (64); **Goals:** Lilley 0/2.
Sin bin: Hardaker (56) - professional foul.
WARRIORS: 1 Sam Tomkins; 5 Dominic Manfredi; 20 Oliver Gildart; 4 Dan Sarginson; 2 Josh Charnley; 6 George Williams; 7 Matty Smith; 8 Dominic Crosby; 16 Sam Powell; 10 Ben Flower; 14 John Bateman; 25 Willie Isa; 13 Sean O'Loughlin (C). Subs (all used): 21 Ryan Sutton; 17 Lee Mossop; 19 Taulima Tautai; 26 Greg Burke.
Tries: Isa (16, 24), Williams (42), Manfredi (44), Flower (52), Gildart (75), Sarginson (77); **Goals:** Smith 6/7.
Rugby Leaguer & League Express Men of the Match:
Rhinos: Adam Cuthbertson; *Warriors:* George Williams.
Penalty count: 8-13; **Half-time:** 4-12;
Referee: Robert Hicks *(replaced by Joe Cobb, 17)*.

Attendance: 39,331 *(at St James' Park, Newcastle)*.

Sunday 22nd May 2016

CATALANS DRAGONS 24
WAKEFIELD TRINITY WILDCATS 25

DRAGONS: 1 Tony Gigot; 2 Jodie Broughton; 12 Justin Horo; 4 Vincent Duport; 5 Pat Richards; 6 Todd Carney; 18 Thomas Bosc; 14 Dave Taylor; 16 Eloi Pelissier; 10 Remi Casty (C); 11 Glenn Stewart; 8 Louis Anderson; 13 Jason Baitieri. Subs: 15 Julian Bousquet; 17 Gregory Mounis; 29 Willie Mason; 28 Alrix Da Costa (not used).
Tries: Horo (18), Broughton (23, 60), Gigot (26), Duport (54); **Goals:** Richards 2/5.
WILDCATS: 21 Max Jowitt; 1 Ben Jones-Bishop; 25 Craig Hall; 18 Joe Arundel; 2 Tom Johnstone; 6 Jacob Miller; 7 Liam Finn; 8 Nick Scruton; 20 Michael Sio; 11 Mickael Simon; 17 Matty Ashurst; 12 Danny Kirmond (C); 13 Anthony Tupou. Subs (all used): 3 Bill Tupou; 16 Tinirau Arona; 23 Scott Anderson; 26 Chris Annakin.
Tries: Jones-Bishop (33, 45), Sio (51), Simon (72); **Goals:** Finn 4/4; Field goal: Miller (77).
Rugby Leaguer & League Express Men of the Match: *Dragons:* Tony Gigot; *Wildcats:* Matty Ashurst.
Penalty count: 10-11; **Half-time:** 14-6;
Referee: Chris Campbell.

HUDDERSFIELD GIANTS 48 ST HELENS 20

GIANTS: 1 Scott Grix; 2 Jermaine McGillvary; 3 Leroy Cudjoe; 18 Jake Connor; 5 Aaron Murphy; 6 Danny Brough; 7 Jamie Ellis; 8 Eorl Crabtree; 9 Ryan Hinchcliffe (C); 21 Nathan Mason; 4 Joe Wardle; 17 Ukuma Ta'ai; 12 Michael Lawrence. Subs (all used): 15 Kyle Wood; 16 Sam Rapira; 22 Oliver Roberts; 36 Sebastine Ikahihifo (D).
Tries: McGillvary (21, 42), Ta'ai (27), Ellis (29), Rapira (50), Murphy (55), Hinchcliffe (74), K Wood (78); **Goals:** Brough 8/9.
SAINTS: 23 Shannon McDonnell; 22 Jack Owens; 30 Calvin Wellington (D); 21 Matty Dawson; 5 Adam Swift; 19 Theo Fages; 7 Luke Walsh; 14 Lama Tasi; 9 James Roby; 10 Kyle Amor; 12 Jon Wilkin (C); 11 Atelea Vea; 13 Louie McCarthy-Scarsbrook. Subs (all used): 3 Jordan Turner; 8 Alex Walmsley; 16 Andre Savelio; 28 Morgan Knowles.
Tries: Dawson (36), Owens (58), Fages (60), Swift (70); **Goals:** Walsh 2/4.
Rugby Leaguer & League Express Men of the Match: *Giants:* Leroy Cudjoe; *Saints:* Theo Fages.
Penalty count: 4-2; **Half-time:** 16-6;
Referee: Ben Thaler.

HULL FC 28 HULL KINGSTON ROVERS 16

HULL FC: 1 Jamie Shaul; 20 Curtis Naughton; 2 Mahe Fonua; 5 Fetuli Talanoa; 24 Kirk Yeaman; 6 Leon Pryce; 7 Marc Sneyd; 8 Scott Taylor; 9 Danny Houghton; 10 Liam Watts; 12 Mark Minichiello; 21 Sika Manu; 11 Gareth Ellis (C). Subs (all used): 3 Carlos Tuimavave; 30 Danny Washbrook; 23 Frank Pritchard; 22 Josh Bowden.
Tries: Fonua (5, 56), Naughton (21), Shaul (60), Minichiello (68); **Goals:** Sneyd 4/5.
ROVERS: 22 Matthew Marsh; 1 Ken Sio; 12 Graeme Horne; 4 Iain Thornley; 21 Thomas Minns; 32 Terry Campese (C); 7 Albert Kelly; 17 Dane Tilse; 24 George Lawler; 10 Mitchell Allgood; 11 Maurice Blair; 20 James Greenwood; 13 Chris Clarkson. Subs (all used): 8 Adam Walker; 9 Shaun Lunt; 15 James Donaldson; 16 James Green.
Tries: Lunt (33), Horne (47); **Goals:** Campese 4/4.
Sin bin: Lunt (20) - dangerous challenge on Watts.
Rugby Leaguer & League Express Men of the Match: *Hull FC:* Mahe Fonua; *Rovers:* Terry Campese.
Penalty count: 5-7; **Half-time:** 10-8;
Referee: Richard Silverwood.

Attendance: 28,945 *(at St James' Park, Newcastle)*.

ROUND 16

Thursday 26th May 2016

CASTLEFORD TIGERS 26 WIGAN WARRIORS 33

TIGERS: 1 Luke Dorn; 34 Paddy Flynn; 19 Ben Crooks; 3 Jake Webster; 5 Denny Solomona; 15 Paul McShane; 7 Luke Gale (C); 32 Larne Patrick; 9 Adam Milner; 10 Grant Millington; 12 Mike McMeeken; 17 Junior Moors; 14 Lee Jewitt. Subs (all used): 13 Danny Tickle; 16 Matt Cook; 22 Gadwin Springer; 18 Ryan Hampshire.
Tries: McShane (9), Solomona (28, 73), Webster (61); **Goals:** Gale 5/6.
Sin bin: Webster (40) - dissent.
WARRIORS: 1 Sam Tomkins; 5 Dominic Manfredi; 4 Dan Sarginson; 20 Oliver Gildart; 2 Josh Charnley; 6 George Williams; 7 Matty Smith (C); 8 Dominic Crosby; 16 Sam Powell; 10 Ben Flower; 14 John Bateman; 25 Willie Isa; 11 Joel Tomkins. Subs (all used): 17 Lee Mossop; 19 Taulima Tautai; 21 Ryan Sutton; 26 Greg Burke.
Tries: Charnley (3, 54), S Tomkins (21), Manfredi (43), Powell (67); **Goals:** Smith 6/7; **Field goal:** Smith (76).
Rugby Leaguer & League Express Men of the Match: *Tigers:* Luke Gale; *Warriors:* Matty Smith.
Penalty count: 8-11; **Half-time:** 12-14;
Referee: Ben Thaler; **Attendance:** 5,558.

Friday 27th May 2016

SALFORD RED DEVILS 38
WAKEFIELD TRINITY WILDCATS 8

RED DEVILS: 14 Gareth O'Brien; 1 Niall Evalds; 33 Josh Jones; 4 Junior Sa'u; 5 Daniel Vidot; 6 Robert Lui; 7 Michael Dobson (C); 8 Craig Kopczak; 19 Logan Tomkins; 10 George Griffin; 11 Ben Murdoch-Masila; 12 Weller Hauraki; 13 Mark Flanagan. Subs (all used): 15 Adam Walne; 17 Phil Joseph; 21 Ryan Lannon; 25 Jake Bibby.
Tries: Evalds (2), Lannon (38, 49), Flanagan (47), Lui (52), G Griffin (65), Sa'u (80);
Goals: O'Brien 4/6, Dobson 1/2.
WILDCATS: 21 Max Jowitt; 25 Craig Hall; 3 Bill Tupou; 18 Joe Arundel; 1 Ben Jones-Bishop; 6 Jacob Miller; 7 Liam Finn; 8 Nick Scruton; 20 Michael Sio; 10 Anthony England; 12 Danny Kirmond (C); 13 Anthony Tupou; 16 Tinirau Arona. Subs (all used): 11 Mickael Simon; 17 Matty Ashurst; 23 Scott Anderson; 26 Chris Annakin.
Tries: A Tupou (27), Jones-Bishop (67); **Goals:** Finn 0/2.
Sin bin: Kirmond (36) - tripping O'Brien; Jones-Bishop (40) - professional foul.
On report: Miller (63) - alleged shoulder charge on O'Brien.
Rugby Leaguer & League Express Men of the Match: *Red Devils:* Robert Lui; *Wildcats:* Jacob Miller.
Penalty count: 12-8; **Half-time:** 10-4;
Referee: Joe Cobb; **Attendance:** 3,022.

WARRINGTON WOLVES 52 LEEDS RHINOS 18

WOLVES: 6 Stefan Ratchford; 22 Gene Ormsby; 3 Rhys Evans; 4 Ryan Atkins; 2 Tom Lineham; 1 Kurt Gidley; 7 Chris Sandow; 8 Chris Hill (C); 9 Daryl Clark; 10 Ashton Sims; 11 Ben Currie; 13 Ben Westwood; 14 Joe Westerman. Subs (all used): 16 Brad Dwyer; 18 George King; 29 Benjamin Jullien; 33 Ryan Bailey.
Tries: Ormsby (6, 48), Lineham (17), Dwyer (30), Atkins (42), Ratchford (56), Gidley (61), Clark (66, 73); **Goals:** Gidley 8/9.
Sin bin: Sims (52) - fighting.
RHINOS: 1 Zak Hardaker; 23 Ashton Golding; 3 Kallum Watkins; 18 Jimmy Keinhorst; 22 Ash Handley; 14 Liam Sutcliffe; 6 Danny McGuire (C); 8 Keith Galloway; 7 Rob Burrow; 16 Brad Singleton; 10 Adam Cuthbertson; 26 Brett Ferres; 15 Brett Delaney. Subs (all used): 11 Jamie Jones-Buchanan; 17 Mitch Garbutt; 19 Mitch Achurch; 25 Jordan Lilley.
Tries: Keinhorst (2), Ferres (34, 69); **Goals:** Sutcliffe 3/3.
Sin bin: Singleton (52) - fighting.
Rugby Leaguer & League Express Men of the Match: *Wolves:* Daryl Clark; *Rhinos:* Brett Ferres.
Penalty count: 8-6; **Half-time:** 18-12;
Referee: Chris Campbell; **Attendance:** 10,317.

Saturday 28th May 2016

HULL FC 32 ST HELENS 24

HULL FC: 1 Jamie Shaul; 20 Curtis Naughton; 2 Mahe Fonua; 24 Kirk Yeaman; 5 Fetuli Talanoa; 3 Carlos Tuimavave; 7 Marc Sneyd; 8 Scott Taylor; 9 Danny Houghton; 10 Liam Watts; 12 Mark Minichiello; 21 Sika Manu; 11 Gareth Ellis (C). Subs (all used): 16 Jordan Thompson; 17 Dean Hadley; 22 Josh Bowden; 30 Danny Washbrook.
Tries: Ellis (10), Fonua (16), Tuimavave (56), Taylor (63), Washbrook (77); **Goals:** Sneyd 6/6.
SAINTS: 1 Jonny Lomax; 22 Jack Owens; 21 Matty Dawson; 3 Jordan Turner; 5 Adam Swift; 19 Theo Fages; 7 Luke Walsh; 13 Louie McCarthy-Scarsbrook; 9 James Roby; 10 Kyle Amor; 12 Jon Wilkin (C); 11 Atelea Vea; 28 Morgan Knowles. Subs (all used): 8 Alex Walmsley; 14 Lama Tasi; 15 Greg Richards; 27 Jack Ashworth.
Tries: Swift (22), Lomax (25), Vea (37), Ashworth (70); **Goals:** Owens 4/4.
Rugby Leaguer & League Express Men of the Match: *Hull FC:* Scott Taylor; *Saints:* Jack Ashworth.
Penalty count: 12-2; **Half-time:** 14-18;
Referee: Gareth Hewer; **Attendance:** 11,247.

CATALANS DRAGONS 34 HULL KINGSTON ROVERS 16

DRAGONS: 1 Tony Gigot; 2 Jodie Broughton; 12 Justin Horo; 4 Vincent Duport; 5 Pat Richards; 6 Todd Carney; 27 Lucas Albert; 14 Dave Taylor; 16 Eloi Pelissier; 10 Remi Casty (C); 8 Louis Anderson; 11 Glenn Stewart; 13 Jason Baitieri. Subs (all used): 15 Julian Bousquet; 17 Gregory Mounis; 18 Thomas Bosc; 22 Antoni Maria.
Tries: Broughton (4), Carney (13), Albert (22), Anderson (31), Gigot (36, 69); **Goals:** Richards 5/7.
ROVERS: 22 Matthew Marsh; 1 Ken Sio; 13 Chris Clarkson (C); 4 Iain Thornley; 29 Joe Wardill; 11 Maurice Blair; 7 Albert Kelly; 17 Dane Tilse; 9 Shaun Lunt; 8 Adam Walker; 15 James Donaldson; 20 James Greenwood; 26 Rob Mulhern. Subs (all used): 14 Kevin Larroyer; 16 James Green; 19 John Boudebza; 24 George Lawler.
Tries: Larroyer (25), Wardill (63), Sio (80);
Goals: Sio 1/2, Kelly 1/1.
Rugby Leaguer & League Express Men of the Match: *Dragons:* Glenn Stewart; *Rovers:* Albert Kelly.
Penalty count: 9-5; **Half-time:** 28-6;
Referee: James Child; **Attendance:** 9,859.

Sunday 29th May 2016

WIDNES VIKINGS 24 HUDDERSFIELD GIANTS 20

VIKINGS: 1 Rhys Hanbury; 2 Corey Thompson; 3 Chris Bridge; 4 Charly Runciman; 17 Stefan Marsh; 7 Joe Mellor; 6 Kevin Brown (C); 18 Gil Dudson; 9 Lloyd White; 13 Hep Cahill; 14 Chris Dean; 11 Chris Houston; 19 Macgraff Leuluai. Subs (all used): 15 Setaimata Sa; 36 Jack Buchanan (D); 10 Manase Manuokafoa; 22 Matt Whitley.
Tries: Thompson (38, 59), Mellor (45, 65), Marsh (56); **Goals:** Hanbury 2/5.
GIANTS: 1 Scott Grix; 2 Jermaine McGillvary; 3 Leroy Cudjoe; 18 Jake Connor; 5 Aaron Murphy; 6 Danny Brough; 7 Jamie Ellis; 8 Eorl Crabtree; 9 Ryan Hinchcliffe (C); 21 Nathan Mason; 4 Joe Wardle; 17 Ukuma Ta'ai; 12 Michael Lawrence. Subs (all used): 15 Kyle Wood; 16 Sam Rapira; 22 Oliver Roberts; 36 Sebastine Ikahihifo.
Tries: Mason (14), Brough (23), Wardle (28), McGillvary (70); **Goals:** Brough 2/4.
Rugby Leaguer & League Express Men of the Match: *Vikings:* Gil Dudson; *Giants:* Joe Wardle.
Penalty count: 6-4; **Half-time:** 4-16;
Referee: Chris Kendall; **Attendance:** 4,683.

ROUND 17

Thursday 2nd June 2016

WAKEFIELD TRINITY WILDCATS 16
HULL KINGSTON ROVERS 54

WILDCATS: 25 Craig Hall; 2 Tom Johnstone; 14 Reece Lyne; 18 Joe Arundel; 3 Bill Tupou; 6 Jacob Miller; 7 Liam Finn; 8 Nick Scruton (C); 20 Michael Sio; 11 Mickael Simon; 13 Anthony Tupou; 17 Matty Ashurst; 19 Jon Molloy. Subs (all used): 23 Scott Anderson; 26 Chris Annakin; 16 Tinirau Arona; 24 Stuart Howarth.
Tries: B Tupou (26), Sio (34), Hall (47); **Goals:** Finn 2/3.
ROVERS: 22 Matthew Marsh; 1 Ken Sio; 13 Chris Clarkson; 4 Iain Thornley; 5 Kieran Dixon; 32 Terry Campese (C); 7 Albert Kelly; 17 Dane Tilse; 9 Shaun Lunt; 8 Adam Walker; 11 Maurice Blair; 20 James Greenwood; 26 Rob Mulhern. Subs (all used): 15 James Donaldson; 16 James Green; 10 Mitchell Allgood; 19 John Boudebza.
Tries: Dixon (3, 56, 59), Kelly (12, 67), Greenwood (18, 63), Lunt (20), Green (30), Blair (75); **Goals:** Sio 7/10.
Rugby Leaguer & League Express Men of the Match: *Wildcats:* Matty Ashurst; *Rovers:* Terry Campese.
Penalty count: 5-6; **Half-time:** 10-26;
Referee: Chris Kendall; **Attendance:** 5,082.

Friday 3rd June 2016

HUDDERSFIELD GIANTS 22 CASTLEFORD TIGERS 30

GIANTS: 1 Scott Grix; 2 Jermaine McGillvary; 3 Leroy Cudjoe; 18 Jake Connor; 5 Aaron Murphy; 15 Kyle Wood; 7 Jamie Ellis; 8 Eorl Crabtree; 9 Ryan Hinchcliffe (C); 19 Josh Johnson; 4 Joe Wardle; 17 Ukuma Ta'ai; 12 Michael Lawrence. Subs (all used): 16 Sam Rapira; 21 Nathan Mason; 22 Oliver Roberts; 34 Ryan Brierley.
Tries: Ellis (10), Cudjoe (35), Brierley (68), Connor (76); **Goals:** Ellis 3/4.
Sin bin: Johnson (20) - fighting.
TIGERS: 1 Luke Dorn; 2 Joel Monaghan; 19 Ben Crooks; 3 Jake Webster; 5 Denny Solomona; 15 Paul McShane; 7 Luke Gale (C); 14 Lee Jewitt; 9 Adam Milner; 33 Danny Tickle; 17 Junior Moors; 12 Mike McMeeken; 13 Nathan Massey. Subs (all used): 10 Grant Millington; 16 Matt Cook; 18 Ryan Hampshire; 22 Gadwin Springer.
Tries: Solomona (5, 43), Webster (22, 63), Gale (31); **Goals:** Gale 5/6.
Sin bin: Jewitt (20) - fighting.
Rugby Leaguer & League Express Men of the Match: *Giants:* Jamie Ellis; *Tigers:* Junior Moors.
Penalty count: 12-8; **Half-time:** 10-16;
Referee: Chris Campbell; **Attendance:** 5,741.

HULL FC 30 WIDNES VIKINGS 10

HULL FC: 1 Jamie Shaul; 19 Steve Michaels; 2 Mahe Fonua; 24 Kirk Yeaman; 5 Fetuli Talanoa; 3 Carlos Tuimavave; 7

Widnes' Matt Whitley races away from Castleford duo Paul McShane and Mike McMeeken

Marc Sneyd; 8 Scott Taylor; 9 Danny Houghton; 22 Josh Bowden; 12 Mark Minichiello; 21 Sika Manu; 11 Gareth Ellis (C). Subs (all used): 15 Chris Green; 16 Jordan Thompson; 17 Dean Hadley; 30 Danny Washbrook.
Tries: Tuimavave (21), Yeaman (50), Bowden (54), Houghton (59), Shaul (61); **Goals:** Sneyd 5/5.
VIKINGS: 1 Rhys Hanbury; 2 Corey Thompson; 4 Charly Runciman; 3 Chris Bridge; 17 Stefan Marsh; 7 Joe Mellor; 6 Kevin Brown (C); 13 Hep Cahill; 9 Lloyd White; 18 Gil Dudson; 11 Chris Houston; 14 Chris Dean; 19 Macgraff Leuluai. Subs (all used): 36 Jack Buchanan; 10 Manase Manuokafoa; 15 Setaimata Sa; 22 Matt Whitley.
Tries: Hanbury (9), Dean (76); **Goals:** Hanbury 1/2.
Rugby Leaguer & League Express Men of the Match: *Hull FC:* Kirk Yeaman; *Vikings:* Chris Houston.
Penalty count: 10-7; **Half-time:** 6-4;
Referee: Jack Smith; **Attendance:** 10,259.

LEEDS RHINOS 12 CATALANS DRAGONS 24

RHINOS: 14 Liam Sutcliffe; 29 Luke Briscoe; 3 Kallum Watkins; 4 Joel Moon; 22 Ash Handley; 6 Danny McGuire (C); 25 Jordan Lilley; 8 Keith Galloway; 9 Beau Falloon; 17 Mitch Garbutt; 15 Brett Delaney; 26 Brett Ferres; 11 Jamie Jones-Buchanan. Subs (all used): 18 Jimmy Keinhorst; 20 Anthony Mullally; 27 Sam Hallas; 21 Josh Walters.
Tries: Ferres (5), Walters (67); **Goals:** Lilley 2/2.
DRAGONS: 21 Morgan Escare; 2 Jodie Broughton; 1 Tony Gigot; 4 Vincent Duport; 20 Fouad Yaha; 6 Todd Carney; 27 Lucas Albert; 29 Willie Mason; 16 Eloi Pelissier; 10 Remi Casty (C); 11 Glenn Stewart; 12 Justin Horo; 13 Jason Baitieri. Subs (all used): 15 Julian Bousquet; 22 Antoni Maria; 18 Thomas Bosc; 30 Romain Navarrete.
Tries: Horo (14), Yaha (28), Baitieri (35), Pelissier (79);
Goals: Carney 4/5.
Rugby Leaguer & League Express Men of the Match: *Rhinos:* Mitch Garbutt; *Dragons:* Justin Horo.
Penalty count: 8-5; **Half-time:** 6-16;
Referee: Ben Thaler; **Attendance:** 14,016.

SALFORD RED DEVILS 20 WIGAN WARRIORS 23

RED DEVILS: 5 Daniel Vidot; 2 Justin Carney; 33 Josh Jones; 4 Junior Sa'u; 25 Jake Bibby; 6 Robert Lui; 7 Michael Dobson (C); 8 Craig Kopczak; 19 Logan Tomkins; 10 George Griffin; 11 Ben Murdoch-Masila; 12 Weller Hauraki; 13 Mark Flanagan. Subs (all used): 15 Adam Walne; 17 Phil Joseph; 21 Ryan Lannon; 31 Connor Williams (D).
Tries: Dobson (18, 26), Jones (73), Vidot (77);
Goals: Dobson 1/3, Lui 1/2.
WARRIORS: 1 Sam Tomkins; 2 Josh Charnley; 20 Oliver Gildart; 4 Dan Sarginson; 5 Dominic Manfredi; 6 George Williams; 7 Matty Smith (C); 8 Dominic Crosby; 16 Sam Powell; 10 Ben Flower; 26 Greg Burke; 25 Willie Isa; 11 Joel Tomkins. Subs (all used): 17 Lee Mossop; 19 Taulima Tautai; 21 Ryan Sutton; 29 Joe Bretherton.
Tries: Charnley (8, 46, 64), Sutton (32);
Goals: Smith 3/5; **Field goal:** Smith (40).
Rugby Leaguer & League Express Men of the Match: *Red Devils:* Justin Carney; *Warriors:* George Williams.
Penalty count: 10-8; **Half-time:** 10-11;
Referee: Gareth Hewer; **Attendance:** 4,096.

ST HELENS 4 WARRINGTON WOLVES 26

SAINTS: 1 Jonny Lomax; 22 Jack Owens; 21 Matty Dawson; 3 Jordan Turner; 5 Adam Swift; 19 Theo Fages; 12 Jon Wilkin (C); 14 Lama Tasi; 9 James Roby; 10 Kyle Amor; 27 Jack Ashworth; 11 Atelea Vea; 13 Louie McCarthy-Scarsbrook. Subs (all used): 8 Alex Walmsley; 15 Greg Richards; 17 Luke Thompson; 20 Joe Greenwood.
Try: Lomax (74); **Goals:** Owens 0/1.
WOLVES: 6 Stefan Ratchford; 22 Gene Ormsby; 3 Rhys Evans; 4 Ryan Atkins; 2 Tom Lineham; 1 Kurt Gidley; 7 Chris Sandow; 8 Chris Hill (C); 9 Daryl Clark; 33 Ryan Bailey; 11 Ben Currie; 29 Benjamin Jullien; 14 Joe Westerman. Subs (all used): 16 Brad Dwyer; 18 George King; 27 Sam Wilde; 32 Jordan Cox.

Tries: Currie (6), Sandow (18), Atkins (33), Ratchford (43), R Evans (48); **Goals:** Gidley 3/5.
Rugby Leaguer & League Express Men of the Match: *Saints:* Jonny Lomax; *Wolves:* Chris Sandow.
Penalty count: 6-7; **Half-time:** 0-16;
Referee: James Child; **Attendance:** 11,353.

ROUND 18

Thursday 9th June 2016

CASTLEFORD TIGERS 28 WIDNES VIKINGS 38

TIGERS: 5 Denny Solomona; 2 Joel Monaghan; 19 Ben Crooks; 3 Jake Webster; 34 Paddy Flynn; 15 Paul McShane; 7 Luke Gale (C); 14 Lee Jewitt; 9 Adam Milner; 32 Larne Patrick; 17 Junior Moors; 12 Mike McMeeken; 13 Nathan Massey. Subs (all used): 10 Grant Millington; 16 Matt Cook; 22 Gadwin Springer; 33 Danny Tickle.
Tries: Flynn (32, 47, 73), Patrick (69), Gale (70);
Goals: Gale 4/5.
VIKINGS: 1 Rhys Hanbury; 2 Corey Thompson; 4 Charly Runciman; 3 Chris Bridge; 5 Patrick Ah Van; 6 Kevin Brown (C); 7 Joe Mellor; 13 Hep Cahill; 9 Lloyd White; 36 Jack Buchanan; 22 Matt Whitley; 14 Chris Dean; 19 Macgraff Leuluai. Subs (all used): 24 Jay Chapelhow; 10 Manase Manuokafoa; 28 Brad Walker (D); 33 Aaron Heremaia.
Tries: Leuluai (8), Ah Van (19, 53), Bridge (39), White (56, 63), Mellor (65); **Goals:** Hanbury 5/7.
Rugby Leaguer & League Express Men of the Match: *Tigers:* Paul McShane; *Vikings:* Lloyd White.
Penalty count: 10-8; **Half-time:** 6-14;
Referee: Jack Smith; **Attendance:** 4,968.

Friday 10th June 2016

HULL KINGSTON ROVERS 18 WIGAN WARRIORS 20

ROVERS: 22 Matthew Marsh; 1 Ken Sio; 21 Thomas Minns;

4 Iain Thornley; 5 Kieran Dixon; 32 Terry Campese (C); 7 Albert Kelly; 17 Dane Tilse; 9 Shaun Lunt; 8 Adam Walker; 11 Maurice Blair; 13 Chris Clarkson; 20 James Greenwood. Subs (all used): 10 Mitchell Allgood; 26 Rob Mulhern; 16 James Green; 19 John Boudebza.
Tries: Kelly (30), Minns (51), Allgood (65); **Goals:** Sio 3/3.
WARRIORS: 1 Sam Tomkins; 5 Dominic Manfredi; 3 Anthony Gelling; 2 Josh Charnley; 22 Lewis Tierney; 6 George Williams; 7 Matty Smith (C); 8 Dominic Crosby; 16 Sam Powell; 10 Ben Flower; 21 Ryan Sutton; 25 Willie Isa; 11 Joel Tomkins. Subs (all used): 17 Lee Mossop; 19 Taulima Tautai; 26 Greg Burke; 29 Joe Bretherton.
Tries: Manfredi (5, 14), Gelling (69), S Tomkins (78);
Goals: Smith 2/4.
Rugby Leaguer & League Express Men of the Match: *Rovers:* Albert Kelly; *Warriors:* Sam Tomkins.
Penalty count: 7-7; **Half-time:** 6-8;
Referee: Ben Thaler; **Attendance:** 7,507.

LEEDS RHINOS 8 SALFORD RED DEVILS 0

RHINOS: 14 Liam Sutcliffe; 29 Luke Briscoe; 3 Kallum Watkins; 4 Joel Moon; 22 Ash Handley; 6 Danny McGuire (C); 7 Rob Burrow; 8 Keith Galloway; 21 Josh Walters; 17 Mitch Garbutt; 26 Brett Ferres; 11 Jamie Jones-Buchanan; 16 Brad Singleton. Subs (all used): 19 Mitch Achurch; 10 Adam Cuthbertson; 9 Beau Falloon; 18 Jimmy Keinhorst.
Try: L Briscoe (5); **Goals:** Sutcliffe 2/3.
RED DEVILS: 14 Gareth O'Brien; 2 Justin Carney; 4 Junior Sa'u; 33 Josh Jones; 25 Jake Bibby; 6 Robert Lui; 7 Michael Dobson (C); 8 Craig Kopczak; 19 Logan Tomkins; 10 George Griffin; 11 Ben Murdoch-Masila; 12 Weller Hauraki; 13 Mark Flanagan. Subs (all used): 21 Ryan Lannon; 5 Daniel Vidot; 15 Adam Walne; 17 Phil Joseph.
Rugby Leaguer & League Express Men of the Match: *Rhinos:* Jamie Jones-Buchanan; *Red Devils:* Robert Lui.
Penalty count: 8-7; **Half time:** 4-0;
Referee: Chris Kendall; **Attendance:** 14,462.

WARRINGTON WOLVES 12 HULL FC 19

WOLVES: 6 Stefan Ratchford; 22 Gene Ormsby; 3 Rhys Evans; 4 Ryan Atkins; 2 Tom Lineham; 1 Kurt Gidley; 7 Chris Sandow; 8 Chris Hill (C); 9 Daryl Clark; 10 Ashton Sims; 11 Ben Currie; 29 Benjamin Jullien; 14 Joe Westerman. Subs (all used): 16 Brad Dwyer; 18 George King; 27 Sam Wilde; 33 Ryan Bailey.
Tries: Ormsby (4), Sandow (20); **Goals:** Gidley 2/3.
HULL FC: 1 Jamie Shaul; 19 Steve Michaels; 2 Mahe Fonua; 24 Kirk Yeaman; 5 Fetuli Talanoa; 3 Carlos Tuimavave; 7 Marc Sneyd; 8 Scott Taylor; 9 Danny Houghton; 10 Liam Watts; 21 Sika Manu; 12 Mark Minichiello; 11 Gareth Ellis (C). Subs (all used): 23 Frank Pritchard; 15 Chris Green; 30 Danny Washbrook; 22 Josh Bowden.
Tries: Talanoa (13), Minichiello (33), Ellis (65);
Goals: Sneyd 3/3; **Field goal:** Sneyd (77).
Rugby Leaguer & League Express Men of the Match: *Wolves:* Ryan Atkins; *Hull FC:* Gareth Ellis.
Penalty count: 8-4; **Half-time:** 10-12;
Referee: James Child; **Attendance:** 10,513.

Saturday 11th June 2016

CATALANS DRAGONS 33 ST HELENS 16

DRAGONS: 21 Morgan Escare; 2 Jodie Broughton; 1 Tony Gigot; 5 Pat Richards; 20 Fouad Yaha; 6 Todd Carney; 27 Lucas Albert; 14 Dave Taylor; 16 Eloi Pelissier; 10 Remi Casty (C); 11 Glenn Stewart; 12 Justin Horo; 13 Jason Baitieri. Subs (all used): 15 Julian Bousquet; 18 Thomas Bosc; 22 Antoni Maria; 30 Romain Navarrete.
Tries: Yaha (21), Albert (35), Broughton (53, 60), Escare (56), Gigot (68); **Goals:** Richards 2/5, Bosc 2/3;
Field goal: Carney (39).
SAINTS: 23 Shannon McDonnell; 22 Jack Owens; 21 Matty Dawson; 4 Mark Percival; 5 Adam Swift; 19 Theo Fages; 3 Jordan Turner; 14 Lama Tasi; 9 James Roby; 10 Kyle Amor; 20 Joe Greenwood; 12 Jon Wilkin (C); 13 Louie McCarthy-Scarsbrook. Subs (all used): 8 Alex Walmsley; 11 Atelea Vea; 17 Luke Thompson; 28 Morgan Knowles.
Tries: McCarthy-Scarsbrook (7), Swift (46), McDonnell (77); **Goals:** Owens 2/3.
Rugby Leaguer & League Express Men of the Match: *Dragons:* Jason Baitieri; *Saints:* James Roby.
Penalty count: 9-5; **Half-time:** 13-6;
Referee: Chris Campbell; **Attendance:** 10,789.

Sunday 12th June 2016

HUDDERSFIELD GIANTS 2
WAKEFIELD TRINITY WILDCATS 10

GIANTS: 34 Ryan Brierley; 2 Jermaine McGillvary; 3 Leroy Cudjoe; 4 Joe Wardle; 5 Aaron Murphy; 6 Danny Brough; 7 Jamie Ellis; 16 Sam Rapira; 20 Kruise Leeming; 21 Nathan Mason; 22 Oliver Roberts; 17 Ukuma Ta'ai; 12 Michael Lawrence. Subs (all used): 8 Eorl Crabtree; 9 Ryan Hinchcliffe (C); 15 Kyle Wood; 19 Josh Johnson.
Goals: Brough 1/2.
On report:
Roberts (50) - alleged dangerous challenge on B Tupou.
WILDCATS: 21 Max Jowitt; 2 Tom Johnstone; 14 Reece Lyne; 3 Bill Tupou; 1 Ben Jones-Bishop; 6 Jacob Miller; 7 Liam Finn; 23 Scott Anderson; 24 Stuart Howarth; 10 Anthony England; 12 Danny Kirmond (C); 17 Matty Ashurst; 20 Michael Sio. Subs (all used): 8 Nick Scruton; 16 Tinirau Arona; 18 Joe Arundel; 26 Chris Annakin.
Try: Kirmond (69); **Goals:** Finn 3/3.
Rugby Leaguer & League Express Men of the Match: *Giants:* Danny Brough; *Wildcats:* Liam Finn.
Penalty count: 6-7; **Half-time:** 0-2;
Referee: Michael Woodhead; **Attendance:** 5,077.

ROUND 19

Thursday 16th June 2016

WIDNES VIKINGS 0 WIGAN WARRIORS 7

VIKINGS: 1 Rhys Hanbury; 2 Corey Thompson; 4 Charly Runciman; 3 Chris Bridge; 5 Patrick Ah Van; 7 Joe Mellor; 6 Kevin Brown (C); 13 Hep Cahill; 9 Lloyd White; 36 Jack Buchanan; 22 Matt Whitley; 14 Chris Dean; 19 Macgraff Leuluai. Subs: 24 Jay Chapelhow (not used); 10 Manase Manuokafoa; 18 Gil Dudson; 33 Aaron Heremaia.
WARRIORS: 22 Lewis Tierney; 2 Josh Charnley; 3 Anthony Gelling; 20 Oliver Gildart; 5 Dominic Manfredi; 28 Jake Shorrocks (D); 7 Matty Smith (C); 8 Dominic Crosby; 16 Sam Powell; 10 Ben Flower; 21 Ryan Sutton; 25 Willie Isa; 17 Lee Mossop. Subs (all used): 19 Taulima Tautai; 26 Greg Burke; 27 Nick Gregson; 29 Joe Bretherton.
Try: Charnley (48); **Goals:** Smith 1/1; **Field goal:** Smith (59).
Rugby Leaguer & League Express Men of the Match: *Vikings:* Chris Dean; *Warriors:* Dominic Manfredi.
Penalty count: 11-12; **Half-time:** 0-0;
Referee: Chris Kendall; **Attendance:** 6,219.

Friday 17th June 2016

SALFORD RED DEVILS 30 HUDDERSFIELD GIANTS 31

RED DEVILS: 14 Gareth O'Brien; 2 Justin Carney; 33 Josh Jones; 4 Junior Sa'u; 5 Daniel Vidot; 6 Robert Lui; 7 Michael Dobson (C); 8 Craig Kopczak; 19 Logan Tomkins; 10 George Griffin; 11 Ben Murdoch-Masila; 12 Weller Hauraki; 13 Mark Flanagan. Subs (all used): 16 Olsi Krasniqi; 20 Jordan Walne; 25 Jake Bibby; 17 Phil Joseph.
Tries: Kopczak (6), Vidot (38, 78), Jones (53, 76);
Goals: O'Brien 5/5.
Sin bin: Carney (70) - dangerous challenge on Brough.
GIANTS: 1 Scott Grix; 2 Jermaine McGillvary; 3 Leroy Cudjoe; 4 Joe Wardle; 18 Jake Connor; 6 Danny Brough (C); 7 Jamie Ellis; 8 Eorl Crabtree; 20 Kruise Leeming; 16 Sam Rapira; 11 Tom Symonds (D); 17 Ukuma Ta'ai; 12 Michael Lawrence. Subs (all used): 15 Kyle Wood; 22 Oliver Roberts; 19 Josh Johnson; 21 Nathan Mason.
Tries: Connor (10), Ta'ai (26), Cudjoe (30), Crabtree (62), Wardle (64); **Goals:** Brough 5/6; **Field goal:** Brough (71).
Rugby Leaguer & League Express Men of the Match: *Red Devils:* Josh Jones; *Giants:* Jamie Ellis.
Penalty count: 8-4; **Half-time:** 12-16;
Referee: Ben Thaler; **Attendance:** 1,958.

ST HELENS 48 HULL KINGSTON ROVERS 16

SAINTS: 1 Jonny Lomax; 23 Shannon McDonnell; 24 Matty Fleming; 4 Mark Percival; 5 Adam Swift; 3 Jordan Turner; 12 Jon Wilkin (C); 8 Alex Walmsley; 9 James Roby; 14 Lama Tasi; 13 Louie McCarthy-Scarsbrook; 18 Dominique Peyroux; 28 Morgan Knowles. Subs (all used): 10 Kyle Amor; 15 Greg Richards; 17 Luke Thompson; 20 Joe Greenwood.
Tries: Swift (34, 39, 46, 53), McDonnell (49), Percival (62), McCarthy-Scarsbrook (73), Peyroux (75), Walmsley (77); **Goals:** Percival 6/9.
ROVERS: 21 Thomas Minns; 29 Joe Wardill; 12 Graeme Horne (C); 4 Iain Thornley; 5 Kieran Dixon; 11 Maurice Blair; 7 Albert Kelly; 17 Dane Tilse; 9 Shaun Lunt; 10 Mitchell Allgood; 20 James Greenwood; 15 James Donaldson; 13 Chris Clarkson. Subs (all used): 8 Adam Walker; 14 Kevin Larroyer; 16 James Green; 24 George Lawler.
Tries: Lunt (5), Clarkson (16), Minns (59);
Goals: Dixon 2/4.
Rugby Leaguer & League Express Men of the Match: *Saints:* Adam Swift; *Rovers:* Shaun Lunt.
Penalty count: 5-6; **Half-time:** 8-12;
Referee: Jack Smith; **Attendance:** 9,488.

WAKEFIELD TRINITY WILDCATS 6 LEEDS RHINOS 32

WILDCATS: 21 Max Jowitt; 1 Ben Jones-Bishop; 14 Reece Lyne; 3 Bill Tupou; 2 Tom Johnstone; 6 Jacob Miller; 7 Liam Finn (C); 10 Anthony England; 24 Stuart Howarth; 23 Scott Anderson; 19 Jon Molloy; 17 Matty Ashurst; 16 Tinirau Arona. Subs (all used): 9 Scott Moore; 11 Mickael Simon; 31 Jason Walton; 35 David Fifita (D).
Try: Jones-Bishop (19); **Goals:** Finn 1/1.
Sin bin: Fifita (39) - retaliation; B Tupou (64) - interference.
On report:
Moore (31) - alleged dangerous challenge on Ferres.
RHINOS: 14 Liam Sutcliffe; 29 Luke Briscoe; 3 Kallum Watkins; 4 Joel Moon; 1 Zak Hardaker; 6 Danny McGuire (C); 7 Rob Burrow; 8 Keith Galloway; 9 Beau Falloon; 17 Mitch Garbutt; 19 Mitch Achurch; 11 Jamie Jones-Buchanan; 16 Brad Singleton. Subs (all used): 5 Ryan Hall; 10 Adam Cuthbertson; 18 Jimmy Keinhorst; 26 Brett Ferres.
Tries: Achurch (2), Singleton (35, 48), Sutcliffe (69);
Goals: Sutcliffe 8/8.
Rugby Leaguer & League Express Men of the Match: *Wildcats:* Max Jowitt; *Rhinos:* Liam Sutcliffe.
Penalty count: 8-14; **Half-time:** 6-16;
Referee: James Child; **Attendance:** 7,161.

WARRINGTON WOLVES 20 CATALANS DRAGONS 18

WOLVES: 6 Stefan Ratchford; 5 Matthew Russell; 3 Rhys Evans; 4 Ryan Atkins; 20 Kevin Penny; 1 Kurt Gidley; 7 Chris Sandow; 8 Chris Hill (C); 9 Daryl Clark; 10 Ashton Sims; 11 Ben Currie; 12 Jack Hughes; 14 Joe Westerman. Subs (all used): 13 Ben Westwood; 16 Brad Dwyer; 32 Jordan Cox; 33 Ryan Bailey.
Tries: Atkins (11), Penny (17), Dwyer (43); **Goals:** Gidley 4/5.
DRAGONS: 21 Morgan Escare; 2 Jodie Broughton; 1 Tony Gigot; 5 Pat Richards; 20 Fouad Yaha; 6 Todd Carney; 27 Lucas Albert; 15 Julian Bousquet; 16 Eloi Pelissier; 22 Antoni Maria; 10 Remi Casty (C); 11 Glenn Stewart; 13 Jason Baitieri. Subs (all used): 18 Thomas Bosc; 24 Thibaut Margalet; 30 Romain Navarrete; 31 Jordan Dezaria (D).
Tries: Bousquet (14), Yaha (29); **Goals:** Richards 5/5.
Sin bin: Gigot (37) - dangerous challenge on Atkins.
Rugby Leaguer & League Express Men of the Match: *Wolves:* Ben Currie; *Dragons:* Todd Carney.
Penalty count: 13-9; **Half-time:** 10-16;
Referee: Chris Campbell; **Attendance:** 9,259.

Sunday 19th June 2016

CASTLEFORD TIGERS 22 HULL FC 24

TIGERS: 1 Luke Dorn (C); 34 Paddy Flynn; 19 Ben Crooks; 2 Joel Monaghan; 5 Denny Solomona; 15 Paul McShane; 10 Grant Millington; 33 Danny Tickle; 9 Adam Milner; 32 Larne Patrick; 17 Junior Moors; 3 Jake Webster; 13 Nathan Massey. Subs (all used): 27 Tom Holmes; 22 Gadwin Springer; 23 Will Maher; 16 Matt Cook.
Tries: Dorn (4), Webster (16), Flynn (57), Solomona (60, 72); **Goals:** McShane 0/2, Tickle 1/3.
HULL FC: 1 Jamie Shaul; 19 Steve Michaels; 2 Mahe Fonua; 24 Kirk Yeaman; 20 Curtis Naughton; 3 Carlos Tuimavave; 7 Marc Sneyd; 8 Scott Taylor; 9 Danny Houghton (C); 10 Liam Watts; 23 Frank Pritchard; 30 Danny Washbrook; 16 Jordan Thompson. Subs (all used): 17 Dean Hadley; 15 Chris Green; 6 Leon Pryce; 22 Josh Bowden.
Tries: Pritchard (19), Houghton (24), Fonua (37), Shaul (63); **Goals:** Sneyd 4/5.
Rugby Leaguer & League Express Men of the Match: *Tigers:* Denny Solomona; *Hull FC:* Scott Taylor.
Penalty count: 8-12; **Half-time:** 8-18;
Referee: Gareth Hewer; **Attendance:** 10,790.

ROUND 20

Thursday 30th June 2016

HUDDERSFIELD GIANTS 22 HULL FC 12

GIANTS: 18 Jake Connor; 2 Jermaine McGillvary; 3 Leroy Cudjoe; 31 Sam Wood; 5 Aaron Murphy; 7 Jamie Ellis; 34 Ryan Brierley; 16 Sam Rapira; 20 Kruise Leeming; 17 Ukuma Ta'ai; 11 Tom Symonds; 12 Michael Lawrence; 9 Ryan Hinchcliffe (C). Subs (all used): 8 Eorl Crabtree; 15 Kyle Wood; 21 Nathan Mason; 22 Oliver Roberts.
Tries: Lawrence (17), Symonds (48), McGillvary (52, 55);
Goals: Ellis 3/5.
HULL FC: 20 Curtis Naughton; 19 Steve Michaels; 2 Mahe Fonua; 3 Carlos Tuimavave; 5 Fetuli Talanoa; 6 Leon Pryce; 7 Marc Sneyd; 8 Scott Taylor; 9 Danny Houghton (C); 15 Chris Green; 21 Sika Manu; 12 Mark Minichiello; 23 Frank Pritchard. Subs (all used): 16 Jordan Thompson; 17 Dean Hadley; 22 Josh Bowden; 30 Danny Washbrook.
Tries: Washbrook (44), Fonua (78); **Goals:** Sneyd 2/2.
Rugby Leaguer & League Express Men of the Match: *Giants:* Jake Connor; *Hull FC:* Danny Washbrook.
Penalty count: 8-11; **Half-time:** 8-0;
Referee: Chris Kendall; **Attendance:** 4,143.

Friday 1st July 2016

**HULL KINGSTON ROVERS 16
WARRINGTON WOLVES 16**

ROVERS: 18 Ben Cockayne; 1 Ken Sio; 21 Thomas Minns; 4 Iain Thornley; 29 Joe Wardill; 11 Maurice Blair; 7 Albert Kelly; 17 Dane Tilse; 9 Shaun Lunt; 10 Mitchell Allgood; 13 Chris Clarkson (C); 15 James Donaldson; 26 Rob Mulhern. Subs (all used): 24 George Lawler; 16 James Green; 8 Adam Walker; 14 Kevin Larroyer.
Tries: Donaldson (40), Minns (46), Thornley (78);
Goals: Cockayne 2/3.
Dismissal: Green (35) - punching Cox.
WOLVES: 6 Stefan Ratchford; 5 Matthew Russell; 3 Rhys Evans; 24 Toby King; 20 Kevin Penny; 26 Declan Patton; 7 Chris Sandow; 8 Chris Hill (C); 9 Daryl Clark; 13 Ben Westwood; 11 Ben Currie; 12 Jack Hughes; 14 Joe Westerman. Subs (all used): 16 Brad Dwyer; 18 George King; 33 Ryan Bailey; 32 Jordan Cox.
Tries: Russell (50), Dwyer (56), Hughes (75);
Goals: Ratchford 2/3.
Rugby Leaguer & League Express Men of the Match:
Rovers: James Donaldson; *Wolves:* Matthew Russell.
Penalty count: 10-9; **Half-time:** 6-0;
Referee: Michael Woodhead; **Attendance:** 6,827.

SALFORD RED DEVILS 22 CASTLEFORD TIGERS 18

RED DEVILS: 14 Gareth O'Brien; 24 Mason Caton-Brown; 3 Josh Griffin; 4 Junior Sa'u; 18 Greg Johnson; 6 Robert Lui; 7 Michael Dobson (C); 8 Craig Kopczak; 19 Logan Tomkins; 10 George Griffin; 11 Ben Murdoch-Masila; 33 Josh Jones; 13 Mark Flanagan. Subs (all used): 12 Weller Hauraki; 20 Jordan Walne; 34 Sean Kenny (D); 15 Adam Walne.
Tries: O'Brien (14), Dobson (20), Caton-Brown (59);
Goals: O'Brien 5/6.
TIGERS: 1 Luke Dorn; 2 Joel Monaghan; 19 Ben Crooks; 3 Jake Webster; 34 Paddy Flynn; 27 Tom Holmes; 7 Luke Gale (C); 33 Danny Tickle; 15 Paul McShane; 32 Larne Patrick; 17 Junior Moors; 12 Mike McMeeken; 13 Nathan Massey. Subs (all used): 9 Adam Milner; 10 Grant Millington; 11 Oliver Holmes; 22 Gadwin Springer.
Tries: Webster (8, 31), Dorn (44); **Goals:** Gale 3/3.
Rugby Leaguer & League Express Men of the Match:
Red Devils: Gareth O'Brien; *Tigers:* Luke Dorn.
Penalty count: 9-3; **Half-time:** 10-12;
Referee: James Child; **Attendance:** 2,275.

Saturday 2nd July 2016

CATALANS DRAGONS 6 WIGAN WARRIORS 26

DRAGONS: 1 Tony Gigot; 2 Jodie Broughton; 33 Benjamin Garcia; 4 Vincent Duport; 5 Pat Richards; 6 Todd Carney; 27 Lucas Albert; 14 Dave Taylor; 16 Eloi Pelissier; 10 Remi Casty (C); 11 Glenn Stewart; 12 Justin Horo; 13 Jason Baitieri. Subs (all used): 15 Julian Bousquet; 18 Thomas Bosc; 22 Antoni Maria; 30 Romain Navarrete.
Try: Horo (43); **Goals:** Richards 1/2.
WARRIORS: 1 Sam Tomkins; 5 Dominic Manfredi; 4 Dan Sarginson; 20 Oliver Gildart; 2 Josh Charnley; 6 George Williams; 7 Matty Smith; 10 Ben Flower; 16 Sam Powell; 17 Lee Mossop; 21 Ryan Sutton; 25 Willie Isa; 13 Sean O'Loughlin (C). Subs (all used): 19 Taulima Tautai; 26 Greg Burke; 28 Jake Shorrocks; 29 Joe Bretherton.
Tries: Sarginson (20), Sutton (24), Gildart (31), Manfredi (58); **Goals:** Smith 5/5.
Sin bin: Mossop (15) - trip on Gigot.
Rugby Leaguer & League Express Men of the Match:
Dragons: Julian Bousquet; *Warriors:* Dan Sarginson.
Penalty count: 12-11; **Half-time:** 2-20;
Referee: Gareth Hewer; **Attendance:** 11,856.

Sunday 3rd July 2016

LEEDS RHINOS 22 WIDNES VIKINGS 23

RHINOS: 14 Liam Sutcliffe; 29 Luke Briscoe; 3 Kallum Watkins; 4 Joel Moon; 5 Ryan Hall; 6 Danny McGuire (C); 7 Rob Burrow; 8 Keith Galloway; 11 Jamie Jones-Buchanan; 17 Mitch Garbutt; 26 Brett Ferres; 19 Mitch Achurch; 16 Brad Singleton. Subs: 10 Adam Cuthbertson; 23 Ashton Golding; 12 Carl Ablett; 18 Jimmy Keinhorst (not used).
Tries: Watkins (6), Hall (23), Moon (26), Garbutt (51);
Goals: Sutcliffe 3/4.
VIKINGS: 1 Rhys Hanbury; 2 Corey Thompson; 4 Charly Runciman; 17 Stefan Marsh; 5 Patrick Ah Van; 7 Joe Mellor; 6 Kevin Brown (C); 13 Hep Cahill; 9 Lloyd White; 36 Jack Buchanan; 11 Chris Houston; 14 Chris Dean; 19 Macgraff Leuluai. Subs (all used): 18 Gil Dudson; 33 Aaron Heremaia; 10 Manase Manuokafoa; 22 Matt Whitley.
Tries: Thompson (15), Mellor (32), Ah Van (56), Hanbury (58); **Goals:** Hanbury 3/4; **Field goal:** Mellor (78).
Rugby Leaguer & League Express Men of the Match:
Rhinos: Liam Sutcliffe; *Vikings:* Kevin Brown.
Penalty count: 7-8; **Half-time:** 16-10;
Referee: Ben Thaler; **Attendance:** 16,130.

WAKEFIELD TRINITY WILDCATS 32 ST HELENS 44

WILDCATS: 21 Max Jowitt; 1 Ben Jones-Bishop; 14 Reece Lyne; 3 Bill Tupou; 2 Tom Johnstone; 6 Jacob Miller; 7 Liam Finn (C); 35 David Fifita; 9 Scott Moore; 10 Anthony England; 31 Jason Walton; 17 Matty Ashurst; 20 Michael Sio. Subs (all used): 16 Tinirau Arona; 18 Joe Arundel; 26 Chris Annakin; 27 Anthony Walker.
Tries: Miller (5, 40, 54), Johnstone (25), Finn (61), Jones-Bishop (67); **Goals:** Finn 4/6.
SAINTS: 1 Jonny Lomax; 23 Shannon McDonnell; 24 Matty Fleming; 4 Mark Percival; 5 Adam Swift; 3 Jordan Turner; 12 Jon Wilkin (C); 8 Alex Walmsley; 9 James Roby; 15 Greg Richards; 18 Dominique Peyroux; 20 Joe Greenwood; 13 Louie McCarthy-Scarsbrook. Subs (all used): 10 Kyle Amor; 11 Atelea Vea; 17 Luke Thompson; 28 Morgan Knowles.
Tries: Percival (9), Richards (18), Lomax (28, 34), Knowles (46), Roby (58), Turner (72), Fleming (80);
Goals: Percival 6/8.
Rugby Leaguer & League Express Men of the Match:
Wildcats: Jacob Miller; *Saints:* Kyle Amor.
Penalty count: 9-4; **Half-time:** 16-22;
Referee: Joe Cobb; **Attendance:** 4,859.

ROUND 21

Thursday 7th July 2016

WARRINGTON WOLVES 40 SALFORD RED DEVILS 14

WOLVES: 6 Stefan Ratchford; 5 Matthew Russell; 3 Rhys Evans; 4 Ryan Atkins; 2 Tom Lineham; 26 Declan Patton; 7 Chris Sandow; 8 Chris Hill (C); 9 Daryl Clark; 10 Ashton Sims; 11 Ben Currie; 12 Jack Hughes; 14 Joe Westerman. Subs (all used): 16 Brad Dwyer; 13 Ben Westwood; 18 George King; 24 Toby King.
Tries: Westerman (21, 60), Atkins (35, 39), Lineham (45), Patton (63), Russell (68);
Goals: Ratchford 1/2, Patton 5/5.
RED DEVILS: 14 Gareth O'Brien; 24 Mason Caton-Brown; 3 Josh Griffin; 4 Junior Sa'u; 18 Greg Johnson; 6 Robert Lui; 7 Michael Dobson (C); 8 Craig Kopczak; 19 Logan Tomkins; 10 George Griffin; 11 Ben Murdoch-Masila; 33 Josh Jones; 13 Mark Flanagan. Subs (all used): 12 Weller Hauraki; 20 Jordan Walne; 34 Sean Kenny; 15 Adam Walne.
Tries: Sa'u (8), J Griffin (50), Lui (70); **Goals:** O'Brien 1/4.
Rugby Leaguer & League Express Men of the Match:
Wolves: Joe Westerman; *Red Devils:* Robert Lui.
Penalty count: 8-8; **Half-time:** 18-4;
Referee: Joe Cobb; **Attendance:** 9,024.

Friday 8th July 2016

HULL FC 15 LEEDS RHINOS 20

HULL FC: 1 Jamie Shaul; 19 Steve Michaels; 2 Mahe Fonua; 24 Kirk Yeaman; 5 Fetuli Talanoa; 3 Carlos Tuimavave; 7 Marc Sneyd; 8 Scott Taylor; 9 Danny Houghton (C); 10 Liam Watts; 21 Sika Manu; 12 Mark Minichiello; 17 Dean Hadley. Subs (all used): 30 Danny Washbrook; 27 Jack Downs; 16 Jordan Thompson; 22 Josh Bowden.
Tries: Tuimavave (20), Yeaman (33); **Goals:** Sneyd 3/3;
Field goal: Sneyd (40).
RHINOS: 14 Liam Sutcliffe; 22 Ash Handley; 3 Kallum Watkins; 4 Joel Moon; 5 Ryan Hall; 25 Jordan Lilley; 7 Rob Burrow (C); 8 Keith Galloway; 30 James Segeyaro (D); 17 Mitch Garbutt; 19 Mitch Achurch; 12 Carl Ablett; 16 Brad Singleton. Subs (all used): 15 Brett Delaney; 18 Jimmy Keinhorst; 11 Jamie Jones-Buchanan; 10 Adam Cuthbertson.
Tries: Sutcliffe (3), Moon (49), Watkins (72, 75);
Goals: Sutcliffe 2/5.
Rugby Leaguer & League Express Men of the Match:
Hull FC: Marc Sneyd; *Rhinos:* Brad Singleton.
Penalty count: 7-7; **Half-time:** 13-4;
Referee: Chris Campbell; **Attendance:** 10,618.

**HULL KINGSTON ROVERS 20
HUDDERSFIELD GIANTS 19**

ROVERS: 18 Ben Cockayne; 1 Ken Sio; 21 Thomas Minns; 4 Iain Thornley; 33 David Thompson (D); 22 Matthew Marsh; 7 Albert Kelly; 17 Dane Tilse; 9 Shaun Lunt; 10 Mitchell Allgood; 13 Chris Clarkson (C); 14 Kevin Larroyer; 24 George Lawler. Subs (all used): 19 John Boudebza; 5 Kieran Dixon; 26 Rob Mulhern; 8 Adam Walker.
Tries: Marsh (13), Kelly (49), Lawler (52);
Goals: Cockayne 4/4.
GIANTS: 18 Jake Connor; 2 Jermaine McGillvary; 3 Leroy Cudjoe; 31 Sam Wood; 5 Aaron Murphy; 34 Ryan Brierley; 7 Jamie Ellis; 16 Sam Rapira; 15 Kyle Wood; 17 Ukuma Ta'ai; 11 Tom Symonds; 12 Michael Lawrence; 9 Ryan Hinchcliffe (C). Subs (all used): 6 Danny Brough; 22 Oliver Roberts; 21 Nathan Mason; 8 Eorl Crabtree.
Tries: Brierley (8), Connor (19, pen), Ellis (26);
Goals: Ellis 3/3; **Field goal:** Brough (49).
Rugby Leaguer & League Express Men of the Match:
Rovers: Ben Cockayne; *Giants:* Jake Connor.
Penalty count: 12-7; **Half-time:** 6-18;
Referee: Ben Thaler; **Attendance:** 6,434.

ST HELENS 12 WIDNES VIKINGS 10

SAINTS: 1 Jonny Lomax; 23 Shannon McDonnell; 24 Matty Fleming; 4 Mark Percival; 22 Jack Owens; 3 Jordan Turner; 12 Jon Wilkin (C); 8 Alex Walmsley; 9 James Roby; 15 Greg Richards; 13 Louie McCarthy-Scarsbrook; 20 Joe Greenwood; 17 Luke Thompson. Subs (all used): 10 Kyle Amor; 11 Atelea Vea; 27 Jack Ashworth; 28 Morgan Knowles.
Tries: Turner (4), Fleming (37); **Goals:** Percival 2/3.
VIKINGS: 1 Rhys Hanbury; 2 Corey Thompson; 4 Charly Runciman; 17 Stefan Marsh; 5 Patrick Ah Van; 7 Joe Mellor; 6 Kevin Brown (C); 13 Hep Cahill; 9 Lloyd White; 36 Jack Buchanan; 11 Chris Houston; 14 Chris Dean; 19 Macgraff Leuluai. Subs (all used): 18 Gil Dudson; 10 Manase Manuokafoa; 22 Matt Whitley; 37 Greg Burke (D).
Tries: Thompson (21), Ah Van (56); **Goals:** Hanbury 1/2.
Rugby Leaguer & League Express Men of the Match:
Saints: James Roby; *Vikings:* Rhys Hanbury.
Penalty count: 10-9; **Half-time:** 10-6;
Referee: Gareth Hewer; **Attendance:** 11,566.

**WIGAN WARRIORS 22
WAKEFIELD TRINITY WILDCATS 18**

WARRIORS: 1 Sam Tomkins; 22 Lewis Tierney; 2 Josh Charnley; 20 Oliver Gildart; 5 Dominic Manfredi; 6 George Williams; 7 Matty Smith; 29 Joe Bretherton; 16 Sam Powell; 10 Ben Flower; 21 Ryan Sutton; 25 Willie Isa; 13 Sean O'Loughlin (C). Subs (all used): 19 Taulima Tautai; 28 Jake Shorrocks; 33 Kyle Shelford (D); 35 Macauley Davies (D).
Tries: Gildart (25), Powell (34), Tierney (67, 79);
Goals: Smith 3/4.
Dismissal: O'Loughlin (39) - high tackle on Annakin.
Sin bin: Manfredi (18) - striking;
Charnley (29) - professional foul.
WILDCATS: 21 Max Jowitt; 25 Craig Hall; 14 Reece Lyne; 3 Bill Tupou; 1 Ben Jones-Bishop; 6 Jacob Miller; 7 Liam Finn (C); 35 David Fifita; 9 Scott Moore; 16 Tinirau Arona; 19 Jon Molloy; 17 Matty Ashurst; 20 Michael Sio. Subs (all used): 18 Joe Arundel; 26 Chris Annakin; 27 Anthony Walker; 31 Jason Walton.
Tries: Jowitt (5), Lyne (42), Jones-Bishop (59);
Goals: Finn 3/4.
Rugby Leaguer & League Express Men of the Match:
Warriors: George Williams; *Wildcats:* Liam Finn.
Penalty count: 9-8; **Half-time:** 10-6;
Referee: James Child; **Attendance:** 11,121.

Sunday 10th July 2016

CASTLEFORD TIGERS 38 CATALANS DRAGONS 24

TIGERS: 1 Luke Dorn; 18 Ryan Hampshire; 19 Ben Crooks; 24 Greg Minikin; 5 Denny Solomona; 15 Paul McShane; 7 Luke Gale (C); 33 Danny Tickle; 9 Adam Milner; 32 Larne Patrick; 11 Oliver Holmes; 17 Junior Moors; 13 Nathan Massey. Subs (all used): 10 Grant Millington; 20 Frankie Mariano; 16 Matt Cook; 22 Gadwin Springer.
Tries: Hampshire (8, 26), Mariano (36), McShane (40), Dorn (44, 55), O Holmes (51); **Goals:** Gale 5/7.
DRAGONS: 21 Morgan Escare; 2 Jodie Broughton; 1 Tony Gigot; 4 Vincent Duport; 20 Fouad Yaha; 18 Thomas Bosc; 7 Richard Myler; 22 Antoni Maria; 28 Alrix Da Costa; 10 Remi Casty (C); 14 Dave Taylor; 12 Justin Horo; 33 Benjamin Garcia. Subs (all used): 15 Julian Bousquet; 16 Eloi Pelissier; 17 Gregory Mounis; 30 Romain Navarrete.
Tries: Horo (12), Yaha (46), Casty (62), Bousquet (80);
Goals: Bosc 3/3, Gigot 1/1.
Rugby Leaguer & League Express Men of the Match:
Tigers: Luke Dorn; *Dragons:* Remi Casty.
Penalty count: 10-8; **Half-time:** 20-6;
Referee: Michael Woodhead; **Attendance:** 5,586.

ROUND 22

Thursday 14th July 2016

HULL FC 36 HULL KINGSTON ROVERS 12

HULL FC: 1 Jamie Shaul; 19 Steve Michaels; 2 Mahe Fonua; 24 Kirk Yeaman; 5 Fetuli Talanoa; 13 Jordan Abdull; 7 Marc Sneyd; 8 Scott Taylor; 9 Danny Houghton; 10 Liam Watts; 21 Sika Manu; 12 Mark Minichiello; 11 Gareth Ellis (C). Subs (all used): 30 Danny Washbrook; 6 Leon Pryce; 16 Jordan Thompson; 22 Josh Bowden.
Tries: Watts (11), Houghton (15), Minichiello (23, 47), Michaels (52, 67); **Goals:** Sneyd 6/6.
ROVERS: 18 Ben Cockayne; 1 Ken Sio; 21 Thomas Minns; 4 Iain Thornley; 2 Josh Mantellato; 11 Maurice Blair; 7 Albert Kelly; 10 Mitchell Allgood; 9 Shaun Lunt; 17 Dane Tilse; 20 James Greenwood; 13 Chris Clarkson (C); 15 James

Donaldson. Subs (all used): 8 Adam Walker; 26 Rob Mulhern; 24 George Lawler; 22 Matthew Marsh.
Tries: Walker (54), Thornley (78); **Goals:** Mantellato 2/2.
Rugby Leaguer & League Express Men of the Match: *Hull FC:* Marc Sneyd; *Rovers:* Ben Cockayne.
Penalty count: 7-9; **Half-time:** 18-0;
Referee: Ben Thaler; **Attendance:** 17,481.

Friday 15th July 2016

LEEDS RHINOS 18 WIGAN WARRIORS 16

RHINOS: 14 Liam Sutcliffe; 2 Tom Briscoe; 3 Kallum Watkins; 4 Joel Moon; 5 Ryan Hall; 25 Jordan Lilley; 7 Rob Burrow (C); 8 Keith Galloway; 30 James Segeyaro; 16 Brad Singleton; 19 Mitch Achurch; 12 Carl Ablett; 11 Jamie Jones-Buchanan. Subs (all used): 15 Brett Delaney; 26 Brett Ferres; 10 Adam Cuthbertson; 18 Jimmy Keinhorst.
Tries: Watkins (11), Cuthbertson (45), Ferres (66);
Goals: Sutcliffe 3/3.
WARRIORS: 22 Lewis Tierney; 2 Josh Charnley; 20 Oliver Gildart; 4 Dan Sarginson; 5 Dominic Manfredi; 6 George Williams; 7 Matty Smith (C); 29 Joe Bretherton; 16 Sam Powell; 10 Ben Flower; 21 Ryan Sutton; 25 Willie Isa; 17 Lee Mossop. Subs (all used): 19 Taulima Tautai; 24 Frank-Paul Nuuausala (D); 28 Jake Shorrocks; 30 Jack Higginson.
Tries: Charnley (14), Higginson (69), Williams (72);
Goals: Smith 2/3.
Rugby Leaguer & League Express Men of the Match: *Rhinos:* Kallum Watkins; *Warriors:* George Williams.
Penalty count: 8-6; **Half time:** 6-4;
Referee: Robert Hicks; **Attendance:** 16,712.

WIDNES VIKINGS 24 SALFORD RED DEVILS 32

VIKINGS: 1 Rhys Hanbury; 2 Corey Thompson; 4 Charly Runciman; 17 Stefan Marsh; 5 Patrick Ah Van; 7 Joe Mellor; 6 Kevin Brown (C); 37 Greg Burke; 9 Lloyd White; 36 Jack Buchanan; 22 Matt Whitley; 14 Chris Dean; 11 Chris Houston. Subs (all used): 13 Hep Cahill; 33 Aaron Heremaia; 10 Manase Manuokafoa; 32 Connor Farrell.
Tries: Whitley (16, 62), Ah Van (35), Thompson (76);
Goals: White 3/3, Thompson 1/1.
Sin bin: Buchanan (70) - fighting.
RED DEVILS: 14 Gareth O'Brien; 2 Justin Carney; 3 Josh Griffin; 4 Junior Sa'u; 24 Mason Caton-Brown; 6 Robert Lui; 7 Michael Dobson (C); 8 Craig Kopczak; 19 Logan Tomkins; 10 George Griffin; 11 Ben Murdoch-Masila; 33 Josh Jones; 13 Mark Flanagan. Subs (all used): 12 Weller Hauraki; 16 Olsi Krasniqi; 1 Niall Evalds; 34 Sean Kenny.
Tries: Caton-Brown (3, 54, 78), Carney (27), Jones (68);
Goals: O'Brien 5/6, Dobson 1/1.
Sin bin: Kopczak (70) - fighting.
Rugby Leaguer & League Express Men of the Match: *Vikings:* Matt Whitley; *Red Devils:* Mason Caton-Brown.
Penalty count: 9-7; **Half-time:** 12-12;
Referee: Gareth Hewer; **Attendance:** 4,636.

Saturday 16th July 2016

CATALANS DRAGONS 28 WAKEFIELD TRINITY WILDCATS 30

DRAGONS: 21 Morgan Escare; 20 Fouad Yaha; 33 Benjamin Garcia; 4 Vincent Duport; 5 Pat Richards; 1 Tony Gigot; 27 Lucas Albert; 22 Antoni Maria; 16 Eloi Pelissier; 10 Remi Casty (C); 14 Dave Taylor; 12 Justin Horo; 13 Jason Baitieri. Subs (all used): 15 Julian Bousquet; 28 Alrix Da Costa; 29 Willie Mason; 30 Romain Navarrete.
Tries: Gigot (18), Taylor (24), Horo (28), Escare (58), Yaha (70); **Goals:** Richards 4/5.
WILDCATS: 21 Max Jowitt; 14 Reece Lyne; 18 Joe Arundel; 3 Bill Tupou; 25 Craig Hall; 6 Jacob Miller; 7 Liam Finn; 11 Mickael Simon; 9 Scott Moore; 16 Tinirau Arona; 17 Matty Ashurst; 19 Jon Molloy; 20 Michael Sio. Subs (all used): 8 Nick Scruton (C); 13 Anthony Tupou; 31 Jason Walton; 35 David Fifita.
Tries: Jowitt (8), Molloy (33), Hall (38), B Tupou (48), Sio (67); **Goals:** Finn 5/5.
Rugby Leaguer & League Express Men of the Match: *Dragons:* Lucas Albert; *Wildcats:* Tinirau Arona.
Penalty count: 9-6; **Half-time:** 18-18;
Referee: Chris Campbell; **Attendance:** 8,562.

Sunday 17th July 2016

HUDDERSFIELD GIANTS 18 ST HELENS 34

GIANTS: 18 Jake Connor; 2 Jermaine McGillvary; 3 Leroy Cudjoe; 5 Aaron Murphy; 35 Gene Ormsby (D2); 6 Danny Brough; 34 Ryan Brierley; 10 Craig Huby; 9 Ryan Hinchcliffe (C); 16 Sam Rapira; 11 Tom Symonds; 12 Michael Lawrence; 17 Ukuma Ta'ai. Subs (all used): 8 Eorl Crabtree; 20 Kruise Leeming; 22 Oliver Roberts; 36 Sebastine Ikahihifo.
Tries: Brough (9), Symonds (19), McGillvary (46);
Goals: Brough 3/3.
SAINTS: 1 Jonny Lomax; 22 Jack Owens; 24 Matty Fleming; 4 Mark Percival; 5 Adam Swift; 3 Jordan Turner; 7 Luke Walsh; 8 Alex Walmsley; 9 James Roby; 15 Greg Richards; 20 Joe Greenwood; 13 Louie McCarthy-Scarsbrook; 12 Jon Wilkin (C). Subs (all used): 10 Kyle Amor; 11 Atelea Vea; 17 Luke Thompson; 28 Morgan Knowles.
Tries: Greenwood (2), Owens (16), McCarthy-Scarsbrook (27), Turner (35), Swift (49), Walmsley (63); **Goals:** Percival 5/6.
Rugby Leaguer & League Express Men of the Match: *Giants:* Tom Symonds; *Saints:* Luke Walsh.
Penalty count: 8-5; **Half-time:** 12-22;
Referee: Joe Cobb; **Attendance:** 5,526.

CASTLEFORD TIGERS 26 WARRINGTON WOLVES 42

TIGERS: 1 Luke Dorn; 18 Ryan Hampshire; 19 Ben Crooks; 24 Greg Minikin; 5 Denny Solomona; 15 Paul McShane; 7 Luke Gale (C); 33 Danny Tickle; 9 Adam Milner; 32 Larne Patrick; 11 Oliver Holmes; 20 Frankie Mariano; 17 Junior Moors. Subs (all used): 10 Grant Millington; 35 Rangi Chase (D2); 16 Matt Cook; 22 Gadwin Springer.
Tries: Mariano (3), Solomona (18, 27, 37, 72), Crooks (80);
Goals: Gale 1/6.
WOLVES: 6 Stefan Ratchford; 5 Matthew Russell; 3 Rhys Evans; 4 Ryan Atkins; 2 Tom Lineham; 1 Kurt Gidley; 7 Chris Sandow; 8 Chris Hill (C); 9 Daryl Clark; 10 Ashton Sims; 11 Ben Currie; 12 Jack Hughes; 14 Joe Westerman. Subs (all used): 24 Toby King; 16 Brad Dwyer; 13 Ben Westwood; 33 Ryan Bailey.
Tries: R Evans (5, 10), Ratchford (35), Dwyer (45), Currie (55), T King (57), Clark (65);
Goals: Sandow 4/4, Gidley 3/4.
Rugby Leaguer & League Express Men of the Match: *Tigers:* Denny Solomona; *Wolves:* Daryl Clark.
Penalty count: 6-4; **Half-time:** 18-16;
Referee: Chris Kendall; **Attendance:** 8,060.

ROUND 23

Thursday 21st July 2016

HULL KINGSTON ROVERS 20 LEEDS RHINOS 24

ROVERS: 18 Ben Cockayne (C); 1 Ken Sio; 21 Thomas Minns; 11 Maurice Blair; 2 Josh Mantellato; 22 Matthew Marsh; 7 Albert Kelly; 17 Dane Tilse; 19 John Boudebza; 8 Adam Walker; 20 James Greenwood; 14 Kevin Larroyer; 24 George Lawler. Subs (all used): 5 Kieran Dixon; 30 Joe Cator; 26 Rob Mulhern; 16 James Green.
Tries: Marsh (15), Blair (36), Sio (42), Dixon (79);
Goals: Mantellato 2/4.
RHINOS: 14 Liam Sutcliffe; 2 Tom Briscoe; 3 Kallum Watkins; 18 Jimmy Keinhorst; 5 Ryan Hall; 25 Jordan Lilley; 7 Rob Burrow (C); 8 Keith Galloway; 30 James Segeyaro; 16 Brad Singleton; 26 Brett Ferres; 12 Carl Ablett; 11 Jamie Jones-Buchanan. Subs: 10 Adam Cuthbertson; 17 Mitch Garbutt; 19 Mitch Achurch; 23 Ashton Golding (not used).
Tries: Keinhorst (18), Burrow (21), Segeyaro (64), Hall (78); **Goals:** Sutcliffe 4/4.
On report:
Segeyaro (33) - alleged shoulder charge on Green.
Rugby Leaguer & League Express Men of the Match: *Rovers:* Ken Sio; *Rhinos:* James Segeyaro.
Penalty count: 8-9; **Half-time:** 10-12;
Referee: Robert Hicks; **Attendance:** 8,109.

Friday 22nd July 2016

SALFORD RED DEVILS 20 HULL FC 28

RED DEVILS: 14 Gareth O'Brien; 1 Niall Evalds; 3 Josh Griffin; 4 Junior Sa'u; 24 Mason Caton-Brown; 6 Robert Lui; 7 Michael Dobson (C); 8 Craig Kopczak; 19 Logan Tomkins; 10 George Griffin; 11 Ben Murdoch-Masila; 33 Josh Jones; 13 Mark Flanagan. Subs (all used): 12 Weller Hauraki; 16 Olsi Krasniqi; 34 Sean Kenny; 15 Adam Walne.
Tries: Dobson (13), Caton-Brown (52), Evalds (65), Lui (68); **Goals:** O'Brien 2/4.
HULL FC: 20 Curtis Naughton; 19 Steve Michaels; 2 Mahe Fonua; 24 Kirk Yeaman; 5 Fetuli Talanoa; 13 Jordan Abdull; 7 Marc Sneyd; 8 Scott Taylor; 9 Danny Houghton; 10 Liam Watts; 21 Sika Manu; 12 Mark Minichiello; 11 Gareth Ellis (C). Subs (all used): 15 Chris Green; 16 Jordan Thompson; 30 Danny Washbrook; 23 Frank Pritchard.
Tries: Michaels (4), Pritchard (23), Green (59), Sneyd (71), Fonua (76); **Goals:** Sneyd 4/5.
Rugby Leaguer & League Express Men of the Match: *Red Devils:* Robert Lui; *Hull FC:* Danny Houghton.
Penalty count: 7-8; **Half-time:** 6-12;
Referee: Chris Campbell; **Attendance:** 3,225.

WIGAN WARRIORS 4 ST HELENS 23

WARRIORS: 1 Sam Tomkins; 22 Lewis Tierney; 4 Dan Sarginson; 20 Oliver Gildart; 5 Dominic Manfredi; 6 George Williams; 7 Matty Smith; 21 Ryan Sutton; 16 Sam Powell; 10 Ben Flower; 25 Willie Isa; 14 John Bateman; 13 Sean O'Loughlin (C). Subs (all used): 8 Dominic Crosby; 17 Lee Mossop; 24 Frank-Paul Nuuausala; 28 Jake Shorrocks.
Try: Tierney (11); **Goals:** Smith 0/1.
Sin bin: Nuuausala (75) - fighting.
SAINTS: 1 Jonny Lomax; 22 Jack Owens; 24 Matty Fleming; 4 Mark Percival; 5 Adam Swift; 3 Jordan Turner; 7 Luke Walsh; 8 Alex Walmsley; 9 James Roby; 15 Greg Richards; 20 Joe Greenwood; 13 Louie McCarthy-Scarsbrook; 12 Jon Wilkin (C). Subs (all used): 10 Kyle Amor; 11 Atelea Vea; 17 Luke Thompson; 28 Morgan Knowles.
Tries: Percival (33), Knowles (38), Roby (80);
Goals: Percival 5/5; **Field goal:** Walsh (73).
Sin bin: McCarthy-Scarsbrook (75) - fighting.
Rugby Leaguer & League Express Men of the Match: *Warriors:* Ryan Sutton; *Saints:* Alex Walmsley.
Penalty count: 10-7; **Half-time:** 4-16;
Referee: Phil Bentham; **Attendance:** 20,049.

Saturday 23rd July 2016

WARRINGTON WOLVES 34 HUDDERSFIELD GIANTS 30

WOLVES: 6 Stefan Ratchford; 5 Matthew Russell; 24 Toby King; 4 Ryan Atkins; 3 Rhys Evans; 1 Kurt Gidley; 7 Chris Sandow; 8 Chris Hill (C); 9 Daryl Clark; 10 Ashton Sims; 11 Ben Currie; 12 Jack Hughes; 14 Joe Westerman. Subs (all used): 16 Brad Dwyer; 13 Ben Westwood; 18 George King; 33 Ryan Bailey.
Tries: Ratchford (7), Currie (14), Westwood (40), Sandow (51), Atkins (56), Clark (76); **Goals:** Gidley 5/6.
GIANTS: 34 Ryan Brierley; 5 Aaron Murphy; 3 Leroy Cudjoe; 18 Jake Connor; 35 Gene Ormsby; 6 Danny Brough; 7 Jamie Ellis; 16 Sam Rapira; 9 Ryan Hinchcliffe (C); 10 Craig Huby; 17 Ukuma Ta'ai; 12 Michael Lawrence; 36 Sebastine Ikahihifo. Subs (all used): 15 Kyle Wood; 22 Oliver Roberts; 21 Nathan Mason; 8 Eorl Crabtree.
Tries: Ormsby (20, 36, 64), Murphy (25), Mason (46), Huby (70); **Goals:** Brough 3/6.
Rugby Leaguer & League Express Men of the Match: *Wolves:* Ben Westwood; *Giants:* Ukuma Ta'ai.
Penalty count: 7-6; **Half-time:** 16-14;
Referee: Jack Smith; **Attendance:** 9,829.

Sunday 24th July 2016

WAKEFIELD TRINITY WILDCATS 20 CASTLEFORD TIGERS 46

WILDCATS: 21 Max Jowitt; 14 Reece Lyne; 3 Bill Tupou; 18 Joe Arundel; 25 Craig Hall; 6 Jacob Miller; 7 Liam Finn; 8 Nick Scruton (C); 20 Michael Sio; 35 David Fifita; 31 Jason Walton; 17 Matty Ashurst; 19 Jon Molloy. Subs (all used): 22 Jordan Crowther; 16 Tinirau Arona; 36 Bradley Moules (D); 13 Anthony Tupou.
Tries: Miller (4), Arundel (12, 28), Lyne (51);
Goals: Finn 2/4.
TIGERS: 18 Ryan Hampshire; 34 Paddy Flynn; 19 Ben Crooks; 11 Oliver Holmes; 24 Greg Minikin; 15 Paul McShane; 7 Luke Gale (C); 22 Gadwin Springer; 9 Adam Milner; 32 Larne Patrick; 20 Frankie Mariano; 10 Grant Millington; 17 Junior Moors. Subs (all used): 36 Andre Savelio (D); 27 Tom Holmes; 16 Matt Cook; 23 Will Maher.
Tries: Minikin (20, 71), O Holmes (25), Savelio (45), Gale (58), Moors (63), T Holmes (75), Hampshire (77);
Goals: Gale 7/8.
Rugby Leaguer & League Express Men of the Match: *Wildcats:* Liam Finn; *Tigers:* Luke Gale.
Penalty count: 6-5; **Half-time:** 16-10;
Referee: Joe Cobb; **Attendance:** 6,855.

WIDNES VIKINGS 32 CATALANS DRAGONS 4

VIKINGS: 2 Corey Thompson; 17 Stefan Marsh; 4 Charly Runciman; 14 Chris Dean; 5 Patrick Ah Van; 7 Joe Mellor; 6 Kevin Brown (C); 37 Greg Burke; 9 Lloyd White; 36 Jack Buchanan; 22 Matt Whitley; 11 Chris Houston; 13 Hep Cahill. Subs (all used): 19 Macgraff Leuluai; 33 Aaron Heremaia; 10 Manase Manuokafoa; 32 Connor Farrell.
Tries: Thompson (8), Ah Van (16), Mellor (60), Heremaia (67), Marsh (78);
Goals: Thompson 3/5, Marsh 3/3.
DRAGONS: 1 Tony Gigot; 2 Jodie Broughton; 33 Benjamin Garcia; 4 Vincent Duport; 20 Fouad Yaha; 6 Todd Carney; 27 Lucas Albert; 14 Dave Taylor; 16 Eloi Pelissier; 10 Remi Casty (C); 11 Glenn Stewart; 12 Justin Horo; 13 Jason Baitieri. Subs (all used): 15 Julian Bousquet; 22 Antoni Maria; 28 Alrix Da Costa; 30 Romain Navarrete.
Try: Taylor (13); **Goals:** Carney 0/1.
Rugby Leaguer & League Express Men of the Match: *Vikings:* Joe Mellor; *Dragons:* Glenn Stewart.
Penalty count: 10-6; **Half-time:** 14-4;
Referee: James Child; **Attendance:** 4,195.

SUPER 8s

ROUND 1

Thursday 4th August 2016

WARRINGTON WOLVES 18 ST HELENS 20

WOLVES: 6 Stefan Ratchford; 5 Matthew Russell; 24 Toby King; 4 Ryan Atkins; 3 Rhys Evans; 1 Kurt Gidley; 7 Chris Sandow; 8 Chris Hill (C); 9 Daryl Clark; 10 Ashton Sims; 11 Ben Currie; 12 Jack Hughes; 14 Joe Westerman. Subs: 16 Brad Dwyer; 13 Ben Westwood; 18 George King; 27 Sam Wilde (not used).
Tries: Clark (30), Hughes (63), Atkins (72);
Goals: Gidley 3/3.
SAINTS: 1 Jonny Lomax; 22 Jack Owens; 18 Dominique Peyroux; 4 Mark Percival; 5 Adam Swift; 3 Jordan Turner; 7 Luke Walsh; 15 Greg Richards; 9 James Roby; 8 Alex Walmsley; 13 Louie McCarthy-Scarsbrook; 20 Joe Greenwood; 12 Jon Wilkin (C). Subs (all used): 10 Kyle Amor; 11 Atelea Vea; 17 Luke Thompson; 28 Morgan Knowles.
Tries: McCarthy-Scarsbrook (20), Lomax (36), Turner (70); **Goals:** Percival 4/4.
Rugby Leaguer & League Express Men of the Match:
Wolves: Daryl Clark; *Saints:* Jordan Turner.
Penalty count: 7-9; **Half-time:** 6-12;
Referee: Phil Bentham; **Attendance:** 10,759.

Friday 5th August 2016

HULL FC 16 CASTLEFORD TIGERS 30

HULL FC: 1 Jamie Shaul; 19 Steve Michaels; 3 Carlos Tuimavave; 24 Kirk Yeaman; 20 Curtis Naughton; 13 Jordan Abdull; 7 Marc Sneyd; 8 Scott Taylor; 9 Danny Houghton; 22 Josh Bowden; 21 Sika Manu; 23 Frank Pritchard; 11 Gareth Ellis (C). Subs (all used): 12 Mark Minichiello; 16 Jordan Thompson; 15 Chris Green; 30 Danny Washbrook.
Tries: Michaels (62), Washbrook (70), Shaul (73);
Goals: Sneyd 2/3.
TIGERS: 1 Luke Dorn; 18 Ryan Hampshire; 19 Ben Crooks; 24 Greg Minikin; 5 Denny Solomona; 35 Rangi Chase; 7 Luke Gale (C); 22 Gadwin Springer; 9 Adam Milner; 32 Larne Patrick; 11 Oliver Holmes; 36 Andre Savelio; 17 Junior Moors. Subs (all used): 14 Lee Jewitt; 15 Paul McShane; 16 Matt Cook; 10 Grant Millington.
Tries: Minikin (3), Hampshire (17, 53), Gale (23), Dorn (29), Milner (79); **Goals:** Gale 3/6.
Rugby Leaguer & League Express Men of the Match:
Hull FC: Danny Houghton; *Tigers:* Luke Gale.
Penalty count: 5-8; **Half-time:** 0-20;
Referee: Jack Smith; **Attendance:** 9,936.

WIGAN WARRIORS 60
WAKEFIELD TRINITY WILDCATS 12

WARRIORS: 1 Sam Tomkins; 2 Josh Charnley; 4 Dan Sarginson; 20 Oliver Gildart; 5 Dominic Manfredi; 6 George Williams; 7 Matty Smith; 8 Dominic Crosby; 16 Sam Powell; 10 Ben Flower; 14 John Bateman; 25 Willie Isa; 13 Sean O'Loughlin (C). Subs (all used): 17 Lee Mossop; 19 Taulima Tautai; 24 Frank-Paul Nuuausala; 28 Jake Shorrocks.
Tries: Williams (5, 57), Powell (9), Charnley (15), S Tomkins (27, 66), Bateman (36), Gildart (38), Manfredi (55), Sarginson (60), Smith (72);
Goals: Smith 3/5, Charnley 0/1, Shorrocks 5/5.
WILDCATS: 21 Max Jowitt; 25 Craig Hall; 14 Reece Lyne; 18 Joe Arundel; 34 Judah Mazive (D); 6 Jacob Miller; 7 Liam Finn; 8 Nick Scruton (C); 9 Scott Moore; 35 David Fifita; 31 Jason Walton; 13 Anthony Tupou; 22 Jordan Crowther. Subs (all used): 16 Tinirau Arona; 20 Michael Sio; 28 Andy Yates; 33 Frazer Morris (D).
Tries: Arundel (32), Hall (67); **Goals:** Finn 2/2.
Rugby Leaguer & League Express Men of the Match:
Warriors: John Bateman; *Wildcats:* Jordan Crowther.
Penalty count: 6-6; **Half-time:** 30-6;
Referee: Scott Mikalauskas; **Attendance:** 10,593.

Saturday 6th August 2016

CATALANS DRAGONS 26 WIDNES VIKINGS 10

DRAGONS: 1 Tony Gigot; 2 Jodie Broughton; 33 Benjamin Garcia; 4 Vincent Duport; 20 Fouad Yaha; 6 Todd Carney; 18 Thomas Bosc; 14 Dave Taylor; 16 Eloi Pelissier; 10 Remi Casty (C); 11 Glenn Stewart; 12 Justin Horo; 13 Jason Baitieri. Subs (all used): 8 Louis Anderson; 9 Paul Aiton; 15 Julian Bousquet; 17 Gregory Mounis.
Tries: Broughton (21), Horo (25), Yaha (50, 58, 68);
Goals: Bosc 3/4, Carney 0/1.
VIKINGS: 1 Rhys Hanbury; 2 Corey Thompson; 4 Charly Runciman; 17 Stefan Marsh; 5 Patrick Ah Van; 6 Kevin Brown (C); 7 Joe Mellor; 37 Greg Burke; 9 Lloyd White; 36 Jack Buchanan; 14 Chris Dean; 11 Chris Houston; 13 Hep Cahill. Subs (all used): 10 Manase Manuokafoa; 19 Macgraff Leuluai; 22 Matt Whitley; 33 Aaron Heremaia.
Tries: Whitley (47), Ah Van (74); **Goals:** White 1/2.
Rugby Leaguer & League Express Men of the Match:
Dragons: Thomas Bosc; *Vikings:* Kevin Brown.
Penalty count: 9-6; **Half-time:** 10-0;
Referee: Robert Hicks; **Attendance:** 8,562.

ROUND 2

Thursday 11th August 2016

WIDNES VIKINGS 0 HULL FC 38

VIKINGS: 7 Joe Mellor; 5 Patrick Ah Van; 2 Corey Thompson; 25 Ed Chamberlain; 26 Ryan Ince (D); 6 Kevin Brown (C); 33 Aaron Heremaia; 36 Jack Buchanan; 9 Lloyd White; 37 Greg Burke; 11 Chris Houston; 22 Matt Whitley; 13 Hep Cahill. Subs (all used): 10 Manase Manuokafoa; 19 Macgraff Leuluai; 24 Jay Chapelhow; 32 Connor Farrell.
HULL FC: 1 Jamie Shaul; 19 Steve Michaels; 2 Mahe Fonua; 24 Kirk Yeaman; 5 Fetuli Talanoa; 13 Jordan Abdull; 3 Carlos Tuimavave; 8 Scott Taylor; 9 Danny Houghton; 10 Liam Watts; 21 Sika Manu; 12 Mark Minichiello; 11 Gareth Ellis (C). Subs (all used): 15 Chris Green; 17 Dean Hadley; 22 Josh Bowden; 23 Frank Pritchard.
Tries: Abdull (22), Talanoa (27, 34, 69), Tuimavave (32), Michaels (52), Hadley (59); **Goals:** Abdull 5/7.
Rugby Leaguer & League Express Men of the Match:
Vikings: Lloyd White; *Hull FC:* Fetuli Talanoa.
Penalty count: 8-12; **Half-time:** 0-22;
Referee: Ben Thaler; **Attendance:** 4,359.

Friday 12th August 2016

CASTLEFORD TIGERS 36 WIGAN WARRIORS 22

TIGERS: 1 Luke Dorn; 18 Ryan Hampshire; 19 Ben Crooks; 24 Greg Minikin; 5 Denny Solomona; 35 Rangi Chase; 7 Luke Gale (C); 22 Gadwin Springer; 9 Adam Milner; 32 Larne Patrick; 11 Oliver Holmes; 36 Andre Savelio; 17 Junior Moors. Subs (all used): 14 Lee Jewitt; 15 Paul McShane; 16 Matt Cook; 10 Grant Millington.
Tries: Solomona (8, 47, 55), McShane (26), Hampshire (77), O Holmes (79); **Goals:** Gale 6/8.
Sin bin: O Holmes (59) - fighting.
WARRIORS: 1 Sam Tomkins (C); 2 Josh Charnley; 3 Anthony Gelling; 4 Dan Sarginson; 5 Dominic Manfredi; 6 George Williams; 7 Matty Smith; 8 Dominic Crosby; 16 Sam Powell; 10 Ben Flower; 14 John Bateman; 25 Willie Isa; 21 Ryan Sutton. Subs (all used): 12 Liam Farrell; 17 Lee Mossop; 19 Taulima Tautai; 24 Frank-Paul Nuuausala.
Tries: Powell (32), Flower (50), Bateman (63), Mossop (65); **Goals:** Smith 3/4.
Sin bin: Crosby (59) - fighting.
Rugby Leaguer & League Express Men of the Match:
Tigers: Luke Gale; *Warriors:* Matty Smith.
Penalty count: 12-9; **Half-time:** 12-6;
Referee: Joe Cobb; **Attendance:** 6,325.

ST HELENS 39 CATALANS DRAGONS 16

SAINTS: 1 Jonny Lomax; 22 Jack Owens; 18 Dominique Peyroux; 4 Mark Percival; 5 Adam Swift; 3 Jordan Turner; 7 Luke Walsh; 8 Alex Walmsley; 9 James Roby; 15 Greg Richards; 13 Louie McCarthy-Scarsbrook; 20 Joe Greenwood; 12 Jon Wilkin (C). Subs (all used): 10 Kyle Amor; 11 Atelea Vea; 17 Luke Thompson; 28 Morgan Knowles.
Tries: Swift (19, 25, 40, 51), Owens (72), Greenwood (76);
Goals: Percival 0/1, Walsh 6/6, Owens 1/1;
Field goal: Walsh (61).
Sin bin: Walsh (31) - dangerous challenge on Albert.
On report:
Thompson (54) - alleged dangerous challenge on Horo.
DRAGONS: 1 Tony Gigot; 2 Jodie Broughton; 33 Benjamin Garcia; 4 Vincent Duport; 20 Fouad Yaha; 6 Todd Carney; 27 Lucas Albert; 14 Dave Taylor; 16 Eloi Pelissier; 10 Remi Casty (C); 11 Glenn Stewart; 12 Justin Horo; 13 Jason Baitieri. Subs (all used): 8 Louis Anderson; 9 Paul Aiton; 15 Julian Bousquet; 17 Gregory Mounis.
Tries: Taylor (7), Baitieri (34), Duport (67);
Goals: Albert 2/3.
Rugby Leaguer & League Express Men of the Match:
Saints: Adam Swift; *Dragons:* Paul Aiton.
Penalty count: 10-8; **Half-time:** 16-12;
Referee: James Child; **Attendance:** 9,440.

Sunday 14th August 2016

WAKEFIELD TRINITY WILDCATS 10
WARRINGTON WOLVES 38

WILDCATS: 25 Craig Hall; 34 Judah Mazive; 14 Reece Lyne; 18 Joe Arundel; 1 Ben Jones-Bishop; 6 Jacob Miller; 7 Liam Finn; 8 Nick Scruton (C); 20 Michael Sio; 16 Tinirau Arona; 19 Jon Molloy; 31 Jason Walton; 22 Jordan Crowther. Subs (all used): 21 Max Jowitt; 28 Andy Yates; 32 James Batchelor (D); 35 David Fifita.
Tries: Molloy (5), Mazive (53); **Goals:** Finn 1/2.
WOLVES: 6 Stefan Ratchford; 3 Rhys Evans; 24 Toby King; 4 Ryan Atkins; 5 Matthew Russell; 1 Kurt Gidley; 7 Chris Sandow; 8 Chris Hill (C); 9 Daryl Clark; 10 Ashton Sims; 12 Jack Hughes; 11 Ben Currie; 14 Joe Westerman. Subs (all used): 16 Brad Dwyer; 13 Ben Westwood; 18 George King; 27 Sam Wilde.
Tries: Currie (19), Hill (24), Atkins (37), Russell (48, 66), Clark (59), Westerman (75); **Goals:** Gidley 5/7.
Rugby Leaguer & League Express Men of the Match:
Wildcats: James Batchelor; *Wolves:* Ben Currie.
Penalty count: 7-8; **Half-time:** 6-16;
Referee: Robert Hicks; **Attendance:** 3,552.

ROUND 3

Thursday 18th August 2016

HULL FC 44 CATALANS DRAGONS 0

HULL FC: 1 Jamie Shaul; 19 Steve Michaels; 2 Mahe Fonua; 24 Kirk Yeaman; 5 Fetuli Talanoa; 3 Carlos Tuimavave; 7 Marc Sneyd; 8 Scott Taylor; 9 Danny Houghton (C); 22 Josh Bowden; 12 Mark Minichiello; 17 Dean Hadley; 30 Danny Washbrook. Subs (all used): 13 Jordan Abdull; 15 Chris Green; 16 Jordan Thompson; 23 Frank Pritchard.
Tries: Hadley (12), Fonua (19, 56), Minichiello (30), Talanoa (43), Sneyd (61), Pritchard (72); **Goals:** Sneyd 8/9.
DRAGONS: 21 Morgan Escare; 20 Fouad Yaha; 33 Benjamin Garcia; 4 Vincent Duport; 26 Jordan Sigismeau; 1 Tony Gigot; 27 Lucas Albert; 15 Julian Bousquet; 9 Paul Aiton; 10 Remi Casty (C); 11 Glenn Stewart; 14 Dave Taylor; 13 Jason Baitieri. Subs (all used): 16 Eloi Pelissier; 17 Gregory Mounis; 19 Olivier Elima; 30 Romain Navarrete.
Sin bin: Casty (75) - high tackle.
Rugby Leaguer & League Express Men of the Match:
Hull FC: Mahe Fonua; *Dragons:* Dave Taylor.
Penalty count: 9-8; **Half-time:** 22-0;
Referee: Phil Bentham; **Attendance:** 10,494.

Friday 19th August 2016

WIGAN WARRIORS 25 ST HELENS 0

WARRIORS: 1 Sam Tomkins (C); 2 Josh Charnley; 3 Anthony Gelling; 4 Dan Sarginson; 20 Oliver Gildart; 6 George Williams; 7 Matty Smith; 8 Dominic Crosby; 16 Sam Powell; 10 Ben Flower; 14 John Bateman; 12 Liam Farrell; 25 Willie Isa. Subs (all used): 19 Taulima Tautai; 21 Ryan Sutton; 24 Frank-Paul Nuuausala; 28 Jake Shorrocks.
Tries: Gelling (3, 30, 65), Williams (78);
Goals: Smith 4/5; **Field goal:** Smith (59).
SAINTS: 1 Jonny Lomax; 22 Jack Owens; 24 Matty Fleming; 18 Dominique Peyroux; 5 Adam Swift; 3 Jordan Turner; 19 Theo Fages; 8 Alex Walmsley; 9 James Roby; 15 Greg Richards; 20 Joe Greenwood; 28 Morgan Knowles; 12 Jon Wilkin (C). Subs (all used): 10 Kyle Amor; 11 Atelea Vea; 13 Louie McCarthy-Scarsbrook; 14 Lama Tasi.
Rugby Leaguer & League Express Men of the Match:
Warriors: Liam Farrell; *Saints:* James Roby.
Penalty count: 6-3; **Half-time:** 12-0;
Referee: Ben Thaler; **Attendance:** 15,265.

Saturday 20th August 2016

WARRINGTON WOLVES 14 CASTLEFORD TIGERS 11

WOLVES: 6 Stefan Ratchford; 5 Matthew Russell; 24 Toby King; 4 Ryan Atkins; 3 Rhys Evans; 1 Kurt Gidley; 7 Chris Sandow; 8 Chris Hill (C); 9 Daryl Clark; 10 Ashton Sims; 11 Ben Currie; 12 Jack Hughes; 14 Joe Westerman. Subs (all used): 16 Brad Dwyer; 13 Ben Westwood; 18 George King; 33 Ryan Bailey.
Tries: Westerman (9), R Evans (60), Hughes (80);
Goals: Gidley 1/3.
TIGERS: 1 Luke Dorn; 18 Ryan Hampshire; 19 Ben Crooks; 24 Greg Minikin; 5 Denny Solomona; 35 Rangi Chase; 7 Luke Gale (C); 22 Gadwin Springer; 9 Adam Milner; 32 Larne Patrick; 11 Oliver Holmes; 36 Andre Savelio; 17 Junior Moors. Subs (all used): 20 Frankie Mariano; 15 Paul McShane; 16 Matt Cook; 10 Grant Millington.
Try: Solomona (26); **Goals:** Gale 3/3; **Field goal:** Gale (77).
Rugby Leaguer & League Express Men of the Match:
Wolves: Ryan Bailey; *Tigers:* Paul McShane.
Penalty count: 5-6; **Half-time:** 6-8;
Referee: Chris Kendall; **Attendance:** 9,228.

Sunday 21st August 2016

WIDNES VIKINGS 40
WAKEFIELD TRINITY WILDCATS 8

VIKINGS: 1 Rhys Hanbury; 2 Corey Thompson; 14 Chris Dean; 17 Stefan Marsh; 5 Patrick Ah Van; 7 Joe Mellor; 6

Kevin Brown (C); 36 Jack Buchanan; 9 Lloyd White; 37 Greg Burke; 11 Chris Houston; 22 Matt Whitley; 13 Hep Cahill. Subs (all used): 18 Gil Dudson; 33 Aaron Heremaia; 24 Jay Chapelhow; 32 Connor Farrell.
Tries: Ah Van (8, 68), Hanbury (15), Whitley (19), Thompson (37), Marsh (45), White (50);
Goals: White 5/7, Thompson 1/1.
WILDCATS: 21 Max Jowitt; 25 Craig Hall; 3 Bill Tupou; 14 Reece Lyne; 1 Ben Jones-Bishop; 6 Jacob Miller; 7 Liam Finn; 8 Nick Scruton (C); 9 Scott Moore; 16 Tinirau Arona; 19 Jon Molloy; 31 Jason Walton; 20 Michael Sio. Subs (all used): 18 Joe Arundel; 28 Andy Yates; 32 James Batchelor; 35 David Fifita.
Tries: Hall (56), Jones-Bishop (75); **Goals:** Hall 0/1, Finn 0/1.
Rugby Leaguer & League Express Men of the Match: *Vikings:* Matt Whitley; *Wildcats:* Craig Hall.
Penalty count: 8-4; **Half-time:** 24-0;
Referee: Gareth Hewer; **Attendance:** 4,010.

ROUND 4

Thursday 1st September 2016

WIGAN WARRIORS 6 WIDNES VIKINGS 8

WARRIORS: 1 Sam Tomkins (C); 2 Josh Charnley; 3 Anthony Gelling; 4 Dan Sarginson; 22 Lewis Tierney; 6 George Williams; 28 Jake Shorrocks; 21 Ryan Sutton; 16 Sam Powell; 10 Ben Flower; 14 John Bateman; 12 Liam Farrell; 25 Willie Isa. Subs (all used): 19 Taulima Tautai; 20 Oliver Gildart; 24 Frank-Paul Nuuausala; 29 Joe Bretherton.
Try: Farrell (50); **Goals:** Shorrocks 1/1.
VIKINGS: 1 Rhys Hanbury; 2 Corey Thompson; 14 Chris Dean; 4 Charly Runciman; 17 Stefan Marsh; 7 Joe Mellor; 6 Kevin Brown (C); 36 Jack Buchanan; 9 Lloyd White; 37 Greg Burke; 11 Chris Houston; 22 Matt Whitley; 13 Hep Cahill. Subs (all used): 18 Gil Dudson; 33 Aaron Heremaia; 24 Jay Chapelhow; 32 Connor Farrell.
Tries: Thompson (10, 29); **Goals:** White 0/2.
Sin bin: Buchanan (56) - interference;
Farrell (64) - late challenge on Tierney.
Rugby Leaguer & League Express Men of the Match: *Warriors:* John Bateman; *Vikings:* Corey Thompson.
Penalty count: 20-9; **Half-time:** 0-8;
Referee: Phil Bentham; **Attendance:** 11,495.

Friday 2nd September 2016

CASTLEFORD TIGERS 46 WAKEFIELD TRINITY WILDCATS 22

TIGERS: 1 Luke Dorn; 18 Ryan Hampshire; 24 Greg Minikin; 3 Jake Webster; 5 Denny Solomona; 35 Rangi Chase; 7 Luke Gale (C); 32 Larne Patrick; 9 Adam Milner; 22 Gadwin Springer; 11 Oliver Holmes; 36 Andre Savelio; 17 Junior Moors. Subs (all used): 15 Paul McShane; 10 Grant Millington; 16 Matt Cook; 23 Will Maher.
Tries: Solomona (7, 22, 27), Chase (15), Dorn (37), McShane (40), Webster (49), Gale (75); **Goals:** Gale 7/8.
Sin bin: Hampshire (60) - holding down.
WILDCATS: 25 Craig Hall; 14 Reece Lyne; 18 Joe Arundel; 3 Bill Tupou; 2 Tom Johnstone; 6 Jacob Miller; 7 Liam Finn; 8 Nick Scruton (C); 9 Scott Moore; 16 Tinirau Arona; 19 Jon Molloy; 13 Anthony Tupou; 38 Ben Harrison (D). Subs (all used): 20 Michael Sio; 11 Mickael Simon; 28 Andy Yates; 23 Scott Anderson.
Tries: Lyne (11), Johnstone (31, 66), B Tupou (43), Scruton (63); **Goals:** Finn 1/5.
Rugby Leaguer & League Express Men of the Match: *Tigers:* Luke Gale; *Wildcats:* Ben Harrison.
Penalty count: 10-7; **Half-time:** 34-8;
Referee: Gareth Hewer; **Attendance:** 6,283.

ST HELENS 31 HULL FC 10

SAINTS: 1 Jonny Lomax; 22 Jack Owens; 18 Dominique Peyroux; 24 Matty Fleming; 5 Adam Swift; 3 Jordan Turner; 19 Theo Fages; 8 Alex Walmsley; 9 James Roby; 15 Greg Richards; 13 Louie McCarthy-Scarsbrook; 20 Joe Greenwood; 12 Jon Wilkin (C). Subs (all used): 10 Kyle Amor; 11 Atelea Vea; 27 Jack Ashworth; 28 Morgan Knowles.
Tries: Owens (22, 76), Fleming (25), Vea (51, 71);
Goals: Owens 5/6; **Field goal:** Turner (74).
HULL FC: 1 Jamie Shaul; 19 Steve Michaels; 2 Mahe Fonua; 5 Fetuli Talanoa; 20 Curtis Naughton; 6 Leon Pryce (C); 13 Jordan Abdull; 22 Josh Bowden; 30 Danny Washbrook; 15 Chris Green; 21 Sika Manu; 17 Dean Hadley; 16 Jordan Thompson. Subs (all used): 10 Liam Watts; 14 Iafeta Palea'aesina; 23 Frank Pritchard; 27 Jack Downs.
Tries: Fonua (4), Manu (54); **Goals:** Naughton 1/2.
Rugby Leaguer & League Express Men of the Match: *Saints:* Adam Swift; *Hull FC:* Sika Manu.
Penalty count: 6-7; **Half-time:** 10-6;
Referee: Chris Campbell; **Attendance:** 10,086.

Saturday 3rd September 2016

CATALANS DRAGONS 22 WARRINGTON WOLVES 26

DRAGONS: 1 Tony Gigot; 2 Jodie Broughton; 33 Benjamin Garcia; 4 Vincent Duport; 20 Fouad Yaha; 11 Glenn Stewart; 7 Richard Myler; 15 Julian Bousquet; 9 Paul Aiton; 19 Olivier Elima; 10 Remi Casty (C); 12 Justin Horo; 13 Jason Baitieri. Subs (all used): 8 Louis Anderson; 16 Eloi Pelissier; 17 Gregory Mounis; 30 Romain Navarrete.
Tries: Duport (44), Myler (50), Garcia (67); **Goals:** Gigot 5/5.
WOLVES: 28 Jack Johnson; 5 Matthew Russell; 24 Toby King; 4 Ryan Atkins; 20 Kevin Penny; 6 Stefan Ratchford; 26 Declan Patton; 8 Chris Hill (C); 16 Brad Dwyer; 10 Ashton Sims; 11 Ben Currie; 12 Jack Hughes; 18 George King. Subs (all used): 27 Sam Wilde; 31 Morgan Smith; 32 Jordan Cox; 33 Ryan Bailey.
Tries: Patton (7, 39), Penny (18), Currie (77);
Goals: Patton 5/5.
Rugby Leaguer & League Express Men of the Match: *Dragons:* Tony Gigot; *Wolves:* Declan Patton.
Penalty count: 10-5; **Half-time:** 0-18;
Referee: Jack Smith; **Attendance:** 7,108.

ROUND 5

Thursday 8th September 2016

ST HELENS 40 CASTLEFORD TIGERS 16

SAINTS: 1 Jonny Lomax; 22 Jack Owens; 18 Dominique Peyroux; 24 Matty Fleming; 5 Adam Swift; 3 Jordan Turner; 7 Luke Walsh; 8 Alex Walmsley; 9 James Roby; 15 Greg Richards; 12 Jon Wilkin (C); 20 Joe Greenwood; 13 Louie McCarthy-Scarsbrook. Subs (all used): 10 Kyle Amor; 11 Atelea Vea; 17 Luke Thompson; 28 Morgan Knowles.
Tries: Fleming (6), Knowles (29), Amor (33), Thompson (36), McCarthy-Scarsbrook (61), Swift (72), Walmsley (80); **Goals:** Walsh 5/6, Owens 1/1.
TIGERS: 1 Luke Dorn; 18 Ryan Hampshire; 19 Ben Crooks; 24 Greg Minikin; 5 Denny Solomona; 35 Rangi Chase; 7 Luke Gale (C); 16 Matt Cook; 15 Paul McShane; 32 Larne Patrick; 3 Jake Webster; 17 Junior Moors; 9 Adam Milner. Subs (all used): 23 Will Maher; 31 Connor Fitzsimmons; 34 Paddy Flynn; 37 Brandon Douglas (D).
Tries: Dorn (2), Hampshire (17), Maher (77); **Goals:** Gale 2/3.
Sin bin: Chase (36) - trip on Lomax.
Rugby Leaguer & League Express Men of the Match: *Saints:* Kyle Amor; *Tigers:* Adam Milner.
Penalty count: 10-6; **Half-time:** 24-10;
Referee: Jack Smith; **Attendance:** 9,448.

Friday 9th September 2016

HULL FC 12 WIGAN WARRIORS 18

HULL FC: 1 Jamie Shaul; 19 Steve Michaels; 2 Mahe Fonua; 24 Kirk Yeaman; 5 Fetuli Talanoa; 3 Carlos Tuimavave; 7 Marc Sneyd; 8 Scott Taylor; 9 Danny Houghton; 10 Liam Watts; 21 Sika Manu; 12 Mark Minichiello; 11 Gareth Ellis (C). Subs (all used): 23 Frank Pritchard; 16 Jordan Thompson; 22 Josh Bowden; 17 Dean Hadley.
Tries: Talanoa (20), Fonua (37); **Goals:** Sneyd 2/3.
WARRIORS: 1 Sam Tomkins (C); 2 Josh Charnley; 3 Anthony Gelling; 4 Dan Sarginson; 22 Lewis Tierney; 6 George Williams; 7 Matty Smith; 24 Frank-Paul Nuuausala; 16 Sam Powell; 10 Ben Flower; 14 John Bateman; 12 Liam Farrell; 25 Willie Isa. Subs (all used): 8 Dominic Crosby; 21 Ryan Sutton; 19 Taulima Tautai; 28 Jake Shorrocks.
Tries: Williams (11), Powell (65), Tautai (77);
Goals: Smith 3/4.
Rugby Leaguer & League Express Men of the Match: *Hull FC:* Mahe Fonua; *Warriors:* John Bateman.
Penalty count: 10-7; **Half-time:** 12-4;
Referee: Ben Thaler; **Attendance:** 11,686.

WAKEFIELD TRINITY WILDCATS 10 CATALANS DRAGONS 14

WILDCATS: 21 Max Jowitt; 2 Tom Johnstone; 3 Bill Tupou; 14 Reece Lyne; 25 Craig Hall; 6 Jacob Miller; 7 Liam Finn; 8 Nick Scruton (C); 20 Michael Sio; 16 Tinirau Arona; 17 Matty Ashurst; 19 Jon Molloy; 38 Ben Harrison. Subs (all used): 11 Mickael Simon; 13 Anthony Tupou; 23 Scott Anderson; 35 David Fifita.
Tries: Jowitt (7), Hall (42); **Goals:** Finn 1/2.
DRAGONS: 1 Tony Gigot; 2 Jodie Broughton; 33 Benjamin Garcia; 4 Vincent Duport; 20 Fouad Yaha; 11 Glenn Stewart; 7 Richard Myler; 19 Olivier Elima; 9 Paul Aiton; 10 Remi Casty (C); 8 Louis Anderson; 12 Justin Horo; 13 Jason Baitieri. Subs (all used): 15 Julian Bousquet; 16 Eloi Pelissier; 17 Gregory Mounis; 35 Paul Seguier (D).
Tries: Baitieri (4), Bousquet (20); **Goals:** Gigot 3/3.
Sin bin: Elima (58) - holding down.
Rugby Leaguer & League Express Men of the Match: *Wildcats:* Max Jowitt; *Dragons:* Tony Gigot.
Penalty count: 9-6; **Half-time:** 4-12;
Referee: James Child; **Attendance:** 2,612.

WARRINGTON WOLVES 30 WIDNES VIKINGS 12

WOLVES: 6 Stefan Ratchford; 5 Matthew Russell; 24 Toby King; 4 Ryan Atkins; 3 Rhys Evans; 1 Kurt Gidley; 26 Declan Patton; 8 Chris Hill (C); 16 Brad Dwyer; 10 Ashton Sims; 11 Ben Currie; 12 Jack Hughes; 18 George King. Subs (all used): 27 Sam Wilde; 31 Morgan Smith; 25 Joe Philbin; 33 Ryan Bailey.
Tries: Hill (11), Sims (28), Smith (34), Philbin (45), Russell (68); **Goals:** Gidley 5/6.
VIKINGS: 1 Rhys Hanbury; 2 Corey Thompson; 14 Chris Dean; 4 Charly Runciman; 5 Patrick Ah Van; 7 Joe Mellor; 6 Kevin Brown (C); 37 Greg Burke; 9 Lloyd White; 36 Jack Buchanan; 22 Matt Whitley; 11 Chris Houston; 13 Hep Cahill. Subs (all used): 24 Jay Chapelhow; 18 Gil Dudson; 33 Aaron Heremaia; 32 Connor Farrell.
Tries: Mellor (51), Thompson (78);
Goals: Thompson 1/1, White 1/1.
Rugby Leaguer & League Express Men of the Match: *Wolves:* Stefan Ratchford; *Vikings:* Joe Mellor.
Penalty count: 10-9; **Half-time:** 20-0;
Referee: Gareth Hewer; **Attendance:** 10,488.

ROUND 6

Thursday 15th September 2016

WAKEFIELD TRINITY WILDCATS 12 HULL FC 18

WILDCATS: 21 Max Jowitt; 14 Reece Lyne; 18 Joe Arundel; 3 Bill Tupou; 2 Tom Johnstone; 25 Craig Hall; 7 Liam Finn (C); 23 Scott Anderson; 20 Michael Sio; 16 Tinirau Arona; 19 Jon Molloy; 17 Matty Ashurst; 38 Ben Harrison. Subs (all used): 11 Mickael Simon; 13 Anthony Tupou; 35 David Fifita; 32 James Batchelor.
Tries: Arundel (16), Johnstone (67); **Goals:** Finn 2/3.
HULL FC: 1 Jamie Shaul; 19 Steve Michaels; 2 Mahe Fonua; 24 Kirk Yeaman; 5 Fetuli Talanoa; 3 Carlos Tuimavave; 7 Marc Sneyd; 8 Scott Taylor; 9 Danny Houghton; 10 Liam Watts; 21 Sika Manu; 30 Danny Washbrook; 11 Gareth Ellis (C). Subs (all used): 15 Chris Green; 22 Josh Bowden; 16 Jordan Thompson; 14 Iafeta Palea'aesina.
Tries: Washbrook (36), Thompson (54), Fonua (72);
Goals: Sneyd 3/4.
Sin bin: Talanoa (14) - professional foul.
Rugby Leaguer & League Express Men of the Match: *Wildcats:* Craig Hall; *Hull FC:* Mahe Fonua.
Penalty count: 9-7; **Half-time:** 8-6;
Referee: Chris Campbell; **Attendance:** 3,413.

Friday 16th September 2016

WARRINGTON WOLVES 28 WIGAN WARRIORS 35

WOLVES: 6 Stefan Ratchford; 5 Matthew Russell; 24 Toby King; 4 Ryan Atkins; 3 Rhys Evans; 1 Kurt Gidley; 26 Declan Patton; 8 Chris Hill (C); 9 Daryl Clark; 10 Ashton Sims; 11 Ben Currie; 12 Jack Hughes; 14 Joe Westerman. Subs (all used): 27 Sam Wilde; 18 George King; 25 Joe Philbin; 16 Brad Dwyer.
Tries: Russell (24), Gidley (33), Hill (36), Westerman (46), Currie (50); **Goals:** Patton 4/5.
Sin bin: Ratchford (30) - late challenge on Tierney.
WARRIORS: 1 Sam Tomkins (C); 2 Josh Charnley; 3 Anthony Gelling; 4 Dan Sarginson; 22 Lewis Tierney; 6 George Williams; 7 Matty Smith; 24 Frank-Paul Nuuausala; 16 Sam Powell; 10 Ben Flower; 14 John Bateman; 12 Liam Farrell; 25 Willie Isa. Subs (all used): 8 Dominic Crosby; 19 Taulima Tautai; 21 Ryan Sutton; 28 Jake Shorrocks.
Tries: Tierney (2, 72), S Tomkins (40), Charnley (60, 64), Gelling (78); **Goals:** Smith 3/5, Shorrocks 2/3;
Field goal: Smith (76).
Dismissal: Flower (57) - late, high challenge on Patton.
Rugby Leaguer & League Express Men of the Match: *Wolves:* Daryl Clark; *Warriors:* Sam Tomkins.
Penalty count: 12-12; **Half-time:** 16-14;
Referee: Robert Hicks; **Attendance:** 13,044.

Saturday 17th September 2016

CATALANS DRAGONS 28 CASTLEFORD TIGERS 34

DRAGONS: 1 Tony Gigot; 2 Jodie Broughton; 33 Benjamin Garcia; 4 Vincent Duport; 26 Jordan Sigismeau; 11 Glenn Stewart; 7 Richard Myler; 19 Olivier Elima; 9 Paul Aiton; 10 Remi Casty (C); 8 Louis Anderson; 12 Justin Horo; 17 Gregory Mounis. Subs (all used): 14 Dave Taylor; 15 Julian Bousquet; 16 Eloi Pelissier; 35 Paul Seguier.
Tries: Elima (18), Stewart (36), Pelissier (65), Anderson (68), Myler (76); **Goals:** Gigot 4/5.
Sin bin: Garcia (61) - punching Webster.
TIGERS: 1 Luke Dorn; 34 Paddy Flynn; 24 Greg Minikin; 3 Jake Webster; 5 Denny Solomona; 18 Ryan Hampshire; 7 Luke Gale (C); 32 Larne Patrick; 15 Paul McShane; 16 Matt Cook; 36 Andre Savelio; 11 Oliver Holmes; 9 Adam Milner. Subs: 12 Mike McMeeken; 19 Ben Crooks; 23 Will Maher; 37 Brandon Douglas (not used).

Tries: Flynn (13, 54), Solomona (20, 23), Crooks (31, 43);
Goals: Gale 5/6.
Rugby Leaguer & League Express Men of the Match:
Dragons: Tony Gigot; *Tigers:* Luke Gale.
Penalty count: 10-7; **Half-time:** 10-24;
Referee: Phil Bentham; **Attendance:** 7,802.

Sunday 18th September 2016

WIDNES VIKINGS 8 ST HELENS 21

VIKINGS: 1 Rhys Hanbury; 2 Corey Thompson; 14 Chris
Dean; 4 Charly Runciman; 5 Patrick Ah Van; 7 Joe Mellor;
6 Kevin Brown (C); 37 Greg Burke; 9 Lloyd White; 36 Jack
Buchanan; 22 Matt Whitley; 11 Chris Houston; 19 Macgraff
Leuluai. Subs (all used): 24 Jay Chapelhow; 10 Manase
Manuokafoa; 33 Aaron Heremaia; 32 Connor Farrell.
Tries: Ah Van (37), Thompson (62);
Goals: White 0/1, Thompson 0/1.
Dismissals: Brown (78) - fighting; Ah Van (78) - fighting.
SAINTS: 23 Shannon McDonnell; 22 Jack Owens; 18
Dominique Peyroux; 24 Matty Fleming; 5 Adam Swift; 3
Jordan Turner; 7 Luke Walsh; 10 Kyle Amor; 9 James Roby; 15
Greg Richards; 12 Jon Wilkin (C); 20 Joe Greenwood; 13 Louie
McCarthy-Scarsbrook. Subs (all used): 8 Alex Walmsley; 11
Atelea Vea; 17 Luke Thompson; 28 Morgan Knowles.
Tries: Swift (3, 9), Fleming (52), Vea (79);
Goals: Walsh 2/5; **Field goal:** Walsh (75).
Sin bin: Greenwood (78) - fighting.
Rugby Leaguer & League Express Men of the Match:
Vikings: Chris Houston; *Saints:* Kyle Amor.
Penalty count: 6-10; **Half-time:** 4-12;
Referee: James Child; **Attendance:** 6,128.

ROUND 7

Friday 23rd September 2016

HULL FC 6 WARRINGTON WOLVES 23

HULL FC: 1 Jamie Shaul; 19 Steve Michaels; 2 Mahe Fonua;
24 Kirk Yeaman; 5 Fetuli Talanoa; 3 Carlos Tuimavave;
7 Marc Sneyd; 8 Scott Taylor; 9 Danny Houghton; 10
Liam Watts; 12 Mark Minichiello; 21 Sika Manu; 11 Gareth
Ellis (C). Subs (all used): 16 Jordan Thompson; 23 Frank
Pritchard; 22 Josh Bowden; 17 Dean Hadley.
Try: Tuimavave (43); **Goals:** Sneyd 1/1.
WOLVES: 5 Matthew Russell; 2 Tom Lineham; 3
Rhys Evans; 4 Ryan Atkins; 20 Kevin Penny; 6 Stefan
Ratchford; 26 Declan Patton; 8 Chris Hill (C); 9 Daryl
Clark; 10 Ashton Sims; 27 Sam Wilde; 12 Jack Hughes; 14
Joe Westerman. Subs (all used): 18 George King; 24 Toby
King; 25 Joe Philbin; 31 Morgan Smith.
Tries: Lineham (6, 75), Penny (13); **Goals:** Patton 5/7;
Field goal: Patton (78).
Rugby Leaguer & League Express Men of the Match:
Hull FC: Gareth Ellis; *Wolves:* Chris Hill.
Penalty count: 0-10; **Half-time:** 0-10;
Referee: Ben Thaler; **Attendance:** 17,453.

ST HELENS 32 WAKEFIELD TRINITY WILDCATS 12

SAINTS: 1 Jonny Lomax; 23 Shannon McDonnell; 4 Mark
Percival; 18 Dominique Peyroux; 22 Jack Owens; 3 Jordan
Turner; 7 Luke Walsh; 11 Atelea Vea; 28 Morgan Knowles;
10 Kyle Amor; 13 Louie McCarthy-Scarsbrook; 20 Joe
Greenwood; 12 Jon Wilkin (C); 19 Theo Fages; 26 Olly Davies.
Subs (all used): 8 Alex
Walmsley; 12 Jon Wilkin (C); 19 Theo Fages; 26 Olly Davies.
Tries: McCarthy-Scarsbrook (21), Owens (39),
McDonnell (48, 65, 71), Fages (70); **Goals:** Walsh 4/6.
WILDCATS: 21 Max Jowitt; 2 Tom Johnstone; 14 Reece
Lyne; 18 Joe Arundel; 3 Bill Tupou; 25 Craig Hall; 7 Liam
Finn (C); 11 Mickael Simon; 20 Michael Sio; 35 David Fifita;
19 Jon Molloy; 17 Matty Ashurst; 13 Anthony Tupou. Subs
(all used): 16 Tinirau Arona; 22 Jordan Crowther; 28 Andy
Yates; 31 Jason Walton.
Tries: Hall (28), Johnstone (58); **Goals:** Finn 2/3.
Rugby Leaguer & League Express Men of the Match:
Saints: Jordan Turner; *Wildcats:* Tinirau Arona.
Penalty count: 6-8; **Half-time:** 12-6;
Referee: Joe Cobb; **Attendance:** 9,516.

WIGAN WARRIORS 48 CATALANS DRAGONS 24

WARRIORS: 4 Dan Sarginson; 2 Josh Charnley; 3 Anthony
Gelling; 20 Oliver Gildart; 22 Lewis Tierney; 6 George
Williams; 7 Matty Smith (C); 24 Frank-Paul Nuuausala; 16
Sam Powell; 21 Ryan Sutton; 14 John Bateman; 12 Liam
Farrell; 8 Dominic Crosby. Subs (all used): 19 Taulima
Tautai; 25 Willie Isa; 28 Jake Shorrocks; 29 Joe Bretherton.
Tries: Gelling (12, 22), Bateman (21),
Bretherton (30), Charnley (33), Smith (43, 54);
Goals: Smith 8/8.
DRAGONS: 1 Tony Gigot; 2 Jodie Broughton; 33 Benjamin
Garcia; 4 Vincent Duport; 26 Jordan Sigismeau; 27 Lucas
Albert; 7 Richard Myler; 15 Julian Bousquet; 9 Paul Aiton;

10 Remi Casty (C); 11 Glenn Stewart; 12 Justin Horo; 8
Louis Anderson. Subs (all used): 14 Dave Taylor; 28 Alrix
Da Costa; 30 Romain Navarrete; 35 Paul Seguier.
Tries: Duport (40), Horo (49), Albert (62), Myler (69),
Sigismeau (77); **Goals:** Gigot 0/1, Myler 2/4.
Sin bin: Horo (73) - professional foul.
Rugby Leaguer & League Express Men of the Match:
Warriors: Matty Smith; *Dragons:* Glenn Stewart.
Penalty count: 11-8; **Half-time:** 36-4;
Referee: Phil Bentham; **Attendance:** 16,140.

Sunday 25th September 2016

CASTLEFORD TIGERS 40 WIDNES VIKINGS 26

TIGERS: 1 Luke Dorn (C); 34 Paddy Flynn; 24 Greg
Minikin; 3 Jake Webster; 5 Denny Solomona; 36 Ryan
Hampshire; 7 Luke Gale; 16 Matt Cook; 15 Paul McShane;
22 Gadwin Springer; 11 Oliver Holmes; 36 Andre Savelio;
9 Adam Milner. Subs (all used): 35 Rangi Chase; 19 Ben
Crooks; 12 Mike McMeeken; 23 Will Maher.
Tries: Dorn (11), Solomona (21, 37, 51), Crooks (47),
Cook (57), McShane (61); **Goals:** Gale 6/7.
Sin bin: McShane (30) - holding down.
VIKINGS: 1 Rhys Hanbury; 2 Corey Thompson; 14 Chris
Dean; 4 Charly Runciman; 5 Patrick Ah Van; 7 Joe Mellor
(C); 21 Tom Gilmore; 24 Jay Chapelhow; 9 Lloyd White;
18 Gil Dudson; 22 Matt Whitley; 32 Connor Farrell; 13 Hep
Cahill. Subs (all used): 23 Ted Chapelhow (D); 19 Macgraff
Leuluai; 33 Aaron Heremaia; 10 Manase Manuokafoa.
Tries: Farrell (11, 76), Thompson (43, 79), Ah Van (72);
Goals: White 3/5.
Sin bin: Farrell (61) - holding down.
Rugby Leaguer & League Express Men of the Match:
Tigers: Denny Solomona; *Vikings:* Lloyd White.
Penalty count: 10-7; **Half-time:** 16-6;
Referee: Jack Smith; **Attendance:** 7,103.

SEMI-FINALS

Thursday 29th September 2016

WARRINGTON WOLVES 18 ST HELENS 10

WOLVES: 6 Stefan Ratchford; 2 Tom Lineham; 3 Rhys
Evans; 4 Ryan Atkins; 5 Matthew Russell; 1 Kurt Gidley; 26
Declan Patton; 8 Chris Hill (C); 9 Daryl Clark; 10 Ashton
Sims; 27 Sam Wilde; 12 Jack Hughes; 14 Joe Westerman.
Subs (all used): 24 Toby King; 18 George King; 25 Joe
Philbin; 31 Morgan Smith.
Tries: Gidley (30), Ratchford (51), Lineham (64);
Goals: Patton 3/4.
SAINTS: 1 Jonny Lomax; 22 Jack Owens; 18 Dominique
Peyroux; 4 Mark Percival; 5 Adam Swift; 3 Jordan Turner; 7
Luke Walsh; 10 Kyle Amor; 9 James Roby; 15 Greg Richards;
20 Joe Greenwood; 13 Louie McCarthy-Scarsbrook; 12 Jon
Wilkin (C). Subs (all used): 8 Alex Walmsley; 11 Atelea Vea;
17 Luke Thompson; 28 Morgan Knowles.

Warrington's Chris Hill halted by St Helens' Joe Greenwood and Kyle Amor

Try: Lomax (38); **Goals:** Walsh 3/3.
Rugby Leaguer & League Express Men of the Match:
Wolves: Stefan Ratchford; *Saints:* Jonny Lomax.
Penalty count: 7-4; **Half-time:** 8-10;
Referee: Ben Thaler; **Attendance:** 12,036.

Friday 30th September 2016

WIGAN WARRIORS 28 HULL FC 18

WARRIORS: 4 Dan Sarginson; 2 Josh Charnley; 3 Anthony
Gelling; 20 Oliver Gildart; 22 Lewis Tierney; 6 George
Williams; 7 Matty Smith (C); 8 Dominic Crosby; 16 Sam
Powell; 24 Frank-Paul Nuuausala; 14 John Bateman; 12 Liam
Farrell; 25 Willie Isa. Subs (all used): 19 Taulima Tautai; 21
Ryan Sutton; 28 Jake Shorrocks; 29 Joe Bretherton.
Tries: Tierney (8, 15), Bateman (39), Powell (72),
Gelling (78); **Goals:** Smith 4/6.
HULL FC: 1 Jamie Shaul; 19 Steve Michaels; 2 Mahe Fonua;
24 Kirk Yeaman; 5 Fetuli Talanoa; 3 Carlos Tuimavave;
7 Marc Sneyd; 8 Scott Taylor; 9 Danny Houghton (C); 10
Liam Watts; 12 Mark Minichiello; 23 Frank Pritchard; 30
Danny Washbrook. Subs (all used): 15 Chris Green; 16
Jordan Thompson; 22 Josh Bowden; 13 Jordan Abdull.
Tries: Bowden (46), Watts (50), Michaels (63);
Goals: Sneyd 3/3.
Rugby Leaguer & League Express Men of the Match:
Warriors: John Bateman; *Hull FC:* Danny Houghton.
Penalty count: 5-4; **Half-time:** 14-0;
Referee: Robert Hicks; **Attendance:** 10,013.

GRAND FINAL

Saturday 8th October 2016

WARRINGTON WOLVES 6 WIGAN WARRIORS 12

WOLVES: 6 Stefan Ratchford; 2 Tom Lineham; 3 Rhys
Evans; 4 Ryan Atkins; 5 Matthew Russell; 1 Kurt Gidley; 26
Declan Patton; 8 Chris Hill (C); 9 Daryl Clark; 10 Ashton
Sims; 27 Sam Wilde; 12 Jack Hughes; 14 Joe Westerman.
Subs (all used): 24 Toby King; 18 George King; 7 Chris
Sandow; 33 Ryan Bailey.
Try: Patton (21); **Goals:** Patton 1/1.
WARRIORS: 4 Dan Sarginson; 2 Josh Charnley; 3 Anthony
Gelling; 20 Oliver Gildart; 22 Lewis Tierney; 6 George
Williams; 7 Matty Smith; 24 Frank-Paul Nuuausala; 16
Sam Powell; 10 Ben Flower; 14 John Bateman; 12 Liam
Farrell; 25 Willie Isa. Subs (all used): 8 Dominic Crosby;
19 Taulima Tautai; 21 Ryan Sutton; 13 Sean O'Loughlin (C).
Tries: Gildart (55), Charnley (63); **Goals:** Smith 2/4.
Rugby Leaguer & League Express Men of the Match:
Wolves: Kurt Gidley; *Warriors:* Liam Farrell.
Penalty count: 4-6; **Half-time:** 6-2;
Referee: Robert Hicks; **Attendance:** 70,202.
(at Old Trafford, Manchester).

Harry Sunderland Trophy winner Liam Farrell takes on Kurt Gidley during the Super League Grand Final

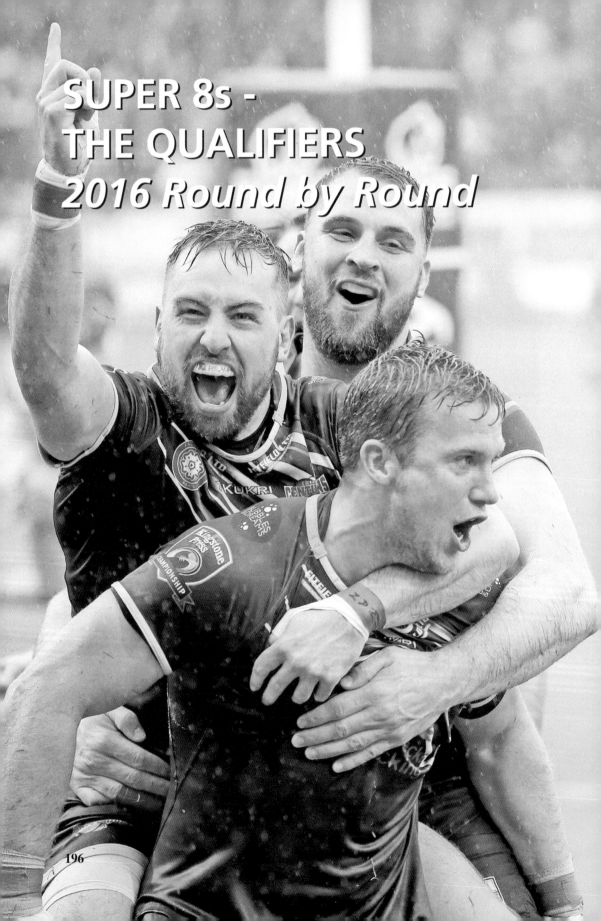

SUPER 8s -
THE QUALIFIERS
2016 Round by Round

ROUND 1

Saturday 6th August 2016

FEATHERSTONE ROVERS 6 LEEDS RHINOS 62

ROVERS: 15 Ian Hardman; 33 James Duckworth; 3 Michael Channing; 4 Misi Taulapapa; 29 Luke Briscoe; 6 Kyle Briggs; 7 Anthony Thackeray; 10 Andrew Bostock; 23 Andy Ellis; 32 Jordan Baldwinson; 11 Steve Snitch; 12 John Davies; 17 Jack Ormondroyd. Subs (all used): 13 Tim Spears; 21 Bradley Knowles-Tagg; 20 Luke Cooper; 8 Darrell Griffin.
Try: Thackeray (28); **Goals:** Briggs 1/1.
RHINOS: 14 Liam Sutcliffe; 2 Tom Briscoe; 3 Kallum Watkins; 4 Joel Moon; 5 Ryan Hall; 6 Danny McGuire (C); 7 Rob Burrow; 8 Keith Galloway; 30 James Segeyaro; 16 Brad Singleton; 26 Brett Ferres; 12 Carl Ablett; 11 Jamie Jones-Buchanan. Subs (all used): 15 Brett Delaney; 17 Mitch Garbutt; 18 Jimmy Keinhorst; 19 Mitch Achurch.
Tries: Watkins (6, 45, 73, 78), Sutcliffe (14, 60), Moon (33, 68), Achurch (48), Ablett (55), T Briscoe (58);
Goals: Sutcliffe 9/12.
Sin bin: Keinhorst (66) - holding down.
Rugby Leaguer & League Express Men of the Match:
Rovers: Bradley Knowles-Tagg; *Rhinos:* Kallum Watkins.
Penalty count: 6-7; **Half-time:** 6-18;
Referee: Joe Cobb; **Attendance:** 6,671.

LEIGH CENTURIONS 34 LONDON BRONCOS 30

CENTURIONS: 1 Gregg McNally; 2 Adam Higson; 41 Mitch Brown; 3 Greg Worthington; 40 Matty Dawson; 6 Martyn Ridyard; 36 Josh Drinkwater; 8 Fuifui Moimoi; 14 Micky Higham; 10 Dayne Weston; 16 Reni Maitua; 13 Cory Paterson; 12 Gareth Hock. Subs (all used): 11 Harrison Hansen; 17 Jamie Acton; 31 Ben Reynolds; 39 Danny Tickle.
Tries: Dawson (22, 68), Brown (37, 62), Maitua (47);
Goals: Ridyard 7/7.
Dismissal: Worthington (72) - fighting.
Sin bin: Paterson (32) - high tackle.
BRONCOS: 24 Alex Walker; 2 Rhys Williams; 1 Ben Hellewell; 32 Elliot Kear; 5 Iliess Macani; 26 Api Pewhairangi; 33 Jamie Soward; 8 Nick Slyney; 14 Andy Ackers; 16 Mark Ioane; 11 Daniel Harrison; 12 Matt Garside; 15 Jack Bussey. Subs (all used): 9 James Cunningham; 10 Eddie Battye; 18 Jamie Thackray; 23 Jon Magrin.
Tries: Hellewell (25), Pewhairangi (72, 75), Ackers (77), Harrison (79); **Goals:** Soward 2/2, Pewhairangi 3/4.
Dismissal: Soward (72) - fighting.
Rugby Leaguer & League Express Men of the Match:
Centurions: Josh Drinkwater; *Broncos:* Jack Bussey.
Penalty count: 10-9; **Half-time:** 14-8;
Referee: Ben Thaler; **Attendance:** 4,041.

Sunday 7th August 2016

HULL KINGSTON ROVERS 58 BATLEY BULLDOGS 18

ROVERS: 18 Ben Cockayne; 1 Ken Sio; 21 Thomas Minns; 4 Iain Thornley; 2 Josh Mantellato; 22 Matthew Marsh; 7 Albert Kelly; 8 Adam Walker; 9 Shaun Lunt; 17 Dane Tilse; 11 Maurice Blair; 20 James Greenwood; 13 Chris Clarkson (C). Subs (all used): 14 Kevin Larroyer; 10 Mitchell Allgood; 15 James Donaldson; 33 David Thompson.
Tries: Thornley (6), Minns (9, 18, 38), Marsh (22), Greenwood (25, 55), Cockayne (51), Blair (59), Mantellato (74); **Goals:** Mantellato 9/10.
BULLDOGS: 22 Dave Scott; 2 Wayne Reittie; 4 Shaun Squires; 3 Chris Ulugia; 5 Shaun Ainscough; 13 Pat Walker; 7 Dominic Brambani; 10 Alex Rowe; 20 Alistair Leak; 15 Adam Gledhill; 11 Brad Day; 19 Alex Bretherton; 17 Joe Chandler. Subs (all used): 14 James Davey; 18 Tom Lillycrop; 21 James Brown; 31 Sam Smeaton.
Tries: Leak (3), Lillycrop (40), Rowe (80);
Goals: Walker 1/1, Brambani 2/2.
Rugby Leaguer & League Express Men of the Match:
Rovers: Albert Kelly; *Bulldogs:* Alistair Leak.
Penalty count: 8-6; **Half-time:** 36-12;
Referee: Gareth Hewer; **Attendance:** 6,684.

SALFORD RED DEVILS 34 HUDDERSFIELD GIANTS 12

RED DEVILS: 14 Gareth O'Brien; 2 Justin Carney; 3 Josh Griffin; 4 Junior Sa'u; 24 Mason Caton-Brown; 6 Robert Lui; 7 Michael Dobson (C); 8 Craig Kopczak; 19 Logan Tomkins; 10 George Griffin; 11 Ben Murdoch-Masila; 36 Feleti Mateo (D); 13 Mark Flanagan. Subs (all used): 12 Weller Hauraki; 16 Olsi Krasniqi; 34 Sean Kenny; 35 Luke Burgess (D).
Tries: G Griffin (6), Caton-Brown (11, 61, 73), Hauraki (38), Murdoch-Masila (52); **Goals:** O'Brien 5/7.
GIANTS: 1 Scott Grix; 35 Gene Ormsby; 3 Leroy Cudjoe; 18 Jake Connor; 5 Aaron Murphy; 6 Danny Brough; 7 Jamie Ellis; 16 Sam Rapira; 9 Ryan Hinchcliffe (C); 10 Craig Huby; 17 Ukuma Ta'ai; 12 Michael Lawrence; 36 Sebastine Ikahihifo. Subs (all used): 15 Kyle Wood; 22 Oliver Roberts; 8 Eorl Crabtree; 21 Nathan Mason.
Tries: Mason (53), Roberts (58); **Goals:** Brough 2/2.
Rugby Leaguer & League Express Men of the Match:
Red Devils: Mason Caton-Brown; *Giants:* Nathan Mason.
Penalty count: 10-10; **Half-time:** 20-0;
Referee: James Child; **Attendance:** 2,184.

ROUND 2

Friday 12th August 2016

LEEDS RHINOS 22 HULL KINGSTON ROVERS 18

RHINOS: 14 Liam Sutcliffe; 2 Tom Briscoe; 3 Kallum Watkins; 4 Joel Moon; 5 Ryan Hall; 6 Danny McGuire (C); 7 Rob Burrow; 8 Keith Galloway; 30 James Segeyaro; 16 Brad Singleton; 26 Brett Ferres; 12 Carl Ablett; 11 Jamie Jones-Buchanan. Subs (all used): 17 Mitch Garbutt; 19 Mitch Achurch; 10 Adam Cuthbertson; 18 Jimmy Keinhorst.
Tries: Watkins (26), Segeyaro (66, 76); **Goals:** Sutcliffe 5/5.
ROVERS: 18 Ben Cockayne; 1 Ken Sio; 21 Thomas Minns; 4 Iain Thornley; 2 Josh Mantellato; 11 Maurice Blair; 7 Albert Kelly; 17 Dane Tilse; 9 Shaun Lunt; 10 Mitchell Allgood; 20 James Greenwood; 13 Chris Clarkson (C); 15 James Donaldson. Subs: 8 Adam Walker; 14 Kevin Larroyer; 24 George Lawler; 33 David Thompson (not used).
Tries: Greenwood (43), Donaldson (73), Lawler (79);
Goals: Mantellato 3/3, Cockayne 0/1.
Rugby Leaguer & League Express Men of the Match:
Rhinos: James Segeyaro; *Rovers:* James Greenwood.
Penalty count: 5-12; **Half time:** 8-0;
Referee: Phil Bentham; **Attendance:** 14,180.

Saturday 13th August 2016

LEIGH CENTURIONS 32 SALFORD RED DEVILS 26

CENTURIONS: 1 Gregg McNally; 2 Adam Higson; 41 Mitch Brown; 4 Willie Tonga; 40 Matty Dawson; 6 Martyn Ridyard; 36 Josh Drinkwater; 20 Sam Hopkins; 14 Micky Higham; 10 Dayne Weston; 16 Reni Maitua; 13 Cory Paterson; 12 Gareth Hock. Subs (all used): 17 Jamie Acton; 32 Liam Hood; 39 Danny Tickle; 11 Harrison Hansen.
Tries: Maitua (7), Paterson (12), McNally (22), Higson (74), Dawson (76); **Goals:** Ridyard 6/7.
RED DEVILS: 14 Gareth O'Brien; 1 Niall Evalds; 4 Junior Sa'u; 3 Josh Griffin; 24 Mason Caton-Brown; 6 Robert Lui; 7 Michael Dobson (C); 8 Craig Kopczak; 19 Logan Tomkins; 10 George Griffin; 11 Ben Murdoch-Masila; 36 Feleti Mateo; 13 Mark Flanagan. Subs (all used): 12 Weller Hauraki; 35 Luke Burgess; 16 Olsi Krasniqi; 34 Sean Kenny.
Tries: Caton-Brown (15, 79), Evalds (31), Lui (55), Murdoch-Masila (77); **Goals:** O'Brien 3/5.
Rugby Leaguer & League Express Men of the Match:
Centurions: Adam Higson; *Red Devils:* Robert Lui.
Penalty count: 8-10; **Half-time:** 20-10;
Referee: Chris Campbell; **Attendance:** 4,547.

Sunday 14th August 2016

HUDDERSFIELD GIANTS 62 FEATHERSTONE ROVERS 16

GIANTS: 18 Jake Connor; 5 Aaron Murphy; 3 Leroy Cudjoe; 4 Joe Wardle; 35 Gene Ormsby; 34 Ryan Brierley; 7 Jamie Ellis; 8 Eorl Crabtree; 9 Ryan Hinchcliffe (C); 10 Craig Huby; 17 Ukuma Ta'ai; 12 Michael Lawrence; 36 Sebastine Ikahihifo. Subs (all used): 15 Kyle Wood; 16 Sam Rapira; 21 Nathan Mason; 22 Oliver Roberts.
Tries: Lawrence (13), Roberts (18, 38), Ormsby (31), Brierley (36, 70), Ta'ai (47, 74), K Wood (50, 64), Hinchcliffe (76); **Goals:** Ellis 9/11.
ROVERS: 15 Ian Hardman; 33 James Duckworth; 21 Bradley Knowles-Tagg; 4 Misi Taulapapa; 29 Luke Briscoe; 6 Kyle Briggs; 1 Danny Craven; 32 Jordan Baldwinson; 7 Anthony Thackeray; 10 Andrew Bostock; 11 Steve Snitch; 12 John Davies; 39 Josh Walters. Subs (all used): 23 Andy Ellis; 8 Darrell Griffin; 20 Luke Cooper; 17 Jack Ormondroyd.
Tries: Davies (24), Briscoe (60), Hardman (68);
Goals: Briggs 2/3.
Sin bin: Davies (65) - dissent.
Rugby Leaguer & League Express Men of the Match:
Giants: Kyle Wood; *Rovers:* Ian Hardman.
Penalty count: 8-6; **Half-time:** 28-6;
Referee: Gareth Hewer; **Attendance:** 3,690.

LONDON BRONCOS 76 BATLEY BULLDOGS 16

BRONCOS: 24 Alex Walker; 2 Rhys Williams; 1 Ben Hellewell; 21 Alex Foster; 5 Iliess Macani; 26 Api Pewhairangi; 33 Jamie Soward; 8 Nick Slyney; 9 James Cunningham; 16 Mark Ioane; 11 Daniel Harrison; 12 Matt Garside; 15 Jack Bussey. Subs (all used): 14 Andy Ackers; 18 Jamie Thackray; 10 Eddie Battye; 34 Lewis Bienek.
Tries: Soward (4), Harrison (8), Macani (10, 27, 44), Ackers (24), Cunningham (35, 72), Garside (42), Williams (54, 60, 74), Bussey (64), Ioane (77);
Goals: Soward 10/14.
BULLDOGS: 22 Dave Scott; 2 Wayne Reittie; 31 Sam Smeaton; 3 Chris Ulugia; 26 Alex Brown; 6 Cain Southernwood; 7 Dominic Brambani; 8 Keegan Hirst; 20 Alistair Leak; 10 Alex Rowe; 11 Brad Day; 19 Alex Bretherton; 15 Adam Gledhill. Subs (all used): 14 James Davey; 17 Joe Chandler; 18 Tom Lillycrop; 21 James Brown.
Tries: J Brown (48), Rowe (51), Ulugia (70);
Goals: Brambani 2/3.
Sin bin: Lillycrop (57) - punching.
Rugby Leaguer & League Express Men of the Match:
Broncos: Mark Ioane; *Bulldogs:* Alex Rowe.
Penalty count: 8-5; **Half-time:** 32-0;
Referee: Chris Kendall; **Attendance:** 674.

ROUND 3

Friday 19th August 2016

SALFORD RED DEVILS 12 HULL KINGSTON ROVERS 29

RED DEVILS: 14 Gareth O'Brien; 18 Greg Johnson; 3 Josh Griffin; 4 Junior Sa'u; 24 Mason Caton-Brown; 6 Robert Lui; 7 Michael Dobson (C); 35 Luke Burgess; 19 Logan Tomkins; 10 George Griffin; 11 Ben Murdoch-Masila; 33 Josh Jones; 13 Mark Flanagan. Subs (all used): 12 Weller Hauraki; 36 Feleti Mateo; 34 Sean Kenny; 8 Craig Kopczak.
Tries: Caton-Brown (20), O'Brien (51); **Goals:** O'Brien 2/3.
ROVERS: 18 Ben Cockayne; 1 Ken Sio; 21 Thomas Minns; 4 Iain Thornley; 2 Josh Mantellato; 22 Matthew Marsh; 7 Albert Kelly; 17 Dane Tilse; 9 Shaun Lunt; 10 Mitchell Allgood; 11 Maurice Blair; 20 James Greenwood; 13 Chris Clarkson (C). Subs (all used): 8 Adam Walker; 24 George Lawler; 15 James Donaldson; 14 Kevin Larroyer.
Tries: Mantellato (3), Greenwood (12), Sio (28), Minns (76);
Goals: Mantellato 6/6; **Field goal:** Kelly (67).
Rugby Leaguer & League Express Men of the Match:
Red Devils: Luke Burgess; *Rovers:* Ben Cockayne.
Penalty count: 7-5; **Half-time:** 6-22;
Referee: Robert Hicks; **Attendance:** 2,074.

Saturday 20th August 2016

LONDON BRONCOS 28 LEEDS RHINOS 42

BRONCOS: 24 Alex Walker; 2 Rhys Williams; 1 Ben Hellewell; 32 Elliot Kear; 5 Iliess Macani; 33 Jamie Soward; 7 William Barthau; 8 Nick Slyney; 9 James Cunningham; 16 Mark Ioane; 11 Daniel Harrison; 12 Matt Garside; 15 Jack Bussey. Subs (all used): 10 Eddie Battye; 14 Andy Ackers; 18 Jamie Thackray; 17 Mark Offerdahl.
Tries: Williams (5), Cunningham (21), Slyney (59), Macani (76), Kear (78); **Goals:** Soward 4/5.
RHINOS: 14 Liam Sutcliffe; 2 Tom Briscoe; 3 Kallum Watkins; 18 Jimmy Keinhorst; 5 Ryan Hall; 6 Danny McGuire (C); 4 Joel Moon; 8 Keith Galloway; 30 James Segeyaro; 17 Mitch Garbutt; 26 Brett Ferres; 12 Carl Ablett; 11 Jamie Jones-Buchanan. Subs (all used): 25 Jordan Lilley; 19 Mitch Achurch; 20 Anthony Mullally; 10 Adam Cuthbertson.
Tries: T Briscoe (12, 25, 63), Sutcliffe (14), Segeyaro (37), Lilley (46), Achurch (50), Watkins (52);
Goals: Sutcliffe 5/8.
Rugby Leaguer & League Express Men of the Match:
Broncos: Eddie Battye; *Rhinos:* Liam Sutcliffe.
Penalty count: 5-3; **Half-time:** 12-20;
Referee: Chris Campbell; **Attendance:** 1,845.

Sunday 21st August 2016

BATLEY BULLDOGS 28 HUDDERSFIELD GIANTS 58

BULLDOGS: 22 Dave Scott; 2 Wayne Reittie; 4 Shaun Squires; 3 Chris Ulugia; 26 Alex Brown; 13 Pat Walker; 7 Dominic Brambani; 8 Keegan Hirst; 20 Alistair Leak; 10 Alex Rowe; 11 Brad Day; 19 Alex Bretherton; 21 James Brown. Subs (all used): 14 James Davey; 18 Tom Lillycrop; 15 Adam Gledhill; 24 James Harrison.
Tries: Squires (55, 71), D Scott (57, 79), Ulugia (77);
Goals: Brambani 4/6.
GIANTS: 18 Jake Connor; 5 Aaron Murphy; 3 Leroy Cudjoe; 4 Joe Wardle; 35 Gene Ormsby; 34 Ryan Brierley; 7 Jamie Ellis; 8 Eorl Crabtree; 9 Ryan Hinchcliffe (C); 10 Craig Huby; 11 Tom Symonds; 12 Michael Lawrence; 17 Ukuma Ta'ai. Subs (all used): 15 Kyle Wood; 22 Oliver Roberts; 36 Sebastine Ikahihifo; 16 Sam Rapira.
Tries: Cudjoe (6, 60), Ormsby (10), Crabtree (17), Symonds (20, 28), Connor (24), Wardle (31), Brierley (33, 37, 70); **Goals:** Ellis 7/11.
Rugby Leaguer & League Express Men of the Match:
Bulldogs: Dominic Brambani; *Giants:* Jake Connor.
Penalty count: 7-3; **Half-time:** 2-48;
Referee: James Child; **Attendance:** 2,201.

Super 8s - The Qualifiers - 2016 Round by Round

FEATHERSTONE ROVERS 18 LEIGH CENTURIONS 30

ROVERS: 1 Danny Craven; 33 James Duckworth; 15 Ian Hardman; 4 Misi Taulapapa; 29 Luke Briscoe; 6 Kyle Briggs; 7 Anthony Thackeray; 8 Darrell Griffin; 23 Andy Ellis; 32 Jordan Baldwinson; 21 Bradley Knowles-Tagg; 39 Josh Walters; 13 Tim Spears. Subs (all used): 19 Sam Day; 11 Steve Snitch; 20 Luke Cooper; 17 Jack Ormondroyd.
Tries: Walters (13), Briscoe (68), Ormondroyd (70);
Goals: Briggs 3/4.
CENTURIONS: 1 Gregg McNally; 2 Adam Higson; 41 Mitch Brown; 24 Tom Armstrong; 40 Matty Dawson; 6 Martyn Ridyard; 36 Josh Drinkwater; 8 Fuifui Moimoi; 14 Micky Higham; 10 Dayne Weston; 16 Reni Maitua; 13 Cory Paterson; 12 Gareth Hock. Subs (all used): 32 Liam Hood; 39 Danny Tickle; 11 Harrison Hansen; 20 Sam Hopkins.
Tries: Maitua (4), Brown (7), Dawson (54), Higham (60), Hock (79); **Goals:** Ridyard 5/6.
Rugby Leaguer & League Express Men of the Match: *Rovers:* Kyle Briggs; *Centurions:* Micky Higham.
Penalty count: 9-8; **Half-time:** 8-12;
Referee: Jack Smith; **Attendance:** 3,644.

ROUND 4

Friday 2nd September 2016

HUDDERSFIELD GIANTS 40 LONDON BRONCOS 4

GIANTS: 18 Jake Connor; 2 Jermaine McGillvary; 3 Leroy Cudjoe; 4 Joe Wardle; 5 Aaron Murphy; 6 Danny Brough; 7 Jamie Ellis; 8 Eorl Crabtree; 9 Ryan Hinchcliffe (C); 10 Craig Huby; 11 Tom Symonds; 12 Michael Lawrence; 17 Ukuma Ta'ai. Subs (all used): 20 Kruise Leeming; 21 Nathan Mason; 22 Oliver Roberts; 36 Sebastine Ikahihifo.
Tries: McGillvary (23), Cudjoe (33, 50), Wardle (42), Lawrence (53), Brough (66), Murphy (75);
Goals: Brough 6/7.
BRONCOS: 24 Alex Walker; 2 Rhys Williams; 1 Ben Hellewell; 32 Elliot Kear; 5 Iliess Macani; 7 William Barthau; 20 Scott Leatherbarrow; 8 Nick Slyney; 9 James Cunningham; 16 Mark Ioane; 11 Daniel Harrison; 12 Matt Garside; 18 Jamie Thackray. Subs (all used): 14 Andy Ackers; 17 Mark Offerdahl; 10 Eddie Battye; 23 Jon Magrin.
Try: Williams (19); **Goals:** Leatherbarrow 0/1.
Rugby Leaguer & League Express Men of the Match: *Giants:* Danny Brough; *Broncos:* William Barthau.
Penalty count: 5-9; **Half-time:** 10-4;
Referee: James Child; **Attendance:** 3,794.

LEEDS RHINOS 30 SALFORD RED DEVILS 8

RHINOS: 14 Liam Sutcliffe; 2 Tom Briscoe; 3 Kallum Watkins; 18 Jimmy Keinhorst; 5 Ryan Hall; 4 Joel Moon; 7 Rob Burrow (C); 8 Keith Galloway; 30 James Segeyaro; 16 Brad Singleton; 26 Brett Ferres; 12 Carl Ablett; 11 Jamie Jones-Buchanan. Subs (all used): 17 Mitch Garbutt; 10 Adam Cuthbertson; 25 Jordan Lilley; 13 Stevie Ward.
Tries: Jones-Buchanan (5), Watkins (38), Segeyaro (56), Ablett (60), Cuthbertson (78);
Goals: Sutcliffe 1/2, Lilley 4/4.
RED DEVILS: 1 Niall Evalds; 3 Josh Griffin; 4 Junior Sa'u; 33 Josh Jones; 5 Daniel Vidot; 14 Gareth O'Brien; 7 Michael Dobson (C); 35 Luke Burgess; 19 Logan Tomkins; 10 George Griffin; 11 Ben Murdoch-Masila; 12 Weller Hauraki; 13 Mark Flanagan. Subs (all used): 8 Craig Kopczak; 16 Olsi Krasniqi; 6 Robert Lui; 21 Ryan Lannon.
Try: G Griffin (8); **Goals:** O'Brien 2/2.
Sin bin: O'Brien (36) - professional foul.
Rugby Leaguer & League Express Men of the Match: *Rhinos:* James Segeyaro; *Red Devils:* Luke Burgess.
Penalty count: 13-7; **Half time:** 10-8;
Referee: Ben Thaler; **Attendance:** 13,996.

Saturday 3rd September 2016

HULL KINGSTON ROVERS 18 LEIGH CENTURIONS 25

ROVERS: 18 Ben Cockayne; 1 Ken Sio; 21 Thomas Minns; 4 Iain Thornley; 2 Josh Mantellato; 22 Matthew Marsh; 11 Maurice Blair; 17 Dane Tilse; 9 Shaun Lunt; 10 Mitchell Allgood; 20 James Greenwood; 13 Chris Clarkson (C); 8 Adam Walker. Subs (all used): 14 Kevin Larroyer; 15 James Donaldson; 24 George Lawler; 26 Rob Mulhern.
Tries: Sio (6), Mantellato (11), Marsh (65);
Goals: Mantellato 3/5.
CENTURIONS: 1 Gregg McNally; 2 Adam Higson; 41 Mitch Brown; 3 Greg Worthington; 40 Matty Dawson; 6 Martyn Ridyard; 36 Josh Drinkwater; 12 Gareth Hock; 14 Micky Higham; 10 Dayne Weston; 16 Reni Maitua; 13 Cory Paterson; 39 Danny Tickle. Subs (all used): 11 Harrison Hansen; 20 Sam Hopkins; 21 Andrew Dixon; 32 Liam Hood.
Tries: Hopkins (25), Dixon (46), Dawson (49), Drinkwater (52); **Goals:** Ridyard 4/5;
Field goal: Ridyard (78).
Rugby Leaguer & League Express Men of the Match: *Rovers:* Mitchell Allgood; *Centurions:* Harrison Hansen.
Penalty count: 10-6; **Half-time:** 12-6;
Referee: Robert Hicks; **Attendance:** 7,363.

Sunday 4th September 2016

BATLEY BULLDOGS 11 FEATHERSTONE ROVERS 10

BULLDOGS: 22 Dave Scott; 2 Wayne Reittie; 4 Shaun Squires; 3 Chris Ulugia; 26 Alex Brown; 13 Pat Walker; 7 Dominic Brambani; 8 Keegan Hirst; 20 Alistair Leak; 10 Alex Rowe; 11 Brad Day; 19 Alex Bretherton; 15 Adam Gledhill. Subs (all used): 31 Sam Smeaton; 18 Tom Lillycrop; 9 Luke Blake; 21 James Brown.
Tries: Reittie (14, 69); **Goals:** Walker 1/3;
Field goal: Brambani (40).
ROVERS: 15 Ian Hardman; 33 James Duckworth; 29 Luke Briscoe; 4 Misi Taulapapa; 27 Jamie Foster; 1 Danny Craven; 7 Anthony Thackeray; 8 Darrell Griffin; 23 Andy Ellis; 32 Jordan Baldwinson; 39 Josh Walters; 13 Tim Spears; 17 Jack Ormondroyd. Subs (all used): 19 Sam Day; 21 Bradley Knowles-Tagg; 20 Luke Cooper; 11 Steve Snitch.
Tries: Briscoe (19), Duckworth (37); **Goals:** Foster 1/3.
Rugby Leaguer & League Express Men of the Match: *Bulldogs:* Alistair Leak; *Rovers:* James Duckworth.
Penalty count: 7-12; **Half-time:** 5-8;
Referee: Joe Cobb; **Attendance:** 1,131.

ROUND 5

Friday 9th September 2016

LEEDS RHINOS 32 BATLEY BULLDOGS 0

RHINOS: 14 Liam Sutcliffe; 2 Tom Briscoe; 3 Kallum Watkins; 18 Jimmy Keinhorst; 5 Ryan Hall; 25 Jordan Lilley; 7 Rob Burrow (C); 8 Keith Galloway; 30 James Segeyaro; 16 Brad Singleton; 26 Brett Ferres; 12 Carl Ablett; 11 Jamie Jones-Buchanan. Subs (all used): 10 Adam Cuthbertson; 13 Stevie Ward; 20 Anthony Mullally; 23 Ashton Golding.
Tries: T Briscoe (17), Watkins (30, 38), Hall (56, 66), Burrow (70); **Goals:** Lilley 4/6.
BULLDOGS: 22 Dave Scott; 2 Wayne Reittie; 31 Sam Smeaton; 3 Chris Ulugia; 5 Shaun Ainscough; 13 Pat Walker; 7 Dominic Brambani; 8 Keegan Hirst; 20 Alistair Leak; 10 Alex Rowe; 11 Brad Day; 19 Alex Bretherton; 9 Luke Blake. Subs (all used): 15 Adam Gledhill; 18 Tom Lillycrop; 14 James Davey; 17 Joe Chandler.
Rugby Leaguer & League Express Men of the Match: *Rhinos:* Brett Ferres; *Bulldogs:* Alistair Leak.
Penalty count: 8-8; **Half-time:** 16-0;
Referee: Joe Cobb; **Attendance:** 15,135.

Saturday 10th September 2016

LEIGH CENTURIONS 48 HUDDERSFIELD GIANTS 40

CENTURIONS: 1 Gregg McNally; 2 Adam Higson; 41 Mitch Brown; 3 Greg Worthington; 40 Matty Dawson; 6 Martyn Ridyard; 36 Josh Drinkwater; 12 Gareth Hock; 14 Micky Higham; 10 Dayne Weston; 16 Reni Maitua; 13 Cory Paterson; 39 Danny Tickle. Subs (all used): 11 Harrison Hansen; 20 Sam Hopkins; 21 Andrew Dixon; 32 Liam Hood.
Tries: Worthington (1), Dawson (7, 12, 32), Ridyard (27, 39), Paterson (35), Brown (48); **Goals:** Ridyard 8/8.
GIANTS: 18 Jake Connor; 2 Jermaine McGillvary; 3 Leroy Cudjoe; 4 Joe Wardle; 5 Aaron Murphy; 6 Danny Brough; 7 Jamie Ellis; 36 Sebastine Ikahihifo; 9 Ryan Hinchcliffe (C); 10 Craig Huby; 12 Michael Lawrence; 17 Ukuma Ta'ai; 22 Oliver Roberts. Subs (all used): 16 Sam Rapira; 19 Josh Johnson; 20 Kruise Leeming; 21 Nathan Mason.
Tries: Lawrence (17), Murphy (24), Connor (53), Cudjoe (63, 65), Ellis (70, 76); **Goals:** Brough 6/7.
Rugby Leaguer & League Express Men of the Match: *Centurions:* Josh Drinkwater; *Giants:* Danny Brough.
Penalty count: 6-6; **Half-time:** 42-10;
Referee: Robert Hicks; **Attendance:** 5,934.

Sunday 11th September 2016

LONDON BRONCOS 18 HULL KINGSTON ROVERS 58

BRONCOS: 24 Alex Walker; 2 Rhys Williams; 1 Ben Hellewell; 32 Elliot Kear; 5 Iliess Macani; 7 William Barthau; 33 Jamie Soward; 8 Nick Slyney; 9 James Cunningham; 16 Mark Ioane; 11 Daniel Harrison; 12 Matt Garside; 15 Jack Bussey. Subs (all used): 14 Andy Ackers; 18 Jamie Thackray; 23 Jon Magrin; 17 Mark Offerdahl.
Tries: Walker (26), Cunningham (32), Barthau (54);
Goals: Soward 3/3.
ROVERS: 18 Ben Cockayne; 5 Kieran Dixon; 4 Iain Thornley; 21 Thomas Minns; 2 Josh Mantellato; 32 Terry Campese (C); 22 Matthew Marsh; 17 Dane Tilse; 9 Shaun Lunt; 10 Mitchell Allgood; 13 Chris Clarkson; 20 James Greenwood; 15 James Donaldson. Subs (all used): 14 Kevin Larroyer; 34 Jamie Peacock (D); 8 Adam Walker; 31 Will Jubb (D).
Tries: Minns (2, 6, 74), Cockayne (11), Dixon (15), Greenwood (41), Marsh (45, 61), Donaldson (59), Jubb (66);
Goals: Mantellato 9/10.
Rugby Leaguer & League Express Men of the Match: *Broncos:* James Cunningham; *Rovers:* Terry Campese.
Penalty count: 6-7; **Half-time:** 12-24;
Referee: Phil Bentham; **Attendance:** 1,215.

SALFORD RED DEVILS 70
FEATHERSTONE ROVERS 16

RED DEVILS: 1 Niall Evalds; 5 Daniel Vidot; 33 Josh Jones; 4 Junior Sa'u; 3 Josh Griffin; 14 Gareth O'Brien; 7 Michael Dobson (C); 35 Luke Burgess; 19 Logan Tomkins; 10 George Griffin; 11 Ben Murdoch-Masila; 12 Weller Hauraki; 13 Mark Flanagan. Subs (all used): 16 Olsi Krasniqi; 15 Adam Walne; 6 Robert Lui; 8 Craig Kopczak.
Tries: Hauraki (2, 53), Sa'u (6, 19), Jones (12, 72), Vidot (15), Evalds (28), Murdoch-Masila (33, 70), Tomkins (37), Krasniqi (50), Dobson (59); **Goals:** O'Brien 9/12, Lui 0/1.
ROVERS: 1 Danny Craven; 33 James Duckworth; 15 Ian Hardman; 4 Misi Taulapapa; 29 Luke Briscoe; 6 Kyle Briggs; 7 Anthony Thackeray; 8 Darrell Griffin; 23 Andy Ellis; 32 Jordan Baldwinson; 39 Josh Walters; 17 Jack Ormondroyd; 12 John Davies. Subs (all used): 19 Sam Day; 20 Luke Cooper; 11 Steve Snitch; 27 Jamie Foster.
Tries: Baldwinson (1), Ormondroyd (25), Walters (45);
Goals: Briggs 2/3.
Rugby Leaguer & League Express Men of the Match: *Red Devils:* Junior Sa'u; *Rovers:* Jordan Baldwinson.
Penalty count: 8-6; **Half-time:** 44-12;
Referee: Chris Campbell; **Attendance:** 1,759.

ROUND 6

Saturday 17th September 2016

LEIGH CENTURIONS 42 BATLEY BULLDOGS 24

CENTURIONS: 26 Lee Smith; 2 Adam Higson; 41 Mitch Brown; 4 Willie Tonga; 40 Matty Dawson; 31 Ben Reynolds; 38 Travis Burns; 8 Fuifui Moimoi; 32 Liam Hood; 10 Dayne Weston; 13 Cory Paterson; 21 Andrew Dixon; 35 Brad Fash. Subs (all used): 11 Harrison Hansen; 18 Tom Spencer; 19 Lewis Foster; 20 Sam Hopkins.
Tries: Moimoi (17), Higson (21), Paterson (31), Foster (35), Burns (46), Tonga (63), Weston (75); **Goals:** Smith 7/7.
BULLDOGS: 22 Dave Scott; 2 Wayne Reittie; 31 Sam Smeaton; 3 Chris Ulugia; 5 Shaun Ainscough; 13 Pat Walker; 7 Dominic Brambani; 8 Keegan Hirst; 20 Alistair Leak; 10 Alex Rowe; 11 Brad Day; 19 Alex Bretherton; 9 Luke Blake. Subs (all used): 14 James Davey; 15 Adam Gledhill; 17 Joe Chandler; 18 Tom Lillycrop.
Tries: D Scott (8), Leak (27), Hirst (70), Reittie (79);
Goals: Walker 4/4.
On report: Bretherton (60) - alleged bite on Weston.
Rugby Leaguer & League Express Men of the Match: *Centurions:* Travis Burns; *Bulldogs:* Alistair Leak.
Penalty count: 9-12; **Half-time:** 24-12;
Referee: Chris Kendall; **Attendance:** 10,556.

SALFORD RED DEVILS 16 LONDON BRONCOS 19

RED DEVILS: 1 Niall Evalds; 18 Greg Johnson; 33 Josh Jones; 4 Junior Sa'u; 3 Josh Griffin; 14 Gareth O'Brien; 7 Michael Dobson (C); 35 Luke Burgess; 19 Logan Tomkins; 10 George Griffin; 11 Ben Murdoch-Masila; 12 Weller Hauraki; 13 Mark Flanagan. Subs (all used): 6 Robert Lui; 8 Craig Kopczak; 15 Adam Walne; 16 Olsi Krasniqi.
Tries: G Griffin (35), J Griffin (74, 77); **Goals:** O'Brien 2/3.
BRONCOS: 32 Elliot Kear; 2 Rhys Williams; 1 Ben Hellewell; 6 Israel Eliab; 31 Kameron Pearce-Paul; 7 William Barthau; 33 Jamie Soward; 8 Nick Slyney; 14 Andy Ackers; 16 Mark Ioane; 11 Daniel Harrison; 12 Matt Garside; 15 Jack Bussey. Subs (all used): 10 Eddie Battye; 17 Mark Offerdahl; 18 Jamie Thackray; 20 Scott Leatherbarrow.
Tries: Barthau (16), Leatherbarrow (39), Soward (58);
Goals: Soward 3/5; **Field goal:** Barthau (70).
Rugby Leaguer & League Express Men of the Match: *Red Devils:* Josh Jones; *Broncos:* William Barthau.
Penalty count: 6-8; **Half-time:** 6-10;
Referee: Joe Cobb; **Attendance:** 2,521.

Sunday 18th September 2016

FEATHERSTONE ROVERS 24
HULL KINGSTON ROVERS 32

ROVERS: 1 Danny Craven; 33 James Duckworth; 15 Ian Hardman; 4 Misi Taulapapa; 29 Luke Briscoe; 6 Kyle Briggs; 7 Anthony Thackeray; 8 Darrell Griffin; 23 Andy Ellis; 32 Jordan Baldwinson; 39 Josh Walters; 12 John Davies; 21 Bradley Knowles-Tagg. Subs (all used): 19 Sam Day; 11 Steve Snitch; 13 Tim Spears; 20 Luke Cooper.
Tries: Walters (8), Duckworth (15), Taulapapa (66, 68);
Goals: Briggs 3/4, Craven 1/1.

Greg Johnson celebrates scoring Salford's last-gasp equalising try against Hull KR in the Million Pound Game

ROBINS: 18 Ben Cockayne; 1 Ken Sio; 21 Thomas Minns; 4 Iain Thornley; 2 Josh Mantellato; 32 Terry Campese (C); 22 Matthew Marsh; 17 Dane Tilse; 9 Shaun Lunt; 10 Mitchell Allgood; 11 Maurice Blair; 20 James Greenwood; 15 James Donaldson. Subs (all used): 34 Jamie Peacock; 8 Adam Walker; 31 Will Jubb; 12 Graeme Horne.
Tries: Mantellato (12, 40), Lunt (38), Minns (46, 53), Greenwood (62); **Goals:** Mantellato 4/6.
Rugby Leaguer & League Express Men of the Match: *Rovers:* Kyle Briggs; *Robins:* Ben Cockayne.
Penalty count: 9-7; **Half-time:** 12-16;
Referee: Gareth Hewer; **Attendance:** 4,034.

HUDDERSFIELD GIANTS 22 LEEDS RHINOS 14

GIANTS: 1 Scott Grix; 2 Jermaine McGillvary; 3 Leroy Cudjoe; 18 Jake Connor; 5 Aaron Murphy; 6 Danny Brough; 34 Ryan Brierley; 10 Craig Huby; 9 Ryan Hinchcliffe (C); 17 Ukuma Ta'ai; 11 Tom Symonds; 4 Joe Wardle; 12 Michael Lawrence. Subs (all used): 15 Kyle Wood; 16 Sam Rapira; 22 Oliver Roberts; 36 Sebastine Ikahihifo.
Tries: Cudjoe (11), Brierley (35), Brough (47);
Goals: Brough 5/6.
RHINOS: 14 Liam Sutcliffe; 2 Tom Briscoe; 3 Kallum Watkins; 18 Jimmy Keinhorst; 22 Ash Handley; 25 Jordan Lilley; 7 Rob Burrow (C); 11 Jamie Jones-Buchanan; 30 James Segeyaro; 16 Brad Singleton; 26 Brett Ferres; 12 Carl Ablett; 13 Stevie Ward. Subs (all used): 4 Joel Moon; 8 Keith Galloway; 10 Adam Cuthbertson; 23 Ashton Golding.
Tries: Cuthbertson (58), T Briscoe (59), Handley (75);
Goals: Sutcliffe 1/3.
On report: Segeyaro (46) - alleged high tackle on Connor.
Rugby Leaguer & League Express Men of the Match: *Giants:* Danny Brough; *Rhinos:* Rob Burrow .
Penalty count: 11-12; **Half-time:** 14-0;
Referee: Ben Thaler; **Attendance:** 6,666.

ROUND 7

Thursday 22nd September 2016

LEEDS RHINOS 37 LEIGH CENTURIONS 12

RHINOS: 23 Ashton Golding; 2 Tom Briscoe; 3 Kallum Watkins; 5 Ryan Hall; 14 Liam Sutcliffe; 4 Joel Moon; 16 Brad Singleton; 30 James Segeyaro; 11 Jamie Jones-Buchanan (C); 26 Brett Ferres; 13 Stevie Ward; 10 Adam Cuthbertson. Subs (all used): 27 Sam Hallas; 22 Ash Handley; 28 Cameron Smith; 31 Josh Jordan-Roberts (D).
Tries: Ferres (13), Keinhorst (25, 29), Segeyaro (34), Golding (49), Moon (54), T Briscoe (67);
Goals: Watkins 4/8; **Field goal:** Moon (7).
Sin bin: Jones-Buchanan (4) - dangerous challenge on Worthington.
CENTURIONS: 26 Lee Smith; 41 Mitch Brown; 3 Greg Worthington; 4 Willie Tonga; 40 Matty Dawson; 6 Martyn Ridyard; 36 Josh Drinkwater; 8 Fuifui Moimoi; 14 Micky

Higham; 10 Dayne Weston; 21 Andrew Dixon; 16 Reni Maitua; 12 Gareth Hock. Subs (all used): 39 Danny Tickle; 11 Harrison Hansen; 20 Sam Hopkins; 38 Travis Burns.
Tries: Hopkins (36), Dawson (57); **Goals:** Ridyard 2/2.
Sin bin: Smith (73) - persistent team offences.
Rugby Leaguer & League Express Men of the Match: *Rhinos:* Adam Cuthbertson; *Centurions:* Willie Tonga.
Penalty count: 13-8; **Half time:** 18-6;
Referee: Gareth Hewer; **Attendance:** 14,747.

Saturday 24th September 2016

HULL KINGSTON ROVERS 22 HUDDERSFIELD GIANTS 23

ROVERS: 18 Ben Cockayne; 1 Ken Sio; 21 Thomas Minns; 4 Iain Thornley; 2 Josh Mantellato; 32 Terry Campese (C); 22 Matthew Marsh; 17 Dane Tilse; 9 Shaun Lunt; 10 Mitchell Allgood; 11 Maurice Blair; 13 Chris Clarkson; 15 James Donaldson. Subs (all used): 20 James Greenwood; 8 Adam Walker; 34 Jamie Peacock; 31 Will Jubb.
Tries: Blair (17), Sio (49), Allgood (52), Thornley (61);
Goals: Mantellato 3/4.
Sin bin: Cockayne (31) - holding down.
GIANTS: 1 Scott Grix; 2 Jermaine McGillvary; 3 Leroy Cudjoe; 18 Jake Connor; 5 Aaron Murphy; 6 Danny Brough; 34 Ryan Brierley; 10 Craig Huby; 9 Ryan Hinchcliffe (C); 17 Ukuma Ta'ai; 11 Tom Symonds; 4 Joe Wardle; 12 Michael Lawrence. Subs (all used): 15 Kyle Wood; 21 Nathan Mason; 22 Oliver Roberts; 36 Sebastine Ikahihifo.
Tries: Brierley (5, 27), Cudjoe (23), Murphy (32);
Goals: Brough 3/5; **Field goal:** Brough (74).
Rugby Leaguer & League Express Men of the Match: *Rovers:* Shaun Lunt; *Giants:* Danny Brough.
Penalty count: 7-5; **Half-time:** 4-22;
Referee: Robert Hicks; **Attendance:** 8,024.

Sunday 25th September 2016

BATLEY BULLDOGS 14 SALFORD RED DEVILS 42

BULLDOGS: 22 Dave Scott; 2 Wayne Reittie; 31 Sam Smeaton; 3 Chris Ulugia; 5 Shaun Ainscough; 6 Cain Southernwood; 7 Dominic Brambani; 8 Keegan Hirst; 20 Alistair Leak; 10 Alex Rowe; 11 Brad Day; 19 Alex Bretherton; 9 Luke Blake. Subs (all used): 13 Pat Walker; 18 Tom Lillycrop; 15 Adam Gledhill; 24 James Harrison.
Tries: Reittie (20, 46), Ulugia (74); **Goals:** Brambani 1/3.
RED DEVILS: 14 Gareth O'Brien; 18 Greg Johnson; 33 Josh Jones; 4 Junior Sa'u; 3 Josh Griffin; 6 Robert Lui; 7 Michael Dobson (C); 35 Luke Burgess; 19 Logan Tomkins; 10 George Griffin; 11 Ben Murdoch-Masila; 12 Weller Hauraki; 13 Mark Flanagan. Subs (all used): 16 Olsi Krasniqi; 15 Adam Walne; 34 Sean Kenny; 5 Daniel Vidot.
Tries: O'Brien (11, 77), Sa'u (13), Hauraki (25, 34), Johnson (29), J Griffin (37), Lui (62); **Goals:** O'Brien 5/8.

Rugby Leaguer & League Express Men of the Match: *Bulldogs:* Keegan Hirst; *Red Devils:* Gareth O'Brien.
Penalty count: 10-10; **Half-time:** 4-34;
Referee: Chris Campbell; **Attendance:** 1,520.

LONDON BRONCOS 46 FEATHERSTONE ROVERS 6

BRONCOS: 32 Elliot Kear; 2 Rhys Williams; 1 Ben Hellewell; 6 Israel Eliab; 31 Kameron Pearce-Paul; 7 William Barthau; 33 Jamie Soward; 8 Nick Slyney; 14 Andy Ackers; 16 Mark Ioane; 11 Daniel Harrison; 12 Matt Garside; 15 Jack Bussey. Subs (all used): 20 Scott Leatherbarrow; 17 Mark Offerdahl; 18 Jamie Thackray; 10 Eddie Battye.
Tries: Williams (4, 34, 65), Harrison (16), Kear (24), Garside (53), Hellewell (70), Bussey (71), Ioane (78);
Goals: Soward 5/8, Thackray 0/1.
ROVERS: 1 Danny Craven; 33 James Duckworth; 15 Ian Hardman; 4 Misi Taulapapa; 29 Luke Briscoe; 6 Kyle Briggs; 7 Anthony Thackeray; 8 Darrell Griffin; 23 Andy Ellis; 32 Jordan Baldwinson; 39 Josh Walters; 12 John Davies; 21 Bradley Knowles-Tagg. Subs (all used): 19 Sam Day; 20 Luke Cooper; 13 Tim Spears; 11 Steve Snitch.
Try: Davies (74); **Goals:** Craven 1/1.
Rugby Leaguer & League Express Men of the Match: *Broncos:* Jamie Soward; *Rovers:* Anthony Thackeray.
Penalty count: 10-8; **Half-time:** 18-0;
Referee: James Child; **Attendance:** 605.

MILLION POUND GAME

Saturday 1st October 2016

HULL KINGSTON ROVERS 18 SALFORD RED DEVILS 19
(after golden point extra-time)

ROVERS: 18 Ben Cockayne; 1 Ken Sio; 21 Thomas Minns; 4 Iain Thornley; 2 Josh Mantellato; 32 Terry Campese (C); 22 Matthew Marsh; 17 Dane Tilse; 9 Shaun Lunt; 8 Adam Walker; 11 Maurice Blair; 13 Chris Clarkson; 15 James Donaldson. Subs (all used): 12 Graeme Horne; 34 Jamie Peacock; 10 Mitchell Allgood; 31 Will Jubb.
Tries: Walker (7), Mantellato (13), Minns (57);
Goals: Mantellato 3/4.
On report:
Clarkson (23) - alleged dangerous contact on Jones.
RED DEVILS: 14 Gareth O'Brien; 18 Greg Johnson; 33 Josh Jones; 4 Junior Sa'u; 3 Josh Griffin; 6 Robert Lui; 7 Michael Dobson (C); 35 Luke Burgess; 19 Logan Tomkins; 10 George Griffin; 11 Ben Murdoch-Masila; 12 Weller Hauraki; 13 Mark Flanagan. Subs (all used): 8 Craig Kopczak; 16 Olsi Krasniqi; 1 Niall Evalds; 34 Sean Kenny.
Tries: Murdoch-Masila (18), Evalds (31, 78), Johnson (80);
Goals: O'Brien 1/4; **Field goal:** O'Brien (81).
Rugby Leaguer & League Express Men of the Match: *Rovers:* Shaun Lunt; *Red Devils:* Mark Flanagan.
Penalty count: 5-4; **Half-time:** 12-10;
Referee: Phil Bentham; **Attendance:** 6,562.

SUPER LEAGUE XXI
Opta Analysis

SUPER LEAGUE XXI TOP PERFORMERS

TACKLES

Danny Houghton	Hull FC	1289
Sam Powell	Wigan	1120
James Roby	St Helens	1067
Glenn Stewart	Catalans	1026
Hep Cahill	Widnes	1023
Jon Wilkin	St Helens	1009
Eloi Pelissier	Catalans	954
Adam Milner	Castleford	932
Chris Hill	Warrington	920
Lloyd White	Widnes	896

OFFLOADS

Ashton Sims	Warrington	64
John Bateman	Wigan	61
Adam Cuthbertson	Leeds	48
Dan Sarginson	Wigan	48
Anthony Gelling	Wigan	47
Mahe Fonua	Hull FC	45
Dave Taylor	Catalans	39
Adam Walker	Hull KR	39
Josh Jones	Salford	38
Mickael Simon	Wakefield	36

CARRIES

Dan Sarginson	Wigan	530
Kyle Amor	St Helens	499
Chris Hill	Warrington	486
Alex Walmsley	St Helens	469
Matthew Russell	Warrington	433
Rhys Hanbury	Widnes	426
Josh Charnley	Wigan	424
Tony Gigot	Catalans	413
John Bateman	Wigan	396
Ashton Sims	Warrington	381

CLEAN BREAKS

Denny Solomona	Castleford	50
Adam Swift	St Helens	27
Josh Charnley	Wigan	26
Joe Mellor	Widnes	26
Rhys Hanbury	Widnes	25
Jermaine McGillvary	Huddersfield	25
Corey Thompson	Widnes	25
Tom Johnstone	Wakefield	24
Jodie Broughton	Catalans	23
Jamie Shaul	Hull FC	22

1289 TACKLES - Danny Houghton

ERRORS

Tony Gigot	Catalans	48
Dan Sarginson	Wigan	44
Ben Crooks	Castleford	42
Jacob Miller	Wakefield	41
Corey Thompson	Widnes	41
Kallum Watkins	Leeds	40
Craig Hall	Wakefield	38
Denny Solomona	Castleford	38
Kevin Brown	Widnes	37
Jamie Shaul	Hull FC	37

METRES

Chris Hill	Warrington	3983
Matthew Russell	Warrington	3774
Kyle Amor	St Helens	3718
Alex Walmsley	St Helens	3691
Josh Charnley	Wigan	3679
Dan Sarginson	Wigan	3561
Tony Gigot	Catalans	3502
Rhys Hanbury	Widnes	3413
Jamie Shaul	Hull FC	3057
Ken Sio	Hull KR	3028

MISSED TACKLES

Jacob Miller	Wakefield	99
Adam Milner	Castleford	81
Lloyd White	Widnes	75
Louie McCarthy-Scarsbrook	St Helens	73
Luke Gale	Castleford	71
Eloi Pelissier	Catalans	70
Glenn Stewart	Catalans	70
Jon Wilkin	St Helens	70
Liam Finn	Wakefield	69
Albert Kelly	Hull KR	69

KICKS IN GENERAL PLAY

Marc Sneyd	Hull FC	342
Luke Gale	Castleford	310
Matty Smith	Wigan	293
Kevin Brown	Widnes	246
Danny Brough	Huddersfield	231
Michael Dobson	Salford	204
Liam Finn	Wakefield	197
Luke Walsh	St Helens	196
Chris Sandow	Warrington	183
Joe Mellor	Widnes	164

QUICK PLAY-THE-BALLS

Josh Charnley	Wigan	67
Jermaine McGillvary	Huddersfield	64
Justin Carney	Salford	62
Matthew Russell	Warrington	62
Ryan Atkins	Warrington	60
Dan Sarginson	Wigan	59
Fetuli Talanoa	Hull FC	57
Chris Hill	Warrington	54
Ken Sio	Hull KR	53
Jamie Shaul	Hull FC	47

PENALTIES CONCEDED

Dave Taylor	Catalans	34
Jon Wilkin	St Helens	34
Chris Houston	Widnes	32
Chris Hill	Warrington	30
Lloyd White	Widnes	27
Adam Milner	Castleford	26
Liam Watts	Hull FC	26
Remi Casty	Catalans	23
Brett Ferres	Leeds	22
Jacob Miller	Wakefield	22

TACKLE BUSTS

Matthew Russell	Warrington	126
Dominic Manfredi	Wigan	119
John Bateman	Wigan	109
Josh Jones	Salford	107
Daryl Clark	Warrington	105
Jamie Shaul	Hull FC	103
Tony Gigot	Catalans	100
Joe Mellor	Widnes	96
Corey Thompson	Widnes	93
Rhys Hanbury	Widnes	91

All statistics in Opta Analysis include Super League regular season & Super 8s/Qualifiers. (except pages 201-202, based on regular season only) Play-offs not included throughout.

SUPER LEAGUE XXI TRIES SCORED/CONCEDED

TOTAL TRIES SCORED
Warrington Wolves 150
Castleford Tigers 147
St Helens...............................131
Hull FC 128
Catalans Dragons 127
Wigan Warriors 117
Widnes Vikings......................110
Wakefield Trinity Wildcats 101
Salford Red Devils 100
Huddersfield Giants.................89
Hull Kingston Rovers 88
Leeds Rhinos 69

TOTAL TRIES CONCEDED
Wakefield Trinity Wildcats 161
Castleford Tigers 144
Catalans Dragons 122
St Helens...............................116
Widnes Vikings......................113
Hull Kingston Rovers 107
Hull FC 104
Leeds Rhinos 100
Salford Red Devils.................100
Huddersfield Giants.................98
Wigan Warriors 97
Warrington Wolves 95

SCORED FROM KICKS
Castleford Tigers 18
Hull FC 17
Warrington Wolves 16
St Helens.................................13
Wigan Warriors 13
Huddersfield Giants..................12
Salford Red Devils 12
Catalans Dragons 11
Wakefield Trinity Wildcats 11
Widnes Vikings........................10
Leeds Rhinos 9
Hull Kingston Rovers 8

Warrington's Ryan Atkins crosses to score against St Helens. The Wolves scored more tries than any other team in Super League XXI

CONCEDED FROM KICKS
Castleford Tigers 17
Catalans Dragons 17
St Helens.................................16
Leeds Rhinos 15
Warrington Wolves 15
Wakefield Trinity Wildcats 13
Wigan Warriors 13
Hull FC 10
Huddersfield Giants....................9
Hull Kingston Rovers 9
Widnes Vikings...........................9
Salford Red Devils......................7

TRIES SCORED FROM OWN HALF
Warrington Wolves 17
Hull Kingston Rovers 15
Wigan Warriors 13
Huddersfield Giants..................12
Salford Red Devils 12
Catalans Dragons 11
Hull FC 11
Castleford Tigers 10
St Helens.................................10
Wakefield Trinity Wildcats 10
Widnes Vikings........................10
Leeds Rhinos 6

TRIES CONCEDED FROM OVER 50M
Wakefield Trinity Wildcats 20
Catalans Dragons 17
St Helens.................................16
Castleford Tigers 14
Hull Kingston Rovers 14
Widnes Vikings........................14
Leeds Rhinos 12
Wigan Warriors 10
Salford Red Devils 9
Hull FC 8
Huddersfield Giants....................5
Warrington Wolves 5

TRIES SCORED FROM UNDER 10M
St Helens.................................65
Hull FC 61
Warrington Wolves 59
Castleford Tigers 55
Catalans Dragons 53
Huddersfield Giants..................48
Salford Red Devils 47
Widnes Vikings........................46
Wigan Warriors 44
Wakefield Trinity Wildcats 42
Hull Kingston Rovers 33
Leeds Rhinos 32

TRIES CONCEDED FROM UNDER 10M
Wakefield Trinity Wildcats 78
Castleford Tigers 61
Widnes Vikings........................59
Hull FC 58
Huddersfield Giants..................56
St Helens.................................52
Catalans Dragons 50
Salford Red Devils 48
Hull Kingston Rovers 46
Leeds Rhinos 44
Warrington Wolves 41
Wigan Warriors 37

SUPER LEAGUE XXI AVERAGES PER MATCH

METRES
Warrington Wolves 1356.9
Wigan Warriors 1280.3
Hull FC 1251.0
Widnes Vikings.................1247.0
Castleford Tigers 1245.7
St Helens...........................1228.0
Catalans Dragons 1200.7
Wakefield Trinity Wildcats..1107.9
Leeds Rhinos 994.9
Hull Kingston Rovers 973.2
Huddersfield Giants............926.7
Salford Red Devils..............926.0

CLEAN BREAKS
Castleford Tigers 6.6
Warrington Wolves 5.9
Hull FC 5.8
Widnes Vikings........................5.8
St Helens.................................5.2
Catalans Dragons 5.1
Wigan Warriors 4.9
Wakefield Trinity Wildcats 4.5
Salford Red Devils....................4.3
Leeds Rhinos 4.0
Hull Kingston Rovers 3.8
Huddersfield Giants..................3.6

OFFLOADS
Warrington Wolves 12.4
Leeds Rhinos 11.5
Castleford Tigers 11.1
Wigan Warriors 10.8
Hull FC 10.0
Widnes Vikings.........................9.8
Wakefield Trinity Wildcats 9.3
St Helens..................................8.3
Hull Kingston Rovers 8.2
Catalans Dragons 7.2
Huddersfield Giants...................7.2
Salford Red Devils.....................5.8

PASSES
St Helens.............................242.0
Wigan Warriors 223.5
Hull FC 212.2
Widnes Vikings...................208.2
Wakefield Trinity Wildcats..203.6
Castleford Tigers 201.7
Catalans Dragons 194.8
Warrington Wolves 191.7
Huddersfield Giants...........166.0
Salford Red Devils..............164.1
Leeds Rhinos 162.2
Hull Kingston Rovers 159.1

TACKLES
Widnes Vikings...................352.0
Wigan Warriors 334.7
Wakefield Trinity Wildcats..325.5
Castleford Tigers 321.7
St Helens............................317.6
Catalans Dragons 312.7
Hull FC 309.9
Warrington Wolves 309.3
Leeds Rhinos 264.2
Huddersfield Giants...........262.7
Hull Kingston Rovers 255.7
Salford Red Devils..............248.8

MISSED TACKLES
Wakefield Trinity Wildcats ...28.6
Catalans Dragons 26.4
St Helens...............................26.2
Wigan Warriors 25.9
Widnes Vikings......................25.3
Castleford Tigers 25.1
Hull FC 24.3
Hull Kingston Rovers 23.3
Leeds Rhinos 22.0
Salford Red Devils.................20.7
Warrington Wolves 20.2
Huddersfield Giants...............18.4

ERRORS
Warrington Wolves 13.3
Widnes Vikings......................13.2
Wakefield Trinity Wildcats ...12.3
Wigan Warriors 12.3
Castleford Tigers 11.6
Hull FC 11.6
Catalans Dragons 11.5
St Helens...............................11.1
Leeds Rhinos 10.8
Huddersfield Giants.................9.6
Hull Kingston Rovers 9.2
Salford Red Devils...................8.4

KICKS IN GENERAL PLAY
St Helens...............................19.2
Hull FC 18.7
Widnes Vikings......................18.3
Wigan Warriors 18.3
Warrington Wolves 16.6
Catalans Dragons 16.5
Wakefield Trinity Wildcats ...16.0
Castleford Tigers 15.5
Huddersfield Giants...............14.4
Salford Red Devils.................14.2
Hull Kingston Rovers 13.7
Leeds Rhinos 12.9

SUPER LEAGUE XXI PENALTIES

TOTAL PENALTIES AWARDED
Wigan Warriors 279
Hull FC 261
Catalans Dragons 257
Wakefield Trinity Wildcats 247
Widnes Vikings 246
Warrington Wolves 240
Castleford Tigers 235
St Helens 214
Leeds Rhinos 196
Salford Red Devils 190
Hull Kingston Rovers 187
Huddersfield Giants 176

TOTAL PENALTIES CONCEDED
Widnes Vikings.......................276
Catalans Dragons 274
Wakefield Trinity Wildcats 271
Wigan Warriors 262
Castleford Tigers 242
St Helens 235
Hull FC 227
Warrington Wolves 224
Huddersfield Giants 196
Salford Red Devils 183
Hull Kingston Rovers 180
Leeds Rhinos 158

FOUL PLAY - AWARDED
Catalans Dragons 63
Castleford Tigers 55
St Helens 52
Wakefield Trinity Wildcats 48
Widnes Vikings........................ 47
Wigan Warriors 47
Salford Red Devils 45
Hull FC 40
Warrington Wolves 40
Hull Kingston Rovers 37
Huddersfield Giants 29
Leeds Rhinos 29

FOUL PLAY - CONCEDED
Catalans Dragons 68
Wakefield Trinity Wildcats 51
Wigan Warriors 50
Widnes Vikings.........................49
Castleford Tigers 47
Hull FC 44
Warrington Wolves 42
Salford Red Devils 40
St Helens 40
Huddersfield Giants 37
Hull Kingston Rovers 35
Leeds Rhinos 29

OFFSIDE - AWARDED
Huddersfield Giants 37
Warrington Wolves 37
St Helens 36
Wigan Warriors 31
Wakefield Trinity Wildcats 30
Widnes Vikings........................30
Castleford Tigers 29
Catalans Dragons 27
Hull FC 22
Salford Red Devils 21
Leeds Rhinos 20
Hull Kingston Rovers 17

OFFSIDE - CONCEDED
St Helens 43
Castleford Tigers 37
Wakefield Trinity Wildcats 35
Catalans Dragons 34
Wigan Warriors 31
Widnes Vikings........................30
Warrington Wolves 27
Huddersfield Giants 26
Salford Red Devils 25
Hull FC 20
Leeds Rhinos 17
Hull Kingston Rovers 12

INTERFERENCE - AWARDED
Wigan Warriors 140
Hull FC 125
Widnes Vikings........................106
Warrington Wolves 98
Catalans Dragons 96
Wakefield Trinity Wildcats 96
Castleford Tigers 85
Leeds Rhinos 78
St Helens 75
Hull Kingston Rovers 73
Huddersfield Giants 67
Salford Red Devils 65

INTERFERENCE - CONCEDED
Widnes Vikings........................121
Wakefield Trinity Wildcats 114
Catalans Dragons 110
Wigan Warriors 103
Hull FC 102
Castleford Tigers 100
Warrington Wolves 88
St Helens 82
Huddersfield Giants 76
Hull Kingston Rovers 74
Leeds Rhinos 71
Salford Red Devils 63

OBSTRUCTION - AWARDED
Wakefield Trinity Wildcats 14
Hull FC 13
Castleford Tigers 12
Catalans Dragons 12
Salford Red Devils 11
Leeds Rhinos 10
St Helens 10
Hull Kingston Rovers 7
Widnes Vikings.........................7
Warrington Wolves 6
Wigan Warriors 6
Huddersfield Giants 3

OBSTRUCTION - CONCEDED
St Helens 11
Wakefield Trinity Wildcats 11
Warrington Wolves 11
Wigan Warriors 11
Castleford Tigers 10
Catalans Dragons 10
Hull Kingston Rovers 10
Hull FC 9
Widnes Vikings......................... 9
Salford Red Devils 8
Huddersfield Giants 7
Leeds Rhinos 4

BALL STEALING - AWARDED
Hull Kingston Rovers 29
Wakefield Trinity Wildcats 28
Hull FC 27
Wigan Warriors 27
Warrington Wolves 24
Huddersfield Giants 23
Widnes Vikings........................ 23
Catalans Dragons 20
Salford Red Devils 20
Castleford Tigers 17
Leeds Rhinos 16
St Helens 14

BALL STEALING - CONCEDED
Widnes Vikings........................29
Wigan Warriors 29
Catalans Dragons 27
Hull Kingston Rovers 25
Wakefield Trinity Wildcats 25
St Helens 24
Warrington Wolves 23
Castleford Tigers 21
Hull FC 20
Huddersfield Giants 18
Salford Red Devils 15
Leeds Rhinos 12

OFFSIDE MARKERS - CONCEDED
St Helens 19
Widnes Vikings........................18
Wigan Warriors 14
Wakefield Trinity Wildcats 12
Huddersfield Giants 11
Leeds Rhinos 11
Salford Red Devils 11
Warrington Wolves 10
Hull FC 9
Castleford Tigers 7
Catalans Dragons 6
Hull Kingston Rovers 5

OFFSIDE FROM KICK - AWARDED
Castleford Tigers 7
Salford Red Devils 6
St Helens 6
Warrington Wolves 5
Catalans Dragons 4
Leeds Rhinos 4
Widnes Vikings......................... 4
Hull FC 3
Hull Kingston Rovers 3
Huddersfield Giants 2
Wakefield Trinity Wildcats 2
Wigan Warriors 1

OFFSIDE FROM KICK - CONCEDED
Wakefield Trinity Wildcats 7
Hull FC 6
Salford Red Devils 6
Warrington Wolves 5
Huddersfield Giants 4
Leeds Rhinos 4
St Helens 4
Wigan Warriors 4
Catalans Dragons 3
Castleford Tigers 2
Widnes Vikings......................... 2
Hull Kingston Rovers 0

DISSENT - AWARDED
Castleford Tigers 5
Huddersfield Giants 4
Wigan Warriors 4
Hull FC 3
Hull Kingston Rovers 3
Leeds Rhinos 3
Wakefield Trinity Wildcats 3
Warrington Wolves 3
Widnes Vikings......................... 3
Catalans Dragons 1
Salford Red Devils 1
St Helens 0

OFFSIDE MARKERS - AWARDED
Leeds Rhinos 17
Hull FC 15
Wakefield Trinity Wildcats 14
Salford Red Devils 13
Warrington Wolves 12
Castleford Tigers 11
Catalans Dragons 11
Widnes Vikings.........................10
Hull Kingston Rovers 9
St Helens 9
Wigan Warriors 8
Huddersfield Giants 4

DISSENT - CONCEDED
Wakefield Trinity Wildcats 6
Castleford Tigers 4
Huddersfield Giants 4
Hull FC 4
Leeds Rhinos 4
Salford Red Devils 4
Hull Kingston Rovers 3
St Helens 2
Widnes Vikings......................... 2
Wigan Warriors 2
Catalans Dragons 0
Warrington Wolves 0

CASTLEFORD TIGERS
SUPER LEAGUE XXI LEADERS

CATALANS DRAGONS
SUPER LEAGUE XXI LEADERS

HUDDERSFIELD GIANTS
SUPER LEAGUE XXI LEADERS

CARRIES		CARRIES		CARRIES	
Grant Millington	355	Tony Gigot	413	Jermaine McGillvary	353
Junior Moors	309	Jason Baitieri	359	Sam Rapira	327
Denny Solomona	304	Julian Bousquet	332	Leroy Cudjoe	294
Matt Cook	303	Glenn Stewart	304	Michael Lawrence	286
Luke Gale	297	Dave Taylor	293	Aaron Murphy	281

OFFLOADS		OFFLOADS		OFFLOADS	
Grant Millington	35	Dave Taylor	39	Leroy Cudjoe	33
Junior Moors	35	Tony Gigot	22	Sam Rapira	26
Mike McMeeken	29	Julian Bousquet	16	Jake Connor	23
Luke Gale	25	Todd Carney	15	Danny Brough	20
Jake Webster	24	Glenn Stewart	14	Aaron Murphy	17

METRES		METRES		METRES	
Denny Solomona	2981	Tony Gigot	3502	Jermaine McGillvary	2965
Junior Moors	2480	Julian Bousquet	2655	Leroy Cudjoe	2438
Matt Cook	2401	Jason Baitieri	2550	Sam Rapira	2415
Grant Millington	2314	Jodie Broughton	2526	Ukuma Ta'ai	2057
Jake Webster	2126	Dave Taylor	2463	Aaron Murphy	1974

TACKLES		TACKLES		TACKLES	
Adam Milner	932	Glenn Stewart	1026	Michael Lawrence	842
Paul McShane	820	Eloi Pelissier	954	Ryan Hinchcliffe	787
Matt Cook	703	Jason Baitieri	854	Ukuma Ta'ai	739
Grant Millington	612	Julian Bousquet	714	Sam Rapira	608
Mike McMeeken	582	Remi Casty	591	Leroy Cudjoe	567

CLEAN BREAKS		CLEAN BREAKS		CLEAN BREAKS	
Denny Solomona	50	Jodie Broughton	23	Jermaine McGillvary	25
Luke Dorn	19	Fouad Yaha	15	Jake Connor	13
Jake Webster	15	Dave Taylor	12	Leroy Cudjoe	9
Ryan Hampshire	12	Tony Gigot	11	Aaron Murphy	9
Greg Minikin	11	Vincent Duport	10	Ryan Brierley	7

TACKLE BUSTS		TACKLE BUSTS		TACKLE BUSTS	
Junior Moors	85	Tony Gigot	100	Leroy Cudjoe	70
Denny Solomona	84	Dave Taylor	82	Jermaine McGillvary	68
Luke Dorn	61	Jodie Broughton	51	Jake Connor	44
Ben Crooks	56	Justin Horo	40	Danny Brough	43
Luke Gale	51	Eloi Pelissier	39	Ukuma Ta'ai	33

MARKER TACKLES		MARKER TACKLES		MARKER TACKLES	
Adam Milner	134	Glenn Stewart	181	Michael Lawrence	150
Matt Cook	127	Eloi Pelissier	150	Ryan Hinchcliffe	131
Paul McShane	105	Jason Baitieri	143	Ukuma Ta'ai	112
Mike McMeeken	94	Julian Bousquet	89	Leroy Cudjoe	109
Nathan Massey	86	Gregory Mounis	87	Eorl Crabtree	73

TRY ASSISTS		TRY ASSISTS		TRY ASSISTS	
Luke Gale	46	Todd Carney	17	Danny Brough	18
Luke Dorn	21	Richard Myler	15	Leroy Cudjoe	13
Paul McShane	11	Tony Gigot	11	Jake Connor	12
Jake Webster	10	Eloi Pelissier	10	Jamie Ellis	9
Denny Solomona	7	Thomas Bosc	7	Aaron Murphy	5

TOTAL OPTA INDEX		TOTAL OPTA INDEX		TOTAL OPTA INDEX	
Denny Solomona	13577	Tony Gigot	13599	Leroy Cudjoe	12699
Luke Gale	12434	Jason Baitieri	13383	Michael Lawrence	12105
Paul McShane	11211	Glenn Stewart	13363	Ukuma Ta'ai	11806
Matt Cook	10898	Julian Bousquet	11964	Jermaine McGillvary	11628
Grant Millington	10358	Eloi Pelissier	11595	Danny Brough	9635

HULL F.C.
SUPER LEAGUE XXI LEADERS

HULL KINGSTON ROVERS
SUPER LEAGUE XXI LEADERS

LEEDS RHINOS
SUPER LEAGUE XXI LEADERS

CARRIES

Hull F.C.		Hull KR		Leeds Rhinos	
Scott Taylor	348	Adam Walker	329	Kallum Watkins	307
Jamie Shaul	337	Ken Sio	320	Rob Burrow	290
Liam Watts	325	Dane Tilse	286	Mitch Garbutt	282
Fetuli Talanoa	317	Iain Thornley	241	Adam Cuthbertson	279
Josh Bowden	302	Albert Kelly	224	Brett Ferres	269

OFFLOADS

Hull F.C.		Hull KR		Leeds Rhinos	
Mahe Fonua	45	Adam Walker	39	Adam Cuthbertson	48
Liam Watts	34	Dane Tilse	30	Brett Ferres	33
Carlos Tuimavave	23	Iain Thornley	22	Kallum Watkins	30
Frank Pritchard	20	Ben Cockayne	19	Carl Ablett	21
Kirk Yeaman	20	James Greenwood	19	Liam Sutcliffe	20

METRES

Hull F.C.		Hull KR		Leeds Rhinos	
Jamie Shaul	3057	Ken Sio	3028	Mitch Garbutt	2368
Scott Taylor	2872	Adam Walker	2353	Rob Burrow	2113
Fetuli Talanoa	2515	Iain Thornley	2024	Kallum Watkins	2098
Liam Watts	2299	Dane Tilse	1946	Brett Ferres	1979
Josh Bowden	2208	Albert Kelly	1606	Keith Galloway	1899

TACKLES

Hull F.C.		Hull KR		Leeds Rhinos	
Danny Houghton	1289	Mitchell Allgood	675	Jamie Jones-Buchanan	794
Scott Taylor	748	Adam Walker	610	Keith Galloway	580
Liam Watts	735	Dane Tilse	571	Kallum Watkins	574
Sika Manu	628	George Lawler	560	Brad Singleton	558
Josh Bowden	601	Chris Clarkson	553	Brett Ferres	522

CLEAN BREAKS

Hull F.C.		Hull KR		Leeds Rhinos	
Jamie Shaul	22	Albert Kelly	15	Rob Burrow	14
Fetuli Talanoa	21	Maurice Blair	11	Liam Sutcliffe	13
Mark Minichiello	15	Kieran Dixon	10	Kallum Watkins	13
Mahe Fonua	13	Ken Sio	10	Ash Handley	8
Steve Michaels	12	Iain Thornley	10	Jordan Lilley	7

TACKLE BUSTS

Hull F.C.		Hull KR		Leeds Rhinos	
Jamie Shaul	103	Maurice Blair	59	Kallum Watkins	75
Mark Minichiello	91	Albert Kelly	59	Rob Burrow	63
Fetuli Talanoa	73	Iain Thornley	49	Zak Hardaker	58
Mahe Fonua	68	Ken Sio	48	Mitch Garbutt	49
Sika Manu	49	Thomas Minns	46	Joel Moon	38

MARKER TACKLES

Hull F.C.		Hull KR		Leeds Rhinos	
Danny Houghton	192	Mitchell Allgood	116	Jamie Jones-Buchanan	172
Liam Watts	141	Adam Walker	90	Brad Singleton	123
Scott Taylor	114	Chris Clarkson	88	Kallum Watkins	111
Sika Manu	97	George Lawler	86	Adam Cuthbertson	94
Gareth Ellis	95	Dane Tilse	78	Mitch Achurch	86

TRY ASSISTS

Hull F.C.		Hull KR		Leeds Rhinos	
Marc Sneyd	22	Ben Cockayne	14	Rob Burrow	11
Danny Houghton	18	Albert Kelly	11	Danny McGuire	7
Mahe Fonua	7	Shaun Lunt	10	Liam Sutcliffe	5
Jamie Shaul	7	Maurice Blair	7	Adam Cuthbertson	3
Kirk Yeaman	7	Iain Thornley	6	Joel Moon	3

TOTAL OPTA INDEX

Hull F.C.		Hull KR		Leeds Rhinos	
Danny Houghton	16029	Adam Walker	10042	Kallum Watkins	11774
Scott Taylor	13035	Ken Sio	9402	Jamie Jones-Buchanan	10502
Jamie Shaul	12858	Maurice Blair	8691	Liam Sutcliffe	8916
Marc Sneyd	12390	Mitchell Allgood	8401	Mitch Garbutt	8729
Sika Manu	10750	James Greenwood	8224	Brett Ferres	8420

SALFORD RED DEVILS
SUPER LEAGUE XXI LEADERS

ST HELENS
SUPER LEAGUE XXI LEADERS

WAKEFIELD TRINITY WILDCATS
SUPER LEAGUE XXI LEADERS

CARRIES

Salford		St Helens		Wakefield	
Justin Carney	314	Kyle Amor	499	Tinirau Arona	350
Craig Kopczak	302	Alex Walmsley	469	Jacob Miller	289
George Griffin	279	Jon Wilkin	363	Mickael Simon	275
Josh Jones	278	Louie McCarthy-Scarsbrook	361	Reece Lyne	257
Junior Sa'u	268	Jack Owens	333	Tom Johnstone	253

OFFLOADS

Salford		St Helens		Wakefield	
Josh Jones	38	Kyle Amor	33	Mickael Simon	36
Robert Lui	26	Alex Walmsley	29	Anthony Tupou	35
Josh Griffin	14	Jon Wilkin	23	Jacob Miller	22
Junior Sa'u	14	Louie McCarthy-Scarsbrook	20	Tinirau Arona	18
Craig Kopczak	10	James Roby	16	Matty Ashurst	16

METRES

Salford		St Helens		Wakefield	
Justin Carney	2807	Kyle Amor	3718	Tom Johnstone	2346
Junior Sa'u	2244	Alex Walmsley	3691	Tinirau Arona	2106
Josh Jones	2070	James Roby	2544	Reece Lyne	2060
Josh Griffin	2034	Jack Owens	2282	Joe Arundel	1898
Craig Kopczak	1942	Adam Swift	2220	Craig Hall	1806

TACKLES

Salford		St Helens		Wakefield	
George Griffin	759	James Roby	1067	Tinirau Arona	751
Logan Tomkins	753	Jon Wilkin	1009	Matty Ashurst	732
Mark Flanagan	700	Louie McCarthy-Scarsbrook	763	Michael Sio	710
Craig Kopczak	681	Kyle Amor	710	Liam Finn	681
Ben Murdoch-Masila	594	Joe Greenwood	612	Nick Scruton	587

CLEAN BREAKS

Salford		St Helens		Wakefield	
Junior Sa'u	18	Adam Swift	27	Tom Johnstone	24
Justin Carney	14	Louie McCarthy-Scarsbrook	12	Craig Hall	18
Robert Lui	12	Jack Owens	12	Ben Jones-Bishop	11
Gareth O'Brien	12	Jonny Lomax	9	Joe Arundel	10
Niall Evalds	11	Mark Percival	9	Jacob Miller	8

TACKLE BUSTS

Salford		St Helens		Wakefield	
Josh Jones	107	Alex Walmsley	76	Jacob Miller	70
Justin Carney	79	Adam Swift	63	Tom Johnstone	66
Ben Murdoch-Masila	49	Louie McCarthy-Scarsbrook	62	Reece Lyne	54
Junior Sa'u	49	Shannon McDonnell	46	David Fifita	47
Gareth O'Brien	43	James Roby	46	Craig Hall	41

MARKER TACKLES

Salford		St Helens		Wakefield	
George Griffin	148	Jon Wilkin	192	Tinirau Arona	117
Mark Flanagan	124	James Roby	178	Matty Ashurst	114
Craig Kopczak	113	Kyle Amor	134	Nick Scruton	105
Logan Tomkins	111	Alex Walmsley	126	Michael Sio	101
Adam Walne	78	Louie McCarthy-Scarsbrook	123	Danny Kirmond	95

TRY ASSISTS

Salford		St Helens		Wakefield	
Gareth O'Brien	22	Luke Walsh	25	Liam Finn	18
Michael Dobson	18	Jon Wilkin	15	Jacob Miller	18
Robert Lui	13	Jordan Turner	14	Craig Hall	10
Junior Sa'u	7	Theo Fages	13	Max Jowitt	8
Ben Murdoch-Masila	5	Jonny Lomax	10	Scott Moore	6

TOTAL OPTA INDEX

Salford		St Helens		Wakefield	
Josh Jones	11915	James Roby	17084	Liam Finn	11144
Craig Kopczak	10788	Jon Wilkin	14378	Matty Ashurst	10453
George Griffin	10110	Kyle Amor	13713	Tinirau Arona	10367
Gareth O'Brien	9655	Alex Walmsley	13100	Jacob Miller	10166
Michael Dobson	9235	Louie McCarthy-Scarsbrook	12260	Tom Johnstone	9622

WARRINGTON WOLVES
SUPER LEAGUE XXI LEADERS

CARRIES

Chris Hill	486
Matthew Russell	433
Ashton Sims	381
Joe Westerman	335
Ben Currie	319

OFFLOADS

Ashton Sims	64
Ben Currie	33
Matthew Russell	33
Daryl Clark	28
Ryan Atkins	27

METRES

Chris Hill	3983
Matthew Russell	3774
Daryl Clark	2905
Ben Currie	2606
Ashton Sims	2553

TACKLES

Chris Hill	920
Joe Westerman	808
Ashton Sims	762
Jack Hughes	734
Ben Currie	721

CLEAN BREAKS

Daryl Clark	18
Kevin Penny	18
Stefan Ratchford	18
Chris Sandow	17
Matthew Russell	15

TACKLE BUSTS

Matthew Russell	126
Daryl Clark	105
Stefan Ratchford	75
Joe Westerman	72
Ryan Atkins	61

MARKER TACKLES

Chris Hill	156
Kurt Gidley	126
Ashton Sims	118
Ben Currie	108
Joe Westerman	105

TRY ASSISTS

Chris Sandow	25
Kurt Gidley	16
Ben Currie	13
Stefan Ratchford	10
Jack Hughes	7

TOTAL OPTA INDEX

Chris Hill	15939
Ben Currie	13900
Joe Westerman	13068
Daryl Clark	12947
Stefan Ratchford	12700

WIDNES VIKINGS
SUPER LEAGUE XXI LEADERS

CARRIES

Rhys Hanbury	426
Hep Cahill	362
Chris Houston	347
Joe Mellor	344
Corey Thompson	310

OFFLOADS

Matt Whitley	32
Gil Dudson	30
Hep Cahill	28
Rhys Hanbury	28
Lloyd White	27

METRES

Rhys Hanbury	3413
Corey Thompson	2861
Hep Cahill	2415
Joe Mellor	2325
Chris Houston	2235

TACKLES

Hep Cahill	1023
Lloyd White	896
Chris Houston	858
Matt Whitley	819
Chris Dean	795

CLEAN BREAKS

Joe Mellor	26
Rhys Hanbury	25
Corey Thompson	25
Patrick Ah Van	17
Stefan Marsh	14

TACKLE BUSTS

Joe Mellor	96
Corey Thompson	93
Rhys Hanbury	91
Patrick Ah Van	35
Kevin Brown	34

MARKER TACKLES

Hep Cahill	217
Chris Dean	164
Matt Whitley	145
Chris Houston	126
Aaron Heremaia	124

TRY ASSISTS

Kevin Brown	22
Joe Mellor	16
Rhys Hanbury	11
Charly Runciman	8
Lloyd White	5

TOTAL OPTA INDEX

Joe Mellor	17209
Hep Cahill	12949
Corey Thompson	12109
Rhys Hanbury	11918
Matt Whitley	11351

WIGAN WARRIORS
SUPER LEAGUE XXI LEADERS

CARRIES

Dan Sarginson	530
Josh Charnley	424
John Bateman	396
Taulima Tautai	330
Anthony Gelling	301

OFFLOADS

John Bateman	61
Dan Sarginson	48
Anthony Gelling	47
Taulima Tautai	30
George Williams	29

METRES

Josh Charnley	3679
Dan Sarginson	3561
John Bateman	2825
Taulima Tautai	2386
Anthony Gelling	2383

TACKLES

Sam Powell	1120
Willie Isa	873
Ryan Sutton	788
John Bateman	705
Ben Flower	600

CLEAN BREAKS

Josh Charnley	26
Dominic Manfredi	21
Anthony Gelling	14
Lewis Tierney	14
John Bateman	13

TACKLE BUSTS

Dominic Manfredi	119
John Bateman	109
Dan Sarginson	82
George Williams	66
Josh Charnley	65

MARKER TACKLES

Sam Powell	185
Willie Isa	152
Ryan Sutton	133
Lee Mossop	119
John Bateman	118

TRY ASSISTS

George Williams	18
Dan Sarginson	12
Matty Smith	11
Sam Tomkins	10
Anthony Gelling	6

TOTAL OPTA INDEX

John Bateman	16111
Dan Sarginson	13642
Josh Charnley	12502
Sam Powell	11813
Taulima Tautai	11047

CHAMPIONSHIP 2016
Club by Club

BATLEY BULLDOGS

DATE	FIXTURE	RESULT	SCORERS	LGE	ATT
7/2/16	Leigh (h)	W24-22	t:J Brown,Ulugia(2),Ainscough g:Walker(3),Brambani	6th	1,678
14/2/16	Featherstone (a)	L14-12	t:D Scott,Reittie g:Walker(2)	7th	2,103
21/2/16	Sheffield (h)	W20-8	t:Brambani(2),Leak g:Walker(3),Brambani	6th	814
28/2/16	Halifax (a)	W12-17	t:Bretherton,Brambani g:Brambani(3),Walker fg:Brambani	5th	2,010
6/3/16	Workington (h)	W44-12	t:Southernwood(2),Ulugia,Bretherton,J Brown,Leak,A Brown g:Walker(8)	1st	658
13/3/16	Bradford (h)	D24-24	t:Ulugia,D Scott,Hirst,A Brown g:Walker(4)	2nd	2,742
19/3/16	Whitehaven (h) (CCR4)	W37-36	t:A Brown,Davey,Rowe(2),Reittie,Chandler g:Walker(6) fg:Brambani	N/A	457
25/3/16	Dewsbury (a)	W30-44	t:Leak(2),Reittie(2),A Brown,Ainscough,Day g:Walker(8)	2nd	2,020
28/3/16	Whitehaven (h)	W24-23	t:D Scott,Gledhill,J Brown,A Brown g:Brambani(2),Walker(2)	2nd	706
3/4/16	Oldham (a)	L28-12	t:Lillycrop,Reittie g:Walker(2)	2nd	814
10/4/16	London Broncos (a)	L32-8	t:D Scott g:Walker(2)	3rd	753
16/4/16	Featherstone (h) (CCR5)	W28-10	t:Squires,Harrison,Ainscough,Brambani,Southernwood g:Walker(4)	N/A	1,461
24/4/16	Swinton (h)	L24-32	t:Gledhill(2),D Scott(2) g:Brambani(4)	4th	726
1/5/16	Leigh (a)	L37-30	t:Ainscough,Leak,Bretherton,Brambani,Harrison g:Brambani(5)	5th	3,389
6/5/16	Catalans Dragons (h) (CCR6)	L4-40	t:A Brown	N/A	1,249
15/5/16	Halifax (h)	W32-16	t:Reittie(2),Ainscough,Walker,D Scott,J Brown g:Walker(4)	5th	1,203
22/5/16	Workington (a)	W24-31	t:Blake,Minikin,A Brown,D Scott,Leak g:Brambani(2),Walker(3) fg:Walker	5th	681
29/5/16	Dewsbury (SB) ●	W28-24	t:Ulugia,Minikin,J Brown,Lillycrop g:Walker(5) fg:Walker,Brambani	3rd	N/A
5/6/16	Oldham (h)	W42-18	t:Blake,J Brown(2),Reittie,Brambani(2),Minikin g:Brambani(2),Walker(6)	3rd	783
10/6/16	Sheffield (a)	W10-24	t:Hirst,Minikin,Reittie,Chandler g:Walker(4)	3rd	651
19/6/16	Bradford (a)	L17-16	t:Southernwood(2),Ulugia g:Walker(2)	5th	4,617
26/6/16	Dewsbury (h)	W18-16	t:A Brown,Ulugia,Bretherton g:Brambani(2),Walker	4th	1,501
2/7/16	Whitehaven (a)	W8-16	t:J Brown,Reittie,Gledhill g:Walker(2)	4th	571
10/7/16	Featherstone (h)	L6-34	t:Ulugia g:Walker	4th	1,351
17/7/16	London Broncos (h)	W31-20	t:Ainscough(2),Squires,Reittie,Brambani,Gledhill g:Walker(3) fg:Brambani	3rd	783
24/7/16	Swinton (a)	W24-62	t:Leak(2),Ulugia(2),Reittie,Squires,Day,J Brown,Ainscough(2),Brambani g:Walker(9)	3rd	1,147
7/8/16	Hull KR (a) (S8-Q)	L58-18	t:Leak,Lillycrop,Rowe g:Walker,Brambani(2)	7th(S8-Q)	6,684
14/8/16	London Broncos (a) (S8-Q)	L76-16	t:J Brown,Rowe,Ulugia g:Brambani(2)	7th(S8-Q)	674
21/8/16	Huddersfield (h) (S8-Q)	L28-58	t:Squires(2),D Scott(2),Ulugia g:Brambani(4)	8th(S8-Q)	2,201
4/9/16	Featherstone (h) (S8-Q)	W11-10	t:Reittie g:Walker fg:Brambani	7th(S8-Q)	1,131
9/9/16	Leeds (a) (S8-Q)	L32-0		7th(S8-Q)	15,135
17/9/16	Leigh (a) (S8-Q)	L42-24	t:D Scott,Leak,Hirst,Reittie g:Walker(4)	7th(S8-Q)	10,556
25/9/16	Salford (h) (S8-Q)	L14-42	t:Reittie(2),Ulugia g:Brambani	7th(S8-Q)	1,520

● *Played at Bloomfield Road, Blackpool*

		APP		TRIES		GOALS		FG		PTS	
	D.O.B.	ALL	Ch	ALL	Ch	ALL	Ch	ALL	Ch	ALL	Ch
Shaun Ainscough	27/11/89	22(1)	17	9	8	0	0	0	0	36	32
Luke Blake	10/8/89	23(2)	17(1)	2	2	0	0	0	0	8	8
Dominic Brambani	10/5/85	33	23	9	8	30	21	5	3	101	77
Alex Bretherton	5/12/82	29(1)	19(1)	4	4	0	0	0	0	16	16
Alex Brown	28/8/87	17(1)	12(1)	8	6	0	0	0	0	32	24
James Brown	6/5/88	14(15)	10(12)	10	9	0	0	0	0	40	36
Callum Casey	6/6/90	1	1	0	0	0	0	0	0	0	0
Joe Chandler	2/11/88	22(4)	19(1)	2	1	0	0	0	0	8	4
Danny Cowling	20/12/92	9	7	0	0	0	0	0	0	0	0
James Davey	21/8/89	6(16)	5(10)	1	0	0	0	0	0	4	0
Brad Day	23/9/94	14(4)	6(4)	2	2	0	0	0	0	8	8
Adam Gledhill	15/2/93	16(13)	13(7)	5	5	0	0	0	0	20	20
James Harrison	15/6/96	2(8)	1(5)	2	1	0	0	0	0	8	4
Sean Hesketh	17/8/86	1	1	0	0	0	0	0	0	0	0
Keegan Hirst	13/12/88	32	23	3	2	0	0	0	0	12	8
Alistair Leak	5/4/92	17(9)	10(7)	10	8	0	0	0	0	40	32
Tom Lillycrop	29/11/91	(31)	(22)	3	2	0	0	0	0	12	8
Frankie Mariano	10/5/87	3(1)	3(1)	0	0	0	0	0	0	0	0
Greg Minikin	29/3/95	7	7	4	4	0	0	0	0	16	16
Dave Petersen	6/3/92	(2)	(1)	0	0	0	0	0	0	0	0
Wayne Reittie	21/1/88	30	20	17	11	0	0	0	0	68	44
Alex Rowe	11/3/85	13(11)	6(9)	4	0	0	0	0	0	16	0
Dave Scott	8/6/93	33	23	11	8	0	0	0	0	44	32
Sam Scott	5/6/90	1	1	0	0	0	0	0	0	0	0
Sam Smeaton	26/10/88	4(2)	0	0	0	0	0	0	0	0	0
Cain Southernwood	4/5/92	25	20	5	4	0	0	0	0	20	16
Shaun Squires	20/3/90	10	6	5	2	0	0	0	0	20	8
Chris Ulugia	15/1/92	26	17	13	10	0	0	0	0	52	40
Pat Walker	24/3/86	19(11)	12(10)	1	1	91	75	2	2	188	156

'Ch' totals include Championship regular season only; 'All' totals also include Super 8s (Qualifiers) & Challenge Cup

Dominic Brambani

LEAGUE RECORD
Championship, before Super 8 split:
P23-W15-D1-L7 (3rd)
F589, A485, Diff+104, 31 points.

S8-Q: P7-W1-D0-L6 (7th)
F111, A318, Diff-207, 2 points.

CHALLENGE CUP
Round Six

ATTENDANCES
Best - v Bradford (Ch - 2,742)
Worst - v Whitehaven (CC - 457)
Total (Championship/S8s only) - 17,797
Average (Championship/S8s only) - 1,271
(Up by 344 on 2015)

CLUB RECORDS	
MATCH RECORDS	Highest score: 100-4 v Gateshead, 17/3/2010 Highest score against: 9-78 v Wakefield, 26/8/67 Record attendance: 23,989 v Leeds, 14/3/25
	Tries: 5 Joe Oakland v Bramley, 19/12/1908; Tommy Brannan v Swinton, 17/1/20; Jim Wale v Bramley, 4/12/26; Jim Wale v Cottingham, 12/2/27;
	Tommy Oldroyd v Highfield, 6/3/94; Ben Feehan v Halifax, 10/8/2008; Jermaine McGillvary v Whitehaven, 24/5/2009
	Goals: 16 Gareth Moore v Gateshead, 17/3/2010 Points: 40 Gareth Moore v Gateshead, 17/3/2010
SEASON RECORDS	Tries: 30 Johnny Campbell 2010 Goals: 144 Barry Eaton 2004 Points: 308 Richard Price 1997
CAREER RECORDS	Tries: 142 Craig Lingard 1998-2008 Goals: 463 Wharton 'Wattie' Davies 1897-1912 Points: 1,297 Wharton 'Wattie' Davies 1897-1912
	Appearances: 421 Wharton 'Wattie' Davies 1897-1912

BRADFORD BULLS

DATE	FIXTURE	RESULT	SCORERS	LGE	ATT
7/2/16	Featherstone (h)	W22-12	t:Gaskell,Caro(3) g:Addy(3)	4th	4,518
13/2/16	Whitehaven (a)	W10-46	t:Clare,Gaskell(3),Pitts(2),Ferguson,O'Brien g:Addy(7)	2nd	878
20/2/16	Swinton (a) ●	W16-48	t:Olbison(2),Welham(3),Caro,Clare,Blythe,Gaskell g:Addy(6)	1st	880
28/2/16	Leigh (h)	D32-32	t:Welham,Clare(2),Purtell,Addy,Caro g:Addy(4)	1st	6,563
13/3/16	Batley (a)	D24-24	t:Caro,Ferguson,Pitts(2) g:Addy(4)	4th	2,742
18/3/16	Dewsbury (a) (CCR4)	L31-30	t:Caro,Lumb,Addy,Blythe(2),Olbison g:Addy(3)	N/A	2,021
24/3/16	London Broncos (h)	W28-20	t:Clare,Blythe,Haggerty(2),Ryan g:Addy(4)	3rd	4,163
28/3/16	Halifax (a)	L14-10	t:Uaisele,Clare g:Addy	4th	4,018
3/4/16	Sheffield (h)	L28-46	t:Addy,Gaskell,Caro,Clare,Welham g:Addy(4)	4th	4,234
10/4/16	Dewsbury (a)	W18-52	t:Welham(5),Gaskell,Caro(2),Mellor,Clare g:Addy(3),Caro(3)	4th	1,954
24/4/16	Workington (h)	W52-16	t:Clark,Williams(2),Purtell,Clare,Welham,Caro(2),Thomas,Ferguson g:Addy(6)	3rd	3,467
1/5/16	London Broncos (a)	L30-16	t:Addy,Welham(2) g:Addy(2)	3rd	1,524
15/5/16	Swinton (h)	W54-8	t:Clare(2),Caro(2),Sidlow,Welham,Addy,Thomas,Olbison,Gaskell g:Addy(6),Thomas	3rd	4,152
20/5/16	Sheffield (a)	W14-25	t:Thomas,Williams,Sidlow,Welham g:Addy(4) fg:Thomas	3rd	995
28/5/16	Leigh (SB) ●●	L20-24	t:Williams,Clark,O'Brien,Addy g:Addy(2)	4th	N/A
5/6/16	Dewsbury (h)	L14-16	t:Pitts,O'Brien g:Addy(3)	6th	4,303
12/6/16	Workington (a)	W22-29	t:O'Brien,Ryan,Sidlow,Clare,Charnock g:Addy(4) fg:Addy	5th	723
15/6/16	Oldham (a)	W4-48	t:Mellor,Thomas,Campbell,Charnock,Clark,O'Brien,Clare(2),Pitts g:Thomas(6)	4th	1,051
19/6/16	Batley (h)	W17-16	t:Clare(2),Pitts g:Haggerty(2) fg:Haggerty	3rd	4,617
26/6/16	Halifax (h)	L24-32	t:Moss,Haggerty,Welham,Ryan g:Addy(4)	5th	6,312
3/7/16	Leigh (a)	L22-20	t:Caro,Moss,Clare,Mellor g:Addy(2)	5th	5,111
10/7/16	Whitehaven (h)	W64-18	t:Ryan(3),Sidlow,Chisholm(2),Moss(2),Philbin,Crossley,Clare g:Addy(5),Chisholm(2),Charnock(3)	5th	4,163
17/7/16	Oldham (h)	W44-12	t:Welham,Caro(5),Haggerty,Philbin,Ryan g:Addy,Charnock(3)	4th	4,235
24/7/16	Featherstone (a)	L20-0		5th	4,554
7/8/16	Whitehaven (a) (CS)	W18-46	t:Addy,Mellor(3),Williams,Blythe,Welham,Moss,Haggerty g:Addy(3),Charnock(2)	1st(CS)	675
14/8/16	Halifax (h) (CS)	W44-22	t:Mellor,Moss(2),Welham,Purtell,Pitts,Williams g:Charnock(6)	1st(CS)	3,498
21/8/16	Oldham (h) (CS)	W82-0	t:Welham(5),Olbison,Pitts(3),Lauaki,Chisholm(2),Keyes,Williams,Ryan g:Keyes(10),Crossley	1st(CS)	3,022
29/8/16	Dewsbury (a) (CS)	W26-36	t:Pitts,Williams(2),Ryan,Welham,Chisholm,Clark g:Keyes(2),Addy(2)	1st(CS)	1,807
4/9/16	Swinton (h) (CS)	W46-28	t:O'Brien(2),Ryan(3),Pitts,Kavanagh,Chisholm g:Keyes(7)	1st(CS)	4,030
11/9/16	Workington (a) (CS)	L30-26	t:Clark,Ryan,Oakes,Moss,Ferguson g:Keyes(3)	1st(CS)	596
18/9/16	Sheffield (h) (CS)	W80-0	t:Charnock,Chisholm(2),Olbison,Moss(4),Ryan(2),Pitts,Oakes(3),Sidlow g:Charnock(5),Chisholm(4),Sidlow	1st(CS)	4,035
25/9/16	Dewsbury (h) (CSSF)	W36-22	t:Chisholm,Mellor(2),Welham,Williams,Moss,Ryan g:Charnock(4)	N/A	2,189
2/10/16	Sheffield (h) (CSF)	W27-16	t:O'Brien(2),Purtell,Welham(2) g:Charnock(3) fg:Chisholm	N/A	3,518

● *Played at Select Security Stadium, Widnes* ●● *Played at Bloomfield Road, Blackpool*

		APP		TRIES		GOALS		FG		PTS	
	D.O.B.	ALL	Ch	ALL	Ch	ALL	Ch	ALL	Ch	ALL	Ch
Danny Addy	15/1/91	31	21	7	5	83	75	1	1	195	171
Jean-Philippe Baile	7/6/87	(1)	(1)	0	0	0	0	0	0	0	0
James Bentley	19/10/97	(1)	0	0	0	0	0	0	0	0	0
Matty Blythe	20/11/88	12(4)	9(4)	5	2	0	0	0	0	20	8
Johnny Campbell	17/7/87	3	3	1	1	0	0	0	0	4	4
Omari Caro	7/3/91	19	18	20	19	3	3	0	0	86	82
Lewis Charnock	2/9/94	12	7	3	2	26	6	0	0	64	20
Dane Chisholm	4/7/90	11	3	9	2	6	2	1	0	49	12
James Clare	13/4/91	23	22	18	18	0	0	0	0	72	72
Mitch Clark	13/3/93	6(18)	5(11)	5	3	0	0	0	0	20	12
Paul Clough	27/9/87	12(1)	11(1)	0	0	0	0	0	0	0	0
Steve Crossley	28/11/89	7(12)	6(9)	1	1	1	0	0	0	6	4
Dale Ferguson	13/4/88	13(9)	11(5)	4	3	0	0	0	0	16	12
Daniel Fleming	8/7/92	2(3)	2(3)	0	0	0	0	0	0	0	0
Lee Gaskell	28/10/90	12	11	8	8	0	0	0	0	32	32
Kurt Haggerty	8/1/89	22(3)	16(3)	5	4	2	2	1	1	25	21
Stuart Howarth	25/1/90	4(5)	3(2)	0	0	0	0	0	0	0	0
Ben Kavanagh	4/3/88	12(3)	4(2)	1	0	0	0	0	0	4	0
Joe Keyes	17/9/95	4	0	1	0	22	0	0	0	48	0
Liam Kirk	26/3/97	(3)	0	0	0	0	0	0	0	0	0
Epalahame Lauaki	27/1/84	(9)	(6)	1	0	0	0	0	0	4	0
Rhys Lovegrove	11/3/87	3(2)	2(2)	0	0	0	0	0	0	0	0
Joe Lumb	21/8/96	2(8)	2(6)	1	0	0	0	0	0	4	0
Richard Mathers	24/10/83	8	8	0	0	0	0	0	0	0	0
Alex Mellor	24/9/94	16(10)	7(9)	9	3	0	0	0	0	36	12
Kieren Moss	6/8/93	16	7	13	4	0	0	0	0	52	16
Adam O'Brien	11/7/93	23(8)	15(7)	9	5	0	0	0	0	36	20
Ross Oakes	12/10/96	3(3)	2	4	0	0	0	0	0	16	0
Tom Olbison	20/3/91	18(11)	14(5)	6	3	0	0	0	0	24	12
Joe Philbin	16/11/94	1(4)	1(4)	2	2	0	0	0	0	8	8
Jay Pitts	9/12/89	26(6)	17(5)	14	7	0	0	0	0	56	28
Adrian Purtell	31/1/85	9	7	4	2	0	0	0	0	16	8
Josh Rickett	20/10/97	1	0	0	0	0	0	0	0	0	0
Ethan Ryan	12/5/96	14	8	16	7	0	0	0	0	64	28
Adam Sidlow	25/10/87	23(3)	15(2)	5	4	1	0	0	0	22	16
Oscar Thomas	3/1/94	11(1)	10(1)	4	4	7	7	1	1	31	31
Jacob Trueman	16/2/99	(1)	(1)	0	0	0	0	0	0	0	0
Etuate Uaisele	8/12/84	2	1	1	1	0	0	0	0	4	4
Jonathan Walker	20/2/91	(3)	(3)	0	0	0	0	0	0	0	0
Lucas Walshaw	4/8/92	3	3	0	0	0	0	0	0	0	0
Kris Welham	12/5/87	30	21	29	17	0	0	0	0	116	68
Danny Williams	26/9/86	15	7	10	4	0	0	0	0	40	16

'Ch' totals include Championship regular season only; 'All' totals also include Championship Shield & Challenge Cup

Kris Welham

LEAGUE RECORD
Championship, before Super 8 split:
P23-W13-D2-L8 (5th)
F717, A446, Diff+271, 28 points.

After Championship Shield:
P30-W19-D2-L9 (1st/Winners)
F1077, A570, Diff+507, 40 points.

CHALLENGE CUP
Round Four

ATTENDANCES
Best - v Leigh (Ch - 6,563)
Worst - v Dewsbury (CSSF - 2,189)
Total (Championship/
Championship Shield only) - 71,019
Average (Championship/
Championship Shield only) - 4,178
(Down by 1,279 on 2015)

CLUB RECORDS	Highest score: 98-6 v Toulouse, 19/4/2008 Highest score against: 6-84 v Wigan, 21/4/2014 Record attendance: 69,429 v Huddersfield, 14/3/53
MATCH RECORDS	Tries: 6 Eric Batten v Leeds, 15/9/45; Trevor Foster v Wakefield, 10/4/48; Steve McGowan v Barrow, 8/11/92; Lesley Vainikolo v Hull, 2/9/2005
	Goals: 15 Iestyn Harris v Toulouse, 15/4/2008 Points: 36 John Woods v Swinton, 13/10/85
SEASON RECORDS	Tries: 63 Jack McLean 1951-52 Goals: 213 (inc 5fg) Henry Paul 2001 Points: 457 Henry Paul 2001
CAREER RECORDS	Tries: 261 Jack McLean 1950-56 Goals: 1,165 (inc 25fg) Paul Deacon 1998-2009 Points: 2,605 Paul Deacon 1998-2009
	Appearances: 588 Keith Mumby 1973-90; 1992-93

DEWSBURY RAMS

DATE	FIXTURE	RESULT	SCORERS	LGE	ATT
7/2/16	Swinton (a) ●	W24-26	t:Guzdek(3),Reynolds,Sykes g:Reynolds(3)	5th	639
14/2/16	Workington (h)	W38-16	t:Crookes(2),Grant(2),Morton,Kain,Guzdek,Trout g:Reynolds(3)	4th	786
21/2/16	Oldham (a)	L38-16	t:Grant(2),Teanby g:Reynolds,Sykes	7th	816
28/2/16	Whitehaven (h)	W20-4	t:Guzdek,Grady,Hale g:Sykes(4)	4th	778
6/3/16	Featherstone (a)	L21-20	t:Guzdek,Grady,Crookes g:Reynolds(4)	6th	1,665
12/3/16	London Broncos (a)	L22-18	t:Grant,Crookes,Trout g:Delaney(2),Sykes	7th	512
18/3/16	Bradford (h) (CCR4)	W31-30	t:Grant,Morton(2),Teanby,Brown g:Sykes(5) fg:Sykes	N/A	2,021
25/3/16	Batley (h)	L30-44	t:L Adamson,Guzdek,Grady,Morton,Sykes,Kain g:Sykes(2),Hemingway	8th	2,020
28/3/16	Sheffield (h)	W34-16	t:Morton(2),Grant,Grady,Farrell,L Adamson g:Sykes(5)	7th	813
3/4/16	Leigh (h)	L18-40	t:L Adamson,Morton,Teanby g:Sykes(3)	8th	1,691
10/4/16	Bradford (h)	L18-52	t:Grant,Farrell(2) g:Sykes(2),Hemingway	8th	1,954
15/4/16	York (h) (CCR5)	W30-16	t:Teanby,Morton(2),Grant,Kain g:Glover(5)	N/A	707
24/4/16	Halifax (a)	L23-14	t:Grant,Uaisele g:Glover(3)	8th	1,453
29/4/16	Sheffield (a)	L32-28	t:L Adamson,Grant,Uaisele,Brown,Conroy g:Glover,Grady,Sykes(2)	9th	441
8/5/16	Wigan (h) (CCR6)	L4-54	t:Sykes	N/A	3,102
14/5/16	Whitehaven (a)	W16-36	t:Hale,Sykes(2),Grady,Guzdek,Grant g:Sykes(6)	8th	684
22/5/16	Featherstone (h)	L0-31		8th	1,281
29/5/16	Batley (SB) ●●	L28-24	t:Crookes,Sykes,Morton,Grant g:Sykes(4)	9th	N/A
5/6/16	Bradford (a)	W14-16	t:Grady,Guzdek g:Sykes(4)	7th	4,303
12/6/16	Oldham (h)	W46-10	t:Grant,Speakman,Crookes,Uaisele,Spicer,Kain,Morton g:Sykes(9)	7th	742
19/6/16	Halifax (h)	L8-24	t:Hale,Morton	7th	1,146
26/6/16	Batley (a)	L18-16	t:Crookes,Kain,Guzdek g:Sykes(2)	8th	1,501
3/7/16	London Broncos (h)	L6-34	t:Guzdek g:Sykes	8th	645
10/7/16	Workington (a)	L22-20	t:Morton,Tonks,Walshaw,Kain g:Sykes(2)	9th	492
17/7/16	Swinton (h)	W34-16	t:Walshaw,Morton,Groat,Kain,Tonks,Sykes g:Sykes(5)	7th	739
24/7/16	Leigh (a)	L58-0		8th	3,498
7/8/16	Swinton (h) (CS)	W36-24	t:Sykes(2),Farrell,Walshaw,Guzdek,Speakman g:Sykes(6)	4th(CS)	674
14/8/16	Workington (a) (CS)	L34-24	t:Morton(2),Guzdek,Sykes g:Sykes(4)	4th(CS)	527
21/8/16	Halifax (a) (CS)	W22-24	t:Uaisele(2),Kain,Tonks g:Sykes(3),Hemingway	4th(CS)	1,133
29/8/16	Bradford (h) (CS)	L26-36	t:Morton(2),Brown,Speakman g:Glover(4),Grady	4th(CS)	1,807
4/9/16	Whitehaven (h) (CS)	L12-56	t:Teanby(2) g:Hemingway(2)	4th(CS)	524
11/9/16	Sheffield (a) (CS)	W22-38	t:Hale,Uaisele,T Adamson,Brown,Walshaw,Hemingway g:Hemingway(3),Grady(4)	4th(CS)	564
18/9/16	Oldham (h) (CS)	W30-12	t:Uaisele,Crookes,Kain,Walshaw,Grady g:Hemingway,Grady(4)	4th(CS)	628
25/9/16	Bradford (a) (CSSF)	L36-22	t:Kain,Crookes,Guzdek,T Adamson g:Grady(3)	N/A	2,189

● *Played at AJ Bell Stadium, Salford* ●● *Played at Bloomfield Road, Blackpool*

APP TRIES GOALS FG PTS

	D.O.B.	ALL	Ch	ALL	Ch	ALL	Ch	ALL	Ch	ALL	Ch
Luke Adamson	17/11/87	22(4)	17(4)	4	4	0	0	0	0	16	16
Toby Adamson	28/5/90	14(1)	8	2	0	0	0	0	0	8	0
Sam Bates	2/12/95	(1)	0	0	0	0	0	0	0	0	0
Aaron Brown	27/7/92	10(14)	5(8)	4	1	0	0	0	0	16	4
Nathan Conroy	6/3/95	5(20)	5(12)	1	1	0	0	0	0	4	4
Jason Crookes	21/4/90	32	23	9	7	0	0	0	0	36	28
Brad Delaney	25/5/95	1	0	0	0	2	2	0	0	4	4
Joel Farrell	15/3/94	11(9)	9(6)	4	3	0	0	0	0	16	12
James Glover	2/12/93	7(1)	4	0	0	13	4	0	0	26	8
Bobbie Goulding	4/3/93	2	2	0	0	0	0	0	0	0	0
Shane Grady	13/12/89	28	20	7	6	13	1	0	0	54	26
Dalton Grant	21/4/90	22	19	14	12	0	0	0	0	56	48
Matt Groat	4/3/92	23(1)	17(1)	1	1	0	0	0	0	4	4
Josh Guzdek	22/4/95	34	23	14	11	0	0	0	0	56	44
Scott Hale	14/12/91	22	14	4	3	0	0	0	0	16	12
Tom Hemingway	6/12/86	16(1)	8(1)	1	0	9	2	0	0	22	4
Ryan Hepworth	16/1/81	8(4)	8(4)	0	0	0	0	0	0	0	0
Paul Jackson	29/9/78	5(2)	4(1)	0	0	0	0	0	0	0	0
Andy Kain	1/9/85	27(1)	17(1)	10	6	0	0	0	0	40	24
Donald Kudangirana	23/5/95	2	0	0	0	0	0	0	0	0	0
Dale Morton	31/10/90	31	21	18	10	0	0	0	0	72	40
Jason Muranka	4/8/89	1(7)	1(6)	0	0	0	0	0	0	0	0
Karl Pryce	27/7/86	1(2)	(2)	0	0	0	0	0	0	0	0
Ben Reynolds	15/1/94	4	4	1	1	11	11	0	0	26	26
Dom Speakman	22/3/94	22(1)	12(1)	3	1	0	0	0	0	12	4
Rob Spicer	22/9/84	8(5)	5(1)	1	1	0	0	0	0	4	4
Mitchell Stringer	1/11/83	8(3)	3(2)	0	0	0	0	0	0	0	0
Paul Sykes	11/8/81	25(3)	19(3)	10	6	71	53	1	0	183	130
Jack Teanby	14/5/96	2(18)	(12)	6	2	0	0	0	0	24	8
Tony Tonks	27/4/85	(22)	(14)	3	2	0	0	0	0	12	8
Kyle Trout	1/3/91	22(7)	14(6)	2	2	0	0	0	0	8	8
Etuate Uaisele	8/12/84	15(1)	9(1)	7	3	0	0	0	0	28	12
Jonathan Walker	20/2/91	2(2)	2	0	0	0	0	0	0	0	0
Lucas Walshaw	4/8/92	10	5	5	2	0	0	0	0	20	8
Ryan Wright	28/10/91	(6)	(6)	0	0	0	0	0	0	0	0

'Ch' totals include Championship regular season only; 'All' totals also include Championship Shield & Challenge Cup

Josh Guzdek

LEAGUE RECORD
Championship, before Super 8 split:
P23-W8-D0-L15 (8th)
F486, A603, Diff-117, 16 points.

After Championship Shield:
P30-W12-D0-L18 (4th/Semi-Finalists)
F676, A809, Diff-133, 24 points.

CHALLENGE CUP
Round Six

ATTENDANCES
Best - v Wigan (CC - 3,102)
Worst - v Whitehaven (CS - 524)
Total (Championship/
Championship Shield only) - 16,228
Average (Championship/
Championship Shield only) - 1,082
(Down by 161 on 2015)

CLUB RECORDS	**Highest score:** 90-5 v Blackpool, 4/4/93 **Highest score against:** 0-82 v Widnes, 30/11/86
	Record attendance: 26,584 v Halifax, 30/10/20 (*Crown Flatt*); 4,068 v Bradford, 6/4/2015 (*Tetley's Stadium*)
MATCH RECORDS	**Tries:** 8 Dai Thomas v Liverpool, 13/4/1907
	Goals: 13 Greg Pearce v Blackpool Borough, 4/4/93; Francis Maloney v Hunslet, 25/3/2007 **Points:** 32 Les Holliday v Barrow, 11/9/94
SEASON RECORDS	**Tries:** 40 Dai Thomas 1906-07 **Goals:** 169 Barry Eaton 2000 **Points:** 394 Barry Eaton 2000
CAREER RECORDS	**Tries:** 144 Joe Lyman 1913-31 **Goals:** 863 Nigel Stephenson 1967-78; 1984-86 **Points:** 2,082 Nigel Stephenson 1967-78; 1984-86
	Appearances: 454 Joe Lyman 1913-31

FEATHERSTONE ROVERS

DATE	FIXTURE	RESULT	SCORERS	LGE	ATT
7/2/16	Bradford (a)	L22-12	t:Craven,Thackeray g:Briggs(2)	9th	4,518
14/2/16	Batley (h)	W14-12	t:Handley,Taulapapa g:Briggs(3)	8th	2,103
28/2/16	Oldham (h)	W20-6	t:Taulapapa,Thackeray,Briggs,Craven g:Briggs(2)	8th	1,739
6/3/16	Dewsbury (h)	W21-20	t:Briggs,Johnson,Taulapapa,Turner g:Briggs(2) fg:Craven	7th	1,665
13/3/16	Swinton (a)	W10-30	t:Turner,Hardman,Johnson,Cording,Briggs,Thackeray g:Briggs(3)	5th	745
19/3/16	London Broncos (a) (CCR4)	W26-48	t:Hardman(5),Ormondroyd,Day,Johnson,Turner g:Johnson(6)	N/A	294
25/3/16	Sheffield (h)	W28-16	t:Taulapapa,Ellis,Cording(2),Briggs g:Briggs(4)	5th	2,052
28/3/16	London Broncos (a)	L20-12	t:Baldwinson,Davies,Craven	5th	428
3/4/16	Halifax (h)	L19-20	t:Lilley,Taulapapa,Turner g:Lilley(3) fg:Lilley	6th	2,129
10/4/16	Workington (a)	W6-52	t:Davies(2),Hardman(2),Turner,Craven,Knowles-Tagg,Ormondroyd,Cording g:Johnson(8)	5th	719
16/4/16	Batley (a) (CCR5)	L28-10	t:Taulapapa,Cording g:Johnson	N/A	1,461
24/4/16	Leigh (h)	L24-30	t:Ellis,Knowles-Tagg,Taulapapa,Johnson g:Johnson(4)	5th	2,731
1/5/16	Oldham (a)	L16-14	t:Hardman,Taulapapa g:Foster(3)	6th	868
7/5/16	Whitehaven (a)	W22-44	t:Taulapapa(3),Johnson,Craven,Roche,Thackeray g:Foster(8)	4th	658
15/5/16	London Broncos (h)	W42-18	t:Foster,Briscoe(2),Ormondroyd,Craven(2),Thackeray g:Foster(7)	4th	1,723
22/5/16	Dewsbury (a)	W0-31	t:Taulapapa(2),Davies,Cording,Hardman g:Foster(5) fg:Briggs	4th	1,281
29/5/16	Halifax (SB) ●	L0-37		5th	N/A
5/6/16	Swinton (a)	W58-12	t:Baldwinson(2),Craven(2),Davies,Cording,Briggs,Johnson,Knowles-Tagg, Hardman g:Briggs(6),Craven(3)	4th	1,381
12/6/16	Leigh (a)	L16-12	t:Ellis,Knowles-Tagg g:Foster(2)	6th	3,503
19/6/16	Whitehaven (h)	W30-18	t:Briggs,Lilley,Ormondroyd,Griffin,Foster g:Foster(5)	6th	1,456
24/6/16	Sheffield (a)	L35-10	t:Cording,Duckworth g:Foster	6th	817
3/7/16	Workington (h)	W44-22	t:Handley,Cording,Briggs,Thackeray,Channing,Foster,Hardman,Spears g:Foster(6)	6th	1,281
10/7/16	Batley (a)	W6-34	t:Bostock,Briggs,Hardman,Golding,Channing g:Briggs(7)	6th	1,351
17/7/16	Halifax (h)	W20-24	t:Ellis,Golding,Taulapapa,Thackeray g:Briggs(4)	5th	2,305
24/7/16	Bradford (h)	W20-0	t:Ellis,Thackeray,Snitch g:Briggs(4)	4th	4,554
6/8/16	Leeds (h) (S8-Q)	L6-62	t:Thackeray g:Briggs	8th(S8-Q)	6,671
14/8/16	Huddersfield (a) (S8-Q)	L62-16	t:Davies,Briscoe,Hardman g:Briggs(2)	8th(S8-Q)	3,690
21/8/16	Leigh (h) (S8-Q)	L18-30	t:Walters,Briscoe,Ormondroyd g:Briggs(3)	7th(S8-Q)	3,644
4/9/16	Batley (a) (S8-Q)	L11-10	t:Briscoe,Duckworth g:Foster	8th(S8-Q)	1,131
11/9/16	Salford (a) (S8-Q)	L70-16	t:Baldwinson,Ormondroyd,Walters g:Briggs(2)	8th(S8-Q)	1,759
18/9/16	Hull KR (h) (S8-Q)	L24-32	t:Walters,Duckworth,Taulapapa(2) g:Briggs(3),Craven	8th(S8-Q)	4,034
25/9/16	London Broncos (a) (S8-Q)	L46-6	t:Davies g:Craven	8th(S8-Q)	605

● Played at Bloomfield Road, Blackpool

	D.O.B.	APP ALL	Ch	TRIES ALL	Ch	GOALS ALL	Ch	FG ALL	Ch	PTS ALL	Ch
Jordan Abdull	5/2/96	4(1)	4(1)	0	0	0	0	0	0	0	0
Mitch Achurch	14/7/88	1(2)	1(2)	0	0	0	0	0	0	0	0
Jordan Baldwinson	10/11/94	20(8)	13(8)	4	3	0	0	0	0	16	12
Liam Blockley	19/9/95	4(2)	3(1)	0	0	0	0	0	0	0	0
Andrew Bostock	25/2/85	21(5)	17(5)	1	1	0	0	0	0	4	4
Kyle Briggs	7/12/87	21(4)	15(4)	8	8	48	37	1	1	129	107
Luke Briscoe	11/3/94	10	3	5	2	0	0	0	0	20	8
Michael Channing	30/6/92	12	10	2	2	0	0	0	0	8	8
Luke Cooper	28/7/94	(16)	(7)	0	0	0	0	0	0	0	0
Jamie Cording	30/12/89	22	20	9	8	0	0	0	0	36	32
Danny Craven	21/11/91	24	16	9	5	3	1	1	47	43	
John Davies	8/1/91	27(2)	20(2)	7	5	0	0	0	0	28	20
Sam Day	12/6/94	(7)	(1)	1	0	0	0	0	0	4	0
James Duckworth	9/4/94	9	2	3	1	0	0	0	0	12	4
Andy Ellis	15/12/84	24(2)	18(1)	5	5	0	0	0	0	20	20
Jamie Foster	27/7/90	10(1)	9	3	3	38	37	0	0	88	86
Ashton Golding	4/9/96	3	3	2	2	0	0	0	0	8	8
Darrell Griffin	19/6/81	19(13)	13(10)	1	1	0	0	0	0	4	4
Ash Handley	16/2/96	3	3	2	2	0	0	0	0	8	8
Ian Hardman	8/12/84	29(1)	20(1)	14	8	0	0	0	0	56	32
Kyran Johnson	23/3/94	15	13	6	5	19	12	0	0	62	44
Bradley Knowles-Tagg	31/7/93	20(5)	14(3)	4	4	0	0	0	0	16	16
Jordan Lilley	4/9/96	3	3	2	2	3	3	1	1	15	15
Will Milner	28/10/94	3(3)	2(3)	0	0	0	0	0	0	0	0
Anthony Mullally	28/6/91	(3)	(3)	0	0	0	0	0	0	0	0
Jack Ormondroyd	7/11/91	11(19)	7(16)	6	3	0	0	0	0	24	12
Colton Roche	23/6/93	3(13)	2(12)	1	1	0	0	0	0	4	4
Steve Snitch	22/2/83	7(5)	5	1	1	0	0	0	0	4	4
Tim Spears	27/7/84	20(7)	16(4)	1	1	0	0	0	0	4	4
Misi Taulapapa	25/1/82	28	20	16	13	0	0	0	0	64	52
Anthony Thackeray	19/2/86	26(1)	18	9	8	0	0	0	0	36	32
Scott Turner	15/4/88	11	9	5	4	0	0	0	0	20	16
Josh Walters	23/12/94	6		3	0	0	0	0	0	12	0
Robbie Ward	27/10/95	(4)	(4)	0	0	0	0	0	0	0	0

'Ch' totals include Championship regular season only; 'All' totals also include Super 8s (Qualifiers) & Challenge Cup

Misi Taulapapa

LEAGUE RECORD
Championship, before Super 8 split:
P23-W15-D0-L8 (4th)
F595, A384, Diff+211, 30 points.

S8-Q: P7-W0-D0-L7 (8th)
F96, A313, Diff-217, 0 points.

CHALLENGE CUP
Round Five

ATTENDANCES
Best - v Leeds (S8 - 6,671)
Worst - v Workington (Ch - 1,281)
Total (Championship/S8s only) - 37,163
Average (Championship/
S8s only) - 2,655
(Up by 671 on 2015)

CLUB RECORDS MATCH RECORDS	**Highest score:** 96-0 v Castleford Lock Lane, 8/2/2004 **Highest score against:** 14-80 v Bradford, 3/4/2005 **Record attendance:** 17,531 v St Helens, 21/3/59
	Tries: 6 Mike Smith v Doncaster, 13/4/68; Chris Bibb v Keighley, 17/9/89
	Goals: 13 Mark Knapper v Keighley, 17/9/89; Liam Finn v Hunslet Old Boys, 25/3/2012; Liam Finn v Swinton, 12/8/2012
	Points: 40 Martin Pearson v Whitehaven, 26/11/95
SEASON RECORDS	**Tries:** 48 Paul Newlove 1992-93 **Goals:** 183 *(inc 2fg)* Liam Finn 2012 **Points:** 436 Liam Finn 2012
CAREER RECORDS	**Tries:** 162 Don Fox 1953-66 **Goals:** 1,210 Steve Quinn 1975-88 **Points:** 2,654 Steve Quinn 1975-88 **Appearances:** 440 Jim Denton 1921-37

HALIFAX

DATE	FIXTURE	RESULT	SCORERS	LGE	ATT
7/2/16	Whitehaven (h)	W52-6	t:Tyrer(4),G Moore,Smeaton,Kaye,Sharp,Saltonstall g:Tyrer(8)	1st	1,785
12/2/16	Sheffield (a)	L26-6	t:Sharp g:Tyrer	6th	1,350
21/2/16	Workington (a)	W0-20	t:Eccleston,Maneely,Ambler,Manning g:Tyrer(2)	2nd	641
28/2/16	Batley (h)	L12-17	t:Manning,G Moore g:Tyrer(2)	7th	2,010
6/3/16	London Broncos (a)	L29-22	t:Ambler,Saltonstall,Murrell(2) g:Tyrer(3)	8th	732
13/3/16	Leigh (h)	L18-26	t:Saxton,Tangata,C Robinson g:Tyrer(3)	8th	2,706
19/3/16	Pilkington Recs (a) (CCR4) ●	W0-78	t:Barber,C Robinson(2),Greenwood,Tangata,G Moore(2),B Moore,Ambler(2),Smeaton, Eccleston,Fairbank,R Moore g:Tyrer(6),G Moore,C Robinson(4)	N/A	837
25/3/16	Oldham (a)	W28-42	t:Saltonstall(2),Eccleston,G Moore(2),Greenwood,Cahalane g:G Moore(6),C Robinson	6th	1,046
28/3/16	Bradford (h)	W14-10	t:Eccleston,Manning g:Tyrer(3)	6th	4,018
3/4/16	Featherstone (a)	W19-20	t:G Moore,Smeaton(2) g:Tyrer(4)	5th	2,129
10/4/16	Swinton (h)	L35-38	t:Greenwood(2),Smeaton,Eccleston,B Moore,Kaye g:Tyrer(5) fg:G Moore	6th	1,551
17/4/16	Castleford Lock Lane (h) (CCR5)	W80-4	t:Johnston(2),Fairbank,Barber(4),Potts(2),C Robinson,G Moore,Bracek,Greenwood, Ambler g:Tyrer(12)	N/A	1,108
24/4/16	Dewsbury (h)	W23-14	t:G Moore,Potts,Tangata g:Tyrer(5) fg:Murrell	6th	1,453
1/5/16	Workington (h)	W36-32	t:Smeaton,Manning,Tyrer,Bennion,Murrell,Saltonstall g:Tyrer(6)	4th	1,293
8/5/16	Widnes (h) (CCR6)	L18-28	t:Saltonstall,A Robinson,Greenwood g:Tyrer(3)	N/A	2,032
15/5/16	Batley (a)	L32-16	t:Tyrer,Sarsfield,Heaton g:Tyrer(2)	6th	1,203
20/5/16	Oldham (h)	W12-6	t:Sarsfield(2) g:Tyrer(2)	6th	1,285
29/5/16	Featherstone (SB) ●●	W0-37	t:Tangata,G Moore,Sarsfield,Johnston,Saltonstall,Tyrer g:Tyrer(6) fg:G Moore	6th	N/A
5/6/16	Sheffield (h)	W60-22	t:Tangata,G Moore(3),Sarsfield(3),Sharp,Greenwood,Fairbank g:Tyrer(10)	5th	1,680
11/6/16	Whitehaven (h)	D12-12	t:Sharp,G Moore g:Tyrer(2)	4th	667
19/6/16	Dewsbury (a)	W8-24	t:G Moore,Saltonstall,Cahalane,C Robinson g:Tyrer(4)	4th	1,146
26/6/16	Bradford (a)	W24-32	t:Tangata,Murrell,Saltonstall,Fairbank,Tyrer,Barber g:Tyrer(4)	3rd	6,312
3/7/16	Swinton (a)	W12-62	t:Johnston(2),Barber(3),Sharp,Murrell,G Moore,Cahalane,Bennion,Ambler g:Tyrer(9)	3rd	1,017
10/7/16	Leigh (a)	L58-18	t:Johnston(2),Sharp g:Tyrer(3)	3rd	4,052
17/7/16	Featherstone (h)	L20-24	t:C Robinson,Johnston,Cahalane g:Tyrer(3),Murrell	6th	2,305
24/7/16	London Broncos (h)	L22-41	t:Johnston,Sharp,Barber(2) g:G Moore(3)	6th	1,559
7/8/16	Sheffield (h) (CS)	L28-48	t:Ambler,Tangata(2),G Moore,Saltonstall g:G Moore(4)	2nd(CS)	1,288
14/8/16	Bradford (a) (CS)	L44-22	t:Tangata(2),B Moore,Saltonstall,Barber g:C Robinson	2nd(CS)	3,498
21/8/16	Dewsbury (h) (CS)	L22-24	t:Greenwood,Murrell,Manning,Fairbank g:Rawsthorne(3)	2nd(CS)	1,133
29/8/16	Whitehaven (a) (CS)	W10-30	t:Butler,Boyle,Rawsthorne,Fairbank,Tangata g:Rawsthorne(5)	2nd(CS)	718
4/9/16	Oldham (h) (CS)	W32-18	t:Heaton(2),Rawsthorne,Greenwood,Murrell,Tangata g:G Moore(4)	2nd(CS)	1,182
11/9/16	Swinton (a) (CS)	L28-26	t:Heaton,Sharp,Nelmes,Rawsthorne(2) g:G Moore(3)	2nd(CS)	582
18/9/16	Workington (h) (CS)	W46-26	t:Barber,Sharp,Morris,Woodburn-Hall(2),Ambler,Cahalane,G Moore g:G Moore(7)	2nd(CS)	1,217
25/9/16	Sheffield (h) (CSSF)	L32-46	t:Woodburn-Hall(3),Barber,B Moore,Cahalane g:G Moore(4)	N/A	946

● Played at Langtree Park, St Helens
●● Played at Bloomfield Road, Blackpool

Gareth Moore

	D.O.B.	APP		TRIES		GOALS		FG		PTS	
		ALL	Ch	ALL	Ch	ALL	Ch	ALL	Ch	ALL	Ch
Luke Ambler	18/12/89	18(13)	12(11)	8	3	0	0	0	0	32	12
Ed Barber	26/4/90	10(8)	5(6)	14	6	0	0	0	0	56	24
Gavin Bennion	31/12/93	8(12)	3(7)	2	2	0	0	0	0	8	8
Ryan Boyle	17/10/87	5(11)	(8)	1	0	0	0	0	0	4	0
Andy Bracek	21/3/84	(4)	(2)	1	0	0	0	0	0	4	0
Chester Butler	10/3/95	4(1)	0	1	0	0	0	0	0	4	0
Mitch Cahalane	5/5/89	29(1)	21(1)	6	4	0	0	0	0	24	16
Ross Divorty	27/11/88	2	2	0	0	0	0	0	0	0	0
Jake Eccleston	24/4/95	9	8	5	4	0	0	0	0	20	16
Jacob Fairbank	4/3/90	29(2)	20(2)	6	2	0	0	0	0	24	8
Miles Greenwood	30/7/87	18	11	9	4	0	0	0	0	36	16
Simon Grix	28/9/85	4(2)	4(2)	0	0	0	0	0	0	0	0
Ben Heaton	12/3/90	21	14	4	1	0	0	0	0	16	4
Ben Johnston	8/3/92	20(4)	12(3)	9	7	0	0	0	0	36	28
Ben Kaye	19/12/88	23(4)	17(2)	2	2	0	0	0	0	8	8
Ryan Maneely	19/10/94	2(7)	1(6)	1	1	0	0	0	0	4	4
Dane Manning	15/4/89	22	18	5	4	0	0	0	0	20	16
Brandon Moore	27/7/96	5(14)	1(8)	4	1	0	0	0	0	16	4
Gareth Moore	3/6/89	32	23	18	13	32	9	2	2	138	72
Richard Moore	2/2/81	3(19)	2(16)	1	0	0	0	0	0	4	0
Elliot Morris	4/1/96	(6)	(1)	1	0	0	0	0	0	4	0
Scott Murrell	5/9/85	29(1)	21(1)	7	5	1	1	1	1	31	23
Luke Nelmes	7/6/93	(5)	0	1	0	0	0	0	0	4	0
Gareth Potts	25/7/90	2	1	3	1	0	0	0	0	12	4
Nick Rawsthorne	30/9/95	7	0	4	0	8	0	0	0	32	0
Adam Robinson	8/4/87	2(11)	1(8)	1	0	0	0	0	0	4	0
Connor Robinson	23/10/94	7(7)	4(4)	6	3	6	1	0	0	36	14
James Saltonstall	27/9/93	22	18	11	8	0	0	0	0	44	32
Matt Sarsfield	10/9/91	9	9	7	7	0	0	0	0	28	28
Tom Saxton	3/10/83	5	4	1	1	0	0	0	0	4	4
Will Sharp	12/5/86	28	18	9	7	0	0	0	0	36	28
Sam Smeaton	26/10/88	12	9	6	5	0	0	0	0	24	20
Adam Tangata	17/3/91	28(4)	19(4)	12	5	0	0	0	0	48	20
Steve Tyrer	16/3/89	24	21	8	8	108	87	0	0	248	206
James Woodburn-Hall	2/2/95	3	0	5	0	0	0	0	0	20	0

'Ch' totals include Championship regular season only; 'All' totals also include Championship Shield & Challenge Cup

LEAGUE RECORD
Championship, before Super 8 split:
P23-W13-D1-L9 (6th)
F615, A484, Diff+131, 27 points.

After Championship Shield:
P30-W16-D1-L13 (2nd/Semi-Finalists)
F821, A682, Diff+139, 33 points.

CHALLENGE CUP
Round Six

ATTENDANCES
Best - v Bradford (Ch - 4,018)
Worst - v Sheffield (CSSF - 946)
Total (Championship/
Championship Shield only) - 27,411
Average (Championship/
Championship Shield only) - 1,713
(Down by 422 on 2015)

CLUB RECORDS	
	Highest score: 94-4 v Myton, 25/3/2012 Highest score against: 6-88 v Hull KR, 23/4/2006
	Record attendance: 29,153 v Wigan, 21/3/59 *(Thrum Hall)*; 9,827 v Bradford, 12/3/2000 *(The Shay)*
MATCH RECORDS	Tries: 8 Keith Williams v Dewsbury, 9/11/57 Goals: 14 Bruce Burton v Hunslet, 27/8/72
	Points: 32 John Schuster v Doncaster, 9/10/94; Steve Tyrer v Whitehaven, 7/2/2016
SEASON RECORDS	Tries: 48 Johnny Freeman 1956-57 Goals: 156 Graham Holroyd 2008 Points: 362 John Schuster 1994-95
CAREER RECORDS	Tries: 290 Johnny Freeman 1954-67 Goals: 1,028 Ronnie James 1961-71 Points: 2,191 Ronnie James 1961-71 Appearances: 482 Stan Kielty 1946-58

LEIGH CENTURIONS

DATE	FIXTURE	RESULT	SCORERS	LGE	ATT
7/2/16	Batley (a)	L24-22	t:Dixon,Armstrong,Higham,Brierley g:Ridyard(3)	8th	1,678
14/2/16	Oldham (h)	W48-18	t:Pownall,Smith,Higson(2),Hopkins(3),Moimoi,Maitua g:Ridyard(4),Smith(2)	5th	3,371
21/2/16	London Broncos (h)	W24-20	t:Hopkins,Acton,Emmitt,Chase g:Smith(4)	5th	3,291
28/2/16	Bradford (a)	D32-32	t:Pownall,Brierley(2),Smith,Maitua g:Smith(6)	6th	6,563
6/3/16	Sheffield (h)	W36-28	t:Weston,Higson,Higham,Charnock,Maitua,Paterson g:Ridyard(6)	4th	3,282
13/3/16	Halifax (a)	W18-26	t:Maitua,Smith,Hock,Higham g:Ridyard(5)	3rd	2,706
19/3/16	Workington (h) (CCR4)	W68-14	t:Paterson(4),Reynolds,Hood,Pownall,Smith,Hansen(2),Acton,Hopkins g:Ridyard(10)	N/A	2,049
24/3/16	Swinton (h)	W42-12	t:Smith,Owen,Weston,Hopkins,Higham,Hansen,Armstrong g:Ridyard(7)	1st	3,230
28/3/16	Workington (a)	W24-40	t:Emmitt,Hansen,Armstrong,Maitua(2),Hopkins,Moimoi g:Ridyard(5),Reynolds	1st	787
3/4/16	Dewsbury (a)	W18-40	t:Hopkins(2),Higson,Reynolds,Kay,Paterson,Whiting g:Ridyard(6)	1st	1,691
10/4/16	Whitehaven (h)	W60-6	t:Paterson(3),Armstrong,Acton,Reynolds,Maitua,Kay(2),Weston,Hood g:Ridyard(8)	1st	3,089
16/4/16	Toulouse (a) (CCR5)	L10-8	t:Hopkins g:Ridyard(2)	N/A	2,133
24/4/16	Featherstone (a)	W24-30	t:Armstrong,Acton,Chase,Smith,Kay g:Ridyard(5)	1st	2,731
1/5/16	Batley (h)	W37-30	t:Kay,Hansen(2),Hood,Smith,Hopkins g:Ridyard(6) fg:Ridyard	1st	3,389
15/5/16	Oldham (a)	W14-56	t:Maitua(2),Smith,Ridyard,Kay,Hood,Armstrong,Reynolds,Acton,Weston g:Ridyard(8)	1st	1,489
22/5/16	Swinton (a)	W6-48	t:Armstrong,Smith(2),Pownall,Whiting,Ridyard,Weston,Reynolds,Drinkwater g:Ridyard(5),Reynolds	1st	1,413
28/5/16	Bradford (SB) ●	W20-24	t:Kay,Drinkwater,Higson,Higham g:Reynolds(4)	1st	N/A
4/6/16	Whitehaven (a)	W12-36	t:Drinkwater,Higson,Burns(2),Paterson,Worthington g:Reynolds(3),Burns(3)	1st	782
12/6/16	Featherstone (h)	W16-12	t:Kay,Worthington,Armstrong g:Burns,Drinkwater	1st	3,503
19/6/16	Workington (h)	W54-12	t:Reynolds(2),Worthington,Drinkwater(2),Kay,Spencer,Higson,Paterson g:Smith(9)	1st	3,002
26/6/16	London Broncos (a)	W12-38	t:Drinkwater,Paterson(2),Worthington(2),Kay,Higson g:Smith(5)	1st	1,234
3/7/16	Bradford (h)	W22-20	t:Smith,Hock,Worthington,Maitua g:Smith(3)	1st	5,111
10/7/16	Halifax (h)	W58-18	t:Paterson(2),Smith,Higson,Worthington,Drinkwater,Dixon(2),Moimoi,Kay g:Ridyard(9)	1st	4,052
15/7/16	Sheffield (a)	W30-34	t:McNally,Armstrong,Ridyard,Dixon,Harper,Hock g:Ridyard(5)	1st	774
24/7/16	Dewsbury (h)	W58-0	t:McNally(3),Maitua,Worthington,Higson(3),Reynolds,Higham g:Ridyard(9)	1st	3,498
6/8/16	London Broncos (h) (S8-Q)	W34-30	t:Dawson(2),Brown(2),Maitua g:Ridyard(7)	4th(S8-Q)	4,041
13/8/16	Salford (h) (S8-Q)	W32-26	t:Maitua,Paterson,McNally,Higson,Dawson g:Ridyard(6)	2nd(S8-Q)	4,547
21/8/16	Featherstone (a) (S8-Q)	W18-30	t:Maitua,Brown,Dawson,Higham,Hock g:Ridyard(5)	2nd(S8-Q)	3,644
3/9/16	Hull KR (a) (S8-Q)	W18-25	t:Hopkins,Dixon,Dawson,Drinkwater g:Ridyard(4) fg:Ridyard	2nd(S8-Q)	7,363
10/9/16	Huddersfield (h) (S8-Q)	W48-40	t:Worthington,Dawson(3),Ridyard(2),Paterson,Brown g:Ridyard(8)	2nd(S8-Q)	5,934
17/9/16	Batley (h) (S8-Q)	W42-24	t:Moimoi,Higson,Paterson,Foster,Burns,Tonga,Weston g:Smith(7)	1st(S8-Q)	10,556
22/9/16	Leeds (a) (S8-Q)	L37-12	t:Hopkins,Dawson g:Ridyard(2)	2nd(S8-Q)	14,747

● Played at Bloomfield Road, Blackpool

APP TRIES GOALS FG PTS

	D.O.B.	ALL	Ch	ALL	Ch	ALL	Ch	ALL	Ch	ALL	Ch
Jamie Acton	4/4/92	3(12)	2(9)	5	4	0	0	0	0	20	16
Tom Armstrong	12/9/89	20	17	9	9	0	0	0	0	36	36
Ryan Brierley	12/3/92	3	3	3	3	0	0	0	0	12	12
Mitch Brown	7/11/87	7	0	4	0	0	0	0	0	16	0
Travis Burns	6/2/84	6(2)	5(1)	3	2	4	4	0	0	20	16
Lewis Charnock	2/9/94	1(1)	1(1)	1	1	0	0	0	0	4	4
Rangi Chase	11/4/86	5	5	2	2	0	0	0	0	8	8
Matty Dawson	2/10/90	8	1	9	0	0	0	0	0	36	0
Andrew Dixon	28/2/90	9(3)	6(1)	5	4	0	0	0	0	20	16
Josh Drinkwater	15/6/92	14(1)	8(1)	8	7	1	1	0	0	34	30
Jake Emmitt	4/10/88	5(10)	4(10)	2	2	0	0	0	0	8	8
Ben Evans	30/10/92	1(2)	1(2)	0	0	0	0	0	0	0	0
Brad Fash	24/1/96	1(7)	(7)	0	0	0	0	0	0	0	0
Lewis Foster	21/12/93	1(6)	1(3)	1	0	0	0	0	0	4	0
Harrison Hansen	26/10/85	15(14)	15(6)	6	4	0	0	0	0	24	16
Eze Harper	7/12/94	3	3	1	1	0	0	0	0	4	4
Micky Higham	18/9/80	23(3)	16(3)	7	6	0	0	0	0	28	24
Adam Higson	19/5/87	30	22	14	12	0	0	0	0	56	48
Gareth Hock	5/9/83	21(2)	14(2)	4	3	0	0	0	0	16	12
Liam Hood	6/1/92	7(12)	5(8)	4	3	0	0	0	0	16	12
Sam Hopkins	17/2/90	4(23)	3(16)	13	9	0	0	0	0	52	36
Liam Kay	17/12/91	18	16	11	11	0	0	0	0	44	44
Reni Maitua	11/6/82	24(5)	17(5)	14	11	0	0	0	0	56	44
Gregg McNally	2/1/91	7	2	5	4	0	0	0	0	20	16
Fuifui Moimoi	26/9/79	18(2)	14(2)	4	3	0	0	0	0	16	12
Richard Owen	25/4/90	2	2	1	1	0	0	0	0	4	4
Cory Paterson	14/7/87	21	13	18	11	0	0	0	0	72	44
Jonny Pownall	22/8/91	8	6	4	3	0	0	0	0	16	12
Ben Reynolds	15/1/94	14(4)	11(3)	8	7	9	9	0	0	50	46
Martyn Ridyard	25/7/86	23(2)	15(2)	5	3	135	91	2	1	292	195
Lee Smith	8/8/86	23	20	12	11	36	29	0	0	120	102
Tom Spencer	2/1/91	3(7)	3(4)	1	1	0	0	0	0	4	4
Danny Tickle	10/3/83	2(5)	(1)	0	0	0	0	0	0	0	0
Willie Tonga	8/7/83	6	3	1	0	0	0	0	0	4	0
Dayne Weston	15/12/86	30(1)	21(1)	6	5	0	0	0	0	24	20
Richard Whiting	20/12/84	12(3)	11(3)	2	2	0	0	0	0	8	8
Greg Worthington	17/7/90	18	13	9	8	0	0	0	0	36	32

'Ch' totals include Championship regular season only; 'All' totals also include Super 8s (Qualifiers) & Challenge Cup

Martyn Ridyard

LEAGUE RECORD
Championship, before Super 8 split:
P23-W21-D1-L1 (1st)
F881, A410, Diff+471, 43 points.

S8-Q: P7-W6-D0-L1 (2nd)
F223, A193, Diff+30, 12 points.

CHALLENGE CUP
Round Five

ATTENDANCES
Best - v Batley (S8 - 10,556)
Worst - v Workington (CC - 2,049)
Total (Championship/S8s only) - 63,896
Average (Championship/S8s only) - 4,260
(Up by 318 on 2015)

CLUB RECORDS	
	Highest score: 92-2 v Keighley, 30/4/86 Highest score against: 4-94 v Workington, 26/2/95
MATCH RECORDS	Record attendance: 31,326 v St Helens, 14/3/53 *(Hilton Park)*; 10,556 v Batley, 17/9/2016 *(Leigh Sports Village)*
	Tries: 6 Jack Wood v York, 4/10/47; Neil Turley v Workington, 31/1/2001
	Goals: 15 Mick Stacey v Doncaster, 28/3/76 Points: 42 Neil Turley v Chorley, 4/4/2004
SEASON RECORDS	Tries: 55 Neil Turley 2001 Goals: 187 Neil Turley 2004 Points: 468 Neil Turley 2004
CAREER RECORDS	Tries: 189 Mick Martyn 1954-67 Goals: 1,043 Jimmy Ledgard 1948-58 Points: 2,492 John Woods 1976-85; 1990-92
	Appearances: 503 Albert Worrall 1920-38

LONDON BRONCOS

DATE	FIXTURE	RESULT	SCORERS	LGE	ATT
7/2/16	Oldham (a)	W0-22	t:Ackers,Bussey,Macani,Hellewell g:Naiqama(3)	3rd	767
14/2/16	Swinton (h)	W38-18	t:Walker(2),Garside,Bussey,Foster,Macani,Keyes g:Naiqama(5)	3rd	653
21/2/16	Leigh (a)	L24-20	t:Foster,Cunningham,Williams,Hellewell g:Naiqama(2)	3rd	3,291
28/2/16	Workington (a)	W13-16	t:Cunningham,Williams,Garside g:Leatherbarrow(2)	3rd	632
6/3/16	Halifax (h)	W29-22	t:Barthau(2),Williams(2),Hellewell,Slyney g:Naiqama,Leatherbarrow fg:Leatherbarrow	2nd	732
12/3/16	Dewsbury (h)	W22-18	t:Williams(2),Barthau,Garside g:Naiqama(3)	1st	512
19/3/16	Featherstone (h) (CCR4)	L26-48	t:Kear,Foster(2),Williams,Barthau g:Leatherbarrow(3)	N/A	294
24/3/16	Bradford (a)	L28-20	t:Cunningham,Thackray,Foster(2) g:Leatherbarrow(2)	4th	4,163
28/3/16	Featherstone (h)	W20-12	t:Williams,Hellewell(2),Foster g:Leatherbarrow(2)	3rd	428
10/4/16	Batley (h)	W32-8	t:Williams(2),Hellewell,Battye,Barthau,Kear,Ioane g:Barthau(2)	2nd	753
17/4/16	Whitehaven (a)	W12-16	t:Barthau(2),Slyney g:Naiqama(2)	2nd	548
22/4/16	Sheffield (a)	W24-56	t:Barthau(3),Naiqama,Williams(2),Garside(2),Ackers,Foster g:Naiqama(7),Barthau	2nd	513
1/5/16	Bradford (h)	W30-16	t:Hellewell,Williams(2),Ackers(2),Cunningham g:Barthau,Bussey(2)	2nd	1,524
15/5/16	Featherstone (a)	L42-18	t:Harrison,Macani,Kear g:Barthau,Naiqama(2)	2nd	1,723
22/5/16	Whitehaven (h)	W62-4	t:Williams(2),Pewhairangi(2),Naiqama(2),Offerdahl,Hellewell(2),Cunningham,Foster g:Naiqama(9)	2nd	675
28/5/16	Sheffield (SB) ●	W32-14	t:Williams,Slyney,Garside,Foster,Offerdahl,Battye g:Naiqama(4)	2nd	N/A
5/6/16	Workington (h)	W50-28	t:Leatherbarrow,Pewhairangi,Foster,Ackers,Kear(2),Ioane,Cunningham,Williams g:Pewhairangi(7)	2nd	650
12/6/16	Swinton (a)	W16-42	t:Harrison,Slyney(2),Offerdahl,Pewhairangi(2),Hellewell g:Naiqama(5),Pewhairangi(2)	2nd	485
19/6/16	Oldham (h)	W56-16	t:Harrison,Kear(2),Williams(3),Macani(2),Hellewell,Offerdahl g:Pewhairangi(8)	2nd	425
26/6/16	Leigh (h)	L12-38	t:Ioane,Pewhairangi g:Pewhairangi(2)	2nd	1,234
3/7/16	Dewsbury (a)	W6-34	t:Naiqama,Eliab(2),Ioane,Williams,Garside g:Naiqama(5)	2nd	645
10/7/16	Sheffield (h)	L14-32	t:Williams,Eliab,Ackers g:Naiqama	2nd	530
17/7/16	Batley (a)	L31-20	t:Kear,Hellewell,Pewhairangi,Offerdahl g:Soward(2)	2nd	783
24/7/16	Halifax (a)	W22-41	t:Battye(2),Garside,Soward,Ioane,Slyney,Adebiyi g:Soward(5),Pewhairangi fg:Soward	2nd	1,559
6/8/16	Leigh (a) (S8-Q)	L34-30	t:Hellewell,Pewhairangi(2),Ackers,Harrison g:Soward(2),Pewhairangi(3)	5th(S8-Q)	4,041
14/8/16	Batley (h) (S8-Q)	W76-16	t:Soward,Harrison,Macani(3),Ackers,Cunningham(2),Garside,Williams(3),Bussey,Ioane g:Soward(10)	3rd(S8-Q)	674
20/8/16	Leeds (h) (S8-Q)	L28-42	t:Williams,Cunningham,Slyney,Macani,Kear g:Soward(4)	5th(S8-Q)	1,845
2/9/16	Huddersfield (a) (S8-Q)	L40-4	t:Williams	5th(S8-Q)	3,794
11/9/16	Hull KR (h) (S8-Q)	L18-58	t:Walker,Cunningham,Barthau g:Soward(3)	6th(S8-Q)	1,215
17/9/16	Salford (a) (S8-Q)	W16-19	t:Barthau,Leatherbarrow,Soward g:Soward(3) fg:Barthau	6th(S8-Q)	2,521
25/9/16	Featherstone (h) (S8-Q)	W46-6	t:Williams(3),Harrison,Kear,Garside,Hellewell,Bussey,Ioane g:Soward(5)	6th(S8-Q)	605

● *Played at Bloomfield Road, Blackpool*

APP TRIES GOALS FG PTS

	D.O.B.	ALL	Ch	ALL	Ch	ALL	Ch	ALL	Ch	ALL	Ch
Andy Ackers	25/12/93	14(14)	10(10)	8	6	0	0	0	0	32	24
Sadiq Adebiyi	8/1/97	(1)	(1)	1	1	0	0	0	0	4	4
William Barthau	30/1/90	17(1)	12	12	9	5	5	1	0	59	46
Eddie Battye	24/7/91	5(24)	5(18)	4	4	0	0	0	0	16	16
Lewis Bienek	11/4/98	(1)	0	0	0	0	0	0	0	0	0
Jack Bussey	17/8/92	23(5)	17(4)	4	2	2	2	0	0	20	12
Callum Bustin	28/2/97	1	1	0	0	0	0	0	0	0	0
James Cunningham	3/4/94	17(9)	13(8)	10	6	0	0	0	0	40	24
Matt Davis	5/7/96	2(6)	1(6)	0	0	0	0	0	0	0	0
Israel Eliab	16/1/91	7(1)	4(1)	3	3	0	0	0	0	12	12
Toby Everett	22/12/95	(1)	0	0	0	0	0	0	0	0	0
Alex Foster	25/9/93	20	18	11	9	0	0	0	0	44	36
Matt Garside	1/10/90	26(3)	19(3)	10	8	0	0	0	0	40	32
Daniel Harrison	15/4/88	28(2)	20(2)	6	3	0	0	0	0	24	12
Ben Hellewell	30/1/92	29	21	14	12	0	0	0	0	56	48
Mark Ioane	3/2/90	18(12)	11(12)	7	5	0	0	0	0	28	20
Elliot Kear	29/11/88	27	20	10	7	0	0	0	0	40	28
Joe Keyes	17/9/95	4	4	1	1	0	0	0	0	4	4
Scott Leatherbarrow	3/9/90	15(2)	13	2	1	10	7	1	1	29	19
Iliess Macani	6/12/93	22	16	9	5	0	0	0	0	36	20
Jon Magrin	8/10/94	5(12)	4(9)	0	0	0	0	0	0	0	0
Wes Naiqama	19/10/82	12(1)	12(1)	4	4	49	49	0	0	114	114
Mark Offerdahl	15/10/87	7(15)	7(9)	5	5	0	0	0	0	20	20
Kameron Pearce-Paul	28/2/97	2	0	0	0	0	0	0	0	0	0
Api Pewhairangi	19/3/92	12	10	9	7	23	20	0	0	82	68
Nick Slyney	11/2/88	28(2)	21(2)	7	6	0	0	0	0	28	24
Jamie Soward	13/11/84	8	2	3	1	34	7	1	1	81	19
Nathan Stapleton	1/12/89	2	2	0	0	0	0	0	0	0	0
Jamie Thackray	30/9/79	7(12)	5(6)	1	1	0	0	0	0	4	4
Alex Walker	4/9/95	14	8	3	2	0	0	0	0	12	8
Rhys Williams	8/12/89	31	23	31	22	0	0	0	0	124	88

'Ch' totals include Championship regular season only; 'All' totals also include Super 8s (Qualifiers) & Challenge Cup

Rhys Williams

LEAGUE RECORD
Championship, before Super 8 split:
P23-W17-D0-L6 (2nd)
F702, A444, Diff+258, 34 points.

S8-Q: P7-W3-D0-L4 (6th)
F221, A212, Diff+9, 6 points.

CHALLENGE CUP
Round Four

ATTENDANCES
Best - v Leeds (S8 - 1,845)
Worst - v Featherstone (CC - 294)
Total (Championship/S8s only) - 12,455
Average (Championship/S8s only) - 830
(Up by 185 on 2015)

CLUB RECORDS	**Highest score:** 82-0 v Highfield, 12/11/95; 82-2 v Barrow, 20/5/2006 **Highest score against:** 6-82 v Warrington, 20/3/2011; 10-82 v Warrington, 8/6/2013
	Record attendance: 15,013 v Wakefield, 15/2/81
MATCH RECORDS	**Tries:** 5 Martin Offiah v Whitehaven, 14/3/99; Sean Morris v Batley, 13/9/2015
	Goals: 13 Rob Purdham v Barrow, 20/5/2006 **Points:** 34 Rob Purdham v Barrow, 20/5/2006
SEASON RECORDS	**Tries:** 43 Mark Johnson 1993-94 **Goals:** 159 John Gallagher 1993-94 **Points:** 384 John Gallagher 1993-94
CAREER RECORDS	**Tries:** 109 Luke Dorn 2005-2006; 2009-2013 **Goals:** 309 Steve Diamond 1981-84 **Points:** 772 Paul Sykes 2001-2007
	Appearances: 202 Steele Retchless 1998-2004

OLDHAM

DATE	FIXTURE	RESULT	SCORERS	LGE	ATT
7/2/16	London Broncos (h)	L0-22		10th	767
14/2/16	Leigh (a)	L48-18	t:Ashton,Clay,Palfrey g:Palfrey(3)	11th	3,371
21/2/16	Dewsbury (h)	W38-16	t:Ashton,Owen(2),Langtree(2),Ward,Clay g:Palfrey(5)	9th	816
28/2/16	Featherstone (a)	L20-6	t:Lepori g:Palfrey	9th	1,739
13/3/16	Workington (a)	L23-12	t:Middlehurst,Joy g:Palfrey(2)	10th	637
20/3/16	Kells (h) (CCR4)	W40-6	t:Chisholm(2),Ford,Middlehurst,Files,Grimshaw,Holmes(2) g:Roper(4)	N/A	385
25/3/16	Halifax (h)	L28-42	t:Hope(2),Chisholm,Clay(2) g:Roper(4)	10th	1,046
28/3/16	Swinton (a)	L28-18	t:Grimshaw,Files,Ford g:Palfrey(3)	10th	823
3/4/16	Batley (h)	W28-12	t:Lepori,Johnson,Chisholm(2),Gee g:Palfrey(4)	10th	814
10/4/16	Sheffield (h)	W21-20	t:Johnson,Ward,Hughes g:Palfrey(4) fg:Palfrey	9th	724
16/4/16	Hull KR (a) (CCR5)	W22-36	t:Hope,Lepori(2),Roper,Clay,Middlehurst g:Palfrey(6)	N/A	3,056
23/4/16	Whitehaven (a)	L14-6	t:Holmes g:Palfrey	11th	615
1/5/16	Featherstone (h)	W16-14	t:Hughes,Holmes,Johnson g:Palfrey(2)	10th	868
7/5/16	Warrington (h) (CCR6)	L10-70	t:Ward,Owen g:Palfrey	N/A	2,394
15/5/16	Leigh (a)	L14-56	t:Grimshaw,Johnson,Langtree g:Roper	10th	1,489
20/5/16	Halifax (a)	L12-6	t:Chisholm g:Gee	10th	1,285
29/5/16	Swinton (SB) ●	L24-25	t:Hughes,Langtree,Files,Clay g:Palfrey(3)	11th	N/A
5/6/16	Batley (a)	L42-18	t:Hughes,Wood,Middlehurst g:Palfrey(3)	11th	783
12/6/16	Dewsbury (a)	L46-10	t:Burke,Chisholm g:Roper	11th	742
15/6/16	Bradford (h)	L4-48	t:Wood	11th	1,051
19/6/16	London Broncos (a)	L56-16	t:Chisholm,Holmes,Ward g:Palfrey(2)	11th	425
26/6/16	Whitehaven (h)	W26-18	t:Chisholm,Langtree(2),Gill,Joy g:Wood(3)	11th	516
1/7/16	Sheffield (a)	W16-24	t:Gill,Hughes,Thompson,Foster g:Palfrey(4)	10th	531
10/7/16	Swinton (h)	W26-24	t:Gill,Ward(2),Clay g:Palfrey(5)	10th	758
17/7/16	Bradford (a)	L44-12	t:Blagbrough,Ward g:Palfrey(2)	10th	4,235
24/7/16	Workington (h)	L30-32	t:Lepori,Owen,Ward,Hughes(2) g:Hewitt(5)	10th	689
7/8/16	Workington (h) (CS)	W30-16	t:Turner(2),Chisholm,Blagbrough,Langtree g:Palfrey(5)	5th(CS)	573
14/8/16	Swinton (a) (CS)	W8-30	t:Hewitt(2),Clay,Langtree g:Palfrey(7)	5th(CS)	693
21/8/16	Bradford (a) (CS)	L82-0		5th(CS)	3,022
29/8/16	Sheffield (h) (CS)	L24-54	t:Gill(2),Hewitt(2) g:Palfrey(4)	6th(CS)	680
4/9/16	Halifax (a) (CS)	L32-18	t:Gill(2),Hughes g:Palfrey(3)	6th(CS)	1,182
11/9/16	Whitehaven (h) (CS)	W20-18	t:Joy,Thompson,Clay g:Palfrey(4)	6th(CS)	843
18/9/16	Dewsbury (a) (CS)	L30-12	t:Hughes,Gill g:Palfrey,Lepori	6th(CS)	628

● *Played at Bloomfield Road, Blackpool*

	D.O.B.	APP ALL	Ch	TRIES ALL	Ch	GOALS ALL	Ch	FG ALL	Ch	PTS ALL	Ch
Tom Ashton	26/6/92	3(1)	3	2	2	0	0	0	0	8	8
Jake Bibby	17/6/96	3	3	0	0	0	0	0	0	0	0
Jack Blagbrough	18/1/94	(7)	(2)	2	1	0	0	0	0	8	4
Craig Briscoe	8/12/92	4(3)	4(2)	0	0	0	0	0	0	0	0
Joe Burke	18/5/90	8(14)	6(10)	1	1	0	0	0	0	4	4
Jamel Chisholm	7/11/92	26	17	10	7	0	0	0	0	40	28
Adam Clay	7/10/90	30	21	9	6	0	0	0	0	36	24
Josh Crowley	24/9/91	2(2)	2(2)	0	0	0	0	0	0	0	0
Tyler Dickinson	18/8/96	15(3)	8(3)	0	0	0	0	0	0	0	0
Adam Files	7/1/93	1(13)	1(8)	3	2	0	0	0	0	12	8
Jonathan Ford	1/11/93	3	2	2	1	0	0	0	0	8	4
Lewis Foster	21/12/93	6(1)	6(1)	1	1	0	0	0	0	4	4
Sam Gee	28/2/87	12(10)	8(8)	1	1	1	1	0	0	6	6
Kieran Gill	4/12/95	12	5	8	3	0	0	0	0	32	12
Danny Grimshaw	25/2/86	19(1)	14(1)	3	2	0	0	0	0	12	8
Dave Hewitt	4/11/95	9	2	4	0	5	5	0	0	26	10
Jack Holmes	5/1/94	14	12	5	3	0	0	0	0	20	12
Will Hope	2/6/93	20(3)	17(2)	3	2	0	0	0	0	12	8
Kenny Hughes	30/3/90	2(25)	2(17)	9	7	0	0	0	0	36	28
Liam Johnson	12/5/97	14	13	4	4	0	0	0	0	16	16
Phil Joy	4/9/91	27(1)	19(1)	3	2	0	0	0	0	12	8
Danny Langtree	18/2/91	25(1)	17(1)	8	6	0	0	0	0	32	24
Kruise Leeming	7/9/95	4	4	0	0	0	0	0	0	0	0
Richard Lepori	22/10/91	23(1)	17	5	3	1	0	0	0	22	12
Darnell McIntosh	5/7/97	1	1	0	0	0	0	0	0	0	0
Gary Middlehurst	24/10/83	24	14	4	2	0	0	0	0	16	8
Gareth Owen	3/7/92	31	21	4	3	0	0	0	0	16	12
Lewis Palfrey	25/2/90	25(1)	16(1)	1	1	76	45	1	1	157	95
Steve Roper	10/11/86	12	9	1	0	10	6	0	0	24	12
Jared Simpson	4/1/96	3	3	0	0	0	0	0	0	0	0
Jack Spencer	21/12/90	12(8)	9(3)	0	0	0	0	0	0	0	0
Tom Spencer	2/1/91	4	4	0	0	0	0	0	0	0	0
Liam Thompson	3/1/92	20(10)	13(8)	2	1	0	0	0	0	8	4
Scott Turner	7/5/94	6	0	2	0	0	0	0	0	8	0
Michael Ward	10/2/91	4(27)	1(22)	8	7	0	0	0	0	32	28
Sam Wood	11/6/97	5	5	2	2	3	3	0	0	14	14

'Ch' totals include Championship regular season only; 'All' totals also include Championship Shield & Challenge Cup

Michael Ward

LEAGUE RECORD
Championship, before Super 8 split:
P23-W7-D0-L16 (10th)
F401, A678, Diff-277, 14 points.

After Championship Shield:
P30-W10-D0-L20 (6th)
F535, A918, Diff-383, 20 points.

CHALLENGE CUP
Round Six

ATTENDANCES
Best - v Warrington (CC - 2,394)
Worst - v Kells (CC - 385)
Total (Championship/
Championship Shield only) - 11,634
Average (Championship/
Championship Shield only) - 831
(Up by 200 on 2015, League 1)

CLUB RECORDS	
	Highest score: 80-6 v Blackwood, 7/3/2010 **Highest score against:** 0-84 v Widnes, 25/7/99
MATCH RECORDS	**Record attendance:** 28,000 v Huddersfield, 24/2/1912 *(Watersheddings)*; 2,394 v Warrington, 7/5/2016 *(Bower Fold)*
	Tries: 7 James Miller v Barry, 31/10/1908 **Goals:** 14 Bernard Ganley v Liverpool City, 4/4/59
SEASON RECORDS	**Points:** 34 Andy Ballard v London Skolars, 2/5/2009; Chris Baines v Hunslet, 20/9/2009; Lewis Palfrey v Hemel, 9/8/2015
	Tries: 49 Reg Farrar 1921-22 **Goals:** 200 Bernard Ganley 1957-58 **Points:** 412 Bernard Ganley 1957-58
CAREER RECORDS	**Tries:** 174 Alan Davies 1950-61 **Goals:** 1,358 Bernard Ganley 1951-61 **Points:** 2,761 Bernard Ganley 1951-61 **Appearances:** 627 Joe Ferguson 1899-1923

SHEFFIELD EAGLES

DATE	FIXTURE	RESULT	SCORERS	LGE	ATT
7/2/16	Workington (a)	W12-42	t:Worrincy,Aston(2),Neal,Yere,Fozard(2) g:Knowles(7)	2nd	813
12/2/16	Halifax (h)	W26-6	t:Worrincy(2),Yere,Aston,Minchella g:Knowles(3)	1st	1,350
21/2/16	Batley (a)	L20-8	t:Yere,Lo	4th	814
26/2/16	Swinton (h)	W48-26	t:Blackmore(2),Tyson,Wheeldon,Laulu-Togagae,Yere,Aston,Stringer g:Knowles(5),Aston	2nd	508
6/3/16	Leigh (a)	L36-28	t:Worrincy(2),Laulu-Togagae(2),Yere g:Knowles(4)	5th	3,282
12/3/16	Whitehaven (h)	L24-26	t:Worrincy(3),Knowles,Laulu-Togagae g:Knowles,Aston	6th	502
19/3/16	Swinton (h) (CCR4)	W32-28	t:Straugheir(2),Yere,Blackmore(2),Aston g:Knowles,Hewitt(3)	N/A	412
25/3/16	Featherstone (a)	L28-16	t:Worrincy,Laulu-Togagae,Carlile g:Knowles(2)	7th	2,052
28/3/16	Dewsbury (a)	L34-16	t:Hewitt,Worrincy,Knowles g:Knowles(2)	8th	813
3/4/16	Bradford (a)	W28-46	t:Aston,Minchella,Millar(2),Lo,Mexico,Straugheir,Tyson g:Aston(7)	7th	4,234
10/4/16	Oldham (a)	L21-20	t:Fozard(2),Yere,James g:Aston(2)	7th	724
15/4/16	Wakefield (a) (CCR5)	L44-10	t:Yere(2) g:Aston	N/A	2,257
22/4/16	London Broncos (h)	L24-56	t:Blackmore,Yere,Worrincy,Aston,Mexico g:Aston,Knowles	7th	513
29/4/16	Dewsbury (h)	W32-28	t:Yere(2),Mexico,Laulu-Togagae,Worrincy(2),Carlile g:Fozard(2)	7th	441
14/5/16	Workington (h)	L30-37	t:Lo(2),Blackmore,Wheeldon,Worrincy,Aston g:Aston(3)	7th	494
20/5/16	Bradford (h)	L14-25	t:Worrincy(2),Aston g:Aston	7th	995
28/5/16	London Broncos (SB) ●	L32-14	t:Laulu-Togagae,Aston,Worrincy g:Aston	8th	N/A
5/6/16	Halifax (a)	L60-22	t:Blackmore(2),James,Millar g:Aston(3)	9th	1,680
10/6/16	Batley (h)	L10-24	t:Laulu-Togagae,Tyson g:Aston	10th	651
19/6/16	Swinton (a)	L22-18	t:Neal,Blackmore,Laulu-Togagae g:Aston(3)	10th	551
24/6/16	Featherstone (h)	W35-10	t:Aston,Wheeldon,Blackmore(2),Lo,Yere,Minchella g:Aston(3) fg:Knowles	9th	817
1/7/16	Oldham (h)	L16-24	t:Aston,Laulu-Togagae,Robin g:Aston(2)	9th	531
10/7/16	London Broncos (a)	W14-32	t:James,Fozard,Robin,Laulu-Togagae,Yere,Straugheir g:Aston(4)	8th	530
15/7/16	Leigh (h)	L30-34	t:Yere(2),Straugheir,Wheeldon,Chappell g:Aston(5)	9th	774
23/7/16	Whitehaven (a)	W14-32	t:Laulu-Togagae,Worrincy,Robin,Thorpe,Chappell,Lo g:Aston(4)	7th	553
7/8/16	Halifax (a) (CS)	W28-48	t:Wheeldon,Laulu-Togagae,Worrincy,Neal,Aston,Robin,Lo(2),James g:Aston(6)	3rd(CS)	1,288
14/8/16	Whitehaven (h) (CS)	W48-16	t:Minchella(2),Laulu-Togagae(3),Fozard,Thorpe,Chappell g:Aston(7),Knowles	3rd(CS)	412
21/8/16	Swinton (h) (CS)	L38-40	t:Straugheir,Worrincy,Robin,Knowles,Chappell(2),Fozard g:Aston(5)	3rd(CS)	466
29/8/16	Oldham (a) (CS)	W24-54	t:Yere(2),Laulu-Togagae,Blackmore,Mexico,Knowles,Fozard,Chappell,Minchella,Thorpe g:Aston(7)	3rd(CS)	680
4/9/16	Workington (h) (CS)	W62-0	t:Knowles,Straugheir,Laulu-Togagae(3),Fozard,Jacks,Lo(3),Margalet g:Aston(9)	3rd(CS)	380
11/9/16	Dewsbury (h) (CS)	L22-38	t:Yere,Millar(2),Aston g:Aston(3)	3rd(CS)	564
18/9/16	Bradford (a) (CS)	L80-0		3rd(CS)	4,035
25/9/16	Halifax (a) (CSSF)	W32-46	t:Jacks,Wheeldon,Neal,Tyson(2),Worrincy,Lo g:Aston(9)	N/A	946
2/10/16	Bradford (a) (CSF)	L27-16	t:Yere,Worrincy g:Aston(4)	N/A	3,518

● *Played at Bloomfield Road, Blackpool*

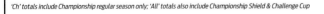

	D.O.B.	APP		TRIES		GOALS		FG		PTS	
		ALL	Ch	ALL	Ch	ALL	Ch	ALL	Ch	ALL	Ch
Cory Aston	1/3/95	34	23	15	12	93	42	0	0	246	132
Ben Blackmore	19/2/93	25	20	12	9	0	0	0	0	48	36
Jack Blagbrough	18/1/94	(6)	(5)	0	0	0	0	0	0	0	0
Greg Burns	25/3/95	(3)	0	0	0	0	0	0	0	0	0
Keal Carlile	20/3/90	31(1)	22(1)	2	2	0	0	0	0	8	8
Nathan Chappell	4/12/89	10	5	6	2	0	0	0	0	24	8
Matty Fozard	3/3/95	11(20)	9(11)	9	5	2	2	0	0	40	24
Dave Hewitt	4/11/95	12(1)	10(1)	1	1	3	0	0	0	10	4
Rhys Jacks	21/1/90	12(3)	8(3)	2	0	0	0	0	0	8	0
Matt James	26/3/87	26(5)	17(5)	4	3	0	0	0	0	16	12
Michael Knowles	2/5/87	24(6)	18(3)	5	2	27	25	1	1	75	59
Quentin Laulu-Togagae	1/12/84	34	23	20	12	0	0	0	0	80	48
Garry Lo	1/11/93	15(1)	10	12	6	0	0	0	0	48	24
Thibaut Margalet	3/1/93	8(1)	3	1	0	0	0	0	0	4	0
Mark Mexico	21/5/89	2(29)	2(19)	4	3	0	0	0	0	16	12
Ryan Millar	12/5/94	8	4	5	3	0	0	0	0	20	12
Elliot Minchella	28/1/96	10(17)	5(12)	6	3	0	0	0	0	24	12
Adam Neal	21/5/90	16(16)	12(9)	4	2	0	0	0	0	16	8
Stan Robin	21/10/90	6(1)	3(1)	5	3	0	0	0	0	20	12
Duane Straugheir	29/9/89	27	16	7	3	0	0	0	0	28	12
Mitchell Stringer	1/11/83	6(7)	4(7)	1	1	0	0	0	0	4	4
Steve Thorpe	26/9/89	26(2)	18(1)	3	1	0	0	0	0	12	4
George Tyson	1/10/93	21(5)	16(3)	5	3	0	0	0	0	20	12
Scott Wheeldon	23/2/86	22(9)	13(9)	6	4	0	0	0	0	24	16
Rob Worrincy	9/7/85	26(3)	16(2)	22	18	0	0	0	0	88	72
Menzie Yere	24/10/83	30	22	20	13	0	0	0	0	80	52

'Ch' totals include Championship regular season only; 'All' totals also include Championship Shield & Challenge Cup

Quentin Laulu-Togagae

LEAGUE RECORD
Championship, before Super 8 split:
P23-W8-D0-L15 (7th)
F583, A617, Diff-34, 16 points.

After Championship Shield:
P30-W12-D0-L18 (3rd/Runners-Up)
F855, A843, Diff+12, 24 points.

CHALLENGE CUP
Round Five

ATTENDANCES
Best - v Halifax (Ch - 1,350)
Worst - v Workington (CS - 380)
Total (Championship/
Championship Shield only) - 9,398
Average (Championship/
Championship Shield only) - 626
(Down by 657 on 2015)

CLUB RECORDS	
MATCH RECORDS	**Highest score:** 112-6 v Leigh East, 7/4/2013 **Highest score against:** 0-88 v Hull, 2/3/2003 **Record attendance:** 10,603 v Bradford, 16/8/97
	Tries: 5 Daryl Powell v Mansfield, 2/1/89; Menzie Yere v Leigh East, 7/4/2013; Quentin Laulu-Togagae v Rochdale, 7/9/2014
	Goals: 14 Dominic Brambani v Leigh East, 7/4/2013 **Points:** 32 Roy Rafferty v Fulham, 21/9/86
SEASON RECORDS	**Tries:** 46 Menzie Yere 2013 **Goals:** 169 *(inc 1fg)* Dominic Brambani 2013 **Points:** 361 Dominic Brambani 2013
CAREER RECORDS	**Tries:** 178 Menzie Yere 2009-2016 **Goals:** 986 Mark Aston 1986-2004 **Points:** 2,142 Mark Aston 1986-2004 **Appearances:** 389 Mark Aston 1986-2004

SWINTON LIONS

DATE	FIXTURE	RESULT	SCORERS	LGE	ATT
7/2/16	Dewsbury (h) ●	L24-26	t:Wilde(2),Lever(2) g:Atkin(4)	7th	639
14/2/16	London Broncos (a)	L38-18	t:White,Lever,Dwyer g:Atkin(3)	9th	653
20/2/16	Bradford (h) ●●	L16-48	t:Barlow,Robinson,Scott g:Atkin(2)	10th	880
26/2/16	Sheffield (a)	L48-26	t:Atkin,Robinson,Scott(2),Hallett g:Atkin(3)	11th	508
5/3/16	Whitehaven (a)	L18-12	t:Robinson,Atkin g:Atkin(2)	11th	517
13/3/16	Featherstone (h)	L10-30	t:Hallett,Atkin g:Atkin	12th	745
19/3/16	Sheffield (a) (CCR4)	L32-28	t:Littler,Hallett(3),Morrison g:Atkin(4)	N/A	412
24/3/16	Leigh (a)	L42-12	t:Marshall(2) g:Atkin(2)	12th	3,230
28/3/16	Oldham (h)	W28-18	t:Lloyd,Atkin,Dwyer(2),Kilday g:Atkin(4)	12th	823
3/4/16	Workington (h)	W26-22	t:Fell,Littler,Lloyd,Marshall,Atkin g:Atkin(3)	11th	501
10/4/16	Halifax (a)	W35-38	t:Marshall(4),Barlow,Atkin,Hallett,Robinson g:Atkin(3)	10th	1,551
24/4/16	Batley (a)	W24-32	t:Robinson,Marshall(2),White,Halafihi,Fell g:Atkin(4)	9th	726
1/5/16	Whitehaven (h)	W32-26	t:White,Hallett(2),Fell,Lloyd,Marshall g:Atkin(4)	8th	711
15/5/16	Bradford (a)	L54-8	t:Marshall,Lloyd	9th	4,152
22/5/16	Leigh (h)	L6-48	t:Nicholson g:Atkin	9th	1,413
29/5/16	Oldham (SB) ●●●	W24-25	t:Hallett,Atkin,Lloyd,Beharrell g:Atkin(4) fg:Beharrell	7th	N/A
5/6/16	Featherstone (a)	L58-12	t:Gregson,Marshall g:Atkin(2)	8th	1,381
12/6/16	London Broncos (h)	L16-42	t:Robinson,Hallett,Lever g:Atkin(2)	8th	485
19/6/16	Sheffield (h)	W22-18	t:Lloyd(2),Dwyer g:Atkin(5)	8th	551
26/6/16	Workington (a)	D10-10	t:Marshall(2) g:Atkin	7th	593
3/7/16	Halifax (h)	L12-62	t:Lloyd,Fell g:Atkin,Beharrell	7th	1,017
10/7/16	Oldham (a)	L26-24	t:White(2),Hallett,Barlow g:Atkin(4)	7th	758
17/7/16	Dewsbury (a)	L34-16	t:Marshall(2),Lloyd g:Atkin(2)	8th	739
24/7/16	Batley (h)	L24-62	t:Robinson,Barlow,Thornley,Beharrell g:Atkin(4)	9th	1,147
7/8/16	Dewsbury (a) (CS)	L36-24	t:Hallett,Barlow,Butt,Lloyd g:Atkin(4)	6th(CS)	674
14/8/16	Oldham (h) (CS)	L8-30	t:Robinson(2)	6th(CS)	693
21/8/16	Sheffield (a) (CS)	W38-40	t:Marshall(3),Dwyer,White,Hallett,Littler g:Atkin(6)	6th(CS)	466
29/8/16	Workington (h) (CS)	W19-12	t:Littler,Marshall,Atkin g:Atkin(3) fg:Atkin	5th(CS)	546
4/9/16	Bradford (a) (CS)	L46-28	t:Hallett(2),White,Atkin,Butt g:Atkin(4)	5th(CS)	4,030
11/9/16	Halifax (h) (CS)	W28-26	t:Atkin,Dwyer,Hallett(2),Fleming g:Atkin(4)	5th(CS)	582
18/9/16	Whitehaven (a) (CS)	L40-18	t:Waterworth,Butt,Atkin g:Atkin(2),Beharrell	5th(CS)	733

● *Played at AJ Bell Stadium, Salford*
●● *Played at Select Security Stadium, Widnes*
●●● *Played at Bloomfield Road, Blackpool*

		APP		TRIES		GOALS		FG		PTS	
	D.O.B.	ALL	Ch	ALL	Ch	ALL	Ch	ALL	Ch	ALL	Ch
Chris Atkin	7/2/93	31	23	11	7	88	61	1	0	221	150
Ben Austin	3/5/95	8(16)	6(12)	0	0	0	0	0	0	0	0
Josh Barlow	15/5/91	5(24)	4(17)	5	4	0	0	0	0	20	16
Matty Beharrell	29/3/94	11(15)	9(10)	2	2	2	1	1	1	13	11
Andy Bracek	21/3/84	7(9)	4(7)	0	0	0	0	0	0	0	0
Mike Butt	6/5/95	14	7	3	0	0	0	0	0	12	0
Connor Dwyer	29/12/93	27(1)	20(1)	6	4	0	0	0	0	24	16
Jake Emmitt	4/10/88	6(1)	0	0	0	0	0	0	0	0	0
Gabriel Fell	12/9/95	11	4	4	4	0	0	0	0	16	16
Daniel Fleming	8/7/92	6(4)	4(1)	1	0	0	0	0	0	4	0
Carl Forster	4/6/92	3(1)	3(1)	0	0	0	0	0	0	0	0
Nick Gregson	17/12/95	1	1	1	1	0	0	0	0	4	4
Vila Halafihi	24/1/94	(5)	(5)	1	1	0	0	0	0	4	4
Macauley Hallett	27/11/95	25	17	17	8	0	0	0	0	68	32
Jordan Hand	13/5/93	18(7)	14(3)	0	0	0	0	0	0	0	0
Liam Hood	6/1/92	4	4	0	0	0	0	0	0	0	0
Tom Hughes	24/3/94	1	1	0	0	0	0	0	0	0	0
Kieran Hyde	10/10/89	4(1)	3(1)	0	0	0	0	0	0	0	0
Zach Johnson	9/3/91	(9)	(7)	0	0	0	0	0	0	0	0
Corbyn Kilday	17/11/94	1(3)	1(3)	1	1	0	0	0	0	4	4
Rob Lever	13/7/95	21(8)	15(6)	4	4	0	0	0	0	16	16
Stuart Littler	19/2/79	25	19	4	1	0	0	0	0	16	4
Rhodri Lloyd	22/7/93	24	22	10	9	0	0	0	0	40	36
Liam Marshall	9/5/96	22	16	20	16	0	0	0	0	80	64
Mike Morrison	9/9/87	13	12	1	0	0	0	0	0	4	0
Stephen Nash	14/1/86	2(8)	2(7)	0	0	0	0	0	0	0	0
Anthony Nicholson	28/11/90	13(2)	12(2)	1	1	0	0	0	0	4	4
Shaun Robinson	13/7/89	29	21	9	7	0	0	0	0	36	28
Greg Scott	21/6/91	5	4	3	3	0	0	0	0	12	12
Kyle Shelford	13/9/96	(1)	(1)	0	0	0	0	0	0	0	0
Jake Shorrocks	26/10/95	1	1	0	0	0	0	0	0	0	0
Andy Thornley	1/3/89	27(4)	19(4)	1	1	0	0	0	0	4	4
Luke Waterworth	20/6/96	11(1)	5	1	0	0	0	0	0	4	0
Ben White	27/10/94	28(1)	20(1)	7	5	0	0	0	0	28	20
Greg Wilde	22/12/93	2	2	2	2	0	0	0	0	8	8

'Ch' totals include Championship regular season only; 'All' totals also include Championship Shield & Challenge Cup

Chris Atkin

LEAGUE RECORD
Championship, before Super 8 split:
P23-W7-D1-L15 (9th)
F449, A813, Diff-364, 15 points.

After Championship Shield:
P30-W10-D1-L19 (5th)
F614, A1041, Diff-427, 21 points.

CHALLENGE CUP
Round Four

ATTENDANCES
Best - v Leigh (Ch - 1,413)
Worst - v London Broncos (Ch - 485)
Total (Championship/
Championship Shield only) - 10,733
Average (Championship/
Championship Shield only) - 767
(Up by 290 on 2015, League 1)

CLUB RECORDS	**Highest score:** 96-4 v Oxford, 12/7/2015 **Highest score against:** 0-112 v Warrington, 20/5/2011
MATCH RECORDS	**Record attendance:** 26,891 v Wigan, 12/2/64 *(Station Road)*; 1,413 v Leigh, 22/5/2016 *(Heywood Road)* **Tries:** 6 Mark Riley v Prescot, 11/8/96 **Goals:** 14 Ian Mort v Oxford, 12/7/2015 **Points:** 48 Ian Mort v Oxford, 12/7/2015
SEASON RECORDS	**Tries:** 42 John Stopford 1963-64 **Goals:** 128 Albert Blan 1960-61 **Points:** 338 Ian Mort 2011
CAREER RECORDS	**Tries:** 197 Frank Evans 1921-31 **Goals:** 970 Ken Gowers 1954-73 **Points:** 2,105 Ken Gowers 1954-73 **Appearances:** 601 Ken Gowers 1954-73

WHITEHAVEN

DATE	FIXTURE	RESULT	SCORERS	LGE	ATT
7/2/16	Halifax (a)	L52-6	t:Miller g:Chamberlain	12th	1,785
13/2/16	Bradford (h)	L10-46	t:J Chapelhow,Holliday g:Jouffret	12th	878
28/2/16	Dewsbury (a)	L20-4	t:McAvoy	12th	778
5/3/16	Swinton (h)	W18-12	t:Brocklebank,Jouffret,Miller g:Brocklebank(3)	10th	517
12/3/16	Sheffield (a)	W24-26	t:Calvert(2),Miller(2),McAvoy,Carberry g:Chamberlain	9th	502
19/3/16	Batley (a) (CCR4)	L37-36	t:Jouffret,Taylor,Carberry,Gore,Newton,Holliday g:Jouffret(6)	N/A	457
25/3/16	Workington (h)	W24-16	t:Miller,Allen,Calvert,Carberry g:Jouffret(4)	9th	1,425
28/3/16	Batley (a)	L24-23	t:Taylor(2),Calvert,Aiye g:Jouffret(3) fg:Gore	9th	706
10/4/16	Leigh (a)	L60-6	t:Riley g:Jouffret	11th	3,089
17/4/16	London Broncos (h)	L12-16	t:Holliday,Calvert g:Jouffret(2)	11th	548
23/4/16	Oldham (h)	W14-6	t:Taylor,Calvert g:Jouffret(3)	10th	615
1/5/16	Swinton (a)	L32-26	t:Parker(2),Jouffret,Burns,Holliday g:Jouffret(3)	11th	711
7/5/16	Featherstone (h)	L22-44	t:Calvert(2),Allen,Parker,Holliday g:Jouffret	11th	658
14/5/16	Dewsbury (h)	L16-36	t:Calvert,Holliday,Ince g:Jouffret(2)	11th	684
22/5/16	London Broncos (a)	L62-4	t:Jouffret	11th	675
28/5/16	Workington (SB) ●	W28-24	t:Allen,Taylor,Parker,Calvert g:Jouffret(6)	10th	N/A
4/6/16	Leigh (h)	L12-36	t:Brocklebank,Jouffret g:Jouffret(2)	10th	782
11/6/16	Halifax (h)	D12-12	t:Chamberlain,Holliday g:Jouffret(2)	9th	667
19/6/16	Featherstone (a)	L30-18	t:Walker,Burns,Parker g:Jouffret,Chamberlain(2)	9th	1,456
26/6/16	Oldham (a)	L26-18	t:Fox,Duffy,Parker g:Chamberlain(3)	10th	516
2/7/16	Batley (h)	L8-16	t:Gore,Calvert	11th	571
10/7/16	Bradford (a)	L64-18	t:J Chapelhow,Newton,Brocklebank g:Brocklebank(3)	11th	4,163
17/7/16	Workington (a)	L30-28	t:Newton,Yates,Calvert,Brocklebank,Gore g:Burns(2),Brocklebank(2)	11th	1,138
23/7/16	Sheffield (h)	L14-32	t:Taylor,Gore g:Gore(3)	12th	553
7/8/16	Bradford (h) (CS)	L18-46	t:Perez,Taylor,Allen g:Jouffret(3)	8th(CS)	675
14/8/16	Sheffield (a) (CS)	L48-16	t:Carberry,Fox,Gore g:Jouffret(2)	8th(CS)	412
21/8/16	Workington (a) (CS)	W24-28	t:Taylor(2),Chamberlain,Parker,Aiye g:Jouffret(4)	8th(CS)	1,058
29/8/16	Halifax (h) (CS)	L10-30	t:Chamberlain,Gore g:Jouffret	8th(CS)	718
4/9/16	Dewsbury (a) (CS)	W12-56	t:Allen(2),Newton,Aiye,Forster(2),Walker,T Chapelhow,Davies,Riley g:Chamberlain(8)	7th(CS)	524
11/9/16	Oldham (a) (CS)	L20-18	t:Perez,Carberry,Newton g:Chamberlain(3)	8th(CS)	843
18/9/16	Swinton (h) (CS)	W40-18	t:T Chapelhow,Chamberlain(2),Ince,Aiye,Gore,Holliday g:Jouffret(6)	7th(CS)	733

● *Played at Bloomfield Road, Blackpool*

		APP		TRIES		GOALS		FG		PTS	
	D.O.B.	ALL	Ch	ALL	Ch	ALL	Ch	ALL	Ch	ALL	Ch
Dion Aiye	6/11/87	27(2)	19(2)	4	1	0	0	0	0	16	4
Dave Allen	15/9/85	27	19	6	3	0	0	0	0	24	12
Richard Beaumont	2/2/88	3	3	0	0	0	0	0	0	0	0
John-Paul Brocklebank	1/11/89	15(3)	15(3)	4	4	8	8	0	0	32	32
Sam Brooks	29/9/93	5(2)	5(2)	0	0	0	0	0	0	0	0
Jordan Burns	2/9/95	13	10	2	2	2	2	0	0	12	12
Craig Calvert	10/2/84	19	18	12	12	0	0	0	0	48	48
Liam Carberry	24/2/93	22(3)	14(3)	5	2	0	0	0	0	20	8
Ed Chamberlain	8/2/96	16(2)	11(2)	5	1	18	7	0	0	56	18
Jay Chapelhow	21/9/95	(6)	(6)	2	2	0	0	0	0	8	8
Ted Chapelhow	21/9/95	14(10)	7(10)	2	0	0	0	0	0	8	0
Thomas Coyle	10/5/88	10(1)	9(1)	0	0	0	0	0	0	0	0
Ben Davies	2/11/89	7(20)	6(14)	1	0	0	0	0	0	4	0
Ryan Duffy	13/5/93	7(13)	7(11)	1	1	0	0	0	0	4	4
Carl Forster	4/6/92	6(1)	0	2	0	0	0	0	0	8	0
Steve Fox	13/2/90	8(15)	6(9)	2	1	0	0	0	0	8	4
Grant Gore	21/11/91	30	22	7	3	3	3	1	1	35	19
Connor Holliday	9/6/95	16(8)	14(5)	8	6	0	0	0	0	32	24
Ryan Ince	16/9/96	16	10	2	1	0	0	0	0	8	4
Louis Jouffret	24/5/95	25	18	5	4	53	31	0	0	126	78
Nathan Lucock	2/10/93	(3)	(2)	0	0	0	0	0	0	0	0
Scott McAvoy	9/4/86	7(1)	6(1)	2	2	0	0	0	0	8	8
Elliott Miller	14/9/90	6	6	5	5	0	0	0	0	20	20
James Newton	20/12/91	10(17)	8(11)	5	2	0	0	0	0	20	8
Jessie Joe Parker	22/8/85	24(1)	18(1)	7	6	0	0	0	0	28	24
Ugo Perez	30/11/94	13(2)	8	2	0	0	0	0	0	8	0
Glenn Riley	21/9/92	20(8)	18(4)	2	1	0	0	0	0	8	4
Almer Salvilla	31/5/96	1	1	0	0	0	0	0	0	0	0
Chris Taylor	25/10/93	22	14	9	5	0	0	0	0	36	20
Anthony Walker	28/12/91	12(1)	5(1)	2	1	0	0	0	0	8	4
Andy Yates	23/2/90	2(1)	2(1)	1	1	0	0	0	0	4	4

'Ch' totals include Championship regular season only; 'All' totals also include Championship Shield & Challenge Cup

Craig Calvert

LEAGUE RECORD
Championship, before Super 8 split:
P23-W5-D1-L17 (12th)
F367, A720, Diff-353, 11 points.

After Championship Shield:
P30-W8-D1-L21 (7th)
F553, A918, Diff-365, 17 points.

CHALLENGE CUP
Round Four

ATTENDANCES
Best - v Workington (Ch - 1,425)
Worst - v Swinton (Ch - 517)
Total (Championship/
Championship Shield only) - 10,024
Average (Championship/
Championship Shield only) - 716
(Down by 154 on 2015)

CLUB RECORDS	
MATCH RECORDS	**Highest score:** 86-6 v Highfield, 25/1/95 **Highest score against:** 8-106 v Wigan, 12/5/2008 **Record attendance:** 18,500 v Wakefield, 19/3/60
SEASON RECORDS	**Tries:** 6 Vince Gribbin v Doncaster, 18/11/84 **Goals:** 13 Lee Anderson v Highfield, 25/1/95 **Points:** 32 Mick Nanyn v Batley, 22/8/2004
CAREER RECORDS	**Tries:** 34 Mike Pechey 1994-95 **Goals:** 141 John McKeown 1956-57 **Points:** 398 Mick Nanyn 2004
	Tries: 232 Craig Calvert 2004-2016 **Goals:** 1,050 John McKeown 1948-61 **Points:** 2,133 John McKeown 1948-61 **Appearances:** 417 John McKeown 1948-61

WORKINGTON TOWN

DATE	FIXTURE	RESULT	SCORERS	LGE	ATT
7/2/16	Sheffield (h)	L12-42	t:Doran,J Murphy g:Forber(2)	11th	813
14/2/16	Dewsbury (a)	L38-16	t:C Phillips,Hulme,Mossop g:Forber(2)	10th	786
21/2/16	Halifax (h)	L0-20		11th	641
28/2/16	London Broncos (h)	L13-16	t:Sammut(2) g:Forber(2) fg:Sammut	10th	632
6/3/16	Batley (a)	L44-12	t:Hulme,Carter g:Forber(2)	12th	658
13/3/16	Oldham (h)	W23-12	t:Sammut(2),J Murphy,C Murphy g:Forber(3) fg:Sammut	11th	637
19/3/16	Leigh (a) (CCR4)	L68-14	t:Sammut,Ritson,Whiteley g:Forber	N/A	2,049
25/3/16	Whitehaven (a)	L24-16	t:Sammut(2),B Phillips g:Forber,Sammut	11th	1,425
28/3/16	Leigh (h)	L24-40	t:C Murphy,Ritson,Sammut,B Phillips,Mossop g:Sammut(2)	11th	787
3/4/16	Swinton (a)	L26-22	t:J Murphy,C Murphy,Mattinson,Sammut g:Forber(3)	12th	501
10/4/16	Featherstone (h)	L6-52	t:B Phillips g:Forber	12th	719
24/4/16	Bradford (a)	L52-16	t:C Murphy(2),J Murphy g:Forber(2)	12th	3,467
1/5/16	Halifax (a)	L36-32	t:C Murphy,Mossop,Stack(2),Whiteley,Mattinson g:Forber(4)	12th	1,293
14/5/16	Sheffield (a)	W30-37	t:Hulme,Whiteley(3),Forber,Coward g:Forber(6) fg:Forber	12th	494
22/5/16	Batley (h)	L24-31	t:B Phillips,Whiteley,Sammut,J Murphy g:Forber(4)	12th	681
28/5/16	Whitehaven (SB) ●	L28-24	t:Sammut(3),C Phillips,Hulme g:Forber(2)	12th	N/A
5/6/16	London Broncos (a)	L50-28	t:Carter,J Murphy,Gee,Sammut,Gordon g:Sammut(4)	12th	650
12/6/16	Bradford (h)	L22-29	t:Sammut(2),Forrester,Hulme g:Sammut(3)	12th	723
19/6/16	Leigh (a)	L54-12	t:Mossop,Whiteley g:Sammut(2)	12th	3,002
26/6/16	Swinton (a)	D10-10	t:Doran g:Sammut(3)	12th	593
3/7/16	Featherstone (a)	L44-22	t:Hulme(2),B Phillips,Shackley g:Sammut(3)	12th	1,281
10/7/16	Dewsbury (h)	W22-20	t:Hulme,Olstrum,Ritson,Gee g:Sammut(3)	12th	492
17/7/16	Whitehaven (h)	W30-28	t:Patrick(2),Sammut,Mossop g:Sammut(7)	12th	1,138
24/7/16	Oldham (a)	W30-32	t:Sammut,Shackley,Walker,Gordon,Hulme g:Sammut(6)	11th	689
7/8/16	Oldham (a) (CS)	L30-16	t:Sammut,Hulme,B Phillips g:Sammut(2)	7th(CS)	573
14/8/16	Dewsbury (h) (CS)	W34-24	t:Gee(2),C Phillips,Walker,Mossop g:Sammut(7)	7th(CS)	527
21/8/16	Whitehaven (h) (CS)	L24-28	t:Shackley,Doran(2),Sammut g:Sammut(4)	7th(CS)	1,058
29/8/16	Swinton (a) (CS)	L19-12	t:Shackley,Mossop g:Sammut(2)	7th(CS)	546
4/9/16	Sheffield (a) (CS)	L62-0		8th(CS)	380
11/9/16	Bradford (h) (CS)	W30-26	t:Shackley,Sammut(3),Ritson g:Sammut(5)	7th(CS)	596
18/9/16	Halifax (a) (CS)	L46-26	t:Ritson,Mossop,Doran,Gee,Hulme g:Sammut(3)	8th(CS)	1,217

● *Played at Bloomfield Road, Blackpool*

		APP		TRIES		GOALS		FG		PTS	
	D.O.B.	ALL	Ch	ALL	Ch	ALL	Ch	ALL	Ch	ALL	Ch
Brett Carter	9/7/88	8	8	2	2	0	0	0	0	8	8
Kris Coward	1/10/81	18(1)	13	1	1	0	0	0	0	4	4
Jamie Doran	8/12/94	20(8)	16(4)	5	2	0	0	0	0	20	8
Carl Forber	17/3/85	26(3)	18(3)	1	1	35	34	1	1	75	73
Sam Forrester	28/6/93	8	8	1	1	0	0	0	0	4	4
Matty Gee	12/12/94	20	14	5	2	0	0	0	0	20	8
Oliver Gordon	27/6/92	24(5)	16(5)	2	2	0	0	0	0	8	8
Declan Hulme	14/1/93	28	20	11	9	0	0	0	0	44	36
Graeme Mattinson	24/4/85	14(7)	12(7)	2	2	0	0	0	0	8	8
Liam McAvoy	24/9/93	23(5)	16(4)	0	0	0	0	0	0	0	0
Jason Mossop	12/9/85	29	21	8	5	0	0	0	0	32	20
Chris Murphy	19/9/89	10(1)	9(1)	6	6	0	0	0	0	24	24
Jack Murphy	18/3/92	29	21	6	6	0	0	0	0	24	24
Karl Olstrum	21/9/91	9(7)	5(7)	1	1	0	0	0	0	4	4
John Patrick	29/11/82	4	4	2	2	0	0	0	0	8	8
Brett Phillips	25/10/88	22	19	6	5	0	0	0	0	24	20
Callum Phillips	19/2/92	14(6)	12(4)	3	2	0	0	0	0	12	8
Theerapol Ritson	7/1/96	20(1)	12(1)	5	2	0	0	0	0	20	8
Daniel Rooney	6/1/90	(2)	(2)	0	0	0	0	0	0	0	0
Jarrod Sammut	15/2/87	23(2)	16(2)	23	17	57	34	2	2	208	138
Steve Scholey	7/1/96	3(13)	2(7)	0	0	0	0	0	0	0	0
Marc Shackley	14/1/89	19(9)	11(9)	5	2	0	0	0	0	20	8
Jarrad Stack	13/2/88	7(2)	7(2)	2	2	0	0	0	0	8	8
Alex Szostak	4/3/86	(8)	(5)	0	0	0	0	0	0	0	0
Ryan Verlinden	18/6/86	2(22)	2(14)	0	0	0	0	0	0	0	0
Tom Walker	25/12/94	8(11)	3(9)	2	1	0	0	0	0	8	4
Perry Whiteley	22/2/93	15(2)	14(2)	7	6	0	0	0	0	28	24

'Ch' totals include Championship regular season only; 'All' totals also include Championship Shield & Challenge Cup

Jarrod Sammut

LEAGUE RECORD
Championship, before Super 8 split:
P23-W5-D1-L17 (11th)
F455, A756, Diff-301, 11 points.

After Championship Shield:
P30-W7-D1-L22 (8th)
F597, A991, Diff-394, 15 points.

CHALLENGE CUP
Round Four

ATTENDANCES
Best - v Whitehaven (Ch - 1,138)
Worst - v Dewsbury (Ch - 492)
Total (Championship/
Championship Shield only) - 10,037
Average (Championship/
Championship Shield only) - 717
(Down by 132 on 2015)

CLUB RECORDS **MATCH RECORDS**	**Highest score:** 94-4 v Leigh, 26/2/95 **Highest score against:** 0-92 v Bradford, 14/2/99 **Record attendance:** 17,741 v Wigan, 3/3/65
	Tries: 7 Ike Southward v Blackpool, 17/9/55 **Goals:** 14 Darren Holt v Gateshead, 12/6/2011
	Points: 42 Dean Marwood v Highfield, 1/11/92; Dean Marwood v Leigh, 26/2/95
SEASON RECORDS	**Tries:** 49 Johnny Lawrenson 1951-52 **Goals:** 186 Lyn Hopkins 1981-82 **Points:** 438 Lyn Hopkins 1981-82
CAREER RECORDS	**Tries:** 274 Ike Southward 1952-68 **Goals:** 809 Iain MacCorquodale 1972-80 **Points:** 1,800 Iain MacCorquodale 1972-80
	Appearances: 419 Paul Charlton 1961-69; 1975-80

CHAMPIONSHIP 2016
Round by Round

ROUND 1

Sunday 7th February 2016

BATLEY BULLDOGS 24 LEIGH CENTURIONS 22

BULLDOGS: 22 Dave Scott; 2 Wayne Reittie; 4 Shaun Squires; 3 Chris Ulugia; 5 Shaun Ainscough; 6 Cain Southernwood; 7 Dominic Brambani; 8 Keegan Hirst; 9 Luke Blake; 15 Adam Gledhill; 12 Sam Scott; 17 Joe Chandler; 13 Pat Walker. Subs (all used): 11 Brad Day; 14 James Davey; 18 Tom Lillycrop; 21 James Brown.
Tries: J Brown (28), Ulugia (40, 68), Ainscough (77); **Goals:** Walker 3/4, Brambani 1/1.
CENTURIONS: 23 Rangi Chase; 2 Adam Higson; 3 Greg Worthington; 24 Tom Armstrong; 5 Liam Kay; 6 Martyn Ridyard; 7 Ryan Brierley; 8 Fuifui Moimoi; 14 Micky Higham; 10 Dayne Weston; 11 Harrison Hansen; 21 Andrew Dixon; 29 Jake Emmitt. Subs (all used): 16 Reni Maitua; 18 Tom Spencer; 19 Lewis Foster; 20 Sam Hopkins.
Tries: Dixon (19), Armstrong (33), Higham (49), Brierley (58); **Goals:** Ridyard 3/4.
Rugby Leaguer & League Express Men of the Match: *Bulldogs:* Chris Ulugia; *Centurions:* Micky Higham.
Penalty count: 6-8; **Half-time:** 12-12;
Referee: Gareth Hewer; **Attendance:** 1,678.

BRADFORD BULLS 22 FEATHERSTONE ROVERS 12

BULLS: 34 Richard Mathers; 22 James Clare; 3 Adrian Purtell; 4 Kris Welham; 2 Omari Caro; 6 Lee Gaskell; 13 Danny Addy; 25 Ben Kavanagh; 9 Adam O'Brien; 10 Adam Sidlow; 11 Tom Olbison; 28 Kurt Haggerty; 14 Jay Pitts. Subs (all used): 15 Matty Blythe; 27 Jonathan Walker; 12 Dale Ferguson; 21 Epalahame Lauaki.
Tries: Gaskell (12), Caro (19, 31, 54); **Goals:** Addy 3/4.
ROVERS: 1 Danny Craven; 33 Ash Handley; 3 Michael Channing; 4 Misi Taulapapa; 5 Scott Turner; 6 Kyle Briggs; 7 Anthony Thackeray; 8 Darrell Griffin; 12 John Davies; 10 Andrew Bostock; 18 Jamie Cording; 13 Tim Spears; 17 Jack Ormondroyd. Subs (all used): 15 Ian Hardman; 34 Mitch Achurch; 32 Jordan Baldwinson; 21 Bradley Knowles-Tagg.
Tries: Craven (6), Thackeray (37); **Goals:** Briggs 2/2.
Rugby Leaguer & League Express Men of the Match: *Bulls:* Adam Sidlow; *Rovers:* Danny Craven.
Penalty count: 12-6; **Half-time:** 16-12;
Referee: George Stokes; **Attendance:** 4,518.

HALIFAX 52 WHITEHAVEN 6

HALIFAX: 1 Ben Johnston; 2 Will Sharp; 20 Sam Smeaton; 3 Steve Tyrer; 5 James Saltonstall; 7 Gareth Moore; 6 Scott Murrell; 10 Luke Ambler; 9 Ben Kaye; 8 Mitch Cahalane; 26 Ed Barber; 11 Dane Manning; 13 Jacob Fairbank. Subs (all used): 14 Adam Tangata; 15 Ryan Maneely; 16 Richard Moore; 21 Adam Robinson.
Tries: Tyrer (12, 21, 39, 53), G Moore (30), Smeaton (47), Kaye (68), Sharp (72), Saltonstall (75); **Goals:** Tyrer 8/9.
WHITEHAVEN: 1 Louis Jouffret; 5 Elliott Miller; 28 Ed Chamberlain; 3 Chris Taylor; 20 Jordan Burns; 6 Dion Aiye; 7 Grant Gore; 10 Richard Beaumont; 9 James Newton; 19 Glenn Riley; 11 Dave Allen; 4 Jessie Joe Parker; 17 Steve Fox. Subs (all used): 26 Ted Chapelhow; 15 Ben Davies; 27 Jay Chapelhow; 21 John-Paul Brocklebank.
Try: Miller (78); **Goals:** Chamberlain 1/1.
Rugby Leaguer & League Express Men of the Match: *Halifax:* Steve Tyrer; *Whitehaven:* Ted Chapelhow.
Penalty count: 8-2; **Half-time:** 24-0;
Referee: Joe Cobb; **Attendance:** 1,785.

OLDHAM 0 LONDON BRONCOS 22

OLDHAM: 1 Richard Lepori; 2 Adam Clay; 25 Tom Ashton; 4 Jack Holmes; 5 Jamel Chisholm; 6 Lewis Palfrey; 7 Steve Roper; 8 Phil Joy; 9 Sam Gee; 10 Jack Spencer; 11 Josh Crowley; 12 Danny Langtree; 24 Will Hope. Subs (all used): 19 Adam Files; 26 Michael Ward; 21 Kenny Hughes; 13 Liam Thompson.
BRONCOS: 1 Ben Hellewell; 2 Rhys Williams; 3 Nathan Stapleton; 4 Wes Naiqama; 5 Iliess Macani; 7 William Barthau; 19 Joe Keyes; 18 Jamie Thackray; 14 Andy Ackers; 8 Nick Slyney; 11 Daniel Harrison; 12 Matt Garside; 21 Alex Foster. Subs (all used): 15 Jack Bussey; 22 Matt Davis; 16 Mark Ioane; 10 Eddie Battye.
Tries: Ackers (15), Bussey (48), Macani (59), Hellewell (66); **Goals:** Naiqama 3/4.
Rugby Leaguer & League Express Men of the Match: *Oldham:* Richard Lepori; *Broncos:* Andy Ackers.
Penalty count: 11-4; **Half-time:** 0-4;
Referee: Michael Woodhead; **Attendance:** 767.

SWINTON LIONS 24 DEWSBURY RAMS 26

LIONS: 1 Chris Atkin; 2 Shaun Robinson; 3 Stuart Littler; 24 Greg Wilde; 5 Greg Scott; 6 Ben White; 7 Matty Beharrell; 8 Mike Morrison; 27 Liam Hood; 10 Jordan Hand; 12 Andy Thornley; 11 Connor Dwyer; 26 Carl Forster. Subs (all used): 13 Rob Lever; 15 Corbyn Kilday; 19 Josh Barlow; 9 Anthony Nicholson.
Tries: Wilde (4, 31), Lever (44, 68); **Goals:** Atkin 4/6.
RAMS: 1 Josh Guzdek; 2 Dale Morton; 4 Shane Grady; 15 Jason Crookes; 5 Dalton Grant; 7 Ben Reynolds; 22 Andy Kain; 8 Matt Groat; 19 Nathan Conroy; 10 Ryan Hepworth; 32 Kyle Trout; 16 Toby Adamson; 13 Aaron Brown. Subs (all used): 31 Ryan Wright; 24 Jack Teanby; 18 Tony Tonks; 6 Paul Sykes.
Tries: Guzdek (18, 24, 73), Reynolds (47), Sykes (63); **Goals:** Reynolds 3/5.
On report: Grady (27) - alleged high tackle on Dwyer.
Rugby Leaguer & League Express Men of the Match: *Lions:* Carl Forster; *Rams:* Josh Guzdek.
Penalty count: 8-5; **Half-time:** 8-12;
Referee: Chris Campbell; **Attendance:** 639
(at AJ Bell Stadium, Salford).

WORKINGTON TOWN 12 SHEFFIELD EAGLES 42

TOWN: 1 Jack Murphy; 2 Sam Forrester; 3 Declan Hulme; 4 Jason Mossop; 5 Brett Carter; 6 Carl Forber; 7 Jamie Doran; 8 Kris Coward; 14 Callum Phillips; 20 Steve Scholey; 16 Perry Whiteley; 15 Karl Olstrum; 13 Liam McAvoy. Subs (all used): 9 Graeme Mattinson; 19 Ryan Verlinden; 21 Oliver Gordon; 23 Daniel Rooney.
Tries: Doran (37), J Murphy (67); **Goals:** Forber 2/2.
On report: Brawl (60).
EAGLES: 1 Quentin Laulu-Togagae; 2 Rob Worrincy; 3 Menzie Yere; 4 George Tyson; 5 Ben Blackmore; 6 Cory Aston; 21 Dave Hewitt; 15 Scott Wheeldon; 9 Keal Carlile; 16 Adam Neal; 11 Michael Knowles; 12 Duane Straugheir; 10 Mitchell Stringer. Subs (all used): 14 Matty Fozard; 8 Steve Thorpe; 13 Matt James; 17 Mark Mexico.
Tries: Worrincy (12), Aston (17, 72), Neal (21), Yere (28), Fozard (50, 63); **Goals:** Knowles 7/7.
On report: Brawl (60).
Rugby Leaguer & League Express Men of the Match: *Town:* Perry Whiteley; *Eagles:* Michael Knowles.
Penalty count: 6-9; **Half-time:** 6-24;
Referee: Sam Ansell; **Attendance:** 813.

ROUND 2

Friday 12th February 2016

SHEFFIELD EAGLES 26 HALIFAX 6

EAGLES: 1 Quentin Laulu-Togagae; 2 Rob Worrincy; 3 Menzie Yere; 4 George Tyson; 5 Ben Blackmore; 6 Cory Aston; 21 Dave Hewitt; 15 Scott Wheeldon; 9 Keal Carlile; 16 Adam Neal; 11 Michael Knowles; 12 Duane Straugheir; 13 Matt James. Subs (all used): 14 Matty Fozard; 10 Mitchell Stringer; 17 Mark Mexico; 18 Elliot Minchella.
Tries: Worrincy (43, 51), Yere (46), Aston (49), Minchella (70); **Goals:** Knowles 3/5.
HALIFAX: 1 Ben Johnston; 2 Will Sharp; 20 Sam Smeaton; 3 Steve Tyrer; 5 James Saltonstall; 7 Gareth Moore; 6 Scott Murrell; 10 Luke Ambler; 9 Ben Kaye; 8 Mitch Cahalane; 11 Dane Manning; 26 Ed Barber; 13 Jacob Fairbank. Subs (all used): 14 Adam Tangata; 15 Ryan Maneely; 16 Richard Moore; 21 Adam Robinson.
Try: Sharp (65); **Goals:** Tyrer 1/1.
Rugby Leaguer & League Express Men of the Match: *Eagles:* Cory Aston; *Halifax:* Gareth Moore.
Penalty count: 11-10; **Half-time:** 0-0;
Referee: Chris Kendall; **Attendance:** 1,350.

Saturday 13th February 2016

WHITEHAVEN 10 BRADFORD BULLS 46

WHITEHAVEN: 1 Louis Jouffret; 5 Elliott Miller; 4 Jessie Joe Parker; 16 Connor Holliday; 28 Ed Chamberlain; 21 John-Paul Brocklebank; 7 Grant Gore; 26 Ted Chapelhow; 14 Thomas Coyle; 19 Glenn Riley; 11 Dave Allen; 6 Dion Aiye; 8 Sam Brooks. Subs (all used): 9 James Newton; 15 Ben Davies; 17 Steve Fox; 27 Jay Chapelhow.
Tries: J Chapelhow (30), Holliday (47); **Goals:** Jouffret 1/2.
BULLS: 34 Richard Mathers; 22 James Clare; 3 Adrian Purtell; 4 Kris Welham; 2 Omari Caro; 6 Lee Gaskell; 13 Danny Addy; 11 Tom Olbison; 9 Adam O'Brien; 10 Adam Sidlow; 12 Dale Ferguson; 28 Kurt Haggerty; 14 Jay Pitts. Subs (all used): 15 Matty Blythe; 35 Rhys Lovegrove; 20 Mitch Clark; 23 Alex Mellor.
Tries: Clare (4), Gaskell (12, 61, 80), Pitts (14, 74), Ferguson (20), O'Brien (50); **Goals:** Addy 7/8.
Rugby Leaguer & League Express Men of the Match: *Whitehaven:* John-Paul Brocklebank; *Bulls:* Lee Gaskell.
Penalty count: 9-11; **Half-time:** 6-24;
Referee: Jon Roberts; **Attendance:** 878.

Sunday 14th February 2016

DEWSBURY RAMS 38 WORKINGTON TOWN 16

RAMS: 1 Josh Guzdek; 2 Dale Morton; 15 Jason Crookes; 4 Shane Grady; 5 Dalton Grant; 7 Ben Reynolds; 22 Andy Kain; 8 Matt Groat; 19 Nathan Conroy; 10 Ryan Hepworth; 16 Toby Adamson; 32 Kyle Trout; 14 Luke Adamson. Subs (all used): 31 Ryan Wright; 13 Aaron Brown; 6 Paul Sykes; 18 Tony Tonks.
Tries: Crookes (1, 49), Grant (23, 58), Morton (52), Kain (55), Guzdek (66), Trout (78); **Goals:** Reynolds 3/8.
TOWN: 1 Jack Murphy; 2 Sam Forrester; 3 Declan Hulme; 4 Jason Mossop; 24 Theerapol Ritson; 6 Carl Forber; 7 Jamie Doran; 8 Kris Coward; 14 Callum Phillips; 19 Ryan Verlinden; 16 Perry Whiteley; 15 Karl Olstrum; 13 Liam McAvoy. Subs (all used): 10 Marc Shackley; 20 Steve Scholey; 9 Graeme Mattinson; 21 Oliver Gordon.
Tries: C Phillips (13), Hulme (28), Mossop (76); **Goals:** Forber 2/3.
Sin bin: Hulme (33) - persistent team offences.
Rugby Leaguer & League Express Men of the Match: *Rams:* Jason Crookes; *Town:* Callum Phillips.
Penalty count: 12-5; **Half-time:** 8-10;
Referee: Gareth Hewer; **Attendance:** 786.

FEATHERSTONE ROVERS 14 BATLEY BULLDOGS 12

ROVERS: 1 Danny Craven; 33 Ash Handley; 3 Michael Channing; 15 Ian Hardman; 5 Scott Turner; 6 Kyle Briggs; 7 Anthony Thackeray; 8 Darrell Griffin; 12 John Davies; 10 Andrew Bostock; 34 Mitch Achurch; 13 Tim Spears; 4 Misi Taulapapa. Subs: 17 Jack Ormondroyd; 19 Sam Day (not used); 21 Bradley Knowles-Tagg; 32 Jordan Baldwinson.
Tries: Handley (17), Taulapapa (20); **Goals:** Briggs 3/3.
BULLDOGS: 22 Dave Scott; 2 Wayne Reittie; 4 Shaun Squires; 3 Chris Ulugia; 5 Shaun Ainscough; 6 Cain Southernwood; 7 Dominic Brambani; 8 Keegan Hirst; 9 Luke Blake; 21 James Brown; 19 Alex Bretherton; 17 Joe Chandler; 13 Pat Walker. Subs (all used): 10 Alex Rowe; 15 Adam Gledhill; 18 Tom Lillycrop; 20 Alistair Leak.
Tries: D Scott (8), Reittie (59); **Goals:** Walker 2/2.
Rugby Leaguer & League Express Men of the Match: *Rovers:* Kyle Briggs; *Bulldogs:* Alex Rowe.
Penalty count: 10-7; **Half-time:** 12-6;
Referee: Michael Woodhead; **Attendance:** 2,103.

LEIGH CENTURIONS 48 OLDHAM 18

CENTURIONS: 26 Lee Smith; 15 Jonny Pownall; 2 Adam Higson; 24 Tom Armstrong; 5 Liam Kay; 6 Martyn Ridyard; 23 Rangi Chase; 8 Fuifui Moimoi; 19 Lewis Foster; 10 Dayne Weston; 11 Harrison Hansen; 21 Andrew Dixon; 12 Gareth Hock. Subs (all used): 14 Micky Higham; 20 Sam Hopkins; 16 Reni Maitua; 29 Jake Emmitt.
Tries: Pownall (11), Smith (23), Higson (31, 36), Hopkins (45, 53, 58), Moimoi (60), Maitua (62); **Goals:** Ridyard 4/7, Smith 2/2.
OLDHAM: 1 Richard Lepori; 2 Adam Clay; 4 Jack Holmes; 25 Tom Ashton; 5 Jamel Chisholm; 6 Lewis Palfrey; 7 Steve Roper; 8 Phil Joy; 20 Gareth Owen; 10 Jack Spencer; 11 Josh Crowley; 12 Danny Langtree; 24 Will Hope. Subs (all used): 9 Sam Gee; 13 Liam Thompson; 19 Adam Files; 26 Michael Ward.
Tries: Ashton (15), Clay (65), Palfrey (77); **Goals:** Palfrey 3/3.
Rugby Leaguer & League Express Men of the Match: *Centurions:* Lee Smith; *Oldham:* Lewis Palfrey.
Penalty count: 8-7; **Half-time:** 20-6;
Referee: Sam Ansell; **Attendance:** 3,371.

LONDON BRONCOS 38 SWINTON LIONS 18

BRONCOS: 24 Alex Walker; 2 Rhys Williams; 3 Nathan Stapleton; 4 Wes Naiqama; 5 Iliess Macani; 7 William Barthau; 19 Joe Keyes; 8 Nick Slyney; 14 Andy Ackers; 18 Jamie Thackray; 11 Daniel Harrison; 12 Matt Garside; 21 Alex Foster. Subs (all used): 10 Eddie Battye; 15 Jack Bussey; 16 Mark Ioane; 22 Matt Davis.
Tries: Walker (21, 33), Garside (45), Bussey (50), Foster (66), Macani (72), Keyes (78); **Goals:** Naiqama 5/7.
LIONS: 1 Chris Atkin; 20 Mike Butt; 23 Rhodri Lloyd; 24 Greg Wilde; 5 Greg Scott; 6 Ben White; 7 Matty Beharrell; 8 Mike Morrison; 9 Anthony Nicholson; 10 Jordan Hand; 12 Andy Thornley; 11 Connor Dwyer; 26 Carl Forster. Subs (all used): 14 Kieran Hyde; 19 Josh Barlow; 15 Corbyn Kilday; 13 Rob Lever.
Tries: White (25), Lever (29), Dwyer (39); **Goals:** Atkin 3/3.
Sin bin: R Lloyd (9) - professional foul.
Rugby Leaguer & League Express Men of the Match: *Broncos:* William Barthau; *Lions:* Ben White.
Penalty count: 8-6; **Half-time:** 12-18;
Referee: Jamie Bloem; **Attendance:** 653.

Championship 2016 - Round by Round

ROUND 3

Saturday 20th February 2016

SWINTON LIONS 16 BRADFORD BULLS 48

LIONS: 20 Mike Butt; 2 Shaun Robinson; 23 Rhodri Lloyd; 4 Macauley Hallett; 5 Greg Scott; 6 Ben White; 1 Chris Atkin; 8 Mike Morrison; 27 Liam Hood; 26 Carl Forster; 12 Andy Thornley; 11 Connor Dwyer; 13 Rob Lever. Subs (all used): 17 Stephen Nash; 10 Jordan Hand; 19 Josh Barlow; 16 Ben Austin.
Tries: Barlow (30), Robinson (58), Scott (63);
Goals: Atkin 2/3.
Sin bin: Dwyer (72) - holding down.
BULLS: 1 Oscar Thomas; 22 James Clare; 3 Adrian Purtell; 4 Kris Welham; 2 Omari Caro; 6 Lee Gaskell; 13 Danny Addy; 10 Adam Sidlow; 9 Adam O'Brien; 11 Tom Olbison; 12 Dale Ferguson; 23 Alex Mellor; 14 Jay Pitts. Subs (all used): 15 Matty Blythe; 35 Rhys Lovegrove; 20 Mitch Clark; 30 Joe Lumb.
Tries: Olbison (3, 68), Welham (17, 26, 55), Caro (34), Clare (39), Blythe (44), Gaskell (75); **Goals:** Addy 6/9.
Rugby Leaguer & League Express Men of the Match: *Lions:* Liam Hood; *Bulls:* Lee Gaskell.
Penalty count: 11-15; **Half-time:** 6-26;
Referee: Chris Kendall; **Attendance:** 880 *(at Select Security Stadium, Widnes).*

Sunday 21st February 2016

BATLEY BULLDOGS 20 SHEFFIELD EAGLES 8

BULLDOGS: 22 Dave Scott; 2 Wayne Reittie; 23 Danny Cowling; 3 Chris Ulugia; 5 Shaun Ainscough; 6 Cain Southernwood; 7 Dominic Brambani; 8 Keegan Hirst; 9 Luke Blake; 21 James Brown; 19 Alex Bretherton; 17 Joe Chandler; 13 Pat Walker. Subs (all used): 18 Tom Lillycrop; 20 Alistair Leak; 15 Adam Gledhill; 10 Alex Rowe.
Tries: Brambani (17, 46), Leak (57);
Goals: Walker 3/3, Brambani 1/1.
Sin bin: Blake (64) - dissent.
EAGLES: 1 Quentin Laulu-Togagae; 19 Garry Lo; 3 Menzie Yere; 4 George Tyson; 5 Ben Blackmore; 6 Cory Aston; 21 Dave Hewitt; 8 Steve Thorpe; 9 Keal Carlile; 15 Scott Wheeldon; 11 Michael Knowles; 13 Matt James; 18 Elliot Minchella. Subs (all used): 14 Matty Fozard; 10 Mitchell Stringer; 16 Adam Neal; 17 Mark Mexico.
Tries: Yere (10), Lo (28); **Goals:** Knowles 0/2.
Rugby Leaguer & League Express Men of the Match: *Bulldogs:* Pat Walker; *Eagles:* Mark Mexico.
Penalty count: 9-11; **Half-time:** 6-8;
Referee: Sam Ansell; **Attendance:** 814.

LEIGH CENTURIONS 24 LONDON BRONCOS 20

CENTURIONS: 26 Lee Smith; 2 Adam Higson; 3 Greg Worthington; 27 Richard Whiting; 15 Jonny Pownall; 23 Rangi Chase; 7 Ryan Brierley; 8 Fuifui Moimoi; 14 Micky Higham; 10 Dayne Weston; 11 Harrison Hansen; 16 Reni Maitua; 12 Gareth Hock. Subs (all used): 19 Lewis Foster; 20 Sam Hopkins; 17 Jamie Acton; 29 Jake Emmitt.
Tries: Hopkins (38), Acton (67), Emmitt (70), Chase (72);
Goals: Smith 4/4.
Sin bin: Weston (20) - holding down; Emmitt (33) - holding down.
BRONCOS: 24 Alex Walker; 2 Rhys Williams; 1 Ben Hellewell; 4 Wes Naiqama; 5 Iliess Macani; 19 Joe Keyes; 20 Scott Leatherbarrow; 8 Nick Slyney; 9 James Cunningham; 16 Mark Ioane; 21 Alex Foster; 12 Matt Garside; 15 Jack Bussey. Subs (all used): 14 Andy Ackers; 11 Daniel Harrison; 18 Jamie Thackray; 10 Eddie Battye.
Tries: Foster (16), Cunningham (25), Williams (34), Hellewell (60); **Goals:** Naiqama 2/4.
Rugby Leaguer & League Express Men of the Match: *Centurions:* Harrison Hansen; *Broncos:* Scott Leatherbarrow.
Penalty count: 14-16; **Half-time:** 6-14;
Referee: George Stokes; **Attendance:** 3,291.

OLDHAM 38 DEWSBURY RAMS 16

OLDHAM: 1 Richard Lepori; 2 Adam Clay; 25 Tom Ashton; 18 Jake Bibby; 4 Jack Holmes; 22 Danny Grimshaw; 6 Lewis Palfrey; 8 Phil Joy; 20 Gareth Owen; 10 Jack Spencer; 12 Danny Langtree; 24 Will Hope; 13 Liam Thompson. Subs (all used): 11 Josh Crowley; 21 Kenny Hughes; 9 Sam Gee; 26 Michael Ward.
Tries: Ashton (5), Owen (17, 70), Langtree (24, 37), Ward (47), Clay (75); **Goals:** Palfrey 5/8.
Sin bin: Lepori (39) - professional foul.
RAMS: 1 Josh Guzdek; 2 Dale Morton; 15 Jason Crookes; 6 Paul Sykes; 5 Dalton Grant; 7 Ben Reynolds; 22 Andy Kain; 8 Matt Groat; 19 Nathan Conroy; 16 Toby Adamson; 32 Kyle Trout; 4 Shane Grady; 14 Luke Adamson. Subs (all used): 31 Ryan Wright; 18 Tony Tonks; 24 Jack Teanby; 25 Joel Farrell.
Tries: Grant (41, 55), Teanby (79);
Goals: Reynolds 1/2, Sykes 1/1.
Sin bin: Grant (23) - tripping; Conroy (69) - dissent; Reynolds (70) - dissent.
Rugby Leaguer & League Express Men of the Match: *Oldham:* Gareth Owen; *Rams:* Ben Reynolds.
Penalty count: 13-10; **Half-time:** 24-0;
Referee: Joe Cobb; **Attendance:** 816.

WORKINGTON TOWN 0 HALIFAX 20

TOWN: 1 Jack Murphy; 2 Sam Forrester; 3 Declan Hulme; 4 Jason Mossop; 24 Theerapol Ritson; 6 Carl Forber; 7 Jamie Doran; 8 Kris Coward; 9 Graeme Mattinson; 21 Oliver Gordon; 11 Brett Phillips; 16 Perry Whiteley; 13 Liam McAvoy. Subs (all used): 20 Steve Scholey; 15 Karl Olstrum; 10 Marc Shackley; 23 Daniel Rooney.
HALIFAX: 2 Will Sharp; 25 Jake Eccleston; 4 Ben Heaton; 3 Steve Tyrer; 5 James Saltonstall; 7 Gareth Moore; 6 Scott Murrell; 10 Luke Ambler; 9 Ben Kaye; 8 Mitch Cahalane; 27 Ross Divorty; 11 Dane Manning; 14 Adam Tangata. Subs (all used): 13 Jacob Fairbank; 15 Ryan Maneely; 16 Richard Moore; 26 Ed Barber.
Tries: Eccleston (19), Maneely (37), Ambler (68), Manning (78); **Goals:** Tyrer 2/4.
Rugby Leaguer & League Express Men of the Match: *Town:* Liam McAvoy; *Halifax:* Ben Kaye.
Penalty count: 9-7; **Half-time:** 0-8;
Referee: Jamie Bloem; **Attendance:** 641.

ROUND 4

Friday 26th February 2016

SHEFFIELD EAGLES 48 SWINTON LIONS 26

EAGLES: 1 Quentin Laulu-Togagae; 2 Rob Worrincy; 3 Menzie Yere; 4 George Tyson; 5 Ben Blackmore; 6 Cory Aston; 21 Dave Hewitt; 8 Steve Thorpe; 9 Keal Carlile; 10 Mitchell Stringer; 11 Michael Knowles; 12 Duane Straugheir; 13 Matt James. Subs (all used): 24 Rhys Jacks; 15 Scott Wheeldon; 16 Adam Neal; 17 Mark Mexico.
Tries: Blackmore (14, 70), Tyson (28), Wheeldon (34), Laulu-Togagae (37), Yere (44), Aston (52, 60), Stringer (80); **Goals:** Knowles 5/8, Aston 1/1.
LIONS: 20 Mike Butt; 2 Shaun Robinson; 23 Rhodri Lloyd; 4 Macauley Hallett; 5 Greg Scott; 6 Ben White; 1 Chris Atkin; 8 Mike Morrison; 27 Liam Hood; 10 Jordan Hand; 12 Andy Thornley; 11 Connor Dwyer; 13 Rob Lever. Subs (all used): 17 Stephen Nash; 26 Carl Forster; 19 Josh Barlow; 16 Ben Austin.
Tries: Atkin (3), Robinson (49), Scott (65, 79), Hallett (68); **Goals:** Atkin 3/5.
Rugby Leaguer & League Express Men of the Match: *Eagles:* Scott Wheeldon; *Lions:* Chris Atkin.
Penalty count: 6-5; **Half-time:** 22-6;
Referee: Michael Woodhead; **Attendance:** 508.

Sunday 28th February 2016

BRADFORD BULLS 32 LEIGH CENTURIONS 32

BULLS: 34 Richard Mathers; 22 James Clare; 3 Adrian Purtell; 4 Kris Welham; 2 Omari Caro; 6 Lee Gaskell; 13 Danny Addy; 10 Adam Sidlow; 9 Adam O'Brien; 35 Rhys Lovegrove; 11 Tom Olbison; 28 Kurt Haggerty; 14 Jay Pitts. Subs (all used): 12 Dale Ferguson; 15 Matty Blythe; 20 Mitch Clark; 27 Jonathan Walker.
Tries: Welham (28), Clare (65, 67), Purtell (71), Addy (75), Caro (78); **Goals:** Addy 4/6.
CENTURIONS: 26 Lee Smith; 15 Jonny Pownall; 3 Greg Worthington; 27 Richard Whiting; 2 Adam Higson; 13 Cory Paterson; 7 Ryan Brierley; 8 Fuifui Moimoi; 14 Micky Higham; 10 Dayne Weston; 11 Harrison Hansen; 12 Gareth Hock; 17 Jamie Acton. Subs (all used): 19 Lewis Foster; 20 Sam Hopkins; 16 Reni Maitua; 29 Jake Emmitt.
Tries: Pownall (3), Brierley (8, 55), Smith (43), Maitua (45); **Goals:** Smith 6/6.
Sin bin: Higson (39) - professional foul.
Rugby Leaguer & League Express Men of the Match: *Bulls:* Kurt Haggerty; *Centurions:* Cory Paterson.
Penalty count: 7-8; **Half-time:** 6-14;
Referee: Richard Silverwood; **Attendance:** 6,563.

DEWSBURY RAMS 20 WHITEHAVEN 4

RAMS: 1 Josh Guzdek; 2 Dale Morton; 15 Jason Crookes; 4 Shane Grady; 5 Dalton Grant; 6 Paul Sykes; 22 Andy Kain; 8 Matt Groat; 9 Tom Hemingway; 10 Ryan Hepworth; 16 Toby Adamson; 12 Scott Hale; 13 Aaron Brown. Subs (all used): 31 Ryan Wright; 18 Tony Tonks; 14 Luke Adamson; 24 Jack Teanby.
Tries: Guzdek (12), Grady (26), Hale (70);
Goals: Sykes 4/5.
WHITEHAVEN: 1 Louis Jouffret; 5 Elliott Miller; 3 Chris Taylor; 4 Jessie Joe Parker; 2 Craig Calvert; 6 Dion Aiye; 7 Grant Gore; 26 Ted Chapelhow; 29 Almer Salvilla; 8 Sam Brooks; 11 Dave Allen; 12 Scott McAvoy; 15 Ben Davies. Subs (all used): 9 James Newton; 27 Jay Chapelhow; 19 Glenn Riley; 28 Ed Chamberlain.
Try: McAvoy (54); **Goals:** Jouffret 0/1.
Rugby Leaguer & League Express Men of the Match: *Rams:* Aaron Brown; *Whitehaven:* Scott McAvoy.
Penalty count: 13-12; **Half-time:** 12-0;
Referee: Sam Ansell; **Attendance:** 778.

FEATHERSTONE ROVERS 20 OLDHAM 6

ROVERS: 15 Ian Hardman; 2 Kyran Johnson; 3 Michael Channing; 4 Misi Taulapapa; 5 Scott Turner; 6 Kyle Briggs; 7 Anthony Thackeray; 8 Darrell Griffin; 1 Danny Craven; 10 Andrew Bostock; 18 Jamie Cording; 13 Tim Spears; 21 Bradley Knowles-Tagg. Subs (all used): 12 John Davies; 16 Colton Roche; 17 Jack Ormondroyd; 14 Will Milner.
Tries: Taulapapa (6), Thackeray (11), Briggs (55), Craven (79); **Goals:** Briggs 2/4.
OLDHAM: 1 Richard Lepori; 2 Adam Clay; 18 Jake Bibby; 4 Jack Holmes; 5 Jamel Chisholm; 6 Lewis Palfrey; 22 Danny Grimshaw; 10 Jack Spencer; 20 Gareth Owen; 8 Phil Joy; 24 Will Hope; 12 Danny Langtree; 13 Liam Thompson. Subs (all used): 21 Kenny Hughes; 26 Michael Ward; 9 Sam Gee; 11 Josh Crowley.
Try: Lepori (25); **Goals:** Palfrey 1/1.
Rugby Leaguer & League Express Men of the Match: *Rovers:* Anthony Thackeray; *Oldham:* Kenny Hughes.
Penalty count: 10-9; **Half-time:** 10-6;
Referee: Chris Kendall; **Attendance:** 1,739.

HALIFAX 12 BATLEY BULLDOGS 17

HALIFAX: 2 Will Sharp; 25 Jake Eccleston; 4 Ben Heaton; 3 Steve Tyrer; 5 James Saltonstall; 7 Gareth Moore; 6 Scott Murrell; 10 Luke Ambler; 9 Ben Kaye; 8 Mitch Cahalane; 27 Ross Divorty; 11 Dane Manning; 14 Adam Tangata. Subs (all used): 13 Jacob Fairbank; 15 Ryan Maneely; 16 Richard Moore; 26 Ed Barber.
Tries: Manning (27), G Moore (46); **Goals:** Tyrer 2/2.
BULLDOGS: 22 Dave Scott; 2 Wayne Reittie; 23 Danny Cowling; 3 Chris Ulugia; 5 Shaun Ainscough; 6 Cain Southernwood; 7 Dominic Brambani; 8 Keegan Hirst; 9 Luke Blake; 21 James Brown; 19 Alex Bretherton; 17 Joe Chandler; 13 Pat Walker. Subs (all used): 18 Tom Lillycrop; 20 Alistair Leak; 15 Adam Gledhill; 10 Alex Rowe.
Tries: Bretherton (38), Brambani (50);
Goals: Brambani 3/4, Walker 1/1;
Field goal: Brambani (80).
Rugby Leaguer & League Express Men of the Match: *Halifax:* Mitch Cahalane; *Bulldogs:* James Brown.
Penalty count: 8-7; **Half-time:** 6-8;
Referee: George Stokes; **Attendance:** 2,010.

WORKINGTON TOWN 13 LONDON BRONCOS 16

TOWN: 1 Jack Murphy; 2 Sam Forrester; 3 Declan Hulme; 4 Jason Mossop; 5 Brett Carter; 6 Carl Forber; 28 Jarrod Sammut; 8 Kris Coward; 9 Graeme Mattinson; 21 Oliver Gordon; 11 Brett Phillips; 12 Jarrad Stack; 13 Liam McAvoy. Subs (all used): 20 Steve Scholey; 15 Karl Olstrum; 16 Perry Whiteley; 19 Ryan Verlinden.
Tries: Sammut (26, 54); **Goals:** Forber 2/2;
Field goal: Sammut (72).
BRONCOS: 24 Alex Walker; 2 Rhys Williams; 32 Elliot Kear; 1 Ben Hellewell; 5 Iliess Macani; 7 William Barthau; 20 Scott Leatherbarrow; 8 Nick Slyney; 9 James Cunningham; 16 Mark Ioane; 11 Daniel Harrison; 12 Matt Garside; 15 Jack Bussey. Subs (all used): 14 Andy Ackers; 22 Matt Davis; 17 Mark Offerdahl; 10 Eddie Battye.
Tries: Cunningham (10), Williams (67), Garside (72);
Goals: Leatherbarrow 2/3.
Rugby Leaguer & League Express Men of the Match: *Town:* Jarrod Sammut; *Broncos:* Matt Garside.
Penalty count: 8-8; **Half-time:** 6-6;
Referee: Chris Campbell; **Attendance:** 632.

ROUND 5

Saturday 5th March 2016

WHITEHAVEN 18 SWINTON LIONS 12

WHITEHAVEN: 1 Louis Jouffret; 5 Elliott Miller; 3 Chris Taylor; 4 Jessie Joe Parker; 2 Craig Calvert; 21 John-Paul Brocklebank; 7 Grant Gore; 10 Richard Beaumont; 9 James Newton; 19 Glenn Riley; 11 Dave Allen; 12 Scott McAvoy; 8 Sam Brooks. Subs (all used): 26 Ted Chapelhow; 28 Ed Chamberlain; 17 Steve Fox; 6 Dion Aiye.
Tries: Brocklebank (10), Jouffret (14), Miller (74);
Goals: Brocklebank 3/3.
LIONS: 1 Chris Atkin; 2 Shaun Robinson; 3 Stuart Littler; 4 Macauley Hallett; - Liam Marshall; 6 Ben White; 7 Matty Beharrell; 8 Mike Morrison; 27 Liam Hood; 10 Jordan Hand; 23 Rhodri Lloyd; 11 Connor Dwyer; 13 Rob Lever. Subs (all used): 9 Anthony Nicholson; 16 Ben Austin; 19 Josh Barlow; 12 Andy Thornley.
Tries: Robinson (20), Atkin (44); **Goals:** Atkin 2/3.

Rugby Leaguer & League Express Men of the Match: *Whitehaven:* James Newton; *Lions:* Chris Atkin.
Penalty count: 14-14; **Half-time:** 12-6;
Referee: Andrew Sweet; **Attendance:** 517.

Sunday 6th March 2016

BATLEY BULLDOGS 44 WORKINGTON TOWN 12

BULLDOGS: 22 Dave Scott; 2 Wayne Reittie; 23 Danny Cowling; 3 Chris Ulugia; 5 Shaun Ainscough; 6 Cain Southernwood; 7 Dominic Brambani; 8 Keegan Hirst; 9 Luke Blake; 21 James Brown; 19 Alex Bretherton; 15 Adam Gledhill; 13 Pat Walker. Subs (all used): 18 Tom Lillycrop; 20 Alistair Leak; 26 Alex Brown; 10 Alex Rowe.
Tries: Southernwood (20, 66), Ulugia (27), Bretherton (42), J Brown (57), Leak (61), A Brown (76);
Goals: Walker 8/8.
TOWN: 1 Jack Murphy; 2 Sam Forrester; 3 Declan Hulme; 4 Jason Mossop; 5 Brett Carter; 6 Carl Forber; 28 Jarrod Sammut; 8 Kris Coward; 9 Graeme Mattinson; 21 Oliver Gordon; 11 Brett Phillips; 16 Perry Whiteley; 13 Liam McAvoy. Subs (all used): 15 Karl Olstrum; 12 Jarrad Stack; 10 Marc Shackley; 19 Ryan Verlinden.
Tries: Hulme (16), Carter (37); **Goals:** Forber 2/2.
Sin bin: Stack (32) - holding down.
Rugby Leaguer & League Express Men of the Match: *Bulldogs:* Pat Walker; *Town:* Jack Murphy.
Penalty count: 13-6; **Half-time:** 14-12;
Referee: Jon Roberts; **Attendance:** 658.

FEATHERSTONE ROVERS 21 DEWSBURY RAMS 20

ROVERS: 15 Ian Hardman; 2 Kyran Johnson; 3 Michael Channing; 4 Misi Taulapapa; 5 Scott Turner; 6 Kyle Briggs; 7 Anthony Thackeray; 8 Darrell Griffin; 1 Danny Craven; 10 Andrew Bostock; 18 Jamie Cording; 21 Bradley Knowles-Tagg; 17 Jack Ormondroyd. Subs (all used): 12 John Davies; 16 Colton Roche; 32 Jordan Baldwinson; 23 Andy Ellis.
Tries: Briggs (31), Johnson (39), Taulapapa (49), Turner (57); **Goals:** Briggs 2/5; **Field goal:** Craven (78).
RAMS: 1 Josh Guzdek; 2 Dale Morton; 4 Shane Grady; 15 Jason Crookes; 5 Dalton Grant; 6 Paul Sykes; 7 Ben Reynolds; 8 Matt Groat; 17 Dom Speakman; 10 Ryan Hepworth; 16 Toby Adamson; 12 Scott Hale; 13 Aaron Brown. Subs (all used): 18 Tony Tonks; 19 Nathan Conroy; 14 Luke Adamson; 32 Kyle Trout.
Tries: Guzdek (1), Grady (25), Crookes (50);
Goals: Reynolds 4/5.
Rugby Leaguer & League Express Men of the Match: *Rovers:* Andy Ellis; *Rams:* Aaron Brown.
Penalty count: 11-8; **Half-time:** 10-14;
Referee: Chris Campbell; **Attendance:** 1,665.

LEIGH CENTURIONS 36 SHEFFIELD EAGLES 28

CENTURIONS: 15 Jonny Pownall; 25 Eze Harper; 2 Adam Higson; 27 Richard Whiting; 30 Richard Owen; 6 Martyn Ridyard; 28 Lewis Charnock; 8 Fuifui Moimoi; 14 Micky Higham; 10 Dayne Weston; 11 Harrison Hansen; 12 Gareth Hock; 13 Cory Paterson. Subs: 19 Lewis Foster (not used); 18 Tom Spencer; 16 Reni Maitua; 29 Jake Emmitt.
Tries: Weston (7), Higson (10), Higham (28), Charnock (39), Maitua (44), Paterson (78);
Goals: Ridyard 6/8.
Sin bin: Hock (58) - shoulder charge on Hewitt.
EAGLES: 1 Quentin Laulu-Togagae; 2 Rob Worrincy; 3 Menzie Yere; 4 George Tyson; 5 Ben Blackmore; 6 Cory Aston; 21 Dave Hewitt; 15 Scott Wheeldon; 9 Keal Carlile; 16 Adam Neal; 11 Michael Knowles; 12 Duane Straugheir; 13 Matt James. Subs (all used): 14 Matty Fozard; 10 Mitchell Stringer; 18 Elliot Minchella; 17 Mark Mexico.
Tries: Worrincy (17, 71), Laulu-Togagae (31, 75), Yere (50);
Goals: Knowles 4/5.
Sin bin: Stringer (58) - punching.
Rugby Leaguer & League Express Men of the Match: *Centurions:* Harrison Hansen; *Eagles:* Cory Aston.
Penalty count: 8-16; **Half-time:** 22-10;
Referee: Chris Kendall; **Attendance:** 3,282.

LONDON BRONCOS 29 HALIFAX 22

BRONCOS: 24 Alex Walker; 2 Rhys Williams; 1 Ben Hellewell; 4 Wes Naiqama; 32 Elliot Kear; 7 William Barthau; 20 Scott Leatherbarrow; 8 Nick Slyney; 9 James Cunningham; 16 Mark Ioane; 21 Alex Foster; 12 Matt Garside; 15 Jack Bussey. Subs (all used): 22 Matt Davis; 11 Daniel Harrison; 17 Mark Offerdahl; 10 Eddie Battye.
Tries: Barthau (13, 17), Williams (26, 76), Hellewell (57), Slyney (69); **Goals:** Naiqama 1/4, Leatherbarrow 1/2;
Field goal: Leatherbarrow (78).
HALIFAX: 1 Ben Johnston; 2 Will Sharp; 20 Sam Smeaton; 3 Steve Tyrer; 5 James Saltonstall; 7 Gareth Moore; 6 Scott Murrell; 8 Mitch Cahalane; 9 Ben Kaye; 10 Luke Ambler; 11 Dane Manning; 17 Gavin Bennion; 13 Jacob Fairbank. Subs (all used): 14 Adam Tangata; 15 Ryan Maneely; 16 Richard Moore; 21 Adam Robinson.
Tries: Ambler (8), Saltonstall (31), Murrell (43, 63);
Goals: Tyrer 3/4.
Rugby Leaguer & League Express Men of the Match: *Broncos:* William Barthau; *Halifax:* Scott Murrell.
Penalty count: 4-4; **Half-time:** 14-10;
Referee: Sam Ansell; **Attendance:** 732.

ROUND 6

Saturday 12th March 2016

LONDON BRONCOS 22 DEWSBURY RAMS 18

BRONCOS: 32 Elliot Kear; 2 Rhys Williams; 1 Ben Hellewell; 4 Wes Naiqama; 5 Iliess Macani; 7 William Barthau; 19 Joe Keyes; 8 Nick Slyney; 9 James Cunningham; 16 Mark Ioane; 11 Daniel Harrison; 12 Matt Garside; 15 Jack Bussey. Subs (all used): 14 Andy Ackers; 22 Matt Davis; 18 Jamie Thackray; 10 Eddie Battye.
Tries: Williams (20, 36), Barthau (58), Garside (65);
Goals: Naiqama 3/4.
Sin bin: Naiqama (69) - punching L Adamson.
RAMS: 1 Josh Guzdek; 2 Dale Morton; 15 Jason Crookes; 4 Shane Grady; 5 Dalton Grant; 6 Paul Sykes; 26 Brad Delaney; 8 Matt Groat; 17 Dom Speakman; 16 Toby Adamson; 14 Luke Adamson; 25 Joel Farrell; 13 Aaron Brown. Subs (all used): 31 Ryan Wright; 24 Jack Teanby; 32 Kyle Trout; 3 Karl Pryce.
Tries: Grant (14), Crookes (32), Trout (77);
Goals: Delaney 2/2, Sykes 1/1.
Rugby Leaguer & League Express Men of the Match: *Broncos:* Rhys Williams; *Rams:* Josh Guzdek.
Penalty count: 4-4; **Half-time:** 10-12;
Referee: Chris Kendall; **Attendance:** 512.

SHEFFIELD EAGLES 24 WHITEHAVEN 26

EAGLES: 1 Quentin Laulu-Togagae; 2 Rob Worrincy; 3 Menzie Yere; 4 George Tyson; 5 Ben Blackmore; 6 Cory Aston; 24 Rhys Jacks; 8 Steve Thorpe; 9 Keal Carlile; 17 Mark Mexico; 11 Michael Knowles; 12 Duane Straugheir; 18 Elliot Minchella. Subs (all used): 14 Matty Fozard; 10 Mitchell Stringer; 13 Matt James; 15 Scott Wheeldon.
Tries: Worrincy (5, 14, 73), Knowles (58), Laulu-Togagae (76); **Goals:** Knowles 1/3, Aston 1/2.
WHITEHAVEN: 1 Louis Jouffret; 5 Elliott Miller; 3 Chris Taylor; 28 Ed Chamberlain; 2 Craig Calvert; 21 John-Paul Brocklebank; 7 Grant Gore; 8 Sam Brooks; 9 James Newton; 19 Glenn Riley; 12 Scott McAvoy; 4 Jessie Joe Parker; 13 Liam Carberry. Subs (all used): 6 Dion Aiye; 16 Connor Holliday; 31 Ryan Duffy; 15 Ben Davies.
Tries: Calvert (10, 30), Miller (39, 51), McAvoy (47), Carberry (65);
Goals: Brocklebank 0/2, Jouffret 0/3, Chamberlain 1/1.
Rugby Leaguer & League Express Men of the Match: *Eagles:* Mark Mexico; *Whitehaven:* Liam Carberry.
Penalty count: 8-6; **Half-time:** 8-12;
Referee: Joe Cobb; **Attendance:** 502.

Sunday 13th March 2016

BATLEY BULLDOGS 24 BRADFORD BULLS 24

BULLDOGS: 22 Dave Scott; 26 Alex Brown; 23 Danny Cowling; 3 Chris Ulugia; 5 Shaun Ainscough; 6 Cain Southernwood; 7 Dominic Brambani; 8 Keegan Hirst; 9 Luke Blake; 21 James Brown; 19 Alex Bretherton; 17 Joe Chandler; 13 Pat Walker. Subs (all used): 18 Tom Lillycrop; 20 Alistair Leak; 15 Adam Gledhill; 10 Alex Rowe.
Tries: Ulugia (17), D Scott (21), Hirst (66), A Brown (76);
Goals: Walker 4/5.
BULLS: 34 Richard Mathers; 22 James Clare; 15 Matty Blythe; 4 Kris Welham; 2 Omari Caro; 6 Lee Gaskell; 13 Danny Addy; 8 Paul Clough; 9 Adam O'Brien; 35 Rhys Lovegrove; 12 Dale Ferguson; 28 Kurt Haggerty; 14 Jay Pitts. Subs (all used): 23 Alex Mellor; 20 Mitch Clark; 1 Oscar Thomas; 19 Steve Crossley.
Tries: Caro (6), Ferguson (31), Pitts (37, 50);
Goals: Addy 4/4.
Rugby Leaguer & League Express Men of the Match: *Bulldogs:* Keegan Hirst; *Bulls:* Jay Pitts.
Penalty count: 9-7; **Half-time:** 12-18;
Referee: Ben Thaler; **Attendance:** 2,742.

HALIFAX 18 LEIGH CENTURIONS 26

HALIFAX: 18 Miles Greenwood; 19 Tom Saxton; 4 Ben Heaton; 3 Steve Tyrer; 5 James Saltonstall; 7 Gareth Moore; 1 Ben Johnston; 16 Richard Moore; 15 Ryan Maneely; 8 Mitch Cahalane; 14 Adam Tangata; 11 Dane Manning; 21 Adam Robinson. Subs (all used): 10 Luke Ambler; 22 Connor Robinson; 17 Gavin Bennion; 24 Andy Bracek.
Tries: Saxton (20), Tangata (52), C Robinson (77);
Goals: Tyrer 3/3.
Sin bin: Manning (78) - fighting.
CENTURIONS: 26 Lee Smith; 15 Jonny Pownall; 27 Richard Whiting; 2 Adam Higson; 5 Liam Kay; 6 Martyn Ridyard; 31 Ben Reynolds; 8 Fuifui Moimoi; 14 Micky Higham; 10 Dayne Weston; 11 Harrison Hansen; 12 Gareth Hock; 13 Cory Paterson. Subs (all used): 32 Liam Hood; 20 Sam Hopkins; 16 Reni Maitua; 29 Jake Emmitt.
Tries: Maitua (46), Smith (60), Hock (63), Higham (72);
Goals: Ridyard 5/6.
Sin bin: Hock (78) - fighting.
Rugby Leaguer & League Express Men of the Match: *Halifax:* Gareth Moore; *Centurions:* Jake Emmitt.
Penalty count: 12-11; **Half-time:** 6-0;
Referee: Richard Silverwood; **Attendance:** 2,706.

SWINTON LIONS 10 FEATHERSTONE ROVERS 30

LIONS: 1 Chris Atkin; 2 Shaun Robinson; 3 Stuart Littler; 4 Macauley Hallett; - Liam Marshall; 6 Ben White; 7 Matty Beharrell; 8 Mike Morrison; 9 Anthony Nicholson; 10 Jordan Hand; 11 Connor Dwyer; 23 Rhodri Lloyd; 13 Rob Lever. Subs (all used): - Vila Halafihi; 12 Andy Thornley; 19 Josh Barlow; 16 Ben Austin.
Tries: Hallett (70), Atkin (73); **Goals:** Atkin 1/2.
Sin bin: Morrison (59) - punching.
ROVERS: 1 Danny Craven; 2 Kyran Johnson; 15 Ian Hardman; 4 Misi Taulapapa; 5 Scott Turner; 6 Kyle Briggs; 7 Anthony Thackeray; 8 Darrell Griffin; 23 Andy Ellis; 10 Andrew Bostock; 18 Jamie Cording; 12 John Davies; 21 Bradley Knowles-Tagg. Subs (all used): 17 Jack Ormondroyd; 16 Colton Roche; 32 Jordan Baldwinson; 14 Will Milner.
Tries: Turner (12), Hardman (19), Johnson (31), Cording (44), Briggs (56), Thackeray (65);
Goals: Craven 0/3, Briggs 3/3.
Rugby Leaguer & League Express Men of the Match: *Lions:* Connor Dwyer; *Rovers:* Anthony Thackeray.
Penalty count: 11-11; **Half-time:** 0-12;
Referee: Sam Ansell; **Attendance:** 745.

WORKINGTON TOWN 23 OLDHAM 12

TOWN: 1 Jack Murphy; 2 Sam Forrester; 16 Perry Whiteley; 4 Jason Mossop; 24 Theerapol Ritson; 6 Carl Forber; 28 Jarrod Sammut; 8 Kris Coward; 9 Graeme Mattinson; 21 Oliver Gordon; 11 Brett Phillips; 12 Jarrad Stack; 13 Liam McAvoy. Subs (all used): 14 Callum Phillips; 10 Marc Shackley; 22 Chris Murphy; 19 Ryan Verlinden.
Tries: Sammut (26, 29), J Murphy (36), C Murphy (80);
Goals: Forber 3/4; **Field goal:** Sammut (78).
OLDHAM: 1 Richard Lepori; 2 Adam Clay; 18 Jake Bibby; 4 Jack Holmes; 5 Jamel Chisholm; 6 Lewis Palfrey; 22 Danny Grimshaw; 8 Phil Joy; 20 Gareth Owen; 10 Jack Spencer; - Gary Middlehurst; 12 Danny Langtree; 24 Will Hope. Subs (all used): 26 Michael Ward; 13 Liam Thompson; 19 Adam Files; 21 Kenny Hughes.
Tries: Middlehurst (8), Joy (72); **Goals:** Palfrey 2/2.
Rugby Leaguer & League Express Men of the Match: *Town:* Jarrod Sammut; *Oldham:* Danny Grimshaw.
Penalty count: 10-10; **Half-time:** 16-6;
Referee: Chris Campbell; **Attendance:** 637.

ROUND 7

Thursday 24th March 2016

BRADFORD BULLS 28 LONDON BRONCOS 20

BULLS: 34 Richard Mathers; 29 Ethan Ryan; 15 Matty Blythe; 22 James Clare; 2 Omari Caro; 6 Lee Gaskell; 13 Danny Addy; 8 Paul Clough; 9 Adam O'Brien; 19 Steve Crossley; 28 Kurt Haggerty; 11 Tom Olbison; 14 Jay Pitts. Subs (all used): 23 Alex Mellor; 16 Daniel Fleming; 20 Mitch Clark; 30 Joe Lumb.
Tries: Clare (3), Blythe (10), Haggerty (16, 50), Ryan (42);
Goals: Addy 4/7.
BRONCOS: 24 Alex Walker; 2 Rhys Williams; 1 Ben Hellewell; 21 Alex Foster; 32 Elliot Kear; 7 William Barthau; 20 Scott Leatherbarrow; 8 Nick Slyney; 9 James Cunningham; 16 Mark Ioane; 11 Daniel Harrison; 12 Matt Garside; 15 Jack Bussey. Subs (all used): 14 Andy Ackers; 17 Mark Offerdahl; 10 Eddie Battye; 18 Jamie Thackray.
Tries: Cunningham (28), Thackray (31), Foster (35, 45);
Goals: Leatherbarrow 2/4.
Rugby Leaguer & League Express Men of the Match: *Bulls:* Steve Crossley; *Broncos:* Alex Walker.
Penalty count: 14-5; **Half-time:** 14-16;
Referee: Jon Roberts; **Attendance:** 4,163.

LEIGH CENTURIONS 42 SWINTON LIONS 12

CENTURIONS: 26 Lee Smith; 30 Richard Owen; 24 Tom Armstrong; 4 Willie Tonga; 2 Adam Higson; 6 Martyn Ridyard; 31 Ben Reynolds; 8 Fuifui Moimoi; 14 Micky Higham; 10 Dayne Weston; 16 Reni Maitua; 21 Andrew Dixon; 11 Harrison Hansen. Subs (all used): 28 Lewis Charnock; 27 Richard Whiting; 20 Sam Hopkins; 29 Jake Emmitt.
Tries: Smith (7), Owen (11), Weston (21), Hopkins (33), Higham (49), Hansen (61), Armstrong (66);
Goals: Ridyard 7/7.
Sin bin: Reynolds (46) - fighting.

Whitehaven's Louis Jouffret takes on the Workington defence

LIONS: 14 Kieran Hyde; 2 Shaun Robinson; 3 Stuart Littler; 4 Macauley Hallett; - Liam Marshall; 6 Ben White; 1 Chris Atkin; 13 Rob Lever; 9 Anthony Nicholson; 10 Jordan Hand; 11 Connor Dwyer; 23 Rhodri Lloyd; 12 Andy Thornley. Subs (all used): 16 Ben Austin; 15 Corbyn Kilday; 19 Josh Barlow; 7 Matty Beharrell.
Tries: Marshall (72, 77); **Goals:** Atkin 2/2.
Sin bin: Littler (46) - fighting.
Rugby Leaguer & League Express Men of the Match: *Centurions:* Martyn Ridyard; *Lions:* Jordan Hand.
Penalty count: 5-10; **Half-time:** 24-0;
Referee: Chris Campbell; **Attendance:** 3,230.

Friday 25th March 2016

WHITEHAVEN 24 WORKINGTON TOWN 16

WHITEHAVEN: 1 Louis Jouffret; 5 Elliot Miller; 3 Chris Taylor; 4 Jessie Joe Parker; 2 Craig Calvert; 6 Dion Aiye; 7 Grant Gore; 19 Glenn Riley; 9 James Newton; 15 Ben Davies; 11 Dave Allen; 12 Scott McAvoy; 13 Liam Carberry. Subs (all used): 22 Nathan Lucock; 16 Connor Holliday; 17 Steve Fox; 31 Ryan Duffy.
Tries: Miller (9), Allen (16), Calvert (56), Carberry (78);
Goals: Jouffret 4/4.
TOWN: 1 Jack Murphy; 22 Chris Murphy; 3 Declan Hulme; 4 Jason Mossop; 24 Theerapol Ritson; 6 Carl Forber; 28 Jarrod Sammut; 8 Kris Coward; 7 Jamie Doran; 10 Marc Shackley; 11 Brett Phillips; 12 Jarrad Stack; 15 Karl Olstrum. Subs: 13 Liam McAvoy; 5 Brett Carter (not used); 16 Perry Whiteley; 21 Oliver Gordon.
Tries: Sammut (20, 79), B Phillips (52);
Goals: Forber 1/4, Sammut 1/1.
Rugby Leaguer & League Express Men of the Match: *Whitehaven:* Jessie Joe Parker; *Town:* Jarrod Sammut.
Penalty count: 10-7; **Half-time:** 12-6;
Referee: Sam Ansell; **Attendance:** 1,425.

OLDHAM 28 HALIFAX 42

OLDHAM: 1 Richard Lepori; 2 Adam Clay; 4 Jack Holmes; 3 Jonathan Ford; 5 Jamel Chisholm; 22 Danny Grimshaw; 7 Steve Roper; 8 Phil Joy; 20 Gareth Owen; 10 Jack Spencer; - Gary Middlehurst; 23 Will Hope. Subs (all used): 26 Michael Ward; 21 Kenny Hughes; 23 Tyler Dickinson; 14 Joe Burke.
Tries: Hope (45, 55), Chisholm (62), Clay (71, 80);
Goals: Roper 4/5.
HALIFAX: 18 Miles Greenwood; 5 James Saltonstall; 20 Sam Smeaton; 4 Ben Heaton; 25 Jake Eccleston; 6 Scott Murrell; 7 Gareth Moore; 8 Mitch Cahalane; 22 Connor Robinson; 16 Richard Moore; 11 Dane Manning; 14 Adam Tangata; 13 Jacob Fairbank. Subs (all used): 10 Luke Ambler; 24 Andy Bracek; 30 Brandon Moore; 21 Adam Robinson.
Tries: Saltonstall (4, 50), Eccleston (10),
G Moore (28, 36), Greenwood (40) Cahalane (71);

Goals: G Moore 6/6, C Robinson 1/1.
Rugby Leaguer & League Express Men of the Match: *Oldham:* Adam Clay; *Halifax:* Scott Murrell.
Penalty count: 6-10; **Half-time:** 0-30;
Referee: Tom Grant; **Attendance:** 1,046.

DEWSBURY RAMS 30 BATLEY BULLDOGS 44

RAMS: 1 Josh Guzdek; 2 Dale Morton; 15 Jason Crookes; 4 Shane Grady; 5 Dalton Grant; 6 Paul Sykes; 17 Dom Speakman; 8 Matt Groat; 9 Tom Hemingway; 10 Ryan Hepworth; 14 Luke Adamson; 32 Kyle Trout; 13 Aaron Brown. Subs (all used): 18 Tony Tonks; 11 Rob Spicer; 22 Andy Kain; 25 Joel Farrell.
Tries: L Adamson (28), Guzdek (30), Grady (49), Morton (59), Sykes (70), Kain (72);
Goals: Sykes 2/4, Hemingway 1/2.
Sin bin: Farrell (35) - holding down;
Grady (55) - interference; Crookes (79) - punching.
BULLDOGS: 22 Dave Scott; 2 Wayne Reittie; 23 Danny Cowling; 5 Shaun Ainscough; 26 Alex Brown; 13 Pat Walker; 7 Dominic Brambani; 8 Keegan Hirst; 20 Alistair Leak; 10 Alex Rowe; 17 Joe Chandler; 11 Brad Day; 9 Luke Blake. Subs (all used): 21 James Brown; 18 Tom Lillycrop; 24 James Harrison; 14 James Davey.
Tries: Leak (2, 5), Reittie (19, 22), A Brown (39), Ainscough (42), Day (75); **Goals:** Walker 8/12.
Rugby Leaguer & League Express Men of the Match: *Rams:* Josh Guzdek; *Bulldogs:* Alex Rowe.
Penalty count: 5-18; **Half-time:** 12-26;
Referee: Chris Kendall; **Attendance:** 2,020.

FEATHERSTONE ROVERS 28 SHEFFIELD EAGLES 16

ROVERS: 15 Ian Hardman; 2 Kyran Johnson; 21 Bradley Knowles-Tagg; 4 Misi Taulapapa; 5 Scott Turner; 6 Kyle Briggs; 1 Danny Craven; 8 Darrell Griffin; 23 Andy Ellis; 10 Andrew Bostock; 18 Jamie Cording; 12 John Davies; 13 Tim Spears. Subs (all used): 17 Jack Ormondroyd; 16 Colton Roche; 32 Jordan Baldwinson; 34 Mitch Achurch.
Tries: Taulapapa (2), Ellis (15), Cording (29, 78), Briggs (76); **Goals:** Briggs 4/8.
EAGLES: 1 Quentin Laulu-Togagae; 2 Rob Worrincy; 3 Menzie Yere; 12 Duane Straugheir; 5 Ben Blackmore; 6 Cory Aston; 21 Dave Hewitt; 8 Steve Thorpe; 9 Keal Carlile; 16 Adam Neal; 11 Michael Knowles; 15 Scott Wheeldon; 14 Matty Fozard. Subs (all used): 24 Rhys Jacks; 13 Matt James; 18 Elliot Minchella; 10 Mitchell Stringer.
Tries: Worrincy (6), Laulu-Togagae (10), Carlile (33);
Goals: Knowles 2/3.
Sin bin: Blackmore (27) - punching Taulapapa.
Rugby Leaguer & League Express Men of the Match: *Rovers:* Misi Taulapapa; *Eagles:* Keal Carlile.
Penalty count: 12-9; **Half-time:** 16-16;
Referee: Michael Woodhead; **Attendance:** 2,052.

ROUND 8

Monday 28th March 2016

SWINTON LIONS 28 OLDHAM 18

LIONS: 14 Kieran Hyde; 2 Shaun Robinson; 3 Stuart Littler; 23 Rhodri Lloyd; 4 Macauley Hallett; 6 Ben White; 1 Chris Atkin; 10 Jordan Hand; 9 Anthony Nicholson; 17 Stephen Nash; 11 Connor Dwyer; 12 Andy Thornley; 13 Rob Lever. Subs (all used): 19 Josh Barlow; 16 Ben Austin; 7 Matty Beharrell; 15 Corbyn Kilday.
Tries: Lloyd (5), Atkin (17), Dwyer (25, 44), Kilday (31);
Goals: Atkin 4/5.
OLDHAM: 9 Sam Gee; 3 Jonathan Ford; 15 Liam Johnson; 4 Jack Holmes; 1 Richard Lepori; 6 Lewis Palfrey; 22 Danny Grimshaw; 8 Phil Joy; 20 Gareth Owen; 23 Tyler Dickinson; - Gary Middlehurst; 10 Jack Spencer; 24 Will Hope. Subs (all used): 26 Michael Ward; 19 Adam Files; 21 Kenny Hughes; 13 Liam Thompson.
Tries: Grimshaw (59), Files (63), Ford (79);
Goals: Palfrey 3/3.
Rugby Leaguer & League Express Men of the Match: *Lions:* Chris Atkin; *Oldham:* Jonathan Ford.
Penalty count: 8-11; **Half-time:** 24-0;
Referee: Sam Ansell; **Attendance:** 823.

BATLEY BULLDOGS 24 WHITEHAVEN 23

BULLDOGS: 22 Dave Scott; 2 Wayne Reittie; 19 Alex Bretherton; 5 Shaun Ainscough; 26 Alex Brown; 6 Cain Southernwood; 7 Dominic Brambani; 8 Keegan Hirst; 20 Alistair Leak; 21 James Brown; 15 Adam Gledhill; 17 Joe Chandler; 9 Luke Blake. Subs (all used): 14 James Davey; 18 Tom Lillycrop; 13 Pat Walker; 10 Alex Rowe.
Tries: D Scott (16), Gledhill (19), J Brown (36), A Brown (67); **Goals:** Brambani 2/3, Walker 2/2.
WHITEHAVEN: 1 Louis Jouffret; 20 Jordan Burns; 3 Chris Taylor; 4 Jessie Joe Parker; 2 Craig Calvert; 6 Dion Aiye; 7 Grant Gore; 19 Glenn Riley; 9 James Newton; 15 Ben Davies; 11 Dave Allen; 12 Scott McAvoy; 13 Liam Carberry. Subs (all used): 22 Nathan Lucock; 17 Steve Fox; 16 Connor Holliday; 31 Ryan Duffy.
Tries: Taylor (11, 41), Calvert (43), Aiye (51);
Goals: Jouffret 3/4; **Field goal:** Gore (73).
Rugby Leaguer & League Express Men of the Match: *Bulldogs:* James Brown; *Whitehaven:* Chris Taylor.
Penalty count: 7-7; **Half-time:** 16-6;
Referee: Andrew Sweet; **Attendance:** 706.

HALIFAX 14 BRADFORD BULLS 10

HALIFAX: 18 Miles Greenwood; 25 Jake Eccleston; 20 Sam Smeaton; 3 Steve Tyrer; 19 Tom Saxton; 6 Scott Murrell; 7 Gareth Moore; 8 Mitch Cahalane; 9 Ben Kaye;

10 Luke Ambler; 11 Dane Manning; 14 Adam Tangata; 13 Jacob Fairbank. Subs (all used): 16 Richard Moore; 30 Brandon Moore; 26 Ed Barber; 31 Elliot Morris.
Tries: Eccleston (13), Manning (26); **Goals:** Tyrer 3/3.
BULLS: 34 Richard Mathers; 32 Johnny Campbell; 22 James Clare; 33 Etuate Uaisele; 2 Omari Caro; 6 Lee Gaskell; 13 Danny Addy; 8 Paul Clough; 9 Adam O'Brien; 20 Mitch Clark; 28 Kurt Haggerty; 11 Tom Olbison; 14 Jay Pitts. Subs (all used): 12 Dale Ferguson; 16 Daniel Fleming; 19 Steve Crossley; 17 Jean-Philippe Baile.
Tries: Uaisele (6), Clare (69); **Goals:** Addy 1/2.
Rugby Leaguer & League Express Men of the Match: *Halifax:* Sam Smeaton; *Bulls:* Dale Ferguson.
Penalty count: 6-9; **Half-time:** 12-4;
Referee: Jon Roberts; **Attendance:** 4,018.

LONDON BRONCOS 20 FEATHERSTONE ROVERS 12

BRONCOS: 32 Elliot Kear; 2 Rhys Williams; 1 Ben Hellewell; 21 Alex Foster; 5 Iliess Macani; 7 William Barthau; 20 Scott Leatherbarrow; 8 Nick Slyney; 9 James Cunningham; 10 Eddie Battye; 11 Daniel Harrison; 12 Matt Garside; 22 Matt Davis. Subs (all used): 14 Andy Ackers; 15 Jack Bussey; 16 Mark Ioane; 17 Mark Offerdahl.
Tries: Williams (24), Hellewell (67, 76), Foster (71);
Goals: Leatherbarrow 2/4.
Sin bin: Foster (78) - fighting.
ROVERS: 15 Ian Hardman; 2 Kyran Johnson; 21 Bradley Knowles-Tagg; 4 Misi Taulapapa; 5 Scott Turner; 1 Danny Craven; 6 Kyle Briggs; 16 Colton Roche; 23 Andy Ellis; 32 Jordan Baldwinson; 18 Jamie Cording; 12 John Davies; 13 Tim Spears. Subs (all used): 19 Sam Day; 10 Andrew Bostock; 17 Jack Ormondroyd; 8 Darrell Griffin.
Tries: Baldwinson (10), Davies (16), Craven (38);
Goals: Briggs 0/2, Johnson 0/1.
Sin bin: Knowles-Tagg (24) - interference;
Hardman (78) - fighting.
Rugby Leaguer & League Express Men of the Match: *Broncos:* Ben Hellewell; *Rovers:* Jordan Baldwinson.
Penalty count: 16-8; **Half-time:** 4-12;
Referee: Jack Smith; **Attendance:** 428.

WORKINGTON TOWN 24 LEIGH CENTURIONS 40

TOWN: 1 Jack Murphy; 22 Chris Murphy; 16 Perry Whiteley; 4 Jason Mossop; 24 Theerapol Ritson; 6 Carl Forber; 28 Jarrod Sammut; 8 Kris Coward; 7 Jamie Doran; 10 Marc Shackley; 11 Brett Phillips; 12 Jarrad Stack; 13 Liam McAvoy. Subs: 21 Oliver Gordon; 19 Ryan Verlinden (not used); 18 Tom Walker (not used); 5 Brett Carter (not used).
Tries: C Murphy (9), Ritson (15), Sammut (32), B Phillips (55), Mossop (78); **Goals:** Forber 0/1, Sammut 2/4.
CENTURIONS: 26 Lee Smith; 2 Adam Higson; 27 Richard Whiting; 24 Tom Armstrong; 25 Eze Harper; 6 Martyn Ridyard; 31 Ben Reynolds; 8 Fuifui Moimoi; 32 Liam Hood; 10 Dayne Weston; 16 Reni Maitua; 21 Andrew Dixon; 29 Jake Emmitt. Subs (all used): 14 Micky Higham; 20 Sam Hopkins; 17 Jamie Acton; 11 Harrison Hansen.
Tries: Emmitt (19), Hansen (25), Armstrong (38), Maitua (60, 69), Hopkins (64), Moimoi (74);
Goals: Ridyard 5/6, Reynolds 1/1.
Rugby Leaguer & League Express Men of the Match: *Town:* Theerapol Ritson; *Centurions:* Jake Emmitt.
Penalty count: 10-10; **Half-time:** 14-16;
Referee: Gareth Hewer; **Attendance:** 787.

DEWSBURY RAMS 34 SHEFFIELD EAGLES 16

RAMS: 1 Josh Guzdek; 2 Dale Morton; 15 Jason Crookes; 6 Paul Sykes; 5 Dalton Grant; 23 James Glover; 22 Andy Kain; 16 Toby Adamson; 19 Nathan Conroy; 33 Paul Jackson; 4 Shane Grady; 12 Scott Hale; 25 Joel Farrell. Subs (all used): 31 Ryan Wright; 24 Jack Teanby; 18 Tony Tonks; 14 Luke Adamson.
Tries: Morton (3, 40), Grant (18), Grady (58), Farrell (62), L Adamson (80); **Goals:** Sykes 5/7.
EAGLES: 1 Quentin Laulu-Togagae; 2 Rob Worrincy; 12 Duane Straugheir; 4 George Tyson; 5 Ben Blackmore; 6 Cory Aston; 21 Dave Hewitt; 8 Steve Thorpe; 9 Keal Carlile; 15 Scott Wheeldon; 11 Michael Knowles; 16 Adam Neal; 14 Matty Fozard. Subs (all used): 24 Rhys Jacks; 10 Mitchell Stringer; 18 Elliot Minchella; 20 Jack Blagbrough.
Tries: Hewitt (30), Worrincy (49), Knowles (67);
Goals: Knowles 2/3.
Rugby Leaguer & League Express Men of the Match: *Rams:* Dalton Grant; *Eagles:* Michael Knowles.
Penalty count: 7-7; **Half-time:** 16-6;
Referee: Jamie Bloem; **Attendance:** 813.

ROUND 9

Sunday 3rd April 2016

BRADFORD BULLS 28 SHEFFIELD EAGLES 46

BULLS: 1 Oscar Thomas; 2 Omari Caro; 22 James Clare; 4 Kris Welham; 32 Johnny Campbell; 6 Lee Gaskell; 3 Adrian Purtell; 8 Paul Clough; 9 Adam O'Brien; 19 Steve Crossley; 28 Kurt Haggerty; 12 Dale Ferguson; 13 Danny Addy. Subs (all used): 11 Tom Olbison; 14 Jay Pitts; 16 Daniel Fleming; 20 Mitch Clark.
Tries: Addy (8), Gaskell (18), Caro (51), Clare (71), Welham (78); **Goals:** Addy 4/5.
EAGLES: 1 Quentin Laulu-Togagae; 19 Garry Lo; 3 Menzie Yere; 4 George Tyson; 22 Ryan Millar; 6 Cory Aston; 24 Rhys Jacks; 8 Steve Thorpe; 9 Keal Carlile; 16 Adam Neal; 13 Matt James; 12 Duane Straugheir; 14 Matty Fozard. Subs (all used): 20 Jack Blagbrough; 17 Mark Mexico; 15 Scott Wheeldon; 18 Elliot Minchella.
Tries: Aston (22), Minchella (29), Millar (38, 68), Lo (43), Mexico (55), Straugheir (64), Tyson (74);
Goals: Aston 7/9.
Rugby Leaguer & League Express Men of the Match: *Bulls:* Kurt Haggerty; *Eagles:* Cory Aston.
Penalty count: 8-7; **Half-time:** 12-18;
Referee: Ben Thaler; **Attendance:** 4,234.

DEWSBURY RAMS 18 LEIGH CENTURIONS 40

RAMS: 1 Josh Guzdek; 2 Dale Morton; 15 Jason Crookes; 38 Etuate Uaisele; 5 Dalton Grant; 23 James Glover; 6 Paul Sykes; 16 Toby Adamson; 17 Dom Speakman; 40 Jonathan Walker; 12 Scott Hale; 4 Shane Grady; 25 Joel Farrell. Subs (all used): 24 Jack Teanby; 14 Luke Adamson; 19 Nathan Conroy; 32 Kyle Trout.
Tries: L Adamson (26), Morton (77), Teanby (79);
Goals: Sykes 3/4.
Sin bin: Crookes (74) - fighting.
CENTURIONS: 26 Lee Smith; 2 Adam Higson; 24 Tom Armstrong; 27 Richard Whiting; 5 Liam Kay; 6 Martyn Ridyard; 31 Ben Reynolds; 20 Sam Hopkins; 14 Micky Higham; 10 Dayne Weston; 16 Reni Maitua; 12 Gareth Hock; 13 Cory Paterson. Subs (all used): 32 Liam Hood; 29 Jake Emmitt; 17 Jamie Acton; 11 Harrison Hansen.
Tries: Hopkins (10, 14), Higson (44), Reynolds (60), Kay (65), Paterson (67), Whiting (69); **Goals:** Ridyard 6/7.
Sin bin: Hock (55) - dangerous challenge;
Acton (74) - fighting.
Rugby Leaguer & League Express Men of the Match: *Rams:* Paul Sykes; *Centurions:* Sam Hopkins.
Penalty count: 15-10; **Half-time:** 8-12;
Referee: Sam Ansell; **Attendance:** 1,691.

FEATHERSTONE ROVERS 19 HALIFAX 20

ROVERS: 15 Ian Hardman; 2 Kyran Johnson; 21 Bradley Knowles-Tagg; 4 Misi Taulapapa; 5 Scott Turner; 1 Danny Craven; 33 Jordan Lilley; 8 Darrell Griffin; 23 Andy Ellis; 17 Jack Ormondroyd; 18 Jamie Cording; 12 John Davies; 13 Tim Spears. Subs (all used): 10 Andrew Bostock; 14 Will Milner; 20 Luke Cooper; 32 Jordan Baldwinson.
Tries: Lilley (23), Taulapapa (42), Turner (68);
Goals: Lilley 3/5; **Field goal:** Lilley (77).
HALIFAX: 18 Miles Greenwood; 25 Jake Eccleston; 20 Sam Smeaton; 3 Steve Tyrer; 19 Tom Saxton; 7 Gareth Moore; 6 Scott Murrell; 8 Mitch Cahalane; 9 Ben Kaye; 10 Luke Ambler; 11 Dane Manning; 14 Adam Tangata; 13 Jacob Fairbank. Subs (all used): 16 Richard Moore; 17 Gavin Bennion; 21 Adam Robinson; 30 Brandon Moore.
Tries: G Moore (8), Smeaton (45, 51); **Goals:** Tyrer 4/4.
Rugby Leaguer & League Express Men of the Match: *Rovers:* Jordan Lilley; *Halifax:* Adam Tangata.
Penalty count: 9-9; **Half-time:** 6-6;
Referee: Chris Kendall; **Attendance:** 2,129.

OLDHAM 28 BATLEY BULLDOGS 12

OLDHAM: 1 Richard Lepori; 2 Adam Clay; 9 Sam Gee; 15 Liam Johnson; 5 Jamel Chisholm; 6 Lewis Palfrey; 7 Steve Roper; 8 Phil Joy; 20 Gareth Owen; 23 Tyler Dickinson; 13 Liam Thompson; 16 Gary Middlehurst; 24 Will Hope. Subs (all used): 14 Joe Burke; 26 Michael Ward; 21 Kenny Hughes; 10 Jack Spencer.
Tries: Lepori (17), Johnson (40), Chisholm (45, 67), Gee (52); **Goals:** Palfrey 4/5.
BULLDOGS: 22 Dave Scott; 2 Wayne Reittie; 19 Alex Bretherton; 5 Shaun Ainscough; 26 Alex Brown; 6 Cain Southernwood; 7 Dominic Brambani; 8 Keegan Hirst; 20 Alistair Leak; 10 Alex Rowe; 17 Joe Chandler; 11 Brad Day; 13 Pat Walker. Subs (all used): 9 Luke Blake; 14 James Davey; 18 Tom Lillycrop; 21 James Brown.
Tries: Lillycrop (67), Reittie (79); **Goals:** Walker 2/3.
Rugby Leaguer & League Express Men of the Match: *Oldham:* Gary Middlehurst; *Bulldogs:* Cain Southernwood.
Penalty count: 6-16; **Half-time:** 12-2;
Referee: Chris Campbell; **Attendance:** 814.

SWINTON LIONS 26 WORKINGTON TOWN 22

LIONS: - Gabriel Fell; 2 Shaun Robinson; 3 Stuart Littler; 23 Rhodri Lloyd; - Liam Marshall; 6 Ben White; 1 Chris Atkin; 8 Mike Morrison; 9 Anthony Nicholson; 10 Jordan Hand; 11 Connor Dwyer; 12 Andy Thornley; 17 Stephen Nash. Subs (all used): 19 Josh Barlow; 7 Matty Beharrell; 13 Rob Lever; 16 Ben Austin.
Tries: Fell (5), Littler (14), Lloyd (21), Marshall (37), Atkin (67); **Goals:** Atkin 3/5.
TOWN: 1 Jack Murphy; 24 Theerapol Ritson; 16 Perry Whiteley; 4 Jason Mossop; 22 Chris Murphy; 6 Carl Forber; 28 Jarrod Sammut; 8 Kris Coward; 7 Jamie Doran; 21 Oliver Gordon; 11 Brett Phillips; 12 Jarrad Stack; 13 Liam McAvoy. Subs (all used): 9 Graeme Mattinson; 10 Marc Shackley; 18 Tom Walker; 19 Ryan Verlinden.
Tries: J Murphy (8), C Murphy (29), Mattinson (43), Sammut (47); **Goals:** Forber 3/4.
Rugby Leaguer & League Express Men of the Match: *Lions:* Gabriel Fell; *Town:* Graeme Mattinson.
Penalty count: 7-7; **Half-time:** 20-10;
Referee: Michael Woodhead; **Attendance:** 501.

ROUND 10

Sunday 10th April 2016

DEWSBURY RAMS 18 BRADFORD BULLS 52

RAMS: 1 Josh Guzdek; 2 Dale Morton; 15 Jason Crookes; 4 Shane Grady; 5 Dalton Grant; 6 Paul Sykes; 22 Andy Kain; 33 Paul Jackson; 9 Tom Hemingway; 10 Ryan Hepworth; 12 Scott Hale; 25 Joel Farrell; 14 Luke Adamson. Subs (all used): 19 Nathan Conroy; 24 Jack Teanby; 32 Kyle Trout; 18 Tony Tonks.
Tries: Grant (2), Farrell (21, 79);
Goals: Sykes 2/2, Hemingway 1/1.
BULLS: 22 James Clare; 2 Omari Caro; 37 Ross Oakes; 4 Kris Welham; 29 Ethan Ryan; 6 Lee Gaskell; 3 Adrian Purtell; 8 Paul Clough; 30 Joe Lumb; 16 Daniel Fleming; 14 Jay Pitts; 12 Dale Ferguson; 13 Danny Addy. Subs (all used): 11 Tom Olbison; 20 Mitch Clark; 9 Adam O'Brien; 23 Alex Mellor.
Tries: Welham (11, 29, 65, 67, 76), Gaskell (38), Caro (42, 46), Mellor (49), Clare (69);
Goals: Addy 3/5, Gaskell 0/1, Caro 3/4.
Rugby Leaguer & League Express Men of the Match: *Rams:* Joel Farrell; *Bulls:* Kris Welham.
Penalty count: 8-12; **Half-time:** 12-14;
Referee: James Child; **Attendance:** 1,954.

HALIFAX 35 SWINTON LIONS 38

HALIFAX: 18 Miles Greenwood; 25 Jake Eccleston; 20 Sam Smeaton; 3 Steve Tyrer; 2 Will Sharp; 7 Gareth Moore; 6 Scott Murrell; 8 Mitch Cahalane; 9 Ben Kaye; 10 Luke Ambler; 11 Dane Manning; 14 Adam Tangata; 13 Jacob Fairbank. Subs (all used): 16 Richard Moore; 17 Gavin Bennion; 21 Adam Robinson; 30 Brandon Moore.
Tries: Greenwood (6, 32), Smeaton (8), Eccleston (11), B Moore (29), Kaye (63); **Goals:** Tyrer 5/6;
Field goal: G Moore (75).
LIONS: 20 Mike Butt; 2 Shaun Robinson; 3 Stuart Littler; 4 Macauley Hallett; - Liam Marshall; 6 Ben White; 1 Chris Atkin; 8 Mike Morrison; 9 Anthony Nicholson; 10 Jordan Hand; 11 Connor Dwyer; 23 Rhodri Lloyd; 12 Andy Thornley. Subs (all used): 27 Vila Halafihi; 17 Stephen Nash; 19 Josh Barlow; 13 Rob Lever.
Tries: Marshall (15, 18, 45, 79), Barlow (35), Atkin (48), Hallett (65), Robinson (72); **Goals:** Atkin 3/9.
Rugby Leaguer & League Express Men of the Match: *Halifax:* Ben Kaye; *Lions:* Liam Marshall.
Penalty count: 6-6; **Half-time:** 28-16;
Referee: Chris Campbell; **Attendance:** 1,551.

LEIGH CENTURIONS 60 WHITEHAVEN 6

CENTURIONS: 26 Lee Smith; 2 Adam Higson; 3 Greg Worthington; 24 Tom Armstrong; 5 Liam Kay; 6 Martyn Ridyard; 31 Ben Reynolds; 18 Tom Spencer; 14 Micky Higham; 10 Dayne Weston; 16 Reni Maitua; 12 Gareth Hock; 13 Cory Paterson. Subs (all used): 32 Liam Hood; 20 Sam Hopkins; 27 Richard Whiting; 17 Jamie Acton.
Tries: Paterson (14, 20, 24), Armstrong (29), Acton (33), Reynolds (38), Maitua (45), Kay (50, 52), Weston (67), Hood (73); **Goals:** Ridyard 8/11.
WHITEHAVEN: 1 Louis Jouffret; 28 Ed Chamberlain; 3 Chris Taylor; 4 Jessie Joe Parker; 2 Craig Calvert; 6 Dion Aiye; 7 Grant Gore; 19 Glenn Riley; 13 Liam Carberry; 26 Ted Chapelhow; 11 Dave Allen; 12 Scott McAvoy; 15 Ben Davies. Subs (all used): 17 Steve Fox; 9 James Newton; 31 Ryan Duffy; 21 John-Paul Brocklebank.
Try: Riley (61); **Goals:** Jouffret 1/1.
Rugby Leaguer & League Express Men of the Match: *Centurions:* Cory Paterson; *Whitehaven:* James Newton.
Penalty count: 7-9; **Half-time:** 36-0;
Referee: Chris Kendall; **Attendance:** 3,089.

LONDON BRONCOS 32 BATLEY BULLDOGS 8

BRONCOS: 32 Elliot Kear; 2 Rhys Williams; 1 Ben

Hellewell; 6 Israel Eliab; 5 Iliess Macani; 15 Jack Bussey; 7 William Barthau; 8 Nick Slyney; 9 James Cunningham; 16 Mark Ioane; 11 Daniel Harrison; 12 Matt Garside; 21 Alex Foster. Subs (all used): 14 Andy Ackers; 23 Jon Magrin; 17 Mark Offerdahl; 10 Eddie Battye.
Tries: Williams (1, 6), Hellewell (29), Battye (33), Barthau (45), Kear (60), Ioane (67);
Goals: Barthau 2/6, Bussey 0/1.
BULLDOGS: 22 Dave Scott; 26 Alex Brown; 23 Danny Cowling; 4 Shaun Squires; 5 Shaun Ainscough; 6 Cain Southernwood; 7 Dominic Brambani; 8 Keegan Hirst; 9 Luke Blake; 15 Adam Gledhill; 11 Brad Day; 19 Alex Bretherton; 13 Pat Walker. Subs (all used): 14 James Davey; 17 Joe Chandler; 18 Tom Lillycrop; 21 James Brown.
Try: D Scott (9); **Goals:** Walker 2/2.
Dismissal: Lillycrop (51) - high tackle on Barthau.
Rugby Leaguer & League Express Men of the Match:
Broncos: William Barthau; *Bulldogs:* Pat Walker.
Penalty count: 6-9; **Half-time:** 20-8;
Referee: Michael Woodhead; **Attendance:** 753.

OLDHAM 21 SHEFFIELD EAGLES 20

OLDHAM: 1 Richard Lepori; 2 Adam Clay; 9 Sam Gee; 15 Liam Johnson; 5 Jamel Chisholm; 6 Lewis Palfrey; 7 Steve Roper; 8 Phil Joy; 20 Gareth Owen; 23 Tyler Dickinson; 13 Liam Thompson; 16 Gary Middlehurst; 24 Will Hope. Subs (all used): 14 Joe Burke; 26 Michael Ward; 21 Kenny Hughes; 10 Jack Spencer.
Tries: Johnson (38), Ward (48), Hughes (51);
Goals: Palfrey 4/4; **Field goal:** Palfrey (78).
On report: Middlehurst (73) - alleged biting.
EAGLES: 1 Quentin Laulu-Togagae; 2 Rob Worrincy; 3 Menzie Yere; 4 George Tyson; 22 Ryan Millar; 6 Cory Aston; 24 Rhys Jacks; 8 Steve Thorpe; 9 Keal Carlile; 16 Adam Neal; 13 Matt James; 12 Duane Straugheir; 14 Matty Fozard. Subs (all used): 18 Elliot Minchella; 20 Jack Blagbrough; 11 Michael Knowles; 17 Mark Mexico.
Tries: Fozard (8, 59), Yere (27), James (75);
Goals: Aston 2/4.
Rugby Leaguer & League Express Men of the Match:
Oldham: Liam Thompson; *Eagles:* Mark Mexico.
Penalty count: 10-5; **Half-time:** 6-12;
Referee: Jon Roberts; **Attendance:** 724.

WORKINGTON TOWN 6 FEATHERSTONE ROVERS 52

TOWN: 1 Jack Murphy; 22 Chris Murphy; 3 Declan Hulme; 4 Jason Mossop; 5 Brett Carter; 6 Carl Forber; 28 Jarrod Sammut; 8 Kris Coward; 7 Jamie Doran; 19 Ryan Verlinden; 11 Brett Phillips; 25 Matty Gee; 9 Graeme Mattinson. Subs (all used): 14 Callum Phillips; 10 Marc Shackley; 18 Tom Walker; 21 Oliver Gordon.
Try: B Phillips (44); **Goals:** Forber 1/1.
Sin bin: Sammut (56) - dissent.
ROVERS: 15 Ian Hardman; 2 Kyran Johnson; 21 Bradley Knowles-Tagg; 4 Misi Taulapapa; 5 Scott Turner; 14 Will Milner; 1 Danny Craven; 10 Andrew Bostock; 23 Andy Ellis; 17 Jack Ormondroyd; 18 Jamie Cording; 12 John Davies; 13 Tim Spears. Subs: 16 Colton Roche; 20 Luke Cooper; 8 Darrell Griffin (not used); 25 Liam Blockley.
Tries: Davies (6, 74), Hardman (18, 20), Turner (23), Craven (40), Knowles-Tagg (41), Ormondroyd (57), Cording (65); **Goals:** Johnson 8/9.
Rugby Leaguer & League Express Men of the Match:
Town: Callum Phillips; *Rovers:* Danny Craven.
Penalty count: 9-7; **Half-time:** 0-28;
Referee: Andrew Sweet; **Attendance:** 719.

ROUND 9

Sunday 17th April 2016

WHITEHAVEN 12 LONDON BRONCOS 16

WHITEHAVEN: 1 Louis Jouffret; 20 Jordan Burns; 3 Chris Taylor; 16 Connor Holliday; 2 Craig Calvert; 6 Dion Aiye; 7 Grant Gore; 19 Glenn Riley; 21 John-Paul Brocklebank; 10 Richard Beaumont; 11 Dave Allen; 4 Jessie Joe Parker; 13 Liam Carberry. Subs (all used): 15 Ben Davies; 12 Scott McAvoy; 17 Steve Fox; 31 Ryan Duffy.
Tries: Holliday (11), Calvert (36); **Goals:** Jouffret 2/2.
BRONCOS: 32 Elliot Kear; 2 Rhys Williams; 1 Ben Hellewell; 4 Wes Naiqama; 5 Iliess Macani; 15 Jack Bussey; 7 William Barthau; 8 Nick Slyney; 9 James Cunningham; 16 Mark Ioane; 11 Daniel Harrison; 21 Alex Foster; 23 Jon Magrin. Subs (all used): 14 Andy Ackers; 17 Mark Offerdahl; 10 Eddie Battye; 12 Matt Garside.
Tries: Barthau (5, 61), Slyney (66); **Goals:** Naiqama 2/3.
Rugby Leaguer & League Express Men of the Match:
Whitehaven: Glenn Riley; *Broncos:* William Barthau.
Penalty count: 10-5; **Half-time:** 12-4;
Referee: Tom Grant; **Attendance:** 548.

ROUND 11

Friday 22nd April 2016

SHEFFIELD EAGLES 24 LONDON BRONCOS 56

EAGLES: 1 Quentin Laulu-Togagae; 2 Rob Worrincy; 3 Menzie Yere; 4 George Tyson; 5 Ben Blackmore; 6 Cory Aston; 21 Dave Hewitt; 8 Steve Thorpe; 14 Matty Fozard; 10 Mitchell Stringer; 11 Michael Knowles; 13 Matt James; 18 Elliot Minchella. Subs (all used): 9 Keal Carlile; 17 Mark Mexico; 16 Adam Neal; 15 Scott Wheeldon.
Tries: Blackmore (25), Yere (30), Worrincy (35), Aston (76), Mexico (78); **Goals:** Aston 1/4, Knowles 1/1.
Sin bin: Aston (78) - fighting.
On report: Tyson (53) - alleged late challenge.
BRONCOS: 32 Elliot Kear; 2 Rhys Williams; 1 Ben Hellewell; 4 Wes Naiqama; 5 Iliess Macani; 15 Jack Bussey; 7 William Barthau; 8 Nick Slyney; 9 James Cunningham; 17 Mark Offerdahl; 11 Daniel Harrison; 21 Alex Foster; 23 Jon Magrin. Subs (all used): 14 Andy Ackers; 12 Matt Garside; 16 Mark Ioane; 10 Eddie Battye.
Tries: Barthau (5, 40, 43), Naiqama (12), Williams (19, 53), Garside (28, 69), Ackers (60), Foster (73); **Goals:** Naiqama 7/9, Barthau 1/1.
Sin bin: Magrin (78) - fighting.
Rugby Leaguer & League Express Men of the Match:
Eagles: Steve Thorpe; *Broncos:* William Barthau.
Penalty count: 4-6; **Half-time:** 12-26;
Referee: Chris Kendall; **Attendance:** 513.

Saturday 23rd April 2016

WHITEHAVEN 14 OLDHAM 6

WHITEHAVEN: 28 Ed Chamberlain; 20 Jordan Burns; 3 Chris Taylor; 16 Connor Holliday; 2 Craig Calvert; 1 Louis Jouffret; 7 Grant Gore; 26 Ted Chapelhow; 21 John-Paul Brocklebank; 19 Glenn Riley; 6 Dion Aiye; 4 Jessie Joe Parker; 13 Liam Carberry. Subs (all used): 15 Ben Davies; 9 James Newton; 27 Jay Chapelhow; 31 Ryan Duffy.
Tries: Taylor (22), Calvert (35); **Goals:** Jouffret 3/3.
OLDHAM: 1 Richard Lepori; 2 Adam Clay; 15 Liam Johnson; 22 Danny Grimshaw; 4 Jack Holmes; 6 Lewis Palfrey; 7 Steve Roper; 8 Phil Joy; 20 Gareth Owen; 10 Jack Spencer; 16 Gary Middlehurst; 12 Danny Langtree; 24 Will Hope. Subs (all used): 26 Michael Ward; 14 Joe Burke; 19 Adam Files; 13 Liam Thompson.
Try: Holmes (5); **Goals:** Palfrey 1/1.
Sin bin: Middlehurst (67) - punching.
Rugby Leaguer & League Express Men of the Match:
Whitehaven: Ed Chamberlain; *Oldham:* Jack Spencer.
Penalty count: 11-8; **Half-time:** 12-6;
Referee: Warren Turley; **Attendance:** 615.

Sunday 24th April 2016

BATLEY BULLDOGS 24 SWINTON LIONS 32

BULLDOGS: 22 Dave Scott; 2 Wayne Reittie; 23 Danny Cowling; 4 Shaun Squires; 5 Shaun Ainscough; 6 Cain Southernwood; 7 Dominic Brambani; 8 Keegan Hirst; 9 Luke Blake; 21 James Brown; 19 Alex Bretherton; 17 Joe Chandler; 13 Pat Walker. Subs (all used): 15 Adam Gledhill; 18 Tom Lillycrop; 20 Alistair Leak; 24 James Harrison.
Tries: Gledhill (27, 49), D Scott (56, 68);
Goals: Brambani 4/4.
LIONS: 22 Gabriel Fell; 2 Shaun Robinson; 3 Stuart Littler; 4 Macauley Hallett; 18 Liam Marshall; 6 Ben White; 1 Chris Atkin; 8 Mike Morrison; 9 Anthony Nicholson; 13 Rob Lever; 23 Rhodri Lloyd; 11 Connor Dwyer; 12 Andy Thornley. Subs (all used): 16 Ben Austin; 19 Josh Barlow; 27 Vila Halafihi; - Zach Johnson.
Tries: Robinson (3), Marshall (17, 58), White (22), Halafihi (45), Fell (73); **Goals:** Atkin 4/6.
Rugby Leaguer & League Express Men of the Match:
Bulldogs: Dave Scott; *Lions:* Chris Atkin.
Penalty count: 11-7; **Half-time:** 6-18;
Referee: Jon Roberts; **Attendance:** 726.

BRADFORD BULLS 52 WORKINGTON TOWN 16

BULLS: 1 Oscar Thomas; 2 Omari Caro; 22 James Clare; 4 Kris Welham; 5 Danny Williams; 3 Adrian Purtell; 13 Danny Addy; 8 Paul Clough; 9 Adam O'Brien; 16 Daniel Fleming; 11 Tom Olbison; 28 Kurt Haggerty; 14 Jay Pitts. Subs (all used): 12 Dale Ferguson; 20 Mitch Clark; 19 Steve Crossley; 23 Alex Mellor.
Tries: Clark (16), Williams (25, 47), Purtell (29), Clare (32), Welham (44), Caro (52, 77), Thomas (68), Ferguson (79); **Goals:** Addy 6/10.
TOWN: 1 Jack Murphy; 22 Chris Murphy; 3 Declan Hulme; 4 Jason Mossop; 5 Brett Carter; 6 Carl Forber; 7 Jamie Doran; 8 Kris Coward; 9 Graeme Mattinson; 21 Oliver Gordon; 11 Brett Phillips; 16 Perry Whiteley; 25 Matty Gee. Subs (all used): 14 Callum Phillips; 19 Ryan Verlinden; 10 Marc Shackley; 18 Tom Walker.
Tries: C Murphy (10, 37), J Murphy (63); **Goals:** Forber 2/3.
Rugby Leaguer & League Express Men of the Match:
Bulls: Mitch Clark; *Town:* Carl Forber.
Penalty count: 8-4; **Half-time:** 22-10;
Referee: Chris Campbell; **Attendance:** 3,467.

FEATHERSTONE ROVERS 24 LEIGH CENTURIONS 30

ROVERS: 15 Ian Hardman; 2 Kyran Johnson; 21 Bradley Knowles-Tagg; 4 Misi Taulapapa; 25 Liam Blockley; 14 Will Milner; 7 Anthony Thackeray; 8 Darrell Griffin; 23 Andy Ellis; 10 Andrew Bostock; 18 Jamie Cording; 12 John Davies; 13 Tim Spears. Subs: 20 Luke Cooper; 33 Curtis MacDonald (not used); 17 Jack Ormondroyd; 32 Jordan Baldwinson.
Tries: Ellis (10), Knowles-Tagg (45), Taulapapa (49), Johnson (59); **Goals:** Johnson 4/5.
CENTURIONS: 26 Lee Smith; 2 Adam Higson; 27 Richard Whiting; 24 Tom Armstrong; 5 Liam Kay; 6 Martyn Ridyard; 23 Rangi Chase; 11 Harrison Hansen; 14 Micky Higham; 10 Dayne Weston; 16 Reni Maitua; 12 Gareth Hock; 13 Cory Paterson. Subs (all used): 32 Liam Hood; 20 Sam Hopkins; 29 Jake Emmitt; 17 Jamie Acton.
Tries: Armstrong (15), Acton (25), Chase (27), Smith (40), Kay (64); **Goals:** Ridyard 5/7.
Sin bin: Hock (38) - interference; Acton (44) - tripping.
On report: Whiting (71) - alleged dissent.
Rugby Leaguer & League Express Men of the Match:
Rovers: Misi Taulapapa; *Centurions:* Martyn Ridyard.
Penalty count: 14-9; **Half-time:** 8-22;
Referee: James Child; **Attendance:** 2,731.

HALIFAX 23 DEWSBURY RAMS 14

HALIFAX: 18 Miles Greenwood; 19 Tom Saxton; 20 Sam Smeaton; 3 Steve Tyrer; 23 Gareth Potts; 7 Gareth Moore; 1 Ben Johnston; 17 Gavin Bennion; 9 Ben Kaye; 10 Luke Ambler; 11 Dane Manning; 26 Ed Barber; 13 Jacob Fairbank. Subs (all used): 6 Scott Murrell; 8 Mitch Cahalane; 14 Adam Tangata; 15 Ryan Maneely.
Tries: G Moore (11), Potts (39), Tangata (45);
Goals: Tyrer 5/5; **Field goal:** Murrell (80).
RAMS: 1 Josh Guzdek; 2 Dale Morton; 38 Etuate Uaisele; 15 Jason Crookes; 5 Dalton Grant; 23 James Glover; 22 Andy Kain; 33 Paul Jackson; 17 Dom Speakman; 40 Jonathan Walker; 12 Scott Hale; 4 Shane Grady; 25 Joel Farrell. Subs (all used): 13 Aaron Brown; 19 Nathan Conroy; 24 Jack Teanby; 32 Kyle Trout.
Tries: Grant (14), Uaisele (53); **Goals:** Glover 3/3.
Rugby Leaguer & League Express Men of the Match:
Halifax: Scott Murrell; *Rams:* Joel Farrell.
Penalty count: 10-10; **Half-time:** 12-8;
Referee: Michael Woodhead; **Attendance:** 1,453.

ROUND 12

Friday 29th April 2016

SHEFFIELD EAGLES 32 DEWSBURY RAMS 28

EAGLES: 1 Quentin Laulu-Togagae; 2 Rob Worrincy; 3 Menzie Yere; 4 George Tyson; 5 Ben Blackmore; 6 Cory Aston; 21 Dave Hewitt; 8 Steve Thorpe; 9 Keal Carlile; 10 Mitchell Stringer; 11 Michael Knowles; 13 Matt James; 18 Elliot Minchella. Subs (all used): 14 Matty Fozard; 17 Mark Mexico; 16 Adam Neal; 15 Scott Wheeldon.
Tries: Yere (14, 80), Mexico (39), Laulu-Togagae (46), Worrincy (56, 72), Carlile (62);
Goals: Knowles 0/2, Aston 0/1, Fozard 2/4.
RAMS: 1 Josh Guzdek; 2 Dale Morton; 15 Jason Crookes; 38 Etuate Uaisele; 5 Dalton Grant; 23 James Glover; 22 Andy Kain; 14 Luke Adamson; 19 Nathan Conroy; 10 Ryan Hepworth; 12 Scott Hale; 4 Shane Grady; 25 Joel Farrell. Subs (all used): 6 Paul Sykes; 13 Aaron Brown; 24 Jack Teanby; 32 Kyle Trout.
Tries: L Adamson (5), Grant (8), Uaisele (31), Brown (36), Conroy (43); **Goals:** Glover 1/2, Grady 1/2, Sykes 2/2.
Sin bin: Conroy (46) - dissent.
Rugby Leaguer & League Express Men of the Match:
Eagles: Keal Carlile; *Rams:* Dalton Grant.
Penalty count: 8-6; **Half-time:** 8-22;
Referee: Jon Roberts; **Attendance:** 441.

Sunday 1st May 2016

HALIFAX 36 WORKINGTON TOWN 32

HALIFAX: 1 Ben Johnston; 2 Will Sharp; 20 Sam Smeaton; 3 Steve Tyrer; 5 James Saltonstall; 7 Gareth Moore; 6 Scott Murrell; 8 Mitch Cahalane; 9 Ben Kaye; 10 Luke Ambler; 11 Dane Manning; 14 Adam Tangata; 13 Jacob Fairbank. Subs (all used): 16 Richard Moore; 17 Gavin Bennion; 26 Ed Barber; 30 Brandon Moore.
Tries: Smeaton (5), Manning (7), Tyrer (26), Bennion (32), Murrell (49), Saltonstall (61); **Goals:** Tyrer 6/6.
TOWN: 1 Jack Murphy; 22 Chris Murphy; 3 Declan Hulme; 4 Jason Mossop; 5 Brett Carter; 6 Carl Forber; 7 Jamie

Doran; 18 Tom Walker; 9 Graeme Mattinson; 10 Marc Shackley; 11 Brett Phillips; 16 Perry Whiteley; 25 Matty Gee. Subs (all used): 12 Jarrad Stack; 13 Liam McAvoy; 14 Callum Phillips; 17 Alex Szostak.
Tries: C Murphy (13), Mossop (18), Stack (44, 74), Whiteley (69), Mattinson (78); **Goals:** Forber 4/6.
Rugby Leaguer & League Express Men of the Match: *Halifax:* Dane Manning; *Town:* Jamie Doran.
Penalty count: 10-4; **Half-time:** 30-10;
Referee: Andrew Sweet; **Attendance:** 1,293.

LEIGH CENTURIONS 37 BATLEY BULLDOGS 30

CENTURIONS: 26 Lee Smith; 2 Adam Higson; 27 Richard Whiting; 24 Tom Armstrong; 5 Liam Kay; 6 Martyn Ridyard; 23 Rangi Chase; 29 Jake Emmitt; 14 Micky Higham; 10 Dayne Weston; 16 Reni Maitua; 12 Gareth Hock; 11 Harrison Hansen. Subs (all used): 17 Jamie Acton; 18 Tom Spencer; 20 Sam Hopkins; 32 Liam Hood.
Tries: Kay (19), Hansen (35, 43), Hood (56), Smith (78), Hopkins (79); **Goals:** Ridyard 6/6;
Field goal: Ridyard (40).
BULLDOGS: 22 Dave Scott; 26 Alex Brown; 30 Greg Minikin; 27 Callum Casey; 5 Shaun Ainscough; 6 Cain Southernwood; 7 Dominic Brambani; 8 Keegan Hirst; 14 James Davey; 16 Sean Hesketh; 17 Joe Chandler; 19 Alex Bretherton; 9 Luke Blake. Subs (all used): 18 Tom Lillycrop; 20 Alistair Leak; 24 James Harrison; 28 Dave Petersen.
Tries: Ainscough (28), Leak (50), Bretherton (65), Brambani (69), Harrison (74); **Goals:** Brambani 5/5.
Rugby Leaguer & League Express Men of the Match: *Centurions:* Martyn Ridyard; *Bulldogs:* Dominic Brambani.
Penalty count: 8-6; **Half-time:** 13-6;
Referee: Chris Campbell; **Attendance:** 3,389.

LONDON BRONCOS 30 BRADFORD BULLS 16

BRONCOS: 32 Elliot Kear; 2 Rhys Williams; 1 Ben Hellewell; 21 Alex Foster; 5 Iliess Macani; 15 Jack Bussey; 7 William Barthau; 8 Nick Slyney; 9 James Cunningham; 17 Mark Offerdahl; 11 Daniel Harrison; 12 Matt Garside; 23 Jon Magrin. Subs (all used): 14 Andy Ackers; 22 Matt Davis; 16 Mark Ioane; 10 Eddie Battye.
Tries: Hellewell (20), Williams (29, 62), Ackers (43, 58), Cunningham (73); **Goals:** Barthau 1/4, Bussey 2/3.
Sin bin: Slyney (80) - fighting.
BULLS: 22 James Clare; 2 Omari Caro; 1 Oscar Thomas; 4 Kris Welham; 5 Danny Williams; 28 Kurt Haggerty; 13 Danny Addy; 8 Paul Clough; 30 Joe Lumb; 19 Steve Crossley; 11 Tom Olbison; 12 Dale Ferguson; 14 Jay Pitts. Subs (all used): 10 Adam Sidlow; 20 Mitch Clark; 9 Adam O'Brien; 23 Alex Mellor.
Tries: Addy (3), Welham (23, 40); **Goals:** Addy 2/4.
Sin bin: Ferguson (62) - high tackle; Clark (80) - fighting.
Rugby Leaguer & League Express Men of the Match: *Broncos:* Elliot Kear; *Bulls:* Danny Addy.
Penalty count: 8-9; **Half-time:** 8-14;
Referee: James Child; **Attendance:** 1,524.

OLDHAM 16 FEATHERSTONE ROVERS 14

OLDHAM: 1 Richard Lepori; 2 Adam Clay; 15 Liam Johnson; 22 Danny Grimshaw; 4 Jack Holmes; 6 Lewis Palfrey; 20 Gareth Owen; 10 Jack Spencer; - Kruise Leeming; 23 Tyler Dickinson; 16 Gary Middlehurst; 13 Liam Thompson; 24 Will Hope. Subs (all used): 26 Michael Ward; 14 Joe Burke; 9 Sam Gee; 21 Kenny Hughes.
Tries: Hughes (31), Holmes (53), Johnson (74);
Goals: Palfrey 2/5.
ROVERS: 15 Ian Hardman; 2 Kyran Johnson; 25 Liam Blockley; 4 Misi Taulapapa; 27 Jamie Foster; 28 Jordan Abdull; 7 Anthony Thackeray; 8 Darrell Griffin; 12 John Davies; 10 Andrew Bostock; 18 Jamie Cording; 11 Steve Snitch; 21 Bradley Knowles-Tagg. Subs: 20 Luke Cooper; 17 Jack Ormondroyd; 32 Jordan Baldwinson; 22 Jack Coventry (not used).
Tries: Hardman (47), Taulapapa (69); **Goals:** Foster 3/3.
Sin bin: Hardman (30) - professional foul.
Rugby Leaguer & League Express Men of the Match: *Oldham:* Gareth Owen; *Rovers:* John Davies.
Penalty count: 10-8; **Half-time:** 6-0;
Referee: Michael Woodhead; **Attendance:** 868.

SWINTON LIONS 32 WHITEHAVEN 26

LIONS: 22 Gabriel Fell; 2 Shaun Robinson; 3 Stuart Littler; 4 Macauley Hallett; 18 Liam Marshall; 6 Ben White; 1 Chris Atkin; 8 Mike Morrison; 9 Anthony Nicholson; 13 Rob Lever; 11 Connor Dwyer; 23 Rhodri Lloyd; 12 Andy Thornley. Subs (all used): 7 Matty Beharrell; 19 Josh Barlow; - Andy Bracek; 16 Ben Austin.
Tries: White (7), Hallett (33, 53), Fell (51), Lloyd (60), Marshall (76); **Goals:** Atkin 4/6.
WHITEHAVEN: 28 Ed Chamberlain; 20 Jordan Burns; 3 Chris Taylor; 4 Jessie Joe Parker; 16 Connor Holliday; 1 Louis Jouffret; 7 Grant Gore; 19 Glenn Riley; 21 John-Paul Brocklebank; 8 Sam Brooks; 11 Dave Allen; 6 Dion Aiye; 13 Liam Carberry. Subs (all used): 9 James Newton; 31 Ryan Duffy; 27 Jay Chapelhow; 26 Ted Chapelhow.
Tries: Parker (3, 29), Jouffret (18), Burns (23), Holliday (40);
Goals: Jouffret 3/5.
Rugby Leaguer & League Express Men of the Match: *Lions:* Ben White; *Whitehaven:* Louis Jouffret.
Penalty count: 7-4; **Half-time:** 10-26;
Referee: Chris Kendall; **Attendance:** 711.

ROUND 3

Saturday 7th May 2016

WHITEHAVEN 22 FEATHERSTONE ROVERS 44

WHITEHAVEN: 1 Louis Jouffret; 20 Jordan Burns; 3 Chris Taylor; 16 Connor Holliday; 2 Craig Calvert; 6 Dion Aiye; 7 Grant Gore; 26 Ted Chapelhow; 9 James Newton; 19 Glenn Riley; 11 Dave Allen; 4 Jessie Joe Parker; 13 Liam Carberry. Subs (all used): 15 Ben Davies; 17 Steve Fox; 21 John-Paul Brocklebank; 31 Ryan Duffy.
Tries: Calvert (13, 20), Allen (28), Parker (64), Holliday (72); **Goals:** Jouffret 1/4, Brocklebank 0/2.
ROVERS: 1 Danny Craven; 2 Kyran Johnson; 15 Ian Hardman; 4 Misi Taulapapa; 27 Jamie Foster; 28 Jordan Abdull; 7 Anthony Thackeray; 32 Jordan Baldwinson; 23 Andy Ellis; 10 Andrew Bostock; 18 Jamie Cording; 12 John Davies; 13 Tim Spears. Subs (all used): 16 Colton Roche; 17 Jack Ormondroyd; 8 Darrell Griffin; 6 Kyle Briggs.
Tries: Taulapapa (18, 24, 33), Johnson (61), Craven (70), Roche (75), Thackeray (78); **Goals:** Foster 8/8.
Rugby Leaguer & League Express Men of the Match: *Whitehaven:* Connor Holliday; *Rovers:* Jamie Foster.
Penalty count: 13-9; **Half-time:** 14-18;
Referee: Warren Turley; **Attendance:** 658.

ROUND 13

Saturday 14th May 2016

SHEFFIELD EAGLES 30 WORKINGTON TOWN 37

EAGLES: 1 Quentin Laulu-Togagae; 19 Garry Lo; 3 Menzie Yere; 4 George Tyson; 5 Ben Blackmore; 6 Cory Aston; 24 Rhys Jacks; 8 Steve Thorpe; 9 Keal Carlile; 16 Adam Neal; 11 Michael Knowles; 13 Matt James; 18 Elliot Minchella. Subs (all used): 2 Rob Worrincy; 17 Mark Mexico; 10 Mitchell Stringer; 15 Scott Wheeldon.
Tries: Lo (4, 15), Blackmore (52), Wheeldon (62), Worrincy (73), Aston (79); **Goals:** Knowles 0/2, Aston 3/4.
TOWN: 1 Jack Murphy; 22 Chris Murphy; 3 Declan Hulme; 16 Perry Whiteley; 5 Brett Carter; 6 Carl Forber; 7 Jamie Doran; 8 Kris Coward; 14 Callum Phillips; 21 Oliver Gordon; 11 Brett Phillips; 12 Jarrad Stack; 25 Matty Gee. Subs (all used): 28 Jarrod Sammut; 13 Liam McAvoy; 18 Tom Walker; 10 Marc Shackley.
Tries: Hulme (12), Whiteley (26, 43, 70), Forber (40), Coward (65); **Goals:** Forber 6/8; **Field goal:** Forber (77).
Sin bin: Sammut (72) - interference.
Rugby Leaguer & League Express Men of the Match: *Eagles:* Rhys Jacks; *Town:* Perry Whiteley.
Penalty count: 11-10; **Half-time:** 8-20;
Referee: Tom Grant; **Attendance:** 494.

WHITEHAVEN 16 DEWSBURY RAMS 36

WHITEHAVEN: 1 Louis Jouffret; 25 Ryan Ince; 4 Jessie Joe Parker; 16 Connor Holliday; 2 Craig Calvert; 21 John-Paul Brocklebank; 7 Grant Gore; 26 Ted Chapelhow; 9 James Newton; 19 Glenn Riley; 11 Dave Allen; 6 Dion Aiye; 13 Liam Carberry. Subs: 15 Ben Davies; 17 Steve Fox; 20 Jordan Burns (not used); 31 Ryan Duffy.
Tries: Calvert (47), Holliday (56), Ince (68);
Goals: Jouffret 2/3.
RAMS: 1 Josh Guzdek; 38 Etuate Uaisele; 15 Jason Crookes; 4 Shane Grady; 5 Dalton Grant; 6 Paul Sykes; 22 Andy Kain; 8 Matt Groat; 9 Tom Hemingway; 14 Luke Adamson; 12 Scott Hale; 32 Kyle Trout; 25 Joel Farrell. Subs (all used): 19 Nathan Conroy; 13 Aaron Brown; 27 Jason Muranka; 18 Tony Tonks.
Tries: Hale (8), Sykes (39, 63), Grady (58), Guzdek (76), Grant (79); **Goals:** Sykes 6/6.
Rugby Leaguer & League Express Men of the Match: *Whitehaven:* Dave Allen; *Rams:* Tom Hemingway.
Penalty count: 10-7; **Half-time:** 0-12;
Referee: Jon Roberts; **Attendance:** 684.

Sunday 15th May 2016

BATLEY BULLDOGS 32 HALIFAX 16

BULLDOGS: 22 Dave Scott; 2 Wayne Reittie; 3 Chris Ulugia; 30 Greg Minikin; 5 Shaun Ainscough; 6 Cain Southernwood; 7 Dominic Brambani; 8 Keegan Hirst; 14 James Davey; 10 Alex Rowe; 17 Joe Chandler; 19 Alex Bretherton; 9 Luke Blake. Subs (all used): 15 Adam Gledhill; 18 Tom Lillycrop; 13 Pat Walker; 21 James Brown.
Tries: Reittie (27, 55), Ainscough (33), Walker (62), D Scott (77), J Brown (79); **Goals:** Walker 4/6.
HALIFAX: 18 Miles Greenwood; 5 James Saltonstall; 4 Ben Heaton; 3 Steve Tyrer; 2 Will Sharp; 7 Gareth Moore; 6 Scott Murrell; 17 Gavin Bennion; 30 Brandon Moore; 14 Adam Tangata; 11 Dane Manning; 33 Matt Sarsfield; 13 Jacob Fairbank. Subs (all used): 9 Ben Kaye; 10 Luke Ambler; 16 Richard Moore; 21 Adam Robinson.
Tries: Tyrer (3), Sarsfield (43), Heaton (66);
Goals: Tyrer 2/3.
Rugby Leaguer & League Express Men of the Match: *Bulldogs:* Wayne Reittie; *Halifax:* Gavin Bennion.
Penalty count: 9-7; **Half-time:** 10-6;
Referee: Michael Woodhead; **Attendance:** 1,203.

BRADFORD BULLS 54 SWINTON LIONS 8

BULLS: 22 James Clare; 2 Omari Caro; 15 Matty Blythe; 4 Kris Welham; 5 Danny Williams; 6 Lee Gaskell; 1 Oscar Thomas; 8 Paul Clough; 9 Adam O'Brien; 10 Adam Sidlow; 11 Tom Olbison; 14 Jay Pitts; 13 Danny Addy. Subs (all used): 19 Steve Crossley; 23 Alex Mellor; 25 Ben Kavanagh; 38 Jacob Trueman.
Tries: Clare (7, 39), Caro (13, 79), Sidlow (19), Welham (43), Addy (46), Thomas (48), Olbison (52), Gaskell (63); **Goals:** Addy 6/9, Thomas 1/1.
Sin bin: Addy (32) - fighting.
LIONS: 22 Gabriel Fell; 2 Shaun Robinson; 3 Stuart Littler; 23 Rhodri Lloyd; 18 Liam Marshall; 6 Ben White; 1 Chris Atkin; 8 Mike Morrison; 9 Anthony Nicholson; - Andy Bracek; 11 Connor Dwyer; 13 Rob Lever; 12 Andy Thornley. Subs (all used): 19 Josh Barlow; 17 Stephen Nash; 7 Matty Beharrell; 16 Ben Austin.
Tries: Marshall (57), Lloyd (60); **Goals:** Atkin 0/2.
Sin bin: Barlow (32) - fighting.
Rugby Leaguer & League Express Men of the Match: *Bulls:* James Clare; *Lions:* Rhodri Lloyd.
Penalty count: 10-6; **Half-time:** 20-0;
Referee: Warren Turley; **Attendance:** 4,152.

FEATHERSTONE ROVERS 42 LONDON BRONCOS 18

ROVERS: 1 Danny Craven; 29 Luke Briscoe; 15 Ian Hardman; 4 Misi Taulapapa; 27 Jamie Foster; 28 Jordan Abdull; 7 Anthony Thackeray; 10 Andrew Bostock; 23 Andy Ellis; 32 Jordan Baldwinson; 18 Jamie Cording; 12 John Davies; 13 Tim Spears. Subs (all used): 16 Colton Roche; 17 Jack Ormondroyd; 6 Kyle Briggs; 8 Darrell Griffin.
Tries: Foster (5), Briscoe (13, 54), Ormondroyd (32), Craven (38, 75), Thackeray (68); **Goals:** Foster 7/9.
BRONCOS: 32 Elliot Kear; 2 Rhys Williams; 1 Ben Hellewell; 21 Alex Foster; 5 Iliess Macani; 15 Jack Bussey; 7 William Barthau; 8 Nick Slyney; 9 James Cunningham; 17 Mark Offerdahl; 11 Daniel Harrison; 12 Matt Garside; 23 Jon Magrin. Subs (all used): 4 Wes Naiqama; 14 Andy Ackers; 16 Mark Ioane; 10 Eddie Battye.
Tries: Harrison (19), Macani (49), Kear (78);
Goals: Barthau 1/1, Naiqama 2/2.
Rugby Leaguer & League Express Men of the Match: *Rovers:* Danny Craven; *Broncos:* Daniel Harrison.
Penalty count: 13-11; **Half-time:** 24-6;
Referee: Sam Ansell; **Attendance:** 1,723.

OLDHAM 14 LEIGH CENTURIONS 56

OLDHAM: - Jared Simpson; 2 Adam Clay; 15 Liam Johnson; 22 Danny Grimshaw; 5 Jamel Chisholm; 7 Steve Roper; 20 Gareth Owen; 8 Phil Joy; 17 Kruise Leeming; 26 Michael Ward; 16 Gary Middlehurst; 13 Liam Thompson; 24 Will Hope. Subs (all used): 14 Joe Burke; 9 Sam Gee; 21 Kenny Hughes; 12 Danny Langtree.
Tries: Grimshaw (14), Johnson (74), Langtree (77);
Goals: Roper 1/3.
CENTURIONS: 26 Lee Smith; 2 Adam Higson; 3 Greg Worthington; 24 Tom Armstrong; 5 Liam Kay; 6 Martyn Ridyard; 31 Ben Reynolds; 17 Jamie Acton; 14 Micky Higham; 10 Dayne Weston; 27 Richard Whiting; 16 Reni Maitua; 12 Gareth Hock. Subs (all used): 11 Harrison Hansen; 32 Liam Hood; 29 Jake Emmitt; 35 Brad Fash.
Tries: Maitua (18, 47), Smith (24), Ridyard (34), Kay (37), Hood (40), Armstrong (50), Reynolds (54), Acton (66), Weston (69); **Goals:** Ridyard 8/10.
Rugby Leaguer & League Express Men of the Match: *Oldham:* Gareth Owen; *Centurions:* Ben Reynolds.
Penalty count: 6-12; **Half-time:** 6-26;
Referee: Scott Mikalauskas; **Attendance:** 1,489.

ROUND 14

Friday 20th May 2016

SHEFFIELD EAGLES 14 BRADFORD BULLS 25

EAGLES: 1 Quentin Laulu-Togagae; 19 Garry Lo; 3 Menzie Yere; 2 Rob Worrincy; 5 Ben Blackmore; 6 Cory Aston; 24

Rhys Jacks; 8 Steve Thorpe; 9 Keal Carlile; 16 Adam Neal; 11 Michael Knowles; 4 George Tyson; 14 Matty Fozard. Subs (all used): 18 Elliot Minchella; 17 Mark Mexico; 13 Matt James; 15 Scott Wheeldon.
Tries: Worrincy (7, 49), Aston (24); **Goals:** Aston 1/3.
BULLS: 22 James Clare; 2 Omari Caro; 15 Matty Blythe; 4 Kris Welham; 5 Danny Williams; 6 Lee Gaskell; 1 Oscar Thomas; 8 Paul Clough; 9 Adam O'Brien; 10 Adam Sidlow; 11 Tom Olbison; 14 Jay Pitts; 13 Danny Addy. Subs (all used): 12 Dale Ferguson; 19 Steve Crossley; 20 Mitch Clark; 30 Joe Lumb.
Tries: Thomas (29), Williams (56), Sidlow (64), Welham (73); **Goals:** Addy 4/4; **Field goal:** Thomas (68).
Rugby Leaguer & League Express Men of the Match: *Eagles:* Menzie Yere; *Bulls:* Adam Sidlow.
Penalty count: 4-9; **Half-time:** 10-6;
Referee: Michael Woodhead; **Attendance:** 995.

HALIFAX 12 OLDHAM 6

HALIFAX: 18 Miles Greenwood; 2 Will Sharp; 3 Steve Tyrer; 4 Ben Heaton; 5 James Saltonstall; 7 Gareth Moore; 6 Scott Murrell; 8 Mitch Cahalane; 9 Ben Kaye; 14 Adam Tangata; 11 Dane Manning; 33 Matt Sarsfield; 13 Jacob Fairbank. Subs (all used): 10 Luke Ambler; 16 Richard Moore; 21 Adam Robinson; 30 Brandon Moore.
Tries: Sarsfield (9, 28); **Goals:** Tyrer 2/4.
OLDHAM: - Jared Simpson; 2 Adam Clay; 9 Sam Gee; 15 Liam Johnson; 5 Jamel Chisholm; 22 Danny Grimshaw; 20 Gareth Owen; 23 Tyler Dickinson; 17 Kruise Leeming; - Tom Spencer; 16 Gary Middlehurst; 12 Danny Langtree; 13 Liam Thompson. Subs (all used): 8 Phil Joy; 14 Joe Burke; 19 Adam Files; 26 Michael Ward.
Try: Chisholm (49); **Goals:** Gee 1/1.
Rugby Leaguer & League Express Men of the Match: *Halifax:* Jacob Fairbank; *Oldham:* Kruise Leeming.
Penalty count: 9-15; **Half-time:** 10-0;
Referee: Warren Turley; **Attendance:** 1,285.

Sunday 22nd May 2016

DEWSBURY RAMS 0 FEATHERSTONE ROVERS 31

RAMS: 1 Josh Guzdek; 38 Etuate Uaisele; 15 Jason Crookes; 4 Shane Grady; 5 Dalton Grant; 6 Paul Sykes; 22 Andy Kain; 8 Matt Groat; 9 Tom Hemingway; 14 Luke Adamson; 12 Scott Hale; 32 Kyle Trout; 25 Joel Farrell. Subs (all used): 19 Nathan Conroy; 13 Aaron Brown; 27 Jason Muranka; 18 Tony Tonks.
Sin bin: Crookes (10) - high tackle on Craven; L Adamson (23) - professional foul.
ROVERS: 1 Danny Craven; 2 Kyran Johnson; 15 Ian Hardman; 4 Misi Taulapapa; 27 Jamie Foster; 28 Jordan Abdull; 7 Anthony Thackeray; 10 Andrew Bostock; 23 Andy Ellis; 32 Jordan Baldwinson; 18 Jamie Cording; 12 John Davies; 13 Tim Spears. Subs (all used): 6 Kyle Briggs; 8 Darrell Griffin; 16 Colton Roche; 17 Jack Ormondroyd.
Tries: Taulapapa (13, 49), Davies (31), Cording (62), Hardman (75); **Goals:** Foster 5/6; **Field goal:** Briggs (58).
Sin bin: Taulapapa (34) - high tackle on Farrell.
Rugby Leaguer & League Express Men of the Match: *Rams:* Matt Groat; *Rovers:* Jordan Abdull.
Penalty count: 7-13; **Half-time:** 0-10;
Referee: Jon Roberts; **Attendance:** 1,281.

LONDON BRONCOS 62 WHITEHAVEN 4

BRONCOS: 24 Alex Walker; 2 Rhys Williams; 1 Ben Hellewell; 4 Wes Naiqama; 32 Elliot Kear; 26 Api Pewhairangi; 20 Scott Leatherbarrow; 8 Nick Slyney; 14 Andy Ackers; 10 Eddie Battye; 11 Daniel Harrison; 21 Alex Foster; 15 Jack Bussey. Subs (all used): 9 James Cunningham; 23 Jon Magrin; 16 Mark Ioane; 17 Mark Offerdahl.
Tries: Williams (11, 52), Pewhairangi (14, 18), Naiqama (26, 64), Offerdahl (34), Hellewell (43, 49), Cunningham (59), Foster (69); **Goals:** Naiqama 9/11.
WHITEHAVEN: 28 Ed Chamberlain; 20 Jordan Burns; 16 Connor Holliday; 21 John-Paul Brocklebank; 25 Ryan Ince; 1 Louis Jouffret; 7 Grant Gore; 19 Glenn Riley; 9 James Newton; 26 Ted Chapelhow; 11 Dave Allen; 4 Jessie Joe Parker; 13 Liam Carberry. Subs (all used): 31 Ryan Duffy; 15 Ben Davies; 8 Sam Brooks; 14 Thomas Coyle.
Try: Jouffret (80); **Goals:** Jouffret 0/1.
Rugby Leaguer & League Express Men of the Match: *Broncos:* Api Pewhairangi; *Whitehaven:* Ed Chamberlain.
Penalty count: 8-5; **Half-time:** 28-0;
Referee: Scott Mikalauskas; **Attendance:** 675.

SWINTON LIONS 6 LEIGH CENTURIONS 48

LIONS: 14 Kieran Hyde; 2 Shaun Robinson; 3 Stuart Littler; 23 Rhodri Lloyd; 20 Mike Butt; 6 Ben White; 1 Chris Atkin; 16 Ben Austin; 9 Anthony Nicholson; - Andy Bracek; 12 Andy Thornley; 11 Connor Dwyer; 19 Josh Barlow. Subs (all used): - Daniel Fleming; 7 Matty Beharrell; 17 Stephen Nash; 28 Zach Johnson.
Try: Nicholson (14); **Goals:** Atkin 1/1.
Dismissal: Johnson (45) - fighting; Barlow (45) - fighting, from the bench.
Sin bin: Butt (45) - fighting; Fleming (77) - fighting.
CENTURIONS: 26 Lee Smith; 2 Adam Higson; 24 Tom Armstrong; 4 Willie Tonga; 15 Jonny Pownall; 6 Martyn Ridyard; 31 Ben Reynolds; 29 Jake Emmitt; 14 Micky Higham; 10 Dayne Weston; 27 Richard Whiting; 16 Reni Maitua; 12 Gareth Hock. Subs (all used): 36 Josh Drinkwater; 35 Brad Fash; 20 Sam Hopkins; 17 Jamie Acton.
Tries: Armstrong (7), Smith (24, 40), Pownall (27), Whiting (34), Ridyard (55), Weston (60), Reynolds (66), Drinkwater (78); **Goals:** Ridyard 5/7, Reynolds 1/2.
Dismissal: Hock (45) - fighting.
Sin bin: Higson (45) - fighting; Emmitt (77) - fighting.
Rugby Leaguer & League Express Men of the Match: *Lions:* Shaun Robinson; *Centurions:* Ben Reynolds.
Penalty count: 12-12; **Half-time:** 6-26;
Referee: Andrew Sweet; **Attendance:** 1,413.

WORKINGTON TOWN 24 BATLEY BULLDOGS 31

TOWN: 1 Jack Murphy; 22 Chris Murphy; 12 Jarrad Stack; 16 Perry Whiteley; 3 Declan Hulme; 6 Carl Forber; 7 Jamie Doran; 10 Marc Shackley; 14 Callum Phillips; 21 Oliver Gordon; 11 Brett Phillips; 25 Matty Gee; 13 Liam McAvoy. Subs (all used): 9 Graeme Mattinson; 18 Tom Walker; 28 Jarrod Sammut; 19 Ryan Verlinden.
Tries: B Phillips (10), Whiteley (42), Sammut (63), J Murphy (66); **Goals:** Forber 4/4.
BULLDOGS: 22 Dave Scott; 2 Wayne Reittie; 30 Greg Minikin; 3 Chris Ulugia; 26 Alex Brown; 6 Cain Southernwood; 7 Dominic Brambani; 8 Keegan Hirst; 20 Alistair Leak; 10 Alex Rowe; 29 Frankie Mariano; 17 Joe Chandler; 9 Luke Blake. Subs (all used): 13 Pat Walker; 15 Adam Gledhill; 19 Alex Bretherton; 21 James Brown.
Tries: Blake (25), Minikin (38), A Brown (56), D Scott (59), Leak (74); **Goals:** Brambani 2/2, Walker 3/5;
Field goal: Walker (74).
Rugby Leaguer & League Express Men of the Match: *Town:* Jack Murphy; *Bulldogs:* James Brown.
Penalty count: 8-10; **Half-time:** 6-14;
Referee: Jack Smith; **Attendance:** 681.

ROUND 15 - SUMMER BASH

Saturday 28th May 2016

LONDON BRONCOS 32 SHEFFIELD EAGLES 14

BRONCOS: 32 Elliot Kear; 2 Rhys Williams; 1 Ben Hellewell; 21 Alex Foster; 4 Wes Naiqama; 26 Api Pewhairangi; 20 Scott Leatherbarrow; 8 Nick Slyney; 14 Andy Ackers; 10 Eddie Battye; 11 Daniel Harrison; 12 Matt Garside; 15 Jack Bussey. Subs (all used): 9 James Cunningham; 23 Jon Magrin; 16 Mark Ioane; 17 Mark Offerdahl.
Tries: Williams (6), Slyney (20), Garside (30), Foster (37), Offerdahl (49), Battye (59); **Goals:** Naiqama 4/6.
EAGLES: 1 Quentin Laulu-Togagae; 19 Garry Lo; 3 Menzie Yere; 5 Ben Blackmore; 2 Rob Worrincy; 6 Cory Aston; 24 Rhys Jacks; 15 Scott Wheeldon; 9 Keal Carlile; 16 Adam Neal; 11 Michael Knowles; 4 George Tyson; 14 Matty Fozard. Subs (all used): 13 Matt James; 20 Jack Blagbrough; 18 Elliot Minchella; 17 Mark Mexico.
Tries: Laulu-Togagae (11), Aston (15), Worrincy (73);
Goals: Aston 1/3.
Rugby Leaguer & League Express Men of the Match: *Broncos:* Nick Slyney; *Eagles:* Cory Aston.
Penalty count: 11-7; **Half-time:** 20-10;
Referee: Jack Smith.

WHITEHAVEN 28 WORKINGTON TOWN 24

WHITEHAVEN: 1 Louis Jouffret; 25 Ryan Ince; 3 Chris Taylor; 4 Jessie Joe Parker; 2 Craig Calvert; 6 Dion Aiye; 7 Grant Gore; 31 Ryan Duffy; 14 Thomas Coyle; 19 Glenn Riley; 11 Dave Allen; 30 Ugo Perez; 15 Ben Davies. Subs (all used): 9 James Newton; 32 Anthony Walker; 26 Ted Chapelhow; 16 Connor Holliday.
Tries: Allen (3), Taylor (12), Parker (23), Calvert (47);
Goals: Jouffret 6/7.
TOWN: 1 Jack Murphy; 22 Chris Murphy; 16 Perry Whiteley; 4 Jason Mossop; 3 Declan Hulme; 6 Carl Forber; 28 Jarrod Sammut; 21 Oliver Gordon; 14 Callum Phillips; 10 Marc Shackley; 11 Brett Phillips; 25 Matty Gee; 13 Liam McAvoy. Subs (all used): 7 Jamie Doran; 15 Karl Olstrum; 18 Tom Walker; 19 Ryan Verlinden.
Tries: Sammut (7, 27, 68), C Phillips (21), Hulme (51);
Goals: Forber 2/4, Sammut 0/1.
Rugby Leaguer & League Express Men of the Match: *Whitehaven:* Dion Aiye; *Town:* Jarrod Sammut.
Penalty count: 7-8; **Half-time:** 22-16;
Referee: Michael Woodhead.

BRADFORD BULLS 20 LEIGH CENTURIONS 24

BULLS: 22 James Clare; 2 Omari Caro; 15 Matty Blythe; 4 Kris Welham; 5 Danny Williams; 1 Oscar Thomas; 34 Richard Mathers; 10 Adam Sidlow; 13 Danny Addy; 20 Mitch Clark; 11 Tom Olbison; 12 Dale Ferguson; 14 Jay Pitts. Subs (all used): 9 Adam O'Brien; 19 Steve Crossley; 23 Alex Mellor; 28 Kurt Haggerty.
Tries: Williams (6), Clark (10), O'Brien (53), Addy (75);
Goals: Addy 2/4.
CENTURIONS: 26 Lee Smith; 2 Adam Higson; 3 Greg Worthington; 24 Tom Armstrong; 5 Liam Kay; 31 Ben Reynolds; 36 Josh Drinkwater; 11 Harrison Hansen; 14 Micky Higham; 10 Dayne Weston; 16 Reni Maitua; 27 Richard Whiting; 12 Gareth Hock. Subs (all used): 32 Liam Hood; 20 Sam Hopkins; 29 Jake Emmitt; 17 Jamie Acton.
Tries: Kay (16), Drinkwater (38), Higson (43), Higham (78);
Goals: Reynolds 4/5.
Rugby Leaguer & League Express Men of the Match: *Bulls:* Mitch Clark; *Centurions:* Ben Reynolds.
Penalty count: 10-10; **Half-time:** 10-10;
Referee: Sam Ansell.

Attendance: 9,521 *(at Bloomfield Road, Blackpool)*.

Sunday 29th May 2016

BATLEY BULLDOGS 28 DEWSBURY RAMS 24

BULLDOGS: 22 Dave Scott; 2 Wayne Reittie; 30 Greg Minikin; 3 Chris Ulugia; 5 Shaun Ainscough; 6 Cain Southernwood; 7 Dominic Brambani; 8 Keegan Hirst; 20 Alistair Leak; 15 Adam Gledhill; 24 James Harrison; 17 Joe Chandler; 9 Luke Blake. Subs (all used): 13 Pat Walker; 18 Tom Lillycrop; 21 James Brown; 29 Frankie Mariano.
Tries: Ulugia (19), Minikin (25), J Brown (50), Lillycrop (55);
Goals: Brambani 0/1, Walker 5/5;
Field goals: Walker (74), Brambani (79).
RAMS: 1 Josh Guzdek; 2 Dale Morton; 38 Etuate Uaisele; 15 Jason Crookes; 5 Dalton Grant; 6 Paul Sykes; 22 Andy Kain; 8 Matt Groat; 25 Joel Farrell; 32 Kyle Trout; 4 Shane Grady; 11 Rob Spicer; 14 Luke Adamson. Subs (all used): 9 Tom Hemingway; 13 Aaron Brown; 27 Jason Muranka; 24 Jack Teanby.
Tries: Crookes (4), Sykes (13), Morton (39), Grant (62);
Goals: Sykes 4/5.
Rugby Leaguer & League Express Men of the Match: *Bulldogs:* James Brown; *Rams:* Joel Farrell.
Penalty count: 12-11; **Half-time:** 12-18;
Referee: Tom Grant.

OLDHAM 24 SWINTON LIONS 25

OLDHAM: - Jared Simpson; 2 Adam Clay; 9 Sam Gee; 15 Liam Johnson; 4 Jack Holmes; 6 Lewis Palfrey; 20 Gareth Owen; - Tom Spencer; 21 Kenny Hughes; 23 Tyler Dickinson; 12 Danny Langtree; 16 Gary Middlehurst; 24 Will Hope. Subs (all used): 26 Michael Ward; 14 Joe Burke; 19 Adam Files; 13 Liam Thompson.
Tries: Hughes (9), Langtree (12), Files (39), Clay (76);
Goals: Palfrey 4/5.
LIONS: 22 Gabriel Fell; 2 Shaun Robinson; 3 Stuart Littler; 4 Macauley Hallett; 18 Liam Marshall; 6 Ben White; 1 Chris Atkin; 16 Ben Austin; 9 Anthony Nicholson; 29 Daniel Fleming; 23 Rhodri Lloyd; 11 Connor Dwyer; 19 Josh Barlow. Subs (all used): 7 Matty Beharrell; 12 Andy Thornley; 13 Rob Lever; - Andy Bracek.
Tries: Hallett (43), Atkin (45), Lloyd (65), Beharrell (68);
Goals: Atkin 4/4; **Field goal:** Beharrell (78).
Rugby Leaguer & League Express Men of the Match: *Oldham:* Danny Langtree; *Lions:* Matty Beharrell.
Penalty count: 8-9; **Half-time:** 20-0;
Referee: Warren Turley.

FEATHERSTONE ROVERS 0 HALIFAX 37

ROVERS: 1 Danny Craven; 29 Luke Briscoe; 15 Ian Hardman; 4 Misi Taulapapa; 27 Jamie Foster; 6 Kyle Briggs; 7 Anthony Thackeray; 8 Darrell Griffin; 23 Andy Ellis; 32 Jordan Baldwinson; 18 Jamie Cording; 12 John Davies; 13 Tim Spears. Subs (all used): 16 Colton Roche; 17 Jack Ormondroyd; 28 Jordan Abdull; 24 Robbie Ward.
Sin bin:
Taulapapa (44) - kicking the ball free in the act of scoring.
HALIFAX: 18 Miles Greenwood; 5 James Saltonstall; 4 Ben Heaton; 3 Steve Tyrer; 2 Will Sharp; 7 Gareth Moore; 6 Scott Murrell; 8 Mitch Cahalane; 9 Ben Kaye; 14 Adam Tangata; 11 Dane Manning; 33 Matt Sarsfield; 13 Jacob Fairbank. Subs (all used): 1 Ben Johnston; 10 Luke Ambler; 16 Richard Moore; 34 Ryan Boyle.
Tries: Tangata (5), G Moore (9), Sarsfield (32), Johnston (35), Saltonstall (56), Tyrer (62);
Goals: Tyrer 6/7; **Field goal:** G Moore (29).
Rugby Leaguer & League Express Men of the Match: *Rovers:* John Davies; *Halifax:* Ben Kaye.
Penalty count: 10-9; **Half-time:** 0-27;
Referee: Chris Campbell.

Attendance: 6,391 *(at Bloomfield Road, Blackpool)*.

Leigh's Lee Smith brought down by Bradford's Jay Pitts and Tom Olbison at the Summer Bash

ROUND 16

Saturday 4th June 2016

WHITEHAVEN 12 LEIGH CENTURIONS 36

WHITEHAVEN: 1 Louis Jouffret; 25 Ryan Ince; 28 Ed Chamberlain; 16 Connor Holliday; 2 Craig Calvert; 6 Dion Aiye; 7 Grant Gore; 32 Anthony Walker; 14 Thomas Coyle; 31 Ryan Duffy; 30 Ugo Perez; 17 Steve Fox; 21 John-Paul Brocklebank. Subs (all used): 4 Jessie Joe Parker; 15 Ben Davies; 13 Liam Carberry; 26 Ted Chapelhow.
Tries: Brocklebank (17), Jouffret (39); **Goals:** Jouffret 2/2.
Sin bin: Calvert (68) - dissent.
CENTURIONS: 26 Lee Smith; 2 Adam Higson; 3 Greg Worthington; 24 Tom Armstrong; 5 Liam Kay; 31 Ben Reynolds; 36 Josh Drinkwater; 8 Fuifui Moimoi; 32 Liam Hood; 10 Dayne Weston; 16 Reni Maitua; 13 Cory Paterson; 11 Harrison Hansen. Subs (all used): 35 Brad Fash; 20 Sam Hopkins; 38 Travis Burns; 27 Richard Whiting.
Tries: Drinkwater (5), Higson (10), Burns (48, 66), Paterson (68), Worthington (79);
Goals: Reynolds 3/3, Burns 3/3.
Sin bin: Weston (38) - use of the knees.
Rugby Leaguer & League Express Men of the Match:
Whitehaven: Ugo Perez; *Centurions:* Travis Burns.
Penalty count: 11-7; **Half-time:** 12-12;
Referee: Jon Roberts; **Attendance:** 782.

Sunday 5th June 2016

BATLEY BULLDOGS 42 OLDHAM 18

BULLDOGS: 22 Dave Scott; 2 Wayne Reittie; 3 Chris Ulugia; 30 Greg Minikin; 26 Alex Brown; 6 Cain Southernwood; 7 Dominic Brambani; 8 Keegan Hirst; 20 Alistair Leak; 15 Adam Gledhill; 17 Joe Chandler; 19 Alex Bretherton; 9 Luke Blake. Subs (all used): 14 James Davey; 18 Tom Lillycrop; 13 Pat Walker; 21 James Brown.
Tries: Blake (20), J Brown (29, 39), Reittie (33), Brambani (48, 77), Minikin (70);
Goals: Brambani 1/1, Walker 6/6.
Rugby Leaguer & League Express Men of the Match:
Bulldogs: James Brown; *Oldham:* Steve Roper.
Penalty count: 7-7; **Half-time:** 24-6;
Referee: Sam Ansell; **Attendance:** 783.
OLDHAM: 6 Lewis Palfrey; 2 Adam Clay; 15 Liam Johnson; - Sam Wood; 4 Jack Holmes; 7 Steve Roper; 20 Gareth Owen; 8 Phil Joy; 21 Kenny Hughes; - Tom Spencer; 16 Gary Middlehurst; 12 Danny Langtree; 13 Liam Thompson. Subs (all used): 26 Michael Ward; 14 Joe Burke; 19 Adam Files; 9 Sam Gee.
Tries: Hughes (7), Wood (56), Middlehurst (79);
Goals: Palfrey 3/3.

BRADFORD BULLS 14 DEWSBURY RAMS 16

BULLS: 22 James Clare; 2 Omari Caro; 24 Lucas Walshaw; 4 Kris Welham; 5 Danny Williams; 34 Richard Mathers; 1 Oscar Thomas; 19 Steve Crossley; 13 Danny Addy; 20 Mitch Clark; 11 Tom Olbison; 12 Dale Ferguson; 14 Jay Pitts. Subs (all used): 9 Adam O'Brien; 10 Adam Sidlow; 21 Epalahame Lauaki; 28 Kurt Haggerty.
Tries: Pitts (25), O'Brien (61); **Goals:** Addy 3/4.
RAMS: 1 Josh Guzdek; 2 Dale Morton; 15 Jason Crookes; 4 Shane Grady; 5 Dalton Grant; 6 Paul Sykes; 22 Andy Kain; 8 Matt Groat; 17 Dom Speakman; 32 Kyle Trout; 11 Rob Spicer; 12 Scott Hale; 14 Luke Adamson. Subs (all used): 13 Aaron Brown; 19 Nathan Conroy; 27 Jason Muranka; 10 Ryan Hepworth.
Tries: Grady (20), Guzdek (36); **Goals:** Sykes 4/4.
Sin bin: Conroy (79) - interference.
Rugby Leaguer & League Express Men of the Match:
Bulls: Adam O'Brien; *Rams:* Paul Sykes.
Penalty count: 16-8; **Half-time:** 6-14;
Referee: Warren Turley; **Attendance:** 4,303.

FEATHERSTONE ROVERS 58 SWINTON LIONS 12

ROVERS: 1 Danny Craven; 2 Kyran Johnson; 15 Ian Hardman; 18 Jamie Cording; 25 Liam Blockley; 6 Kyle Briggs; 7 Anthony Thackeray; 8 Darrell Griffin; 23 Andy Ellis; 32 Jordan Baldwinson; 13 Tim Spears; 12 John Davies; 21 Bradley Knowles-Tagg. Subs (all used): 16 Colton Roche; 17 Jack Ormondroyd; 10 Andrew Bostock; 8 Darrell Griffin.
Tries: Baldwinson (4, 16), Craven (27, 60), Davies (44), Cording (49), Briggs (57), Johnson (74), Knowles-Tagg (75), Hardman (80); **Goals:** Briggs 6/7, Craven 3/3.
Sin bin: Knowles-Tagg (22) - fighting.
LIONS: 22 Gabriel Fell; 2 Shaun Robinson; 3 Stuart Littler; 4 Macauley Hallett; 18 Liam Marshall; 1 Chris Atkin; - Jake Shorrocks; - Andy Bracek; 9 Anthony Nicholson; 16 Ben Austin; 23 Rhodri Lloyd; - Nick Gregson; 12 Andy Thornley. Subs (all used): 7 Matty Beharrell; 11 Connor Dwyer; 10 Jordan Hand; 28 Zach Johnson.
Tries: Gregson (9), Marshall (23); **Goals:** Atkin 2/2.
Sin bin: Robinson (22) - fighting;
Beharrell (69) - interference.
Rugby Leaguer & League Express Men of the Match:
Rovers: Kyle Briggs; *Lions:* Anthony Nicholson.
Penalty count: 13-7; **Half-time:** 16-12;
Referee: Tom Grant; **Attendance:** 1,381.

HALIFAX 60 SHEFFIELD EAGLES 22

HALIFAX: 18 Miles Greenwood; 2 Will Sharp; 3 Steve Tyrer; 4 Ben Heaton; 5 James Saltonstall; 7 Gareth Moore; 6 Scott Murrell; 8 Mitch Cahalane; 9 Ben Kaye; 14 Adam Tangata; 11 Dane Manning; 33 Matt Sarsfield; 13 Jacob Fairbank. Subs (all used): 1 Ben Johnston; 10 Luke Ambler; 16 Richard Moore; 34 Ryan Boyle.
Tries: Tangata (2), G Moore (16, 37, 64), Sarsfield (27, 47, 50), Sharp (42), Greenwood (60), Fairbank (70); **Goals:** Tyrer 10/10.
EAGLES: 1 Quentin Laulu-Togagae; 2 Rob Worrincy; 3 Menzie Yere; 5 Ben Blackmore; 22 Ryan Millar; 6 Cory Aston; 24 Rhys Jacks; 15 Scott Wheeldon; 9 Keal Carlile; 16 Adam Neal; 11 Michael Knowles; 4 George Tyson; 13

Matt James. Subs (all used): 17 Mark Mexico; 18 Eliot Minchella; 20 Jack Blagbrough; 21 Dave Hewitt.
Tries: Blackmore (12, 74), James (55), Millar (57); **Goals:** Aston 3/4.
Sin bin: Wheeldon (61) - dissent.
Rugby Leaguer & League Express Men of the Match:
Halifax: Ben Heaton; *Eagles:* Quentin Laulu-Togagae.
Penalty count: 3-8; **Half-time:** 24-4;
Referee: Scott Mikalauskas; **Attendance:** 1,680.

LONDON BRONCOS 50 WORKINGTON TOWN 28

BRONCOS: 32 Elliot Kear; 2 Rhys Williams; 1 Ben Hellewell; 21 Alex Foster; 5 Iliess Macani; 26 Api Pewhairangi; 20 Scott Leatherbarrow; 8 Nick Slyney; 14 Andy Ackers; 17 Mark Offerdahl; 11 Daniel Harrison; 12 Matt Garside; 15 Jack Bussey. Subs (all used): 9 James Cunningham; 23 Jon Magrin; 16 Mark Ioane; 10 Eddie Battye.
Tries: Leatherbarrow (3), Pewhairangi (9), Foster (20), Ackers (25), Kear (29, 51), Ioane (37), Cunningham (53), Williams (64); **Goals:** Pewhairangi 7/9.
TOWN: 1 Jack Murphy; 2 Sam Forrester; 3 Declan Hulme; 4 Jason Mossop; 5 Brett Carter; 7 Jamie Doran; 28 Jarrod Sammut; 18 Tom Walker; 14 Callum Phillips; 21 Oliver Gordon; 25 Matty Gee; 13 Liam McAvoy; 9 Graeme Mattinson. Subs (all used): 24 Theerapol Ritson; 6 Carl Forber; 17 Alex Szostak; 19 Ryan Verlinden.
Tries: Carter (9), J Murphy (12), Gee (46), Sammut (71), Gordon (75); **Goals:** Sammut 4/5.
Rugby Leaguer & League Express Men of the Match:
Broncos: Api Pewhairangi; *Town:* Jack Murphy.
Penalty count: 8-6; **Half-time:** 34-12;
Referee: Andrew Bentham; **Attendance:** 650.

ROUND 17

Friday 10th June 2016

SHEFFIELD EAGLES 10 BATLEY BULLDOGS 24

EAGLES: 1 Quentin Laulu-Togagae; 2 Rob Worrincy; 3 Menzie Yere; 5 Ben Blackmore; 22 Ryan Millar; 6 Cory Aston; 24 Rhys Jacks; 8 Steve Thorpe; 9 Keal Carlile; 16 Adam Neal; 13 Matt James; 12 Duane Straugheir; 11 Michael Knowles. Subs (all used): 14 Matty Fozard; 15 Scott Wheeldon; 4 George Tyson; 17 Mark Mexico.
Tries: Laulu-Togagae (11), Tyson (47); **Goals:** Aston 1/2.
BULLDOGS: 22 Dave Scott; 2 Wayne Reittie; 30 Greg Minikin; 3 Chris Ulugia; 26 Alex Brown; 6 Cain Southernwood; 7 Dominic Brambani; 8 Keegan Hirst; 14 James Davey; 15 Adam Gledhill; 17 Joe Chandler; 19 Alex Bretherton; 9 Luke Blake. Subs (all used): 11 Brad Day; 13 Pat Walker; 18 Tom Lillycrop; 21 James Brown.
Tries: Hirst (23), Minikin (40), Reittie (53), Chandler (73); **Goals:** Walker 4/5.
Rugby Leaguer & League Express Men of the Match:
Eagles: Steve Thorpe; *Bulldogs:* Keegan Hirst.
Penalty count: 11-10; **Half-time:** 6-14;
Referee: Callum Straw; **Attendance:** 651.

Championship 2016 - Round by Round

Saturday 11th June 2016

WHITEHAVEN 12 HALIFAX 12

WHITEHAVEN: 1 Louis Jouffret; 25 Ryan Ince; 28 Ed Chamberlain; 16 Connor Holliday; 2 Craig Calvert; 6 Dion Aiye; 7 Grant Gore; 32 Anthony Walker; 14 Thomas Coyle; 31 Ryan Duffy; 30 Ugo Perez; 11 Dave Allen; 21 John-Paul Brocklebank. Subs (all used): 19 Glenn Riley; 17 Steve Fox; 13 Liam Carberry; 26 Ted Chapelhow.
Tries: Chamberlain (30), Holliday (43); **Goals:** Jouffret 2/3.
HALIFAX: 18 Miles Greenwood; 2 Will Sharp; 3 Steve Tyrer; 4 Ben Heaton; 25 Jake Eccleston; 7 Gareth Moore; 6 Scott Murrell; 8 Mitch Cahalane; 9 Ben Kaye; 14 Adam Tangata; 11 Dane Manning; 33 Matt Sarsfield; 13 Jacob Fairbank. Subs (all used): 1 Ben Johnston; 10 Luke Ambler; 12 Simon Grix; 34 Ryan Boyle.
Tries: Sharp (52), G Moore (79); **Goals:** Tyrer 2/2.
Rugby Leaguer & League Express Men of the Match: *Whitehaven:* Grant Gore; *Halifax:* Will Sharp.
Penalty count: 6-13; **Half time:** 6-0;
Referee: Tom Grant; **Attendance:** 667.

Sunday 12th June 2016

DEWSBURY RAMS 46 OLDHAM 10

RAMS: 1 Josh Guzdek; 2 Dale Morton; 15 Jason Crookes; 4 Shane Grady; 5 Dalton Grant; 6 Paul Sykes; 22 Andy Kain; 8 Matt Groat; 17 Dom Speakman; 32 Kyle Trout; 12 Scott Hale; 11 Rob Spicer; 14 Luke Adamson. Subs (all used): 19 Nathan Conroy; 13 Aaron Brown; 10 Ryan Hepworth; 38 Etuate Uaisele.
Tries: Grant (6), Speakman (16), Crookes (32), Uaisele (43), Spicer (53), Kain (61), Morton (64); **Goals:** Sykes 9/9.
OLDHAM: - Darnell McIntosh; 2 Adam Clay; 15 Liam Johnson; - Sam Wood; 5 Jamel Chisholm; 7 Steve Roper; 20 Gareth Owen; 8 Phil Joy; - Lewis Foster; - Tom Spencer; 16 Gary Middlehurst; 12 Danny Langtree; 13 Liam Thompson. Subs (all used): 14 Joe Burke; 21 Kenny Hughes; 26 Michael Ward; 22 Danny Grimshaw.
Tries: Burke (48), Chisholm (72);
Goals: Roper 1/1, Wood 0/1.
Sin bin: Owen (60) - high tackle.
Rugby Leaguer & League Express Men of the Match: *Rams:* Paul Sykes; *Oldham:* Michael Ward.
Penalty count: 15-9; **Half-time:** 22-0;
Referee: Joe Cobb; **Attendance:** 742.

LEIGH CENTURIONS 16 FEATHERSTONE ROVERS 12

CENTURIONS: 26 Lee Smith; 2 Adam Higson; 24 Tom Armstrong; 3 Greg Worthington; 5 Liam Kay; 38 Travis Burns; 36 Josh Drinkwater; 8 Fuifui Moimoi; 32 Liam Hood; 10 Dayne Weston; 16 Reni Maitua; 13 Cory Paterson; 11 Harrison Hansen. Subs (all used): 20 Sam Hopkins; 31 Ben Reynolds; 35 Brad Fash; 37 Ben Evans.
Tries: Kay (23), Worthington (53), Armstrong (76);
Goals: Burns 1/3, Drinkwater 1/1.
ROVERS: 1 Danny Craven; 2 Kyran Johnson; 15 Ian Hardman; 18 Jamie Cording; 27 Jamie Foster; 6 Kyle Briggs; 7 Anthony Thackeray; 8 Darrell Griffin; 23 Andy Ellis; 32 Jordan Baldwinson; 13 Tim Spears; 12 John Davies; 21 Bradley Knowles-Tagg. Subs (all used): 16 Colton Roche; 17 Jack Ormondroyd; 10 Andrew Bostock; 24 Robbie Ward.
Tries: Ellis (28), Knowles-Tagg (78); **Goals:** Foster 2/3.
Rugby Leaguer & League Express Men of the Match: *Centurions:* Harrison Hansen; *Rovers:* Tim Spears.
Penalty count: 7-11; **Half-time:** 6-4;
Referee: Sam Ansell; **Attendance:** 3,503.

SWINTON LIONS 16 LONDON BRONCOS 42

LIONS: 22 Gabriel Fell; 2 Shaun Robinson; 3 Stuart Littler; 4 Macauley Hallett; 18 Liam Marshall; 6 Ben White; 1 Chris Atkin; 8 Mike Morrison; 7 Matty Beharrell; 10 Jordan Hand; 23 Rhodri Lloyd; 11 Connor Dwyer; 12 Andy Thornley. Subs (all used): - Andy Bracek; 13 Rob Lever; - Kyle Shelford; 27 Vila Halafihi.
Tries: Robinson (38), Hallett (47), Lever (80);
Goals: Atkin 2/3.
BRONCOS: 32 Elliot Kear; 2 Rhys Williams; 1 Ben Hellewell; 21 Alex Foster; 4 Wes Naiqama; 26 Api Pewhairangi; 20 Scott Leatherbarrow; 8 Nick Slyney; 14 Andy Ackers; 16 Mark Ioane; 11 Daniel Harrison; 12 Matt Garside; 15 Jack Bussey. Subs (all used): 9 James Cunningham; 18 Jamie Thackray; 10 Eddie Battye; 17 Mark Offerdahl.
Tries: Harrison (12), Slyney (19, 64), Offerdahl (28), Pewhairangi (33, 76), Hellewell (67);
Goals: Naiqama 5/5, Pewhairangi 2/2.
Sin bin:
Naiqama (62) - dangerous challenge on Marshall.
Rugby Leaguer & League Express Men of the Match: *Lions:* Vila Halafihi; *Broncos:* Api Pewhairangi.
Penalty count: 9-8; **Half-time:** 4-24;
Referee: Scott Mikalauskas; **Attendance:** 485.

WORKINGTON TOWN 22 BRADFORD BULLS 29

TOWN: 1 Jack Murphy; 2 Sam Forrester; 3 Declan Hulme; 4 Jason Mossop; 24 Theerapol Ritson; 7 Jamie Doran; 28 Jarrod Sammut; 8 Kris Coward; 14 Callum Phillips; 21 Oliver Gordon; 13 Liam McAvoy; 25 Matty Gee; 9 Graeme Mattinson. Subs (all used): 6 Carl Forber; 20 Steve Scholey; 10 Marc Shackley; 19 Ryan Verlinden.
Tries: Sammut (10, 47), Forrester (38), Hulme (53);
Goals: Sammut 3/4.
BULLS: 39 Kieren Moss; 29 Ethan Ryan; 4 Kris Welham; 37 Ross Oakes; 22 James Clare; 13 Danny Addy; 40 Lewis Charnock; 20 Mitch Clark; 9 Adam O'Brien; 10 Adam Sidlow; 23 Alex Mellor; 12 Dale Ferguson; 14 Jay Pitts. Subs (all used): 30 Joe Lumb; 8 Paul Clough; 21 Epalahame Lauaki; 28 Kurt Haggerty.
Tries: O'Brien (8), Ryan (18), Sidlow (22), Clare (64), Charnock (73); **Goals:** Addy 4/5; **Field goal:** Addy (77).
Rugby Leaguer & League Express Men of the Match: *Town:* Jarrod Sammut; *Bulls:* Danny Addy.
Penalty count: 8-10; **Half-time:** 10-18;
Referee: Andrew Sweet; **Attendance:** 723.

ROUND 5

Wednesday 15th June 2016

OLDHAM 4 BRADFORD BULLS 48

OLDHAM: 9 Sam Gee; 2 Adam Clay; 15 Liam Johnson; - Sam Wood; 5 Jamel Chisholm; 6 Lewis Palfrey; 20 Gareth Owen; 8 Phil Joy; 17 Lewis Foster; 14 Joe Burke; 12 Danny Langtree; 16 Gary Middlehurst; 24 Will Hope. Subs (all used): 26 Michael Ward; 13 Liam Thompson; 21 Kenny Hughes; 23 Craig Briscoe.
Try: Wood (77); **Goals:** Palfrey 0/1.
BULLS: 22 James Clare; 32 Johnny Campbell; 4 Kris Welham; 24 Lucas Walshaw; 29 Ethan Ryan; 1 Oscar Thomas; 40 Lewis Charnock; 19 Steve Crossley; 9 Adam O'Brien; 10 Adam Sidlow; 23 Alex Mellor; 28 Kurt Haggerty; 11 Tom Olbison. Subs (all used): 30 Joe Lumb; 20 Mitch Clark; 14 Jay Pitts; 27 Jonathan Walker.
Tries: Mellor (5), Thomas (7), Campbell (14), Charnock (34), Clark (47), O'Brien (51), Clare (61, 72), Pitts (74);
Goals: Thomas 6/8, Haggerty 0/1.
Rugby Leaguer & League Express Men of the Match: *Oldham:* Sam Gee; *Bulls:* Oscar Thomas.
Penalty count: 4-11; **Half-time:** 0-20;
Referee: Callum Straw; **Attendance:** 1,051.

ROUND 18

Sunday 19th June 2016

BRADFORD BULLS 17 BATLEY BULLDOGS 16

BULLS: 39 Kieren Moss; 22 James Clare; 24 Lucas Walshaw; 4 Kris Welham; 5 Danny Williams; 28 Kurt Haggerty; 40 Lewis Charnock; 10 Adam Sidlow; 9 Adam O'Brien; 20 Mitch Clark; 23 Alex Mellor; 14 Jay Pitts; 8 Paul Clough. Subs (all used): 11 Tom Olbison; 19 Steve Crossley; 21 Epalahame Lauaki; 30 Joe Lumb.
Tries: Clare (16, 21), Pitts (67); **Goals:** Haggerty 2/4;
Field goal: Haggerty (76).
BULLDOGS: 22 Dave Scott; 2 Wayne Reittie; 30 Greg Minikin; 3 Chris Ulugia; 26 Alex Brown; 6 Cain Southernwood; 7 Dominic Brambani; 8 Keegan Hirst; 14 James Davey; 15 Adam Gledhill; 17 Joe Chandler; 19 Alex Bretherton; 9 Luke Blake. Subs (all used): 13 Pat Walker; 18 Tom Lillycrop; 21 James Brown; 11 Brad Day.
Tries: Southernwood (28, 71), Ulugia (35);
Goals: Walker 2/4.
Rugby Leaguer & League Express Men of the Match: *Bulls:* Jay Pitts; *Bulldogs:* James Brown.
Penalty count: 10-5; **Half-time:** 8-10;
Referee: Joe Cobb; **Attendance:** 4,617.

DEWSBURY RAMS 8 HALIFAX 24

RAMS: 1 Josh Guzdek; 2 Dale Morton; 15 Jason Crookes; 4 Shane Grady; 5 Dalton Grant; 6 Paul Sykes; 22 Andy Kain; 8 Matt Groat; 17 Dom Speakman; 33 Paul Jackson; 12 Scott Hale; 27 Jason Muranka; 14 Luke Adamson. Subs (all used): 19 Nathan Conroy; 24 Jack Teanby; 3 Karl Pryce; 18 Tony Tonks.
Tries: Hale (28), Morton (32); **Goals:** Sykes 0/2.
Sin bin: Groat (57) - fighting.
HALIFAX: 1 Ben Johnston; 5 James Saltonstall; 4 Ben Heaton; 3 Steve Tyrer; 2 Will Sharp; 7 Gareth Moore; 6 Scott Murrell; 8 Mitch Cahalane; 9 Ben Kaye; 14 Adam Tangata; 11 Dane Manning; 33 Matt Sarsfield; 13 Jacob Fairbank. Subs (all used): 10 Luke Ambler; 12 Simon Grix; 22 Connor Robinson; 34 Ryan Boyle.
Tries: G Moore (36), Saltonstall (39), Cahalane (49), C Robinson (75); **Goals:** Tyrer 4/5.
Sin bin: Cahalane (57) - fighting.
Rugby Leaguer & League Express Men of the Match: *Rams:* Scott Hale; *Halifax:* Scott Murrell.
Penalty count: 6-10; **Half-time:** 8-10;
Referee: Michael Woodhead; **Attendance:** 1,146.

FEATHERSTONE ROVERS 30 WHITEHAVEN 18

ROVERS: 1 Danny Craven; 33 James Duckworth; 3 Michael Channing; 18 Jamie Cording; 27 Jamie Foster; 6 Kyle Briggs; 35 Jordan Lilley; 10 Andrew Bostock; 23 Andy Ellis; 32 Jordan Baldwinson; 11 Steve Snitch; 13 Tim Spears; 21 Bradley Knowles-Tagg. Subs (all used): 8 Darrell Griffin; 20 Luke Cooper; 17 Jack Ormondroyd; 24 Robbie Ward.
Tries: Briggs (35), Lilley (53), Ormondroyd (67), Griffin (72), Foster (76); **Goals:** Foster 5/6.
WHITEHAVEN: 4 Jessie Joe Parker; 20 Jordan Burns; 16 Connor Holliday; 28 Ed Chamberlain; 25 Ryan Ince; 6 Dion Aiye; 1 Louis Jouffret; 31 Ryan Duffy; 14 Thomas Coyle; 32 Anthony Walker; 11 Dave Allen; 30 Ugo Perez; 21 John-Paul Brocklebank. Subs (all used): 13 Liam Carberry; 26 Ted Chapelhow; 19 Glenn Riley; 15 Ben Davies.
Tries: Walker (25), Burns (60), Parker (80);
Goals: Jouffret 1/1, Chamberlain 2/2.
Dismissal: Allen (16) - dissent.
Sin bin: Allen (16) - dissent.
Rugby Leaguer & League Express Men of the Match: *Rovers:* Jordan Baldwinson; *Whitehaven:* Ryan Duffy.
Penalty count: 12-3; **Half-time:** 8-6;
Referee: Callum Straw; **Attendance:** 1,456.

LEIGH CENTURIONS 54 WORKINGTON TOWN 12

CENTURIONS: 26 Lee Smith; 2 Adam Higson; 24 Tom Armstrong; 3 Greg Worthington; 5 Liam Kay; 36 Josh Drinkwater; 38 Travis Burns; 8 Fuifui Moimoi; 31 Ben Reynolds; 10 Dayne Weston; 16 Reni Maitua; 13 Cory Paterson; 37 Ben Evans. Subs (all used): 6 Martyn Ridyard; 11 Harrison Hansen; 35 Brad Fash; 18 Tom Spencer.
Tries: Reynolds (14, 75), Worthington (18), Drinkwater (20, 56), Kay (35), Spencer (61), Higson (70), Paterson (77); **Goals:** Smith 9/9.
TOWN: 1 Jack Murphy; 24 Theerapol Ritson; 3 Declan Hulme; 16 Perry Whiteley; 4 Jason Mossop; 7 Jamie Doran; 28 Jarrod Sammut; 21 Oliver Gordon; 14 Callum Phillips; 10 Marc Shackley; 11 Brett Phillips; 25 Matty Gee; 13 Liam McAvoy. Subs (all used): 9 Graeme Mattinson; 15 Karl Olstrum; 17 Alex Szostak; 19 Ryan Verlinden.
Tries: Mossop (45), Whiteley (52); **Goals:** Sammut 2/2.
Rugby Leaguer & League Express Men of the Match: *Centurions:* Ben Reynolds; *Town:* Jason Mossop.
Penalty count: 6-4; **Half-time:** 24-0;
Referee: Scott Mikalauskas; **Attendance:** 3,002.

LONDON BRONCOS 56 OLDHAM 16

BRONCOS: 32 Elliot Kear; 2 Rhys Williams; 1 Ben Hellewell; 21 Alex Foster; 5 Iliess Macani; 26 Api Pewhairangi; 20 Scott Leatherbarrow; 8 Nick Slyney; 9 James Cunningham; 16 Mark Ioane; 11 Daniel Harrison; 12 Matt Garside; 17 Mark Offerdahl. Subs (all used): 6 Israel Eliab; 23 Jon Magrin; 10 Eddie Battye; 18 Jamie Thackray.
Tries: Harrison (7), Kear (15, 24), Williams (17, 33, 36), Macani (47, 61), Hellewell (58), Offerdahl (69);
Goals: Pewhairangi 8/10.
OLDHAM: 1 Richard Lepori; 4 Jack Holmes; 9 Sam Gee; 15 Liam Johnson; 5 Jamel Chisholm; - Sam Wood; 20 Gareth Owen; 8 Phil Joy; - Lewis Foster; 14 Joe Burke; 13 Liam Thompson; 12 Danny Langtree; 24 Will Hope. Subs (all used): 26 Michael Ward; 21 Kenny Hughes; 6 Lewis Palfrey; 23 Craig Briscoe.
Tries: Chisholm (44), Holmes (76), Ward (80);
Goals: Palfrey 2/3.
Rugby Leaguer & League Express Men of the Match: *Broncos:* Elliot Kear; *Oldham:* Lewis Palfrey.
Penalty count: 4-9; **Half-time:** 34-0;
Referee: Jamie Bloem; **Attendance:** 425.

SWINTON LIONS 22 SHEFFIELD EAGLES 18

LIONS: 22 Gabriel Fell; 2 Shaun Robinson; 23 Rhodri Lloyd; 4 Macaulay Hallett; 18 Liam Marshall; 6 Ben White; 1 Chris Atkin; 10 Jordan Hand; 7 Matty Beharrell; 13 Rob Lever; 12 Andy Thornley; 11 Connor Dwyer; 29 Daniel Fleming. Subs (all used): - Andy Bracek; 16 Ben Austin; 19 Josh Barlow; 27 Vila Halafihi.
Tries: Lloyd (5, 60), Dwyer (70); **Goals:** Atkin 5/5.
Sin bin: Hallett (54) - punching.
EAGLES: 1 Quentin Laulu-Togagae; 2 Rob Worrincy; 3 Menzie Yere; 4 George Tyson; 5 Ben Blackmore; 6 Cory Aston; 21 Dave Hewitt; 8 Steve Thorpe; 9 Keal Carlile; 17 Mark Mexico; 13 Matt James; 12 Duane Straugheir; 11 Michael Knowles. Subs (all used): 14 Matty Fozard; 15 Scott Wheeldon; 16 Adam Neal; 18 Elliot Minchella.
Tries: Neal (29), Blackmore (31), Laulu-Togagae (42);
Goals: Aston 3/4.
Dismissal: Tyson (54) - dangerous challenge on Atkin.

Rugby Leaguer & League Express Men of the Match:
Lions: Rob Lever; *Eagles:* Matt James.
Penalty count: 12-10; **Half-time:** 10-12;
Referee: Tom Grant; **Attendance:** 551.

ROUND 19

Friday 24th June 2016

SHEFFIELD EAGLES 35 FEATHERSTONE ROVERS 10

EAGLES: 1 Quentin Laulu-Togagae; 19 Garry Lo; 3 Menzie Yere; 25 Nathan Chappell; 5 Ben Blackmore; 6 Cory Aston; 14 Matty Fozard; 8 Steve Thorpe; 9 Keal Carlile; 15 Scott Wheeldon; 13 Matt James; 12 Duane Straugheir; 11 Michael Knowles. Subs (all used): 18 Elliot Minchella; 2 Rob Worrincy; 4 George Tyson; 17 Mark Mexico.
Tries: Aston (11), Wheeldon (18), Blackmore (31, 60), Lo (37), Yere (57), Minchella (76); **Goals:** Aston 3/7;
Field goal: Knowles (67).
Sin bin: Mexico (36) - use of the elbow;
Straugheir (49) - repeated team offences.
ROVERS: 3 Michael Channing; 33 James Duckworth; 18 Jamie Cording; 4 Misi Taulapapa; 27 Jamie Foster; 35 Jordan Lilley; 7 Anthony Thackeray; 8 Darrell Griffin; 23 Andy Ellis; 32 Jordan Baldwinson; 13 Tim Spears; 12 John Davies; 21 Bradley Knowles-Tagg. Subs (all used): 6 Kyle Briggs; 16 Colton Roche; 17 Jack Ormondroyd; 10 Andrew Bostock.
Tries: Cording (40), Duckworth (52); **Goals:** Foster 1/2.
Sin bin: Bostock (75) - interference.
Rugby Leaguer & League Express Men of the Match:
Eagles: Cory Aston; *Rovers:* Anthony Thackeray.
Penalty count: 8-12; **Half-time:** 20-6;
Referee: Andrew Sweet; **Attendance:** 817.

Sunday 26th June 2016

BATLEY BULLDOGS 18 DEWSBURY RAMS 16

BULLDOGS: 22 Dave Scott; 2 Wayne Reittie; 3 Chris Ulugia; 29 Frankie Mariano; 26 Alex Brown; 6 Cain Southernwood; 7 Dominic Brambani; 8 Keegan Hirst; 14 James Davey; 21 James Brown; 19 Alex Bretherton; 17 Joe Chandler; 15 Adam Gledhill. Subs (all used): 10 Alex Rowe; 11 Brad Day; 13 Pat Walker; 18 Tom Lillycrop.
Tries: A Brown (22), Ulugia (24), Bretherton (32);
Goals: Brambani 2/2, Walker 1/3.
Sin bin: Reittie (67) - kicking out.
RAMS: 1 Josh Guzdek; 2 Dale Morton; 42 Lucas Walshaw; 15 Jason Crookes; 5 Dalton Grant; 6 Paul Sykes; 22 Andy Kain; 8 Matt Groat; 17 Dom Speakman; 32 Kyle Trout; 11 Rob Spicer; 12 Scott Hale; 14 Luke Adamson. Subs (all used): 10 Ryan Hepworth; 19 Nathan Conroy; 27 Jason Muranka; 45 Mitchell Stringer.
Tries: Crookes (3), Kain (10), Guzdek (42); **Goals:** Sykes 2/5.
Rugby Leaguer & League Express Men of the Match:
Bulldogs: Dave Scott; *Rams:* Paul Sykes.
Penalty count: 6-6; **Half-time:** 16-10;
Referee: Jack Smith; **Attendance:** 1,501.

BRADFORD BULLS 24 HALIFAX 32

BULLS: 39 Kieren Moss; 22 James Clare; 4 Kris Welham; 15 Matty Blythe; 29 Ethan Ryan; 13 Danny Addy; 40 Lewis Charnock; 8 Paul Clough; 9 Adam O'Brien; 10 Adam Sidlow; 23 Alex Mellor; 28 Kurt Haggerty; 14 Jay Pitts. Subs (all used): 19 Steve Crossley; 25 Ben Kavanagh; 41 Joe Philbin; 42 Stuart Howarth.
Tries: Moss (6), Haggerty (51), Welham (77), Ryan (80);
Goals: Addy 4/4.
HALIFAX: 1 Ben Johnston; 2 Will Sharp; 4 Ben Heaton; 3 Steve Tyrer; 5 James Saltonstall; 7 Gareth Moore; 6 Scott Murrell; 8 Mitch Cahalane; 9 Ben Kaye; 14 Adam Tangata; 12 Simon Grix; 33 Matt Sarsfield; 13 Jacob Fairbank. Subs (all used): 10 Luke Ambler; 22 Connor Robinson; 26 Ed Barber; 34 Ryan Boyle.
Tries: Tangata (20), Murrell (35), Saltonstall (48), Fairbank (57), Tyrer (70), Barber (75); **Goals:** Tyrer 4/6.
Rugby Leaguer & League Express Men of the Match:
Bulls: Jay Pitts; *Halifax:* Gareth Moore.
Penalty count: 7-3; **Half-time:** 6-12;
Referee: Chris Kendall; **Attendance:** 6,312.

LONDON BRONCOS 12 LEIGH CENTURIONS 38

BRONCOS: 32 Elliot Kear; 2 Rhys Williams; 1 Ben Hellewell; 21 Alex Foster; 5 Iliess Macani; 26 Api Pewhairangi; 20 Scott Leatherbarrow; 8 Nick Slyney; 9 James Cunningham; 16 Mark Ioane; 11 Daniel Harrison; 12 Matt Garside; 17 Mark Offerdahl. Subs (all used): 15 Jack Bussey; 23 Jon Magrin; 10 Eddie Battye; 18 Jamie Thackray.
Tries: Ioane (43), Pewhairangi (65);
Goals: Pewhairangi 2/2.
Sin bin: Ioane (22) - dangerous challenge on Higson.
On report: Bussey (40) - alleged dangerous challenge.
CENTURIONS: 26 Lee Smith; 2 Adam Higson; 3 Greg Worthington; 24 Tom Armstrong; 5 Liam Kay; 36 Josh Drinkwater; 38 Travis Burns; 8 Fuifui Moimoi; 14 Micky Higham; 10 Dayne Weston; 16 Reni Maitua; 13 Cory Paterson; 12 Gareth Hock. Subs (all used): 32 Liam Hood; 11 Harrison Hansen; 20 Sam Hopkins; 37 Ben Evans.
Tries: Drinkwater (3), Paterson (10, 25), Worthington (35, 72), Kay (39), Higson (58);
Goals: Smith 5/9.
Sin bin: Hood (61) - high tackle on Cunningham.
Rugby Leaguer & League Express Men of the Match:
Broncos: Api Pewhairangi; *Centurions:* Greg Worthington.
Penalty count: 8-10; **Half-time:** 0-28;
Referee: Joe Cobb; **Attendance:** 1,234.

OLDHAM 26 WHITEHAVEN 18

OLDHAM: 1 Richard Lepori; 2 Adam Clay; - Kieran Gill; - Sam Wood; 5 Jamel Chisholm; 22 Danny Grimshaw; 20 Gareth Owen; 8 Phil Joy; 17 Kruise Leeming; 14 Joe Burke; 12 Danny Langtree; 23 Craig Briscoe; 13 Liam Thompson. Subs (all used): 26 Michael Ward; 9 Sam Gee; 10 Jack Spencer; - Lewis Foster.
Tries: Chisholm (20), Langtree (25, 29), Gill (39), Joy (62);
Goals: Wood 3/5.
WHITEHAVEN: 4 Jessie Joe Parker; 25 Ryan Ince; 28 Ed Chamberlain; 16 Connor Holliday; 2 Craig Calvert; 6 Dion Aiye; 7 Grant Gore; 31 Ryan Duffy; 13 Liam Carberry; 32 Anthony Walker; 11 Dave Allen; 17 Steve Fox; 21 John-Paul Brocklebank. Subs (all used): 9 James Newton; 8 Sam Brooks; 19 Glenn Riley; 15 Ben Davies.
Tries: Fox (5), Duffy (7), Parker (74);
Goals: Chamberlain 3/3.
Rugby Leaguer & League Express Men of the Match:
Oldham: Liam Thompson; *Whitehaven:* Steve Fox.
Penalty count: 7-8; **Half-time:** 20-12;
Referee: Scott Mikalauskas; **Attendance:** 516.

WORKINGTON TOWN 10 SWINTON LIONS 10

TOWN: 28 Jarrod Sammut; 4 Jason Mossop; 3 Declan Hulme; 16 Perry Whiteley; 26 John Patrick; 7 Jamie Doran; 6 Carl Forber; 21 Oliver Gordon; 14 Callum Phillips; 10 Marc Shackley; 11 Brett Phillips; 25 Matty Gee; 13 Liam McAvoy. Subs (all used): 9 Graeme Mattinson; 15 Karl Olstrum; 19 Ryan Verlinden; 17 Alex Szostak.
Try: Doran (11); **Goals:** Sammut 3/5.
Sin bin: McAvoy (22) - tripping.
LIONS: 20 Mike Butt; 2 Shaun Robinson; 3 Stuart Littler; 4 Macauley Hallett; 18 Liam Marshall; 6 Ben White; 1 Chris Atkin; 10 Jordan Hand; - Luke Waterworth; 16 Ben Austin; 12 Andy Thornley; 23 Rhodri Lloyd; 13 Rob Lever. Subs (all used): - Andy Bracek; 19 Josh Barlow; 28 Zach Johnson; 7 Matty Beharrell.
Tries: Marshall (14, 77); **Goals:** Atkin 1/3.
Sin bin: Beharrell (39) - delaying restart.
Rugby Leaguer & League Express Men of the Match:
Town: Jarrod Sammut; *Lions:* Liam Marshall.
Penalty count: 12-11; **Half-time:** 6-6;
Referee: Tom Grant; **Attendance:** 593.

ROUND 20

Friday 1st July 2016

SHEFFIELD EAGLES 16 OLDHAM 24

EAGLES: 1 Quentin Laulu-Togagae; 19 Garry Lo; 3 Menzie Yere; 25 Nathan Chappell; 5 Ben Blackmore; 6 Cory Aston; 14 Matty Fozard; 8 Steve Thorpe; 9 Keal Carlile; 15 Scott Wheeldon; 13 Matt James; 12 Duane Straugheir; 11 Michael Knowles. Subs (all used): 18 Elliot Minchella; 26 Stan Robin; 16 Adam Neal; 17 Mark Mexico.
Tries: Aston (2), Laulu-Togagae (24), Robin (56);
Goals: Aston 2/3.
OLDHAM: 1 Richard Lepori; 2 Adam Clay; 22 Danny Grimshaw; - Kieran Gill; 5 Jamel Chisholm; 6 Lewis Palfrey; 20 Gareth Owen; 8 Phil Joy; - Lewis Foster; 14 Joe Burke; 23 Craig Briscoe; 12 Danny Langtree; 13 Liam Thompson. Subs (all used): 26 Michael Ward; 21 Kenny Hughes; - Tyler Dickinson; 24 Will Hope.
Tries: Gill (5), Hughes (31), Thompson (43), Foster (76);
Goals: Palfrey 4/6.
Rugby Leaguer & League Express Men of the Match:
Eagles: Stan Robin; *Oldham:* Kenny Hughes.
Penalty count: 10-11; **Half-time:** 12-14;
Referee: Tom Grant; **Attendance:** 531.

Saturday 2nd July 2016

WHITEHAVEN 8 BATLEY BULLDOGS 16

WHITEHAVEN: 4 Jessie Joe Parker; 25 Ryan Ince; 3 Chris Taylor; 6 Dion Aiye; 2 Craig Calvert; 14 Thomas Coyle; 7 Grant Gore; 19 Glenn Riley; 13 Liam Carberry; 32 Andy Yates; 30 Ugo Perez; 21 John-Paul Brocklebank; 17 Steve Fox. Subs (all used): 16 Connor Holliday; 9 James Newton; 15 Ben Davies; 26 Ted Chapelhow.
Tries: Gore (10), Calvert (65); **Goals:** Brocklebank 0/2.
Sin bin: T Chapelhow (22) - holding down.
BULLDOGS: 22 Dave Scott; 2 Wayne Reittie; 3 Chris Ulugia; 17 Joe Chandler; 5 Shaun Ainscough; 6 Cain Southernwood; 7 Dominic Brambani; 8 Keegan Hirst; 20 Alistair Leak; 21 James Brown; 19 Alex Bretherton; 29 Frankie Mariano; 15 Adam Gledhill. Subs (all used): 14 James Davey; 10 Alex Rowe; 13 Pat Walker; 18 Tom Lillycrop.
Tries: J Brown (23), Reittie (50), Gledhill (61);
Goals: Walker 2/3.
Rugby Leaguer & League Express Men of the Match:
Whitehaven: Grant Gore; *Bulldogs:* Alistair Leak.
Penalty count: 7-10; **Half time:** 4-4;
Referee: Jamie Bloem; **Attendance:** 571.

Sunday 3rd July 2016

DEWSBURY RAMS 6 LONDON BRONCOS 34

RAMS: 1 Josh Guzdek; 2 Dale Morton; 42 Lucas Walshaw; 4 Shane Grady; 15 Jason Crookes; 6 Paul Sykes; 36 Bobbie Goulding; 8 Matt Groat; 17 Dom Speakman; 32 Kyle Trout; 11 Rob Spicer; 12 Scott Hale; 14 Luke Adamson. Subs (all used): 19 Nathan Conroy; 25 Joel Farrell; 45 Mitchell Stringer; 33 Paul Jackson.
Try: Guzdek (68); **Goals:** Sykes 1/1.
BRONCOS: 32 Elliot Kear; 2 Rhys Williams; 1 Ben Hellewell; 6 Israel Eliab; 4 Wes Naiqama; 26 Api Pewhairangi; 20 Scott Leatherbarrow; 18 Jamie Thackray; 14 Andy Ackers; 10 Eddie Battye; 11 Daniel Harrison; 21 Alex Foster; 15 Jack Bussey. Subs (all used): 9 James Cunningham; 12 Matt Garside; 8 Nick Slyney; 16 Mark Ioane.
Tries: Naiqama (15), Eliab (24, 50), Ioane (55), Williams (58), Garside (79); **Goals:** Naiqama 5/6.
Rugby Leaguer & League Express Men of the Match:
Rams: Josh Guzdek; *Broncos:* Israel Eliab.
Penalty count: 10-4; **Half-time:** 0-12;
Referee: Scott Mikalauskas; **Attendance:** 645.

FEATHERSTONE ROVERS 44 WORKINGTON TOWN 22

ROVERS: 15 Ian Hardman; 36 Ash Handley; 3 Michael Channing; 4 Misi Taulapapa; 27 Jamie Foster; 6 Kyle Briggs; 7 Anthony Thackeray; 10 Andrew Bostock; 23 Andy Ellis; 32 Jordan Baldwinson; 18 Jamie Cording; 12 John Davies; 16 Colton Roche. Subs (all used): 8 Darrell Griffin; 13 Tim Spears; 17 Jack Ormondroyd; 24 Robbie Ward.
Tries: Handley (5), Cording (14), Briggs (18), Thackeray (27), Channing (37), Foster (50), Hardman (55), Spears (58); **Goals:** Foster 6/8.
Sin bin: Roche (22) - professional foul.
TOWN: 28 Jarrod Sammut; 24 Theerapol Ritson; 4 Jason Mossop; 25 Matty Gee; 3 Declan Hulme; 6 Carl Forber; 7 Jamie Doran; 21 Oliver Gordon; 14 Callum Phillips; 10 Marc Shackley; 11 Brett Phillips; 13 Liam McAvoy; 20 Steve Scholey. Subs (all used): 19 Ryan Verlinden; 18 Tom Walker; 9 Graeme Mattinson; 17 Alex Szostak.
Tries: Hulme (10, 65), B Phillips (70), Shackley (73);
Goals: Sammut 3/4.
Rugby Leaguer & League Express Men of the Match:
Rovers: Anthony Thackeray; *Town:* Brett Phillips.
Penalty count: 10-12; **Half-time:** 28-4;
Referee: Jon Roberts; **Attendance:** 1,281.

LEIGH CENTURIONS 22 BRADFORD BULLS 20

CENTURIONS: 26 Lee Smith; 2 Adam Higson; 24 Tom Armstrong; 3 Greg Worthington; 5 Liam Kay; 36 Josh Drinkwater; 38 Travis Burns; 8 Fuifui Moimoi; 14 Micky Higham; 10 Dayne Weston; 16 Reni Maitua; 13 Cory Paterson; 12 Gareth Hock. Subs (all used): 6 Martyn Ridyard; 11 Harrison Hansen; 20 Sam Hopkins; 35 Brad Fash.
Tries: Smith (3), Hock (15), Worthington (27), Maitua (78);
Goals: Smith 3/5.
BULLS: 39 Kieren Moss; 22 James Clare; 15 Matty Blythe; 4 Kris Welham; 2 Omari Caro; 13 Danny Addy; 1 Oscar Thomas; 25 Ben Kavanagh; 42 Stuart Howarth; 10 Adam Sidlow; 41 Joe Philbin; 28 Kurt Haggerty; 11 Tom Olbison. Subs (all used): 9 Adam O'Brien; 14 Jay Pitts; 21 Epalahame Lauaki; 23 Alex Mellor.
Tries: Caro (19), Moss (34), Clare (51), Mellor (56);
Goals: Addy 2/4.
Rugby Leaguer & League Express Men of the Match:
Centurions: Lee Smith; *Bulls:* Adam Sidlow.
Penalty count: 5-8; **Half-time:** 16-10;
Referee: Chris Campbell; **Attendance:** 5,111.

SWINTON LIONS 12 HALIFAX 62

LIONS: 22 Gabriel Fell; 2 Shaun Robinson; 3 Stuart Littler; 4 Macauley Hallett; 18 Liam Marshall; 1 Chris Atkin; 7 Matty Beharrell; 29 Daniel Fleming; - Luke Waterworth; 16 Ben Austin; 23 Rhodri Lloyd; 12 Andy Thornley; 13 Rob Lever. Subs (all used): 6 Ben White; 10 Jordan Hand; 19 Josh Barlow; 28 Zach Johnson.
Tries: Lloyd (34), Fell (62); **Goals:** Atkin 1/1, Beharrell 1/1.

Oldham's Kieran Gill makes a break against Swinton

HALIFAX: 1 Ben Johnston; 5 James Saltonstall; 26 Ed Barber; 3 Steve Tyrer; 2 Will Sharp; 7 Gareth Moore; 6 Scott Murrell; 8 Mitch Cahalane; 9 Ben Kaye; 10 Luke Ambler; 12 Simon Grix; 14 Adam Tangata; 13 Jacob Fairbank. Subs (all used): 16 Richard Moore; 17 Gavin Bennion; 22 Connor Robinson; 34 Ryan Boyle.
Tries: Johnston (1, 22), Barber (8, 15, 60), Sharp (30), Murrell (48), G Moore (68), Cahalane (72), Bennion (76), Ambler (80); **Goals:** Tyrer 9/11.
Sin bin: Fairbank (65) - trip on Beharrell.
Rugby Leaguer & League Express Men of the Match: *Lions:* Matty Beharrell; *Halifax:* Scott Murrell.
Penalty count: 6-11; **Half-time:** 6-28;
Referee: Warren Turley; **Attendance:** 1,017.

ROUND 21

Sunday 10th July 2016

BATLEY BULLDOGS 6 FEATHERSTONE ROVERS 34

BULLDOGS: 22 Dave Scott; 2 Wayne Reittie; 17 Joe Chandler; 3 Chris Ulugia; 26 Alex Brown; 6 Cain Southernwood; 7 Dominic Brambani; 8 Keegan Hirst; 20 Alistair Leak; 21 James Brown; 19 Alex Bretherton; 11 Brad Day; 15 Adam Gledhill. Subs (all used): 10 Alex Rowe; 13 Pat Walker; 14 James Davey; 18 Tom Lillycrop.
Try: Ulugia (78); **Goals:** Walker 1/1.
ROVERS: 15 Ian Hardman; 37 Ashton Golding; 3 Michael Channing; 18 Jamie Cording; 4 Misi Taulapapa; 6 Kyle Briggs; 7 Anthony Thackeray; 10 Andrew Bostock; 23 Andy Ellis; 32 Jordan Baldwinson; 11 Steve Snitch; 12 John Davies; 17 Jack Ormondroyd. Subs (all used): 8 Darrell Griffin; 13 Tim Spears; 20 Luke Cooper; 38 Anthony Mullally.
Tries: Bostock (8), Briggs (42), Hardman (47), Golding (50), Channing (53); **Goals:** Briggs 7/7.
Rugby Leaguer & League Express Men of the Match: *Bulldogs:* James Brown; *Rovers:* Andrew Bostock.
Penalty count: 6-8; **Half-time:** 0-10;
Referee: Scott Mikalauskas; **Attendance:** 1,351.

BRADFORD BULLS 64 WHITEHAVEN 18

BULLS: 39 Kieren Moss; 22 James Clare; 15 Matty Blythe; 4 Kris Welham; 29 Ethan Ryan; 40 Lewis Charnock; 7 Dane Chisholm; 25 Ben Kavanagh; 42 Stuart Howarth; 10 Adam Sidlow; 23 Alex Mellor; 28 Kurt Haggerty; 13 Danny Addy. Subs (all used): 9 Adam O'Brien; 14 Jay Pitts; 19 Steve Crossley; 41 Joe Philbin.
Tries: Ryan (3, 30, 42), Sidlow (7), Chisholm (9, 35), Moss (14, 24), Philbin (33), Crossley (39), Clare (46);
Goals: Addy 5/5, Chisholm 2/3, Charnock 3/3.
Sin bin: Welham (53) - punching.
WHITEHAVEN: 7 Grant Gore; 2 Craig Calvert; 16 Connor Holliday; 30 Ugo Perez; 25 Ryan Ince; 21 John-Paul Brocklebank; 14 Thomas Coyle; 31 Ryan Duffy; 13 Liam

Carberry; 19 Glenn Riley; 11 Dave Allen; 17 Steve Fox; 32 Andy Yates. Subs (all used): 26 Ted Chapelhow; 27 Jay Chapelhow; 15 Ben Davies; 9 James Newton.
Tries: J Chapelhow (55), Newton (59), Brocklebank (69);
Goals: Brocklebank 3/3.
Rugby Leaguer & League Express Men of the Match: *Bulls:* Dane Chisholm; *Whitehaven:* James Newton.
Penalty count: 11-12; **Half-time:** 52-0;
Referee: Tom Grant; **Attendance:** 4,163.

LEIGH CENTURIONS 58 HALIFAX 18

CENTURIONS: 31 Ben Reynolds; 2 Adam Higson; 3 Greg Worthington; 26 Lee Smith; 5 Liam Kay; 6 Martyn Ridyard; 36 Josh Drinkwater; 20 Sam Hopkins; 32 Liam Hood; 18 Tom Spencer; 21 Andrew Dixon; 13 Cory Paterson; 11 Harrison Hansen. Subs (all used): 8 Fuifui Moimoi; 10 Dayne Weston; 12 Gareth Hock; 14 Micky Higham.
Tries: Paterson (4, 47), Smith (18), Higson (20), Worthington (25), Drinkwater (30), Dixon (38, 64), Moimoi (75), Kay (77); **Goals:** Ridyard 9/10.
HALIFAX: 1 Ben Johnston; 5 James Saltonstall; 4 Ben Heaton; 3 Steve Tyrer; 2 Will Sharp; 7 Gareth Moore; 6 Scott Murrell; 8 Mitch Cahalane; 22 Connor Robinson; 14 Adam Tangata; 12 Simon Grix; 33 Matt Sarsfield; 13 Jacob Fairbank. Subs (all used): 10 Luke Ambler; 17 Gavin Bennion; 26 Ed Barber; 30 Brandon Moore.
Tries: Johnston (14, 49), Sharp (56); **Goals:** Tyrer 3/3.
Rugby Leaguer & League Express Men of the Match: *Centurions:* Josh Drinkwater; *Halifax:* Ben Johnston.
Penalty count: 8-9; **Half-time:** 34-6;
Referee: Robert Hicks; **Attendance:** 4,052.

LONDON BRONCOS 14 SHEFFIELD EAGLES 32

BRONCOS: 32 Elliot Kear; 2 Rhys Williams; 1 Ben Hellewell; 6 Israel Eliab; 4 Wes Naiqama; 26 Api Pewhairangi; 20 Scott Leatherbarrow; 18 Jamie Thackray; 14 Andy Ackers; 10 Eddie Battye; 11 Daniel Harrison; 12 Matt Garside; 15 Jack Bussey. Subs (all used): 9 James Cunningham; 23 Jon Magrin; 8 Nick Slyney; 16 Mark Ioane.
Tries: Williams (7), Eliab (65), Ackers (79);
Goals: Naiqama 1/3.
EAGLES: 1 Quentin Laulu-Togagae; 19 Garry Lo; 3 Menzie Yere; 25 Nathan Chappell; 5 Ben Blackmore; 6 Cory Aston; 26 Stan Robin; 8 Steve Thorpe; 9 Keal Carlile; 15 Scott Wheeldon; 13 Matt James; 12 Duane Straugheir; 27 Thibaut Margalet. Subs (all used): 14 Matty Fozard; 17 Mark Mexico; 16 Adam Neal; 11 Michael Knowles.
Tries: James (15), Fozard (28), Robin (35), Laulu-Togagae (55), Yere (61), Straugheir (69);
Goals: Aston 4/6.
Rugby Leaguer & League Express Men of the Match: *Broncos:* Matt Garside; *Eagles:* Cory Aston.
Penalty count: 7-8; **Half-time:** 4-18;
Referee: Tom Crashley; **Attendance:** 530.

OLDHAM 26 SWINTON LIONS 24

OLDHAM: 1 Richard Lepori; 2 Adam Clay; 22 Danny Grimshaw; - Kieran Gill; 5 Jamel Chisholm; 6 Lewis Palfrey; 20 Gareth Owen; 8 Phil Joy; - Lewis Foster; 14 Joe Burke; 12 Danny Langtree; 23 Craig Briscoe; 13 Liam Thompson. Subs (all used): 26 Michael Ward; 21 Kenny Hughes; - Tyler Dickinson; 24 Will Hope.
Tries: Gill (22), Ward (51, 54), Clay (69); **Goals:** Palfrey 5/5.
Sin bin: Lepori (58) - dissent.
LIONS: 22 Gabriel Fell; 2 Shaun Robinson; 3 Stuart Littler; 4 Macauley Hallett; 18 Liam Marshall; 6 Ben White; 1 Chris Atkin; 29 Daniel Fleming; - Luke Waterworth; - Andy Bracek; 23 Rhodri Lloyd; 11 Connor Dwyer; 19 Josh Barlow. Subs (all used): 7 Matty Beharrell; 12 Andy Thornley; 13 Rob Lever; 17 Stephen Nash.
Tries: White (12, 15), Hallett (58), Barlow (72);
Goals: Atkin 4/5.
Rugby Leaguer & League Express Men of the Match: *Oldham:* Michael Ward; *Lions:* Stuart Littler.
Penalty count: 11-7; **Half-time:** 6-14;
Referee: Chris Kendall; **Attendance:** 758.

WORKINGTON TOWN 22 DEWSBURY RAMS 20

TOWN: 1 Jack Murphy; 24 Theerapol Ritson; 4 Jason Mossop; 3 Declan Hulme; 26 John Patrick; 28 Jarrod Sammut; 14 Callum Phillips; 18 Tom Walker; 9 Graeme Mattinson; 10 Marc Shackley; 11 Brett Phillips; 25 Matty Gee; 15 Karl Olstrum. Subs (all used): 19 Ryan Verlinden; 20 Steve Scholey; 6 Carl Forber; 7 Jamie Doran.
Tries: Hulme (9), Olstrum (48), Ritson (59), Gee (78);
Goals: Sammut 3/4.
RAMS: 1 Josh Guzdek; 2 Dale Morton; 15 Jason Crookes; 4 Shane Grady; 38 Etuate Uaisele; 6 Paul Sykes; 22 Andy Kain; 45 Mitchell Stringer; 9 Tom Hemingway; 32 Kyle Trout; 10 Ryan Hepworth; 42 Lucas Walshaw; 14 Luke Adamson. Subs (all used): 17 Dom Speakman; 25 Joel Farrell; 18 Tony Tonks; 8 Matt Groat.
Tries: Morton (12), Tonks (33), Walshaw (38), Kain (65);
Goals: Sykes 2/4.
Rugby Leaguer & League Express Men of the Match: *Town:* Karl Olstrum; *Rams:* Andy Kain.
Penalty count: 9-6; **Half-time:** 6-14;
Referee: Jack Smith; **Attendance:** 492.

ROUND 22

Friday 15th July 2016

SHEFFIELD EAGLES 30 LEIGH CENTURIONS 34

EAGLES: 1 Quentin Laulu-Togagae; 19 Garry Lo; 3 Menzie Yere; 25 Nathan Chappell; 5 Ben Blackmore; 26 Stan Robin; 6 Cory Aston; 8 Steve Thorpe; 9 Keal Carlile; 15

Scott Wheeldon; 13 Matt James; 12 Duane Straugheir; 27 Thibaut Margalet. Subs (all used): 14 Matty Fozard; 16 Adam Neal; 17 Mark Mexico; 11 Michael Knowles.
Tries: Yere (4, 66), Straugheir (17), Wheeldon (21), Chappell (52); **Goals:** Aston 5/6.
CENTURIONS: 1 Gregg McNally; 25 Eze Harper; 26 Lee Smith; 24 Tom Armstrong; 5 Liam Kay; 6 Martyn Ridyard; 38 Travis Burns; 18 Tom Spencer; 32 Liam Hood; 20 Sam Hopkins; 21 Andrew Dixon; 16 Reni Maitua; 11 Harrison Hansen. Subs (all used): 31 Ben Reynolds; 12 Gareth Hock; 35 Brad Fash; 18 Fuifui Moimoi.
Tries: McNally (13), Armstrong (31), Ridyard (35), Dixon (56), Harper (64), Hock (79); **Goals:** Ridyard 5/7.
Rugby Leaguer & League Express Men of the Match:
Eagles: Cory Aston; Centurions: Gareth Hock.
Penalty count: 8-6; **Half-time:** 16-18;
Referee: Callum Straw; **Attendance:** 774.

Sunday 17th July 2016

BATLEY BULLDOGS 31 LONDON BRONCOS 20

BULLDOGS: 22 Dave Scott; 2 Wayne Reittie; 4 Shaun Squires; 3 Chris Ulugia; 5 Shaun Ainscough; 13 Pat Walker; 7 Dominic Brambani; 8 Keegan Hirst; 20 Alistair Leak; 10 Alex Rowe; 11 Brad Day; 19 Alex Bretherton; 15 Adam Gledhill. Subs (all used): 14 James Davey; 18 Tom Lillycrop; 21 James Brown; 24 James Harrison.
Tries: Ainscough (28, 39), Squires (35), Reittie (48), Brambani (51), Gledhill (64); **Goals:** Walker 3/6.
Field goal: Brambani (79).
BRONCOS: 24 Alex Walker; 2 Rhys Williams; 1 Ben Hellewell; 32 Elliot Kear; 5 Iliess Macani; 26 Api Pewhairangi; 33 Jamie Soward; 8 Nick Slyney; 14 Andy Ackers; 18 Jamie Thackray; 15 Jack Bussey; 12 Matt Garside; 17 Mark Offerdahl. Subs (all used): 9 James Cunningham; 10 Eddie Battye; 16 Mark Ioane; 23 Jon Magrin.
Tries: Kear (19), Hellewell (44), Pewhairangi (58), Offerdahl (68); **Goals:** Soward 2/4.
Rugby Leaguer & League Express Men of the Match:
Bulldogs: Dominic Brambani; Broncos: Jack Bussey.
Penalty count: 11-5; **Half-time:** 14-4;
Referee: Jack Smith; **Attendance:** 783.

BRADFORD BULLS 44 OLDHAM 12

BULLS: 39 Kieren Moss; 2 Omari Caro; 22 James Clare; 4 Kris Welham; 29 Ethan Ryan; 40 Lewis Charnock; 7 Dane Chisholm; 10 Adam Sidlow; 42 Stuart Howarth; 19 Steve Crossley; 12 Dale Ferguson; 28 Kurt Haggerty; 13 Danny Addy. Subs (all used): 9 Adam O'Brien; 11 Tom Olbison; 21 Epalahame Lauaki; 41 Joe Philbin.
Tries: Welham (12), Caro (15, 42, 54, 56, 67), Haggerty (29), Philbin (32), Ryan (79).
Goals: Addy 1/3, Chisholm 0/1, Charnock 3/5.
OLDHAM: 1 Richard Lepori; 2 Adam Clay; 22 Danny Grimshaw; - Kieran Gill; 5 Jamel Chisholm; - Dave Hewitt; 6 Lewis Palfrey; 16 Joe Burke; 19 Adam Files; - Tyler Dickinson; 23 Craig Briscoe; 12 Danny Langtree; 24 Will Hope. Subs (all used): 9 Sam Gee; 21 Kenny Hughes; 26 Michael Ward; - Jack Blagbrough.
Tries: Blagbrough (22), Ward (37); **Goals:** Palfrey 2/2.
Rugby Leaguer & League Express Men of the Match:
Bulls: Omari Caro; Oldham: Jack Blagbrough.
Penalty count: 10-7; **Half-time:** 18-12;
Referee: Phil Bentham; **Attendance:** 4,235.

DEWSBURY RAMS 34 SWINTON LIONS 16

RAMS: 1 Josh Guzdek; 2 Dale Morton; 15 Jason Crookes; 6 Paul Sykes; 38 Etuate Uaisele; 17 Dom Speakman; 22 Andy Kain; 8 Matt Groat; 9 Tom Hemingway; 45 Mitchell Stringer; 42 Lucas Walshaw; 32 Kyle Trout; 14 Luke Adamson. Subs (all used): 24 Jack Teanby; 18 Tony Tonks; 25 Joel Farrell; 27 Jason Muranka.
Tries: Walshaw (3), Morton (7), Groat (11), Kain (31), Tonks (63), Sykes (79); **Goals:** Sykes 5/8.
Sin bin: Crookes (27) - fighting.
LIONS: 22 Gabriel Fell; 20 Mike Butt; 3 Stuart Littler; 23 Rhodri Lloyd; 18 Liam Marshall; 1 Chris Atkin; 7 Matty Beharrell; 16 Ben Austin; - Luke Waterworth; 10 Jordan Hand; 11 Connor Dwyer; 12 Andy Thornley; 13 Rob Lever. Subs (all used): 19 Josh Barlow; 17 Stephen Nash; 28 Zach Johnson; - Andy Bracek.
Tries: Marshall (20, 50), Lloyd (35); **Goals:** Atkin 2/3.
Sin bin: Littler (27) - fighting.
Rugby Leaguer & League Express Men of the Match:
Rams: Paul Sykes; Lions: Chris Atkin.
Penalty count: 10-6; **Half-time:** 24-10;
Referee: Michael Woodhead; **Attendance:** 739.

HALIFAX 20 FEATHERSTONE ROVERS 24

HALIFAX: 1 Ben Johnston; 2 Will Sharp; 4 Ben Heaton; 3 Steve Tyrer; 5 James Saltonstall; 7 Gareth Moore; 6 Scott Murrell; 8 Mitch Cahalane; 22 Connor Robinson; 14

Adam Tangata; 12 Simon Grix; 33 Matt Sarsfield; 13 Jacob Fairbank. Subs (all used): 10 Luke Ambler; 16 Richard Moore; 30 Brandon Moore; 34 Ryan Boyle.
Tries: C Robinson (30), Johnston (38), Cahalane (60);
Goals: Tyrer 3/3, Murrell 1/1.
Sin bin: Fairbank (18) - fighting.
ROVERS: 15 Ian Hardman; 37 Ashton Golding; 3 Michael Channing; 21 Bradley Knowles-Tagg; 4 Misi Taulapapa; 6 Kyle Briggs; 7 Anthony Thackeray; 10 Andrew Bostock; 23 Andy Ellis; 32 Jordan Baldwinson; 11 Steve Snitch; 12 John Davies; 17 Jack Ormondroyd. Subs (all used): 8 Darrell Griffin; 13 Tim Spears; 20 Luke Cooper; 38 Anthony Mullally.
Tries: Ellis (22), Golding (25), Taulapapa (54), Thackeray (67); **Goals:** Briggs 4/6.
Sin bin: Hardman (18) - fighting.
Rugby Leaguer & League Express Men of the Match:
Halifax: Adam Tangata; Rovers: Misi Taulapapa.
Penalty count: 7-7; **Half-time:** 14-12;
Referee: James Child; **Attendance:** 2,305.

ROUND 23

Saturday 23rd July 2016

WHITEHAVEN 14 SHEFFIELD EAGLES 32

WHITEHAVEN: 20 Jordan Burns; 16 Connor Holliday; 3 Chris Taylor; 30 Ugo Perez; 2 Craig Calvert; 6 Dion Aiye; 7 Grant Gore; 19 Glenn Riley; 14 Thomas Coyle; 32 Anthony Walker; 11 Dave Allen; 17 Steve Fox; 15 Ben Davies. Subs: 31 Ryan Duffy; 9 James Newton; 13 Liam Carberry (not used); 1 Louis Jouffret (not used).
Tries: Taylor (12), Gore (25); **Goals:** Gore 3/5.
EAGLES: 1 Quentin Laulu-Togagae; 19 Garry Lo; 3 Menzie Yere; 25 Nathan Chappell; 2 Rob Worrincy; 26 Stan Robin; 6 Cory Aston; 8 Steve Thorpe; 9 Keal Carlile; 15 Scott Wheeldon; 13 Matt James; 12 Duane Straugheir; 27 Thibaut Margalet. Subs (all used): 14 Matty Fozard; 4 George Tyson; 16 Adam Neal; 17 Mark Mexico.
Tries: Laulu-Togagae (6), Worrincy (33), Robin (53), Thorpe (68), Chappell (72), Lo (79); **Goals:** Aston 4/6.
Rugby Leaguer & League Express Men of the Match:
Whitehaven: Anthony Walker; Eagles: Garry Lo.
Penalty count: 10-7; **Half-time:** 12-10;
Referee: Tom Crashley; **Attendance:** 553.

Sunday 24th July 2016

FEATHERSTONE ROVERS 20 BRADFORD BULLS 0

ROVERS: 15 Ian Hardman; 37 Ashton Golding; 3 Michael Channing; 4 Misi Taulapapa; 29 Luke Briscoe; 6 Kyle Briggs; 7 Anthony Thackeray; 10 Andrew Bostock; 23 Andy Ellis; 32 Jordan Baldwinson; 11 Steve Snitch; 12 John Davies; 17 Jack Ormondroyd. Subs (all used): 8 Darrell Griffin; 21 Bradley Knowles-Tagg; 13 Tim Spears; 38 Anthony Mullally.
Tries: Ellis (6), Thackeray (23), Snitch (32);
Goals: Briggs 4/5.
BULLS: 39 Kieren Moss; 2 Omari Caro; 15 Matty Blythe; 4 Kris Welham; 29 Ethan Ryan; 40 Lewis Charnock; 7 Dane Chisholm; 10 Adam Sidlow; 13 Danny Addy; 25 Ben Kavanagh; 28 Kurt Haggerty; 23 Alex Mellor; 12 Dale Ferguson. Subs (all used): 11 Tom Olbison; 14 Jay Pitts; 41 Joe Philbin; 42 Stuart Howarth.
Sin bin: Haggerty (71) - interference.
Rugby Leaguer & League Express Men of the Match:
Rovers: Steve Snitch; Bulls: Kris Welham.
Penalty count: 13-6; **Half-time:** 18-0;
Referee: Ben Thaler; **Attendance:** 4,554.

HALIFAX 22 LONDON BRONCOS 41

HALIFAX: 1 Ben Johnston; 2 Will Sharp; 4 Ben Heaton; 25 Jake Eccleston; 5 James Saltonstall; 7 Gareth Moore; 6 Scott Murrell; 8 Mitch Cahalane; 22 Connor Robinson; 10 Luke Ambler; 26 Ed Barber; 14 Adam Tangata; 13 Jacob Fairbank. Subs (all used): 9 Ben Kaye; 16 Richard Moore; 17 Gavin Bennion; 34 Ryan Boyle.
Tries: Johnston (10), Sharp (54), Barber (56, 59);
Goals: G Moore 3/4.
BRONCOS: 24 Alex Walker; 2 Rhys Williams; 32 Elliot Kear; 6 Israel Eliab; 5 Iliess Macani; 26 Api Pewhairangi; 33 Jamie Soward; 16 Mark Ioane; 14 Andy Ackers; 30 Callum Bustin; 11 Daniel Harrison; 12 Matt Garside; 8 Nick Slyney. Subs (all used): 9 James Cunningham; 10 Eddie Battye; 23 Jon Magrin; 29 Sadiq Adebiyi.
Tries: Battye (19, 27), Garside (37), Soward (45), Ioane (62), Slyney (73), Adebiyi (80); **Goals:** Soward 5/6, Pewhairangi 1/1.
Field goal: Soward (71).
Sin bin: Soward (53) - high tackle on Heaton.
Rugby Leaguer & League Express Men of the Match:
Halifax: Luke Ambler; Broncos: Mark Ioane.
Penalty count: 8-5; **Half-time:** 6-16;
Referee: Gareth Hewer; **Attendance:** 1,559.

LEIGH CENTURIONS 58 DEWSBURY RAMS 0

CENTURIONS: 1 Gregg McNally; 2 Adam Higson; 4 Willie Tonga; 3 Greg Worthington; 40 Matty Dawson; 6 Martyn Ridyard; 36 Josh Drinkwater; 8 Fuifui Moimoi; 14 Micky Higham; 10 Dayne Weston; 16 Reni Maitua; 13 Cory Paterson; 11 Harrison Hansen. Subs (all used): 31 Ben Reynolds; 17 Jamie Acton; 21 Andrew Dixon; 39 Danny Tickle.
Tries: McNally (3, 15, 18), Maitua (12), Worthington (32), Higson (45, 55, 58), Reynolds (65), Higham (68);
Goals: Ridyard 9/10.
RAMS: 1 Josh Guzdek; 2 Dale Morton; 6 Paul Sykes; 15 Jason Crookes; 38 Etuate Uaisele; 17 Dom Speakman; 36 Bobbie Goulding; 45 Mitchell Stringer; 9 Tom Hemingway; 8 Matt Groat; 32 Kyle Trout; 42 Lucas Walshaw; 14 Luke Adamson. Subs (all used): 18 Tony Tonks; 25 Joel Farrell; 19 Nathan Conroy; 10 Ryan Hepworth.
Rugby Leaguer & League Express Men of the Match:
Centurions: Gregg McNally; Rams: Lucas Walshaw.
Penalty count: 9-10; **Half-time:** 28-0;
Referee: Tom Grant; **Attendance:** 3,498.

OLDHAM 30 WORKINGTON TOWN 32

OLDHAM: 1 Richard Lepori; 2 Adam Clay; 22 Danny Grimshaw; - Kieran Gill; 5 Jamel Chisholm; - Dave Hewitt; 20 Gareth Owen; 8 Phil Joy; - Lewis Foster; 23 Tyler Dickinson; 12 Danny Langtree; 16 Gary Middlehurst; 24 Will Hope. Subs (all used): 26 Michael Ward; 21 Kenny Hughes; 13 Liam Thompson; - Jack Blagbrough.
Tries: Lepori (17), Owen (39), Ward (41), Hughes (75, 78);
Goals: Hewitt 5/5.
TOWN: 1 Jack Murphy; 24 Theerapol Ritson; 3 Declan Hulme; 4 Jason Mossop; 26 John Patrick; 6 Carl Forber; 28 Jarrod Sammut; 21 Oliver Gordon; 9 Graeme Mattinson; 10 Marc Shackley; 11 Brett Phillips; 25 Matty Gee; 13 Liam McAvoy. Subs (all used): 7 Jamie Doran; 15 Karl Olstrum; 18 Tom Walker; 20 Steve Scholey.
Tries: Sammut (5), Shackley (14), Walker (22), Gordon (59), Hulme (67); **Goals:** Sammut 6/6.
Rugby Leaguer & League Express Men of the Match:
Oldham: Kenny Hughes; Town: Jarrod Sammut.
Penalty count: 7-7; **Half-time:** 12-20;
Referee: Michael Woodhead; **Attendance:** 689.

SWINTON LIONS 24 BATLEY BULLDOGS 62

LIONS: 1 Chris Atkin; 2 Shaun Robinson; 3 Stuart Littler; 4 Macauley Hallett; 18 Tom Hughes; 6 Ben White; 7 Matty Beharrell; 13 Rob Lever; - Luke Waterworth; 10 Jordan Hand; 11 Connor Dwyer; 23 Rhodri Lloyd; 12 Andy Thornley. Subs (all used): 16 Ben Austin; - Andy Bracek; 19 Josh Barlow; 28 Zach Johnson.
Tries: Robinson (5), Barlow (36), Thornley (64), Beharrell (73); **Goals:** Atkin 4/4.
Sin bin: Thornley (18) - holding down;
Barlow (66) - punching Brambani.
BULLDOGS: 22 Dave Scott; 2 Wayne Reittie; 4 Shaun Squires; 3 Chris Ulugia; 5 Shaun Ainscough; 13 Pat Walker; 7 Dominic Brambani; 8 Keegan Hirst; 20 Alistair Leak; 10 Alex Rowe; 11 Brad Day; 19 Alex Bretherton; 15 Adam Gledhill. Subs (all used): 14 James Davey; 18 Tom Lillycrop; 21 James Brown; 24 James Harrison.
Tries: Leak (10, 22), Ulugia (13, 42), Reittie (15), Squires (32), Day (46), J Brown (54), Ainscough (68, 75), Brambani (80); **Goals:** Walker 9/12.
Rugby Leaguer & League Express Men of Match:
Lions: Matty Beharrell; Bulldogs: Dominic Brambani.
Penalty count: 5-11; **Half-time:** 12-30;
Referee: Scott Mikalauskas; **Attendance:** 1,147.

CHAMPIONSHIP SHIELD
2016 *Round by Round*

ROUND 1

Sunday 7th August 2016

WHITEHAVEN 18 BRADFORD BULLS 46

WHITEHAVEN: 1 Louis Jouffret; 25 Ryan Ince; 3 Chris Taylor; 13 Liam Carberry; 16 Connor Holliday; 6 Dion Aiye; 7 Grant Gore; 19 Glenn Riley; 9 James Newton; 26 Ted Chapelhow; 30 Ugo Perez; 11 Dave Allen; 32 Anthony Walker. Subs (all used): 31 Ryan Duffy; 37 Carl Forster; 15 Ben Davies; 17 Steve Fox.
Tries: Perez (31), Taylor (36), Allen (75); **Goals:** Jouffret 3/3.
BULLS: 39 Kieren Moss; 15 Matty Blythe; 23 Alex Mellor; 4 Kris Welham; 5 Danny Williams; 40 Lewis Charnock; 7 Dane Chisholm; 25 Ben Kavanagh; 9 Adam O'Brien; 10 Adam Sidlow; 28 Kurt Haggerty; 14 Jay Pitts; 13 Danny Addy. Subs (all used): 11 Tom Olbison; 21 Epalahame Lauaki; 19 Steve Crossley; 42 Stuart Howarth.
Tries: Addy (4), Mellor (7, 39, 43), Williams (12), Blythe (17), Welham (58), Moss (62), Haggerty (78);
Goals: Addy 3/4, Charnock 2/5.
Rugby Leaguer & League Express Men of the Match:
Whitehaven: Ugo Perez; *Bulls:* Alex Mellor.
Penalty count: 5-3; **Half-time:** 12-26;
Referee: Tom Crashley; **Attendance:** 675.

DEWSBURY RAMS 36 SWINTON LIONS 24

RAMS: 1 Josh Guzdek; 2 Dale Morton; 6 Paul Sykes; 15 Jason Crookes; 38 Etuate Uaisele; 17 Dom Speakman; 22 Andy Kain; 8 Matt Groat; 9 Tom Hemingway; 45 Mitchell Stringer; 12 Scott Hale; 42 Lucas Walshaw; 32 Kyle Trout. Subs (all used): 13 Aaron Brown; 33 Paul Jackson; 25 Joel Farrell; 11 Rob Spicer.
Tries: Sykes (5, 20), Farrell (33), Walshaw (37), Guzdek (57), Speakman (64); **Goals:** Sykes 6/7.
Sin bin: Crookes (40) - high tackle.
LIONS: 1 Chris Atkin; 2 Shaun Robinson; 23 Rhodri Lloyd; 4 Macauley Hallett; 20 Mike Butt; 6 Ben White; 7 Matty Beharrell; 29 Daniel Fleming; 19 Josh Barlow; - Jake Emmitt; 11 Connor Dwyer; 12 Andy Thornley; 13 Rob Lever. Subs (all used): - Andy Bracek; 28 Zach Johnson; 10 Jordan Hand; - Luke Waterworth.
Tries: Hallett (45), Barlow (68), Butt (71), Lloyd (79);
Goals: Atkin 4/4.
Rugby Leaguer & League Express Men of the Match:
Rams: Andy Kain; *Lions:* Jake Emmitt.
Penalty count: 9-10; **Half-time:** 22-0;
Referee: Chris Kendall; **Attendance:** 674.

HALIFAX 28 SHEFFIELD EAGLES 48

HALIFAX: 1 Ben Johnston; 2 Will Sharp; 4 Ben Heaton; 26 Ed Barber; 5 James Saltonstall; 7 Gareth Moore; 6 Scott Murrell; 8 Mitch Cahalane; 9 Ben Kaye; 34 Ryan Boyle; 17 Gavin Bennion; 14 Adam Tangata; 10 Luke Ambler. Subs (all used): 16 Richard Moore; 29 Chester Butler; 30 Brandon Moore; 31 Elliot Morris.
Tries: Ambler (5), Tangata (7, 50), G Moore (25), Saltonstall (57); **Goals:** G Moore 4/5.
Sin bin: Heaton (38) - professional foul.
EAGLES: 1 Quentin Laulu-Togagae; 19 Garry Lo; 3 Menzie Yere; 25 Nathan Chappell; 2 Rob Worrincy; 26 Stan Robin; 6 Cory Aston; 8 Steve Thorpe; 9 Keal Carlile; 15 Scott Wheeldon; 13 Matt James; 12 Duane Straugheir; 27 Thibaut Margalet. Subs (all used): 14 Matty Fozard; 4 George Tyson; 16 Adam Neal; 17 Mark Mexico.
Tries: Wheeldon (3), Laulu-Togagae (14), Worrincy (18), Neal (27), Aston (30), Robin (36), Lo (46, 70), James (68);
Goals: Aston 6/9.
Rugby Leaguer & League Express Men of the Match:
Halifax: Adam Tangata; *Eagles:* Garry Lo.
Penalty count: 8-6; **Half-time:** 18-32;
Referee: Andrew Sweet; **Attendance:** 1,288.

OLDHAM 30 WORKINGTON TOWN 16

OLDHAM: - Scott Turner; 2 Adam Clay; 22 Danny Grimshaw; - Kieran Gill; 5 Jamel Chisholm; 6 Lewis Palfrey; - Dave Hewitt; 14 Joe Burke; 20 Gareth Owen; - Tyler Dickinson; 12 Danny Langtree; 16 Gary Middlehurst; 13 Liam Thompson. Subs (all used): 9 Sam Gee; 23 Craig Briscoe; 21 Kenny Hughes; - Jack Blagbrough.
Tries: Turner (5, 77), Chisholm (15), Blagbrough (28), Langtree (36); **Goals:** Palfrey 5/5.
TOWN: 1 Jack Murphy; 24 Theerapol Ritson; 25 Matty Gee; 4 Jason Mossop; 3 Declan Hulme; 6 Carl Forber; 28 Jarrod Sammut; 21 Oliver Gordon; 9 Graeme Mattinson; 10 Marc Shackley; 11 Brett Phillips; 13 Liam McAvoy; 18 Tom Walker. Subs (all used): 7 Jamie Doran; 14 Callum Phillips; 19 Ryan Verlinden; 20 Steve Scholey.
Tries: Sammut (33), Hulme (63), B Phillips (70);
Goals: Sammut 2/3.
Rugby Leaguer & League Express Men of the Match:
Oldham: Scott Turner; *Town:* Carl Forber.
Penalty count: 4-8; **Half-time:** 24-6;
Referee: Chris Campbell; **Attendance:** 573.

ROUND 2

Sunday 14th August 2016

BRADFORD BULLS 44 HALIFAX 22

BULLS: 39 Kieren Moss; 15 Matty Blythe; 3 Adrian Purtell; 4 Kris Welham; 5 Danny Williams; 40 Lewis Charnock; 7 Dane Chisholm; 10 Adam Sidlow; 9 Adam O'Brien; 19 Steve Crossley; 28 Kurt Haggerty; 23 Alex Mellor; 13 Danny Addy. Subs (all used): 25 Ben Kavanagh; 11 Tom Olbison; 14 Jay Pitts; 42 Stuart Howarth.
Tries: Mellor (15), Moss (21, 80), Welham (27, 65), Purtell (33), Pitts (35), Williams (42); **Goals:** Charnock 6/8.
HALIFAX: 1 Ben Johnston; 2 Will Sharp; 36 Nick Rawsthorne; 29 Chester Butler; 5 James Saltonstall; 6 Scott Murrell; 7 Gareth Moore; 8 Mitch Cahalane; 30 Brandon Moore; 34 Ryan Boyle; 14 Adam Tangata; 17 Gavin Bennion; 10 Luke Ambler. Subs (all used): 21 Adam Robinson; 22 Connor Robinson; 26 Ed Barber; 31 Elliot Morris.
Tries: Tangata (7, 56), B Moore (19), Saltonstall (40), Barber (76); **Goals:** G Moore 0/2, Murrell 0/1, C Robinson 1/2.
Rugby Leaguer & League Express Men of the Match:
Bulls: Dane Chisholm; *Halifax:* Brandon Moore.
Penalty count: 8-7; **Half-time:** 30-12;
Referee: Michael Woodhead; **Attendance:** 3,498.

SHEFFIELD EAGLES 48 WHITEHAVEN 16

EAGLES: 1 Quentin Laulu-Togagae; 19 Garry Lo; 3 Menzie Yere; 25 Nathan Chappell; 2 Rob Worrincy; 6 Cory Aston; 26 Stan Robin; 8 Steve Thorpe; 9 Keal Carlile; 15 Scott Wheeldon; 13 Matt James; 12 Duane Straugheir; 27 Thibaut Margalet. Subs (all used): 16 Adam Neal; 11 Michael Knowles; 14 Matty Fozard; 18 Elliot Minchella.
Tries: Minchella (18, 68), Laulu-Togagae (31, 48, 80), Fozard (43), Thorpe (58), Chappell (70);
Goals: Aston 7/7, Knowles 1/1.
WHITEHAVEN: 1 Louis Jouffret; 20 Jordan Burns; 3 Chris Taylor; 30 Ugo Perez; 16 Connor Holliday; 6 Dion Aiye; 7 Grant Gore; 32 Anthony Walker; 14 Thomas Coyle; 26 Ted Chapelhow; 11 Dave Allen; 37 Carl Forster; 13 Liam Carberry. Subs (all used): 9 James Newton; 15 Ben Davies; 31 Ryan Duffy; 17 Steve Fox.
Tries: Carberry (12), Fox (13), Gore (40); **Goals:** Jouffret 2/3.
Rugby Leaguer & League Express Men of the Match:
Eagles: Quentin Laulu-Togagae;
Whitehaven: Anthony Walker.
Penalty count: 4-7; **Half-time:** 12-16;
Referee: Jack Smith; **Attendance:** 412.

SWINTON LIONS 8 OLDHAM 30

LIONS: 20 Mike Butt; 2 Shaun Robinson; 6 Ben White; 4 Macauley Hallett; 18 Liam Marshall; 1 Chris Atkin; 7 Matty Beharrell; 29 Daniel Fleming; - Luke Waterworth; - Jake Emmitt; 13 Rob Lever; 12 Andy Thornley; 16 Ben Austin. Subs (all used): 19 Josh Barlow; - Andy Bracek; 10 Jordan Hand; 28 Zach Johnson.
Tries: Robinson (30, 75); **Goals:** Atkin 0/2.
OLDHAM: - Scott Turner; 2 Adam Clay; 9 Sam Gee; - Kieran Gill; 5 Jamel Chisholm; 6 Lewis Palfrey; - Dave Hewitt; 8 Phil Joy; 20 Gareth Owen; 23 Tyler Dickinson; 12 Danny Langtree; 16 Gary Middlehurst; 13 Liam Thompson. Subs (all used): 21 Kenny Hughes; 14 Joe Burke; 10 Jack Spencer; 24 Will Hope.
Tries: Hewitt (5, 80), Clay (34), Langtree (63);
Goals: Palfrey 7/8.
Rugby Leaguer & League Express Men of the Match:
Lions: Mike Butt; *Oldham:* Danny Langtree.
Penalty count: 10-12; **Half-time:** 4-16;
Referee: Tom Crashley; **Attendance:** 693.

WORKINGTON TOWN 34 DEWSBURY RAMS 24

TOWN: 1 Jack Murphy; 3 Declan Hulme; 25 Matty Gee; 4 Jason Mossop; 24 Theerapol Ritson; 6 Carl Forber; 28 Jarrod Sammut; 21 Oliver Gordon; 14 Callum Phillips; 10 Marc Shackley; 11 Brett Phillips; 18 Tom Walker; 13 Liam McAvoy. Subs (all used): 7 Jamie Doran; 8 Kris Coward; 19 Ryan Verlinden; 20 Steve Scholey.
Tries: Gee (4, 70), C Phillips (54), Walker (64), Mossop (67);
Goals: Sammut 7/8.
Sin bin: B Phillips (39) - retaliation.
RAMS: 1 Josh Guzdek; 2 Dale Morton; 6 Paul Sykes; 15 Jason Crookes; 38 Etuate Uaisele; 17 Dom Speakman; 22 Andy Kain; 8 Matt Groat; 9 Tom Hemingway; 45 Mitchell Stringer; 12 Scott Hale; 32 Kyle Trout; 13 Aaron Brown. Subs (all used): 25 Joel Farrell; 16 Toby Adamson; 11 Rob Spicer; 18 Tony Tonks.
Tries: Morton (29, 47), Guzdek (36), Sykes (42);
Goals: Sykes 4/5.
Dismissal: Farrell (39) - use of the knee on B Phillips.
Sin bin: Tonks (24) - high tackle;
Groat (63) - professional foul; Sykes (79) - dissent.
Rugby Leaguer & League Express Men of the Match:
Town: Liam McAvoy; *Rams:* Josh Guzdek.
Penalty count: 17-10; **Half-time:** 8-10;
Referee: Tom Grant; **Attendance:** 527.

ROUND 3

Sunday 21st August 2016

BRADFORD BULLS 82 OLDHAM 0

BULLS: 39 Kieren Moss; 5 Danny Williams; 23 Alex Mellor; 4 Kris Welham; 29 Ethan Ryan; 43 Joe Keyes; 7 Dane Chisholm; 10 Adam Sidlow; 9 Adam O'Brien; 25 Ben Kavanagh; 14 Jay Pitts; 13 Danny Addy; 11 Tom Olbison. Subs (all used): 20 Mitch Clark; 21 Epalahame Lauaki; 19 Steve Crossley; 44 James Bentley.
Tries: Welham (4, 26, 54, 57, 69), Olbison (12), Pitts (30, 33, 74), Lauaki (37), Chisholm (43, 48), Keyes (60), Williams (63), Ryan (76);
Goals: Keyes 10/14, Crossley 1/1.
OLDHAM: - Scott Turner; 1 Richard Lepori; 9 Sam Gee; - Kieran Gill; 5 Jamel Chisholm; 6 Lewis Palfrey; - Dave Hewitt; 8 Phil Joy; 20 Gareth Owen; 23 Tyler Dickinson; 16 Gary Middlehurst; 12 Danny Langtree; 24 Will Hope. Subs (all used): 19 Adam Files; - Jack Blagbrough; 26 Michael Ward; 10 Jack Spencer.
Sin bin: Owen (64) - high tackle;
Middlehurst (67) - interference.
Rugby Leaguer & League Express Men of the Match:
Bulls: Joe Keyes; *Oldham:* Scott Turner.
Penalty count: 15-9; **Half-time:** 34-0;
Referee: Callum Straw; **Attendance:** 3,022.

HALIFAX 22 DEWSBURY RAMS 24

HALIFAX: 18 Miles Greenwood; 5 James Saltonstall; 36 Nick Rawsthorne; 4 Ben Heaton; 2 Will Sharp; 7 Gareth Moore; 6 Scott Murrell; 8 Mitch Cahalane; 30 Brandon Moore; 34 Ryan Boyle; 11 Dane Manning; 14 Adam Tangata; 13 Jacob Fairbank. Subs (all used): 17 Gavin Bennion; 21 Adam Robinson; 22 Connor Robinson; 26 Ed Barber.
Tries: Greenwood (9), Murrell (30), Manning (35), Fairbank (66); **Goals:** Rawsthorne 3/4.
RAMS: 1 Josh Guzdek; 2 Dale Morton; 6 Paul Sykes; 15 Jason Crookes; 38 Etuate Uaisele; 17 Dom Speakman; 22 Andy Kain; 45 Mitchell Stringer; 9 Tom Hemingway; 32 Kyle Trout; 12 Scott Hale; 42 Lucas Walshaw; 13 Aaron Brown. Subs (all used): 11 Rob Spicer; 18 Tony Tonks; 23 James Glover; 24 Jack Teanby.
Tries: Uaisele (18, 50), Kain (23), Tonks (46);
Goals: Sykes 3/4, Hemingway 1/1.
Rugby Leaguer & League Express Men of the Match:
Halifax: Nick Rawsthorne; *Rams:* Andy Kain.
Penalty count: 10-8; **Half-time:** 16-10;
Referee: Michael Woodhead; **Attendance:** 1,133.

SHEFFIELD EAGLES 38 SWINTON LIONS 40

EAGLES: 1 Quentin Laulu-Togagae; 2 Rob Worrincy; 4 George Tyson; 25 Nathan Chappell; 5 Ben Blackmore; 6 Cory Aston; 26 Stan Robin; 15 Scott Wheeldon; 9 Keal Carlile; 16 Adam Neal; 13 Matt James; 12 Duane Straugheir; 27 Thibaut Margalet. Subs (all used): 14 Matty Fozard; 11 Michael Knowles; 18 Elliot Minchella; 17 Mark Mexico.
Tries: Straugheir (16), Worrincy (24), Robin (31), Knowles (37), Chappell (44, 61), Fozard (64);
Goals: Aston 5/7.
LIONS: 20 Mike Butt; 2 Shaun Robinson; 3 Stuart Littler; 4 Macauley Hallett; 18 Liam Marshall; 6 Ben White; 1 Chris Atkin; - Jake Emmitt; - Luke Waterworth; - Andy Bracek; 11 Connor Dwyer; 12 Andy Thornley; 13 Rob Lever. Subs (all used): 7 Matty Beharrell; 19 Josh Barlow; 10 Jordan Hand; 29 Daniel Fleming.
Tries: Marshall (5, 56, 75), Dwyer (37), White (53), Hallett (69), Littler (78); **Goals:** Atkin 6/8.
Rugby Leaguer & League Express Men of the Match:
Eagles: Cory Aston; *Lions:* Chris Atkin.
Penalty count: 12-11; **Half-time:** 22-14;
Referee: Tom Grant; **Attendance:** 466.

WORKINGTON TOWN 24 WHITEHAVEN 28

TOWN: 1 Jack Murphy; 24 Theerapol Ritson; 25 Matty Gee; 4 Jason Mossop; 3 Declan Hulme; 6 Carl Forber; 28 Jarrod Sammut; 21 Oliver Gordon; 14 Callum Phillips; 8 Kris Coward; 10 Marc Shackley; 13 Liam McAvoy; 15 Karl Olstrum. Subs (all used): 7 Jamie Doran; 18 Tom Walker; 19 Ryan Verlinden; 20 Steve Scholey.
Tries: Shackley (2), Doran (63, 74), Sammut (68);
Goals: Sammut 4/5.

Championship Shield 2016 - Round by Round

WHITEHAVEN: 1 Louis Jouffret; 25 Ryan Ince; 3 Chris Taylor; 4 Jessie Joe Parker; 28 Ed Chamberlain; 6 Dion Aiye; 7 Grant Gore; 32 Anthony Walker; 13 Liam Carberry; 26 Ted Chapelhow; 17 Steve Fox; 37 Carl Forster; 11 Dave Allen. Subs (all used): 9 James Newton; 15 Ben Davies; 19 Glenn Riley; 30 Ugo Perez.
Tries: Taylor (18, 54), Chamberlain (24), Parker (36), Aiye (48); **Goals:** Jouffret 4/5.
Sin bin: Davies (62) - headbutt.
Rugby Leaguer & League Express Men of the Match: *Town:* Jack Murphy; *Whitehaven:* Chris Taylor.
Penalty count: 9-9; **Half-time:** 8-16;
Referee: Joe Cobb; **Attendance:** 1,058.

ROUND 4

Monday 29th August 2016

WHITEHAVEN 10 HALIFAX 30

WHITEHAVEN: 1 Louis Jouffret; 25 Ryan Ince; 3 Chris Taylor; 4 Jessie Joe Parker; 28 Ed Chamberlain; 6 Dion Aiye; 7 Grant Gore; 32 Anthony Walker; 13 Liam Carberry; 26 Ted Chapelhow; 17 Steve Fox; 11 Dave Allen; 37 Carl Forster. Subs (all used): 9 James Newton; 15 Ben Davies; 19 Glenn Riley; 30 Ugo Perez.
Tries: Chamberlain (26), Gore (45); **Goals:** Jouffret 1/2.
Sin bin: Allen (71) - dissent.
HALIFAX: 18 Miles Greenwood; 4 Ben Heaton; 29 Chester Butler; 36 Nick Rawsthorne; 2 Will Sharp; 1 Ben Johnston; 6 Scott Murrell; 8 Mitch Cahalane; 30 Brandon Moore; 34 Ryan Boyle; 14 Adam Tangata; 11 Dane Manning; 13 Jacob Fairbank. Subs (all used): 9 Ben Kaye; 17 Gavin Bennion; 31 Elliot Morris; 35 Luke Nelmes.
Tries: Butler (11), Boyle (22), Rawsthorne (37), Fairbank (58), Tangata (78); **Goals:** Rawsthorne 5/5.
Rugby Leaguer & League Express Men of the Match: *Whitehaven:* Louis Jouffret; *Halifax:* Nick Rawsthorne.
Half-time: 4-18; **Referee:** Tom Grant; **Attendance:** 718.

DEWSBURY RAMS 26 BRADFORD BULLS 36

RAMS: 1 Josh Guzdek; 2 Dale Morton; 15 Jason Crookes; 4 Shane Grady; 34 Donald Kudangirana; 23 James Glover; 22 Andy Kain; 45 Mitchell Stringer; 17 Dom Speakman; 16 Toby Adamson; 32 Kyle Trout; 12 Scott Hale; 13 Aaron Brown. Subs (all used): 24 Jack Teanby; 19 Nathan Conroy; 11 Rob Spicer; 18 Tony Tonks.
Tries: Morton (6, 75), Brown (22), Speakman (71);
Goals: Glover 4/7, Grady 1/1.
BULLS: 39 Kieren Moss; 5 Danny Williams; 23 Alex Mellor; 4 Kris Welham; 29 Ethan Ryan; 7 Dane Chisholm; 43 Joe Keyes; 10 Adam Sidlow; 9 Adam O'Brien; 25 Ben Kavanagh; 14 Jay Pitts; 28 Kurt Haggerty; 13 Danny Addy. Subs (all used): 11 Tom Olbison; 20 Mitch Clark; 21 Epalahame Lauaki; 30 Joe Lumb.
Tries: Pitts (12), Williams (19, 35), Ryan (32), Welham (53), Chisholm (67), Clark (79);
Goals: Keyes 2/5, Addy 2/2.
Rugby Leaguer & League Express Men of the Match: *Rams:* Dale Morton; *Bulls:* Dane Chisholm.
Half-time: 14-18; **Referee:** Scott Mikalauskas;
Attendance: 1,807.

OLDHAM 24 SHEFFIELD EAGLES 54

OLDHAM: 1 Richard Lepori; 2 Adam Clay; - Kieran Gill; 15 Liam Johnson; 5 Jamel Chisholm; 6 Lewis Palfrey; - Dave Hewitt; 14 Joe Burke; 20 Gareth Owen; 23 Tyler Dickinson; 12 Danny Langtree; 16 Gary Middlehurst; 13 Liam Thompson. Subs (all used): - Jack Blagbrough; 26 Michael Ward; 19 Adam Files; 10 Jack Spencer.
Tries: Gill (14, 75), Hewitt (20, 78); **Goals:** Palfrey 4/4.
Dismissal: Lepori (38) - punching.
EAGLES: 1 Quentin Laulu-Togagae; 2 Rob Worrincy; 3 Menzie Yere; 25 Nathan Chappell; 5 Ben Blackmore; 6 Cory Aston; 18 Elliot Minchella; 8 Steve Thorpe; 9 Keal Carlile; 15 Scott Wheeldon; 13 Matt James; 12 Duane Straugheir; 11 Michael Knowles. Subs (all used): 14 Matty Fozard; 4 George Tyson; 16 Adam Neal; 17 Mark Mexico.
Tries: Yere (22, 58), Laulu-Togagae (25), Blackmore (29), Mexico (38), Knowles (39), Fozard (64), Chappell (68), Minchella (74), Thorpe (80); **Goals:** Aston 7/10.
Sin bin: Chappell (8) - trip on Gill.
Rugby Leaguer & League Express Men of the Match: *Oldham:* Lewis Palfrey; *Eagles:* Cory Aston.
Half-time: 12-26; **Referee:** Tom Crashley;
Attendance: 680.

SWINTON LIONS 19 WORKINGTON TOWN 12

LIONS: 20 Mike Butt; 2 Shaun Robinson; 3 Stuart Littler; 4 Macauley Hallett; 18 Liam Marshall; 6 Ben White; 1 Chris Atkin; - Jake Emmitt; - Luke Waterworth; - Andy Bracek; 11 Connor Dwyer; 12 Andy Thornley; 13 Rob Lever. Subs (all used): 7 Matty Beharrell; 19 Josh Barlow; 10 Jordan Hand; 16 Ben Austin.
Tries: Littler (5), Marshall (11), Atkin (21); **Goals:** Atkin 3/4;
Field goal: Atkin (75).
TOWN: 1 Jack Murphy; 24 Theerapol Ritson; 15 Karl Olstrum; 4 Jason Mossop; 3 Declan Hulme; 6 Carl Forber; 28 Jarrod Sammut; 8 Kris Coward; 7 Jamie Doran; 21 Oliver Gordon; 10 Marc Shackley; 13 Liam McAvoy; 18 Tom Walker. Subs: 20 Steve Scholey; 19 Ryan Verlinden; 17 Alex Szostak; 26 John Patrick (not used).
Tries: Shackley (14), Mossop (71); **Goals:** Sammut 2/2.
Rugby Leaguer & League Express Men of the Match: *Lions:* Stuart Littler; *Town:* Marc Shackley.
Penalty count: 12-12; **Half-time:** 16-6;
Referee: Callum Straw; **Attendance:** 546.

ROUND 5

Sunday 4th September 2016

BRADFORD BULLS 46 SWINTON LIONS 28

BULLS: 39 Kieren Moss; 5 Danny Williams; 23 Alex Mellor; 4 Kris Welham; 29 Ethan Ryan; 7 Dane Chisholm; 43 Joe Keyes; 10 Adam Sidlow; 9 Adam O'Brien; 25 Ben Kavanagh; 14 Jay Pitts; 28 Kurt Haggerty; 13 Danny Addy. Subs (all used): 11 Tom Olbison; 12 Dale Ferguson; 20 Mitch Clark; 42 Stuart Howarth.
Tries: O'Brien (10, 28), Ryan (17, 57, 80), Pitts (21), Kavanagh (41), Chisholm (55); **Goals:** Keyes 7/8.
Dismissal: Haggerty (35) - fighting.
Sin bin: Welham (49) - dissent.
LIONS: 20 Mike Butt; 2 Shaun Robinson; 3 Stuart Littler; 4 Macauley Hallett; 18 Liam Marshall; 6 Ben White; 1 Chris Atkin; 10 Jordan Hand; - Luke Waterworth; 16 Ben Austin; 11 Connor Dwyer; 12 Andy Thornley; - Andy Bracek. Subs (all used): 7 Matty Beharrell; 19 Josh Barlow; 13 Rob Lever; - Jake Emmitt.
Tries: Hallett (35, 64), White (49), Atkin (53), Butt (70);
Goals: Atkin 4/5.
Sin bin: Littler (9) - dissent; Thornley (35) - fighting.
Rugby Leaguer & League Express Men of the Match: *Bulls:* Adam O'Brien; *Lions:* Mike Butt.
Penalty count: 9-10; **Half-time:** 22-6;
Referee: Tom Crashley; **Attendance:** 4,030.

DEWSBURY RAMS 12 WHITEHAVEN 56

RAMS: 1 Josh Guzdek; 2 Dale Morton; 15 Jason Crookes; 4 Shane Grady; 38 Etuate Uaisele; 23 James Glover; 22 Andy Kain; 16 Toby Adamson; 9 Tom Hemingway; 45 Mitchell Stringer; 12 Scott Hale; 42 Lucas Walshaw; 32 Kyle Trout. Subs (all used): 13 Aaron Brown; 19 Nathan Conroy; 24 Jack Teanby; 18 Tony Tonks.
Tries: Teanby (31, 47); **Goals:** Hemingway 2/2.
WHITEHAVEN: 28 Ed Chamberlain; 25 Ryan Ince; 3 Chris Taylor; 4 Jessie Joe Parker; 1 Louis Jouffret; 6 Dion Aiye; 7 Grant Gore; 32 Anthony Walker; 13 Liam Carberry; 26 Ted Chapelhow; 11 Dave Allen; 30 Ugo Perez; 37 Carl Forster. Subs (all used): 17 Steve Fox; 19 Glenn Riley; 9 James Newton; 15 Ben Davies.
Tries: Allen (1, 21), Newton (51), Aiye (57), Forster (62, 74), Walker (68), T Chapelhow (71), Davies (77), Riley (80);
Goals: Chamberlain 8/10.
Rugby Leaguer & League Express Men of the Match: *Rams:* Jack Teanby; *Whitehaven:* Carl Forster.
Penalty count: 9-7; **Half-time:** 6-10;
Referee: Callum Straw; **Attendance:** 524.

HALIFAX 32 OLDHAM 18

HALIFAX: 18 Miles Greenwood; 4 Ben Heaton; 29 Chester Butler; 36 Nick Rawsthorne; 2 Will Sharp; 1 Ben Johnston; 7 Gareth Moore; 8 Mitch Cahalane; 9 Ben Kaye; 34 Ryan Boyle; 14 Adam Tangata; 13 Jacob Fairbank; 6 Scott Murrell. Subs (all used): 10 Luke Ambler; 17 Gavin Bennion; 30 Brandon Moore; 35 Luke Nelmes.
Tries: Heaton (10, 52), Rawsthorne (14), Greenwood (56), Murrell (74), Tangata (77);
Goals: Rawsthorne 0/3, G Moore 4/4.
OLDHAM: - Scott Turner; 2 Adam Clay; - Kieran Gill; 16 Gary Middlehurst; 1 Richard Lepori; 6 Lewis Palfrey; - Dave Hewitt; 8 Phil Joy; 20 Gareth Owen; 23 Tyler Dickinson; 13 Liam Thompson; 12 Danny Langtree; 26 Michael Ward. Subs (all used): - Jack Blagbrough; 10 Jack Spencer; 14 Joe Burke; 21 Kenny Hughes.
Tries: Gill (6, 46), Hughes (49); **Goals:** Palfrey 3/3.
Rugby Leaguer & League Express Men of the Match: *Halifax:* Ben Heaton; *Oldham:* Kieran Gill.
Penalty count: 11-5; **Half-time:** 8-6;
Referee: Michael Woodhead; **Attendance:** 1,182.

SHEFFIELD EAGLES 62 WORKINGTON TOWN 0

EAGLES: 1 Quentin Laulu-Togagae; 19 Garry Lo; 3 Menzie Yere; 12 Duane Straugheir; 2 Rob Worrincy; 6 Cory Aston; 24 Rhys Jacks; 8 Steve Thorpe; 14 Matty Fozard; 27 Thibaut Margalet; 11 Michael Knowles; 15 Scott Wheeldon; 13 Matt James. Subs (all used): 18 Elliot Minchella; 23 Greg Burns; 16 Adam Neal; 17 Mark Mexico.
Tries: Knowles (4), Straugheir (10), Laulu-Togagae (12, 26, 67), Fozard (17), Jacks (24), Lo (54, 58, 60), Margalet (65); **Goals:** Aston 9/11.
TOWN: 1 Jack Murphy; 3 Declan Hulme; 4 Jason Mossop; 25 Matty Gee; 24 Theerapol Ritson; 6 Carl Forber; 7 Jamie Doran; 8 Kris Coward; 15 Karl Olstrum; 21 Oliver Gordon; 10 Marc Shackley; 13 Liam McAvoy; 18 Tom Walker. Subs (all used, only three named): 20 Steve Scholey; 19 Ryan Verlinden; 17 Alex Szostak.
Rugby Leaguer & League Express Men of the Match: *Eagles:* Quentin Laulu-Togagae; *Town:* Theerapol Ritson.
Penalty count: 8-10; **Half-time:** 36-0;
Referee: Jon Roberts; **Attendance:** 380.

ROUND 6

Sunday 11th September 2016

OLDHAM 20 WHITEHAVEN 18

OLDHAM: - Scott Turner; 2 Adam Clay; 22 Danny Grimshaw; - Kieran Gill; 5 Jamel Chisholm; 6 Lewis Palfrey; - Dave Hewitt; 8 Phil Joy; 20 Gareth Owen; 23 Tyler Dickinson; 12 Danny Langtree; 16 Gary Middlehurst; 13 Liam Thompson. Subs (all used): 10 Jack Spencer; 14 Joe Burke; 26 Michael Ward; 21 Kenny Hughes.
Tries: Joy (9), Thompson (26), Clay (49); **Goals:** Palfrey 4/4.
WHITEHAVEN: 28 Ed Chamberlain; 25 Ryan Ince; 3 Chris Taylor; 4 Jessie Joe Parker; 20 Jordan Burns; 6 Dion Aiye; 7 Grant Gore; 32 Anthony Walker; 13 Liam Carberry; 26 Ted Chapelhow; 11 Dave Allen; 30 Ugo Perez; 37 Carl Forster. Subs (all used): 17 Steve Fox; 19 Glenn Riley; 9 James Newton; 16 Connor Holliday.
Tries: Perez (4), Carberry (54), Newton (63);
Goals: Chamberlain 3/4.
Rugby Leaguer & League Express Men of the Match: *Oldham:* Adam Clay; *Whitehaven:* Dave Allen.
Penalty count: 5-7; **Half-time:** 14-6;
Referee: Tom Crashley; **Attendance:** 843.

SHEFFIELD EAGLES 22 DEWSBURY RAMS 38

EAGLES: 1 Quentin Laulu-Togagae; 22 Ryan Millar; 3 Menzie Yere; 12 Duane Straugheir; 2 Rob Worrincy; 6 Cory Aston; 24 Rhys Jacks; 8 Steve Thorpe; 14 Matty Fozard; 27 Thibaut Margalet; 11 Michael Knowles; 15 Scott Wheeldon; 13 Matt James. Subs (all used): 18 Elliot Minchella; 23 Greg Burns; 16 Adam Neal; 17 Mark Mexico.
Tries: Yere (12), Millar (35, 60), Aston (68);
Goals: Aston 3/4.
Sin bin: Thorpe (76) - dissent.
RAMS: 1 Josh Guzdek; 2 Dale Morton; 42 Lucas Walshaw; 4 Shane Grady; 38 Etuate Uaisele; 17 Dom Speakman; 22 Andy Kain; 8 Matt Groat; 9 Tom Hemingway; 16 Toby Adamson; 11 Rob Spicer; 12 Scott Hale; 14 Luke Adamson. Subs (all used): 19 Nathan Conroy; 13 Aaron Brown; 24 Jack Teanby; 18 Tony Tonks.
Tries: Hale (3), Uaisele (5), T Adamson (27), Brown (31), Walshaw (38), Hemingway (72);
Goals: Hemingway 3/4, Grady 4/4.
Rugby Leaguer & League Express Men of the Match: *Eagles:* Ryan Millar; *Rams:* Matt Groat.
Penalty count: 8-9; **Half-time:** 10-28;
Referee: Michael Woodhead; **Attendance:** 564.

SWINTON LIONS 28 HALIFAX 26

LIONS: 20 Mike Butt; 2 Shaun Robinson; 3 Stuart Littler; 4 Macauley Hallett; 18 Liam Marshall; 1 Chris Atkin; 6 Ben White; - Jake Emmitt; - Luke Waterworth; 10 Jordan Hand; 11 Connor Dwyer; 12 Andy Thornley; 13 Rob Lever. Subs (all used): 7 Matty Beharrell; 16 Ben Austin; 19 Josh Barlow; 29 Daniel Fleming.
Tries: Atkin (11), Dwyer (29), Hallett (35, 75), Fleming (50);
Goals: Atkin 4/6.
HALIFAX: 32 James Woodburn-Hall; 4 Ben Heaton; 36 Nick Rawsthorne; 29 Chester Butler; 2 Will Sharp; 1 Ben Johnston; 7 Gareth Moore; 8 Mitch Cahalane; 9 Ben Kaye; 10 Luke Ambler; 14 Adam Tangata; 13 Jacob Fairbank; 6 Scott Murrell. Subs (all used): 17 Gavin Bennion; 30 Brandon Moore; 34 Ryan Boyle; 35 Luke Nelmes.
Tries: Heaton (4), Sharp (40), Nelmes (43), Rawsthorne (61, 71); **Goals:** Rawsthorne 0/2, G Moore 3/3.
Rugby Leaguer & League Express Men of the Match: *Lions:* Connor Dwyer; *Halifax:* Adam Tangata.
Penalty count: 9-9; **Half-time:** 16-8;
Referee: Tom Grant; **Attendance:** 582.

WORKINGTON TOWN 30 BRADFORD BULLS 26

TOWN: 1 Jack Murphy; 3 Declan Hulme; 25 Matty Gee; 4 Jason Mossop; 24 Theerapol Ritson; 6 Carl Forber; 28 Jarrod Sammut; 8 Kris Coward; 7 Jamie Doran; 21 Oliver Gordon; 10 Marc Shackley; 13 Liam McAvoy; 15 Karl Olstrum. Subs (all used): 18 Tom Walker; 19 Ryan Verlinden; 20 Steve Scholey; 17 Alex Szostak.

Bradford's Adam Sidlow looks for a way past Sheffield's Steve Thorpe during the Championship Shield Final

Tries: Shackley (15), Sammut (33, 36, 54), Ritson (78); **Goals:** Sammut 5/6.
BULLS: 39 Kieren Moss; 45 Josh Rickett; 23 Alex Mellor; 37 Ross Oakes; 29 Ethan Ryan; 13 Danny Addy; 43 Joe Keyes; 20 Mitch Clark; 42 Stuart Howarth; 25 Ben Kavanagh; 14 Jay Pitts; 28 Kurt Haggerty; 11 Tom Olbison. Subs (all used): 9 Adam O'Brien; 12 Dale Ferguson; 46 Liam Kirk; 10 Adam Sidlow.
Tries: Clark (4), Ryan (26), Oakes (50), Moss (63), Ferguson (74); **Goals:** Keyes 3/5.
Rugby Leaguer & League Express Men of the Match: *Town:* Jarrod Sammut; *Bulls:* Kurt Haggerty.
Penalty count: 12-9; **Half-time:** 18-12;
Referee: Scott Mikalauskas; **Attendance:** 596.

ROUND 7

Sunday 18th September 2016

BRADFORD BULLS 80 SHEFFIELD EAGLES 0

BULLS: 39 Kieren Moss; 5 Danny Williams; 23 Alex Mellor; 4 Kris Welham; 29 Ethan Ryan; 7 Dane Chisholm; 40 Lewis Charnock; 10 Adam Sidlow; 9 Adam O'Brien; 25 Ben Kavanagh; 14 Jay Pitts; 13 Danny Addy; 11 Tom Olbison. Subs (all used): 12 Dale Ferguson; 20 Mitch Clark; 37 Ross Oakes; 46 Liam Kirk.
Tries: Charnock (2), Chisholm (13, 47), Olbison (15), Moss (25, 68, 71, 79), Ryan (31, 75), Pitts (33), Oakes (58, 61, 66), Sidlow (77);
Goals: Charnock 5/7, Chisholm 4/7, Sidlow 1/1.
EAGLES: 1 Quentin Laulu-Togagae; 19 Garry Lo; 4 George Tyson; 5 Ben Blackmore; 22 Ryan Millar; 6 Cory Aston; 18 Elliot Minchella; 8 Steve Thorpe; 9 Keal Carlile; 16 Adam Neal; 11 Michael Knowles; 12 Duane Straugheir; 15 Scott Wheeldon. Subs (all used): 2 Rob Worrincy; 14 Matty Fozard; 17 Mark Mexico; 23 Greg Burns.
Rugby Leaguer & League Express Men of the Match: *Bulls:* Ross Oakes; *Eagles:* Garry Lo.
Penalty count: 7-3; **Half-time:** 32-0;
Referee: Andrew Sweet; **Attendance:** 4,035.

DEWSBURY RAMS 30 OLDHAM 12

RAMS: 1 Josh Guzdek; 2 Dale Morton; 15 Jason Crookes; 4 Shane Grady; 38 Etuate Uaisele; 17 Dom Speakman; 22 Andy Kain; 8 Matt Groat; 9 Tom Hemingway; 16 Toby Adamson; 11 Rob Spicer; 42 Lucas Walshaw; 14 Luke Adamson. Subs (all used): 19 Nathan Conroy; 13 Aaron Brown; 45 Mitchell Stringer; 18 Tony Tonks.
Tries: Uaisele (21), Crookes (26), Kain (33), Walshaw (55), Grady (65); **Goals:** Hemingway 1/1, Grady 4/6.
OLDHAM: - Scott Turner; 2 Adam Clay; 16 Gary Middlehurst; - Kieran Gill; 5 Jamel Chisholm; 6 Lewis Palfrey; - Dave Hewitt; 8 Phil Joy; 20 Gareth Owen; 23 Tyler Dickinson; 10 Jack Spencer; 13 Liam Thompson; 26 Michael Ward. Subs (all used): 21 Kenny Hughes; 14 Joe Burke; 1 Richard Lepori; - Jack Blagbrough.
Tries: Hughes (51), Gill (77); **Goals:** Palfrey 1/1, Lepori 1/1.
Sin bin: Lepori (20) - professional foul; Chisholm (62) - punching.
Rugby Leaguer & League Express Men of the Match: *Rams:* Shane Grady; *Oldham:* Lewis Palfrey.
Penalty count: 11-9; **Half-time:** 16-0;
Referee: Jack Smith; **Attendance:** 628.

HALIFAX 46 WORKINGTON TOWN 26

HALIFAX: 1 Ben Johnston; 18 Miles Greenwood; 32 James Woodburn-Hall; 36 Nick Rawsthorne; 2 Will Sharp; 22 Connor Robinson; 7 Gareth Moore; 8 Mitch Cahalane; 9 Ben Kaye; 10 Luke Ambler; 26 Ed Barber; 17 Gavin Bennion; 13 Jacob Fairbank. Subs (all used): 30 Brandon Moore; 31 Elliot Morris; 34 Ryan Boyle; 35 Luke Nelmes.
Tries: Barber (11), Sharp (20), Morris (38), Woodburn-Hall (40), Ambler (66), Cahalane (72), G Moore (74); **Goals:** G Moore 7/8.
TOWN: 1 Jack Murphy; 3 Declan Hulme; 25 Matty Gee; 4 Jason Mossop; 24 Theerapol Ritson; 6 Carl Forber; 28 Jarrod Sammut; 18 Tom Walker; 7 Jamie Doran; 21 Oliver Gordon; 10 Marc Shackley; 13 Liam McAvoy; 20 Steve Scholey. Sub (used, only one named): 19 Ryan Verlinden.
Tries: Ritson (14), Mossop (26), Doran (56), Gee (62), Hulme (77); **Goals:** Sammut 3/6.
Sin bin: McAvoy (48) - punching; Shackley (69) - dissent.
Rugby Leaguer & League Express Men of the Match: *Halifax:* Gareth Moore; *Town:* Jarrod Sammut.
Penalty count: 13-8; **Half-time:** 22-12;
Referee: Tom Grant; **Attendance:** 1,217.

WHITEHAVEN 40 SWINTON LIONS 18

WHITEHAVEN: 1 Louis Jouffret; 25 Ryan Ince; 4 Jessie Joe Parker; 3 Chris Taylor; 28 Ed Chamberlain; 6 Dion Aiye; 7 Grant Gore; 32 Anthony Walker; 13 Liam Carberry; 26 Ted Chapelhow; 11 Dave Allen; 30 Ugo Perez; 37 Carl Forster. Subs (all used): 15 Ben Davies; 17 Steve Fox; 16 Connor Holliday; 9 James Newton.
Tries: T Chapelhow (3), Chamberlain (30, 72), Ince (44), Aiye (52), Gore (61), Holliday (76);
Goals: Jouffret 6/6, Perez 0/1.
LIONS: 20 Mike Butt; 2 Shaun Robinson; 3 Stuart Littler; 4 Macauley Hallett; 18 Liam Marshall; 1 Chris Atkin; 6 Ben White; - Jake Emmitt; - Luke Waterworth; 10 Jordan Hand; 11 Connor Dwyer; 12 Andy Thornley; 13 Rob Lever. Subs (all used): 7 Matty Beharrell; 16 Ben Austin; 19 Josh Barlow; 29 Daniel Fleming.
Tries: Waterworth (11), Butt (23), Atkin (67);
Goals: Atkin 2/2, Beharrell 1/1.
Rugby Leaguer & League Express Men of the Match: *Whitehaven:* Anthony Walker; *Lions:* Ben White.
Penalty count: 11-8; **Half-time:** 12-12;
Referee: Scott Mikalauskas; **Attendance:** 733.

SEMI-FINALS

Sunday 25th September 2016

BRADFORD BULLS 36 DEWSBURY RAMS 22

BULLS: 39 Kieren Moss; 5 Danny Williams; 23 Alex Mellor; 4 Kris Welham; 29 Ethan Ryan; 7 Dane Chisholm; 40 Lewis Charnock; 10 Adam Sidlow; 9 Adam O'Brien; 25 Ben Kavanagh; 14 Jay Pitts; 13 Danny Addy; 12 Dale Ferguson. Subs (all used): 11 Tom Olbison; 20 Mitch Clark; 37 Ross Oakes; 46 Liam Kirk.
Tries: Chisholm (3), Mellor (12, 28), Welham (40), Williams (48), Moss (52), Ryan (80); **Goals:** Charnock 4/7.
RAMS: 1 Josh Guzdek; 2 Dale Morton; 6 Paul Sykes; 4 Shane Grady; 15 Jason Crookes; 17 Dom Speakman; 22 Andy Kain; 8 Matt Groat; 9 Tom Hemingway; 16 Toby

Adamson; 11 Rob Spicer; 32 Kyle Trout; 14 Luke Adamson. Subs (all used): 13 Aaron Brown; 18 Tony Tonks; 19 Nathan Conroy; 24 Jack Teanby.
Tries: Kain (18), Crookes (44), Guzdek (59), T Adamson (75); **Goals:** Hemingway 0/1, Grady 3/3.
Rugby Leaguer & League Express Men of the Match: *Bulls:* Alex Mellor; *Rams:* Shane Grady.
Penalty count: 11-11; **Half-time:** 20-4;
Referee: Scott Mikalauskas; **Attendance:** 2,189.

HALIFAX 32 SHEFFIELD EAGLES 46

HALIFAX: 1 Ben Johnston; 4 Ben Heaton; 32 James Woodburn-Hall; 36 Nick Rawsthorne; 2 Will Sharp; 6 Scott Murrell; 7 Gareth Moore; 8 Mitch Cahalane; 9 Ben Kaye; 10 Luke Ambler; 26 Ed Barber; 14 Adam Tangata; 13 Jacob Fairbank. Subs (all used): 17 Gavin Bennion; 30 Brandon Moore; 34 Ryan Boyle; 35 Luke Nelmes.
Tries: Woodburn-Hall (32, 58, 65), Barber (42), B Moore (49), Cahalane (77); **Goals:** G Moore 4/6.
Dismissal: G Moore (79) - punching.
EAGLES: 1 Quentin Laulu-Togagae; 2 Rob Worrincy; 4 George Tyson; 25 Nathan Chappell; 5 Ben Blackmore; 6 Cory Aston; 24 Rhys Jacks; 15 Scott Wheeldon; 9 Keal Carlile; 16 Adam Neal; 13 Matt James; 12 Duane Straugheir; 18 Elliot Minchella. Subs (all used): 11 Michael Knowles; 14 Matty Fozard; 17 Mark Mexico; 19 Garry Lo.
Tries: Jacks (4), Wheeldon (9), Neal (16), Tyson (28, 75), Worrincy (62), Lo (71); **Goals:** Aston 9/11.
Sin bin: Wheeldon (79) - high tackle.
Rugby Leaguer & League Express Men of the Match: *Halifax:* James Woodburn-Hall; *Eagles:* Keal Carlile.
Penalty count: 10-12; **Half-time:** 6-28;
Referee: Callum Straw; **Attendance:** 946.

FINAL

Sunday 2nd October 2016

BRADFORD BULLS 27 SHEFFIELD EAGLES 16

BULLS: 39 Kieren Moss; 5 Danny Williams; 23 Alex Mellor; 4 Kris Welham; 3 Adrian Purtell; 7 Dane Chisholm; 40 Lewis Charnock; 10 Adam Sidlow; 9 Adam O'Brien; 25 Ben Kavanagh; 28 Kurt Haggerty; 13 Danny Addy; 14 Jay Pitts. Subs (all used): 37 Ross Oakes; 11 Tom Olbison; 12 Dale Ferguson; 20 Mitch Clark.
Tries: O'Brien (1, 22), Purtell (12), Welham (71, 77); **Goals:** Charnock 3/5; **Field goal:** Chisholm (74).
EAGLES: 1 Quentin Laulu-Togagae; 19 Garry Lo; 3 Menzie Yere; 4 George Tyson; 2 Rob Worrincy; 6 Cory Aston; 24 Rhys Jacks; 15 Scott Wheeldon; 9 Keal Carlile; 16 Adam Neal; 13 Matt James; 12 Duane Straugheir; 18 Elliot Minchella. Subs (all used): 14 Matty Fozard; 8 Steve Thorpe; 27 Thibaut Margalet; 17 Mark Mexico.
Tries: Yere (26), Worrincy (32); **Goals:** Aston 4/4.
Rugby Leaguer & League Express Men of the Match: *Bulls:* Adam O'Brien; *Eagles:* Quentin Laulu-Togagae.
Penalty count: 7-7; **Half-time:** 18-12;
Referee: Jack Smith; **Attendance:** 3,518.

LEAGUE 1 2016
Club by Club

BARROW RAIDERS

DATE	FIXTURE	RESULT	SCORERS	LGE	ATT
21/2/16	Rochdale (h) (L1CR1)	L4-14	t:Ward	N/A	659
28/2/16	Hunslet (a) (CCR3)	L46-12	t:Ward,Duerden g:Ward(2)	N/A	354
6/3/16	North Wales (a)	W18-37	t:Harrison(2),Wiper,Hankinson,Litherland(2) g:Ward(6) fg:Ward	4th	543
13/3/16	Hunslet (h)	W40-6	t:Fieldhouse(2),Harrison,Pitman,Wiper,D Toal,Abram g:Ward(6)	2nd	1,003
25/3/16	Newcastle (h)	D24-24	t:Holmes,Duerden,Ward,Wiper g:Ward(4)	2nd	1,033
10/4/16	Coventry (a)	W0-38	t:Harrison,Fleming,Litherland,Duerden,Haney,Abram,Bullock g:Ward(5)	2nd	425
24/4/16	Doncaster (a)	L21-18	t:Hankinson,Haney,Bate g:Ward(3)	5th	540
1/5/16	Rochdale (h)	L4-18	t:Pitman	7th	793
8/5/16	York (h)	W50-12	t:Bullock,Dallimore,Litherland,Morrow,Pitman(2),S Toal,D Toal,Hankinson g:Hankinson(7)	5th	977
15/5/16	South Wales (a)	W4-44	t:Marwood,Wiper,S Toal(2),While,Abram,Hankinson(2) g:Hankinson(6)	5th	180
22/5/16	Toulouse (h)	L16-44	t:Wiper,Wilkes(2) g:Hankinson(2)	6th	1,050
5/6/16	Gloucestershire All Golds (a)	W16-52	t:Pitman(3),Dawson,Hankinson,D Toal,Harrison,Wiper,Dallimore g:Hankinson(8)	6th	122
11/6/16	London Skolars (a)	L42-34	t:Fieldhouse(3),Wiper,S Toal g:Hankinson(6),Dallimore	6th	364
19/6/16	Hemel (h)	W62-4	t:Harper(2),Harrison,Litherland,Fleming,Pitman(2),Mossop(2),D Toal,Aspinwall g:Hankinson(8),Ward	6th	714
26/6/16	Keighley (a)	W32-34	t:Fieldhouse,Hankinson,Harper,Dallimore,Pitman,Harrison g:Hankinson(5)	5th	716
3/7/16	Oxford (h)	W76-12	t:Wilkes,Dallimore,Litherland(4),Morrow(2),Hankinson(2),Bate,D Toal,Fleming g:Fleming(12)	5th	857
24/7/16	Rochdale (a) (S8)	W34-12	t:Fieldhouse,Brennan(2),Dallimore,Bullock,Fleming g:Hankinson(5)	3rd	913
31/7/16	Doncaster (a) (S8)	W12-40	t:Harper(2),Harrison,Litherland,D Toal(2) g:Hankinson(8)	3rd	622
7/8/16	York (a) (S8)	W6-20	t:Hankinson,Harper(2),Crellin g:Hankinson(2)	3rd	664
14/8/16	Hunslet (h) (S8)	W44-26	t:Fleming(2),Hankinson(2),Wiper,Wilkes,Aspinwall(2) g:Hankinson(6)	3rd	1,003
20/8/16	London Skolars (a) (S8)	W4-54	t:Mossop,Brennan(2),Hankinson,Holmes,Pitman(2),Harper,Ashall g:Hankinson(8),Wilkes	2nd	227
4/9/16	Keighley (h) (S8)	W26-18	t:Harper,Harrison,Fieldhouse,Bate g:Hankinson(5)	2nd	1,173
10/9/16	Toulouse (a) (S8)	L44-22	t:Harper,Fleming,Harrison,Pitman g:Hankinson(3)	3rd	1,161
25/9/16	Doncaster (h) (SF)	W46-6	t:Wiper,Fleming(2),Bate,D Toal(2),Ashall,Fieldhouse g:Hankinson(6),Harrison	N/A	1,117
1/10/16	Toulouse (a) (POF)	L32-22	t:Harper,Fleming(2),Fieldhouse g:Hankinson(3)	N/A	1,213

		APP		TRIES		GOALS		FG		PTS	
	D.O.B.	ALL	L1	ALL	L1	ALL	L1	ALL	L1	ALL	L1
Dan Abram	11/11/95	2(13)	2(11)	3	3	0	0	0	0	12	12
Karl Ashall	3/11/89	19	19	2	2	0	0	0	0	8	8
Martin Aspinwall	21/10/81	22(1)	20(1)	3	3	0	0	0	0	12	12
Anthony Bate	28/4/93	3(15)	3(15)	4	4	0	0	0	0	16	16
Brad Brennan	18/1/93	(9)	(9)	4	4	0	0	0	0	16	16
Joe Bullock	27/11/92	22(3)	20(3)	3	3	0	0	0	0	12	12
Liam Campbell	5/6/86	2	0	0	0	0	0	0	0	0	0
Bradd Crellin	2/7/89	8	6	1	1	0	0	0	0	4	4
Luke Cresswell	5/5/95	1	1	0	0	0	0	0	0	0	0
Jamie Dallimore	20/8/88	22	22	5	5	1	1	0	0	22	22
Andrew Dawson	12/3/89	4(10)	4(8)	1	1	0	0	0	0	4	4
James Duerden	9/10/91	1(11)	1(9)	3	2	0	0	0	0	12	8
Ryan Fieldhouse	10/4/88	23	21	10	10	0	0	0	0	40	40
Chris Fleming	11/1/91	16	16	11	11	12	12	0	0	68	68
Joe Hambley	2/12/95	(1)	(1)	0	0	0	0	0	0	0	0
Lee Haney	11/6/88	3	3	2	2	0	0	0	0	8	8
Chris Hankinson	30/11/93	24	22	13	13	88	88	0	0	228	228
Eze Harper	7/12/94	12	12	11	11	0	0	0	0	44	44
Liam Harrison	3/12/82	22	20	10	10	1	1	0	0	42	42
Matty Holmes	24/4/94	6(5)	6(5)	2	2	0	0	0	0	8	8
Andy Litherland	15/5/90	13	13	10	10	0	0	0	0	40	40
Brad Marwood	4/11/93	5(1)	5(1)	1	1	0	0	0	0	4	4
Danny Morrow	30/4/90	10	10	3	3	0	0	0	0	12	12
Nathan Mossop	21/2/88	4(10)	2(10)	3	3	0	0	0	0	12	12
Cameron Pitman	9/7/89	23	21	13	13	0	0	0	0	52	52
Dan Toal	22/9/89	1(19)	1(17)	9	9	0	0	0	0	36	36
Shane Toal	11/11/95	8	6	4	4	0	0	0	0	16	16
Josh Ward	16/6/95	9	7	3	1	27	25	1	1	67	55
Matty While	25/11/96	(2)	(2)	1	1	0	0	0	0	4	4
Oliver Wilkes	2/5/80	23	21	4	4	1	1	0	0	18	18
Max Wiper	18/9/90	17	15	9	9	0	0	0	0	36	36

'L1' totals include Super 8s & play-offs; 'All' totals also include League 1 Cup & Challenge Cup

Chris Hankinson

LEAGUE RECORD
P21-W15-D1-L5
(3rd/Losers, Play-off Final)
F769, A375, Diff+394, 31 points.

LEAGUE 1 CUP
Round One

CHALLENGE CUP
Round Three

ATTENDANCES
Best - v Keighley (S8 - 1,173)
Worst - v Rochdale (L1C - 659)
Total (all home games
included) - 11,292
Average (all home games
included) - 941
(Up by 36 on 2015)

CLUB RECORDS MATCH RECORDS	**Highest score:** 138-0 v Nottingham City, 27/11/94 **Highest score against:** 0-90 v Leeds, 11/2/90 **Record attendance:** 21,651 v Salford, 15/4/38 **Tries:** 6 Val Cumberbatch v Batley, 21/11/36; Jim Thornburrow v Maryport, 19/2/38; Steve Rowan v Nottingham City, 15/11/92 **Goals:** 17 Darren Carter v Nottingham City, 27/11/94 **Points:** 42 Darren Carter v Nottingham City, 27/11/94
SEASON RECORDS CAREER RECORDS	**Tries:** 50 Jim Lewthwaite 1956-57 **Goals:** 135 Joe Ball 1956-57 **Points:** 323 Jamie Rooney 2010 **Tries:** 352 Jim Lewthwaite 1943-57 **Goals:** 1,099 (inc 63fg) Darren Holt 1998-2002; 2004-2009; 2012 **Points:** 2,403 Darren Holt 1998-2002; 2004-2009; 2012 **Appearances:** 500 Jim Lewthwaite 1943-57

COVENTRY BEARS

DATE	FIXTURE	RESULT	SCORERS	LGE	ATT
21/2/16	Gloucestershire All Golds (h) (L1CR1)	L24-48	t:Bass,Medforth,Freeman(2),Hunte g:Weston,White	N/A	146
28/2/16	Keighley (a) (CCR3)	L54-28	t:Holland,Warrilow,O'Mara,Lobwein,Milizewski g:James(4)	N/A	421
5/3/16	Toulouse (a)	L54-6	t:Reid g:James	14th	2,284
13/3/16	Rochdale (h)	L16-58	t:Hughes(2),Reid g:White(2)	15th	250
25/3/16	Gloucestershire All Golds (a)	W28-29	t:Morrison,Medforth,Freeman,Reid,Hughes g:James(4) fg:James	12th	167
10/4/16	Barrow (h)	L0-38		13th	425
23/4/16	London Skolars (a)	L52-20	t:Barratt,Hughes,Beecham,O'Mara g:James(2)	12th	365
8/5/16	Keighley (h) ●	L16-36	t:Geurtjens,Beecham,Barratt g:James(2)	13th	1,097
14/5/16	Doncaster (h)	L20-32	t:Freeman,Medforth(2),O'Mara g:James(2)	12th	373
22/5/16	Hemel (a)	W14-50	t:Milizewski(3),Barratt,Lobwein,Brennan,O'Mara(3),Thompson g:James(5)	11th	149
1/6/16	York (a)	L32-14	t:Redman,Chapman,Bass g:James	11th	451
11/6/16	Oxford (h)	W48-10	t:James,Morrison,Medforth(2),Brennan,Thompson,Milizewski,Batchelor, Barratt g:James(6)	11th	444
19/6/16	Hunslet (a)	L38-18	t:Lobwein,Batchelor,Reid g:James(3)	11th	446
25/6/16	Newcastle (h)	L14-32	t:Beecham,O'Mara,Medforth g:James	11th	266
3/7/16	North Wales (a) ●●	D20-20	t:Reid,Bass,Beddows,Morrison g:James(2)	11th	359
9/7/16	South Wales (h)	W18-16	t:Hughes(2),Morrison g:James(3)	11th	545
23/7/16	Oxford (h) (L1S)	W48-6	t:O'Mara,Hughes(2),Medforth(3),Reid,Beddows,Morrison g:James(6)	3rd(L1S)	253
6/8/16	South Wales (h) (L1S)	L14-18	t:Bass,Batchelor g:James(3)	3rd(L1S)	497
14/8/16	North Wales (a) (L1S) ●●	W28-30	t:Beecham,Batchelor,Lobwein,Hunte,Hughes g:James(5)	3rd(L1S)	297
21/8/16	Gloucestershire All Golds (h) (L1S)	W33-20	t:Freeman,Price(2),Hunte,Lobwein,Bass g:James(4) fg:James	3rd(L1S)	392
3/9/16	Newcastle (a) (L1S)	L46-10	t:Medforth,Morrison g:James	3rd(L1S)	456
10/9/16	Hemel (a) (L1S)	W12-22	t:Morrison,Milizewski,Hunte,Price g:James(3)	3rd(L1S)	307

● Played at Ricoh Arena
●● Played at Hare Lane, Chester

	D.O.B.	APP ALL	APP L1	TRIES ALL	TRIES L1	GOALS ALL	GOALS L1	FG ALL	FG L1	PTS ALL	PTS L1
John Aldred	3/10/89	(4)	(2)	0	0	0	0	0	0	0	0
Dylan Bale	23/5/96	(2)		0	0	0	0	0	0	0	0
Brett Barlow	29/8/96	1	0	0	0	0	0	0	0	0	0
Chris Barratt	7/2/93	19(3)	12(2)	4	4	0	0	0	0	16	16
Jason Bass	10/5/96	17	10	5	2	0	0	0	0	20	8
Joe Batchelor	28/10/94	5(6)	1(5)	4	2	0	0	0	0	16	8
Alex Beddows	1/8/94	14(1)	8	2	1	0	0	0	0	8	4
Grant Beecham	25/10/94	13(4)	7(4)	4	3	0	0	0	0	16	12
Brad Brennan	18/1/93	(3)	(3)	2	2	0	0	0	0	8	8
Harry Chapman	15/7/97	1(1)	1	1	1	0	0	0	0	4	4
Hayden Freeman	20/8/97	10	6	5	2	0	0	0	0	20	8
James Geurtjens	28/4/86	6(11)	5(5)	1	1	0	0	0	0	4	4
Tommy Holland	28/8/95	2(1)	1(1)	1	0	0	0	0	0	4	0
Elliot Holton	22/7/96	1(1)	(1)	0	0	0	0	0	0	0	0
Richard Hughes	28/3/93	12(4)	8(3)	9	6	0	0	0	0	36	24
Jamahl Hunte	27/4/94	9	4	4	0	0	0	0	0	16	0
Joel James	17/2/95	20(1)	13	1	1	58	32	2	1	122	69
Elliot Liku	21/4/96	1(2)	(2)	0	0	0	0	0	0	0	0
Jay Lobwein	13/4/92	18(3)	13	5	2	0	0	0	0	20	8
Eddie Medforth	30/3/95	19	14	11	6	0	0	0	0	44	24
Jonathan Milizewski	17/4/91	18(3)	11(2)	6	4	0	0	0	0	24	16
Jack Morrison	16/9/92	21	14	7	4	0	0	0	0	28	16
Elliot Norman	11/10/96	1(1)	1	0	0	0	0	0	0	0	0
Charlie O'Mara	11/9/96	14(2)	9(2)	8	6	0	0	0	0	32	24
Trae O'Sullivan	7/9/96	3(16)	1(10)	0	0	0	0	0	0	0	0
Dan Price	5/10/92	7(3)	3(3)	3	0	0	0	0	0	12	0
James Redman	8/3/95	13(1)	12(1)	1	1	0	0	0	0	4	4
Matt Reid	16/9/92	16	11	6	5	0	0	0	0	24	20
Adam Saynor	7/11/89	2(4)	1(3)	0	0	0	0	0	0	0	0
Liam Thompson	7/2/91	17	14	2	2	0	0	0	0	8	8
Andy Unsworth	14/9/92	1(5)	(2)	0	0	0	0	0	0	0	0
Ben Warrilow	24/1/94	5	4	1	0	0	0	0	0	4	0
Dave Weston	11/2/91	1	0	0	0	1	0	0	0	2	0
Craig White	13/1/88	3(1)	2(1)	0	0	3	2	0	0	6	4

'L1' totals include League 1 regular season only; 'All' totals also include League 1 Shield, League 1 Cup & Challenge Cup

Eddie Medforth

LEAGUE RECORD
League 1, before Super 8 split:
P14-W4-D1-L9 (11th)
F289, A460, Diff-171, 9 points.

After League 1 Shield:
P20-W8-D1-L11 (3rd)
F446, A590, Diff-144, 17 points.

LEAGUE 1 CUP
Round One

CHALLENGE CUP
Round Three

ATTENDANCES
Best - v Keighley (L1 - 1,097)
Worst - v Gloucestershire All Golds (L1C - 146)
Total (all home games included) - 4,688
Average (all home games included) - 426
(Down by 32 on 2015)

CLUB RECORDS Highest score: 52-16 v Hemel, 19/4/2015 Highest score against: 8-78 v Swinton, 14/6/2015 Record attendance: 1,097 v Keighley, 8/5/2016
MATCH RECORDS Tries: 3 (5 players) Goals: 8 Connor Robinson v Hemel, 19/4/2015 Points: 22 Dan Parker v London Skolars, 7/6/2015
SEASON RECORDS Tries: 13 Jamahl Hunte 2015 Goals: 60 (inc 2fg) Joel James 2016 Points: 122 Joel James 2016
CAREER RECORDS Tries: 17 Richard Hughes 2015-2016; Jamahl Hunte 2015-2016 Goals: 60 (inc 2fg) Joel James 2015-2016
Points: 126 Joel James 2015-2016 Appearances: 46 Chris Barratt 2015-2016

DONCASTER
RUGBY LEAGUE CLUB

DONCASTER

DATE	FIXTURE	RESULT	SCORERS	LGE	ATT
21/2/16	North Wales (h) (L1CR1)	W35-28	t:L Welham,Abdull,Hedges(2),Foggin-Johnston(2),Cross g:Hedges(3) fg:Hedges	N/A	513
28/2/16	West Hull (a) (CCR3)	W0-54	t:L Welham,Scott(2),Jones-Bishop(2),M Nicholson,Hedges,M Welham,Walton g:Carr(9)	N/A	268
6/3/16	Gloucestershire All Golds (h)	W40-8	t:Sheriff,Cross(3),Yeaman,L Welham,Foggin-Johnston g:Carr(6)	3rd	538
13/3/16	Keighley (a)	W28-44	t:Sheriff,M Welham(2),Dean(2),Hedges,Tonks,Braham g:Carr(5),Hedges	4th	791
18/3/16	Hunslet (a) (CCR4)	L48-6	t:Braham g:Hedges	N/A	337
25/3/16	York (h)	L16-46	t:M Welham,Sheriff,Aizue g:Dean(2)	7th	946
3/4/16	London Skolars (h) (L1CQF)	L12-24	t:L Welham,Tonks g:Dean(2)	N/A	367
10/4/16	North Wales (h)	W30-14	t:Castle,Tali(2),Tonks(2),Kelly g:Carr(3)	6th	580
24/4/16	Barrow (h)	W21-18	t:Castle,Tali(2) g:Carr(4) fg:Carr	5th	540
1/5/16	Hunslet (a)	W22-30	t:Kelly,B Delaney(2),Tali,Castle g:Carr(5)	2nd	385
8/5/16	Newcastle (a)	L35-34	t:B Nicholson,Foggin-Johnston,Tali(3),B Delaney g:Carr(5)	3rd	552
14/5/16	Coventry (a)	W20-32	t:B Nicholson,Palea'aesina(2),Carr,Doherty,Tali g:Carr(4)	3rd	373
22/5/16	Oxford (h)	W54-14	t:L Welham(3),Aizue,Carr,Kesik,Sheriff(2),Hedges,Wright g:Carr(7)	2nd	744
4/6/16	Toulouse (a)	L46-26	t:Wright,Braham,Sheriff,Doherty,Howden g:Carr(3)	5th	2,218
12/6/16	South Wales (h) ●	W54-4	t:M Nicholson,Hedges,Castle,Tali,Howden,B Nicholson,Sheriff,Foster,Milton g:Carr(9)	5th	450
25/6/16	London Skolars (a)	W10-30	t:Kesik,Sheriff,Doherty(3) g:Carr(5)	4th	425
3/7/16	Hemel (h) ●	W80-18	t:Scott(3),Jones-Bishop(2),Doherty(2),Cross(2),Tali(2),Carr,L Welham,Foggin-Johnston g:Carr(12)	4th	562
10/7/16	Rochdale (a)	L21-8	t:Scott g:Hedges(2)	4th	591
31/7/16	Barrow (h) (S8)	L12-40	t:Castle,Foggin-Johnston g:Carr(2)	5th	622
5/8/16	Hunslet (a) (S8)	W24-36	t:Sheriff(2),Carr,Foggin-Johnston(2),Aizue g:Carr(6)	4th	541
14/8/16	Keighley (h) (S8)	L18-38	t:Foggin-Johnston,Aizue,B Nicholson g:Carr(3)	5th	573
21/8/16	Keighley (h) (S8)	W26-24	t:B Nicholson,Sheriff,Castle,Hedges g:Carr(5)	4th	609
4/9/16	Rochdale (a) (S8)	L38-22	t:Foggin-Johnston,Sheriff,Jones-Bishop(2) g:Carr(3)	5th	392
8/9/16	York (a) (S8)	W28-36	t:Scott,Doherty(2),Palea'aesina,B Nicholson,Howden(2) g:Carr(4)	4th	540
11/9/16	London Skolars (h) (S8)	W34-30	t:Sheriff,Doherty,Scott,Kesik,Foggin-Johnston,Howden g:Carr(5)	4th	587
25/9/16	Barrow (a) (SF)	L46-6	t:Kesik g:Carr	N/A	1,117

● *Played at Keepmoat Athletics Ground*

Tom Carr

		APP		TRIES		GOALS		FG		PTS	
	D.O.B.	ALL	L1	ALL	L1	ALL	L1	ALL	L1	ALL	L1
Jordan Abdull	5/2/96	1	0	1	0	0	0	0	0	4	0
Makali Aizue	30/12/77	13(8)	11(7)	4	4	0	0	0	0	16	16
Zac Braham	14/1/95	4(12)	3(10)	3	2	0	0	0	0	12	8
Tom Carr	16/7/91	21	20	4	4	106	97	1	1	229	211
Mark Castle	19/2/86	8(11)	8(10)	6	6	0	0	0	0	24	24
Mathew Cook	28/6/94	2	1	0	0	0	0	0	0	0	0
Kieran Cross	18/2/95	4(10)	4(6)	6	5	0	0	0	0	24	20
Reece Dean	30/11/96	4	3	2	2	4	2	0	0	16	12
Brad Delaney	25/5/95	5	5	3	3	0	0	0	0	12	12
James Delaney	4/5/92	(2)	(2)	0	0	0	0	0	0	0	0
Sam Doherty	14/11/93	19	18	10	10	0	0	0	0	40	40
Brad Fash	24/1/96	1	0	0	0	0	0	0	0	0	0
David Foggin-Johnston	19/8/96	19	17	11	9	0	0	0	0	44	36
Brad Foster	28/8/95	13	11	1	1	0	0	0	0	4	4
Ben Frankland	13/4/96	3	1	0	0	0	0	0	0	0	0
Jordie Hedges	4/8/95	18	14	7	4	7	3	1	0	43	22
Jordan Howden	6/5/96	16	16	5	5	0	0	0	0	20	20
Aaron Jones-Bishop	18/1/90	9	7	6	4	0	0	0	0	24	16
Michael Kelly	23/5/89	5	3	2	2	0	0	0	0	8	8
Kyle Kesik	3/6/89	21(2)	18(2)	4	4	0	0	0	0	16	16
Callum Lancaster	13/10/96	1	0	0	0	0	0	0	0	0	0
George Milton	4/9/95	16(2)	14(1)	1	1	0	0	0	0	4	4
Brad Nicholson	20/8/95	9(8)	9(8)	6	6	0	0	0	0	24	24
Matt Nicholson	11/9/91	9(4)	8(2)	2	1	0	0	0	0	8	4
Iafeta Palea'aesina	10/2/82	(11)	(10)	3	3	0	0	0	0	12	12
Joe Pickets-O'Donnell	27/11/90	3(9)	2(8)	0	0	0	0	0	0	0	0
Connor Scott	27/5/93	20(4)	17(4)	8	6	0	0	0	0	32	24
Louis Sheriff	6/9/92	25	21	13	13	0	0	0	0	52	52
Jason Tali	7/7/89	14	13	12	12	0	0	0	0	48	48
Mason Tonks	11/10/94	12	8	4	3	0	0	0	0	16	12
Jansin Turgut	8/3/96	1	1	0	0	0	0	0	0	0	0
Harry Tyson-Wilson	29/12/96	2	1	0	0	0	0	0	0	0	0
Mitch Vincent	14/3/94	(1)	0	0	0	0	0	0	0	0	0
Jack Walton	7/5/95	13(5)	12(3)	1	0	0	0	0	0	4	0
Liam Welham	11/11/88	18(2)	14(2)	8	5	0	0	0	0	32	20
Matty Welham	1/2/93	5(2)	3(2)	4	3	0	0	0	0	16	12
Ryan Wright	28/10/91	2(11)	2(11)	2	2	0	0	0	0	8	8
Kirk Yeaman	15/9/83	2	1	1	1	0	0	0	0	4	4

'L1' totals include Super 8s & play-offs; 'All' totals also include League 1 Cup & Challenge Cup

LEAGUE RECORD
P21-W14-D0-L7
(4th/Semi-Finalists)
F683, A526, Diff+157, 28 points.

LEAGUE 1 CUP
Quarter Finalists

CHALLENGE CUP
Round Four

ATTENDANCES
Best - v York (L1 - 946)
Worst - v London Skolars (L1CQF - 367)
Total (all home games included) - 7,631
Average (all home games included) - 587
(Down by 523 on 2015, Championship)

CLUB RECORDS	**Highest score:** 96-0 v Highfield, 20/3/94 **Highest score against:** 4-90 v Widnes, 10/6/2007 **Record attendance:** 10,000 v Bradford, 16/2/52 *(York Road)*; 6,528 v Castleford, 12/4/2007 *(Keepmoat Stadium)*
MATCH RECORDS	**Tries:** 6 Kane Epati v Oldham, 30/7/2006; Lee Waterman v Sharlston, 24/3/2012 **Goals:** 12 Tony Zelei v Nottingham City, 1/9/91; Robert Turner v Highfield, 20/3/94; Tom Carr v Hemel, 3/7/2016 **Points:** 32 Tony Zelei v Nottingham City, 1/9/91; Lee Waterman v Sharlston, 24/3/2012
SEASON RECORDS	**Tries:** 36 Lee Waterman 2012 **Goals:** 129 Jonny Woodcock 2002 **Points:** 306 Jonny Woodcock 2002
CAREER RECORDS	**Tries:** 112 Mark Roache 1985-97 **Goals:** 850 David Noble 1976-77; 1980-89; 1992 **Points:** 1,751 David Noble 1976-77; 1980-89; 1992 **Appearances:** 327 Audley Pennant 1980-83; 1985-97

241

GLOUCESTERSHIRE ALL GOLDS

ALL GOLDS

DATE	FIXTURE	RESULT	SCORERS	LGE	ATT
21/2/16	Coventry (a) (L1CR1)	W24-48	t:Newton(2),Elliott,Cowburn(3),Evans,Kidd,Allison g:Davies(5),Lombardo	N/A	146
28/2/16	North Wales (a) (CCR3)	W36-40	t:Murphy,Leather(2),Davies,Elliott,Cowburn,Kidd g:Davies(6)	N/A	324
6/3/16	Doncaster (a)	L40-8	t:Cowburn,Murphy	13th	538
16/3/16	South Wales (h)	W44-22	t:Parry,Elliott,Davidson(2),Leather,Barlow(2),Newton(2) g:Lombardo(4)	9th	160
19/3/16	Toulouse (a) (CCR4)	L62-28	t:Davidson,Parry(3),Leather g:Davies(4)	N/A	1,053
25/3/16	Coventry (h)	L28-29	t:Davies,Parry(2),Bryan,Barlow g:Davies(4)	9th	167
3/4/16	Newcastle (h) (L1CQF)	W36-28	t:Allison,Elliott,Leather,Cowburn,Parry,Reece,Purslow g:Davies(3),Murphy	N/A	102
10/4/16	Rochdale (a)	L38-16	t:Murphy,Cowburn,Leather g:Murphy(2)	9th	430
17/4/16	Keighley (a)	L42-18	t:Rowland,Kislingbury,McClean,Bryan g:Murphy	10th	527
24/4/16	Newcastle (h)	L18-21	t:Bryan,Barlow,Davidson g:Bradley(3)	11th	105
1/5/16	York (a) (L1CSF)	L58-14	t:Barlow,Cowburn,Parry g:Davies	N/A	469
22/5/16	Hunslet (h)	L18-26	t:Allison,Barlow,Bryan g:Bradley(3)	12th	134
28/5/16	Toulouse (a)	L48-16	t:Parry,Barlow(2) g:Bradley(2)	12th	1,335
5/6/16	Barrow (h)	L16-52	t:Newton,McClean,Whittel g:Newton(2)	12th	122
12/6/16	Hemel (a)	W18-48	t:Mitchell(2),Reece(3),Allison,Hyde,Agoro,Parry g:Mitchell,Hyde(5)	12th	124
19/6/16	North Wales (h)	L18-30	t:Parry(2),Cowburn g:Hyde(3)	12th	171
26/6/16	York (a)	L56-12	t:Parry(2) g:Hyde(2)	12th	585
3/7/16	London Skolars (h)	L22-23	t:Reece(2),Parry,Bryan g:Hyde(3)	12th	190
10/7/16	Oxford (a)	W34-52	t:McClean(4),Uren,Walter(2),Reece,Cowburn(2) g:Hyde(4),Reece(2)	12th	185
24/7/16	Newcastle (a) (L1S)	L50-24	t:Parry,Hyde,Williams,Bryan g:Hyde(2),Rowland(2)	4th(L1S)	482
31/7/16	Oxford (h) (L1S)	L26-28	t:Evans,McClean,Bryan,Kislingbury,Parry g:Reece,Rowland(2)	4th(L1S)	105
14/8/16	Hemel (h) (L1S)	W74-18	t:Uren,Newton(4),McClean,Rowland(2),Williams,Cowburn(2),Allison,Whittel g:Hyde(11)	4th(L1S)	101
21/8/16	Coventry (a) (L1S)	L33-20	t:Mitchell,Parry,Uren,Williams g:Hyde(2)	4th(L1S)	392
3/9/16	North Wales (a) (L1S) ●	L18-4	t:Parry	4th(L1S)	270
10/9/16	South Wales (h) (L1S)	W33-18	t:Mitchell,Parry,Walter,Rowland,Cowburn,Allison g:Hyde(4) fg:Rowland	4th(L1S)	115

● Played at Queensway Stadium, Wrexham

	D.O.B.	APP ALL	APP L1	TRIES ALL	TRIES L1	GOALS ALL	GOALS L1	FG ALL	FG L1	PTS ALL	PTS L1
Mo Agoro	29/1/93	8	5	1	1	0	0	0	0	4	4
Josh Allison	5/4/93	24	14	6	2	0	0	0	0	24	8
Chris Barlow	24/10/95	11	9	8	7	0	0	0	0	32	28
Callum Bradbury	3/8/96	(1)	(1)	0	0	0	0	0	0	0	0
Matt Bradley	2/8/91	3(1)	3(1)	0	0	8	8	0	0	16	16
Lamont Bryan	12/4/88	18(4)	10(4)	7	5	0	0	0	0	28	20
Phil Cowburn	15/10/90	24	13	14	5	0	0	0	0	56	20
Dale Cunniffe	25/3/87	(2)	(2)	0	0	0	0	0	0	0	0
Alex Davidson	1/11/92	6(5)	3(4)	4	3	0	0	0	0	16	12
Courtney Davies	1/7/94	9	4	2	1	23	4	0	0	54	12
Harrison Elliott	16/3/92	13(5)	6(2)	4	1	0	0	0	0	16	4
Morgan Evans	23/3/92	13(10)	9(4)	2	0	0	0	0	0	8	0
Jamel Goodall	7/9/97	1(2)	1(2)	0	0	0	0	0	0	0	0
Mick Govin	5/11/84	4(3)	1(2)	0	0	0	0	0	0	0	0
Brad Hill	18/2/93	1(3)	1(3)	0	0	0	0	0	0	0	0
Kieran Hyde	10/10/89	9	5	2	1	36	17	0	0	80	38
Richard Jones	7/7/89	3(7)	3(1)	0	0	0	0	0	0	0	0
Jose Kenga	3/5/95	(2)	(2)	0	0	0	0	0	0	0	0
Harry Kidd	12/6/95	(7)	(3)	2	0	0	0	0	0	8	0
Brad Kislingbury	2/2/96	10(2)	4	2	1	0	0	0	0	8	4
Jonny Leather	29/7/89	8	3	6	2	0	0	0	0	24	8
Jayson Lombardo	28/3/91	3(3)	2(1)	0	0	5	4	0	0	10	8
Joe McClean	10/8/89	23	12	8	6	0	0	0	0	32	24
Zack McComb	9/9/95	3(1)	3(1)	0	0	0	0	0	0	0	0
Jack Mitchell	16/3/95	8	5	4	2	1	1	0	0	18	10
Jamie Murphy	29/12/89	8	4	3	2	4	3	0	0	20	14
Brendon Newton	18/2/93	15(2)	9(1)	9	3	2	2	0	0	40	16
Charles Nies	3/8/94	(2)	(2)	0	0	0	0	0	0	0	0
Graham O'Keeffe	13/5/91	(1)	(1)	0	0	0	0	0	0	0	0
Steve Parry	19/10/88	24(1)	13(1)	20	10	0	0	0	0	80	40
Dan Poulton	17/11/81	(1)	(1)	0	0	0	0	0	0	0	0
Oliver Purslow	17/9/87	17(8)	9(5)	1	0	0	0	0	0	4	0
Lewis Reece	17/6/91	18	11	7	6	3	2	0	0	34	28
Jimmy Rowland	8/4/94	9(1)	5	4	1	4	0	1	0	25	4
Luke Stephens	21/11/96	(4)	(1)	0	0	0	0	0	0	0	0
Almer Tagayuna	31/5/96	2(6)	2(4)	0	0	0	0	0	0	0	0
Jack Uren	3/1/98	4	1	3	1	0	0	0	0	12	4
James Walter	11/9/91	3(7)	1(2)	3	2	0	0	0	0	12	8
Emmerson Whittel	13/9/94	20(4)	11(2)	2	1	0	0	0	0	8	4
Kadeem Williams	23/3/95	3(5)	(3)	3	0	0	0	0	0	12	0

Oliver Purslow

LEAGUE RECORD
League 1, before Super 8 split:
P14-W3-D0-L11 (12th)
F334, A479, Diff-145, 6 points.

After League 1 Shield:
P20-W5-D0-L15 (4th)
F515, A644, Diff-129, 10 points.

LEAGUE 1 CUP
Semi-Finalists

CHALLENGE CUP
Round Four

ATTENDANCES
Best - v London Skolars (L1 - 190)
Worst - v Hemel (L1S - 101)
Total (all home games
included) - 1,472
Average (all home games
included) - 134
(Down by 108 on 2015)

'L1' totals include League 1 regular season only; 'All' totals also include League 1 Shield, League 1 Cup & Challenge Cup

CLUB RECORDS
MATCH RECORDS — Highest score: 74-18 v Hemel, 14/8/2016 Highest score against: 6-82 v Salford, 21/4/2013 Record attendance: 867 v Salford, 21/4/2013
Tries: 4 Joe McClean v Oxford, 10/7/2016; Brendon Newton, 14/8/2016
Goals: 11 Kieran Hyde v Hemel, 14/8/2016 Points: 24 Matt Bradley v Coventry, 16/5/2015

SEASON RECORDS — Tries: 20 Steve Parry 2016 Goals: 76 Matt Bradley 2015 Points: 172 Matt Bradley 2015
CAREER RECORDS — Tries: 40 Steve Parry 2013-2016 Goals: 161 Matt Bradley 2013-2016 Points: 354 Matt Bradley 2013-2016 Appearances: 87 Phil Cowburn 2013-2016

HEMEL STAGS

DATE	FIXTURE	RESULT	SCORERS	LGE	ATT
21/2/16	Oxford (a) (L1CR1) ●	L34-12	t:Stewart,Ellis g:Stead(2)	N/A	155
27/2/16	Kells (a) (CCR3)	L12-6	t:Rance g:Stead	N/A	250
12/3/16	Toulouse (a)	L74-0		14th	1,784
25/3/16	London Skolars (h)	L12-38	t:Greene,Swindells g:Stead(2)	15th	425
10/4/16	York (h)	L6-60	t:Stead g:Stead	15th	152
17/4/16	South Wales (a)	W14-30	t:Hrbek,Rance(2),Egodo,Stead,Stewart g:Swindells(3)	13th	215
24/4/16	North Wales (h)	L10-38	t:Ross,Pearce-Paul g:Stead	13th	150
8/5/16	Hunslet (a)	L44-28	t:Clough,Rance,Stewart(2),Pearce-Paul g:Stead(4)	14th	469
15/5/16	Keighley (a)	L74-6	t:Hall g:Stead	14th	421
22/5/16	Coventry (h)	L14-50	t:Munnelly,Rance,Hall g:Stead	14th	149
5/6/16	Oxford (a)	L24-18	t:Lloyd-Jones,Munnelly,Everett g:Swindells(2),Toms	14th	125
12/6/16	Gloucestershire All Golds (h)	L18-48	t:Swindells,O'Callaghan(2) g:Swindells(3)	14th	124
19/6/16	Barrow (a)	L62-4	t:Brough	15th	714
26/6/16	Rochdale (h)	L6-60	t:Bryan g:Swindells	15th	115
3/7/16	Doncaster (a) ●●	L80-18	t:Hall,Ross,Readman g:Swindells(3)	15th	562
10/7/16	Newcastle (h)	L20-52	t:Rance,Spearing,Hall,Ross g:B Delaney(2)	15th	115
31/7/16	North Wales (h) (L1S)	L18-42	t:Vincent,Stewart,Readman g:Stead(3)	7th(L1S)	147
7/8/16	Oxford (a) (L1S)	L46-10	t:Lloyd-Jones,Brough g:Stead	7th(L1S)	103
14/8/16	Gloucestershire All Golds (a) (L1S)	L74-18	t:Stead,Williams,Vincent g:Stead(3)	7th(L1S)	101
21/8/16	Newcastle (h) (L1S)	L10-66	t:Vincent(2) g:Stead	7th(L1S)	112
4/9/16	South Wales (a) (L1S) ●●●	W8-16	t:Stewart,Stewart-Beckett,Burns g:Stead(2)	7th(L1S)	178
10/9/16	Coventry (h) (L1S)	L12-22	t:Stead,Burns g:Stead(2)	7th(L1S)	307

● Played at Braywick Park, Maidenhead ●● Played at Keepmoat Athletics Ground ●●● Played at Glan-yr-Afon Park, Blackwood

		APP		TRIES		GOALS		FG		PTS	
	D.O.B.	ALL	L1	ALL	L1	ALL	L1	ALL	L1	ALL	L1
Brad Adams	31/3/95	5	3	0	0	0	0	0	0	0	0
Sadiq Adebiyi	8/1/97	1(1)	1(1)	0	0	0	0	0	0	0	0
Jordan Aitchison	6/8/93	4	4	0	0	0	0	0	0	0	0
Jack Asher	20/1/94	1	1	0	0	0	0	0	0	0	0
Joe Barron	6/5/98	1	0	0	0	0	0	0	0	0	0
Adam Booth	13/12/91	(3)	(2)	0	0	0	0	0	0	0	0
Rhys Bowditch	18/3/91	3(3)	1(3)	0	0	0	0	0	0	0	0
Harrison Brough	15/10/96	9(1)	5	2	1	0	0	0	0	8	4
Dom Bryan	28/4/95	2(1)	2(1)	1	1	0	0	0	0	4	4
Jono Burns	22/8/92	6	0	2	0	0	0	0	0	8	0
Chris Clough	20/1/87	4	4	1	1	0	0	0	0	4	4
Victor Coker	28/6/91	2(5)	1(4)	0	0	0	0	0	0	0	0
Matt Davis	5/7/96	1	1	0	0	0	0	0	0	0	0
Brad Delaney	25/5/95	5	3	0	0	2	2	0	0	4	4
James Delaney	4/5/92	2	2	0	0	0	0	0	0	0	0
Tuoyo Egodo	16/2/97	9	7	1	1	0	0	0	0	4	4
Scott Ellis	20/7/91	2	0	1	0	0	0	0	0	4	0
Toby Everett	22/12/95	1	1	1	1	0	0	0	0	4	4
Will Forsyth	6/6/95	2	2	0	0	0	0	0	0	0	0
Alex Gilbey	14/8/95	1(1)	1(1)	0	0	0	0	0	0	0	0
James Glover	2/12/93	1	1	0	0	0	0	0	0	0	0
Kyal Greene	1/10/94	20	14	1	1	0	0	0	0	4	4
Aaron Hall	19/2/93	14	10	4	4	0	0	0	0	16	16
Josh Halstead	13/9/90	2(4)	2(4)	0	0	0	0	0	0	0	0
Simon Hrbek	15/10/94	2	2	1	1	0	0	0	0	4	4
Chad Isles	7/2/87	7	5	0	0	0	0	0	0	0	0
Andrew Joy	7/2/94	1(3)	1(3)	0	0	0	0	0	0	0	0
Rick Joy	13/9/90	1(1)	1(1)	0	0	0	0	0	0	0	0
Andy Kay	1/6/86	2	0	0	0	0	0	0	0	0	0
Donald Kudangirana	23/5/95	1	1	0	0	0	0	0	0	0	0
Scott Leatherbarrow	3/9/90	2	2	0	0	0	0	0	0	0	0
Malikhi Lloyd-Jones	29/8/94	3(8)	1(5)	2	1	0	0	0	0	8	4
Dominic Maloney	12/3/87	4(1)	0	0	0	0	0	0	0	0	0
Elliot Munnelly	28/7/94	2	2	2	2	0	0	0	0	8	8
Will O'Brien	26/9/97	(1)	0	0	0	0	0	0	0	0	0
Liam O'Callaghan	24/9/94	5(8)	3(5)	2	2	0	0	0	0	8	8
Dave O'Conner	13/4/91	2(9)	1(5)	0	0	0	0	0	0	0	0
Andy Parrott	28/4/87	(3)	(3)	0	0	0	0	0	0	0	0
Luke Patterson	17/6/95	3(2)	3	0	0	0	0	0	0	0	0
Kameron Pearce-Paul	28/2/97	11	8	2	2	0	0	0	0	8	8
Tala Petelo	25/4/82	4	3	0	0	0	0	0	0	0	0
Reece Rance	17/7/93	15	13	6	5	0	0	0	0	24	20
Dylan Readman	5/11/95	8(5)	7	2	1	0	0	0	0	8	4
Matt Ross	2/9/92	16(2)	10(1)	3	3	0	0	0	0	12	12
Rory Sharratt	26/3/92	1	1	0	0	0	0	0	0	0	0
James Shaw	28/2/95	1(2)	1(2)	0	0	0	0	0	0	0	0
Josh Spearing	7/6/96	14	8	1	1	0	0	0	0	4	4
Ben Stead	13/10/92	16	8	4	2	25	10	0	0	66	28
Mitch Stephenson	29/7/94	(2)	(1)	0	0	0	0	0	0	0	0
Mike Stewart	14/2/89	5(14)	2(9)	6	3	0	0	0	0	24	12
Paul Stewart-Beckett	28/10/88	5	1	1	0	0	0	0	0	4	0
Marcus Stock	1/5/96	6(3)	2(3)	0	0	0	0	0	0	0	0
Barry-John Swindells	6/4/82	19(1)	14	2	2	12	12	0	0	32	32
Oli Toms	9/1/96	14	12	0	0	1	1	0	0	2	2
Reece Trout	29/4/94	(4)	(2)	0	0	0	0	0	0	0	0
Mitch Vincent	14/3/94	7	1	4	0	0	0	0	0	16	0
Alex Walker	4/9/95	2	2	0	0	0	0	0	0	0	0
Ben Waud	1/10/94	3	1	0	0	0	0	0	0	0	0
Reece Williams	28/2/95	6	0	1	0	0	0	0	0	4	0

Barry-John Swindells

LEAGUE RECORD
League 1, before Super 8 split:
P14-W1-D0-L13 (15th).
F190, A718, Diff-528, 2 points.

After League 1 Shield:
P20-W2-D0-L18 (7th)
F274, A976, Diff-702, 4 points.

LEAGUE 1 CUP
Round One

CHALLENGE CUP
Round Three

ATTENDANCES
Best - v London Skolars (L1 - 425)
Worst - v Newcastle (L1S - 112)
Total (all home games included) - 1,796
Average (all home games included) - 180
(Down by 24 on 2015)

'L1' totals include League 1 regular season only;
'All' totals also include League 1 Shield,
League 1 Cup & Challenge Cup

CLUB RECORDS	
MATCH RECORDS	Highest score: 52-24 v South Wales, 26/5/2013 Highest score against: 18-80 v Doncaster, 3/7/2016 Record attendance: 679 v Oldham, 12/5/2013
	Tries: 3 (3 players) Goals: 8 Mike Bishay v South Wales, 26/5/2013; Jy-mel Coleman v Oldham, 8/6/2014
	Points: 16 Mike Bishay v South Wales, 26/5/2013; Jy-mel Coleman v Oldham, 8/6/2014
SEASON RECORDS	Tries: 14 Alex Anthony 2015 Goals: 62 Barry-John Swindells 2014 Points: 160 Barry-John Swindells 2014
CAREER RECORDS	Tries: 19 Barry-John Swindells 2013-2016 Goals: 138 Barry-John Swindells 2013-2016
	Points: 352 Barry-John Swindells 2013-2016 Appearances: 76 Barry-John Swindells 2013-2016

HUNSLET HAWKS

DATE	FIXTURE	RESULT	SCORERS	LGE	ATT
21/2/16	York (h) (L1CR1)	L4-24	t:Barnett	N/A	464
28/2/16	Barrow (h) (CCR3)	W46-12	t:Barnett(2),Ansell(2),Watson(2),Carbutt,Reed g:Brown(7)	N/A	354
6/3/16	Rochdale (a)	L28-18	t:Barnett(2),Flanagan,Agoro g:Brown	10th	610
13/3/16	Barrow (a)	L40-6	t:Barnett g:Brown	12th	1,003
18/3/16	Doncaster (h) (CCR4)	W48-6	t:Lee(2),Barnett(4),Faal,Waterman,Mvududu g:Brown(6)	N/A	337
25/3/16	Keighley (h)	L16-24	t:Faal,Carbutt,Lee g:Brown(2)	14th	707
10/4/16	Newcastle (a)	W24-28	t:Ansell(2),Carbutt,Barnett,Flanagan,Faal g:Ansell(2)	10th	604
17/4/16	Salford (h) (CCR5)	L14-50	t:Lee,Flanagan,Duckworth g:Ansell	N/A	834
24/4/16	Oxford (a)	W14-40	t:Mvududu(3),Flanagan,Agoro,Reed,Barnett,Crane g:Brown(4)	9th	225
1/5/16	Doncaster (h)	L22-30	t:Duckworth,Watson,Normington,Barnett g:Brown(3)	9th	385
8/5/16	Hemel (h)	W44-28	t:Duckworth,Faal,Flanagan(3),Mackay(2),Watson g:Brown(6)	9th	469
15/5/16	Toulouse (h)	L24-46	t:Mackay,Normington,Lee,Reed g:Brown(4)	10th	328
22/5/16	Gloucestershire All Golds (a)	W18-26	t:Faal(2),Flanagan,Haley,Lee g:Ansell,Flanagan(2)	9th	134
5/6/16	London Skolars (h)	W26-18	t:Watson,Duckworth(2),Ansell g:Ansell(5)	8th	382
12/6/16	York (a)	L32-24	t:Watson,Reed,Duckworth,Mapals g:Brown(2),Ansell(2)	8th	778
19/6/16	Coventry (h)	W38-18	t:Mapals,Normington,Lee,Ansell,Mackay,Mvududu g:Brown(7)	8th	446
26/6/16	South Wales (a)	W24-36	t:Mvududu(2),Williams,Thomas,Flanagan,Reed g:Brown(6)	8th	259
10/7/16	North Wales (h)	W35-30	t:Williams,Haley,Faal,Flanagan(2),Ansell g:Brown(5) fg:Brown	7th	462
23/7/16	London Skolars (h) (S8)	W30-26	t:Sanderson(2),Mvududu,Normington,Watson g:Brown(5)	7th	414
31/7/16	Keighley (a) (S8)	W8-18	t:Ansell,K Johnson,Sanderson g:Ansell(3)	6th	384
5/8/16	Doncaster (h) (S8)	L24-36	t:Ansell,K Johnson,Reed,Thomas g:Ansell(4)	6th	541
14/8/16	Barrow (a) (S8)	L44-26	t:Coventry,Barnett(2),Flanagan,K Johnson g:Brown(3)	7th	1,003
21/8/16	York (a) (S8)	W12-33	t:Ansell,Mvududu,Watson,Flanagan,Lee g:Ansell(6) fg:Ansell	6th	702
3/9/16	Toulouse (h) (S8)	L12-16	t:Barnett,Flanagan g:Brown(2)	6th	379
11/9/16	Rochdale (a) (S8)	L34-18	t:Ansell(2),Lee,Barnett g:Brown	7th	690

		APP		TRIES		GOALS		FG		PTS	
	D.O.B.	ALL	L1	ALL	L1	ALL	L1	ALL	L1	ALL	L1
Mo Agoro	29/1/93	6	4	2	2	0	0	0	0	8	8
Danny Ansell	9/10/91	22	19	12	10	24	23	1	1	97	87
Richie Barnett	26/4/81	25	21	17	10	0	0	0	0	68	40
Austin Bell	6/9/91	(13)	(10)	0	0	0	0	0	0	0	0
Simon Brown	23/6/89	18(1)	15(1)	0	0	65	52	1	1	131	105
Chris Buttery	23/12/85	(3)	(2)	0	0	0	0	0	0	0	0
Matt Carbutt	3/10/85	15(9)	13(8)	3	2	0	0	0	0	12	8
Callum Casey	6/6/90	3(2)	3(2)	0	0	0	0	0	0	0	0
Jack Coventry	5/3/94	3(7)	3(7)	1	1	0	0	0	0	4	4
Ben Crane	30/12/91	7(1)	4(1)	1	1	0	0	0	0	4	4
James Duckworth	9/4/94	14	10	6	5	0	0	0	0	24	20
Ayden Faal	12/12/86	12	10	7	6	0	0	0	0	28	24
George Flanagan	8/10/86	1(21)	1(17)	14	13	2	2	0	0	60	56
Michael Haley	19/9/87	15(6)	13(4)	2	2	0	0	0	0	8	8
Kyran Johnson	23/3/94	8	8	3	3	0	0	0	0	12	12
Zach Johnson	9/3/91	(3)	(3)	0	0	0	0	0	0	0	0
Jose Kenga	3/5/95	(3)	(3)	0	0	0	0	0	0	0	0
Jack Lee	1/11/82	24(1)	20(1)	9	6	0	0	0	0	36	24
Liam Mackay	26/10/90	13	11	4	4	0	0	0	0	16	16
Lee Mapals	17/7/85	2(3)	2(3)	2	2	0	0	0	0	8	8
Jamie Milburn	11/6/91	2(3)	2(3)	0	0	0	0	0	0	0	0
Mufaro Mvududu	29/8/91	23	19	9	8	0	0	0	0	36	32
Jake Normington	11/10/91	25	21	4	4	0	0	0	0	16	16
Lewis Reed	24/3/91	19(4)	15(4)	6	5	0	0	0	0	24	20
Craig Robinson	30/7/85	2(13)	2(11)	0	0	0	0	0	0	0	0
Stewart Sanderson	10/4/85	7	7	3	3	0	0	0	0	12	12
Danny Thomas	21/12/83	11(3)	9(2)	2	2	0	0	0	0	8	8
Lee Waterman	13/4/87	2(1)	1	1	0	0	0	0	0	4	0
Jimmy Watson	9/9/91	24	20	8	6	0	0	0	0	32	24
Daniel Williams	26/8/89	20(3)	18(2)	2	2	0	0	0	0	8	8
Aston Wilson	23/10/90	2	2	0	0	0	0	0	0	0	0

'L1' totals include Super 8s; 'All' totals also include League 1 Cup & Challenge Cup

Jake Normington

LEAGUE RECORD
P21-W11-D0-L10 (7th)
F544, A550, Diff-6, 22 points.

LEAGUE 1 CUP
Round One

CHALLENGE CUP
Round Five

ATTENDANCES
Best - v Salford (CC - 834)
Worst - v Toulouse (L1 - 328)
Total (excluding Challenge Cup) - 4,977
Average (excluding Challenge Cup) - 452
(Down by 375 on 2015, Championship)

CLUB RECORDS	
	Highest score: 82-0 v Highfield, 21/1/96 **Highest score against:** 0-82 v Bradford, 2/3/2003
	Record attendance: 24,700 v Wigan, 15/3/24 *(Parkside)*; 2,454 v Wakefield, 13/4/98 *(South Leeds Stadium)*
MATCH RECORDS	**Tries:** 7 George Dennis v Bradford, 20/1/34 **Goals:** 12 Billy Langton v Keighley, 18/8/59 **Points:** 30 Simon Wilson v Highfield, 21/1/96
SEASON RECORDS	**Tries:** 34 Alan Snowden 1956-57 **Goals:** 181 Billy Langton 1958-59 **Points:** 380 Billy Langton 1958-59
CAREER RECORDS	**Tries:** 154 Fred Williamson 1943-55 **Goals:** 1,044 Billy Langton 1955-66 **Points:** 2,202 Billy Langton 1955-66 **Appearances:** 579 Geoff Gunney 1951-73

PRIDE OF KEIGHLEY

KEIGHLEY COUGARS

DATE	FIXTURE	RESULT	SCORERS	LGE	ATT
20/2/16	Wath Brow (a) (L1CR1)	W4-10	t:Feather,Law g:Brook	N/A	300
28/2/16	Coventry (h) (CCR3)	W54-28	t:R Hawkyard,Barnes(3),Oakes,Ollett,Gabriel,White,Martin(2) g:Brook(7)	N/A	421
6/3/16	South Wales (a)	W4-60	t:Law,Barnes,Martin,D Hawkyard,Oakes(2),R Hawkyard,Rawlins,Lawton, White,Ollett g:Brook(7),Handforth	1st	210
13/3/16	Doncaster (h)	L28-44	t:White(2),Barnes(2),Ollett,Peltier g:Brook(2)	5th	791
20/3/16	York (a) (CCR4)	L20-12	t:Brook,Feather g:Brook(2)	N/A	624
25/3/16	Hunslet (a)	W16-24	t:Barnes(2),Martin(2) g:Brook(4)	4th	707
3/4/16	Oxford (h) (L1CQF)	W54-14	t:White(2),R Sheriffe,Barnes,Finigan,Darville,D Hawkyard,Feather,Peltier, R Hawkyard g:Brook(7)	N/A	402
10/4/16	Oxford (h)	W70-10	t:R Hawkyard(2),J Sheriffe,D Hawkyard(2),Handforth(3),White,Rawlins,Law, Finigan(2) g:Brook(8),Handforth	4th	671
17/4/16	Gloucestershire All Golds (h)	W42-18	t:Barnes(2),Martin,R Hawkyard,Lindsay,Law,Gabriel g:Brook(7)	1st	527
30/4/16	London Skolars (a) (L1CSF)	W22-31	t:Barnes,Law,D Hawkyard,R Hawkyard(2) g:Brook(5) fg:Brook	N/A	436
8/5/16	Coventry (a) ●	W16-36	t:Brook,Finigan,Martin,Peltier,Lindsay,White,Barnes g:Brook(4)	2nd	1,097
15/5/16	Hemel (h)	W74-6	t:D Hawkyard,White,Rawlins(3),Finigan(3),Barnes,R Sheriffe,Lynam,Peltier, Bailey,R Hawkyard,Oakes g:Handforth(7)	2nd	421
21/5/16	London Skolars (a)	L30-20	t:Peltier,R Hawkyard,Finigan,Feather g:Brook(2)	4th	352
28/5/16	York (L1CF) ●●	W22-18	t:White,R Sheriffe,Oakes,Martin g:Handforth(3)	N/A	N/A
4/6/16	Newcastle (h)	W36-14	t:Handforth(3),Finigan,R Sheriffe(2),Darville g:Handforth,Martin(3)	4th	827
12/6/16	North Wales (a)	W22-30	t:Law(2),R Sheriffe(2),Feather g:Brook(5)	4th	504
18/6/16	Toulouse (a)	L84-6	t:Bailey g:Brook	4th	1,167
26/6/16	Barrow (h)	L32-34	t:White(2),Campbell,Peltier,Rawlins,Gabriel g:Lawton(4)	6th	716
3/7/16	Rochdale (a)	L42-28	t:Peltier,Feather,Martin(2),Rawlins g:Lawton(4)	6th	558
10/7/16	York (h)	W34-28	t:Gabriel,Rawlins,Campbell,Lindsay,Feather g:Lawton(5)	6th	631
23/7/16	Toulouse (a) (S8)	L40-4	t:Martin	6th	1,214
31/7/16	Hunslet (h) (S8)	L8-18	t:Brook,White	7th	384
7/8/16	Rochdale (a) (S8)	L18-4	t:Brook	7th	510
14/8/16	London Skolars (h) (S8)	W30-10	t:Lawton,Brook,R Hawkyard,Peltier,Gabriel,Feather g:Lawton(3)	6th	297
21/8/16	Doncaster (a) (S8)	L26-24	t:Martin,Gabriel,R Hawkyard,Ollett g:Lawton(4)	7th	609
4/9/16	Barrow (a) (S8)	L26-18	t:R Hawkyard,Milner,Peltier g:Lawton(3)	7th	1,173
11/9/16	York (h) (S8)	W50-8	t:Lawton(3),Ollett,Milner,R Hawkyard(2),Handforth,White g:Lawton(5),Lindsay,White	6th	658

● Played at Ricoh Arena
●● Played at Bloomfield Road, Blackpool

		APP		TRIES		GOALS		FG		PTS	
	D.O.B.	ALL	L1	ALL	L1	ALL	L1	ALL	L1	ALL	L1
Matthew Bailey	1/12/91	8(16)	7(13)	2	2	0	0	0	0	8	8
Hamish Barnes	22/5/92	15	10	14	9	0	0	0	0	56	36
Adam Brook	29/9/94	21(1)	16(1)	5	4	62	40	1	0	145	96
Johnny Campbell	17/7/87	3	3	3	3	0	0	0	0	12	12
Neil Cherryholme	20/12/86	8(12)	7(8)	0	0	0	0	0	0	0	0
Liam Darville	7/7/94	7	4	2	1	0	0	0	0	8	4
Tyler Dickinson	18/8/96	(1)	0	0	0	0	0	0	0	0	0
Sonny Esslemont	29/12/93	1(3)	1	0	0	0	0	0	0	0	0
James Feather	15/4/84	26(1)	20(1)	9	6	0	0	0	0	36	24
Vinny Finigan	4/8/89	13	9	9	8	0	0	0	0	36	32
Andy Gabriel	21/12/93	17	15	6	5	0	0	0	0	24	20
Jamel Goodall	7/9/97	1(1)	1(1)	0	0	0	0	0	0	0	0
Paul Handforth	6/10/81	19	15	7	7	13	10	0	0	54	48
Darren Hawkyard	14/10/84	17(3)	14(1)	6	4	0	0	0	0	24	16
Ritchie Hawkyard	21/1/86	24	18	15	11	0	0	0	0	60	44
Scott Law	19/2/85	19(1)	14	7	5	0	0	0	0	28	20
Danny Lawton	10/3/90	8(2)	8(2)	5	5	28	28	0	0	76	76
Ashley Lindsay	31/7/83	17(3)	14(2)	3	3	1	1	0	0	14	14
Josh Lynam	16/2/93	10(5)	6(5)	1	1	0	0	0	0	4	4
Charlie Martin	2/12/92	23(1)	18(1)	12	9	3	3	0	0	54	42
Will Milner	28/10/94	7(1)	7(1)	2	2	0	0	0	0	8	8
John Oakes	12/2/88	15(8)	10(8)	5	4	0	0	0	0	20	12
Aaron Ollett	19/11/92	10(15)	7(12)	5	4	0	0	0	0	20	16
Ross Peltier	24/4/92	(23)	(20)	8	7	0	0	0	0	32	28
Brendan Rawlins	28/1/86	19(2)	14(1)	8	8	0	0	0	0	32	32
Jode Sheriffe	4/7/86	1(8)	1(7)	1	1	0	0	0	0	4	4
Rikki Sheriffe	5/5/84	14	12	7	5	0	0	0	0	28	20
Jonathan Walker	20/2/91	4	4	0	0	0	0	0	0	0	0
Paul White	7/12/82	24	18	14	10	1	1	0	0	58	42

'L1' totals include Super 8s; 'All' totals also include League 1 Cup & Challenge Cup

Ritchie Hawkyard

LEAGUE RECORD
P21-W11-D0-L10 (6th)
F658, A514, Diff+144, 22 points.

LEAGUE 1 CUP
Winners

CHALLENGE CUP
Round Four

ATTENDANCES
Best - v Newcastle (L1 - 827)
Worst - v London Skolars (S8 - 297)
Total (excluding Challenge Cup) - 6,325
Average (excluding Challenge Cup) - 575
(Down by 451 on 2015)

CLUB RECORDS	
MATCH RECORDS	**Highest score:** 104-4 v Highfield, 23/4/95 **Highest score against:** 2-92 v Leigh, 30/4/86 **Record attendance:** 14,500 v Halifax, 3/3/51
	Tries: 6 Jason Critchley v Widnes, 18/8/96
	Goals: 15 John Wasyliw v Nottingham City, 1/11/92; Martyn Wood v Lancashire Lynx, 1/5/2000 **Points:** 36 John Wasyliw v Nottingham City, 1/11/92
SEASON RECORDS	**Tries:** 45 Nick Pinkney 1994-95 **Goals:** 187 John Wasyliw 1992-93 **Points:** 490 John Wasyliw 1992-93
CAREER RECORDS	**Tries:** 155 Sam Stacey 1904-20 **Goals:** 967 Brian Jefferson 1965-77 **Points:** 2,116 Brian Jefferson 1965-77
	Appearances: 372 Hartley Tempest 1902-15; David McGoun 1925-38

LONDON SKOLARS

DATE	FIXTURE	RESULT	SCORERS	LGE	ATT
20/2/16	South Wales (h) (L1CR1)	W44-6	t:Kear(2),Lawrence,Dollapi,Anthony,Mbaraga,Small,Pointer,Nash g:Lawrence(4)	N/A	100
27/2/16	Pilkington Recs (a) (CCR3)	L13-0		N/A	500
6/3/16	York (a)	L28-12	t:Dollapi,Anthony g:Lawrence(2)	11th	554
12/3/16	Oxford (h)	W26-16	t:Lovell,Paxton,Pointer,Magrin,Mbaraga g:Lawrence,Bishay(2)	8th	331
25/3/16	Hemel (a)	W12-38	t:Anthony,Bishay,Nash(2),Small,Mbaraga g:Lawrence(2),Bishay(5)	6th	425
3/4/16	Doncaster (a) (L1CQF)	W12-24	t:Nash,Williams,Mbaraga(2) g:Bishay(4)	N/A	367
17/4/16	North Wales (a)	W24-31	t:Williams,Walker,Chester,Nash(2),Eliab g:Bishay(2),Jy-mel Coleman fg:Jy-mel Coleman	7th	448
23/4/16	Coventry (h)	W52-20	t:Walker(2),Jy-mel Coleman,Dollapi(2),Paxton,Bishay,Eliab g:Bishay(10)	4th	365
30/4/16	Keighley (h) (L1CSF)	L22-31	t:Paxton,Small(2),Pointer g:Bishay(3)	N/A	436
8/5/16	Rochdale (a)	L40-12	t:Juma,Fatouri g:Bishay(2)	7th	513
14/5/16	Newcastle (h)	L26-46	t:Jy-mel Coleman,Nash,Gray,Lawrence,Bishay g:Bishay(3)	8th	339
21/5/16	Keighley (a)	W30-20	t:Dollapi,Small,Eliab,Druce,Williams g:Lawrence(5)	7th	352
5/6/16	Hunslet (a)	L26-18	t:Driver,Eliab,Woodburn-Hall g:Lawrence(3)	7th	382
11/6/16	Barrow (h)	W42-34	t:Williams,Everett,Driver,Walker,Mbaraga g:Druce(2),Jy-mel Coleman(9)	7th	364
19/6/16	South Wales (a)	W6-22	t:Walker,Sykes,Nash g:Jy-mel Coleman(3)	7th	170
25/6/16	Doncaster (h)	L10-30	t:Worrincy,Lovell g:Jy-mel Coleman	7th	425
3/7/16	Gloucestershire All Golds (a)	W22-23	t:Williams,Lovell,Dollapi,Nash g:Jy-mel Coleman(3) fg:Jy-mel Coleman	7th	190
9/7/16	Toulouse (h)	L12-52	t:Mbaraga,Chester g:Lawrence(2)	8th	550
23/7/16	Hunslet (a) (S8)	L30-26	t:Jy-mel Coleman,Juma,Dollapi(2),Driver g:Jy-mel Coleman(3)	8th	414
30/7/16	Rochdale (a) (S8)	L28-38	t:O Thomas,Driver,Paxton(2),Dollapi g:O Thomas(4)	8th	308
14/8/16	Keighley (a) (S8)	L30-10	t:Hill(2) g:O Thomas	8th	297
20/8/16	Barrow (h) (S8)	L4-54	t:Juma	8th	227
26/8/16	Toulouse (h) (S8)	L14-58	t:Jy-mel Coleman,Juma,Paxton g:O Thomas	8th	974
4/9/16	York (a) (S8)	L30-4	t:Hill	8th	448
11/9/16	Doncaster (a) (S8)	L34-30	t:Robinson,Small,Mbaraga(2),Hill,Juma g:O Thomas(3)	8th	587

APP TRIES GOALS FG PTS

	D.O.B.	ALL	L1	ALL	L1	ALL	L1	ALL	L1	ALL	L1
Alex Anthony	24/12/91	9	5	3	2	0	0	0	0	12	8
Steve Bannister	10/10/87	3	3	0	0	0	0	0	0	0	0
Mike Bishay	8/2/93	18	14	3	3	31	24	0	0	74	60
Dion Chapman	16/2/92	1	1	0	0	0	0	0	0	0	0
Ryan Chester	19/3/92	11(4)	9(4)	2	2	0	0	0	0	8	8
Jermaine Coleman	17/6/82	6	3	0	0	0	0	0	0	0	0
Jy-mel Coleman	13/10/88	18	17	4	4	20	20	2	2	58	58
Erjon Dollapi	16/3/93	6(17)	6(13)	9	8	0	0	0	0	36	32
Billy Driver	18/9/90	2(13)	2(13)	4	4	0	0	0	0	16	16
Sam Druce	23/9/93	10(1)	8(1)	1	1	2	2	0	0	8	8
Israel Eliab	16/1/91	6	6	4	4	0	0	0	0	16	16
Toby Everett	22/12/95	12(5)	9(5)	1	1	0	0	0	0	4	4
Kazeem Fatouri	22/10/93	5(5)	5(4)	1	1	0	0	0	0	4	4
Ben Gray	12/11/95	4(14)	3(12)	1	1	0	0	0	0	4	4
Mike Greenhalgh	8/6/94	3	3	0	0	0	0	0	0	0	0
James Hill	11/6/93	4	4	4	4	0	0	0	0	16	16
Lameck Juma	6/12/90	12	12	5	5	0	0	0	0	20	20
Elliot Kear	29/11/88	1	0	2	0	0	0	0	0	8	0
Joe Keyes	17/9/95	1	0	0	0	0	0	0	0	0	0
Charlie Lawrence	6/10/94	14	12	2	1	19	15	0	0	46	34
Will Lovell	10/5/93	21	17	3	3	0	0	0	0	12	12
Jon Magrin	8/10/94	(3)	(2)	1	1	0	0	0	0	4	4
Eddie Mbaraga	9/9/87	14(7)	14(4)	9	6	0	0	0	0	36	24
Sam Nash	1/5/89	24	20	9	7	0	0	0	0	36	28
John Paxton	20/4/85	16	13	6	5	0	0	0	0	24	20
Ben Pointer	25/5/96	5(12)	5(8)	3	1	0	0	0	0	12	4
Joe Price	7/10/85	7(1)	3(1)	0	0	0	0	0	0	0	0
Joe Ridley	14/4/91	1	0	0	0	0	0	0	0	0	0
Louis Robinson	9/1/91	3(3)	3(3)	1	1	0	0	0	0	4	4
Aaron Small	28/10/91	22	19	6	3	0	0	0	0	24	12
Michael Sykes	10/12/86	8(10)	5(9)	1	1	0	0	0	0	4	4
Jamie Thackray	30/9/79	2	2	0	0	0	0	0	0	0	0
Oscar Thomas	3/1/94	6	6	1	1	9	9	0	0	22	22
Rob Thomas	9/10/90	1	0	0	0	0	0	0	0	0	0
Alex Walker	4/9/95	7	7	6	6	0	0	0	0	24	24
Dave Williams	29/1/87	25	21	5	4	0	0	0	0	20	16
Andy Winfield	8/7/91	4	4	0	0	0	0	0	0	0	0
James Woodburn-Hall	2/2/95	3	3	1	1	0	0	0	0	4	4
Michael Worrincy	16/2/86	10(5)	8(5)	1	1	0	0	0	0	4	4

'L1' totals include Super 8s; 'All' totals also include League 1 Cup & Challenge Cup

Dave Williams

LEAGUE RECORD
P21-W8-D0-L13 (8th)
F470, A650, Diff-180, 16 points.

LEAGUE 1 CUP
Semi-Finalists

CHALLENGE CUP
Round Three

ATTENDANCES
Best - v Toulouse (S8 - 974)
Worst - v South Wales (L1C - 100)
Total (all home games included) - 4,771
Average (all home games included) - 398
(Up by 56 on 2015)

CLUB RECORDS
MATCH RECORDS Highest score: 70-28 v St Albans, 19/3/2006 Highest score against: 4-98 v Sheffield, 3/8/2003 Record attendance: 1,427 v Keighley, 29/8/2008
Tries: 5 Mark Cantoni v Gateshead, 27/6/2004
Goals: 10 Jake Johnstone v Gateshead, 24/8/2003; Dylan Skee v South Wales, 29/7/2012; Dylan Skee v Rochdale, 5/8/2012; Mike Bishay v Coventry, 23/4/2016
Points: 28 Dylan Skee v South Wales, 29/7/2012
SEASON RECORDS Tries: 20 Mark Cantoni 2004; James Anthony 2013 Goals: 100 Dylan Skee 2013 Points: 248 Dylan Skee 2013
CAREER RECORDS Tries: 57 Austen Aggrey 2004-2012 Goals: 230 (inc 1fg) Dylan Skee 2011-2013 Points: 579 Dylan Skee 2011-2013
Appearances: 198 Gareth Honor 2003-2011

NEWCASTLE THUNDER

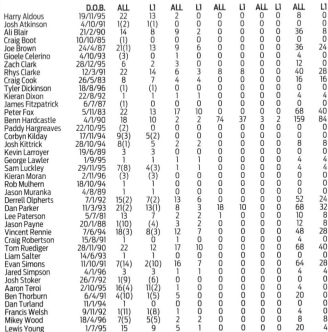

DATE	FIXTURE	RESULT	SCORERS	LGE	ATT
20/2/16	Leigh Miners Rangers (h) (L1CR1)	W36-12	t:Ruediger,Aldous,Welsh,Simons(2),Olpherts,Rennie g:Hardcastle(4)	N/A	200
27/2/16	Siddal (a) (CCR3)	L30-4	t:Parker	N/A	405
6/3/16	Oxford (a) ●	W22-30	t:Luckley,Cook(2),Parker,Paterson g:Hardcastle(5)	7th	120
13/3/16	North Wales (h)	L20-24	t:Brown,Simons,Rennie,Kittrick g:Hardcastle(2)	7th	926
25/3/16	Barrow (a)	D24-24	t:Cook,Hardcastle,Ruediger,Rennie g:Hardcastle(4)	8th	1,033
3/4/16	Gloucestershire All Golds (a) (L1CQF)	L36-28	t:Parker,Ruediger,Blair(2),Olpherts,Rennie g:Hardcastle,Parker	N/A	102
10/4/16	Hunslet (h)	L24-28	t:Ruediger,Rennie,Olpherts,Simpson,R Clarke g:Hardcastle(2)	8th	604
24/4/16	Gloucestershire All Golds (a)	W18-21	t:Blair,Simons,Brown g:Hardcastle(4) fg:Hardcastle	8th	105
8/5/16	Doncaster (h)	W35-34	t:Rennie,Hardcastle,Brown(2),Paterson,Fox g:Hardcastle(5) fg:Hardcastle	8th	552
14/5/16	London Skolars (a)	W26-46	t:Brown,Rennie(2),Ruediger,Dixon,Simons,Fox,Cook g:Hardcastle(3),Parker(4)	7th	339
20/5/16	York (h)	L4-36	t:Ruediger	8th	3,033
4/6/16	Keighley (a)	L36-14	t:Young,Fox,Ruediger g:Parker	10th	827
12/6/16	Toulouse (h)	L22-32	t:Fox,Olpherts,Brown,Lawler g:Parker(3)	10th	902
19/6/16	Rochdale (h)	L30-38	t:Ruediger,Fox(2),R Clarke(2),Olpherts g:Parker(2),Hardcastle	10th	1,076
25/6/16	Coventry (a)	W14-32	t:Fox(2),Simons,Rennie,Blair,Parker g:Hardcastle(4)	10th	266
3/7/16	South Wales (h)	W50-16	t:Ruediger(4),Payne,Olpherts(2),Kittrick,Wood g:Hardcastle(7)	9th	782
10/7/16	Hemel (a)	W20-52	t:Wood,Payne,Olpherts,Simons(3),Fox(2),Parker g:R Clarke(8)	9th	115
24/7/16	Gloucestershire All Golds (h) (L1S)	W50-24	t:Z Clark(2),Fox(2),Olpherts,Simons(2),Parker,Rennie g:Parker(7)	1st(L1S)	482
31/7/16	South Wales (a) (L1S)	W16-28	t:Young,Fox,Simons,Olpherts(2) g:Hardcastle(4)	1st(L1S)	151
7/8/16	North Wales (h) (L1S)	W30-14	t:Fox,Ruediger,Rennie,Olpherts,Simons,Thorburn g:Hardcastle(3)	1st(L1S)	408
13/8/16	Oxford (a) (L1S)	W18-62	t:Blair(3),Simons(2),Ruediger(2),R Clarke,Payne,Thorburn,Olpherts g:Hardcastle(9)	1st(L1S)	121
21/8/16	Hemel (a) (L1S)	W10-66	t:Blair,Young(3),Brown(2),Thorburn,Celerino,Robertson,Aldous,R Clarke, Ruediger,Rennie g:Hardcastle(6),Paterson	1st(L1S)	112
3/9/16	Coventry (h) (L1S)	W46-10	t:Z Clark,Fox,Parker,Thorburn(2),Blair,Teroi,Brown,Simons g:Hardcastle(5)	1st(L1S)	456
18/9/16	North Wales (h) (L1S-F)	W31-26	t:Fox(2),Parker,Ruediger,R Clarke g:Hardcastle(5) fg:Hardcastle	N/A	300

● Played at Iffley Road

	D.O.B.	APP ALL	APP L1	TRIES ALL	TRIES L1	GOALS ALL	GOALS L1	FG ALL	FG L1	PTS ALL	PTS L1
Harry Aldous	19/11/95	22	13	2	0	0	0	0	0	8	0
Josh Atkinson	4/10/91	1(2)	1(1)	0	0	0	0	0	0	0	0
Ali Blair	21/2/90	14	8	9	2	0	0	0	0	36	8
Craig Boot	10/10/85	(1)		0		0		0		0	
Joe Brown	24/4/87	21(1)	13	9	6	0	0	0	0	36	24
Gioele Celerino	4/10/93	(3)		1	0	0	0	0	0	4	0
Zach Clark	28/12/95	6	2	3	0	0	0	0	0	12	0
Rhys Clarke	12/3/91	22	14	6	3	8	8	0	0	40	28
Craig Cook	26/5/83	8	7	4	4	0	0	0	0	16	16
Tyler Dickinson	18/8/96	(1)	(1)	0	0	0	0	0	0	0	0
Kieran Dixon	22/8/92	1	1	1	1	0	0	0	0	4	4
James Fitzpatrick	6/7/87	(1)	0	0	0	0	0	0	0	0	0
Peter Fox	5/11/83	22	13	17	10	0	0	0	0	68	40
Benn Hardcastle	4/1/90	18	10	2	2	74	37	3	2	159	84
Paddy Hargreaves	22/10/95	(2)		0	0	0	0	0	0	0	0
Corbyn Kilday	17/11/94	9(3)	5(2)	0	0	0	0	0	0	0	0
Josh Kittrick	28/10/94	8(1)	5	2	2	0	0	0	0	8	8
Kevin Larroyer	19/6/89	3	3	0	0	0	0	0	0	0	0
George Lawler	1/9/95	1	1	1	1	0	0	0	0	4	4
Sam Luckley	29/11/95	7(8)	4(3)	1	1	0	0	0	0	4	4
Kieran Moran	2/11/96	(3)	(3)	0	0	0	0	0	0	0	0
Rob Mulhern	18/10/94	1	1	0	0	0	0	0	0	0	0
Jason Muranka	4/8/89	1	1	0	0	0	0	0	0	0	0
Derrell Olpherts	7/1/92	15(2)	7(2)	13	6	0	0	0	0	52	24
Dan Parker	11/3/93	21(2)	13(1)	8	3	18	10	0	0	68	32
Lee Paterson	5/7/81	13	7	2	2	1	0	0	0	10	8
Jason Payne	20/1/88	1(10)	(4)	3	2	0	0	0	0	12	8
Vincent Rennie	7/6/94	18(3)	8(3)	12	7	0	0	0	0	48	28
Craig Robertson	15/8/91	1	0	1	0	0	0	0	0	4	0
Tom Ruediger	28/11/90	22	12	17	10	0	0	0	0	68	40
Liam Salter	14/6/93	1	1	0	0	0	0	0	0	0	0
Evan Simons	11/10/91	7(14)	2(10)	16	7	0	0	0	0	64	28
Jared Simpson	4/1/96	3	3	1	1	0	0	0	0	4	4
Josh Stoker	26/7/92	1(9)	(6)	0	0	0	0	0	0	0	0
Aaron Teroi	2/10/95	16(4)	11(2)	1	0	0	0	0	0	4	0
Ben Thorburn	6/4/91	4(10)	1(5)	5	0	0	0	0	0	20	0
Dan Turland	11/1/94	1	0	0	0	0	0	0	0	0	0
Francis Welsh	9/11/92	1(11)	1(8)	1	0	0	0	0	0	4	0
Mikey Wood	18/4/96	7(5)	5(5)	2	2	0	0	0	0	8	8
Lewis Young	1/7/95	15	9	5	1	0	0	0	0	20	4

Benn Hardcastle

LEAGUE RECORD
League 1, before Super 8 split:
P14-W7-D1-L6 (9th)
F404, A368, Diff+36, 15 points.

After League 1 Shield:
P20-W13-D1-L6 (1st/Winners)
F686, A460, Diff+226, 27 points.

LEAGUE 1 CUP
Quarter Finalists

CHALLENGE CUP
Round Three

ATTENDANCES
Best - v York (L1 - 3,033)
Worst - v Leigh Miners Rangers
(LIC - 200)
Total (all home games
included) - 9,721
Average (all home games
included) - 810
(Down by 134 on 2015)

'L1' totals include League 1 regular season only; 'All' totals also include League 1 Shield, League 1 Cup & Challenge Cup

CLUB RECORDS	**Highest score:** 66-6 v Wakefield, 5/9/99; 66-6 v London Skolars, 29/6/2014; 66-10 v Hemel, 21/8/2016
	Highest score against: 0-132 v Blackpool Panthers, 16/5/2010 **Record attendance:** 6,631 v Bradford, 16/5/99
MATCH RECORDS	**Tries:** 5 Andy Walker v London Skolars, 22/6/2003 **Goals:** 11 Ian Herron v Wakefield, 5/9/99 **Points:** 26 Ian Herron v Wakefield, 5/9/99
SEASON RECORDS	**Tries:** 25 Matt Daylight 1999 **Goals:** 129 *(inc 1fg)* Dan Russell 2008 **Points:** 293 Dan Russell 2008
CAREER RECORDS	**Tries:** 74 Kevin Neighbour 2001-2006; 2008-2010 **Goals:** 184 *(inc 5fg)* Benn Hardcastle 2013-2016 **Points:** 443 Benn Hardcastle 2013-2016
	Appearances: 218 Robin Peers 2002-2012

NORTH WALES CRUSADERS

DATE	FIXTURE	RESULT	SCORERS	LGE	ATT
21/2/16	Doncaster (a) (L1CR1)	L35-28	t:Turner(3),Massam,Duffy g:Johnson(3),Turner	N/A	513
28/2/16	Gloucestershire All Golds (h) (CCR3)	L36-40	t:Turner,Dallimore(3),Wild,Andrade,Massam g:Turner(4)	N/A	324
6/3/16	Barrow (h)	L18-37	t:Saunders,Massam,Burke g:Johnson(3)	12th	543
13/3/16	Newcastle (a)	W20-24	t:Smith(2),Hurst,Caton-Brown g:Johnson(4)	9th	926
25/3/16	Rochdale (h)	L16-42	t:Massam,Hurst,Thompson g:Johnson(2)	10th	634
10/4/16	Doncaster (a)	L30-14	t:Hansen,Johnson,Davies g:Johnson	11th	580
17/4/16	London Skolars (h)	L24-31	t:Thompson(2),Smith,Turner g:Johnson(4)	11th	448
24/4/16	Hemel (a)	W10-38	t:Wild,Atherton,Baker,Thompson,Moulsdale,Turner,Hudson g:Johnson(5)	10th	150
8/5/16	Oxford (h)	W40-18	t:Baker,Smith,Bibby,Turner(2),Massam,Wild,Hurst g:Johnson(4)	10th	411
15/5/16	York (a)	D16-16	t:Turner,Atherton,Hansen g:Johnson(2)	9th	535
4/6/16	South Wales (a) ●	W16-30	t:Johnson,Massam(3),Turner,Atherton g:Johnson(3)	9th	927
12/6/16	Keighley (h)	L22-30	t:Massam,Reardon,Brickhill,Turner g:Johnson(3)	9th	504
19/6/16	Gloucestershire All Golds (a)	W18-30	t:Turner(2),Massam,Hansen,Brickhill g:Johnson(5)	9th	171
26/6/16	Toulouse (h)	L14-32	t:Massam(2),Turner g:Johnson	9th	486
3/7/16	Coventry (h) ●●	D20-20	t:Warburton,Wild,Joseph,Johnson g:Johnson(2)	10th	359
10/7/16	Hunslet (a)	L35-30	t:Thompson,Smith,Oakden,Massam,Baker g:Johnson(5)	10th	462
23/7/16	South Wales (h) (L1S) ●●	W30-26	t:Thompson,Massam,Oakden,Hansen,Atherton,Smith g:Johnson(3)	2nd(L1S)	343
31/7/16	Hemel (a) (L1S)	W18-42	t:Massam,Smith(2),Andrade,Baker,Hansen,Thompson g:Johnson(7)	2nd(L1S)	147
7/8/16	Newcastle (a) (L1S)	L30-14	t:Oakden,Wilkinson,Massam g:Johnson	2nd(L1S)	408
14/8/16	Coventry (h) (L1S) ●●	L28-30	t:Massam,Thompson,Wild,Smith,Aaronson g:Johnson(4)	2nd(L1S)	297
3/9/16	Gloucestershire All Golds (h) (L1S) ●●●	W18-4	t:Massam,Thompson(2),Hansen g:Johnson	2nd(L1S)	270
11/9/16	Oxford (a) (L1S)	W6-37	t:Holland,Massam(3),Atherton,Baker,Thompson g:Johnson(4) fg:Smith	2nd(L1S)	120
18/9/16	Newcastle (a) (L1S-F)	L31-26	t:Hansen,Massam,Oakden,Smith,Walker g:Johnson(3)	N/A	300

● Played at Cardiff Arms Park ●● Played at Hare Lane, Chester ●●● Played at Queensway Stadium, Wrexham

Tommy Johnson

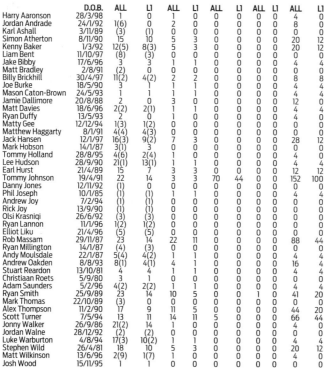

		APP		TRIES		GOALS		FG		PTS	
	D.O.B.	ALL	L1	ALL	L1	ALL	L1	ALL	L1	ALL	L1
Harry Aaronson	28/3/98	1	0	1	0	0	0	0	0	4	0
Jordan Andrade	24/1/92	1(6)	0	2	0	0	0	0	0	8	0
Karl Ashall	3/11/89	(3)	(1)	0	0	0	0	0	0	0	0
Simon Atherton	8/11/90	15	10	5	3	0	0	0	0	20	12
Kenny Baker	1/3/92	12(5)	8(3)	5	3	0	0	0	0	20	12
Liam Bent	11/10/97	(8)	(3)	0	0	0	0	0	0	0	0
Jake Bibby	17/6/96	3	3	1	1	0	0	0	0	4	4
Matt Bradley	2/8/91	(2)	0	0	0	0	0	0	0	0	0
Billy Brickhill	30/4/97	11(2)	4(2)	2	2	0	0	0	0	8	8
Joe Burke	18/5/90	3	1	1	1	0	0	0	0	4	4
Mason Caton-Brown	24/5/93	1	1	1	1	0	0	0	0	4	4
Jamie Dallimore	20/8/88	2	0	3	0	0	0	0	0	12	0
Matt Davies	18/6/96	2(2)	2(1)	1	1	0	0	0	0	4	4
Ryan Duffy	13/5/93	2	0	1	0	0	0	0	0	4	0
Matty Gee	12/12/94	1(3)	1(2)	0	0	0	0	0	0	0	0
Matthew Haggarty	8/1/91	4(4)	4(3)	0	0	0	0	0	0	0	0
Jack Hansen	12/1/97	16(3)	9(2)	7	3	0	0	0	0	28	12
Mark Hobson	14/1/87	3(1)	3	0	0	0	0	0	0	0	0
Tommy Holland	28/8/95	4(6)	2(4)	1	0	0	0	0	0	4	0
Lee Hudson	28/9/90	21(1)	13(1)	1	1	0	0	0	0	4	4
Earl Hurst	21/4/89	15	7	3	3	0	0	0	0	12	12
Tommy Johnson	19/4/91	22	14	3	3	70	44	0	0	152	100
Danny Jones	12/11/92	(1)	0	0	0	0	0	0	0	0	0
Phil Joseph	10/1/85	(1)	(1)	1	1	0	0	0	0	4	4
Andrew Joy	7/2/94	(1)	(1)	0	0	0	0	0	0	0	0
Rick Joy	13/9/90	(1)	(1)	0	0	0	0	0	0	0	0
Olsi Krasniqi	26/6/92	(3)	(3)	0	0	0	0	0	0	0	0
Ryan Lannon	11/1/96	1(2)	1(2)	0	0	0	0	0	0	0	0
Elliot Liku	21/4/96	(5)	(5)	0	0	0	0	0	0	0	0
Rob Massam	29/11/87	23	14	22	11	0	0	0	0	88	44
Ryan Millington	14/1/87	(4)	(3)	0	0	0	0	0	0	0	0
Andy Moulsdale	22/1/87	5(4)	4(2)	1	1	0	0	0	0	4	4
Andrew Oakden	8/8/93	8(1)	4(1)	4	1	0	0	0	0	16	4
Stuart Reardon	13/10/81	4	4	1	1	0	0	0	0	4	4
Christiaan Roets	5/9/80	3	1	0	0	0	0	0	0	0	0
Adam Saunders	5/2/96	4(2)	2(2)	1	1	0	0	0	0	4	4
Ryan Smith	25/9/89	23	14	10	5	0	0	1	0	41	20
Mark Thomas	22/10/89	(3)	(3)	0	0	0	0	0	0	0	0
Alex Thompson	11/2/90	17	9	11	5	0	0	0	0	44	20
Scott Turner	7/5/94	13	11	14	11	5	0	0	0	66	44
Jonny Walker	26/9/86	21(2)	14	1	0	0	0	0	0	4	0
Jordan Walne	28/12/92	(2)	(2)	0	0	0	0	0	0	0	0
Luke Warburton	4/8/94	17(3)	10(2)	1	1	0	0	0	0	4	4
Stephen Wild	26/4/81	18	10	5	3	0	0	0	0	20	12
Matt Wilkinson	13/6/96	2(9)	1(7)	1	0	0	0	0	0	4	0
Josh Wood	15/11/95	1	0	0	0	0	0	0	0	0	0

'L1' totals include League 1 regular season only; 'All' totals also include League 1 Shield, League 1 Cup & Challenge Cup

LEAGUE RECORD
League 1, before Super 8 split:
P14-W5-D2-L7 (10th)
F336, A355, Diff-19, 12 points.

After League 1 Shield:
P20-W9-D2-L9 (2nd/Runners-Up)
F505, A469, Diff+36, 20 points.

LEAGUE 1 CUP
Round One

CHALLENGE CUP
Round Three

ATTENDANCES
Best - v Rochdale (L1 - 634)
Worst - v Gloucestershire All Golds (L1S - 270)
Total (excluding Challenge Cup) - 4,295
Average (excluding Challenge Cup) - 430
(Down by 211 on 2015)

CLUB RECORDS MATCH RECORDS	Highest score: 82-6 v West Hull, 6/4/2013 Highest score against: 4-98 v Wigan, 15/4/2012 Record attendance: 1,562 v South Wales, 1/9/2013 Tries: 5 Rob Massam v Rochdale, 30/6/2013; Jono Smith v Hemel, 16/5/2015 Goals: 11 Tommy Johnson v West Hull, 6/4/2013; Ian Mort v Hemel, 16/5/2015 Points: 30 Tommy Johnson v West Hull, 6/4/2013
SEASON RECORDS CAREER RECORDS	Tries: 29 Rob Massam 2015 Goals: 109 Tommy Johnson 2015 Points: 266 Tommy Johnson 2015 Tries: 97 Rob Massam 2012-2016 Goals: 390 Tommy Johnson 2012-2016 Points: 932 Tommy Johnson 2012-2016 Appearances: 120 Tommy Johnson 2012-2016

OXFORD

DATE	FIXTURE	RESULT	SCORERS	LGE	ATT
21/2/16	Hemel (h) (L1CR1) ●	W34-12	t:Hoggins,Canterbury,Holmes,Greene,Nathaniel,Decaro g:Richardson(4),Kitson	N/A	155
28/2/16	Castleford Lock Lane (h) (CCR3) ●	L22-37	t:Kitson,Hoggins,Dobek,Nathaniel g:Kitson(3)	N/A	55
6/3/16	Newcastle (h) ●●	L22-30	t:Nathaniel,Dobek,K Gill,Kitson g:Kitson(3)	9th	120
12/3/16	London Skolars (a)	L26-16	t:Canterbury,Burnett,Holmes g:Kitson(2)	10th	331
25/3/16	South Wales (h) ●●	L20-38	t:Hughes,Dobek,Hoggins,Allan g:Hughes(2)	13th	152
3/4/16	Keighley (a) (L1CQF)	L54-14	t:Canterbury,Kitson,Nathaniel g:Kitson	N/A	402
10/4/16	Keighley (a)	L70-10	t:Canterbury,McComb g:Kitson	14th	671
24/4/16	Hunslet (h)	L14-40	t:Kitson,Holmes,Smith g:Kitson	15th	225
30/4/16	Toulouse (a)	L54-8	t:Cryer,Greene	15th	738
8/5/16	North Wales (a)	L40-18	t:Brooker,Kitson,Canterbury,Siddons g:Kitson	15th	411
15/5/16	Rochdale (h)	L24-52	t:Nathaniel,Burnett,Siddons,Canterbury g:Kitson(2),Allan(2)	15th	352
22/5/16	Doncaster (a)	L54-14	t:Nicholson,McAllister,Burnett g:Kitson	15th	744
5/6/16	Hemel (h)	W24-18	t:Nathaniel,Canterbury,Hoggins,Brooker g:Allan(4)	13th	125
11/6/16	Coventry (a)	L48-10	t:Nicholson,Allan g:Allan	13th	444
19/6/16	York (h)	L6-50	t:Gardiner g:Allan	13th	126
3/7/16	Barrow (a)	L76-12	t:J Gill(2) g:Allan,Kitson	13th	857
10/7/16	Gloucestershire All Golds (h)	L34-52	t:J Gill(2),Gardiner,Adebiyi,Greene(2),Cryer g:Kitson(3)	14th	185
23/7/16	Coventry (a) (L1S)	L48-6	t:Canterbury g:Fleming	7th(L1S)	253
31/7/16	Gloucestershire All Golds (a) (L1S)	W26-28	t:Hoggins,Greene,Nathaniel,Fleming(2),Kitson g:Kitson,Backhouse	5th(L1S)	105
7/8/16	Hemel (h) (L1S)	W46-10	t:Siddons,Fleming(2),Brooker,Kitson(3),Nathaniel,Flintham g:Kitson(5)	5th(L1S)	103
13/8/16	Newcastle (h) (L1S)	L18-62	t:Griffith,Nathaniel(2),Nicholson g:Allan	5th(L1S)	121
21/8/16	South Wales (a) (L1S)	W12-20	t:Nicholson,Hoggins,Griffith,Kitson g:Kitson(2)	5th(L1S)	410
11/9/16	North Wales (h) (L1S)	L6-37	t:Kitson g:Kitson	5th(L1S)	120

● *Played at Braywick Park, Maidenhead* ●● *Played at Iffley Road*

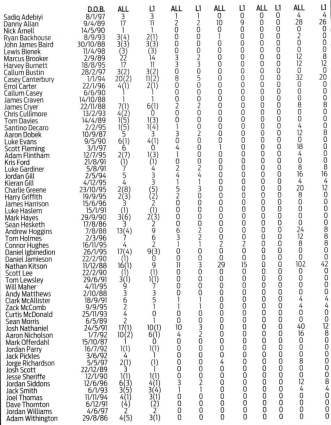

		APP		TRIES		GOALS		FG		PTS	
	D.O.B.	ALL	L1	ALL	L1	ALL	L1	ALL	L1	ALL	L1
Sadiq Adebiyi	8/1/97	3	3	1	1	0	0	0	0	4	4
Danny Allan	9/4/89	17	11	2	2	10	9	0	0	28	26
Nick Arnell	14/5/90	1	1	0	0	0	0	0	0	0	0
Ryan Backhouse	8/9/93	3(4)	2(1)	0	0	1	0	0	0	2	0
John James Baird	30/10/88	3(3)	3(3)	0	0	0	0	0	0	0	0
Lewis Bienek	11/4/98	(3)	(3)	0	0	0	0	0	0	0	0
Marcus Brooker	2/9/89	22	14	3	2	0	0	0	0	12	8
Harvey Burnett	18/8/95	17	11	3	3	0	0	0	0	12	12
Callum Bustin	28/2/97	3(2)	3(2)	0	0	0	0	0	0	0	0
Casey Canterbury	1/1/94	20(2)	11(2)	8	5	0	0	0	0	32	20
Errol Carter	22/1/96	4(1)	2(1)	0	0	0	0	0	0	0	0
Callum Casey	6/6/90	1		0		0	0	0	0	0	
James Craven	14/10/88	1	1	0	0	0	0	0	0	0	0
James Cryer	22/11/88	7(1)	6(1)	2	2	0	0	0	0	8	8
Chris Cullimore	13/2/93	4(2)	0	0	0	0	0	0	0	0	0
Tom Davies	14/4/89	1(5)	1(3)	0	0	0	0	0	0	0	0
Santino Decaro	2/2/95	1(5)	1(4)	1	0	0	0	0	0	4	0
Aaron Dobek	10/9/87	5		3	2	0	0	0	0	12	8
Luke Evans	9/5/90	6(1)	4(1)	0	0	0	0	0	0	0	0
Scott Fleming	3/1/97	6	0	4	0	1	0	0	0	18	0
Adam Flintham	12/7/95	2(7)	1(3)	1	0	0	0	0	0	4	0
Kris Ford	21/8/91	(1)	(1)	0	0	0	0	0	0	0	0
Luke Gardiner	5/8/91	7	4	2	2	0	0	0	0	8	8
Jordan Gill	2/5/94	5	4	4	4	0	0	0	0	16	16
Kieran Gill	4/12/95	4	3	1	1	0	0	0	0	4	4
Charlie Greene	23/10/95	2(8)	(5)	5	3	0	0	0	0	20	12
Harry Griffith	19/9/95	2(3)	(2)	2	2	0	0	0	0	8	0
James Harrison	15/6/96	3	2	0	0	0	0	0	0	0	0
Luke Haslem	15/1/91	(1)	(1)	0	0	0	0	0	0	0	0
Mark Hayes	29/9/90	3(6)	2(3)	0	0	0	0	0	0	0	0
Sean Hesketh	17/8/86	3	2	0	0	0	0	0	0	0	0
Andrew Hoggins	7/8/88	13(4)	9	6	2	0	0	0	0	24	8
Tom Holmes	2/3/96	7	6	3	2	0	0	0	0	12	8
Connor Hughes	16/11/95	4	2	1	1	2	2	0	0	8	8
Daniel Igbinedion	26/1/95	17(4)	9(3)	0	0	0	0	0	0	0	0
Daniel Jamieson	22/2/90	(1)	0	0	0	0	0	0	0	0	0
Nathan Kitson	11/12/88	16(1)	9	11	3	29	15	0	0	102	42
Scott Lee	22/2/90	(1)	(1)	0	0	0	0	0	0	0	0
Tom Lewsley	29/6/91	3(1)	1(1)	0	0	0	0	0	0	0	0
Will Maher	4/11/95	9	7	0	0	0	0	0	0	0	0
Andy Matthews	2/10/88	3	3	0	0	0	0	0	0	0	0
Clark McAllister	18/9/91	6	5	1	1	0	0	0	0	4	4
Zack McComb	9/9/95	2	1	1	1	0	0	0	0	4	4
Curtis McDonald	25/11/93	4	0	0	0	0	0	0	0	0	0
Sean Morris	6/5/89	2	1	0	0	0	0	0	0	0	0
Josh Nathaniel	24/5/91	17(1)	10(1)	10	3	0	0	0	0	40	12
Aaron Nicholson	1/7/92	10(2)	6(1)	4	2	0	0	0	0	16	8
Mark Offerdahl	15/10/87	1	0	0	0	0	0	0	0	0	0
Jordan Parry	16/7/92	1(1)	1(1)	0	0	0	0	0	0	0	0
Jack Pickles	3/6/92	4	1	0	0	0	0	0	0	0	0
Jorge Richardson	5/5/97	2(1)	0	0	0	4	0	0	0	8	0
Josh Scott	22/12/89	3	1	0	0	0	0	0	0	0	0
Jesse Sheriffe	12/1/90	1(1)	1(1)	0	0	0	0	0	0	0	0
Jordan Siddons	12/6/96	6(3)	4(1)	3	2	0	0	0	0	12	8
Jack Smith	6/1/93	3(5)	3(4)	1	1	0	0	0	0	4	4
Joel Thomas	11/11/94	4(1)	3(1)	0	0	0	0	0	0	0	0
Dave Thornton	6/12/91	(4)	(2)	0	0	0	0	0	0	0	0
Jordan Williams	4/6/97	2	2	0	0	0	0	0	0	0	0
Adam Withington	29/8/86	4(5)	3(1)	0	0	0	0	0	0	0	0

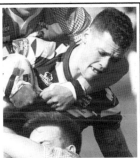

Josh Nathaniel

LEAGUE RECORD
League 1, before Super 8 split:
P14-W1-D0-L13 (14th)
F232, A648, Diff-416, 2 points.

After League 1 Shield:
P20-W4-D0-L16 (5th)
F356, A843, Diff-487, 8 points.

LEAGUE 1 CUP
Quarter Finalists

CHALLENGE CUP
Round Three

ATTENDANCES
Best - v Rochdale (L1 - 352)
Worst - v Castleford Lock Lane (CC - 55)
Total (excluding Challenge Cup) - 1,784
Average (excluding Challenge Cup) - 162
(Down by 122 on 2015)

'L1' totals include League 1 regular season only;
'All' totals also include League 1 Shield,
League 1 Cup & Challenge Cup

CLUB RECORDS **MATCH RECORDS**	**Highest score:** 46-10 v Hemel, 7/8/2016 **Highest score against:** 4-96 v Swinton, 12/7/2015 **Record attendance:** 502 v Coventry, 27/6/2015 **Tries:** 3 *(4 players)* **Goals:** 6 Jonny Leather v Gloucestershire All Golds, 29/3/2013; Nathan Kitson v South Wales, 23/8/2015 **Points:** 22 Nathan Kitson v Hemel, 7/8/2016
SEASON RECORDS **CAREER RECORDS**	**Tries:** 17 Sean Morris 2014 **Goals:** 46 *(inc 2fg)* Jimmy Rowland 2014 **Points:** 118 Jimmy Rowland 2014 **Tries:** 29 Sean Morris 2013-2016 **Goals:** 64 Nathan Kitson 2015-2016 **Points:** 204 Nathan Kitson 2015-2016 **Appearances:** 73 Andrew Hoggins

ROCHDALE HORNETS

DATE	FIXTURE	RESULT	SCORERS	LGE	ATT
21/2/16	Barrow (a) (L1CR1)	W4-14	t:Lee,Dandy,Riley g:Crook	N/A	659
27/2/16	Rochdale Mayfield (a) (CCR3)	W14-40	t:Tilley,Walpole,English(2),Hadden,Thompson,Yates g:Crook(6)	N/A	937
6/3/16	Hunslet (h)	W28-18	t:Philbin(2),English,Tahraoui,Biscomb g:Crook(4)	6th	610
13/3/16	Coventry (a)	W16-58	t:Riley(2),Taira(3),Yates(2),Case(2),Lee,English g:Crook(7)	3rd	250
20/3/16	Siddal (h) (CCR4)	W48-20	t:Biscomb,Tilley(2),Bloomfield,Hadden,McClurg,Tahraoui,Moores,Lee g:Crook(5),Yates	N/A	653
25/3/16	North Wales (a)	W16-42	t:Case(2),Bloomfield,Moores,Crook(2),Hadden g:Crook(7)	1st	634
3/4/16	York (h) (L1CQF)	L16-40	t:Case,Jullien,Crook g:Crook(2)	N/A	451
10/4/16	Gloucestershire All Golds (h)	W38-16	t:Case,Bloomfield,Yates,Johnson,Ratu(2),Trumper g:Yates(5)	1st	430
17/4/16	Widnes (h) (CCR5)	L6-62	t:Crook g:Crook	N/A	1,242
24/4/16	Toulouse (a)	D28-28	t:Tilley,Lineham(2),Smith,Yates g:Crook(4)	1st	536
1/5/16	Barrow (a)	W4-18	t:Bloomfield,Smith g:Crook(5)	1st	793
8/5/16	London Skolars (h)	W40-12	t:Case,Crook,McClurg,Smith(2),English,Riley g:Crook(6)	1st	513
15/5/16	Oxford (a)	W24-52	t:Riley(2),Smith(2),Moores,Tahraoui,Ratu,Thompson,Trumper g:Crook(8)	1st	352
22/5/16	South Wales (h)	W70-6	t:Bloomfield(3),Riley(2),Smith(2),Philbin,Wilde,Yates(2),Crook(2),English g:Crook(7)	1st	455
5/6/16	York (a)	L40-12	t:Bloomfield,Smith g:Crook(2)	2nd	613
19/6/16	Newcastle (a)	W30-38	t:King,Yates,Wilde,D Cookson,Thompson,Riley,Bloomfield g:Crook(5)	3rd	1,076
26/6/16	Hemel (a)	W6-60	t:Yates(2),Lee(3),Smith,Tilley,Case,Maneely,Galbraith(2) g:Crook(8)	3rd	115
3/7/16	Keighley (h)	W42-28	t:Tilley,Jullien(2),English,Bloomfield,Smith,Moores g:Crook(7)	2nd	558
10/7/16	Doncaster (h)	W21-8	t:Moores,Lee,Yates,Jullien g:Crook(2) fg:Yates	2nd	591
24/7/16	Barrow (a) (S8)	L34-12	t:Yates,Penny g:Crook,Yates	2nd	913
30/7/16	London Skolars (a) (S8)	W28-38	t:Thompson,Smith(3),Tilley,English g:Yates(7)	2nd	308
7/8/16	Keighley (h) (S8)	W18-4	t:Case,Thompson,Tahraoui g:Yates(3)	2nd	510
14/8/16	York (h) (S8)	L16-36	t:Smith,Moores,Case g:Yates(2)	2nd	413
20/8/16	Toulouse (a) (S8)	L46-6	t:Smith g:Crook	3rd	1,572
4/9/16	Doncaster (h) (S8)	W38-22	t:D Cookson(2),Riley,Galbraith,Tahraoui,Moores,Crook g:Crook(5)	3rd	392
11/9/16	Hunslet (h) (S8)	W34-18	t:D Cookson(2),Maneely,Riley(2),Tahraoui,Galbraith g:Crook(3)	2nd	690
17/9/16	Toulouse (a) (PF)	W22-24	t:Holmes,Galbraith,D Cookson,Riley g:Crook(4)	N/A	3,513

APP TRIES GOALS FG PTS

	D.O.B.	ALL	L1	ALL	L1	ALL	L1	ALL	L1	ALL	L1
Stuart Biscomb	16/12/91	4(5)	1(4)	2	1	0	0	0	0	8	4
Dale Bloomfield	24/10/87	18	16	10	9	0	0	0	0	40	36
Harry Cartwright	15/4/95	(2)	(2)	0	0	0	0	0	0	0	0
Jordan Case	10/4/93	20(3)	15(3)	10	9	0	0	0	0	40	36
Dave Cookson	1/10/88	8	6	6	6	0	0	0	0	24	24
John Cookson	12/12/84	(2)	0	0	0	0	0	0	0	0	0
Paul Crook	28/8/86	23	18	8	6	101	86	0	0	234	196
Josh Crowley	24/9/91	8(2)	8(2)	0	0	0	0	0	0	0	0
James Dandy	23/5/90	1(5)	(3)	1	0	0	0	0	0	4	0
Wayne English	8/3/80	18(1)	14(1)	8	6	0	0	0	0	32	24
Ben Evans	30/10/92	1(1)	(1)	0	0	0	0	0	0	0	0
Harry Files	6/2/95	(2)	(1)	0	0	0	0	0	0	0	0
Jack Francis	17/12/92	(4)	(2)	0	0	0	0	0	0	0	0
Lewis Galbraith	1/2/95	16	15	5	5	0	0	0	0	20	20
Matty Hadden	7/6/90	1(26)	(22)	3	1	0	0	0	0	12	4
Jack Holmes	5/1/94	7	7	1	1	0	0	0	0	4	4
Jack Johnson	25/4/96	2	2	1	1	0	0	0	0	4	4
Benjamin Jullien	1/3/95	4	3	4	3	0	0	0	0	16	12
Toby King	9/7/96	1	1	1	1	0	0	0	0	4	4
Corey Lee	10/9/93	12(1)	7(1)	7	5	0	0	0	0	28	20
Tom Lineham	21/9/91	3	3	2	2	0	0	0	0	8	8
Ryan Maneely	19/10/94	1(9)	1(9)	2	2	0	0	0	0	8	8
Alex McClurg	28/8/89	(12)	(8)	2	1	0	0	0	0	8	4
Ben Moores	6/12/93	26	21	7	6	0	0	0	0	28	24
Daniel Murray	21/3/96	1(3)	1(3)	0	0	0	0	0	0	0	0
Declan Patton	23/5/95	1	1	0	0	0	0	0	0	0	0
Kevin Penny	3/10/87	1	1	1	1	0	0	0	0	4	4
Joe Philbin	16/11/94	3(3)	2(3)	3	3	0	0	0	0	12	12
Mike Ratu	16/10/87	12(1)	11(1)	3	3	0	0	0	0	12	12
Chris Riley	22/2/88	18	15	13	12	0	0	0	0	52	48
Steve Roper	10/11/86	2(2)	2(2)	0	0	0	0	0	0	0	0
Jake Shoel	30/12/93	3	3	0	0	0	0	0	0	0	0
Jono Smith	12/11/88	20	19	16	16	0	0	0	0	64	64
Samir Tahraoui	28/12/90	20(6)	15(6)	6	5	0	0	0	0	24	20
Jovili Taira	30/3/89	12(6)	11(5)	3	3	0	0	0	0	12	12
Warren Thompson	24/2/90	24(3)	20(2)	5	4	0	0	0	0	20	16
James Tilley	11/11/93	22(2)	18(2)	7	4	0	0	0	0	28	16
Alex Trumper	5/4/91	9(5)	6(4)	2	2	0	0	0	0	8	8
Kieran Walpole	23/8/97	1	0	1	0	0	0	0	0	4	0
Sam Wilde	8/9/95	1(2)	1(1)	2	2	0	0	0	0	8	8
Danny Yates	28/5/94	27	22	12	11	19	18	1	1	87	81

'L1' totals include Super 8s & play-offs; 'All' totals also include League 1 Cup & Challenge Cup

Paul Crook

LEAGUE RECORD
P21-W16-D1-L4
(2nd/Winners, Promotion Final)
F709, A440, Diff+269, 33 points.

LEAGUE 1 CUP
Quarter Finalists

CHALLENGE CUP
Round Five

ATTENDANCES
Best - v Widnes (CC - 1,242)
Worst - v Doncaster (S8 - 392)
Total (excluding
Challenge Cup) - 6,149
Average (excluding
Challenge Cup) - 512
(Down by 4 on 2015)

CLUB RECORDS
Highest score: 120-4 v Illingworth, 13/3/2005 Highest score against: 0-106 v Castleford, 9/9/2007
Record attendance: 26,664 v Oldham, 25/3/22 (*Athletic Grounds*); 8,061 v Oldham, 26/12/89 (*Spotland*)

MATCH RECORDS
Tries: 5 Jack Corsi v Barrow, 31/12/21; Jack Corsi v Broughton Moor, 25/2/22; Jack Williams v St Helens, 4/4/33; Norman Brelsford v Whitehaven, 3/9/73; Marlon Billy v York, 8/4/2001 Goals: 18 Lee Birdseye v Illingworth, 13/3/2005 Points: 44 Lee Birdseye v Illingworth, 13/3/2005

SEASON RECORDS
Tries: 31 Marlon Billy 2001 Goals: 150 Martin Strett 1994-95 Points: 350 Mick Nanyn 2003

CAREER RECORDS
Tries: 103 Jack Williams 1931-37 Goals: 741 Walter Gowers 1922-36
Points: 1,497 Walter Gowers 1922-36; Paul Crook 2010-2016 Appearances: 456 Walter Gowers 1922-36

SOUTH WALES SCORPIONS

DATE	FIXTURE	RESULT	SCORERS	LGE	ATT
20/2/16	London Skolars (a) (L1CR1)	L44-6	t:Farrer g:Emanuelli	N/A	100
27/2/16	Featherstone Lions (a) (CCR3)	L37-20	t:Evans(2),Vitalini,R Davies g:Emanuelli(2)	N/A	400
6/3/16	Keighley (h)	L4-60	t:Newbury	15th	210
16/3/16	Gloucestershire All Golds (a)	L44-22	t:Roets,Farrer,Wilde,O Phillips g:Emanuelli(3)	14th	160
25/3/16	Oxford (a) ●	W20-38	t:Nelmes,Evans(2),Sheridan,Roets,Wilde,Parker g:Emanuelli(5)	11th	152
10/4/16	Toulouse (h)	L0-64		12th	241
17/4/16	Hemel (h)	L14-30	t:Roets,Rawsthorne,Parker g:Emanuelli	14th	215
24/4/16	York (a)	L40-6	t:Roets g:Emanuelli	14th	643
15/5/16	Barrow (h)	L4-44	t:Gregory	13th	180
22/5/16	Rochdale (a)	L70-6	t:S Jones g:Emanuelli	13th	455
4/6/16	North Wales (h) ●●	L16-30	t:Roets,Farrer,Scrivens g:Emanuelli(2)	15th	927
12/6/16	Doncaster (a) ●●●	L54-4	t:Murphy	15th	450
19/6/16	London Skolars (h)	L6-22	t:Sheridan g:Emanuelli	14th	170
26/6/16	Hunslet (h)	L24-36	t:Sheridan,Roets,Evans(2),Newbury g:Emanuelli(2)	14th	259
3/7/16	Newcastle (a)	L50-16	t:R Jones,Murphy,Davidson g:Emanuelli(2)	14th	782
9/7/16	Coventry (a)	L18-16	t:Murphy,Gaylor,Baller g:Emanuelli(2)	13th	545
23/7/16	North Wales (a) (L1S) ●●●●	L30-26	t:S Jones,Farrer(2),Stringer g:Emanuelli(5)	5th(L1S)	343
31/7/16	Newcastle (h) (L1S)	L16-28	t:Farrer,Newbury(2) g:Murphy(2)	6th(L1S)	151
6/8/16	Coventry (a) (L1S)	W14-18	t:Newbury,Vitalini(2) g:Emanuelli(3)	6th(L1S)	497
21/8/16	Oxford (h) (L1S)	L12-20	t:Vitalini,Roets g:Emanuelli(2)	6th(L1S)	410
4/9/16	Hemel (h) (L1S) ●●●●●	L8-16	t:S Jones,Scrivens	6th(L1S)	178
10/9/16	Gloucestershire All Golds (a) (L1S)	L33-18	t:O Phillips,Newbury,Duffy g:Emanuelli(3)	6th(L1S)	115

● *Played at Iffley Road* ●● *Played at Cardiff Arms Park* ●●● *Played at Keepmoat Athletics Ground*
●●●● *Played at Hare Lane, Chester* ●●●●● *Played at Glan-yr-Afon Park, Blackwood*

		APP		TRIES		GOALS		FG		PTS	
	D.O.B.	ALL	L1	ALL	L1	ALL	L1	ALL	L1	ALL	L1
Kristian Baller	18/2/87	5(8)	4(4)	1	1	0	0	0	0	4	4
Mike Connor	27/3/94	4(4)	3(3)	0	0	0	0	0	0	0	0
Alex Davidson	1/11/92	8	3	1	1	0	0	0	0	4	4
Chris Davies	24/12/91	8(1)	6(1)	0	0	0	0	0	0	0	0
Courtney Davies	1/7/94	8	3	0	0	0	0	0	0	0	0
Rhys Davies	9/6/96	(4)	(3)	1	0	0	0	0	0	4	0
Izaak Duffy	16/2/89	15(2)	11	1	0	0	0	0	0	4	0
Paul Emanuelli	3/1/84	20	13	0	0	36	20	0	0	72	40
Dai Evans	30/7/92	11	9	6	4	0	0	0	0	24	16
Connor Farrer	6/6/95	11(3)	5(2)	6	2	0	0	0	0	24	8
Rhys Gant	15/11/95	4	1	0	0	0	0	0	0	0	0
Billy Gaylor	30/4/97	3(4)	3(3)	1	1	0	0	0	0	4	4
Scott Gregory	24/7/90	12	9	1	1	0	0	0	0	4	4
Kristian Hawkes	11/12/90	3	1	0	0	0	0	0	0	0	0
Daffyd Hellard	21/2/85	(3)	(2)	0	0	0	0	0	0	0	0
Aiden Hema	27/10/95	3	3	0	0	0	0	0	0	0	0
Bradley Hill	14/11/92	5(1)	5(1)	0	0	0	0	0	0	0	0
Robert Holroyd	12/7/96	1	1	0	0	0	0	0	0	0	0
Jamie I'Anson	19/6/87	2(1)		0	0	0	0	0	0	0	0
Ben Jones	7/9/96	1	1	0	0	0	0	0	0	0	0
Richard Jones	7/7/89	4(1)	4(1)	1	1	0	0	0	0	4	4
Sion Jones	16/12/97	8(3)	2(3)	3	1	0	0	0	0	12	4
Chris Leyshon	24/12/94	1	0	0	0	0	0	0	0	0	0
Joe Martin	28/3/95	1	1	0	0	0	0	0	0	0	0
Tom Morgan	18/10/89	3	2	0	0	0	0	0	0	0	0
Jamie Murphy	29/12/89	10	6	3	3	2	0	0	0	16	12
Luke Nelmes	7/6/93	4(3)	4(3)	1	1	0	0	0	0	4	4
Ian Newbury	17/9/86	14	8	6	2	0	0	0	0	24	8
Yannic Parker	29/12/90	13	11	2	2	0	0	0	0	8	8
Barrie Phillips	27/5/86	5(10)	3(7)	0	0	0	0	0	0	0	0
Osian Phillips	2/5/94	5(14)	3(8)	2	1	0	0	0	0	8	4
Nick Rawsthorne	30/9/95	3	3	1	1	0	0	0	0	4	4
Martyn Reilly	5/1/96	1(2)	1(2)	0	0	0	0	0	0	0	0
Christiaan Roets	5/9/80	19	13	7	6	0	0	0	0	28	24
Kyle Scrivens	7/8/88	16(2)	9(2)	2	1	0	0	0	0	8	4
Jordan Sheridan	19/7/94	16	9	3	3	0	0	0	0	12	12
James Stringer	6/12/94	3	1	1	0	0	0	0	0	4	0
Jordan Syme	14/11/96	(1)	(1)	0	0	0	0	0	0	0	0
Anthony Symons	1/6/90	7(6)	1(4)	0	0	0	0	0	0	0	0
Jake Thomas	7/1/96	(1)	0	0	0	0	0	0	0	0	0
Cian Timmins	2/4/96	1	1	0	0	0	0	0	0	0	0
Chris Vitalini	5/5/87	17(2)	9(2)	4	0	0	0	0	0	16	0
Greg Wilde	22/12/93	3	3	2	2	0	0	0	0	8	8
Zak Williams	17/9/96	8(10)	7(4)	0	0	0	0	0	0	0	0

Chris Vitalini

LEAGUE RECORD
League 1, before Super 8 split:
P14-W1-D0-L13 (13th)
F176, A582, Diff-406, 2 points.

After League 1 Shield:
P20-W2-D0-L18 (6th)
F274, A723, Diff-449, 4 points.

LEAGUE 1 CUP
Round One

CHALLENGE CUP
Round Three

ATTENDANCES
Best - v North Wales (L1 - 927)
Worst - v Newcastle (L1S - 151)
Total (all home games included) - 2,941
Average (all home games included) - 294
(Up by 5 on 2015)

'L1' totals include League 1 regular season only;
'All' totals also include League 1 Shield,
League 1 Cup & Challenge Cup

CLUB RECORDS
Highest score: 70-22 v London Skolars, 23/5/2010; 70-16 v Gateshead, 11/7/2010 **Highest score against:** 6-94 v Swinton, 13/9/2015
Record attendance: 1,025 v North Wales, 10/5/2015

MATCH RECORDS **Tries:** 4 Dalton Grant v Gateshead, 22/5/2011 **Goals:** 11 Lewis Reece v Gateshead, 11/7/2010 **Points:** 30 Lewis Reece v Gateshead, 11/7/2010
SEASON RECORDS **Tries:** 19 Steve Parry 2010 **Goals:** 55 Lewis Reece 2011 **Points:** 130 Lewis Reece 2011
CAREER RECORDS **Tries:** 43 Steve Parry 2010-2013 **Goals:** 115 *(inc 2fg)* Paul Emanuelli 2014-2016 **Points:** 236 Paul Emanuelli 2014-2016
Appearances: 101 Ashley Bateman 2010-2014

TOULOUSE OLYMPIQUE

DATE	FIXTURE	RESULT	SCORERS	LGE	ATT
27/2/16	Wath Brow (a) (CCR3)	W14-32	t:Kheirallah(4),Ford,Minga g:Kheirallah(4)	N/A	400
5/3/16	Coventry (h)	W54-6	t:Hulme(4),Kriouache,Maurel,White,Kheirallah(2) g:Kheirallah(9)	2nd	2,284
12/3/16	Hemel (h)	W74-0	t:Maurel(2),Minga(2),Hulme(2),Ader,Masselot,Kheirallah(2),Hepi,White(2), Canet g:Kheirallah(9)	1st	1,784
19/3/16	Gloucestershire All Golds (h) (CCR4)	W62-28	t:Kheirallah(3),Ford(2),White,Minga(2),Kriouache,Maurel,Boyer g:Kheirallah(9)	N/A	1,053
10/4/16	South Wales (a)	W0-64	t:Minga(4),Gonzalez-Trique(2),Ford,Marguerite,Canet,Maurel,K Bentley, Kheirallah g:Kheirallah(8)	3rd	241
16/4/16	Leigh (h) (CCR5)	W10-8	t:Canet g:Kheirallah(3)	N/A	2,133
24/4/16	Rochdale (a)	D28-28	t:Curran(3),Minga,White g:Kheirallah(4)	6th	536
30/4/16	Oxford (h)	W54-8	t:K Bentley,Boyer,White,Curran,Marguerite,Gonzalez-Trique,Maurel,Kriouache, Masselot,Marcon g:Kheirallah(7)	3rd	738
8/5/16	Wakefield (a) (CCR6)	L40-22	t:Marguerite,Kriouache,Hulme,Minga g:Kheirallah(3)	N/A	2,539
15/5/16	Hunslet (a)	W24-46	t:Maurel(3),Kheirallah(2),Curran,Minga,Marguerite,Ford g:Kheirallah(5)	4th	328
22/5/16	Barrow (a)	W16-44	t:Curran,Canet,Minga(2),Kheirallah(2),Ford,Maurel g:Kheirallah(6)	3rd	1,050
28/5/16	Gloucestershire All Golds (h)	W48-16	t:Curran,Minga(2),Hulme,Kriouache(2),White,Ford g:Kheirallah(5),Kriouache(3)	2nd	1,335
4/6/16	Doncaster (h)	W46-26	t:Canet,Minga,Maurel,Curran,Hulme(2),White,Marion g:Kheirallah(7)	1st	2,218
12/6/16	Newcastle (a)	W22-32	t:Ader(2),Hulme(2),Marion(2) g:Kheirallah(4)	1st	902
18/6/16	Keighley (h)	W84-6	t:Minga,Kheirallah(4),Planas,Boyer(2),Ader(2),Kriouache(2),Maurel,Hulme, Marion g:Kheirallah(12)	1st	1,167
26/6/16	North Wales (a)	W14-32	t:Minga(2),Kriouache,Ford,Kheirallah,Planas g:Kheirallah(4)	1st	486
2/7/16	York (h)	W44-6	t:Planas(2),Curran,Mika,Minga(2),Canet(2) g:Kheirallah(6)	1st	1,254
9/7/16	London Skolars (a)	W12-52	t:Canet(2),White,Minga,Masselot,Curran,Hepi,K Bentley,Kheirallah g:Kheirallah(8)	1st	550
23/7/16	Keighley (h) (S8)	W40-4	t:Marion,Ader,Canet,White,Maurel,Hulme,Curran g:Kheirallah(6)	1st	1,214
30/7/16	York (h) (S8)	W46-16	t:Hulme,Puech,Minga(2),Curran,White,Boyer,Canet g:Kheirallah(7)	1st	1,327
14/8/16	Doncaster (a) (S8)	W18-38	t:Minga,Curran(3),Ford,Hepi,Kheirallah g:Kheirallah(5)	1st	573
20/8/16	Rochdale (h) (S8)	W46-6	t:Kheirallah,Minga(3),Maurel,Hulme(2),Planas g:Kheirallah(7)	1st	1,572
26/8/16	London Skolars (a) (S8)	W14-58	t:Marguerite(2),Kheirallah(4),Minga(2),Ford,Maurel,Mika g:Kheirallah(7)	1st	974
3/9/16	Hunslet (a) (S8)	W12-16	t:Minga,Maurel,Hulme g:Kheirallah(2)	1st	379
10/9/16	Barrow (h) (S8)	W44-22	t:K Bentley,White,Minga,Boyer,Hulme,Mika(2),Canet g:Kheirallah(6)	1st	1,161
17/9/16	Rochdale (h) (PF)	L22-24	t:Canet,Curran,White,Ader g:Kheirallah(3)	N/A	3,513
24/9/16	York (h) (SF)	W62-10	t:Maurel(2),K Bentley,Kheirallah(2),Minga(2),Ferret(2),Marguerite(2) g:Kheirallah(9)	N/A	400
1/10/16	Barrow (h) (POF)	W32-22	t:Maurel,Marguerite,Hulme,Minga,Kheirallah g:Kheirallah(6)	N/A	1,213

		APP		TRIES		GOALS		FG		PTS	
	D.O.B.	ALL	L1	ALL	L1	ALL	L1	ALL	L1	ALL	L1
Bastien Ader	6/6/91	19	16	7	7	0	0	0	0	28	28
Andrew Bentley	13/5/85	6	3	0	0	0	0	0	0	0	0
Kane Bentley	16/4/87	18(3)	15(2)	5	5	0	0	0	0	20	20
Clement Boyer	27/7/94	24(2)	22(1)	6	5	0	0	0	0	24	20
Bastian Canet	26/6/93	21(1)	17(1)	13	12	0	0	0	0	52	48
Rhys Curran	7/7/89	25	21	16	16	0	0	0	0	64	64
Christopher Denis	6/11/96	(2)	(2)	0	0	0	0	0	0	0	0
Etienne Ferret	23/3/96	5	5	2	2	0	0	0	0	8	8
Jonathon Ford	17/8/89	27	23	10	7	0	0	0	0	40	28
Arthur Gonzalez-Trique	21/4/94	6(1)	5(1)	3	3	0	0	0	0	12	12
Tyla Hepi	15/6/93	1(24)	1(22)	3	3	0	0	0	0	12	12
Danny Hulme	15/2/91	18(1)	15(1)	20	19	0	0	0	0	80	76
Mark Kheirallah	15/2/90	28	24	31	24	171	152	0	0	466	400
Mourad Kriouache	10/5/91	6(21)	5(18)	9	7	3	3	0	0	42	34
Kalausa Leha	26/3/94	(10)	(10)	0	0	0	0	0	0	0	0
Paul Marcon	10/7/95	1	1	1	1	0	0	0	0	4	4
Gavin Marguerite	12/8/96	14(1)	13(1)	9	8	0	0	0	0	36	32
Anthony Marion	12/1/94	18(8)	17(5)	5	5	0	0	0	0	20	20
Samy Masselot	1/9/89	6(13)	6(9)	3	3	0	0	0	0	12	12
Tony Maurel	21/4/93	28	24	19	18	0	0	0	0	76	72
Cedric Mazars	23/7/96	1(2)	1(2)	0	0	0	0	0	0	0	0
Constantine Mika	14/9/89	5(7)	5(7)	4	4	0	0	0	0	16	16
Kuni Minga	2/2/93	27	23	36	32	0	0	0	0	144	128
Sebastien Planas	5/5/84	24	20	5	5	0	0	0	0	20	20
Maxime Puech	16/3/94	13(9)	11(7)	1	1	0	0	0	0	4	4
Justin Sangare	7/3/98	(6)	(6)	0	0	0	0	0	0	0	0
Gregory White	28/8/88	23(1)	19(1)	13	12	0	0	0	0	52	48

'L1' totals include Super 8s & play-offs; 'All' totals also include Challenge Cup

Mark Kheirallah

LEAGUE RECORD
P21-W20-D1-L0
(1st/Winners, Play-off Final)
F990, A276, Diff+714, 41 points.

LEAGUE 1 CUP
Not entered

CHALLENGE CUP
Round Six

ATTENDANCES
Best - v Rochdale (PF - 3,513)
Worst - v York (SF - 400)
Total (excluding
Challenge Cup) - 21,180
Average (excluding
Challenge Cup) - 1,513

CLUB RECORDS MATCH RECORDS	**Highest score:** 84-6 v Keighley, 18/6/2016 **Highest score against:** 10-90 v Featherstone, 3/7/2011 **Record attendance:** 3,513 v Rochdale, 17/9/2016 **Tries:** 4 Mark Kheirallah v Wath Brow, 27/2/2016; Danny Hulme v Coventry, 5/3/2016; Kuni Minga v South Wales, 10/4/2016; Mark Kheirallah v Keighley, 18/6/2016; Mark Kheirallah v London Skolars, 26/8/2016 **Goals:** 12 Mark Kheirallah v Keighley, 18/6/2016 **Points:** 40 Mark Kheirallah v Keighley, 18/6/2016
SEASON RECORDS CAREER RECORDS	**Tries:** 36 Kuni Minga 2016 **Goals:** 171 Mark Kheirallah 2016 **Points:** 466 Mark Kheirallah 2016 **Tries:** 36 Kuni Minga 2016 **Goals:** 171 Mark Kheirallah 2016 **Points:** 466 Mark Kheirallah 2016 **Appearances:** 86 Sebastien Planas 2009-2011; 2016

● *Records only include seasons when the club competed in the British game (2009-2011 & 2016)*

YORK CITY KNIGHTS

DATE	FIXTURE	RESULT	SCORERS	LGE	ATT
21/2/16	Hunslet (a) (L1CR1)	W4-24	t:Turner,Morrison,Spiers,Wilkinson g:Nicklas(4)	N/A	464
28/2/16	York Acorn (h) (CCR3)	W66-0	t:Mallinder(2),Presley,E Smith,Morland(2),Carter,Wilkinson,Craig,Bower, Nicklas,Turner,Brining g:Nicklas(2),Wilkinson(5)	N/A	2,293
6/3/16	London Skolars (h)	W28-12	t:Brining,Morland(2),Turner,Hey,Applegarth g:Nicklas(2)	5th	554
20/3/16	Keighley (h) (CCR4)	W20-12	t:Emmett,Morland,Buchanan,Nicklas g:Nicklas(2)	N/A	624
25/3/16	Doncaster (a)	W16-46	t:Hey,Emmett,E Smith,Wilkinson,Brining,Crowther(2),Waller,Nicklas g:Nicklas(5)	5th	946
3/4/16	Rochdale (a) (L1CQF)	W16-40	t:Tonks,B Dent(2),Morland,Turner(2),Spiers g:Nicklas(6)	N/A	451
10/4/16	Hemel (h)	W6-60	t:E Smith,Wilkinson(2),Brining(3),Crowther,A Dent,Craig,Tonks,P Smith g:Nicklas(8)	5th	152
15/4/16	Dewsbury (a) (CCR5)	L30-16	t:Wilkinson,Brining,Buchanan g:Nicklas(2)	N/A	707
24/4/16	South Wales (h)	W40-6	t:Craig,Carter,Tonks,Brining(2),Applegarth,P Smith g:Nicklas(6)	2nd	643
1/5/16	Gloucestershire All Golds (h) (L1CSF)	W58-14	t:Craig(2),E Smith,Turner(2),Morland,Spiers,Buchanan,Crowther,Presley, Nicklas,Mallinder g:Nicklas(5)	N/A	469
8/5/16	Barrow (a)	L50-12	t:A Dent,Morland,Brining	6th	977
15/5/16	North Wales (h)	D16-16	t:Buchanan,B Dent,Craig g:Craig(2)	6th	535
20/5/16	Newcastle (a)	W4-36	t:Presley,P Smith,Turner(2),Tonks,Saxton,E Smith g:Craig,Nicklas,Turner(2)	5th	3,033
28/5/16	Keighley (L1CF) ●	L22-18	t:Aldous,Presley,E Smith g:Turner(3)	N/A	N/A
1/6/16	Coventry (h)	W32-14	t:E Smith(3),Brining(2),Presley g:Nicklas(4)	4th	451
5/6/16	Rochdale (h)	W40-12	t:Buchanan(2),Nicklas,B Dent,Brining,Tonks(2),Emmett g:Nicklas(4)	3rd	613
12/6/16	Hunslet (h)	W32-24	t:Applegarth,Morland,Nicklas(2) g:Nicklas(6)	3rd	778
19/6/16	Oxford (a)	W6-50	t:Robinson(2),Morland,Buchanan,Tyson-Wilson,A Dent,P Smith,Crowther, Anderson g:Nicklas,Tyson-Wilson(6)	2nd	126
26/6/16	Gloucestershire All Golds (h)	W56-12	t:Tyson-Wilson(3),Emmett(2),Brining(2),E Smith,Tonks,Robinson g:Tyson-Wilson(8)	2nd	585
2/7/16	Toulouse (a)	L44-6	t:Brining g:Nicklas	3rd	1,254
10/7/16	Keighley (a)	L34-28	t:Morland(2),Saxton,A Smith,Applegarth,Smeaton g:Nicklas(2)	3rd	631
30/7/16	Toulouse (a) (S8)	L46-16	t:Emmett,Carter,Presley g:Morland(2)	4th	664
7/8/16	Barrow (h) (S8)	L6-20	t:Spiers g:Morland	4th	413
14/8/16	Rochdale (a) (S8)	W16-36	t:Waller,Haynes,Brining,Craig,Spiers,Emmett g:Craig(6)	5th	702
21/8/16	Hunslet (h) (S8)	L12-33	t:Buchanan,Morland,Nicklas	4th	448
4/9/16	London Skolars (h) (S8)	W30-4	t:E Smith,Nicklas,Westerman(2),Waller g:Craig(5)	5th	540
8/9/16	Doncaster (h) (S8)	L28-36	t:Aldous,Brining,Nicklas,Haynes,A Smith g:Craig(4)	5th	658
11/9/16	Keighley (a) (S8)	L50-8	t:Saxton,Aldous	N/A	400
24/9/16	Toulouse (a) (SF)	L62-10	t:E Smith,Brining g:B Dent		

● *Played at Bloomfield Road, Blackpool*

		APP		TRIES		GOALS		FG		PTS	
	D.O.B.	ALL	L1	ALL	L1	ALL	L1	ALL	L1	ALL	L1
Jack Aldous	3/4/91	25(1)	18(1)	3	2	0	0	0	0	12	8
Jack Anderson	20/11/94	1(6)	1(5)	1	1	0	0	0	0	4	4
Mark Applegarth	10/12/84	8(13)	5(10)	4	4	0	0	0	0	16	16
Connor Bower	18/1/97	5	2	1	0	0	0	0	0	4	0
Kris Brining	16/11/93	8(18)	7(13)	22	20	0	0	0	0	88	80
Austin Buchanan	22/5/84	16	11	8	5	0	0	0	0	32	20
Harry Carter	10/2/94	10(8)	6(6)	3	2	0	0	0	0	12	8
Tyler Craig	4/7/93	11(1)	10	7	4	18	18	0	0	64	52
Jordan Crowther	19/2/97	2(8)	1(7)	5	4	0	0	0	0	20	16
Matty Dale	10/10/86	2(4)	2(4)	0	0	0	0	0	0	0	0
Adam Dent	2/11/93	9	8	3	3	0	0	0	0	12	12
Ben Dent	27/9/91	16	13	4	2	1	1	0	0	18	10
Ross Divorty	27/11/88	4	4	0	0	0	0	0	0	0	0
Mike Emmett	13/5/87	27	20	7	6	0	0	0	0	28	24
James Haynes	22/3/89	5(1)	5(1)	2	2	0	0	0	0	8	8
Brad Hey	4/9/94	11(5)	8(4)	2	2	0	0	0	0	8	8
Mick Learmonth	8/2/95	2(2)	2(2)	0	0	0	0	0	0	0	0
Ryan Mallinder	17/7/88	6(3)	2(2)	3	0	0	0	0	0	12	0
James Morland	29/6/95	18	11	11	6	3	3	0	0	50	30
Nev Morrison	27/5/90	1	1	1	0	0	0	0	0	4	0
Brad Nicholson	20/8/95	(1)	0	0	0	0	0	0	0	0	0
Danny Nicklas	29/6/91	25	18	10	7	61	40	0	0	162	108
Ross Osborne	7/7/97	1(6)	1(3)	0	0	0	0	0	0	0	0
Jon Presley	8/7/84	26	19	6	3	0	0	0	0	24	12
Adam Robinson	8/4/87	3(1)	3(1)	3	3	0	0	0	0	12	12
Tom Saxton	3/10/83	13	13	3	3	0	0	0	0	12	12
Sam Smeaton	26/10/88	3	1	1	0	0	0	0	0	4	4
Andy Smith	6/7/84	4(5)	4(5)	2	2	0	0	0	0	8	8
Ed Smith	12/11/92	26	19	12	9	0	0	0	0	48	36
Pat Smith	4/3/90	14(1)	13(1)	4	4	0	0	0	0	16	16
Russ Spiers	28/4/91	10(13)	8(9)	5	2	0	0	0	0	20	8
Josh Tonks	14/8/91	21(4)	18(1)	7	6	0	0	0	0	28	24
Brett Turner	1/12/87	10	5	9	3	5	2	0	0	46	16
Harry Tyson-Wilson	29/12/96	2(1)	2(1)	4	4	14	14	0	0	44	44
Brett Waller	3/7/87	13(8)	9(6)	3	3	0	0	0	0	12	12
Brandon Westerman	26/2/97	5	5	2	2	0	0	0	0	8	8
Richard Wilkinson	26/10/93	13	9	6	3	5	0	0	0	34	12

Kris Brining

'L1' totals include Super 8s & play-offs; 'All' totals also include League 1 Cup & Challenge Cup

LEAGUE RECORD
P21-W12-D1-L8
(5th/Semi-Finalists)
F618, A461, Diff+157, 25 points.

LEAGUE 1 CUP
Runners-Up

CHALLENGE CUP
Round Five

ATTENDANCES
Best - v York Acorn (CC - 2,293)
Worst - v London Skolars (S8 - 448)
Total (excluding
Challenge Cup) - 6,982
Average (excluding
Challenge Cup) - 582
(Up by 152 on 2015)

CLUB RECORDS	**Highest score:** 132-0 v Northumbria University, 6/3/2011 **Highest score against:** 0-98 v Rochdale, 8/4/2001
MATCH RECORDS	**Record attendance:** 14,689 v Swinton, 10/2/34 *(Clarence Street)*; 4,977 v Halifax, 5/1/90 *(Ryedale/Huntington Stadium)* **Tries:** 7 Brad Davis v Highfield, 17/9/95 **Goals:** 20 Chris Thorman v Northumbria University, 6/3/2011 **Points:** 56 Chris Thorman v Northumbria University, 6/3/2011
SEASON RECORDS	**Tries:** 35 John Crossley 1980-81 **Goals:** 178 *(inc 4fg)* Danny Brough 2004 **Points:** 412 Danny Brough 2004
CAREER RECORDS	**Tries:** 167 Peter Foster 1955-67 **Goals:** 1,060 Vic Yorke 1954-67 **Points:** 2,159 Vic Yorke 1954-67 **Appearances:** 449 Willie Hargreaves 1952-65

LEAGUE 1 2016
Round by Round

ROUND 1

Saturday 5th March 2016

TOULOUSE OLYMPIQUE 54 COVENTRY BEARS 6

OLYMPIQUE: 1 Mark Kheirallah; 2 Tony Maurel; 3 Bastien Ader; 4 Gregory White; 5 Kuni Minga; 6 Johnathon Ford; 22 Danny Hulme; 16 Bastien Canet; 14 Mourad Kriouache; 15 Maxime Puech; 11 Sebastien Planas; 12 Rhys Curran; 13 Andrew Bentley. Subs (all used): 9 Kane Bentley; 10 Samy Masselot; 18 Tyla Hepi; 17 Anthony Marion.
Tries: Hulme (4, 10, 35, 39), Kriouache (18), Maurel (21), White (45), Kheirallah (53, 79); **Goals:** Kheirallah 9/9.
BEARS: 1 Joel James; 2 Jamahl Hunte; 3 Eddie Medforth; 4 Matt Reid; 5 Hayden Freeman; 6 Charlie O'Mara; 7 Jay Lobwein; 8 James Geurtjens; 9 Richard Hughes; 10 Jack Morrison; 11 Liam Thompson; 12 Chris Barratt; 13 Jonathan Milizewski. Subs (all used): 14 James Redman; 15 Elliot Liku; 16 Tommy Holland; 17 Adam Saynor.
Try: Reid (31); **Goals:** James 1/1.
Rugby Leaguer & League Express Men of the Match: *Olympique:* Mourad Kriouache; *Bears:* Tommy Holland.
Penalty count: 7-6; **Half-time:** 36-6; **Referee:** Tom Grant; **Attendance:** 2,284.

Sunday 6th March 2016

NORTH WALES CRUSADERS 18 BARROW RAIDERS 37

CRUSADERS: 1 Tommy Johnson; 2 Scott Turner; 3 Adam Saunders; 4 Christiaan Roets; 5 Rob Massam; 6 Jack Hansen; 7 Ryan Smith; 8 Jonny Walker; 9 Lee Hudson; 10 Joe Burke; 11 Mark Hobson; 12 Luke Warburton; 13 Matty Gee. Subs (both used, only two named): 14 Karl Ashall; 15 Andrew Oakden.
Tries: Saunders (55), Massam (58), Burke (68); **Goals:** Johnson 3/3.
RAIDERS: 1 Ryan Fieldhouse; 5 Cameron Pitman; 4 Andy Litherland; 16 Max Wiper; 23 Chris Fleming; 3 Chris Hankinson; 6 Josh Ward; 10 Oliver Wilkes; 21 Dan Abram; 17 Andrew Dawson; 11 Liam Harrison; 27 Matty Holmes; 13 Martin Aspinwall. Subs (all used): 8 Joe Bullock; 12 Dan Toal; 18 James Duerden; 20 Joe Hambley.
Tries: Harrison (5, 42), Wiper (14), Hankinson (30), Litherland (40, 76); **Goals:** Ward 6/7; **Field goal:** Ward (75).
Rugby Leaguer & League Express Men of the Match: *Crusaders:* Tommy Johnson; *Raiders:* Liam Harrison.
Penalty count: 6-4; **Half-time:** 0-22; **Referee:** Jack Smith; **Attendance:** 543.

OXFORD 22 NEWCASTLE THUNDER 30

OXFORD: 1 Nathan Kitson; 2 Tom Lewsley; 3 Kieran Gill; 4 Harvey Burnett; 5 Josh Nathaniel; 6 Tom Holmes; 7 Aaron Dobek; 8 Daniel Igbinedion; 9 Casey Canterbury; 10 Joel Thomas; 11 Mark Hayes; 12 Andrew Hoggins; 13 Marcus Brooker. Subs (all used): 14 Santino Decaro; 15 Dave Thornton; 16 Jorge Richardson; 17 Tom Davies.
Tries: Nathaniel (4), Dobek (24), K Gill (45), Kitson (76); **Goals:** Kitson 3/4.
THUNDER: 1 Tom Ruediger; 2 Joe Brown; 3 Derrell Olpherts; 4 Dan Parker; 5 Peter Fox; 6 Aaron Teroi; 7 Benn Hardcastle; 8 Rhys Clarke; 9 Craig Cook; 10 Vincent Rennie; 11 Harry Aldous; 12 Sam Luckley; 13 Lee Paterson. Subs (all used): 14 Evan Simons; 15 Josh Stoker; 16 Francis Welsh; 17 Jason Payne.
Tries: Luckley (14), Cook (18, 74), Parker (59), Paterson (65); **Goals:** Hardcastle 5/5.
Rugby Leaguer & League Express Men of the Match: *Oxford:* Tom Holmes; *Thunder:* Vincent Rennie.
Penalty count: 8-8; **Half-time:** 10-12; **Referee:** Michael Woodhead; **Attendance:** 120 (at Iffley Road).

DONCASTER 40 GLOUCESTERSHIRE ALL GOLDS 8

DONCASTER: 1 Tom Carr; 2 David Foggin-Johnston; 3 Liam Welham; 4 Kirk Yeaman; 5 Aaron Jones-Bishop; 6 Louis Sheriff; 7 Jordie Hedges; 8 Connor Scott; 9 Kieran Cross; 10 Makali Aizue; 11 Mason Tonks; 12 Brad Foster; 13 George Milton. Subs (all used): 14 Kyle Kesik; 15 Jack Walton; 16 Matt Nicholson; 17 Iafeta Palea'aesina.
Tries: Sheriff (11), Cross (14, 69, 73), Yeaman (32), L Welham (75), Foggin-Johnston (78); **Goals:** Carr 6/7.
ALL GOLDS: 1 Jonny Leather; 2 Jamie Murphy; 3 Josh Allison; 4 Brad Kislingbury; 5 Phil Cowburn; 6 Courtney Davies; 7 Brandon Newton; 8 Oliver Purslow; 9 Steve Parry; 10 Morgan Evans; 11 Lamont Bryan; 12 Lewis Reece; 13 Emmerson Whittel. Subs (all used): 14 Jayson Lombardo; 15 Harrison Elliott; 16 Harry Kidd; 17 Alex Davidson.
Tries: Cowburn (50), Murphy (57); **Goals:** Leather 0/1, Murphy 0/1.
Sin bin: Whittel (48) - persistent team offences.
Rugby Leaguer & League Express Men of the Match: *Doncaster:* Kieran Cross; *All Golds:* Morgan Evans.
Penalty count: 14-9; **Half-time:** 16-0; **Referee:** Callum Straw; **Attendance:** 538.

ROCHDALE HORNETS 28 HUNSLET HAWKS 18

HORNETS: 1 Wayne English; 2 Chris Riley; 3 Jovili Taira; 4 Jack Johnson; 5 Corey Lee; 6 Paul Crook; 7 Danny Yates; 8 Samir Tahraoui; 9 Ben Moores; 10 Warren Thompson; 11 Joe Philbin; 12 Jordan Case; 13 James Tilley. Subs (all used): 14 Alex McClurg; 15 Matty Hadden; 16 Stuart Biscomb; 17 Ben Evans.
Tries: Philbin (10, 35), English (49), Tahraoui (57), Biscomb (61); **Goals:** Crook 4/6.
HAWKS: 1 Jimmy Watson; 2 Mo Agoro; 5 James Duckworth; 15 Mufaro Mvududu; 28 Richie Barnett; 6 Simon Brown; 7 Danny Ansell; 8 Michael Haley; 9 Jack Lee; 10 Lewis Reed; 12 Ben Crane; 3 Jake Normington; 29 Daniel Williams. Subs (all used): 14 George Flanagan; 26 Austin Bell; 19 Matt Carbutt; 39 Zach Johnson.
Tries: Barnett (2, 65), Flanagan (29), Agoro (39); **Goals:** Brown 1/4.
Rugby Leaguer & League Express Men of the Match: *Hornets:* James Tilley; *Hawks:* Richie Barnett.
Penalty count: 10-11; **Half-time:** 10-14; **Referee:** Dave Merrick; **Attendance:** 610.

SOUTH WALES SCORPIONS 4 KEIGHLEY COUGARS 60

SCORPIONS: 15 Jordan Sheridan; 2 Ian Newbury; 21 Scott Gregory; 4 Yannic Parker; 5 Dai Evans; 30 Greg Wilde; 7 Paul Emanuelli; 8 Chris Davies; 24 Zak Williams; 14 Osian Phillips; 11 Bradley Hill; 12 Tom Morgan; 13 Chris Vitalini. Subs (all used): 9 Connor Farrer; 17 Mike Connor; 27 Rhys Davies; 28 Sion Jones.
Try: Newbury (52); **Goals:** Emanuelli 0/1.
COUGARS: 22 Ritchie Hawkyard; 2 Andy Gabriel; 23 Charlie Martin; 29 Hamish Barnes; 5 Paul White; 14 Adam Brook; 7 Paul Handforth; 8 Scott Law; 9 James Feather; 12 Brendan Rawlins; 17 John Oakes; 25 Darren Hawkyard; 20 Aaron Ollett. Subs (all used): 4 Danny Lawton; 15 Neil Cherryholme; 19 Matthew Bailey; 35 Ross Peltier.
Tries: Law (7), Barnes (20), Martin (28), D Hawkyard (32), Oakes (37, 71), R Hawkyard (43), Rawlins (62), Lawton (65), White (75), Ollett (80); **Goals:** Brook 7/8, Handforth 1/2, Lawton 0/1.
Rugby Leaguer & League Express Men of the Match: *Scorpions:* Jordan Sheridan; *Cougars:* John Oakes.
Penalty count: 5-7; **Half-time:** 0-26; **Referee:** Jamie Bloem; **Attendance:** 210.

YORK CITY KNIGHTS 28 LONDON SKOLARS 12

CITY KNIGHTS: 1 Richard Wilkinson; 2 Brett Turner; 3 Brad Hey; 4 Connor Bower; 5 James Morland; 6 Jon Presley; 7 Danny Nicklas; 8 Brett Waller; 9 Kris Brining; 10 Jack Aldous; 11 Ed Smith; 12 Josh Tonks; 13 Mike Emmett. Subs (all used): 14 Harry Carter; 15 Mark Applegarth; 16 Russ Spiers; 17 Jordan Crowther.
Tries: Brining (10), Morland (29, 45), Turner (58), Hey (70), Applegarth (79); **Goals:** Nicklas 2/6.
SKOLARS: 1 Alex Anthony; 2 Sam Nash; 3 Aaron Small; 4 Joe Price; 5 John Paxton; 6 Jermaine Coleman; 7 Charlie Lawrence; 8 Toby Everett; 9 Mike Bishay; 10 Dave Williams; 11 Michael Worrincy; 12 Will Lovell; 13 Eddie Mbaraga. Subs (all used): 14 Ben Pointer; 15 Jon Magrin; 16 Louis Robinson; 17 Erjon Dollapi.
Tries: Dollapi (63), Anthony (80); **Goals:** Lawrence 2/2.
Dismissal: Lovell (73) - dissent.
Rugby Leaguer & League Express Men of the Match: *City Knights:* Harry Carter; *Skolars:* Jermaine Coleman.
Penalty count: 9-7; **Half-time:** 10-0; **Referee:** Scott Mikalauskas; **Attendance:** 554.

ROUND 2

Saturday 12th March 2016

LONDON SKOLARS 26 OXFORD 16

SKOLARS: 1 Alex Anthony; 2 Sam Nash; 3 Aaron Small; 4 Joe Price; 5 John Paxton; 6 Jermaine Coleman; 7 Mike Bishay; 8 Michael Sykes; 9 Charlie Lawrence; 10 Toby Everett; 11 Eddie Mbaraga; 12 Will Lovell; 13 Dave Williams. Subs (all used): 14 Ben Pointer; 15 Erjon Dollapi; 16 Jon Magrin; 17 Louis Robinson.
Tries: Lovell (4), Paxton (8), Pointer (35), Magrin (44), Mbaraga (72); **Goals:** Lawrence 1/2, Bishay 2/3.
OXFORD: 1 Nathan Kitson; 2 Connor Hughes; 3 Andrew Hoggins; 4 Harvey Burnett; 5 Josh Nathaniel; 6 Tom Holmes; 7 Aaron Dobek; 8 Daniel Igbinedion; 9 Casey Canterbury; 10 Sean Hesketh; 11 Mark Hayes; 12 James Harrison; 13 Marcus Brooker. Subs (all used): 14 Santino Decaro; 15 Tom Davies; 16 Adam Flintham; 17 Joel Thomas.
Tries: Canterbury (17), Burnett (62), Holmes (70); **Goals:** Kitson 2/3.
Rugby Leaguer & League Express Men of the Match: *Skolars:* Jermaine Coleman; *Oxford:* Casey Canterbury.
Penalty count: 8-10; **Half-time:** 16-6; **Referee:** Warren Turley; **Attendance:** 331.

TOULOUSE OLYMPIQUE 74 HEMEL STAGS 0

OLYMPIQUE: 1 Mark Kheirallah; 2 Tony Maurel; 3 Bastien Ader; 4 Gregory White; 5 Kuni Minga; 6 Johnathon Ford; 22 Danny Hulme; 16 Bastien Canet; 14 Mourad Kriouache; 15 Maxime Puech; 17 Sebastien Planas; 12 Rhys Curran; 17 Anthony Marion. Subs (all used): 8 Clement Boyer; 10 Samy Masselot; 18 Tyla Hepi; 20 Christopher Denis.
Tries: Maurel (3, 30), Minga (6, 16), Hulme (20, 53), Ader (33), Masselot (37), Kheirallah (53, 68), Hepi (56), White (62, 74), Canet (77); **Goals:** Kheirallah 9/14.
Sin bin: Planas (64) - fighting.
On report: Maurel (33) - alleged spitting.
STAGS: 1 Paul Stewart-Beckett; 2 Ben Waud; 3 Oli Toms; 4 Barry-John Swindells; 5 Reece Rance; 6 Chad Isles; 7 Ben Stead; 8 Mike Stewart; 9 James Delaney; 10 Matt Ross; 11 Kyal Greene; 12 Luke Patterson; 13 Rhys Bowditch. Subs (all used): 14 Victor Coker; 15 Mitch Stephenson; 16 Dave O'Conner; 17 Liam O'Callaghan.
Sin bin: Swindells (64) - fighting.
Rugby Leaguer & League Express Men of the Match: *Olympique:* Johnathon Ford; *Stags:* James Delaney.
Penalty count: 8-6; **Half-time:** 34-0; **Referee:** Andrew Sweet; **Attendance:** 1,784.

Sunday 13th March 2016

COVENTRY BEARS 16 ROCHDALE HORNETS 58

BEARS: 1 Ben Warrilow; 2 Jamahl Hunte; 3 Eddie Medforth; 4 Matt Reid; 5 Hayden Freeman; 6 James Redman; 7 Jay Lobwein; 8 Tommy Holland; 9 Richard Hughes; 10 Jack Morrison; 11 Liam Thompson; 12 Chris Barratt; 13 Jonathan Milizewski. Subs (all used): 14 Craig White; 15 Elliot Liku; 16 James Geurtjens; 17 Trae O'Sullivan.
Tries: Hughes (51), Reid (66); **Goals:** White 2/3.
HORNETS: 1 Wayne English; 2 Chris Riley; 3 Jovili Taira; 4 Alex Trumper; 5 Corey Lee; 6 Paul Crook; 7 Danny Yates; 8 Samir Tahraoui; 9 Ben Moores; 10 Warren Thompson; 11 Stuart Biscomb; 12 Jordan Case; 13 James Tilley. Subs (all used): 14 Alex McClurg; 15 Matty Hadden; 16 James Dandy; 17 Jack Francis.
Tries: Riley (5, 63), Taira (9, 30, 44), Yates (12, 26), Case (24, 49), Lee (73), English (80); **Goals:** Crook 7/11.
Rugby Leaguer & League Express Men of the Match: *Bears:* Jack Morrison; *Hornets:* Jovili Taira.
Penalty count: 8-4; **Half-time:** 0-32; **Referee:** Jack Smith; **Attendance:** 250.

KEIGHLEY COUGARS 28 DONCASTER 44

COUGARS: 22 Ritchie Hawkyard; 2 Andy Gabriel; 23 Charlie Martin; 29 Hamish Barnes; 5 Paul White; 14 Adam Brook; 7 Paul Handforth; 8 Scott Law; 9 James Feather; 12 Brendan Rawlins; 17 John Oakes; 25 Darren Hawkyard; 13 Ashley Lindsay. Subs (all used): 15 Neil Cherryholme; 19 Matthew Bailey; 20 Aaron Ollett; 35 Ross Peltier.
Tries: White (3, 42), Barnes (18, 29), Ollett (39), Peltier (77); **Goals:** Brook 2/6.
DONCASTER: 1 Tom Carr; 2 Marty Welham; 3 Liam Welham; 4 Jansin Turgut; 5 Louis Sheriff; 6 Reece Dean; 7 Jordie Hedges; 8 Connor Scott; 9 Kieran Cross; 10 Matt Nicholson; 11 Mason Tonks; 12 Brad Foster; 13 George Milton. Subs (all used): 14 Zac Braham; 15 Kyle Kesik; 16 Iafeta Palea'aesina; 17 Makali Aizue.
Tries: Sheriff (8), M Welham (12, 80), Dean (22, 25), Hedges (35), Cross (44), Tonks (52), Braham (66); **Goals:** Carr 5/6, Hedges 1/2.
Rugby Leaguer & League Express Men of the Match: *Cougars:* Charlie Martin; *Doncaster:* Makali Aizue.
Penalty count: 10-7; **Half-time:** 18-28; **Referee:** Dave Merrick; **Attendance:** 791.

NEWCASTLE THUNDER 20 NORTH WALES CRUSADERS 24

THUNDER: 1 Ali Blair; 2 Joe Brown; 3 Aaron Teroi; 4 Dan Parker; 5 Peter Fox; 6 Josh Kittrick; 7 Benn Hardcastle; 8 Vincent Rennie; 9 Craig Cook; 10 Rhys Clarke; 11 Harry Aldous; 12 Jason Muranka; 13 Lee Paterson. Subs (all used): 14 Evan Simons; 15 Sam Luckley; 16 Josh Stoker; 17 Josh Atkinson.
Tries: Brown (40), Simons (51), Rennie (55), Kittrick (66); **Goals:** Hardcastle 2/4.
CRUSADERS: 1 Tommy Johnson; 2 Scott Turner; 3 Earl Hurst; 4 Stuart Reardon; 5 Rob Massam; 6 Ryan Smith; 7 Josh Wood; 8 Mark Hobson; 9 Lee Hudson; 10 Jonny Walker; 11 Alex Thompson; 12 Luke Warburton; 13 Mason Caton-Brown. Subs (all used): 14 Jack Hansen; 15 Matty Gee; 16 Adam Saunders; 17 Olsi Krasniqi.
Tries: Smith (14, 35), Hurst (45), Caton-Brown (76); **Goals:** Johnson 4/4.
Rugby Leaguer & League Express Men of the Match: *Thunder:* Evan Simons; *Crusaders:* Ryan Smith.
Penalty count: 7-6; **Half-time:** 4-12; **Referee:** Callum Straw; **Attendance:** 926.

BARROW RAIDERS 40 HUNSLET HAWKS 6

RAIDERS: 1 Ryan Fieldhouse; 23 Chris Fleming; 3 Chris Hankinson; 16 Max Wiper; 5 Cameron Pitman; 31 Jamie Dallimore; 6 Josh Ward; 10 Oliver Wilkes; 30 Karl Ashall; 17 Andrew Dawson; 11 Liam Harrison; 27 Matty Holmes; 13 Martin Aspinwall. Subs (all used): 21 Dan Abram; 8 Joe Bullock; 12 Dan Toal; 18 James Duerden.
Tries: Fieldhouse (7, 74), Harrison (12), Pitman (19), Wiper (30), D Toal (35), Abram (50); **Goals:** Ward 6/8.
Sin bin: Fieldhouse (48) - late challenge.
HAWKS: 1 Jimmy Watson; 2 Mo Agoro; 5 James Duckworth; 15 Mufaro Mvududu; 28 Richie Barnett; 6 Simon Brown; 20 Danny Thomas; 8 Michael Haley; 9 Jack Lee; 10 Lewis Reed; 29 Daniel Williams; 3 Jake Normington; 19 Matt Carbutt. Subs (all used): 14 George Flanagan; 26 Austin Bell; 23 Chris Buttery; 39 Zach Johnson.
Try: Barnett (48); **Goals:** Brown 1/1.
Sin bin: Watson (78) - punching.
Rugby Leaguer & League Express Men of the Match: *Raiders:* Karl Ashall; *Hawks:* Richie Barnett.
Penalty count: 10-5; **Half-time:** 28-0;
Referee: Tom Grant; **Attendance:** 1,003.

Wednesday 16th March 2016

**GLOUCESTERSHIRE ALL GOLDS 44
SOUTH WALES SCORPIONS 22**

ALL GOLDS: 1 Jonny Leather; 2 Chris Barlow; 3 Josh Allison; 4 Brad Kislingbury; 5 Phil Cowburn; 6 Jayson Lombardo; 7 Brendon Newton; 8 Oliver Purslow; 9 Steve Parry; 10 Morgan Evans; 11 Lamont Bryan; 12 Joe McClean; 13 Harrison Elliott. Subs (all used): 14 Dan Poulton; 15 Emmerson Whittel; 16 Alex Davidson; 17 Harry Kidd.
Tries: Parry (3), Elliott (19), Davidson (27, 74), Leather (37), Barlow (44, 79), Newton (59, 66);
Goals: Lombardo 4/9.
SCORPIONS: 2 Ian Newbury; 5 Dai Evans; 22 Christiaan Roets; 12 Tom Morgan; 4 Yannic Parker; 30 Greg Wilde; 7 Paul Emanuelli; 8 Chris Davies; 9 Connor Farrer; 10 Izaak Duffy; 11 Bradley Hill; 17 Mike Connor; 13 Chris Vitalini. Subs (all used): 14 Osian Phillips; 23 Barrie Phillips; 24 Zak Williams; 27 Rhys Davies.
Tries: Roets (14), Farrer (57), Wilde (64), O Phillips (70);
Goals: Emanuelli 3/4.
Rugby Leaguer & League Express Men of the Match: *All Golds:* Brendon Newton; *Scorpions:* Chris Davies.
Penalty count: 5-6; **Half-time:** 18-6;
Referee: Jamie Bloem; **Attendance:** 160.

ROUND 3

Friday 25th March 2016

HUNSLET HAWKS 16 KEIGHLEY COUGARS 24

HAWKS: 1 Jimmy Watson; 5 James Duckworth; 4 Ayden Faal; 15 Mufaro Mvududu; 28 Richie Barnett; 6 Simon Brown; 20 Danny Thomas; 19 Matt Carbutt; 9 Jack Lee; 10 Lewis Reed; 27 Lee Waterman; 3 Jake Normington; 29 Daniel Williams. Subs (all used): 14 George Flanagan; 23 Chris Buttery; 26 Austin Bell; 39 Zach Johnson.
Tries: Faal (59), Carbutt (65), Lee (71); **Goals:** Brown 2/3.
COUGARS: 22 Ritchie Hawkyard; 26 Vinny Finigan; 23 Charlie Martin; 29 Hamish Barnes; 5 Paul White; 14 Adam Brook; 7 Paul Handforth; 8 Scott Law; 9 James Feather; 15 Neil Cherryholme; 12 Brendan Rawlins; 17 John Oakes; 13 Ashley Lindsay. Subs (all used): 20 Aaron Ollett; 19 Matthew Bailey; 35 Ross Peltier; 25 Darren Hawkyard.
Tries: Barnes (17, 48), Martin (32, 44); **Goals:** Brook 4/4.
Rugby Leaguer & League Express Men of the Match: *Hawks:* Danny Thomas; *Cougars:* Paul Handforth.
Penalty count: 6-6; **Half-time:** 0-12;
Referee: Scott Mikalauskas; **Attendance:** 707.

HEMEL STAGS 12 LONDON SKOLARS 38

STAGS: 1 Reece Rance; 2 Jordan Aitchison; 3 Barry-John Swindells; 4 Oli Toms; 5 Simon Hrbek; 6 Chad Isles; 7 Ben Stead; 8 Malikhi Lloyd-Jones; 9 James Delaney; 10 Matt Ross; 11 Tala Petelo; 12 Kyal Greene; 13 Luke Patterson. Subs (all used): 14 Mike Stewart; 15 Rhys Bowditch; 16 Liam O'Callaghan; 17 Victor Coker.
Tries: Greene (2), Swindells (47); **Goals:** Stead 2/2.
Sin bin: Greene (39) - high tackle;
Swindells (79) - high tackle.
SKOLARS: 1 Alex Anthony; 2 Sam Nash; 3 Aaron Small; 4 Joe Price; 5 John Paxton; 6 Jermaine Coleman; 7 Mike Bishay; 8 Dion Chapman; 9 Charlie Lawrence; 10 Dave Williams; 11 Eddie Mbaraga; 12 Will Lovell; 13 Michael Sykes. Subs (all used): 14 Ben Pointer; 15 Ben Gray; 16 Ryan Chester; 17 Erjon Dollapi.
Tries: Anthony (18), Bishay (24), Nash (51, 69), Small (61), Mbaraga (64); **Goals:** Lawrence 2/2, Bishay 5/5.
Rugby Leaguer & League Express Men of the Match: *Stags:* Simon Hrbek; *Skolars:* Mike Bishay.
Penalty count: 7-11; **Half-time:** 6-14;
Referee: Jack Smith; **Attendance:** 425.

**NORTH WALES CRUSADERS 16
ROCHDALE HORNETS 42**

CRUSADERS: 1 Tommy Johnson; 2 Scott Turner; 3 Earl Hurst; 4 Andrew Oakden; 5 Rob Massam; 6 Ryan Smith; 7 Jack Hansen; 8 Tommy Holland; 9 Matt Wilkinson; 10 Jonny Walker; 11 Alex Thompson; 12 Mark Hobson; 13 Luke Warburton. Subs (all used): 14 Lee Hudson; 15 Matty Gee; 16 Matthew Haggarty; 17 Jordan Walne.
Tries: Massam (19), Hurst (32), Thompson (38);
Goals: Johnson 2/3.
HORNETS: 1 Wayne English; 2 Chris Riley; 3 Jovili Taira; 4 Jordan Case; 5 Dale Bloomfield; 6 Paul Crook; 7 Danny Yates; 8 Warren Thompson; 9 Ben Moores; 10 Samir Tahraoui; 11 Jono Smith; 12 Alex Trumper; 13 James Tilley. Subs (all used): 14 Alex McClurg; 15 Matty Hadden; 16 Daniel Murray; 17 Corey Lee.
Tries: Case (10, 69), Bloomfield (14), Moores (23), Crook (29, 58), Hadden (46); **Goals:** Crook 7/8.
Rugby Leaguer & League Express Men of the Match: *Crusaders:* Rob Massam; *Hornets:* Paul Crook.
Penalty count: 6-6; **Half-time:** 16-22;
Referee: John McMullen; **Attendance:** 634.

OXFORD 20 SOUTH WALES SCORPIONS 38

OXFORD: 1 Sean Morris; 2 Connor Hughes; 3 Harvey Burnett; 4 Josh Nathaniel; 5 Errol Carter; 6 Aaron Dobek; 7 Danny Allan; 8 Josh Scott; 9 Casey Canterbury; 10 Tom Davies; 11 Santino Decaro; 12 Andrew Hoggins; 13 Marcus Brooker. Subs (all used): 14 Adam Flintham; 15 Dave Thornton; 16 Mark Hayes; 17 Tom Lewsley.
Tries: Hughes (31), Dobek (35), Hoggins (57), Allan (72);
Goals: Hughes 2/4.
SCORPIONS: - Nick Rawsthorne; 4 Yannic Parker; 22 Christiaan Roets; 15 Jordan Sheridan; 5 Dai Evans; 30 Greg Wilde; 7 Paul Emanuelli; 8 Chris Davies; 24 Zak Williams; 26 Luke Nelmes; 11 Bradley Hill; 29 Aiden Hema; 13 Chris Vitalini. Subs (all used): 14 Osian Phillips; 23 Barrie Phillips; 25 Billy Gaylor; 27 Rhys Davies.
Tries: Nelmes (14), Evans (21, 53), Sheridan (45), Roets (50), Wilde (63), Parker (80); **Goals:** Emanuelli 5/7.
Rugby Leaguer & League Express Men of the Match: *Oxford:* Sean Morris; *Scorpions:* Dai Evans.
Penalty count: 6-8; **Half-time:** 10-10;
Referee: Jamie Bloem; **Attendance:** 152 *(at Iffley Road)*.

BARROW RAIDERS 24 NEWCASTLE THUNDER 24

RAIDERS: 1 Ryan Fieldhouse; 23 Chris Fleming; 4 Andy Litherland; 16 Max Wiper; 5 Cameron Pitman; 31 Jamie Dallimore; 6 Josh Ward; 10 Oliver Wilkes; 30 Karl Ashall; 17 Andrew Dawson; 11 Liam Harrison; 27 Matty Holmes; 13 Martin Aspinwall. Subs (all used): 21 Dan Abram; 8 Joe Bullock; 12 Dan Toal; 18 James Duerden.
Tries: Holmes (15), Duerden (50), Ward (53), Wiper (70);
Goals: Ward 4/4.
THUNDER: 1 Tom Ruediger; 2 Joe Brown; 3 Derrell Olpherts; 4 Josh Atkinson; 5 Peter Fox; 6 Aaron Teroi; 7 Benn Hardcastle; 8 Vincent Rennie; 9 Craig Cook; 10 Rhys Clarke; 11 Harry Aldous; 12 Dan Parker; 13 Francis Welsh. Subs (all used): 14 Evan Simons; 15 Josh Stoker; 16 Mikey Wood; 17 Jason Payne.
Tries: Cook (1), Hardcastle (10), Ruediger (67), Rennie (75); **Goals:** Hardcastle 4/5.
Rugby Leaguer & League Express Men of the Match: *Raiders:* Andy Litherland; *Thunder:* Derrell Olpherts.
Penalty count: 13-9; **Half-time:** 6-12;
Referee: Andrew Sweet; **Attendance:** 1,033.

DONCASTER 16 YORK CITY KNIGHTS 46

DONCASTER: 1 Reece Dean; 2 Louis Sheriff; 3 Liam Welham; 4 Mathew Cook; 5 Matty Welham; 6 Harry Tyson-Wilson; 7 Jordie Hedges; 8 Matt Nicholson; 9 Ben Frankland; 10 Makali Aizue; 11 Mason Tonks; 12 Brad Foster; 13 Joe Pickets-O'Donnell. Subs (all used): 14 Kieran Cross; 15 Connor Scott; 16 Zac Braham; 17 Jack Walton.
Tries: M Welham (14), Sheriff (24), Aizue (80);
Goals: Dean 2/3.
Sin bin: Tonks (51) - dissent;
Pickets-O'Donnell (59) - late challenge.
CITY KNIGHTS: 1 Richard Wilkinson; 2 Brett Turner; 3 James Morland; 4 Brad Hey; 5 Austin Buchanan; 6 Jon Presley; 7 Danny Nicklas; 8 Brett Waller; 9 Harry Carter; 10 Jack Aldous; 11 Ryan Mallinder; 12 Ed Smith; 13 Mike Emmett. Subs (all used): 14 Kris Brining; 15 Mark Applegarth; 16 Russ Spiers; 17 Jordan Crowther.
Tries: Hey (3), Emmett (10), E Smith (29), Wilkinson (35), Brining (49), Crowther (52, 76), Waller (61), Nicklas (69); **Goals:** Nicklas 5/7, Turner 0/2.
Rugby Leaguer & League Express Men of the Match: *Doncaster:* Makali Aizue; *City Knights:* Danny Nicklas.
Penalty count: 8-13; **Half-time:** 10-18;
Referee: Callum Straw; **Attendance:** 946.

**GLOUCESTERSHIRE ALL GOLDS 28
COVENTRY BEARS 29**

ALL GOLDS: 1 Brendon Newton; 2 Chris Barlow; 3 Josh Allison; 4 Brad Kislingbury; 5 Phil Cowburn; 6 Courtney Davies; 7 Jayson Lombardo; 8 Oliver Purslow; 9 Steve Parry; 10 Harrison Elliott; 11 Lewis Reece; 12 Joe McClean; 13 Emmerson Whittel. Subs (all used): 14 Almer Tagayuna; 15 Lamont Bryan; 16 Alex Davidson; 17 Morgan Evans.
Tries: Davies (6), Parry (9, 74), Bryan (32), Barlow (69);
Goals: Davies 4/6.
Sin bin: McClean (51) - high tackle.
BEARS: 1 Jason Bass; 2 Jamahl Hunte; 3 Eddie Medforth; 4 Matt Reid; 5 Hayden Freeman; 6 James Redman; 7 Joel James; 8 Trae O'Sullivan; 9 Jay Lobwein; 10 Jack Morrison; 11 Liam Thompson; 12 Chris Barratt; 13 Richard Hughes. Subs (all used): 14 Charlie O'Mara; 15 Adam Saynor; 16 James Geurtjens; 17 Jonathan Milizewski.
Tries: Morrison (22), Medforth (45), Freeman (60), Reid (64), Hughes (72); **Goals:** James 4/5;
Field goal: James (79).
Rugby Leaguer & League Express Men of the Match: *All Golds:* Lamont Bryan; *Bears:* Joel James.
Penalty count: 12-16; **Half-time:** 16-6;
Referee: Tom Crashley; **Attendance:** 167.

ROUND 4

Sunday 10th April 2016

HEMEL STAGS 6 YORK CITY KNIGHTS 60

STAGS: 1 Josh Spearing; 2 Tala Petelo; 3 Oli Toms; 4 Alex Gilbey; 5 Reece Rance; 6 Chad Isles; 7 Ben Stead; 8 Mike Stewart; 9 Rory Sharratt; 10 Matt Ross; 11 Kyal Greene; 12 Luke Patterson; 13 Barry-John Swindells. Subs (all used): 14 Victor Coker; 15 Reece Bowditch; 16 Adam Booth; 17 Liam O'Callaghan.
Try: Stead (65); **Goals:** Stead 1/1.
CITY KNIGHTS: 1 Richard Wilkinson; 2 Ben Dent; 3 Connor Bower; 4 Tyler Craig; 5 Adam Dent; 6 Jon Presley; 7 Danny Nicklas; 8 Brett Waller; 9 Kris Brining; 10 Russ Spiers; 11 Josh Tonks; 12 Ed Smith; 13 Mike Emmett. Subs (all used): 14 Pat Smith; 15 Matty Dale; 16 Jordan Crowther; 17 Ross Osborne.
Tries: E Smith (5), Wilkinson (9, 68), Brining (13, 16, 71), Crowther (24), A Dent (28), Craig (38), Tonks (46), P Smith (54); **Goals:** Nicklas 8/11.
Rugby Leaguer & League Express Men of the Match: *Stags:* Ben Stead; *City Knights:* Kris Brining.
Penalty count: 8-8; **Half-time:** 0-38;
Referee: Liam Moore; **Attendance:** 152.

COVENTRY BEARS 0 BARROW RAIDERS 38

BEARS: 1 Joel James; 2 Jamahl Hunte; 3 Eddie Medforth; 4 Matt Reid; 5 Jason Bass; 6 Craig White; 7 James Redman; 8 Chris Barratt; 9 Jay Lobwein; 10 Jack Morrison; 11 Liam Thompson; 12 Jonathan Milizewski; 13 Richard Hughes. Subs (all used): 14 Charlie O'Mara; 15 James Geurtjens; 16 Adam Saynor; 17 Grant Beecham.
RAIDERS: 1 Ryan Fieldhouse; 22 Lee Haney; 3 Chris Hankinson; 4 Andy Litherland; 23 Chris Fleming; 31 Jamie Dallimore; 6 Josh Ward; 8 Joe Bullock; 30 Karl Ashall; 17 Andrew Dawson; 11 Liam Harrison; 26 Danny Morrow; 13 Martin Aspinwall. Subs (all used): 21 Dan Abram; 12 Dan Toal; 18 James Duerden; 19 Anthony Bate.
Tries: Harrison (5), Fleming (15), Litherland (26), Duerden (39), Haney (62), Abram (68), Bullock (79);
Goals: Ward 5/7.
Rugby Leaguer & League Express Men of the Match: *Bears:* Chris Barratt; *Raiders:* Jamie Dallimore.
Penalty count: 8-11; **Half-time:** 0-22;
Referee: Callum Straw; **Attendance:** 425.

DONCASTER 30 NORTH WALES CRUSADERS 14

DONCASTER: 1 Tom Carr; 2 Louis Sheriff; 3 Liam Welham; 4 Jason Tali; 5 Sam Doherty; 6 Reece Dean; 7 Brad Delaney; 8 Connor Scott; 9 Kyle Kesik; 10 Mark Castle; 11 Mason Tonks; 12 Michael Kelly; 13 Joe Picketts-O'Donnell. Subs (all used): 14 James Delaney; 15 Matt Nicholson; 16 Zac Braham; 17 Makali Aizue.
Tries: Castle (14), Tali (19, 35), Tonks (64, 80), Kelly (67);
Goals: Carr 3/6.
CRUSADERS: 1 Tommy Johnson; 2 Andrew Oakden; 3 Earl Hurst; 4 Matt Davies; 5 Rob Massam; 6 Ryan Smith; 7 Jack Hansen; 8 Jonny Walker; 9 Lee Hudson; 10 Tommy Holland; 11 Alex Thompson; 12 Stephen Wild; 13 Luke Warburton. Subs (all used): 14 Ryan Millington; 15 Kenny Baker; 16 Andrew Joy; 17 Elliot Liku.

Tries: Hansen (25), Johnson (30), Davies (79);
Goals: Johnson 1/3.
Rugby Leaguer & League Express Men of the Match:
Doncaster: Jason Tali; *Crusaders:* Jack Hansen.
Penalty count: 8-5; **Half-time:** 16-10;
Referee: Jack Smith; **Attendance:** 580.

KEIGHLEY COUGARS 70 OXFORD 10

COUGARS: 22 Ritchie Hawkyard; 26 Vinny Finigan; 23 Charlie Martin; 3 Rikki Sheriffe; 5 Paul White; 14 Adam Brook; 7 Paul Handforth; 8 Scott Law; 9 James Feather; 16 Jode Sheriffe; 17 John Oakes; 25 Darren Hawkyard; 12 Brendan Rawlins. Subs (all used): 11 Josh Lynam; 13 Ashley Lindsay; 19 Matthew Bailey; 35 Ross Peltier.
Tries: R Hawkyard (3, 73), J Sheriffe (7), D Hawkyard (9, 37), Handforth (26, 39, 44), White (50), Rawlins (63), Law (70), Finigan (76, 78); **Goals:** Brook 8/12, Handforth 1/1.
OXFORD: 1 James Craven; 2 Clark McAllister; 3 Zack McComb; 4 Harvey Burnett; 5 Andy Matthews; 6 Nathan Kitson; 7 Marcus Brooker; 8 Sean Hesketh; 9 Casey Canterbury; 10 Joel Thomas; 11 Daniel Igbinedion; 12 Andrew Hoggins; 13 Danny Allan. Subs (all used): 14 Josh Nathaniel; 15 Charlie Greene; 16 Luke Haslem; 17 Kris Ford.
Tries: Canterbury (17), McComb (66); **Goals:** Kitson 1/2.
Rugby Leaguer & League Express Men of the Match:
Cougars: Paul Handforth; *Oxford:* Marcus Brooker.
Penalty count: 7-6; **Half-time:** 36-4;
Referee: Jamie Bloem; **Attendance:** 671.

NEWCASTLE THUNDER 24 HUNSLET HAWKS 28

THUNDER: 1 Tom Ruediger; 2 Peter Fox; 3 Ali Blair; 4 Derrell Olpherts; 5 Jared Simpson; 6 Lee Paterson; 7 Benn Hardcastle; 8 Rhys Clarke; 9 Aaron Teroi; 10 Vincent Rennie; 11 Harry Aldous; 12 Dan Parker; 13 Ben Thorburn. Subs (all used): 14 Evan Simons; 15 Josh Stoker; 16 Mikey Wood; 17 Francis Welsh.
Tries: Ruediger (23), Rennie (37), Olpherts (48), Simpson (53), R Clarke (68); **Goals:** Hardcastle 2/5.
Sin bin: Olpherts (55) - dangerous challenge.
HAWKS: 1 Jimmy Watson; 5 James Duckworth; 4 Ayden Faal; 15 Mufaro Mvududu; 28 Richie Barnett; 20 Danny Thomas; 7 Danny Ansell; 19 Matt Carbutt; 9 Jack Lee; 8 Michael Haley; 29 Daniel Williams; 3 Jake Normington; 13 Liam Mackay. Subs (all used): 14 George Flanagan; 26 Austin Bell; 22 Craig Robinson; 12 Ben Crane.
Tries: Ansell (5, 79), Carbutt (19), Barnett (40), Flanagan (47), Faal (58); **Goals:** Ansell 2/6.
Rugby Leaguer & League Express Men of the Match:
Thunder: Tom Ruediger; *Hawks:* Danny Ansell.
Penalty count: 4-5; **Half-time:** 12-14;
Referee: John McMullen; **Attendance:** 604.

ROCHDALE HORNETS 38
GLOUCESTERSHIRE ALL GOLDS 16

HORNETS: 1 Wayne English; 2 Chris Riley; 3 Jack Johnson; 4 Mike Ratu; 5 Dale Bloomfield; 6 Declan Patton; 7 Danny Yates; 8 Daniel Murray; 9 Ben Moores; 10 Warren Thompson; 11 Jono Smith; 12 Jordan Case; 13 James Tilley. Subs (all used): 14 Alex McClurg; 15 Matty Hadden; 16 Alex Trumper; 17 James Dandy.
Tries: Case (5), Bloomfield (21), Yates (25), Johnson (37), Ratu (53, 78), Trumper (76);
Goals: Patton 0/1, Yates 5/6.
ALL GOLDS: 1 Jamie Murphy; 2 Jonny Leather; 3 Josh Allison; 4 Joe McClean; 5 Phil Cowburn; 6 Courtney Davies; 7 Brendon Newton; 8 Alex Davidson; 9 Almer Tagayuna; 10 Harrison Elliott; 11 Lamont Bryan; 12 Richard Jones; 13 Emmerson Whittel. Subs (all used): 14 Steve Parry; 15 Graham O'Keeffe; 16 Oliver Purslow; 17 Morgan Evans.
Tries: Murphy (14), Cowburn (65), Leather (70);
Goals: Davies 0/1, Murphy 2/2.
Rugby Leaguer & League Express Men of the Match:
Hornets: Jono Smith; *All Golds:* Almer Tagayuna.
Penalty count: 13-7; **Half-time:** 20-4;
Referee: Scott Mikalauskas; **Attendance:** 430.

SOUTH WALES SCORPIONS 0
TOULOUSE OLYMPIQUE 64

SCORPIONS: - Nick Rawsthorne; 4 Yannic Parker; 22 Christiaan Roets; 15 Jordan Sheridan; 5 Dai Evans; 25 Billy Gaylor; 7 Paul Emanuelli; 8 Chris Davies; 9 Connor Farrer; 10 Izaak Duffy; 29 Aiden Hema; 3 Kyle Scrivens; 13 Chris Vitalini. Subs (all used): 17 Mike Connor; 23 Barrie Phillips; 24 Zak Williams; 26 Luke Nelmes.
Sin bin: Nelmes (75) - punching.
OLYMPIQUE: 1 Mark Kheirallah; 2 Tony Maurel; 21 Gavin Marguerite; 4 Gregory White; 5 Kuni Minga; 6 Jonathon Ford; 7 Arthur Gonzalez-Trique; 8 Clement Boyer; 14 Mourad Kriouache; 16 Bastien Canet; 11 Sebastien Planas; 12 Rhys Curran; 13 Andrew Bentley. Subs (all used): 9 Kane Bentley; 15 Maxime Puech; 18 Tyla Hepi; 17 Anthony Marion.
Tries: Minga (3, 59, 67, 79), Gonzalez-Trique (7, 57), Ford (11), Marguerite (21), Canet (24), Maurel (31), K Bentley (51), Kheirallah (69); **Goals:** Kheirallah 8/12.
Rugby Leaguer & League Express Men of the Match:
Scorpions: Christiaan Roets; *Olympique:* Kuni Minga.
Penalty count: 2-8; **Half-time:** 0-32;
Referee: Warren Turley; **Attendance:** 241.

ROUND 5

Sunday 17th April 2016

NORTH WALES CRUSADERS 24 LONDON SKOLARS 31

CRUSADERS: 1 Tommy Johnson; 2 Scott Turner; 3 Simon Atherton; 4 Earl Hurst; 5 Rob Massam; 6 Ryan Smith; 7 Jack Hansen; 8 Jonny Walker; 9 Lee Hudson; 10 Kenny Baker; 11 Alex Thompson; 12 Stephen Wild; 13 Luke Warburton. Subs (all used): 14 Ryan Millington; 15 Tommy Holland; 16 Elliot Liku; 17 Matt Davies.
Tries: Thompson (22, 80), Smith (24), Turner (51);
Goals: Johnson 4/5.
SKOLARS: 1 Alex Walker; 2 Sam Nash; 3 Aaron Small; 4 Israel Eliab; 5 John Paxton; 6 Jy-mel Coleman; 7 Mike Bishay; 8 Toby Everett; 9 Sam Druce; 10 Ben Gray; 11 Dave Williams; 12 Will Lovell; 13 Ryan Chester. Subs (all used): 14 Erjon Dollapi; 15 Eddie Mbaraga; 16 Michael Sykes; 17 Ben Pointer.
Tries: Williams (7), Walker (18), Chester (20), Nash (35, 54), Eliab (61); **Goals:** Bishay 2/5, Jy-mel Coleman 1/1;
Field goal: Jy-mel Coleman (71).
Rugby Leaguer & League Express Men of the Match:
Crusaders: Kenny Baker; *Skolars:* Dave Williams.
Penalty count: 5-8; **Half-time:** 14-20;
Referee: Scott Mikalauskas; **Attendance:** 448.

KEIGHLEY COUGARS 42
GLOUCESTERSHIRE ALL GOLDS 18

COUGARS: 22 Ritchie Hawkyard; 2 Andy Gabriel; 29 Hamish Barnes; 23 Charlie Martin; 5 Paul White; 14 Adam Brook; 7 Paul Handforth; 8 Scott Law; 9 James Feather; 15 Neil Cherryholme; 17 John Oakes; 12 Brendan Rawlins; 13 Ashley Lindsay. Subs (all used): 16 Jode Sheriffe; 19 Matthew Bailey; 20 Aaron Ollett; 35 Ross Peltier.
Tries: Barnes (10, 46), Martin (26), R Hawkyard (31), Lindsay (66), Law (75), Gabriel (79); **Goals:** Brook 7/8.
ALL GOLDS: 1 Jamie Murphy; 2 Chris Barlow; 3 Lewis Reece; 4 Brad Kislingbury; 5 Josh Allison; 6 Courtney Davies; 7 Jimmy Rowland; 8 Oliver Purslow; 9 Steve Parry; 10 James Walter; 11 Joe McClean; 12 Richard Jones; 13 Lamont Bryan. Subs (all used): 14 Emmerson Whittel; 15 Harrison Elliott; 16 Harry Kidd; 17 Morgan Evans.
Tries: Rowland (14), Kislingbury (21), McClean (42), Bryan (53); **Goals:** Davies 0/1, Murphy 1/3.
Rugby Leaguer & League Express Men of the Match:
Cougars: Hamish Barnes; *All Golds:* Jimmy Rowland.
Penalty count: 9-6; **Half-time:** 18-8;
Referee: Jack Smith; **Attendance:** 527.

SOUTH WALES SCORPIONS 14 HEMEL STAGS 30

SCORPIONS: - Nick Rawsthorne; 4 Yannic Parker; 22 Christiaan Roets; 15 Jordan Sheridan; 5 Dai Evans; 6 Kristian Hawkes; 7 Paul Emanuelli; 26 Luke Nelmes; 24 Zak Williams; 10 Izaak Duffy; 11 Bradley Hill; 29 Aiden Hema; 8 Chris Davies. Subs (all used): 14 Osian Phillips; 13 Chris Vitalini; 3 Kyle Scrivens; 23 Barrie Phillips.
Tries: Roets (27), Rawsthorne (31), Parker (57);
Goals: Emanuelli 1/3.
STAGS: 1 Josh Spearing; 2 Simon Hrbek; 3 Kameron Pearce-Paul; 4 Tuoyo Egodo; 5 Reece Rance; 6 Chad Isles; 7 Ben Stead; 8 Aaron Hall; 9 Liam O'Callaghan; 10 Matt Ross; 11 Barry-John Swindells; 12 Oli Toms; 13 Kyal Greene. Subs (all used): 14 Mike Stewart; 15 Rhys Bowditch; 16 Marcus Stock; 17 Sadiq Adebiyi.
Tries: Hrbek (9), Rance (15, 67), Egodo (21), Stead (45), Stewart (53); **Goals:** Swindells 3/5, Hrbek 0/1.
Rugby Leaguer & League Express Men of the Match:
Scorpions: Kristian Hawkes; *Stags:* Tuoyo Egodo.
Penalty count: 5-7; **Half-time:** 10-16;
Referee: Callum Straw; **Attendance:** 215.

ROUND 6

Saturday 23rd April 2016

LONDON SKOLARS 52 COVENTRY BEARS 20

SKOLARS: 1 Alex Walker; 2 Sam Nash; 3 Aaron Small; 4 Israel Eliab; 5 John Paxton; 6 Jy-mel Coleman; 7 Mike Bishay; 8 Michael Sykes; 9 Sam Druce; 10 Toby Everett; 11 Eddie Mbaraga; 12 Will Lovell; 13 Dave Williams. Subs (all used): 14 Ben Pointer; 15 Erjon Dollapi; 16 Ben Gray; 17 Joe Price.
Tries: Walker (10, 40), Jy-mel Coleman (30), Dollapi (44, 47), Paxton (61), Bishay (67), Eliab (78);
Goals: Bishay 10/10.
BEARS: 1 Joel James; 2 Ben Warrilow; 3 Eddie Medforth; 4 Matt Reid; 5 Jason Bass; 6 Craig White; 7 James Redman; 8 James Geurtjens; 9 Jay Lobwein; 10 Jack Morrison; 11 Liam Thompson; 12 Chris Barratt; 13 Richard Hughes. Subs (all used): 14 Charlie O'Mara; 15 Adam Saynor; 16 Jonathan Milizewski; 17 Grant Beecham.
Tries: Barratt (16), Hughes (57), Beecham (72), O'Mara (75); **Goals:** James 2/2, White 0/2.
Rugby Leaguer & League Express Men of the Match:
Skolars: Mike Bishay; *Bears:* Grant Beecham.
Penalty count: 14-8; **Half-time:** 20-6;
Referee: Andrew Bentham; **Attendance:** 365.

Sunday 24th April 2016

HEMEL STAGS 10 NORTH WALES CRUSADERS 38

STAGS: 1 Josh Spearing; 2 Reece Rance; 3 Tuoyo Egodo; 4 Kameron Pearce-Paul; 5 Harrison Brough; 6 Chad Isles; 7 Scott Leatherbarrow; 8 Matt Ross; 9 Ben Stead; 10 Aaron Hall; 11 Barry-John Swindells; 12 Kyle Greene; 13 Matt Davis. Subs (all used): 14 Mike Stewart; 15 Malikhi Lloyd-Jones; 16 Josh Halstead; 17 Liam O'Callaghan.
Tries: Ross (24), Pearce-Paul (40); **Goals:** Stead 1/2.
Sin bin: Greene (76) - fighting.
CRUSADERS: 1 Tommy Johnson; 2 Scott Turner; 3 Alex Thompson; 4 Earl Hurst; 5 Rob Massam; 6 Ryan Smith; 7 Jack Hansen; 8 Jonny Walker; 9 Lee Hudson; 10 Matthew Haggarty; 11 Simon Atherton; 12 Stephen Wild; 13 Kenny Baker. Subs (all used): 14 Matt Wilkinson; 15 Tommy Holland; 16 Andy Moulsdale; 17 Elliot Liku.
Tries: Wild (12), Atherton (15), Baker (21), Thompson (49), Moulsdale (61), Turner (71), Hudson (79);
Goals: Johnson 5/7.
Sin bin: Haggarty (76) - fighting.
Rugby Leaguer & League Express Men of the Match:
Stags: Ben Stead; *Crusaders:* Andy Moulsdale.
Penalty count: 6-6; **Half-time:** 10-18;
Referee: Tom Crashley; **Attendance:** 150.

OXFORD 14 HUNSLET HAWKS 40

OXFORD: 1 Josh Nathaniel; 2 Andy Matthews; 3 Kieran Gill; 4 Harvey Burnett; 5 James Cryer; 6 Tom Holmes; 7 Danny Allan; 8 Joel Thomas; 9 Nathan Kitson; 10 Will Mayer; 11 Marcus Brooker; 12 Andrew Hoggins; 13 Sadiq Adebiyi. Subs (all used): 14 Casey Canterbury; 15 John James Baird; 16 Adam Withington; 17 Jack Smith.
Tries: Kitson (15), Holmes (22), Smith (66);
Goals: Kitson 1/3.
Sin bin: Smith (46) - punching;
Nathaniel (52) - professional foul.
HAWKS: 1 Jimmy Watson; 2 Mo Agoro; 18 Aston Wilson; 15 Mufaro Mvududu; 28 Richie Barnett; 6 Simon Brown; 7 Danny Ansell; 19 Matt Carbutt; 14 George Flanagan; 29 Daniel Williams; 12 Ben Crane; 3 Jake Normington; 13 Liam Mackay. Subs (all used): 9 Jack Lee; 10 Lewis Reed; 22 Craig Robinson; 30 Jamie Milburn.
Tries: Mvududu (4, 12, 50), Flanagan (19), Agoro (38), Reed (47), Barnett (52), Crane (72); **Goals:** Brown 4/8.
Rugby Leaguer & League Express Men of the Match:
Oxford: Tom Holmes; *Hawks:* Mufaro Mvududu.
Penalty count: 3-6; **Half-time:** 8-18;
Referee: Scott Mikalauskas; **Attendance:** 225.

DONCASTER 21 BARROW RAIDERS 18

DONCASTER: 1 Tom Carr; 2 Louis Sheriff; 3 Liam Welham; 4 Jason Tali; 5 Sam Doherty; 6 Jordan Howden; 7 Brad Delaney; 8 Mark Castle; 9 Kyle Kesik; 10 Makali Aizue; 11 Mason Tonks; 12 Brad Foster; 13 Matt Nicholson. Subs (all used): 14 James Delaney; 15 Zac Braham; 16 Brad Nicholson; 17 Connor Scott.
Tries: Castle (7), Tali (42, 52); **Goals:** Carr 4/4;
Field goal: Carr (72).
Dismissal: Scott (27) - punching Dallimore.
RAIDERS: 1 Ryan Fieldhouse; 2 Shane Toal; 3 Chris Hankinson; 16 Max Wiper; 22 Lee Haney; 31 Jamie Dallimore; 6 Josh Ward; 8 Joe Bullock; 30 Karl Ashall; 10 Oliver Wilkes; 4 Andy Litherland; 26 Danny Morrow; 13 Martin Aspinwall. Subs (all used): 21 Dan Abram; 12 Dan Toal; 18 James Duerden; 19 Anthony Bate.
Tries: Hankinson (33), Haney (59), Bate (78);
Goals: Ward 3/4.
Rugby Leaguer & League Express Men of the Match:
Doncaster: Jason Tali; *Raiders:* Chris Hankinson.
Penalty count: 11-8; **Half-time:** 6-6;
Referee: Andrew Sweet; **Attendance:** 540.

GLOUCESTERSHIRE ALL GOLDS 18
NEWCASTLE THUNDER 21

ALL GOLDS: 1 Jamie Murphy; 2 Chris Barlow; 3 Josh

Allison; 4 Lewis Reece; 5 Phil Cowburn; 6 Jimmy Rowland; 7 Matt Bradley; 8 Oliver Purslow; 9 Steve Parry; 10 Harrison Elliott; 11 Lamont Bryan; 12 Joe McClean; 13 Emmerson Whittel. Subs (all used): 14 Almer Tagayuna; 15 Morgan Evans; 16 Richard Jones; 17 Alex Davidson.
Tries: Bryan (3), Barlow (24), Davidson (47);
Goals: Bradley 3/4.
Sin bin: Murphy (32) - dissent.
THUNDER: 1 Tom Ruediger; 2 Jared Simpson; 3 Joe Brown; 4 Ali Blair; 5 Peter Fox; 6 Lewis Young; 7 Benn Hardcastle; 8 Rhys Clarke; 9 Craig Cook; 10 Vincent Rennie; 11 Harry Aldous; 12 Dan Parker; 13 Lee Paterson. Subs (all used): 14 Evan Simons; 15 Mikey Wood; 16 Josh Stoker; 17 Francis Welsh.
Tries: Blair (16), Simons (31), Brown (41);
Goals: Hardcastle 4/4; **Field goal:** Hardcastle (70).
Rugby Leaguer & League Express Men of the Match: *All Golds:* Lamont Bryan; *Thunder:* Vincent Rennie.
Penalty count: 11-8; **Half-time:** 10-12;
Referee: Callum Straw; **Attendance:** 105.

ROCHDALE HORNETS 28 TOULOUSE OLYMPIQUE 28

HORNETS: 1 Wayne English; 2 Tom Lineham; 3 Mike Ratu; 4 Lewis Galbraith; 5 Chris Riley; 6 Paul Crook; 7 Danny Yates; 8 Samir Tahraoui; 9 Ben Moores; 10 Warren Thompson; 11 Jono Smith; 12 Jordan Case; 13 James Tilley. Subs (all used): 14 Alex McClurg; 15 Matty Hadden; 16 Joe Philbin; 17 Jovili Taira.
Tries: Tilley (18), Lineham (30, 35), Smith (47), Yates (54);
Goals: Crook 4/7.
Sin bin: Smith (73) - fighting.
OLYMPIQUE: 1 Mark Kheirallah; 2 Tony Maurel; 3 Bastien Ader; 4 Gregory White; 5 Kuni Minga; 6 Jonathon Ford; 7 Arthur Gonzalez-Trique; 8 Clement Boyer; 9 Kane Bentley; 16 Bastien Canet; 11 Sebastien Planas; 12 Rhys Curran; 13 Andrew Bentley. Subs (all used): 14 Mourad Kriouache; 22 Danny Hulme; 18 Tyla Hepi; 10 Samy Masselot.
Tries: Curran (2, 10, 74), Minga (7), White (60);
Goals: Kheirallah 4/5.
Sin bin: Planas (73) - fighting.
Rugby Leaguer & League Express Men of the Match: *Hornets:* Samir Tahraoui; *Olympique:* Jonathon Ford.
Penalty count: 10-7; **Half-time:** 16-16;
Referee: Tom Grant; **Attendance:** 536.

YORK CITY KNIGHTS 40 SOUTH WALES SCORPIONS 6

CITY KNIGHTS: 1 Richard Wilkinson; 2 Ben Dent; 3 Tyler Craig; 4 Brad Hey; 5 Austin Buchanan; 6 Pat Smith; 7 Danny Nicklas; 8 Brett Waller; 9 Harry Carter; 10 Jack Aldous; 11 Josh Tonks; 12 Jack Anderson; 13 Mike Emmett. Subs (all used): 14 Kris Brining; 15 Mark Applegarth; 16 Ross Osborne; 17 Jordan Crowther.
Tries: Craig (10), Carter (18), Tonks (28), Brining (32, 40), Applegarth (37), P Smith (46); **Goals:** Nicklas 6/7.
SCORPIONS: - Joe Martin; 5 Dai Evans; 22 Christiaan Roets; 21 Scott Gregory; 4 Yannic Parker; 25 Billy Gaylor; 7 Paul Emanuelli; 10 Izaak Duffy; 24 Zak Williams; 14 Osian Phillips; 11 Bradley Hill; 3 Kyle Scrivens; 13 Chris Vitalini. Subs (all used): 8 Chris Davies; 17 Mike Connor; 26 Luke Nelmes; 19 Kristian Baller.
Try: Roets (51); **Goals:** Emanuelli 1/1.
Rugby Leaguer & League Express Men of the Match: *City Knights:* Mark Applegarth; *Scorpions:* Paul Emanuelli.
Penalty count: 8-8; **Half-time:** 34-0;
Referee: Jack Smith; **Attendance:** 643.

ROUND 5

Saturday 30th April 2016

TOULOUSE OLYMPIQUE 54 OXFORD 8

OLYMPIQUE: 1 Mark Kheirallah; 2 Tony Maurel; 21 Gavin Marguerite; 4 Gregory White; - Paul Marcon; 6 Johnathon Ford; 7 Arthur Gonzalez-Trique; 8 Clement Boyer; 9 Kane Bentley; 16 Bastien Canet; 11 Sebastien Planas; 12 Rhys Curran; 17 Anthony Marion. Subs (all used): 14 Mourad Kriouache; 15 Maxime Puech; 10 Samy Masselot; 18 Tyla Hepi.
Tries: K Bentley (5), Boyer (19), White (25), Curran (28), Marguerite (30), Gonzalez-Trique (44), Maurel (46), Kriouache (60), Masselot (65), Marcon (68);
Goals: Kheirallah 7/10.
Sin bin: Marguerite (2) - professional foul.
OXFORD: 1 Adam Flintham; 2 Andy Matthews; 3 Kieran Gill; 4 Harvey Burnett; 5 Clark McAllister; 6 Tom Holmes; 7 Marcus Brooker; 8 Daniel Igbinedion; 9 Casey Canterbury; 10 Jack Smith; 11 John James Baird; 12 Andrew Hoggins; 13 Luke Evans. Subs (all used): 14 Scott Lee; 15 Santino Decaro; 16 James Cryer; 17 Charlie Greene.
Tries: Cryer (14), Greene (75);
Goals: Holmes 0/1, McAllister 0/1.
Rugby Leaguer & League Express Men of the Match: *Olympique:* Johnathon Ford; *Oxford:* John James Baird.
Penalty count: 7-7; **Half-time:** 28-4;
Referee: Jack Smith; **Attendance:** 738.

Sunday 1st May 2016

HUNSLET HAWKS 22 DONCASTER 30

HAWKS: 1 Jimmy Watson; 2 Mo Agoro; 5 James Duckworth; 15 Mufaro Mvududu; 28 Richie Barnett; 6 Simon Brown; 7 Danny Ansell; 8 Michael Haley; 9 Jack Lee; 10 Lewis Reed; 12 Ben Crane; 3 Jake Normington; 13 Liam Mackay. Subs (all used): 14 George Flanagan; 26 Austin Bell; 19 Matt Carbutt; 29 Daniel Williams.
Tries: Duckworth (16), Watson (48), Normington (52), Barnett (65); **Goals:** Brown 3/5.
DONCASTER: 1 Tom Carr; 2 Louis Sheriff; 3 Liam Welham; 4 Jason Tali; 5 Sam Doherty; 6 Jordan Howden; 7 Brad Delaney; 8 Makali Aizue; 9 Kyle Kesik; 10 Mark Castle; 11 Brad Foster; 12 Michael Kelly; 13 Matt Nicholson. Subs (all used): 14 Ryan Wright; 15 Iafeta Palea'aesina; 16 Connor Scott; 17 Brad Nicholson.
Tries: Kelly (7), B Delaney (20, 33), Tali (68), Castle (78);
Goals: Carr 5/5.
Rugby Leaguer & League Express Men of the Match: *Hawks:* George Flanagan; *Doncaster:* Jordan Howden.
Penalty count: 11-5; **Half-time:** 4-18;
Referee: Warren Turley; **Attendance:** 385.

BARROW RAIDERS 4 ROCHDALE HORNETS 18

RAIDERS: 1 Ryan Fieldhouse; 22 Lee Haney; 3 Chris Hankinson; 4 Andy Litherland; 5 Cameron Pitman; 31 Jamie Dallimore; 6 Josh Ward; 8 Joe Bullock; 30 Karl Ashall; 10 Oliver Wilkes; 11 Liam Harrison; 26 Danny Morrow; 13 Martin Aspinwall. Subs (all used): 14 Brad Marwood; 12 Dan Toal; 18 James Duerden; 19 Anthony Bate.
Try: Pitman (39); **Goals:** Ward 0/1.
Sin bin: Haney (10) - fighting, (23) - holding down.
HORNETS: 1 Wayne English; 2 Dale Bloomfield; 3 Mike Ratu; 4 Lewis Galbraith; 5 Chris Riley; 6 Paul Crook; 7 Danny Yates; 8 Samir Tahraoui; 9 Ben Moores; 10 Warren Thompson; 11 Jono Smith; 12 Jordan Case; 13 James Tilley. Subs (all used): 14 Alex McClurg; 15 Matty Hadden; 16 Stuart Biscomb; 17 Jack Francis.
Tries: Bloomfield (26), Smith (52); **Goals:** Crook 5/5.
Sin bin: Moores (10) - fighting.
Rugby Leaguer & League Express Men of the Match: *Raiders:* Liam Harrison; *Hornets:* Paul Crook.
Penalty count: 15-13; **Half-time:** 4-10;
Referee: Tom Crashley; **Attendance:** 793.

ROUND 7

Sunday 8th May 2016

NORTH WALES CRUSADERS 40 OXFORD 18

CRUSADERS: 1 Tommy Johnson; 2 Scott Turner; 3 Stuart Reardon; 4 Earl Hurst; 5 Rob Massam; 6 Ryan Smith; 7 Andy Moulsdale; 8 Jonny Walker; 9 Lee Hudson; 10 Kenny Baker; 11 Jake Bibby; 12 Stephen Wild; 13 Simon Atherton. Subs (all used): 14 Matt Wilkinson; 15 Ryan Millington; 16 Tommy Holland; 17 Elliot Liku.
Tries: Baker (10), Smith (12), Bibby (18), Turner (20, 76), Massam (48), Wild (56), Hurst (63); **Goals:** Johnson 4/8.
OXFORD: 1 Nathan Kitson; 2 Josh Nathaniel; 3 Jordan Williams; 4 Marcus Brooker; 5 Clark McAllister; 6 Tom Holmes; 7 Danny Allan; 8 Jack Smith; 9 Casey Canterbury; 10 Will Maher; 11 John James Baird; 12 Andrew Hoggins; 13 Luke Evans. Subs (all used): 14 Callum Bustin; 15 Daniel Igbinedion; 16 Jordan Siddons; 17 Charlie Greene.
Tries: Brooker (28), Kitson (33), Canterbury (37), Siddons (72); **Goals:** Kitson 1/4.
Rugby Leaguer & League Express Men of the Match: *Crusaders:* Scott Turner; *Oxford:* Nathan Kitson.
Penalty count: 14-19; **Half-time:** 22-14;
Referee: Tom Crashley; **Attendance:** 411.

COVENTRY BEARS 16 KEIGHLEY COUGARS 36

BEARS: 1 Charlie O'Mara; 2 Ben Warrilow; 3 Eddie Medforth; 4 Matt Reid; 5 Jason Bass; 6 James Redman; 7 Joel James; 8 Alex Beddows; 9 Jay Lobwein; 10 Jack Morrison; 11 Liam Thompson; 12 Chris Barratt; 13 Richard Hughes. Subs (all used): 14 James Geurtjens; 15 Grant Beecham; 16 Jonathan Milizewski; 17 Trae O'Sullivan.
Tries: Geurtjens (32), Beecham (50), Barratt (54);
Goals: James 2/3.
Sin bin: James (71) - fighting.
COUGARS: 5 Paul White; 2 Andy Gabriel; 3 Rikki Sheriffe; 29 Hamish Barnes; 26 Vinny Finigan; 24 Liam Darville; 14 Adam Brook; 15 Neil Cherryholme; 9 James Feather; 12 Brendan Rawlins; 25 Darren Hawkyard; 23 Charlie Martin; 13 Ashley Lindsay. Subs (all used): 20 Aaron Ollett; 11 Josh Lynam; 35 Ross Peltier; 19 Matthew Bailey.
Tries: Brook (12), Finigan (24), Martin (38), Peltier (46), Lindsay (72), White (76), Barnes (79); **Goals:** Brook 4/7.
Sin bin: Darville (71) - fighting.
Rugby Leaguer & League Express Men of the Match: *Bears:* Richard Hughes; *Cougars:* Ross Peltier.
Penalty count: 14-9; **Half-time:** 4-14;
Referee: John McMullen; **Attendance:** 1,097 *(at Ricoh Arena)*.

HUNSLET HAWKS 44 HEMEL STAGS 28

HAWKS: 1 Jimmy Watson; 5 James Duckworth; 4 Ayden Faal; 18 Aston Wilson; 28 Richie Barnett; 6 Simon Brown; 7 Danny Ansell; 8 Michael Haley; 9 Jack Lee; 22 Craig Robinson; 30 Jamie Milburn; 3 Jake Normington; 13 Liam Mackay. Subs (all used): 14 George Flanagan; 19 Matt Carbutt; 20 Danny Thomas; 10 Lewis Reed.
Tries: Duckworth (2), Faal (6), Flanagan (32, 36, 56), Mackay (48, 80), Watson (79); **Goals:** Brown 6/8.
STAGS: 1 Josh Spearing; 2 Reece Rance; 3 Tuoyo Egodo; 4 Kameron Pearce-Paul; 5 Harrison Brough; 6 Barry-John Swindells; 7 Ben Stead; 8 Aaron Hall; 9 Liam O'Callaghan; 10 Matt Ross; 11 Chris Clough; 12 Oli Toms; 13 Kyal Greene. Subs (all used): 14 Mike Stewart; 15 Dave O'Conner; 16 Josh Halstead; 17 Alex Gilbey.
Tries: Clough (9), Rance (16), Stewart (28, 52), Pearce-Paul (40); **Goals:** Stead 4/5.
Rugby Leaguer & League Express Men of the Match: *Hawks:* George Flanagan; *Stags:* Oli Toms.
Penalty count: 6-6; **Half-time:** 22-22;
Referee: Jack Smith; **Attendance:** 469.

NEWCASTLE THUNDER 35 DONCASTER 34

THUNDER: 1 Jared Simpson; 2 Ali Blair; 3 Joe Brown; 4 Dan Parker; 5 Peter Fox; 6 Lewis Young; 7 Benn Hardcastle; 8 Vincent Rennie; 9 Craig Cook; 10 Rhys Clarke; 11 Mikey Wood; 12 Harry Aldous; 13 Lee Paterson. Subs (all used): 14 Aaron Teroi; 15 Kieran Moran; 16 Evan Simons; 17 Francis Welsh.
Tries: Rennie (19), Hardcastle (21), Brown (27, 44), Paterson (48), Fox (56); **Goals:** Hardcastle 5/7;
Field goal: Hardcastle (78).
DONCASTER: 1 Tom Carr; 2 Louis Sheriff; 3 Sam Doherty; 4 Jason Tali; 5 David Foggin-Johnston; 6 Jordan Howden; 7 Brad Delaney; 8 Brad Nicholson; 9 Kyle Kesik; 10 Mark Castle; 11 Jack Walton; 12 Brad Foster; 13 Matt Nicholson. Subs (all used): 14 Ryan Wright; 15 Connor Scott; 16 Iafeta Palea'aesina; 17 Zac Braham.
Tries: B Nicholson (7), Foggin-Johnston (12), Tali (40, 61, 64), B Delaney (80); **Goals:** Carr 5/6.
Rugby Leaguer & League Express Men of the Match: *Thunder:* Lee Paterson; *Doncaster:* Jason Tali.
Penalty count: 11-18; **Half-time:** 14-18;
Referee: Andrew Sweet; **Attendance:** 552.

ROCHDALE HORNETS 40 LONDON SKOLARS 12

HORNETS: 1 Wayne English; 2 Dale Bloomfield; 3 Mike Ratu; 4 Lewis Galbraith; 5 Chris Riley; 6 Paul Crook; 7 Danny Yates; 8 Samir Tahraoui; 9 Ben Moores; 10 Warren Thompson; 11 Jono Smith; 12 Jordan Case; 13 James Tilley. Subs (all used): 14 Alex McClurg; 15 Matty Hadden; 16 Stuart Biscomb; 17 Alex Trumper.
Tries: Case (25), Crook (34), McClurg (45), Smith (61, 64), English (75), Riley (80); **Goals:** Crook 6/7.
SKOLARS: 1 Alex Anthony; 2 Sam Nash; 3 Aaron Small; 4 Lameck Juma; 5 John Paxton; 6 Jy-mel Coleman; 7 Mike Bishay; 8 Toby Everett; 9 Ben Pointer; 10 Ben Gray; 11 Dave Williams; 12 Eddie Mbaraga; 13 Ryan Chester. Subs (all used): 14 Michael Sykes; 15 Erjon Dollapi; 16 Kazeem Fatouri; 17 Billy Driver.
Tries: Juma (12), Fatouri (55); **Goals:** Bishay 2/2.
Rugby Leaguer & League Express Men of the Match: *Hornets:* Paul Crook; *Skolars:* Jy-mel Coleman.
Penalty count: 14-7; **Half-time:** 12-6;
Referee: Sam Ansell; **Attendance:** 513.

BARROW RAIDERS 50 YORK CITY KNIGHTS 12

RAIDERS: 1 Ryan Fieldhouse; 2 Shane Toal; 3 Chris Hankinson; 4 Andy Litherland; 5 Cameron Pitman; 28 Jamie Dallimore; 14 Brad Marwood; 8 Joe Bullock; 29 Karl Ashall; 10 Oliver Wilkes; 11 Liam Harrison; 26 Danny Morrow; 13 Martin Aspinwall. Subs (all used): 17 Andrew Dawson; 12 Dan Toal; 21 Dan Abram; 19 Anthony Bate.
Tries: Bullock (9), Dallimore (15), Litherland (32), Morrow (42), Pitman (50, 76), S Toal (65), D Toal (74), Hankinson (79); **Goals:** Hankinson 7/9.
Sin bin: Morrow (55) - dangerous challenge.
CITY KNIGHTS: 1 Brett Turner; 2 James Morland; 3 Tyler Craig; 4 Brad Hey; 5 Adam Dent; 6 Jon Presley; 7 Danny Nicklas; 8 Brett Waller; 9 Harry Carter; 10 Russ Spiers; 11 Ryan Mallinder; 12 Mark Applegarth; 13 Jack Aldous. Subs (all used): 14 Kris Brining; 15 Ross Osborne; 16 Matty Dale; 17 Jack Anderson.

Tries: A Dent (20), Morland (23), Brining (58);
Goals: Nicklas 0/3.
Rugby Leaguer & League Express Men of the Match: *Raiders:* Jamie Dallimore; *City Knights:* Jon Presley.
Penalty count: 7-7; **Half time:** 16-8;
Referee: Tom Grant; **Attendance:** 977.

ROUND 8

Saturday 14th May 2016

COVENTRY BEARS 20 DONCASTER 32

BEARS: 1 Charlie O'Mara; 2 Hayden Freeman; 3 Eddie Medforth; 4 Jonathan Milizewski; 5 Jason Bass; 6 Joel James; 7 James Redman; 8 Alex Beddows; 9 Jay Lobwein; 10 Jack Morrison; 11 Liam Thompson; 12 Chris Barratt; 13 Richard Hughes. Subs (all used): 14 James Geurtjens; 15 Grant Beecham; 16 Joe Batchelor; 17 Trae O'Sullivan.
Tries: Freeman (18), Medforth (44, 71), O'Mara (59);
Goals: James 2/4.
DONCASTER: 1 Tom Carr; 2 David Foggin-Johnston; 3 Sam Doherty; 4 Jason Tali; 5 Louis Sheriff; 6 Jordan Howden; 7 Brad Delaney; 8 Makali Aizue; 9 Kyle Kesik; 10 Mark Castle; 11 Brad Nicholson; 12 Jack Walton; 13 Connor Scott. Subs (all used): 14 Kieran Cross; 15 Iafeta Palea'aesina; 16 Zac Braham; 17 Liam Welham.
Tries: B Nicholson (8), Palea'aesina (28, 47), Carr (32), Doherty (53), Tali (75); **Goals:** Carr 4/6.
Rugby Leaguer & League Express Men of the Match: *Bears:* Charlie O'Mara; *Doncaster:* Iafeta Palea'aesina.
Penalty count: 5-5; **Half-time:** 4-18;
Referee: Liam Moore; **Attendance:** 373.

LONDON SKOLARS 26 NEWCASTLE THUNDER 46

SKOLARS: 1 Israel Eliab; 2 Sam Nash; 3 Aaron Small; 4 Lameck Juma; 5 John Paxton; 6 Jy-mel Coleman; 7 Mike Bishay; 8 Toby Everett; 9 Charlie Lawrence; 10 Ben Gray; 11 Dave Williams; 12 Eddie Mbaraga; 13 Ryan Chester. Subs (all used): 14 Billy Driver; 15 Michael Worrincy; 16 Michael Sykes; 17 Erjon Dollapi.
Tries: Jy-mel Coleman (21), Nash (32), Gray (52), Lawrence (58), Bishay (79);
Goals: Bishay 3/5, Lawrence 0/1.
THUNDER: 1 Tom Ruediger; 2 Kieran Dixon; 3 Ali Blair; 4 Joe Brown; 5 Peter Fox; 6 Lewis Young; 7 Benn Hardcastle; 8 Vincent Rennie; 9 Craig Cook; 10 Rhys Clarke; 11 Harry Aldous; 12 Dan Parker; 13 Evan Simons. Subs (all used): 14 Aaron Teroi; 15 Ben Thorburn; 16 Josh Stoker; 17 Francis Welsh.
Tries: Brown (13), Rennie (18, 38), Ruediger (40), Dixon (42), Simons (45), Fox (55), Cook (72);
Goals: Hardcastle 3/4, Parker 4/4.
Rugby Leaguer & League Express Men of the Match: *Skolars:* Charlie Lawrence; *Thunder:* Vincent Rennie.
Penalty count: 9-7; **Half-time:** 12-22;
Referee: John McMullen; **Attendance:** 339.

Sunday 15th May 2016

OXFORD 24 ROCHDALE HORNETS 52

OXFORD: 1 Nathan Kitson; 2 Clark McAllister; 3 Marcus Brooker; 4 Andrew Hoggins; 5 Josh Nathaniel; 6 Tom Holmes; 7 Danny Allan; 8 Callum Bustin; 9 Harvey Burnett; 10 Luke Evans; 11 Jordan Siddons; 12 Jordan Williams; 13 Will Maher. Subs (all used): 14 Casey Canterbury; 15 Daniel Igbinedion; 16 John James Baird; 17 Aaron Nicholson.
Tries: Nathaniel (12), Burnett (22), Siddons (43), Canterbury (57); **Goals:** Kitson 2/2, Allan 2/2.
Sin bin:
Nathaniel (69) - dangerous contact, (80) - fighting.
HORNETS: 1 Chris Riley; 2 Dale Bloomfield; 3 Jake Shoel; 4 Lewis Galbraith; 5 Mike Ratu; 6 Paul Crook; 7 Danny Yates; 8 Samir Tahraoui; 9 Ben Moores; 10 Warren Thompson; 11 Jono Smith; 12 Jordan Case; 13 Alex Trumper. Subs (all used): 14 Harry Files; 15 Stuart Biscomb; 16 Matty Hadden; 17 Wayne English.
Tries: Riley (8, 71), Smith (24, 53), Moores (31), Tahraoui (43), Ratu (64), Thompson (76), Trumper (77);
Goals: Crook 8/9.
Sin bin: Galbraith (80) - fighting.
Rugby Leaguer & League Express Men of the Match: *Oxford:* Tom Holmes; *Hornets:* Chris Riley.
Penalty count: 4-7; **Half-time:** 12-18;
Referee: Tom Hudson; **Attendance:** 352.

HUNSLET HAWKS 24 TOULOUSE OLYMPIQUE 46

HAWKS: 1 Jimmy Watson; 5 James Duckworth; 4 Ayden Faal; 15 Mufaro Mvududu; 28 Richie Barnett; 6 Simon Brown; 7 Danny Ansell; 8 Michael Haley; 9 Jack Lee; 10 Lewis Reed; 12 Ben Crane; 3 Jake Normington; 13 Liam Mackay. Subs (all used): 19 Matt Carbutt; 26 Austin Bell; 22 Craig Robinson; 29 Daniel Williams.
Tries: Mackay (32), Normington (37), Lee (62), Reed (75);
Goals: Brown 4/4.
Sin bin: Reed (59) - fighting.
OLYMPIQUE: 1 Mark Kheirallah; 2 Tony Maurel; 21 Gavin Marguerite; 4 Gregory White; 5 Kuni Minga; 6 Johnathon Ford; 7 Arthur Gonzalez-Trique; 18 Tyla Hepi; 9 Kane Bentley; 16 Bastien Canet; 8 Clement Boyer; 12 Rhys Curran; 17 Anthony Marion. Subs (all used): 14 Mourad Kriouache; 15 Maxime Puech; 10 Samy Masselot; 24 Justin Sangare.
Tries: Maurel (5, 43, 46), Kheirallah (7, 52), Curran (14), Minga (65), Marguerite (70), Ford (73);
Goals: Kheirallah 5/9.
Sin bin: Canet (58) - professional foul; Masselot (59) - fighting.
Rugby Leaguer & League Express Men of the Match: *Hawks:* Jake Normington; *Olympique:* Johnathon Ford.
Penalty count: 9-7; **Half-time:** 12-14;
Referee: Andrew Sweet; **Attendance:** 328.

KEIGHLEY COUGARS 74 HEMEL STAGS 6

COUGARS: 22 Ritchie Hawkyard; 26 Vinny Finigan; 29 Hamish Barnes; 3 Rikki Sheriffe; 5 Paul White; 24 Liam Darville; 7 Paul Handforth; 8 Scott Law; 20 Aaron Ollett; 12 Brendan Rawlins; 11 Josh Lynam; 25 Darren Hawkyard; 13 Ashley Lindsay. Subs (all used): 9 James Feather; 17 John Oakes; 19 Matthew Bailey; 35 Ross Peltier.
Tries: D Hawkyard (4), White (6), Rawlins (8, 41, 64), Finigan (18, 37, 53), Barnes (31), R Sheriffe (33), Lynam (40), Peltier (46), Bailey (49), R Hawkyard (68), Oakes (80); **Goals:** Handforth 7/14, R Sheriffe 0/1.
Sin bin: Feather (73) - fighting.
STAGS: 1 Alex Walker; 2 Josh Spearing; 3 Kameron Pearce-Paul; 4 Tuoyo Egodo; 5 Reece Rance; 6 Ben Stead; 7 Scott Leatherbarrow; 8 Aaron Hall; 9 Barry-John Swindells; 10 Matt Ross; 11 Kyal Greene; 12 Oli Toms; 13 Chris Clough. Subs (all used): 14 Adam Booth; 15 Liam O'Callaghan; 16 Malikhi Lloyd-Jones; 17 Josh Halstead.
Try: Hall (11); **Goals:** Stead 1/1.
Sin bin: Clough (73) - fighting.
Rugby Leaguer & League Express Men of the Match: *Cougars:* Paul Handforth; *Stags:* Tuoyo Egodo.
Penalty count: 6-5; **Half-time:** 38-6;
Referee: Andrew Bentham; **Attendance:** 421.

SOUTH WALES SCORPIONS 4 BARROW RAIDERS 44

SCORPIONS: - James Stringer; 4 Yannic Parker; 22 Christiaan Roets; 21 Scott Gregory; 5 Dai Evans; - Cian Timmins; 7 Paul Emanuelli; 8 Chris Davies; 24 Zak Williams; 10 Izaak Duffy; 3 Kyle Scrivens; 17 Mike Connor; 13 Chris Vitalini. Subs (all used): 14 Osian Phillips; 19 Kristian Baller; - Martyn Reilly; 23 Barrie Phillips.
Try: Gregory (46); **Goals:** Emanuelli 0/1.
Sin bin: Duffy (36) - punching.
RAIDERS: 1 Ryan Fieldhouse; 2 Shane Toal; 3 Chris Hankinson; 16 Max Wiper; 5 Cameron Pitman; 28 Jamie Dallimore; 14 Brad Marwood; 8 Joe Bullock; 29 Karl Ashall; 18 James Duerden; 11 Liam Harrison; 12 Dan Toal; 13 Martin Aspinwall. Subs (all used): 21 Dan Abram; 19 Anthony Bate; 24 Matty While; 17 Andrew Dawson.
Tries: Marwood (7), Wiper (14), S Toal (26, 38), While (57), Abram (66), Hankinson (71, 78);
Goals: Hankinson 6/8.
Rugby Leaguer & League Express Men of the Match: *Scorpions:* Christiaan Roets; *Raiders:* Chris Hankinson.
Penalty count: 7-10; **Half-time:** 0-24;
Referee: James Callaghan; **Attendance:** 180.

YORK CITY KNIGHTS 16 NORTH WALES CRUSADERS 16

CITY KNIGHTS: 1 Brett Turner; 2 Ben Dent; 3 Tyler Craig; 4 James Morland; 5 Austin Buchanan; 6 Jon Presley; 7 Danny Nicklas; 8 Mark Applegarth; 9 Pat Smith; 10 Ross Osborne; 11 Josh Tonks; 12 Ed Smith; 13 Jack Aldous. Subs (all used): 14 Kris Brining; 15 Russ Spiers; 16 Brett Waller; 17 Ryan Mallinder.
Tries: Buchanan (6), B Dent (53), Craig (79);
Goals: Craig 2/3.
CRUSADERS: 1 Tommy Johnson; 2 Scott Turner; 3 Stuart Reardon; 4 Earl Hurst; 5 Rob Massam; 6 Ryan Smith; 7 Jack Hansen; 8 Jonny Walker; 9 Lee Hudson; 10 Kenny Baker; 11 Jake Bibby; 12 Stephen Wild; 13 Simon Atherton. Subs (all used): 14 Matt Wilkinson; 15 Rick Joy; 16 Matthew Haggarty; 17 Luke Warburton.
Tries: Turner (11), Atherton (16), Hansen (62);
Goals: Johnson 2/3.
Rugby Leaguer & League Express Men of the Match: *City Knights:* Tyler Craig; *Crusaders:* Lee Hudson.
Penalty count: 7-5; **Half-time:** 6-10;
Referee: Jack Smith; **Attendance:** 535.

ROUND 9

Friday 20th May 2016

NEWCASTLE THUNDER 4 YORK CITY KNIGHTS 36

THUNDER: 1 Tom Ruediger; 2 Joe Brown; 3 Liam Salter; 4 Dan Parker; 5 Peter Fox; 6 Lewis Young; 7 Aaron Teroi; 8 Vincent Rennie; 9 Craig Cook; 10 Rhys Clarke; 11 Harry Aldous; 12 Kevin Larroyer; 13 Lee Paterson. Subs (all used): 14 Evan Simons; 15 Kieran Moran; 16 Corbyn Kilday; 17 Francis Welsh.
Try: Ruediger (40); **Goals:** Salter 0/1.
CITY KNIGHTS: 1 Richard Wilkinson; 2 Brett Turner; 3 James Morland; 4 Tyler Craig; 5 Tom Saxton; 6 Jon Presley; 7 Danny Nicklas; 8 Russ Spiers; 9 Pat Smith; 10 Jack Aldous; 11 Josh Tonks; 12 Ed Smith; 13 Mike Emmett. Subs (all used): 14 Kris Brining; 15 Ryan Mallinder; 16 Mark Applegarth; 17 Brett Waller.
Tries: Presley (11), P Smith (37), Turner (40, 51), Tonks (59), Saxton (65), E Smith (72);
Goals: Craig 1/1, Nicklas 1/3, Wilkinson 0/1, Turner 2/2.
Rugby Leaguer & League Express Men of the Match: *Thunder:* Lewis Young; *City Knights:* Josh Tonks.
Penalty count: 5-9; **Half-time:** 4-16;
Referee: Sam Ansell; **Attendance:** 3,033.

Saturday 21st May 2016

LONDON SKOLARS 30 KEIGHLEY COUGARS 20

SKOLARS: 1 Alex Anthony; 2 Sam Nash; 3 Aaron Small; 4 Israel Eliab; 5 Lameck Juma; 6 Jy-mel Coleman; 7 Charlie Lawrence; 8 Erjon Dollapi; 9 Sam Druce; 10 Jamie Thackray; 11 Steve Bannister; 12 Eddie Mbaraga; 13 Dave Williams. Subs (all used): 14 Billy Driver; 15 Ben Gray; 16 Michael Sykes; 17 Michael Worrincy.
Tries: Dollapi (3), Small (22), Eliab (37), Druce (67), Williams (73); **Goals:** Lawrence 5/6.
Sin bin: Thackray (59) - dissent.
COUGARS: 22 Ritchie Hawkyard; 2 Andy Gabriel; 3 Rikki Sheriffe; 4 Danny Lawton; 26 Vinny Finigan; 14 Adam Brook; 7 Paul Handforth; 8 Scott Law; 9 James Feather; 15 Neil Cherryholme; 25 Darren Hawkyard; 23 Charlie Martin; 13 Ashley Lindsay. Subs (all used): 19 Mathew Bailey; 12 Brendan Rawlins; 35 Ross Peltier; 20 Aaron Ollett.
Tries: Peltier (46), R Hawkyard (49), Finigan (62), Feather (65); **Goals:** Brook 2/4.
Sin bin: R Hawkyard (78) - punching.
Rugby Leaguer & League Express Men of the Match: *Skolars:* Aaron Small; *Cougars:* Ross Peltier.
Penalty count: 8-12; **Half-time:** 18-0;
Referee: Tom Grant; **Attendance:** 352.

Sunday 22nd May 2016

HEMEL STAGS 14 COVENTRY BEARS 50

STAGS: 1 Jordan Aitchison; 2 Reece Rance; 3 Barry-John Swindells; 4 Kameron Pearce-Paul; 5 Elliot Munnelly; 6 Chris Clough; 7 Ben Stead; 8 Josh Halstead; 9 Dylan Readman; 10 Aaron Hall; 11 Oli Toms; 12 Kyal Greene; 13 Sadiq Adebiyi. Subs (all used): 14 Marcus Stock; 15 Malikhi Lloyd-Jones; 16 Matt Ross; 17 Mike Stewart.
Tries: Munnelly (9), Rance (13), Hall (51);
Goals: Stead 1/3.
BEARS: 1 Charlie O'Mara; 2 Ben Warrilow; 3 Eddie Medforth; 4 Jonathan Milizewski; 5 Jason Bass; 6 Joel James; 7 James Redman; 8 James Geurtjens; 9 Jay Lobwein; 10 Alex Beddows; 11 Liam Thompson; 12 Grant Beecham; 13 Jack Morrison. Subs (all used): 14 Brad Brennan; 15 Chris Barratt; 16 Joe Batchelor; 17 Trae O'Sullivan.
Tries: Milizewski (23, 71, 77), Barratt (31), Lobwein (34), Brennan (43), O'Mara (47, 57, 80), Thompson (68);
Goals: James 5/10.
Rugby Leaguer & League Express Men of the Match: *Stags:* Jordan Aitchison; *Bears:* Charlie O'Mara.
Penalty count: 5-7; **Half-time:** 8-14;
Referee: Brandon Robinson; **Attendance:** 149.

DONCASTER 54 OXFORD 14

DONCASTER: 1 Tom Carr; 2 Louis Sheriff; 3 Sam Doherty; 4 Jason Tali; 5 David Foggin-Johnston; 6 Jordan Howden; 7 Jordie Hedges; 8 Makali Aizue; 9 Kyle Kesik; 10 Connor Scott; 11 Michael Kelly; 12 Brad Foster; 13 Brad Nicholson. Subs (all used): 14 Ryan Wright; 15 Iafeta Palea'aesina; 16 Mark Castle; 17 Liam Welham.
Tries: L Welham (2, 5, 48), Aizue (8), Carr (23), Kesik (29), Sheriff (44, 69), Hedges (65), Wright (78);
Goals: Carr 7/10.
OXFORD: 1 Nathan Kitson; 2 Josh Nathaniel; 3 Aaron Nicholson; 4 Marcus Brooker; 5 Clark McAllister; 6 Harvey Burnett; 7 Danny Allan; 8 Will Maher; 9 Casey Canterbury; 10 Callum Bustin; 11 Jordan Siddons; 12 Adam Withington; 13 Jack Smith. Subs (all used): 14 Luke Evans; 15 John James Baird; 16 Daniel Igbinedion; 17 Lewis Bienek.

Tries: Nicholson (13), McAllister (16), Burnett (59);
Goals: Kitson 1/2, Allan 0/1.
Sin bin: Siddons (32) - holding down;
Allan (69) - interference.
Rugby Leaguer & League Express Men of the Match:
Doncaster: Liam Welham; *Oxford:* Clark McAllister.
Penalty count: 11-10; **Half-time:** 28-10;
Referee: Andrew Bentham; **Attendance:** 744.

GLOUCESTERSHIRE ALL GOLDS 18
HUNSLET HAWKS 26

ALL GOLDS: 1 Brendon Newton; 2 Chris Barlow; 3 Josh Allison; 4 Lewis Reece; 5 Phil Cowburn; 6 Jimmy Rowland; 7 Matt Bradley; 8 Morgan Evans; 9 Steve Parry; 10 Harrison Elliott; 11 Lamont Bryan; 12 Joe McClean; 13 Emmerson Whittel. Subs (all used): 14 Almer Tagayuna; 15 Zack McComb; 16 Charles Nies; 17 Oliver Purslow.
Tries: Allison (21), Barlow (50), Bryan (79);
Goals: Bradley 3/3.
Dismissal: Parry (49) - fighting.
HAWKS: 1 Jimmy Watson; 5 James Duckworth; 4 Ayden Faal; 15 Mufaro Mvududu; 28 Richie Barnett; 20 Danny Thomas; 7 Danny Ansell; 8 Michael Haley; 9 Jack Lee; 19 Matt Carbutt; 29 Daniel Williams; 3 Jake Normington; 13 Liam Mackay. Subs (all used): 14 George Flanagan; 22 Craig Robinson; 31 Lee Mapals; 10 Lewis Reed.
Tries: Faal (12, 33), Flanagan (36), Haley (46), Lee (74);
Goals: Ansell 1/2, Flanagan 2/3.
Dismissal: Flanagan (49) - fighting.
Rugby Leaguer & League Express Men of the Match:
All Golds: Matt Bradley; *Hawks:* Lewis Reed.
Penalty count: 8-10; **Half-time:** 6-16;
Referee: James Callaghan; **Attendance:** 134.

ROCHDALE HORNETS 70
SOUTH WALES SCORPIONS 6

HORNETS: 1 Wayne English; 2 Dale Bloomfield; 3 Mike Ratu; 4 Lewis Galbraith; 5 Chris Riley; 6 Paul Crook; 7 Danny Yates; 8 Samir Tahraoui; 9 Ben Moores; 10 Warren Thompson; 11 Jono Smith; 12 Alex Trumper; 13 James Tilley. Subs (all used): 14 Daniel Murray; 15 Matty Hadden; 16 Sam Wilde; 17 Joe Philbin.
Tries: Bloomfield (4, 61, 74), Riley (14, 57), Smith (19, 29), Philbin (31), Wilde (35), Yates (37, 76), Crook (52, 71), English (54); **Goals:** Crook 7/13, Smith 0/1.
SCORPIONS: 15 Jordan Sheridan; 2 Ian Newbury; 21 Scott Gregory; 22 Christiaan Roets; 4 Yannic Parker; 25 Billy Gaylor; 7 Paul Emanuelli; - Robert Holroyd; 19 Kristian Baller; 26 Luke Nelmes; 28 Sion Jones; 3 Kyle Scrivens; 13 Chris Vitalini. Subs (all used): 24 Zak Williams; 23 Barrie Phillips; - Martyn Reilly; 20 Anthony Symons.
Try: S Jones (25); **Goals:** Emanuelli 1/1.
Rugby Leaguer & League Express Men of the Match:
Hornets: Dale Bloomfield; *Scorpions:* Luke Nelmes.
Penalty count: 12-4; **Half-time:** 34-6;
Referee: Tom Hudson; **Attendance:** 455.

BARROW RAIDERS 16 TOULOUSE OLYMPIQUE 44

RAIDERS: 1 Ryan Fieldhouse; 2 Shane Toal; 3 Chris Hankinson; 16 Max Wiper; 5 Cameron Pitman; 28 Jamie Dallimore; 14 Brad Marwood; 8 Joe Bullock; 29 Karl Ashall; 10 Oliver Wilkes; 11 Liam Harrison; 15 Bradd Crellin; 13 Martin Aspinwall. Subs (all used): 18 James Duerden; 12 Dan Toal; 21 Dan Abram; 19 Anthony Bate.
Tries: Wiper (52), Wilkes (72, 76); **Goals:** Hankinson 2/3.
Sin bin: Harrison (45) - tripping.
OLYMPIQUE: 1 Mark Kheirallah; 2 Tony Maurel; 21 Gavin Marguerite; 4 Gregory White; 5 Kuni Minga; 6 Johnathon Ford; 7 Arthur Gonzalez-Trique; 15 Maxime Puech; 9 Kane Bentley; 16 Bastien Canet; 8 Clement Boyer; 12 Rhys Curran; 17 Anthony Marion. Subs (all used): 14 Mourad Kriouache; - Cedric Mazars; 10 Samy Masselot; 24 Justin Sangare.
Tries: Curran (6), Canet (18), Minga (26, 54), Kheirallah (34, 68), Ford (45), Maurel (65);
Goals: Kheirallah 6/8.
Rugby Leaguer & League Express Men of the Match:
Raiders: Chris Hankinson; *Olympique:* Mark Kheirallah.
Penalty count: 5-8; **Half-time:** 0-22;
Referee: Tom Crashley; **Attendance:** 1,050.

ROUND 7

Saturday 28th May 2016

TOULOUSE OLYMPIQUE 48
GLOUCESTERSHIRE ALL GOLDS 16

OLYMPIQUE: 1 Mark Kheirallah; 2 Tony Maurel; 21 Gavin Marguerite; 4 Gregory White; 5 Kuni Minga; 6 Johnathon Ford; 22 Danny Hulme; 15 Maxime Puech; 9 Kane Bentley; 10 Samy Masselot; 8 Clement Boyer; 12 Rhys Curran; 17 Anthony Marion. Subs (all used): 14 Mourad Kriouache; 18 Tyla Hepi; - Kalausa Leha; 23 Cedric Mazars.
Tries: Curran (4), Minga (6, 79), Hulme (8), Kriouache (32, 38), White (68), Ford (74);
Goals: Kheirallah 5/5, Kriouache 3/3.
ALL GOLDS: 1 Brendon Newton; 2 Chris Barlow; 3 Josh Allison; 4 Lewis Reece; 5 Phil Cowburn; 6 Jimmy Rowland; 7 Matt Bradley; 8 Morgan Evans; 9 Steve Parry; 10 Alex Davidson; 11 Zack McComb; 12 Joe McClean; 13 Emmerson Whittel. Subs (all used): 14 Almer Tagayuna; 15 Lamont Bryan; 16 Charles Nies; 17 Oliver Purslow.
Tries: Parry (16), Barlow (26, 50); **Goals:** Bradley 2/3.
Rugby Leaguer & League Express Men of the Match:
Olympique: Mourad Kriouache; *All Golds:* Matt Bradley.
Penalty count: 10-9; **Half-time:** 30-12;
Referee: Liam Moore; **Attendance:** 1,335.

ROUND 5

Wednesday 1st June 2016

YORK CITY KNIGHTS 32 COVENTRY BEARS 14

CITY KNIGHTS: 1 Ben Dent; 2 Adam Dent; 3 Ed Smith; 4 Brad Hey; 5 Tom Saxton; 6 Jon Presley; 7 Danny Nicklas; 8 Brett Waller; 9 Pat Smith; 10 Jack Aldous; 11 Josh Tonks; 12 Ross Divorty; 13 Mike Emmett. Subs (all used): 14 Kris Brining; 15 Jack Anderson; 16 Russ Spiers; 17 Mark Applegarth.
Tries: E Smith (4, 30, 68), Brining (37, 42), Presley (63);
Goals: Nicklas 4/6.
BEARS: 1 Jason Bass; 2 Harry Chapman; 3 Eddie Medforth; 4 Joe Batchelor; 5 Hayden Freeman; 6 Joel James; 7 James Redman; 8 Jack Morrison; 9 Elliot Norman; 10 Alex Beddows; 11 Liam Thompson; 12 Chris Barratt; 13 Grant Beecham. Subs (all used): 14 Brad Brennan; 15 Trae O'Sullivan; 16 Elliot Holton; 17 Dan Price.
Tries: Redman (9), Chapman (13), Bass (78);
Goals: James 1/3.
Sin bin: Chapman (34) – late challenge.
Rugby Leaguer & League Express Men of the Match:
City Knights: Ed Smith; *Bears:* James Redman.
Penalty count: 8-10; **Half-time:** 14-10;
Referee: Tom Crashley; **Attendance:** 451.

ROUND 10

Saturday 4th June 2016

SOUTH WALES SCORPIONS 16
NORTH WALES CRUSADERS 30

SCORPIONS: 15 Jordan Sheridan; 2 Ian Newbury; 21 Scott Gregory; 22 Christiaan Roets; 4 Yannic Parker; 30 Jamie Murphy; 7 Paul Emanuelli; 14 Osian Phillips; 24 Zak Williams; 10 Izaak Duffy; 17 Mike Connor; 3 Kyle Scrivens; 13 Chris Vitalini. Subs (all used): 9 Connor Farrer; 20 Anthony Symons; 23 Barrie Phillips; 28 Richard Jones.
Tries: Roets (9), Farrer (32), Scrivens (70);
Goals: Emanuelli 2/3.
CRUSADERS: 1 Tommy Johnson; 2 Scott Turner; 3 Matt Davies; 4 Adam Saunders; 5 Rob Massam; 6 Ryan Smith; 7 Jack Hansen; 8 Jonny Walker; 9 Lee Hudson; 10 Matthew Haggarty; 11 Luke Warburton; 12 Simon Atherton; 13 Kenny Baker. Subs (all used): 14 Andy Moulsdale; 15 Billy Brickhill; 16 Jordan Walne; 17 Olsi Krasniqi.
Tries: Johnson (25), Massam (28, 44, 62), Turner (36), Atherton (57); **Goals:** Johnson 3/6.
Rugby Leaguer & League Express Men of the Match:
Scorpions: Chris Vitalini; *Crusaders:* Rob Massam.
Penalty count: 8-7; **Half-time:** 12-16;
Referee: James Callaghan; **Attendance:** 927
(at Cardiff Arms Park).

KEIGHLEY COUGARS 36 NEWCASTLE THUNDER 14

COUGARS: 22 Ritchie Hawkyard; 26 Vinny Finigan; 23 Charlie Martin; 3 Rikki Sheriffe; 5 Paul White; 24 Liam Darville; 7 Paul Handforth; 8 Scott Law; 9 James Feather; 34 Jamel Goodall; 25 Darren Hawkyard; 17 John Oakes; 13 Ashley Lindsay. Subs (all used): 15 Neil Cherryholme; 19 Matthew Bailey; 20 Aaron Ollett; 35 Ross Peltier.
Tries: Handforth (10, 56, 58), Finigan (48), R Sheriffe (50, 53), Darville (60);
Goals: Handforth 1/4, Martin 3/3.
THUNDER: 1 Tom Ruediger; 2 Derrell Olpherts; 3 Joe Brown; 4 Dan Parker; 5 Peter Fox; 6 Lewis Young; 7 Josh Kittrick; 8 Rhys Clarke; 9 Aaron Teroi; 10 Mikey Wood; 11 Harry Aldous; 12 Lee Paterson; 13 Evan Simons. Subs (all used): 14 Ben Thorburn; 15 Corbyn Kilday; 16 Kieran Moran; 17 Tyler Dickinson.
Tries: Young (18), Fox (38), Ruediger (66);
Goals: Parker 1/3.
Rugby Leaguer & League Express Men of the Match:
Cougars: Paul Handforth; *Thunder:* Mikey Wood.
Penalty count: 9-7; **Half-time:** 6-10;
Referee: Jamie Bloem; **Attendance:** 827.

TOULOUSE OLYMPIQUE 46 DONCASTER 26

OLYMPIQUE: 1 Mark Kheirallah; 2 Tony Maurel; 3 Bastien Ader; 4 Gregory White; 5 Kuni Minga; 6 Johnathon Ford; 22 Danny Hulme; 15 Maxime Puech; 9 Kane Bentley; 16 Bastien Canet; 8 Clement Boyer; 12 Rhys Curran; 17 Anthony Marion. Subs (all used): 14 Mourad Kriouache; 18 Tyla Hepi; - Kalausa Leha; 21 Gavin Marguerite.
Tries: Canet (16), Minga (22), Maurel (29), Curran (36), Hulme (39, 73), White (61), Marion (70);
Goals: Kheirallah 7/9.
On report: Canet (11) - alleged dangerous challenge.
DONCASTER: 1 Tom Carr; 2 Louis Sheriff; 3 Sam Doherty; 4 Jason Tali; 5 David Foggin-Johnston; 6 Jordan Howden; 7 Jordie Hedges; 8 Makali Aizue; 9 Kyle Kesik; 10 Connor Scott; 11 Liam Welham; 12 Brad Foster; 13 Matt Nicholson. Subs (all used): 14 Ryan Wright; 15 Brad Nicholson; 16 Zac Braham; 17 George Milton.
Tries: Wright (32), Braham (44), Sheriff (55), Doherty (58), Howden (76); **Goals:** Carr 3/5.
Rugby Leaguer & League Express Men of the Match:
Olympique: Bastien Canet; *Doncaster:* Jordan Howden.
Penalty count: 11-6; **Half-time:** 28-6;
Referee: Andrew Sweet; **Attendance:** 2,218.

Sunday 5th June 2016

OXFORD 24 HEMEL STAGS 18

OXFORD: 1 Harvey Burnett; 2 Josh Nathaniel; 3 Aaron Nicholson; 4 Andrew Hoggins; 5 James Cryer; 6 Marcus Brooker; 7 Danny Allan; 8 Daniel Igbinedion; 9 Casey Canterbury; 10 Jordan Siddons; 11 Sadiq Adebiyi; 12 John James Baird; 13 Will Maher. Subs (all used): 14 Callum Bustin; 15 Lewis Bienek; 16 Adam Flintham; 17 Jack Smith.
Tries: Nathaniel (9), Canterbury (33), Hoggins (36), Brooker (53); **Goals:** Allan 4/4.
Dismissal: Smith (37) - fighting.
Sin bin: Igbinedion (20) - punching.
STAGS: 1 Alex Walker; 2 Reece Rance; 3 Tuoyo Egodo; 4 Kameron Pearce-Paul; 5 Elliot Munnelly; 6 Jordan Aitchison; 7 Dylan Readman; 8 Aaron Hall; 9 Oli Toms; 10 Matt Ross; 11 Barry-John Swindells; 12 Kyal Greene; 13 Toby Everett. Subs (all used): 14 Josh Halstead; 15 Malikhi Lloyd-Jones; 16 Mike Stewart; 17 Marcus Stock.
Tries: Lloyd-Jones (39), Munnelly (43), Everett (74);
Goals: Swindells 2/2, Toms 1/1.
Dismissal: Stewart (37) - fighting.
Rugby Leaguer & League Express Men of the Match:
Oxford: Casey Canterbury; *Stags:* Elliot Munnelly.
Penalty count: 7-5; **Half-time:** 18-6;
Referee: Steve Race; **Attendance:** 125.

GLOUCESTERSHIRE ALL GOLDS 16
BARROW RAIDERS 52

ALL GOLDS: 1 Brendon Newton; 2 Josh Allison; 3 Lewis Reece; 4 Joe McClean; 5 Phil Cowburn; 6 Jack Mitchell; 7 Jimmy Rowland; 8 Morgan Evans; 9 Steve Parry; 10 Alex Davidson; 11 Zack McComb; 12 Emmerson Whittel; 13 Almer Tagayuna. Subs (all used): 14 Matt Bradley; 15 Lamont Bryan; 16 Oliver Purslow; 17 James Walter.
Tries: Newton (8), McClean (19), Whittel (25);
Goals: Newton 2/3.
RAIDERS: 1 Ryan Fieldhouse; 2 Shane Toal; 3 Chris Hankinson; 16 Max Wiper; 5 Cameron Pitman; 28 Jamie Dallimore; 14 Brad Marwood; 8 Joe Bullock; 29 Karl Ashall; 10 Oliver Wilkes; 11 Liam Harrison; 27 Matty Holmes; 13 Martin Aspinwall. Subs (all used): 12 Dan Toal; 17 Andrew Dawson; 19 Anthony Bate; 21 Dan Abram.
Tries: Pitman (2, 54, 78), Dawson (22), Hankinson (32), D Toal (41), Harrison (44), Wiper (70), Dallimore (74);
Goals: Hankinson 8/10.
Sin bin: Fieldhouse (29) - tripping Mitchell.
Rugby Leaguer & League Express Men of the Match:
All Golds: Jack Mitchell; *Raiders:* Chris Hankinson.
Penalty count: 8-10; **Half-time:** 16-16;
Referee: Liam Moore; **Attendance:** 122.

HUNSLET HAWKS 26 LONDON SKOLARS 18

HAWKS: 1 Jimmy Watson; 5 James Duckworth; 4 Ayden Faal; 15 Mufaro Mvududu; 28 Richie Barnett; 20 Danny Thomas; 7 Danny Ansell; 8 Michael Haley; 9 Jack Lee; 10 Lewis Reed; 29 Daniel Williams; 3 Jake Normington; 13 Liam Mackay. Subs (all used): 19 Matt Carbutt; 26 Austin Bell; 6 Simon Brown; 31 Lee Mapals.
Tries: Watson (9), Duckworth (37, 63), Ansell (43);
Goals: Ansell 5/5.
SKOLARS: 1 James Woodburn-Hall; 2 Sam Nash; 3 Israel Eliab; 4 Aaron Small; 5 Lameck Juma; 6 Jy-mel Coleman; 7 Charlie Lawrence; 8 Jamie Thackray; 9 Ben Pointer; 10 Dave Williams; 11 Eddie Mbaraga; 12 Will Lovell; 13 Ryan Chester. Subs (all used): 14 Billy Driver; 15 Ben Gray; 16 Michael Worrincy; 17 Erjon Dollapi.

Tries: Driver (50), Eliab (74), Woodburn-Hall (76);
Goals: Lawrence 3/3.
Rugby Leaguer & League Express Men of the Match:
Hawks: Danny Ansell; *Skolars:* Billy Driver.
Penalty count: 6-9; **Half-time:** 12-0;
Referee: John McMullen; **Attendance:** 382.

YORK CITY KNIGHTS 40 ROCHDALE HORNETS 12

CITY KNIGHTS: 1 Ben Dent; 2 Tom Saxton; 3 James Morland; 4 Ed Smith; 5 Austin Buchanan; 6 Jon Presley; 7 Danny Nicklas; 8 Brett Waller; 9 Pat Smith; 10 Jack Aldous; 11 Josh Tonks; 12 Ross Divorty; 13 Mike Emmett. Subs (all used): 14 Kris Brining; 15 Matty Dale; 16 Mark Applegarth; 17 Russ Spiers.
Tries: Buchanan (11, 25), Nicklas (34), B Dent (39), Brining (43), Tonks (48, 66), Emmett (78);
Goals: Nicklas 4/8, B Dent 0/1.
HORNETS: 1 Wayne English; 2 Dale Bloomfield; 3 Mike Ratu; 4 Lewis Galbraith; 5 Chris Riley; 6 Paul Crook; 7 Danny Yates; 8 Samir Tahraoui; 9 Ben Moores; 10 Warren Thompson; 11 Jono Smith; 12 Joe Philbin; 13 James Tilley. Subs (all used): 14 Alex McClurg; 15 Matty Hadden; 16 Alex Trumper; 17 Daniel Murray.
Tries: Bloomfield (63), Smith (72); **Goals:** Crook 2/2.
Sin bin: Moores (65) - off the ball challenge.
Rugby Leaguer & League Express Men of the Match:
City Knights: Josh Tonks; *Hornets:* Jono Smith.
Penalty count: 7-5; **Half-time:** 22-0;
Referee: Callum Straw; **Attendance:** 613.

ROUND 11

Saturday 11th June 2016

LONDON SKOLARS 42 BARROW RAIDERS 34

SKOLARS: 1 Alex Walker; 2 Sam Nash; 3 Will Lovell; 4 Israel Eliab; 5 Andy Winfield; 6 James Woodburn-Hall; 7 Jy-mel Coleman; 8 Mike Greenhalgh; 9 Sam Druce; 10 Dave Williams; 11 Steve Bannister; 12 Eddie Mbaraga; 13 Michael Worrincy. Subs (all used): 14 Billy Driver; 15 Ben Gray; 16 Toby Everett; 17 Ryan Chester.
Tries: Williams (21), Everett (25), Driver (43), Walker (46), Mbaraga (66); **Goals:** Druce 2/2, Jy-mel Coleman 9/9.
RAIDERS: 1 Ryan Fieldhouse; 2 Shane Toal; 3 Chris Hankinson; 16 Max Wiper; 5 Cameron Pitman; 28 Jamie Dallimore; 14 Brad Marwood; 8 Joe Bullock; 29 Karl Ashall; 10 Oliver Wilkes; 11 Liam Harrison; 15 Bradd Crellin; 13 Martin Aspinwall. Subs (all used): 21 Dan Abram; 12 Dan Toal; 17 Andrew Dawson; 19 Anthony Bate.
Tries: Fieldhouse (9, 11, 32), Wiper (52), S Toal (77);
Goals: Hankinson 6/6, Dallimore 1/1.
Dismissal: Dallimore (80) - dissent.
Sin bin: Dallimore (80) - dissent.
Rugby Leaguer & League Express Men of the Match:
Skolars: Jy-mel Coleman; *Raiders:* Ryan Fieldhouse.
Penalty count: 13-12; **Half-time:** 14-20;
Referee: Tom Crashley; **Attendance:** 364.

COVENTRY BEARS 48 OXFORD 10

BEARS: 1 Dan Price; 2 Jonathan Milizewski; 3 Matt Reid; 4 Eddie Medforth; 5 Hayden Freeman; 6 Joel James; 7 James Redman; 8 James Geurtjens; 9 Jay Lobwein; 10 Jack Morrison; 11 Liam Thompson; 12 Chris Barratt; 13 Grant Beecham. Subs (all used): 14 Trae O'Sullivan; 15 Brad Brennan; 16 Joe Batchelor; 17 Richard Hughes.
Tries: James (8), Morrison (11), Medforth (17, 40), Brennan (29), Thompson (44), Milizewski (47), Batchelor (53), Barratt (75); **Goals:** James 6/9.
OXFORD: 1 Harvey Burnett; 2 Jordan Parry; 3 James Cryer; 4 Josh Nathaniel; 5 Luke Gardiner; 6 Marcus Brooker; 7 Danny Allan; 8 Daniel Igbinedion; 9 Casey Canterbury; 10 Will Maher; 11 Jordan Siddons; 12 Aaron Nicholson; 13 Luke Evans. Subs (all used): 14 Santino Decaro; 15 Tom Davies; 16 Ryan Backhouse; 17 Jack Smith.
Tries: Nicholson (34), Allan (57); **Goals:** Allan 1/2.
Rugby Leaguer & League Express Men of the Match:
Bears: Eddie Medforth; *Oxford:* Danny Allan.
Penalty count: 9-7; **Half-time:** 26-6;
Referee: Brandon Robinson; **Attendance:** 444.

Sunday 12th June 2016

HEMEL STAGS 18 GLOUCESTERSHIRE ALL GOLDS 48

STAGS: 1 Josh Spearing; 2 Tala Petelo; 3 Oli Toms; 4 Barry-John Swindells; 5 Reece Rance; 6 Chris Clough; 7 Dylan Readman; 8 Aaron Hall; 9 Liam O'Callaghan; 10 Josh Halstead; 11 Kyal Greene; 12 Dave O'Conner; 13 Jack Asher. Subs (all used): 14 Rick Joy; 15 Andrew Joy; 16 Andy Parrott; 17 Victor Coker.
Tries: Swindells (3) O'Callaghan (13, 37);
Goals: Swindells 3/4.
Sin bin: Swindells (63) - fighting; Hall (65) - punching.
ALL GOLDS: 1 Phil Cowburn; 2 Mo Agoro; 3 Josh Allison; 4 Lewis Reece; 5 Chris Barlow; 6 Jack Mitchell; 7 Kieran Hyde; 8 Oliver Purslow; 9 Steve Parry; 10 Morgan Evans; 11 Lamont Bryan; 12 Joe McClean; 13 Emmerson Whittel. Subs (all used): 14 Mick Govin; 15 Dale Cunniffe; 16 Jamel Goodall; 17 Brad Hill.
Tries: Mitchell (8, 21), Reece (26, 57, 72), Allison (40), Hyde (46), Agoro (48), Parry (80);
Goals: Mitchell 1/3, Hyde 5/7.
Sin bin: Cunniffe (34) - shoulder charge on Readman, (63) - fighting.
Rugby Leaguer & League Express Men of the Match:
Stags: Reece Rance; *All Golds:* Kieran Hyde.
Penalty count: 8-16; **Half-time:** 18-20;
Referee: John McMullen; **Attendance:** 124.

NEWCASTLE THUNDER 22
TOULOUSE OLYMPIQUE 32

THUNDER: 1 Tom Ruediger; 2 Derrell Olpherts; 3 Joe Brown; 4 Dan Parker; 5 Peter Fox; 6 Lewis Young; 7 Josh Kittrick; 8 Corbyn Kilday; 9 Aaron Teroi; 10 Kevin Larroyer; 11 Harry Aldous; 12 Rhys Clarke; 13 George Lawler. Subs (all used): 14 Ben Thorburn; 15 Mikey Wood; 16 Sam Luckley; 17 Francis Welsh.
Tries: Fox (2), Olpherts (15), Brown (50), Lawler (72);
Goals: Parker 3/4.
OLYMPIQUE: 1 Mark Kheirallah; 2 Tony Maurel; 3 Bastien Ader; 4 Gregory White; 5 Kuni Minga; 6 Johnathon Ford; 22 Danny Hulme; 8 Clement Boyer; 14 Mourad Kriouache; 16 Bastien Canet; 11 Sebastien Planas; 12 Rhys Curran; 17 Anthony Marion. Subs (all used): 7 Arthur Gonzalez-Trique; 15 Maxime Puech; 18 Tyla Hepi; 25 Kalausa Leha.
Tries: Ader (13, 46), Hulme (39, 54), Marion (60, 76);
Goals: Kheirallah 4/6.
Rugby Leaguer & League Express Men of the Match:
Thunder: Joe Brown; *Olympique:* Anthony Marion.
Penalty count: 6-7; **Half-time:** 12-12;
Referee: Jamie Bloem; **Attendance:** 902.

NORTH WALES CRUSADERS 22
KEIGHLEY COUGARS 30

CRUSADERS: 1 Tommy Johnson; 2 Scott Turner; 3 Stuart Reardon; 4 Alex Thompson; 5 Rob Massam; 6 Ryan Smith; 7 Jack Hansen; 8 Jonny Walker; 9 Lee Hudson; 10 Kenny Baker; 11 Simon Atherton; 12 Stephen Wild; 13 Luke Warburton. Subs (all used): 14 Billy Brickhill; 15 Matthew Haggarty; 16 Matt Wilkinson; 17 Liam Bent.
Tries: Massam (11), Reardon (42), Brickhill (59), Turner (76); **Goals:** Johnson 3/4.
COUGARS: 5 Paul White; 2 Andy Gabriel; 3 Rikki Sheriffe; 23 Charlie Martin; 26 Vinny Finigan; 14 Adam Brook; 7 Paul Handforth; 8 Scott Law; 9 James Feather; 15 Neil Cherryholme; 17 John Oakes; 12 Brendan Rawlins; 13 Ashley Lindsay. Subs (all used): 11 Josh Lynam; 19 Matthew Bailey; 20 Aaron Ollett; 35 Ross Peltier.
Tries: Law (19, 25), R Sheriffe (29, 53), Feather (72);
Goals: Brook 5/7.
Rugby Leaguer & League Express Men of the Match:
Crusaders: Scott Turner; *Cougars:* Scott Law.
Penalty count: 9-7; **Half-time:** 6-16;
Referee: Jon Roberts; **Attendance:** 504.

DONCASTER 54 SOUTH WALES SCORPIONS 4

DONCASTER: 1 Tom Carr; 2 David Foggin-Johnston; 3 Liam Welham; 4 Jason Tali; 5 Louis Sheriff; 6 Jordan Howden; 7 Jordie Hedges; 8 Makali Aizue; 9 Kyle Kesik; 10 Matt Nicholson; 11 Brad Foster; 12 Jack Walton; 13 George Milton. Subs (all used): 14 Ryan Wright; 15 Brad Nicholson; 16 Mark Castle; 17 Zac Braham.
Tries: M Nicholson (11), Hedges (16), Castle (31), Tali (35), Howden (42), B Nicholson (48), Sheriff (60), Foster (73), Milton (76); **Goals:** Carr 9/9.
SCORPIONS: - Ben Jones; 4 Yannic Parker; 3 Kyle Scrivens; 21 Scott Gregory; 5 Dai Evans; 30 Jamie Murphy; 19 Kristian Baller; - Martyn Reilly; 9 Connor Farrer; 10 Izaak Duffy; 28 Richard Jones; 22 Christiaan Roets; 26 Luke Nelmes. Subs (all used): 14 Osian Phillips; 16 Dafydd Hellard; 24 Zak Williams; - Jordan Syme.
Try: Murphy (53); **Goals:** Murphy 0/1.
Rugby Leaguer & League Express Men of the Match:
Doncaster: Tom Carr; *Scorpions:* Jamie Murphy.
Penalty count: 16-7; **Half-time:** 24-0;
Referee: Liam Moore; **Attendance:** 450
(at Keepmoat Athletics Ground).

YORK CITY KNIGHTS 32 HUNSLET HAWKS 24

CITY KNIGHTS: 1 Ben Dent; 2 Adam Dent; 3 James Morland; 4 Ed Smith; 5 Austin Buchanan; 6 Jon Presley; 7 Danny Nicklas; 8 Brett Waller; 9 Pat Smith; 10 Jack Aldous; 11 Josh Tonks; 12 Ross Divorty; 13 Mike Emmett. Subs (all used): 14 Kris Brining; 15 Jordan Crowther; 16 Mark Applegarth; 17 Russ Spiers.
Tries: Applegarth (22), Brining (33, 53), Nicklas (49, 69);
Goals: Nicklas 6/6.
Sin bin: Tonks (62) - dangerous contact;
B Dent (72) - high tackle; Aldous (72) - punching.
HAWKS: 1 Jimmy Watson; 5 James Duckworth; 4 Ayden Faal; 15 Mufaro Mvududu; 28 Richie Barnett; 6 Simon Brown; 7 Danny Ansell; 8 Michael Haley; 9 Jack Lee; 10 Lewis Reed; 29 Daniel Williams; 3 Jake Normington; 13 Liam Mackay. Subs (all used): 19 Matt Carbutt; 20 Danny Thomas; 31 Lee Mapals; 26 Austin Bell.
Tries: Watson (7), Reed (11), Duckworth (39), Mapals (65);
Goals: Brown 2/2, Ansell 2/2.
Dismissal: Normington (72) - dissent.
Rugby Leaguer & League Express Men of the Match:
City Knights: Danny Nicklas; *Hawks:* Lewis Reed.
Penalty count: 6-12; **Half-time:** 12-18;
Referee: Warren Turley; **Attendance:** 778.

ROUND 12

Saturday 18th June 2016

TOULOUSE OLYMPIQUE 84 KEIGHLEY COUGARS 6

OLYMPIQUE: 1 Mark Kheirallah; 2 Tony Maurel; 3 Bastien Ader; 4 Greg White; 5 Kuni Minga; 6 Johnathon Ford; 22 Danny Hulme; 15 Maxime Puech; 17 Anthony Marion; 10 Samy Masselot; 11 Sebastien Planas; 12 Rhys Curran; 8 Clement Boyer. Subs (all used): 14 Mourad Kriouache; 18 Tyla Hepi; 25 Kalausa Leha; 24 Justin Sangare.
Tries: Minga (9), Kheirallah (11, 14, 46, 70), Planas (22), Boyer (28, 74), Ader (35, 41), Kriouache (44, 53), Maurel (50), Hulme (58), Marion (78);
Goals: Kheirallah 12/15.
COUGARS: 22 Ritchie Hawkyard; 26 Vinny Finigan; 23 Charlie Martin; 3 Rikki Sheriffe; 5 Paul White; 14 Adam Brook; 7 Paul Handforth; 8 Scott Law; 9 James Feather; 15 Neil Cherryholme; 12 Brendan Rawlins; 17 John Oakes; 13 Ashley Lindsay. Subs (all used): 20 Aaron Ollett; 19 Matthew Bailey; 35 Ross Peltier; 11 Josh Lynam.
Try: Bailey (39); **Goals:** Brook 1/1.
Rugby Leaguer & League Express Men of the Match:
Olympique: Mark Kheirallah; *Cougars:* Ritchie Hawkyard.
Penalty count: 8-2; **Half-time:** 36-6;
Referee: Tom Crashley; **Attendance:** 1,167.

Sunday 19th June 2016

OXFORD 6 YORK CITY KNIGHTS 50

OXFORD: 1 James Cryer; 2 Luke Gardiner; 3 Jordan Gill; 4 Callum Casey; 5 Josh Nathaniel; 6 Harvey Burnett; 7 Danny Allan; 8 Ryan Backhouse; 9 Casey Canterbury; 10 James Harrison; 11 Aaron Nicholson; 12 Daniel Igbinedion; 13 Marcus Brooker. Subs (all used): 14 Adam Withington; 15 Mark Hayes; 16 Errol Carter; 17 Harry Griffith.
Try: Gardiner (67); **Goals:** Allan 1/1.
CITY KNIGHTS: 1 Ben Dent; 2 Adam Dent; 3 Sam Smeaton; 4 James Morland; 5 Austin Buchanan; 6 Harry Tyson-Wilson; 7 Danny Nicklas; 8 Mark Applegarth; 9 Pat Smith; 10 Jordan Crowther; 11 Adam Robinson; 12 Ross Divorty; 13 Mike Emmett. Subs (all used): 14 Harry Carter; 15 Matty Dale; 16 Brad Hey; 17 Jack Anderson.
Tries: Robinson (13, 31), Morland (19), Buchanan (40), Tyson-Wilson (44), A Dent (47), P Smith (49), Crowther (61), Anderson (77);
Goals: Nicklas 1/3, Tyson-Wilson 6/6.
Rugby Leaguer & League Express Men of the Match:
Oxford: Danny Allan; *City Knights:* Mark Applegarth.
Penalty count: 6-8; **Half-time:** 0-20;
Referee: Billy Pearson; **Attendance:** 126.

GLOUCESTERSHIRE ALL GOLDS 18
NORTH WALES CRUSADERS 30

ALL GOLDS: 1 Phil Cowburn; 2 Mo Agoro; 3 Josh Allison; 4 Lewis Reece; 5 Chris Barlow; 6 Jack Mitchell; 7 Kieran Hyde; 8 Oliver Purslow; 9 Steve Parry; 10 Morgan Evans; 11 Lamont Bryan; 12 Joe McClean; 13 Emmerson Whittel. Subs (all used): 14 Kadeem Williams; 15 Dale Cunniffe; 16 Brad Hill; 17 Jamel Goodall.
Tries: Parry (3, 46), Cowburn (50); **Goals:** Hyde 3/3.
CRUSADERS: 1 Tommy Johnson; 2 Scott Turner; 3 Simon Atherton; 4 Alex Thompson; 5 Rob Massam; 6 Ryan Smith; 7 Jack Hansen; 8 Jonny Walker; 9 Lee Hudson; 10 Matthew Haggarty; 11 Luke Warburton; 12 Stephen Wild; 13 Billy Brickhill. Subs (all used): 14 Matt Wilkinson; 15 Kenny Baker; 16 Liam Bent; 17 Ryan Lannon.
Tries: Turner (12, 28), Massam (17), Hansen (25), Brickhill (79); **Goals:** Johnson 5/6.
Rugby Leaguer & League Express Men of the Match:
All Golds: Steve Parry; *Crusaders:* Jack Hansen.
Penalty count: 12-9; **Half-time:** 6-22;
Referee: Steve Race; **Attendance:** 171.

HUNSLET HAWKS 38 COVENTRY BEARS 18

HAWKS: 1 Jimmy Watson; 31 Lee Mapals; 4 Ayden Faal; 15 Mufaro Mvududu; 28 Richie Barnett; 6 Simon Brown; 7 Danny Ansell; 19 Matt Carbutt; 9 Jack Lee; 10 Lewis Reed; 29 Daniel Williams; 3 Jake Normington; 13 Liam Mackay. Subs (all used): 14 George Flanagan; 26 Austin Bell; 22 Craig Robinson; 32 Jack Coventry.
Tries: Mapals (10), Normington (15), Lee (25), Ansell (28), Mackay (32), Mvududu (68); **Goals:** Brown 7/7.
BEARS: 1 Charlie O'Mara; 2 Dan Price; 3 Matt Reid; 4 Eddie Medforth; 5 Jonathan Milizewski; 6 Joel James; 7 James Redman; 8 Alex Beddows; 9 Jay Lobwein; 10 Jack Morrison; 11 Liam Thompson; 12 Chris Barratt; 13 Grant Beecham. Subs (all used): 14 Trae O'Sullivan; 15 James Geurtjens; 16 Joe Batchelor; 17 Richard Hughes.
Tries: Lobwein (7), Batchelor (37), Reid (70);
Goals: James 3/3.
Rugby Leaguer & League Express Men of the Match:
Hawks: Lee Mapals; *Bears:* Jay Lobwein.
Penalty count: 11-11; **Half-time:** 30-12;
Referee: Brandon Robinson; **Attendance:** 446.

NEWCASTLE THUNDER 30 ROCHDALE HORNETS 38

THUNDER: 1 Tom Ruediger; 2 Ali Blair; 3 Joe Brown; 4 Dan Parker; 5 Peter Fox; 6 Lewis Young; 7 Benn Hardcastle; 8 Corbyn Kilday; 9 Aaron Teroi; 10 Rob Mulhern; 11 Harry Aldous; 12 Rhys Clarke; 13 Sam Luckley. Subs (all used): 14 Ben Thorburn; 15 Mikey Wood; 16 Derrell Olpherts; 17 Francis Welsh.
Tries: Ruediger (6), Fox (24, 54), R Clarke (35, 67), Olpherts (77); **Goals:** Parker 2/4, Hardcastle 1/2.
HORNETS: 1 Chris Riley; 2 Dale Bloomfield; 3 Dave Cookson; 4 Toby King; 5 Lewis Galbraith; 6 Paul Crook; 7 Danny Yates; 8 Jovili Taira; 9 Ben Moores; 10 Warren Thompson; 11 Jono Smith; 12 Sam Wilde; 13 James Tilley. Subs (all used): 14 Ryan Maneely; 15 Samir Tahraoui; 16 Matty Hadden; 17 Joe Philbin.
Tries: King (11), Yates (16), Wilde (41), D Cookson (47), Thompson (69), Riley (72), Bloomfield (79);
Goals: Crook 5/7.
Rugby Leaguer & League Express Men of the Match:
Thunder: Rhys Clarke; *Hornets:* Paul Crook.
Penalty count: 12-10; **Half-time:** 14-12;
Referee: Jon Roberts; **Attendance:** 1,076.

SOUTH WALES SCORPIONS 6 LONDON SKOLARS 22

SCORPIONS: 15 Jordan Sheridan; 2 Ian Newbury; 21 Scott Gregory; 22 Christiaan Roets; 4 Yannic Parker; 30 Jamie Murphy; 7 Paul Emanuelli; 20 Anthony Symons; 9 Connor Farrer; 10 Izaak Duffy; 23 Barrie Phillips; 28 Richard Jones; 24 Zak Williams. Subs (all used): 3 Kyle Scrivens; 14 Osian Phillips; 16 Dafydd Hellard; 19 Kristian Baller.
Try: Sheridan (36); **Goals:** Emanuelli 1/2.
Sin bin: Farrer (50) - punching.
SKOLARS: 1 Alex Walker; 2 Sam Nash; 3 Will Lovell; 4 Kazeem Fatouri; 5 Andy Winfield; 6 Jy-mel Coleman; 7 Joe Keyes; 8 Mike Greenhalgh; 9 Charlie Lawrence; 10 Dave Williams; 11 Eddie Mbaraga; 12 Steve Bannister; 13 Michael Worrincy. Subs (all used): 14 Billy Driver; 15 Ben Gray; 16 Michael Sykes; 17 Ryan Chester.
Tries: Walker (4, 8), Sykes (33), Nash (70);
Goals: Jy-mel Coleman 3/4.
Rugby Leaguer & League Express Men of the Match:
Scorpions: Zak Williams; *Skolars:* Alex Walker.
Penalty count: 10-7; **Half-time:** 6-16;
Referee: Marcus Griffiths; **Attendance:** 170.

BARROW RAIDERS 62 HEMEL STAGS 4

RAIDERS: 1 Ryan Fieldhouse; 23 Chris Fleming; 3 Chris Hankinson; 5 Cameron Pitman; 31 Eze Harper; 28 Jamie Dallimore; 6 Josh Ward; 8 Joe Bullock; 21 Dan Abram; 10 Oliver Wilkes; 11 Liam Harrison; 4 Andy Litherland; 13 Martin Aspinwall. Subs (all used): 24 Matty While; 12 Dan Toal; 9 Nathan Mossop; 32 Brad Brennan.
Tries: Harper (12, 22), Harrison (17), Litherland (19), Fleming (26), Pitman (33, 45), Mossop (35, 38), D Toal (56), Aspinwall (65); **Goals:** Hankinson 8/10, Ward 1/1.
STAGS: 1 Josh Spearing; 2 Reece Rance; 3 Dom Bryan; 4 Barry-John Swindells; 5 Harrison Brough; 6 Jordan Aitchison; 7 Brad Delaney; 8 Rick Joy; 9 Dylan Readman; 10 Victor Coker; 11 Brad Adams; 12 Kyal Greene; 13 Andrew Joy. Subs (all used): 14 Reece Trout; 15 James Shaw; 16 Dave O'Conner; 17 Andy Parrott.
Try: Brough (62); **Goals:** B Delaney 0/1.
Rugby Leaguer & League Express Men of the Match:
Raiders: Chris Hankinson; *Stags:* Brad Delaney.
Penalty count: 12-6; **Half-time:** 46-0;
Referee: Liam Moore; **Attendance:** 714.

ROUND 13

Saturday 25th June 2016

COVENTRY BEARS 14 NEWCASTLE THUNDER 32

BEARS: 1 Charlie O'Mara; 2 Jason Bass; 3 Matt Reid; 4 Eddie Medforth; 5 Jonathan Milizewski; 6 Joel James; 7 James Redman; 8 Alex Beddows; 9 Jay Lobwein; 10 Jack Morrison; 11 Liam Thompson; 12 Grant Beecham; 13 Richard Hughes. Subs (all used): 14 Chris Barratt; 15 Dan Price; 16 Joe Batchelor; 17 Trae O'Sullivan.
Tries: Beecham (10), O'Mara (22), Medforth (30);
Goals: James 1/3.
THUNDER: 1 Tom Ruediger; 2 Ali Blair; 3 Dan Parker; 4 Joe Brown; 5 Peter Fox; 6 Lewis Young; 7 Benn Hardcastle; 8 Mikey Wood; 9 Aaron Teroi; 10 Corbyn Kilday; 11 Harry Aldous; 12 Rhys Clarke; 13 Kevin Larroyer. Subs (all used): 14 Evan Simons; 15 Derrell Olpherts; 16 Sam Luckley; 17 Vincent Rennie.
Tries: Fox (16, 80), Simons (27), Rennie (40), Blair (42), Parker (66); **Goals:** Hardcastle 4/6.
Rugby Leaguer & League Express Men of the Match:
Bears: Jack Morrison; *Thunder:* Derrell Olpherts.
Penalty count: 9-8; **Half-time:** 14-16;
Referee: John McMullen; **Attendance:** 266.

LONDON SKOLARS 10 DONCASTER 30

SKOLARS: 1 Alex Walker; 2 Sam Nash; 3 Will Lovell; 4 Aaron Small; 5 John Paxton; 6 Jy-mel Coleman; 7 James Woodburn-Hall; 8 Erjon Dollapi; 9 Charlie Lawrence; 10 Toby Everett; 11 Dave Williams; 12 Michael Worrincy; 13 Ryan Chester. Subs (all used): 14 Michael Sykes; 15 Eddie Mbaraga; 16 Billy Driver; 17 Ben Gray.
Tries: Worrincy (37), Lovell (64);
Goals: Jy-mel Coleman 1/2.
Sin bin: Lawrence (76) - dissent.
DONCASTER: 1 Tom Carr; 2 Louis Sheriff; 3 Sam Doherty; 4 Liam Welham; 5 David Foggin-Johnston; 6 Jordan Howden; 7 Jordie Hedges; 8 Connor Scott; 9 Kyle Kesik; 10 Matt Nicholson; 11 Jack Walton; 12 Brad Foster; 13 George Milton. Subs (all used): 14 Ryan Wright; 15 Brad Nicholson; 16 Mark Castle; 17 Joe Picketts-O'Donnell.
Tries: Kesik (11), Sheriff (29), Doherty (57, 71, 79);
Goals: Carr 5/7.
Rugby Leaguer & League Express Men of the Match:
Skolars: Billy Driver; *Doncaster:* Sam Doherty.
Penalty count: 6-11; **Half-time:** 6-14;
Referee: Callum Straw; **Attendance:** 425.

Sunday 26th June 2016

HEMEL STAGS 6 ROCHDALE HORNETS 60

STAGS: 1 Will Forsyth; 2 Donald Kudangirana; 3 Brad Adams; 4 Dom Bryan; 5 Harrison Brough; 6 Oli Toms; 7 Brad Delaney; 8 James Shaw; 9 Dylan Readman; 10 Aaron Hall; 11 Marcus Stock; 12 Barry-John Swindells; 13 Kyal Greene. Subs (all used): 14 Malikhi Lloyd-Jones; 15 Dave O'Conner; 16 Mike Stewart; 17 Andrew Joy.
Try: Bryan (16); **Goals:** Swindells 1/1.
HORNETS: 1 Chris Riley; 2 Dale Bloomfield; 3 Dave Cookson; 4 Lewis Galbraith; 5 Corey Lee; 6 Paul Crook; 7 Danny Yates; 8 Jovili Taira; 9 Ben Moores; 10 Warren Thompson; 11 Jono Smith; 12 Jordan Case; 13 James Tilley. Subs (all used): 14 Ryan Maneely; 15 Matty Hadden; 16 Samir Tahraoui; 17 Josh Crowley.
Tries: Yates (4, 70), Lee (10, 40, 64), Smith (19), Tilley (24), Case (41), Maneely (45), Galbraith (48, 76);
Goals: Crook 8/11.
Sin bin: D Cookson (80) - punching.
Rugby Leaguer & League Express Men of the Match:
Stags: Donald Kudangirana; *Hornets:* Corey Lee.
Penalty count: 7-9; **Half-time:** 6-26;
Referee: Jamie Bloem; **Attendance:** 115.

NORTH WALES CRUSADERS 14
TOULOUSE OLYMPIQUE 32

CRUSADERS: 1 Tommy Johnson; 2 Scott Turner; 3 Simon Atherton; 4 Alex Thompson; 5 Rob Massam; 6 Ryan Smith; 7 Andy Moulsdale; 8 Jonny Walker; 9 Lee Hudson; 10 Matthew Haggarty; 11 Luke Warburton; 12 Stephen Wild; 13 Billy Brickhill. Subs (all used): 14 Matt Wilkinson; 15 Liam Bent; 16 Kenny Baker; 17 Adam Saunders.
Tries: Massam (7, 70), Turner (68); **Goals:** Johnson 1/3.
OLYMPIQUE: 1 Mark Kheirallah; 2 Tony Maurel; 3 Bastien Ader; 21 Gavin Marguerite; 5 Kuni Minga; 6 Johnathon Ford; 22 Danny Hulme; 15 Maxime Puech; 17 Anthony Marion; 10 Samy Masselot; 11 Sebastien Planas; 12 Rhys Curran; 8 Clement Boyer. Subs (all used): 14 Mourad Kriouache; 24 Justin Sangare; 25 Kalausa Leha; 18 Tyla Hepi.
Tries: Minga (3, 10), Kriouache (28), Ford (36), Kheirallah (42), Planas (64); **Goals:** Kheirallah 4/6.
Rugby Leaguer & League Express Men of the Match:
Crusaders: Lee Hudson; *Olympique:* Johnathon Ford.
Penalty count: 6-2; **Half-time:** 4-22;
Referee: Tom Crashley; **Attendance:** 486.

KEIGHLEY COUGARS 32 BARROW RAIDERS 34

COUGARS: 38 Johnny Campbell; 2 Andy Gabriel; 23 Charlie Martin; 4 Danny Lawton; 5 Paul White; 24 Liam Darville; 7 Paul Handforth; 8 Scott Law; 9 James Feather; 12 Brendan Rawlins; 11 Josh Lynam; 17 John Oakes; 20 Aaron Ollett. Subs (all used): 15 Neil Cherryholme; 19 Matthew Bailey; 35 Ross Peltier; 37 Will Milner.
Tries: White (5, 40), Campbell (25), Peltier (31), Rawlins (62), Gabriel (72); **Goals:** Lawton 4/7.
RAIDERS: 1 Ryan Fieldhouse; 31 Eze Harper; 5 Cameron Pitman; 4 Andy Litherland; 23 Chris Fleming; 3 Chris Hankinson; 28 Jamie Dallimore; 8 Joe Bullock; 29 Karl Ashall; 10 Oliver Wilkes; 11 Liam Harrison; 26 Danny Morrow; 13 Martin Aspinwall. Subs (all used): 9 Nathan Mossop; 12 Dan Toal; 19 Anthony Bate; 32 Brad Brennan.
Tries: Fieldhouse (12), Hankinson (16), Harper (22), Dallimore (33), Pitman (54), Harrison (68);
Goals: Hankinson 5/7.
Sin bin: Pitman (38) - dissent.
Rugby Leaguer & League Express Men of the Match:
Cougars: Johnny Campbell; *Raiders:* Chris Hankinson.
Penalty count: 9-7; **Half-time:** 20-22;
Referee: Warren Turley; **Attendance:** 716.

SOUTH WALES SCORPIONS 24 HUNSLET HAWKS 36

SCORPIONS: 30 Jamie Murphy; 2 Ian Newbury; 22 Christiaan Roets; 15 Jordan Sheridan; 5 Dai Evans; 27 Courtney Davies; 7 Paul Emanuelli; 28 Richard Jones; 9 Connor Farrer; 10 Izaak Duffy; 3 Kyle Scrivens; 23 Barrie Phillips; - Alex Davidson. Subs (all used): 11 Bradley Hill; 14 Osian Phillips; 19 Kristian Baller; - Sion Jones.
Tries: Sheridan (43), Roets (48), Evans (51, 79), Newbury (77); **Goals:** Emanuelli 2/5.
HAWKS: 31 Lee Mapals; 20 Danny Thomas; 15 Mufaro Mvududu; 4 Ayden Faal; 28 Richie Barnett; 6 Simon Brown; 7 Danny Ansell; 19 Matt Carbutt; 9 Jack Lee; 10 Lewis Reed; 29 Daniel Williams; 3 Jake Normington; 13 Liam Mackay. Subs (all used): 14 George Flanagan; 22 Craig Robinson; 26 Austin Bell; 32 Jack Coventry.
Tries: Mvududu (4, 14), Williams (29), Thomas (38), Flanagan (66), Reed (73); **Goals:** Brown 6/6.
Rugby Leaguer & League Express Men of the Match:
Scorpions: Sion Jones; *Hawks:* Lee Mapals.
Penalty count: 8-11; **Half-time:** 0-24;
Referee: Liam Moore; **Attendance:** 259.

YORK CITY KNIGHTS 56
GLOUCESTERSHIRE ALL GOLDS 12

CITY KNIGHTS: 1 Richard Wilkinson; 2 Tom Saxton; 3 Sam Smeaton; 4 Ed Smith; 5 Austin Buchanan; 6 Jon Presley; 7 Harry Tyson-Wilson; 8 Jack Aldous; 9 Harry Carter; 10 Russ Spiers; 11 Josh Tonks; 12 Adam Robinson; 13 Mike Emmett. Subs (all used): 14 Kris Brining; 15 Jack Anderson; 16 Jordan Crowther; 17 Andy Smith.
Tries: Tyson-Wilson (2, 18, 42), Emmett (6, 12), Brining (35, 55), E Smith (52), Tonks (69), Robinson (75);
Goals: Tyson-Wilson 8/10.
ALL GOLDS: 1 Phil Cowburn; 2 Mo Agoro; 3 Josh Allison; 4 Zack McComb; 5 Chris Barlow; 6 Jack Mitchell; 7 Kieran Hyde; 8 Morgan Evans; 9 Steve Parry; 10 Oliver Purslow; 11 Emmerson Whittel; 12 Jamel Goodall; 13 Lamont Bryan. Subs (all used): 14 Brendon Newton; 15 Kadeem Williams; 16 Brad Hill; 17 Jose Kenga.
Tries: Parry (31, 65); **Goals:** Hyde 2/2.
Rugby Leaguer & League Express Men of the Match:
City Knights: Harry Tyson-Wilson; *All Golds:* Steve Parry.
Penalty count: 12-8; **Half-time:** 28-6;
Referee: Jon Roberts; **Attendance:** 585.

ROUND 14

Saturday 2nd July 2016

TOULOUSE OLYMPIQUE 44 YORK CITY KNIGHTS 6

OLYMPIQUE: 1 Mark Kheirallah; 2 Tony Maurel; 3 Bastien Ader; 4 Gregory White; 5 Kuni Minga; 22 Danny Hulme; 6 Johnathon Ford; 15 Maxime Puech; 9 Kane Bentley; 16 Bastien Canet; 11 Sebastien Planas; 12 Rhys Curran; 8 Clement Boyer. Subs (all used): 14 Mourad Kriouache; 18 Tyla Hepi; 25 Kalausa Leha; 26 Constantine Mika.
Tries: Planas (26, 63), Curran (40), Mika (49), Minga (52, 54), Canet (63, 69); **Goals:** Kheirallah 6/8.
CITY KNIGHTS: 1 Ben Dent; 2 Tom Saxton; 3 Ed Smith; 4 Andy Smith; 5 Austin Buchanan; 6 Jon Presley; 7 Danny Nicklas; 8 Russ Spiers; 9 Pat Smith; 10 Jack Aldous; 11 Josh Tonks; 12 Adam Robinson; 13 Mike Emmett. Subs (all used): 14 Kris Brining; 15 Mark Applegarth; 16 Jordan Crowther; 17 Harry Tyson-Wilson.
Try: Brining (37); **Goals:** Nicklas 1/1.
Rugby Leaguer & League Express Men of the Match:
Olympique: Rhys Curran; *City Knights:* Danny Nicklas.
Penalty count: 10-8; **Half-time:** 12-6;
Referee: Callum Straw; **Attendance:** 1,254.

Sunday 3rd July 2016

NORTH WALES CRUSADERS 20 COVENTRY BEARS 20

CRUSADERS: 1 Tommy Johnson; 2 Andrew Oakden; 3 Simon Atherton; 4 Jake Bibby; 5 Rob Massam; 6 Ryan Smith; 7 Andy Moulsdale; 8 Jonny Walker; 9 Lee Hudson; 10 Kenny Baker; 11 Luke Warburton; 12 Stephen Wild; 13 Billy Brickhill. Subs (all used): 14 Jack Hansen; 15 Ryan Lannon; 16 Olsi Krasniqi; 17 Phil Joseph.
Tries: Warburton (19), Wild (39), Joseph (45), Johnson (52);
Goals: Johnson 2/4.
BEARS: 1 Charlie O'Mara; 2 Jason Bass; 3 Eddie Medforth; 4 Matt Reid; 5 Jonathan Milizewski; 6 Joel James; 7 James Redman; 8 Alex Beddows; 9 Jay Lobwein; 10 Jack Morrison; 11 Liam Thompson; 12 Chris Barratt; 13 Grant Beecham. Subs (all used): 14 Dan Price; 15 Andy Unsworth; 16 John Aldred; 17 Trae O'Sullivan.
Tries: Reid (2), Bass (8), Beddows (60), Morrison (79);
Goals: James 2/4.
Rugby Leaguer & League Express Men of the Match:
Crusaders: Stephen Wild; *Bears:* Joel James.
Penalty count: 7-9; **Half-time:** 10-8;
Referee: Andrew Sweet; **Attendance:** 359
(at Hare Lane, Chester).

DONCASTER 80 HEMEL STAGS 18

DONCASTER: 1 Tom Carr; 2 David Foggin-Johnston; 3 Sam Doherty; 4 Jason Tali; 5 Aaron Jones-Bishop; 6 Jordan Howden; 7 Jordie Hedges; 8 Makali Aizue; 9 Kyle Kesik; 10 Connor Scott; 11 Jack Walton; 12 Liam Welham; 13 George Milton. Subs (all used): 14 Mark Castle; 15 Kieran Cross; 16 Joe Pickets-O'Donnell; 17 Brad Nicholson.
Tries: Scott (2, 73, 77), Jones-Bishop (5, 18), Doherty (26, 28), Cross (34, 44), Tali (40, 61), Carr (53), L Welham (56), Foggin-Johnston (80); **Goals:** Carr 12/14.
STAGS: 1 Will Forsyth; 2 Reece Rance; 3 Kameron Pearce-Paul; 4 Tuoyo Egodo; 5 Harrison Brough; 6 Oli Toms; 7 James Glover; 8 Matt Ross; 9 Dylan Readman; 10 Aaron Hall; 11 Marcus Stock; 12 Barry-John Swindells; 13 Kyal Greene. Subs (all used): 14 Dave O'Conner; 15 Andy Parrott; 16 Andrew Joy; 17 Mike Stewart.
Tries: Hall (18), Ross (22), Readman (64);
Goals: Swindells 3/3.
Rugby Leaguer & League Express Men of the Match:
Doncaster: Jack Walton; *Stags:* Aaron Hall.
Penalty count: 6-8; **Half-time:** 40-12;
Referee: James Callaghan; **Attendance:** 562
(at Keepmoat Athletics Ground).

GLOUCESTERSHIRE ALL GOLDS 22
LONDON SKOLARS 23

ALL GOLDS: 1 Kieran Hyde; 2 Mo Agoro; 3 Josh Allison; 4 Lewis Reece; 5 Phil Cowburn; 6 Brendon Newton; 7 Jack Mitchell; 8 Brad Hill; 9 Steve Parry; 10 Morgan Evans; 11 Lamont Bryan; 12 Joe McClean; 13 Emmerson Whittel. Subs (all used): 14 Mick Govin; 15 Kadeem Williams; 16 Oliver Purslow; 17 Jose Kenga.
Tries: Reece (14, 64), Parry (17), Bryan (53);
Goals: Hyde 3/4.
SKOLARS: 1 Alex Walker; 2 Sam Nash; 3 Aaron Small; 4 Lameck Juma; 5 John Paxton; 6 Jy-mel Coleman; 7 Sam Druce; 8 Dave Williams; 9 Billy Driver; 10 Mike Greenhalgh; 11 Michael Worrincy; 12 Will Lovell; 13 Ryan Chester. Subs (all used): 14 Ben Pointer; 15 Erjon Dollapi; 16 Toby Everett; 17 Eddie Mbaraga.
Tries: Williams (23), Lovell (28), Dollapi (31), Nash (71);
Goals: Jy-mel Coleman 3/5;
Field goal: Jy-mel Coleman (75).
Rugby Leaguer & League Express Men of the Match:
All Golds: Steve Parry; *Skolars:* Jy-mel Coleman.
Penalty count: 5-5; **Half-time:** 10-16;
Referee: Robert Hicks; **Attendance:** 190.

NEWCASTLE THUNDER 50
SOUTH WALES SCORPIONS 16

THUNDER: 1 Tom Ruediger; 2 Ali Blair; 3 Derrell Olpherts; 4 Joe Brown; 5 Zach Clark; 6 Josh Kittrick; 7 Benn Hardcastle; 8 Corbyn Kilday; 9 Aaron Teroi; 10 Mikey Wood; 11 Dan Parker; 12 Rhys Clarke; 13 Sam Luckley. Subs (all used): 14 Evan Simons; 15 Vincent Rennie; 16 Jason Payne; 17 Ben Thorburn.
Tries: Ruediger (5, 13, 58, 65), Payne (30), Olpherts (42, 75), Kittrick (54), Wood (79); **Goals:** Hardcastle 7/9.
SCORPIONS: 30 Jamie Murphy; 2 Ian Newbury; 15 Jordan Sheridan; 22 Christiaan Roets; 21 Scott Gregory; 27 Courtney Davies; 7 Paul Emanuelli; 10 Izaak Duffy; 19 Kristian Baller; 28 Richard Jones; 23 Barrie Phillips; 3 Kyle Scrivens; - Alex Davidson. Subs (all used): 25 Billy Gaylor; 13 Chris Vitalini; - Sion Jones; 20 Anthony Symons.
Tries: R Jones (18), Murphy (62), Davidson (68);
Goals: Emanuelli 2/3.
Rugby Leaguer & League Express Men of the Match:
Thunder: Tom Ruediger; *Scorpions:* Richard Jones.
Penalty count: 5-8; **Half-time:** 16-6;
Referee: Andrew Bentham; **Attendance:** 782.

ROCHDALE HORNETS 42 KEIGHLEY COUGARS 28

HORNETS: 1 Wayne English; 2 Tom Lineham; 3 Dave Cookson; 4 Benjamin Jullien; 5 Dale Bloomfield; 6 Paul Crook; 7 Danny Yates; 8 Jovili Taira; 9 Ben Moores; 10 Warren Thompson; 11 Jono Smith; 12 Jordan Case; 13 James Tilley. Subs (all used): 14 Ryan Maneely; 15 Samir Tahraoui; 16 Matty Hadden; 17 Josh Crowley.
Tries: Tilley (2), Jullien (14, 77), English (19), Bloomfield (22), Smith (54), Moores (62); **Goals:** Crook 7/9.
Sin bin: Tilley (73) - professional foul.
COUGARS: 22 Ritchie Hawkyard; 38 Johnny Campbell; 23 Charlie Martin; 4 Danny Lawton; 5 Paul White; 37 Will Milner; 7 Paul Handforth; 19 Matthew Bailey; 9 James Feather; 12 Brendan Rawlins; 11 Josh Lynam; 18 Sonny Esslemont; 20 Aaron Ollett. Subs (all used): 14 Adam Brook; 15 Neil Cherryholme; 17 John Oakes; 35 Ross Peltier.
Tries: Peltier (32), Feather (57), Martin (65, 71), Rawlins (74); **Goals:** Lawton 4/5.
Rugby Leaguer & League Express Men of the Match:
Hornets: Jovili Taira; *Cougars:* Ross Peltier.
Penalty count: 10-12; **Half-time:** 26-6;
Referee: Tom Crashley; **Attendance:** 558.

BARROW RAIDERS 76 OXFORD 12

RAIDERS: 23 Chris Fleming; 31 Eze Harper; 4 Andy Litherland; 11 Liam Harrison; 5 Cameron Pitman; 3 Chris Hankinson; 28 Jamie Dallimore; 8 Joe Bullock; 29 Karl Ashall; 10 Oliver Wilkes; 27 Matty Holmes; 26 Danny Morrow; 13 Martin Aspinwall. Subs (all used): 18 James Duerden; 12 Dan Toal; 9 Nathan Mossop; 19 Anthony Bate.
Tries: Wilkes (4), Dallimore (18), Litherland (25, 40, 52, 70), Morrow (30, 45), Hankinson (34, 59), Bate (42), D Toal (48), Fleming (66); **Goals:** Fleming 12/13.
OXFORD: 1 James Cryer; 2 Luke Gardiner; 3 Jordan Gill; 4 Marcus Brooker; 5 Nick Arnell; 6 Jesse Sheriffe; 7 Danny Allan; 8 Ryan Backhouse; 9 Nathan Kitson; 10 Daniel Igbinedion; 11 Aaron Nicholson; 12 Adam Withington; 13 Will Maher. Subs (all used): 14 Charlie Greene; 15 Harry Griffith; 16 Mark Hayes; 17 Jordan Parry.
Tries: J Gill (23, 75); **Goals:** Allan 1/1, Kitson 1/1.
Sin bin: Cryer (60) - dissent; Withington (79) - high tackle.
Rugby Leaguer & League Express Men of the Match:
Raiders: Andy Litherland; *Oxford:* Danny Allan.
Penalty count: 10-5; **Half-time:** 36-6;
Referee: John McMullen; **Attendance:** 857.

ROUND 15

Saturday 9th July 2016

COVENTRY BEARS 18 SOUTH WALES SCORPIONS 16

BEARS: 1 Charlie O'Mara; 2 Jonathan Milizewski; 3 Eddie Medforth; 4 Matt Reid; 5 Jason Bass; 6 Dan Price; 7 Joel James; 8 Alex Beddows; 9 Jay Lobwein; 10 Jack Morrison; 11 Liam Thompson; 12 Chris Barratt; 13 Grant Beecham. Subs (all used): 14 Andy Unsworth; 15 Trae O'Sullivan; 16 John Aldred; 17 Richard Hughes.
Tries: Hughes (45, 49), Morrison (59);
Goals: James 3/3, Price 0/1.
SCORPIONS: 30 Jamie Murphy; 2 Ian Newbury; 22 Christiaan Roets; 21 Scott Gregory; - Rhys Gant; 27 Courtney Davies; 7 Paul Emanuelli; - Alex Davidson; 19 Kristian Baller; 10 Izaak Duffy; 3 Kyle Scrivens; 28 Sion Jones; 13 Chris Vitalini. Subs (all used): 14 Osian Phillips; 25 Billy Gaylor; 26 Luke Nelmes; 20 Anthony Symons.
Tries: Murphy (10), Gaylor (20), Baller (76);
Goals: Emanuelli 2/3.
Sin bin: Roets (45) - high tackle.
Rugby Leaguer & League Express Men of the Match:
Bears: Richard Hughes; *Scorpions:* Jamie Murphy.
Penalty count: 11-7; **Half-time:** 0-12;
Referee: Andrew Bentham; **Attendance:** 545.

LONDON SKOLARS 12 TOULOUSE OLYMPIQUE 52

SKOLARS: 1 Alex Walker; 2 Sam Nash; 3 Aaron Small; 4 Lameck Juma; 5 John Paxton; 6 Sam Druce; 7 Charlie Lawrence; 10 Dave Williams; 9 Ben Pointer; 11 Toby Everett; 13 Eddie Mbaraga; 12 Will Lovell; 16 Ryan Chester. Subs (all used): 14 Billy Driver; 23 Ben Gray; 19 Erjon Dollapi; 17 Kazeem Fatouri.
Tries: Mbaraga (45), Chester (52); **Goals:** Lawrence 2/2.
OLYMPIQUE: 1 Mark Kheirallah; 2 Tony Maurel; 21 Gavin Marguerite; 4 Gregory White; 5 Kuni Minga; 6 Johnathon Ford; 19 Etienne Ferret; 8 Clement Boyer; 9 Kane Bentley; 16 Bastien Canet; 11 Sebastien Planas; 12 Rhys Curran; 17 Anthony Marion. Subs (all used): 14 Mourad Kriouache; 18 Tyla Hepi; 10 Samy Masselot; 26 Constantine Mika.
Tries: Canet (2, 72), White (9), Minga (17), Masselot (36), Curran (61), Hepi (65), K Bentley (69), Kheirallah (73);
Goals: Kheirallah 8/9.
Rugby Leaguer & League Express Men of the Match:
Skolars: Charlie Lawrence; *Olympique:* Mark Kheirallah.
Penalty count: 6-6; **Half-time:** 0-24;
Referee: Warren Turley; **Attendance:** 550.

Sunday 10th July 2016

HEMEL STAGS 20 NEWCASTLE THUNDER 52

STAGS: 1 Mitch Vincent; 2 Josh Spearing; 3 Tuoyo Egodo; 4 Kameron Pearce-Paul; 5 Reece Rance; 6 Oli Toms; 7 Brad Delaney; 8 Matt Ross; 9 Dylan Readman; 10 Aaron Hall; 11 Brad Adams; 12 Barry-John Swindells; 13 Kyal Greene. Subs (all used): 14 Reece Trout; 15 James Shaw; 16 Mike Stewart; 17 Dom Bryan.
Tries: Rance (17), Spearing (41), Hall (67), Ross (77);
Goals: B Delaney 2/4.
THUNDER: 1 Tom Ruediger; 2 Zach Clark; 3 Joe Brown; 4 Derrell Olpherts; 5 Peter Fox; 6 Lewis Young; 7 Josh Kittrick; 8 Corbyn Kilday; 9 Aaron Teroi; 10 Mikey Wood; 11 Harry Aldous; 12 Rhys Clarke; 13 Sam Luckley. Subs (all used): 14 Evan Simons; 15 Jason Payne; 16 Vincent Rennie; 17 Dan Parker.
Tries: Wood (11), Payne (33), Olpherts (36), Simons (48, 53, 60), Fox (51, 62), Parker (64);
Goals: R Clarke 8/9.
Rugby Leaguer & League Express Men of the Match:
Stags: Brad Delaney; *Thunder:* Evan Simons.
Penalty count: 5-9; **Half-time:** 6-18;
Referee: Nick Bennett; **Attendance:** 115.

OXFORD 34 GLOUCESTERSHIRE ALL GOLDS 52

OXFORD: 1 James Cryer; 2 Luke Gardiner; 3 Jordan Gill; 4 Marcus Brooker; 5 Errol Carter; 6 Nathan Kitson; 7 Danny Allan; 8 Callum Bustin; 9 Casey Canterbury; 10 Sadiq Adebiyi; 11 Aaron Nicholson; 12 Daniel Igbinedion; 13 Jack Pickles. Subs (all used): 14 Jesse Sheriffe; 15 Lewis Bienek; 16 Jack Smith; 17 Charlie Greene.
Tries: J Gill (10, 30), Gardiner (27), Adebiyi (49), Greene (53, 56), Cryer (74); **Goals:** Kitson 3/7.
ALL GOLDS: 1 Brendon Newton; 2 Mo Agoro; 3 Josh Allison; 4 Phil Cowburn; 5 Jack Uren; 6 Kieran Hyde; 7 Mick Govin; 8 Oliver Purslow; 9 Steve Parry; 10 Harrison Elliott; 11 Lewis Reece; 12 Joe McClean; 13 Richard Jones. Subs (all used): 14 Luke Stephens; 15 Lamont Bryan; 16 Callum Bradbury; 17 James Walter.
Tries: McClean (2, 4, 15, 66), Uren (20), Walter (36, 45), Reece (41), Cowburn (63, 72); **Goals:** Hyde 4/8, Reece 2/2.
Rugby Leaguer & League Express Men of the Match:
Oxford: Daniel Igbinedion; *All Golds:* Joe McClean.
Penalty count: 10-10; **Half-time:** 14-24;
Referee: John McMullen; **Attendance:** 185.

HUNSLET HAWKS 35 NORTH WALES CRUSADERS 30

HAWKS: 1 Jimmy Watson; 33 Kyran Johnson; 4 Ayden Faal; 15 Mufaro Mvududu; 28 Richie Barnett; 6 Simon Brown; 7 Danny Ansell; 19 Matt Carbutt; 9 Jack Lee; 10 Lewis Reed; 29 Daniel Williams; 3 Jake Normington; 13 Liam Mackay. Subs (all used): 14 George Flanagan; 8 Michael Haley; 22 Craig Robinson; 32 Jack Coventry.
Tries: Williams (16), Haley (31), Faal (34), Flanagan (39, 41), Ansell (56); **Goals:** Brown 5/6; **Field goal:** Brown (62).
CRUSADERS: 1 Tommy Johnson; 2 Andrew Oakden; 3 Alex Thompson; 4 Simon Atherton; 5 Rob Massam; 6 Ryan Smith; 7 Andy Moulsdale; 8 Jonny Walker; 9 Lee Hudson; 10 Kenny Baker; 11 Ryan Lannon; 12 Stephen Wild; 13 Billy Brickhill. Subs (all used): 14 Matt Wilkinson; 15 Luke Warburton; 16 Elliot Liku; 17 Tommy Holland.
Tries: Thompson (8), Smith (13), Oakden (21), Massam (74), Baker (79); **Goals:** Johnson 5/5.
Rugby Leaguer & League Express Men of the Match:
Hawks: George Flanagan; *Crusaders:* Ryan Smith.
Penalty count: 8-9; **Half-time:** 22-18;
Referee: Phil Bentham; **Attendance:** 462.

KEIGHLEY COUGARS 34 YORK CITY KNIGHTS 28

COUGARS: 22 Ritchie Hawkyard; 2 Andy Gabriel; 4 Danny Lawton; 23 Charlie Martin; 38 Johnny Campbell; 14 Adam Brook; 37 Will Milner; 39 Jonathan Walker; 9 James Feather; 12 Brendan Rawlins; 25 Darren Hawkyard; 20 Aaron Ollett; 13 Ashley Lindsay. Subs (all used): 15 Neil Cherryholme; 17 John Oakes; 19 Matthew Bailey; 35 Ross Peltier.
Tries: Gabriel (1), Rawlins (24), Campbell (34, 43), Lindsay (63), Feather (69); **Goals:** Lawton 5/7.
CITY KNIGHTS: 1 Ben Dent; 2 Andy Smith; 3 Sam Smeaton; 4 James Morland; 5 Tom Saxton; 6 Jon Presley; 7 Danny Nicklas; 8 Russ Spiers; 9 Harry Carter; 10 Jack Aldous; 11 Josh Tonks; 12 Ed Smith; 13 Mike Emmett. Subs (all used): 14 Kris Brining; 15 Mark Applegarth; 16 Adam Robinson; 17 Brad Hey.

Tries: Morland (3, 47), Saxton (11), A Smith (39), Applegarth (53), Smeaton (66); **Goals:** Nicklas 2/6.
Rugby Leaguer & League Express Men of the Match: *Cougars:* Johnny Campbell; *City Knights:* James Morland.
Penalty count: 4-5; **Half-time:** 16-14;
Referee: Jamie Bloem; **Attendance:** 631.

ROCHDALE HORNETS 21 DONCASTER 8

HORNETS: 1 Wayne English; 2 Corey Lee; 3 Jake Shoel; 4 Benjamin Jullien; 5 Lewis Galbraith; 6 Paul Crook; 7 Danny Yates; 8 Jovili Taira; 9 Ben Moores; 10 Samir Tahraoui; 11 Jono Smith; 12 Josh Crowley; 13 James Tilley. Subs (all used): 14 Ryan Maneely; 15 Matty Hadden; 16 Warren Thompson; 17 Jordan Case.
Tries: Moores (6), Lee (45), Yates (54), Jullien (75); **Goals:** Crook 2/4; **Field goal:** Yates (78).
DONCASTER: 1 Matty Welham; 2 David Foggin-Johnston; 3 Sam Doherty; 4 Jason Tali; 5 Aaron Jones-Bishop; 6 Louis Sheriff; 7 Jordie Hedges; 8 Makali Aizue; 9 Ryan Wright; 10 Connor Scott; 11 Jack Walton; 12 Liam Welham; 13 George Milton. Subs (all used): 14 Kieran Cross; 15 Zac Braham; 16 Mark Castle; 17 Joe Pickets-O'Donnell.
Try: Scott (12); **Goals:** Hedges 2/3.
Rugby Leaguer & League Express Men of the Match: *Hornets:* Jono Smith; *Doncaster:* Jack Walton.
Penalty count: 7-7; **Half-time:** 6-8;
Referee: Callum Straw; **Attendance:** 591.

SUPER 8s

ROUND 1

Saturday 23rd July 2016

HUNSLET HAWKS 30 LONDON SKOLARS 26

HAWKS: 1 Jimmy Watson; 36 Stewart Sanderson; 33 Kyran Johnson; 15 Mufaro Mvududu; 28 Richie Barnett; 6 Simon Brown; 7 Danny Ansell; 32 Jack Coventry; 9 Jack Lee; 10 Lewis Reed; 29 Daniel Williams; 3 Jake Normington; 19 Matt Carbutt. Subs (all used): 14 George Flanagan; 8 Michael Haley; 22 Craig Robinson; 30 Jamie Milburn.
Tries: Sanderson (10, 15), Mvududu (33), Normington (37), Watson (52); **Goals:** Brown 5/6.
SKOLARS: 1 John Paxton; 2 Sam Nash; 3 Aaron Small; 4 Lameck Juma; 5 Billy Driver; 6 Jy-mel Coleman; 7 Mike Bishay; 8 Michael Sykes; 9 Sam Druce; 10 Dave Williams; 11 Michael Worrincy; 12 Will Lovell; 13 Ryan Chester. Subs (all used): 14 Ben Pointer; 15 Erjon Dollapi; 16 Ben Gray; 17 Eddie Mbaraga.
Tries: Jy-mel Coleman (20), Juma (26), Dollapi (51, 79), Driver (74); **Goals:** Jy-mel Coleman 3/5.
Rugby Leaguer & League Express Men of the Match: *Hawks:* Stewart Sanderson; *Skolars:* Mike Bishay.
Penalty count: 11-6; **Half-time:** 22-12;
Referee: John McMullen; **Attendance:** 414.

TOULOUSE OLYMPIQUE 40 KEIGHLEY COUGARS 4

OLYMPIQUE: 1 Mark Kheirallah; 2 Tony Maurel; 3 Bastien Ader; 4 Gregory White; 5 Kuni Minga; 19 Etienne Ferret; 22 Danny Hulme; 8 Clement Boyer; 9 Kane Bentley; 16 Bastien Canet; 11 Sebastien Planas; 12 Rhys Curran; 17 Anthony Marion. Subs (all used): 14 Mourad Kriouache; 18 Tyla Hepi; 15 Maxime Puech; 26 Constantine Mika.
Tries: Marion (10), Ader (15), Canet (20), White (37), Maurel (51), Hulme (58), Curran (62); **Goals:** Kheirallah 6/8.
COUGARS: 22 Ritchie Hawkyard; 2 Andy Gabriel; 29 Hamish Barnes; 23 Charlie Martin; 5 Paul White; 14 Adam Brook; 37 Will Milner; 39 Jonathan Walker; 9 James Feather; 19 Matthew Bailey; 25 Darren Hawkyard; 11 Josh Lynam; 20 Aaron Ollett. Subs (all used): 15 Neil Cherryholme; 17 John Oakes; 34 Jamel Goodall; 35 Ross Peltier.
Try: Martin (31); **Goals:** Brook 0/1.
Rugby Leaguer & League Express Men of the Match: *Olympique:* Danny Hulme; *Cougars:* Adam Brook.
Penalty count: 9-7; **Half-time:** 26-4;
Referee: Callum Straw; **Attendance:** 1,214.

Sunday 24th July 2016

BARROW RAIDERS 34 ROCHDALE HORNETS 12

RAIDERS: 1 Ryan Fieldhouse; 31 Eze Harper; 5 Cameron Pitman; 4 Andy Litherland; 23 Chris Fleming; 3 Chris Hankinson; 28 Jamie Dallimore; 8 Joe Bullock; 29 Karl Ashall; 10 Oliver Wilkes; 11 Liam Harrison; 26 Danny Morrow; 13 Martin Aspinwall. Subs (all used): 9 Nathan Mossop; 12 Dan Toal; 32 Brad Brennan; 27 Matty Holmes.
Tries: Fieldhouse (9), Brennan (24, 63), Dallimore (28), Bullock (51), Fleming (58); **Goals:** Hankinson 5/6.
Dismissal: Morrow (38) - dangerous challenge on Case.
HORNETS: 1 Kevin Penny; 2 Tom Lineham; 3 Jack Holmes; 4 Benjamin Jullien; 5 Lewis Galbraith; 6 Paul Crook; 7 Danny Yates; 8 Samir Tahraoui; 9 Ben Moores; 10 Jovili Taira; 11 Jono Smith; 12 Josh Crowley; 13 James Tilley. Subs (all used): 14 Ryan Maneely; 15 Warren Thompson; 16 Matty Hadden; 17 Jordan Case.
Tries: Yates (17), Penny (79); **Goals:** Crook 1/1, Yates 1/1.
Rugby Leaguer & League Express Men of the Match: *Raiders:* Brad Brennan; *Hornets:* Danny Yates.
Penalty count: 8-12; **Half-time:** 16-6;
Referee: Jamie Bloem; **Attendance:** 913.

ROUND 2

Saturday 30th July 2016

LONDON SKOLARS 28 ROCHDALE HORNETS 38

SKOLARS: 1 Oscar Thomas; 2 Sam Nash; 3 Aaron Small; 4 Lameck Juma; 5 John Paxton; 6 Jy-mel Coleman; 7 Mike Bishay; 8 Michael Sykes; 9 Charlie Lawrence; 10 Dave Williams; 11 Michael Worrincy; 12 Will Lovell; 13 Ryan Chester. Subs (all used): 14 Erjon Dollapi; 15 Toby Everett; 16 Kazeem Fatouri; 17 Billy Driver.
Tries: O Thomas (32), Driver (43), Paxton (60, 78), Dollapi (80); **Goals:** O Thomas 4/5.
Sin bin: Small (39) - punching; Williams (50) - interference.
HORNETS: 1 Wayne English; 2 Corey Lee; 3 Mike Ratu; 4 Lewis Galbraith; 5 Dale Bloomfield; 6 James Tilley; 7 Danny Yates; 8 Jovili Taira; 9 Ben Moores; 10 Warren Thompson; 11 Jono Smith; 12 Jordan Case; 13 Alex Trumper. Subs (all used): 14 Ryan Maneely; 15 Matty Hadden; 16 Harry Cartwright; 17 Samir Tahraoui.
Tries: Thompson (11), Smith (17, 28, 36), Tilley (40), English (65); **Goals:** Yates 7/7.
Rugby Leaguer & League Express Men of the Match: *Skolars:* Oscar Thomas; *Hornets:* Jono Smith.
Penalty count: 6-12; **Half-time:** 6-30;
Referee: Tom Grant; **Attendance:** 308.

TOULOUSE OLYMPIQUE 46 YORK CITY KNIGHTS 16

OLYMPIQUE: 1 Mark Kheirallah; 2 Tony Maurel; 3 Bastien Ader; 4 Gregory White; 5 Kuni Minga; 6 Johnathon Ford; 22 Danny Hulme; 8 Clement Boyer; 9 Kane Bentley; 16 Bastien Canet; 11 Sebastien Planas; 12 Rhys Curran; 17 Anthony Marion. Subs (all used): 14 Mourad Kriouache; 18 Tyla Hepi; 15 Maxime Puech; 26 Constantine Mika.
Tries: Hulme (28), Puech (31), Minga (34, 59), Curran (37), White (51), Boyer (70), Canet (76);
Goals: Kheirallah 7/8.
CITY KNIGHTS: 1 Richard Wilkinson; 2 Tom Saxton; 3 Brad Hey; 4 James Morland; 5 Adam Dent; 6 Jon Presley; 7 Pat Smith; 8 Matty Dale; 9 Harry Carter; 10 Jack Aldous; 11 Josh Tonks; 12 Ed Smith; 13 Mike Emmett. Subs (both used, only two named): 14 James Haynes; 15 Andy Smith.
Tries: Emmett (3), Carter (7), Presley (66);
Goals: Morland 2/3.
Rugby Leaguer & League Express Men of the Match: *Olympique:* Johnathon Ford; *City Knights:* Pat Smith.
Penalty count: 4-10; **Half-time:** 24-10;
Referee: Scott Mikalauskas; **Attendance:** 1,327.

Sunday 31st July 2016

DONCASTER 12 BARROW RAIDERS 40

DONCASTER: 1 Tom Carr; 2 David Foggin-Johnston; 3 Liam Welham; 4 Jason Tali; 5 Sam Doherty; 6 Louis Sheriff; 7 Kyle Kesik; 8 Makali Aizue; 9 Ryan Wright; 10 Connor Scott; 11 Brad Foster; 12 Jack Walton; 13 George Milton. Subs (all used): 14 Brad Nicholson; 15 Joe Pickets-O'Donnell; 16 Zac Braham; 17 Mark Castle.
Tries: Castle (55), Foggin-Johnston (75); **Goals:** Carr 2/2.
Sin bin: Wright (35) - late challenge;
Castle (43) - late challenge.
RAIDERS: 1 Ryan Fieldhouse; 31 Eze Harper; 5 Cameron Pitman; 4 Andy Litherland; 23 Chris Fleming; 28 Jamie Dallimore; 3 Chris Hankinson; 8 Joe Bullock; 29 Karl Ashall; 10 Oliver Wilkes; 11 Liam Harrison; 26 Danny Morrow; 19 Anthony Bate. Subs (all used): 9 Nathan Mossop; 12 Dan Toal; 27 Matty Holmes; 32 Brad Brennan.
Tries: Harper (3, 38), Harrison (26), Litherland (44), D Toal (62, 69); **Goals:** Hankinson 8/9.
Rugby Leaguer & League Express Men of the Match: *Doncaster:* David Foggin-Johnston; *Raiders:* Chris Hankinson.
Penalty count: 5-9; **Half-time:** 0-22;
Referee: Jack Smith; **Attendance:** 622.

KEIGHLEY COUGARS 8 HUNSLET HAWKS 18

COUGARS: 22 Ritchie Hawkyard; 2 Andy Gabriel; 29 Hamish Barnes; 3 Rikki Sheriffe; 5 Paul White; 14 Adam Brook; 7 Paul Handforth; 39 Jonathan Walker; 9 James Feather; 19 Matthew Bailey; 17 John Oakes; 25 Darren Hawkyard; 11 Josh Lynam. Subs (all used): 4 Danny Lawton; 15 Neil Cherryholme; 23 Charlie Martin; 16 Jode Sheriffe.
Tries: Brook (30), White (39); **Goals:** Brook 0/2.
HAWKS: 1 Jimmy Watson; 36 Stewart Sanderson; 33 Kyran Johnson; 15 Mufaro Mvududu; 28 Richie Barnett; 20 Danny Thomas; 7 Danny Ansell; 32 Jack Coventry; 9 Jack Lee; 10 Lewis Reed; 29 Daniel Williams; 3 Jake Normington; 19 Matt Carbutt. Subs (all used): 8 Michael Haley; 14 George Flanagan; 22 Craig Robinson; 30 Jamie Milburn.
Tries: Ansell (5), K Johnson (24), Sanderson (48);
Goals: Ansell 3/3.
Sin bin: Normington (58) - punching.
Rugby Leaguer & League Express Men of the Match: *Cougars:* Ritchie Hawkyard; *Hawks:* Danny Ansell.
Penalty count: 13-9; **Half-time:** 8-12;
Referee: Andrew Sweet; **Attendance:** 384.

ROUND 3

Friday 5th August 2016

HUNSLET HAWKS 24 DONCASTER 36

HAWKS: 1 Jimmy Watson; 36 Stewart Sanderson; 33 Kyran Johnson; 15 Mufaro Mvududu; 28 Richie Barnett; 20 Danny Thomas; 7 Danny Ansell; 32 Jack Coventry; 9 Jack Lee; 10 Lewis Reed; 29 Daniel Williams; 3 Jake Normington; 30 Jamie Milburn. Subs (all used): 14 George Flanagan; 19 Matt Carbutt; 37 Callum Casey; 8 Michael Haley.
Tries: Ansell (10), K Johnson (47), Reed (63), Thomas (78);
Goals: Ansell 4/4.
Sin bin: Normington (39) - punching.
DONCASTER: 1 Tom Carr; 2 David Foggin-Johnston; 3 Liam Welham; 4 Sam Doherty; 5 Louis Sheriff; 6 Jordan Howden; 7 Kieran Cross; 8 Connor Scott; 9 Kyle Kesik; 10 Mark Castle; 11 Mason Tonks; 12 Jack Walton; 13 George Milton. Subs (all used): 14 Ryan Wright; 15 Brad Nicholson; 16 Makali Aizue; 17 Joe Pickets-O'Donnell.
Tries: Sheriff (6, 52), Carr (14), Foggin-Johnston (20, 75), Aizue (35); **Goals:** Carr 6/6.
Sin bin: Pickets-O'Donnell (40) - dissent;
Walton (69) - interference.
Rugby Leaguer & League Express Men of the Match: *Hawks:* Danny Ansell; *Doncaster:* Jordan Howden.
Penalty count: 19-9; **Half-time:** 6-24;
Referee: Jon Roberts; **Attendance:** 541.

Sunday 7th August 2016

ROCHDALE HORNETS 18 KEIGHLEY COUGARS 4

HORNETS: 1 Wayne English; 2 Corey Lee; 3 Mike Ratu; 4 Jack Holmes; 5 Dale Bloomfield; 6 Steve Roper; 7 Danny Yates; 8 Jovili Taira; 9 Ben Moores; 10 Warren Thompson; 11 Josh Crowley; 12 Jordan Case; 13 James Tilley. Subs (all used): 14 Ryan Maneely; 15 Matty Hadden; 16 Samir Tahraoui; 17 Harry Cartwright.
Tries: Case (51), Thompson (60), Tahraoui (80);
Goals: Yates 3/3.
COUGARS: 22 Ritchie Hawkyard; 2 Andy Gabriel; 29 Hamish Barnes; 3 Rikki Sheriffe; 5 Paul White; 14 Adam Brook; 7 Paul Handforth; 39 Jonathan Walker; 9 James Feather; 19 Matthew Bailey; 25 Darren Hawkyard; 23 Charlie Martin; 20 Aaron Ollett. Subs (all used): 13 Ashley Lindsay; 17 John Oakes; 16 Jode Sheriffe; 35 Ross Peltier.
Try: Brook (11); **Goals:** Brook 0/1.
Dismissal: White (21) - punching Lee.
Rugby Leaguer & League Express Men of the Match: *Hornets:* Josh Crowley; *Cougars:* Adam Brook.
Penalty count: 10-8; **Half-time:** 0-4;
Referee: Callum Straw; **Attendance:** 510.

YORK CITY KNIGHTS 6 BARROW RAIDERS 20

CITY KNIGHTS: 1 Richard Wilkinson; 2 Tom Saxton; 3 Ed Smith; 4 James Morland; 5 Ben Dent; 6 Jon Presley; 7 Pat Smith; 8 Mark Applegarth; 9 Kris Brining; 10 Jack Aldous; 11 Josh Tonks; 12 Matty Dale; 13 Mike Emmett. Subs (all used): 14 Harry Carter; 15 Russ Spiers; 16 Andy Smith; 17 Brad Hey.
Try: Spiers (43); **Goals:** Morland 1/1.
RAIDERS: 1 Ryan Fieldhouse; 31 Eze Harper; 5 Cameron Pitman; 16 Max Wiper; 23 Chris Fleming; 3 Chris Hankinson; 28 Jamie Dallimore; 8 Joe Bullock; 9 Nathan Mossop; 10 Oliver Wilkes; 11 Liam Harrison; 15 Bradd Crellin; 13 Martin Aspinwall. Subs (all used): 21 Dan Abram; 19 Anthony Bate; 27 Matty Holmes; 32 Brad Brennan.
Tries: Hankinson (33), Harper (72, 75), Crellin (80);
Goals: Hankinson 2/4.
Rugby Leaguer & League Express Men of the Match: *City Knights:* Ed Smith; *Raiders:* Jamie Dallimore.
Penalty count: 7-3; **Half-time:** 0-6;
Referee: Scott Mikalauskas; **Attendance:** 664.

ROUND 4

Sunday 14th August 2016

DONCASTER 18 TOULOUSE OLYMPIQUE 38

DONCASTER: 1 Tom Carr; 2 David Foggin-Johnston; 3

Liam Welham; 4 Sam Doherty; 5 Louis Sheriff; 6 Jordan Howden; 7 Kieran Cross; 8 Mark Castle; 9 Kyle Kesik; 10 Connor Scott; 11 Brad Nicholson; 12 Jack Walton; 13 George Milton. Subs (all used): 14 Ryan Wright; 15 Makali Aizue; 16 Iafeta Palea'aesina; 17 Joe Pickets-O'Donnell.
Tries: Foggin-Johnston (13), Aizue (48), B Nicholson (59); **Goals:** Carr 3/3.
OLYMPIQUE: 1 Mark Kheirallah; 2 Tony Maurel; 3 Bastien Ader; 21 Gavin Marguerite; 5 Kuni Minga; 6 Johnathon Ford; 19 Etienne Ferret; 8 Clement Boyer; 14 Mourad Kriouache; 15 Maxime Puech; 11 Sebastien Planas; 12 Rhys Curran; 26 Constantine Mika. Subs (all used): 18 Tyla Hepi; 25 Kalausa Leha; 16 Bastien Canet; 17 Anthony Marion.
Tries: Minga (9), Curran (25, 54, 64), Ford (43), Hepi (62), Kheirallah (77); **Goals:** Kheirallah 5/7.
Rugby Leaguer & League Express Men of the Match: *Doncaster:* Brad Nicholson; *Olympique:* Johnathon Ford.
Penalty count: 10-5; **Half-time:** 6-12;
Referee: Callum Straw; **Attendance:** 573.

KEIGHLEY COUGARS 30 LONDON SKOLARS 10

COUGARS: 22 Ritchie Hawkyard; 2 Andy Gabriel; 4 Danny Lawton; 3 Rikki Sheriffe; 5 Paul White; 14 Adam Brook; 37 Will Milner; 8 Scott Law; 9 James Feather; 19 Matthew Bailey; 25 Darren Hawkyard; 23 Charlie Martin; 13 Ashley Lindsay. Subs (all used): 16 Jode Sheriffe; 17 John Oakes; 20 Aaron Ollett; 35 Ross Peltier.
Tries: Lawton (21), Brook (25), R Hawkyard (34), Peltier (52), Gabriel (56), Feather (77);
Goals: Brook 0/2, Lawton 3/4.
SKOLARS: 1 Andy Winfield; 2 Sam Nash; 3 Aaron Small; 4 Will Lovell; 5 James Hill; 6 Oscar Thomas; 7 Mike Bishay; 8 Toby Everett; 9 Ben Pointer; 10 Dave Williams; 11 Michael Worrincy; 12 Kazeem Fatouri; 13 Jy-mel Coleman. Subs (all used): 14 Billy Driver; 15 Ryan Chester; 16 Ben Gray; 17 Erjon Dollapi.
Tries: Hill (9, 64); **Goals:** O Thomas 1/3.
Rugby Leaguer & League Express Men of the Match: *Cougars:* Adam Brook; *Skolars:* James Hill.
Penalty count: 5-9; **Half-time:** 14-6;
Referee: Jamie Bloem; **Attendance:** 297.

ROCHDALE HORNETS 16 YORK CITY KNIGHTS 36

HORNETS: 1 Wayne English; 2 Jack Holmes; 3 Alex Trumper; 4 Mike Ratu; 5 Dale Bloomfield; 6 Steve Roper; 7 Danny Yates; 8 Jovili Taira; 9 Ben Moores; 10 Warren Thompson; 11 Josh Crowley; 12 Jono Smith; 13 James Tilley. Subs (all used): 14 James Dandy; 15 Matty Hadden; 16 Jordan Case; 17 Samir Tahraoui.
Tries: Smith (41), Moores (70), Case (72); **Goals:** Yates 2/3.
CITY KNIGHTS: 1 James Haynes; 2 Tom Saxton; 3 Brandon Westerman; 4 Tyler Craig; 5 Austin Buchanan; 6 Jon Presley; 7 Danny Nicklas; 8 Russ Spiers; 9 Pat Smith; 10 Jack Aldous; 11 Josh Tonks; 12 Ed Smith; 13 Mike Emmett. Subs (all used): 14 Kris Brining; 15 Mick Learmonth; 16 Andy Smith; 17 Brett Waller.
Tries: Waller (21), Haynes (37), Brining (39), Craig (55), Spiers (60), Emmett (67); **Goals:** Craig 6/7.
Rugby Leaguer & League Express Men of the Match: *Hornets:* Jovili Taira; *City Knights:* Kris Brining.
Penalty count: 7-12; **Half-time:** 0-18;
Referee: Jon Roberts; **Attendance:** 413.

BARROW RAIDERS 44 HUNSLET HAWKS 26

RAIDERS: 1 Ryan Fieldhouse; 31 Eze Harper; 5 Cameron Pitman; 16 Max Wiper; 23 Chris Fleming; 3 Chris Hankinson; 28 Jamie Dallimore; 8 Joe Bullock; 9 Nathan Mossop; 10 Oliver Wilkes; 4 Andy Litherland; 15 Bradd Crellin; 13 Martin Aspinwall. Subs (all used): 21 Dan Abram; 27 Matty Holmes; 32 Brad Brennan; 19 Anthony Bate.
Tries: Fleming (4, 8), Hankinson (12, 57), Wiper (19), Wilkes (44), Aspinwall (33, 67); **Goals:** Hankinson 6/8.
HAWKS: 1 Jimmy Watson; 36 Stewart Sanderson; 33 Kyran Johnson; 15 Mufaro Mvududu; 28 Richie Barnett; 6 Simon Brown; 7 Danny Ansell; 8 Michael Haley; 9 Jack Lee; 19 Matt Carbutt; 29 Daniel Williams; 3 Jake Normington; 22 Craig Robinson. Subs (all used): 14 George Flanagan; 37 Callum Casey; 32 Jack Coventry; 10 Lewis Reed.
Tries: Coventry (27), Barnett (37, 39), Flanagan (52), K Johnson (62); **Goals:** Brown 3/5.
Rugby Leaguer & League Express Men of the Match: *Raiders:* Martin Aspinwall; *Hawks:* Jimmy Watson.
Penalty count: 7-9; **Half-time:** 26-14;
Referee: Andrew Sweet; **Attendance:** 1,003.

ROUND 5

Saturday 20th August 2016

LONDON SKOLARS 4 BARROW RAIDERS 54

SKOLARS: 1 Oscar Thomas; 2 Sam Nash; 3 Aaron Small; 4 Lameck Juma; 5 James Hill; 6 Jy-mel Coleman; 7 Mike Bishay; 8 Erjon Dollapi; 9 Ben Pointer; 10 Dave Williams; 11 Kazeem Fatouri; 12 Will Lovell; 13 Louis Robinson. Subs (all used): 14 Billy Driver; 15 Toby Everett; 16 Michael Sykes; 17 Michael Worrincy.
Try: Juma (6); **Goals:** O Thomas 0/1.
Sin bin: Dollapi (19) - dissent; Lovell (21) - fighting; Fatouri (35) - high tackle.
RAIDERS: 1 Ryan Fieldhouse; 31 Eze Harper; 16 Max Wiper; 5 Cameron Pitman; 23 Chris Fleming; 3 Chris Hankinson; 28 Jamie Dallimore; 8 Joe Bullock; 29 Karl Ashall; 10 Oliver Wilkes; 27 Matty Holmes; 15 Bradd Crellin; 19 Anthony Bate. Subs (all used): 9 Nathan Mossop; 17 Andrew Dawson; 13 Martin Aspinwall; 32 Brad Brennan.
Tries: Mossop (35), Brennan (45, 72), Hankinson (48), Holmes (50), Pitman (57, 67), Harper (76), Ashall (80);
Goals: Hankinson 8/10, Wilkes 1/1.
Sin bin: Dallimore (21) - fighting.
Rugby Leaguer & League Express Men of the Match: *Skolars:* Aaron Small; *Raiders:* Nathan Mossop.
Penalty count: 2-13; **Half-time:** 4-8;
Referee: Andrew Sweet; **Attendance:** 227.

TOULOUSE OLYMPIQUE 46 ROCHDALE HORNETS 6

OLYMPIQUE: 1 Mark Kheirallah; 2 Tony Maurel; 3 Bastien Ader; 21 Gavin Marguerite; 5 Kuni Minga; 6 Johnathon Ford; 22 Danny Hulme; 8 Clement Boyer; 9 Kane Bentley; 10 Samy Masselot; 11 Sebastien Planas; 12 Rhys Curran; 26 Constantine Mika. Subs (all used): 14 Mourad Kriouache; 17 Anthony Marion; 18 Tyla Hepi; 25 Kalausa Leha.
Tries: Kheirallah (7), Minga (10, 53, 72), Maurel (37), Hulme (45, 59), Planas (64); **Goals:** Kheirallah 7/8.
HORNETS: 1 Jack Holmes; 2 Mike Ratu; 3 Jake Shoel; 4 Lewis Galbraith; 5 Dale Bloomfield; 6 Paul Crook; 7 Danny Yates; 8 Samir Tahraoui; 9 Ben Moores; 10 Warren Thompson; 11 Jono Smith; 12 Josh Crowley; 13 Jordan Case. Subs (all used): 14 Steve Roper; 15 Jovili Taira; 16 Matty Hadden; 17 Alex Trumper.
Try: Smith (34); **Goals:** Crook 1/1.
Sin bin: Taira (21) - interference; Galbraith (62) - dissent; Moores (70) - dissent.
Rugby Leaguer & League Express Men of the Match: *Olympique:* Kuni Minga; *Hornets:* Samir Tahraoui.
Penalty count: 7-7; **Half-time:** 16-6;
Referee: Jamie Bloem; **Attendance:** 1,572.

Sunday 21st August 2016

DONCASTER 26 KEIGHLEY COUGARS 24

DONCASTER: 1 Tom Carr; 2 David Foggin-Johnston; 3 Aaron Jones-Bishop; 4 Sam Doherty; 5 Louis Sheriff; 6 Jordan Howden; 7 Jordie Hedges; 8 Mark Castle; 9 Kyle Kesik; 10 Connor Scott; 11 Jack Walton; 12 Brad Nicholson; 13 George Milton. Subs (all used): 14 Kieran Cross; 15 Iafeta Palea'aesina; 16 Joe Pickets-O'Donnell; 17 Matty Welham.
Tries: B Nicholson (5), Sheriff (27), Castle (68), Hedges (71);
Goals: Carr 5/5.
COUGARS: 22 Ritchie Hawkyard; 2 Andy Gabriel; 4 Danny Lawton; 3 Rikki Sheriffe; 26 Vinny Finigan; 14 Adam Brook; 37 Will Milner; 8 Scott Law; 9 James Feather; 19 Matthew Bailey; 25 Darren Hawkyard; 23 Charlie Martin; 13 Ashley Lindsay. Subs (all used): 20 Aaron Ollett; 11 Josh Lynam; 16 Jode Sheriffe; 35 Ross Peltier.
Tries: Martin (11), Gabriel (19), R Hawkyard (37), Ollett (54);
Goals: Lawton 4/6.
Rugby Leaguer & League Express Men of the Match: *Doncaster:* Louis Sheriff; *Cougars:* Danny Lawton.
Penalty count: 8-8; **Half-time:** 12-18;
Referee: Greg Dolan; **Attendance:** 609.

YORK CITY KNIGHTS 12 HUNSLET HAWKS 33

CITY KNIGHTS: 1 James Haynes; 2 Austin Buchanan; 3 Brandon Westerman; 4 Tyler Craig; 5 Tom Saxton; 6 Jon Presley; 7 Danny Nicklas; 8 Russ Spiers; 9 Pat Smith; 10 Jack Aldous; 11 Josh Tonks; 12 Ed Smith; 13 Mike Emmett. Subs (all used): 14 Kris Brining; 15 Andy Smith; 16 Brett Waller; 17 Mick Learmonth.
Tries: Buchanan (3), Brining (53), Nicklas (64);
Goals: Craig 0/3.
Dismissal: Emmett (74) - use of the knees.
Sin bin: Saxton (75) - dissent.
On report: Buchanan (78) - alleged dangerous contact.
HAWKS: 1 Jimmy Watson; 36 Stewart Sanderson; 33 Kyran Johnson; 15 Mufaro Mvududu; 28 Richie Barnett; 20 Danny Thomas; 7 Danny Ansell; 8 Michael Haley; 9 Jack Lee; 19 Matt Carbutt; 37 Callum Casey; 3 Jake Normington; 29 Daniel Williams. Subs (all used): 14 George Flanagan; 22 Craig Robinson; 32 Jack Coventry; - Jose Kenga.
Tries: Ansell (14), Mvududu (21), Watson (30), Flanagan (39), Lee (74); **Goals:** Ansell 6/6;
Field goal: Ansell (80).
Rugby Leaguer & League Express Men of the Match: *City Knights:* Kris Brining; *Hawks:* Danny Ansell.
Penalty count: 8-15; **Half-time:** 4-24;
Referee: John McMullen; **Attendance:** 702.

ROUND 3

Friday 26th August 2016

LONDON SKOLARS 14 TOULOUSE OLYMPIQUE 58

SKOLARS: 1 Oscar Thomas; 2 Sam Nash; 3 Aaron Small; 4 Lameck Juma; 5 John Paxton; 6 Jy-mel Coleman; 7 Mike Bishay; 8 Erjon Dollapi; 9 Sam Druce; 10 Dave Williams; 11 Eddie Mbaraga; 12 Will Lovell; 13 Kazeem Fatouri. Subs (all used): 14 Billy Driver; 15 Toby Everett; 16 Louis Robinson; 17 Michael Worrincy.
Tries: Jy-mel Coleman (10), Juma (31), Paxton (71);
Goals: O Thomas 1/3.
OLYMPIQUE: 1 Mark Kheirallah; 2 Tony Maurel; 3 Bastien Ader; 21 Gavin Marguerite; 5 Kuni Minga; 6 Johnathon Ford; 19 Etienne Ferret; 15 Maxime Puech; 17 Anthony Marion; 10 Samy Masselot; 11 Sebastien Planas; 8 Clement Boyer; 26 Constantine Mika. Subs (all used): 18 Tyla Hepi; 25 Kalausa Leha; 24 Justin Sangare; 20 Christopher Denis.
Tries: Marguerite (15, 56), Kheirallah (24, 35, 44, 61), Minga (27, 76), Ford (42), Maurel (50), Mika (67);
Goals: Kheirallah 7/11.
Rugby Leaguer & League Express Men of the Match: *Skolars:* Erjon Dollapi; *Olympique:* Mark Kheirallah.
Penalty count: 7-6; **Half-time:** 10-22;
Referee: Robert Hicks; **Attendance:** 974.

ROUND 6

Saturday 3rd September 2016

HUNSLET HAWKS 12 TOULOUSE OLYMPIQUE 16

HAWKS: 1 Jimmy Watson; 36 Stewart Sanderson; 33 Kyran Johnson; 15 Mufaro Mvududu; 28 Richie Barnett; 6 Simon Brown; 7 Danny Ansell; 8 Michael Haley; 9 Jack Lee; 10 Lewis Reed; 37 Callum Casey; 3 Jake Normington; 29 Daniel Williams. Subs (all used): 14 George Flanagan; 19 Matt Carbutt; - Jose Kenga; 32 Jack Coventry.
Tries: Barnett (9), Flanagan (44); **Goals:** Brown 2/2.
OLYMPIQUE: 1 Mark Kheirallah; 2 Tony Maurel; 3 Bastien Ader; 21 Gavin Marguerite; 5 Kuni Minga; 6 Johnathon Ford; 22 Danny Hulme; 8 Clement Boyer; 17 Anthony Marion; 10 Samy Masselot; 11 Sebastien Planas; 23 Cedric Mazars; 26 Constantine Mika. Subs (all used): 14 Mourad Kriouache; 4 Gregory White; 24 Justin Sangare; 18 Tyla Hepi.
Tries: Minga (15), Maurel (38), Hulme (78);
Goals: Kheirallah 2/3.
Rugby Leaguer & League Express Men of the Match: *Hawks:* Simon Brown; *Olympique:* Mark Kheirallah.
Penalty count: 5-8; **Half-time:** 6-10;
Referee: Scott Mikalauskas; **Attendance:** 379.

Sunday 4th September 2016

ROCHDALE HORNETS 38 DONCASTER 22

HORNETS: 1 Chris Riley; 2 Jack Holmes; 3 Dave Cookson; 4 Lewis Galbraith; 5 Corey Lee; 6 Paul Crook; 7 Danny Yates; 8 Samir Tahraoui; 9 Ben Moores; 10 Warren Thompson; 11 Josh Crowley; 12 Jono Smith; 13 Jordan Case. Subs (all used): 14 Ryan Maneely; 15 Matty Hadden; 16 Jovili Taira; 17 James Tilley.
Tries: D Cookson (1, 35), Riley (40), Galbraith (47), Tahraoui (56), Moores (63), Crook (80); **Goals:** Crook 5/7.
DONCASTER: 1 Tom Carr; 2 David Foggin-Johnston; 3 Aaron Jones-Bishop; 4 Sam Doherty; 5 Louis Sheriff; 6 Jordan Howden; 7 Jordie Hedges; 8 Brad Nicholson; 9 Kyle Kesik; 10 Connor Scott; 11 Mason Tonks; 12 Jack Walton; 13 George Milton. Subs (all used): 14 Ryan Wright; 15 Matty Welham; 16 Mark Castle; 17 Joe Pickets-O'Donnell.
Tries: Foggin-Johnston (15), Sheriff (18), Jones-Bishop (25, 79); **Goals:** Carr 3/4.
Rugby Leaguer & League Express Men of the Match: *Hornets:* Lewis Galbraith; *Doncaster:* Aaron Jones-Bishop.
Penalty count: 11-10; **Half-time:** 16-16;
Referee: Tom Grant; **Attendance:** 392.

YORK CITY KNIGHTS 30 LONDON SKOLARS 4

CITY KNIGHTS: 1 James Haynes; 2 Austin Buchanan; 3 Tyler Craig; 4 Ed Smith; 5 Tom Saxton; 6 Jon Presley; 7 Danny Nicklas; 8 Mick Learmonth; 9 Kris Brining; 10 Jack Aldous; 11 Josh Tonks; 12 Brandon Westerman; 13 Mike Emmett. Subs (all used): 14 Harry Carter; 15 Mark Applegarth; 16 Brett Waller; 17 Russ Spiers.
Tries: E Smith (21), Nicklas (27), Westerman (47, 68), Waller (73); **Goals:** Craig 5/5.
SKOLARS: 1 Oscar Thomas; 2 Sam Nash; 3 Aaron Small; 4 Lameck Juma; 5 James Hill; 6 Jy-mel Coleman; 7 Charlie Lawrence; 8 Erjon Dollapi; 9 Mike Bishay; 10 Dave Williams; 11 Kazeem Fatouri; 12 Eddie Mbaraga; 13 Louis Robinson. Subs (all used): 14 Billy Driver; 15 Ben Gray; 16 Michael Sykes; 17 Sam Druce.
Try: Hill (78); **Goals:** O Thomas 0/1.

Rugby Leaguer & League Express Men of the Match:
City Knights: Brandon Westerman; *Skolars:* Eddie Mbaraga.
Penalty count: 11-7; **Half-time:** 12-0;
Referee: Greg Dolan; **Attendance:** 448.

BARROW RAIDERS 26 KEIGHLEY COUGARS 18

RAIDERS: 1 Ryan Fieldhouse; 31 Eze Harper; 5 Cameron Pitman; 16 Max Wiper; 23 Chris Fleming; 3 Chris Hankinson; 28 Jamie Dallimore; 8 Joe Bullock; 29 Karl Ashall; 10 Oliver Wilkes; 11 Liam Harrison; 4 Andy Litherland; 13 Martin Aspinwall. Subs (all used): 9 Nathan Mossop; 17 Andrew Dawson; 32 Brad Brennan; 19 Anthony Bate.
Tries: Harper (3), Harrison (21), Fieldhouse (30), Bate (65);
Goals: Hankinson 5/5.
COUGARS: 22 Ritchie Hawkyard; 2 Andy Gabriel; 4 Danny Lawton; 3 Rikki Sheriffe; 5 Paul White; 14 Adam Brook; 37 Will Milner; 12 Brendan Rawlins; 9 James Feather; 19 Matthew Bailey; 11 Josh Lynam; 23 Charlie Martin; 13 Ashley Lindsay. Subs (all used): 20 Aaron Ollett; 17 John Oakes; 16 Jode Sheriffe; 35 Ross Peltier.
Tries: R Hawkyard (48), Milner (76), Feather (80);
Goals: Lawton 3/3.
Rugby Leaguer & League Express Men of the Match:
Raiders: Andy Litherland; *Cougars:* James Feather.
Penalty count: 6-13; **Half-time:** 18-0;
Referee: Liam Moore; **Attendance:** 1,173.

ROUND 1

Thursday 8th September 2016

YORK CITY KNIGHTS 28 DONCASTER 36

CITY KNIGHTS: 1 James Haynes; 2 Ben Dent; 3 Ed Smith; 4 Tyler Craig; 5 Tom Saxton; 6 Jon Presley; 7 Danny Nicklas; 8 Andy Smith; 9 Kris Brining; 10 Jack Aldous; 11 Josh Tonks; 12 Brandon Westerman; 13 Mike Emmett. Subs (all used): 14 Harry Carter; 15 Russ Spiers; 16 Brett Waller; 17 Brad Hey.
Tries: Aldous (64), Brining (69), Nicklas (72), Haynes (74), A Smith (79); **Goals:** Craig 4/5.
DONCASTER: 1 Tom Carr; 2 David Foggin-Johnston; 3 Aaron Jones-Bishop; 4 Sam Doherty; 5 Louis Sheriff; 6 Jordan Howden; 7 Jordie Hedges; 8 Zac Braham; 9 Kyle Kesik; 10 Connor Scott; 11 Brad Nicholson; 12 Jack Walton; 13 George Milton. Subs (all used): 14 Ryan Wright; 15 Makali Aizue; 16 Iafeta Palea'aesina; 17 Mark Castle.
Tries: Scott (4), Doherty (10,15), Palea'aesina (26), B Nicholson (45), Howden (59, 80); **Goals:** Carr 4/7.
Rugby Leaguer & League Express Men of the Match:
City Knights: Kris Brining; *Doncaster:* Jordan Howden.
Penalty count: 8-5; **Half-time:** 0-20;
Referee: Andrew Sweet; **Attendance:** 540.

ROUND 7

Saturday 10th September 2016

TOULOUSE OLYMPIQUE 44 BARROW RAIDERS 22

OLYMPIQUE: 1 Mark Kheirallah; 2 Tony Maurel; 3 Bastien Ader; 4 Gregory White; 5 Kuni Minga; 6 Johnathon Ford; 22 Danny Hulme; 15 Maxime Puech; 9 Kane Bentley; 16 Bastien Canet; 11 Sebastien Planas; 8 Clement Boyer; 17 Anthony Marion. Subs (all used): 14 Mourad Kriouache; 18 Tyla Hepi; 26 Constantine Mika; 25 Kalausa Leha.
Tries: K Bentley (3), White (5), Minga (11), Boyer (21), Hulme (30), Mika (55, 64), Canet (77);
Goals: Kheirallah 6/8.
RAIDERS: 30 Luke Cresswell; 31 Eze Harper; 16 Max Wiper; 5 Cameron Pitman; 23 Chris Fleming; 3 Chris Hankinson; 28 Jamie Dallimore; 8 Joe Bullock; 29 Karl Ashall; 10 Oliver Wilkes; 11 Liam Harrison; 15 Bradd Crellin; 19 Anthony Bate. Subs (all used): 9 Nathan Mossop; 17 Andrew Dawson; 18 James Duerden; 27 Matty Holmes.
Tries: Harper (30), Fleming (40), Harrison (44), Pitman (64); **Goals:** Hankinson 3/4.
Rugby Leaguer & League Express Men of the Match:
Olympique: Kane Bentley; *Raiders:* Oliver Wilkes.
Penalty count: 10-9; **Half-time:** 28-12;
Referee: Chris Kendall; **Attendance:** 1,161.

Sunday 11th September 2016

DONCASTER 34 LONDON SKOLARS 30

DONCASTER: 1 Tom Carr; 2 David Foggin-Johnston; 3 Sam Doherty; 4 Jason Tali; 5 Louis Sheriff; 6 Jordan Howden; 7 Jordie Hedges; 8 Zac Braham; 9 Kyle Kesik; 10 Connor Scott; 11 Brad Nicholson; 12 Aaron Jones-Bishop; 13 George Milton. Subs (all used): 14 Kieran Cross; 15 Makali Aizue; 16 Mark Castle; 17 Jack Walton.
Tries: Sheriff (8), Doherty (14), Scott (17), Kesik (30), Foggin-Johnston (55), Howden (64); **Goals:** Carr 5/6.

SKOLARS: 1 Oscar Thomas; 2 James Hill; 3 Aaron Small; 4 Lameck Juma; 5 Andy Winfield; 6 Jy-mel Coleman; 7 Charlie Lawrence; 8 Erjon Dollapi; 9 Mike Bishay; 10 Dave Williams; 11 Eddie Mbaraga; 12 Will Lovell; 13 Louis Robinson. Subs (all used): 14 Ben Pointer; 15 Ben Gray; 16 Michael Sykes; 17 Kazeem Fatouri.
Tries: Robinson (3), Small (37), Mbaraga (48, 61), Hill (70), Juma (78);
Goals: O Thomas 3/5, Jy-mel Coleman 0/1.
Sin bin: Robinson (63) - holding down.
Rugby Leaguer & League Express Men of the Match:
Doncaster: Jordan Howden; *Skolars:* Aaron Small.
Penalty count: 11-7; **Half-time:** 24-12;
Referee: John McMullen; **Attendance:** 587.

KEIGHLEY COUGARS 50 YORK CITY KNIGHTS 8

COUGARS: 22 Ritchie Hawkyard; 2 Andy Gabriel; 4 Danny Lawton; 29 Hamish Barnes; 5 Paul White; 37 Will Milner; 7 Paul Handforth; 8 Scott Law; 9 James Feather; 15 Neil Cherryholme; 25 Darren Hawkyard; 12 Brendan Rawlins; 13 Ashley Lindsay. Subs (all used): 16 Jode Sheriffe; 17 John Oakes; 20 Aaron Ollett; 35 Ross Peltier.
Tries: Lawton (2, 35, 60), Ollett (26), Milner (38), R Hawkyard (53, 75), Handforth (77), White (80);
Goals: Lawton 5/6, Lindsay 1/1, White 1/1, Cherryholme 0/1.
CITY KNIGHTS: 1 Ben Dent; 2 Tom Saxton; 3 Tyler Craig; 4 Andy Smith; 5 Adam Dent; 6 Richard Wilkinson; 7 Danny Nicklas; 8 Mick Learmonth; 9 Kris Brining; 10 Mike Emmett; 11 Brad Hey; 12 Ed Smith; 13 Pat Smith. Subs (all used): 14 Jack Aldous; 15 Harry Carter; 16 Jack Anderson; 17 Josh Tonks.
Tries: Saxton (14), Aldous (29); **Goals:** Craig 0/2.
Rugby Leaguer & League Express Men of the Match:
Cougars: Danny Lawton; *City Knights:* Pat Smith.
Penalty count: 3-5; **Half-time:** 24-8;
Referee: Callum Straw; **Attendance:** 658.

ROCHDALE HORNETS 34 HUNSLET HAWKS 18

HORNETS: 1 Chris Riley; 2 Jack Holmes; 3 Dave Cookson; 4 Lewis Galbraith; 5 Dale Bloomfield; 6 Paul Crook; 7 Danny Yates; 8 Samir Tahraoui; 9 Ryan Maneely; 10 Warren Thompson; 11 Josh Crowley; 12 Jono Smith; 13 Jordan Case. Subs (all used): 14 Steve Roper; 15 Matty Hadden; 16 Jovili Taira; 17 James Tilley.
Tries: D Cookson (2, 42), Maneely (15), Riley (25, 67), Tahraoui (61), Galbraith (72); **Goals:** Crook 3/7, Roper 0/1.
Sin bin: Tahraoui (22) - fighting;
Galbraith (30) - fighting; Taira (33) - punching.
HAWKS: 1 Jimmy Watson; 36 Stewart Sanderson; 33 Kyran Johnson; 37 Callum Casey; 28 Richie Barnett; 6 Simon Brown; 7 Danny Ansell; 8 Michael Haley; 9 Jack Lee; 10 Lewis Reid; 29 Daniel Williams; 3 Jake Normington; 19 Matt Carbutt. Subs (all used): 14 George Flanagan; 22 Craig Robinson; 32 Jack Coventry; - Jose Kenga.
Tries: Ansell (45, 79), Lee (52), Barnett (59);
Goals: Brown 1/4.
Sin bin: Williams (22) - fighting; Carbutt (30) - fighting.
Rugby Leaguer & League Express Men of the Match:
Hornets: Chris Riley; *Hawks:* Danny Ansell.
Penalty count: 7-11; **Half-time:** 16-0;
Referee: Jon Roberts; **Attendance:** 690.

PROMOTION FINAL

Saturday 17th September 2016

TOULOUSE OLYMPIQUE 22 ROCHDALE HORNETS 24

OLYMPIQUE: 1 Mark Kheirallah; 2 Tony Maurel; 3 Bastien Ader; 4 Gregory White; 5 Kuni Minga; 6 Johnathon Ford; 22 Danny Hulme; 8 Clement Boyer; 9 Kane Bentley; 16 Bastien Canet; 11 Sebastien Planas; 12 Rhys Curran; 26 Constantine Mika. Subs (all used): 14 Mourad Kriouache; 15 Maxime Puech; 17 Anthony Marion; 18 Tyla Hepi.
Tries: Canet (11), Curran (15), White (17), Ader (79);
Goals: Kheirallah 3/4.
Sin bin: Kriouache (60) - dangerous challenge.
HORNETS: 1 Chris Riley; 2 Jack Holmes; 3 Dave Cookson; 4 Lewis Galbraith; 5 Dale Bloomfield; 6 Paul Crook; 7 Danny Yates; 8 Samir Tahraoui; 9 Ben Moores; 10 Warren Thompson; 11 Jono Smith; 12 Josh Crowley; 13 James Tilley. Subs (all used): 14 Ryan Maneely; 15 Jovili Taira; 16 Matty Hadden; 17 Mike Ratu.
Tries: Holmes (21), Galbraith (50), D Cookson (72), Riley (74); **Goals:** Crook 4/5.
Sin bin: Smith (46) - dissent.
Rugby Leaguer & League Express Men of the Match:
Olympique: Kane Bentley; *Hornets:* Paul Crook.
Penalty count: 15-13; **Half-time:** 16-8;
Referee: Tom Crashley; **Attendance:** 3,513.

SEMI-FINALS

Saturday 24th September 2016

TOULOUSE OLYMPIQUE 62 YORK CITY KNIGHTS 10

OLYMPIQUE: 1 Mark Kheirallah; 2 Tony Maurel; 21 Gavin Marguerite; 4 Gregory White; 5 Kuni Minga; 6 Johnathon Ford; 19 Etienne Ferret; 8 Clement Boyer; 9 Kane Bentley; 16 Bastien Canet; 11 Sebastien Planas; 12 Rhys Curran; 17 Anthony Marion. Subs (all used): 14 Mourad Kriouache; 18 Tyla Hepi; 10 Samy Masselot; 26 Constantine Mika.
Tries: Maurel (8, 59), K Bentley (10), Kheirallah (14, 67), Minga (37, 66), Ferret (50, 71), Marguerite (53, 76);
Goals: Kheirallah 9/11.
CITY KNIGHTS: 1 James Haynes; 2 Ben Dent; 3 Ed Smith; 4 Brad Hey; 5 Adam Dent; 6 Jon Presley; 7 Mark Applegarth; 8 Kris Brining; 9 Brett Waller; 10 Josh Tonks; 11 Brandon Westerman; 12 Mike Emmett. No Subs (only 12 players named).
Tries: E Smith (21), Brining (54);
Goals: Haynes 0/1, B Dent 1/1.
Rugby Leaguer & League Express Men of the Match:
Olympique: Gavin Marguerite; *City Knights:* Kris Brining.
Penalty count: 2-5; **Half-time:** 24-4;
Referee: Chris Kendall; **Attendance:** 400.

Sunday 25th September 2016

BARROW RAIDERS 46 DONCASTER 6

RAIDERS: 1 Ryan Fieldhouse; 31 Eze Harper; 5 Cameron Pitman; 16 Max Wiper; 23 Chris Fleming; 3 Chris Hankinson; 28 Jamie Dallimore; 8 Joe Bullock; 29 Karl Ashall; 10 Oliver Wilkes; 11 Liam Harrison; 26 Danny Morrow; 13 Martin Aspinwall. Subs (all used): 9 Nathan Mossop; 12 Dan Toal; 32 Brad Brennan; 19 Anthony Bate.
Tries: Wiper (4), Fleming (10, 62), Bate (31), D Toal (45, 50), Ashall (78), Fieldhouse (80);
Goals: Hankinson 6/8, Harrison 1/1.
DONCASTER: 1 Tom Carr; 2 David Foggin-Johnston; 3 Sam Doherty; 4 Jason Tali; 5 Louis Sheriff; 6 Jordan Howden; 7 Jordie Hedges; 8 Zac Braham; 9 Kyle Kesik; 10 Connor Scott; 11 Mason Tonks; 12 Brad Nicholson; 13 George Milton. Subs (all used): 14 Ryan Wright; 15 Mark Castle; 16 Iafeta Palea'aesina; 17 Makali Aizue.
Try: Kesik (18); **Goals:** Carr 1/1.
Sin bin: Kesik (61) - high tackle.
Rugby Leaguer & League Express Men of the Match:
Raiders: Chris Fleming; *Doncaster:* Tom Carr.
Penalty count: 11-8; **Half-time:** 18-6;
Referee: Tom Crashley; **Attendance:** 1,117.

PLAY-OFF FINAL

Saturday 1st October 2016

TOULOUSE OLYMPIQUE 32 BARROW RAIDERS 22

OLYMPIQUE: 1 Mark Kheirallah; 2 Tony Maurel; 21 Gavin Marguerite; 4 Gregory White; 5 Kuni Minga; 6 Johnathon Ford; 22 Danny Hulme; 8 Clement Boyer; 9 Kane Bentley; 16 Bastien Canet; 11 Sebastien Planas; 12 Rhys Curran; 17 Anthony Marion. Subs (all used): 14 Mourad Kriouache; 18 Tyla Hepi; 10 Samy Masselot; 26 Constantine Mika.
Tries: Maurel (38), Marguerite (48), Hulme (50), Minga (54), Kheirallah (60); **Goals:** Kheirallah 6/6.
RAIDERS: 1 Ryan Fieldhouse; 31 Eze Harper; 5 Cameron Pitman; 16 Max Wiper; 23 Chris Fleming; 3 Chris Hankinson; 28 Jamie Dallimore; 8 Joe Bullock; 29 Karl Ashall; 10 Oliver Wilkes; 11 Liam Harrison; 26 Danny Morrow; 13 Martin Aspinwall. Subs (all used): 9 Nathan Mossop; 12 Dan Toal; 17 Anthony Dawson; 19 Anthony Bate.
Tries: Harper (5), Fleming (69, 78), Fieldhouse (71);
Goals: Hankinson 3/4.
Sin bin: D Toal (32) - high tackle;
Fieldhouse (36) - professional foul.
Rugby Leaguer & League Express Men of the Match:
Olympique: Mark Kheirallah; *Raiders:* Martin Aspinwall.
Penalty count: 9-8; **Half-time:** 6-4;
Referee: Gareth Hewer; **Attendance:** 1,213.

266

LEAGUE 1 SHIELD 2016
Round by Round

League 1 Shield 2016 - Round by Round

ROUND 1

Saturday 23rd July 2016

NORTH WALES CRUSADERS 30 SOUTH WALES SCORPIONS 26

CRUSADERS: 1 Tommy Johnson; 2 Andrew Oakden; 3 Alex Thompson; 4 Earl Hurst; 5 Rob Massam; 6 Ryan Smith; 7 Andy Moulsdale; 8 Jonny Walker; 9 Lee Hudson; 10 Kenny Baker; 11 Luke Warburton; 12 Simon Atherton; 13 Billy Brickhill. Subs (all used): 14 Jack Hansen; 15 Matthew Haggarty; 16 Ryan Millington; 17 Jordan Andrade.
Tries: Thompson (3), Massam (35), Oakden (45), Hansen (58), Atherton (67), Smith (75);
Goals: Johnson 3/6.
SCORPIONS: 30 Jamie Murphy; - James Stringer; 22 Christiaan Roets; 15 Jordan Sheridan; 3 Kyle Scrivens; 7 Paul Emanuelli; 27 Courtney Davies; - Alex Davidson; 19 Kristian Baller; 14 Osian Phillips; 23 Barrie Phillips; 28 Sion Jones; 13 Chris Vitalini. Subs (all used): 24 Zak Williams; 9 Connor Farrer; - Jamie I'Anson; 20 Anthony Symons.
Tries: S Jones (15), Farrer (31, 42), Stringer (52);
Goals: Emanuelli 5/6.
Rugby Leaguer & League Express Men of the Match: *Crusaders:* Ryan Smith; *Scorpions:* Connor Farrer.
Penalty count: 14-12; **Half-time:** 8-14;
Referee: Brandon Robinson; **Attendance:** 343 *(at Hare Lane, Chester).*

COVENTRY BEARS 48 OXFORD 6

BEARS: 1 Charlie O'Mara; 2 Jonathan Milizewski; 3 Eddie Medforth; 4 Matt Reid; 5 Jason Bass; 6 Dan Price; 7 Joel James; 8 Alex Beddows; 9 Richard Hughes; 10 Jack Morrison; 11 Joe Batchelor; 12 Chris Barratt; 13 Grant Beecham. Subs (all used): 14 Jay Lobwein; 15 James Geurtjens; 16 Andy Unsworth; 17 Trae O'Sullivan.
Tries: O'Mara (9), Hughes (18, 42), Medforth (28, 63, 66), Reid (51), Beddows (57), Morrison (60); **Goals:** James 6/9.
Sin bin: Price (78) - fighting.
OXFORD: 1 Harvey Burnett; 2 Luke Gardiner; 3 Jordan Gill; 4 Curtis McDonald; 5 James Cryer; 6 Scott Fleming; 7 Nathan Kitson; 8 Ryan Backhouse; 9 Casey Canterbury; 10 Josh Scott; 11 Daniel Igbinedion; 12 Jordan Siddons; 13 Jack Pickles. Subs (all used): 14 Chris Cullimore; 15 Andrew Hoggins; 16 Charlie Greene; 17 Jack Smith.
Try: Canterbury (32); **Goals:** Fleming 1/1.
Sin bin: Smith (78) - fighting.
Rugby Leaguer & League Express Men of the Match: *Bears:* Eddie Medforth; *Oxford:* Casey Canterbury.
Penalty count: 6-10; **Half-time:** 16-6;
Referee: Nick Bennett; **Attendance:** 253.

Sunday 24th July 2016

NEWCASTLE THUNDER 50 GLOUCESTERSHIRE ALL GOLDS 24

THUNDER: 1 Tom Ruediger; 2 Zach Clark; 3 Joe Brown; 4 Derrell Olpherts; 5 Peter Fox; 6 Josh Kittrick; 7 Lewis Young; 8 Vincent Rennie; 9 Aaron Teroi; 10 Mikey Wood; 11 Harry Aldous; 12 Dan Parker; 13 Sam Luckley. Subs (all used): 14 Evan Simons; 15 Jason Payne; 16 James Fitzpatrick; 17 Ben Thorburn.
Tries: Z Clark (6, 56), Fox (15, 44), Olpherts (17), Simons (32, 53), Parker (48), Rennie (59);
Goals: Parker 7/9.
Sin bin: Teroi (4) - dangerous contact; Brown (76) - dissent.
ALL GOLDS: 1 Jack Uren; 2 Mo Agoro; 3 Lewis Reece; 4 Kadeem Williams; 5 Phil Cowburn; 6 Kieran Hyde; 7 Mick Govin; 8 Morgan Evans; 9 Steve Parry; 10 James Walter; 11 Lamont Bryan; 12 Joe McClean; 13 Harrison Elliott. Subs (all used): 14 Jimmy Rowland; 15 Emmerson Whittel; 16 Richard Jones; 17 Oliver Purslow.
Tries: Parry (10), Hyde (38, pen), Williams (64), Bryan (79);
Goals: Hyde 2/2, Rowland 2/2.
Sin bin: Hyde (55) - dissent.
Rugby Leaguer & League Express Men of the Match: *Thunder:* Zach Clark; *All Golds:* Steve Parry.
Penalty count: 6-8; **Half-time:** 20-12;
Referee: Andrew Bentham; **Attendance:** 482.

ROUND 2

Sunday 31st July 2016

HEMEL STAGS 18 NORTH WALES CRUSADERS 42

STAGS: 1 Mitch Vincent; 2 Harrison Brough; 3 Tuoyo Egodo; 4 Kameron Pearce-Paul; 5 Josh Spearing; 6 Ben Stead; 7 Brad Delaney; 8 Reece Williams; 9 Jono Burns; 10 Matt Ross; 11 Marcus Stock; 12 Brad Adams; 13 Kyal Greene. Subs (all used): 14 Barry-John Swindells; 15 Mike Stewart; 16 Dave O'Conner; 17 Dylan Readman.
Tries: Vincent (16), Stewart (40), Readman (47);
Goals: Stead 3/3.
Sin bin: Greene (66) - dangerous challenge.
CRUSADERS: 1 Tommy Johnson; 2 Rob Massam; 3 Earl Hurst; 4 Alex Thompson; 5 Andrew Oakden; 6 Ryan Smith; 7 Jack Hansen; 8 Jonny Walker; 9 Lee Hudson; 10 Kenny Baker; 11 Simon Atherton; 12 Stephen Wild; 13 Billy Brickhill. Subs (all used): 14 Matt Bradley; 15 Luke Warburton; 16 Jordan Andrade; 17 Tommy Holland.
Tries: Massam (6), Smith (23, 43), Andrade (36), Baker (51), Hansen (59), Thompson (72); **Goals:** Johnson 7/7.
Rugby Leaguer & League Express Men of the Match: *Stags:* Mitch Vincent; *Crusaders:* Simon Atherton.
Penalty count: 12-12; **Half-time:** 12-18;
Referee: Jon Roberts; **Attendance:** 147.

GLOUCESTERSHIRE ALL GOLDS 26 OXFORD 28

ALL GOLDS: 1 Brendon Newton; 2 Josh Allison; 3 Lewis Reece; 4 Brad Kislingbury; 5 Phil Cowburn; 6 Mick Govin; 7 Jimmy Rowland; 8 Morgan Evans; 9 Steve Parry; 10 James Walter; 11 Lamont Bryan; 12 Joe McClean; 13 Harrison Elliott. Subs (all used): 14 Luke Stephens; 15 Emmerson Whittel; 16 Richard Jones; 17 Oliver Purslow.
Tries: Evans (19), McClean (34), Bryan (43), Kislingbury (53), Parry (71); **Goals:** Reece 1/2, Rowland 2/3.
On report: Bryan (76) - alleged dangerous challenge.
OXFORD: 1 Scott Fleming; 2 Luke Gardiner; 3 Marcus Brooker; 4 Harvey Burnett; 5 Josh Nathaniel; 6 Casey Canterbury; 7 Nathan Kitson; 8 Daniel Igbinedion; 9 Danny Allan; 10 Will Maher; 11 Charlie Greene; 12 Andrew Hoggins; 13 Jack Pickles. Subs (all used): 14 Chris Cullimore; 15 Ryan Backhouse; 16 Jordan Siddons; 17 Aaron Nicholson.
Tries: Hoggins (3), Greene (24), Nathaniel (37), Fleming (46, 49), Kitson (59);
Goals: Kitson 1/4, Backhouse 1/2.
Rugby Leaguer & League Express Men of the Match: *All Golds:* Brad Kislingbury; *Oxford:* Nathan Kitson.
Penalty count: 7-6; **Half-time:** 10-14;
Referee: Callum Straw; **Attendance:** 105.

SOUTH WALES SCORPIONS 16 NEWCASTLE THUNDER 28

SCORPIONS: 15 Jordan Sheridan; 2 Ian Newbury; 3 Kyle Scrivens; 22 Christiaan Roets; - Rhys Gant; 27 Courtney Davies; 30 Jamie Murphy; - Jamie I'Anson; 9 Connor Farrer; - Alex Davidson; 20 Anthony Symons; 28 Sion Jones; 13 Chris Vitalini. Subs (all used): 14 Osian Phillips; 10 Izaak Duffy; 23 Barrie Phillips; 24 Zak Williams.
Tries: Farrer (57), Newbury (60, 70); **Goals:** Murphy 2/3.
THUNDER: 1 Tom Ruediger; 2 Zach Clark; 3 Derrell Olpherts; 4 Dan Parker; 5 Peter Fox; 6 Lewis Young; 7 Benn Hardcastle; 8 Vincent Rennie; 9 Evan Simons; 10 Mikey Wood; 11 Harry Aldous; 12 Rhys Clarke; 13 Sam Luckley. Subs (all used): 14 Ben Thorburn; 15 Corbyn Kilday; 16 Jason Payne; 17 Gioele Celerino.
Tries: Young (14), Fox (33), Simons (49), Olpherts (64, 67);
Goals: Hardcastle 4/5.
Sin bin: Simons (30) - high tackle.
Rugby Leaguer & League Express Men of the Match: *Scorpions:* Anthony Symons; *Thunder:* Evan Simons.
Penalty count: 6-5; **Half-time:** 0-10;
Referee: Nick Bennett; **Attendance:** 151.

ROUND 3

Saturday 6th August 2016

COVENTRY BEARS 14 SOUTH WALES SCORPIONS 18

BEARS: 1 Charlie O'Mara; 2 Jonathan Milizewski; 3 Eddie Medforth; 4 Matt Reid; 5 Jason Bass; 6 Joe Batchelor; 7 Joel James; 8 Alex Beddows; 9 Richard Hughes; 10 Jack Morrison; 11 Liam Thompson; 12 Chris Barratt; 13 Grant Beecham. Subs (all used): 14 Jay Lobwein; 15 James Geurtjens; 16 Andy Unsworth; 17 Trae O'Sullivan.
Tries: Bass (2), Batchelor (63); **Goals:** James 3/3.
SCORPIONS: 15 Jordan Sheridan; 2 Ian Newbury; 3 Kyle Scrivens; 22 Christiaan Roets; - James Stringer; 30 Jamie Murphy; 7 Paul Emanuelli; - Alex Davidson; 24 Zak Williams; - Jamie I'Anson; 28 Sion Jones; 20 Anthony Symons; 13 Chris Vitalini. Subs (all used): 14 Osian Phillips; 25 Billy Gaylor; - Jake Thomas; 21 Scott Gregory.
Tries: Newbury (13), Vitalini (50, 53); **Goals:** Emanuelli 3/3.
Rugby Leaguer & League Express Men of the Match: *Bears:* Joe Batchelor; *Scorpions:* Chris Vitalini.
Penalty count: 13-4; **Half-time:** 8-6;
Referee: Michael Woodhead; **Attendance:** 497.

Sunday 7th August 2016

OXFORD 46 HEMEL STAGS 10

OXFORD: 1 Scott Fleming; 2 Jordan Gill; 3 Harvey Burnett; 4 Marcus Brooker; 5 Josh Nathaniel; 6 Casey Canterbury; 7 Nathan Kitson; 8 Daniel Igbinedion; 9 Chris Cullimore; 10 Aaron Nicholson; 11 Curtis McDonald; 12 Jordan Siddons; 13 Danny Allan. Subs (all used): 14 Adam Flintham; 15 Adam Withington; 16 Charlie Greene; 17 Ryan Backhouse.
Tries: Siddons (12), Fleming (20, 71), Brooker (25), Kitson (38, 57, 76), Nathaniel (54), Flintham (61);
Goals: Kitson 5/9.
STAGS: 1 Mitch Vincent; 2 Harrison Brough; 3 Joe Barron; 4 Brad Adams; 5 Josh Spearing; 6 Ben Stead; 7 Brad Delaney; 8 Dominic Maloney; 9 Jono Burns; 10 Matt Ross; 11 Marcus Stock; 12 Kyal Greene; 13 Reece Williams. Subs (all used): 14 Malikhi Lloyd-Jones; 15 Dylan Readman; 16 Reece Trout; 17 Mike Stewart.
Tries: Lloyd-Jones (28), Brough (74); **Goals:** Stead 1/2.
Rugby Leaguer & League Express Men of the Match: *Oxford:* Nathan Kitson; *Stags:* Malikhi Lloyd-Jones.
Penalty count: 11-11; **Half-time:** 20-6;
Referee: Brandon Robinson; **Attendance:** 103.

NEWCASTLE THUNDER 30 NORTH WALES CRUSADERS 14

THUNDER: 1 Tom Ruediger; 2 Zach Clark; 3 Joe Brown; 4 Derrell Olpherts; 5 Peter Fox; 6 Lewis Young; 7 Benn Hardcastle; 8 Vincent Rennie; 9 Aaron Teroi; 10 Corbyn Kilday; 11 Harry Aldous; 12 Dan Parker; 13 Rhys Clarke. Subs (all used): 14 Evan Simons; 15 Sam Luckley; 16 Jason Payne; 17 Ben Thorburn.
Tries: Fox (5), Ruediger (10), Rennie (13), Olpherts (17), Simons (40), Thorburn (67); **Goals:** Hardcastle 3/6.
Sin bin: Parker (28) - fighting.
CRUSADERS: 1 Tommy Johnson; 2 Andrew Oakden; 3 Luke Warburton; 4 Earl Hurst; 5 Rob Massam; 6 Ryan Smith; 7 Jack Hansen; 8 Jonny Walker; 9 Matt Wilkinson; 10 Kenny Baker; 11 Simon Atherton; 12 Stephen Wild; 13 Billy Brickhill. Subs (all used): 14 Matt Bradley; 15 Mark Thomas; 16 Liam Bent; 17 Jordan Andrade.
Tries: Oakden (63), Wilkinson (73), Massam (76);
Goals: Johnson 1/3.
Sin bin: Atherton (28) - fighting.
Rugby Leaguer & League Express Men of the Match: *Thunder:* Benn Hardcastle; *Crusaders:* Andrew Oakden.
Penalty count: 14-16; **Half-time:** 24-0;
Referee: Liam Moore; **Attendance:** 408.

ROUND 4

Saturday 13th August 2016

OXFORD 18 NEWCASTLE THUNDER 62

OXFORD: 1 Scott Fleming; 2 Josh Nathaniel; 3 Marcus Brooker; 4 Harvey Burnett; 5 Harry Griffith; 6 Casey Canterbury; 7 Danny Allan; 8 Daniel Igbinedion; 9 Chris Cullimore; 10 Aaron Nicholson; 11 Charlie Greene; 12 Curtis McDonald; 13 Jack Pickles. Subs (all used): 14 Adam Withington; 15 Ryan Backhouse; 16 Adam Flintham; 17 Andrew Hoggins.
Tries: Griffith (30), Nathaniel (50, 53), Nicholson (62);
Goals: Allan 1/4.
THUNDER: 1 Tom Ruediger; 2 Ali Blair; 3 Derrell Olpherts; 4 Joe Brown; 5 Peter Fox; 6 Josh Kittrick; 7 Benn Hardcastle; 8 Vincent Rennie; 9 Evan Simons; 10 Corbyn Kilday; 11 Harry Aldous; 12 Rhys Clarke; 13 Lee Paterson. Subs (all used): 14 Ben Thorburn; 15 Jason Payne; 16 Sam Luckley; 17 Dan Parker.
Tries: Blair (2, 65, 76), Simons (15, 45), Ruediger (20, 70), R Clarke (27), Payne (42), Thorburn (57), Olpherts (68);
Goals: Hardcastle 9/11.
Rugby Leaguer & League Express Men of the Match: *Oxford:* Aaron Nicholson; *Thunder:* Benn Hardcastle.
Penalty count: 4-7; **Half-time:** 4-22;
Referee: Warren Turley; **Attendance:** 121.

Sunday 14th August 2016

NORTH WALES CRUSADERS 28 COVENTRY BEARS 30

CRUSADERS: 1 Tommy Johnson; 2 Harry Aaronson; 3 Alex Thompson; 4 Earl Hurst; 5 Rob Massam; 6 Ryan Smith; 7 Jack Hansen; 8 Jonny Walker; 9 Lee Hudson; 10 Kenny Baker; 11 Luke Warburton; 12 Stephen Wild; 13 Billy Brickhill. Subs (all used): 14 Andy Moulsdale; 15 Mark Thomas; 16 Jordan Andrade; 17 Liam Bent.
Tries: Massam (9), Thompson (28), Wild (32), Smith (63), Aaronson (68); **Goals:** Johnson 4/5.
BEARS: 1 Jason Bass; 2 Jonathan Milizewski; 3 Eddie Medforth; 4 Matt Reid; 5 Jamahl Hunte; 6 Joe Batchelor; 7 Joel James; 8 Alex Beddows; 9 Richard Hughes; 10 Jack Morrison; 11 Liam Thompson; 12 Chris Barratt; 13 Grant Beecham. Subs (all used): 14 Jay Lobwein; 15 James Geurtjens; 16 Andy Unsworth; 17 Trae O'Sullivan.
Tries: Beecham (17), Batchelor (36), Lobwein (49), Hunte (56), Hughes (73); **Goals:** James 5/6.

Rugby Leaguer & League Express Men of the Match:
Crusaders: Stephen Wild; *Bears:* Jack Morrison.
Penalty count: 10-8; **Half-time:** 18-12;
Referee: John McMullen; **Attendance:** 297
(at Hare Lane, Chester).

GLOUCESTERSHIRE ALL GOLDS 74 HEMEL STAGS 18

ALL GOLDS: 1 Brendon Newton; 2 Jack Uren; 3 Josh Allison; 4 Brad Kislingbury; 5 Phil Cowburn; 6 Kieran Hyde; 7 Jimmy Rowland; 8 Oliver Purslow; 9 Steve Parry; 10 Harrison Elliott; 11 Emmerson Whittel; 12 Lewis Reece; 13 Joe McClean. Subs (all used): 14 Luke Stephens; 15 Kadeem Williams; 16 Morgan Evans; 17 James Walter.
Tries: Uren (5), Newton (9, 20, 31, 64), McClean (11), Rowland (34, 38), Williams (36), Cowburn (40, 52), Allison (43), Whittel (46); **Goals:** Hyde 11/13.
STAGS: 1 Mitch Vincent; 2 Harrison Brough; 3 Kyal Greene; 4 Tuoyo Egodo; 5 Josh Spearing; 6 Dylan Readman; 7 Ben Stead; 8 Matt Ross; 9 Jono Burns; 10 Aaron Hall; 11 Marcus Stock; 12 Reece Williams; 13 Malikhi Lloyd-Jones. Subs (all used): 14 Mike Stewart; 15 Dominic Maloney; 16 Liam O'Callaghan; 17 Reece Trout.
Tries: Stead (25), Williams (57), Vincent (67);
Goals: Stead 3/3.
Rugby Leaguer & League Express Men of the Match:
All Golds: Brendon Newton; *Stags:* Ben Stead.
Penalty count: 6-7; **Half-time:** 52-6;
Referee: Nick Bennett; **Attendance:** 101.

ROUND 5

Sunday 21st August 2016

HEMEL STAGS 10 NEWCASTLE THUNDER 66

STAGS: 1 Josh Spearing; 2 Paul Stewart-Beckett; 3 Harrison Brough; 4 Barry-John Swindells; 5 Tala Petelo; 6 Mitch Vincent; 7 Ben Stead; 8 Dominic Maloney; 9 Jono Burns; 10 Aaron Hall; 11 Dave O'Conner; 12 Reece Williams; 13 Malikhi Lloyd-Jones. Subs (all used): 14 Dylan Readman; 15 Liam O'Callaghan; 16 Mike Stewart; 17 Matt Ross.
Tries: Vincent (14, 75); **Goals:** Stead 1/2.
THUNDER: 1 Tom Ruediger; 2 Craig Robertson; 3 Derrell Olpherts; 4 Joe Brown; 5 Ali Blair; 6 Lewis Young; 7 Benn Hardcastle; 8 Vincent Rennie; 9 Ben Thorburn; 10 Corbyn Kilday; 11 Rhys Clarke; 12 Harry Aldous; 13 Lee Paterson. Subs (all used): 14 Paddy Hargreaves; 15 Gioele Celerino; 16 Sam Luckley; 17 Josh Stoker.
Tries: Blair (4), Young (6, 21, 70), Brown (26, 44), Thorburn (35), Celerino (37), Robertson (46), Aldous (54), R Clarke (57), Ruediger (63), Rennie (65);
Goals: Hardcastle 6/12, Paterson 1/1.
Rugby Leaguer & League Express Men of the Match:
Stags: Mitch Vincent; *Thunder:* Lewis Young.
Penalty count: 4-7; **Half-time:** 6-30;
Referee: Nick Bennett; **Attendance:** 112.

COVENTRY BEARS 33
GLOUCESTERSHIRE ALL GOLDS 20

BEARS: 1 Jason Bass; 2 Hayden Freeman; 3 Jonathan Milizewski; 4 Grant Beecham; 5 Jamahl Hunte; 6 Dan Price; 7 Joel James; 8 Alex Beddows; 9 Jay Lobwein; 10 Trae O'Sullivan; 11 Andy Unsworth; 12 Chris Barratt; 13 Jack Morrison. Subs (all used): 14 Harry Chapman; 15 James Geurtjens; 16 John Aldred; 17 Dylan Bale.
Tries: Freeman (2), Price (31, 75), Hunte (34), Lobwein (37), Bass (54); **Goals:** James 4/6;
Field goal: James (72).
ALL GOLDS: 1 Phil Cowburn; 2 Jack Uren; 3 Josh Allison; 4 Brad Kislingbury; 5 Kadeem Williams; 6 Jack Mitchell; 7 Kieran Hyde; 8 Oliver Purslow; 9 Steve Parry; 10 Harrison Elliott; 11 Emmerson Whittel; 12 Lewis Reece; 13 Joe McClean. Subs (all used): 14 Luke Stephens; 15 Richard Jones; 16 Morgan Evans; 17 James Walter.
Tries: Mitchell (16), Parry (44), Uren (59), Williams (66);
Goals: Hyde 2/3, Mitchell 0/1.
Rugby Leaguer & League Express Men of the Match:
Bears: Jay Lobwein; *All Golds:* Steve Parry.
Penalty count: 9-7; **Half-time:** 22-6;
Referee: Jon Roberts; **Attendance:** 392.

SOUTH WALES SCORPIONS 12 OXFORD 20

SCORPIONS: 30 Jamie Murphy; 2 Ian Newbury; 21 Scott Gregory; 22 Christiaan Roets; 3 Kyle Scrivens; 27 Courtney Davies; 7 Paul Emanuelli; - Alex Davidson; 9 Connor Farrer; 23 Barrie Phillips; 20 Anthony Symons; 28 Sion Jones; 13 Chris Vitalini. Subs (all used): 10 Izaak Duffy; 14 Osian Phillips; 19 Kristian Baller; 24 Zak Williams.
Tries: Vitalini (26), Roets (39); **Goals:** Emanuelli 2/3.
OXFORD: 1 Scott Fleming; 2 Errol Carter; 3 Harvey Burnett; 4 Marcus Brooker; 5 Luke Gardiner; 6 Nathan Kitson; 7 Casey Canterbury; 8 Daniel Igbinedion; 9 Chris Cullimore; 10 Aaron Nicholson; 11 Adam Withington; 12 Andrew Hoggins; 13 Danny Allan. Subs (all used): 14 Mark Hayes; 15 Harry Griffith; 16 Adam Flintham; 17 Daniel Jamieson.
Tries: Nicholson (14), Hoggins (72), Griffith (76), Kitson (80); **Goals:** Kitson 2/4.
Rugby Leaguer & League Express Men of the Match:
Scorpions: Christiaan Roets; *Oxford:* Nathan Kitson.
Penalty count: 11-11; **Half-time:** 10-4;
Referee: James Callaghan; **Attendance:** 410.

ROUND 6

Saturday 3rd September 2016

NORTH WALES CRUSADERS 18
GLOUCESTERSHIRE ALL GOLDS 4

CRUSADERS: 1 Tommy Johnson; 2 Adam Saunders; 3 Alex Thompson; 4 Earl Hurst; 5 Rob Massam; 6 Ryan Smith; 7 Jack Hansen; 8 Jonny Walker; 9 Lee Hudson; 10 Jordan Andrade; 11 Stephen Wild; 12 Luke Warburton; 13 Billy Brickhill. Subs (all used): 14 Matt Wilkinson; 15 Matt Davies; 16 Liam Bent; 17 Tommy Holland.
Tries: Massam (29), Thompson (39, 53), Hansen (78);
Goals: Johnson 1/3, Hansen 0/1.
ALL GOLDS: 1 Mick Govin; 2 Mo Agoro; 3 Josh Allison; 4 Brad Kislingbury; 5 Phil Cowburn; 6 Jack Mitchell; 7 Jimmy Rowland; 8 Oliver Purslow; 9 Steve Parry; 10 Harrison Elliott; 11 Lamont Bryan; 12 Joe McClean; 13 Emmerson Whittel. Subs (all used): 14 Richard Jones; 15 Kadeem Williams; 16 James Walter; 17 Morgan Evans.
Try: Parry (66); **Goals:** Rowland 0/1.
Rugby Leaguer & League Express Men of the Match:
Crusaders: Alex Thompson; *All Golds:* Steve Parry.
Penalty count: 4-6; **Half-time:** 8-0;
Referee: Matt Rossleigh; **Attendance:** 270
(at Queensway Stadium, Wrexham).

NEWCASTLE THUNDER 46 COVENTRY BEARS 10

THUNDER: 1 Tom Ruediger; 2 Zach Clark; 3 Ali Blair; 4 Joe Brown; 5 Peter Fox; 6 Lewis Young; 7 Benn Hardcastle; 8 Vincent Rennie; 9 Evan Simons; 10 Rhys Clarke; 11 Harry Aldous; 12 Dan Parker; 13 Lee Paterson. Subs (all used): 14 Aaron Teroi; 15 Jason Payne; 16 Sam Luckley; 17 Ben Thorburn.
Tries: Z Clark (8), Fox (10), Parker (14), Thorburn (35, 38), Blair (41), Teroi (50), Brown (57), Simons (74);
Goals: Hardcastle 5/8, Parker 0/1.
BEARS: 1 Charlie O'Mara; 2 Jason Bass; 3 Eddie Medforth; 4 Jonathan Milizewski; 5 Jamahl Hunte; 6 Dan Price; 7 Joel James; 8 Alex Beddows; 9 Jay Lobwein; 10 Trae O'Sullivan; 11 Grant Beecham; 12 Chris Barratt; 13 Jack Morrison. Subs (all used): 14 Richard Hughes; 15 James Geurtjens; 16 Joe Batchelor; 17 John Aldred.
Tries: Medforth (31), Morrison (66); **Goals:** James 1/2.
Sin bin: Hughes (53) - professional foul.
Rugby Leaguer & League Express Men of the Match:
Thunder: Lewis Young; *Bears:* Jamahl Hunte.
Penalty count: 11-6; **Half-time:** 24-6;
Referee: John McMullen; **Attendance:** 456.

Sunday 4th September 2016

SOUTH WALES SCORPIONS 8 HEMEL STAGS 16

SCORPIONS: 15 Jordan Sheridan; 2 Ian Newbury; 3 Kyle Scrivens; 22 Christiaan Roets; - Rhys Gant; 27 Courtney Davies; 7 Paul Emanuelli; - Alex Davidson; 9 Connor Farrer; 10 Izaak Duffy; 20 Anthony Symons; 28 Sion Jones; 13 Chris Vitalini. Subs (all used): 14 Osian Phillips; 23 Barrie Phillips; 24 Zak Williams; 19 Kristian Baller.
Tries: S Jones (18), Scrivens (32); **Goals:** Emanuelli 0/2.
STAGS: 1 Kameron Pearce-Paul; 2 Josh Spearing; 3 Reece Williams; 4 Barry-John Swindells; 5 Paul Stewart-Beckett; 6 Mitch Vincent; 7 Ben Stead; 8 Dominic Maloney; 9 Jono Burns; 10 Aaron Hall; 11 Mike Stewart; 12 Liam O'Callaghan; 13 Matt Ross. Subs (all used): 14 Dylan Readman; 15 Malikhi Lloyd-Jones; 16 Will O'Brien; 17 Dave O'Conner.
Tries: Stewart (54), Stewart-Beckett (59), Burns (74);
Goals: Stead 2/3.
Rugby Leaguer & League Express Men of the Match:
Scorpions: Christiaan Roets; *Stags:* Dominic Maloney.
Penalty count: 8-6; **Half-time:** 8-0;
Referee: Brandon Robinson; **Attendance:** 178
(at Glan-yr-Afon Park, Blackwood).

ROUND 7

Saturday 10th September 2016

HEMEL STAGS 12 COVENTRY BEARS 22

STAGS: 1 Kameron Pearce-Paul; 2 Mitch Vincent; 3 Barry-John Swindells; 4 Reece Williams; 5 Josh Spearing; 6 Kyal Greene; 7 Ben Stead; 8 Dominic Maloney; 9 Jono Burns; 10 Aaron Hall; 11 Marcus Stock; 12 Liam O'Callaghan; 13 Matt Ross. Subs (all used): 14 Dave O'Conner; 15 Malikhi Lloyd-Jones; 16 Mike Stewart; 17 Dylan Readman.
Tries: Stead (16), Burns (24); **Goals:** Stead 2/3.
BEARS: 1 Charlie O'Mara; 2 Hayden Freeman; 3 Jason Bass; 4 Jonathan Milizewski; 5 Jamahl Hunte; 6 Dan Price; 7 Joel James; 8 Alex Beddows; 9 Jay Lobwein; 10 Jack Morrison; 11 Joe Batchelor; 12 Chris Barratt; 13 Grant Beecham. Subs (all used, only three named): 14 Dylan Bale; 15 Trae O'Sullivan; 16 James Geurtjens.
Tries: Morrison (4), Milizewski (36), Hunte (66), Price (71);
Goals: James 3/4.
Rugby Leaguer & League Express Men of the Match:
Stags: Ben Stead; *Bears:* Jack Morrison.
Penalty count: 5-7; **Half-time:** 12-12;
Referee: Matt Rossleigh; **Attendance:** 307.

GLOUCESTERSHIRE ALL GOLDS 33
SOUTH WALES SCORPIONS 18

ALL GOLDS: 1 Kieran Hyde; 2 Mo Agoro; 3 Josh Allison; 4 Phil Cowburn; 5 Kadeem Williams; 6 Jack Mitchell; 7 Jimmy Rowland; 8 Oliver Purslow; 9 Steve Parry; 10 Harrison Elliott; 11 Emmerson Whittel; 12 Joe McClean; 13 Lamont Bryan. Subs (all used): 14 Mick Govin; 15 Richard Jones; 16 James Walter; 17 Harry Kidd.
Tries: Mitchell (5), Parry (20), Walter (27), Rowland (46), Cowburn (71), Allison (80); **Goals:** Hyde 4/6;
Field goal: Rowland (68).
Dismissal: Govin (57) - fighting.
SCORPIONS: 15 Jordan Sheridan; 2 Ian Newbury; 3 Kyle Scrivens; 21 Scott Gregory; - Rhys Gant; 27 Courtney Davies; 7 Paul Emanuelli; 14 Osian Phillips; 9 Connor Farrer; 10 Izaak Duffy; 28 Sion Jones; 22 Christiaan Roets; 13 Chris Vitalini. Subs (all used): 19 Kristian Baller; 20 Anthony Symons; 23 Barrie Phillips; 24 Zak Williams.
Tries: O Phillips (32), Newbury (49), Duffy (58);
Goals: Emanuelli 3/3.
Dismissal: Farrer (57) - fighting.
Rugby Leaguer & League Express Men of the Match:
All Golds: Jimmy Rowland; *Scorpions:* Osian Phillips.
Penalty count: 10-10; **Half-time:** 18-6;
Referee: Brandon Robinson; **Attendance:** 115.

Sunday 11th September 2016

OXFORD 6 NORTH WALES CRUSADERS 37

OXFORD: 1 Scott Fleming; 2 Josh Nathaniel; 3 Marcus Brooker; 4 Harvey Burnett; 5 Errol Carter; 6 Casey Canterbury; 7 Nathan Kitson; 8 Aaron Nicholson; 9 Chris Cullimore; 10 Mark Hayes; 11 Harry Griffith; 12 Curtis McDonald; 13 Danny Allan. Subs (all used): 14 Andrew Hoggins; 15 Daniel Igbinedion; 16 Jordan Siddons; 17 Adam Withington.
Try: Kitson (5); **Goals:** Kitson 1/1.
CRUSADERS: 1 Tommy Johnson; 2 Adam Saunders; 3 Alex Thompson; 4 Earl Hurst; 5 Rob Massam; 6 Ryan Smith; 7 Jack Hansen; 8 Jonny Walker; 9 Lee Hudson; 10 Tommy Holland; 11 Stephen Wild; 12 Simon Atherton; 13 Billy Brickhill. Subs (all used): 14 Matt Wilkinson; 15 Liam Bent; 16 Kenny Baker; 17 Mark Thomas.
Tries: Holland (5), Massam (28, 36, 71), Atherton (48), Baker (60), Thompson (73); **Goals:** Johnson 4/7;
Field goal: Smith (80).
Rugby Leaguer & League Express Men of the Match:
Oxford: Nathan Kitson; *Crusaders:* Rob Massam.
Penalty count: 9-10; **Half-time:** 6-16;
Referee: Greg Dolan; **Attendance:** 120.

FINAL

Sunday 18th September 2016

NEWCASTLE THUNDER 31
NORTH WALES CRUSADERS 26

THUNDER: 1 Tom Ruediger; 2 Ali Blair; 3 Dan Parker; 4 Joe Brown; 5 Peter Fox; 6 Lewis Young; 7 Benn Hardcastle; 8 Vincent Rennie; 9 Evan Simons; 10 Corbyn Kilday; 11 Harry Aldous; 12 Rhys Clarke; 13 Lee Paterson. Subs (all used): 14 Aaron Teroi; 15 Jason Payne; 16 Sam Luckley; 17 Josh Stoker.
Tries: Fox (10, 14), Parker (11), Ruediger (20), R Clarke (53);
Goals: Hardcastle 5/5; **Field goal:** Hardcastle (77).
CRUSADERS: 1 Tommy Johnson; 2 Andrew Oakden; 3 Simon Atherton; 4 Alex Thompson; 5 Rob Massam; 6 Ryan Smith; 7 Jack Hansen; 8 Jonny Walker; 9 Lee Hudson; 10 Tommy Holland; 11 Luke Warburton; 12 Stephen Wild; 13 Billy Brickhill. Subs (all used): 14 Andy Moulsdale; 15 Liam Bent; 16 Jordan Andrade; 17 Kenny Baker.
Tries: Hansen (38), Massam (46), Oakden (56), Smith (61), Walker (70); **Goals:** Johnson 3/5.
Rugby Leaguer & League Express Men of the Match:
Thunder: Benn Hardcastle; *Crusaders:* Ryan Smith.
Penalty count: 6-7; **Half-time:** 24-6;
Referee: Jon Roberts; **Attendance:** 300.

iPRO Sport Cup 2016
Round by Round

ROUND 1

Saturday 20th February 2016

WATH BROW HORNETS 4 KEIGHLEY COUGARS 10

HORNETS: 1 Karl Dixon; 2 Luke Davidson; 3 Adam Ramsden; 4 Peter Caddy; 5 Conner Molyneaux; 6 Fran King; 7 Dean Rooney; 8 Richard Huby; 9 Cole Walker-Taylor; 10 Charlie Tomlinson; 11 Callum Farrer; 12 Matt Huby; 13 Mark Watson. Subs (all used): 14 Owen McCartney; 15 Rhys Pritchard; 16 James Dixon; 17 Paul Murphy.
Try: Caddy (73); **Goals:** Walker-Taylor 0/1.
COUGARS: 22 Ritchie Hawkyard; 2 Andy Gabriel; 23 Charlie Martin; 29 Hamish Barnes; 5 Paul White; 14 Adam Brook; 7 Paul Handforth; 8 Scott Law; 9 James Feather; 12 Brendan Rawlins; 11 Josh Lynam; 17 John Oakes; 20 Aaron Ollett. Subs (all used): 15 Neil Cherryholme; 10 Tyler Dickinson; 19 Matthew Bailey; 18 Sonny Esslemont.
Tries: Feather (24), Law (59); **Goals:** Brook 1/2.
Rugby Leaguer & League Express Men of the Match:
Hornets: Charlie Tomlinson; *Cougars:* Paul Handforth.
Penalty count: 7-6; **Half-time:** 0-4;
Referee: Callum Straw; **Attendance:** 300.

LONDON SKOLARS 44 SOUTH WALES SCORPIONS 6

SKOLARS: 1 Alex Anthony; 2 Sam Nash; 3 Aaron Small; 4 Joe Price; 5 Elliot Kear; 6 Jermaine Coleman; 7 Charlie Lawrence; 8 Michael Sykes; 9 Mike Bishay; 10 Toby Everett; 11 Dave Williams; 12 Will Lovell; 13 Michael Worricy. Subs (all used): 14 Ben Pointer; 15 Erjon Dollapi; 16 Jon Magrin; 17 Eddie Mbaraga.
Tries: Kear (17, 52), Lawrence (34), Dollapi (38), Anthony (44), Mbaraga (50), Small (59), Pointer (63), Nash (71); **Goals:** Lawrence 4/9.
SCORPIONS: 15 Jordan Sheridan; 5 Dai Evans; 3 Kyle Scrivens; 4 Yannic Parker; 1 Chris Leyshon; 6 Kristian Hawkes; 7 Paul Emanuelli; 8 Chris Davies; 9 Connor Farrer; 10 Izaak Duffy; 20 Anthony Symons; 17 Mike Connor; 13 Chris Vitalini. Subs (all used): 16 Dafydd Hellard; 19 Kristian Baller; 14 Osian Phillips; 21 Scott Gregory.
Try: Farrer (12); **Goals:** Emanuelli 1/1.
Rugby Leaguer & League Express Men of the Match:
Skolars: Ben Pointer; *Scorpions:* Connor Farrer.
Penalty count: 7-5; **Half-time:** 16-6;
Referee: Jack Smith; **Attendance:** 100.

NEWCASTLE THUNDER 36 LEIGH MINERS RANGERS 12

THUNDER: 1 Tom Ruediger; 2 Joe Brown; 3 Derrell Olpherts; 4 Dan Parker; 5 Peter Fox; 6 Aaron Teroi; 7 Benn Hardcastle; 8 Vincent Rennie; 9 Craig Cook; 10 Rhys Clarke; 11 Lee Paterson; 12 Harry Aldous; 13 Sam Luckley. Subs (all used): 14 Evan Simons; 15 Francis Welsh; 16 Josh Kittrick; 17 Craig Boot.
Tries: Ruediger (17), Aldous (24), Welsh (35), Simons (39, 74), Olpherts (45), Rennie (52);
Goals: Hardcastle 4/7.
MINERS RANGERS: 1 Andrew Groves; 2 Gareth Pain; 3 Connor Ratcliffe; 4 Lee Gittins; 5 Harry Gagen; 6 Tom Farrimond; 7 Scott O'Brien; 8 Martin Gray; 9 Jordan Hill; 10 Darryl Kay; 11 Tommy Parkinson; 12 Mick O'Boyle; 13 Mark Nicholson. Subs (all used): 14 Gary Gittins; 15 Ellis Grimes; 16 Chris Bower; 17 Chris Mayren.
Tries: Hill (42), Parkinson (47), Gagen (66);
Goals: O'Brien 0/3.
Rugby Leaguer & League Express Men of the Match:
Thunder: Tom Ruediger;
Miners Rangers: Tommy Parkinson.
Penalty count: 10-8; **Half-time:** 20-0;
Referee: Stephen Race; **Attendance:** 200.

Sunday 21st February 2016

COVENTRY BEARS 24
GLOUCESTERSHIRE ALL GOLDS 48

BEARS: 1 Dave Weston; 2 Jamahl Hunte; 3 Eddie Medforth; 4 Jason Bass; 5 Hayden Freeman; 6 Craig White; 7 Jay Lobwein; 8 James Geurtjens; 9 Richard Hughes; 10 Jack Morrison; 11 Liam Thompson; 12 Matt Reid; 13 Adam Saynor. Subs (all used): 14 Joel James; 15 Jonathan Milizewski; 16 Trae O'Sullivan; 17 Chris Barratt.
Tries: Bass (6), Medforth (10), Freeman (15, 72), Hunte (78); **Goals:** Weston 1/3, White 1/2.
ALL GOLDS: 1 Jonny Leather; 2 Jamie Murphy; 3 Josh Allison; 4 Brad Kislingbury; 5 Phil Cowburn; 6 Brendon Newton; 7 Courtney Davies; 8 Oliver Purslow; 9 Steve Parry; 10 Alex Davidson; 11 Lewis Reece; 12 Joe McClean; 13 Emmerson Whittel. Subs (all used): 14 Jayson Lombardo; 15 Harrison Elliott; 16 Harry Kidd; 17 Morgan Evans.
Tries: Newton (1, 65), Elliott (24), Cowburn (38, 47, 62), Evans (44), Kidd (53), Allison (56);
Goals: Davies 5/7, Murphy 0/1, Lombardo 1/1.
Rugby Leaguer & League Express Men of the Match:
Bears: Hayden Freeman; *All Golds:* Courtney Davies.
Penalty count: 9-10; **Half-time:** 14-18;
Referee: Tom Grant; **Attendance:** 146.

OXFORD 34 HEMEL STAGS 12

OXFORD: 1 Connor Hughes; 2 Tom Lewsley; 3 Andrew Hoggins; 4 Marcus Brooker; 5 Josh Nathaniel; 6 Tom Holmes; 7 Jorge Richardson; 8 Mark Offerdahl; 9 Casey Canterbury; 10 Will Mayer; 11 Josh Scott; 12 Daniel Igbinedion; 13 Luke Evans. Subs (all used): 14 Santino Decaro; 15 Charlie Greene; 16 Nathan Kitson; 17 Dave Thornton.
Tries: Hoggins (4), Canterbury (25), Holmes (39), Greene (42), Nathaniel (65), Decaro (67);
Goals: Richardson 4/4, Kitson 1/2.
STAGS: 1 Scott Ellis; 5 Paul Stewart-Beckett; 3 Oli Toms; 18 Ben Waud; 2 Reece Rance; 6 Chad Isles; 7 Ben Stead; 10 Matt Ross; 9 Andy Kay; 8 Mike Stewart; 12 Kyal Greene; 11 Barry-John Swindells; 13 Rhys Bowditch. Subs (all used): 14 Dave O'Conner; 17 Liam O'Callaghan; 16 Luke Patterson; 19 Victor Coker.
Tries: Stewart (10), Ellis (54); **Goals:** Stead 2/2.
Rugby Leaguer & League Express Men of the Match: *Oxford:* Casey Canterbury; *Stags:* Andy Kay.
Penalty count: 8-7; **Half-time:** 18-6;
Referee: Gareth Hewer; **Attendance:** 155
(at Braywick Park, Maidenhead).

DONCASTER 35 NORTH WALES CRUSADERS 28

DONCASTER: 1 Louis Sheriff; 2 Matty Welham; 3 Liam Welham; 4 Kirk Yeaman; 5 David Foggin-Johnston; 6 Jordan Abdull; 7 Jordie Hedges; 8 Connor Scott; 9 Kyle Kesik; 10 Zac Braham; 11 Mason Tonks; 12 Brad Foster; 13 George Milton. Subs (all used): 14 Kieran Cross; 15 Matt Nicholson; 16 Makali Aizue; 17 Iafeta Palea'aesina.
Tries: L Welham (8), Abdull (17), Hedges (28, 49), Foggin-Johnston (33, 79), Cross (52);
Goals: Abdull 0/1, Hedges 3/7; **Field goal:** Hedges (66).
CRUSADERS: 1 Tommy Johnson; 2 Scott Turner; 3 Christiaan Roets; 4 Earl Hurst; 5 Rob Massam; 6 Ryan Smith; 7 Jamie Dallimore; 8 Ryan Duffy; 9 Lee Hudson; 10 Joe Burke; 11 Alex Thompson; 12 Stephen Wild; 13 Luke Warburton. Subs (all used): 14 Karl Ashall; 15 Danny Jones; 16 Jonny Walker; 17 Mark Hobson.
Tries: Turner (3, 22, 30), Massam (37), Duffy (61);
Goals: Johnson 3/5, Turner 1/1.
Rugby Leaguer & League Express Men of the Match: *Doncaster:* Louis Sheriff; *Crusaders:* Scott Turner.
Penalty count: 13-9; **Half-time:** 18-22;
Referee: Andrew Sweet; **Attendance:** 513.

HUNSLET HAWKS 4 YORK CITY KNIGHTS 24

HAWKS: 1 Jimmy Watson; 2 Mo Agoro; 5 James Duckworth; 15 Mufaro Mvududu; 28 Richie Barnett; 6 Simon Brown; 7 Danny Ansell; 10 Lewis Reed; 9 Jack Lee; 19 Matt Carbutt; 12 Ben Crane; 3 Jake Normington; 13 Liam Mackay. Subs (all used): 14 George Flanagan; 8 Michael Haley; 22 Craig Robinson; 27 Lee Waterman.
Try: Barnett (50); **Goals:** Brown 0/1.
CITY KNIGHTS: 1 Richard Wilkinson; 2 Nev Morrison; 3 James Morland; 4 Connor Bower; 5 Brett Turner; 6 Jon Presley; 7 Danny Nicklas; 8 Mark Applegarth; 9 Mike Emmett; 10 Russ Spiers; 11 Ryan Mallinder; 12 Ed Smith; 13 Jack Aldous. Subs (all used): 14 Harry Carter; 15 Brad Nicholson; 16 Brett Waller; 17 Josh Tonks.
Tries: Turner (5), Morrison (44), Spiers (64), Wilkinson (78); **Goals:** Nicklas 4/5.
Rugby Leaguer & League Express Men of the Match: *Hawks:* Jimmy Watson; *City Knights:* Russ Spiers.
Penalty count: 11-14; **Half-time:** 0-4;
Referee: Dave Merrick; **Attendance:** 464.

BARROW RAIDERS 4 ROCHDALE HORNETS 14

RAIDERS: 1 Ryan Fieldhouse; 2 Shane Toal; 3 Chris Hankinson; 16 Max Wiper; 5 Cameron Pitman; 6 Josh Ward; 7 Liam Campbell; 8 Joe Bullock; 9 Nathan Mossop; 10 Oliver Wilkes; 11 Liam Harrison; 15 Bradd Crellin; 13 Martin Aspinwall. Subs (all used): 21 Dan Abram; 12 Dan Toal; 17 Andrew Dawson; 18 James Duerden.
Try: Ward (32); **Goals:** Ward 0/1.
HORNETS: 1 Wayne English; 2 Chris Riley; 3 Dave Cookson; 4 Lewis Galbraith; 5 Corey Lee; 6 Paul Crook; 7 Danny Yates; 8 Samir Tahraoui; 9 Ben Moores; 10 Matty Hadden; 11 Jordan Case; 12 Alex Trumper; 13 James Tilley. Subs (all used): 14 Warren Thompson; 15 Jack Francis; 16 Harry Files; 17 James Dandy.
Tries: Lee (21), Dandy (56), Riley (73); **Goals:** Crook 1/3.
Rugby Leaguer & League Express Men of the Match: *Raiders:* Liam Harrison; *Hornets:* Wayne English.
Penalty count: 6-8; **Half time:** 4-4;
Referee: Scott Mikalauskas; **Attendance:** 659.

QUARTER FINALS

Sunday 3rd April 2016

DONCASTER 12 LONDON SKOLARS 24

DONCASTER: 1 Reece Dean; 2 Louis Sheriff; 3 Liam Welham; 4 Jason Tali; 5 Callum Lancaster; 6 Harry Tyson-Wilson; 7 Jordie Hedges; 8 Makali Aizue; 9 Ben Frankland; 10 Brad Fash; 11 Mason Tonks; 12 Michael Kelly; 13 Joe Picketts-O'Donnell. Subs (all used): 14 Kieran Cross; 15 Jack Walton; 16 Mark Castle; 17 Mitch Vincent.
Tries: L Welham (1), Tonks (19); **Goals:** Dean 2/2.
SKOLARS: 1 Alex Anthony; 2 Sam Nash; 3 Aaron Small; 4 Joe Price; 5 John Paxton; 6 Jermaine Coleman; 7 Mike Bishay; 8 Michael Sykes; 9 Sam Druce; 10 Toby Everett; 11 Dave Williams; 12 Will Lovell; 13 Ryan Chester. Subs (all used): 14 Ben Pointer; 15 Erjon Dollapi; 16 Eddie Mbaraga; 17 Ben Gray.
Tries: Nash (12), Williams (26), Mbaraga (48, 79);
Goals: Bishay 4/4, Druce 0/1.
Rugby Leaguer & League Express Men of the Match: *Doncaster:* Liam Welham; *Skolars:* Eddie Mbaraga.
Penalty count: 9-7; **Half-time:** 12-14;
Referee: Jon Roberts; **Attendance:** 367.

GLOUCESTERSHIRE ALL GOLDS 36 NEWCASTLE THUNDER 28

ALL GOLDS: 1 Jamie Murphy; 2 Jonny Leather; 3 Josh Allison; 4 Lewis Reece; 5 Phil Cowburn; 6 Courtney Davies; 7 Brendon Newton; 8 Alex Davidson; 9 Steve Parry; 10 Morgan Evans; 11 Lamont Bryan; 12 Joe McClean; 13 Emmerson Whittel. Subs (all used): 14 Almer Tagayuna; 15 Richard Jones; 16 Oliver Purslow; 17 Harrison Elliott.
Tries: Allison (14), Elliott (32), Leather (43), Cowburn (45), Parry (62), Reece (66), Purslow (79);
Goals: Davies 3/6, Murphy 1/1.
THUNDER: 1 Tom Ruediger; 2 Joe Brown; 3 Derrell Olpherts; 4 Ali Blair; 5 Peter Fox; 6 Lee Paterson; 7 Benn Hardcastle; 8 Vincent Rennie; 9 Aaron Teroi; 10 Josh Stoker; 11 Harry Aldous; 12 Dan Parker; 13 Ben Thorburn. Subs (all used): 14 Evan Simons; 15 Gioele Celerino; 16 Francis Welsh; 17 Josh Atkinson.
Tries: Parker (19), Ruediger (36), Blair (50, 76), Olpherts (55), Rennie (70); **Goals:** Hardcastle 1/3, Parker 1/3.
Rugby Leaguer & League Express Men of the Match: *All Golds:* Lewis Reece; *Thunder:* Lee Paterson.
Penalty count: 6-12; **Half-time:** 10-10;
Referee: Scott Mikalauskas; **Attendance:** 102.

KEIGHLEY COUGARS 54 OXFORD 14

COUGARS: 22 Ritchie Hawkyard; 26 Vinny Finigan; 29 Hamish Barnes; 3 Rikki Sheriffe; 5 Paul White; 14 Adam Brook; 24 Liam Darville; 8 Scott Law; 9 James Feather; 15 Neil Cherryholme; 11 Josh Lynam; 25 Darren Hawkyard; 20 Aaron Ollett. Subs: 7 Paul Handforth (not used); 12 Brendan Rawlins; 18 Sonny Esslemont; 35 Ross Peltier.
Tries: White (7, 73), R Sheriffe (13), Barnes (20), Finigan (30), Darville (35), D Hawkyard (42), Feather (47), Peltier (50), R Hawkyard (63); **Goals:** Brook 7/10.
OXFORD: 1 Nathan Kitson; 2 Sean Morris; 3 Zack McComb; 4 Marcus Brooker; 5 Josh Nathaniel; 6 Adam Flintham; 7 Aaron Dobek; 8 Sean Hesketh; 9 Casey Canterbury; 10 Joel Thomas; 11 James Harrison; 12 Daniel Igbinedion; 13 Danny Allan. Subs (all used): 14 Adam Withington; 15 Mark Hayes; 16 Andrew Hoggins; 17 Tom Davies.
Tries: Canterbury (26), Kitson (39), Nathaniel (79);
Goals: Kitson 1/3.
Rugby Leaguer & League Express Men of the Match: *Cougars:* Ritchie Hawkyard; *Oxford:* James Harrison.
Penalty count: 9-8; **Half-time:** 26-10;
Referee: Callum Straw; **Attendance:** 402.

ROCHDALE HORNETS 16 YORK CITY KNIGHTS 40

HORNETS: 1 Wayne English; 2 Chris Riley; 3 Benjamin Jullien; 4 Jordan Case; 5 Corey Lee; 6 Paul Crook; 7 Danny Yates; 8 Ben Evans; 9 Ben Moores; 10 Samir Tahraoui; 11 Jono Smith; 12 Joe Philbin; 13 Warren Thompson. Subs (all used): 14 Alex McClurg; 15 Stuart Biscomb; 16 Matty Hadden; 17 Sam Wilde.
Tries: Case (2), Jullien (6), Crook (40); **Goals:** Crook 2/3.
Dismissal: Riley (78) - dissent.
CITY KNIGHTS: 1 Brett Turner; 2 Ben Dent; 3 James Morland; 4 Brad Hey; 5 Austin Buchanan; 6 Jon Presley; 7 Danny Nicklas; 8 Russ Spiers; 9 Harry Carter; 10 Jack Aldous; 11 Josh Tonks; 12 Ed Smith; 13 Mike Emmett. Subs (all used): 14 Kris Brining; 15 Jack Anderson; 16 Ryan Mallinder; 17 Jordan Crowther.
Tries: Tonks (13), B Dent (26, 75), Morland (35), Turner (45, 72), Spiers (68); **Goals:** Nicklas 6/8.
Rugby Leaguer & League Express Men of the Match: *Hornets:* Jono Smith; *City Knights:* Jon Presley.
Penalty count: 7-6; **Half-time:** 16-16;
Referee: Andrew Sweet; **Attendance:** 451.

SEMI-FINALS

Saturday 30th April 2016

LONDON SKOLARS 22 KEIGHLEY COUGARS 31

SKOLARS: 1 Alex Anthony; 2 Sam Nash; 3 Aaron Small; 4 Joe Price; 5 John Paxton; 6 Jy-mel Coleman; 7 Mike Bishay; 8 Ben Gray; 9 Sam Druce; 10 Toby Everett; 11 Daye Williams; 12 Will Lovell; 13 Ryan Chester. Subs (all used): 14 Ben Pointer; 15 Michael Sykes; 16 Erjon Dollapi; 17 Kazeem Fatouri.
Tries: Paxton (16), Small (35, 68), Pointer (52);
Goals: Bishay 3/4.
Sin bin: Dollapi (80) - fighting.
COUGARS: 22 Ritchie Hawkyard; 26 Vinny Finigan; 23 Charlie Martin; 29 Hamish Barnes; 5 Paul White; 14 Adam Brook; 24 Liam Darville; 8 Scott Law; 9 James Feather; 12 Brendan Rawlins; 11 Josh Lynam; 17 John Oakes; 13 Ashley Lindsay. Subs (all used): 20 Aaron Ollett; 16 Jode Sheriffe; 15 Neil Cherryholme; 25 Darren Hawkyard.
Tries: Barnes (5), Law (22), D Hawkyard (41), R Hawkyard (57, 71); **Goals:** Brook 5/5;
Field goal: Brook (79).
Sin bin: R Hawkyard (80) - fighting.
Rugby Leaguer & League Express Men of the Match: *Skolars:* Aaron Small; *Cougars:* Adam Brook.
Penalty count: 11-10; **Half-time:** 10-12;
Referee: Tom Grant; **Attendance:** 436.

Sunday 1st May 2016

YORK CITY KNIGHTS 58 GLOUCESTERSHIRE ALL GOLDS 14

CITY KNIGHTS: 1 Brett Turner; 2 James Morland; 3 Jordan Crowther; 4 Tyler Craig; 5 Austin Buchanan; 6 Jon Presley; 7 Danny Nicklas; 8 Brett Waller; 9 Harry Carter; 10 Jack Aldous; 11 Ryan Mallinder; 12 Ed Smith; 13 Mike Emmett. Subs (all used): 14 Kris Brining; 15 Mark Applegarth; 16 Russ Spiers; 17 Ross Osborne.
Tries: Craig (2, 30), E Smith (7), Turner (33, 80), Morland (37), Spiers (50), Buchanan (55), Crowther (65), Presley (69), Nicklas (72), Mallinder (75);
Goals: Nicklas 5/12.
ALL GOLDS: 1 Jonny Leather; 2 Chris Barlow; 3 Josh Allison; 4 Lewis Reece; 5 Phil Cowburn; 6 Brendon Newton; 7 Courtney Davies; 8 Oliver Purslow; 9 Steve Parry; 10 Morgan Evans; 11 Joe McClean; 12 Lamont Bryan; 13 Emmerson Whittel. Subs (all used): 14 Almer Tagayuna; 15 Brad Kislingbury; 16 Harry Kidd; 17 James Walter.
Tries: Barlow (13), Cowburn (19), Parry (59);
Goals: Davies 1/3.
Rugby Leaguer & League Express Men of the Match: *City Knights:* Jon Presley; *All Golds:* Brendon Newton.
Penalty count: 9-3; **Half time:** 22-10;
Referee: Scott Mikalauskas; **Attendance:** 469.

FINAL

Saturday 28th May 2016

KEIGHLEY COUGARS 22 YORK CITY KNIGHTS 18

COUGARS: 22 Ritchie Hawkyard; 26 Vinny Finigan; 3 Rikki Sheriffe; 23 Charlie Martin; 5 Paul White; 24 Liam Darville; 7 Paul Handforth; 8 Scott Law; 9 James Feather; 12 Brendan Rawlins; 11 Josh Lynam; 17 John Oakes; 13 Ashley Lindsay. Subs (all used): 25 Darren Hawkyard; 19 Matthew Bailey; 35 Ross Peltier; 20 Aaron Ollett.
Tries: White (20), R Sheriffe (26), Oakes (44), Martin (78);
Goals: Handforth 3/4.
CITY KNIGHTS: 1 Ben Dent; 2 Brett Turner; 3 James Morland; 4 Ed Smith; 5 Austin Buchanan; 6 Jon Presley; 7 Danny Nicklas; 8 Brett Waller; 9 Pat Smith; 10 Jack Aldous; 11 Josh Tonks; 12 Mark Applegarth; 13 Mike Emmett. Subs (all used): 14 Kris Brining; 15 Russ Spiers; 16 Ross Osborne; 17 Brad Hey.
Tries: Aldous (10), Presley (57), E Smith (75);
Goals: Turner 3/3.
Rugby Leaguer & League Express Men of the Match: *Cougars:* Paul Handforth; *City Knights:* Brett Turner.
Penalty count: 8-5; **Half-time:** 10-6;
Referee: Scott Mikalauskas.
(at Bloomfield Road, Blackpool).

CHALLENGE CUP 2016
Round by Round

ROUND 3

Saturday 27th February 2016

FEATHERSTONE LIONS 37 SOUTH WALES SCORPIONS 20

LIONS: 1 Ian Jackson; 2 Kieran Redfearn; 3 John Hardcastle; 4 Ricky Williams; 5 Reece Dyas; 6 Matthew Johnson; 7 Sam Candlin; 8 Adam Curtis; 9 Dean Gamble; 10 Sam Millard; 11 Joe Fox; 12 Gareth Gale; 13 Richard Frankland. Subs (all used): 14 Davi Garahan; 15 George Nuttall; 16 Brendan Gibbins; 17 Connor Walker.
Tries: Hardcastle (7), Redfearn (11), Dyas (17, 44, 63), Fox (32), Gamble (68); **Goals:** Jackson 4/7;
Field goal: Gamble (80).
Sin bin: Fox (36) - punching.
SCORPIONS: 15 Jordan Sheridan; 2 Ian Newbury; 21 Scott Gregory; 4 Yannic Parker; 5 Dai Evans; 6 Kristian Hawkes; 7 Paul Emanuelli; 8 Chris Davies; 9 Connor Farrer; 10 Izaak Duffy; 20 Anthony Symons; 12 Tom Morgan; 13 Chris Vitalini. Subs (all used): 14 Osian Phillips; 17 Mike Connor; 24 Zak Williams; 27 Rhys Davies.
Tries: Evans (25, 53), Vitalini (48), R Davies (75);
Goals: Emanuelli 2/4.
Sin bin: Davies (15) - punching.
Rugby Leaguer & League Express Men of the Match: *Lions:* Reece Dyas; *Scorpions:* Dai Evans.
Penalty count: 10-9; **Half-time:** 22-4;
Referee: Scott Mikalauskas; **Attendance:** 400.

KELLS 12 HEMEL STAGS 6

KELLS: 1 Lewis Smith; 2 Reece O'Neil; 3 Craig Benson; 4 Martin O'Neil; 5 Daniel Joyce; 6 Tyrone Dalton; 7 Ross Crawford; 8 Dave Lowery; 9 Nathan Doran; 10 Ross Ainley; 11 Scott Lofthouse; 12 Paul Cullnean; 13 Carl Sice. Subs (all used): 14 Dominic Wear; 15 Lewis Wilson; 16 David Ford; 17 Alan McGuinness.
Tries: Crawford (7), Cullnean (13); **Goals:** Crawford 2/3.
STAGS: 1 Scott Ellis; 2 Paul Stewart-Beckett; 3 Ben Waud; 4 Oli Toms; 5 Reece Rance; 6 Chad Isles; 7 Ben Stead; 8 Victor Coker; 9 Andy Kay; 10 Mike Stewart; 11 Kyal Greene; 12 Barry-John Swindells; 13 Rhys Bowditch. Subs (all used): 14 Mitch Stephenson; 15 Adam Booth; 16 Luke Patterson; 17 Harrison Brough.
Try: Rance (8); **Goals:** Stead 1/1.
Rugby Leaguer & League Express Men of the Match: *Kells:* Scott Lofthouse; *Stags:* Mitch Stephenson.
Penalty count: 5-7; **Half-time:** 12-6;
Referee: James Callaghan; **Attendance:** 250.

PILKINGTON RECS 13 LONDON SKOLARS 0

PILKINGTON RECS: 1 Ryan Hillard; 2 Kyran Knapper; 3 Ian Stanley; 4 John Rees; 5 Andrew Knapper; 6 Greg Smith; 7 Danny Lynch; 8 Jamie Smith; 9 Ryan Liptrot; 10 Steve Charlson; 11 Mike Garrity; 12 Tom Roughley; 13 Jonathan Keys. Subs (all used): 14 Liam Bostock; 15 Jonathan Peers; 16 Ben Gravener; 17 Luke Riley.
Tries: K Knapper (42), A Knapper (73);
Goals: G Smith 2/2; **Field goal:** G Smith (70).
SKOLARS: 1 Alex Anthony; 2 Sam Nash; 3 Joe Ridley; 4 Joe Price; 5 John Paxton; 6 Jermaine Coleman; 7 Charlie Lawrence; 8 Rob Thomas; 9 Mike Bishay; 10 Dave Williams; 11 Michael Sykes; 12 Will Lovell; 13 Michael Worrincy. Subs (all used): 14 Erjon Dollapi; 15 Ben Gray; 16 Ben Pointer; 17 Eddie Mbaraga.
Sin bin: Dollapi (37) - tripping.
Rugby Leaguer & League Express Men of the Match: *Pilkington Recs:* Jamie Smith; *Skolars:* Alex Anthony.
Penalty count: 8-15; **Half-time:** 0-0;
Referee: Liam Moore; **Attendance:** 500.

ROCHDALE MAYFIELD 14 ROCHDALE HORNETS 40

MAYFIELD: 1 Declan Sheridan; 2 Jack Sampson; 3 Liam Whalley; 4 Matt Calland; 5 Komai Namulnatua; 6 Paul Brearley; 7 Sam Butterworth; 8 Sean Mulcahy; 9 Callum Ogden; 10 Aide Gleeson; 11 Sean Watkins; 12 Callum Marriott; 13 Lewis Sheridan. Subs (all used): 14 Steve Campbell; 15 Jack Rush; 16 Simon Moore; 17 Nick Hargreaves.
Tries: Watkins (54), D Sheridan (55);
Goals: Butterworth 3/3.
HORNETS: 1 Wayne English; 2 Kieran Walpole; 3 Dave Cookson; 4 Alex Trumper; 5 Corey Lee; 6 Paul Crook; 7 Danny Yates; 8 Warren Thompson; 9 Ben Moores; 10 Samir Tahraoui; 11 Stuart Biscomb; 12 Jordan Case; 13 James Tilley. Subs (all used): 14 Alex McClurg; 15 John Cookson; 16 Matty Hadden; 17 Jack Francis.
Tries: Tilley (21), Walpole (28), English (30, 32), Hadden (60), Thompson (69), Yates (78); **Goals:** Crook 6/7.
Rugby Leaguer & League Express Men of the Match: *Mayfield:* Paul Brearley; *Hornets:* James Tilley.
Penalty count: 14-16; **Half-time:** 2-22;
Referee: Gareth Hewer; **Attendance:** 937.

SIDDAL 30 NEWCASTLE THUNDER 4

SIDDAL: 1 Freddie Walker; 2 Taniela Bakosa; 3 Billy Hammond; 4 Scott Caley; 5 Gareth Blackburn; 6 Shaun Garrod; 7 Chris Brooke; 8 George Ambler; 9 Craig Sanderson; 10 Iain Davies; 11 Canaan Smithies; 12 Tom Garratt; 13 Byron Smith. Subs (all used): 14 Dominic Booth; 15 Ben Hinsley; 16 Gareth English; 17 Jason Boults.
Tries: Garratt (4), Smith (27, 45), Walker (62), Garrod (71);
Goals: Blackburn 2/2, Brooke 3/4.
Sin bin: Blackburn (26) - fighting.
THUNDER: 1 Tom Ruediger; 2 Ali Blair; 3 Derrell Olpherts; 4 Aaron Teroi; 5 Peter Fox; 6 Ben Thorburn; 7 Josh Kittrick; 8 Vincent Rennie; 9 Evan Simons; 10 Rhys Clarke; 11 Dan Parker; 12 Dan Turland; 13 Jason Payne. Subs (all used): 14 Paddy Hargreaves; 15 Joe Brown; 16 Francis Welsh; 17 Josh Stoker.
Try: Parker (76); **Goals:** Parker 0/1.
Sin bin: Olpherts (26) - fighting.
Rugby Leaguer & League Express Men of the Match: *Siddal:* Tom Garratt; *Thunder:* Jason Payne.
Penalty count: 9-9; **Half-time:** 14-0;
Referee: Billy Pearson; **Attendance:** 405.

WATH BROW HORNETS 14 TOULOUSE OLYMPIQUE 32

HORNETS: 1 Karl Dixon; 2 Luke Davidson; 3 Ryan Amor; 4 Peter Caddy; 5 Conner Molyneaux; 6 Fran King; 7 Dean Rooney; 8 James Dixon; 9 Cole Walker-Taylor; 10 Matt Huby; 11 Callum Farrer; 12 Lewis McCarron; 13 Charlie Tomlinson. Subs (all used): 14 Owen McCartney; 15 Rhys Pritchard; 16 Ben Agnew; 17 Paul Murphy.
Tries: Davidson (11), K Dixon (22, 53);
Goals: Walker-Taylor 0/2, King 1/1.
OLYMPIQUE: 1 Mark Kheirallah; 2 Tony Maurel; 3 Bastien Ader; 4 Gregory White; 5 Kuni Minga; 6 Johnathan Ford; 22 Danny Hulme; 15 Maxime Puech; 14 Mourad Kriouache; 16 Bastien Canet; 11 Sebastien Planas; 12 Rhys Curran; 13 Andrew Bentley. Subs (all used): 9 Kane Bentley; 18 Tyla Hepi; 10 Samy Masselot; 17 Anthony Marion.
Tries: Kheirallah (15, 43, 68, 72), Ford (27), Minga (37);
Goals: Kheirallah 4/6.
Rugby Leaguer & League Express Men of the Match: *Hornets:* James Dixon; *Olympique:* Mark Kheirallah.
Penalty count: 10-5; **Half-time:** 8-14;
Referee: Dave Merrick; **Attendance:** 400.

Sunday 28th February 2016

NORTH WALES CRUSADERS 36 GLOUCESTERSHIRE ALL GOLDS 40

CRUSADERS: 1 Ryan Smith; 2 Scott Turner; 3 Earl Hurst; 4 Christiaan Roets; 5 Rob Massam; 6 Jack Hansen; 7 Jamie Dallimore; 8 Ryan Duffy; 9 Lee Hudson; 10 Joe Burke; 11 Alex Thompson; 12 Stephen Wild; 13 Luke Warburton. Subs (all used): 14 Karl Ashall; 15 Matt Gee; 16 Jordan Andrade; 17 Jonny Walker.
Tries: Turner (3), Dallimore (12, 50, 54), Wild (20), Andrade (39), Massam (57); **Goals:** Turner 4/7.
ALL GOLDS: 1 Jonny Leather; 2 Jamie Murphy; 3 Josh Allison; 4 Brad Kislingbury; 5 Phil Cowburn; 6 Courtney Davies; 7 Jayson Lombardo; 8 Oliver Purslow; 9 Steve Parry; 10 Alex Davidson; 11 Lamont Bryan; 12 Joe McClean; 13 Emmerson Whittel. Subs (all used): 14 Brendon Newton; 15 Harrison Elliott; 16 Harry Kidd; 17 Morgan Evans.
Tries: Murphy (24), Leather (27, 76), Davies (35), Elliott (64), Cowburn (72), Kidd (80); **Goals:** Davies 6/7.
Rugby Leaguer & League Express Men of the Match: *Crusaders:* Jamie Dallimore; *All Golds:* Courtney Davies.
Penalty count: 6-9; **Half-time:** 20-16;
Referee: Jamie Bloem; **Attendance:** 324.

OXFORD 22 CASTLEFORD LOCK LANE 37

OXFORD: 1 Connor Hughes; 2 Tom Lewsley; 3 Kieran Gill; 4 Clark McAllister; 5 Josh Nathaniel; 6 Nathan Kitson; 7 Aaron Dobek; 8 Luke Evans; 9 Casey Canterbury; 10 Daniel Igbinedion; 11 Andrew Hoggins; 12 Marcus Brooker; 13 Jorge Richardson. Subs (all used): 14 Dave Thornton; 15 Mark Hayes; 16 Adam Flintham; 17 Tom Davies.
Tries: Kitson (12), Hoggins (20), Dobek (61), Nathaniel (77); **Goals:** Kitson 3/3, Richardson 0/1.
LOCK LANE: 1 Mikey Hayward; 2 Adam Garlick; 3 Nicky Saxton; 4 Lewis Price; 5 Connor Turner; 6 Nathan Fozzard; 7 Danny Rowse; 8 Craig Jones; 9 Callum Butler; 10 Chris Siddons; 11 Royce Geoffrey; 12 Danny Lidbury; 13 Karl Robinson. Subs (all used): 14 Mitchell Platt; 15 Paul Brown; 16 Oliver Bloomer; 17 James Woods.
Tries: Geoffrey (8), Butler (16), Garlick (29, 65), Fozzard (32), Saxton (52); **Goals:** Rowse 6/6;
Field goal: Rowse (38).
Rugby Leaguer & League Express Men of the Match: *Oxford:* Marcus Brooker; *Lock Lane:* Danny Rowse.
Penalty count: 10-8; **Half-time:** 12-25;
Referee: Brandon Robinson; **Attendance:** 55
(at Braywick Park, Maidenhead).

WEST HULL 0 DONCASTER 54

WEST HULL: 1 Matt Plummer; 2 Jack Watts; 3 Callum King; 4 Josh Nicklin; 5 Jimmy Goulsbra-Miller; 6 Ben Arbon; 7 Callum Windley; 8 Scott Howlett; 9 Alex Shepherdson; 10 James Garmston; 11 Jack Lazenby; 12 Jacob Moore; 13 Ryan Steen. Subs (all used): 14 Elliott Windley; 15 Calvin Parker; 16 Ryan Wilson; 17 Liam Garside.
DONCASTER: 1 Louis Sheriff; 2 Aaron Jones-Bishop; 3 Mathew Cook; 4 Liam Welham; 5 Matty Welham; 6 Tom Carr; 7 Jordie Hedges; 8 Connor Scott; 9 Kyle Kesik; 10 Makali Aizue; 11 Brad Foster; 12 Mason Tonks; 13 George Milton. Subs (all used): 14 Kieran Cross; 15 Zac Braham; 16 Matt Nicholson; 17 Jack Walton.
Tries: L Welham (2), Scott (18, 69), Jones-Bishop (21, 25), M Nicholson (28), Hedges (48), M Welham (56), Walton (61); **Goals:** Carr 9/10.
Rugby Leaguer & League Express Men of the Match: *West Hull:* Ryan Steen; *Doncaster:* Connor Scott.
Penalty count: 10-12; **Half-time:** 0-30;
Referee: Tom Crashley; **Attendance:** 268.

HUNSLET HAWKS 46 BARROW RAIDERS 12

HAWKS: 1 Jimmy Watson; 2 Mo Agoro; 5 James Duckworth; 15 Mufaro Mvududu; 28 Richie Barnett; 6 Simon Brown; 7 Danny Ansell; 8 Michael Haley; 9 Jack Lee; 10 Lewis Reed; 12 Ben Crane; 3 Jake Normington; 29 Daniel Williams. Subs (all used): 14 George Flanagan; 26 Austin Bell; 19 Matt Carbutt; 20 Danny Thomas.
Tries: Barnett (14, 51), Ansell (23, 60), Watson (34, 41), Carbutt (37), Reed (80); **Goals:** Brown 7/8.
RAIDERS: 1 Ryan Fieldhouse; 2 Shane Toal; 3 Chris Hankinson; 16 Max Wiper; 5 Cameron Pitman; 6 Josh Ward; 7 Liam Campbell; 8 Joe Bullock; 9 Nathan Mossop; 10 Oliver Wilkes; 11 Liam Harrison; 15 Bradd Crellin; 13 Martin Aspinwall. Subs (all used): 21 Dan Abram; 18 James Duerden; 12 Dan Toal; 17 Andrew Dawson.
Tries: Ward (28), Duerden (68); **Goals:** Ward 2/2.
Rugby Leaguer & League Express Men of the Match: *Hawks:* Mufaro Mvududu; *Raiders:* Ryan Fieldhouse.
Penalty count: 10-7; **Half-time:** 22-6;
Referee: Tom Grant; **Attendance:** 354.

KEIGHLEY COUGARS 54 COVENTRY BEARS 28

COUGARS: 22 Ritchie Hawkyard; 2 Andy Gabriel; 23 Charlie Martin; 29 Hamish Barnes; 5 Paul White; 14 Adam Brook; 7 Paul Handforth; 8 Scott Law; 9 James Feather; 12 Brendan Rawlins; 17 John Oakes; 25 Darren Hawkyard; 13 Ashley Lindsay. Subs (all used): 15 Neil Cherryholme; 19 Matthew Bailey; 20 Aaron Ollett; 35 Ross Peltier.
Tries: R Hawkyard (25), Barnes (30, 40, 48), Oakes (51), Ollett (54), Gabriel (58), White (61), Martin (65, 67);
Goals: Brook 7/10.
BEARS: 1 Joel James; 2 Ben Warrilow; 3 Brett Barlow; 4 Matt Reid; 5 Hayden Freeman; 6 Charlie O'Mara; 7 Jay Lobwein; 8 Tommy Holland; 9 James Redman; 10 Elliot Liku; 11 Elliot Holton; 12 Chris Barratt; 13 Jonathan Milizewski. Subs (all used): 14 Elliot Norman; 15 Alex Beddows; 16 Trae O'Sullivan; 17 Adam Saynor.
Tries: Holland (2), Warrilow (17), O'Mara (22), Lobwein (76), Milizewski (79); **Goals:** James 4/5.
Rugby Leaguer & League Express Men of the Match: *Cougars:* Hamish Barnes; *Bears:* Jonathan Milizewski.
Penalty count: 11-7; **Half-time:** 16-18;
Referee: Jon Roberts; **Attendance:** 421.

YORK CITY KNIGHTS 66 YORK ACORN 0

CITY KNIGHTS: 1 Richard Wilkinson; 2 Brett Turner; 3 James Morland; 4 Connor Bower; 5 Adam Dent; 6 Jon Presley; 7 Danny Nicklas; 8 Mark Applegarth; 9 Kris Brining; 10 Jack Aldous; 11 Ryan Mallinder; 12 Ed Smith; 13 Mike Emmett. Subs (all used): 14 Harry Carter; 15 Brett Waller; 16 Tyler Craig; 17 Josh Tonks.
Tries: Mallinder (12, 39), Presley (16), E Smith (22), Morland (29, 32), Carter (45), Wilkinson (48), Craig (51), Bower (61), Nicklas (67), Turner (75), Brining (80);
Goals: Nicklas 2/6, Wilkinson 5/6
(last conversion attempt declined).
Sin bin: Nicklas (70) - fighting.
ACORN: 1 Jake Calam; 2 Joel Johnson; 3 Ryan Gallacher; 4 Jordan Myers; 5 Josh Thompson; 6 Anthony Chilton; 7 Joe Budd; 8 Daryl North; 9 Nick Speck; 10 Joe Porter; 11 Elliot Bulmer; 12 Tom Hill; 13 Josh Mortimer. Subs (all used): 14 Tim Stubbs; 15 Reece Rushworth; 16 Harry Bromwich; 17 Jack Byrnes.
Sin bin: Thompson (70) - fighting.
Rugby Leaguer & League Express Men of the Match: *City Knights:* Ed Smith; *Acorn:* Tom Hill.
Penalty count: 12-8; **Half-time:** 28-0;
Referee: Andrew Sweet; **Attendance:** 2,293.

ROUND 4

Friday 18th March 2016

HUNSLET HAWKS 48 DONCASTER 6

HAWKS: 1 Jimmy Watson; 5 James Duckworth; 4 Ayden Faal; 15 Mufaro Mvududu; 28 Richie Barnett; 6 Simon Brown; 20 Danny Thomas; 19 Matt Carbutt; 9 Jack Lee; 10 Lewis Reed; 27 Lee Waterman; 3 Jake Normington; 29 Daniel Williams. Subs (all used): 8 Michael Haley; 14 George Flanagan; 23 Chris Buttery; 26 Austin Bell.
Tries: Lee (7, 63), Barnett (25, 30, 74, 78), Faal (47), Waterman (57), Mvududu (69); **Goals:** Brown 6/9.
DONCASTER: 1 Louis Sheriff; 2 Aaron Jones-Bishop; 3 Sam Doherty; 4 Liam Welham; 5 David Foggin-Johnston; 6 Kyle Kesik; 7 Jordie Hedges; 8 Connor Scott; 9 Ben Frankland; 10 Matt Nicholson; 11 Mason Tonks; 12 Michael Kelly; 13 Jack Walton. Subs (all used): 14 Zac Braham; 15 Kieran Cross; 16 Joe Pickets-O'Donnell; 17 George Milton.
Try: Braham (43); **Goals:** Hedges 1/1.
Dismissal: Pickets-O'Donnell (28) - stamping.
Rugby Leaguer & League Express Men of the Match: *Hawks:* Danny Thomas; *Doncaster:* Ben Frankland.
Penalty count: 13-7; **Half-time:** 14-0;
Referee: Andrew Sweet; **Attendance:** 337.

DEWSBURY RAMS 31 BRADFORD BULLS 30

RAMS: 1 Josh Guzdek; 2 Dale Morton; 15 Jason Crookes; 4 Shane Grady; 5 Dalton Grant; 6 Paul Sykes; 17 Dom Speakman; 8 Matt Groat; 9 Tom Hemingway; 16 Toby Adamson; 12 Scott Hale; 14 Luke Adamson; 13 Aaron Brown. Subs (all used): 19 Nathan Conroy; 24 Jack Teanby; 25 Joel Farrell; 32 Kyle Trout.
Tries: Grant (19), Morton (25, 31), Teanby (44), Brown (69); **Goals:** Sykes 5/5; **Field goal:** Sykes (73).
BULLS: 22 James Clare; 33 Etuate Uaisele; 15 Matty Blythe; 4 Kris Welham; 2 Omari Caro; 6 Lee Gaskell; 1 Oscar Thomas; 8 Paul Clough; 13 Danny Addy; 35 Rhys Lovegrove; 11 Tom Olbison; 12 Dale Ferguson; 14 Jay Pitts. Subs (all used): 19 Steve Crossley; 20 Mitch Clark; 23 Alex Mellor; 30 Joe Lumb.
Tries: Caro (10), Lumb (33), Addy (40), Blythe (51, 60), Olbison (57); **Goals:** Addy 3/6.
Rugby Leaguer & League Express Men of the Match: *Rams:* Aaron Brown; *Bulls:* Mitch Clark.
Penalty count: 6-10; **Half-time:** 18-16;
Referee: Chris Campbell; **Attendance:** 2,021.

Saturday 19th March 2016

FEATHERSTONE LIONS 16 CASTLEFORD LOCK LANE 30

LIONS: 1 Ian Jackson; 2 Jake Perkins; 3 Josh Hardcastle; 4 Ricky Williams; 5 Gareth Gale; 6 Matthew Johnson; 7 Richard Frankland; 8 Adam Curtis; 9 Dean Gamble; 10 Scott Glassell; 11 Joe Fox; 12 Davi Garahan; 13 Danny Glassell. Subs (all used): 14 Reece Dyas; 15 Adam Hepworth; 16 George Nuttall; 17 Brendan Gibbins.
Tries: Williams (5, 49), Jackson (53); **Goals:** Williams 2/3.
Sin bin: Hardcastle (31) - repeated team offences.
LOCK LANE: 1 Mikey Hayward; 2 James Cryer; 3 Nicky Saxton; 4 Lewis Price; 5 Adam Garlick; 6 Nathan Fozzard; 7 Danny Rowse; 8 Craig Jones; 9 Paul Brown; 10 Chris Siddons; 11 Royce Geoffrey; 12 Jordan Siddons; 13 Karl Robinson. Subs (all used): 14 Callum Butler; 15 Mitchell Platt; 16 Danny Lidbury; 17 James Woods.
Tries: Fozzard (18, 73), Price (26), Lidbury (38), Hayward (44); **Goals:** Rowse 5/6.
Rugby Leaguer & League Express Men of the Match: *Lions:* Ricky Williams; *Lock Lane:* Chris Siddons.
Penalty count: 13-15; **Half-time:** 4-18;
Referee: Callum Straw; **Attendance:** 1,738 *(at BigFellas Stadium)*.

PILKINGTON RECS 0 HALIFAX 78

PILKINGTON RECS: 1 Kyran Knapper; 2 Andrew Knapper; 3 Danny Hallsall; 4 Ian Stanley; 5 Kelvin Duffy; 6 Greg Smith; 7 Danny Lynch; 8 Jamie Smith; 9 Liam Bostock; 10 Steve Charlson; 11 John Rees; 12 Tom Roughley; 13 Mike Garrity. Subs (all used): 14 Andrew Nesbit; 15 Ben Gravener; 16 Jonathan Keys; 17 Jonathan Peers.
HALIFAX: 18 Miles Greenwood; 25 Jake Eccleston; 20 Sam Smeaton; 3 Steve Tyrer; 2 Will Sharp; 7 Gareth Moore; 22 Connor Robinson; 21 Adam Robinson; 15 Ryan Maneely; 16 Richard Moore; 26 Ed Barber; 14 Adam Tangata; 13 Jacob Fairbank. Subs (all used): 10 Luke Ambler; 24 Andy Bracek; 30 Brandon Moore; 31 Elliot Morris.
Tries: Barber (8), C Robinson (24, 47), Greenwood (28), Tangata (31), G Moore (38, 77), B Moore (39), Ambler (45, 70), Smeaton (55), Eccleston (61), Fairbank (65), R Moore (72); **Goals:** Tyrer 6/7, G Moore 1/2, C Robinson 4/5.
Rugby Leaguer & League Express Men of the Match: *Pilkington Recs:* Mike Garrity; *Halifax:* Connor Robinson.
Penalty count: 3-10; **Half-time:** 0-34;
Referee: Tom Crashley; **Attendance:** 837 *(at Langtree Park, St Helens)*.

BATLEY BULLDOGS 37 WHITEHAVEN 36

BULLDOGS: 22 Dave Scott; 2 Wayne Reittie; 23 Danny Cowling; 3 Chris Ulugia; 26 Alex Brown; 6 Cain Southernwood; 7 Dominic Brambani; 8 Keegan Hirst; 9 Luke Blake; 21 James Brown; 19 Alex Bretherton; 17 Joe Chandler; 13 Pat Walker. Subs (all used): 14 James Davey; 5 Shaun Ainscough; 15 Adam Gledhill; 10 Alex Rowe.
Tries: A Brown (5), Davey (29), Rowe (33, 44), Reittie (36), Chandler (55); **Goals:** Walker 6/6;
Field goal: Brambani (75).
WHITEHAVEN: 1 Louis Jouffret; 20 Jordan Burns; 3 Chris Taylor; 4 Jessie Joe Parker; 2 Craig Calvert; 6 Dion Aiye; 7 Grant Gore; 19 Glenn Riley; 9 James Newton; 15 Ben Davies; 11 Dave Allen; 12 Scott McAvoy; 13 Liam Carberry. Subs: 22 Nathan Lucock; 17 Steve Fox; 16 Connor Holliday; 21 John-Paul Brocklebank (not used).
Tries: Jouffret (10), Taylor (17), Carberry (22), Gore (49), Newton (60), Holliday (65); **Goals:** Jouffret 6/6.
Rugby Leaguer & League Express Men of the Match: *Bulldogs:* James Davey; *Whitehaven:* Glenn Riley.
Penalty count: 6-7; **Half-time:** 24-18;
Referee: Joe Cobb; **Attendance:** 457.

SHEFFIELD EAGLES 32 SWINTON LIONS 28

EAGLES: 1 Quentin Laulu-Togagae; 22 Ryan Millar; 3 Menzie Yere; 5 Ben Blackmore; 2 Rob Worrincy; 6 Cory Aston; 21 Dave Hewitt; 8 Steve Thorpe; 9 Keal Carlile; 10 Mitchell Stringer; 11 Michael Knowles; 12 Duane Straugheir; 18 Elliot Minchella. Subs (all used): 14 Matty Fozard; 17 Mark Mexico; 16 Adam Neal; 20 Jack Blagbrough.
Tries: Straugheir (25, 55), Yere (32), Blackmore (46, 68), Aston (72); **Goals:** Knowles 1/2, Hewitt 3/5.
Sin bin: Blackmore (77) - punching.
LIONS: 14 Kieran Hyde; 2 Shaun Robinson; 3 Stuart Littler; 4 Macauley Hallett; 5 Greg Scott; 6 Ben White; 1 Chris Atkin; 8 Mike Morrison; 9 Anthony Nicholson; 10 Jordan Hand; 11 Connor Dwyer; 23 Rhodri Lloyd; 12 Andy Thornley. Subs (all used): 13 Rob Lever; 16 Ben Austin; 19 Josh Barlow; 17 Stephen Nash.
Tries: Littler (7), Hallett (14, 42, 61), Morrison (18);
Goals: Atkin 4/5.
Rugby Leaguer & League Express Men of the Match: *Eagles:* Quentin Laulu-Togagae; *Lions:* Macauley Hallett.
Penalty count: 12-7; **Half-time:** 10-18;
Referee: Tom Grant; **Attendance:** 412.

TOULOUSE OLYMPIQUE 62 GLOUCESTERSHIRE ALL GOLDS 28

OLYMPIQUE: 1 Mark Kheirallah; 2 Tony Maurel; 3 Bastien Ader; 4 Gregory White; 5 Kuni Minga; 6 Johnathon Ford; 22 Danny Hulme; 16 Bastien Canet; 9 Kane Bentley; 15 Maxime Puech; 11 Sebastien Planas; 12 Rhys Curran; 13 Andrew Bentley. Subs (all used): 14 Mourad Kriouache; 10 Samy Masselot; 8 Clement Boyer; 17 Anthony Marion.
Tries: Kheirallah (4, 61, 69), Ford (14, 49), White (18), Minga (20, 45), Kriouache (32), Maurel (37), Boyer (64);
Goals: Kheirallah 9/11.
ALL GOLDS: 1 Jonny Leather; 2 Chris Barlow; 3 Josh Allison; 4 Phil Cowburn; 5 Jamie Murphy; 6 Courtney Davies; 7 Brendon Newton; 8 Oliver Purslow; 9 Steve Parry; 10 Harrison Elliott; 11 Lamont Bryan; 12 Joe McClean; 13 Emmerson Whittel. Subs (all used): 14 Jayson Lombardo; 15 Brad Kislingbury; 16 Alex Davidson; 17 Morgan Evans.
Tries: Davidson (23), Parry (42, 54, 76), Leather (58);
Goals: Davies 4/5.
Rugby Leaguer & League Express Men of the Match: *Olympique:* Mark Kheirallah; *All Golds:* Steve Parry.
Penalty count: 6-6; **Half-time:** 32-6;
Referee: Michael Woodhead; **Attendance:** 1,053.

LEIGH CENTURIONS 68 WORKINGTON TOWN 14

CENTURIONS: 26 Lee Smith; 15 Jonny Pownall; 2 Adam Higson; 24 Tom Armstrong; 5 Liam Kay; 6 Martyn Ridyard; 31 Ben Reynolds; 17 Jamie Acton; 32 Liam Hood; 10 Dayne Weston; 21 Andrew Dixon; 12 Gareth Hock; 13 Cory Paterson. Subs (all used): 19 Lewis Foster; 18 Tom Spencer; 20 Sam Hopkins; 11 Harrison Hansen.
Tries: Paterson (3, 10, 21, 68), Reynolds (6), Hood (12), Pownall (16), Smith (45), Hansen (54, 63), Acton (70), Hopkins (79); **Goals:** Ridyard 10/12.
TOWN: 1 Jack Murphy; 22 Chris Murphy; 3 Declan Hulme; 4 Jason Mossop; 24 Theerapol Ritson; 6 Carl Forber; 28 Jarrod Sammut; 8 Kris Coward; 9 Graeme Mattinson; 21 Oliver Gordon; 11 Brett Phillips; 16 Perry Whiteley; 10 Marc Shackley. Subs (all used): 13 Liam McAvoy; 19 Ryan Verlinden; 7 Jamie Doran; 14 Callum Phillips.
Tries: Sammut (25), Ritson (36), Whiteley (59);
Goals: Forber 1/3.
Rugby Leaguer & League Express Men of the Match: *Centurions:* Dayne Weston; *Town:* Jarrod Sammut.
Penalty count: 7-5; **Half-time:** 32-10;
Referee: Chris Kendall; **Attendance:** 2,049.

LONDON BRONCOS 26 FEATHERSTONE ROVERS 48

BRONCOS: 24 Alex Walker; 2 Rhys Williams; 1 Ben Hellewell; 32 Elliot Kear; 5 Iliess Macani; 6 Israel Eliab; 20 Scott Leatherbarrow; 18 Jamie Thackray; 14 Andy Ackers; 23 Jon Magrin; 11 Daniel Harrison; 21 Alex Foster; 22 Matt Davis. Subs (all used): 7 William Barthau; 15 Jack Bussey; 17 Mark Offerdahl; 25 Toby Everett.
Tries: Kear (6), Foster (16, 60), Williams (29), Barthau (69); **Goals:** Leatherbarrow 3/5.
ROVERS: 15 Ian Hardman; 2 Kyran Johnson; 3 Michael Channing; 25 Liam Blockley; 5 Scott Turner; 1 Danny Craven; 7 Anthony Thackeray; 8 Darrell Griffin; 12 John Davies; 10 Andrew Bostock; 18 Jamie Cording; 13 Tim Spears; 21 Bradley Knowles-Tagg. Subs (all used): 19 Sam Day; 20 Luke Cooper; 17 Jack Ormondroyd; 16 Colton Roche.
Tries: Hardman (34, 52, 65, 72, 77), Ormondroyd (42), Day (48), Johnson (57), Turner (63); **Goals:** Johnson 6/9.
Rugby Leaguer & League Express Men of the Match: *Broncos:* Alex Foster; *Rovers:* Ian Hardman.
Penalty count: 9-11; **Half-time:** 14-4;
Referee: Sam Ansell; **Attendance:** 294.

Sunday 20th March 2016

OLDHAM 40 KELLS 6

OLDHAM: 1 Richard Lepori; 2 Adam Clay; 4 Jack Holmes; 3 Jonathan Ford; 5 Jamel Chisholm; 22 Danny Grimshaw; 7 Steve Roper; 8 Phil Joy; 20 Gareth Owen; 10 Jack Spencer; - Gary Middlehurst; 12 Danny Langtree; 9 Sam Gee. Subs (all used): 19 Adam Files; 26 Michael Ward; 21 Kenny Hughes; 13 Liam Thompson.
Tries: Chisholm (5, 78), Ford (19), Middlehurst (29), Files (37), Grimshaw (42), Holmes (54, 59);
Goals: Roper 4/8.
KELLS: 1 Lewis Smith; 2 Reece O'Neil; 3 Craig Benson; 4 Scott Lofthouse; 5 Daniel Joyce; 6 Tyrone Dalton; 7 Ross Gainford; 8 Dave Lowery; 9 Carl Sice; 10 David Ford; 11 Ryan Watson; 12 Paul Cullnean; 13 Tony Burns. Subs (all used): 14 Dominic Wear; 15 Martin O'Neil; 16 Lewis Wilson; 17 Ross Ainley.
Try: Watson (40); **Goals:** Gainford 1/1.
Rugby Leaguer & League Express Men of the Match: *Oldham:* Danny Grimshaw; *Kells:* Carl Sice.
Penalty count: 6-6; **Half-time:** 20-6;
Referee: Jamie Bloem; **Attendance:** 385.

ROCHDALE HORNETS 48 SIDDAL 20

HORNETS: 1 Chris Riley; 2 Corey Lee; 3 Jovili Taira; 4 Alex Trumper; 5 Dale Bloomfield; 6 Paul Crook; 7 Danny Yates; 8 Samir Tahraoui; 9 Ben Moores; 10 Warren Thompson; 11 Jordan Case; 12 Stuart Biscomb; 13 James Tilley. Subs (all used): 14 John Cookson; 15 Matty Hadden; 16 Alex McClurg; 17 James Dandy.
Tries: Biscomb (2), Tilley (16, 24), Bloomfield (29), Hadden (34), McClurg (38), Tahraoui (58), Moores (66), Lee (69); **Goals:** Crook 5/8, Yates 1/1.
SIDDAL: 1 Freddie Walker; 2 Stephen Hope; 3 Tom Garratt; 4 Ben West; 5 Taniela Bakosa; 6 Shaun Garrod; 7 Chris Brooke; 8 George Ambler; 9 Craig Sanderson; 10 Iain Davies; 11 Mark Boothroyd; 12 Jason Boults; 13 Byron Smith. Subs (all used): 14 Dominic Booth; 15 Canaan Smithies; 16 Ben Hinsley; 17 Gareth English.
Tries: Bakosa (12), Garratt (20), Boults (43), Boothroyd (47); **Goals:** Brooke 2/4.
Rugby Leaguer & League Express Men of the Match: *Hornets:* Ben Moores; *Siddal:* Mark Boothroyd.
Penalty count: 9-7; **Half-time:** 32-10;
Referee: Jamie Bloem; **Attendance:** 653.

YORK CITY KNIGHTS 20 KEIGHLEY COUGARS 12

CITY KNIGHTS: 1 Richard Wilkinson; 2 Austin Buchanan; 3 Connor Bower; 4 Brad Hey; 5 James Morland; 6 Jon Presley; 7 Danny Nicklas; 8 Brett Waller; 9 Harry Carter; 10 Jack Aldous; 11 Ryan Mallinder; 12 Ed Smith; 13 Mike Emmett. Subs (all used): 14 Kris Brining; 15 Mark Applegarth; 16 Russ Spiers; 17 Josh Tonks.
Tries: Emmett (10), Morland (12), Buchanan (19), Nicklas (30); **Goals:** Nicklas 2/5.
COUGARS: 22 Ritchie Hawkyard; 26 Vinny Finigan; 23 Charlie Martin; 29 Hamish Barnes; 5 Paul White; 14 Adam Brook; 7 Paul Handforth; 19 Matthew Bailey; 9 James Feather; 12 Brendan Rawlins; 17 John Oakes; 25 Darren Hawkyard; 20 Aaron Ollett. Subs (all used): 8 Scott Law; 13 Ashley Lindsay; 15 Neil Cherryholme; 18 Sonny Esslemont.
Tries: Brook (45), Feather (66); **Goals:** Brook 2/3.
Rugby Leaguer & League Express Men of the Match: *City Knights:* Richard Wilkinson; *Cougars:* John Oakes.
Penalty count: 13-8; **Half-time:** 20-0;
Referee: Jon Roberts; **Attendance:** 624.

ROUND 5

Friday 15th April 2016

DEWSBURY RAMS 30 YORK CITY KNIGHTS 16

RAMS: 1 Josh Guzdek; 2 Dale Morton; 3 Karl Pryce; 4 Shane Grady; 5 Dalton Grant; 23 James Glover; 22 Andy Kain; 33 Paul Jackson; 17 Dom Speakman; 24 Jack Teanby; 32 Kyle Trout; 25 Joel Farrell; 13 Aaron Brown. Subs (all used): 19 Nathan Conroy; 21 Sam Bates; 40 Jonathan Walker; 18 Tony Tonks.
Tries: Teanby (16), Morton (20, 42), Grant (67), Kain (77); **Goals:** Glover 5/7.
CITY KNIGHTS: 1 Richard Wilkinson; 2 Austin Buchanan; 3 Brad Hey; 4 James Morland; 5 Ben Dent; 6 Jon Presley; 7 Danny Nicklas; 8 Brett Waller; 9 Harry Carter; 10 Jack Aldous; 11 Josh Tonks; 12 Ed Smith; 13 Mike Emmett. Subs (all used): 14 Kris Brining; 15 Mark Applegarth; 16 Russ Spiers; 17 Ross Osborne.
Tries: Wilkinson (29), Brining (33), Buchanan (40); **Goals:** Nicklas 2/3.
Rugby Leaguer & League Express Men of the Match: *Rams:* James Glover; *City Knights:* Danny Nicklas.
Penalty count: 11-7; **Half-time:** 10-16;
Referee: Andrew Sweet; **Attendance:** 707.

WAKEFIELD TRINITY WILDCATS 44 SHEFFIELD EAGLES 10

WILDCATS: 25 Craig Hall; 1 Ben Jones-Bishop; 4 Ashley Gibson; 18 Joe Arundel; 2 Tom Johnstone; 6 Jacob Miller; 7 Liam Finn (C); 10 Anthony England; 24 Stuart Howarth; 16 Tinirau Arona; 13 Anthony Tupou; 17 Matty Ashurst; 20 Michael Sio. Subs (all used): 11 Mickael Simon; 26 Chris Annakin; 28 Andy Yates; 31 Jason Walton.
Tries: Finn (12, 21), Johnstone (16), Jones-Bishop (24), Arona (33), Simon (38, 79), Sio (50); **Goals:** Finn 6/8.
EAGLES: 1 Quentin Laulu-Togagae; 2 Rob Worrincy; 3 Menzie Yere; 4 George Tyson; 22 Ryan Millar; 6 Cory Aston; 21 Dave Hewitt; 8 Steve Thorpe; 9 Keal Carlile; 10 Mitchell Stringer; 13 Matt James; 12 Duane Straugheir; 11 Michael Knowles. Subs (all used): 14 Matty Fozard; 18 Elliot Minchella; 16 Adam Neal; 17 Mark Mexico.
Tries: Yere (3, 24); **Goals:** Aston 1/2.
Rugby Leaguer & League Express Men of the Match: *Wildcats:* Liam Finn; *Eagles:* Menzie Yere.
Penalty count: 10-3; **Half-time:** 32-10;
Referee: Ben Thaler; **Attendance:** 2,257.

Saturday 16th April 2016

HULL KINGSTON ROVERS 22 OLDHAM 36

ROVERS: 18 Ben Cockayne; 29 Joe Wardill; 1 Ken Sio; 4 Iain Thornley; 5 Kieran Dixon; 11 Maurice Blair; 22 Matthew Marsh; 17 Dane Tilse; 9 Shaun Lunt; 16 James Green; 20 James Greenwood; 13 Chris Clarkson (C); 8 Adam Walker. Subs: 26 Rob Mulhern; 15 James Donaldson; 19 John Boudebza (not used); 24 George Lawler.
Tries: Tilse (16, 68), Lunt (47), Blair (58), Wardill (65); **Goals:** Cockayne 1/3, Sio 0/2.
Sin bin: Cockayne (77) - punching.
OLDHAM: 1 Richard Lepori; 2 Adam Clay; 9 Sam Gee; 22 Danny Grimshaw; 5 Jamel Chisholm; 6 Lewis Palfrey; 7 Steve Roper; 8 Phil Joy; 20 Gareth Owen; 10 Jack Spencer; 16 Gary Middlehurst; 12 Danny Langtree; 24 Will Hope. Subs (all used): 26 Michael Ward; 21 Kenny Hughes; 19 Adam Files; 13 Liam Thompson.
Tries: Hope (3), Lepori (23, 79), Roper (33), Clay (38), Middlehurst (56); **Goals:** Palfrey 6/7.
Rugby Leaguer & League Express Men of the Match: *Rovers:* Shaun Lunt; *Oldham:* Steve Roper.
Penalty count: 9-7; **Half-time:** 6-24;
Referee: Sam Ansell; **Attendance:** 3,056.

BATLEY BULLDOGS 28 FEATHERSTONE ROVERS 10

BULLDOGS: 22 Dave Scott; 2 Wayne Reittie; 23 Danny Cowling; 4 Shaun Squires; 5 Shaun Ainscough; 6 Cain Southernwood; 7 Dominic Brambani; 8 Keegan Hirst; 9 Luke Blake; 21 James Brown; 11 Brad Day; 19 Alex Bretherton; 13 Pat Walker. Subs (all used): 20 Alistair Leak; 18 Tom Lillycrop; 15 Adam Gledhill; 24 James Harrison.
Tries: Squires (8), Harrison (59), Ainscough (61), Brambani (63), Southernwood (65); **Goals:** Walker 4/6.
ROVERS: 15 Ian Hardman; 2 Kyran Johnson; 21 Bradley Knowles-Tagg; 4 Misi Taulapapa; 5 Scott Turner; 14 Will Milner; 1 Danny Craven; 10 Andrew Bostock; 12 John Davies; 17 Jack Ormondroyd; 18 Jamie Cording; 13 Tim Spears; 16 Colton Roche. Subs (all used): 20 Luke Cooper; 8 Darrell Griffin; 25 Liam Blockley; 7 Anthony Thackeray.
Tries: Taulapapa (24), Cording (72); **Goals:** Johnson 1/3.
Rugby Leaguer & League Express Men of the Match: *Bulldogs:* Dominic Brambani; *Rovers:* Danny Craven.
Penalty count: 10-6; **Half-time:** 4-6;
Referee: Gareth Hewer; **Attendance:** 1,461.

TOULOUSE OLYMPIQUE 10 LEIGH CENTURIONS 8

OLYMPIQUE: 1 Mark Kheirallah; 5 Kuni Minga; 3 Bastien Ader; 4 Gregory White; 2 Tony Maurel; 6 Johnathon Ford; 7 Arthur Gonzales-Trique; 16 Bastien Canet; 9 Kane Bentley; 8 Clement Boyer; 11 Sebastien Planas; 12 Rhys Curran; 13 Andrew Bentley. Subs (all used): 14 Mourad Kriouache; 10 Samy Masselot; 15 Maxime Puech; 17 Anthony Marion.
Try: Canet (5); **Goals:** Kheirallah 3/3.
CENTURIONS: 15 Jonny Pownall; 2 Adam Higson; 3 Greg Worthington; 24 Tom Armstrong; 5 Liam Kay; 6 Martyn Ridyard; 31 Ben Reynolds; 29 Jake Emmitt; 14 Micky Higham; 10 Dayne Weston; 27 Richard Whiting; 16 Reni Maitua; 13 Cory Paterson. Subs (all used): 19 Lewis Foster; 18 Tom Spencer; 17 Jamie Acton; 20 Sam Hopkins.
Try: Hopkins (44); **Goals:** Ridyard 2/2.
Rugby Leaguer & League Express Men of the Match: *Olympique:* Sebastien Planas; *Centurions:* Cory Paterson.
Penalty count: 10-11; **Half-time:** 8-0;
Referee: Chris Kendall; **Attendance:** 2,133.

Sunday 17th April 2016

HALIFAX 80 CASTLEFORD LOCK LANE 4

HALIFAX: 18 Miles Greenwood; 19 Tom Saxton; 20 Sam Smeaton; 3 Steve Tyrer; 23 Gareth Potts; 7 Gareth Moore; 1 Ben Johnston; 17 Gavin Bennion; 9 Ben Kaye; 10 Luke Ambler; 11 Dane Manning; 26 Ed Barber; 13 Jacob Fairbank. Subs (all used): 15 Ryan Maneely; 16 Richard Moore; 22 Connor Robinson; 24 Andy Bracek.
Tries: Johnston (10, 78), Fairbank (16), Barber (18, 38, 53, 64), Potts (22, 26), C Robinson (35), G Moore (51), Bracek (55), Greenwood (59), Ambler (69); **Goals:** Tyrer 12/14.
LOCK LANE: 1 Mikey Hayward; 2 Adam Garlick; 3 Nicky Saxton; 4 Lewis Price; 5 Connor Turner; 6 Nathan Fozzard; 7 Danny Rowse; 8 Ben Lawson; 9 Callum Butler; 10 Chris Siddons; 11 Royce Geoffrey; 12 Jordan Siddons; 13 Karl Robinson. Subs (all used): 14 Mitchell Platt; 15 Josh Steels; 16 Luke Tagg; 17 Craig Jones.
Try: Robinson (44); **Goals:** Rowse 0/1.
Rugby Leaguer & League Express Men of the Match: *Halifax:* Ed Barber; *Lock Lane:* Nicky Saxton.
Penalty count: 9-4; **Half-time:** 40-0;
Referee: Jamie Bloem; **Attendance:** 1,108.

HUNSLET HAWKS 14 SALFORD RED DEVILS 50

HAWKS: 1 Jimmy Watson; 5 James Duckworth; 4 Ayden Faal; 15 Mufaro Mvududu; 28 Richie Barnett; 20 Danny Thomas; 7 Danny Ansell; 8 Michael Haley; 9 Jack Lee; 10 Lewis Reed; 12 Ben Crane; 3 Jake Normington; 13 Liam Mackay. Subs (all used): 14 George Flanagan; 26 Austin Bell; 22 Craig Robinson; 29 Daniel Williams.
Tries: Lee (21), Flanagan (39), Duckworth (68); **Goals:** Ansell 1/4.
RED DEVILS: 14 Gareth O'Brien; 1 Niall Evalds; 4 Junior Sa'u; 3 Josh Griffin; 25 Jake Bibby; 6 Robert Lui; 7 Michael Dobson (C); 15 Adam Walne; 26 Josh Wood; 17 Phil Joseph; 20 Jordan Walne; 22 Matt Sarsfield; 21 Ryan Lannon. Subs (all used): 16 Olsi Krasniqi; 12 Weller Hauraki; 33 Josh Jones; 27 Matthew Haggarty (D).
Tries: Lannon (3), Bibby (7, 54), J Griffin (10, 20, 79), Wood (28), Lui (32, 50); **Goals:** Dobson 3/3, O'Brien 4/6 .
Rugby Leaguer & League Express Men of the Match: *Hawks:* Danny Ansell; *Red Devils:* Josh Griffin.
Penalty count: 9-8; **Half-time:** 8-32;
Referee: Chris Campbell; **Attendance:** 834.

ROCHDALE HORNETS 6 WIDNES VIKINGS 62

HORNETS: 1 Wayne English; 2 Corey Lee; 3 Mike Ratu; 4 James Dandy; 5 Dale Bloomfield; 6 Paul Crook; 7 Danny Yates; 8 Samir Tahraoui; 9 Ben Moores; 10 Warren Thompson; 11 Stuart Biscomb; 12 Jordan Case; 13 James Tilley. Subs (all used): 14 Alex McClurg; 15 Matty Hadden; 16 Alex Trumper; 17 Jovili Taira.
Try: Crook (20); **Goals:** Crook 1/1.
Sin bin: Taira (35) - high tackle on Johnstone.
VIKINGS: 2 Corey Thompson; 16 Paddy Flynn; 3 Chris Bridge; 25 Ed Chamberlain; 17 Stefan Marsh; 21 Tom Gilmore; 6 Kevin Brown (C); 10 Manase Manuokafoa; 9 Lloyd White; 18 Gil Dudson; 22 Matt Whitley; 14 Chris Dean; 19 Macgraff Leuluai. Subs (all used): 34 Sam Brooks; 24 Jay Chapelhow; 35 Jordan Johnstone; 13 Hep Cahill.
Tries: Bridge (4, 43, 74), Johnstone (25), Brown (29, 38, 69), Dean (36), Thompson (41), Marsh (45), Manuokafoa (63), Whitley (79); **Goals:** Bridge 7/12.
Rugby Leaguer & League Express Men of the Match: *Hornets:* Wayne English; *Vikings:* Corey Thompson.
Penalty count: 9-11; **Half-time:** 6-28;
Referee: James Child; **Attendance:** 1,242.

ROUND 6

Friday 6th May 2016

BATLEY BULLDOGS 4 CATALANS DRAGONS 40

BULLDOGS: 22 Dave Scott; 2 Wayne Reittie; 3 Chris Ulugia; 19 Alex Bretherton; 26 Alex Brown; 6 Cain Southernwood; 7 Dominic Brambani; 8 Keegan Hirst; 14 James Davey; 21 James Brown; 17 Joe Chandler; 24 James Harrison; 9 Luke Blake. Subs (all used): 20 Alistair Leak; 18 Tom Lillycrop; 10 Alex Rowe; 28 Dave Petersen.
Try: A Brown (65); **Goals:** Brambani 0/1.
DRAGONS: 1 Tony Gigot; 20 Fouad Yaha; 12 Justin Horo; 4 Vincent Duport; 5 Pat Richards; 27 Lucas Albert; 7 Richard Myler; 14 Dave Taylor; 16 Eloi Pelissier; 10 Remi Casty (C); 11 Glenn Stewart; 8 Louis Anderson; 13 Jason Baitieri. Subs (all used): 15 Julian Bousquet; 17 Gregory Mounis; 18 Thomas Bosc; 29 Willie Mason.
Tries: Yaha (5), Duport (25, 45), Myler (47), Taylor (55), Gigot (57, 70); **Goals:** Richards 6/7.
On report: Baitieri and Taylor (63) - alleged dangerous challenge on Hirst.
Rugby Leaguer & League Express Men of the Match: *Bulldogs:* Dave Scott; *Dragons:* Vincent Duport.
Penalty count: 10-2; **Half-time:** 0-12;
Referee: Gareth Hewer; **Attendance:** 1,249.

HUDDERSFIELD GIANTS 36 LEEDS RHINOS 22

GIANTS: 34 Ryan Brierley; 2 Jermaine McGillvary; 3 Leroy Cudjoe; 5 Aaron Murphy; 18 Jake Connor; 6 Danny Brough; 15 Kyle Wood; 8 Eorl Crabtree; 9 Ryan Hinchcliffe (C); 19 Josh Johnson; 4 Joe Wardle; 17 Ukuma Ta'ai; 12 Michael Lawrence. Subs (all used): 16 Sam Rapira; 21 Nathan Mason; 22 Oliver Roberts; 31 Sam Wood.
Tries: Ta'ai (13), McGillvary (20), Brierley (37), K Wood (49), Brough (66); **Goals:** Brough 6/7;
Field goals: Connor (40), Brough (69, 72, 79).
RHINOS: 1 Zak Hardaker; 23 Ashton Golding; 3 Kallum Watkins; 18 Jimmy Keinhorst; 22 Ash Handley; 14 Liam Sutcliffe; 25 Jordan Lilley; 8 Keith Galloway; 7 Rob Burrow (C); 17 Mitch Garbutt; 21 Josh Walters; 26 Brett Ferres; 11 Jamie Jones-Buchanan. Subs (all used): 10 Adam Cuthbertson; 19 Mitch Achurch; 20 Anthony Mullally; 29 Luke Briscoe.
Tries: Keinhorst (1, 52), Sutcliffe (45), Mullally (75); **Goals:** Lilley 3/4.
Sin bin: Ferres (37) - dissent.
Rugby Leaguer & League Express Men of the Match: *Giants:* Kyle Wood; *Rhinos:* Ashton Golding.
Penalty count: 11-11; **Half-time:** 19-6;
Referee: Ben Thaler; **Attendance:** 4,979.

Saturday 7th May 2016

CASTLEFORD TIGERS 32 SALFORD RED DEVILS 18

TIGERS: 18 Ryan Hampshire; 2 Joel Monaghan; 19 Ben Crooks; 3 Jake Webster; 5 Denny Solomona; 10 Grant Millington (C); 15 Paul McShane; 32 Larne Patrick; 9 Adam Milner; 14 Lee Jewitt; 17 Junior Moors; 12 Mike McMeeken; 13 Nathan Massey. Subs (all used): 16 Matt Cook; 22 Gadwin Springer; 25 Jy Hitchcox; 33 Danny Tickle (D).
Tries: McMeeken (11, 37), Webster (35), Solomona (41, 75), McShane (52); **Goals:** McShane 4/6.
RED DEVILS: 14 Gareth O'Brien; 2 Justin Carney; 4 Junior Sa'u; 33 Josh Jones; 5 Daniel Vidot (D); 6 Robert Lui; 7 Michael Dobson (C); 8 Craig Kopczak; 17 Phil Joseph; 10 George Griffin; 11 Ben Murdoch-Masila; 12 Weller Hauraki; 13 Mark Flanagan. Subs (all used): 20 Jordan Walne; 15 Adam Walne; 16 Olsi Krasniqi; 1 Niall Evalds.
Tries: Sa'u (11, 28), Lui (48); **Goals:** O'Brien 3/3.
Rugby Leaguer & League Express Men of the Match: *Tigers:* Paul McShane; *Red Devils:* Junior Sa'u.
Penalty count: 5-9; **Half-time:** 18-12;
Referee: James Child; **Attendance:** 3,317.

OLDHAM 10 WARRINGTON WOLVES 70

OLDHAM: 1 Richard Lepori; 2 Adam Clay; 4 Jack Holmes; 22 Danny Grimshaw; 5 Jamel Chisholm; 6 Lewis Palfrey; 7 Steve Roper; 8 Phil Joy; 20 Gareth Owen; 26 Michael Ward; 13 Liam Thompson; 16 Gary Middlehurst; 24 Will Hope. Subs (all used): 9 Sam Gee; 19 Adam Files; 21 Kenny Hughes; 25 Tom Ashton.
Tries: Ward (7), Owen (80); **Goals:** Palfrey 1/1, Roper 0/1.
WOLVES: 20 Kevin Penny; 22 Gene Ormsby; 3 Rhys Evans; 29 Benjamin Jullien; 2 Tom Lineham; 1 Kurt Gidley; 6 Stefan Ratchford; 8 Chris Hill (C); 9 Daryl Clark; 10 Ashton Sims; 25 Joe Philbin; 11 Ben Currie; 14 Joe Westerman. Subs (all used): 18 George King; 27 Sam Wilde; 31 Morgan Smith (D); 32 Jordan Cox.
Tries: Hill (16), Jullien (29, 73), Currie (32, 59), R Evans (36), G King (41, 44, 47), Lineham (51), Ormsby (53, 64), Smith (69); **Goals:** Gidley 6/9, Ratchford 3/4.

Rugby Leaguer & League Express Men of the Match: *Oldham:* Adam Clay; *Wolves:* Ben Currie.
Penalty count: 4-6; **Half-time:** 6-22;
Referee: Jon Roberts; **Attendance:** 2,394.

Sunday 8th May 2016

WAKEFIELD TRINITY WILDCATS 40
TOULOUSE OLYMPIQUE 22

WILDCATS: 21 Max Jowitt; 1 Ben Jones-Bishop; 31 Jason Walton; 25 Craig Hall; 2 Tom Johnstone; 6 Jacob Miller; 7 Liam Finn; 10 Anthony England; 24 Stuart Howarth; 16 Tinirau Arona; 12 Danny Kirmond (C); 17 Matty Ashurst; 20 Michael Sio. Subs (all used): 11 Mickael Simon; 22 Jordan Crowther; 28 Andy Yates; 23 Scott Anderson.
Tries: Johnstone (3, 15, 72, 78), Miller (9), Hall (13), Ashurst (57); **Goals:** Finn 6/7.
OLYMPIQUE: 1 Mark Kheirallah; 2 Tony Maurel; 21 Gavin Marguerite; 4 Gregory White; 5 Kuni Minga; 6 Jonathon Ford; 22 Danny Hulme; 8 Clement Boyer; 9 Kane Bentley; 16 Bastien Canet; 11 Sebastien Planas; 12 Rhys Curran; 17 Anthony Marion. Subs (all used): 14 Mourad Kriouache; 15 Maxime Puech; 10 Samy Masselot; 18 Tyla Hepi.
Tries: Marguerite (27), Kriouache (33), Hulme (62), Minga (67); **Goals:** Kheirallah 3/4.
Rugby Leaguer & League Express Men of the Match: *Wildcats:* Tom Johnstone; *Olympique:* Danny Hulme.
Penalty count: 8-7; **Half-time:** 22-10;
Referee: Chris Kendall; **Attendance:** 2,539.

DEWSBURY RAMS 4 WIGAN WARRIORS 54

RAMS: 1 Josh Guzdek; 34 Donald Kudangirana; 15 Jason Crookes; 4 Shane Grady; 5 Dalton Grant; 6 Paul Sykes; 22 Andy Kain; 14 Luke Adamson; 17 Dom Speakman; 24 Jack Teanby; 12 Scott Hale; 32 Kyle Trout; 25 Joel Farrell. Subs (all used): 19 Nathan Conroy; 13 Aaron Brown; 27 Jason Muranka; 40 Jonathan Walker.
Try: Sykes (24); **Goals:** Sykes 0/1.
WARRIORS: 4 Dan Sarginson; 5 Dominic Manfredi; 3 Anthony Gelling; 20 Oliver Gildart; 2 Josh Charnley; 6 George Williams; 7 Matty Smith; 8 Dominic Crosby; 16 Sam Powell; 17 Lee Mossop; 14 John Bateman; 25 Willie Isa; 13 Sean O'Loughlin (C). Subs (all used): 19 Taulima Tautai; 21 Ryan Sutton; 22 Lewis Tierney; 26 Greg Burke.
Tries: Charnley (2, 11), Williams (5), Gildart (15, 43), Sarginson (18), Bateman (31, 37), Sutton (41), Tierney (56); **Goals:** Smith 0/2, Charnley 7/8.
Rugby Leaguer & League Express Men of the Match: *Rams:* Paul Sykes; *Warriors:* Anthony Gelling.
Penalty count: 8-6; **Half-time:** 4-36;
Referee: Chris Campbell; **Attendance:** 3,102.

HALIFAX 18 WIDNES VIKINGS 28

HALIFAX: 18 Miles Greenwood; 2 Will Sharp; 3 Steve Tyrer; 20 Sam Smeaton; 5 James Saltonstall; 22 Connor Robinson; 6 Scott Murrell; 17 Gavin Bennion; 30 Brandon Moore; 14 Adam Tangata; 11 Dane Manning; 4 Ben Heaton; 13 Jacob Fairbank. Subs (all used): 1 Ben Johnston; 9 Ben Kaye; 16 Richard Moore; 21 Adam Robinson.
Tries: Saltonstall (9), A Robinson (40), Greenwood (46); **Goals:** Tyrer 3/3.
VIKINGS: 1 Rhys Hanbury; 2 Corey Thompson; 4 Charly Runciman; 14 Chris Dean; 25 Ed Chamberlain; 7 Joe Mellor (C); 33 Aaron Heremaia; 13 Hep Cahill; 9 Lloyd White; 18 Gil Dudson; 11 Chris Houston; 15 Setaimata Sa; 19 Macgraff Leuluai. Subs (all used): 10 Manase Manuokafoa; 22 Matt Whitley; 24 Jay Chapelhow; 35 Jordan Johnstone.
Tries: Heremaia (4), White (23), Houston (30), Runciman (64), J Chapelhow (74); **Goals:** Hanbury 4/5.
Rugby Leaguer & League Express Men of the Match: *Halifax:* Jacob Fairbank; *Vikings:* Hep Cahill.
Penalty count: 7-8; **Half-time:** 12-18;
Referee: Michael Woodhead; **Attendance:** 2,032.

ST HELENS 18 HULL FC 47

SAINTS: 1 Jonny Lomax; 21 Matty Dawson; 18 Dominique Peyroux; 4 Mark Percival; 22 Jack Owens; 19 Theo Fages; 7 Luke Walsh; 8 Alex Walmsley; 9 James Roby; 10 Kyle Amor; 11 Atelea Vea; 20 Joe Greenwood; 12 Jon Wilkin (C). Subs (all used): 13 Louie McCarthy-Scarsbrook; 14 Lama Tasi; 15 Greg Richards; 28 Morgan Knowles.
Tries: Percival (5), McCarthy-Scarsbrook (33), Walsh (46); **Goals:** Walsh 3/3.
HULL FC: 1 Jamie Shaul; 20 Curtis Naughton; 2 Mahe Fonua; 24 Kirk Yeaman; 5 Fetuli Talanoa; 6 Leon Pryce; 7 Marc Sneyd; 8 Scott Taylor; 9 Danny Houghton; 10 Liam Watts; 30 Danny Washbrook; 12 Mark Minichiello; 11 Gareth Ellis (C). Subs (all used): 15 Chris Green; 16 Jordan Thompson; 17 Dean Hadley; 22 Josh Bowden.
Tries: Houghton (11), Taylor (14, 69), Ellis (21), Shaul (36), Naughton (53), Yeaman (64), Talanoa (75); **Goals:** Sneyd 7/9; **Field goal:** Sneyd (39).

Rugby Leaguer & League Express Men of the Match: *Saints:* Mark Percival; *Hull FC:* Danny Houghton.
Penalty count: 3-6; **Half-time:** 12-25;
Referee: Richard Silverwood; **Attendance:** 7,094.

QUARTER FINALS

Thursday 23rd June 2016

HUDDERSFIELD GIANTS 16
WAKEFIELD TRINITY WILDCATS 28

GIANTS: 1 Scott Grix; 2 Jermaine McGillvary; 3 Leroy Cudjoe; 4 Joe Wardle; 18 Jake Connor; 6 Danny Brough; 7 Jamie Ellis; 8 Eorl Crabtree; 9 Ryan Hinchcliffe (C); 16 Sam Rapira; 11 Tom Symonds; 17 Ukuma Ta'ai; 12 Michael Lawrence. Subs (all used): 5 Aaron Murphy; 15 Kyle Wood; 19 Josh Johnson; 21 Nathan Mason.
Tries: Grix (19), Connor (25), McGillvary (57, 78); **Goals:** Ellis 0/2, Brough 0/2.
Sin bin: Brough (13) - high challenge on Lyne.
WILDCATS: 21 Max Jowitt; 2 Tom Johnstone; 14 Reece Lyne; 3 Bill Tupou; 1 Ben Jones-Bishop; 6 Jacob Miller; 7 Liam Finn (C); 35 David Fifita; 9 Scott Moore; 10 Anthony England; 19 Jon Molloy; 17 Matty Ashurst; 20 Michael Sio. Subs (all used): 16 Tinirau Arona; 23 Scott Anderson; 26 Chris Annakin; 31 Jason Walton.
Tries: Fifita (2, 55), Jones-Bishop (14), Johnstone (44); **Goals:** Finn 6/7.
Rugby Leaguer & League Express Men of the Match: *Giants:* Jake Connor; *Wildcats:* David Fifita.
Penalty count: 7-9; **Half-time:** 8-14;
Referee: Gareth Hewer; **Attendance:** 3,289.

Friday 24th June 2016

WARRINGTON WOLVES 20 WIDNES VIKINGS 18

WOLVES: 6 Stefan Ratchford; 5 Matthew Russell; 3 Rhys Evans; 4 Ryan Atkins; 20 Kevin Penny; 1 Kurt Gidley; 7 Chris Sandow; 8 Chris Hill (C); 9 Daryl Clark; 13 Ben Westwood; 11 Ben Currie; 12 Jack Hughes; 14 Joe Westerman. Subs (all used): 16 Brad Dwyer; 18 George King; 32 Jordan Cox; 33 Ryan Bailey.
Tries: Hughes (4), Penny (36), Dwyer (59); **Goals:** Gidley 4/5.
VIKINGS: 1 Rhys Hanbury; 2 Corey Thompson; 4 Charly Runciman; 3 Chris Bridge; 5 Patrick Ah Van; 7 Joe Mellor; 6 Kevin Brown (C); 13 Hep Cahill; 9 Lloyd White; 36 Jack Buchanan; 11 Chris Houston; 14 Chris Dean; 19 Macgraff Leuluai. Subs (all used): 10 Manase Manuokafoa; 18 Gil Dudson; 22 Matt Whitley; 33 Aaron Heremaia.
Tries: Mellor (27), Whitley (29), Runciman (65); **Goals:** Hanbury 3/3.
Rugby Leaguer & League Express Men of the Match: *Wolves:* Kurt Gidley; *Vikings:* Rhys Hanbury.
Penalty count: 9-6; **Half-time:** 10-12;
Referee: James Child; **Attendance:** 7,773.

Saturday 25th June 2016

HULL FC 22 CATALANS DRAGONS 8

HULL FC: 1 Jamie Shaul; 19 Steve Michaels; 2 Mahe Fonua; 24 Kirk Yeaman; 5 Fetuli Talanoa; 3 Carlos Tuimavave; 7 Marc Sneyd; 8 Scott Taylor; 9 Danny Houghton; 10 Liam Watts; 21 Sika Manu; 12 Mark Minichiello; 11 Gareth Ellis (C). Subs (all used): 15 Chris Green; 22 Josh Bowden; 23 Frank Pritchard; 30 Danny Washbrook.
Tries: Michaels (21), Pritchard (33), Houghton (50); **Goals:** Sneyd 5/5.
DRAGONS: 21 Morgan Escare; 2 Jodie Broughton; 33 Benjamin Garcia (D2); 5 Pat Richards; 20 Fouad Yaha; 6 Todd Carney; 27 Lucas Albert; 29 Willie Mason; 16 Eloi Pelissier; 10 Remi Casty (C); 11 Glenn Stewart; 12 Justin Horo; 13 Jason Baitieri. Subs (all used): 14 Dave Taylor; 15 Julian Bousquet; 17 Gregory Mounis; 18 Thomas Bosc.
Tries: Garcia (13), Yaha (57); **Goals:** Richards 0/2.
Rugby Leaguer & League Express Men of the Match: *Hull FC:* Scott Taylor; *Dragons:* Glenn Stewart.
Penalty count: 10-6; **Half-time:** 12-4;
Referee: Ben Thaler; **Attendance:** 9,639.

WIGAN WARRIORS 26 CASTLEFORD TIGERS 12

WARRIORS: 1 Sam Tomkins; 2 Josh Charnley; 4 Dan Sarginson; 20 Oliver Gildart; 5 Dominic Manfredi; 6 George Williams; 7 Matty Smith; 17 Lee Mossop; 16 Sam Powell; 10 Ben Flower; 21 Ryan Sutton; 25 Willie Isa; 13 Sean O'Loughlin (C). Subs (all used): 11 Joel Tomkins; 19 Taulima Tautai; 26 Greg Burke; 29 Joe Bretherton.
Tries: Sarginson (6), S Tomkins (15), Charnley (29, 35), Manfredi (66); **Goals:** Smith 3/5.
TIGERS: 1 Luke Dorn; 2 Joel Monaghan; 19 Ben Crooks; 24 Greg Minikin; 5 Denny Solomona; 10 Grant Millington; 7 Luke Gale (C); 14 Lee Jewitt; 15 Paul McShane; 32 Larne Patrick; 17 Junior Moors; 12 Mike McMeeken; 13 Nathan Massey. Subs (all used): 9 Adam Milner; 33 Danny Tickle; 11 Oliver Holmes; 16 Matt Cook.
Tries: Gale (59), Crooks (80); **Goals:** Gale 2/2.
Rugby Leaguer & League Express Men of the Match: *Warriors:* Sam Tomkins; *Tigers:* Junior Moors.
Penalty count: 8-13; **Half-time:** 22-0;
Referee: Chris Campbell; **Attendance:** 8,010.

SEMI-FINALS

Friday 29th July 2016

HULL FC 16 WIGAN WARRIORS 12

HULL FC: 1 Jamie Shaul; 19 Steve Michaels; 2 Mahe Fonua; 24 Kirk Yeaman; 5 Fetuli Talanoa; 3 Carlos Tuimavave; 7 Marc Sneyd; 8 Scott Taylor; 9 Danny Houghton; 10 Liam Watts; 21 Sika Manu; 12 Mark Minichiello; 11 Gareth Ellis (C). Subs (all used): 16 Jordan Thompson; 23 Frank Pritchard; 30 Danny Washbrook; 15 Chris Green.
Tries: Michaels (47), Talanoa (51); **Goals:** Sneyd 4/4.
WARRIORS: 1 Sam Tomkins; 22 Lewis Tierney; 4 Dan Sarginson; 20 Oliver Gildart; 5 Dominic Manfredi; 6 George Williams; 7 Matty Smith; 21 Ryan Sutton; 16 Sam Powell; 10 Ben Flower; 25 Willie Isa; 14 John Bateman; 13 Sean O'Loughlin (C). Subs (all used): 8 Dominic Crosby; 17 Lee Mossop; 19 Taulima Tautai; 29 Joe Bretherton.
Tries: Williams (16), Isa (70); **Goals:** Smith 2/3.
Rugby Leaguer & League Express Men of the Match: *Hull FC:* Sika Manu; *Warriors:* George Williams.
Penalty count: 7-10; **Half-time:** 2-6;
Referee: Ben Thaler; **Attendance:** 10,488 *(at Keepmoat Stadium, Doncaster)*.

Saturday 30th July 2016

WAKEFIELD TRINITY WILDCATS 12
WARRINGTON WOLVES 56

WILDCATS: 21 Max Jowitt; 1 Ben Jones-Bishop; 14 Reece Lyne; 18 Joe Arundel; 25 Craig Hall; 6 Jacob Miller; 7 Liam Finn; 8 Nick Scruton; 9 Scott Moore; 35 David Fifita; 31 Jason Walton; 13 Anthony Tupou; 20 Michael Sio. Subs (all used): 22 Jordan Crowther; 12 Danny Kirmond (C); 16 Tinirau Arona; 28 Andy Yates.
Tries: Hall (4), Jowitt (66); **Goals:** Finn 2/2.
Sin bin: Fifita (50) - high tackle on Sandow.
WOLVES: 6 Stefan Ratchford; 5 Matthew Russell; 24 Toby King; 4 Ryan Atkins; 3 Rhys Evans; 1 Kurt Gidley; 7 Chris Sandow; 8 Chris Hill (C); 9 Daryl Clark; 10 Ashton Sims; 11 Ben Currie; 12 Jack Hughes; 14 Joe Westerman. Subs (all used): 18 George King; 16 Brad Dwyer; 13 Ben Westwood; 33 Ryan Bailey.
Tries: Hughes (15), Clark (23), R Evans (26), Gidley (39), Sandow (46), Ratchford (49), Currie (53), T King (55, 78), Westwood (63); **Goals:** Gidley 7/9, Ratchford 1/2.
Rugby Leaguer & League Express Men of the Match: *Wildcats:* Jordan Crowther; *Wolves:* Chris Sandow.
Penalty count: 5-7; **Half-time:** 6-24;
Referee: Gareth Hewer; **Attendance:** 10,358 *(at Leigh Sports Village)*.

FINAL

Saturday 27th August 2016

HULL FC 12 WARRINGTON WOLVES 10

HULL FC: 1 Jamie Shaul; 19 Steve Michaels; 2 Mahe Fonua; 24 Kirk Yeaman; 5 Fetuli Talanoa; 3 Carlos Tuimavave; 7 Marc Sneyd; 8 Scott Taylor; 9 Danny Houghton; 10 Liam Watts; 21 Sika Manu; 12 Mark Minichiello; 11 Gareth Ellis (C). Subs (all used): 22 Josh Bowden; 23 Frank Pritchard; 30 Danny Washbrook; 15 Chris Green.
Tries: Fonua (61), Shaul (73); **Goals:** Sneyd 2/2.
WOLVES: 6 Stefan Ratchford; 5 Matthew Russell; 24 Toby King; 4 Ryan Atkins; 3 Rhys Evans; 1 Kurt Gidley; 7 Chris Sandow; 8 Chris Hill (C); 9 Daryl Clark; 10 Ashton Sims; 11 Ben Currie; 12 Jack Hughes; 14 Joe Westerman. Subs (all used): 18 George King; 16 Brad Dwyer; 13 Ben Westwood; 33 Ryan Bailey.
Tries: Russell (34), Currie (54); **Goals:** Gidley 1/3.
Rugby Leaguer & League Express Men of the Match: *Hull FC:* Danny Houghton; *Wolves:* Daryl Clark.
Penalty count: 3-3; **Half-time:** 0-6;
Referee: Gareth Hewer; **Attendance:** 76,235 *(at Wembley Stadium)*.

Hull FC's Jamie Shaul beats Warrington's Daryl Clark to score the winning try in the Challenge Cup Final

GRAND FINALS
1998-2015

1998

DIVISION ONE GRAND FINAL

Saturday 26th September 1998

FEATHERSTONE ROVERS 22 WAKEFIELD TRINITY 24

ROVERS: 1 Steve Collins; 2 Carl Hall; 3 Shaun Irwin; 4 Danny Baker; 5 Karl Pratt; 6 Jamie Coventry; 7 Ty Fallins; 8 Chico Jackson; 9 Richard Chapman; 10 Stuart Dickens; 11 Gary Price; 12 Neil Lowe; 13 Richard Slater. Subs: 14 Paddy Handley for Coventry (70); 15 Asa Amone for Lowe (50); 16 Micky Clarkson for Jackson (50); 17 Steve Dooler (not used). **Tries:** Baker (15), Jackson (45), Collins (49), Hall (69); **Goals:** Chapman 3.
TRINITY: 1 Martyn Holland; 2 Josh Bostock; 3 Adam Hughes; 4 Martin Law; 5 Kevin Gray; 6 Garen Casey; 7 Roger Kenworthy; 8 Francis Stephenson; 9 Roy Southernwood; 10 Gary Lord; 11 Ian Hughes; 12 Sonny Whakarau; 13 Matt Fuller. Subs: 14 Sean Richardson for I Hughes (32); 15 Andy Fisher for Lord (26); 16 David Mycoe (not used); 17 Wayne McDonald for Whakarau (70); Lord for Stephenson (40); Stephenson for Lord (70).
Tries: Southernwood (2), Bostock (7, 25), Casey (58), Stephenson (76); **Goals:** Casey 2.
League Express Men of the Match:
Rovers: Richard Chapman; *Trinity:* Garen Casey.
Penalty count: 8-3; **Half-time:** 6-12;
Referee: Nick Oddy (Halifax); **Attendance:** 8,224
(at McAlpine Stadium, Huddersfield).

SUPER LEAGUE GRAND FINAL

Saturday 24th October 1998

LEEDS RHINOS 4 WIGAN WARRIORS 10

RHINOS: 1 Iestyn Harris (C); 22 Leroy Rivett; 3 Richie Blackmore; 4 Brad Godden; 5 Francis Cummins; 13 Daryl Powell; 7 Ryan Sheridan; 8 Martin Masella; 21 Terry Newton; 25 Darren Fleary; 11 Adrian Morley; 17 Anthony Farrell; 12 Marc Glanville. Subs: 20 Jamie Mathiou for Masella (25); 24 Marcus St Hilaire for Powell (40); 14 Graham Holroyd for Newton (49); 27 Andy Hay for Fleary (54); Powell for Godden (58); Masella for Mathiou (71).
Try: Blackmore (20).
WARRIORS: 1 Kris Radlinski; 2 Jason Robinson; 3 Danny Moore; 4 Gary Connolly; 5 Mark Bell; 6 Henry Paul; 7 Tony Smith; 16 Terry O'Connor; 9 Robbie McCormack; 10 Tony Mestrov; 20 Lee Gilmour; 17 Stephen Holgate; 13 Andy Farrell (C). Subs: 8 Neil Cowie for O'Connor (18BB, rev 48); 14 Mick Cassidy for McCormack (19BB, rev 27); 25 Paul Johnson for Moore (37); 12 Simon Haughton for Gilmour (27BB, rev 33); Haughton for Holgate (33); Cowie for Mestrov (54); Cassidy for Haughton (64); Holgate for Cowie (68); Haughton for Gilmour (71BB, rev 75); Mestrov for O'Connor (75BB).
Try: Robinson (37); **Goals:** Farrell 3.
League Express Men of the Match:
Rhinos: Iestyn Harris; *Warriors:* Jason Robinson.
Penalty count: 7-13; **Half-time:** 4-6;
Referee: Russell Smith (Castleford); **Attendance:** 43,553
(at Old Trafford, Manchester).

1999

NORTHERN FORD PREMIERSHIP GRAND FINAL

Saturday 25th September 1999

DEWSBURY RAMS 11 HUNSLET HAWKS 12

RAMS: 1 Nathan Graham; 2 Alex Godfrey; 3 Paul Evans; 4 Brendan O'Meara; 5 Adrian Flynn; 6 Richard Agar; 7 Barry Eaton; 8 Alan Boothroyd; 9 Paul Delaney; 10 Matthew Long; 11 Andy Spink; 12 Mark Haigh; 13 Damian Ball. Subs: 14 Brendan Williams for Eaton (5BB, rev 15); 15 Sean Richardson for Haigh (50); 16 Simon Hicks for Long (25); 17 Paul Medley for Spink (50); Williams for Evans (61); Long for Boothroyd (71); Spink for Long (78).
Tries: Flynn (27), Ball (54); **Goal:** Eaton; **Field goal:** Agar.
HAWKS: 1 Abraham Fatnowna; 2 Chris Ross; 3 Shaun Irwin; 4 Paul Cook; 5 Iain Higgins; 6 Marcus Vassilakopoulos; 7 Latham Tawhai; 8 Richard Hayes; 9 Richard Pachniuk; 10 Steve Pryce; 11 Rob Wilson; 12 Jamie Leighton; 13 Lee St Hilaire. Subs: 14 Mick Coyle for Wilson (57); 15 Phil Kennedy for Pryce (35); 16 Jamie Thackray for St Hilaire (25); 17 Richard Baker for Higgins (55); Higgins for Fatnowna (62); Pryce for Kennedy (65).
Tries: Cook (31), Higgins (46); **Goal:** Ross;
Field goals: Tawhai, Leighton.
League Express Men of the Match:
Rams: Barry Eaton; *Hawks:* Latham Tawhai.
Penalty count: 8-5; **Half-time:** 7-7;
Referee: Steve Ganson (St Helens); **Attendance:** 5,783
(at Headingley Stadium, Leeds).

SUPER LEAGUE GRAND FINAL

Saturday 9th October 1999

BRADFORD BULLS 6 ST HELENS 8

BULLS: 28 Stuart Spruce; 2 Tevita Vaikona; 20 Scott Naylor; 5 Michael Withers; 17 Leon Pryce; 6 Henry Paul; 1 Robbie Paul (C); 10 Paul Anderson; 9 James Lowes; 29 Stuart Fielden; 15 David Boyle; 23 Bernard Dwyer; 13 Steve McNamara. Subs: 14 Paul Deacon for R Paul (53); 4 Nathan McAvoy (not used); 12 Mike Forshaw for McNamara (18); 22 Brian McDermott for Anderson (18); Anderson for Fielden (61); Fielden for Dwyer (65); R Paul for Deacon (72).
Try: H Paul (18); **Goal:** H Paul.
SAINTS: 1 Paul Atcheson; 14 Chris Smith; 3 Kevin Iro; 4 Paul Newlove; 5 Anthony Sullivan; 13 Paul Sculthorpe; 20 Tommy Martyn; 8 Apollo Perelini; 9 Keiron Cunningham; 10 Julian O'Neill; 2 Fereti Tuilagi; 21 Sonny Nickle; 11 Chris Joynt (C). Subs: 26 Paul Wellens for Newlove (43); 16 Vila Matautia for O'Neill (20); 7 Sean Long for Perelini (24); Perelini for Matautia (46); O'Neill for Perelini (69).
Tries: Iro (65); **Goals:** Long 2.
League Express Men of the Match:
Bulls: Henry Paul; *Saints:* Kevin Iro.
Penalty count: 4-7; **Half-time:** 6-2;
Referee: Stuart Cummings (Widnes);
Attendance: 50,717 *(at Old Trafford, Manchester).*

2000

NORTHERN FORD PREMIERSHIP GRAND FINAL

Saturday 29th July 2000

DEWSBURY RAMS 13 LEIGH CENTURIONS 12

RAMS: 1 Nathan Graham; 2 Richard Baker; 4 Dan Potter; 3 Brendan O'Meara; 5 Adrian Flynn; 6 Richard Agar; 7 Barry Eaton; 8 Shayne Williams; 9 David Mycoe; 10 Mark Haigh; 11 Sean Richardson; 12 Daniel Frame; 13 Damian Ball. Subs: 14 Gavin Wood (not used); 15 Paul Delaney for Mycoe (53); 16 Ryan McDonald for Haigh (30); 17 Matthew Long for Williams (23); Haigh for McDonald (64).
Tries: Eaton (2), Long (23); **Goals:** Eaton 2;
Field goal: Agar.
Sin bin: Williams (66) - use of the elbow.
On report: Richardson (20) - high tackle on Donlan.
CENTURIONS: 1 Stuart Donlan; 5 David Ingram; 3 Paul Anderson; 4 Andy Fairclough; 2 Alan Cross; 6 Liam Bretherton; 7 Kieron Purtill; 8 Tim Street; 9 Mick Higham; 10 Andy Leatham; 11 Chris Baldwin; 12 Heath Cruckshank; 13 Adam Bristow. Subs: 14 James Arkwright for Cross (68); 15 Paul Norman for Street (36); 16 Radney Bowker (not used); 17 David Whittle for Leathem (24); Street for Norman (62).
Tries: Higham (29, 69); **Goals:** Bretherton 2.
Sin bin: Whittle (66) - retaliation.
League Express Men of the Match:
Rams: Richard Agar; *Centurions:* Mick Higham.
Penalty count: 4-4; **Half-time:** 10-6;
Referee: Robert Connolly (Wigan); **Attendance:** 8,487
(at Gigg Lane, Bury).

SUPER LEAGUE GRAND FINAL

Saturday 14th October 2000

ST HELENS 29 WIGAN WARRIORS 16

SAINTS: 17 Paul Wellens; 24 Steve Hall; 3 Kevin Iro; 15 Sean Hoppe; 5 Anthony Sullivan; 20 Tommy Martyn; 7 Sean Long; 8 Apollo Perelini; 9 Keiron Cunningham; 10 Julian O'Neill; 11 Chris Joynt (C); 22 Tim Jonkers; 13 Paul Sculthorpe. Subs: 14 Fereti Tuilagi for O'Neill (20); 12 Sonny Nickle for Perelini (28); 26 John Stankevitch for Jonkers (50); 23 Scott Barrow (not used); Perelini for Nickle (52); Jonkers for Stankevitch (66); Stankevitch for Perelini (67BB); O'Neill for Hall (74).
Tries: Hoppe (7), Joynt (28, 50), Tuilagi (69), Jonkers (80); **Goals:** Long 4; **Field goal:** Sculthorpe.
WARRIORS: 5 Jason Robinson; 2 Brett Dallas; 1 Kris Radlinski; 3 Steve Renouf; 26 David Hodgson; 6 Tony Smith; 7 Willie Peters; 8 Terry O'Connor; 9 Terry Newton; 10 Neil Cowie; 11 Mick Cassidy; 12 Denis Betts; 13 Andy Farrell (C). Subs: 23 Brady Malam for Cowie (30); 17 Tony Mestrov for O'Connor (43); 19 Chris Chester for Cassidy (47BB, rev 69); 14 Lee Gilmour for Betts (51); O'Connor for Mestrov (61); Cowie for Malam (67); Chester for Newton (75).
Tries: Farrell (13), Hodgson (58), Smith (61);
Goals: Farrell 2.
League Express Men of the Match:
Saints: Chris Joynt; *Warriors:* Andy Farrell.
Penalty count: 10-6; **Half-time:** 11-4;
Referee: Russell Smith (Castleford); **Attendance:** 58,132
(at Old Trafford, Manchester).

2001

NORTHERN FORD PREMIERSHIP GRAND FINAL

Saturday 28th July 2001

OLDHAM 14 WIDNES VIKINGS 24

OLDHAM: 1 Mark Sibson; 2 Joey Hayes; 3 Anthony Gibbons; 4 Pat Rich; 5 Joe McNicholas; 6 David Gibbons; 7 Neil Roden; 8 Leo Casey; 9 Keith Brennan; 10 Paul Norton; 11 Phil Farrell; 12 Bryan Henare; 13 Kevin Mannion. Subs: 14 Mike Ford for Mannion (27); 15 Jason Clegg for Casey (18); 16 John Hough for Brennan (44); 17 Danny Guest for Norton (40BB, rev 54); Mannion for Henare (65); Guest for Clegg (73).
Tries: Brennan (9), Ford (74), Mannion (80); **Goal:** Rich.
VIKINGS: 1 Paul Atcheson; 2 Damian Munro; 3 Craig Weston; 4 Jason Demetriou; 5 Chris Percival; 6 Richard Agar; 7 Martin Crompton; 8 Simon Knox; 9 Phil Cantillon; 10 Stephen Holgate; 11 Steve Gee; 12 Sean Richardson; 13 Tommy Hodgkinson. Subs: 14 Andy Craig for Percival (65); 15 Chris McKinney for Crompton (18); 16 Joe Faimalo for Knox (32); 17 Matthew Long for Holgate (23); Knox for Long (49BB, rev 61); Holgate for Long (74).
Tries: Gee (17), Demetriou (38, 60), Cantillon (50), Munro (69); **Goals:** Weston 2.
League Express Men of the Match:
Oldham: Jason Clegg; *Vikings:* Phil Cantillon.
Penalty count: 8-5; **Half-time:** 4-10;
Referee: Steve Ganson (St Helens); **Attendance:** 8,974
(at Spotland, Rochdale).

SUPER LEAGUE GRAND FINAL

Saturday 13th October 2001

BRADFORD BULLS 37 WIGAN WARRIORS 6

BULLS: 5 Michael Withers; 2 Tevita Vaikona; 20 Scott Naylor; 23 Graham Mackay; 3 Leon Pryce; 6 Henry Paul; 1 Robbie Paul (C); 8 Joe Vagana; 9 James Lowes; 22 Brian McDermott; 11 Daniel Gartner; 19 Jamie Peacock; 12 Mike Forshaw. Subs: 29 Stuart Fielden for McDermott (21BB, rev 65); 10 Paul Anderson for Vagana (22); 15 Shane Rigon for Pryce (40); 7 Paul Deacon for R Paul (69); Vagana for Anderson (53); Fielden for Gartner (72); Anderson for Vagana (74).
Tries: Lowes (9), Withers (11, 27, 31), Fielden (65), Mackay (72); **Goals:** H Paul 5, Mackay; **Field goal:** H Paul.
WARRIORS: 1 Kris Radlinski; 2 Brett Dallas; 4 Gary Connolly; 3 Steve Renouf; 5 Brian Carney; 6 Matthew Johns; 7 Adrian Lam; 8 Terry O'Connor; 9 Terry Newton; 20 Harvey Howard; 11 Mick Cassidy; 14 David Furner; 13 Andy Farrell (C). Subs: 15 Paul Johnson for Carney (12BB); 10 Neil Cowie for Howard (17); 12 Denis Betts for O'Connor (32); 19 Chris Chester for Farrell (59); O'Connor for Cowie (55); Howard for Newton (64); Cowie for Cassidy (72).
Try: Lam (63); **Goal:** Furner.
League Express Men of the Match:
Bulls: Michael Withers; *Warriors:* Adrian Lam.
Penalty count: 6-7; **Half-time:** 26-0;
Referee: Stuart Cummings (Widnes);
Attendance: 60,164 *(at Old Trafford, Manchester)*.

2002

NORTHERN FORD PREMIERSHIP GRAND FINAL

Saturday 12th October 2002

HUDDERSFIELD GIANTS 38 LEIGH CENTURIONS 16

GIANTS: 1 Ben Cooper; 2 Hefin O'Hare; 3 Eorl Crabtree; 4 Graeme Hallas; 5 Marcus St Hilaire; 6 Stanley Gene; 7 Chris Thorman; 8 Michael Slicker; 9 Paul March; 10 Jeff Wittenberg; 11 David Atkins; 12 Robert Roberts; 13 Steve McNamara. Subs: 14 Heath Cruckshank for Roberts (24BB); 15 Chris Molyneux for Slicker (53); 16 Darren Turner for March (21); 17 Andy Rice for Cruckshank (57); Roberts for Wittenberg (34); Wittenberg for Roberts (74).
Tries: O'Hare (12, 78), St Hilaire (34, 53), Thorman (46), Gene (57); **Goals:** McNamara 7.
Sin bin: Roberts (47) - fighting.
CENTURIONS: 1 Neil Turley; 2 Leon Felton; 4 Jon Roper; 3 Dale Cardoza; 5 Oliver Marns; 6 Willie Swann; 7 Bobbie Goulding; 8 Vila Matautia; 9 Paul Rowley; 10 David Bradbury; 11 Simon Baldwin; 12 Andrew Isherwood; 13 Adam Bristow. Subs: 14 Gareth Price for Bradbury (24BB, rev 35); 15 John Duffy for Swann (32); 16 John Hamilton for Bristow (46BB, rev 57); 17 David Whittle for Matautia (22); Matautia for Bradbury (53BB); Swann for Goulding (58); Hamilton for Whittle (67); Bradbury for Turley (72); Goulding for Swann (75).
Tries: Cardoza (9), Marns (18), Hamilton (70);
Goals: Turley 2.
Sin bin: Whittle (47) - fighting; Bristow (74) - interference.
On report: Isherwood (66) - high tackle on Roberts.
Rugby League & League Express Men of the Match:
Giants: Chris Thorman; *Centurions:* Adam Bristow.
Penalty count: 11-11; **Half-time:** 14-10;
Referee: Karl Kirkpatrick (Warrington);
Attendance: 9,051 *(at Halton Stadium, Widnes)*.

SUPER LEAGUE GRAND FINAL

Saturday 19th October 2002

BRADFORD BULLS 18 ST HELENS 19

BULLS: 6 Michael Withers; 2 Tevita Vaikona; 20 Scott Naylor; 15 Brandon Costin; 5 Lesley Vainikolo; 1 Robbie Paul (C); 7 Paul Deacon; 8 Joe Vagana; 9 James Lowes; 29 Stuart Fielden; 11 Daniel Gartner; 12 Jamie Peacock; 13 Mike Forshaw. Subs: 14 Lee Gilmour for Gartner (21); 10 Paul Anderson for Vagana (25); 22 Brian McDermott for Fielden (34); 3 Leon Pryce for Vainikolo (53); Fielden for Anderson (55); Vainikolo for Paul (77).
Tries: Naylor (3), Paul (44), Withers (47); **Goals:** Deacon 3.
SAINTS: 1 Paul Wellens; 5 Darren Albert; 3 Martin Gleeson; 4 Paul Newlove; 19 Anthony Stewart; 13 Paul Sculthorpe; 7 Sean Long; 8 Darren Britt; 9 Keiron Cunningham; 10 Barry Ward; 23 Mike Bennett; 15 Tim Jonkers; 11 Chris Joynt (C). Subs: 2 Sean Hoppe for Wellens (3); 12 Peter Shiels for Ward (27); 14 John Stankevitch for Britt (31BB, rev 58); 17 Mick Higham for Joynt (54); Stankevitch for Shiels (58); Joynt for Britt (75); Shiels for Jonkers (77).
Tries: Bennett (24), Long (32), Gleeson (56);
Goals: Long 3; **Field goal:** Long.
Rugby League & League Express Men of the Match:
Bulls: Paul Deacon; *Saints:* Mike Bennett.
Penalty count: 5-4; **Half-time:** 12-8;
Referee: Russell Smith (Castleford); **Attendance:** 61,138 *(at Old Trafford, Manchester)*.

2003

NATIONAL LEAGUE TWO GRAND FINAL

Sunday 5th October 2003

KEIGHLEY COUGARS 13 SHEFFIELD EAGLES 11

COUGARS: 1 Matt Foster; 2 Max Tomlinson; 3 David Foster; 4 James Rushforth; 5 Andy Robinson; 6 Paul Ashton; 7 Matt Firth; 8 Phil Stephenson; 9 Simeon Hoyle; 10 Danny Ekis; 11 Oliver Wilkes; 12 Ian Sinfield; 13 Lee Patterson. Subs (all used): 14 Chris Wainwright; 15 Richard Mervill; 16 Mick Durham; 17 Jason Ramshaw.
Tries: M Foster (7), Robinson (74); **Goals:** Ashton 2;
Field goal: Firth.
EAGLES: 1 Andy Poynter; 2 Tony Weller; 3 Richard Goddard; 4 Tom O'Reilly; 5 Greg Hurst; 6 Gavin Brown; 7 Mark Aston; 8 Jack Howieson; 9 Gareth Stanley; 10 Dale Laughton; 11 Andy Raleigh; 12 Craig Brown; 13 Wayne Flynn. Subs (all used): 14 Peter Reilly; 15 Simon Tillyer; 16 Nick Turnbull; 17 Mitchell Stringer.
Try: O'Reilly (51); **Goals:** G Brown 3; **Field goal:** Reilly.
Rugby League & League Express Men of the Match:
Cougars: Simeon Hoyle; *Eagles:* Andy Raleigh.
Penalty count: 6-8; **Half-time:** 9-4;
Referee: Peter Taberner (Wigan).
(at Halton Stadium, Widnes).

NATIONAL LEAGUE ONE GRAND FINAL

Sunday 5th October 2003

LEIGH CENTURIONS 14 SALFORD CITY REDS 31

CENTURIONS: 1 Neil Turley; 2 Damian Munro; 3 Alan Hadcroft; 4 Danny Halliwell; 5 Leroy Rivett; 6 John Duffy; 7 Tommy Martyn; 8 Sonny Nickle; 9 Patrick Weisner; 10 Paul Norman; 11 Sean Richardson; 12 Willie Swann; 13 Adam Bristow. Subs (all used): 14 David Bradbury; 15 Lee Sanderson; 16 Bryan Henare; 17 Ricky Bibey.
Tries: Richardson (33), Halliwell (38), Swann (65);
Goal: Turley.
On report: Nickle (60) - late tackle on Clinch.
CITY REDS: 1 Jason Flowers; 2 Danny Arnold; 3 Stuart Littler; 4 Alan Hunte; 5 Andy Kirk; 6 Cliff Beverley; 7 Gavin Clinch; 8 Neil Baynes; 9 Malcolm Alker; 10 Andy Coley; 11 Simon Baldwin; 12 Paul Highton; 13 Chris Charles. Subs (all used): 14 Steve Blakeley; 15 David Highton; 16 Martin Moana; 17 Gareth Haggerty.
Tries: Hunte (3, 52), Beverley (23), Littler (73);
Goals: Charles 6, Blakeley; **Field goal:** Blakeley.
Rugby League & League Express Men of the Match:
Centurions: Willie Swann; *City Reds:* Gavin Clinch.
Penalty count: 10-10; **Half-time:** 10-16;
Referee: Richard Silverwood (Dewsbury);
Attendance: 9,186 *(at Halton Stadium, Widnes)*.

SUPER LEAGUE GRAND FINAL

Saturday 18th October 2003

BRADFORD BULLS 25 WIGAN WARRIORS 12

BULLS: 17 Stuart Reardon; 2 Tevita Vaikona; 6 Michael Withers; 4 Shontayne Hape; 5 Lesley Vainikolo; 15 Karl Pratt; 7 Paul Deacon; 8 Joe Vagana; 9 James Lowes; 29 Stuart Fielden; 11 Daniel Gartner; 12 Jamie Peacock; 13 Mike Forshaw. Subs (all used): 10 Paul Anderson; 18 Lee Radford; 3 Leon Pryce; 1 Robbie Paul (C).
Tries: Reardon (51), Hape (59), Lowes (75);
Goals: Deacon 6/6; **Field goal:** Deacon.
WARRIORS: 1 Kris Radlinski; 5 Brian Carney; 18 Martin Aspinwall; 14 David Hodgson; 2 Brett Dallas; 15 Sean O'Loughlin; 20 Luke Robinson; 30 Quentin Pongia; 9 Terry Newton; 10 Craig Smith; 11 Mick Cassidy; 12 Danny Tickle; 13 Andy Farrell (C). Subs (all used): 4 Paul Johnson; 8 Terry O'Connor; 23 Gareth Hock; 17 Mark Smith.
Tries: Tickle (17), Radlinski (72); **Goals:** Farrell 2/3.
Rugby League & League Express Men of the Match:
Bulls: Stuart Reardon; *Warriors:* Kris Radlinski.
Penalty count: 7-6; **Half-time:** 4-6;
Referee: Karl Kirkpatrick (Warrington);
Attendance: 65,537 *(at Old Trafford, Manchester)*.

2004

NATIONAL LEAGUE ONE GRAND FINAL

Sunday 10th October 2004

LEIGH CENTURIONS 32 WHITEHAVEN 16
(after extra-time)

CENTURIONS: 1 Neil Turley; 2 Rob Smyth; 3 Danny Halliwell; 4 Ben Cooper; 5 David Alstead; 6 John Duffy; 7 Tommy Martyn; 8 Simon Knox; 9 Paul Rowley; 10 Matt Sturm; 11 David Larder; 12 Oliver Wilkes; 13 Ian Knott. Subs (all used): 14 Dave McConnell; 15 Heath Cruckshank; 16 Richard Marshall; 17 Willie Swann.
Tries: Cooper (27, 83), Martyn (61), Turley (87);
Goals: Turley 6/8; **Field goals:** Turley 2, Rowley, Martyn.
WHITEHAVEN: 1 Gary Broadbent; 2 Craig Calvert; 3 David Seeds; 4 Mick Nanyn; 5 Wesley Wilson; 6 Leroy Joe; 7 Sam Obst; 8 Marc Jackson; 9 Aaron Lester; 10 David Fatialofa; 11 Paul Davidson; 12 Howard Hill; 13 Craig Walsh. Subs (all used): 14 Spencer Miller; 15 Carl Sice; 16 Chris McKinney; 17 Ryan Tandy.
Tries: Wilson (2, 71), Calvert (45); **Goals:** Nanyn 2/6.
Rugby League & League Express Men of the Match:
Centurions: Neil Turley; *Whitehaven:* Aaron Lester.
Penalty count: 5-9; **Half-time:** 7-6; **Full-time:** 16-16;
Referee: Ronnie Laughton (Barnsley);
Attendance: 11,005 *(at Halton Stadium, Widnes)*.

SUPER LEAGUE GRAND FINAL

Saturday 16th October 2004

BRADFORD BULLS 8 LEEDS RHINOS 16

BULLS: 6 Michael Withers; 17 Stuart Reardon; 16 Paul Johnson; 4 Shontayne Hape; 5 Lesley Vainikolo; 18 Iestyn Harris; 7 Paul Deacon; 8 Joe Vagana; 1 Robbie Paul (C); 29 Stuart Fielden; 12 Jamie Peacock; 13 Logan Swann; 11 Lee Radford. Subs: 10 Paul Anderson for Vagana (14); 15 Karl Pratt for Paul (23); 27 Rob Parker for Anderson (24); 19 Jamie Langley for Peacock (32); Paul for Withers (ht); Peacock for Radford (48); Radford for Swann (54); Vagana for Parker (56); Parker for Fielden (63); Fielden for Vagana (67); Swann for Langley (68).
Tries: Vainikolo (7), Hape (43); **Goals:** Deacon 0/2.
RHINOS: 21 Richard Mathers; 18 Mark Calderwood; 5 Chev Walker; 4 Keith Senior; 22 Marcus Bai; 13 Kevin Sinfield (C); 6 Danny McGuire; 19 Danny Ward; 9 Matt Diskin; 8 Ryan Bailey; 3 Chris McKenna; 29 Ali Lauitiiti; 11 David Furner. Subs: 16 Willie Poching for Furner (19); 10 Barrie McDermott for Ward (22); Ward for Bailey (29); 7 Rob Burrow for Lauitiiti (30); Bailey for McDermott (41); 20 Jamie Jones-Buchanan for McKenna (48); Lauitiiti for Ward (50); Furner for Sinfield (60); McKenna for Poching (63); Sinfield for Diskin (67); Poching for McKenna (72); Ward for Bailey (73).
Tries: Diskin (15), McGuire (75); **Goals:** Sinfield 4/4.
Rugby League & League Express Men of the Match:
Bulls: Lesley Vainikolo; *Rhinos:* Richard Mathers.
Penalty count: 5-5; **Half-time:** 4-10;
Referee: Steve Ganson (St Helens);
Attendance: 65,547 *(at Old Trafford, Manchester)*.

2005

NATIONAL LEAGUE ONE GRAND FINAL

Sunday 9th October 2005

CASTLEFORD TIGERS 36 WHITEHAVEN 8

TIGERS: 1 Michael Platt; 2 Waine Pryce; 3 Michael Shenton; 4 Jon Hepworth; 5 Damien Blanch; 6 Brad Davis; 7 Andrew Henderson; 8 Adam Watene; 9 Aaron Smith; 10 Richard Fletcher; 11 Tom Haughey; 12 Steve Crouch; 13 Deon Bird. Subs (all used): 14 Paul Handforth; 15 Craig Huby; 16 Adrian Vowles; 17 Frank Watene.
Tries: Huby (22), Crouch (24), Blanch (26), Davis (33, 45), Haughey (52); **Goals:** Fletcher 2/3, Huby 3/4, Hepworth 1/1.
WHITEHAVEN: 1 Gary Broadbent; 2 Craig Calvert; 3 David Seeds; 4 Mick Nanyn; 5 Wesley Wilson; 6 Leroy Joe; 7 Joel Penny; 8 Ryan Tandy; 9 Carl Sice; 10 David Fatialofa; 11 Spencer Miller; 12 Howard Hill; 13 Aaron Lester. Subs (all used): 14 Carl Rudd; 15 Aaron Summers; 16 Craig Chambers; 17 Marc Jackson.
Tries: Seeds (56), Calvert (78); **Goals:** Nanyn 0/2.
Sin bin: Joe (16) - late tackle on Davis.
On report: Joe (16) - late tackle on Davis;
Sice (40) - alleged biting.
Rugby League & League Express Men of the Match:
Tigers: Brad Davis; *Whitehaven:* Wesley Wilson.
Penalty count: 4-9; **Half-time:** 26-0;
Referee: Steve Ganson (St Helens);
Attendance: 13,300 *(at Halton Stadium, Widnes)*.

SUPER LEAGUE GRAND FINAL

Saturday 15th October 2005

BRADFORD BULLS 15 LEEDS RHINOS 6

BULLS: 6 Michael Withers; 3 Leon Pryce; 13 Ben Harris; 4 Shontayne Hape; 5 Lesley Vainikolo; 18 Iestyn Harris; 7 Paul Deacon; 12 Jamie Peacock (C); 9 Ian Henderson; 29 Stuart Fielden; 16 Paul Johnson; 10 Brad Meyers; 11 Lee Radford. Subs (all used): 24 Adrian Morley for Johnson (5); 19 Jamie Langley for Peacock (24); 8 Joe Vagana for Fielden (24); Johnson for Radford (24); 1 Robbie Paul for Henderson (31); Peacock for Vagana (45); Fielden for Morley (49); Henderson for Paul (54); Radford for Meyers (60); Morley for Peacock (62); Meyers for Langley (73); Peacock for Johnson (74).
Tries: L Pryce (29), Vainikolo (53); **Goals:** Deacon 3/5;
Field goal: I Harris.

RHINOS: 1 Richard Mathers; 2 Mark Calderwood; 3 Chev Walker; 12 Chris McKenna; 5 Marcus Bai; 6 Danny McGuire; 7 Rob Burrow; 8 Ryan Bailey; 14 Andrew Dunemann; 15 Danny Ward; 20 Gareth Ellis; 16 Willie Poching; 13 Kevin Sinfield (C). Subs (all used): 10 Barrie McDermott for Ward (17); 11 Ali Lauitiiti for Poching (21); 18 Jamie Jones-Buchanan for Bailey (31); Ward for McDermott (34); 9 Matt Diskin for Ellis (48); Poching for Lauitiiti (48); McDermott for Ward (54); Ellis for Poching (54); Lauitiiti for McDermott (61); Poching for Dunemann (65); Ward for Jones-Buchanan (68); Dunemann for Ellis (71).
Try: McGuire (22); **Goals:** Sinfield 1/2.
Rugby Leaguer & League Express Men of the Match: *Bulls:* Leon Pryce; *Rhinos:* Danny McGuire.
Penalty count: 6-8; **Half-time:** 8-6;
Referee: Ashley Klein (Keighley); **Attendance:** 65,537 *(at Old Trafford, Manchester).*

2006

NATIONAL LEAGUE TWO GRAND FINAL

Sunday 8th October 2006

SHEFFIELD EAGLES 35 SWINTON LIONS 10

EAGLES: 1 Johnny Woodcock; 5 Greg Hurst; 4 Jimmy Walker; 3 James Ford; 2 Rob Worrincy; 6 Brendon Lindsay; 7 Gavin Brown; 8 Jack Howieson; 9 Paul Pickering; 10 Mitchell Stringer; 11 Andy Hay; 12 Dale Holdstock; 13 Andy Smith. Subs (all used): 14 Craig Poucher; 15 Martin Ostler; 16 Sean Dickinson; 17 Waisale Sovatabua.
Tries: Worrincy (21, 43), Lindsay (38), Woodcock (39), Walker (51), Hay (60); **Goals:** Woodcock 5/6;
Field goal: G Brown.
LIONS: 1 Wayne English; 2 Andy Saywell; 3 Darren Woods; 4 David Alstead; 5 Marlon Billy; 6 Martin Moana; 7 Chris Hough; 8 Bruce Johnson; 9 Phil Wood; 10 Dave Newton; 11 Kris Smith; 12 Ian Sinfield; 13 Lee Marsh. Subs (all used): 14 Liam McGovern; 15 Chris Morley; 16 Danny Aboushakra; 17 Ian Parry.
Tries: Saywell (35), Alstead (74); **Goals:** McGovern 1/2.
Rugby Leaguer & League Express Men of the Match: *Eagles:* Johnny Woodcock; *Lions:* Wayne English.
Penalty count: 3-4; **Half-time:** 16-4;
Referee: Peter Taberner (Wigan).
(at Halliwell Jones Stadium, Warrington).

Dewsbury Rams were National League Two Champions in 2006. This game was to determine who took the second promotion place.

NATIONAL LEAGUE ONE GRAND FINAL

Sunday 8th October 2006

HULL KINGSTON ROVERS 29 WIDNES VIKINGS 16

ROVERS: 1 Ben Cockayne; 2 Leroy Rivett; 3 Gareth Morton; 4 Jon Goddard; 5 Byron Ford; 6 Scott Murrell; 7 James Webster; 8 Makali Aizue; 9 Ben Fisher; 10 David Tangata-Toa; 11 Iain Morrison; 12 Michael Smith; 13 Tommy Gallagher. Subs (all used): 14 Pat Weisner; 15 Dwayne Barker; 16 Jason Netherton; 17 Dave Wilson.
Tries: Ford (6), Goddard (18, 36), Murrell (24), Weisner (43); **Goals:** Morton 4/6; **Field goal:** Murrell.
VIKINGS: 1 Gavin Dodd; 2 Damien Blanch; 3 Sean Gleeson; 4 Daryl Cardiss; 5 John Kirkpatrick; 6 Dennis Moran; 7 Ian Watson; 8 Terry O'Connor; 9 Mark Smith; 10 Barrie McDermott; 11 Mick Cassidy; 12 David Allen; 13 Bob Beswick. Subs (all used): 14 Aaron Summers; 15 Oliver Wilkes; 16 Jordan James; 17 Ryan Tandy.
Tries: Dodd (32), Tandy (57), Blanch (70);, **Goals:** Dodd 2/3.
Rugby Leaguer & League Express Men of the Match: *Rovers:* James Webster; *Vikings:* Mark Smith.
Penalty count: 8-5; **Half-time:** 22-4;
Referee: Phil Bentham (Warrington); **Attendance:** 13,024 *(at Halliwell Jones Stadium, Warrington).*

SUPER LEAGUE GRAND FINAL

Saturday 14th October 2006

HULL FC 4 ST HELENS 26

HULL: 1 Shaun Briscoe; 14 Motu Tony; 4 Sid Domic; 3 Kirk Yeaman; 5 Gareth Raynor; 13 Paul Cooke; 7 Richard Horne; 8 Ewan Dowes; 9 Richard Swain (C); 10 Garreth Carvell; 11 Lee Radford; 12 Shayne McMenemy; 24 Danny Washbrook. Subs: 15 Paul King for Carvell (17); 19 Graeme Horne for Radford (23); 26 Scott Wheeldon for Dowes (27); 6 Richard Whiting for McMenemy (29); Dowes for Wheeldon (49); Carvell for King (49); Radford for G Horne (51); McMenemy for Whiting (54); King for Carvell (68); Wheeldon for Dowes (73); Whiting for Tony (76); G Horne for Radford (77).
Try: Domic (24); **Goals:** Cooke 0/1.

SAINTS: 1 Paul Wellens; 2 Ade Gardner; 3 Jamie Lyon; 4 Willie Talau; 5 Francis Meli; 6 Leon Pryce; 7 Sean Long (C); 17 Paul Anderson; 9 Keiron Cunningham; 10 Jason Cayless; 11 Lee Gilmour; 12 Jon Wilkin; 16 Jason Hooper. Subs: 23 Maurie Fa'asavalu for P Anderson (12); 19 James Graham for Cayless (25); 15 Mike Bennett for Fa'asavalu (28); 14 James Roby for Cunningham (31); P Anderson for Wilkin (33); Cunningham for Gilmour (49); Cayless for P Anderson (52); Wilkin for Hooper (56); Fa'asavalu for Cayless (58); Gilmour for Graham (66); Cayless for Fa'asavalu (72); P Anderson for Wilkin (75).
Tries: Meli (17), Pryce (29), Talau (49), Gardner (52), Cunningham (62); **Goals:** Lyon 3/5.
Rugby Leaguer & League Express Men of the Match: *Hull:* Shaun Briscoe; *Saints:* Paul Wellens.
Penalty count: 4-2; **Half-time:** 4-10;
Referee: Karl Kirkpatrick (Warrington);
Attendance: 72,582 *(at Old Trafford, Manchester).*

2007

NATIONAL LEAGUE TWO GRAND FINAL

Sunday 7th October 2007

FEATHERSTONE ROVERS 24 OLDHAM 6

ROVERS: 1 Loz Wildbore; 2 Danny Kirmond; 3 Jon Whittle; 4 Wayne McHugh; 5 Ade Adebisi; 6 Andy Kain; 7 Paul Handforth; 8 Gareth Handford; 9 Joe McLocklan; 10 Stuart Dickens; 11 Jamie Field; 12 Richard Blakeway; 13 Tom Haughey. Subs (all used): 14 Jamie Benn; 15 Ian Tonks; 16 James Houston; 17 Gavin Swinson.
Tries: McHugh (39, 49), Handforth (46);
Goals: Dickens 5/6; **Field goals:** Wildbore (66, 70).
Dismissal: Blakeway (64) – head butt on Roberts.
OLDHAM: 1 Gareth Langley; 2 Byron Ford; 3 Craig Littler; 4 Adam Hughes; 5 Lucas Onyango; 6 Neil Roden; 7 James Coyle; 8 Anthony Tonks; 9 Simeon Hoyle; 10 Richard Mervill; 11 Ian Sinfield; 12 Robert Roberts; 13 Geno Costin. Subs (all used): 14 Ian Hodson; 15 Alex Wilkinson; 16 Said Tamghart; 17 Matty Brooks.
Try: Hughes (31); **Goals:** Langley 1/2.
Rugby Leaguer & League Express Men of the Match: *Rovers:* Paul Handforth; *Oldham:* Robert Roberts.
Penalty count: 9-5; **Half-time:** 10-6;
Referee: Gareth Hewer. *(at Headingley Carnegie, Leeds).*

Celtic Crusaders were National League Two Champions in 2007. This game was to determine who took the second promotion place.

NATIONAL LEAGUE ONE GRAND FINAL

Sunday 7th October 2007

CASTLEFORD TIGERS 42 WIDNES VIKINGS 10

TIGERS: 1 Stuart Donlan; 2 Danny Williams; 3 Michael Shenton; 4 Ryan McGoldrick; 5 Kirk Dixon; 6 Anthony Thackeray; 7 Danny Brough; 8 Liam Higgins; 9 Andrew Henderson; 10 Awen Guttenbeil; 11 Joe Westerman; 12 Ryan Clayton; 13 Peter Lupton. Subs (all used): 14 Mark Leafa; 15 Chris Charles; 16 Michael Wainwright; 17 Ryan Boyle.
Tries: Wainwright (20), McGoldrick (29), Guttenbeil (44, 76), M Shenton (52), Westerman (62), Clayton (66);
Goals: Brough 6/9; **Field goals:** Brough (25, 55).
VIKINGS: 1 Scott Grix; 2 Damien Blanch; 3 Toa Kohe-Love; 4 Mick Nanyn; 5 Gavin Dodd; 6 Dennis Moran; 7 Joel Penny; 8 Mick Cassidy; 9 Mark Smith; 10 Oliver Wilkes; 11 Joel Tomkins; 12 Paul Noone; 13 Bob Beswick. Subs (all used): 14 Aaron Summers; 15 Jordan James; 16 Ian Webster; 17 Lee Doran.
Tries: Nanyn (35), Wilkes (69); **Goals:** Nanyn 1/2.
Rugby Leaguer & League Express Men of the Match: *Tigers:* Danny Brough; *Vikings:* Scott Grix.
Penalty count: 7-2; **Half-time:** 13-4;
Referee: Phil Bentham; **Attendance:** 20,814 *(at Headingley Carnegie, Leeds).*

SUPER LEAGUE GRAND FINAL

Saturday 13th October 2007

LEEDS RHINOS 33 ST HELENS 6

RHINOS: 1 Brent Webb; 5 Lee Smith; 3 Clinton Toopi; 4 Keith Senior; 2 Scott Donald; 6 Danny McGuire; 7 Rob Burrow; 8 Kylie Leuluai; 9 Matt Diskin; 10 Jamie Peacock; 11 Jamie Jones-Buchanan; 12 Gareth Ellis; 13 Kevin Sinfield (C). Subs (all used): 14 Ali Lauitiiti for Diskin (23); 16 Ryan Bailey for Leuluai (18); 18 Ian Kirke for Jones-Buchanan (33); 22 Carl Ablett for Kirke (57); Leuluai for Bailey (55); Jones-Buchanan for Lauitiiti (60); Diskin for Ablett (63); Kirke for Leuluai (65); Bailey for Kirke (76).
Tries: Webb (19), Lauitiiti (50), Donald (52), Smith (69), Jones-Buchanan (80); **Goals:** Sinfield 6/7;
Field goal: Burrow (55).

SAINTS: 1 Paul Wellens; 2 Ade Gardner; 3 Matt Gidley; 4 Willie Talau; 5 Francis Meli; 6 Leon Pryce; 7 Sean Long; 8 Nick Fozzard; 9 Keiron Cunningham (C); 10 Jason Cayless; 11 Lee Gilmour; 30 Chris Flannery; 12 Jon Wilkin. Subs (all used): 17 James Graham for Cayless (15); 14 James Roby for Cunningham (23); 23 Maurie Fa'asavalu for Fozzard (23); 15 Mike Bennett for Wilkin (31); Cayless for Fa'asavalu (34); Cunningham for Flannery (51); Wilkin for Bennett (55); Fa'asavalu for Cayless (55); Fozzard for Graham (57); Cayless for Fozzard (68); Graham for Fa'asavalu (68); Bennett for Gilmour (72).
Try: Roby (27); **Goals:** Long 1/2.
Rugby Leaguer & League Express Men of the Match: *Rhinos:* Rob Burrow; *Saints:* Sean Long.
Penalty count: 4-5; **Half-time:** 8-6; **Referee:** Ashley Klein;
Attendance: 71,352 *(at Old Trafford, Manchester).*

2008

NATIONAL LEAGUE TWO GRAND FINAL

Sunday 28th September 2008

DONCASTER 18 OLDHAM 10

DONCASTER: 1 Zebastian Luisi; 2 Dean Colton; 3 Andreas Bauer; 4 Shaun Leaf; 5 Wayne Reittie; 6 Kyle Wood; 7 Luke Gale; 8 Nathan Freer; 9 Corey Lawrie; 10 Alex Benson; 11 Peter Green; 12 Craig Lawton; 13 Josh Weeden. Subs (all used): 14 Kyle Briggs; 15 Chris Buttery; 16 Michael Haley; 17 Mark Castle.
Tries: Buttery (44), Gale (49), Briggs (73); **Goals:** Gale 3/4.
OLDHAM: 1 Paul O'Connor; 2 Gareth Langley; 3 Marcus St Hilaire; 4 Mick Nanyn; 5 Daryl Cardiss; 6 Phil Joseph; 7 James Coyle; 8 Adam Robinson; 9 Matty Brooks; 10 Richard Mervill; 11 Tommy Goulden; 12 Danny Halliwell; 13 Robert Roberts. Subs (all used): 14 Ian Hodson; 15 Luke Menzies; 16 Chris Baines; 17 Said Tamghart.
Tries: Hodson (34), Nanyn (62); **Goals:** Nanyn 1/4.
Rugby Leaguer & League Express Men of the Match: *Doncaster:* Luke Gale; *Oldham:* Adam Robinson.
Penalty count: 7-8; **Half-time:** 2-6;
Referee: Ronnie Laughton.
(at Halliwell Jones Stadium, Warrington).

Gateshead Thunder were National League Two Champions in 2008. This game was to determine who took the second promotion place.

NATIONAL LEAGUE ONE GRAND FINAL

Sunday 28th September 2008

CELTIC CRUSADERS 18 SALFORD CITY REDS 36
(after extra-time)

CRUSADERS: 1 Tony Duggan; 2 Luke Dyer; 3 Josh Hannay; 4 Mark Dalle Cort; 5 Anthony Blackwood; 6 Damien Quinn; 7 Jace Van Dijk; 8 Jordan James; 9 Neil Budworth; 10 David Tangata-Toa; 11 Chris Beasley; 12 Darren Mapp; 13 Terry Martin. Subs (all used): 14 Aaron Summers; 15 Ian Webster; 16 Mark Lennon; 17 Neale Wyatt.
Tries: Blackwood (38), Dyer (50), J James (54), Tangata-Toa (66); **Goals:** Hannay 0/1, Lennon 1/3.
CITY REDS: 1 Karl Fitzpatrick; 2 Matt Gardner; 3 Stuart Littler; 4 John Wilshere; 5 Paul White; 6 Robbie Paul; 7 Richard Myler; 8 Paul Highton; 9 Malcolm Alker; 10 Craig Stapleton; 11 Ian Sibbit; 12 Luke Adamson; 13 Jordan Turner. Subs (all used): 14 Stefan Ratchford; 15 Steve Bannister; 16 Lee Jewitt; 17 Phil Leuluai.
Tries: White (5, 86), Gardner (26), Fitzpatrick (63), Sibbit (83), Myler (99); **Goals:** Wilshere 6/7.
Rugby Leaguer & League Express Men of the Match: *Crusaders:* Tony Duggan; *City Reds:* John Wilshere.
Penalty count: 5-5; **Half-time:** 4-10; **Full-time:** 18-18;
Referee: Ben Thaler; **Attendance:** 7,104
(at Halliwell Jones Stadium, Warrington).

SUPER LEAGUE GRAND FINAL

Saturday 4th October 2008

LEEDS RHINOS 24 ST HELENS 16

RHINOS: 5 Lee Smith; 22 Ryan Hall; 19 Carl Ablett; 4 Keith Senior; 2 Scott Donald; 6 Danny McGuire; 7 Rob Burrow; 8 Kylie Leuluai; 9 Matt Diskin; 10 Jamie Peacock; 11 Jamie Jones-Buchanan; 12 Gareth Ellis; 13 Kevin Sinfield (C). Subs (all used): 17 Nick Scruton; 14 Ali Lauitiiti; 18 Ian Kirke; 16 Ryan Bailey.
Tries: Smith (23), Hall (37), McGuire (49, 63);
Goals: Sinfield 4/4.
SAINTS: 1 Paul Wellens; 2 Ade Gardner; 3 Matt Gidley; 4 Willie Talau; 5 Francis Meli; 6 Leon Pryce; 7 Sean Long; 18 Bryn Hargreaves; 9 Keiron Cunningham (C); 17 James Graham; 11 Lee Gilmour; 12 Jon Wilkin; 16 Chris Flannery. Subs (all used): 8 Nick Fozzard; 21 Paul Clough; 14 James Roby; 23 Maurie Fa'asavalu.

Tries: Graham (6), Gidley (43), Gardner (59);
Goals: Long 2/3.
Rugby Leaguer & League Express Men of the Match:
Rhinos: Jamie Peacock; *Saints:* Sean Long.
Penalty count: 6-8; **Half-time:** 12-6;
Referee: Ashley Klein; **Attendance:** 68,810
(at Old Trafford, Manchester).

2009

CHAMPIONSHIP ONE GRAND FINAL

Sunday 4th October 2009

KEIGHLEY COUGARS 28 OLDHAM 26

COUGARS: 1 George Rayner; 2 Sam Gardner; 3 Dan Potter; 4 Oliver Pursglove; 5 Gavin Duffy; 6 Jon Presley; 7 Danny Jones; 17 Scott Law; 14 Jamaine Wray; 8 Andy Shickell; 11 Will Cartledge; 18 Greg Nicholson; 13 Carl Hughes. Subs (all used): 21 Ryan Smith; 28 Ryan Benjafield; 9 James Feather; 16 Brendan Rawlins.
Tries: Gardner (24), Jones (42, 50), Presley (63), Pursglove (67); **Goals:** Jones 4/5.
OLDHAM: 4 Paul Reilly; 21 Lucas Onyango; 24 Marcus St Hilaire; 22 Phil Joseph; 1 Paul O'Connor; 18 Neil Roden; 7 Thomas Coyle; 15 Jason Boults; 30 Martin Roden; 16 Wayne Kerr; 23 Chris Baines; 12 Tommy Goulden; 28 Craig Lawton. Subs (all used): 10 Jamie I'Anson; 25 Luke Menzies; 27 Matt Ashe; 29 Ben Heaton.
Tries: Menzies (35, 76), N Roden (54), St Hilaire (70), Kerr (78); **Goals:** Baines 3/4, Ashe 0/1.
Rugby Leaguer & League Express Men of the Match:
Cougars: Danny Jones; *Oldham:* Luke Menzies.
Penalty count: 9-2; **Half-time:** 4-6;
Referee: Ronnie Laughton.
(at Halliwell Jones Stadium, Warrington).

Dewsbury Rams were Championship One Champions in 2009. This game was to determine who took the second promotion place.

CHAMPIONSHIP GRAND FINAL

Sunday 4th October 2009

BARROW RAIDERS 26 HALIFAX 18

RAIDERS: 1 Gary Broadbent; 36 Andy Ballard; 32 Andreas Bauer; 4 Liam Harrison; 5 James Nixon; 24 Jamie Rooney; 31 James Coyle; 34 Rob Roberts; 9 Andy Ellis; 8 Brett McDermott; 33 Dave Allen; 22 Ned Catic; 26 Zebastian Luisi. Subs (all used): 15 Chris Young; 3 Andy Bracek; 35 Danny Halliwell; 14 Paul Noone.
Tries: Harrison (33), Ballard (37), Allen (61), Bauer (66, 78); **Goals:** Rooney 3/5.
HALIFAX: 4 Shad Royston; 5 James Haley; 15 Mark Roberts; 2 Lee Paterson; 23 Rob Worricy; 19 Mick Govin; 7 Ben Black; 21 Neil Cherryholme; 9 Sean Penkywicz; 22 David Wrench; 11 David Larder; 27 Steve Bannister; 12 Paul Smith. Subs (all used): 13 Bob Beswick; 14 Mark Gleeson; 16 Said Tamghart; 26 Dominic Maloney.
Tries: Haley (12), Royston (31), Black (45), Govin (70); **Goals:** Paterson 1/5.
Rugby Leaguer & League Express Men of the Match:
Raiders: Gary Broadbent; *Halifax:* Mick Govin.
Penalty count: 8-5; **Half-time:** 10-10;
Referee: Phil Bentham; **Attendance:** 11,398
(at Halliwell Jones Stadium, Warrington).

SUPER LEAGUE GRAND FINAL

Saturday 10th October 2009

LEEDS RHINOS 18 ST HELENS 10

RHINOS: 1 Brent Webb; 2 Scott Donald; 3 Lee Smith; 4 Keith Senior; 5 Ryan Hall; 6 Danny McGuire; 7 Rob Burrow; 8 Kylie Leuluai; 14 Matt Diskin; 10 Jamie Peacock; 11 Jamie Jones-Buchanan; 18 Carl Ablett; 13 Kevin Sinfield (C). Subs (all used): 16 Ryan Bailey for Leuluai (19); 19 Luke Burgess for Peacock (29); 17 Ian Kirke for Jones-Buchanan (29); 12 Ali Lauitiiti for Ablett (29); Jones-Buchanan for Lauitiiti (36); Peacock for Burgess (46); Leuluai for Bailey (53); Ablett for Kirke (57); Burgess for Diskin (62); Bailey for Leuluai (67); Diskin for Burgess (69); Kirke for Jones-Buchanan (76).
Tries: Diskin (30), Smith (37, 72); **Goals:** Sinfield 2/4;
Field goals: Sinfield (42), Burrow (78).
SAINTS: 1 Paul Wellens; 2 Ade Gardner; 3 Matt Gidley; 18 Kyle Eastmond; 5 Francis Meli; 6 Leon Pryce; 7 Sean Long; 10 James Graham; 9 Keiron Cunningham (C); 16 Tony Puletua; 12 Jon Wilkin; 11 Lee Gilmour; 13 Chris Flannery. Subs (all used): 14 James Roby for Cunningham (25); 15 Bryn Hargreaves for Puletua (24); 17 Paul Clough for Gilmour (31); 23 Maurie Fa'asavalu for Graham (31); Graham for Fa'asavalu (48); Puletua for Hargreaves (50); Gilmour for Wilkin (55); Cunningham for Clough (61); Wilkin for Roby (65); Roby for Flannery (73).

Try: Eastmond (13); **Goals:** Eastmond 3/3.
Rugby Leaguer & League Express Men of the Match:
Rhinos: Kevin Sinfield; *Saints:* James Graham.
Penalty count: 8-7; **Half-time:** 8-8;
Referee: Steve Ganson; **Attendance:** 63,259
(at Old Trafford, Manchester).

2010

CHAMPIONSHIP ONE GRAND FINAL

Sunday 26th September 2010

OLDHAM 4 YORK CITY KNIGHTS 25

OLDHAM: 1 Paul O'Connor; 2 Lucas Onyango; 24 Marcus St Hilaire; 4 Mick Fogerty; 5 John Gillam; 6 Neil Roden; 28 Gregg McNally; 8 Jason Boults; 9 Martin Roden; 16 Wayne Kerr; 18 Chris Clarke; 13 Joe Chandler; 21 Valu Bentley. Subs (all used): 10 Dave Ellison; 19 Ben Heaton; 17 Danny Whitmore; 7 Matt Ashe.
Try: Fogerty (20); **Goals:** McNally 0/1.
CITY KNIGHTS: 31 James Haynes; 2 Wayne Reittie; 3 Mike Mitchell; 4 Lee Waterman; 28 Danny Wilson; 6 Chris Thorman; 1 Danny Ratcliffe; 17 Nathan Freer; 33 Jack Lee; 10 Alex Benson; 11 Jordan Ross; 29 Ryan Esders; 15 Luke Hardbottle. Subs (all used): 32 Paul Stamp; 36 Callum Dinsdale; 26 Steve Lewis; 30 Jack Stearman.
Tries: Reittie (7), Haynes (26), Thorman (64), Lewis (74); **Goals:** Waterman 2/3, Thorman 2/2;
Field goal: Thorman (69).
Rugby Leaguer & League Express Men of the Match:
Oldham: Neil Roden; *City Knights:* Chris Thorman.
Penalty count: 2-7; **Half-time:** 4-10;
Referee: Gareth Hewer.
(at Halliwell Jones Stadium, Warrington).

Hunslet Hawks were Championship One Champions in 2010. This game was to determine who took the second promotion place.

CHAMPIONSHIP GRAND FINAL

Sunday 26th September 2010

FEATHERSTONE ROVERS 22 HALIFAX 23

(after golden point extra-time)

ROVERS: 1 Ian Hardman; 26 Zak Hardaker; 3 Sam Smeaton; 4 Liam Welham; 2 Tom Saxton; 6 Kyle Briggs; 4 Liam Finn; 17 Tony Tonks; 31 Ben Kaye; 10 Stuart Dickens; 18 Tim Spears; 13 Jamie Field; 11 Matty Dale. Subs (all used): 19 Ross Divorty; 16 Dane Manning; 12 Jon Grayshon; 7 Andy Kain.
Tries: Briggs (28), Hardaker (30, 52), Dale (45);
Goals: Briggs 3/4.
HALIFAX: 4 Shad Royston; 2 Lee Paterson; 6 Luke Branighan; 18 Dylan Nash; 23 Rob Worricy; 26 Graham Holroyd; 7 Ben Black; 10 Neil Cherryholme; 13 Bob Beswick; 8 Makali Aizue; 11 David Larder; 22 David Wrench; 27 Sam Barlow. Subs (all used): 9 Sean Penkywicz; 17 Frank Watene; 19 Dane Manning; 24 Steve Bannister.
Tries: Worricy (20), Black (58), Branighan (60), Bannister (75); **Goals:** Paterson 3/4; **Field goal:** Black (82).
On report: Barlow (35) - alleged high tackle on Divorty.
Rugby Leaguer & League Express Men of the Match:
Rovers: Tom Saxton; *Halifax:* Ben Black.
Penalty count: 6-3; **Half-time:** 12-4; **Full-time:** 22-22;
Referee: Robert Hicks; **Attendance:** 9,443
(at Halliwell Jones Stadium, Warrington).

SUPER LEAGUE GRAND FINAL

Saturday 2nd October 2010

ST HELENS 10 WIGAN WARRIORS 22

SAINTS: 1 Paul Wellens; 30 Jamie Foster; 3 Matt Gidley; 5 Francis Meli; 24 Jonny Lomax; 12 Jon Wilkin; 34 Matty Smith; 10 James Graham; 9 Keiron Cunningham (C); 15 Bryn Hargreaves; 4 Iosia Soliola; 13 Chris Flannery; 11 Tony Puletua. Subs (all used): 17 Paul Clough; 14 James Roby; 22 Andrew Dixon; 25 Jacob Emmitt.
Tries: Dixon (28), Meli (74); **Goals:** Foster 1/2.
WARRIORS: 6 Sam Tomkins; 24 Darrell Goulding; 3 Martin Gleeson; 4 George Carmont; 5 Pat Richards; 19 Paul Deacon; 7 Thomas Leuluai; 8 Stuart Fielden; 15 Michael McIlorum; 10 Andy Coley; 11 Harrison Hansen; 12 Joel Tomkins; 13 Sean O'Loughlin (C). Subs (all used): 9 Mark Riddell; 17 Iafeta Palea'aesina; 25 Liam Farrell; 14 Paul Prescott.
Tries: Gleeson (4, 16), Goulding (20), S Tomkins (53);
Goals: Richards 2/3, Riddell 1/3, S Tomkins 0/1.
Rugby Leaguer & League Express Men of the Match:
Saints: Tony Puletua; *Warriors:* Thomas Leuluai.
Penalty count: 6-11; **Half-time:** 6-16;
Referee: Richard Silverwood; **Attendance:** 71,526
(at Old Trafford, Manchester).

2011

CHAMPIONSHIP ONE GRAND FINAL

Sunday 2nd October 2011

KEIGHLEY COUGARS 32 WORKINGTON TOWN 12

COUGARS: 18 James Haythornthwaite; 4 Danny Lawton; 22 Ben Sagar; 33 Jake Normington; 5 Gavin Duffy; 6 Jason Demetriou; 36 Jy-Mel Coleman; 17 Ryan Benjafield; 9 James Feather; 10 Scott Law; 11 Will Cartledge; 12 Oliver Pursglove; 21 Richard Jones. Subs (all used): 14 Jamaine Wray; 8 Andy Shickell; 16 Brendan Rawlins; 7 Ryan Smith.
Tries: Lawton (5), Feather (20), Rawlins (25), Pursglove (32), Normington (69, 77); **Goals:** Lawton 4/6.
TOWN: 1 Brett Carter; 2 Elliott Miller; 3 Jason Mossop; 4 Aaron Low; 5 Neil Frazer; 24 Darren Holt; 7 Scott Kaighan; 10 Kris Coward; 13 Karl Olstrum; 29 Dave Armitstead; 11 Mike Whitehead; 18 Joe McKenna; 12 Jarrad Stack. Subs (all used): 23 Marc Bainbridge; 15 Ruairi McGoff; 32 Chris Clough; 17 James Robinson.
Tries: Kaighan (65), Frazer (74); **Goals:** Holt 2/2.
Rugby Leaguer & League Express Men of the Match:
Cougars: Jason Demetriou; *Town:* Jarrad Stack.
Penalty count: 7-5; **Half-time:** 22-0; **Referee:** Tim Roby.
(at Halliwell Jones Stadium, Warrington).

Swinton Lions were Championship One Champions in 2011. This game was to determine who took the second promotion place.

CHAMPIONSHIP GRAND FINAL

Sunday 2nd October 2011

FEATHERSTONE ROVERS 40 SHEFFIELD EAGLES 4

ROVERS: 1 Ian Hardman; 33 Ben Cockayne; 3 Sam Smeaton; 17 Greg Worthington; 5 Tom Saxton; 6 Andy Kain; 7 Liam Finn; 8 Tony Tonks; 9 Ben Kaye; 10 Stuart Dickens; 11 Jon Grayshon; 12 Tim Spears; 28 Jon Hepworth. Subs (all used): 18 Ross Divorty; 13 Matty Dale; 4 Andrew Bostock; 30 Kirk Netherton.
Tries: Spears (4), Finn (7, 39), Hardman (42), Cockayne (56), Hepworth (59), Saxton (79); **Goals:** Finn 6/7.
Sin bin: Netherton (54) - fighting.
EAGLES: 6 Quentin Laulu-Togagae; 5 Tim Bergin; 26 Corey Hanson; 1 Misi Taulapapa; 14 Vinny Finigan; 13 Dane McDonald; 7 Simon Brown; 8 Jack Howieson; 9 Andrew Henderson; 10 Mitchell Stringer; 11 Alex Szostak; 12 Peter Green; 19 Joe Hirst. Subs (all used): 22 Ryan Hepworth; 30 Sam Scott; 20 Pat Smith; 14 Jonny Woodcock.
Try: McDonald (12); **Goals:** Brown 0/1.
Sin bin: Hirst (54) - fighting.
Rugby Leaguer & League Express Men of the Match:
Rovers: Liam Finn; *Eagles:* Joe Hirst.
Penalty count: 7-11; **Half-time:** 18-4;
Referee: Matthew Thomason; **Attendance:** 7,263
(at Halliwell Jones Stadium, Warrington).

SUPER LEAGUE GRAND FINAL

Saturday 8th October 2011

LEEDS RHINOS 32 ST HELENS 16

RHINOS: 1 Brent Webb; 23 Ben Jones-Bishop; 27 Zak Hardaker; 12 Carl Ablett; 5 Ryan Hall; 13 Kevin Sinfield (C); 6 Danny McGuire; 8 Kylie Leuluai; 9 Danny Buderus; 10 Jamie Peacock; 11 Jamie Jones-Buchanan; 3 Brett Delaney; 21 Chris Clarkson. Subs (all used): 7 Rob Burrow; 16 Ryan Bailey; 17 Ian Kirke; 14 Ali Lauitiiti.
Tries: Burrow (34), Webb (65), Hall (70), Ablett (74), Hardaker (80); **Goals:** Sinfield 6/7.
SAINTS: 1 Paul Wellens (C); 28 Tom Makinson; 3 Michael Shenton; 5 Francis Meli; 22 Jamie Foster; 25 Lee Gaskell; 20 Jonny Lomax; 10 James Graham (C); 9 James Roby; 11 Tony Puletua; 12 Jon Wilkin; 4 Iosia Soliola; 16 Paul Clough. Subs (all used): 19 Andrew Dixon; 14 Scott Moore; 15 Louie McCarthy-Scarsbrook; 17 Gary Wheeler.
Tries: Makinson (50), Shenton (55); **Goals:** Foster 4/5.
Rugby Leaguer & League Express Men of the Match:
Rhinos: Rob Burrow; *Saints:* Lee Gaskell.
Penalty count: 5-7; **Half-time:** 8-2;
Referee: Phil Bentham; **Attendance:** 69,107
(at Old Trafford, Manchester).

2012

CHAMPIONSHIP ONE GRAND FINAL

Sunday 30th September 2012

BARROW RAIDERS 13 DONCASTER 16

RAIDERS: 1 Andy Ballard; 2 Lee Haney; 3 Chris Larkin; 4 Aaron Low; 5 James Nixon; 6 Scott Kaighan; 7 Liam Campbell; 8 Jamie Butler; 9 James Dandy; 10 Ryan Duffy;

11 Liam Harrison; 12 James Gordon; 13 Daniel Toal. **Subs** (all used): 14 Liam Finch; 15 Martin Ostler; 16 Ruairi McGoff; 17 Andrew Dawson.
Tries: Larkin (4), Low (77); **Goals:** Ballard 2/3;
Field goal: Kaighan (39).
DONCASTER: 1 Lee Waterman; 2 Tom Hodson; 3 Chris Spurr; 4 Danny Cowling; 5 Stewart Sanderson; 6 Kyle Kesik; 7 Craig Fawcett; 8 Mark Castle; 9 Mike Emmett; 10 Russ Spiers; 11 Lucas Walshaw; 12 Michael Kelly; 13 Carl Hughes. **Subs** (all used): 14 Nathan Powley; 15 Craig Robinson; 16 Grant Edwards; 17 Liam Cunningham.
Tries: Sanderson (11), Waterman (46), Fawcett (57);
Goals: Hodson 2/3.
Rugby Leaguer & League Express Men of the Match:
Raiders: Liam Harrison; *Doncaster:* Craig Fawcett.
Penalty count: 4-5; **Half-time:** 7-4; **Referee:** Jamie Leahy.
(at Halliwell Jones Stadium, Warrington).

CHAMPIONSHIP GRAND FINAL

Sunday 30th September 2012

FEATHERSTONE ROVERS 16 SHEFFIELD EAGLES 20

ROVERS: 1 Ian Hardman; 2 Tangi Ropati; 3 Nathan Chappell; 4 Greg Worthington; 5 Tom Saxton; 6 Andy Kain; 7 Liam Finn; 8 Anthony England; 9 Ben Kaye; 10 James Lockwood; 11 Matty Dale; 12 Tim Spears; 13 Kyle Briggs. **Subs** (all used): 14 Dominic Maloney; 15 Stuart Dickens; 16 Andrew Bostock; 17 Jon Hepworth.
Tries: Hardman (17), Hepworth (51); **Goals:** Finn 4/4.
On report:
Maloney (57) - alleged use of the elbow on Turner.
EAGLES: 1 Quentin Laulu-Togagae; 2 Misi Taulapapa; 3 Duane Straugheir; 4 Menzie Yere; 5 Scott Turner; 6 Simon Brown; 7 Dominic Brambani; 8 Jack Howieson; 9 Andrew Henderson; 10 Mitchell Stringer; 11 Michael Knowles; 12 Sam Scott; 13 Alex Szostak. **Subs** (all used): 14 James Davey; 15 Peter Green; 16 Dane McDonald; 17 Liam Higgins.
Tries: Turner (9), Laulu-Togagae (32), McDonald (46), Taulapapa (57); **Goals:** Brown 2/5.
Rugby Leaguer & League Express Men of the Match:
Rovers: Ian Hardman; *Eagles:* Michael Knowles.
Penalty count: 4-6; **Half-time:** 8-10; **Referee:** Tim Roby.
Attendance: 6,409
(at Halliwell Jones Stadium, Warrington).

SUPER LEAGUE GRAND FINAL

Saturday 6th October 2012

LEEDS RHINOS 26 WARRINGTON WOLVES 18

RHINOS: 4 Zak Hardaker; 2 Ben Jones-Bishop; 3 Kallum Watkins; 12 Carl Ablett; 5 Ryan Hall; 13 Kevin Sinfield (C); 6 Danny McGuire; 8 Kylie Leuluai; 7 Rob Burrow; 10 Jamie Peacock; 11 Jamie Jones-Buchanan; 15 Brett Delaney; 16 Ryan Bailey. **Subs** (all used): 17 Ian Kirke; 20 Darrell Griffin; 25 Stevie Ward; 31 Shaun Lunt.
Tries: Sinfield (19), Jones-Bishop (28), Ablett (59), Hall (72); **Goals:** Sinfield 5/5.
WOLVES: 1 Brett Hodgson; 5 Joel Monaghan; 19 Stefan Ratchford; 4 Ryan Atkins; 2 Chris Riley; 6 Lee Briers; 7 Richard Myler; 20 Chris Hill; 14 Mick Higham; 13 Ben Harrison; 12 Ben Westwood; 11 Trent Waterhouse; 15 Simon Grix. **Subs** (all used): 8 Adrian Morley (C); 9 Michael Monaghan; 16 Paul Wood; 17 Michael Cooper.
Tries: Myler (4), J Monaghan (38), Atkins (45);
Goals: Hodgson 3/4.
Rugby Leaguer & League Express Men of the Match:
Rhinos: Kevin Sinfield; *Wolves:* Richard Myler.
Penalty count: 6-5; **Half-time:** 14-14;
Referee: Richard Silverwood; **Attendance:** 70,676
(at Old Trafford, Manchester).

2013

CHAMPIONSHIP ONE GRAND FINAL

Sunday 29th September 2013

OLDHAM 18 ROCHDALE HORNETS 32

OLDHAM: 1 Richard Lepori; 2 Mo Agoro; 21 David Cookson; 25 Jonathan Ford; 5 Dale Bloomfield; 23 Lewis Palfrey; 16 Kenny Hughes; 18 Phil Joy; 9 Sam Gee; 10 Jason Boults; 11 Josh Crowley; 12 Danny Langtree; 13 Mark Hobson. **Subs** (all used): 14 Adam Files; 19 Michael Ward; 22 Liam Thompson; 28 Matthew Haggarty.
Tries: Ford (12), Hughes (38), Cookson (44);
Goals: Palfrey 3/3.
HORNETS: 1 Wayne English; 2 Gareth Langley; 20 Daniel Davies; 23 Dave Hull; 17 Martin Waring; 6 Paul Crook; 7 Steve Roper; 29 Carl Forster; 31 Chris Hough; 10 Warren Thompson; 26 Dave Llewellyn; 24 Alex Trumper; 18 Joe Greenwood. **Subs** (all used): 8 John Cookson; 9 Alex McClurg; 11 Chris Baines; 13 Jordan Case.

Tries: Llewellyn (5), Davies (20), Hull (58), Cookson (71), English (78); **Goals:** Crook 6/6.
Rugby Leaguer & League Express Men of the Match:
Oldham: Lewis Palfrey; *Hornets:* Paul Crook.
Penalty count: 1-2; **Half-time:** 12-12;
Referee: Chris Leatherbarrow. *(at Leigh Sports Village).*

North Wales Crusaders were Championship One Champions in 2013. This game was to determine who took the second promotion place.

CHAMPIONSHIP GRAND FINAL

Sunday 29th September 2013

BATLEY BULLDOGS 12 SHEFFIELD EAGLES 19

BULLDOGS: 1 Miles Greenwood; 5 Johnny Campbell; 3 Jason Walton; 4 Danny Maun; 21 Greg Johnson; 6 Ben Black; 7 Gareth Moore; 8 Byron Smith; 9 Paul Mennell; 28 Anthony Mullally; 11 Alex Bretherton; 16 John Davies; 13 Ashley Lindsay. **Subs** (all used): 14 George Flanagan; 15 Keegan Hirst; 19 Alex Rowe; 17 Liam Walmsley.
Try: Campbell (13); **Goals:** Moore 4/5.
EAGLES: 1 Quentin Laulu-Togagae; 5 Misi Taulapapa; 4 Tom Armstrong; 3 Menzie Yere; 2 Scott Turner; 6 Pat Walker; 7 Dominic Brambani; 25 Eddie Battye; 9 Andrew Henderson; 10 Mitchell Stringer; 11 Michael Knowles; 15 Alex Szostak; 13 Joe Hirst. **Subs** (all used): 14 James Davey; 12 Peter Green; 16 Duane Straugheir; 21 Matt Garside.
Tries: Turner (56, 67), Yere (61), Laulu-Togagae (70);
Goals: Brambani 1/5; **Field goal:** Walker (74).
Rugby Leaguer & League Express Men of the Match:
Bulldogs: Keegan Hirst; *Eagles:* Dominic Brambani.
Penalty count: 6-7; **Half-time:** 12-0.
Referee: Matthew Thomason; **Attendance:** 6,374
(at Leigh Sports Village).

SUPER LEAGUE GRAND FINAL

Saturday 5th October 2013

WARRINGTON WOLVES 16 WIGAN WARRIORS 30

WOLVES: 19 Stefan Ratchford; 5 Joel Monaghan; 3 Chris Bridge; 4 Ryan Atkins; 2 Chris Riley; 6 Lee Briers; 7 Richard Myler; 16 Paul Wood; 14 Mick Higham; 18 Chris Hill; 13 Ben Harrison; 12 Ben Westwood; 15 Simon Grix. **Subs** (all used): 9 Michael Monaghan; 8 Adrian Morley (C); 17 Michael Cooper; 10 Garreth Carvell.
Tries: J Monaghan (20), Grix (24), Westwood (27);
Goals: Ratchford 2/3.
On report: Westwood (2) - alleged punch on Green.
WARRIORS: 1 Sam Tomkins; 2 Josh Charnley; 3 Darrell Goulding; 17 Iain Thornley; 5 Pat Richards; 6 Blake Green; 7 Matty Smith; 10 Lee Mossop; 9 Michael McIlorum; 20 Gil Dudson; 11 Harrison Hansen; 12 Liam Farrell; 13 Sean O'Loughlin (C). **Subs** (all used): 15 Ben Flower; 4 Jack Hughes; 26 Dominic Crosby; 21 Scott Taylor.
Tries: Goulding (37), McIlorum (47), Charnley (53), Green (65), Richards (74); **Goals:** Richards 5/6.
Rugby Leaguer & League Express Men of the Match:
Wolves: Chris Hill; *Warriors:* Michael McIlorum.
Penalty count: 7-10; **Half-time:** 16-6;
Referee: Richard Silverwood; **Attendance:** 66,281
(at Old Trafford, Manchester).

2014

CHAMPIONSHIP ONE GRAND FINAL

Sunday 5th October 2014

HUNSLET HAWKS 17 OLDHAM 16
(after golden point extra-time)

HAWKS: 2 Jimmy Watson; 36 Gavin Duffy; 4 Danny Maun; 3 Lee Brickwood; 37 James Duckworth; 6 Thomas Coyle; 20 Danny Ansell; 38 Richard Moore; 9 David March; 10 James Houston; 11 John Oakes; 12 Aaron Lyons; 31 Luke Briscoe. **Subs** (all used): 27 Liam Hood; 8 Michael Haley; 1 Stuart Kain; 40 Luke Hardbottle.
Tries: Watson (22), Duckworth (45), T Coyle (53);
Goals: March 2/3; **Field goal:** T Coyle (85).
OLDHAM: 4 Steven Nield; 29 Adam Clay; 21 David Cookson; 25 Jonathan Ford; 5 Dale Bloomfield; 6 Lewis Palfrey; 26 Steve Roper; 8 Phil Joy; 30 Gareth Owen; 10 Jason Boults; 11 Josh Crowley; 12 Danny Langtree; 22 Liam Thompson. **Subs** (all used): 19 Michael Ward; 28 Nathan Mason; 16 Kenny Hughes; 20 George Tyson.
Tries: Roper (5), Bloomfield (31), Langtree (74);
Goals: Roper 2/3.
Rugby Leaguer & League Express Men of the Match:
Hawks: Liam Hood; *Oldham:* Jonathan Ford.
Penalty count: 4-3; **Half-time:** 6-10; **Referee:** Joe Cobb.
(at Headingley Carnegie, Leeds).

CHAMPIONSHIP GRAND FINAL

Sunday 5th October 2014

FEATHERSTONE ROVERS 12 LEIGH CENTURIONS 36

ROVERS: 2 Will Sharp; 35 Jason Crookes; 1 Ian Hardman; 18 Jamie Cording; 36 Ben Blackmore; 23 Andy Kain; 7 Gareth Moore; 8 Steve Crossley; 9 Andy Ellis; 13 Matt James; 31 Shaun Pick; 11 James Lockwood; 12 Tim Spears. **Subs** (all used): 30 Luke Teasdale; 6 Jack Bussey; 42 Chris Annakin; 10 Keegan Hirst.
Tries: Sharp (27, 51); **Goals:** Moore 2/2.
Sin bin: Crookes (68) - high tackle on Armstrong.
CENTURIONS: 1 Gregg McNally; 22 Adam Higson; 34 Michael Platt; 4 Tom Armstrong; 15 Liam Kay; 6 Martyn Ridyard; 7 Ryan Brierley; 29 Jake Emmitt; 14 Sean Penkywicz; 10 Oliver Wilkes; 11 Matt Sarsfield; 30 Kurt Haggerty; 13 Sam Barlow. **Subs** (all used): 9 Bob Beswick; 18 Jamie Acton; 16 Martin Aspinwall; 33 Jonathan Walker.
Tries: Sarsfield (5), McNally (17), Armstrong (22), Higson (65), Barlow (70), Brierley (80);
Goals: Ridyard 6/8.
Sin bin: Penkywicz (68) - retaliation.
Rugby Leaguer & League Express Men of the Match:
Rovers: Jack Bussey; *Centurions:* Tom Armstrong.
Penalty count: 6-8; **Half-time:** 6-20;
Referee: Matthew Thomason; **Attendance:** 9,164
(at Headingley Carnegie, Leeds).

SUPER LEAGUE GRAND FINAL

Saturday 11th October 2014

ST HELENS 14 WIGAN WARRIORS 6

SAINTS: 17 Paul Wellens (C); 2 Tom Makinson; 22 Mark Percival; 4 Josh Jones; 5 Adam Swift; 15 Mark Flanagan; 6 Lance Hohaia; 16 Kyle Amor; 9 James Roby; 8 Mose Masoe; 10 Louie McCarthy-Scarsbrook; 11 Iosia Soliola; 3 Jordan Turner. **Subs** (all used): 28 Luke Thompson; 13 Willie Manu; 18 Alex Walmsley; 27 Greg Richards.
Tries: Soliola (54), Makinson (69); **Goals:** Percival 3/3.
WARRIORS: 1 Matt Bowen; 2 Josh Charnley; 5 Anthony Gelling; 23 Dan Sarginson; 32 Joe Burgess; 6 Blake Green; 7 Matty Smith; 10 Ben Flower; 19 Sam Powell; 17 Dominic Crosby; 11 Joel Tomkins; 12 Liam Farrell; 13 Sean O'Loughlin (C). **Subs** (all used): 22 Eddy Pettybourne; 24 Tony Clubb; 25 John Bateman; 27 George Williams.
Try: Burgess (40); **Goals:** Smith 1/3.
Dismissal: Flower (2) - punching Hohaia.
Rugby Leaguer & League Express Men of the Match:
Saints: James Roby; *Warriors:* Liam Farrell.
Penalty count: 9-7; **Half-time:** 2-6;
Referee: Phil Bentham; **Attendance:** 70,102
(at Old Trafford, Manchester).

2015

SUPER LEAGUE GRAND FINAL

Saturday 10th October 2015

LEEDS RHINOS 22 WIGAN WARRIORS 20

RHINOS: 1 Zak Hardaker; 2 Tom Briscoe; 3 Kallum Watkins; 4 Joel Moon; 5 Ryan Hall; 13 Kevin Sinfield (C); 6 Danny McGuire; 30 Mitch Garbutt; 7 Rob Burrow; 10 Jamie Peacock; 12 Carl Ablett; 15 Brett Delaney; 19 Brad Singleton. **Subs** (all used): 8 Kylie Leuluai; 17 Adam Cuthbertson; 20 Jimmy Keinhorst; 21 Josh Walters.
Tries: McGuire (7, 35), Moon (27), Walters (64);
Goals: Sinfield 3/4.
WARRIORS: 1 Matt Bowen; 22 Dominic Manfredi; 14 John Bateman; 34 Oliver Gildart; 5 Joe Burgess; 6 George Williams; 7 Matty Smith; 8 Dominic Crosby; 9 Michael McIlorum; 10 Ben Flower; 11 Joel Tomkins; 12 Liam Farrell; 13 Sean O'Loughlin (C). **Subs** (all used): 16 Sam Powell; 17 Tony Clubb; 23 Lee Mossop; 25 Larne Patrick.
Tries: Burgess (4), Manfredi (46), Bowen (49);
Goals: Bowen 4/4.
Rugby Leaguer & League Express Men of the Match:
Rhinos: Danny McGuire; *Warriors:* Matt Bowen.
Penalty count: 5-4; **Half-time:** 16-6;
Referee: Ben Thaler; **Attendance:** 73,512
(at Old Trafford, Manchester).

2016 SEASON
Stats round-up

SUPER LEAGUE CLUBS - AVERAGES

	2016 Avg	2015 Avg	Diff
Leeds Rhinos	15,478	15,724	-246
Wigan Warriors	13,235	13,151	+84
Hull FC	11,590	11,173	+417
Warrington Wolves	11,095	9,458	+1,637
St Helens	10,711	11,863	-1,152
Catalans Dragons	9,348	8,635	+713
Hull Kingston Rovers	7,610	7,784	-174
Castleford Tigers	7,458	7,097	+361
Widnes Vikings	5,471	5,976	-505
Huddersfield Giants	5,271	5,942	-671
Wakefield Trinity Wildcats	4,992	4,103	+889
Salford Red Devils	3,228	4,106	-878
2016 Average	8,791		
2015 Average	8,751		
Difference	+40		

CHAMPIONSHIP CLUBS - AVERAGES

	2016 Avg	2015 Avg	Diff
Leigh Centurions	4,260	3,942	+318
Bradford Bulls	4,178	5,457	-1,279
Featherstone Rovers	2,655	1,984	+671
Halifax	1,713	2,135	-422
Batley Bulldogs	1,271	927	+344
Dewsbury Rams	1,082	1,243	-161
Oldham	831	631	+200
			(League 1)
London Broncos	830	645	+185
Swinton Lions	767	477	+290
			(League 1)
Workington Town	717	849	-132
Whitehaven	716	870	-154
Sheffield Eagles	626	1,283	-657
2016 Average	1,637		
2015 Average	1,773		
Difference	-136		

LEAGUE 1 CLUBS - AVERAGES

	2016 Avg	2015 Avg	Diff
Toulouse Olympique	1,513	N/A	N/A
Barrow Raiders	941	905	+36
Newcastle Thunder	810	944	-134
Doncaster	587	1,110	-523
			(Championship)
York City Knights	582	430	+152
Keighley Cougars	575	1,026	-451
Rochdale Hornets	512	516	-4
Hunslet Hawks	452	827	-375
			(Championship)
North Wales Crusaders	430	641	-211
Coventry Bears	426	458	-32
London Skolars	398	342	+56
South Wales Scorpions	294	289	+5
Hemel Stags	180	204	-24
Oxford	162	284	-122
Gloucestershire All Golds	134	242	-108
2016 Average	533		
2015 Average	528		
Difference	+5		

BEST ATTENDANCES

		Round	Date
76,235	Hull FC v Warrington	CCF	27/8/16
		(at Wembley Stadium)	
70,202	Warrington v Wigan	SLGF	8/10/16
		(at Old Trafford, Manchester)	
20,049	Wigan v St Helens	SLR23	22/7/16
19,778	Leeds v North Queensland	WCC	21/2/16
19,103	Wigan v Brisbane	WCS	20/2/16
17,890	St Helens v Wigan	SLR7	25/3/16
17,481	Hull FC v Hull KR	SLR22	14/7/16
17,480	Wigan v Warrington	SLR9	1/4/16
17,453	Hull FC v Warrington	SLS8R7	23/9/16
17,213	Leeds v Castleford	SLR14	12/5/16
17,131	Leeds v St Helens	SLR6	18/3/16
16,712	Leeds v Wigan	SLR22	15/7/16
16,314	Leeds v Wakefield	SLR8	28/3/16
16,168	Leeds v Warrington	SLR1	4/2/16
16,140	Wigan v Catalans Dragons	SLS8R7	23/9/16
16,130	Leeds v Widnes	SLR20	3/7/16
15,888	Leeds v Hull FC	SLR11	15/4/16
15,384	Leeds v Hull KR	SLR9	1/4/16
15,265	Wigan v St Helens	SLS8R3	19/8/16
15,135	Leeds v Batley	S8-QR5	9/9/16

LEADING SCORERS

CHAMPIONSHIP *(Regular season only)*

TRIES

1	Rhys Williams	London Broncos	22
2	Omari Caro	Bradford Bulls	19
3	James Clare	Bradford Bulls	18
	Rob Worrincy	Sheffield Eagles	18
5	Kris Welham	Bradford Bulls	17
	Jarrod Sammut	Workington Town	17
7	Liam Marshall	Swinton Lions	16
8	Misi Taulapapa	Featherstone Rovers	13
	Gareth Moore	Halifax	13
	Menzie Yere	Sheffield Eagles	13

GOALS

1	Martyn Ridyard	Leigh Centurions	91
2	Steve Tyrer	Halifax	87
3	Danny Addy	Bradford Bulls	75
	Pat Walker	Batley Bulldogs	75
5	Chris Atkin	Swinton Lions	61
6	Paul Sykes	Dewsbury Rams	53
7	Wes Naiqama	London Broncos	49
8	Lewis Palfrey	Oldham	45
9	Cory Aston	Sheffield Eagles	42
10	Kyle Briggs	Featherstone Rovers	37
	Jamie Foster	Featherstone Rovers	37

POINTS

			T	G	FG	Pts
1	Steve Tyrer	Halifax	8	87	0	206
2	Martyn Ridyard	Leigh Centurions	3	91	1	195
3	Danny Addy	Bradford Bulls	5	75	1	171
4	Pat Walker	Batley Bulldogs	1	75	2	156
5	Chris Atkin	Swinton Lions	7	61	0	150
6	Jarrod Sammut	Workington Town	17	34	2	138
7	Cory Aston	Sheffield Eagles	12	42	0	132
8	Paul Sykes	Dewsbury Rams	6	53	0	130
9	Wes Naiqama	London Broncos	4	49	0	114
10	Kyle Briggs	Featherstone Rovers	8	37	1	107

CHALLENGE CUP

TRIES

1	Mark Kheirallah	Toulouse Olympique	7
2	Tom Johnstone	Wakefield Trinity Wildcats	6
	Richie Barnett	Hunslet Hawks	6
4	Ian Hardman	Featherstone Rovers	5
	Ed Barber	Halifax	5

GOALS

1	Steve Tyrer	Halifax	21
2	Liam Finn	Wakefield Trinity Wildcats	20
3	Mark Kheirallah	Toulouse Olympique	19
4	Kurt Gidley	Warrington Wolves	18
	Marc Sneyd	Hull FC	18

POINTS

			T	G	FG	Pts
1	Mark Kheirallah	Toulouse Olympique	7	19	0	66
2	Liam Finn	Wakefield Trinity Wildcats	2	20	0	48
3	Steve Tyrer	Halifax	0	21	0	42
4	Kurt Gidley	Warrington Wolves	1	18	0	40
5	Marc Sneyd	Hull FC	0	18	1	37

Rhys Williams

Martyn Ridyard

Steve Tyrer

CHAMPIONSHIP SHIELD

TRIES

1	Kris Welham	Bradford Bulls	12
2	Kieren Moss	Bradford Bulls	9
	Ethan Ryan	Bradford Bulls	9
4	Quentin Laulu-Togagae	Sheffield Eagles	8
5	Dane Chisholm	Bradford Bulls	7
	Jay Pitts	Bradford Bulls	7

GOALS

1	Cory Aston	Sheffield Eagles	50
2	Lewis Palfrey	Oldham	24
3	Chris Atkin	Swinton Lions	23
	Jarrod Sammut	Workington Town	23
5	Joe Keyes	Bradford Bulls	22
	Gareth Moore	Halifax	22

POINTS

			T	G	FG	Pts
1	Cory Aston	Sheffield Eagles	2	50	0	108
2	Jarrod Sammut	Workington Town	5	23	0	66
3	Chris Atkin	Swinton Lions	4	23	1	63
4	Gareth Moore	Halifax	2	22	0	52
5	Joe Keyes	Bradford Bulls	1	22	0	48
	Lewis Palfrey	Oldham	0	24	0	48
	Kris Welham	Bradford Bulls	12	0	0	48

LEAGUE 1 CUP

TRIES

1	Phil Cowburn	Gloucestershire All Golds	5
	Brett Turner	York City Knights	5
3	Ritchie Hawkyard	Keighley Cougars	3
	Paul White	Keighley Cougars	3
	Eddie Mbaraga	London Skolars	3
	Aaron Small	London Skolars	3
	Scott Turner	North Wales Crusaders	3
	Russ Spiers	York City Knights	3

GOALS

1	Danny Nicklas	York City Knights	15
2	Adam Brook	Keighley Cougars	13
3	Courtney Davies	Gloucestershire All Golds	9
4	Mike Bishay	London Skolars	7
5	Benn Hardcastle	Newcastle Thunder	5

POINTS

			T	G	FG	Pts
1	Danny Nicklas	York City Knights	1	15	0	34
2	Adam Brook	Keighley Cougars	0	13	1	27
3	Brett Turner	York City Knights	5	3	0	26
4	Phil Cowburn	Gloucestershire All Golds	5	0	0	20
5	Courtney Davies	Gloucestershire All Golds	0	9	0	18

LEADING SCORERS

SUPER LEAGUE
(Regular season, Super 8s, Semi-finals & Grand Final.
Super 8s (Qualifiers) not included)

TRIES

1	Denny Solomona	Castleford Tigers	40
2	Corey Thompson	Widnes Vikings	27
3	Josh Charnley	Wigan Warriors	20
4	Jodie Broughton	Catalans Dragons	19
5	Jermaine McGillvary	Huddersfield Giants	17
	Adam Swift	St Helens	17
	Ryan Atkins	Warrington Wolves	17
	Ben Currie	Warrington Wolves	17
9	Fetuli Talanoa	Hull FC	15
	Tom Lineham	Warrington Wolves	15

GOALS

1	Luke Gale	Castleford Tigers	118
2	Marc Sneyd	Hull FC	113
3	Matty Smith	Wigan Warriors	89
4	Kurt Gidley	Warrington Wolves	87
5	Liam Finn	Wakefield Trinity Wildcats	83
6	Luke Walsh	St Helens	74
7	Pat Richards	Catalans Dragons	69
8	Danny Brough	Huddersfield Giants	56
9	Rhys Hanbury	Widnes Vikings	55
10	Gareth O'Brien	Salford Red Devils	51

Denny
Solomona

Luke
Gale

SUPER 8s - THE QUALIFIERS

TRIES

1	Thomas Minns	Hull Kingston Rovers	10
2	Kallum Watkins	Leeds Rhinos	9
	Matty Dawson	Leigh Centurions	9
4	Ryan Brierley	Huddersfield Giants	8
	Leroy Cudjoe	Huddersfield Giants	8
	Rhys Williams	London Broncos	8

GOALS

1	Josh Mantellato	Hull Kingston Rovers	40
2	Martyn Ridyard	Leigh Centurions	32
3	Gareth O'Brien	Salford Red Devils	29
4	Jamie Soward	London Broncos	27
5	Danny Brough	Huddersfield Giants	22

POINTS

			T	G	FG	Pts
1	Josh Mantellato	Hull Kingston Rovers	6	40	0	104
2	Martyn Ridyard	Leigh Centurions	2	32	1	73
3	Gareth O'Brien	Salford Red Devils	3	29	1	71
4	Jamie Soward	London Broncos	2	27	0	62
5	Liam Sutcliffe	Leeds Rhinos	3	21	0	54

GOALS PERCENTAGE

			G	Att	%
1	Tony Gigot	Catalans Dragons	13	15	86.66
2	Declan Patton	Warrington Wolves	23	27	85.18
3	Jordan Lilley	Leeds Rhinos	27	32	84.37
4	Thomas Bosc	Catalans Dragons	16	19	84.21
5	Marc Sneyd	Hull FC	113	135	83.70
6	Kurt Gidley	Warrington Wolves	87	110	79.09
7	Luke Walsh	St Helens	74	94	78.72
8	Mark Percival	St Helens	28	36	77.77
9	Luke Gale	Castleford Tigers	118	153	77.12
10	Liam Sutcliffe	Leeds Rhinos	33	43	76.74

(10 minimum attempts to qualify)

POINTS

			T	G	FG	Pts
1	Luke Gale	Castleford Tigers	6	118	2	262
2	Marc Sneyd	Hull FC	4	113	5	247
3	Matty Smith	Wigan Warriors	5	89	9	207
4	Kurt Gidley	Warrington Wolves	8	87	0	206
5	Liam Finn	Wakefield Trinity Wildcats	2	83	0	174
	Pat Richards	Catalans Dragons	9	69	0	174
7	Luke Walsh	St Helens	2	74	5	161
8	Denny Solomona	Castleford Tigers	40	0	0	160
9	Rhys Hanbury	Widnes Vikings	12	55	0	158
10	Danny Brough	Huddersfield Giants	4	56	4	132

CONSECUTIVE APPEARANCES *(all club games included)*

1	Chris Hill	Warrington Wolves	83
2	Ukuma Ta'ai	Huddersfield Giants	70
3	Adam Milner	Castleford Tigers	50
4	Michael Lawrence	Huddersfield Giants	47
5	Sam Powell	Wigan Warriors	46
6	Leroy Cudjoe	Huddersfield Giants	45
7	Julian Bousquet	Catalans Dragons	44
8	Louie McCarthy-Scarsbrook	St Helens	40
9	Kyle Amor	St Helens	39
10	Jon Wilkin	St Helens	38

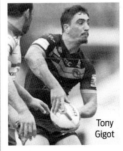

Tony
Gigot

Chris
Hill

Thomas
Minns

Josh
Mantellato

LEADING SCORERS

LEAGUE 1 *(Regular season, Super 8s & play-offs)*

TRIES

1	Kuni Minga	Toulouse Olympique	32
2	Mark Kheirallah	Toulouse Olympique	24
3	Kris Brining	York City Knights	20
4	Danny Hulme	Toulouse Olympique	19
5	Tony Maurel	Toulouse Olympique	18
6	Jono Smith	Rochdale Hornets	16
	Rhys Curran	Toulouse Olympique	16
8	Chris Hankinson	Barrow Raiders	13
	Cameron Pitman	Barrow Raiders	13
	Louis Sheriff	Doncaster	13
	George Flanagan	Hunslet Hawks	13

GOALS

1	Mark Kheirallah	Toulouse Olympique	152
2	Tom Carr	Doncaster	97
3	Chris Hankinson	Barrow Raiders	88
4	Paul Crook	Rochdale Hornets	86
5	Simon Brown	Hunslet Hawks	52
6	Tommy Johnson	North Wales Crusaders	44
7	Adam Brook	Keighley Cougars	40
	Danny Nicklas	York City Knights	40
9	Benn Hardcastle	Newcastle Thunder	37
10	Joel James	Coventry Bears	32

POINTS

			T	G	FG	Pts
1	Mark Kheirallah	Toulouse Olympique	24	152	0	400
2	Chris Hankinson	Barrow Raiders	13	88	0	228
3	Tom Carr	Doncaster	4	97	1	211
4	Paul Crook	Rochdale Hornets	6	86	0	196
5	Kuni Minga	Toulouse Olympique	32	0	0	128
6	Danny Nicklas	York City Knights	7	40	0	108
7	Simon Brown	Hunslet Hawks	0	52	1	105
8	Tommy Johnson	North Wales Crusaders	3	44	0	100
9	Adam Brook	Keighley Cougars	4	40	0	96
10	Danny Ansell	Hunslet Hawks	10	23	1	87

LEAGUE 1 SHIELD

TRIES

1	Rob Massam	North Wales Crusaders	9
2	Peter Fox	Newcastle Thunder	7
	Evan Simons	Newcastle Thunder	7
4	Alex Thompson	North Wales Crusaders	6
	Nathan Kitson	Oxford	6

GOALS

1	Benn Hardcastle	Newcastle Thunder	32
2	Tommy Johnson	North Wales Crusaders	23
3	Joel James	Coventry Bears	22
4	Kieran Hyde	Gloucestershire All Golds	19
5	Paul Emanuelli	South Wales Scorpions	13

POINTS

			T	G	FG	Pts
1	Benn Hardcastle	Newcastle Thunder	0	32	1	65
2	Tommy Johnson	North Wales Crusaders	0	23	0	46
3	Joel James	Coventry Bears	0	22	1	45
4	Kieran Hyde	Gloucestershire All Golds	1	19	0	42
	Nathan Kitson	Oxford	6	9	0	42

Denny Solomona

Mark Kheirallah

ALL COMPETITIONS

TRIES

1	Denny Solomona	Castleford Tigers	42
2	Kuni Minga	Toulouse Olympique	36
3	Rhys Williams	London Broncos	31
	Mark Kheirallah	Toulouse Olympique	31
5	Kris Welham	Bradford Bulls	29
6	Corey Thompson	Widnes Vikings	28
7	Josh Charnley	Wigan Warriors	24
8	Jarrod Sammut	Workington Town	23
9	Rob Worrincy	Sheffield Eagles	22
	Rob Massam	North Wales Crusaders	22
	Kris Brining	York City Knights	22

GOALS

1	Mark Kheirallah	Toulouse Olympique	171
2	Martyn Ridyard	Leigh Centurions	135
3	Marc Sneyd	Hull FC	131
4	Luke Gale	Castleford Tigers	120
5	Steve Tyrer	Halifax	108
6	Tom Carr	Doncaster	106
7	Kurt Gidley	Warrington Wolves	105
8	Liam Finn	Wakefield Trinity Wildcats	103
9	Paul Crook	Rochdale Hornets	101
10	Matty Smith	Wigan Warriors	95

POINTS

			T	G	FG	Pts
1	Mark Kheirallah	Toulouse Olympique	31	171	0	466
2	Martyn Ridyard	Leigh Centurions	5	135	2	292
3	Marc Sneyd	Hull FC	4	131	6	284
4	Luke Gale	Castleford Tigers	7	120	2	270
5	Steve Tyrer	Halifax	8	108	0	248
6	Kurt Gidley	Warrington Wolves	9	105	0	246
	Cory Aston	Sheffield Eagles	15	93	0	246
8	Paul Crook	Rochdale Hornets	8	101	0	234
9	Tom Carr	Doncaster	4	106	1	229
10	Chris Hankinson	Barrow Raiders	13	88	0	228

FIELD GOALS

1	Matty Smith	Wigan Warriors	9
2	Danny Brough	Huddersfield Giants	8
3	Marc Sneyd	Hull FC	6
4	Luke Walsh	St Helens	5
	Dominic Brambani	Batley Bulldogs	5

FINAL TABLES

SUPER LEAGUE - SUPER 8s

	P	W	D	L	F	A	D	Pts
Warrington Wolves	30	21	1	8	852	541	311	43
Wigan Warriors	30	21	0	9	669	560	109	42
Hull FC	30	20	0	10	749	579	170	40
St Helens	30	20	0	10	756	641	115	40
Castleford Tigers	30	15	1	14	830	808	22	31
Catalans Dragons	30	15	0	15	723	716	7	30
Widnes Vikings	30	12	0	18	603	643	-40	24
Wakefield Trinity Wildcats	30	10	0	20	571	902	-331	20

SUPER 8s - THE QUALIFIERS

	P	W	D	L	F	A	D	Pts
Leeds Rhinos	7	6	0	1	239	94	145	12
Leigh Centurions	7	6	0	1	223	193	30	12
Huddersfield Giants	7	5	0	2	257	166	91	10
Hull Kingston Rovers	7	4	0	3	235	142	93	8
Salford Red Devils	7	3	0	4	208	152	56	6
London Broncos	7	3	0	4	221	212	9	6
Batley Bulldogs	7	1	0	6	111	318	-207	2
Featherstone Rovers	7	0	0	7	96	313	-217	0

CHAMPIONSHIP SHIELD

	P	W	D	L	F	A	D	Pts
Bradford Bulls	30	19	2	9	1077	570	507	40
Halifax	30	16	1	13	821	682	139	33
Sheffield Eagles	30	12	0	18	855	843	12	24
Dewsbury Rams	30	12	0	18	676	809	-133	24
Swinton Lions	30	10	1	19	614	1041	-427	21
Oldham	30	10	0	20	535	918	-383	20
Whitehaven	30	8	1	21	553	918	-365	17
Workington Town	30	7	1	22	597	991	-394	15

LEAGUE 1 - SUPER 8s

	P	W	D	L	F	A	D	Pts
Toulouse Olympique	21	20	1	0	990	276	714	41
Rochdale Hornets	21	16	1	4	709	440	269	33
Barrow Raiders	21	15	1	5	769	375	394	31
Doncaster	21	14	0	7	683	526	157	28
York City Knights	21	12	1	8	618	461	157	25
Keighley Cougars	21	11	0	10	658	514	144	22
Hunslet Hawks	21	11	0	10	544	550	-6	22
London Skolars	21	8	0	13	470	650	-180	16

LEAGUE 1 SHIELD

	P	W	D	L	F	A	D	Pts
Newcastle Thunder	20	13	1	6	686	460	226	27
North Wales Crusaders	20	9	2	9	505	469	36	20
Coventry Bears	20	8	1	11	446	590	-144	17
Gloucestershire All Golds	20	5	0	15	515	644	-129	10
Oxford	20	4	0	16	356	843	-487	8
South Wales Scorpions	20	2	0	18	274	723	-449	4
Hemel Stags	20	2	0	18	274	976	-702	4

SUPER LEAGUE - REGULAR SEASON

	P	W	D	L	F	A	D	Pts
Hull FC	23	17	0	6	605	465	140	34
Warrington Wolves	23	16	1	6	675	425	250	33
Wigan Warriors	23	16	0	7	455	440	15	32
St Helens	23	14	0	9	573	536	37	28
Catalans Dragons	23	13	0	10	593	505	88	26
Castleford Tigers	23	10	1	12	617	640	-23	21
Widnes Vikings	23	10	0	13	499	474	25	20
Wakefield Trinity Wildcats	23	10	0	13	485	654	-169	20
Leeds Rhinos	23	8	0	15	404	576	-172	16
Salford Red Devils *	23	10	0	13	560	569	-9	14
Hull Kingston Rovers	23	6	2	15	486	610	-124	14
Huddersfield Giants	23	6	0	17	511	569	-58	12

* Six points deducted for salary cap breaches in 2014 & 2015

CHAMPIONSHIP - REGULAR SEASON

	P	W	D	L	F	A	D	Pts
Leigh Centurions	23	21	1	1	881	410	471	43
London Broncos	23	17	0	6	702	444	258	34
Batley Bulldogs	23	15	1	7	589	485	104	31
Featherstone Rovers	23	15	0	8	595	384	211	30
Bradford Bulls	23	13	2	8	717	446	271	28
Halifax	23	13	1	9	615	484	131	27
Sheffield Eagles	23	8	0	15	583	617	-34	16
Dewsbury Rams	23	8	0	15	486	603	-117	16
Swinton Lions	23	7	1	15	449	813	-364	15
Oldham	23	7	0	16	401	678	-277	14
Workington Town	23	5	1	17	455	756	-301	11
Whitehaven	23	5	1	17	367	720	-353	11

LEAGUE 1 - REGULAR SEASON

	P	W	D	L	F	A	D	Pts
Toulouse Olympique	14	13	1	0	702	184	518	27
Rochdale Hornets	14	12	1	1	547	252	295	25
York City Knights	14	10	1	3	482	256	226	21
Doncaster	14	10	0	4	499	304	195	20
Barrow Raiders	14	9	1	4	529	253	276	19
Keighley Cougars	14	9	0	5	520	368	152	18
Hunslet Hawks	14	8	0	6	383	374	9	16
London Skolars	14	8	0	6	354	376	-22	16
Newcastle Thunder	14	7	1	6	404	368	36	15
North Wales Crusaders	14	5	2	7	336	355	-19	12
Coventry Bears	14	4	1	9	289	460	-171	9
Gloucestershire All Golds	14	3	0	11	334	479	-145	6
South Wales Scorpions	14	1	0	13	176	582	-406	2
Oxford	14	1	0	13	232	648	-416	2
Hemel Stags	14	1	0	13	190	718	-528	2